HANDBOOK
of
PSYCHOLOGY

HANDBOOK
of
PSYCHOLOGY

VOLUME 7
EDUCATIONAL PSYCHOLOGY

William M. Reynolds
Gloria E. Miller

Volume Editors

Irving B. Weiner

Editor-in-Chief

John Wiley & Sons, Inc.

Copyright © 2003 by John Wiley & Sons, Inc., Hoboken, New Jersey. All rights reserved.

Published simultaneously in Canada.

No part of this publication may be reproduced, stored in a retrieval system, or transmitted in any form or by any means, electronic, mechanical, photocopying, recording, scanning, or otherwise, except as permitted under Section 107 or 108 of the 1976 United States Copyright Act, without either the prior written permission of the Publisher, or authorization through payment of the appropriate per-copy fee to the Copyright Clearance Center, Inc., 222 Rosewood Drive, Danvers, MA 01923, (978) 750-8400, fax (978) 750-4470, or on the web at www.copyright.com. Requests to the Publisher for permission should be addressed to the Permissions Department, John Wiley & Sons, Inc., 111 River Street, Hoboken, NJ 07030, (201) 748-6011, fax (201) 748-6008, e-mail: permcoordinator@wiley.com.

Limit of Liability/Disclaimer of Warranty: While the publisher and author have used their best efforts in preparing this book, they make no representations or warranties with respect to the accuracy or completeness of the contents of this book and specifically disclaim any implied warranties of merchantability or fitness for a particular purpose. No warranty may be created or extended by sales representatives or written sales materials. The advice and strategies contained herein may not be suitable for your situation. You should consult with a professional where appropriate. Neither the publisher nor author shall be liable for any loss of profit or any other commercial damages, including but not limited to special, incidental, consequential, or other damages.

This publication is designed to provide accurate and authoritative information in regard to the subject matter covered. It is sold with the understanding that the publisher is not engaged in rendering professional services. If legal, accounting, medical, psychological or any other expert assistance is required, the services of a competent professional person should be sought.

Designations used by companies to distinguish their products are often claimed as trademarks. In all instances where John Wiley & Sons, Inc. is aware of a claim, the product names appear in initial capital or all capital letters. Readers, however, should contact the appropriate companies for more complete information regarding trademarks and registration.

For general information on our other products and services please contact our Customer Care Department within the U.S. at (800) 762-2974, outside the United States at (317) 572-3993 or fax (317) 572-4002.

Wiley also publishes its books in a variety of electronic formats. Some content that appears in print may not be available in electronic books.

Library of Congress Cataloging-in-Publication Data:

Handbook of psychology / Irving B. Weiner, editor-in-chief.
     p. cm.
     Includes bibliographical references and indexes.
     Contents: v. 1. History of psychology / edited by Donald K. Freedheim — v. 2. Research methods in psychology / edited by John A. Schinka, Wayne F. Velicer — v. 3. Biological psychology / edited by Michela Gallagher, Randy J. Nelson — v. 4. Experimental psychology / edited by Alice F. Healy, Robert W. Proctor — v. 5. Personality and social psychology / edited by Theodore Millon, Melvin J. Lerner — v. 6. Developmental psychology / edited by Richard M. Lerner, M. Ann Easterbrooks, Jayanthi Mistry — v. 7. Educational psychology / edited by William M. Reynolds, Gloria E. Miller — v. 8. Clinical psychology / edited by George Stricker, Thomas A. Widiger — v. 9. Health psychology / edited by Arthur M. Nezu, Christine Maguth Nezu, Pamela A. Geller — v. 10. Assessment psychology / edited by John R. Graham, Jack A. Naglieri — v. 11. Forensic psychology / edited by Alan M. Goldstein — v. 12. Industrial and organizational psychology / edited by Walter C. Borman, Daniel R. Ilgen, Richard J. Klimoski.
     ISBN 0-471-17669-9 (set) — ISBN 0-471-38320-1 (cloth : alk. paper : v. 1) — ISBN 0-471-38513-1 (cloth : alk. paper : v. 2) — ISBN 0-471-38403-8 (cloth : alk. paper : v. 3) — ISBN 0-471-39262-6 (cloth : alk. paper : v. 4) — ISBN 0-471-38404-6 (cloth : alk. paper : v. 5) — ISBN 0-471-38405-4 (cloth : alk. paper : v. 6) — ISBN 0-471-38406-2 (cloth : alk. paper : v. 7) — ISBN 0-471-39263-4 (cloth : alk. paper : v. 8) — ISBN 0-471-38514-X (cloth : alk. paper : v. 9) — ISBN 0-471-38407-0 (cloth : alk. paper : v. 10) — ISBN 0-471-38321-X (cloth : alk. paper : v. 11) — ISBN 0-471-38408-9 (cloth : alk. paper : v. 12)
     1. Psychology. I. Weiner, Irving B.

BF121.H1955 2003
150—dc21

2002066380

Printed in the United States of America.

10 9 8 7 6 5 4 3 2 1

Editorial Board

To our parents,

Hugh and Martha Reynolds

and

Joseph and Victoria Miller

and to our
former and current Teachers, Students, and Colleagues
who have continued to fuel and inspire
our desire for life-long learning.

William M. Reynolds, PhD
Department of Psychology
Humboldt State University

&

Gloria E. Miller, PhD
College of Education
University of Denver

Handbook of Psychology Preface

Psychology at the beginning of the twenty-first century has become a highly diverse field of scientific study and applied technology. Psychologists commonly regard their discipline as the science of behavior, and the American Psychological Association has formally designated 2000 to 2010 as the "Decade of Behavior." The pursuits of behavioral scientists range from the natural sciences to the social sciences and embrace a wide variety of objects of investigation. Some psychologists have more in common with biologists than with most other psychologists, and some have more in common with sociologists than with most of their psychological colleagues. Some psychologists are interested primarily in the behavior of animals, some in the behavior of people, and others in the behavior of organizations. These and other dimensions of difference among psychological scientists are matched by equal if not greater heterogeneity among psychological practitioners, who currently apply a vast array of methods in many different settings to achieve highly varied purposes.

Psychology has been rich in comprehensive encyclopedias and in handbooks devoted to specific topics in the field. However, there has not previously been any single handbook designed to cover the broad scope of psychological science and practice. The present 12-volume *Handbook of Psychology* was conceived to occupy this place in the literature. Leading national and international scholars and practitioners have collaborated to produce 297 authoritative and detailed chapters covering all fundamental facets of the discipline, and the *Handbook* has been organized to capture the breadth and diversity of psychology and to encompass interests and concerns shared by psychologists in all branches of the field.

Two unifying threads run through the science of behavior. The first is a common history rooted in conceptual and empirical approaches to understanding the nature of behavior. The specific histories of all specialty areas in psychology trace their origins to the formulations of the classical philosophers and the methodology of the early experimentalists, and appreciation for the historical evolution of psychology in all of its variations transcends individual identities as being one kind of psychologist or another. Accordingly, Volume 1 in the *Handbook* is devoted to the history of psychology as it emerged in many areas of scientific study and applied technology.

A second unifying thread in psychology is a commitment to the development and utilization of research methods suitable for collecting and analyzing behavioral data. With attention both to specific procedures and their application in particular settings, Volume 2 addresses research methods in psychology.

Volumes 3 through 7 of the *Handbook* present the substantive content of psychological knowledge in five broad areas of study: biological psychology (Volume 3), experimental psychology (Volume 4), personality and social psychology (Volume 5), developmental psychology (Volume 6), and educational psychology (Volume 7). Volumes 8 through 12 address the application of psychological knowledge in five broad areas of professional practice: clinical psychology (Volume 8), health psychology (Volume 9), assessment psychology (Volume 10), forensic psychology (Volume 11), and industrial and organizational psychology (Volume 12). Each of these volumes reviews what is currently known in these areas of study and application and identifies pertinent sources of information in the literature. Each discusses unresolved issues and unanswered questions and proposes future directions in conceptualization, research, and practice. Each of the volumes also reflects the investment of scientific psychologists in practical applications of their findings and the attention of applied psychologists to the scientific basis of their methods.

The *Handbook of Psychology* was prepared for the purpose of educating and informing readers about the present state of psychological knowledge and about anticipated advances in behavioral science research and practice. With this purpose in mind, the individual *Handbook* volumes address the needs and interests of three groups. First, for graduate students in behavioral science, the volumes provide advanced instruction in the basic concepts and methods that define the fields they cover, together with a review of current knowledge, core literature, and likely future developments. Second, in addition to serving as graduate textbooks, the volumes offer professional psychologists an opportunity to read and contemplate the views of distinguished colleagues concerning the central thrusts of research and leading edges of practice in their respective fields. Third, for psychologists seeking to become conversant with fields outside their own specialty and for persons outside of psychology seeking information about psychological matters, the *Handbook* volumes serve as a reference source for expanding their knowledge and directing them to additional sources in the literature.

The preparation of this *Handbook* was made possible by the diligence and scholarly sophistication of the 25 volume editors and co-editors who constituted the Editorial Board. As Editor-in-Chief, I want to thank each of them for the pleasure of their collaboration in this project. I compliment them for having recruited an outstanding cast of contributors to their volumes and then working closely with these authors to achieve chapters that will stand each in their own right as

valuable contributions to the literature. I would like finally to express my appreciation to the editorial staff of John Wiley and Sons for the opportunity to share in the development of this project and its pursuit to fruition, most particularly to Jennifer Simon, Senior Editor, and her two assistants, Mary Porterfield and Isabel Pratt. Without Jennifer's vision of the *Handbook* and her keen judgment and unflagging support in producing it, the occasion to write this preface would not have arrived.

IRVING B. WEINER
Tampa, Florida

Volume Preface

SCOPE AND SIGNIFICANCE OF THIS VOLUME

This volume of the *Handbook of Psychology* is dedicated to the field of educational psychology. Educational psychology is focused largely on the application of psychological principles to the study of human learning and development in educational settings. Educational psychology traces its roots to the beginnings of psychology as a field of study in the United States with the pioneering work of William James. Research in the field of educational psychology has progressed over the past century with an explosion of research across numerous domains of this field in the last quarter of the twentieth century.

A careful reading of this volume will show that researchers in educational psychology are actively engaged in studying the complexity of learning and learner characteristics across multiple systems and sociocultural settings. We suggest that more than any other area of psychology, the field of educational psychology has had a major impact in helping to prepare children for living in an increasingly diverse, global world of rapid change. Educational psychologists over the last two decades have contributed to a burgeoning literature on individual and internal cognitive processes related to learning. Along with our greater knowledge of cognitive processes and learner characteristics has come a concomitant increase in our understanding of the roles played by culture, ethnicity, and gender and how learning is affected by the social context of the classroom. This has led to an improved science of instruction, assessment, evaluation, and how we train our teachers, as well as to a more comprehensive view of the complex role of teachers, the instructional process, and factors across home and school environments that lead to behavioral, academic, and social success of a diverse population of students.

The chapter topics selected for inclusion in this volume reflect the field's unique concern for and methods of studying human learning and development in educational settings. The structure and organization of this book provide a window on the current thinking about individual learners, instructional strategies, the dynamics of classroom interaction, social structures that operate in educational settings, and educational programs for exceptional learners. We have included chapters that provide a glimpse of how the field of educational psychology has impacted and will continue to impact reforms in teacher preparation, educational research, and policy. The five major sections of this volume cover significant cognitive contributions to learning, development, and instruction; what we know about sociocultural, instructional, and relational processes critical to successful learning; the design of effective curriculum applications; and models of teacher preparation and educational research that will influence educational reform in the future.

The chapters in this volume include many of the core domains of research that have fostered and are currently fostering major advances in the knowledge base and the basic and applied endeavors in the field of educational psychology. Several conscious editorial decisions were made to shape the scope of this volume in order to minimize overlap with other volumes in this Handbook. First, although prior handbooks in the field of educational psychology have provided one or more chapters on the historical precedents that have shaped the field, such a chapter was omitted here because much of this content was included in Volume 1 of the Handbook, *History of Psychology*. Similarly, although educational research and assessment chapters are typically included more comprehensively within handbooks representing the field of educational psychology, only one chapter was included here because these topics are extensively covered in two other Handbook volumes: Volume 2, *Research Methods in Psychology*, and Volume 10, *Assessment Psychology*, respectively. Finally, developmental issues, especially as they relate to issues of individual learning, interpersonal relationships, and schooling are embedded within and across many of the chapters included in this volume. This helped to lessen the overlap with coverage of normal development topics that are the focus of Volume 6, *Developmental Psychology*. Limited coverage was given also to areas associated with child and adolescent psychological disorders and mental health and to wellness and prevention issues pertinent to creating safe and healthy school and community environments. These topics are covered in Volume 8, *Clinical Psychology*, and Volume 9, *Health Psychology*, respectively.

The field of educational psychology has a rich heritage. As the chapters in this book attest, the field had shown a near exponential growth in the examination of complex learning; cognitive, instructional, sociocultural, motivational, and individual differences; and learner characteristics. The sum total of this research contribution to the understanding of learners and the instructional and learning process represents an important application of psychology to education and the needs of the learner.

The chapters in this book illustrate the dynamic nature of educational psychology as a field of scientific inquiry within psychology. Although we often conceptualize educational psychology as an applied field of study, what can be more basic than understanding the process by which we learn? This book examines what we know about learners in classroom settings—their cognitions, behaviors, interactions with teachers and peers, and the context of learning—as well as learner characteristics, systems of motivation and self-regulation, and other variables that inform us as to the complex interactions that are part of the learning process.

OUR INTERESTS IN THE FIELD OF EDUCATIONAL PSYCHOLOGY AND ACKNOWLEDGMENTS

W. M. R.

My interest in educational psychology dates back to my undergraduate days in the early 1970s at the University of California at Berkeley where faculty such as Read Tuddenham, Arthur Jensen, and Marjorie Honzik stimulated my interest in the study of intelligence, cognitive assessment, and individual differences. During this time I was active as a volunteer and later student director of the Richmond Project, a UC Berkeley student organization in which students worked as volunteer aides in the Richmond, California, public schools. For nearly two years I spent one to two days a week at Cortez School, an inner-city school where Mary Carbone, a progressive third-grade teacher, allowed me to work with small groups of children and apply what I was learning in my psychology courses to the elementary school classroom. This interest in the field continued when I was a graduate student in the Department of Educational Psychology at the University of Oregon, where Richard Rankin provided guidance in understanding the psychometric foundations underlying the evaluation of intelligence and the application of scientific methods to the study of individual differences and encouraged my teaching the graduate course titled "Mental Testing." This experience, along with mentoring and coursework in clinical psychology provided by Norm Sundberg, additional course work in psychometrics and test construction with Lew Goldberg, and collaboration in test construction with Paul Raffeld and Larry Irvin, triggered a switch in graduate-school goals from a career as a school psychologist to that of a university professor.

My subsequent employment in the field of educational psychology has stretched over nearly a quarter of a century as a faculty member in departments of educational psychology at the State University of New York at Albany (1976–1980), the University of Wisconsin-Madison (1980–1991), where 20 years ago I was pleased to serve on the dissertation committee of my esteemed coeditor, and the University of British Columbia (1991–2000).

I wish to acknowledge the influence and example provided by my colleagues and friends in the Department of Educational Psychology at the UW-Madison during my years of teaching there. The intellectual stimulation and positive interactions provided by my colleagues and the graduate students in the educational psychology department at UW-Madison were an unlisted job benefit. I am exceptionally pleased that several of these colleagues and good friends—Joel Levin, Tom Kratochwill, Rich Lehrer, Chris McCormick, and Mike Pressley (who spent many summers working at UW-Madison during this time)—have contributed directly to this volume. I am also pleased that a number of my colleagues from the University of British Columbia, including Linda Siegel, Hillel Goelman, Ricki Goldman (now at New Jersey Institute of Technology), and Marion Porath, also contributed to chapters for this volume.

I especially wish to thank my coeditor, Gloria Miller, my colleague of over 20 years, for her excellent work on this volume and her friendship these many years. Although there is an order to the editorship of this volume on the title page, equal editorship should be understood. Gloria was instrumental in maintaining work on this volume during the months that I was out due to serious illness.

Finally, and most important, I wish to thank and acknowledge the meaningful and much appreciated support of my wife Margaret, a very special person who was understanding of the many late nights spent working on this project, and to my parents for their example and guidance and who amazingly continue to be survivors.

G. E. M.

I began my undergraduate program in the early 1970s as a biology major but very quickly became enthralled by the field of psychology after my first introductory class. I can still recall my fascination and the intellectual stimulation that accompanied my learning about the exciting new advances in learning, cognition, and behavioral neuroscience, which was still in its infancy. My dissecting skills as a biology major led to an invitation to become a psychology "rat" lab assistant. I worked with an older professor who, while trained in Skinnerian conditioning techniques, was more interested in neuroanatomy, brain chemistry, and the effects of environmental learning conditions on brain functioning. The field of medicine and neuropsychology appeared as my niche—that was, until I took my first (of many) summer jobs working as a counselor at a camp for children with Down's syndrome and other forms of mental retardation. From then on my interests leaned further away from basic neuroanatomy and more toward applied research in cognition. After three years of teaching reading to students with severe learning disabilities, my interest in learning and development drew me to reexamine the different graduate program opportunities within psychology. How happy I was to "discover" that in fact there actually was a domain of study called educational psychology that was so closely aligned to my applied instructional research interests.

I had the great fortune of entering the field of educational psychology at a most dynamic and opportune time. The earlier passage of the federal law PL 99-142, which guaranteed free and appropriate education to all handicapped students, ensured that funding for educational research was at an all-time high in the late 1970s. As a graduate student at the University of Wisconsin, I worked closely with some of the top educational researchers of the time on several nationally funded projects housed at the Wisconsin Educational Research Center. Through the excellent research mentorship of professors Joel Levin and Steve Yussen, I developed a strong empirical and theoretical foundation in human learning and development, which contributed to my eventual switch into the closely related field of school psychology.

I would like to thank the many individuals who have contributed significantly to my own learning and development over the years. Although it is not possible due to space limitations to mention everyone here, my list would include many of my K–12 teachers, university professors, and peers, all of whom have been skillful mentors, dynamic instructors, patient collaborators, and steady influences during my quest to apply educational psychology theory to benefit students and teachers.

I would not be where I am today without the total support and affection of my deceased parents. And to my spouse, thank you Joseph—you have added depth and breadth to each and every day. I also want to thank my daughter, Erica, for understanding and accepting the many long evenings and weekends when Mom was back at work—yet again—and so missed the hustle and bustle of our evening goodnight routines. I am certain that the work highlighted here will touch your life and others after you in many as-yet-unforeseen ways.

A special thanks goes to my colleague and coeditor, William (Bill) Reynolds, who honored me with the invitation to collaborate on this exciting project. Finally, I would like to acknowledge several colleagues who provided excellent critical yet constructive feedback during the preparation of this volume: Martin L. Tomabari, University of Denver, Christine B. McCormick, University of New Mexico, and Joseph M. Czajka, Personnel Department for the State of Colorado.

W. M. R. and G. E. M.

It is an honor and a pleasure for us to acknowledge the significant and meaningful contributions of the authors of chapters in this book. Through their own busy schedules, family and personal illness, requests for revisions, and other unforeseen events that impacted our lives, the contributors have been wonderful to work with and magnanimous in their time, effort, and scholarship in creating this book. Their work is a reflection of the best in the field and will be instrumental in establishing the important role of educational psychologists in the next century. To our chapter authors, you have our sincere thanks and appreciation.

A most important acknowledgement and note of appreciation goes Dr. Irving Weiner, Editor-in-Chief of the *Handbook of Psychology*. The completion of this enormous undertaking was facilitated greatly by his exceptional editorial leadership. We have never experienced the level of support, continued guidance, effort, and organization as that presented by Irv toward the realization of this Handbook. We also wish to thank the staff at John Wiley & Sons, and in particular Jennifer Simon—their great support and assistance helped to make this book possible.

WILLIAM M. REYNOLDS
GLORIA E. MILLER

Contents

PART ONE
INTRODUCTION

PART TWO
COGNITIVE CONTRIBUTIONS TO LEARNING, DEVELOPMENT, AND INSTRUCTION

PART THREE
SOCIOCULTURAL, INSTRUCTIONAL, AND RELATIONAL PROCESSES

PART FOUR
CURRICULUM APPLICATIONS

PART FIVE
EXCEPTIONAL LEARNER PROGRAMS AND STUDENTS

PART SIX
EDUCATIONAL PROGRAM, RESEARCH, AND POLICY

Contributors

Catherine J. Andersen
Faculty of Education
University of British Columbia
Vancouver, British Columbia, Canada

James Anderson, PhD
Department of Language and Literacy Education
University of British Columbia
Vancouver, British Columbia, Canada

Kristen Bogner
Department of Educational Psychology
University of Minnesota
Minneapolis, Minnesota

Catherine Bohn
Department of Psychology
Notre Dame University
Notre Dame, Indiana

Anne Chamberlain
Success for All Foundation
Baltimore, Maryland

Sara Dolezal
Department of Psychology
Notre Dame University
Notre Dame, Indiana

Hillel Goelman, PhD
Department of Educational and Counseling Psychology
    and Special Education
Faculty of Education
University of British Columbia
Vancouver, British Columbia, Canada

Ricki Goldman-Segall, PhD
College of Computing Sciences
New Jersey Institute of Technology
Newark, New Jersey

Peter Gouzouasis, PhD
Department of Curriculum Studies
University of British Columbia
Vancouver, British Columbia, Canada

Frank M. Gresham, PhD
Graduate School of Education
University of California–Riverside
Riverside, California

Bridget Hamre
School Psychology Program
University of Virginia
Charlottesville, Virginia

Kass Hogan
Institute of Ecosystem Studies
Milbrook, New York

Eric A. Hurley, PhD
Teacher's College
Columbia University
New York, New York

Vera John-Steiner, PhD
Department of Language, Literacy, and Sociocultural Studies
University of New Mexico
Albuquerque, New Mexico

Maureen Kendrick, PhD
Department of Language and Literacy Education
University of British Columbia
Vancouver, British Columbia, Canada

Anna M. Kindler, PhD
Department of Curriculum Studies
University of British Columbia
Vancouver, British Columbia, Canada

Janice Koch, PhD
Special Programs in Mathematics Science
    and Technology
Hofstra University
Hempstead, New York

Jinyoung Koh
Department of Educational and Counseling Psychology
    and Special Education
University of British Columbia
Vancouver, British Columbia, Canada

Thomas R. Kratochwill, PhD
Department of Educational Psychology
University of Wisconsin–Madison
Madison, Wisconsin

Richard Lehrer, PhD
Department of Teaching and Learning
Peabody College
Vanderbilt University
Nashville, Tennessee

Richard Lesh
Mathematics and Science Center
School of Education
Purdue University
West Lafayette, Indiana

Joel R. Levin, PhD
Department of Educational Psychology
University of Arizona
Tucson, Arizona

Holbrook Mahn, PhD
Department of Language, Literacy, and Sociocultural Studies
University of New Mexico
Albuquerque, New Mexico

John W. Maxwell, MA
College of Education
University of British Columbia
Vancouver, British Columbia, Canada

Richard E. Mayer, PhD
Department of Psychology
University of California
Santa Barbara, California

Barbara L. McCombs, PhD
Human Motivation, Learning and Development Center
University of Denver Research Institute
Denver, Colorado

Christine B. McCormick, PhD
College of Education
University of New Mexico
Albuquerque, New Mexico

Gloria E. Miller, PhD
College of Education
University of Denver
Denver, Colorado

Lindsey Mohan
Department of Psychology
Notre Dame University
Notre Dame, Indiana

Angela M. O'Donnell
Department of Educational Psychology
Rutgers, The State University of New Jersey
New Brunswick, New Jersey

Paula Olszewski-Kubilius, PhD
Center for Talent Development
Northwestern University
Evanston, Illinois

Robert C. Pianta, PhD
Curry Programs in Clinical and School Psychology
University of Virginia
Charlottesville, Virginia

Paul R. Pintrich, PhD
Program in Education and Psychology
University of Michigan
Ann Arbor, Michigan

Marion Porath, PhD
Department of Educational and Counseling Psychology and Special Education
University of British Columbia
Vancouver, British Columbia, Canada

Michael Pressley, PhD
College of Education
Michigan State University

Lisa Raphael
Department of Psychology
Notre Dame University
Notre Dame, Indiana

Daniel J. Reschly, PhD
Department of Special Education
Vanderbilt University
Nashville, Tennessee

William M. Reynolds, PhD
Department of Psychology
Humboldt State University
Arcata, California

Alysia D. Roehrig
Department of Psychology
Notre Dame University
Notre Dame, Indiana

Dale H. Schunk, PhD
School of Education
University of North Carolina–Greensboro
Greensboro, North Carolina

Linda S. Siegel, PhD
Department of Educational and Counseling Psychology
   and Special Education
University of British Columbia
Vancouver, British Columbia, Canada

Robert E. Slavin, PhD
Center for Social Organization of Schools
Johns Hopkins University
Baltimore, Maryland

Robert J. Sternberg, PhD
Department of Psychology
Yale University
New Haven, Connecticut

Megan Stuhlman
School Psychology Program
University of Virginia
Charlottesville, Virginia

Hill M. Walker, PhD
Center on Human Development and Institute on Violence and
   Destructive Behavior
University of Oregon
Eugene, Oregon

Irving Weiner, PhD
University of South Florida
Tampa, Florida

Kathryn R. Wentzel, PhD
Human Development
University of Maryland
College Park, Maryland

Ruth Wharton-McDonald
Department of Education
University of New Hampshire
Durham, New Hampshire

Jennifer A. Whitcomb
College of Education
University of Colorado
Boulder, Colorado

Barry J. Zimmerman, PhD
Department of Psychology
City University of New York
New York, New York

PART ONE

INTRODUCTION

CHAPTER 1

Current Perspectives in Educational Psychology

WILLIAM M. REYNOLDS AND GLORIA E. MILLER

The field of educational psychology traces its roots to some of the major figures in psychology at the turn of the past century. William James at Harvard University is often associated with the founding of psychology in the United States with his influential books of the late 1800s. Other major theorists and thinkers that figure in the early history of the field of educational psychology include G. Stanley Hall, John Dewey, and Edward L. Thorndike. Hall, cofounder of the American Psychological Association and its first president, was a student of James. Dewey at the University of Chicago was one of Hall's students and introduced major educational reforms in the United States. Thorndike, whom we often associate with theories of intelligence and learning, was also one of James's students and went on to start the *Journal of Educational Psychology* in 1910. Similarly, the impact of Lewis Terman (Terman & Childs, 1912) on the field of educational psychology and the assessment of intelligence (as well as related areas

such as educational tracking) was monumental at that time and throughout much of the twentieth century.

Other influences on educational psychology, and its impact on the field of education, have been linked to European philosophers of the mid- and late nineteenth century. For example, the impact of Herbart on educational reforms and teacher preparation in the United States has been described by Hilgard (1996) in his history of educational psychology. Largely ignored by Western psychologists until the 1980s, the work of Russian psychologists in the early twentieth century—in particular the work of Lev Vygotsky (1978, 1926/ 1997)—also contributed to the field of educational psychology. As readers of this volume will find, the work and influence of Vygotsky permeate research in educational psychology in the United States at the end of the twentieth and into the twenty-first century.

This volume of the *Handbook of Psychology* does not delve into the historical foundations of educational psychology, but rather deals with exemplar research and practice domains of educational psychology in the latter part of the twentieth century, with a focus on research and trends that have promise as we begin the twenty-first century. Historical antecedents of this field of psychology are presented in volume 1 of this Handbook.

It is evident from the chapters in this volume that much of the research in educational psychology has been conducted in classroom settings. This research encompasses a broad range of related topics, including children's learning and abilities, classroom processes, and teacher effectiveness. Educational psychology has been described as a discipline uniquely focused upon "the systematic study of the individual in context" (Berliner & Calfee, 1996, p. 6). The long-term focus on the study of children in classroom situations assists in the direct translation of research to practice.

From a pedagogical perspective, educational psychology differs from most fields of psychology in that it is most often found as a separate department in universities and colleges. To some extent this reflects the diversity of research and academic domains within educational psychology, as well as the rich and applied nature of this field of study. Departments of educational psychology are most often found in colleges of education, and courses in educational psychology are typically required for students in teacher education programs and related majors.

The field of educational psychology has ties to many professional organizations and professional societies in the United States and other countries. In the United States, the two major organizations that represent the field of educational psychology are the American Psychological Association (APA) and the American Educational Research Association (AERA). In the APA, educational psychology has as its primary affiliation Division 15 (Educational Psychology) with secondary affiliations in Divisions 5 (Evaluation, Measurement, and Statistics), 7 (Developmental Psychology), and 16 (School Psychology). In the AERA, Division C (Learning and Instruction) largely represents educational psychology with additional representation in Division D (Measurement and Research Methodology), Division E (Counseling and Human Development), and Division H (School Evaluation and Program Development). We also note that a number of educational psychologists, including Lee Cronbach and Frank Farley, have served as president of both APA and AERA, with Cronbach also serving as president of the Psychometric Society. Other professional organizations that have substantial overlap with educational psychology include the International Reading Association, the Council for Exceptional Children, the National Association of School Psychologists, the Psychometric Society, the Society for Re-

search in Child Development, and the Society for Research on Adolescence.

Contemporary educational psychology encompasses a broad and complex array of topics, research, and social policies. Research in educational psychology is most often designed to provide insights into authentic educational problems, using empirical rather than normative or subjective judgments. The field of educational psychology—possibly more than any other—has been shaped by many multidisciplinary factors. The impact of the cognitive revolution, for example, has been broadened by incorporation of other subdisciplines, including sociology, linguistics, the sciences, philosophy, and the associated fields of psychology. The major focus of educational psychology, however, is on individuals and their development, especially within educational settings. Another important characteristic of the field of educational psychology is that issues of concern are not mutually exclusive and in fact tend to overlap and interrelate more than stand as isolated domains of knowledge.

The field of educational psychology includes a rich heritage in the domains of research design and methodology, including statistics and measurement. For most of the twentieth century, educational psychologists have contributed to enhancing statistical and measurement procedures. In the 1950s educational psychologists published two articles reporting on statistical and measurement procedures; these articles have become among the most frequently cited ones in psychology. Cronbach's (1951) classic paper on the internal structure of tests and the derivation of coefficient alpha as an internal measurement of reliability continues to be one of the most cited papers in the behavioral sciences and most used procedure for the measurement of test reliability. Henry Kaiser's (1958) dissertation in educational psychology at the University of California at Berkeley provided the basis for an orthogonal rotation procedure in factor analysis that he called varimax factor rotation, with various little jiffy procedures to follow. These are but two of the many statistical, measurement, and methodological contributions that have been and continue to be made to the fields of psychology and behavioral and social sciences by educational psychologists.

CURRENT PRESENTATIONS OF THE FIELD

A comprehensive review of major work across the field of educational psychology was presented in the publication entitled *Handbook of Educational Psychology,* edited by Berliner and Calfee in 1996. This influential handbook, sponsored by the APA division of Educational Psychology (Division 15), was commissioned to reflect the current state of the field up to the early 1990s. Berliner and Calfee provided a powerful synthesis of the scholarship that defined the scope and relevancy of educational psychology as a discipline up until this time. The major goals of this volume were to offer a vigorous defense of educational psychology as a discipline and to forward the distinctive viewpoints that educational psychologists maintain when explaining educational events. Chapters were organized to represent the major domains within the discipline. Authors were asked to discuss how coverage of these topics changed from 1970 to 1990 and to summarize significant changes in research design within the discipline. The following domains were covered: learning and transfer, motivation, physical and psychological development, intelligence, exceptionality, psychology of learning within subject matters, assessment, processes of teacher growth and development, the psychology underlying instructional strategies, educational technology, and the methodological, philosophical, and historical foundations of the field.

Several consistent conceptual threads ran through the majority of invited chapters. One was the critical paradigm shift from behaviorism to cognitive psychology that shaped the discipline over the period covered. Another commonality across topics was that this conceptual shift resulted in a vigorous debate regarding research methods. What has emerged is a greater range of analytical tools—a methodological pluralism marked by some promising new practices such as exploratory data analysis (Jaeger & Bond, 1996) and design experiments (Brown, 1992). In drawing conclusions about the field, Berliner and Calfee suggested that the discipline's bread-and-butter issues had not changed as dramatically as did the conceptual and methodological tools that educational psychologists employ to understand educational phenomena. They also concluded on a note of congratulatory celebration at what educational psychology as a discipline has contributed, and they looked optimistically to its future.

More recently, Pressley and Roehrig (2002) provided a synopsis of the major domains reflected in the field of educational psychology during the last 40 years. These researchers categorized all research articles published in the 1960–1961 and the 1997–1998 issues of the *Journal of Educational Psychology,* the leading journal serving the field. Domains of information reflected in three contemporary handbooks and textbooks were also categorized, and editorial board members of the *Journal of Educational Psychology* were surveyed for their opinions of texts and articles that had the most significant impact on the field. The consensus of these reviews is amazingly similar in that at least 11 consistent domains appear: cognition, learning, development, motivation, individual differences, teaching and instruction, classroom and sociocultural processes, social relations in education, psychological foundations of curriculum, educational technology, and educational research methods and assessment.

These authors also noted that behaviorism and then the cognitive revolution were two critical forces driving the field, with the former more prevalent before the 1960s and the latter dominating the last 40 years (Pressley & Roehrig, 2002). Many significant changes were noted that led up to this change, beginning with the idea that an internal processing system and internal mechanisms could be objectified and studied (Miller, Galanter, & Pribram, 1960, *Plans and the Structure of Behavior*) and followed by work centered on memory (Tulving & Donaldson, 1972), imagery (Levin, 1973; Paivio, 1971) and other learning processes (Rohwer, 1970; Schank & Abelson, 1977).

Instructional theory and innovations were impacted by Bruner's writings (1960, 1966), as well as the work of J. M. Hunt (1961) and J. Flavell (1963), who together with others (Brainerd, 1978; Inhelder, Sinclair, & Bovet, 1974) helped introduce and transform Piaget's ideas into work on children's thinking. Others' work was more directly linked to educational application, especially in regards to observational and social learning (Bandura, 1969; Rosenthal & Zimmerman, 1978), text comprehension (Anderson & Pearson, 1984; Kintsch, 1989), writing (Flower & Hayes, 1980), problem solving, and mathematics (Mayer, 1976; Polya, 1957; Schoenfeld, 1985).

Sociocultural and cross-cultural contexts were introduced as important factors influencing learning and cognition. Schooling and other critical contexts have been more prominent in the field since the pioneering work of Scribner and Cole (1981) in the 1980s and the influence of Vygotsky's work with the 1978 translation of *Mind in Society.* This work has helped to reconceptualize instruction and teacher training as well as related domains of cognitive psychology. It has moved the field from an individual focus to a broader interpersonal framework. Much of the current research reflects the idea that the child, adults, and the contexts surrounding an event are responsible for forwarding cognitive activity and building competence. These ideas have been inspired by Vygotskiian theory and have contributed to substantial reforms reshaping contemporary school environments. They have had a direct impact on the design of instruction and have had a profound influence on educational research innovation. The linkages between theory and teacher learning, teacher and student relations, and the social climate in classrooms have all become more significant domains of study within the field of educational psychology. We find it of interest to note the extensive citations to the work of Vygotsky across many of the chapters in this volume.

Theories of motivation and its effect on cognition, learning, and social relations have also been more prominent. Historically, the work in educational psychology was dominated by an emphasis on cognition; motivation was ignored. Recent work has pointed to the importance of motivational constructs that apply to all individuals and that can explain important individual differences in cognition. The seminal work of Bernard Weiner (1979) has been instrumental in promoting research that linked cognition and motivation. Ames in the early 1980s also helped connect goal theory with classroom performance (Ames, 1984; Ames & Archer, 1988); others have looked at classroom structures that make a difference in student performance and have refocused on educational motivation as a cognitive enterprise.

Over the past two decades, education and educational issues have dominated both state and national agendas. More federally funded studies of educational issues have been completed in the last 25 years than in any other period of history. It is no surprise that educational psychologists have been involved in or have directed many of these studies that have become a major force in crafting federal policies and legislation. For example, in the 1990s a group of psychologists who were members of the Division of Educational Psychology (Division 15) of the APA were instrumental in producing a collaborative document outlining critical learning principles for all students (*Learner-Centered Psychological Guidelines for School Redesign and Reform;* Lambert & McCombs, 1998). Barbara McCombs, one of the original editors of this publication, reviews in this volume the issues addressed in this document and the impact it has had on recent federal educational policy and reforms.

Distinctiveness of This Volume

Published early in the twenty-first century, this volume looks toward the new century and considers how the discipline of educational psychology will shape the next generation of learners and teachers. Three immediate contextual factors have begun to influence the evolving role of educational psychology in educational practice. First, the gossamer threads of the Internet, a symbol of the information age, will expand increasingly to reach all sectors of our society—in particular, education. Learners and teachers in the information age will more than ever need to be flexible, reflective, motivated learners. Second, in the next decade a significant number of individuals will go through formal teacher education and begin careers. How they use the knowledge, concepts, and methods of educational psychology as they engage in essential acts of teaching (Grant & Murray, 1999) will be critical.

Third, the policy community will have a powerful impact on the funding of research programs sponsored by both the federal government and foundations.

This volume builds upon the optimistic future that Berliner and Calfee (1996) foreshadowed regarding the discipline of educational psychology. Although their handbook provided a systematic overview of the field of educational psychology and legitimized the relevance of this distinct discipline, this volume seeks to highlight key concepts of ongoing research conducted at the turn of the twentieth century. A second goal of this volume is to identify more exclusively the key promising areas for continued research over the next two decades.

This volume both elaborates upon and departs from previous handbook domains. There are distinct overlaps in the following areas of cognition, learning, and motivation, and in reviews of applications of educational psychology to curriculum, classroom, and teaching processes and exceptional learners. We depart, however, in that our intent was to selectively focus on topics that have strongly influenced the field since the mid-1990s. We also choose to de-emphasize traditional school subject domains and instead selected four areas—early childhood, literacy, mathematics learning, and new technologies. These curriculum areas have not only increasingly taken the forefront in the quantity of research conducted, but they also have repeatedly been in the public and policy spotlight influencing many areas of school reform.

Another departure from prior handbooks is that we did not have a separate section or chapters in development or research methodologies because independent volumes in this handbook are devoted to these topics (see Vols. 2 and 6 in this Handbook). Instead, many of the authors here reviewed contemporary developmental findings and elaborated on contemporary research methodologies within their respective domains of study. A final distinct departure is that we have two chapters—rather than an entire section—focused on teaching and classroom processes; this is because this volume is one of a handbook that focuses on the field of psychology. We acknowledge the impact of educational psychology on teaching by including chapters on teaching processes and a more contemporary chapter on teacher learning and teacher education and preparation, which again are issues on whose policy educational psychology research may have a strong influence in the future.

Overview of This Volume

Five major domains of contemporary research in educational psychology are identified in this volume. Within the part entitled "Cognitive Contributions to Learning, Development, and Instruction," contributing authors focus on processes and factors affecting the learner and learning, including individual differences and contextual influences in intellectual processes, memory, metacognition, self-regulation, and motivation. The part entitled "Sociocultural, Instruction, and Relational Processes" emphasizes instructional, interpersonal, and relational processes between teachers and students in culturally situated settings for learning. The part entitled "Curriculum Applications" highlights psychological contributions to curriculum and instruction in early childhood, in literacy, in mathematics, and with new media technologies. The part entitled "Exceptional Learner Programs and Students" focuses on understanding the school-based and developmental needs of exceptional learners. Finally, the part entitled "Educational Program, Research, and Policy" presents current practices in teacher preparation and educational research, and it underscores the pressing need to transform the immense knowledge base established by educational psychology researchers into sound educational policy and reform in the future.

The authors of this volume were selected not only because they have made important and long-standing research contributions, but also because their work reflected the most current areas of research defining their respective fields of scientific inquiry within educational psychology. These authors demonstrate domain mastery by their ability to integrate and synthesize research as well as formulate meaningful directions and suggestions for further scientific study. Each of the chapters in this volume provides a unique examination of an important domain within educational psychology. Yet one finds significant communalities across chapters that highlight the connectedness and consistency of educational psychology as a field of study.

COGNITIVE CONTRIBUTIONS TO LEARNING, DEVELOPMENT, AND INSTRUCTION

The focus of this section is on cognitive processes within the learner and teacher, and it includes the development of such processes and developmental directions for future research. Developmental theory is not singled out here, because Volume 6 in this Handbook is dedicated exclusively to this topic. Prominent in this work is a focus on individual differences in intellectual processes, memory, metacognition, self-regulation, and motivation. The chapters in this section also exemplify the field of educational psychology by relating theory to instruction and factors affecting individual learners and teachers within classrooms.

Contemporary Theories of Intelligence

The field of educational psychology has a long history of research and interest in the theory and study of intelligence. In the early part of the twentieth century, the *Journal of Educational Psychology* was the primary scientific journal in this country for research on the study of intelligence. In addition to theories, a major emphasis in this field of inquiry was its measurement, which continues to occupy a significant place in the study of intelligence. Sternberg (this volume) reviews both classical and contemporary intelligence theories and their profound implications on practical life and societies. He critically evaluates classical intelligence theories that have had a strong impact on education and goes on to present challenges to these and to current conceptions of intelligence. Intelligence-related abilities permeate many areas of society. In the United States and many other Westernized nations, these are most visibly represented in a multitude of educational and occupational tests shown to relate to societal success. Competing views about the sorting influence of intelligence are presented. Sternberg concludes that societies often choose a similar array of criteria to sort people, but he cautions that such correlations may simply be an artifact of societally preferred groups rather than a result of some natural processes.

Sternberg describes the need for psychometrically sound measures of intelligence as a necessary prerequisite for the validation of theories of intelligence. A significant trend in the last two decades of the twentieth century has been the development of intelligence tests based on cognitive and information processing theories of intelligence. Literature is presented on implicit views of intelligence that have served as the basis for explicit conceptions and tests of intelligence. The early biological theories of Halstead (1951), Hebb (1949), and Luria (1980) are reviewed and contrasted with more contemporary biological findings and theories that are poised to have a substantial influence on psychometric work in the future.

Memory and Information Processes

In the 1950s, information processing theorists provided an alternative to behaviorism and offered a rebirth for cognitive psychology. Mayer (this volume) reviews the dominant influence of information processing theories of cognition over the past several decades. A major premise underlying information processing theory is that the human mind seeks to build and manipulate mental representations and that these cognitive processes can be accessed and studied through physiological responses—and more recently, by using introspective interviews and other learning-based observations. Work is reviewed that supports two contrasting views developed within an information-processing paradigm. Classical theorists use the computer-as-mind metaphor with ideas that the human mind is like a complex machine that can be captured through increasingly complex algorithms. Alternatively, constructivist theorists view the human mind as a place where learners actively build their own knowledge structures by integrating new information with the old (see chapter by Mayer in this volume). Each of these approaches has contributed to somewhat independent streams of research for analyzing fundamental cognitive processes, characterizing key types of mental representations, and proposing integrative systems of learning. Nevertheless, work within each of these paradigms reveals that meaningful learning is a generative process in which the learner must actively engage in cognitive processing rather than passively receive or store information (Wittrock, 1990). The components and underlying assumptions of a comprehensive representative model of information processing are presented. Finally, information-processing contributions are reviewed across three content areas—reading, writing, and mathematics learning—and future implications of this work are outlined.

Self-Regulation and Learning

Schunk and Zimmerman (this volume) discuss the role of self-generated or self-directed activities that students use during learning. These notions strongly suggest that students are actively constructing and exercising control over their learning and social goals. Five theoretical perspectives are reviewed that have characterized work within this area: operant theory, information processing theory, developmental theory, social constructivist theory, and social cognitive theory. Research to support the role of self-regulatory processes is reviewed, as is a well-documented intervention that has been successfully linked to improvements in self-regulation in a variety of learners and across different learning contexts. It is of interest to note that the vast majority of the research presented in this chapter focuses on the examination of psychological constructs within the context of the school classroom. The importance of self-regulation in the learning enterprise is presented and reinforces the critical application of educational psychology toward understanding how children learn and how we can enhance the learning process.

Metacognition and Learning

McCormick (this volume) reviews work focused exclusively on metacognition and learning. First, various historical definitions of metacognition are reviewed and contrasted with the more precise definitions currently in use. Clear distinctions are made between metacognition and self-regulation. Metacognition is viewed as one aspect of the larger concept of self-regulation. The latter field of inquiry and its relation to learning is examined by Schunk and Zimmerman elsewhere in this volume. Theoretical issues that have driven researchers over the years are presented, as well as the current unresolved debates. Research paradigms used to assess such abilities are reviewed, including feeling of knowing, pretest judgments, and judgments after retesting. An argument is made that work in metacognition is best viewed as a bridge between theory and practice. Much of the empirical work in this area has been conducted with authentic academic tasks such as reading, writing, and problem solving in science and math.

Motivation and Learning

Pintrich (this volume) presents a comprehensive review of the substantial advances in our scientific knowledge of motivational constructs and their impact on student cognition and learning, especially in classroom settings. Rather than review separate motivational theories, four general outcomes and three key theoretical constructs that cut across theories are highlighted to build a more integrative synthesis of current work in the field. The four motivational outcomes include (a) why individuals choose one activity over another (e.g., to do school work or to play with friends); (b) why individuals become more or less involved in a task either overtly (e.g., taking more detailed notes) or covertly (e.g., using more self-regulation strategies); (c) why individuals persist on a task or are willing to try hard; and (d) what motivational constructs contribute to learning and achievement. The three key constructs are organized into expectancy, value, and affective components of motivation. *Expectancy components,* defined as beliefs about one's ability to control, perform, or accomplish a task, are substantial predictors of learning and achievement outcomes. Three subtypes have been studied: capacity-personal, strategy/means-ends, and outcome-control expectancies. Most research evidence points to the importance of outcome-control expectancies—in particular, self-efficacy—and their link to later learning and achievement. *Value components* are defined as goal orientations or cognitive representations of the purpose of a task as well as task value beliefs about the importance of a task, one's interest in a task, and one's ideas about the ultimate utility of a task. *Affective components* are defined as general feelings of self and one's emotional reactions to a task that affect cognitive resources and performance.

INSTRUCTIONAL, INTERPERSONAL, AND RELATIONAL PROCESSES

Contemporary educational psychology draws substantial inspiration and guidance—directly and indirectly—from social learning theory and in particular from the work of Bandura (1969, 1977, 1982). This work reflects a strong sociocultural perspective in which the emphasis is on interpersonal, motivational, and social processes that occur in classrooms and other culturally situated settings. Work reviewed here focuses on group structures, cooperative learning, and interpersonal relationships, and on the role of personal motivation, goals, and other internalized social processes that contribute to academic, behavioral, and social adaptation. The impact of gender is explored, as is the question of how instruction is affected by important sociocultural contexts.

Sociocultural Contexts for Teaching and Learning

Social and cultural contexts are important considerations for the understanding of learning and development. The influence of Vygotsky in the latter part of the twentieth century has provided a scaffold for the development of theories of language acquisition, writing, assessment, concept formation, and other domains of learning. Vygotsky's work and that of other Russian psychologists such as Luria in the early part of the twentieth century created a major paradigm shift in Western psychology in the 1960s and 1970s (Luria, 1961; Vygotsky, 1962, 1978). This body of work—in particular, the concepts of internal dialogue and the verbal mediation of behavior—greatly influenced the field of learning and also the emerging field of cognitive behavior modification, as evidenced in the work of Donald Meichenbaum in the development of self-instructional training (1977).

John-Steiner, one of the original editors of Vygotsky's (1978) major work *Mind in Society: The Development of Higher Psychological Processes,* and her colleague Mahn (this volume) describe the social and cultural contexts for instruction and learning. They discuss sociocultural approaches in educational psychology with an emphasis on the contributions of Vygotsky and his notions of the individual in the creation of contexts and the internalization of person and environment interactions. The broad interdisciplinary applications of Vygotsky's work and theories are presented in this chapter as John-Steiner and Mahn clarify the philosophical underpinnings of this framework and how it addresses a range of learning outcomes. The breadth of Vygotsky's ideas and their implications for understanding the context and processes of learning are presented, along with the nature of

his dialectic method as applied to cognitive processes. The role of Vygotsky's work and theories for educational reform, including children with special needs, assessment—in particular, dynamic assessment—and collaborative efforts in education are also highlighted.

Teaching Processes in Elementary and Secondary Education

There is little doubt that teachers in most cases play the ultimate role in the education of children, a responsibility of enormous importance. For the education of young people, teachers are expected to be experts in classroom management, curriculum, and instruction; in creating classroom environments that are physically and psychologically motivating; and in transmitting knowledge. Pressley and his colleagues (this volume) review and synthesize the research on what makes effective teachers. Investigations of teaching processes provide us with information on what makes effective teachers.

Pressley et al. examine the research and evidence on teachers' direct transmission of information to students—what we traditionally view as teacher-directed, didactic instruction—along with teacher questioning, explanations, and interactions and feedback to students. An alternative to this approach is constructivist teaching processes, including procedures that focus on discovery learning (pure and guided), problem solving, and related activities that challenge and actively engage students in the learning enterprise. There has been great debate in American education regarding the efficacy of direct transmission versus constructivist teaching processes, and Pressley et al. note how these two approaches can be melded to provide a scaffold of instruction and student learning.

Critical to teaching and learning outcomes is the motivation of learners. The manner in which teachers motivate students to engage in learning-related activities is an important variable in determining teacher effectiveness. Pressley et al. note such factors as rewarding achievement, encouraging moderate risk taking, focusing on self-improvement rather than performance comparisons with others, encouraging cooperative group learning, increasing curiosity and cognitive challenge, creating interesting learning tasks and materials, increasing attributions to effort rather than ability, reinforcing the modifiability of intelligence or cognitive ability, bolstering students' self-efficacy for academics, and enhancing students' healthy sense of self. Research shows that effective teachers are active in their promotion of student and classroom motivation (Brophy, 1986).

To better understand the teaching process, Pressley et al. describe how research in the latter part of the twentieth century has provided information on teachers' thinking as they teach, on their knowledge, and on their beliefs about teaching. This research base allows for the examination of factors related to expert teaching. As pointed out by Pressley and colleagues, teachers' behaviors in creating physical and psychological classroom environments that assist in motivating students and provide for good classroom management are characteristics of highly effective teachers. Pressley et al.'s review serves to provide hypotheses as to the meaningful differences between typical and excellent teachers and at the same time acknowledges the immense challenges faced by teachers, particularly as they begin the teaching profession.

Cooperative Learning

After reviewing literature conducted over the past 30 years, Slavin, Hurley, and Chamberlain (this volume) present an integrative model of the relationships among variables involved in cooperative learning. These researchers move beyond a review that establishes the effectiveness of cooperative learning to focus more specifically on conditions under which it is optimally effective. Slavin et al. review recent empirical work on cooperative learning directed at identifying critical factors that motivate and impede learning outcomes. The work in this area primarily has been framed within four theoretical perspectives: motivational, social cohesion, cognitive, and developmental perspectives. Critical group processes, teaching practices, or classroom structures are evaluated within each of these frameworks. Although several comparative studies have been conducted to contrast alternative theoretical formats of cooperative learning or to isolate essential elements, this work has been hindered due to the variety of factors examined and the different measures, durations, and subjects that have been used.

Much of the research conducted over the last decade has focused on how to structure interactions and incentives among students in cooperative groups. One consistent finding is that cooperative learning is most effective when groups are recognized or rewarded for individual as well as group learning goals (Slavin, 1995). Although the specific forms and means of implementing group incentives and individual accountability have varied widely across studies, evidence overwhelmingly points to the need to include both to obtain the greatest long-standing impact on students' learning. Slavin et al. also point out work that demonstrates the times when group goals and individual accountability may not be necessary. For example, when students are working collaboratively on higher level cognitive tasks that lack a single right answer, when students are already strongly motivated to perform (as in voluntarily formed study groups), or when the tasks are so structured that learning is likely to result simply from participating. Another context in which group goals and individual accountability may not be essential is during communal learning groups composed of homogeneous ethnic minority members, possibly because of an already high level of interdependence functioning within African American communities (Hurley, 1997).

Relationships Between Teachers and Children

Pianta, Hamre, and Stuhlman (this volume) assert that classroom research on teacher processes and teacher-student relationships has moved far beyond its original focus on teachers' and students' expectations and instructional interactions, classroom discipline and management, socially mediated learning, school belonging and caring, and teacher support. They point out that many of these topics have roots in many sources and disciplines, a sampling of which include the original work of Brophy and Good (1974) on teacher-child interactions, Rosenthal (1969) on classroom interpersonal perceptions and expectations that influence student performance, Vygotsky (1978) on socially constructed development, Bronfenbrenner and Morris (1998) on the influence of multiple contexts on development, Bowlby (1969) and Ainsworth, Blehar, Waters, and Wall (1978) on attachment processes between parents and children, the clinical work investigating marital and familial processes (Bakeman & Gottman, 1986), the role of adult relationships in promoting resiliency (Pederson, Faucher, & Eaton, 1978; Werner & Smith, 1980), and finally the longitudinal contributions of developmental systems theory and longitudinal studies of health and psychopathology (Loeber, 1990; Rutter, 1987).

As conceptualized by Pianta and colleagues (this volume), child-teacher relationships not only involve the study of verbal and nonverbal communication processes for exchanging information between two individuals, but also embody biologically determined characteristics and attributes of the individuals involved (i.e., age, gender, ethnicity, temperament, developmental history, and experience), individuals' views of the relationship and their own and the other's role in the relationship, and the external systems within which these interactions are embedded. Educational psychologists have been instrumental in demonstrating that such relationships are a central school-based relational resource that has a positive and reciprocal effect on students' learning, achievement, enjoyment, involvement, and school retention as well as on teachers' sense of well-being, efficacy, job satisfaction, and retention in teaching (Pianta, 1999). Pianta et al.'s chapter reviews current work on teacher-student relationships that has evolved into a dynamic field of study based on developmental systems theory (Lerner, 1998) in which relationships are viewed as part of holistic, multilevel interrelated units functioning reciprocally to motivate successful adaptation and developmental change.

School Adjustment

Wentzel (this volume) has reviewed work demonstrating the importance of social competencies to overall school adjustment and the interrelationships of social, motivational, and academic success. An ecological approach is adopted as a framework to understand how students formulate goals that result in social integration (group cohesion, functioning, responsiveness) and personal social competence (self-determination, persistence, inquisitiveness, and other prosocial skills). She reviews research on school adjustment—defined by motivation of social goal pursuit, behavioral competence, and interpersonal relationships—and focuses on how these assets form a profile of interrelated competencies that are directly related to academic achievement. Research has demonstrated that socially adjusted individuals are able to set and achieve personally valued goals that are sanctioned by the larger community as relevant and desirable. Educational psychology researchers have been at the forefront of work identifying what motivates and mediates such personal goals, the impact of these on personal and school adjustment, and the classroom-school factors that support and promote the expression of these attributes (this volume). Critical factors related to social and school adjustment have been identified. In one study, teachers described ideal students as having socially integrative (helpfulness, sharing), learning (persistence, intrinsic motivation, interest), and performance characteristics (completing assignments, organization).

Gender Issues in the Classroom

Koch (this volume) reviews important literature on gendered socialization of students as they participate in the social and academic culture of the classroom. She suggests that work on social relations in classrooms has led to contemporary efforts to examine curricula through the eyes of gender. She reviews classroom research, practices, and policies that differentiate gender experiences in ways that limit opportunity for females and males in the classroom.

Researchers have shown that the socialization of boys and girls promotes gender stereotypes that in many cases are supported by classroom practices. The work of educational psychologists and others has begun to address the content of the formal curriculum, classroom interaction, and classroom climates that promote gender equity. She explores the attributes of gender-equitable classrooms that foster equitable learning environments for males and females; she also points to the need for a heightened awareness of the impact of gender issues on student learning and self-concept. *Gender equity* in education refers to educational practices that are fair and just toward both females and males. This work has led to improvements in classroom learning environments and has led to ideas about how to change teachers' attitudes through increased awareness of hidden curriculum and gender-differentiated instruction. Researchers have begun to bypass the oversimplification that sometimes has characterized the field of gender equity. Research on equitable environments seeks to uncover the differential needs and social issues behind gendered behavior. Rather than simply advocating equal treatment, equitable interventions are designed to encourage all children to see themselves as contributors to the class environments. The result may in fact lead to the offering of different experiences to girls and boys in the effort to level the playing field for all students.

CURRICULUM APPLICATIONS

Educational psychology has always concentrated on the improvement of educational programs and instruction through the application of psychological theories, processes, and research. In this manner, teaching and curriculum materials and technologies are informed by educational psychologists. Work reported in this section centers on the psychological contributions to curriculum and instruction in early childhood, literacy, mathematics, and computers; it also addresses new media and technologies for learning. Rather than cover all of the traditional school subject curriculum domains, we selected four broad areas in which educational psychologists have had a major and continuing influence over the past two decades. These selected areas have received increasing attention by politicians due to societal pressures and have taken the forefront both in the quantity of research conducted and in their influence on key areas of school reform.

Early Childhood Education

According to Goelman and his coauthors (this volume), research in early childhood education has grown dramatically over the last two decades in concert with our increased knowledge about the significance of the birth-to-five period; the fact that there has not been a chapter on early childhood education in any prior handbook of psychology was duly noted. The authors provide a brief but important overview of how historical issues in early childhood education have set the stage for contemporary research. Research in early childhood education has contributed to a new understanding of preschool learning and development and the settings in which young children participate. Important discoveries are reviewed about the role of play in all aspects of development, likely progressions in play, and the relationship of play behavior to a multitude of interrelated skills such as communication, artistic and musical ability, and early literacy and mathematical skills. Contemporary use of art, play, and music in early childhood education is reviewed, including how teachers might use play to create an environment to nurture and enhance children's mental and moral development (originally proposed by Dewey in 1916). In the first section, the authors review important research contributions in learning and teaching across the domains of play, art, music and literacy. In the second section, issues of diversity and cultural pluralism and their impact on the field of early education are explored through a review of literature associated with giftedness, language learning, attachment, and temperament. The final section is devoted to an integrative model that reflects current thinking about best practices in compensatory education and early child care programs.

Psychology of Literacy and Literacy Instruction

Perhaps no other single educational issue has received as much national and international attention as literacy development. Pressley (this volume) reviews this enormous multidimensional domain of literature by focusing on issues most directly influenced and studied by psychologists and educational psychologists. He directs readers who want a broadly informed opinion and more historical background to several comprehensive volumes on reading research. Pressley emphasizes replicable findings that have been complemented by descriptive methods of classroom practices and reviews key findings beginning in late infancy through early adulthood. With regard to early literacy, it is now widely acknowledged that a great deal of learning occurs before children enter school. Key issues associated with the preschool years include the study of early adult-child interactions that promote emergent literacy and the study of phonemic awareness (i.e., the awareness that words are composed of sounds blended together). Research has convincingly pointed to early verbal interactions, shared reading events, and phonemic awareness as important prerequisites to learning to read and write. Psychologists also have been at the forefront of addressing early word recognition processes and researching the benefits of different methods for teaching beginning readers how to sound out and spell words.

Descriptive classroom studies by Pressley and others have lead to enormous insights about how exceptional primary teachers motivate, instruct, and support continued progress in literacy. Significant progress has been made in understanding basic reading comprehension processes with concomitant research on specific approaches to stimulate fluency, improve vocabulary, and foster the use of critical comprehension strategies before, during, and after reading. Research parallels to writing development and instruction also are reviewed. Finally, work on adult literacy difficulties in word analysis, comprehension, and writing are presented as well as current findings on effective adult literacy instruction. Debates exist as to whether and how our increased knowledge about literacy should be translated to instructional contexts and into educational policy. Notwithstanding these debates and concerns, contemporary findings regarding early, beginning, and advanced literacy skills have fundamentally altered the way that reading and writing instruction is conceived.

Mathematics Learning

We often take precursors to the development of mathematics and mathematics learning for granted. The psychology of mathematics learning is a broad field of study. To provide a meaningful discourse on some of the major developments and research in this field, Lehrer and Lesh (this volume) systematically examine the development argument and inscription as these domains relate to mathematics learning. From these basic structures, the authors examine how generalizations evolve in the areas of geometry-measurement and mathematical modeling—the former drawing from the related domain of spatial visualization and the latter from an area of needed research in mathematics learning and education. To support their treatise, Lehrer and Lesh utilize cognitive and sociocultural perspectives to examine research and theory in these fields of scientific inquiry.

Lehrer and Lesh formulate and present rationale that describes the development of conversational argument, including such concepts as analogy and the development of relations, conditions, and reasoning and how these provide routes to the formulation of mathematical argument as well as mathematical proof. The role of inscription systems or marks on paper and other media is described as a mediator to mathematics learning. From a developmental perspective, the growth of inscription ability and skills allows for the differentiation of numbers from letters, forms, maps, diagrams, and other aspects of symbolic representation.

Geometry as a spatial mathematics is anchored in the development of spatial reasoning. Lehrer and Lesh argue for the inclusion of measurement in geometry education and provide evidence for their relationship. This is examined by investigations of children's reasoning as it relates to the measurement of space, including classic developmental studies of Piaget, Inhelder, and Szeminska (1960) to recent cognitive science investigations.

Lehrer and Lesh call for a broadened scope in what we consider to be mathematics, taking a cognitive developmental perspective with particular relevance to classroom-based research and its application to mathematics education. The case is presented for mathematics learning as a complex realm of inquiry that draws from many cognitive domains. They review significant recent work emphasizing classroom practices that can support productive mathematical thinking even in early elementary classrooms, such as pretend play, setting norms for classroom conversations that emphasize the need for proof, and the orchestration of guided dialogic experiences generated from collective and shared everyday knowledge.

Computers, the Internet, and New Media Technologies for Learning

Goldman-Segall and Maxwell (this volume) present a historical review and creative prospective insights into how technological advances have been shaped and have helped shape our current notions of learners, learning, and teaching. These researchers review the dynamic field of new and emerging medias and technologies that have the potential of creating unique—possibly until now unfathomable—themes of research in educational psychology. They trace instructional technology from its behavioristic, computer-administered drill and practice roots, to the influence of the cognitive science revolution, with its focus on artificial intelligence and analogies to information-processing computing paradigms, to more contemporary situated models of contextualized learning, in which cognition is not viewed in a straightforward algorithm, but rather as the emergent property of complex systems working in parallel. They review different analogies used to characterize the influence of computers in education. These perspectives independently have viewed the computer as an information source, as a curriculum domain, as a communication medium, as a cognitive tool, as an alternative learning environment, as learning partner, as means of scaffolding learning, and most recently as a perspectivity tool. They go on to point out significant newly emerging paradigms and the concomitant challenges that will ensue from these dynamic new applications. The idea of perspectivity technologies and their points of viewing theoretical ideas will be developed over the coming decade with expansions to notions the computers allow for elastic knowledge construction.

EXCEPTIONAL LEARNER PROGRAMS AND STUDENTS

Exceptional students have long been a major focus of research in educational psychology and a major recipient of the applications of research to practice in educational psychology. From the very early applications of Binet and colleagues in France (Binet, 1898; Binet & Henri, 1896; Binet & Simon, 1905) and efforts in the United States (Terman & Childs, 1912; Woolley, 1915) in the development of intelligence tests for the identification of students with exceptional needs who would benefit from special education, educational psychology has informed and addressed the needs of exceptional learners.

Work here focuses on the contributions of educational psychology on understanding the school-based and developmental needs of exceptional learners. Within this domain we include the field of school psychology, which includes a major emphasis on the evaluation and development of programs and interventions for exceptional learners. Educational psychology has had an impact on the study of individuals with learning disabilities as well as those of high cognitive ability. Investigations in these areas have ranged from basic processes to applied research on intervention programs. Students who demonstrate behavioral excess represent another important target population for the application of research on classroom management and behavior change supported by educational psychology.

School Psychology

School psychology is a field of psychology that is closely aligned with educational psychology. School psychology is an applied field of psychology, represented in APA by Division 16 (School Psychology) and by other professional organizations, the most visible being the National Association of School Psychologists (NASP). School psychology is dedicated to providing for and ensuring that the educational, behavioral, and mental health needs of children are met in accordance with federal and state legislation. The vast majority of school psychology graduate programs are located in departments of educational psychology or schools of education, with most of the remainder found in psychology departments. Reschly (this volume) describes how societal events and trends have had a hand in the shaping of school psychology practice and focus over the past century, including events of the last decade of the twentieth century.

School psychology has been an area of psychology that has experienced a tremendous increase in the number of professionals in the field. As presented by Reschly, over the past

25 years, the number of school psychologists as estimated by the U.S. Office of Education has witnessed an increase of over 150%, and data suggest that there is a continued need for school psychologists in the United States. Much of the emphasis in the training and practice of school psychology has been directed by the needs of exceptional children in school settings and the guidelines for the provision of services provided by the Individuals with Disabilities Education Act (IDEA) and other federal legislation. There are over 5 million children and adolescents with educational and emotional disabilities in the nations schools, representing approximately one out of nine children. The approximately 26,000 school psychologists in the United States have a major role in the direct evaluation and provision of psychological services to these children, illustrating the importance of this branch of psychology to the welfare of young people.

Reschly provides a description and discussion of the legal requirements that shape the practice of school psychology, as well as the current characteristics and conditions that illustrate the practice of school psychologists in the United States. The infrastructure of school psychology, including a description of relevant journals in this field, is also provided. Finally, contemporary and future challenges to school psychology are presented, focusing on issues of disability determination and special education placement, the need for empirically supported interventions (see also chapter by Levin, O'Donnell, & Kratochwill in this volume), personnel needs, and the recognition of mental health needs of school children. Reschly's chapter serves to illustrate the importance of school psychology in the education of children and an important application of psychology to education.

Learning Disabilities

Learning disabilities represent one of the most prevalent forms of learner problems; it is also a field of study that is replete with controversy as to classification, assessment, and intervention. It is also a domain that crosses over a wide range of professionals and research perspectives—educators, psychologists, neurologists, pediatricians, neuropsychologists, and others. Siegel (this volume) describes the issues and controversies related to the definition of learning disabilities, including that of using intelligence for defining criteria for diagnosis. She makes the point that the use of intelligence tests is limited in this application, given problems with the anchoring of these tests in knowledge-based domains, as well as the given that youngsters with learning disabilities will by definition often have deficits in skills that are required of the intelligence test. Siegel describes the issues related to the question of whether learning disability is a specific, possibly

neurological type of dysfunction, as well as whether there are multiple subtypes of learning disabilities specific to academic problem domains.

Siegel addresses some of these controversies by critically examining the research and providing insights into the current status of learning disability subtypes. She then provides a critical examination of the research on reading and arithmetic disabilities and a description of assessment requirements. A number of recommendations and accommodations for the remediation of learning problems are given.

Gifted Education Programs and Procedures

Olszewski-Kubilius (this volume) reviews work focused on defining characteristics of gifted children as well as research that demonstrates important implications for education. In addition to more knowledge of the striking capabilities of gifted children, there is increasing evidence of considerable inter- and intra-individual variance or asynchronous development (Morelock & Feldman, 1993). Gifted students are a heterogeneous group whose members differ from each other in their developmental pathways and in their distinct profiles of abilities. At the same time, researchers have consistently confirmed the stability of exceptional abilities over time. Difficulties associated with assessing younger children and the limitations of traditional and standardized intelligence measures are discussed. Such issues have led researchers to conclude that early identification of giftedness may be compromised with typical cognitive assessments because development in some areas may be more closely related to ceilings set by chronological versus conceptual maturity. Programs and practices are reviewed that are currently employed across the country to address the needs of these students.

School-Related Behavior Disorders

The field of behavior disorders in children and adolescents has emerged as a major focus of psychologists, teachers, administrators, state and federal governments, and the general public. With the publication and dissemination of the Surgeon General's report derived from a year-2000 national conference on children's mental health and the needs of this population, there was an increased national awareness of the psychological needs of children and adolescents with behavior problems. As Walker and Gresham (this volume) describe, the widely publicized cases of school shootings and violence by students has galvanized the general public and professionals toward actions aimed at creating safe school environments and an increased acknowledgment of students with extreme emotional and behavioral disturbances.

Walker and Gresham provide a critical examination of behavior disorders in children and adolescents by first delineating the current status of the field. This is followed by a discussion of current trends in research and practice in this field that the authors consider to be indicative of best practices, including functional assessment of behavior, interventions that utilize positive behavioral support, research examining teacher interactions with students with behavior disorders, the association between language deficits and behavior disorders in children, the utility of office referrals as a critical indicator of potential behavior disorders, and resistance to intervention as a cardinal symptom for the determination of treatment eligibility and selection. Walker and Gresham also describe a number of problems in the field of behavior disorders, most of which are at a policy or practice level. These include political turmoil in the field of behavior disorders as a specialty area; limited translation of quality research on major problems in the field to everyday practice; the larger role of creating safe and healthy school environments; the propensity for postmodern and deconstructivist perspectives that devalue scientific research to be adopted by behavior disorder professionals; the general failure of schools to serve the needs of students with behavior disabilities, in part due to interpretation of federal education legislation; and finally, the relative lack of attention by professionals and leaders in the field to early identification and prevention activities.

Instrumental to the provision of appropriate services is the utilization of well-researched interventions for the treatment of behavior disorders in children and adolescents in school settings. The authors provide an argument for the use of social skills instruction with appropriate inclusion of procedures to modify maladaptive behaviors.

EDUCATIONAL PROGRAMS, RESEARCH, AND POLICY

Educational psychology has had a significant role in the development and reform of educational practices. An important contribution of educational psychology is the knowledge and guidance provided to the education of teachers. As noted earlier, courses in educational psychology are required in most university teacher preparation programs. An examination of introductory textbooks in educational psychology shows a strong preference toward teachers as their primary audience. Hoy (2000) observes that it is through textbooks in educational psychology that we can see what the general public and teachers learn about the application of psychology to teaching and related educational activities. The significant breadth of methodological knowledge that educational

psychologists bring to the political reform table has been influential in stressing the need for credible school-based intervention research. In this respect, educational psychology acts as the conduit to introduce and apply research and principles of psychology to educational practices. The role of educational psychologists will continue to be an important and credible voice in resolving ongoing controversies critical to the advancement and application of knowledge for educational practice.

Teacher Learning, Education, and Curriculum

Learning to teach is arguably one of the most cognitively and emotionally challenging efforts one can undertake, and new teachers face greater challenges than ever before with today's diverse student needs, public scrutiny, and political pressures (see chapter by Whitcomb in this volume). Concurrently, there is a critical need to prepare more teachers than ever before and there are deeply divided ideas about best practice for initial teacher preparation (National Commission on Teaching and America's Future, 1996). Whitcomb asserts that there is a critical need for rigorous empirical work on initial teacher preparation. Until recently, scholarly analyses of this pedagogy have been surprisingly limited.

What do initial teachers need to know? Whitcomb reviews and synthesizes that large body of work dedicated to establishing teaching as a learning profession (Darling-Hammond & Sykes, 1999). Teaching is now viewed as a profession with a complex and distinguished knowledge base. Current research is focused on the integrated processes and judgments teachers use to navigate this breadth of information. Whitcomb narrows the focus of this chapter to a critical review of cognitively oriented studies of new teacher's learning. There is an emphasis on what is known about the essential knowledge base for new teachers and how teachers learn across diverse contexts.

The chapter begins with an overview of prior research conducted to identify a knowledge base associated with what an effective beginning teacher needs to know, to do, and to value (Ball & Cohen, 1999). Theoretical shifts in studies of teaching have followed much the same route as that observed in the broader field of educational psychology. Views of a good teacher have moved from a focus on discrete knowledge and skills, to studies of the cognitions and decisions that occur during teaching, to more recent studies on the interplay of personal beliefs, knowledge, skills, and situational or contextual mediators of initial teachers' learning.

From the early 1980s educational researchers have focused on building an understanding of the specialized knowledge base required to effectively teach content in multiple ways to diverse learners. This work has been strongly influenced by the work of educational psychologists working within social constructivist models that view physical and social contexts as integral parts of any cognitive endeavor. Research within this tradition stresses that the situations and the social environments within which they are learned influence skills and that such situated knowledge becomes a fundamental part of what is learned.

Currently there is a move away from studying individual teachers' knowledge to studies that focus on interactive systems as the unit of analysis (Putnam & Borko, 2000). Recent work has focused on the dispositions that underlie good teaching—how teachers become committed to students, to meeting individual student needs, and to monitoring their own and their students' learning. In this respect, teaching and teachers are viewed as part of learning communities that require judgment and ongoing, flexible decision making to support student learning in culturally inclusive settings. Researchers are now examining how teachers learn to teach—how they actively construct a personal knowledge base and then use it to guide everyday classroom judgments and learning. These contemporary efforts are critically relevant to initial teacher preparation.

Whitcomb goes on to highlight key features of effective initial teacher preparation programs. This work supports the critical role of prior beliefs, content knowledge, mentors, colleagues, and the setting in which teacher candidates learn to teach. Two promising lines of research are summarized that embody some of these essential characteristics—research on how initial teachers learn to teach writing and research on the impact of case methodology in teacher preparation.

The chapter ends with a critical analysis of the limits of current research and the need for stronger empirical work to enhance our understanding of initial teacher pedagogy in the future. The conclusion drawn from this review is that educational psychologists are in a unique position to influence and conduct rigorous inquiry that will further unravel the complexity of teaching and contribute to the development of effective initial teacher preparation models.

A Case for Enhancing the Credibility of Educational-Psychological Intervention Research

Educational psychology has for over a century been at the forefront in the development of research methodologies and statistics. Educational psychologists have been active in the fields of educational measurement, statistics, and research designs. Notable journals include the *Journal of Educational Measurement, Educational and Psychological Measurement, Journal of Educational Statistics, Applied Psychological Measurement, Educational Assessment,* and others that have as a primary focus the presentation of new measurement, statistical, and research methodologies. In the chapter by Levin et al. (this volume), a very provocative argument is forwarded that stresses the need for more credible, rigorous standards in the conceptualization, design, and evaluation of instructional educational research. These authors follow up on the work of Levin and O'Donnell (1999), who—after reviewing the thoughts of many prior editors and presidents representing the field of educational psychology—noted collective concerns about the nature and quality of educational research and the preparation of the next generation of researchers.

Educational psychology more than ever before is expected to improve our ability to understand, predict, and control human behavior as well as our ability to design instructional practices with potential applications to problems of schooling. Recognizing the inherent difficulties in conducting educational research and the importance of bridging many different communities across a wide array of academic disciplines, there is a call for a broader array of naturalistic and empirical methodologies, ranging from case studies and observations to multivariate designs and analyses (Wittrock, 1994). Contemporary methodological debates about qualitative and quantitative or applied and basic inquiry oversimplify and trivialize the issue of how to best obtain quality supportive evidence using a variety of rigorous inquiry standards that could be reflected in any methodological orientation.

The acronym CAREful (Comparison, Again and Again, Relationship and Eliminate) research is used to review components of scientific integrity that can enhance the evidence credibility of educational research. A framework for conceptualizing different stages of such research is forwarded, and promising methodological developments in instructional research are reviewed. Preliminary phases of inquiry place a fundamental value on subjective reflection, intuition, and observation as important steps for guiding further inquiry using objective, scientifically credible methodology in order to make valid prescriptions for future intervention. Trustworthy and credible instructional research to assess the relative impact of educational and psychological treatments or interventions is of critical importance for policy makers. Indeed, as Levin (1994) eloquently argued previously, the future viability of the field will depend on our ability to craft educational intervention research that is both credible and creditable. The development of such innovative methodological continua should become a top priority for future educational researchers.

From Credible Research to Policy and Educational Reform

Educational psychology as a discipline has from its inception sought to inform and help guide the education of students and the development of local and national education policies and reforms. Educational psychology has accomplished this goal by maintaining a strong linkage to credible school-based research and associated methodologies. McCombs (this volume) illustrates how research in educational psychology can be translated to changes in educational practice, with a particular reference to how teachers can be informed by research to modify and enhance their classroom and instructional procedures.

McCombs discusses the learner-centered psychological principles (McCombs & Whisler, 1997), a set of practices that are designed to enable teachers to gain an understanding of cognitive and metacognitive factors in learning, motivational and emotional influences on learning, developmental and social influences on learning, and individual differences in learning and evaluation (APA Work Group of the Board of Educational Affairs, 1997). These principles were designed to provide teachers with a set of practices that focus on the learner, including an understanding of individual differences and diversity of learners and learner styles. The principles originated with the 1990 appointment by the APA of the Task Force on Psychology in Education, which sought to provide for the application of psychological research and theory to learning in educational contexts. McCombs also delineates significant contributions of educational psychology to educational reforms. McCombs notes that educational psychology is an applied science, with knowledge created that drives the practice of teaching and the study of learner characteristics. It also informs policy and educational reform, particularly as we enter the twenty-first century.

Future Perspectives in Educational Psychology

In writing their chapters for this book, contributors were asked to provide insight as to what future trends and directions were anticipated for their respective fields of inquiry. By synthesizing these ideas, Miller and Reynolds (this volume) sought to highlight critical theoretical, research, and practical issues likely to inform and direct the field of educational psychology well into the twenty-first century. Future issues that uniformly surfaced across a majority of chapters were reviewed for their potential of advancing our understanding of individual learners and learning contexts; interpersonal, relational, and instructional processes; curriculum development; and teacher

preparation. Implications are presented for translating theory into educational practice that increases student learning, enhances teacher preparation, and improves schooling practices. Contemporary educational research issues, methodological advances, and the impact of educational research on learning, teaching practice, and educational policies are supported by exemplars posed by authors in this volume.

The chapter concludes with an overview of prospective issues relevant to transforming a vast empirical knowledge base into sound educational policy and practice. Significant contributions of educational psychologists are highlighted, as is the need for trustworthy and credible instructional research to assess the relative impact of educational and psychological treatments or interventions. Future educational psychology researchers must take a leadership role to reduce the tendency to overgeneralize when looking for solutions to very complex challenges in education. There is a strong sense that the field of educational psychology will continue to enhance our understanding of critical educational issues and—most important—will lead to higher standards of quality and credibility to guide future educational policy and reform.

SUMMARY

Educational psychology, broadly described, focuses on the application of psychology to the understanding of learners and the learning environment. However, such a broad generalization of the field does not do justice to the myriad of domains and applications represented by this field of psychology. As this introduction to the field and to this volume of the Handbook illustrates, the field of educational psychology represents an important area of psychological research, theory, and practice.

The five major areas of contemporary research and practice in educational psychology covered in this volume include cognitive contributions to learning; development and instruction; sociocultural, instruction, and relational processes; curriculum applications; exceptional learner programs and students; and educational programs, research, and policy. Within these areas, individual chapters provided for broad coverage of nearly all the domains identified by Pressley and Roehrig as having the most significant impact on the field of educational psychology.

Individually, each chapter describes a rich domain of research; almost universally, they note a burgeoning of new research paradigms, perspectives, theories, and major conceptualizations that have emerged over the last quarter of a century. It is noteworthy that some of these so-called new insights into human behavior and psychology applied to education have been predicated on newly recognized and acknowledged contributions made by psychologists (e.g., Vygotsky, etc.) in the early part of the twentieth century. Although the scope of educational psychology as a field of psychology is quite broad, numerous communalities can be seen across the varied chapters of this volume. These communalities suggest a connectedness that supports educational psychology as a rich and vital field of scientific inquiry.

The influence and impact of research in educational psychology on society are probably best recognized by applications to the education and training of teachers and the development of procedures to enhance classroom instruction and learning, ways to motivate learners, and the integration of technology into the classroom. These and other applications in educational psychology are buttressed by an empirical rigor of research methods in the design of both basic and applied experiments and field-based investigations. It is evident that researchers in educational psychology are addressing major issues related to the education of learners in regular and special education contexts. In addition to the impact of educational psychology on learning and learners, it has also played a major role in informing policy and educational reform.

The mosaic of educational psychology is well represented by the authors of this volume and their respective chapter contributions. The sum of knowledge presented in the chapters of this volume illustrates the diversity of research and practice domains. This introduction to current perspectives in educational psychology provides a snapshot of the breadth and scope of this field but does not do justice to the depth of research and applications. For the latter, the following chapters provide excellent description, evaluation, and synthesis. The dynamic nature of this field of psychology is evident across the chapters and serves to illustrate the importance of educational psychology research and practice to individuals and society. It is our expectation that this importance will continue and grow throughout the twenty-first century.

REFERENCES

Ainsworth, M. D., Blehar, M. C., Waters, E., & Wall, D. (1978). *Patterns of attachment: A psychological study of the strange situation.* Hillsdale, NJ: Erlbaum.

Ames, C. (1984). Competitive, cooperative, and individualistic goal structures: A motivational analysis. In R. Ames & C. Ames (Eds.), *Research in motivation in education* (Vol. 1, pp. 117–207). New York: Academic Press.

Ames, C., & Archer, J. (1988). Achievement goals in the classroom: Students' learning strategies and motivational processes. *Journal of Educational Psychology, 80,* 260–270.

Anderson, R. C., & Pearson, P. D. (1984). A schema-theoretic view of basic processes in reading comprehension. In P. D. Pearson (Ed.), *Handbook of reading research* (pp. 225–291). New York: Longman.

Bakeman, R., & Gottman, J. M. (1986). *Observing interaction: An introduction to sequential analysis.* Cambridge, MA: Cambridge University Press.

Ball, D. L., & Cohen, D. K. (1999). Developing practice, developing practitioners: Toward a practice-based theory of professional education. In L. Darling-Hammond & G. Sykes (Eds.), *Teaching as the learning profession: Handbook of policy and practice* (pp. 3–32). San Francisco: Jossey-Bass.

Bandura, A. (1969). *Principles of behavior modification.* New York: Holt.

Bandura, A. (1977). Self-efficacy: Toward a unifying theory of behavior change. *Psychological Review, 84,* 191–215.

Bandura, A. (1982). Self-efficacy mechanisms in human agency. *American Psychologist, 37,* 122–147.

Berliner, D. C., & Calfee, R. (Eds.). (1996). *Handbook of educational psychology.* New York: Macmillan.

Binet, A. (1898). La mesure en psychologie individuelle. *Revue Philosophique, 46,* 113–123.

Binet, A., & Henri, V. (1896). La psychologie individuelle. *L'Annee Psychologique, 2,* 411–465.

Binet, A., & Simon, T. (1905). Application des methodes nouvelles au diagnostic du niveau intellectuel chez des enfants normaux et anormaux d'hospice et d'ecole primaire. *L'Annee Psychologique, 11,* 255–336.

Bowlby, J. (1969). *Attachment and loss: Vol. 1. Attachment.* New York: Basic Books.

Brainerd, C. J. (1978). Cognitive development and instructional theory. *Contemporary Educational Psychology, 3,* 37–50.

Bronfenbrenner, U., & Morris, P. A. (1998). The ecology of developmental processes. In W. Damon & R. M. Lerner (Eds.), *Handbook of child psychology: Vol. 1, Theoretical models of human development* (5th ed., pp. 993–1028). New York: Wiley.

Brophy, J. (1986). Teacher influences on student achievement. *American Psychologist, 41,* 1069–1077.

Brophy, J., & Good, J. L. (1974). *Teacher-student relationships.* New York: Holt, Rinehart, and Winston.

Brown, A. L. (1992). Design experiments: Theoretical and methodological challenges in creating complex interventions in classroom settings. *Journal of the Learning Sciences, 2,* 141–178.

Bruner, J. S. (1960). *The process of education.* Cambridge, MA: Harvard University Press.

Bruner, J. S. (1966). *Toward a theory of instruction.* London: Belnap.

Cronbach, L. J. (1951). Coefficient alpha and the internal structure of tests. *Psychometrika, 16,* 297–301.

Darling-Hammond, L., & Sykes, G. (Eds.). (1999). *Teaching as the learning profession: Handbook of policy and practice.* San Francisco: Jossey-Bass.

Dewey, J. (1916). *Democracy and education.* New York: Macmillan.

Flavell, J. H. (1963). *The developmental psychology of Jean Piaget.* Princeton, NJ: van Nostrand.

Flower, L., & Hayes, J. R. (1980). The dynamics of composing: Making plans and juggling contraints. In L. Gregg & E. Steinberg (Eds.), *Cognitive processes in writing* (pp. 31–50). Hillsdale, NJ: Erlbaum.

Grant, G., & Murray, C. (1999). *Teaching in America: The slow revolution.* Cambridge, MA: Harvard University Press.

Halstead, W. C. (1951). Biological intelligence. *Journal of Personality, 20,* 118–130.

Hebb, D. O. (1949). *The organization of behavior: A neuropsychological theory.* New York: Wiley.

Hilgard, E. R. (1996). History of educational psychology. In D. C. Berliner & R. Calfee (Eds.), *Handbook of educational psychology* (pp. 990–1004). New York: Macmillan.

Hoy, A. W. (2000). Educational psychology in teacher education. *Educational Psychologist, 35,* 257–270.

Hunt, J. M. (1961). *Intelligence and experience.* New York: Roland Press.

Hurley, E. A. (1997, April). *The interaction of communal orientation in African-American children with group processes in cooperative learning: Pedagogical and theoretical implications.* Paper presented at the annual meeting of the American Educational Research Association, Chicago, IL.

Inhelder, B., Sinclair, H., & Bovet, M. (1974). *Learning and the development of cognition* (S. Wedgwood, trans.). Cambridge, MA: Harvard University Press.

Jaeger, R. M., & Bond, L. (1996). Quantitative research methods and design. In D. C. Berliner & R. Calfee (Eds.), *Handbook of educational psychology* (pp. 877–898). New York: Macmillan.

Kaiser, H. F. (1958). The varimax criterion for analytic rotation in factor analysis. *Psychometrika, 23,* 187–200.

Kintsch, W. (1989). Learning from text. In L. B. Resnick (Ed.), *Knowing, learning, and instruction: Essays in honor of Robert Glaser* (pp. 25–46). Hillsdale, NJ: Erlbaum.

Lambert, N., McCombs, B. L. (1998). *How students learn: Reforming schools through learner-centered education.* Washington, DC: APA Books

Lerner, R. M. (1998). Theories of human development: Contemporary perspectives. In W. Damon & R. M. Lerner (Eds.), *Handbook of child psychology: Theoretical models of human development* (5th ed., pp. 1–24). New York: Wiley.

Levin, J. R. (1973). Inducing comprehension in poor readers: A test of a recent model. *Journal of Educational Psychology, 65,* 19–24.

Levin, J. R. (1994). Crafting educational intervention research that's both credible and creditable. *Educational Psychology Review, 6,* 231–243.

Levin, J. R., & O'Donnell, A. M. (1999). What to do about educational research's credibility gaps? *The Issues in Education: Contribution from Educational Psychology, 5,* 177–229.

Loeber, R. (1990). Development and risk factors of juvenile antisocial behavior and delinquency. *Clinical Psychology Review, 10,* 1–41.

Luria, A. R. (1961). *The role of speech in the regulation of normal and abnormal behaviors.* New York: Liverwright.

Luria, A. R. (1980). *Higher cortical functions in man* (2nd ed.). New York: Basic Books.

Mayer, R. E. (1976). Integration of information during problem solving due to a meaningful context of learning. *Memory and Cognition, 4,* 603–608.

McCombs, B. L., & Whisler, J. S. (1997). *The learner-centered classroom and school: Strategies for increasing student motivation and achievement.* San Francisco: Jossey-Bass.

Meichenbaum, D. (1977). *Cognitive behavior modification: An integrative approach.* New York: Plenum.

Miller, G. A., Galanter, G. A., & Pribram, K. H. (1960). Plans and the structure of behavior. New York: Adams Bannister Cox.

Morelock, M. J., & Feldman, D. H. (1993). Prodigies and savants: What they have to tell us about giftedness and human cognition. In K. A. Heller, F. J. Monks, & A. H. Passow (Eds.), *International handbook of research and development of giftedness and talent* (pp. 161–181). Elmsford, NY: Pergamon.

National Commission on Teaching and America's Future. (1996). *What matters most: Teaching for America's future.* New York: Author.

Paivio, A. (1971). *Imagery and verbal processes.* New York: Holt, Rinehart, and Winston.

Pederson, E., Faucher, T. A., & Eaton, W. W. (1978). A new perspective on the effects of first grade teachers on children's subsequent adult status. *Harvard Educational Review, 48,* 1–31.

Piaget, J., Inhelder, B., & Szeminska, A. (1960). *The child's conception of geometry.* New York: Basic Books.

Pianta, R. C. (1999). *Enhancing relationships between children and teachers.* Washington, DC: American Psychological Association.

Polya, G. (1957). *How to solve it* (2nd ed.). Princeton, NJ: Princeton University Press.

Pressley, M., & Roehrig, A. (2002). Educational psychology in the modern era: 1960 to the present. In B. Zimmerman & D. Schunk (Eds.), *Educational psychology: A century of contributions.* Mahwah, NJ: Erlbaum.

Putnam, R., & Borko, H. (2000). What do new views of knowledge and thinking have to say about research on teacher learning? *Educational Researcher, 29,* 4–15.

Rohwer, W. D. (1970). Images and pictures in children's learning: Research results and educational implications. *Psychological Bulletin, 73,* 393–403.

Rosenthal, R. (1969). Interpersonal expectations effects of the experimenter's hypothesis. In R. Rosenthal & R. L. Rosnow (Eds.), *Artifact in behavioral research* (pp. 182–279). New York: Academic Press.

Rosenthal, T. L., & Zimmerman, B. J. (1978). *Social learning and cognition.* New York: Academic Press.

Rutter, M. (1987). Psychosocial resilience and protective mechanisms. *American Journal of Orthopsychiatry, 57,* 316–331.

Schank, R. C., & Abelson, R. P. (1977). *Scripts, plans, goals and understanding: An inquiry into human knowledge structures.* Hillsdale, NJ: Erlbaum.

Schoenfeld, A. H. (1985). Making sense of "out loud" problem-solving protocols. *Journal of Mathematical Behavior, 4,* 171–191.

Scribner, S., & Cole, M. (1981). *The psychology of literacy.* Cambridge, MA: Harvard University Press.

Slavin, R. E. (1995). *Cooperative learning: Theory, research, and practice* (2nd ed.). Boston: Allyn and Bacon.

Terman, L. M., & Childs, H. G. (1912). Tentative revision and extension of the Binet-Simon measuring scale of intelligence. *Journal of Educational Psychology, 3,* 61, 133, 198, 277.

Tulving, E., & Donaldson, W. (1972). *Organization of memory.* New York: Academic Press.

Vygotsky, L. S. (1962). *Thought and language.* Cambridge, MA: MIT Press.

Vygotsky, L. S. (1978). *Mind in society: The development of higher psychological processes.* Cambridge, MA: Harvard University Press.

Vygotsky, L. S. (1997). *Educational psychology.* Jamaica Hills, NY: Saint Lucie Press. (Original work published 1926)

Weiner, B. (1979). A theory of motivation for some classroom experiences. *Journal of Educational Psychology, 71,* 3–25.

Werner, E., & Smith, R. (1980). *Vulnerable but invincible.* New York: Wiley.

Wittrock, M. C. (1990). Generative processes of comprehension. *Educational Psychologist, 24,* 345–376.

Wittrock, M. C. (1994). An empowering conception of educational psychology. *Educational Psychologist, 27,* 129–141.

Woolley, H. T. (1915). A new scale of mental and physical measurements for adolescents and some of its uses. *Journal of Educational Psychology, 6,* 521–550.

PART TWO

COGNITIVE CONTRIBUTIONS TO LEARNING, DEVELOPMENT, AND INSTRUCTION

CHAPTER 2

Contemporary Theories of Intelligence

ROBERT J. STERNBERG

Hundreds of tests of intelligence are currently available to those who wish to test intelligence. Some are household names; others are known only to small groups of aficionados. Can such tests be justified in terms of psychological theory? If so, what are the theories, and what is the evidence in favor of them? Do all the theories lead to the same kinds of tests, or might alternative theories lead to different kinds of tests? And if alternative theories lead to different kinds of tests, might people's fates be changed if other types of tests are used? These are the kinds of questions that are addressed in this chapter.

The chapter is divided into four parts following this introduction. First, I argue that theories of intelligence matter not only in theory, but also in practical everyday life. The ways in which these theories matter has a profound effect on societies, including that of the United States. Second, classical theories of intelligence are presented and critically evaluated.

They are presented not only for historical purposes. Rather, they are presented because these theories continue to be highly influential in the contemporary world, much more so than many contemporary theories. Their influence is contemporary, even though their origins are in the past. Third, contemporary theories of intelligence are presented and critically evaluated. There are many such theories, but consistent with the topic of the volume in which this chapter is embedded, the emphasis is on those theories that have some kind of educational impact. Fourth and finally, the chapter presents some challenges to all current conceptions of intelligence and draws some conclusions.

The second and third parts of the chapter are each divided into two sections. One section considers *implicit theories* of intelligence, or people's informal conceptions of what intelligence is. A second section considers *explicit theories* of intelligence, or experts' formal conceptions of what intelligence is. Each part considers the extent to which implicit and explicit theories correspond, and why the correspondence is, at best, partial.

WHY THEORIES OF INTELLIGENCE MATTER TO SOCIETY

Underlying every measurement of intelligence is a theory. The theory may be transparently obvious, or it may be hidden. It may be a formal explicit theory or an informal implicit one. But there is always a theory of some kind lurking

Preparation of this article was supported by Grant REC-9979843 from the National Science Foundation and by a grant under the Javits Act Program (Grant No. R206R950001) as administered by the Office of Educational Research and Improvement, U.S. Department of Education. Grantees undertaking such projects are encouraged to express freely their professional judgment. This article, therefore, does not necessarily represent the position or policies of the National Science Foundation, the Office of Educational Research and Improvement, or the U.S. Department of Education, and no official endorsement should be inferred.

beneath the test. And in the United States and some other countries, tests seem to be everywhere.

The Pervasiveness of Intelligence-Related Measurements

Students who apply to competitive independent schools in many locations and notably in New York City must present an impressive array of credentials. Among these credentials, for many of these schools, is a set of scores on either the Wechsler Preschool and Primary Scale of Intelligence–Revised (WPPSI-R; Wechsler, 1980) or the Stanford-Binet Intelligence Scale–Fourth Edition (Thorndike, Hagen, & Sattler, 1985). If the children are a bit older, they may take instead the Wechsler Intelligence Scale for Children–Third Edition (WISC-3; Wechsler, 1991). The lower level version of the Wechsler test is used only for children ages 3 to 7 1/2 years. The higher level version of the Wechsler test is used for somewhat older children ages 6 to 16 years, 11 months of age. The Stanford-Binet test is used across a wider range of ages, from 2 years through adult.

Children applying to independent schools in other locations are likely to take either these or similar tests. The names may be different, and the construct they are identified as measuring may differ as well: intelligence, intellectual abilities, mental abilities, scholastic aptitude, and so forth. But the tests will be highly correlated with each other, and ultimately, one will serve the schools' purposes about as well as another. These tests will henceforth be referred to as measuring *intelligence-related abilities* in order to group them together but to distinguish them from tests explicitly purported to measure intelligence.

The need to take tests such as these will not end with primary school. For admission to independent schools, in general, regardless of level, the children may take one of the Wechsler tests, the Stanford-Binet test, or some other intelligence test. More likely, they will take either the Educational Records Bureau (ERB) or the Secondary School Admissions Test (SSAT).

Of course, independent schools are supported by fees, not tax dollars. But children attending public schools will be exposed to a similar regimen. At one time, these children would have been likely to take group intelligence (IQ) tests, which likely would have been used to track them or, at the very least, predict their futures. Today, the students are less likely to take intelligence tests, unless they are being considered for special services, such as services for educable mentally retarded (EMR) children, learning-disabled (LD) children, or gifted children. If the children wish to go to a competitive college or university, they will likely take the SAT (an acronym originally standing for Scholastic Aptitude Test, then for Scholastic

Assessment Test, and now for nothing in particular) or the American College Test (ACT), the two most widely used tests used for college admissions. If individuals' scores are within the normal range of a particular college or university to which they apply for admission, the scores may not much affect their admission prospects. But if their scores are outside this range, they may be a crucial factor in determining acceptance, in the case of high scores, or rejection, in the case of low scores. These tests may be required whether the school is publicly or privately funded. The story still is not over.

If the individuals (now adults) wish to puruse further study, they will have to take tests of various kinds. These include the Graduate Record Examination (GRE) for graduate school, the Law School Admission Test (LSAT) for law, the Graduate Management Admission Test (GMAT) for business school, the Medical College Admission Test (MCAT) for medical school, and so forth. And the story of intelligence testing may not end with graduate-level study: Many kinds of occupational placements, especially in business, may require applicants to take intelligence tests as well.

This rather lengthy introduction to the everyday world of tests of intelligence-related abilities shows the extent to which such tests permeate U.S. society, and some other contemporary societies as well. It is hard not to take such tests very seriously because they can be influential in or even determinative of a person's educational and even occupational fate.

The Societal System Created by Tests

Tests of intelligence-related skills are related to success in many cultures. People with higher test scores seem to be more successful in a variety of ways, and those with lower test scores seem to be less successful (Herrnstein & Murray, 1994; Hunt, 1995). Why are scores on intelligence-related tests closely related to societal success? Consider two points of view.

According to Herrnstein and Murray (1994), Wigdor and Garner (1982), and others, conventional tests of intelligence account for about 10% of the variation, on average, in various kinds of real-world outcomes. This figure increases if one makes various corrections to it (e.g., for attenuation in measures or for restriction of range in particular samples). Although this percentage is not particularly large, it is not trivial either. Indeed, it is difficult to find any other kind of predictor that fares as well. Clearly, the tests have some value (Gottfredson, 1986, 1997; Hunt, 1995; Schmidt & Hunter, 1981, 1998). They predict success in many jobs and predict success even better in schooling for jobs. Rankings of jobs by prestige usually show higher prestige jobs associated with higher levels of intelligence-related skills. Theorists of intelligence differ as to why the tests have some success in prediction of job level and competency.

The Discovery of an Invisible Hand of Nature?

Some theorists believe that the role of intelligence is society is along the lines of some kind of natural law. In their book, Herrnstein and Murray (1994) refer to an "invisible hand of nature" guiding events such that people with high IQs tend to rise toward the top socioeconomic strata of a society and people with low IQs tend to fall toward the bottom strata. Jensen (1969, 1998) has made related arguments, as have many others (see, e.g., the largely unfavorable reviews by Gould, 1981; Lemann, 1999; Sacks, 1999; Zenderland, 1998). Herrnstein and Murray presented data to support their argument, although many aspects of their data and their interpretations of these data are arguable (Fraser, 1995; Gould, 1995; Jacoby & Glauberman, 1995; Sternberg, 1995).

This point of view has a certain level of plausibility to it. First, more complex jobs almost certainly do require higher levels of intelligence-related skills. Presumably, lawyers need to do more complex mental tasks than do street cleaners. Second, reaching the complex jobs via the educational system almost certainly requires a higher level of mental performance than does reaching less complex jobs. Finally, there is at least some heritable component of intelligence (Plomin, DeFries, McClearn, & Rutter, 1997), so nature must play some role in who gets what mental skills. Despite this plausibility, there is an alternative point of view.

A Societal Invention?

An alternative point of view is that the sorting influence of intelligence in society is more a societal invention than a discovery of an invisible hand of nature (Sternberg, 1997). The United States and some other countries have created societies in which test scores matter profoundly. High test scores may be needed for placement in higher tracks in elementary and secondary school. They may be needed for admission to selective undergraduate programs. They may be needed again for admission to selective graduate and professional programs. Test scores help individuals gain the access routes to many of the highest paying and most prestigious jobs. Low GRE scores, for example, may exclude an individual not only from one selective graduate school, but from many others as well. To the extent that there is error of measurement, there will be comparable effects in many schools.

According to this point of view, there are many able people who may be disenfranchised because the kinds of abilities that they have are not important for test performance, even though they may be important for job performance. For example, the kinds of creative and practical skills that matter to success on the job typically are not measured on the tests used for admissions to educational programs. At the same time, society may be overvaluing those who have a fairly narrow range of skills, and a range of skills that may not serve these individuals particularly well on the job, even if they do lead to success in school and on the tests.

On this view, it is scarcely surprising that ability tests predict school grades, because the tests originally were designed explicitly for this purpose (Binet & Simon, 1905/1916). In effect, U.S. society and other societies have created closed systems: Certain abilities are valued in instruction (e.g., memory and analytical abilities). Ability tests are then created that measure these abilities and thus predict school performance. Then assessments of achievement are designed that also assess for these abilities. Little wonder that ability tests are more predictive in school than in the work place: Within the closed system of the school, a narrow range of abilities leads to success on ability tests, in instruction, and on achievement tests. But these same abilities are less important later on in life.

According to the societal-invention view, closed systems can be and have been constructed to value almost any set of attributes at all. In some societies, caste is used. Members of certain castes are allowed to rise to the top; members of other castes have no chance. Of course, the members of the successful castes believe they are getting their due, much as did members of the nobility in the Middle Ages when they rose to the top and subjugated their serfs. Even in the United States, if one were born a slave in the early 1800s, one's IQ would make little difference: One would die a slave. Slave owners and others rationalized the system, as social Darwinists always have, by believing that the fittest were in the roles in which they rightfully belonged.

The general conclusion is that societies can and do choose a variety of criteria to sort people. Some societies have used or continue to use caste systems, whether explicit, as in India, or implicit, as in the United States. Others use or have used race, religion, or wealth of parents as bases for sorting people. Many societies use a combination of criteria. Once a system is in place, those who gain access to the power structure, whether via their passage through elite education or elsewhere, are likely to look for others like themselves to enter into positions of power. The reason, quite simply, is that there probably is no more powerful basis of interpersonal attraction than similarity, so that people in a power structure look for others similar to themselves. The result is a potentially endlessly looping closed system.

A Synthesis?

It seems fair to say that some closed systems may be better, in some sense, than are others. For example, scores on intelligence-related measures would seem more relevant to school or job performance than would social class. But it is hard to draw definitive conclusions because the various attributes that are favored by a society often tend to correlate with each other. Socialization advantages may lead people of societally preferred racial, ethnic, religious, or other groups to have higher test scores. Thus, the extent to which correlations between test scores and status attributes are natural versus manufactured is unknown because it has not been possibly to conduct a study that would look systematically and comparatively at predictors of success across societies. The closest to doing so probably comes from the work of Ogbu (1978, 1991, 1994; Ogbu & Stern, 2001), who has compared the performance of groups that in one society are of low caste but in another society are of high caste. Ogbu found that performance varies not with group but with caste: When a group is of high social caste, it performs well; when it is of low social caste, it does not.

In sum, there may be some work by an invisible hand of nature, although this hand of nature almost certainly sorts on many attributes in addition to intelligence (such as height, beauty, health, and so forth). There also may be some work through societal inventions, although societies, like nature, sort on many attributes. The role of intelligence in society needs further (and unbiased) research.

Studies of sorting use psychological tests of intelligence and intelligence-related skills. What are the psychological theories on which these tests are based? Consider first some of the classical theories and then some contemporary ones.

CLASSICAL THEORIES OF INTELLIGENCE AND THEIR CONTEMPORARY COUNTERPARTS

Implicit Theories

Implicit theories are people's conceptions of intelligence. Why even bother to study or report on implicit theories of intelligence? There are several reasons.

First, people's day-to-day interactions are far more likely to be affected by their implicit theories than by any explicit theories. In job interviews, admission interviews, and even daily conversations, people are continually judging each other's intelligence, based not on any formal and explicit theories but on their own implicit theories of intelligence. Second, implicit theories are of interest in their own right. Part of the study of psychology is seeking an understanding

how people think, and given the importance of intelligence to society, learning how people think about intelligence is a worthy endeavor. Third, implicit theories often serve as the basis for generating explicit theories. The formal explicit theories of many psychologists (and other scientists) had their origins in these individual's implicit theories.

How have psychologists conceived of intelligence? Almost none of these views are adequately expressed by Boring's (1923) operationistic view of intelligence as what intelligence tests test. For example, a symposium on experts' definitions of intelligence ("Intelligence and its measurement: A symposium," 1921) asked leading researchers how they conceptualized intelligence. Among those asked were leaders in the field such as Edward L. Thorndike, Lewis M. Terman, Lewis L. Thurstone, and Herbert Woodrow. The researchers emphasized the importance of the ability to learn and the ability to adapt to the environment. These skills seem important. Are they the skills that play a major role in explicit theories of intelligence?

Explicit Theories

We consider here the three classical theories that today have the most influence: *g* theory, the theory of primary mental abilities, and the theory of fluid and crystallized abilities.

g Theory

Probably the most influential theory in the history of intelligence research is the two-factor theory, which was first proposed by Spearman (1904, 1927) but has been carried forth by many modern theorists as *g* theory. Jensen (1998), himself a *g* theorist, summarizes much of this work.

Spearman (1904) noticed that tests purported to measure intelligence exhibit a *positive manifold:* They tend to correlate positively with each other. He invented a technique called *factor analysis* that was designed to analyze these intercorrelations in order to identify the purported sources of individual differences underlying the observed patterns of test scores. His factor analyses revealed two types of factors (hence the original name of his theory): the general factor (*g*), whose influence pervades all tests of mental abilities, and specific factors (*s*), whose influence is limited to a single test.

Spearman proposed two separate theories to explain the pervasive presence of g. One theory (Spearman, 1927) attributed the general factor to *mental energy,* a concept that he believed originated with Aristotle. The other theory was a more cognitive theory. Spearman (1923) suggested that three information-processing components (termed *qualitative principles of cognition*) were common to all of the tests. The three components were *apprehension of experience,* or encoding of stimuli; *eduction of relations,* or inferring the relation between two terms; and *eduction of correlates,* or applying the inferred relation in a new domain. In the analogy BLACK : WHITE :: HIGH : ?, for example, apprehension of experience would be used to encode the terms; eduction of relations is used to infer the relation between BLACK and WHITE; and eduction of correlates is used to apply the inferred relation from HIGH to produce LOW.

Spearman's *g* theory continues today in more modern form. Indeed, two books published in the late 1990s both were called *The g Factor* (Brand, 1996; Jensen, 1998). Jensen (1998, 2002) has defined *g* as a distillate of the common source of individual differences in all mental tests. He has proposed that underlying *g* are individual differences in the speed or efficiency of the neural processes that affect the kinds of behavior measured by tests of mental ability.

Jensen (1998) has built his argument in terms of converging operations that, to him, seem to indicate unequivocally the presence of some biologically based common source of variation in performance on mental tests. For example, he cited eight studies prior to 1998 using magnetic resonance imaging (MRI) that showed a correlation between IQ and brain volume (p. 147). A number of other studies have shown correlations between aspects of spontaneously measured electroencephalogram (EEG) waves and IQ and between averaged evoked potentials (AEPs) and IQ (pp. 152–157). Other studies using positron-emission tomography (PET) scanning also have shown correlations with IQ (pp. 157–159), as have studies of peripheral nerve conduction velocity (pp. 159–160) and brain-nerve conduction velocity (pp. 160–162). Some of these kinds of works are described in more detail later.

Other studies have also suggested the viability of the general factor. One example is the heritability study (see Bouchard, 1997; Jensen, 1998; Petrill, in press; Plomin, 1997; Plomin et al., 1997; Scarr, 1997). Such studies typically are designed to study identical twins separated at or near birth, to study identical versus fraternal twins, or to study adopted children (of known biological parentage) and biological children living in the same household. These kinds of studies enable investigators to separate, to some extent, genetic from environmental contributions to intelligence. Today it is recognized, however, that pure influences of genetics and environment are extremely difficult to disentangle (Sternberg & Grigorenko, 1997).

As mentioned earlier, the theory of general intelligence has been the longest lasting and perhaps the most widely accepted in all of the psychological literature. The evidence is impressive—certainly more so than that garnered for any competing theory. Nevertheless, the available evidence requires at least some skepticism.

First, some theorists (e.g., Gardner, 1983, 1999; Sternberg, 1997, 1999a, 1999c, 1999d; whose work is described later) suggest that a general factor is obtained in tests of intelligence because the tests are limited to a class of fairly academic and somewhat artificial tasks. They argue that the general factor disappears or at least is greatly weakened when a broader range of tasks is used.

Second, contrary to the claim of Jensen (1998), a general factor does tend to appear as a mathematical regularity when factorial solutions are left unrotated. Such a factor tends to be produced because the methods of both common-factor and principal-components analysis in widespread use today maximize the amount of variance that they place in each successive factor, with the most possible variance going into the first factor. Thus, the first factor maximizes the loadings of variables on it.

Third, the sheer number of studies supporting a general factor does not necessarily engender support of the theory in proportion to the number of studies (Sternberg, 1999a). The large majority of these studies tends to use a somewhat restricted range of tasks, situations in which intelligence is tested, and even participants.

The Theory of Primary Mental Abilities

Thurstone (1938) proposed a theory of primary mental abilities. Although this theory is not widely used today, the theory forms the basis of many contemporary theories, including two contemporary theories discussed later, those of Gardner (1983) and Carroll (1993). It is also the basis for many contemporary group tests of intelligence, which comprise items roughly of the types described next.

Thurstone (1938) analyzed the data from 56 different tests of mental abilities and concluded that to the extent that there is a general factor of intelligence, it is unimportant and possibly epiphenomenal. From this point of view there are seven *primary mental abilities:*

- *Verbal comprehension.* This factor involves a person's ability to understand verbal material. It is measured by tests such as vocabulary and reading comprehension.
- *Verbal fluency.* This ability is involved in rapidly producing words, sentences, and other verbal material. It is measured by tests such as one that requires the examinee to produce as many words as possible beginning with a particular letter in a short amount of time.
- *Number.* This ability is involved in rapid arithmetic computation and in solving simple arithmetic word problems.

- *Perceptual speed.* This ability is involved in proofreading and in rapid recognition of letters and numbers. It is measured by tests such as those requiring the crossing out of As in a long string of letters or in tests requiring recognition of which of several pictures at the right is identical to the picture at the left.
- *Inductive reasoning.* This ability requires generalization—reasoning from the specific to the general. It is measured by tests, such as letter series, number series, and word classifications, in which the examinee must indicate which of several words does not belong with the others.
- *Spatial visualization.* This ability is involved in visualizing shapes, rotations of objects, and how pieces of a puzzle fit together. An example of a test would be the presentation of a geometric form followed by several other geometric forms. Each of the forms that follows the first is either the same rotated by some rigid transformation or the mirror image of the first form in rotation. The examinee has to indicate which of the forms at the right is a rotated version of the form at the left, rather than a mirror image.

Today, Thurstone's theory is not used as often in its original form, but it has served as a basis for many subsequent theories of intelligence, including hierarchical theories and modern theories such as Gardner's (1983). Thus, to the extent that a theory is judged by its heuristic value, Thurstone's has been one of the most important in the field.

Fluid-Crystallized Ability Theory

The theory of fluid and crystallized abilities is one of a class of hierarchical theories of intelligence (Burt, 1949; Gustafsson, 1988; Jensen, 1970; Vernon, 1971), not all of which can be described here. The theory is still current. It was proposed by Cattell (1971) but now has been proposed in a contemporary and elaborated form by Horn (1994). Only the simple form is described here.

According to this theory, *fluid ability* (Gf) is flexibility of thought and the ability to reason abstractly. It is measured by tests such as number series, abstract analogies, matrix problems, and the like. *Crystallized ability* (Gc), which is alleged to derive from fluid ability, is essentially the accumulation of knowledge and skills through the life course. It is measured by tests of vocabulary, reading comprehension, and general information. Sometimes a further distinction is made between fluid and crystallized abilities and a third ability, *visual ability* (Gv), which is the ability to manipulate representations mentally, such as those found in tests of spatial ability (as described earlier for Thurstone's theory).

A number of contemporary tests of intelligence are based on this theory. One is the Test of *g:* Culture Fair (Cattell & Cattell, 1963), which seeks to capture general ability through tests of fluid abilities. Two other such tests are the Kaufman Adolescent and Adult Intelligence Test (KAIT; Kaufman & Kaufman, 1993) and the Woodcock-Johnson Tests of Cognitive Ability–Revised (Woodcock & Johnson, 1989; see Daniel, 2000, for a review of these and other tests).

The theory of fluid and crystallized intelligence has been extremely influential in the psychological literature on intelligence. If one includes visual ability (Gv), the theory seems to capture three of the most pervasive abilities constituting intelligence. Some questions remain unresolved.

First, it is unclear whether fluid ability is statistically separable from general intelligence (Gustafsson, 1984, 1988). Such a separation appears to be difficult, and even Cattell's own allegedly culture-fair test of *g* is actually a test of fluid ability, as is the Raven's Progressive Matrices test.

Second, it is unclear whether crystallized ability really derives from or somehow springs out of fluid ability. Such a view seemed plausible when Cattell and many others could argue persuasively that tests of fluid ability were culture-fair and that fluid ability is largely unaffected by environmental factors. It now appears that both these views are erroneous. Fluid-ability tests often show greater differences between cultural groups than do crystallized ability tests; more important, they are more susceptible to the Flynn effect (considered later) than are tests of crystallized abilities. This effect refers to secular increases in scores over time. If fluid-ability scores are increasing over time more rapidly than crystallized-ability scores, one can hardly argue that they are unaffected by enculturation or, most likely, by schooling. Indeed, Ceci (1991, 1996; Ceci & Williams, 1997) has suggested that schooling has a large effect on measured intelligence of all kinds.

Third, it appears likely that there are other kinds of abilities beyond those specified by the theory of fluid and crystallized abilities. Some of the contemporary theories considered next attempt to specify what these abilities might be.

CONTEMPORARY THEORIES OF INTELLIGENCE

Implicit Theories

Expert Views

Sixty-five years after the symposium in the *Journal of Educational Psychology* on intelligence, Sternberg and Detterman (1986) conducted a similar symposium, again asking experts about their views on intelligence. Experts such as Earl Butterfield, Douglas Detterman, Earl Hunt, Arther Jensen, and Robert Sternberg gave their views. Learning and adaptive abilities retained their importance, and a new emphasis crept in—metacognition, or the ability to understand and control one's self. Of course, the name is new, but the idea is not, because long ago Aristotle emphasized the importance for intelligence of knowing oneself.

The 1921 and 1986 symposia could be criticized for being overly Western in the composition of their contributors. In some cases, Western notions about intelligence are not shared by other cultures. For example, the Western emphasis on speed of mental processing (Sternberg, Conway, Ketron, & Bernstein, 1981) is absent in many cultures. Other cultures may even be suspicious of the quality of work that is done very quickly. Indeed, other cultures emphasize depth rather than speed of processing. They are not alone: Some prominent Western theorists have pointed out the importance of depth of processing for full command of material (e.g., Craik & Lockhart, 1972). Even L. L. Thurstone (1924) emphasized the importance to human intelligence of withholding a quick, instinctive response, a view that Stenhouse (1973) argued is supported by evolutionary theory. Today, unlike in the past, psychologists have a better idea of the implicit theories of people in diverse cultures.

Laypersons' Views (Across Cultures)

Yang and Sternberg (1997a) reviewed Chinese philosophical conceptions of intelligence. The Confucian perspective emphasizes the characteristic of benevolence and of doing what is right. As in the Western notion, the intelligent person spends much effort in learning, enjoys learning, and persists in lifelong learning with a great deal of enthusiasm. The Taoist tradition, in contrast, emphasizes the importance of humility, freedom from conventional standards of judgment, and full knowledge of oneself as well as of external conditions.

The difference between Eastern and Western conceptions of intelligence may persist even in the present day. Yang and Sternberg (1997b) studied contemporary Taiwanese Chinese conceptions of intelligence and found five factors underlying these conceptions: (a) a general cognitive factor, much like the g factor in conventional Western tests; (b) interpersonal intelligence; (c) intrapersonal intelligence; (d) intellectual self-assertion; and (d) intellectual self-effacement. In a related study but with different results, Chen (1994) found three factors underlying Chinese conceptualizations of intelligence: nonverbal reasoning ability, verbal reasoning ability, and rote memory. The difference may be due to different subpopulations of Chinese, to differences in methodology, or to differences in when the studies were done.

The factors uncovered in both studies differ substantially from those identified in U.S. people's conceptions of intelligence by Sternberg et al. (1981). The factors uncovered by this study were (a) practical problem solving, (b) verbal ability, and (c) social competence, although in both cases people's implicit theories of intelligence seem to go far beyond what conventional psychometric intelligence tests measure. Of course, comparing the Chen (1994) to the Sternberg et al. (1981) study simultaneously varies both language and culture.

Chen and Chen (1988) varied only language. They explicitly compared the concepts of intelligence of Chinese graduates from Chinese-language versus English-language schools in Hong Kong. They found that both groups considered nonverbal reasoning skills as the most relevant skill for measuring intelligence. Verbal reasoning and social skills came next, and then numerical skill. Memory was seen as least important. The Chinese-language group, however, tended to rate verbal skills as less important than did the English-language group. Moreover, in an earlier study, Chen, Braithwaite, and Huang (1982) found that Chinese students viewed memory for facts as important for intelligence, whereas Australian students viewed these skills as being of only trivial importance.

Das (1994), also reviewing Eastern notions of intelligence, has suggested that in Buddhist and Hindu philosophies, intelligence involves waking up, noticing, recognizing, understanding, and comprehending, but also includes such things as determination, mental effort, and even feelings and opinions in addition to more intellectual elements.

Differences between cultures in conceptions of intelligence have been recognized for some time. Gill and Keats (1980) noted that Australian university students value academic skills and the ability to adapt to new events as critical to intelligence, whereas Malay students value practical skills, as well as speed and creativity. Dasen (1984) found Malay students to emphasize both social and cognitive attributes in their conceptions of intelligence.

The differences between East and West may be due to differences in the kinds of skills valued by the two kinds of cultures (Srivastava & Misra, 1996). Western cultures and their schools emphasize what might be called *technological intelligence* (Mundy-Castle, 1974), so things like artificial intelligence and so-called smart bombs are viewed, in some sense, as intelligent, or smart.

Western schooling emphasizes other things as well (Srivastava & Misra, 1996), such as generalization, or going beyond the information given (Connolly & Bruner, 1974; Goodnow, 1976), speed (Sternberg, 1985), minimal moves to a solution (Newell & Simon, 1972), and creative thinking (Goodnow, 1976). Moreover, silence is interpreted as a lack of knowledge (Irvine, 1978). In contrast, the Wolof tribe in

Africa views people of higher social class and distinction as speaking less (Irvine, 1978). This difference between the Wolof and Western notions suggests the usefulness of looking at African notions of intelligence as a possible contrast to U.S. notions.

In fact, studies in Africa provide yet another window on the substantial differences. Ruzgis and Grigorenko (1994) have argued that, in Africa, conceptions of intelligence revolve largely around skills that help to facilitate and maintain harmonious and stable intergroup relations; intragroup relations are probably equally important and at times more important. For example, Serpell (1974, 1982, 1993) found that Chewa adults in Zambia emphasize social responsibilities, cooperativeness, and obedience as important to intelligence; intelligent children are expected to be respectful of adults. Kenyan parents also emphasize responsible participation in family and social life as important aspects of intelligence (Super, 1983; Super & Harkness, 1982). In Zimbabwe, the word for intelligence, *ngware,* actually means to be prudent and cautious, particularly in social relationships. Among the Baoule, service to the family and community and politeness toward and respect for elders are seen as key to intelligence (Dasen, 1984).

Similar emphasis on social aspects of intelligence has been found as well among two other African groups, the Songhay of Mali and the Samia of Kenya (Putnam & Kilbride, 1980). The Yoruba, another African tribe, emphasize the importance of depth—of listening rather than just talking—to intelligence, and of being able to see all aspects of an issue and of being able to place the issue in its proper overall context (Durojaiye, 1993).

The emphasis on the social aspects of intelligence is not limited to African cultures. Notions of intelligence in many Asian cultures also emphasize the social aspect of intelligence more than does the conventional Western or IQ-based notion (Azuma & Kashiwagi, 1987; Lutz, 1985; Poole, 1985; White, 1985).

It should be noted that neither African nor Asian cultures emphasize exclusively social notions of intelligence. In one village in Kenya (near Kisumu), many and probably most of the children are at least moderately infected with a variety of parasitic infections. As a result, they experience stomachaches quite frequently. Traditional medicine suggests the usefulness of a large variety (actually, hundreds) of natural herbal medicines that can be used to treat such infections. It appears that at least some of these—although perhaps a small percentage—actually work. More important for our purposes, however, children who learn how to self-medicate via these natural herbal medicines are viewed as being at an adaptive advantage over those who do not have this kind of informal knowledge. Clearly, the kind of adaptive advantage

that is relevant in this culture would be viewed as totally irrelevant in the West, and vice versa.

Grigorenko and her colleagues (2001) have studied conceptions of intelligence in this village in some detail. There appear to be four parts to the conception.

First, the concept of *rieko* can be translated as intelligence, smartness, knowledge, ability, skill, competence, and power. Along with the general concept of *rieko,* the Luo people distinguish among various specialized representations of this concept. Some representations are characterized by the source of *rieko: rieko mar sikul* (knowledge acquired in school), or *rieko mzungu* (the White man's technical powers); others by different domains of action: *rieko mar ot* (competence in household tasks, including planning skills and resource management), or *rieko mar kite* (being versed in traditional customs and rules). Other representations are characterized by specific outcomes, such as *rieko mar lupo* (fishing skills, including knowledge of magic to provide rich catches), *rieko mar yath* (knowledge of healing with herbal medicines), and so forth.

Luoro is the second main quality of children and people in general. It encompasses a whole field of concepts roughly corresponding to social qualities such as respect and care for others, obedience, diligence, consideration, and readiness to share. *Luoro* has an unequivocal positive meaning and was always mentioned as a necessity in response to questions such as "What is most important for a good child to have?" and "What should people have to lead a happy life?" When people were asked to compare the relative importance for an individual's life of *rieko* and *luoro,* respondents generally gave preference to *luoro.* It is interesting that the only two respondents ranking *rieko* higher than *luoro* were outsiders to the local community who had a tertiary education and considerable wealth by village standards. *Rieko* and *luoro* are complementary. *Rieko* is a positive attribute only if *luoro* is also present. Ideally, the power of pure individual abilities should be kept under control by social rules.

Third, *paro* overlaps with both *luoro* and *rieko* and, roughly translated, means *thinking.* Specifically, *paro* refers to the thought processes required to identify a problem and its solution and to the thought processes involved in caring for other people. A child with good thinking (*paro maber*) could thus, for example, be a child who is able to react rationally in case of another person's accident or one who is able to collect wood, burn charcoal, and sell it favorably in order to help his old grandmother. The concept of *paro* stresses the procedural nature of intelligence. In essence, *paro* occupies an intermediate position between the potentiality of *rieko* (its ability aspects) and the partially moral connotation of an outcome (the deed) done with or without *luoro.* *Paro* also reflects the idea of initiative and innovation, for example, in designing a new technical device. *Paro* encompasses the process of thinking, the ability to think, and the specific kind of thinking that an individual demonstrates.

Fourth, *winjo,* like *paro,* is linked to both *rieko* and *luoro.* *Winjo* means comprehending and understanding. It points to the child's abilities to comprehend, that is, to process what is said or what is going on. But it also involves the ability to grasp what is appropriate and inappropriate in a situation, that is, to understand and do what you are told by adults or to derive from the situation what is appropriate to do. It shares with the other key terms the feature that its meaning is a function of context. For a teacher in school it means that a child runs an errand as told. In contrast, a grandmother teaching a child about healing might emphasize the aspect of procedural learning combined with attention to another person.

A "good child" as well as a "good community member" needs a balanced mixture of all positive qualities, in which the contradictory aspects counterbalance each other. Specifically, the ambiguous powers of individual *rieko* (which could be either positive or negative) need to be controlled by social values and rules (*luoro*).

These conceptions of intelligence emphasize social skills much more than do conventional U.S. conceptions of intelligence, but at the same time they recognize the importance of cognitive aspects of intelligence. It is important to realize, again, that there is no one overall U.S. conception of intelligence. Indeed, Okagaki and Sternberg (1993) found that different ethnic groups in San Jose, California, had rather different conceptions of what it means to be intelligent. For example, Latino parents of schoolchildren tended to emphasize the importance of social-competence skills in their conceptions of intelligence, whereas Asian parents tended rather heavily to emphasize the importance of cognitive skills. Anglo parents also emphasized cognitive skills more. Teachers, representing the dominant culture, emphasized cognitive skills more than social-competence skills. The rank order of children of various groups' performances (including subgroups within the Latino and Asian groups) could be perfectly predicted by the extent to which parents shared the teachers' conceptions of intelligence. In other words, teachers tended to reward those children who were socialized into a view of intelligence that happened to correspond to the teachers' own.

Explicit Theories

A Psychometric Theory

The psychometric approach to intelligence is among the oldest of approaches, dating back to Galton's (1883) psychophysical theory of intelligence in terms of psychophysical

abilities (such as strength of hand grip or visual acuity) and later to Binet and Simon's (1905/1916) theory of intelligence as judgment, involving adaptation to the environment, direction of one's efforts, and self-criticism.

Carroll (1993) has proposed a hierarchical model of intelligence, based on a factor analysis of more than 460 data sets obtained between 1927 and 1987. His analysis encompasses more than 130,000 people from diverse walks of life and even countries of origin (although non-English-speaking countries are poorly represented among his data sets). The model Carroll proposed, based on his monumental undertaking, is a hierarchy comprising three strata: Stratum I, which includes many narrow, specific abilities (e.g., spelling ability, speed of reasoning); Stratum II, which includes various group-factor abilities (e.g., fluid intelligence, involved in flexible thinking and seeing things in novel ways; and crystallized intelligence, the accumulated knowledge base); and Stratum III, which is just a single general intelligence, much like Spearman's (1904) general intelligence factor.

Of these strata, the most interesting is perhaps the middle stratum, which includes (in addition to fluid and crystallized abilities) learning and memory processes, visual perception, auditory perception, facile production of ideas (similar to verbal fluency), and speed (which includes both sheer speed of response and speed of accurate responding). Although Carroll does not break much new ground, in that many of the abilities in his model have been mentioned in other theories, he does masterfully integrate a large and diverse factor-analytic literature, thereby giving great authority to his model. At the same time, his meta-analysis assumes that conventional psychometric tests cover the entire domain of intelligence that needs to be covered by a theory of intelligence. Some theorists, discussed next, question this assumption.

Cognitive Theories

Cronbach (1957) called for a merging of the two disciplines of scientific psychology: the differential and experimental approaches. The idea is that the study of individual differences (differential psychology) and of cross-individual commonalities (experimental psychology) need not be separate disciplines. They can be merged.

Serious responses to Cronbach came in the 1970s, with cognitive approaches to intelligence attempting this merger. Two of the responses were the cognitive-correlates approach to intelligence and the cognitive-correlates approach.

Hunt, Frost, and Lunneborg (1973; see also Hunt, Lunneborg, & Lewis, 1975) introduced the cognitive-correlates approach, whereby scores on laboratory cognitive tests were correlated with scores on psychometric intelligence tests. The theory underlying this work was that fairly simple components of information processing studied in the laboratory—such as the time to retrieve lexical information from long-term memory—could serve as a basis for understanding human intelligence. Intelligence tests, on this view, present complex problems whose solution nevertheless relies on fairly simple information processing. Thus, a participant in a cognitive study might be asked whether two letters, *A* and *a*, are identical in identity (answer: yes) or identical in case (answer: no). The tasks were directly out of the literature of experimental psychology, including the letter-comparison task, which is based on work by Posner and Mitchell (1967).

Sternberg (1977; see also Sternberg, 1983) introduced the cognitive-components approach, whereby performance on complex psychometric tasks was decomposed into elementary information-processing components. The underlying theory was that intelligence comprises a series of component information processes. In contrast to the cognitive-correlates approach, however, the underlying components were seen as complex rather than as simple. For example, solving an analogy of the form A : B :: C : ? involves components such as encoding the terms, inferring the relation between A and B, applying this relation from C to ?, and so forth (see review by Lohman, 2000).

The cognitive approaches of Hunt and Sternberg are now primarily of historical interest. Both authors have expanded their conceptualizations of intelligence since this work. They were forced to do so. Neither approach yielded consistently high correlations between the tasks and task components and psychometric tests of intelligence used as criteria. Moreover, sometimes the components showing the highest correlations were the ones least expected to show them. Sternberg and Gardner (1983), for example, consistently found the regression-constant component to have the highest correlations with psychometric test scores, leading them to wonder whether they had rediscovered through information-processing analysis the general factor that had been discovered through psychometric analysis.

In the 1990s cognitive and biological approaches (discussed next) began to merge (Vernon, Wickett, Bazana, & Stelmack, 2000). A prototypical example is the inspection-time task (Nettlebeck, 1982; see reviews by Deary, 2000; Deary & Stough, 1996). In this task, two adjacent vertical lines are presented tachistoscopically or by computer, followed by a visual mask (to destroy the image in visual iconic memory). The two lines differ in length, as do the lengths of time for which the two lines are presented. The participant's task is to say which line is longer. But instead of using raw response time as the dependent variable, investigators typically use measures derived from a psychophysical function estimated after many trials. For example, the measure might be

the duration of a single inspection trial at which 50% accuracy is achieved. Correlations between this task and measures of IQ appear to be about .4, a bit higher than is typical in psychometric tasks. Much of this correlation may be mediated by the visual ability component of intelligence (Gv). There are differing theories as to why such correlations are obtained. All such theories generally attempt to relate the cognitive function of visual inspection time to some kind of biological function, such as speed of neuronal conduction. Let us consider, then, some of the biological functions that may underlie intelligence.

Biological Theories

An important approach to studying intelligence is to understand it in terms of the functioning of the brain, in particular, and of the nervous system, in general. Earlier theories relating the brain to intelligence tended to be global in nature, although they were not necessarily backed by strong empirical evidence. Because these earlier theories are still used in contemporary writings and, in the case of Halstead and Luria, form the bases for test batteries still in contemporary use, they are described here briefly.

Early Biological Theories.   Halstead (1951) suggested that there are four biologically based abilities, which he called (a) the integrative field factor, (b) the abstraction factor, (c) the power factor, and (d) the directional factor. Halstead attributed all four of these abilities primarily to the functioning of the cortex of the frontal lobes.

More influential than Halstead has been Hebb (1949), who distinguished between two basic types of intelligence: Intelligence A and Intelligence B. Hebb's distinction is still used by some theorists. According to Hebb, Intelligence A is innate potential, and Intelligence B is the functioning of the brain as a result of the actual development that has occurred. These two basic types of intelligence should be distinguished from Intelligence C, or intelligence as measured by conventional psychometric tests of intelligence. Hebb also suggested that learning, an important basis of intelligence, is built up through cell assemblies, by which successively more and more complex connections among neurons are constructed as learning takes place.

A third biologically based theory is that of Luria (1973, 1980), which has had a major impact on tests of intelligence (Kaufman & Kaufman, 1983; Naglieri & Das, 1997). According to Luria, the brain comprises three main units with respect to intelligence: (a) a unit of arousal in the brain stem and midbrain structures; (b) a sensory-input unit in the temporal, parietal, and occipital lobes; and (c) an organization and planning unit in the frontal cortex. The more modern form of this theory is PASS theory (Das, Kirby, & Jarman, 1979; Naglieri & Das, 1990, 2002), which distinguishes among planning, attentional, successive processing, and simultaneous processing abilities. These latter two abilities are subsets of the sensory-input abilities referred to by Luria.

The early biological theories continue to have an influence on theories of intelligence. Oddly, their influence on contemporary psychometric work is substantially greater than their influence on contemporary biological work, which largely (although not wholly) has left these theories behind.

Contemporary Biological Theories. More recent theories have dealt with more specific aspects of brain or neural functioning. One contemporary biological theory is based on *speed of neuronal conduction.* For example, one theory has suggested that individual differences in nerve-conduction velocity are a basis for individual differences in intelligence (e.g., Reed & Jensen, 1992; Vernon & Mori, 1992). Two procedures have been used to measure conduction velocity, either centrally (in the brain) or peripherally (e.g., in the arm).

Reed and Jensen (1992) tested brain-nerve conduction velocities via two medium-latency potentials, N70 and P100, which were evoked by pattern-reversal stimulation. Subjects saw a black-and-white checkerboard pattern in which the black squares would change to white and the white squares to black. Over many trials, responses to these changes were analyzed via electrodes attached to the scalp in four places. Correlations of derived latency measures with IQ were small (generally in the .1 to .2 range of absolute value), but were significant in some cases, suggesting at least a modest relation between the two kinds of measures.

Vernon and Mori (1992) reported on two studies investigating the relation between nerve-conduction velocity in the arm and IQ. In both studies nerve-conduction velocity was measured in the median nerve of the arm by attaching electrodes to the arm. In the second study, conduction velocity from the wrist to the tip of the finger was also measured. Vernon and Mori found significant correlations with IQ in the .4 range, as well as somewhat smaller correlations (around .2) with response-time measures. They interpreted their results as supporting the hypothesis of a relation between speed of information transmission in the peripheral nerves and intelligence. However, these results must be interpreted cautiously, as Wickett and Vernon (1994) later tried unsuccessfully to replicate these earlier results.

Other work has emphasized P300 as a measure of intelligence. Higher amplitudes of P300 are suggestive of higher levels of extraction of information from stimuli (Johnson, 1986, 1988) and also more rapid adjustment to novelty in stimuli (Donchin, Ritter, & McCallum, 1979). However, attempts to relate P300 and other measures of amplitudes of evoked potentials to scores on tests of intelligence have led to inconclusive results (Vernon et al., 2000). Indeed, the field has gotten a mixed reputation because so many successful attempts have later been met with failures to replicate.

There could be a number of reasons for these failures. One is almost certainly that there are just so many possible sites, potentials to measure, and ways of quantifying the data that the huge number of possible correlations creates a greater likelihood of Type I errors than would be the case for more typical cases of test-related measurements. Investigators using such methods therefore have to take special care to guard against Type II errors.

Another approach has been to study *glucose metabolism.* The underlying theory is that when a person processes information, there is more activity in a certain part of the brain. The better the person is at the behavioral activity, the less is the effort required by the brain. Some of the most interesting recent studies of glucose metabolism have been done by Richard Haier and his colleagues. For example, Haier et al. (1988) showed that cortical glucose metabolic rates as revealed by PET scan analysis of subjects solving Raven Progressive Matrices problems were lower for more intelligent than for less intelligent subjects. These results suggest that the more intelligent participants needed to expend less effort than the less intelligent ones in order to solve the reasoning problems. A later study (Haier, Siegel, Tang, Abel, & Buchsbaum, 1992) showed a similar result for more versus less practiced performers playing the computer game of Tetris. In other words, smart people or intellectually expert people do not have to work as hard as less smart or intellectually expert people at a given problem.

What remains to be shown, however, is the causal direction of this finding. One could sensibly argue that the smart people expend less glucose (as a proxy for effort) because they are smart, rather than that people are smart because they expend less glucose. Or both high IQ and low glucose metabolism may be related to a third causal variable. In other words, we cannot always assume that the biological event is a cause (in the reductionist sense). It may be, instead, an effect.

Another approach considers *brain size.* The theory is simply that larger brains are able to hold more neurons and, more important, more complex intersynaptic connections between neurons. Willerman, Schultz, Rutledge, and Bigler (1991) correlated brain size with Wechsler Adult Intelligence Scale–Revised (WAIS-R) IQs, controlling for body size. They found that IQ correlated .65 in men and .35 in women, with a correlation of .51 for both sexes combined. A follow-up analysis of the same 40 subjects suggested that, in men, a relatively larger left hemisphere better predicted WAIS-R verbal than it predicted nonverbal ability, whereas in women a larger left hemisphere predicted nonverbal ability better than it predicted verbal ability (Willerman, Schultz, Rutledge, & Bigler, 1992). These brain-size correlations are suggestive, but it is difficult to say what they mean at this point.

Yet another approach that is at least partially biologically based is that of behavior genetics. A fairly complete review of this extensive literature is found in Sternberg and Grigorenko (1997). The basic idea is that it should be possible to disentangle genetic from environmental sources of variation in intelligence. Ultimately, one would hope to locate the genes responsible for intelligence (Plomin, McClearn, & Smith, 1994, 1995; Plomin & Neiderhiser, 1992; Plomin & Petrill, 1997). The literature is complex, but it appears that about half the total variance in IQ scores is accounted for by genetic factors (Loehlin, 1989; Plomin, 1997). This figure may be an underestimate because the variance includes error variance and because most studies of heritability have been with children, but we know that heritability of IQ is higher for adults than for children (Plomin, 1997). Also, some studies, such as the Texas Adoption Project (Loehlin, Horn, & Willerman, 1997), suggest higher estimates: .78 in the Texas Adoption Project, .75 in the Minnesota Study of Twins Reared Apart (Bouchard, 1997; Bouchard, Lykken, McGue, Segal, & Tellegen, 1990), and .78 in the Swedish Adoption Study of Aging (Pedersen, Plomin, Nesselroade, & McClearn, 1992).

At the same time, some researchers argue that effects of heredity and environment cannot be clearly and validly separated (Bronfenbrenner & Ceci, 1994; Wahlsten & Gottlieb, 1997). Perhaps, the direction of future research should be to figure out how heredity and environment work together to produce phenotypic intelligence (Scarr, 1997), concentrating especially on within-family environmental variation, which appears to be more important than between-family variation (Jensen, 1997). Such research requires, at the very least, very carefully prepared tests of intelligence, perhaps some of the newer tests described in the next section.

Systems Theories

Many contemporary theories of intelligence can be viewed as systems theories because they are more complex, in many respects, than past theories, and attempt to deal with intelligence as a complex system.

The Theory of Multiple Intelligences. Gardner (1983, 1993, 1999) proposed that there is no single, unified intelligence, but rather a set of relatively distinct, independent, and modular multiple intelligences. His theory of multiple intelligences (MI theory) originally proposed seven multiple intelligences: (a) linguistic, as used in reading a book or writing a poem; (b) logical-mathematical, as used in deriving a logical proof or solving a mathematical problem; (c) spatial, as used in fitting suitcases into the trunk of a car; (d) musical, as used in singing a song or composing a symphony; (e) bodily-kinesthetic, as used in dancing or playing football; (f) interpersonal, as used in understanding and interacting with other people; and (g) intrapersonal, as used in understanding oneself.

Recently, Gardner (1999) has proposed an additional intelligence as a confirmed part of his theory: naturalist intelligence, the kind shown by people who are able to discern patterns in nature. Charles Darwin would be a notable example. Gardner has also suggested that there may be two other intelligences: spiritual intelligence and existential intelligence. Spiritual intelligence involves a concern with cosmic or existential issues and the recognition of the spiritual as the achievement of a state of being. Existential intelligence involves a concern with ultimate issues. Gardner believes that the evidence for these latter two intelligences is less powerful than the evidence for the other eight intelligences. Whatever the evidence may be for the other eight, we agree that the evidence for these two new intelligences is speculative at this point.

Most activities will involve some combination of these different intelligences. For example, dancing might involve both musical and bodily-kinesthetic intelligences. Reading a mathematical textbook might require both linguistic and logical-mathematical intelligences. Often it will be hard to separate these intelligences in task performance.

In the past, factor analysis served as the major criterion for identifying abilities. Gardner (1983, 1999) proposed a new set of criteria, including but not limited to factor analysis, for identifying the existence of a discrete kind of intelligence: (a) potential isolation by brain damage, in that the destruction or sparing of a discrete area of the brain may destroy or spare a particular kind of intelligent behavior; (b) the existence of exceptional individuals who demonstrate extraordinary ability (or deficit) in a particular kind of intelligent behavior; (c) an identifiable core operation or set of operations that are essential to performance of a particular kind of intelligent behavior; (d) a distinctive developmental history leading from novice to master, along with disparate levels of expert performance; (e) a distinctive evolutionary history, in which increases in intelligence may be plausibly associated with enhanced adaptation to the environment; (f) supportive evidence from cognitive-experimental research; (g) supportive evidence from psychometric tests; and (h) susceptibility to encoding in a symbol system.

Gardner (1993, 1995, 1997) has suggested that the multiple intelligences can be understood as bases not only for understanding intelligence, but for understanding other kinds of constructs as well, such as creativity and leadership. For example, Gardner has analyzed some of the great creative thinkers of the twentieth century in terms of their multiple intelligences, arguing that many of them were extraordinarily creative by virtue of extremely high levels of one of the intelligences. For example, Martha Graham was very high in bodily-kinesthetic intelligence, T. S. Eliot in linguistic intelligence, and so forth.

The theory of multiple intelligences has proved to be enormously successful in capturing the attention both of the psychological public and of the public in general. Nevertheless, some caution must be observed before accepting the theory.

First, since the theory was proposed in 1983, there have been no published empirical tests of the theory as a whole. Given that a major goal of science is empirically to test theories, this fact is something of a disappointment, but it certainly suggests the need for such testing.

Second, the theory has been justified by Gardner on the basis of post hoc reviews of various literatures. Although these reviews are persuasive, they are also highly selective. For example, there is virtually no overlap between the literatures reviewed by Gardner in his various books and the literatures reviewed by Carroll (1993) or Jensen (1998). This is not to say that his literature is wrong or that theirs is right. Rather, all literature reviews are selective and probably tend more to dwell on studies that support the proposed point of view. A difference between the literature reviewed by Gardner and that reviewed by Carroll and Jensen is that the literature Gardner reviews was not intended to test his theory of intelligence or anything like it. In contrast, the literatures reviewed by Carroll and Jensen largely comprise studies designed specifically to test psychometric theories of intelligence.

Third, even if one accepts Gardner's criteria for defining an intelligence, it is not clear whether the eight or ten intelligences proposed by Gardner are the only ones that would fit. For example, might there be a sexual intelligence? And are these intelligences really *intelligences,* per se, or are some of them better labeled *talents?* Obviously, the answer to this question is definitional, and hence there may be no ultimate answer at all.

Finally, there is a real need for psychometrically strong assessments of the various intelligences, because without such assessments it will be difficult ever to validate the theory.

Assessments exist (Gardner, Feldman, & Krechevsky, 1998), but they seem not to be psychometrically strong. Without strong assessments, the theory is likely to survive without or because of the lack of serious attempts at disconfirmation.

Since the theory was first proposed, a large number of educational interventions have arisen that are based on the theory, sometimes closely and other times less so (Gardner, 1993). Many of the programs are unevaluated, and evaluations of other programs seem still to be ongoing, so it is difficult to say at this point what the results will be. In one particularly careful evaluation of a well-conceived program in a large southern city, there were no significant gains in student achievement or changes in student self-concept as a result of an intervention program based on Gardner's (1983, 1999) theory (Callahan, Tomlinson, & Plucker, 1997). There is no way of knowing whether these results are representative of such intervention programs, however.

Successful Intelligence. Sternberg (1997, 1999c, 1999d) has suggested that we may wish to pay less attention to conventional notions of intelligence and more to what he terms *successful intelligence,* or the ability to adapt to, shape, and select environments to accomplish one's goals and those of one's society and culture. A successfully intelligent person balances adaptation, shaping, and selection, doing each as necessary. The theory is motivated in part by repeated findings that conventional tests of intelligence and related tests do not predict meaningful criteria of success as well as they predict scores on other similar tests and school grades (e.g., Sternberg & Williams, 1997).

Successful intelligence involves an individual's discerning his or her pattern of strengths and weaknesses and then figuring out ways to capitalize on the strengths and at the same time compensate for or correct the weaknesses. People attain success, in part, in idiosyncratic ways that involve their finding how best to exploit their own patterns of strengths and weaknesses.

According to the proposed theory of human intelligence and its development (Sternberg, 1980, 1984, 1985, 1990, 1997, 1999a, 1999b), a common set of processes underlies all aspects of intelligence. These processes are hypothesized to be universal. For example, although the solutions to problems that are considered intelligent in one culture may be different from the solutions considered to be intelligent in another culture, the need to define problems and translate strategies to solve these problems exists in any culture.

Metacomponents, or executive processes, plan what to do, monitor things as they are being done, and evaluate things after they are done. Examples of metacomponents are recognizing the existence of a problem, defining the nature of the problem, deciding on a strategy for solving the problem, monitoring the solution of the problem, and evaluating the solution after the problem is solved.

Performance components execute the instructions of the metacomponents. For example, inference is used to decide how two stimuli are related, and application is used to apply what one has inferred (Sternberg, 1977). Other examples of performance components are comparison of stimuli, justification of a given response as adequate although not ideal, and actually making the response.

Knowledge-acquisition components are used to learn how to solve problems or simply to acquire declarative knowledge in the first place (Sternberg, 1985). Selective encoding is used to decide what information is relevant in the context of one's learning. Selective comparison is used to bring old information to bear on new problems. Selective combination is used to put together the selectively encoded and compared information into a single and sometimes insightful solution to a problem.

Although the same processes are used for all three aspects of intelligence universally, these processes are applied to different kinds of tasks and situations depending on whether a given problem requires analytical thinking, creative thinking, practical thinking, or a combination of these kinds of thinking. Data supporting the theory cannot be presented fully here but are summarized elsewhere (Sternberg, 1977, 1985; Sternberg et al., 2000).

Three broad abilities are important to successful intelligence: analytical, creative, and practical abilities.

Analytical abilities are required to analyze and evaluate the options available to oneself in life. They include things such as identifying the existence of a problem, defining the nature of the problem, setting up a strategy for solving the problem, and monitoring one's solution processes.

Creative abilities are required to generate problem-solving options in the first place. Creative individuals typically "buy low and sell high" in the world of ideas (Sternberg & Lubart, 1995, 1996): They are willing to generate ideas that, like stocks with low price-earnings ratios, are unpopular and perhaps even deprecated. Having convinced at least some people of the value of these ideas, they then sell high, meaning that they move on to the next unpopular idea. Research shows that these abilities are at least partially distinct from conventional IQ and that they are moderately domain specific, meaning that creativity in one domain (such as art) does not necessarily imply creativity in another (such as writing; Sternberg & Lubart, 1995). Not all creative work is crowd defying, of course. Some work is creative by virtue of extending existing paradigms (see Sternberg, 1999b).

Practical abilities are required to implement options and to make them work. Practical abilities are involved when intelligence is applied to real-world contexts. A key aspect of practical intelligence is the acquisition and use of tacit knowledge, which is knowledge of what one needs to know to succeed in a given environment that is not explicitly taught and that usually is not verbalized. Research shows several generalizations about tacit knowledge. First, it is acquired through mindful utilization of experience. What matters, however, is not the experience, per se, but how much one profits from it. Second, tacit knowledge is relatively domain specific, although people who are likely to acquire it in one domain are likely to acquire it in another domain. Third, acquisition and utilization are relatively independent of conventional abilities. Fourth, tacit knowledge predicts criteria of job success about as well as and sometimes better than does IQ. Fifth, tacit knowledge predicts these criteria incrementally over IQ and other kinds of measures, such as of personality and of styles of learning and thinking (McClelland, 1973; Sternberg et al., 2000; Sternberg & Wagner, 1993; Sternberg, Wagner, Williams, & Horvath, 1995).

The separation of practical intelligence from IQ has been shown in a number of different ways in a number of different studies (see Sternberg et al., 2000, for a review). Scribner (1984, 1986) showed that experienced assemblers in a milk-processing plant used complex strategies for combining partially filled cases in a manner that minimized the number of moves required to complete an order. Although the assemblers were the least educated workers in the plant, they were able to calculate in their heads quantities expressed in different base number systems, and they routinely outperformed the more highly educated white-collar workers who substituted when the assemblers were absent. Scribner found that the order-filling performance of the assemblers was unrelated to measures of academic skills, including intelligence test scores, arithmetic test scores, and grades.

Ceci and Liker (1986) carried out a study of expert racetrack handicappers and found that expert handicappers used a highly complex algorithm for predicting post time odds that involved interactions among seven kinds of information. Use of a complex interaction term in their implicit equation was unrelated to the handicappers' IQs.

A series of studies showed that shoppers in California grocery stores were able to choose which of several products represented the best buy for them (Lave, Murtaugh, & de la Roche, 1984; Murtaugh, 1985). They were able to do so even though they did very poorly on the same kinds of problems when the problems were presented in the form of a paper-and-pencil arithmetic computation test. The same principle that applies to adults appears to apply to children as well: Carraher, Carraher, and Schliemann (1985) found that Brazilian street children who could apply sophisticated mathematical strategies in their street vending were unable to do the same in a classroom setting (see also Ceci & Roazzi, 1994; Nuñes, 1994).

One more example of a study of practical intelligence was provided by individuals asked to play the role of city managers for the computer-simulated city of Lohhausen (Dörner & Kreuzig, 1983; Dörner, Kreuzig, Reither, & Staudel, 1983). A variety of problems were presented to these individuals, such as how best to raise revenue to build roads. The simulation involved more than one thousand variables. No relation was found between IQ and complexity of strategies used.

There is also evidence that practical intelligence can be taught (Gardner, Krechevsky, Sternberg, & Okagaki, 1994; Sternberg, Okagaki, & Jackson, 1990), at least in some degree. For example, middle-school children given a program for developing their practical intelligence for school (strategies for effective reading, writing, execution of homework, and taking of tests) improved more from pretest to posttest than did control students who received an alternative but irrelevant treatment.

None of these studies suggest that IQ is unimportant for school or job performance or other kinds of performance; indeed, the evidence suggests the contrary (Barrett & Depinet, 1991; Gottfredson, 1986, 1997; Hunt, 1995; Hunter & Hunter, 1984; Schmidt & Hunter, 1981, 1993, 1998; Wigdor & Garner, 1982). What the studies do suggest, however, is that there are other aspects of intelligence that are relatively independent of IQ, and that are important as well. A multiple-abilities prediction model of school or job performance would probably be most satisfactory.

According to the theory of successful intelligence, children's multiple abilities are underutilized in educational institutions because teaching tends to value analytical (as well as memory) abilities at the expense of creative and practical abilities. Sternberg, Ferrari, Clinkenbeard, and Grigorenko (1996; Sternberg, Grigorenko, Ferrari, & Clinkenbeard, 1999) designed an experiment in order to illustrate this point. They identified 199 high school students from around the United States who were strong in either analytical, creative, or practical abilities, or all three kinds of abilities, or none of the kinds of abilities. Students were then brought to Yale University to take a college-level psychology course that was taught in a way that emphasized either memory, analytical, creative, or practical abilities. Some students were matched, and others mismatched, to their own strengths. All students were evaluated for memory-based, analytical, creative, and practical achievements.

Sternberg and his colleagues found that students whose instruction matched their pattern of abilities performed significantly better than did students who were mismatched. They also found that prediction of course performance was improved by taking into account creative and practical as well as analytical abilities.

In subsequent studies (Grigorenko, Jarvin, & Sternberg, 2002; Sternberg, Torff, & Grigorenko, 1998), students were taught a subject matter in a variety of ways in order to compare instruction based on the theory of successful intelligence with other forms of instruction. For example, one set of studies compared such instruction with instruction based on critical thinking and instruction based on traditional, memory-based learning in social studies and science (Sternberg et al., 1998). Another study compared instruction based on successful intelligence to traditional instruction in reading (Grigorenko et al., 2002). Participants in these experiments ranged from middle-school to high-school levels and covered the range of socioeconomic levels from very low to very high. In general, instruction based on the theory of successful intelligence was superior to the other forms of instruction, even if tests of achievement measured only memory-based learning.

At a theoretical level, why should instruction based on the theory of successful intelligence be more effective than conventional or other forms of instruction? Five reasons have been proffered. First, instruction based on the theory of successful intelligence encourages students to capitalize on strengths. Second, it encourages them to correct or to compensate for weaknesses. Third, it enables them to encode material in three different ways, which, by increasing the number of retrieval routes to the information, facilitates memory retrieval later on. Fourth, it encourages elaborative rather than maintenance rehearsal, which results in more elaborated memory traces for the material. Fifth, it is more motivating to students because it typically renders the material more interesting than do conventional forms of presentation.

The theory of successful intelligence has been tested more extensively than many other contemporary theories of intelligence. Nevertheless, questions remain. For example, even some who might accept the existence of distinctive creative and practical abilities might argue that they represent psychological attributes distinct from intelligence. Second, the pervasiveness of the general factor in psychological investigations must make one wary of Type I errors in accepting the notion that the general factor is not truly general, but rather applies primarily to academic kinds of tasks. Third, there is as yet no published test that measures the triarchic abilities, and the research-based tests clearly need further development. Without published tests, it will be difficult for laboratories other than those of the principal proponents of the theory to test the theory adequately.

True Intelligence.   Perkins (1995) proposed a theory of what he refers to as *true intelligence,* which he believes synthesizes classic views as well as new ones. According to Perkins, there are three basic aspects to intelligence: neural, experiential, and reflective.

Neural intelligence concerns what Perkins believes to be the fact that some people's neurological systems function better than do the neurological systems of others, running faster and with more precision. He mentions "more finely tuned voltages" and "more exquisitely adapted chemical catalysts" as well as a "better pattern of connectivity in the labyrinth of neurons" (Perkins, 1995, p. 97), although it is not entirely clear what any of these phrases means. Perkins believes this aspect of intelligence to be largely genetically determined and unlearnable. This kind of intelligence seems to be somewhat similar to Cattell's (1971) idea of fluid intelligence. The experiential aspect of intelligence is what has been learned from experience. It is the extent and organization of the knowledge base, and thus is similar to Cattell's (1971) notion of crystallized intelligence. The reflective aspect of intelligence refers to the role of strategies in memory and problem solving and appears to be similar to the construct of metacognition or cognitive monitoring (Brown & DeLoache, 1978; Flavell, 1981).

There have been no published empirical tests of the theory of true intelligence, so it is difficult to evaluate the theory at this time. Like Gardner's (1983) theory, Perkins's theory is based on literature review, and as noted earlier, such literature reviews often tend to be selective and then interpreted in a way to maximize the theory's fit to the available data.

The Bioecological Model of Intelligence.   Ceci (1996) proposed a bioecological model of intelligence, according to which multiple cognitive potentials, context, and knowledge all are essential bases of individual differences in performance. Each of the multiple cognitive potentials enables relationships to be discovered, thoughts to be monitored, and knowledge to be acquired within a given domain. Although these potentials are biologically based, their development is closely linked to environmental context, and hence it is difficult if not impossible cleanly to separate biological from environmental contributions to intelligence. Moreover, abilities may express themselves very differently in different contexts. For example, children given essentially the same task in the context of a video game and in the context of a laboratory cognitive task performed much better when the task was presented in the context of the video game.

The bioecological model appears in many ways to be more a framework than a theory. At some level, the theory must be right. Certainly, both biological and ecological factors contribute to the development and manifestation of intelligence. Perhaps what the theory needs most at this time are specific and clearly falsifiable predictions that would set it apart from other theories.

Emotional Intelligence.   Emotional intelligence is the ability to perceive accurately, appraise, and express emotion; the ability to access or generate feelings when they facilitate thought; the ability to understand emotion and emotional knowledge; and the ability to regulate emotions to promote emotional and intellectual growth (Mayer et al., 2000). The concept was introduced by Salovey and Mayer (Mayer & Salovey, 1993; Salovey & Mayer, 1990) and popularized and expanded by Goleman (1995).

There is some evidence—though still tentative—for the existence of emotional intelligence. For example, Mayer and Gehr (1996) found that emotional perception of characters in a variety of situations correlated with SAT scores, with empathy, and with emotional openness. Full convergent-discriminant validation of the construct, however, appears to be needed. The results to date are mixed, with some studies supportive (Mayer, Salovey, & Caruso, 2000) and others not (Davies, Stankov, & Roberts, 1998).

CONCLUSIONS

The study of intelligence has come far in the century since Spearman (1904) published his seminal paper on general intelligence. Although there is no consensus as to what intelligence is or how to measure it, there are many viable alternatives. More research needs to distinguish among these alternatives rather than simply adducing evidence for any one of the alternatives.

Among the psychometric theories, Carroll's (1993) has achieved fairly widespread acclaim, perhaps because it is based on a meta-analysis of so much empirical work. Because of its complexity, however, it is likely to have less influence on measurement than simpler theories, such as the theory of fluid and crystallized abilities (Cattell, 1971; Horn, 1994). History suggests that very complicated theories (e.g., Guilford, 1967, 1982; Guilford & Hoepfner, 1971; Guttman, 1954) tend not to have a long shelf life. In Guilford's case, however, it is more a compliment to than a criticism of his theory, because the demise of Guilford's theory is related to its falsifiability (Horn & Knapp, 1973), a property that not all modern theories have shown themselves to possess.

There are some questions that no existing theories of intelligence answer. Consider a few of these.

Challenges to Traditional Theories and Beliefs About Intelligence

Within recent years, several challenges from unexpected quarters have been proposed to theories and conceptions of intelligence. Two such challenges are the Flynn effect and dynamic testing.

The Flynn Effect. An empirical phenomenon challenges many theories of intelligence that view intelligence as some kind of fixed, largely genetically based trait. We know that the environment has powerful effects on cognitive abilities. Perhaps the simplest and most potent demonstration of this effect is what is called the *Flynn effect* (Flynn, 1984, 1987, 1994, 1998). The basic phenomenon is that IQ has increased over successive generations around the world through most of the century—at least since 1930. The effect must be environmental because a successive stream of genetic mutations obviously could not have taken hold and exerted such an effect over such a short period of time. The effect is powerful—about 15 points of IQ per generation for tests of fluid intelligence. And it occurs all over the world. The effect has been greater for tests of fluid intelligence than for tests of crystallized intelligence. The difference, if linearly extrapolated (a hazardous procedure, obviously), would suggest that a person who in 1892 fell at the 90th percentile on the Raven Progressive Matrices Test, a test of fluid intelligence, would, in 1992, score at the 5th percentile.

There have been many potential explanations of the Flynn effect, and in 1996 Ulric Neisser organized a conference at Emory University to try to explain the effect (Neisser, 1998). Some of the possible explanations include increased schooling, greater educational attainment of parents, better nutrition, and less childhood disease. A particularly interesting explanation is that of more and better parental attention to children (see Bronfenbrenner & Ceci, 1994). Whatever the answer, the Flynn effect suggests that we need to think carefully about the view that IQ is fixed. It probably is not fixed within individuals (Campbell & Ramey, 1994; Ramey, 1994), and it is certainly not fixed across generations.

Dynamic Assessment. In dynamic assessment, individuals learn at the time of test. If they answer an item correctly, they are given guided feedback to help them solve the item, either until they get it correct or until the examiner has run out of clues to give them.

The notion of dynamic testing appears to have originated with Vygotsky (1934/1962, 1978) and was developed independently by Feuerstein, Rand, Haywood, Hoffman, and Jensen (1985). Dynamic assessment is generally based on the notion that cognitive abilities are modifiable and that there is some zone of proximal development (Vygotsky, 1978), which represents the difference between actually developed ability and latent capacity. Dynamic assessments attempt to measure this zone of proximal development, or an analogue to it.

Dynamic assessment is cause for both celebration and caution (Grigorenko & Sternberg, 1998). On the one hand, it represents a break from conventional psychometric notions of a more or less fixed level of intelligence. On the other hand, it is more a promissory note than a realized success. The Feuerstein test, the Learning Potential Assessment Device (Feuerstein et al., 1985), is of clinical use but is not psychometrically normed or validated. There is only one formally normed test available in the United States (Swanson, 1995). This test yields scores for working memory before and at various points during and after training, as well as scores for amount of improvement with intervention, number of hints that have been given, and a subjective evaluation by the examiner of the examinee's use of strategies. Other tests are perhaps on the horizon (Guthke & Stein, 1996), but their potential for standardization and validity, too, remains to be shown.

Intelligence as Typical Performance. Traditionally, intelligence has been thought of as something to be conceptualized and measured in terms of maximum performance. The tests of intelligence have been maximum-performance tests, requiring examinees to work as hard as they can to maximize their scores. Ackerman (1994; Ackerman & Heggestad, 1997; Goff & Ackerman, 1992) has recently argued that typical-performance tests—which, like personality tests, do not require extensive intellectual effort—ought to supplement maximal-performance ones. On such tests individuals might be asked to what extent statements like "I prefer my life to be filled with puzzles I must solve" or "I enjoy work that requires conscientious, exacting skills" match their attitudes. A factor analysis of such tests yielded five factors: intellectual engagement, openness, conscientiousness, directed activity, and science-technology interest.

Ackerman's data suggest a weak relationship between his measures of typical performance and more conventional measures of maximum performance. What is needed most at this time are incremental validity studies that show that this theory provides significant incremental validity with respect to real-world task performance over the validity provided by

40 Contemporary Theories of Intelligence

available measures of intelligence. Because our intelligence so often is used in typical performance settings (Sternberg et al., 1981), future theorists will need to cope with the challenge of typical performance, following Ackerman's lead.

REFERENCES

Ackerman, P. (1994). Intelligence, attention, and learning: Maximal and typical performance. In D. K. Detterman (Ed.), *Current topics in human intelligence: Theories of intelligence* (Vol. 4, pp. 1–27). Norwood, NJ: Ablex.

Ackerman, P. L., & Heggestad, E. D. (1997). Intelligence, personality, and interests: Evidence for overlapping traits. *Psychological Bulletin, 121,* 219–245.

Azuma, H., & Kashiwagi, K. (1987). Descriptions for an intelligent person: A Japanese study. *Japanese Psychological Research, 29,* 17–26.

Barrett, G. V., & Depinet, R. L. (1991). A reconsideration of testing for competence rather than for intelligence. *American Psychologist, 46,* 1012–1024.

Binet, A., & Simon, T. (1916). *The development of intelligence in children.* Baltimore: Williams & Wilkins. (Originally published 1905)

Boring, E. G. (1923, June 6). Intelligence as the tests test it. *New Republic,* 35–37.

Bouchard, T. J., Jr. (1997). IQ similarity in twins reared apart: Findings and responses to critics. In R. J. Sternberg & E. L. Grigorenko (Eds.), *Intelligence, heredity, and environment* (pp. 126–160). New York: Cambridge University Press.

Bouchard, T. J., Jr., Lykken, D. T., McGue, M., Segal, N. L., & Tellegen, A. (1990). Sources of human psychological differences: The Minnesota study of twins reared apart. *Science, 250,* 223–228.

Brand, C. (1996). *The g factor: General intelligence and its implications.* Chichester, England: Wiley.

Bronfenbrenner, U., & Ceci, S. J. (1994). Nature-nurture reconceptualized in developmental perspective: A bioecological model. *Psychological Review, 101,* 568–586.

Brown, A. L., & DeLoache, J. S. (1978). Skills, plans, and self-regulation. In R. Siegler (Ed.), *Children's thinking: What develops?* Hillsdale, NJ: Erlbaum.

Burt, C. (1949). Alternative methods of factor analysis and their relations to Pearson's method of "principal axis." *British Journal of Psychology, Statistical Section, 2,* 98–121.

Callahan, C. M., Tomlinson, C. A., & Plucker, J. (1997). *Project START using a multiple intelligences model in identifying and promoting talent in high-risk students* (Research Monograph 95136). Storrs: University of Connecticut, National Research Center on the Gifted and Talented.

Campbell, F. A., & Ramey, C. T. (1994). Effects of early intervention on intellectual and academic achievement: A follow-up study of children from low-income families. *Child Development, 65,* 684–698.

Carraher, T. N., Carraher, D., & Schliemann, A. D. (1985). Mathematics in the streets and in schools. *British Journal of Developmental Psychology, 3,* 21–29.

Carroll, J. B. (1993). *Human cognitive abilities: A survey of factor-analytic studies.* New York: Cambridge University Press.

Cattell, R. B. (1971). *Abilities: Their structure, growth and action.* Boston: Houghton Mifflin.

Cattell, R. B., & Cattell, A. K. (1963). *Test of g: Culture fair, scale 3.* Champaign, IL: Institute for Personality and Ability Testing.

Ceci, S. J. (1991). How much does schooling influence general intelligence and its cognitive components? A reassessment of the evidence. *Developmental Psychology, 27,* 703–722.

Ceci, S. J. (1996). *On intelligence . . . More or less.* Cambridge, MA: Harvard University Press.

Ceci, S. J., & Liker, J. (1986). Academic and nonacademic intelligence: An experimental separation. In R. J. Sternberg & R. K. Wagner (Eds.), *Practical intelligence: Nature and origins of competence in the everyday world* (pp. 119–142). New York: Cambridge University Press.

Ceci, S. J., & Roazzi, A. (1994). The effects of context on cognition: Postcards from Brazil. In R. J. Sternberg & R. K. Wagner (Eds.), *Mind in context: Interactionist perspectives on human intelligence* (pp. 74–101). New York: Cambridge University Press.

Ceci, S. J., & Williams, W. M. (1997). Schooling, intelligence, and income. *American Psychologist, 52*(10), 1051–1058.

Chen, M. J. (1994). Chinese and Australian concepts of intelligence. *Psychology and Developing Societies, 6,* 101–117.

Chen, M. J., Braithwaite, V., & Huang, J. T. (1982). Attributes of intelligent behaviour: Perceived relevance and difficulty by Australian and Chinese students. *Journal of Cross-Cultural Psychology, 13,* 139–156.

Chen, M. J., & Chen, H. C. (1988). Concepts of intelligence: A comparison of Chinese graduates from Chinese and English schools in Hong Kong. *International Journal of Psychology, 223,* 471–487.

Connolly, H., & Bruner, J. (1974). Competence: Its nature and nurture. In K. Connolly & J. Bruner (Eds.), *The growth of competence.* New York: Academic Press.

Craik, F. I. M., & Lockhart, R. S. (1972). Levels of processing: A framework for memory research. *Journal of Verbal Learning and Verbal Behavior, 11,* 671–684.

Cronbach, L. J. (1957). The two disciplines of scientific psychology. *American Psychologist, 12,* 671–684.

Daniel, M. H. (2000). Interpretation of intelligence test scores. In R. J. Sternberg (Ed.), *Handbook of intelligence.* New York: Cambridge University Press.

Das, J. P. (1994). Eastern views of intelligence. In R. J. Sternberg (Ed.), *Encyclopedia of human intelligence* (Vol. 1, p. 391). New York: Macmillan.

Das, J. P., Kirby, J. R., & Jarman, R. F. (1979). *Simultaneous and successive cognitive processes.* New York: Academic Press.

Dasen, P. (1984). The cross-cultural study of intelligence: Piaget and the Baoule. *International Journal of Psychology, 19,* 407–434.

Davies, M., Stankov, L., & Roberts, R. D. (1998). Emotional intelligence: In search of an elusive construct. *Journal of Personality & Social Psychology, 75,* 989–1015.

Deary, I. J. (2000). Simple information processing. In R. J. Sternberg (Ed.), *Handbook of intelligence* (pp. 267–284). New York: Cambridge University Press.

Deary, I. J., & Stough, C. (1996). Intelligence and inspection time: Achievements, prospects, and problems. *American Psychologist, 51,* 599–608.

Donchin, E., Ritter, W., & McCallum, W. C. (1979). Cognitive psychophysiology: The endogenous components of the ERP. In E. Callaway, P. Teuting, & S. H. Koslow (Eds.), *Event-related potentials in man* (pp. 349–441). San Diego: Academic Press.

Dörner, D., & Kreuzig, H. (1983). Problemlosefahigkeit und intelligenz [Problem-solving ability and intelligence]. *Psychologische Rundschaus, 34,* 185–192.

Dörner, D., Kreuzig, H., Reither, F., & Staudel, T. (1983). *Lohhausen: Vom Umgang mit Unbestimmtheir und Komplexitat* [Lonhauser: On handling uncertainty and complexity]. Bern: Huber.

Durojaiye, M. O. A. (1993). Indigenous psychology in Africa. In U. Kim & J. W. Berry (Eds.), *Indigenous psychologies: Research and experience in cultural context.* Newbury Park, CA: Sage.

Feuerstein, R., Rand, Y., Haywood, H. C., Hoffman, M., & Jensen, M. (1985). *The learning potential assessment device (LPAD): Examiners' Manual.* Jerusalem: Hadassah–Wizo–Canada Research Institute.

Flavell, J. H. (1981). Cognitive monitoring. In W. P. Dickson (Ed.), *Children's oral communication skills* (pp. 35–60). New York: Academic Press.

Flynn, J. R. (1984). The mean IQ of Americans: Massive gains 1932 to 1978. *Psychological Bulletin, 95,* 29–51.

Flynn, J. R. (1987). Massive IQ gains in 14 nations. *Psychological Bulletin, 101,* 171–191.

Flynn, J. R. (1994). Giving g a fair chance: How to define intelligence, survive falsification, and resist behaviorism. *Psychological Inquiry, 5,* 204–208.

Flynn, J. R. (1998). WAIS-III and WISC-III gains in the United States from 1972 to 1995: How to compensate for obsolete norms. *Perceptual & Motor Skills, 86,* 1231–1239.

Fraser, S. (Ed.). (1995). *The bell curve wars: Race, intelligence and the future of America.* New York: Basic Books.

Galton, F. (1883). *Inquiry into human faculty and its development.* London: Macmillan.

Gardner, H. (1983). *Frames of mind: The theory of multiple intelligences.* New York: Basic Books.

Gardner, H. (1993). *Multiple intelligences: The theory in practice.* New York: Basic Books.

Gardner, H. (1995). *Leading minds.* New York: Basic Books.

Gardner, H. (1997). *Extraordinary minds: Portraits of exceptional individuals and an examination of our extraordinariness.* New York: Basic Books.

Gardner, H. (1999). *Intelligence reframed: Multiple intelligences for the 21st century.* New York: Basic Books.

Gardner, H., Feldman, D., & Krechevsky, M. (Eds.) (1998). *Project Zero frameworks for early childhood education* (3 vols.). New York: Teachers College Press.

Gardner, H., Krechevsky, M., Sternberg, R. J., & Okagaki, L. (1994). Intelligence in context: Enhancing students' practical intelligence for school. In K. McGilly (Ed.), *Classroom lessons: Integrating cognitive theory and classroom practice* (pp. 105–127). Cambridge, MA: MIT Press.

Gill, R., & Keats, D. M. (1980). Elements of intellectual competence: Judgments by Australian and Malay university students. *Journal of Cross-Cultural Psychology, 11,* 233–243.

Goff, M., & Ackerman, P. L. (1992). Personality-intelligence relations: Assessment of typical intellectual engagement. *Journal of Educational Psychology, 84,* 537–552.

Goleman, D. (1995). *Emotional intelligence.* New York: Bantam Books.

Goodnow, J. J. (1976). The nature of intelligent behavior: Questions raised by cross-cultural studies. In L. Resnick (Ed.), *The nature of intelligence* (pp. 169–188). Hillsdale, NJ: Erlbaum.

Gottfredson, L. S. (Ed.). (1986). The g factor in employment [Special issue]. *Journal of Vocational Behavior, 29,* 293–450.

Gottfredson, L. S. (1997). Why g matters: The complexity of everyday life. *Intelligence, 24,* 79–132.

Gould, S. J. (1981). *The mismeasure of man.* New York: Norton.

Gould, S. J. (1995). Curveball. In S. Fraser (Ed.), *The bell curve wars* (pp. 11–22). New York: Basic Books.

Grigorenko, E. L., Geissler, P. W., Prince, R., Okatcha, F., Nokes, C., Kenny, D. A., Bundy, D. A., & Sternberg, R. J. (2001). The organization of Luo conceptions of intelligence: A study of implicit theories in a Kenyan village. *International Journal of Behavioral Development, 25*(4), 367–378.

Grigorenko, E. L., Jarvin, L., & Sternberg, R. J. (2002). School-based tests of the triarchic theory of intelligence: Three settings, three samples, three syllabi. *Contemporary Educational Psychology, 27,* 167–208.

Grigorenko, E. L., & Sternberg, R. J. (1998). Dynamic testing. *Psychological Bulletin, 124,* 75–111.

Guilford, J. P. (1967). *The nature of human intelligence.* New York: McGraw-Hill.

Guilford, J. P. (1982). Is some creative thinking irrational? *Journal of Creative Behavior, 16,* 151–154.

Guilford, J. P., & Hoepfner, R. (1971). *The analysis of intelligence.* New York: McGraw-Hill.

Gustafsson, J. E. (1984). A unifying model for the structure of intellectual abilities. *Intelligence, 8,* 179–203.

Gustafsson, J. E. (1988). Hierarchical models of the structure of cognitive abilities. In R. J. Sternberg (Ed.), *Advances in the psychology of human intelligence* (Vol. 4, pp. 35–71). Hillsdale, NJ: Erlbaum.

Guthke, J., & Stein, H. (1996). Are learning tests the better version of intelligence tests? *European Journal of Psychological Assessment, 12,* 1–13.

Guttman, L. (1954). A new approach to factor analysis: The radex. In P. F. Lazarsfeld (Ed.), *Matermatical thinking in the social sciences* (pp. 258–348). New York: Free Press.

Haier, R. J., Nuechterlein, K. H., Hazlett, E., Wu, J. C., Pack, J., Browning, H. L., & Buchsbaum, M. S. (1988). Cortical glucose metabolic rate correlates of abstract reasoning and attention studied with positron emission tomography. *Intelligence, 12,* 199–217.

Haier, R. J., Siegel, B., Tang, C., Abel, L., & Buchsbaum, M. S. (1992). Intelligence and changes in regional cerebral glucose metabolic rate following learning. *Intelligence, 16,* 415–426.

Halstead, W. C. (1951). Biological intelligence. *Journal of Personality, 20,* 118–130.

Hebb, D. O. (1949). *The organization of behavior: A neuropsychological theory.* New York: Wiley.

Herrnstein, R., & Murray, C. (1994). *The bell curve.* New York: Free Press.

Horn, J. L. (1994). Theory of fluid and crystallized intelligence. In R. J. Sternberg (Ed.), *The encyclopedia of human intelligence* (Vol. 1, pp. 443–451). New York: Macmillan.

Horn, J. L., & Knapp, J. R. (1973). On the subjective character of the empirical base of Guilford's structure-of-intellect model. *Psychological Bulletin, 80,* 33–43.

Hunt, E. (1995). *Will we be smart enough? A cognitive analysis of the coming workforce.* New York: Russell Sage Foundation.

Hunt, E., Frost, N., & Lunneborg, C. (1973). Individual differences in cognition: A new approach to intelligence. In G. Bower (Ed.), *The psychology of learning and motivation* (Vol. 7, pp. 87–122). New York: Academic Press.

Hunt, E. B., Lunneborg, C., & Lewis, J. (1975). What does it mean to be high verbal? *Cognitive Psychology, 7,* 194–227.

Hunter, J. E., & Hunter, R. F. (1984). Validity and utility of alternative predictors of job performance. *Psychological Bulletin, 96,* 72–98.

"Intelligence and its measurement": A symposium. (1921). *Journal of Educational Psychology, 12,* 123–147, 195–216, 271–275.

Irvine, J. T. (1978). "Wolof magical thinking": Culture and conservation revisited. *Journal of Cross-Cultural Psychology, 9,* 300–310.

Jacoby, R., & Glauberman, N. (Eds.). (1995). *The bell curve debate.* New York: Times Books.

Jensen, A. R. (1969). How much can we boost IQ and scholastic achievement? *Harvard Educational Review, 39,* 1–123.

Jensen, A. R. (1970). Hierarchical theories of mental ability. In W. B. Dockrell (Ed.), *On intelligence* (pp. 119–190). Toronto, Ontario, Canada: Ontario Institute for Studies in Education.

Jensen, A. R. (1997). The puzzle of nongenetic variance. In R. J. Sternberg & E. L. Grigorenko (Eds.), *Intelligence, heredity, and environment* (pp. 42–88). New York: Cambridge University Press.

Jensen, A. R. (1998). *The g factor: The science of mental ability.* Westport, CT: Praeger/Greenwoood.

Jensen, A. R. (2002). Psychometric g: Definition and substantiation. In R. J. Sternberg & E. L. Grigorenko (Eds.), *General factor of intelligence: Fact or fiction.* Mahwah, NJ: Erlbaum.

Johnson, R., Jr. (1986). A triarchic model of P300 amplitude. *Psychophysiology, 23,* 367–384.

Johnson, R., Jr. (1988). The amplitude of the P300 component of the vent-related potential: Review and synthesis. In P. K. Ackles, J. R. Jennings, & M. G. H. Coles (Eds.), *Advances in psychophysiology: A research manual* (Vol. 3, pp. 69–138). Greenwich, CT: CAI Press.

Kaufman, A. S., & Kaufman, N. L. (1983). *Kaufman assessment battery for children: Interpretive manual.* Circle Pines, MN: American Guidance Service.

Kaufman, A. S., & Kaufman, N. L. (1993). *Kaufman Adolescent and Adult Intelligence Test.* Circle Pines, MN: American Guidance Service.

Lave, J., Murtaugh, M., & de la Roche, O. (1984). The dialectic of arithmetic in grocery shopping. In B. Rogoff & J. Lace (Eds.), *Everyday cognition: Its development in social context* (pp. 67–94). Cambridge, MA: Harvard University Press.

Lemann, N. (1999). *The big test: The secret history of the American meritocracy.* New York: Farrar, Straus, & Giroux.

Loehlin, J. C. (1989). Partitioning environmental and genetic contributions to behavioral development. *American Psychologist, 44,* 1285–1292.

Loehlin, J. C., Horn, J. M., & Willerman, L. (1997). Heredity, environment, and IQ in the Texas adoption project. In R. J. Sternberg & E. L. Grigorenko (Eds.), *Intelligence, heredity, and environment* (pp. 105–125). New York: Cambridge University Press.

Lohman, D. F. (2000). Complex information processing and intelligence. In R. J. Sternberg (Ed.), *Handbook of intelligence* (pp. 285–340). New York: Cambridge University Press.

Luria, A. R. (1973). *The working brain.* New York: Basic Books.

Luria, A. R. (1980). *Higher cortical functions in man* (2nd ed., rev. & expanded). New York: Basic.

Lutz, C. (1985). Ethnopsychology compared to what? Explaining behaviour and consciousness among the Ifaluk. In G. M. White & J. Kirkpatrick (Eds.), *Person, self, and experience: Exploring Pacific ethnopsychlogoies* (pp. 35–79). Berkeley: University of California Press.

Mayer, J. D., & Gehr, G. (1996). Emotional intelligence and the identification of emotion. *Intelligence, 22,* 89–114.

Mayer, J. D., & Salovey, P. (1993). The intelligence of emotional intelligence. *Intelligence, 17,* 433–442.

Mayer, J. D., Salovey, P., & Caruso, D. (2000). Emotional intelligence. In R. J. Sternberg (Ed.), *Handbook of intelligence* (pp. 396–421). New York: Cambridge University Press.

McClelland, D. C. (1973). Testing for competence rather than for "intelligence." *American Psychologist, 28,* 1–14.

Mundy-Castle, A. C. (1974). Social and technological intelligence in Western or Nonwestern cultures. *Universitas, 4,* 46–52.

Murtaugh, M. (1985). The practice of arithmetic by American grocery shoppers. *Anthropology and Education Quarterly, 16,* 186–192.

Naglieri, J. A., & Das, J. P. (1990). Planning, attention, simultaneous, and successive cognitive processes as a model for intelligence. *Journal of Psychoeducational Assessment, 8,* 303–337.

Naglieri, J. A., & Das, J. P. (1997). *Cognitive Assessment System.* Itasca, IL: Riverside Publishing.

Naglieri, J. A., & Das, J. P. (2002). Practical implications of general intelligence and PASS cognitive processes. In R. J. Sternberg & E. L. Grigorenko (Eds.), *The general factor of intelligence: Fact or fiction.* Mahwah, NJ: Erlbaum.

Neisser, U. (Ed.). (1998). *The rising curve.* Washington, DC: American Psychological Association.

Nettlebeck, T. (1982). Inspection time: An index for intelligence. *Quarterly Journal of Experimental Psychology, 34,* 299–312.

Newell, A., & Simon, H. A. (1972). *Human problem solving.* Englewood Cliffs, NJ: Prentice-Hall.

Nuñes, T. (1994). Street intelligence. In R. J. Sternberg (Ed.), *Encyclopedia of human intelligence* (Vol. 2, pp. 1045–1049). New York: Macmillan.

Ogbu, J. U. (1978). *Minority education and caste: The American system in cross-cultural perspective.* New York: Academic Press.

Ogbu, J. U. (1991). Low school performance as an adaptation: The case of blacks in Stockton, CA. In M. A. Gibson & J. U. Ogbu (Eds.), *Minority status and schooling: A comparative study of immigrant and involuntary minorities* (pp. 249–286). New York: Garland.

Ogbu, J. U. (1994). From cultural differences to differences in cultural frame of reference. In P. M. Greenfield & R. R. Cocking (Ed.), *Cross-cultural roots of minority child development* (pp. 365–391). Hillsdale, NJ: Erlbaum.

Ogbu, J. U., & Stern, P. (2001). Caste status and intellectual development. In R. S. Sternberg & E. L. Grigorenko (Eds.), *Environmental effects on intellectual functioning* (pp. 3–37). Hillsdale, NJ: Erlbaum.

Okagaki, L., & Sternberg, R. J. (1993). Parental beliefs and children's school performance. *Child Development, 64,* 36–56.

Pedersen, N. L., Plomin, R., Nesselroade, J. R., & McClearn, G. E. (1992). A quantitative genetic analysis of cognitive abilities during the second half of the life span. *Psychological Science, 3,* 346–353.

Perkins, D. N. (1995). *Outsmarting IQ: The emerging science of learnable intelligence.* New York: Free Press.

Petrill, S. A. (in press). The case for general intelligence: A behavioral genetic perspective. In R. J. Sternberg & E. L. Grigorenko (Eds.), *General factor of intelligence: Fact or fiction.* Mahwah, NJ: Erlbaum.

Plomin, R. (1997). Identifying genes for cognitive abilities and disabilities. In R. J. Sternberg & E. L. Grigorenko (Eds.), *Intelligence, heredity, and environment* (pp. 89–104). New York: Cambridge University Press.

Plomin, R., DeFries, J. C., McClearn, G. E., & Rutter, M. (1997). *Behavioral genetics* (3rd ed.). New York: W. H. Freeman.

Plomin, R., McClearn, D. L., & Smith, D. L. (1994). DNA markers associated with high versus low IQ: The IQ QTL Project. *Behavior Genetics, 24,* 107–118.

Plomin, R., McClearn, D. L., & Smith, D. L. (1995). Allelic associations between 100 DNA markers and high versus low IQ. *Intelligence, 21,* 31–48.

Plomin, R., & Neiderhiser, J. M. (1992). Quantitative genetics, molecular genetics, and intelligence. *Intelligence, 15,* 369–387.

Plomin, R., & Petrill, S. A. (1997). Genetics and intelligence: What is new? *Intelligence, 24,* 53–78.

Poole, F. J. P. (1985). Coming into social being: Cultural images of infants in Bimin-Kuskusmin folk psychology. In G. M. White & J. Kirkpatrick (Eds.), *Person, self, and experience: Exploring Pacific ethnopsychologies* (pp. 183–244). Berkeley: University of California Press.

Posner, M. I., & Mitchell, R. F. (1967). Chronometric analysis of classification. *Psychological Review, 74,* 392–409.

Putnam, D. B., & Kilbride, P. L. (1980). *A relativistic understanding of social intelligence among the Songhay of Mali and Smaia of Kenya.* Paper presented at the meeting of the Society for Cross-Cultural Research, Philadelphia, PA.

Ramey, C. T. (1994). Abecedarian Project. In R. J. Sternberg (Ed.), *Encyclopedia of human intelligence* (Vol. 1, pp. 1–2). New York: Macmillan.

Reed, T. E., & Jensen, A. R. (1992). Conduction velocity in a brain nerve pathway of normal adults correlates with intelligence level. *Intelligence, 16,* 259–272.

Ruzgis, P. M., & Grigorenko, E. L. (1994). Cultural meaning systems, intelligence and personality. In R. J. Sternberg & P. Ruzgis (Eds.), *Personality and intelligence* (pp. 248–270). New York: Cambridge.

Sacks, P. (1999). *Standardized minds: The high price of America's testing culture and what we can do to change it.* Cambridge, MA: Perseus Books.

Salovey, P., & Mayer, J. D. (1990). Emotional intelligence. *Imagination, Cognition, and Personality, 9,* 185–211.

Scarr, S. (1997). Behavior-genetic and socialization theories of intelligence: Truce and reconciliation. In R. J. Sternberg & E. L. Grigorenko (Eds.), *Intelligence, heredity and environment* (pp. 3–41). New York: Cambridge University Press.

Schmidt, F. L., & Hunter, J. E. (1981). Employment testing: Old theories and new research findings. *American Psychologist, 36,* 1128–1137.

Schmidt, F. L., & Hunter, J. E. (1993). Tacit knowledge, practical intelligence, general mental ability, and job knowledge. *Current Directions in Psychological Science, 1,* 8–9.

Schmidt, F., & Hunter, J. (1998). The validity and utility of selection methods in personnel psychology: Practical and theoretical implications of 85 years of research findings. *Psychological Bulletin, 124,* 262–274.

Scribner, S. (1984). Studying working intelligence. In B. Rogoff & J. Lave (Eds.), *Everyday cognition: Its development in social context* (pp. 9–40). Cambridge, MA: Harvard University Press.

Scribner, S. (1986). Thinking in action: Some characteristics of practical thought. In R. J. Sternberg & R. K. Wagner (Eds.), *Practical intelligence: Nature and origins of competence in the everyday world* (pp. 13–30). New York: Cambridge University Press.

Serpell, R. (1974). Aspects of intelligence in a developing country. *African Social Research, 17,* 576–596.

Serpell, R. (1982). Measures of perception, skills, and intelligence. In W. W. Hartup (Ed.), *Review of child development research* (Vol. 6, pp. 392–440). Chicago: University of Chicago Press.

Serpell, R. (1993). *The significance of schooling: Life journeys in an African society.* New York: Cambridge University Press.

Spearman, C. (1904). "General intelligence," objectively determined and measured. *American Journal of Psychology, 15*(2), 201–293.

Spearman, C. (1923). *The nature of "intelligence" and the principles of cognition* (2nd ed.). London: Macmillan.

Spearman, C. (1927). *The abilities of man.* London: Macmillan.

Srivastava, A. K., & Misra, G. (1996). Changing perspectives on understanding intelligence: An appraisal. *Indian Psychological Abstracts and Review, 3,* 1–34.

Stenhouse, D. (1973). *The evolution of intelligence: A general theory and some of its implications.* New York: Harper & Row.

Sternberg, R. J. (1977). *Intelligence, information processing, and analogical reasoning: The componential analysis of human abilities.* Hillsdale, NJ: Erlbaum.

Sternberg, R. J. (1980). Representation and process in linear syllogistic reasoning. *Journal of Experimental Psychology: General, 109,* 119–159.

Sternberg, R. J. (1983). Components of human intelligence. *Cognition, 15,* 1–48.

Sternberg, R. J. (1984). Toward a triarchic theory of human intelligence. *Behavioral and Brain Sciences, 7,* 269–287.

Sternberg, R. J. (1985). *Beyond IQ: A triarchic theory of human intelligence.* New York: Cambridge University Press.

Sternberg, R. J. (1990). *Metaphors of mind: Conceptions of the nature of intelligence.* New York: Cambridge University Press.

Sternberg, R. J. (1995). For whom the Bell Curve tolls: A review of *The Bell Curve. Psychological Science, 6,* 257–261.

Sternberg, R. J. (1997). *Successful intelligence.* New York: Plume.

Sternberg, R. J. (1999a). Human intelligence: A case study of how more and more research can lead us to know less and less about a psychological phenomenon, until finally we know much less than we did before we started doing research. In E. Tulving (Ed.), *Memory, consciousness, and the brain: The Tallinn Conference* (pp. 363–373). Philadelphia: Psychology Press.

Sternberg, R. J. (1999b). A propulsion model of types of creative contributions. *Review of General Psychology, 3,* 83–100.

Sternberg, R. J. (1999c). Successful intelligence: Finding a balance. *Trends in Cognitive Sciences, 3,* 436–442.

Sternberg, R. J. (1999d). The theory of successful intelligence. *Review of General Psychology, 3,* 292–316.

Sternberg, R. J., Conway, B. E., Ketron, J. L., & Bernstein, M. (1981). People's conceptions of intelligence. *Journal of Personality and Social Psychology, 41,* 37–55.

Sternberg, R. J., & Detterman, D. K. (1986). *What is intelligence?* Norwood, NJ: Ablex Publishing.

Sternberg, R. J., Ferrari, M., Clinkenbeard, P. R., & Grigorenko, E. L. (1996). Identification, instruction, and assessment of gifted children: A construct validation of a triarchic model. *Gifted Child Quarterly, 40,* 129–137.

Sternberg, R. J., Forsythe, G. B., Hedlund, J., Horvath, J., Snook, S., Williams, W. M., Wagner, R. K., & Grigorenko, E. L. (2000). *Practical intelligence.* New York: Cambridge University Press.

Sternberg, R. J., & Gardner, M. K. (1983). Unities in inductive reasoning. *Journal of Experimental Psychology: General, 112,* 80–116.

Sternberg, R. J., & Grigorenko, E. L. (Eds.). (1997). *Intelligence, heredity, and environment.* New York: Cambridge University Press.

Sternberg, R. J., Grigorenko, E. L., Ferrari, M., & Clinkenbeard, P. (1999). A triarchic analysis of an aptitude-treatment interaction. *European Journal of Psychological Assessment, 15,* 1–11.

Sternberg, R. J., & Lubart, T. I. (1995). *Defying the crowd: Cultivating creativity in a culture of conformity.* New York: Free Press.

Sternberg, R. J., & Lubart, T. I. (1996). Investing in creativity. *American Psychologist, 51,* 677–688.

Sternberg, R. J., Okagaki, L., & Jackson, A. (1990). Practical intelligence for success in school. *Educational Leadership, 48,* 35–39.

Sternberg, R. J., Torff, B., & Grigorenko, E. L. (1998). Teaching triarchically improves school achievement. *Journal of Educational Psychology, 90,* 1–11.

Sternberg, R. J., & Wagner, R. K. (1993). The g-ocentric view of intelligence and job performance is wrong. *Current Directions in Psychological Science, 2,* 1–4.

Sternberg, R. J., Wagner, R. K., Williams, W. M., & Horvath, J. A. (1995). Testing common sense. *American Psychologist, 50,* 912–927.

Sternberg, R. J., & Williams, W. M. (1997). Does the Graduate Record Examination predict meaningful success in the graduate training of psychologists? A case study. *American Psychologist, 52,* 630–641.

Super, C. M. (1983). Cultural variation in the meaning and uses of children's intelligence. In J. B. Deregowski, S. Dziurawiec, & R. C. Annis (Eds.), *Expiscations in cross-cultural psychology* (pp. 199–212). Lisse, the Netherlands: Swets and Zeitlinger.

Super, C. M., & Harkness, S. (1982). The development of affect in infancy and early childhood. In D. Wagnet & H. Stevenson (Eds.), *Cultural perspectives on child development* (pp. 1–19). San Francisco: W. H. Freeman.

Swanson, H. L. (1995). Effects of dynamic testing on the classification of learning disabilities: The predictive and discriminant validity of the Swanson Cognitive Processing Test. *Journal of Psychoeducational Assessment, 1,* 204–229.

Thorndike, R. L., Hagen, E., & Sattler, J. (1985). *Stanford-Binet Intelligence Scale.* Boston: Houghton-Mifflin.

Thurstone, L. L. (1924). *The nature of intelligence.* New York: Harcourt Brace.

Thurstone, L. L. (1938). *Primary mental abilities.* Chicago: University of Chicago Press.

Vernon, P. A., & Mori, M. (1992). Intelligence, reaction times, and peripheral nerve conduction velocity. *Intelligence, 8,* 273–288.

Vernon, P. E. (1971). *The structure of human abilities.* London: Methuen.

Vernon, P. A., Wickett, J. C., Bazana, P. G., & Stelmack, R. M. (2000). The neuropsychology and psycholophysiology of human intelligence In R. J. Sternberg (Ed.), *Handbook of intelligence* (pp. 245–264). New York: Cambridge University Press.

Vygotsky, L. S. (1962). *Thought and language.* Cambridge, MA: MIT Press. (Original work published 1934)

Vygotsky, L. S. (1978). *Mind in society: The development of higher psychological processes.* Cambridge, MA: Harvard University Press.

Wahlsten, D., & Gottlieb, G. (1997). The invalid separation of effects of nature and nurture: Lessons from animal experimentation. In R. J. Sternberg & E. L. Grigorenko (Eds.), *Intelligence, heredity, and environment* (pp. 163–192). New York: Cambridge University Press.

Wechsler, D. (1980). *Wechsler Preschool and Primary Scale of Intelligence–Revised.* San Antonio, TX: The Psychological Corporation.

Wechsler, D. (1991). *Manual for the Wechsler Intelligence Scales for Children* (3rd ed.). San Antonio, TX: Psychological Corporation.

White, G. M. (1985). Premises and purposes in a Solomon Islands ethnopsychology. In G. M. White & J. Kirkpatrick (Eds.), *Person, self, and experience: Exploring Pacific ethnopsychologies* (pp. 328–366). Berkeley: University of California Press.

Wickett, J. C., & Vernon, P. A. (1994). Peripheral nerve conduction velocity, reaction time, and intelligence: An attempt to replicate Vernon and Mori. *Intelligence, 18,* 127–132.

Wigdor, A. K., & Garner, W. R. (Eds.). (1982). *Ability testing: Uses, consequences, and controversies.* Washington, DC: National Academy Press.

Willerman, L., Schultz, R., Rutledge, J. N., & Bigler, E. D. (1991). In vivo brain size and intelligence. *Intelligence, 15,* 223– 228.

Willerman, L., Schultz, R., Rutledge, J. N., & Bigler, E. D. (1992). Hemisphere size asymmetry predicts relative verbal and nonverbal intelligence differently in the sexes: An MRI study of structure function relations. *Intelligence, 16,* 315–328.

Woodcock, R. W., & Johnson, M. B. (1989). *Woodcock-Johnson Tests of Cognitive Ability–Revised.* Itasca, IL: Riverside.

Yang, S., & Sternberg, R. J. (1997a). Conceptions of intelligence in ancient Chinese philosophy. *Journal of Theoretical and Philosophical Psychology, 17*(2), 101–119.

Yang, S., & Sternberg, R. J. (1997b). Taiwanese Chinese people's conceptions of intelligence. *Intelligence, 25*(1), 21–36.

Zenderland, L. (1998). *Measuring minds: Henry Goddard and the origins of American intelligence testing.* New York: Cambridge University Press.

CHAPTER 3

Memory and Information Processes

RICHARD E. MAYER

AN INFORMATION PROCESSING VIEW OF LEARNING AND COGNITION

How does the human mind work? What happens when someone learns or when someone solves a problem? According to the information processing view, the human mind works by forming mental representations and applying cognitive processes to them. This definition has two elements: (a) The content of cognition is mental representations, and (b) the activity of cognition involves cognitive processes. In learning, the learner takes incoming information received through the eyes or ears and applies a series of cognitive processes to the incoming information, resulting in the construction of a series of mental representations. For example, as you read the words in this paragraph you form a series of mental representations by applying appropriate cognitive processes such as mentally selecting important ideas, mentally organizing them into a coherent cognitive structure, and mentally relating them with prior knowledge. In this chapter I provide a brief historical overview of the precursors to the information processing view of learning and cognition, describe two versions of the information processing view, examine three major contributions of the information processing view, and then exemplify how it contributes to theories of learning and cognition.

HISTORICAL OVERVIEW

For more than 100 years psychologists have conducted research aimed at understanding how knowledge is represented and processed in human minds. Such issues fell under the domain of science as psychology entered the twentieth century, heralded by the publication of Ebbinghaus's pioneering memory studies in 1885 (Ebbinghaus, 1964) and Thorndike's pioneering learning studies in 1898 (Thorndike, 1965). During the first half of the twentieth century two competing views of learning emerged—the associationist view of learning as strengthening of associations and the Gestalt view of learning as building cognitive structures.

Associationist View

According to the associationist view, the content of cognition consists of nodes and associations between them and the process of cognition consists of the strengthening and weakening of associations. For example, in Thorndike's (1965) classic study of animal learning, a hungry cat was placed in a wooden box. The cat could escape by pulling a hanging loop of string that opened a door allowing the cat to get out and eat some nearby food. Thorndike noted that on the first day, the cat engaged in many extraneous behaviors before accidentally pulling the string, but on successive days the number of extraneous behaviors decreased. After many days, the cat pulled the loop of string shortly after being placed in the box. According to Thorndike, the cat began with a habit family hierarchy—an ordered set of responses associated with being placed in an enclosed box. The cat would try the most strongly associated response first (e.g., thrusting its paw through the slats of the box), and when it failed, the strength of the association to that response would be weakened. Eventually, the cat would pull the loop of string and get out, thus increasing the association to that response. Over many days, the extraneous responses became very weakly associated with being in the box, and pulling the string became very strongly associated with being in the box. Thus, Thorndike offered a clear vision of learning as the strengthening and weakening of stimulus-response (S-R) associations and memory as the processing of linked nodes in a network—a vision that dominated psychology through the 1950s and still flourishes today in revised form.

Gestalt View

According to the Gestalt view, the content of cognition consists of coherent structures, and the process of cognition consists of building them. For example, Kohler (1925) placed an ape in a pen with crates on the ground and a bunch of bananas hanging overhead out of reach. Kohler observed that the ape looked around and then suddenly placed the crates on top of one another to form a ladder leading to the bananas, allowing the ape to climb the stairs and grasp the bananas. According to Kohler, the ape learned by insight—mentally reorganizing the objects in the situation so they fit together in a way that accomplished the goal. Thus, insight is a process of structure building (Mayer, 1995). The Gestalt approach rose to prominence in the 1930s and 1940s but is rarely mentioned today. Nonetheless, the Gestalt theme of cognition as structure building underlies core topics in cognitive science including the idea of schemas, analogical reasoning, and meaningful learning.

By the 1950s and 1960s, the associationist and Gestalt views were reshaped into a new view of cognition, called *information processing* (Lachman, Lachman, & Butterfield, 1979). The information processing view eventually became the centerpiece of *cognitive science*—the interdisciplinary study of cognition. A core premise in cognitive science is that cognition involves computation; that is, cognition occurs when you begin with a representation as input, apply a process, and create a representation as output. For example, in a review of the field of cognitive science, Johnson-Laird (1988, p. 9) noted, "Cognitive science, sometime explicitly and sometimes

implicitly, tries to elucidate the workings of the mind by treating them as computations." Human cognition on any task can be described as a series of cognitive processes (i.e., a description of the computations that were carried out) or as a series of transformations of mental representations (i.e., a description of the inputs and outputs for each computation).

TWO VIEWS OF INFORMATION PROCESSING THEORY

A central problem of the information processing approach is to clarify the nature of mental representations and the nature of cognitive processes. This task is made more difficult by the fact that researchers cannot directly observe the mental representations and cognitive processes of other people. Rather, researchers must devise methods that allow them to infer the mental representations and cognitive processes of others based on their behavior (including physiological responses). In the evolution of the information processing approach to learning and memory, there have been two contrasting versions: the classical and constructivist view (Mayer, 1992a, 1996a).

Leary (1990) showed how progress in psychological theories can be described as a progression of metaphors, and Mayer (1992a, 2001) described several major metaphors of learning and memory that have emerged during the last century, including viewing knowledge as information versus viewing knowledge as cognitive structure. A major challenge of the information processing view—and the field of cognitive science that it serves—is to clarify the status of the knowledge as information metaphor (which is part of the classical view) and the knowledge as cognitive structure metaphor (which is part of the constructivist view).

Classical View

The classic view is based on a human-machine metaphor in which the human mind is like a computer; knowledge is represented as data that can be processed by a computer, and cognition is represented as a program that specifies how data are processed. According to the classical view, humans are processors of information. Information is a commodity that can be transferred from one mind to another as a series of symbols. Processing involves applying an algorithm to information such that a series of symbols is manipulated according to a step-by-step procedure. For example, when given a problem such as "$x + 2 = 4$, solve for x," a learner forms a mental representation of the problem such as "$x + 2 = 4$" and applies operators such as mentally subtracting 2 to both sides in order to generate a new mental representation, namely "$x = 2$."

The classical information processing approach developed in the 1950s, 1960s, and 1970s, although its roots predate psychology (Lachman et al., 1979). For example, more than 250 years ago De La Mettrie (1748/1912) explored the idea that the human mind works like a complex machine, and the classical information processing view can be seen in Atkinson and Shiffrin's (1968) theory of the human memory system and Newell and Simon's (1972) theory of human problem solving.

For example, Newell and Simon (1972) developed a computer simulation designed to solve a variety of problems ranging from chess to logic to cryptarithmetic. In the problem-solving program, information consists of "symbol structures" (p. 23) such as a list, tree, or network, and processing consists of "executing sequences of elementary information process" (p. 30) on symbol structures. A problem is represented as a *problem space* consisting of the initial state, the goal state, and all possible intervening states with links among them. The process of searching the space is accomplished by a problem-solving strategy called *means-ends analysis,* in which the problem solver sets a goal and carries it out if possible or determines an obstacle that must be overcome if it is not (see Mayer, 1992b). Thus, problem solving involves applying processes to a symbolic representation of a problem: If the application is successful, the representation is changed; if it is not successful, a new process is selected based on a means-ends analysis strategy. In a complex problem, a long series of information processes may be applied, and many successive representations of the problem state may be created.

Two limitations of the classical view—humans as information processors—concern the characterization of information as an objective commodity and the characterization of processing as the application of algorithms. Although such characterizations may mesh well with highly contrived laboratory tasks, they appear too limited to account for the full range of human learning in complex real-world situations. For example, Metcalfe (1986a, 1986b; Metcalfe & Wiebe, 1987) showed that people use different cognitive processing for insight problems (requiring a major reorganization of the problem) and noninsight problems (requiring the step-by-step application of a series of cognitive processes). For insight problems people are not able to predict how close they are to solving the problem (inconsistent with the step-by-step thinking posited by the classical view), but for noninsight problems they are able to gage how close they are to solution (consistent with the step-by-step thinking posited by the classical view). Apparently, the classical view may offer a reasonable account of how people think about noninsight problems but not how they think about insight problems.

Constructivist View

The constructivist view is based on the knowledge construction metaphor, in which the human mind is a sort of construction zone in which learners actively create their own knowledge based on integrating what is presented and what they already know. According to the constructivist view, learners are sense makers who construct knowledge. Knowledge is a mental representation that exists in a human mind. Unlike information, which is an objective entity that can be moved from one mind to another, knowledge is a personal construction that cannot be moved directly from one mind to another. Construction involves cognitive processing aimed at sense making, including attending to relevant portions of the presented material, mentally organizing the material into a coherent structure, and mentally integrating the material with relevant existing knowledge. Unlike the view of cognitive processing as applying algorithms, cognitive processing involves orchestrating cognitive strategies aimed at sense making. For example, as you read this section, you may mentally select relevant ideas such as the classical view of information and processing and the constructivist view of knowledge and construction; you may organize them into a matrix with classical and constructivist as rows and nature of information and nature of processing as columns; and you may integrate this material with your previous knowledge about these topics.

The constructivist approach developed in the 1980s and 1990s, although its earlier proponents include Bartlett's (1932) theory of how people remember stories and Piaget's (1971) theory of how children learn. For example, Bartlett argued that when learners are presented with a folk story, they assimilate story elements to their existing schemas and mentally reorganize the story in a way that makes sense to them. Similarly, Piaget showed how children assimilate their experiences with their existing schemas in an attempt to make sense of their environment. More recently, the constructivist view can be seen in Ausubel's (1968) theory of assimilative learning and Wittrock's (1990) theory of generative learning. In both theories, learning involves connecting what is presented with what the learner already knows, so the outcome of learning depends both on the material presented by the instructor and the schemas used by the learner.

Although the constructivist view addresses some of the limitations of the classical view, major limitations of the constructivist view include the need to account for the social and cultural context of cognition and the need to account for the biological and affective bases of cognition. In particular, the constructivist view focuses on cognitive changes within individual learners, but this view can be expanded by considering how the learner's cognitive processing is mediated by the learner's surrounding social and cultural environment. The constructivist view focuses on what can be called *cold cognition* (i.e., cognitive processing in isolation), but this view can be expanded by also considering the role of the learner's emotional and motivational state.

MAJOR CONTRIBUTIONS OF INFORMATION PROCESSING THEORY

Three important contributions of the information processing approach are techniques for analyzing cognitive processing (e.g., "What are the cognitive processes involved in carrying out a cognitive task?"), techniques for analyzing mental representations (e.g., "How is knowledge represented in memory?"), and a general description of the architecture of the human cognitive system (e.g., "How does information flow through the human memory system?").

Cognitive Processes: Cognitive Task Analysis

A fundamental contribution of information processing theory is cognitive task analysis—techniques for describing the cognitive processes that a person must carry out to accomplish a cognitive task. For example, consider the analogy problem dog : bark :: cat : ____, which can be read as "dog is to bark as cat is to what?" and in which the a-term is "dog," the b-term is "bark," the c-term is "cat," and the d-term is unknown. What are the cognitive processes that a problem solver must go through to solve this problem? Based on a cognitive task analysis, solving an analogy problem can be broken down into five basic steps (Mayer, 1987; Sternberg, 1977):

1. *Encoding*—that is, reading and forming a mental representation of the words and accompanying punctuation,
2. *Inferring*—that is, determining the relation between the a-term and the b-term (e.g., the b-term is the sound that the a-term makes),
3. *Mapping*—this is, determining what the c-term is and how it corresponds to the a-term (e.g., the a-term is a kind of animal that makes sounds, and the c-term is another kind of animal that makes sounds),
4. *Applying*—that is, generating a d-term based on applying the relational rule to the c-term (e.g., the sound that the c-term makes is ____), and

5. *Responding*—that is, physically making the response such as writing "meow" or circling the correct answer ("meow") on a list.

Cognitive task analysis has useful educational applications because it suggests specific cognitive processes that students need to learn. For example, the cognitive task analysis of analogy problems suggests that students would benefit from instruction in how to infer the relation between the a-term and the b-term (Sternberg, 1977).

To test this idea, Sternberg and Ketron (1982) taught college students how to solve analogy problems by showing them how to infer the change from the a-term to the b-term and how to apply that change to the c-term. On a subsequent test of analogical reasoning involving new problems, trained students solved the problems twice as fast and committed half as many errors as did students who had not received training.

Cognitive task analysis also offers advantages in evaluating student learning outcomes. For example, instead of measuring the percentage correct on a test, it is possible to specify more precisely the knowledge that a student possesses—including incomplete or incorrect components. For example, suppose a student gives the following answers on an arithmetic test:

234	678	456	545
−156	−434	−327	−295
122	244	131	350

A traditional evaluation would reveal that the student correctly solved 25% of the problems. However, a cognitive task analysis reveals that the student seems to be consistently applying a subtraction procedure that has one incorrect step, or bug—namely, subtracting the smaller number from the larger number in each column (Brown & Burton, 1978). In specifying the procedure that the student is using, it becomes clear that instruction is needed to help the student replace this *smaller-from-larger bug*.

Mental Representations: Types of Knowledge

According to the information processing approach, knowledge is at the center of cognition: Learning is the construction of knowledge; memory is the storage of knowledge; and thinking is the logical manipulation of knowledge. Therefore, information processing theorists have analyzed the types of knowledge (or mental representations): factual, conceptual, procedural, and metacognitive (Anderson et al., 2001). Factual knowledge consists of facts—that is, simple descriptions of an object or element (e.g., "apples are red"). Conceptual

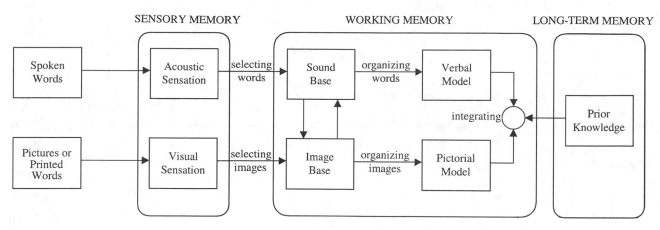

Figure 3.1   An information processing model of how the human mind works.

knowledge involves relations among elements within a coherent structure that enables them to function together, and includes classification hierarchies, cause-and-effect models, explanatory principles, and organizing generalizations (e.g., the model presented in Figure 3.1). Procedural knowledge involves a procedure, method, or algorithm—that is, a step-by-step specification of how to do something (e.g., the procedure for how to carry out long division). Metacognitive knowledge involves strategies for how to coordinate one's cognitive processing (e.g., knowing how to monitor the quality of one's essay-writing activity). As you can see, factual and conceptual knowledge are knowledge of "what" (i.e., data structures), whereas procedural and metacognitive knowledge are knowledge of "how to" (i.e., processes for manipulating data structures).

Knowledge is a mental representation: It is mental because it exists only in human minds; it is a representation because it is intended to denote or signify something. Representations can be classified based on the coding system used to represent them in the cognitive system such as motoric (e.g., bodily movement images), pictorial (e.g., mental images), verbal (e.g., words), or symbolic (e.g., some higher level coding system). Representations can be classified based on the input modality including haptic/kinesthetic/vestibular (e.g., bodily sensations), visual (e.g., imagery sensations), or auditory (e.g., acoustic sensations).

Cognitive System: Architecture of the Cognitive System

An Information Processing Model

Figure 3.1 presents a model of the human information processing system, consisting of three memory stores (represented as labeled boxes), five basic cognitive processes (represented as labeled arrows), and two channels of knowl-

edge representation (represented as the top and bottom rows). The three memory stores are sensory memory, where sensory input is stored briefly in its original form; working memory, where a limited number of elements of the presented material are stored and manipulated within one's conscious awareness; and long-term memory, where large amounts of knowledge are stored for long periods of time. The five cognitive processes presented in Figure 3.1 are selecting images, selecting words, organizing images, organizing words, and integrating. The two channels are the auditory-verbal channel (in the top row of Figure 3.1), in which material enters the cognitive system through the ears and eventually is represented in verbal code, and the visual/pictorial channel (in the bottom row of Figure 3.1), in which material enters the cognitive system through the eyes and eventually is represented in pictorial code.

On the left side of the top row, spoken words enter the cognitive system through the ears, resulting in a short-lasting acoustic sensation in auditory sensory memory. If the learner pays attention, parts of the sensation are transferred to verbal working memory for further processing. The arrow from acoustic sensation in auditory sensory memory to sound base in verbal working memory represents the cognitive process of selecting sounds, and the resulting representation in verbal working memory is a collection of sounds that can be called a sound base. If the learner generates visual representations based on the sounds (e.g., imagining a dog when the word "dog" is spoken), this process is represented by the arrow from sound base to image base. The arrow from sound base to verbal model in verbal working memory represents the cognitive process of organizing sounds, and the resulting representation in verbal working memory is a coherent structure that can be called a verbal model.

On the left side of the bottom row, printed words and pictures enter the cognitive system through the eyes, resulting in in a short-lasting visual sensation in visual sensory memory. If the learner pays attention, parts of the sensation are transferred to visual working memory for further processing. The arrow from visual sensation in visual sensory memory to image base in visual working memory represents the cognitive process of selecting images, and the resulting representation in visual working memory is a collection of images that can be called an image base. If the learner generates verbal representations based on the images (e.g., mentally saying "dog" when a picture of a dog is processed or the printed letters for "dog" are read silently), this process is represented by the arrow from image base to sound base. The arrow from image base to pictorial model in visual working memory represents the cognitive process of organizing images, and the resulting representation in visual working memory is a coherent structure that can be called a pictorial model.

The final cognitive process—integrating—is represented by arrows connecting pictorial model from visual working memory, verbal model from verbal working memory, and prior knowledge from long-term memory. The result is an integrated representation based on visual and verbal representations of the presented material as well as relevant prior knowledge. Overall, the construction of knowledge requires that the learner select relevant images and sounds from the presented material, organize them into coherent pictorial and verbal representations, and integrate the pictorial and verbal representations with each other and with prior knowledge.

Three Assumptions Underlying the Model

The information processing model presented in Figure 3.1 is based on three assumptions from the cognitive science of learning: the dual channel assumption, the limited capacity assumption, and the active learning assumption (Mayer, 2001). The dual channel assumption is that humans possess separate information processing channels for visual-pictorial material and auditory-verbal material (Baddeley, 1998; Paivio, 1986). For example, printed words and pictorial material (e.g., illustrations, graphics, animation, and video) are processed as visual images (at least initially) in the visual-pictorial channel whereas spoken words are processed as sounds (at least initially) in the auditory-verbal channel. Eventually, printed words and pictures may be represented in the verbal channel even if they were presented visually, and spoken words may be represented in the visual channel if they elicit images in the learner. However, the way that verbal and pictorial material is represented in working memory is different, so there is a verbal code and a pictorial code. An important aspect of controlling the flow of visual and verbal information is for learners to build connections between cor-

responding visual and verbal representations of the same material—an accomplishment that Paivio (1986) calls building *referential connections.*

For example, Mayer (2001) reported research in which students learned about how a scientific system works (e.g., a bicycle tire pump, a car's braking system, or the process of lightning formation) and then took a transfer test that measured their depth of understanding. Students performed better on the transfer test when they listened to an explanation and viewed a corresponding animation than when they only listened to the explanation. This *multimedia effect* is consistent with the idea that people process visual and verbal material in separate channels.

The limited capacity assumption concerns constraints on the amount of material that can be processed at one time in working memory (Baddeley, 1998; Sweller, 1999). Thus, only a few images can be held and organized into a coherent visual model at one time, and only a few words can be held and organized into a coherent verbal model at one time. An important aspect of the limited capacity assumption is that the learner's cognitive system easily can become overloaded, such as by presenting a great amount of information simultaneously.

For example, Mayer (2001) reported research in which students learned about how lightning storms develop by receiving a narrated animation and then took transfer tests. When the presentation contained extraneous words (e.g., interesting facts about people being struck by lightning), pictures (e.g., interesting video clips of lightning storms), and sounds (e.g., background music), students performed more poorly on subsequent transfer tests than when extraneous material was excluded. This *coherence effect* is consistent with the idea that the extra material overloaded the learners' working memories, thus making it more difficult to construct a mental representation of the cause-and-effect system.

The active learning assumption is that meaningful learning (or understanding) occurs when learners engage in appropriate cognitive processing during learning—including selecting relevant information, organizing the material into a coherent representation, and integrating incoming visual and verbal material with each other and with prior knowledge (Mayer, 1996b, 1999). The balanced and coordinated activation of these kinds of processes leads to the construction of a meaningful learning outcome that can be stored in long-term memory for future use. In short, meaningful learning is a generative process in which the learner must actively engage in cognitive processing rather than passively receive information for storage (Wittrock, 1990).

For example, signaling (Loman & Mayer, 1983; Lorch, 1989; Meyer, 1975) is a technique intended to improve students' understanding of prose in which the key material is highlighted (thus fostering the process of selecting) and the organizational structure is highlighted (thus fostering the process of organizing). For example, Mautone and Mayer (2001) presented a narrated animation on how airplanes achieve lift and then asked students to solve some transfer problems that required applying what they had learned. Some students received a signaled version that included a short outline stating the main three steps, headings keyed to the three steps, and connecting words such as "because of this" or "first . . . second . . . third." The signals were part of the narration and added no new content information. Other students received a nonsignaled version. On the transfer test, there was a *signaling effect* in which the students in the signaled group performed better than students in the nonsignaled group. Thus, techniques intended to prime active cognitive processing (e.g., selecting and organizing relevant material) resulted in better understanding.

INFORMATION PROCESSING AND INSTRUCTION

In this section I examine three examples of how the information processing approach can be applied to instructional issues in three subject matter domains: reading, writing, and mathematics. In each domain the driving question concerns the cognitive processes or knowledge that a student needs to perform competently as an authentic academic task such as comprehending a passage, creating an essay, or solving an arithmetic word problem. I focus on these three domains because they represent exemplary educational tasks that have been studied extensively in research.

Information Processing in Reading a Passage

What are the cognitive processes involved in comprehending a passage? Mayer (1996b, 1999) analyzed the reading-comprehension task into four component processes: selecting, organizing, integrating, and monitoring.

Selecting involves paying attention to the most relevant portions of the passage. This involves being able to tell what is important and what is not (Brown & Smiley, 1977). For example, Brown and Smiley (1977) broke stories into idea units (e.g., single events or simple facts) and asked children to sort them into four categories ranging from most to least important. Third-graders seemed to sort randomly, such that an important idea unit was no more likely than an unimportant idea unit to be sorted into the important category. However, college students were extremely accurate, such that important idea units were usually classified as important and unimportant idea units were usually classified as unimportant. Apparently,

as students acquire more experience in reading for comprehension, they develop skill in selecting important information.

Organizing involves taking the relevant pieces of information and mentally connecting them into a coherent structure. For example, some possible structures are to organize the material as cause-and-effect sequence, classification hierarchy, compare-and-contrast matrix, description network, or simple list (Chambliss & Calfee, 1998; Cook & Mayer, 1988; Meyer & Poon, 2001). In an exemplary study, Taylor (1980) asked fourth- and sixth-grade students to read and recall a short passage. The sixth-graders recalled much more superordinate material than subordinate material, indicating that they used the higher level structure to help them organize and remember the lower level material. In contrast, fourth-grade readers recalled more subordinate material than superordinate material, indicating that they did not make much use of the higher level structure to help them mentally organize the passage. Apparently, as students acquire more experience in reading for comprehension, they develop skill in organizing the material into a high-level structure.

Integrating involves connecting the incoming knowledge with existing knowledge from one's long-term memory. This involves activating relevant prior knowledge and assimilating the incoming information to it (Ausubel, 1968). For example, Bransford and Johnson (1972) asked college students to read an abstract passage about a procedure. If students were told beforehand that the passage was about washing clothes, they remembered twice as much as when they were told the topic afterward. Apparently, priming appropriate prior knowledge before reading a new passage is a powerful aid to comprehension.

Monitoring involves a metacognitive process of judging whether the newly constructed knowledge makes sense. For example, in comprehension monitoring readers continually ask themselves whether the passage makes, whether parts contradict one another, and whether parts contradict their past experiences (Markman, 1979). In an exemplary study, Vosniadou, Pearson, and Rogers (1988) asked third and fifth graders to read stories that had inconsistent statements. When prompted to point out anything wrong with the passage, the fifth graders recognized more than twice as many of the inconsistencies as did third graders. Apparently, students develop skill in comprehension monitoring as they gain more experience in reading.

There is overwhelming evidence that the cognitive processes underlying reading comprehension can be taught (Pressley & Woloshyn, 1995). For example, Cook and Mayer (1988) taught students how to outline paragraphs from their chemistry textbooks based on some of the structures just listed. Thus, the training focused on the organizing process.

Initially, most students organized passages as lists of facts, but with training they were able to distinguish between passages that best fit within the structure of a cause-and-effect sequence, a classification hierarchy, and so forth. When students were tested on their comprehension of passages from a biology textbook, the structure-trained students performed much better than did students who had not received training. Research on teaching of organizing strategies offers one useful demonstration of the positive consequences of teaching specific ways to process information.

Information Processing in Writing an Essay

What are the cognitive processes involved in writing an essay, such as "how I spent my summer vacation"? Hayes and Flower (1980; Hayes, 1996) analyzed the essay-writing task in three component processes: planning, translating, and reviewing.

Planning involves mentally creating ideas for the essay (i.e., generating), developing an outline structure for the essay (i.e., organizing), and considering how best to communicate with the intended audience (i.e., evaluating). For example, the learner may remember specific events from his or her summer vacation, may decide to present them in chronological order under the theme "too much of a good thing," and may decide that the best way to communicate is through humor.

In a study of the role of planning, Gould (1980) asked people to write (or dictate) a routine business letter for a specific purpose. People spent about one third of their time writing (or speaking) and two thirds of their time in silence—presumably as they planned what to write (or say) next. It is interesting to note that people began writing (or speaking) immediately, indicating that they engaged in no global planning. These results suggest that writers spend most of their time in local planning and therefore point to the need for training in global planning.

Translating involves actually putting words on paper, such as through writing, typing, or dictating. For example, the learner may sit at a word processor and begin to type. In a study of the role of translating, Glynn, Britton, Muth, and Dogan (1982) asked students to write a first draft and then a final draft of a persuasive letter. Some students were told to write a polished first draft paying attention to grammar and spelling, whereas other students were told to write an unpolished first draft minimizing attention to grammar and spelling. Students wrote a higher quality final draft when they were told to write an unpolished rather than a polished first draft. Apparently, the process of translating places a heavy cognitive load on the writers' working memories, so if they have to pay attention to low-level aspects of writing (e.g., spelling and grammar), they are less able to pay attention to high-level aspects of writing (e.g., writing a persuasive argument). These findings suggest the need to minimize cognitive load when students are translating.

Reviewing involves detecting and correcting errors in what has been written. For example, the learner may read over a sentence and decide it needs to be made more specific. In a study of the role of reviewing, Bartlett (1982) found that middle-school students performed poorly on detecting errors in their own essays but well on detecting errors in their peers' essays. Less than half of the detected errors were corrected properly. These results point to the need for training in how to detect and correct errors.

Research on writing shows that learners often have difficulty in the planning and reviewing phases of writing, but these cognitive processes can be taught with success (Kellogg, 1994; Levy & Ransdell, 1996; Mayer, 1999). For example, Kellogg (1994) asked college students to write an essay on the pros and cons of pledging to give all of one's income over a certain level to poor families in the community. One group of students was not asked to engage in any prewriting activity (no-prewriting group), whereas another group was asked to begin by producing an outline containing the relevant ideas (outlining group). The outlining group, therefore, was encouraged to engage in planning processes such as generating ideas, organizing ideas, and evaluating whether the message is appropriate for the audience. When judges were asked to rate the quality of the essays on a 10-point scale, the essays written by the outlining group received much higher quality ratings than did those written by the no-prewriting group. Apparently, students often ignore the cognitive processes in planning, but when they are encouraged to engage in planning processes, their writing is much improved.

Information Processing in Solving a Mathematics Problem

What are the cognitive processes involved in solving an arithmetic word problem, such as, "At ARCO gas sells for $1.13 per gallon. This is 5 cents less per gallon than gas at Chevron. How much do 5 gallons of gas cost at Chevron?" (Lewis & Mayer, 1987). Mayer (1992b) analyzed the task in four component processes: translating, integrating, planning, and executing.

Translating involves building a mental representation for each sentence in the problem. For example, for the first sentence the learner may build a mental representation such as "ARCO = 1.13"; and for the second sentence the learner may build a mental representation such as "ARCO = CHEVRON − .05." In an exemplary study, Soloway, Lochhead, and Clement (1982) asked college students to write equations for statements such as, "There are six times as many students as professors at this university." Approximately one third of the students translated the statement incorrectly, yielding answers such as "6S = P." Students need training in how to represent some of the sentences in word problems.

Integrating involves building a mental representation of the entire situation presented in the problem. For example, the learner may visualize a number line with ARCO at the 1.13 point on the line and Chevron .05 spaces to the right. In an exemplary study, Paige and Simon (1966) gave students a problem with an internal inconsistency, such as: "The number of quarters a man has is seven times the number of dimes he has. The value of the dimes exceeds the value of the quarters by $2.50. How many of each coin does he have?" Most students failed to recognize the inconsistency; some constructed equations such as Q = 7D and D (.10) = 2.50 + Q(.25), and solved for Q. Students need training in how to integrate the information into a meaningful representation that can be called a *situation model* (Kintsch & Greeno, 1985; Mayer & Hegarty, 1996).

Planning involves creating a strategy for solving the problem, such as breaking a problem into parts. For example, the learner may develop the plan: Add .05 to 1.13, then multiply the result by 5. Reed (1987) has shown that giving students worked examples with commentary can help them apply appropriate strategies when they receive new problems. Chi, Bassok, Lewis, Reimann, and Glaser (1989) found that students who spontaneously produced self-explanations as they read worked examples in textbooks tended to excel on subsequent problem-solving tests. Students need practice in understanding the strategies used to solve example problems.

Executing involves carrying out a plan, resulting in the production of an answer. For example, the learner may compute .05 + 1.13 = 1.18, 1.18 × 5 = 5.90. An accompanying process is monitoring, in which the learner evaluates whether the plan is being successfully applied. Fuson (1992) has identified four stages in the development of simple addition for problems (such as 3 + 5 = ___): counting all, in which the student counts 1-2-3, and then 4-5-6-7-8; counting on, in which the student starts with 3 and then counts 4-5-6-7-8; derived facts, in which the student changes the problem into 4 + 4 and gives 8 as the answer; and known facts, in which the student simply retrieves 8 as the answer. When the lower-level skill is automatic—requiring minimal attention—the student can devote more cognitive resources to understanding the problem and planning the problem solution.

Together, translating and integrating constitute the phase of problem understanding, whereas planning and executing constitute the phase of problem solution. Research shows that learners have difficulty with problem understanding—translating and integrating—although instruction emphasizes problem solution, particularly executing (Mayer, Sims, & Tajika, 1995).

An important contribution of the information processing approach to mathematical cognition is the design of programs to teach students how to process mathematics problems. For example, Lewis (1989) taught students how to represent arithmetic word problems in pictorial form as variables along a number line. A sentence like "Megan has $420" is represented by placing "Megan" along a number line along with "$420." Then, the sentence, "She saved one fifth as much as James saved" means that "James" should be placed on the number line to the right of "Megan," indicating that the amount James saved is greater than the amount Megan saved. By converting the sentences into an integrated number line, students learn how to engage in the cognitive processes of translating and integrating. Students who practiced these processes on a variety of problems for approximately 60 min performed much better on tests of solving new arithmetic word problems than did students who spent the same amount of time working with the problems without explicit training in converting them into number-line representations. These findings encourage the idea that students can learn to improve the way they process mathematics problems.

Future research on the psychology of subject matter (Mayer, 1999) is likely to provide detailed analyses of the cognitive processes needed for success on a variety of academic tasks, to uncover individual differences, and to discover instructional techniques for fostering the development of appropriate learning skills.

CONCLUSION

The premise underlying information processing theory is that human mental life consists of building and manipulating mental representations. The information processing view has important implications for education, including implications for how to improve instruction in subject matter areas such as reading, writing, and mathematics. Research and theory on human information processing points to the reciprocal relation between psychology and education: Educational practice can be improved when it is informed by an understanding of how the human mind works, and theories of how the human mind works can be improved when they are informed by studies involving how students perform on authentic academic tasks.

Admittedly, the information processing approach is limited. For example, by focusing mainly on cognition in individual learners, it fails to incorporate affective, motivational, emotional, social, and biological aspects of learning and instruction. All of these aspects must eventually be integrated into a far-reaching theory of how the human mind works. One promising approach is to include motivational strategies along with cognitive strategies in teaching students how to learn (Mayer, 2002).

Yet the information processing approach—now a dominant force in psychology for nearly half a century—also leaves a worthwhile legacy. The information processing approach enabled the rebirth of cognitive psychology by providing an alternative to behaviorism, created a unified framework that stimulated useful research and theory, highlighted the role of mental representations and cognitive processes, and fostered the transition toward studying cognition in more authentic contexts. Many of the current advances in educational research—ranging from cognitive strategy instruction to the psychology of subject matter—were enabled by the information processing approach in psychology. Examples were provided in the foregoing sections, but much more work is needed.

Overall, the information processing approach continues to play a constructive role in the development of educationally relevant theories of how the human mind works. In particular, the constructivist view of learners as sense makers and mental model builders offers a potentially powerful conception of human cognition. A particularly useful approach involves the refinement of techniques for analyzing academic tasks into constituent processes that can be evaluated and taught.

REFERENCES

Anderson, L. W., Krathwohl, D. R., Airasian, P. W., Cruickshank, K. A., Mayer, R. E., Pintrich, P. R., Raths, J., & Wittrock, M. C. (2001). *A taxonomy of learning, teaching, and assessing.* New York: Longman.

Atkinson, R. C., & Shiffrin, R. M. (1968). Human memory: A proposed system and its control processes. In K. W. Spence & J. T. Spence (Eds.), *Advances in the psychology of learning and motivation research and theory* (Vol. 2, pp. 89–195). New York: Academic Press.

Ausubel, D. P. (1968). *Educational psychology: A cognitive view.* New York: Holt, Rinehart, & Winston.

Baddeley, A. L. (1998). *Human memory.* Boston: Allyn and Bacon.

Bartlett, E. J. (1982). Learning to revise: Some component processes. In M. Nystrand (Ed.), *What readers know.* New York: Academic Press.

Bartlett, F. C. (1932). *Remembering.* Cambridge, England: Cambridge University Press.

Bransford, J. D., & Johnson, M. K. (1972). Contextual prerequisites for understanding: Some investigations of comprehension and recall. *Journal of Verbal Learning and Verbal Behavior, 11,* 717–726.

Brown, J. S., & Burton, R. R. (1978). Diagnostic models for procedural bugs in basic mathematical skills. *Cognitive Science, 2,* 155–192.

Brown, A. L., & Smiley, S. S. (1977). Rating the importance of structural units of prose passages: A problem of metacognitive development. *Cognitive Development, 48,* 1–8.

Chambliss, M. J., & Calfee, R. C. (1998). *Textbooks for learning.* Oxford, England: Blackwell.

Chi, M. T. H., Bassok, M., Lewis, M. W., Reimann, P., & Glaser, R. (1989). Self-explanations: How students study and use examples in learning to solve problems. *Cognitive Science, 13,* 145–182.

Cook, L. K., & Mayer, R. E. (1988). Teaching readers about the structure of scientific text. *Journal of Educational Psychology, 80,* 448–456.

De La Mettrie, J. O. (1912). *Man a machine.* La Salle, IL: Open Court. (Original work published 1748)

Ebbinghaus, H. (1964). *Memory.* New York: Dover.

Fuson, K. C. (1992). Research on whole number addition and subtraction. In D. A. Grouws (Ed.), *Handbook of research on mathematics teaching and learning* (pp. 243–275). New York: Macmillan.

Glynn, S. M., Britton, B. K., Muth, D., & Dogan, N. (1982). Writing and revising persuasive documents: Cognitive demands. *Journal of Educational Psychology, 74,* 557–567.

Gould, J. D. (1980). Experiments on composing letters: Some facts, some myths, and some observations. In L. W. Gregg & E. R. Steinberg (Eds.), *Cognitive processes in writing* (pp. 97–128). Hillsdale, NJ: Erlbaum.

Hayes, J. R. (1996). A new framework for understanding cognition and affect in writing. In C. M. Levy & S. Ransdell (Eds.), *The science of writing.* Mahwah, NJ: Erlbaum.

Hayes, J. R., & Flower, L. S. (1980). Identifying the organization of writing processes. In L. W. Gregg & E. R. Steinberg (Eds.), *Cognitive processes in writing.* Hillsdale, NJ: Erlbaum.

Johnson-Laird, P. N. (1988). *The computer and the mind.* Cambridge, MA: Harvard University Press.

Kellogg, R. T. (1994). *The psychology of writing.* New York: Oxford University Press.

Kintsch, W., & Greeno, J. G. (1985). Understanding and solving word problems. *Psychological Review, 92,* 109–129.

Kohler, W. (1925). *The mentality of apes.* New York: Liveright.

Lachman, R., Lachman, J. L., & Butterfield, E. C. (1979). *Cognitive psychology and information processing.* Hillsdale, NJ: Erlbaum.

Leary, D. E. (1990). *Metaphors in the history of psychology.* New York: Cambridge University Press.

Levy, C. M., & Ransdall, S. (Eds.). (1996). *The science of writing.* Mahwah, NJ: Erlbaum.

Lewis, A. B. (1989). Training students to represent arithmetic word problems. *Journal of Educational Psychology, 79,* 363–371.

Lewis, A. B., & Mayer, R. E. (1987). Students' miscomprehension of relational statements in arithmetic word problems. *Journal of Educational Psychology, 79,* 363–371.

Loman, N. L., & Mayer, R. E. (1983). Signaling techniques that increase the understandability of expository prose. *Journal of Educational Psychology, 75,* 402–412.

Lorch, R. F. (1989). Text signaling devices and their effects on reading and memory processes. *Educational Psychology Review, 1,* 209–234.

Markman, E. (1979). Realizing that you don't understand: Elementary school children's awareness of inconsistencies. *Child Development, 50,* 643–655.

Mautone, P. D., & Mayer, R. E. (2001). Signaling as a cognitive guide to multimedia learning. *Journal of Educational Psychology, 93,* 377–389.

Mayer, R. E. (1987). *Educational psychology: A cognitive approach.* New York: HarperCollins.

Mayer, R. E. (1992a). Cognition and instruction: On their historic meeting within educational psychology. *Journal of Educational Psychology, 84,* 405–412.

Mayer, R. E. (1992b). *Thinking, problem solving, cognition.* New York: Freeman.

Mayer, R. E. (1995). The search for insight: Grappling with Gestalt psychology's unanswered questions. In R. J. Sternberg & J. E. Davidson (Eds.), *The nature of insight* (pp. 1–32). Cambridge: MIT Press.

Mayer, R. E. (1996a). Learners as information processors: Legacies and limitations of educational psychology's second metaphor. *Educational Psychologist, 31,* 151–161.

Mayer, R. E. (1996b). Learning strategies for making sense out of expository text: The SOI model for guiding three cognitive processes in knowledge construction. *Educational Psychology Review, 8,* 357–371.

Mayer, R. E. (1999). *The promise of educational psychology: Learning in the content areas.* Upper Saddle River, NJ: Prentice-Hall.

Mayer, R. E. (2001). *Multimedia learning.* New York: Cambridge University Press.

Mayer, R. E. (2002). *The promise of educational psychology: Teaching for meaningful learning.* Upper Saddle River, NJ: Prentice-Hall.

Mayer, R. E., & Hegarty, M. (1996). The process of understanding mathematics problems. In R. J. Sternberg & T. Ben-Zeev (Eds.), *The nature of mathematical thinking* (pp. 29–54). Mahwah, NJ: Erlbaum.

Mayer, R. E., Sims, V. K., & Tajika, H. (1995). A comparison of how textbooks teach mathematical problem solving in Japan and the United States. *American Educational Research Journal, 32,* 443–460.

Metcalfe, J. (1986a). Feeling of knowing in memory and problem solving. *Journal of Experimental Psychology: Learning, Memory, and Cognition, 12,* 288–294.

Metcalfe, J. (1986b). Premonitions of insight predict impending error. *Journal of Experimental Psychology: Learning, Memory, and Cognition, 12,* 623–634.

Metcalfe, J., & Wiebe, D. (1987). Intuition in insight and noninsight problem solving. *Memory & Cognition, 15,* 238–246.

Meyer, B. J. F. (1975). *The organization of prose and its effects on memory.* New York: Elsevier.

Meyer, B. J. F., & Poon, L. W. (2001). Effects of structure strategy training and signaling on recall of text. *Journal of Educational Psychology, 93,* 141–159.

Newell, A., & Simon, H. A. (1972). *Human problem solving.* Englewood Cliffs, NJ: Prentice-Hall.

Paige, J. M., & Simon, H. A. (1966). Cognitive processes in solving algebra word problems. In B. Kleinmuntz (Ed.), *Problem solving: Research, method, and theory* (pp. 51–118). New York: Wiley.

Paivio, A. (1986). *Mental representations.* Oxford, England: Oxford University Press.

Piaget, J. (1971). *Science of education and the psychology of the child.* New York: Viking Press.

Pressley, M., & Woloshyn, V. (1995). *Cognitive strategy instruction that really improves children's academic performance.* Cambridge, MA: Brookline Books.

Reed, S. K. (1987). A structure-mapping model for word problems. *Journal of Experimental Psychology: Learning, Memory, and Cognition, 13,* 124–139.

Soloway, E., Lochhead, J., & Clement, J. (1982). Does computer programming enhance problem solving ability? Some positive evidence on algebra word problems. In R. J. Seidel, R. E. Anderson, & B. Hunter (Eds.), *Computer literacy* (pp. 171–189). New York: Academic Press.

Sternberg, R. J. (1977). *Intelligence, information processing, and analogical reasoning.* Hillsdale, NJ: Erlbaum.

Sternberg, R. J., & Ketron, J. L. (1982). Selection and implementation of strategies in reasoning by analogy. *Journal of Educational Psychology, 74,* 399–413.

Sweller, J. (1999). *Instructional design in technical areas.* Camberwell, Australia: ACER Press.

Taylor, B. (1980). Children's memory for expository text after reading. *Reading Research Quarterly, 15,* 399–411.

Thorndike, E. L. (1965). *Animal intelligence.* New York: Hafner.

Vosniadou, S., Pearson, P. D., & Rogers, T. (1988). What causes children's failures to detect inconsistencies in text? Representation versus comparison difficulties. *Journal of Educational Psychology, 80,* 27–39.

Wittrock, M. C. (1990). Generative processes of comprehension. *Educational Psychologist, 24,* 345–376.

CHAPTER 4

Self-Regulation and Learning

DALE H. SCHUNK AND BARRY J. ZIMMERMAN

Current theoretical accounts of learning view students as active seekers and processors of information. Learners' cognitions can influence the instigation, direction, and persistence of achievement behaviors (Bandura, 1997; Schunk, 1995; Zimmerman, 1998).

This chapter discusses the role of self-regulation during learning. *Self-regulation* (or *self-regulated learning*) refers to learning that results from students' self-generated thoughts and behaviors that are systematically oriented toward the attainment of their learning goals. Self-regulated learning involves goal-directed activities that students instigate, modify, and sustain (Zimmerman, 1994, 1998)—for example, attending to instruction, processing of information, rehearsing and relating new learning to prior knowledge, believing that one is capable of learning, and establishing productive social relationships and work environments (Schunk, 1995). Self-regulated learning fits well with the notion that rather than being passive recipients of information, students contribute actively to their learning goals and exercise control over goal attainment. As we show in this chapter, theory and research attest to the links between self-regulation and achievement processes.

We begin by explaining five theoretical perspectives on self-regulation: operant theory, information processing theory, developmental theory, social constructivist theory, and social cognitive theory. With this theoretical background in place, we discuss self-regulation research that identified self-regulatory processes and examined how self-regulatory processes operate during learning. We also describe in detail an intervention designed to enhance students' self-regulation. We conclude by suggesting that future research address such topics as the links between self-regulation and volition, the development of self-regulation in children, the integration of self-regulation into educational curricula, and self-regulation across the life span.

THEORETICAL FORMULATIONS

Operant Theory

The views of operant psychologists about self-regulation derive primarily from the work of Skinner (1953). Operant behavior is emitted in the presence of discriminative stimuli. Whether behavior becomes more or less likely to occur in the future depends on its consequences. Behaviors that are reinforced are more likely to occur, whereas those punished become less likely. For example, a teacher might praise a student after the student studies hard during a class period. The praise may encourage the student to continue studying hard. Conversely, if a teacher criticizes a student after the student misbehaves, the criticism may decrease the likelihood of disruptive behavior.

Operant theorists have studied how individuals establish discriminative stimuli and reinforcement contingencies (Brigham, 1982). Self-regulated behavior involves choosing among alternative courses of action (Mace, Belfiore, & Shea, 1989), typically by deferring an immediate reinforcer in favor of a different and usually greater future reinforcer (Rachlin, 1991). For example, assume that Brad is having difficulty studying; he spends insufficient time studying and is easily distracted. A key to changing his behavior is to establish discriminative stimuli (cues) for studying. With the assistance of his school counselor, Brad establishes a definite time and place for studying (6:00 to 9:00 p.m. in his room with two 10-min breaks). To eliminate distracting cues, Brad agrees not to use the phone, CD player, or TV during this period. For reinforcement, Brad will award himself one point for each night he successfully accomplishes his routine. When he receives 10 points, he has earned a night off.

From an operant theory perspective, one decides which behaviors to regulate, establishes discriminative stimuli for their occurrence, evaluates performance according to whether it matches the standard, and administers reinforcement. The three key subprocesses are self-monitoring, self-instruction, and self-reinforcement.

Self-Monitoring

Self-monitoring refers to deliberate attention to some aspect of one's behavior, and often is accompanied by recording its frequency or intensity (Mace & Kratochwill, 1988). People cannot regulate their actions if they are not aware of what they do. Behaviors can be assessed on such dimensions as quality, rate, quantity, and originality. While writing a term paper, students may periodically assess their work to determine whether it states important ideas, whether they will finish it by the due date, whether it will be long enough, and whether it integrates their ideas in unusual fashion. One can engage in self-monitoring in such diverse areas as motor skills (how fast one runs the 100-m dash), art (how original one's pen-and-ink drawings are), and social behavior (how much one talks at social functions).

Often students must be taught self-monitoring methods (Belfiore & Hornyak, 1998; Lan, 1998; Ollendick & Hersen, 1984; Shapiro, 1987). Methods include narrations, frequency counts, duration measures, time-sampling measures, behavior ratings, and behavioral traces and archival records (Mace et al., 1989). *Narrations* are written accounts of behavior and the context in which it occurs. Narrations can range from very detailed to open-ended (Bell & Low, 1977). *Frequency counts* are used to self-record instances of specific behaviors during a given period (e.g., number of times a student turns around in his or her seat during a 30-min seatwork exercise). *Duration measures* record the amount of time a behavior occurs during a given period (e.g., number of minutes a student

studies during 30 min). *Time-sampling measures* divide a period into shorter intervals and record how often a behavior occurs during each interval. A 30-min study period might be divided into six 5-min periods; for each 5-min period, students record whether they studied the entire time. *Behavior ratings* require estimates of how often a behavior occurs during a given time (e.g., always, sometimes, never). *Behavioral traces* and *archival records* are permanent records that exist independently of other assessments (e.g., number of worksheets completed, number of problems solved correctly).

When self-recording is not used, people's memory of successes and failures becomes more selective and their beliefs about outcomes do not faithfully reflect actual outcomes. Self-recording often yields surprising results. Students having difficulties studying who keep a written record of their activities may learn they are wasting most of their study time on nonacademic tasks.

Two important self-monitoring criteria are regularity and proximity (Bandura, 1986). *Regularity* means observing behavior continually rather than intermittently, such as by keeping a daily record rather than recording behavior once a week. Nonregular observation requires accurate memory and often yields misleading results. *Proximity* means observing behavior close in time to its occurrence rather than long afterwards. It is better to write down what we do at the time it occurs rather than wait until the end of the day to reconstruct events.

Self-monitoring places responsibility for behavioral assessment on the person doing the monitoring (Belfiore & Hornyak, 1998). Self-monitored responses are consequences of behaviors; like other consequences, they affect future responding. Self-recordings are immediate responses that serve to mediate the relationship between preceding behavior and longer-term consequences (Mace & West, 1986; Nelson & Hayes, 1981). Students who monitor their completion of assignments provide themselves with immediate reinforcers that mediate the link between the work and distant consequences (e.g., teacher praise, high grades).

Self-Instruction

Self-instruction refers to discriminative stimuli that set the occasion for self-regulatory responses leading to reinforcement (Mace et al., 1989). One type of self-instruction involves arranging the environment to produce discriminative stimuli. Students who realize they need to review class notes the next day might write themselves a reminder before going to bed. The written reminder serves as a cue to review, which makes reinforcement (i.e., a good grade on a quiz) more likely.

Another type of self-instruction takes the form of statements that serve as discriminative stimuli to guide behavior. Self-instructional statements have been used to teach a variety of academic, social, and motor skills. Strategy instruction is an effective means of enhancing comprehension and achievement beliefs among remedial readers. Schunk and Rice (1987) taught remedial readers the following strategy, and they verbalized the individual steps prior to applying them to reading comprehension passages:

- What do I have to do?
- Read the questions.
- Read the passage to find out what it is mostly about.
- Think about what the details have in common.
- Think about what would make a good title.
- Reread the story if I don't know the answer to a question.

Verbalizing statements keeps students focused on a task, which may be especially beneficial for learners with attention deficits. Kosiewicz, Hallahan, Lloyd, and Graves (1982) used the following self-instruction procedure to improve the handwriting of a student with learning disabilities:

- Say aloud the word to be written.
- Say the first syllable.
- Name each of the letters in that syllable three times.
- Repeat each letter as it is written down.
- Repeat Steps 2 through 4 for each succeeding syllable.

Self-Reinforcement

Self-reinforcement is the process whereby people provide themselves with reinforcement contingent on performing a response, and the reinforcement increases the likelihood of future responding (Mace et al., 1989). Much research shows that reinforcement contingencies improve academic performance (Bandura, 1986), but it is unclear whether self-reinforcement is more effective than externally administered reinforcement (such as that given by the teacher). Studies investigating self-reinforcement often contain problems (Brigham, 1982; Martin, 1980). In academic settings, the reinforcement contingency too often is set in a context that includes instruction and classroom rules. Students typically do not work on materials when they choose but rather when told to do so by the teacher. Students may stay on task primarily because of the teacher's classroom control rather than because of reinforcement.

Self-reinforcement is hypothesized to be an effective component of self-regulated behavior (O'Leary & Dubey, 1979),

but the reinforcement may be more important than its agent. Although self-reinforcement may enhance behavioral maintenance over time, during the acquisition of self-regulatory skills, explicitly providing reinforcement may be more important.

Information Processing Theory

Information processing theories view learning as the encoding of information in long-term memory (LTM). Learners activate relevant portions of LTM and relate new knowledge to existing information in working memory (WM). Organized, meaningful information is easier to integrate with existing knowledge and more likely to be remembered.

From an information processing perspective, self-regulation is roughly equivalent to *metacognitive awareness* (Gitomer & Glaser, 1987). This awareness includes knowledge of the task (what is to be learned and when and how it is to be learned), as well as self-knowledge of personal capabilities, interests, and attitudes. Self-regulated learning requires learners to have knowledge about task demands, personal qualities, and strategies for completing the task.

Metacognitive awareness also includes procedural knowledge or productions that regulate learning of the material by monitoring one's level of learning, deciding when to take a different task approach, and assessing readiness for a test. Self-regulatory (metacognitive) activities are types of *control processes* under the learner's direction. They facilitate processing and movement of information through the system.

The basic (superordinate) unit of self-regulation may be a *problem-solving production system,* in which the problem is to reach the goal and the monitoring serves to ascertain whether the learner is making progress (Anderson, 1990). This system compares the present situation against a standard and attempts to reduce discrepancies.

An early formulation was Miller, Galanter, and Pribham's (1960) *test-operate-test-exit (TOTE) model.* The initial test phase compares the present situation against a standard. If they are the same, no further action is required. If they do not match, control is switched to the operate function to change behavior to resolve the discrepancy. One perceives a new state of affairs that is compared with the standard during the second test phase. Assuming that these match, one exits the model. If they do not match, further behavioral changes and comparisons are necessary.

To illustrate, assume that Jenny is reading her history text and stops periodically to summarize what she has read. She recalls information from LTM pertaining to what she has read and compares the information to her internal standard of an adequate summary. This standard also may be a production characterized by rules (e.g., be precise, include information on all topics covered, be accurate) developed through experiences in summarizing. She continues reading if her summary matches her standard. If they do not, she evaluates where the problem lies (in her understanding of the second paragraph) and executes a correction strategy (rereads the second paragraph).

Information processing models differ, but two central features are (a) comparisons of present activity against standards and (b) steps taken to resolve discrepancies (Carver & Scheier, 1982). A key aspect of these models is knowledge of learning strategies, including their procedures and conditional knowledge of when and why to employ the strategies.

Learning Strategies

Learning strategies are cognitive plans oriented toward successful task performance (Pressley et al., 1990; Weinstein & Mayer, 1986). Strategies include such activities as selecting and organizing information, rehearsing material to be learned, relating new material to information in memory, and enhancing meaningfulness of material. Strategies also include techniques to create and maintain a positive learning climate—for example, ways to overcome test anxiety, enhance self-efficacy, appreciate the value of learning, and develop positive outcome expectations and attitudes (Weinstein & Mayer, 1986). Use of strategies is an integral part of self-regulated learning because strategies give learners better control over information processing.

From an information-processing perspective, learning involves meaningful integration of new material into LTM networks. To encode (learn) information, learners attend to relevant task information and transfer it from the sensory register to WM. Learners also activate related knowledge in LTM. In WM, learners build connections (links) between new information and prior knowledge and integrate these links into LTM networks. Learning strategies assist encoding in each of these phases.

One important strategy is *rehearsal,* which includes repeating information, underlining, and summarizing. Repeating information aloud, subvocally (whispering), or covertly is an effective procedure for tasks requiring rote memorization. To learn the names of the 50 state capitals, Tim might say the name of each state followed by the name of its capital. Rehearsal also can help learners memorize lines to a song or poem and or learn English translations of foreign-language words.

Rehearsal that repeats information by rote does not link information with what one already knows. Rehearsal also does not organize information in a hierarchical or other fashion. As a consequence, LTM does not store rehearsed information in any meaningful sense, and retrieval after some time is often difficult.

Rehearsal can be useful for complex learning, but it must involve more than merely repeating information. One useful rehearsal procedure is *underlining (highlighting),* which improves learning if employed judiciously (Snowman, 1986). When too much material is underlined, underlining loses its effectiveness because less-important material is underlined along with more-important ideas. Underlined material should represent points most relevant to learning goals.

Summarizing is another popular rehearsal procedure. In summaries (oral or written), students put into their own words the main ideas expressed in the text. As with underlining, summarizing loses its effectiveness if it includes too much information (Snowman, 1986). Limiting the length of students' summaries forces them to identify main ideas.

A second class of learning strategies is *elaboration,* which means using imagery, mnemonics, questioning, and note taking to expand information by adding something to make learning more meaningful. *Imagery* produces a mental picture, which often is more meaningful than a verbal description. *Mnemonics* make information meaningful by relating it to what one knows. *Acronyms* combine the first letters of the material to be remembered into a meaningful word; for example, *HOMES* is an acronym for the five Great Lakes (Huron, Ontario, Michigan, Erie, Superior). Sentence mnemonics use the first letters of the material to be learned as the first letters of words in a sentence (e.g., *every good boy does fine* is a sentence mnemonic for the notes on the treble clef staff: E, G, B, D, and F).

The *method of loci* is a mnemonic in which learners imagine a familiar scene, such as a room in their house, after which they take a mental walk around the room and stop at each prominent object. Each new item to be learned is paired mentally with one object in the room. Assuming that the room contains (in order) a table, a lamp, and a TV, and that Tammy must buy butter, milk, and apples at a grocery store, she might first imagine butter on the table, a milky-colored lamp, and apples on top of the TV. To recall the grocery list, she mentally retraces the path around the room and recalls the appropriate object at each stop.

Questioning requires that learners stop periodically as they read text and ask themselves questions. To address higher order learning outcomes, learners might ask *How does this information relate to what the author discussed in the preceding section?* (synthesis) or *How can this idea be applied in a school setting?* (application).

During *note taking* learners construct meaningful paraphrases of the most important ideas. While taking notes, students might integrate new textual material with other information in personally meaningful ways. To be effective, notes must not reflect verbatim textual information. Copying material is a form of rehearsal and may improve recall, but it is not elaboration. The intent of note taking is to integrate and apply information.

Another learning strategy is *organization.* Two useful organization techniques are outlining and mapping. *Outlining* requires that learners establish headings. One way to teach outlining is to use a text with headings set off from the text or in the margins, along with embedded (**boldface** or *italic*) headings interspersed throughout the text. Another way is to have students identify topic sentences and points that relate to each sentence. Simply telling students to outline a passage does not facilitate learning if students do not understand the procedure.

Mapping improves learners' awareness of text structure because it involves identifying important ideas and their interrelationship. Concepts or ideas are identified, categorized, and related to one another. A map is conceptually akin to a *propositional network,* because mapping involves creating a hierarchy, with main ideas or superordinate concepts listed at the top, followed by supporting points, examples, and subordinate concepts.

Comprehension Monitoring

Comprehension monitoring helps learners determine whether they are properly applying declarative and procedural knowledge to material to be learned, evaluate whether they understand the material, decide whether their strategy is effective or whether a better strategy is needed, and know why strategy use will improve learning. Self-questioning, rereading, checking consistencies, and paraphrasing are monitoring processes (Baker & Brown, 1984; Borkowski & Cavanaugh, 1979; Paris, Lipson, & Wixson, 1983).

Some textual material periodically provides students with questions about content. Students who answer these questions as they read the material are engaging in *self-questioning.* When questions are not provided, students must generate their own. As a means of training, teachers can instruct students to stop periodically while reading and ask themselves questions (i.e., who, what, when, where, why, how).

Rereading is often accomplished in conjunction with self-questioning; when students cannot answer questions about the text or otherwise doubt their understanding, these cues prompt them to reread. *Checking for consistencies* involves determining whether the text is internally consistent—that is, whether parts of the text contradict others and whether conclusions that are drawn follow from what has been discussed.

A belief that textual material is inconsistent serves as a cue for rereading to determine whether the author is inconsistent or whether the reader has failed to comprehend the content. Students who periodically stop and *paraphrase* material are checking their level of understanding. Being able to paraphrase is a cue that rereading is unnecessary (Paris & Oka, 1986).

Developmental Theory

Developmental theorists conceive of self-regulation in terms of progressive cognitive changes in learners that allow them to exert greater control over their thoughts, feelings, and actions (Schunk & Zimmerman, 1994). It involves such actions as beginning and ending actions, altering the frequency and intensity of verbal and motor acts, delaying action on a goal, and acting in socially approved ways (Kopp, 1982).

Developmental Periods

Kopp (1982) presented a framework that links developmental periods with behaviors and cognitive mediators. From birth to approximately 3 months, control is limited to states of arousal and activation of early, rudimentary behaviors (e.g., reaching). During this neurophysiological modulation stage, the important mediators are maturation and parent routines (e.g., feeding) and interactions. Sensorimotor modulation occurs from 3 to 9 months and is marked by changes in ongoing behaviors in response to events and environmental stimuli. Toward the end of the first year (9–12 months), the earliest form of voluntary control over behavior appears in the form of infant compliance to caregivers' requests. The mediators are receptivity of social behaviors and the quality of the mother-child relationship.

Impulse control appears during the second year of life (12–18 months); it is characterized by an awareness of social demands of situations and the initiation, maintenance, and cessation of physical acts and communications. Signs of intentionality and goal-directed actions become apparent. The second year is critical for the shifting of external to internal control of behavior (Kochanska, Tjebkes, & Forman, 1998). Parental discipline expands and child compliance is linked with future internalization of rules.

The self-control phase, which emerges during the third year (24–36 months), is characterized by greater reactivity to adult commands and increased communicative and social interactions through the growth of language and the directive functions of speech. Internalization of adult guidance becomes increasingly prevalent. Finally, children enter a period of self-regulation during the fourth year (36 months and

TABLE 4.1 Social Cognitive Model of the Development of Self-Regulatory Competence

Level of Development	Social Influences	Self Influences
Observational.	Models. Verbal description.	
Emulative.	Social guidance. Feedback.	
Self-controlled.		Internal standards. Self-reinforcement.
Self-regulated.		Self-regulatory processes. Self-efficacy beliefs.

older). Milestones of this period are adoption of rules that guide behavior, greater internalization of guidance by others, emergence of cognitive mediation of behavior (e.g., thought processes), and adaptation of behavior to changes in environmental demands.

Schunk and Zimmerman (1997) postulated that self-regulation develops initially from social sources and shifts to self sources in a series of levels (Table 4.1). At the outset, novice learners acquire learning strategies most rapidly from teaching, social modeling, task structuring, and encouragement (Zimmerman & Rosenthal, 1974). At this observational level, many learners can induce the major features of learning strategies from observing models; however, most of them also need practice to fully incorporate the skill into their behavioral repertoires. Motoric accuracy can be improved if models provide guidance, feedback, and social reinforcement during practice. During participant (mastery) modeling (Bandura, 1986), models repeat aspects of the strategy and guide enactment based on learners' imitative accuracy.

Learners attain an emulative level of skill when their performances approximate the general form of the model's. Observers are not copying the model; rather, they imitate general patterns or styles. For example, they may imitate the type of question that the model asks but not mimic the model's words.

The source of learning skills is primarily social for the first two levels of academic competence but shifts to self-influences at more advanced levels. The third, self-controlled level is characterized by learners' ability to use strategies independently while performing transfer tasks. Students' use of strategies becomes internalized but is affected by representational standards of modeled performances (e.g., covert images and verbal meanings) and self-reinforcement processes (Bandura & Jeffery, 1973).

When students reach adolescence, they need to attain a self-regulated level of academic skill so they can systematically adapt strategies to changes in personal and situational conditions (Bandura, 1986). At this level, learners initiate use of strategies, incorporate adjustments based on features of situations, and are motivated to achieve by goals and perceptions of self-efficacy. Learners choose when to use particular strategies and adapt them to changing conditions with little or no guidance from models.

Triadic reciprocality is evident throughout the phases. Social factors in the environment influence behaviors and personal factors, which in turn affect the social environment. In the early stages of learning, teachers who observe problems in learners' performances offer correction, learners who do not fully comprehend how to perform a skill or strategy at the emulative level may ask teachers for assistance, and learners' performances affect their self-efficacy. At more advanced levels, learners mentally and overtly practice skills and seek out teachers, coaches, and tutors to help refine their skills.

Social influences do not disappear with advancing skill acquisition. Although self-controlled and self-regulated learners use social sources less frequently, they nonetheless continue to rely on such sources (Zimmerman, 2000). Self-regulation does not mean social independence.

This is not a stage model and learners may not necessarily progress in this fashion. Students without access to relevant models may nonetheless learn on their own. For example, one may learn to play a musical instrument by ear or develop a unique method for correctly solving mathematical word problems. Despite the frequent success of self-teaching, it fails to reap the benefits of the social environment on learning. Furthermore, failing to use the social environment may limit overall skill acquisition unless learners possess good self-regulatory skills.

In summary, this four-level analysis of self-regulatory development extends from acquiring knowledge of learning skills (observation), to using these skills (emulation), to internalizing them (self-control), and finally to using them adaptively (self-regulation). Although this conceptualization results from socialization research, it is useful in guiding instructional efforts to teach students how to acquire and self-regulate academic learning (Schunk & Zimmerman, 1997).

Private Speech

Cognitive developmental theory establishes a strong link between private speech and the development of self-regulation (Berk, 1986; Frauenglass & Diaz, 1985). *Private speech* refers to the set of speech phenomena that has a self-regulatory function but is not socially communicative (Fuson, 1979). The historical impetus derives in part from work by Pavlov (1927), who distinguished the first (perceptual) from the second (linguistic) signal systems. Pavlov realized that animal conditioning results do not completely generalize to humans; human conditioning often occurs quickly with one or a few pairings of conditioned stimulus and unconditioned stimulus, in contrast to the multiple pairings required with animals. Pavlov believed that conditioning differences between humans and animals were due to the human capacity for language and thought. Stimuli may not produce conditioning automatically; people interpret stimuli in light of their prior experiences. Although Pavlov did not conduct research on the second signal system, subsequent investigations have validated his beliefs that human conditioning is complex and that language plays a mediational role.

Luria (1961) focused on the child's transition from the first to the second signal system. Luria postulated three stages in the development of verbal control of motor behavior. Initially, the speech of others directed the child's behavior (ages 1.5–2.5). During the second stage (ages 3–4), the child's overt verbalizations initiated motor behaviors but did not necessarily inhibit them. In the third stage, the child's private speech became capable of initiating, directing, and inhibiting motor behaviors (ages 4.5–5.5). Luria believed this private, self-regulatory speech directed behavior through neurophysiological mechanisms. The mediational and self-directing role of the second signal system is embodied in Vygotsky's theory (discussed later).

Production, Mediational, and Continued-Use Deficiencies

Many investigations have attempted to determine what factors determine why children do not use private speech when doing so would be desirable. A distinction is drawn between production and mediational deficiencies in spontaneous use of private speech (Flavell, Beach, & Chinsky, 1966). A *production deficiency* is a failure to generate task-relevant verbalizations (e.g., rules, strategies, information to be remembered) when they could improve performance. A *mediational deficiency* occurs when task-relevant verbalizations are produced, but they do not affect subsequent behaviors (Fuson, 1979).

Young children produce verbalizations that do not necessarily mediate performance. Children eventually develop the ability to verbalize statements that mediate performance, but they may not produce relevant verbalizations at the appropriate times. With development, children learn to verbalize when it might benefit their performances. This developmental model fits better in situations calling for simple types of verbal self-regulation (e.g., rote rehearsal) than it does when complex verbalizations are required. For the latter, production and mediational deficiencies may coexist and may not follow a simple progression (Fuson, 1979).

Ample research demonstrates that after children are trained to produce verbalizations to aid performance, they often discontinue use of private speech when no longer required to verbalize (Schunk, 1982b). A continued-use deficiency arises when students have an inadequate understanding of the strategy, as they might when they receive insufficient instruction and practice using the strategy (Borkowski & Cavanaugh, 1979). Teachers can remedy this problem by providing repeated instruction and practice with spaced review sessions. A *continued-use deficiency* also might arise when students associate the strategy with the training context and do not understand how to transfer it to other tasks. Use of multiple tasks during training helps students understand uses of the strategy. Strategies often must be modified to apply to different tasks. When slight modifications prove troublesome, students benefit from explicit training on strategy modification.

Continued-use deficiencies can also occur when learners do not understand that use of private speech benefits their performances. They might believe that verbal self-regulation is useful, but that it is not as important for success as such factors as personal effort or time available (Fabricius & Hagen, 1984). To promote maintenance of verbal self-regulators, researchers suggest providing learners with strategy value information, or information that links strategy use with improved performance (Baker & Brown, 1984; Paris et al., 1983; Schunk & Rice, 1987).

Strategy value can be conveyed by instructing students to use the strategy because it will help them perform better, informing them that strategy use benefited other students, and providing feedback linking strategy use with progress in skill acquisition (Borkowski & Cavanaugh, 1979). Research shows that strategy value information enhances performance, continued strategy use, and strategy transfer to other tasks (Lodico, Ghatala, Levin, Pressley, & Bell, 1983; Paris, Newman, & McVey, 1982).

Strategy value information also raises self-efficacy, which promotes performance through increased effort and persistence (Schunk & Rice, 1987). Students who benefit most from strategy training are those who work at tasks nonsystematically and who doubt their academic capabilities (Licht & Kistner, 1986). Strategy value information implicitly conveys to students that they are capable of learning and successfully applying the strategy, which engenders a sense of control over learning outcomes and enhances self-efficacy for skill improvement.

Social Constructivist Theory

Social constructivist theory of self-regulation is grounded in theories of cognitive development. These developmental theories have certain core assumptions (Paris & Byrnes, 1989).

Developmental theories stress the notion that people are intrinsically motivated to learn. From birth onward, people are motivated to actively explore, understand, and control their environments. Understanding transcends the literal information acquired. People impose meaning on their perceptions and form beliefs according to their prior experiences.

Mental representations change with development. Infants and toddlers represent their worlds in terms of action and sights. With development, learners use verbal codes (e.g., language, mathematical notation) to represent what they know.

There are progressive refinements in levels of understanding. The process of reconciling what one knows and what one encounters never ends. Progressive refinements are stimulated by internal reorganizations and reflections, as well as by physical experiences, social guidance, and exposure to new information.

Development places limits on learning. Readiness for learning includes maturation and prior experiences. Learning proceeds best when learners have the potential to learn and are exposed to information commensurate with their readiness.

Finally, reflection and reconstruction stimulate learning. Although formal teaching methods can produce learning, the primary motivation behind learning comes from within and involves an intrinsic need to reexamine one's knowledge and behaviors. Learners construct theories about what they are able to do and why.

Construction of Theories

Social constructivists view self-regulation as the process of acquiring beliefs and theories about their abilities and competencies, the structure and difficulty of learning tasks, and the way to regulate effort and strategy use to accomplish goals (Paris & Byrnes, 1989). These theories and beliefs are constrained by development and change as a consequence of development and experience.

For example, research shows that children's earliest *attributions* (perceived causes of outcomes) are nondifferentiated, but that with development a distinct conception of ability emerges (Nicholls, 1978). After this differentiation occurs, children realize that performance may not match abilities and that other factors (e.g., effort, help from others) influence performance. Children's theories about the causes of academic outcomes reflect this developmental progression.

In like fashion, researchers have shown how children construct theories about the use and value of *strategies*. Children are taught methods to use on different tasks and construct their own versions about what works best for them. Strategy

information includes the strategy's goals, the tasks for which it is appropriate, how it improves performance, and how much effort it requires to use (Borkowski, Johnston, & Reid, 1987). Although strategies typically are task specific, there are common elements across different strategies such as goal setting and evaluation of progress (Pressley et al., 1990).

In the course of theory construction it often happens that learners are erroneous because not all instances are provided as examples and children must often improvise solutions. In mathematics, for example, erroneous strategies that nonetheless lead to solutions (albeit inaccurate) are known as *buggy algorithms* (Brown & Burton, 1978). When learning subtraction, children may acquire the belief that column by column, they take the smaller number away from the larger number regardless of whether that means they subtract from top to bottom or from bottom to top. This buggy algorithm generates solutions and can lead to a false sense of perceived competence for subtraction, which yields gross mismatches between what children believe they can do and their actual successes.

Vygotsky's Theory

The Russian psychologist Vygotsky's work is relevant to the social constructivist tradition. Vygotsky emphasized the role that language plays in self-regulation. Vygotsky (1962) believed that private speech helped to develop thought by organizing behavior. Children employed private speech to understand situations and surmount difficulties. Private speech occurred in conjunction with children's interactions in the social environment. As children's language facility developed, words spoken by others acquired meaning independent of their phonological and syntactical qualities. Children internalized word meanings and used them to direct their behaviors.

Vygotsky hypothesized that private speech followed a curvilinear developmental pattern: Overt verbalization (thinking aloud) increased until age 6 or 7, after which it declined and became primarily covert (internal) by ages 8–10. However, overt verbalization could occur at any age when people encountered problems or difficulties. Research shows that although the amount of private speech decreases from about ages 4 or 5 to 8, the proportion of private speech that is self-regulating increases with age (Fuson, 1979). In many research investigations, the actual amount of private speech is small, and many children do not verbalize at all. Thus, the developmental pattern of private speech seems more complex than the pattern originally hypothesized by Vygotsky.

Another Vygotskiian concept is the *zone of proximal development,* or the amount of learning possible by a student given the proper instructional conditions. Tasks that a student cannot do alone but can with some assistance fall into the zone. As teachers or peers provide *scaffolding* to assist in the process, learners are increasingly able to operate independently. Eventually the zone is changed to reflect new, higher-order learning.

Social Cognitive Theory

In the social cognitive theoretical framework, self-regulation is construed as situationally specific—that is, learners are not expected to engage in self-regulation equally in all domains. Although some self-regulatory processes (e.g., goal setting) may generalize across settings, learners must understand how to adapt processes to specific domains and must feel efficacious about doing so. This situational specificity is captured in Zimmerman's (1994, 1998) conceptual framework comprising six areas in which one can use self-regulatory processes: motives, methods, time, outcomes, physical environment, and social environment. Self-regulation is possible to the extent that learners have some *choice* in one or more of these areas. When all aspects of a task are predetermined, students may learn, but the source of control is external (i.e., teachers, parents, computers).

Reciprocal Interactions

According to Bandura (1986), human functioning involves reciprocal interactions between behaviors, environmental variables, and cognitions and other personal factors (Figure 4.1). This reciprocity is exemplified with an important construct in Bandura's theory: *perceived self-efficacy,* or beliefs about one's capabilities to learn or perform behaviors at designated levels (Bandura, 1997). Research shows that students' self-efficacy beliefs influence such actions as choice of tasks, persistence, effort, and achievement (Schunk, 1995). In turn, students' behaviors modify their efficacy beliefs. For example, as students work on tasks they note their progress toward their learning goals (e.g., completing sections of a term paper). Progress indicators convey to students that they are capable of performing well, which enhances self-efficacy for continued learning.

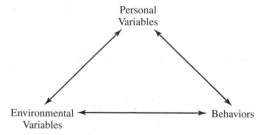

Figure 4.1   Reciprocal interactions in human functioning.

The interaction between self-efficacy and environmental factors has been demonstrated in research on students with learning disabilities, many of whom hold low self-efficacy for performing well (Licht & Kistner, 1986). Individuals in students' social environments may react to them based on attributes typically associated with them rather than based on what students actually do. Teachers may judge such students as less capable than average learners and hold lower academic expectations for them, even in content areas in which students with learning disabilities are performing adequately (Bryan & Bryan, 1983). In turn, teacher feedback can affect self-efficacy. Persuasive statements (e.g., *I know that you can do this*) can raise self-efficacy.

Students' behaviors and classroom environments influence one another. Consider a typical instructional sequence in which the teacher presents information and asks students to direct their attention to an overhead. Environmental influence on behavior occurs when students turn their heads without much conscious deliberation. Students' behaviors often alter the instructional environment. If the teacher asks questions and students give incorrect answers, the teacher may reteach some points rather than continue the lesson.

Subprocesses of Self-Regulated Learning

Self-regulation has been conceptualized as involving three key subprocesses: self-observation, self-judgment, and self-reaction (Bandura, 1986; Kanfer & Gaelick, 1986; Karoly, 1982). These subprocesses are not mutually exclusive; rather, they interact. While observing aspects of one's behavior, one may judge them against standards and react positively or negatively. One's evaluations and reactions set the stage for additional observations of the same behavioral aspects or others. These subprocesses also do not operate independently of the learning environment; environmental factors can assist the development of self-regulation. We discuss only the latter two subprocesses because self-observation is substantially similar to self-monitoring (described earlier).

Self-Judgment

Self-judgment refers to comparing present performance with one's goal. The belief that one is making goal progress enhances self-efficacy and sustains motivation. Students who find a task to be easy may think that they set their goal too low and may set it higher the next time. Furthermore, knowing that similar others performed a task can promote self-efficacy and motivation; students are apt to believe that if others can succeed, they can as well (Schunk, 1987). Students who believe they have not made acceptable progress will not become discouraged if they feel efficacious about succeeding and believe that a different strategy will produce better results.

Self-Reaction

Self-reactions to goal progress exert motivational effects (Bandura, 1986). Students who judge goal progress as acceptable and who anticipate satisfaction from goal accomplishment will feel efficacious about continuing to improve and motivated to complete the task. Negative evaluations will not necessarily decrease motivation if students believe they are capable of improving, such as by working harder. Motivation will not increase if students believe they lack the ability to succeed or to improve.

Instructions to people to respond evaluatively to their performances can affect motivation. People who believe they can perform better persist longer and work harder (Kanfer & Gaelick, 1986). Evaluations are not intimately tied to level of performance. Some students are content with a B in a course, whereas others want only an A. Assuming that people believe they are capable of improving, higher goals lead to greater effort and persistence than do lower goals (Locke & Latham, 1990).

Cyclical Nature of Self-Regulation

The interaction of personal, behavioral, and environmental factors during self-regulation is a cyclical process because these factors typically change during learning and must be monitored (Bandura, 1986, 1997; Zimmerman, 1994). Such monitoring leads to changes in an individual's strategies, cognitions, affects, and behaviors.

This cyclical nature is captured in Zimmerman's (1998) three-phase self-regulation model (Table 4.2). The *forethought* phase precedes actual performance and refers to processes that set the stage for action. The *performance (volitional) control* phase involves processes that occur during learning and affect attention and action. During the *self-reflection* phase—which occurs after performance—people respond to their efforts.

Table 4.2 shows that various self-regulatory processes come into play during the different phases. Social cognitive theorists postulate that students enter learning situations with goals and varying degrees of self-efficacy for attaining these goals. During performance control, they implement learning strategies that affect motivation and learning. During periods of self-reflection, learners engage in self-evaluation.

RESEARCH FOCUS AREAS

This section reviews some key areas of research on self-regulation. A comprehensive review is beyond the scope of this chapter; readers should consult other sources (Bandura, 1986, 1997; Boekaerts, Pintrich, & Zeidner, 2000; Schunk & Zimmerman, 1994, 1998). The research in this section focuses on self-regulation in learning settings. We begin by reviewing research that sought to identify self-regulatory processes; then we discuss research exploring the relation of processes to one another and to achievement outcomes. We conclude by describing an intervention project.

Identification of Self-Regulatory Processes

A number of researchers have sought to identify the types of self-regulatory processes that students use while engaged in academic tasks. Many of these studies also have determined whether the use of processes varies as a function of individual difference variables.

Zimmerman and Martinez-Pons (1986) developed a structured interview in which students were presented with eight different learning contexts (e.g., writing a short paper, taking a test, completing a homework assignment). For each, they were asked to state the methods they would use. Fourteen categories of self-regulated learning processes were identified (Table 4.3).

TABLE 4.3   Categories of Self-Regulated Learning Processes

Category	Example
Self-evaluating.	Checking work to ensure it is correct.
Organizing and transforming.	Making an outline before writing.
Goal-setting and planning.	Start studying 2 weeks before a test.
Seeking information.	Do library research before writing a paper.
Keeping records and monitoring.	Keep a list of words missed.
Environmental structuring.	Isolate oneself from distractions.
Self-consequating.	Reward oneself after a high test score.
Rehearsing and memorizing.	Write down formulas until they are learned.
Seeking peer assistance.	Ask a friend how to do an assignment.
Seeking teacher assistance.	Ask the teacher to reexplain a concept.
Seeking adult assistance.	Ask a parent to check homework.
Reviewing tests.	Determine correct answers on items missed.
Reviewing notes.	Study notes prior to a test.
Reviewing texts.	Study text prior to a test.

TABLE 4.2   Key Processes During Phases of Self-Regulation

Forethought	Performance Control	Self-Reflection
Goal setting.	Social comparisons.	Progress feedback and self-evaluation.
Social modeling.	Attributional feedback.	Self-monitoring.
	Strategy instruction and self-verbalization.	Reward contingencies.

In subsequent research, Zimmerman and Martinez-Pons (1990) found evidence of developmental trends among 5th, 8th, and 11th graders. Older students reviewed notes more and texts less compared with younger children. With development, students sought more assistance from teachers and less from parents. Older students also displayed greater use of record keeping and monitoring, organizing and transforming, and goal setting and planning. The researchers found that compared with boys, girls made greater use of record keeping and monitoring, environmental structuring, and goal setting and planning; they also found that compared with regular students, gifted students displayed greater organizing and transforming, self-consequating, seeking peer assistance, reviewing notes, and seeking adult assistance (fifth grade only).

Various aspects of self-regulation were addressed by Pintrich and De Groot (1990). Seventh graders were administered the Motivated Strategies for Learning Questionnaire (MSLQ). This instrument includes two categories: motivational beliefs (self-efficacy, intrinsic value, test anxiety) and self-regulated learning strategies (cognitive strategy use, self-regulation). Sample items tapping motivational beliefs are *Compared with other students in this class I expect to do well* and *I think I will be able to use what I learn in this class in other classes;* for self-regulation, some sample items are *When I study I put important ideas into my own words* and *I ask myself questions to make sure I know the material I have been studying.* Although the authors distinguished between motivational beliefs and self-regulated strategies, establishing and maintaining positive beliefs about learning is an effective self-regulatory strategy (Zimmerman, 2000). The MSLQ categories and those identified by Zimmerman and Martinez-Pons (1986) show some overlap.

Operation of Self-Regulatory Processes During Learning

In this section we review research on self-regulatory processes as students are engaged in academic tasks. Although there is some overlap between areas, the review is organized according to Zimmerman's (1998) forethought, performance control, and self-reflection phases (Table 4.2).

Goal Setting

Goal setting is an integral component of the forethought phase. Allowing students to set learning goals can enhance their commitment to attaining them, which is necessary for goals to affect performance (Locke & Latham, 1990). Schunk (1985) found that self-set goals promoted self-efficacy. Children with learning disabilities in mathematics received

subtraction instruction and practice over sessions. Some set session performance goals; others had comparable goals assigned; those in a third condition did not set or receive goals. Self-set goals led to the highest self-efficacy and achievement. Children in the two goal conditions demonstrated greater motivation during self-regulated practice than did no-goal students. Self-set children judged themselves more efficacious for attaining their goals than did assigned-goals students.

To test the idea that proximal goals enhance achievement outcomes better than do distant goals, Bandura and Schunk (1981) provided children with subtraction instruction and self-regulated problem solving over sessions. Some set a proximal goal of completing one set of materials each session; others pursued a distant goal of completing all sets of materials by the end of the last session; a third group was advised to work productively (general goal). Proximal goals led to the most productive self-regulated practice and to the highest subtraction self-efficacy and achievement; the distant goal resulted in no benefits compared with the general goal.

Schunk (1983c) tested the effects of goal difficulty. During a long division instructional program, children received either difficult but attainable or easier goals of completing a given number of problems each session. Within each goal condition, children either were given direct attainment information by an adult (i.e., *You can do this*) or received social comparative information indicating that other similar children had been able to complete that many problems. Difficult goals enhanced motivation during self-regulated practice and achievement; direct goal attainment information promoted self-efficacy.

Schunk and Swartz (1993a, 1993b) investigated how goals and progress feedback affected achievement outcomes and self-regulation. Children received paragraph-writing instruction and self-directed practice over sessions. An adult modeled a writing strategy, after which children practiced applying it to compose paragraphs. Process- (learning-) goal children were told to learn to use the strategy; product- (performance-) goal children were advised to write paragraphs; general-goal students were told to do their best. Half of the process-goal students periodically received progress feedback that linked strategy use with improved performance.

The process-goal-plus-feedback condition was the most effective, and some benefits were obtained from the process goal alone. Process-goal-plus-feedback students outperformed product- and general-goal students on self-efficacy, writing achievement, self-evaluated learning progress, and self-regulated strategy use. Gains were maintained after 6 weeks; children applied self-regulated composing strategies to types of paragraphs on which they had received no instruction.

Zimmerman and Kitsantas (1996, 1997) found that providing process goals (similar to learning goals) raised self-efficacy and self-regulation during dart throwing. Ninth and 10th-grade girls were assigned to a process-goal condition and advised to focus on the steps in dart throwing. Others were assigned to a product- (performance-) goal condition and told to concentrate on their scores. Some girls engaged in self-monitoring by writing down after each throw the steps they accomplished properly or their throw's outcome.

In the first study (Zimmerman & Kitsantas, 1996), process-goal girls attained higher self-efficacy and performance than did product-goal girls. Self-recording also enhanced these outcomes. The second study replicated these results (Zimmerman & Kitsantas, 1997); however, a shifting-goal condition was included in which girls pursued a process goal, but after they could perform the steps automatically they switched to a product goal of attaining high scores. The shifting goal led to the highest self-efficacy and performance.

Social Modeling

Modeling studies provide evidence on how information conveyed socially can be internalized by students and used in self-regulation to produce greater learning. In addition to their benefits on learning, models convey that observers can succeed if they follow the same sequence. Students who believe they know how to perform a skill or strategy feel more efficacious and motivated to succeed (Schunk, 1987).

An important means of acquiring self-evaluative standards is through observation of models. When children observe modeled standards, they are more likely to adopt these standards, and model similarity can increase adoption of standards (Davidson & Smith, 1982).

Zimmerman and Ringle (1981) found that models affected children's self-efficacy and achievement behaviors. Children observed an adult model unsuccessfully try to solve a wire-puzzle problem for a long or short period; the model also verbalized statements of confidence or pessimism. Children who observed a pessimistic model persist for a long time lowered their self-efficacy judgments for performing well.

Schunk (1981) provided children with either adult modeling or written instruction on mathematical division, followed by guided and self-directed practice over sessions. The adult model verbalized division solution steps while applying these steps to problems. Both treatments enhanced self-efficacy, persistence, and achievement, but modeling led to higher achievement and more accurate correspondence between self-efficacy and actual performance. Path analysis showed that modeling enhanced self-efficacy and achievement, self-efficacy directly affected persistence and achievement, and persistence raised achievement.

Schunk and his colleagues investigated the role of perceived similarity in competence by comparing mastery with coping models. Coping models initially demonstrate problems in learning but gradually improve and gain confidence. They illustrate how effort and positive thoughts can overcome difficulties. In addition to the modeled skills and strategies, observers learn and internalize these motivational beliefs and self-regulatory actions. Coping models contrast with mastery models, who demonstrate competent performance throughout the modeled sequence. In the early stages of learning, many students may perceive themselves more similar in competence to coping models.

Schunk and Hanson (1985) had children observe models solving subtraction problems. Peer mastery models solved subtraction problems correctly and verbalized statements reflecting high efficacy and ability, low task difficulty, and positive attitudes. Peer coping models initially made errors and verbalized negative statements, but then verbalized coping statements and eventually verbalized and performed as well as mastery models did. After observing a peer mastery model, peer coping model, adult mastery model, or no model, children received instruction and self-regulated practice over sessions. Peer mastery and coping models increased self-efficacy and achievement better than did adult and no models; adult-model children outperformed no-model students.

Schunk, Hanson, and Cox (1987) further explored mastery-coping differences and found that observing peer coping models enhanced children's self-efficacy and achievement more than did observing peer mastery models. Unlike the Schunk and Hanson (1985) study, this project used fractions—a task at which children previously had not been successful. Coping models may be more effective when students have little task familiarity or have had previous learning difficulties. Schunk et al. also found that multiple peer coping or mastery models promoted outcomes as well as did a single coping model and better than did a single mastery model. With multiple models, learners are apt to perceive themselves as similar to at least one model.

Schunk and Hanson (1989) investigated *self-modeling,* or cognitive and behavioral changes brought about by observing one's own performances (Dowrick, 1983). Children were videotaped while solving mathematical problems and then observed their tapes, after which they engaged in self-regulated practice. These children displayed higher self-efficacy, motivation, and self-regulated strategy use than did children who had been taped but did not observe their tapes and children who had not been taped.

Social Comparisons

Social comparisons provide normative information for assessing one's capabilities during the performance control phase. During long-division instructional sessions, Schunk (1983b) gave some children performance goals; the others were advised to work productively. Within each goal condition, half of the students were told the number of problems that other similar children had completed—which matched the session goal—to convey that the goals were attainable; the other half were not given comparative information. Goals enhanced self-efficacy; comparative information promoted self-regulated problem solving. Students receiving goals and comparative information demonstrated the highest mathematical achievement. These results suggest that the perception of progress toward a goal enhances motivation for self-directed learning and skill acquisition.

Attributional Feedback

Self-regulation is facilitated by providing learners with attributional feedback, or information linking performance with one or more causes. Providing effort feedback for prior successes supports students' perceptions of their progress, sustains motivation, and increases self-efficacy for learning. Feedback linking early successes with ability (e.g., *That's correct. You're really good at this.*) should enhance learning efficacy. Effort feedback for early successes may be more credible when students lack skills and must expend effort to succeed. As they develop skills, switching to ability feedback sustains self-efficacy and self-regulation.

Schunk (1982a) found that linking children's prior achievements with effort (e.g., *You've been working hard.*) led to higher self-directed learning, self-efficacy, and achievement than did linking future achievement with effort (e.g., *You need to work hard.*). Schunk (1983a) showed that ability feedback for prior successes (e.g., *You're good at this.*) enhanced self-efficacy and achievement better than did effort feedback or ability-plus-effort feedback. Children in the latter condition may have discounted some ability information in favor of effort. Schunk (1984b) found that providing children with ability feedback for initial learning successes led to higher ability attributions, self-efficacy, and achievement than did effort feedback for early successes.

Schunk and Cox (1986) gave children with learning disabilities effort feedback during the first or second half of a subtraction instructional program or no effort feedback. Attributional feedback promoted self-efficacy, achievement, and effort attributions better than did no feedback. Students who received effort feedback during the first half of the program judged effort as a more important cause of success than did learners who received feedback during the second half. Over a longer period, effort feedback for successes on the same task could lead students to doubt their capabilities and wonder why they still have to work hard to succeed.

Collectively, these results suggest that the credibility of attributional feedback may be more important than the type. Feedback that students believe is likely to enhance their self-efficacy, motivation, and achievement. When feedback is not credible, students may doubt their learning capabilities, and motivation and achievement will suffer.

Strategy Instruction and Self-Verbalization

Learners' verbalizations of self-regulatory strategies can guide their learning during the performance control phase. Schunk (1982b) provided modeled instruction on long division and self-directed practice to children with low mathematical achievement. Adult models verbalized strategy descriptors (e.g., *multiply, check*) at appropriate places. During self-directed practice, some children verbalized the descriptors, others constructed their own verbalizations, those in a third group overtly verbalized strategies and self-constructions, and children in a fourth group did not verbalize.

Self-constructed verbalizations yielded the highest self-directed practice and mathematical achievement. Children who verbalized strategies and self-constructions judged self-efficacy the highest. Self-constructions typically included the strategies and were oriented toward successful problem solving.

Schunk and Cox (1986) examined the role of verbalization during learning of subtraction problem solving strategies among children with learning disabilities. While solving problems, continuous-verbalization students verbalized aloud problem-solving operations. Midway through the instructional program, discontinued-verbalization children were asked to no longer verbalize aloud. No-verbalization children did not verbalize aloud.

Continuous verbalization led to the highest self-efficacy and achievement. When instructed to discontinue verbalizing aloud, these students may have not continued to use the verbal mediators to regulate their academic performances. For verbal mediators to become internalized, students may need to be taught to fade overt verbalizations to a covert level.

Progress Feedback and Self-Evaluation

As learners pursue goals, it is important that they believe they are making progress. During periods of self-reflection, learners can evaluate their progress on tasks having clear criteria; however, on many tasks it is difficult to determine goal progress, especially when standards are not clear or progress is slow. Feedback indicating progress can substantiate self-efficacy and motivation. As learners become more skillful, they become better at self-evaluating progress.

Schunk (1996) investigated how goals and self-evaluation affected self-regulated learning and achievement outcomes. Children received instruction and self-directed practice on fractions over sessions. Students worked under conditions involving either a goal of learning how to solve problems or a goal of merely solving them. Half of the students in each goal condition evaluated their problem-solving capabilities after each session. The learning goal with or without self-evaluation and the performance goal with self-evaluation led to higher self-efficacy, skill, and motivation than did the performance goal without self-evaluation. In a second study, all students in each goal condition evaluated their progress once. The learning goal led to higher motivation and achievement outcomes than did the performance goal.

Frequent opportunities for self-evaluation of capabilities or progress raised achievement outcomes regardless of whether students received learning or performance goals. Conversely, infrequent opportunities for self-evaluation promoted self-regulated learning and self-efficacy only among students receiving learning goals. Under these conditions, self-evaluation may complement learning goals better than it does performance goals.

Schunk and Ertmer (1999) replicated these results with college students during instruction on computer skills. When opportunities for self-evaluation were minimal, the learning goal led to higher self-efficacy, self-evaluated learning progress, and self-regulatory competence and strategy use; self-evaluation promoted self-efficacy. Conversely, frequent self-evaluation produced comparable outcomes when coupled with a learning or performance goal.

Self-Monitoring

The effects of self-monitoring have been studied extensively (Mace et al., 1989; Zimmerman, Bonner, & Kovach, 1996). In an early study (Sagotsky, Patterson, & Lepper, 1978), fifth- and sixth-grade students periodically monitored their work during mathematics sessions and recorded whether they were working on appropriate materials. Other students set daily performance goals, and students in a third condition received self-monitoring and goal setting. Self-monitoring significantly increased students' time on task and mathematical achievement; goal setting had minimal effects. The authors suggested that children may have needed training on how to set challenging but attainable goals.

Schunk (1983d) found benefits of monitoring with children during mathematics learning. Self-monitoring students recorded their progress at the end of each session; external-monitoring students had their progress recorded by an adult; no-monitoring students were not monitored and did not self-monitor. Self- and external monitoring enhanced self-efficacy and achievement equally well, and both produced better results than did no monitoring. Effects of monitoring did not depend on session performance because the three conditions did not differ in work completed during self-directed practice. The key was monitoring of progress rather than who performed it.

Reward Contingencies

Performance-contingent rewards during self-reflection can enhance self-regulation and learning. During mathematical division instruction with self-directed practice, performance-contingent reward children were told they would earn points for each problem solved correctly and that they could exchange their points for prizes (Schunk, 1983e). Task-contingent reward students were told that they would receive prizes for participating. Unexpected-reward children were allowed to choose prizes after completing the project to disentangle the effects of reward anticipation from those of reward receipt. Performance-contingent rewards led to the highest self-regulated problem solving, self-efficacy, and achievement. The other two conditions did not differ. In other research, Schunk (1984) found that combining performance-contingent rewards with proximal goals enhanced self-efficacy and achievement better than did either treatment alone.

INTERVENTIONS TO ENHANCE SELF-REGULATION

Self-regulation does not develop automatically with maturation, nor is it acquired passively from the environment. Systematic interventions assist the development and acquisition of self-regulatory skills. In this section we describe in depth an intervention project.

This project involved strategy instruction in paragraph writing with elementary school children (Schunk & Swartz, 1993a, 1993b). The interventions used goal setting, progress feedback, and self-evaluation of progress; the primary outcome variables were achievement, self-regulated strategy use, and self-efficacy.

Children received instruction and practice during twenty 45-min sessions over consecutive school days. The format for each session was identical. The first 10 min were devoted to *modeled demonstration* in which the teacher (a member of the research team) modeled the writing strategy by verbalizing the strategy's steps and applying them to sample topics and paragraphs. Students then received *guided practice* (15 min), during which time they applied the steps under the guidance of the teacher. The final 20 min of each session were for *self-regulated practice;* students worked alone while the teacher monitored their work.

The five-step writing strategy, which was displayed on a board in front of the room during the sessions, was as follows:

What do I have to do?

1. Choose a topic to write about.
2. Write down ideas about the topic.
3. Pick the main ideas.
4. Plan the paragraph.
5. Write down the main idea and the other sentences.

Four different types of paragraphs were covered during the instructional program; five sessions were devoted to each paragraph type. The four types of paragraphs were *descriptive* (e.g., describe a bird); *informative* (e.g., write about something you like to do after school); *narrative story* (e.g., tell a story about visiting a friend or relative); and *narrative descriptive* (e.g., describe how to play your favorite game).

The daily content coverage was the same for each of the four types of paragraphs: Session 1, strategy Steps 1, 2, and 3; Session 2, strategy Step 4; Session 3, strategy Step 5; Session 4, review of entire strategy; Session 5, review of entire strategy without the modeled demonstration. Children worked on two or three paragraph topics per session.

Children were assigned randomly to one of four experimental conditions: product goal, process goal, process goal plus progress feedback, and general goal (instructional control). Children assigned to the same condition met in small groups with a member of the research team.

Prior to the start of instruction children were pretested on writing achievement and self-efficacy. At the start of the first instructional session for each of the four paragraph types, children received a self-efficacy for improvement test, which was identical to the self-efficacy pretest except children judged capabilities for improving their skills at the five tasks for the paragraph type to be covered during the sessions rather than how well they could perform the tasks. On completion of instruction, children received a posttest that was comparable to the pretest and evaluated their progress in using the strategy compared with when the project began.

At the beginning of the first five sessions, the teacher verbalized to children assigned to the process-goal and to the process-goal-plus-feedback conditions the goal of learning to use the strategy's steps to write a descriptive paragraph.

These goal instructions were identical for the other sessions, except that the teacher substituted the name of the appropriate type of paragraph.

Children assigned to the product-goal condition were told at the start of the first five sessions to keep in mind that they were trying to write a descriptive paragraph. For the remaining sessions the teacher substituted the name of the appropriate paragraph type. These instructions controlled for the effects of goal properties included in the process-goal treatment.

The teacher told general-goal students at the start of every session to try to do their best. This condition controlled for the effects of receiving writing instruction, practice, and goal instructions, included in the other conditions.

Each child assigned to the process-goal-plus-progress feedback condition received verbal feedback three to four times during each session; this feedback conveyed to children that they were making progress toward their goal of learning to use the strategy to write paragraphs. Teachers delivered feedback to each child privately during self-regulated practice with such statements as, *You're learning to use the steps* and *You're doing well because you followed the steps in order.*

An important aim of these projects was to determine whether students would maintain their use of the strategy over time and apply it to types of paragraphs not covered during instruction. Maintenance and generalization were facilitated in several ways. The progress feedback was designed to convey to students that the strategy was useful for writing paragraphs and would help promote their writing achievement. Linking the strategy with four types of paragraphs demonstrated how it was useful on different writing tasks. The periods of self-regulated practice provided independent practice using the strategy and built self-efficacy. Succeeding on one's own leads to attributions of successes to ability and effort and strengthens self-efficacy. Results showed that the process goal with progress feedback had the greatest impact on achievement and self-efficacy to include maintenance after 6 weeks and generalization to other types of paragraphs; some benefits were also due to the process goal alone.

AREAS OF FUTURE RESEARCH

Research on self-regulation has advanced tremendously in the past few years, and we expect this trend to continue. At the same time, there is much work to be done. In this section we suggest some profitable areas for future research that will contribute to our understanding of self-regulation processes and that have implications for practice.

Self-Regulation and Volition

Volition has been of interest for a long time. Ach (1910) conceived of volition as the process of dealing with implementing actions designed to attain goals. More recently, action control theorists (Heckhausen, 1991; Kuhl, 1984) proposed differentiating predecisional processing (cognitive activities involved in making decisions and setting goals) from postdecisional processing (activities engaged in after goal setting). Predecisional analyses involve decision making and are motivational; postdecisional analyses deal with implementing goals and are volitional. Thus, volition mediates the relation between goals and actions and helps learners accomplish their goals.

Self-regulation is a broader process than is volition because self-regulation encompasses activities before, during, and after performance (Zimmerman, 2000). Thus, volition may be the aspect of self-regulation that occurs during performance. Corno (1993) noted that volition helps keep learners on track and thwarts distractions.

From a practical perspective, students can be taught volitional processes, such as metacognitive monitoring, emotion control, and management of environmental resources. There also may be different types of volitional styles or stable, individual differences in volition (Snow, 1989). Clearly more research is needed on volition to show how it is part of a self-regulatory system and on ways to enhance volition in students.

Development of Self-Regulation in Children

We recommend greater exploration of self-regulatory processes in children. Developmental psychologists have studied extensively how various cognitive functions (e.g., memory, metacognition) change with development (Meece, 1997). There also have been many studies conducted on teaching self-regulation strategies to children. A better link is needed between these two literatures.

For example, constructivists contend that individuals form or construct much of what they learn and understand (Bruning, Schraw, & Ronning, 1995). In this view, children are active learners and will try to discover meaning in material to be learned and impose organization as needed. An important question is whether it is better to teach children self-regulation strategies or facilitate their discovering these strategies on their own.

This question could be investigated in various ways. One means would be to compare the effectiveness of direct and constructivist teaching approaches for acquiring self-regulatory study methods. In the direct method, a teacher might explain and demonstrate self-regulation methods, after which students practice the methods and receive feedback. In the constructivist context, the teacher might form student groups and ask them to develop methods for studying given material. To control for the effects of type of model, the direct approach also could include peers as teachers.

As informative as this research might be, it does not address the key role of home influence in self-regulation development. There are wide variations in the extent to which parents and caregivers use self-regulatory skills and attempt to teach these skills to children. We recommend that longitudinal observational research be conducted. This research also would show how much parents stress the importance of self-regulation and encourage and reward their children for attempts at self-regulation. The longitudinal nature of such research could identify how parents' teaching and children's skills change as a function of children's developmental status.

Self-Regulation and the Curriculum

Research is needed on self-regulation in curriculum areas. When self-regulatory processes are linked with academic content, students learn how to apply these processes in a learning context. It is worthwhile to teach students to set goals, organize their schedules, rehearse information to be remembered, and the like, but such instruction may not transfer beyond the context in which it is provided.

Studies are needed in academic settings in which students are taught self-regulatory activities and how to modify those activities to fit different situations. These studies have the added benefit of showing students the value of self-regulation. Students who learn strategies but feel they are not especially useful are not likely to use them. Linking self-regulation with the curriculum raises its perceived value as students compare their work with prior efforts that did not benefit from self-regulation.

An assignment that lends itself well to teaching self-regulation and cuts across different curriculum areas is writing a term paper. In middle schools it is common for teachers to team for instruction; for example, a team of two or three teachers might teach the same students language arts, social studies, and science. Strategies for completing a term paper could be taught by the language arts teacher and would include such practices as setting goals and timelines, deciding on a topic, organizing ideas, collecting information, outlining, writing, and revising. The science and social studies teachers could pick up on these ideas and show students how the ideas can be applied in these classes and what modifications are needed. This approach has practical significance for teaching and provides insight into methods for facilitating transfer of self-regulation methods.

Self-Regulation Across the Life Span

We expect that self-regulation—like other processes—continues to change across the life span, yet there is little research on this point. We might ask how people regulate their finances, family life, work schedules, and so forth. Unfortunately there is little self-regulation research on individuals after they leave formal schooling.

A fruitful area to examine—and one that receives much publicity—is how adults use self-regulation to balance their personal and professional lives. How well do they use goal setting, monitoring of time spent, self-evaluation of the process, and other strategies? What are good ways to teach these skills? This research would have important developmental and practical implications.

CONCLUSION

Self-regulation has become an integral topic in the study of human learning. Various theoretical perspectives on self-regulation have been advanced, and each has important implications for research and practice. As self-regulation research continues, we expect that the knowledge base of self-regulation will be greatly expanded, and we will learn much more about the operation of self-regulatory processes. More intervention studies will show how to best improve individuals' self-regulatory skills. In sum, we believe that research on self-regulation will enhance our understanding of achievement processes and have important implications for teaching and learning in and out of school.

REFERENCES

Ach, N. (1910). *Uber den Willensakt und das Temperament* [On the will and temperament]. Leipzig, Germany: Quelle & Meyer.

Anderson, J. R. (1990). *Cognitive psychology and its implications* (3rd ed.). New York: Freeman.

Baker, L., & Brown, A. L. (1984). Metacognitive skills and reading. In P. D. Pearson (Ed.), *Handbook of reading research* (pp. 353–394). New York: Longman.

Bandura, A. (1986). *Social foundations of thought and action: A social cognitive theory.* Englewood Cliffs, NJ: Prentice Hall.

Bandura, A. (1997). *Self-efficacy: The exercise of control.* New York: Freeman.

Bandura, A., & Jeffery, R. W. (1973). Role of symbolic coding and rehearsal processes in observational learning. *Journal of Personality and Social Psychology, 26,* 122–130.

Bandura, A., & Schunk, D. H. (1981). Cultivating competence, self-efficacy, and intrinsic interest through proximal self-motivation. *Journal of Personality and Social Psychology, 41,* 586–598.

Belfiore, P. J., & Hornyak, R. S. (1998). Operant theory and application to self-monitoring in adolescents. In D. H. Schunk & B. J. Zimmerman (Eds.), *Self-regulated learning: From teaching to self-reflective practice* (pp. 184–202). New York: Guilford Press.

Bell, D. R., & Low, R. M. (1977). *Observing and recording children's behavior.* Richland, WA: Performance.

Berk, L. E. (1986). Relationship of elementary school children's private speech to behavioral accompaniment to task, attention, and task performance. *Developmental Psychology, 22,* 671–680.

Boekaerts, M., Pintrich, P. R., & Zeidner, M. (2000). *Handbook of self-regulation.* San Diego, CA: Academic Press.

Borkowski, J. G., & Cavanaugh, J. C. (1979). Maintenance and generalization of skills and strategies by the retarded. In N. R. Ellis (Ed.), *Handbook of mental deficiency, psychological theory and research* (2nd ed., pp. 569–617). Hillsdale, NJ: Erlbaum.

Borkowski, J. G., Johnston, M. B., & Reid, M. K. (1987). Metacognition, motivation, and controlled performance. In S. J. Ceci (Ed.), *Handbook of cognitive, social, and neuropsychological aspects of learning disabilities* (Vol. 2, pp. 147–173). Hillsdale, NJ: Erlbaum.

Brigham, T. A. (1982). Self-management: A radical behavioral perspective. In P. Karoly & F. H. Kanfer (Eds.), *Self-management and behavior change: From theory to practice* (pp. 32–59). New York: Pergamon.

Brown, J. S., & Burton, R. R. (1978). Diagnostic models for procedural bugs in basic mathematical skills. *Cognitive Science, 2,* 155–192.

Bruning, R. H., Schraw, G. J., & Ronning, R. R. (1995). *Cognitive psychology and instruction* (2nd ed.). Upper Saddle River, NJ: Merrill/Prentice Hall.

Bryan, J. H., & Bryan, T. H. (1983). The social life of the learning disabled youngster. In J. D. McKinney & L. Feagans (Eds.), *Current topics in learning disabilities* (Vol. 1, pp. 57–85). Norwood, NJ: Ablex.

Carver, C. S., & Scheier, M. F. (1982). An information processing perspective on self-management. In P. Karoly & F. H. Kanfer (Eds.), *Self-management and behavior change: From theory to practice* (pp. 93–128). New York: Pergamon.

Corno, L. (1993). The best-laid plans: Modern conceptions of volition and educational research. *Educational Researcher, 22*(2), 14–22.

Davidson, E. S., & Smith, W. P. (1982). Imitation, social comparison, and self-reward. *Child Development, 53,* 928–932.

Dowrick, P. W. (1983). Self-modelling. In P. W. Dowrick & S. J. Biggs (Eds.), *Using video: Psychological and social applications* (pp. 105–124). Chichester, UK: Wiley.

Fabricius, W. V., & Hagen, J. W. (1984). Use of causal attributions about recall performance to assess metamemory and predict strategic memory behavior in young children. *Developmental Psychology, 20,* 975–987.

Flavell, J. H., Beach, D. R., & Chinsky, J. M. (1966). Spontaneous verbal rehearsal in a memory task as a function of age. *Child Development, 37,* 283–299.

Frauenglass, M. H., & Diaz, R. M. (1985). Self-regulatory functions of children's private speech: A critical analysis of recent challenges to Vygotsky's theory. *Developmental Psychology, 21,* 357–364.

Fuson, K. C. (1979). The development of self-regulating aspects of speech: A review. In G. Zivin (Ed.), *The development of self-regulation through private speech* (pp. 135–217). New York: Wiley.

Gitomer, D. H., & Glaser, R. (1987). If you don't know it work on it: Knowledge, self-regulation and instruction. In R. E. Snow & M. J. Farr (Eds.), *Aptitude, learning, and instruction* (Vol. 3, pp. 301–325). Hillsdale, NJ: Erlbaum.

Heckhausen, H. (1991). *Motivation and action.* Berlin, Germany: Springer-Verlag.

Kanfer, F. H., & Gaelick, K. (1986). Self-management methods. In F. H. Kanfer & A. P. Goldstein (Eds.), *Helping people change: A textbook of methods* (3rd ed., pp. 283–345). New York: Pergamon.

Karoly, P. (1982). Perspectives on self-management and behavior change. In P. Karoly & F. H. Kanfer (Eds.), *Self-management and behavior change: From theory to practice* (pp. 3–31). New York: Pergamon.

Kochanska, G., Tjebkes, T. L., & Forman, D. R. (1998). Children's emerging regulation of conduct: Restraint, compliance, and internalization from infancy to the second year. *Child Development, 69,* 1378–1389.

Kopp, C. B. (1982). Antecedents of self-regulation: A developmental perspective. *Developmental Psychology, 18,* 199–214.

Kosiewicz, M. M., Hallahan, D. P., Lloyd, J., & Graves, A. W. (1982). Effects of self-instruction and self-correction procedures on handwriting performance. *Learning Disability Quarterly, 5,* 71–78.

Kuhl, J. (1984). Volitional aspects of achievement motivation and learned helplessness: Toward a comprehensive theory of action control. In B. A. Maher (Ed.), *Progress in experimental personality research* (Vol. 13, pp. 99–171). New York: Academic Press.

Lan, W. Y. (1998). Teaching self-monitoring skills in statistics. In D. H. Schunk & B. J. Zimmerman (Eds.), *Self-regulated learning: From teaching to self-reflective practice* (pp. 86–105). New York: Guilford Press.

Licht, B. G., & Kistner, J. A. (1986). Motivational problems of learning-disabled children: Individual differences and their implications for treatment. In J. K. Torgesen & B. W. L. Wong (Eds.), *Psychological and educational perspectives on learning disabilities* (pp. 225–255). Orlando: Academic Press.

Locke, E. A., & Latham, G. P. (1990). *A theory of goal setting and task performance.* Englewood Cliffs, NJ: Prentice Hall.

Lodico, M. G., Ghatala, E. S., Levin, J. R., Pressley, M., & Bell, J. A. (1983). The effects of strategy-monitoring training on children's selection of effective memory strategies. *Journal of Experimental Child Psychology, 35,* 263–277.

Luria, A. R. (1961). *The role of speech in the regulation of normal and abnormal behavior* (J. Tizard, Trans.). New York: Liveright.

Mace, F. C., Belfiore, P. J., & Shea, M. C. (1989). Operant theory and research on self-regulation. In B. J. Zimmerman & D. H. Schunk (Eds.), *Self-regulated learning and academic achievement: Theory, research, and practice* (pp. 27–50). New York: Springer-Verlag.

Mace, F. C., & Kratochwill, T. R. (1988). Self-monitoring: Applications and issues. In J. Witt, S. Elliott, & F. Gresham (Eds.), *Handbook of behavior therapy in education* (pp. 489–502). New York: Pergamon.

Mace, F. C., & West, B. J. (1986). Unresolved theoretical issues in self-management: Implications for research and practice. *Professional School Psychology, 1,* 149–163.

Martin, J. (1980). External versus self-reinforcement: A review of methodological and theoretical issues. *Canadian Journal of Behavioural Science, 12,* 111–125.

Meece, J. L. (1997). *Child and adolescent development for educators.* New York: McGraw-Hill.

Miller, G. A., Galanter, E., & Pribham, K. H. (1960). *Plans and the structure of behavior.* New York: Holt, Rinehart, and Winston.

Nelson, R. O., & Hayes, S. C. (1981). Theoretical explanations for reactivity in self-monitoring. *Behavior Modification, 5,* 3–14.

Nicholls, J. G. (1978). The development of the concepts of effort and ability, perception of academic attainment, and the understanding that difficult tasks require more ability. *Child Development, 49,* 800–814.

O'Leary, S. G., & Dubey, D. R. (1979). Applications of self-control procedures by children: A review. *Journal of Applied Behavior Analysis, 12,* 449–466.

Ollendick, T. H., & Hersen, M. (1984). *Child behavioral assessment: Principles and procedures.* New York: Pergamon.

Paris, S. G., & Byrnes, J. P. (1989). The constructivist approach to self-regulation and learning in the classroom. In B. J. Zimmerman & D. H. Schunk (Eds.), *Self-regulated learning and academic achievement: Theory, research, and practice* (pp. 169–200). New York: Springer-Verlag.

Paris, S. G., Lipson, M. Y., & Wixson, K. K. (1983). Becoming a strategic reader. *Contemporary Educational Psychology, 8,* 293–316.

Paris, S. G., Newman, R. S., & McVey, K. A. (1982). Learning the functional significance of mnemonic actions: A microgenetic study of strategy acquisition. *Journal of Experimental Child Psychology, 34,* 490–509.

Paris, S. G., & Oka, E. R. (1986). Children's reading strategies, metacognition, and motivation. *Developmental Review, 6,* 25–56.

Pavlov, I. P. (1927). *Conditioned reflexes* (G. V. Anrep, Trans.). New York: International Publishers.

Pintrich, P. R., & De Groot, E. V. (1990). Motivational and self-regulated learning components of classroom academic performance. *Journal of Educational Psychology, 82,* 33–40.

Pressley, M., Woloshyn, V., Lysynchuk, L. M., Martin, V., Wood, E., & Willoughby, T. (1990). A primer of research on cognitive strategy instruction: The important issues and how to address them. *Educational Psychology Review, 2,* 1–58.

Rachlin, H. (1991). *Introduction to modern behaviorism* (3rd ed.). New York: Freeman.

Sagotsky, G., Patterson, C. J., & Lepper, M. R. (1978). Training children's self-control: A field experiment in self-monitoring and goal-setting in the classroom. *Journal of Experimental Child Psychology, 25,* 242–253.

Schunk, D. H. (1981). Modeling and attributional effects on children's achievement: A self-efficacy analysis. *Journal of Educational Psychology, 73,* 93–105.

Schunk, D. H. (1982a). Effects of effort attributional feedback on children's perceived self-efficacy and achievement. *Journal of Educational Psychology, 74,* 548–556.

Schunk, D. H. (1982b). Verbal self-regulation as a facilitator of children's achievement and self-efficacy. *Human Learning, 1,* 265–277.

Schunk, D. H. (1983a). Ability versus effort attributional feedback: Differential effects on self-efficacy and achievement. *Journal of Educational Psychology, 75,* 848–856.

Schunk, D. H. (1983b). Developing children's self-efficacy and skills: The roles of social comparative information and goal setting. *Contemporary Educational Psychology, 8,* 76–86.

Schunk, D. H. (1983c). Goal difficulty and attainment information: Effects on children's achievement behaviors. *Human Learning, 2,* 107–117.

Schunk, D. H. (1983d). Progress self-monitoring: Effects on children's self-efficacy and achievement. *Journal of Experimental Education, 51,* 89–93.

Schunk, D. H. (1983e). Reward contingencies and the development of children's skills and self-efficacy. *Journal of Educational Psychology, 75,* 511–518.

Schunk, D. H. (1984). Enhancing self-efficacy and achievement through rewards and goals: Motivational and informational effects. *Journal of Educational Research, 78,* 29–34.

Schunk, D. H. (1985). Participation in goal setting: Effects on self-efficacy and skills of learning disabled children. *Journal of Special Education, 19,* 307–317.

Schunk, D. H. (1987). Peer models and children's behavioral change. *Review of Educational Research, 57,* 149–174.

Schunk, D. H. (1995). Self-efficacy and education and instruction. In J. E. Maddux (Ed.), *Self-efficacy, adaptation, and adjustment: Theory, research, and application* (pp. 281–303). New York: Plenum.

Schunk, D. H. (1996). Goal and self-evaluative influences during children's cognitive skill learning. *American Educational Research Journal, 33,* 359–382.

Schunk, D. H., & Cox, P. D. (1986). Strategy training and attributional feedback with learning disabled students. *Journal of Educational Psychology, 78,* 201–209.

Schunk, D. H., & Ertmer, P. A. (1999). Self-regulatory processes during computer skill acquisition: Goal and self-evaluative influences. *Journal of Educational Psychology, 91,* 251–260.

Schunk, D. H., & Hanson, A. R. (1985). Peer models: Influence on children's self-efficacy and achievement. *Journal of Educational Psychology, 77,* 313–322.

Schunk, D. H., & Hanson, A. R. (1989). Self-modeling and children's cognitive skill learning. *Journal of Educational Psychology, 81,* 155–163.

Schunk, D. H., Hanson, A. R., & Cox, P. D. (1987). Peer-model attributes and children's achievement behaviors. *Journal of Educational Psychology, 79,* 54–61.

Schunk, D. H., & Rice, J. M. (1987). Enhancing comprehension skill and self-efficacy with strategy value information. *Journal of Reading Behavior, 19,* 285–302.

Schunk, D. H., & Swartz, C. W. (1993a). Goals and progress feedback: Effects on self-efficacy and writing instruction. *Contemporary Educational Psychology, 18,* 337–354.

Schunk, D. H., & Swartz, C. W. (1993b). Writing strategy instruction with gifted students: Effects of goals and feedback on self-efficacy and skills. *Roeper Review, 15,* 225–230.

Schunk, D. H., & Zimmerman, B. J. (Eds.). (1994). *Self-regulation of learning and performance: Issues and educational applications.* Hillsdale, NJ: Erlbaum.

Schunk, D. H., & Zimmerman, B. J. (1997). Social origins of self-regulatory competence. *Educational Psychologist, 32,* 195–208.

Schunk, D. H., & Zimmerman, B. J. (Eds.). (1998). *Self-regulated learning: From teaching to self-reflective practice.* New York: Guilford Press.

Shapiro, E. S. (1987). *Behavioral assessment in school psychology.* Hillsdale, NJ: Erlbaum.

Skinner, B. F. (1953). *Science and human behavior.* New York: Macmillan.

Snow, R. E. (1989). Toward assessment of cognitive and conative structures in learning. *Educational Researcher, 18*(9), 8–14.

Snowman, J. (1986). Learning tactics and strategies. In G. D. Phye & T. Andre (Eds.), *Cognitive classroom learning: Understanding, thinking, and problem solving* (pp. 243–275). Orlando, FL: Academic Press.

Vygotsky, L. S. (1962). *Thought and language.* Cambridge, MA: MIT Press.

Weinstein, C. E., & Mayer, R. E. (1986). The teaching of learning strategies. In M. C. Wittrock (Ed.), *Handbook of research on teaching* (3rd ed., pp. 315–327). New York: Macmillan.

Zimmerman, B. J. (1994). Dimensions of academic self-regulation: A conceptual framework for education. In D. H. Schunk & B. J. Zimmerman (Eds.), *Self-regulation of learning and performance: Issues and educational applications* (pp. 3–21). Hillsdale, NJ: Erlbaum.

Zimmerman, B. J. (1998). Developing self-fulfilling cycles of academic regulation: An analysis of exemplary instructional models. In D. H. Schunk & B. J. Zimmerman (Eds.), *Self-regulated learning: From teaching to self-reflective practice* (pp. 1–19). New York: Guilford Press.

Zimmerman, B. J. (2000). Attaining self-regulation: A social cognitive perspective. In M. Boekaerts, P. R. Pintrich, & M. Zeidner (Eds.), *Handbook of self-regulation* (pp. 13–39). San Diego, CA: Academic Press.

Zimmerman, B. J., Bonner, S., & Kovach, R. (1996). *Developing self-regulated learners: Beyond achievement to self-efficacy.* Washington, DC: American Psychological Association.

Zimmerman, B. J., & Kitsantas, A. (1996). Self-regulated learning of a motoric skill: The role of goal setting and self-monitoring. *Journal of Applied Sport Psychology, 8,* 60–75.

Zimmerman, B. J., & Kitsantas, A. (1997). Developmental phases in self-regulation: Shifting from process goals to outcome goals. *Journal of Educational Psychology, 89,* 29–36.

Zimmerman, B. J., & Martinez-Pons, M. (1986). Development of a structured interview for assessing students' use of self-regulated learning strategies. *American Educational Research Journal, 23,* 614–628.

Zimmerman, B. J., & Martinez-Pons, M. (1990). Student differences in self-regulated learning: Relating grade, sex, and giftedness to self-efficacy and strategy use. *Journal of Educational Psychology, 82,* 51–59.

Zimmerman, B. J., & Ringle, J. (1981). Effects of model persistence and statements of confidence on children's self-efficacy and problem solving. *Journal of Educational Psychology, 73,* 485–493.

Zimmerman, B. J., & Rosenthal, T. L. (1974). Observational learning of rule governed behavior by children. *Psychological Bulletin, 81,* 29–42.

CHAPTER 5

Metacognition and Learning

CHRISTINE B. McCORMICK

A useful convention for beginning a chapter on any topic is to define that topic clearly. An unambiguous definition assures the establishment of clear communication pathways between the writer and the audience. That makes it obvious from the outset what the chapter will and will not be about. Unfortunately, this is not an easy task for a chapter about *metacognition*. This entire chapter could focus solely on an attempt to reconcile what researchers, teacher-educators, and practicing educators mean when they use this term. One deceptively simple definition, "thinking about thinking," is really very complicated as evident from the blank stares I receive when I present that definition to a roomful of preservice teachers. Because the title of this chapter is "Metacognition and Learning," I decided to attempt to define metacognition as succinctly as I can and then move on to a discussion of research on the role of metacognition in classroom learning. I begin with a presentation of more basic research on metacognition, followed by a summary of research on three classroom skills: reading, writing, and problem solving. Finally, I review research on classroom interventions designed to facilitate the development of metacognition.

METACOGNITION: IN SEARCH OF A DEFINITION

Metacognition emerged as an explicit focus of research in psychology (with an initial focus on metamemory) in the early 1970s, but psychologists and educators have long been aware of the knowledge and skills encompassed by this term (Baker & Brown, 1984). John Flavell (1976) offered an early commonly accepted definition of metacognition as "knowledge concerning one's own cognitive processes and products or anything related to them" (p. 232). More than a decade later, Paris and Winograd (1990) asserted that most theorists emphasize two aspects of metacognition, *knowledge* about cognition and *control* over cognition.

Knowledge Versus Control Distinction

Metacognitive knowledge is typically characterized as being comparatively stable and usually statable (Baker & Brown, 1984; Garner, 1987). Jacobs and Paris (1987) further delineated the knowledge component of metacognition into declarative, procedural, and conditional aspects of knowledge.

Declarative metacognitive knowledge refers to knowledge that a person may have about his or her abilities and about the salient learning characteristics that affect cognitive processing. Learners vary in the quality of their declarative knowledge depending on a variety of factors including age and ability. Flavell (1979) distinguished between types of declarative knowledge along the dimensions of knowledge of person, task, and strategy. *Procedural metacognitive knowledge* refers to knowledge of how to execute procedures such as learning strategies. The procedural knowledge of skilled learners is more automatic, accurate, and effective than that of unskilled learners. *Conditional metacognitive knowledge* refers to knowledge about when and why to use procedures or strategies. The conditional knowledge of successful learners makes them very facile and flexible in their strategy use.

Metacognitive control, sometimes also referred to as executive control, is described in various ways by different researchers, but the similarity among the definitions is fairly evident. Jacobs and Paris (1987) demarcated metacognitive control into the processes of planning, evaluation, and regulation. Planning includes the selection of a strategy to achieve a goal. Evaluation is monitoring of the progress made toward achieving the goal. Regulation refers to the revision or modification of the strategies to achieve the goal. Hacker (1998a) described executive control as consisting of both monitoring and regulating. Monitoring includes identifying the task, checking the progress of task completion, and predicting the eventual outcome. Regulation includes allocation of resources, specifying the number of steps to complete a task, and the intensity and speed with which it will be completed. Paris and Lindauer (1982) described metacognitive control during reading and writing as consisting of planning, monitoring, and evaluation. In this case, planning refers to the selection of strategies and the allocation of resources, monitoring to comprehension monitoring, and evaluation to the examination of progress toward goals that can lead back to more planning and more monitoring. What is common to all of these articulations of the control process is some initial analysis of what to do, making a plan to do something, evaluating the usefulness of that plan, and then making appropriate revisions or modifications to the original plan.

Garner (1987) described boundaries between research on metacognition and research on executive control. These areas of research have developed from different theoretical orientations, make dissimilar assumptions, and rely on diverse methodological tools. Much of the work on metacognition emerged from Piagetian developmental research, whereas research on executive control originated in the information-processing model. Researchers from the two traditions differ in the emphasis placed on metacognitive knowledge rather than metacognitive control.

Alternative Perspectives

There are, however, alternative perspectives on metacognition. For example, Schraw and Moshman (1995) focused on learners' theories about their own cognition and on how well developed these knowledge structures are. These theories are "systematic frameworks used to explain and direct cognition, metacognitive knowledge, and regulatory skills" (p. 351). Schraw and Moshman distinguished between tacit, informal, and formal metacognitive theories. *Tacit theories* are implicit, "acquired or constructed without any explicit awareness" (p. 358). Because learners are not aware of them, these implicit frameworks are not accessible for verification and may persist even when incorrect or maladaptive. *Informal theories* are fragmentary. Learners are aware of some of their beliefs and assumptions but "have not yet constructed an explicit theoretical structure that integrates and justifies these beliefs" (p. 359). Unlike tacit theorists, however, informal theorists do have some degree of explicit metacognition and thus can judge the value of their framework. *Formal theories* are "highly systematized accounts of phenomenon involving explicit theoretical structures" (p. 361). According to Schraw and Moshman, the Good Strategy User as outlined by Pressley, Borkowski, and Schneider (1987) would be an example of a formal metacognitive theory. Formal theorists are explicitly aware of their "purposeful efforts to construct and modify metacognitive theories" (Schraw & Moshman, 1995, p. 361), so they can use formal theory to assess and interpret observations. Schraw and Moshman suggested that learners develop metacognitive theories through cultural learning, individual construction, and peer interaction. Cornoldi (1998) echoed the perspective of Schraw and Moshman in his definition of metacognitive attitude as the "general tendency of a person to develop reflection about the nature of his or her own cognitive ability and to think about the possibility of extending and using this reflection" (p. 144).

Critical Distinctions

Sometimes in order to get a more focused view of what something is, theorists and researchers try to elucidate what it is not—a nonexample using the terminology of the concept-learning literature. One key discrimination for understanding the concept of metacognition is to articulate the distinction between cognition and metacognition (Nelson, 1999; Nelson & Narens, 1994). Nelson (1999) defined metacognition as "the scientific study of an individual's cognitions about his or her own cognitions" (p. 625). Thus, metacognition is a subset of cognition, a particular kind of cognition. Garner and Alexander (1989) identified *cognitive strategies* as activities for cognitive enhancement and *metacognitive strategies* as activities for monitoring cognitive processes. In other words, cognitive skills facilitate task achievement, and metacognitive skills help to regulate task achievement. Some research has supported the distinction between cognition and metacognition. For example, there is evidence that metamemory deficits can exist without memory impairment, so memory and metamemory are distinct (Nelson, 1999). Swanson (1990) provided evidence for the independence of metacognition from general aptitude by finding that fifth- and sixth-grade students with high levels of metacognitive skill outperformed students with low levels of metacognitive skills on problem-solving tasks regardless of overall aptitude. Although Hacker (1998a) referred to the "debatable issue" of whether thoughts that were initially metacognitive but are now nonconscious and automatic can still be considered metacognition (see also Nelson, 1996), he suggested that most researchers consider metacognitive thought to be conscious and purposeful thinking (about thinking). Paris and Winograd (1990) limited their conception of metacognition to "knowledge about cognitive states and abilities that can be shared among people" (p. 21).

Another important distinction is that between metacognition and self-regulation. Paris and Winograd (1990) noted that some researchers also include an affective component in their definitions of metacognition such as metacognitive beliefs or attributions. Borkowski (1996), for example, described three interrelated aspects of metacognition: knowledge, judgments and monitoring, and self-regulation. Borkowski's view of metacognitive knowledge corresponds to Flavell's (1979) categories of person, task, and strategy. Judgments and monitoring refer to processes occurring while performing a task, such as a feeling of knowing or comprehension monitoring. Self-regulation refers to adapting skills and strategies to meet changing demands. Zimmerman (1995), however, argued that self-regulation "involves more than metacognitive knowledge and skill, it involves an underlying sense of self-efficacy and personal agency and the motivational and behavioral processes to put these self beliefs into effect" (p. 217). A learner could have well-developed metacognitive knowledge but be unable to self-regulate in a specific context. Self-regulated learning refers to the "capability to mobilize, direct, and sustain one's instructional efforts" (p. 217). Thus, self-regulated learning is "more than metacognitive knowledge and skill, it involves a sense of personal agency to regulate other sources of personal influence (e.g., emotional processes and behavioral and social-environmental sources of influence)" (p. 218; for a further discussion of self-regulated learning, see chapter by Schunk and Zimmerman in this volume).

Relevance to Cognitive Development, Expertise, and Intelligence

How does the concept of metacognition fit into theories of cognitive development? Although the basic idea of metacognition, "thinking about thinking," has been traditionally associated with Piaget's stage of formal operations, the concept has relevance for other theoretical perspectives in cognitive development (Yussen, 1985). The centrality of metacognition to cognitive development was highlighted by Flavell in 1979 when he argued that the "nature and development of metacognition and of cognitive monitoring/regulation is currently emerging as an interesting and promising new area of investigation" (p. 906). He described young children as being limited in their knowledge about cognitive phenomena (metacognition) and as failing to monitor memory and comprehension. He developed a model of cognitive monitoring that he hoped would serve as a target for development. According to this model, development occurs through interactions among metacognitive knowledge, metacognitive experiences, goals (or tasks), and actions (or strategies). Metacognitive knowledge is stored knowledge about person, task, and strategy variables. Metacognitive experiences are the "items of metacognitive knowledge that have entered consciousness" (p. 908). Through metacognitive experiences, the stored metacognitive knowledge can be altered by adding, deleting, or revising information. Paris and Winograd (1990) elaborated on the integral role of metacognition in cognitive development by arguing that metacognition is "both a product and producer of cognitive development" (p. 19).

Kuhn (1999, 2000) extended the discussion of the role of metacognition in cognitive development by focusing on the link between metacognition and the development of higher order thinking skills. She characterized the skills that most consider to be critical thinking skills as being metacognitive rather than cognitive. Higher order thinking or critical thinking by definition involves reflecting on what is known and how that knowledge can be verified—clearly metacognitive processes. Kuhn talked about metaknowing in three broad categories: metacognitive, metastrategic, and epistemological. Metacognitive knowing is declarative knowledge, knowledge about cognition. Metastrategic knowing refers to the selection and monitoring of strategies (procedural knowledge). Epistemological knowledge refers to the general philosophical questions underlying a thoughtful examination of knowledge itself.

What is the role of metacognition in the development of expertise? Experts differ from novices in a variety of ways, some of which are metacognitive. They are more skilled than novices at time allocation, strategy selection, prediction of task difficulty, and monitoring (Sternberg, 2001). Ertmer and

Newby (1996) presented a model of expertise, describing experts as strategic, self-regulated, and reflective. They argued that the key to developing expertise is the facilitation of the growth of reflection. Kruger and Dunning (1999) demonstrated that college-aged novices possess poorer metacognition than college-aged experts in three different domains of expertise: humor, logical reasoning, and grammar. When learners are incompetent in a domain (as indicated by making poor choices and reaching invalid conclusions), this incompetence robs them even of the ability to recognize their faulty thinking. Thus, these novices were unskilled and unaware of it. Ironically, in this study the highly competent tended to underestimate how well they had performed.

What is the relationship of metacognition to "intelligence"? Metacognition is a key component in at least one theory of intelligence—Sternberg's Triarchic Theory (1985). The triarchic theory is composed of three subtheories: contextual, experiential, and componential. The contextual subtheory highlights the sociocultural context of an individual's life. The experiential subtheory emphasizes the role of experience in intelligent behavior. The componential subtheory specifies the mental structures that underlie intelligent behavior. These are broken down into metacomponents, performance components, and knowledge-acquisition components. The metacomponents described by Sternberg include primary metacognitive processes such as planning and monitoring (see also chapter by Sternberg in this volume for an analysis of contemporary theories of intelligence).

Is metacognition a domain-general or a domain-specific skill? Research on expertise often emphasizes domain specificity, whereas theories of intelligence imply a generalized skill. Schraw, Dunkle, Bendixen, and Roedel (1995) explored the generality of monitoring by comparing correlations and principal component structures among multiple tests with four different criterion measures. Their findings provided qualified support for the domain-general hypothesis. Schraw and Nietfeld (1998), however, concluded that there may be separate general monitoring skills for tasks requiring fluid and crystallized reasoning, and Schraw and Moshman (1995) suggested that informal metacognitive theories likely begin tied to a specific domain. More recently, Kelemen, Frost, and Weaver (2000) compared the performance of college students across a number of different metacognitive tasks. Their results indicated that individual differences in memory and confidence were stable across both sessions and tasks but that differences in metacognitive accuracy were not.

Summary

In 1981 Flavell characterized metacognition as a "fuzzy concept" (p. 37). It is not certain that work in this area has greatly reduced this fuzziness in the two decades that have elapsed since his paper was published. The boundaries between what is metacognitive and what is not are not clearly defined. Hacker (1998a) declared that this field of investigation is "made even fuzzier by a ballooning corpus of research that has come from researchers of widely varying disciplines and for widely varying purposes" (p. 2). Borkowski (1996) described the theoretical work on metacognition as "weakly related mini-theories, whose boundary conditions are so poorly delineated that any attempt at empirical and/or theoretical synthesis is nearly impossible" (p. 400).

When I teach introductory educational psychology classes, I am confronted with the problem of conveying the complex concept of metacognition to students planning to become teachers. What ideas will be useful to them in their current roles as students? What can they take with them into the classroom in their future roles as teachers? How can we reduce the "fuzziness"? What kinds of classroom skills are we talking about? What can be applied to classroom tasks from theory and research on metacognition? What I present to my class is the following list of topics in metacognition.

- Knowing about cognition generally ("thinking about thinking").
  - Metacognition about memory.
  - Metacognition about reading.
  - Metacognition about writing.
  - Metacognition about problem solving.
- Knowing when you do or don't understand.
  - Also known as comprehension monitoring.
  - As in *reading*.
- Knowing how well you have learned something.
  - As in *studying*.
- Knowing how well you have performed on a test.
- Knowing about skills and procedures you can use to improve your cognitive performance.
  - Knowledge *about* strategies (declarative knowledge—your repertoire).
  - Knowing *how* to use strategies (procedural knowledge—the steps).
  - Knowing *when* to use strategies (conditional knowledge—when to use which strategy).

It would be impossible to do justice to all of these aspects of metacognition in a single chapter. Many topics within metacognition are deserving of their own chapters, as attested to by the recent publication of entire books on metacognition and educational theory and practice (Hacker, Dunlosky, & Graesser, 1998; Hartman, 2001a). The remaining portions of this chapter describe research exploring the application of metacognition to selected learning situations.

BASIC RESEARCH ON METACOGNITION

There is an extensive research literature exploring metacognitive processes as they occur in controlled learning situations on specific types of learning tasks. Much of this research examines basic metacognitive processes in paired-associate-type learning tasks. Although this research does have relevance to the subset of classroom learning tasks that require learning associations (e.g., vocabulary learning), it is unclear whether conclusions drawn from this research can be generalized to classroom learning tasks involving connected discourse. What follows is a brief summary of the metacognitive processes studied in this research paradigm.

Nelson (1999) described three types of prospective monitoring, that is, monitoring of future memory performance. The *ease-of-learning judgment* (EOL) refers to a judgment before study. The learner evaluates how easy or difficult an item will be to learn. For example, someone learning French vocabulary might predict that learning that "chateau" means "castle" would be easier than learning that "boite" means "box." These EOL predictions tend to be moderately correlated with actual recall.

A second type of monitoring is assessed by a *judgment of learning* (JOL), which is a judgment during or soon after study about future recall. It is the prediction of the likelihood that an item will be remembered correctly on a future test. Typically, learners are more accurate in their JOL predictions than in their EOL predictions. One interesting finding is that if JOL is delayed (e.g., 5 min after study), the prediction is more accurate than immediate JOL (e.g., Nelson & Dunlosky, 1991). Delayed JOL is more accurate if and only if learners are provided with the cue-only prompt (in the French vocabulary example, the cue of "chateau?") and not when provided with a cue-plus-target prompt (e.g., "chateau-castle?").

The third type of monitoring is assessed by a *feeling of knowing* (FOK), which refers to rating the likelihood of future recognition of currently forgotten information after a recall attempt. Some studies elicit FOK for only incorrect items. Klin, Guzman, and Levine (1997) reported that FOK judgments for items that cannot be recalled are often good predictors of future recognition accuracy. This indicates that exploring more about "knowing that you don't know" is a promising avenue for future investigations.

There is also research on retrospective confidence judgments, which are predictions that occur after a recall or recognition performance. On these tasks, there is a strong tendency for overconfidence—especially on recognition

tasks (Nelson, 1999). A developmental pattern has also been observed in that with increasing age, knowledge about information available in memory becomes more accurate (Hacker, 1998a).

The body of research on monitoring of learning in these basic learning tasks is growing rapidly and contributing greatly to our understanding of basic monitoring processes. Because the focus of this chapter is on the role of metacognition in learning situations that most often occur in classrooms, we now turn to a discussion of research on metacognition and reading. Reading is arguably the cognitive skill that underlies the majority of classroom learning tasks.

RESEARCH ON METACOGNITION AND READING SKILLS

Pearson and Stephens (1994) summarized the contributions of the disparate fields of linguistics, psychology, and sociolinguistics to the scientific study of the processes comprising the complex task of reading. One indication of the importance of research on metacognition to this endeavor is the inclusion of metacognition as a separate category in an edited volume titled *Theoretical Models and Processes of Reading* (4th edition) published by the International Reading Association (Ruddell, Ruddell, & Singer, 1994; for a thorough treatment of literacy research, see chapter by Pressley in this volume).

Metacognition about reading is a developmental phenomenon. In an early study, Myers and Paris (1978) questioned 8- and 12-year-old children about factors influencing reading and found age-related differences in metacognitive knowledge about reading. The younger children were less sensitive to different goals of reading, to the structure of paragraphs, and to strategies that can be used to resolve comprehension failures. Knowledge of text structure also develops. Englert and Hiebert (1984) found that third and sixth graders' knowledge of expository text structure was related to age and reading ability. Although many aspects of metacognition involved in reading have been explored, unquestionably the focus of many researchers studying metacognition in reading has been on the process of monitoring comprehension.

Comprehension Monitoring

Much of the early research investigating comprehension monitoring employed the error detection paradigm. In this research paradigm learners are asked to read textual material that contains some kind of inconsistency or error. Whether learners notice the error is an indication of the quality of their comprehension monitoring. Adult readers typically do not excel at comprehension monitoring as indicated by the many studies reporting failures to detect errors (for reviews, see Baker, 1989; Pressley & Ghatala, 1990). As Baker (1989) reported, "detection rates tend to average about 50% across studies" (p. 13). The likelihood with which adults may detect errors in text is influenced by a variety of factors. These include whether they were informed about the likelihood of errors being present, whether the errors were found in details or in the main point of the text, and perhaps most important, what standards they use to evaluate their comprehension (Baker, 1985, 1989).

Baker (1985) described three basic types of standards that readers use to evaluate their comprehension of text: lexical, syntactic, and semantic. The *lexical* standard focuses on the understanding of the meaning of words. The *syntactic* standard concentrates on the appropriateness of the grammar and syntax. The *semantic* standard encompasses evaluation of the meaning of the text and can be further delineated into five subcategories. The first of these is external consistency, that is, the plausibility of the text. The second, propositional cohesiveness, refers to whether adjacent propositions can be integrated for meaning. The third, structural cohesiveness, focuses on thematic relatedness of the ideas in the text. The fourth, internal consistency, refers to whether the ideas in the text are logically consistent. Finally, the fifth, informational completeness, emphasizes how thoroughly ideas are developed in the text.

Much of the research using the error detection paradigm has employed texts requiring the application of the semantic standard of internal consistency. There is considerable evidence, however, that readers differ in the ease with which they apply these standards depending on age and reading ability. For example, less able readers may rely on lexical standards but can be prompted to use other standards (Baker, 1984). The most important consideration, however, is that failure to detect an error in text may not be due to a pervasive failure to monitor comprehension as much as to the application of a different standard of comprehension than the one intended by the researcher.

There are still other explanations of why readers may fail to detect errors or inconsistencies in text (Baker, 1989; Baker & Brown, 1984; Hacker, 1998b; Winograd & Johnston, 1982). According to Grice's Cooperativeness Principle (1975), readers normally expect that text will be complete and informative and therefore are not looking for errors, would be hesitant to criticize, and are more likely to blame themselves rather than the text for any inconsistency noted. Readers might also notice the error but continue to read, expecting a resolution of the inconsistency later in the text. They might lack the linguistic or topic knowledge to detect the error. They might make infer-

ences that allow them to construct a valid interpretation of the text that is different from the one intended by the author. In response to these criticisms of the error detection paradigm, researchers have developed other techniques for evaluating comprehension monitoring such as eye movements, adaptation of reading speed, and even changes in galvanic skin response (GSR) that may indicate some level of awareness of inconsistencies that are not otherwise reported (Baker, 1989; Baker & Brown, 1984).

Beyond the Error Detection Paradigm

Hacker (1998b) outlined differences in the approaches used in cognitive psychology and educational psychology to study the metacognitive processes involved in processing textual material. As we have seen, researchers trained in the field of educational psychology most often use the term *comprehension monitoring* to refer to this phenomenon. Their view of metacognition and textual processing is multidimensional, involving both evaluation and regulation. Evaluation is the monitoring of the understanding of text during reading, and regulation is the control of reading processes to resolve comprehension problems. Much of the research in this tradition has employed the error detection paradigm, but educational psychologists are moving to the study of more natural reading situations, where they look at learners' abilities to construct meaningful representations of text.

On the other hand, researchers trained in cognitive psychology typically use terms such as *metamemory for text, calibration of comprehension,* or *metacomprehension* for the phenomena. They operationalize the construct by relating readers' predictions of comprehension with actual performance on a test. If they find a high correlation, they report good calibration or metacomprehension. If they find a low correlation, they report poor calibration or metacomprehension. If learners overestimate their level of comprehension, this is termed *illusion of knowing* (Glenberg, Wilkinson, & Epstein, 1982).

Metacomprehension, as studied by those trained in this tradition, has considerable relevance for classroom learning. After reading texts assigned in school (which we would expect to be relatively error free), students need to be able to make judgments about how well they have learned the material and about how well they expect they will perform on a test. In a typical study using this paradigm, Maki and Berry (1984) asked college students to read paragraphs from an introductory psychology text. After reading each paragraph, they predicted (on a Likert-type scale), how well they would perform on a multiple-choice test. For the students who scored above the median (the better learners), the mean ratings of material related to questions answered correctly were higher than ratings of material related to questions answered incorrectly. On the other hand, Glenberg and Epstein (1985) asked college students to rate how well they would be able to use what they learned from textual material to draw an inference. They calculated point biserial correlations between the rating given each text and performance on that text. These correlations were not greater than 0 regardless of whether the ratings were made either immediately after reading or following delay. In this study, the only judgments more accurate than chance were postdictions (those made after responding to the inference questions). Weaver (1990) found that the correlation between rated confidence and subsequent performance on comprehension questions (the mean calibration) on an expository passage was typically near zero when only one test question was used but that prediction accuracy was higher when more questions were used per prediction. Weaver and Bryant (1995) also reported that "metamemory for text" or "calibration of comprehension" was more accurate when learners made multiple judgments (see also Schwartz & Metcalfe, 1994).

Maki (1998) discussed several different processes that are likely to be involved in these predictions. One hypothesis is that students may be relying on their judgments of domain familiarity, using their prereading familiarity with the topic to make predictions. Maki (1998), however, reported data indicating that students use more than prereading familiarity with text topics to help them make more accurate predictions. Another hypothesis is that students may base their judgments on their perceived ease of comprehension. Maki (1998), however, summarized studies comparing student ratings of their comprehension of text (ease of comprehension) versus their prediction of the amount of information they would recall (future performance). Generally, there was a stronger relationship between predictions and actual performance than between comprehension ratings and actual performance. So, explicit predictions are based on something more than just ease of comprehension. After weighing the research evidence, Maki (1998) concluded that "accurate predictions are based on aspects of learning from the text, including ease of comprehension, perceived level of learning, and perceived amount of forgetting" (p. 141).

Maki (1998) also pointed out that in the body of research on paired-associate learning, delayed predictions and delayed tests produce the highest prediction accuracy. This is the classic delayed JOL described earlier in this chapter. With text material, however, immediate predictions and immediate tests produce the greatest prediction accuracy. This is a troubling finding for educators because most classroom tasks involve delayed tests.

Maki (1998) reported that the mean gamma correlation between predictions of test performance and actual test performance across many studies emanating from her lab is .27. Is it that the metacomprehension abilities of college students are so poor, or do we need a better paradigm for studying metacomprehension? Maki argued that we need to develop a more stable and less noisy measure of metacomprehension accuracy. Alternatively, Rawson, Dunlosky, and Thiede (2000) contended that researchers need to integrate theories of metacognitive monitoring with theories of text comprehension. In this study, they asked college students to reread texts before predicting performance. Rereading was expected to facilitate the construction of a situation model of the text, leading to the creation of cues that would be more predictive of future performance. In accordance with their predictions, they found that rereading produced better metacomprehension, reporting a median gamma of .60.

Testing Effect

Pressley and Ghatala (1990) summarized a series of studies designed to see if and how tests influence students' awareness of learning from text. They found that although students can monitor during study and attempt to regulate study activity, their evaluations of their learning are not fairly accurate until after they have taken a test. They called this finding of more accurate predictions of learning after testing the *testing effect.* Similarly, in her review of research on metacomprehension, Maki (1998) reported that many studies indicate that predictions made after taking a test (postdictions) were more accurate than predictions preceding a test. This is called the postdiction superiority effect in the metacomprehension research literature.

Exposure to and experience with the types of questions asked can also lead to better judgments of learning. For example, Pressley, Snyder, Levin, Murray, and Ghatala (1987) found that answering adjunct questions embedded in text can improve the monitoring performance of college students. Maki (1998) summarized a group of studies indicating that whether practice tests improve prediction depends on whether performance on the practice tests is correlated with performance on the criterion measure. Moreover, practice test questions are more effective if answered following a delay after reading. More recently, Pierce and Smith (2001) reported that postdictions do not improve with successive tests. Thus, they argued that the superior postdiction effect found in their study, as well as in many other studies, is likely due to students' remembering how well they answered questions rather than increasing knowledge of tests as a result of exposure to successive tests.

Question type also influences student monitoring of learning from text. Pressley, Ghatala, Woloshyn, and Pirie (1990) found that college students had more accurate perceptions of the correctness of their responses to short-answer questions than of their responses to multiple-choice questions. In this study, accuracy of monitoring was measured by whether the students choose to study more after testing. Maki (1998) suggested that true-false questions may be even less helpful to student monitoring than short answer and multiple choice questions (see also Schwartz & Metcalfe, 1994).

The type of content assessed by questions also influences the size of the testing effect. Pressley and Ghatala (1988) found that postdictions of college students were more accurate for multiple-choice questions on opposites and analogies than for multiple-choice comprehension test questions. Moreover, Pressley et al. (1990) reported that college students had greater confidence that their answers to thematic questions (rather than questions on details) were correct, even when their responses were actually wrong.

There is also evidence that the ability to benefit from the information obtained by taking a test improves with development. In a study by Pressley and Ghatala (1989), seventh and eighth graders demonstrated the testing effect, whereas younger children did not. The type of test question also influences children's monitoring abilities. Ghatala, Levin, Foorman, and Pressley (1989) found that fourth graders overestimated their mastery of the material more on multiple-choice tests with plausible distractors than in their responses to short-answer questions.

Development of Comprehension Monitoring

Since Ellen Markman's pioneering studies (1977, 1979) using the error detection paradigm, the poor comprehension-monitoring skills of young children have been demonstrated under varying instructions and circumstances (see Markman, 1985, for a review). For example, Markman (1977) found that although third graders noticed the inadequacy of oral instructions with minimal probing, first graders did not until they saw a demonstration or acted out the instructions themselves. Markman (1979) reported that third through sixth graders failed to notice some inconsistencies in essays that were read to them, even though probing indicated that they had the required logical capacity to detect them. Markman and Gorin (1981) found that specific instructions helped 8- and 10-year-olds find problems with texts that were read to them. They suggested that the instructions enabled the children to adjust their standards of evaluation. Baker (1984) examined children's abilities to apply three standards of evaluation (lexical, internal consistency, and external consistency) when explicitly asked to find

errors in text. In the first experiment 5-, 7-, and 9-year-old children listened to text, whereas in the second experiment 11-year-olds read the texts themselves. The older children used all three standards more effectively than the younger children, and the internal consistency standard was applied least effectively across all age groups. Baker (1984) argued that these results support the view that comprehension-monitoring skills are multidimensional rather than a unitary phenomenon.

Using an on-line measure of reading speed in addition to the traditional verbal-report error detection paradigm, Harris, Kruithof, Terwogt, and Visser (1981) found that children in two age groups (8- and 11-year olds) read inconsistent text more slowly but that the older students were more likely to report inconsistent text. Similarly, Zabrucky and Ratner (1986) found that both third and sixth graders read inconsistent text more slowly than other information in the text, but sixth graders were more likely to use a strategy (look backs) and more likely to report errors in text.

There are also developmental differences in students' sensitivities to text characteristics as they monitor their comprehension. For example, Bonitatibus and Beal (1996) asked second and fourth graders to read stories with two alternative interpretations. The older students were more likely to notice and report both interpretations, and the two interpretations were more likely to be noticed in narrative rather than expository prose. McCormick and Barnett (1984) asked eighth graders, 11th graders, and college students to read passages (both signaled and nonsignaled) that contained inconsistencies. The presence of text signals improved the comprehension monitoring of the college students in passages where contradictions were presented across paragraphs rather than within paragraphs. The younger students did not benefit from the text signals.

Individual difference variables may moderate the developmental differences in comprehension monitoring ability. Pratt and Wickens (1983) found that kindergartners and second graders who were more reflective were more effective detectors of referential ambiguity in text than were impulsive children. Similarly, Walczyk and Hall (1989b) reported that reflective third and fifth graders detected more inconsistencies than did impulsive children across both grade levels. By far the most frequently investigated individual difference variable has been reading ability.

As might be predicted, in studies where the comprehension monitoring of good and poor readers is compared, good readers were more skilled than poor readers. Garner (1980) found that good readers at the junior high level noticed inconsistencies in text and that the poor readers did not. In a study replicating these findings, Garner and Reis (1981) asked students of varying ages (Grade 4 through Grade 10) to read texts that contained obstacles (questions inserted in text). The poor readers mostly failed to monitor their comprehension and mostly failed to use look backs as a strategy. Garner and Kraus (1981–82) suggested that good and poor readers approach reading with widely varying purposes that affect their comprehension monitoring. They interviewed good and poor seventh-grade readers and asked them to read narrative passages (one containing inconsistencies). In their interviews, the good comprehenders described reading as more of a meaning-getting task; the poor readers described reading as more of a decoding task. The poor readers did not detect the inconsistencies in the text. In contrast, good readers could detect inconsistencies but were better with within-sentence inconsistencies than with between-sentence inconsistencies.

Paris and Myers (1981) used multiple measures to indicate comprehension monitoring and also interpreted their results as indicating that poor readers focus more on decoding the text than on determining the meaning of text. Poor fourth-grade readers monitored difficult and inconsistent information significantly less than did good readers as indicated by self-corrections during oral reading, by directed underlining, and by study behaviors. Zabrucky and Ratner (1989) used on-line measures of monitoring along with verbal reports of inconsistencies. They found that all of the sixth-grade students in their study slowed down when reading the portion of the text with inconsistencies but that good readers were more likely to look back at the problem portion of the text and to report inconsistencies verbally. In a replication of these results comparing narrative and expository texts, Zabrucky and Ratner (1992) reported that students were more likely to look back at problems in the narrative texts than at problems in the expository text. Zabrucky and Ratner interpreted their findings as evidence of rudimentary comprehension monitoring in the poor readers even though they may tend to ignore or skip portions of text that cause them problems. Rubman and Waters (2000) were able to increase the error detection of third and sixth graders (both skilled and less skilled) by the use of storyboard construction. They argued that representing stories through storyboard construction enhanced integration of the text propositions. The effect of the storyboard construction was particularly beneficial for the less skilled readers.

Baker and Brown (1984) distinguished between reading for meaning (comprehension) and reading for remembering (studying). They argued that younger and poorer readers look at reading as a decoding process rather than as a meaning-getting process and do not monitor their comprehension as effectively as do older and better readers. Baker (1989) also suggested that there is some evidence that good readers use comprehension strategies, whereas poor readers use study strategies. Yet, those who investigate students' study behav-

iors would argue that students skilled in studying techniques use complex strategies focusing on understanding. For those interested in contemporary views of studying, consult recent integrative reviews detailing metacognitive processes in studying and recent research investigating the study strategies of skilled learners (Hadwin, Winne, Stockley, Nesbit, & Woszczyna, 2001; Loranger, 1994; Pressley, Van Etten, Yokoi, Freebern, & Van Meter, 1998; Son & Metcalfe, 2000; Winne & Hadwin, 1998).

In conclusion, metacognitive processes are central to skilled reading. Although reading is perhaps the primary skill underlying classroom learning, two sets of cognitive skills— those required in writing and in problem solving—also figure prominently in classroom activities. The next section presents research on the role of metacognition in effective writing skills, followed by a section on metacognitive skills in problem solving.

RESEARCH ON METACOGNITION AND WRITING SKILLS

Flower and Hayes (1981) developed an influential model of the composing processes from their analyses of think-aloud protocols of expert and novice writers. The act of writing is assumed to be a goal-directed thinking process in which the writer engages in four kinds of mental processes. These mental processes are *planning, translating* ideas and images into words, *reviewing* what has been written, and *monitoring* the entire process. There is considerable interactivity between the four processes so that the act of writing is recursive rather than linear.

Another theoretical model that has had tremendous influence on theorists and researchers is the model of writing expertise developed by Scardamalia and Bereiter (1986; Bereiter & Scardamalia, 1987). This model describes two broad strategies of composing: knowledge telling and knowledge transforming. In *knowledge telling,* a strategy used more often by novice writers, what is known about a topic is presented in a paper until the supply of knowledge is exhausted. In *knowledge transforming* the writer consciously reworks the text—diagnosing problems, planning solutions, and monitoring the effectiveness of solutions. In both of these influential models of writing, metacognitive processes, particularly monitoring, have a primary role.

Research focusing on the role of metacognition in writing has explored both the knowledge and the control aspects of metacognition (see Sitko, 1998, for a recent review). These include knowledge of the writing process and knowledge and control of strategies for these processes, including planning, drafting, revising, and editing. Research comparing novice and expert writers indicates that in general, expert writers are more metacognitively aware, making more decisions about planning and monitoring and evaluating more as they write. Stolarek (1994) found that when novice writers are given a model of an unfamiliar prose form to imitate, they become more reflective, evaluative, and metacognitive (more like experts) than do novices not given a model.

Englert, Raphael, Fear, and Anderson (1988) investigated the development of metacognitive knowledge about writing in children. They assessed the metacognitive knowledge of fourth and fifth graders (with learning disabilities, low-achieving, and high-achieving) with an interview composed of three vignettes. The first vignette evaluated students' knowledge and strategies related to planning and organizing information relevant to specific expository topics. The second vignette focused on the role of text structure in the editing of expository text and on the general processes of planning, drafting, and editing. The third vignette evaluated students' understanding of editing and revising skills (within text structure and generally). The students with learning disabilities differed from low-achieving and high-achieving students in that they had less knowledge of writing strategies and less knowledge of how to organize ideas. In general, metacognitive knowledge was positively correlated to the quality of texts written by the students.

Knowledge of text structure plays an important role in the development of writing skills. Englert, Stewart, and Hiebert (1988) found that both third and sixth graders were largely insensitive to text structure. The more proficient writers, however, seemed to possess a more generalized knowledge of expository text structure. Durst (1989) demonstrated that the characteristics of the text assignment influences the metacognitive strategies used by students during writing. His analysis of the think-aloud protocols of 11th-grade students for metacognitive processes used during composing revealed much more monitoring and reflecting when students were writing analyses than when they were writing summaries.

Instruction designed to enhance students' awareness of text characteristics (e.g., the underlying structure of expository and narrative text structures) improves writing skill. Taylor and Beach (1984) taught seventh-grade students a reading study strategy focusing on expository text structure and found positive effects in terms of the quality of the students' expository writing. Likewise, Graham and Harris (1989b) found that self-instruction training focusing on a type of expository writing (argumentative essays) given to sixth-grade students with learning disabilities resulted in better writing performance and higher self-efficacy for writing essays. Instruction in narrative text structure has also proved to be beneficial. Fitzgerald and

Teasley (1986) provided direct instruction of story structure to fourth graders and found a strong positive effect on the organization and quality of the students' narrative writing. Similarly, Graham and Harris (1989a) provided self-instruction training in story grammar to normally achieving fifth and sixth graders and to those with learning disabilities and found that the training improved the students' composition skills and increased their self-efficacy.

Well-developed comprehension-monitoring skills are a key part of the revision process. Writers need to monitor how well the text that they have already produced matches the text that they had intended to produce. Inconsistencies between the produced text and the intended text must be noted and then resolved in some manner. Successful comprehension monitoring during the revision process may be especially difficult for writers because they may not be appropriately evaluating the meaning conveyed by their texts because of their awareness of what they had intended to write. Even if they recognize comprehension problems, they may not be able to generate appropriate solutions to those problems. As Carole Beal (1996) noted in her review of research on comprehension monitoring in children's revision of writing, effective comprehension monitory is *necessary but not sufficient* for successful revision. Children are likely to overestimate the comprehensibility of the text they have produced. Background knowledge and experience with a particular text genre influence children's abilities to monitor text adequately. By the end of the elementary school period, however, most children can evaluate text adequately and are aware of the types of problems that affect comprehension and indicate the need to revise.

Children are also able to benefit from instruction designed to increase their evaluation skills. Beal, Garrod, and Bonitatibus (1990) trained third and sixth graders in a self-questioning text-evaluation strategy. After training, these students located and revised more errors in text. They also benefited from their exposure to problematic texts and practice in applying different standards for evaluating comprehension. Children also mature in terms of the quality of the evaluative criteria that they apply to pieces of writing. In a longitudinal study of students' use of criteria to evaluate the quality of writing, McCormick, Busching, and Potter (1992) reported differences in the criteria used by low-achieving and high-achieving fifth graders to evaluate texts that they had written versus texts written by others. A year later, when these students were sixth graders, they demonstrated progression in the sophistication of their evaluative criteria.

Researchers have also reported success with broad-based instructional programs designed to improve writing skills. Raphael, Englert, and Kirschner (1989) assessed fifth and sixth graders' metacognitive knowledge of the writing process before, during, and following participation in different writing programs. The writing programs focused on different aspects of the writing process, metacognitive knowledge of text structures, audience, and purpose in writing. The results indicated improvement in the quality of student writing and increased metacognitive awareness in the areas on which the instructional programs focused. Englert, Raphael, Anderson, Anthony, and Stevens (1991) investigated the effects of an instructional program titled Cognitive Strategy Instruction in Writing (CSIW) on fourth and fifth graders' metacognitive knowledge and writing performance. In CSIW, self-instructional techniques and student-teacher dialogues are used to encourage effective strategies for planning, organizing, writing, editing, and revising. Their findings indicate the facilitation of students' expository writing abilities on the two types of expository writing included in the programs and some evidence of transfer to another text structure that was not part of the instruction.

In yet another demonstration of the effectiveness of writing programs that support the development of metacognitive skills, Graham and Harris (1994) summarized their program of research evaluating a writing intervention they call Self-Regulated Strategy Development (SRSD). Students are explicitly instructed in the writing process, in general, as well as in specific strategies for planning and revising and procedures for regulating strategies. This instruction utilizes a dialectical constructivist approach in which students actively collaborate with teachers and peers. Metacognitive information about strategies is emphasized, particularly self-regulation skills such as self-monitoring, goal setting, and self-instruction (see Zimmerman & Risemberg, 1997, for a review of self-regulation in writing). At the end of the instructional program, the students usually adopt the processes emphasized in the program, and the quality (in terms of both length and structure) of their writing typically improves. In addition, the students typically exhibit increases in their metacognition about writing and their self-efficacy for writing.

This section has focused on research exploring the role of metacognition in writing. When students sit down to write an essay, a paper, or even just a short essay response, they are essentially trying to solve a problem—and an ill-defined problem at that. In the next section of this chapter, the role of metacognition in problem solving is discussed.

RESEARCH ON METACOGNITION AND PROBLEM-SOLVING SKILLS

A very concise definition of problem solving is goal-directed behavior. Metacognition in problem solving refers to the knowledge and processes used to guide the thinking directed toward successful resolution of the problem. Problems differ from each other both in terms of specificity and structure. If the goal of the problem is clearly stated, all the information needed to solve the problem is available, and there is only one solution to the problem, then the problem is considered *well defined.* An *ill-defined* problem, on the other hand, is one in which the goal is not clear, in which information needed to solve the problem is missing or obscured, and in which it is difficult to evaluate the correctness of a solution. According to Davidson, Sternberg, and their colleagues (Davidson, Deuser, & Sternberg, 1994; Davidson & Sternberg, 1998), metacognitive skills help learners to define what the problem is, to select an appropriate solution strategy, to monitor the effectiveness of the solution strategy, and to identify and overcome obstacles to solving the problem.

Problem definition includes the formation of a mental representation that would be helpful to solving the problem (Davidson & Sternberg, 1998). An effective mental representation allows the problem solver to organize and combine information (thus decreasing memory demands), to monitor solution strategies, and to allow generalizations across problems. A mental representation that encourages generalization would be based on essential, rather than surface, features of the problem. Experts in a specific domain spend proportionately more time planning than do novices, and their problem representations tend to be more abstract than those of novices (Davidson et al., 1994). Davidson and Sternberg (1998) argued that metacognition also plays a role in representational change through selective encoding (looking for previously overlooked information), selective combination (looking for previously overlooked ways of combining information), and selective comparison (looking for previously overlooked connections to prior knowledge). Not all problem solving, however, requires restructuring. Some problems can be solved simply by remembering previous solutions—as long as the mental representation allows the problem solver to generalize across problems. When there is a seemingly spontaneous change in understanding, this is typically referred to as an instance of insight (for a discussion of insight problem solving and metacognition, see Metcalfe, 1998).

Next, the problem solver selects a solution strategy (or set of solution strategies) that would facilitate goal attainment. Metacognitive awareness of what is already known is critical in the selection of an appropriate strategy. The problem solver needs to be able to monitor the effectiveness of the solution strategies and needs to be cognizant of other potentially useful plans or of likely modifications to the selected strategies. Metacognition also comes into play in terms of being aware of obstacles to solving the problem.

Bransford, Sherwood, Vye, and Rieser (1986) described two approaches to teaching thinking and problem solving. The first approach emerged from the study of experts and focuses on the role of domain-specific knowledge. The second approach emphasizes general strategic and metacognitive knowledge. Bransford et al. suggested that metacognitive training may be able to help people improve their ability to think and learn. To that end, Davidson and Sternberg (1998) proposed a variety of approaches for training metacognition in problem solving, including modeling, peer interaction, and integration of techniques into curriculum and textbooks. Mayer (2001) emphasized the importance of teaching through modeling of how and when to use metacognitive skills in realistic academic tasks.

There is evidence that problem solvers can benefit from interventions designed to facilitate their monitoring and evaluation skills. Delclos and Harrington (1991) found that fifth and sixth graders who received problem-solving training combined with self-monitoring training solved more complex problems and took less time to solve them than did control students and those who received only problem-solving training. King (1991) taught fifth-grade students to ask themselves questions designed to prompt the metacognitive processes of planning, monitoring, and evaluating as they worked in pairs to solve problems. The students in this guided questioning group performed better on a written test of problem solving and on a novel problem-solving task than did students in an unguided questioning group and a control group. Berardi-Coletta, Buyer, Dominowski, and Rellinger (1995) found that college students given process-oriented (metacognitive) verbalization instructions performed better on training and transfer problem-solving tasks than did students given problem-oriented verbalization instructions and those given simple think-aloud instructions. The process-oriented instructions induced metacognitive processing by asking students questions designed to focus their attention on monitoring and evaluating their problem-solving efforts. In contrast, the problem-oriented instructions focused students' attention on the goals, steps, and current state of the problem-solving effort. Berardi-Coletta et al. suggested that future problem-solving research should emphasize the critical role of metacognition in successful problem solving.

RESEARCH ON METACOGNITION AND INSTRUCTION

Since it has become increasingly clear that metacognitive awareness and skills are a central part of many academic tasks, a critical question for educators is how we foster the development of metacognition in students. What follows is a description of successful interventions, many of which were designed to improve comprehension and comprehension monitoring, but the principles underlying these interventions can and have been extended to other learning contexts. These interventions can be grouped into two categories: those using an individual approach and those using a group-based approach. This section concludes with a presentation of general recommendations for instruction and classroom practice.

Individual Interventions

One of the most promising types of interventions for facilitating the development of metacognitive skills involves *self-instruction* as a technique to make thinking processes more visible. Miller (1985) reported that fourth graders who received either general or specific self-instructions were able to identify more text inconsistencies when reading aloud than could a control group that received practice and feedback. Moreover, the benefits of the self-instruction were maintained three weeks later. Miller, Giovenco, and Rentiers (1987) designed self-instruction training that helped students define the task ("What am I supposed to do?"), determine an approach to the task ("How am I going to do this; what is my plan?"), evaluate the approach ("How is my plan working so far?"), reinforce their efforts ("I am really doing good work"), and evaluate the completion of the task ("Think back—did I find any problems in this story?"). Fourth and fifth graders who received three training sessions in this self-instruction program increased their ability to detect errors in expository texts. Both above- and below-average readers in the self-instruction condition outperformed the students in the control group.

In another effort to help students monitor their comprehension using self-questioning techniques, Elliott-Faust and Pressley (1986) trained third graders to compare different portions of text. In the comparison training, students learned to ask themselves questions such as, "Do these parts make sense together?" For some students, the comparison training included additional self-instruction such as "What is my plan? Am I using my plan? How did I do?" Long-term improvements in the students' ability to monitor their listening comprehension, as indicated by the detection of text inconsistencies, came *only* with the addition of the self-instruction control instructions.

Another technique that has been demonstrated to improve comprehension monitoring is *embedded questions*. Pressley et al. (1987) hypothesized that having to respond to questions inserted in text as they read may make students more aware of what is and what is not being understood. As predicted, they found that college students who read texts with adjunct questions monitored their learning better than did students who did not receive questions in the text. Walczyk and Hall (1989a) asked college students to read expository text with illustrative examples (presenting abstract principles in concrete terms) or embedded questions (encouraging self-questioning). If students received both examples and questions, they assessed their own comprehension more accurately (as indicated by a rating on a Likert-type scale) and made more accurate posttest predictions of test performance. In an informal classroom demonstration, Weir (1998) employed embedded questions to improve middle-school students' reading comprehension. The questions were designed to facilitate interaction with texts, asking students to engage in activities such as making predictions, raising unanswered questions, or determining what is confusing. An interview indicated increased metacognitive awareness, and standardized test scores demonstrated greater than expected growth in reading comprehension from the beginning of the school year until the end of the school year.

Other researchers have found that strategy instruction can benefit from the inclusion of features designed to improve metacognition. For example, El-Hindi (1997) asked first-year college students from underrepresented minorities who were at risk for not completing their degree programs to use *reflective journals* to record their thought processes as they were taught metacognitive strategies for both reading and writing during a six-week summer residential program. The purpose of the reflective journals was to help make covert thought processes more overt and open to reflection and discussion. Pre- and postquestionnaires indicated a significant gain in students' metacognitive awareness of reading at the end of the program. In addition, qualitative analysis of the reflective journal entries indicated a growth in the sophistication of the students' metacognitive thought throughout the program.

Baumann, Seifert-Kessell, and Jones (1992) used a *think-aloud* procedure to teach fourth-grade students a predict-verify strategy for reading, which included self-questioning, prediction, retelling, and rereading. These students were compared to students taught a prediction strategy (a comprehension monitoring strategy) and to a control group taught with traditional methods from the basal reader (such as introducing new vocabulary, activating prior knowledge, and summarizing) that did not include explicit metacognitive or monitoring instruction. The dependent measures included an error detection task, a comprehension monitoring questionnaire, and a modified cloze test. Both groups who received comprehension monitoring/metacognitive training demonstrated better comprehension monitoring abilities on all three dependent measures than did the control students. The students who received the think-aloud training exhibited better metacognitive

awareness than did those taught only the strategy (as measured by the questionnaire and a qualitative interview).

Dewitz, Carr, and Patberg (1987) investigated the effectiveness of a *cloze strategy with a self-monitoring checklist* to induce fifth-grade students to integrate text with prior knowledge. In comparison to students taught a procedure to organize text information (a structured overview) and a control group, students taught the cloze strategy plus self-monitoring (either alone or in combination with a structured overview) improved their reading comprehension (as measured by both literal and inferential questions). These students also demonstrated greater metacognitive awareness as indicated by pre-post differences in responses to a metacognitive interview than did students who did not receive this instruction.

Group-Based Interventions

According to Paris and Winograd (1990), the reflection required to develop sophisticated metacognition can "come from within the individual or from other people" (p. 21). Thus, researchers have explored techniques for fostering metacognition that utilize interactions between learners to encourage the development of metacognitive thought (see also the chapter on cooperative learning by Slavin, Hurley, and Chamberlain and the chapter on sociocultural contexts for learning by John-Steiner and Mahn in this volume).

Perhaps the most well-known technique using peer-interaction is *reciprocal teaching,* an instructional model designed for teaching comprehension strategies in the context of a reading group (Brown & Palincsar, 1989; Palincsar & Brown, 1984). Students learn to make predictions during reading, to question themselves about the text, to seek clarification when confused, and to summarize content. Initially, the teacher models and explains the four strategies. Then the students take turns being the leader, the one who supervises the group's use of the strategies during reading. Peers model to each other, and the teacher provides support on an as-needed basis, progressively becoming less involved. The underlying premise is that by participating in the group, the students eventually internalize the strategies, and the evidence is that reciprocal teaching is generally effective (Rosenshine & Meister, 1994).

Based on a theoretical model of dyadic cooperative learning focusing on the acquisition of cognitive (C), affective (A), metacognitive (M), and social (S) skills (CAMS), O'Donnell, Dansereau, Hall, and Rocklin (1987) asked college students to read textual material working in scripted dyads, in unscripted dyads, or as a group of individuals. Scripted dyads were given instructions in how to interact with their partners. Specifically, they were taught to take turns as they read, having one person summarize the text section while the other tried to detect errors and omissions in the summary. O'Donnell et al. found that students who worked in dyads recalled more of the texts than individuals did. Scripted dyads, however, demonstrated greater metacognitive awareness in that they were more accurate in rating their performance than were the other students.

McInerney, McInerney, and Marsh (1997) explored the benefits of training in self-questioning within a cooperative learning context. College students received modeling from the instructor and practice in the use of higher order questions designed to induce metacognitive strategies in cooperative groups. These researchers reported better achievement as a result of the questioning training in the cooperative group as compared to a group who received traditional direct instruction.

King (1998; King, Staffieri, & Adelgais, 1998) developed the ASK to THINK—TEL WHY®© model of peer tutoring to promote higher level thinking (including metacognition), which also featured training in questioning techniques. Learning partners are trained in communication skills, explanation and elaboration skills, question-asking skills, and skills of sequencing those questions. Students learn to use a variety of questions, including review questions, thinking questions, probing questions, hint questions, and metacognitive "thinking about thinking questions." A preliminary investigation (King, 1997) indicated that thinking about thinking questions made a significant contribution to the effectiveness of the model in that students constructed more knowledge and increased their awareness of thinking processes.

Cooperative learning contexts also can be engineered so that the partner is a computer rather than another student. In a study by Salomon, Globerson, and Guterman (1989), a Computer Reading Partner presented four reading principles and metacognitive-like questions to seventh graders as they read texts. The reading principles taught by the Computer Reading Partner included generating inferences, identifying key sentences, creating images, and summarizing. Those students who worked with the Computer Reading Partner reported more mental effort, showed far better metacognitive reconstruction, and improved more in reading comprehension and quality of written essays than did those who received embedded factual or inferential questions in the text or who simply read the texts.

General Recommendations for Instruction

Sitko (1998) described the overall theme of metacognitive instruction as "making thinking visible." To this end, she suggested incorporating introspection, on-line thinking-aloud protocols, and retrospective interviews or questionnaires into classroom practice. Fusco and Fountain (1992) provided a shopping list of teaching techniques that they suggest are likely to foster the development of metacognition, including extended wait time, metacognitive questions, concept mapping, writing in journals, and think-aloud techniques in cooperative groups. They cautioned, however, that "unless these self-reflective strategies become a part of daily classroom tools, there is little chance that they will become students' strategies" (p. 240). Winograd and Gaskins (1992) emphasized that "metacognition is most likely to be invoked when individuals are pursuing goals they consider important" (p. 232). Thus, they argued for authentic activities and thoughtful assessment in classrooms. In addition, they recommended a combination of teaching methods, including cooperative learning and direct explanation for strategy instruction (Duffy & Roehler, 1989; Roehler & Duffy, 1984).

Schraw (2001) encouraged teachers to use an instructional aid he calls the Strategy Evaluation Matrix (SEM) for the development of metacognitive knowledge related to strategy instruction. In this matrix, students list their accessible strategies and include information on How to Use, When to Use, and Why to Use each strategy. The idea is to foster the development of explicit declarative, procedural, and conditional knowledge about each strategy. In classroom practice a teacher can ask students to complete a SEM for strategies in their repertory. Then the students can compare strategies in their matrix and compare their SEM to the matrices of other students. Schraw conceptualized the SEM as an aid to improve metacognitive knowledge and proposed the Regulatory Checklist (RC; modeled after King, 1991) for improving metacognitive control. The RC is a framework for self-questioning under the general categories of planning, monitoring, and evaluating. Schraw emphasized that providing students with the opportunity to practice and reflect is critical for successful implementation of these instructional aids.

Meichenbaum and Biemiller (1992) proposed that educational growth in a particular skill or content domain has two dimensions: the traditional curriculum sequence or "basic skills" dimension and the dimension of "classroom expertise," where students overtly plan, monitor, and evaluate their work. To foster growth in the second dimension (the development of metacognition), they advised teachers to pay attention to pacing, to explicit labeling of task components, and to clear modeling of how to carry out tasks and problem solve. They cautioned that students should engage in tasks that vary along a range of complexity. Tasks that are too simple will not require extensive metacognitive processing, and excessively complex tasks will inhibit a student's ability to self-talk metacognitively or to talk to others due to limits of attentional capacity.

CONCLUSIONS AND FUTURE DIRECTIONS

This chapter concludes with a brief summary of directions for future research. The first of these, the assessment of metacognition, is an issue with which researchers have been grappling for more than a decade. The second is the potential of advances in neuropsychology for increasing our understanding of metacognitive processes. The third is the complex role that metacognition plays in bilingualism and in the education of bilingual students. Finally, perhaps the most significant direction for future research for educational psychologists is the integration of metacognition into teacher preparation and the professional development of in-service teachers.

Assessment of Metacognition

In 1989 Ruth Garner and Patricia Alexander raised a set of unanswered questions about metacognition. One of these questions was how we can measure "knowing about knowing" more accurately. Unfortunately, more than a decade later, this question is as relevant today as ever. Garner (1988) described two prominent verbal report methods to externalize metacognitive knowledge—interviews and think-aloud protocols. Interviews are retrospective verbalizations; think-alouds are concurrent verbalizations. Verbal-report methods are vulnerable to several valid criticisms, one being the accessibility of metacognitive processes. As cognitive activity becomes more practiced and more automated, the associated metacognitive process, if present, is difficult to report (Garner, 1988). Another potential problem is the verbal facility or linguistic competence of the responder (Cornoldi, 1998; Garner, 1988). The responder, especially a child, may be mimicking the language of teachers rather than truly aware of complex cognitive processing.

Other concerns raised by Garner (1988) include the stability of responses over time and the accuracy of the report. One source of inaccuracy for interviews is that they take place at a time distant from the actual processing. One attempt to remedy this problem is to use concurrent think-alouds. This solution, however, creates its own problems because the process of describing the cognition as it occurs may actually disrupt the cognitive activity. Another methodology is to include hypothetical situations in the interview protocol to elicit responses, but considering hypothetical situations is likely to be more difficult for children. Another potential solution is to stimulate recall by having students comment as they watch a videotape of a previous cognitive activity. In this interview combined with stimulated recall method, the cognitive activity is real, not hypothetical, and although the interview is distant, vivid memory prompts are available in the videotape. In

general, researchers recommend employing multiple methods, converging dependent measures (Cornoldi, 1998). In particular, Garner and Alexander (1989) suggested combining verbal report techniques with behavior- or performance-based methods.

Cornoldi (1998) identified another limitation to the study of metacognition: the low psychometric properties of available scales. What measures are currently available for the measurement of metacognition in classroom contexts? One well-known broad-based measure of study skills is the Learning and Study Strategies Inventory (LASSI; Weinstein, Zimmerman, & Palmer, 1988). The LASSI was developed for undergraduate learning-to-learn or study skills courses with the purpose of diagnosing student strengths and weaknesses. It is a 77-item, self-report, Likert-type scale, with 10 subscales (anxiety, attitude, concentration, information processing, motivation, time management, selecting main ideas, self-testing, study aids, and test strategies). A high school version of the LASSI has also been developed. None of the subscales, however, specifically targets metacognition (although some of the questions in the self-testing subscale address monitoring skills).

The Motivated Strategies for Learning Questionnaire (MSLQ) developed by Pintrich, Smith, Garcia, and McKeachie (1993) to assess motivation and use of learning strategies by college students does include a subscale for metacognition. It is a self-report instrument containing 81 items, using a 7-point Likert-type scale, 1 (not at all true of me) to 7 (very true of me). The MSLQ has Motivational scales (31 items) and Learning Strategies scales (50 items, which assess cognitive, metacognitive, and resource management strategies). Pintrich et al. make a clear distinction between cognitive and metacognitive activities. Cognitive strategies include rehearsal, elaboration, organization, and critical thinking; metacognitive strategies include planning, monitoring, and regulating. Resource management refers to managing time and the study environment, the regulation of effort, peer learning, and help-seeking behavior. The authors report that scale reliabilities are "robust", particularly for the motivational scales (a "reasonable alpha" is reported for the metacognitive strategies subscale).

Schraw and Dennison (1994) developed the Metacognitive Awareness Inventory (MAI) to measure the knowledge of cognition and the regulation of cognition in adolescents and adults. Using a method derived from the multidimensional scaling literature, ratings for each of the 52 items in the MAI are made on a 100-mm scale. The students are asked to draw a slash across the rating scale at a point that best represents *how* true or false each statement is about them (the left end indicates that the statement is true; the right end indicates that the statement is false). Factor analysis indicated that the two factors (knowledge and regulation of metacognition) were reliable and intercorrelated.

Utilizing the conceptual framework of Sternberg's componential theory of intelligence, Armour-Thomas and Haynes (1988) developed a scale to measure metacognition in problem solving for high school students called the Student Thinking About Problem Solving Scale (STAPSS). The STAPSS is a 37-item Likert-type scale, ranging from 1 (not at all like me) to 7 (extremely like me). A factor analysis revealed six factors—Planning, Organizing, Accommodating, Evaluating, Strategizing, and Recapitulating. Armour-Thomas and Haynes reported the reliability to be "acceptable" and to have "modest" predictive validity with SAT scores.

Jacobs and Paris (1987) designed a multiple-choice instrument to assess third and fifth graders' metacognitive knowledge about reading, the Index of Reading Awareness (IRA). The IRA contains questions to measure evaluation, planning, and regulation and also questions to measure conditional knowledge about reading strategies. There are a total of 20 questions, each with three alternatives—inappropriate answer (0 points), partially adequate (1 point), strategic response (2 points)—so scores can range from 0 to 40 points.

Everson and Tobias (2001) developed a measure of metacognitive word knowledge called the Knowledge Monitoring Ability (KMA). The KMA measures the difference between college students' estimates of knowledge and their actual knowledge. Students are given a list of vocabulary words in a content domain and are asked to indicate the words that they know and those that they do not know. This estimate of knowledge is followed by a vocabulary test on the same words. The accurate metacognitive judgments of college students (items that they said they knew and did *and* items that they said they did not know and did not) are positively correlated with standardized measures of language skills. There is also some evidence that KMA is related to college grade point average.

Although there have been some advances in the measurement of metacognition, more work is needed establishing the reliability and validity of the available measures. In addition, there are relatively few measures developed for school-aged children. Finally, teachers need efficient, easy-to-use assessments for classroom purposes. There is some evidence, however, that researchers are turning their attention to issues related to the measurement of metacognition (for more information, see Schraw & Impara, 2000).

Promise of Neuropsychology

A natural question for neuropsychologists to ask is where executive control processes might be situated in the brain.

Darling, Della Sala, Gray, and Trivelli (1998) reviewed the search for the site of executive control in the human brain and found that as early as 1876, Ferrier attributed an executive function to the prefrontal lobes. There are clear indications that the prefrontal lobes are critical to higher order functioning. For example, the percentage of prefrontal cortex in humans "represents an enormous increase" even in comparison to chimps (p. 60). Moreover, the prefrontal lobe is one of the last portions of the brain to mature. There are two primary types of research evidence supporting the role of the prefrontal lobe in metacognition: research on individuals with brain damage and, given relatively recent advances in techniques, research on normally functioning individuals.

Shimamura (1994) described examples of neurological disorders that cause impairment in metacognition. For instance, individuals with Korsokoff's syndrome exhibit poor knowledge of memory strategies and an impaired feeling of knowing (a failure to be aware of what they knew and did not know). They exhibit knowledge of facts but cannot evaluate the accuracy of that knowledge. Other patients with amnesia do not necessarily exhibit this impairment in metamemory, but it has been found in other patients with widespread cortical damage such as in Alzheimer's patients. Individuals with frontal lobe lesions also display feeling-of-knowing problems, but individuals with Korsokoff's syndrome exhibit the most extensive metacognitive limitations.

Darling et al. (1998) remarked that the "basis for location of the central executive within the prefrontal lobe in humans has been strengthened by work that has used modern brain imaging techniques" (p. 78). Brain imagery studies provide evidence that the frontal cortex is involved as normal people complete tasks that require reflection. Although the results hold promise, Darling et al. indicated that more research is needed and cautioned that there may not be a single site for executive control in the brain.

Metacognition and Bilingualism

In recent years there has been considerable interest in the psychology of bilingualism. For example, Francis (1999) conducted a quantitative and qualitative review of over 100 cognitive studies of language integration in bilingual samples and reached the conclusion that "the two languages of a bilingual tap a common semantic-conceptual system" (p. 214). Why might it be beneficial to be bilingual? Some have argued that bilinguals would have increased opportunity to reflect on the nature of language as a result of their experiences with two languages (Vygotsky, 1986), and linguists have found evidence of greater metalinguistic knowledge in bilinguals than in monolinguals (Lambert, 1981). Bialystok and Ryan (1985) reported that children who do well in metalinguistic tasks typically learn also to read quickly and easily. They suggested that "using more than one language may alert the child to the structure of form-meaning relation and promote the ability to deliberately consider these separate aspects of propositions" (p. 217).

Summarizing a program of research conducted in school contexts, Garcia, Jimenez, and Pearson (1998) reported that children use knowledge and strategies developed in reading and writing in one language to facilitate literacy in a second language. Successful bilingual readers mention specific metacognitive strategies that could be transferred from one language to another. In contrast, monolingual readers do not identify as many comprehension strategies as do bilingual readers. Garcia, Jimenez, and Pearson's (1998) analysis indicated that a developmental advantage for bilinguals in literacy tasks surfaces in preschool and seems to disappear with schooling. They noted, however, that there are few instructional programs "explicitly designed to build upon, enhance, and promote the cognitive and metalinguistic advantage of bilingual children" (p. 198). They suggested that increased metacognitive awareness is not an automatic outcome of bilingualism or bilingual education and recommended that educators focus on instruction that fosters metacognitive awareness and strategic reading.

Goh (1997) examined the metacognition of 40 college-aged English as a Second Language (ESL) learners from the People's Republic of China. The students were asked to keep a diary as they learned English and were prompted by questions to reflect on their learning. Using categories in the metacognitive literature, the diary entries were classified into person knowledge, task knowledge, and strategic knowledge. The analysis of the entries revealed that the students had a clear understanding about their own role and performance as second-language listeners, about the demands and procedures of second-language listening, and about strategies for listening. Drawing on the results of this study, Goh advocated the incorporation of process-based discussions about strategy use and beliefs into ESL curriculum.

Carrell, Gajdusek, and Wise (2001) proposed that what is important in learning to read in a second language is metacognition about strategies, specifically, having a strategy repertory and knowing when and how to use the strategies. They analyzed second language reading strategies training studies in terms of the amount of metacognitive training provided in the instruction. Their analysis revealed the presence or absence of the following metacognitive components: declarative knowledge (what and why of strategy use), procedural knowledge (how to use a strategy), conditional

knowledge (when and where to use), and a regulation component of evaluating or monitoring strategy implementation. Their review indicated a significant positive effect of strategy training when compared to control or traditional approaches, but the available data did not reveal which metacognitive components are critical to successful language learning.

Ellis and Zimmeran (2001) described research demonstrating that instruction in self-monitoring led to improvements in the pronunciation of native and nonnative speakers of English enrolled in a remedial speech course. The self-monitoring instruction included teaching students to self-observe, self-evaluate, and self-repair more carefully. They posited that there is a "growing body of research indicating that linguistic novices are handicapped by their inability to self-monitor accurately and make appropriate linguistic corrections in a new language and dialect" (p. 225).

Given the changing demographics of the United States and the increasing multicultural and multilingual nature of today's classrooms, there will be continued interest in the role that metacognition plays in bilingualism and in language learning. Moreover, given that some languages are more similar to each other than others, researchers will need to attend to whether increased metalinguistic knowledge and understanding depend on how similar languages are. As stated by Francis (1999), it is "reasonable to ask whether the particular language combination influences the degree of integration between languages in semantic representations" (p. 214).

Integration of Metacognition Into Teacher Preparation

Why should metacognition be an important part of teacher preparation programs? I have noticed the benefits of the development of expertise in my introductory educational psychology classes even if only in terms of being able to understand and use the term *metacognition*. I frequently ask my students to write a "one minute paper" at the end of a class session in response to two questions. The first is, "What in this course interests you the most?" The second is, "What in this course confuses you the most?" In the early part of the semester, metacognition is repeatedly mentioned as one of the most confusing topics. In particular, the students complain about the term itself, characterizing metacognition as an example of jargon created by educators to confuse those who are not indoctrinated into the educational endeavor. As the course continues, the students begin to realize, as happens with the development of expertise in any field, that terminology allows one to represent complex ideas with a single word. They discover its usefulness as they talk to each other in small groups, participate in class discussions, and write papers. By the end of the semester, many students consider metacognition to be one of the most valuable parts of the course and communicate their desire to help students become more metacognitively aware (often in reaction to what they perceive as a dismal failure on the part of those who taught them).

It is encouraging that there is growing recognition that a central part of the teachers' role is to foster the development of metacognition in students and to apply metacognition to their own instruction. There is also a considerable challenge facing us: how to make sure that what researchers and theorists have learned about metacognition and its role in learning has an impact on standard classroom practice. Hartman (2001b) referred to the dual role of metacognition in teaching as *teaching with metacognition* (reflection on goals, student characteristics, content, etc.) and *teaching for metacognition* (how to activate and develop metacognition in students).

What does happen in classrooms? Can we observe teachers embracing this dual role? Artzt and Armour-Thomas (2001) examined the instructional practice of seven experienced and seven inexperienced teachers of high school mathematics. Throughout one semester, these researchers observed the teachers, looked at their lesson plans, and analyzed videotapes and audiotapes of their classrooms. They developed the Teacher Metacognitive Framework (TMF) to examine the mental activities of the teachers, particularly teachers' knowledge, beliefs, goals, planning, monitoring and regulating, assessing, and revising. Their analysis revealed three general categories: teachers who focused on student learning with understanding (a metacognitive orientation), teachers who focused on their own practices, and teachers who exhibited a mixture of the two foci of attention.

Zohar (1999) evaluated the effectiveness of a "Thinking in Science" course designed to increase in-service teachers' understanding of metacognition. Zohar assessed teachers' intuitive (preinstructional) knowledge of metacognition of thinking skills and then analyzed class discussions, lesson plans, and written reports from the teachers throughout the course. Teachers who had been teaching higher order thinking before taking the course were not explicitly aware that they had been teaching thinking skills and did not consciously plan for engagement in metacognitive activities with their students. The development of thinking skills in their students had not been an explicit goal of their instruction. Zohar (1999) found that participation in the course did encourage teachers consciously to design learning activities rich in higher order thinking goals and activities.

Instructional interventions have also been demonstrated to facilitate the development of metacognition in preservice teachers. Matanzo and Harris (1999) found that preservice reading methodology students had a limited knowledge of the role of metacognition in reading. After course instruction designed to develop more metacognitive awareness, the preservice teachers who became more metacognitive also fostered the development of metacognition in students with whom they interacted as indicated by classroom observations.

What would be our ultimate goal for teachers' understandings about metacognition? Borkowski and Muthukrishna (1992) argued that teachers must develop internal models of what it means to be reflective and strategic—essentially a good thinker. The hypothesis is that teachers who possess a "working model" of their students' metacognitive development are more likely to be teachers who focus on the development of metacognition. A working model is a schema for organizing knowledge—a framework. It can react to opportunities and challenges, thereby growing and developing. Teacher preparation can provide a broad framework and practical suggestions for the development of the mental model, but every mental model must be the result of an active personal construction. Each individual teacher must create his or her own model based on experiences.

In 1987 Jacobs and Paris noted that it would be more difficult to incorporate what we know about metacognition into classroom practice "now that the first glow of metacognition as a new approach to reading has faded" (p. 275). It may be even more difficult today. For the past six years the International Reading Association has asked 25 literacy leaders to indicate "What's hot, what's not" for reading research and practice for the coming year (Cassidy & Cassidy, 2001/2002). They were asked to rate a topic as "hot" or "not hot" and to indicate whether a given topic "should be hot" or "should be not hot." The list of topics was generated from professional journals, conference programs, newspaper and magazine articles, and more general educational publications. For 2002, metacognition was not even on the list to consider, and reading comprehension was rated by the literacy leaders as "not hot, but should be hot."

Any attempt to disseminate more completely what we know about metacognition into teacher preparation and, ultimately, into classrooms must be developed with an awareness of potential constraints due to the demands that such instruction would place on teachers and students. Sitko (1998) articulated the costs of metacognitive instruction from the teacher's perspective. It typically requires more class time and demands more of teachers in terms of content knowledge, task analysis, and planning time. Gourgey (2001) described student reactions as she introduced metacognitive instruction in college-level remedial classes. Baldly stated, the students were not happy about metacognitive teaching. They were not used to being asked to be thoughtful and did not appreciate having to expend the extra effort to do so. Nevertheless, the research reviewed in this chapter provides a strong mandate for infusing practices that support metacognitive processes into classrooms. This is a goal worth pursuing.

REFERENCES

Armour-Thomas, E., & Haynes, N. M. (1988). Assessment of metacognition in problem solving. *Journal of Instructional Psychology, 15,* 87–93.

Artzt, A., & Armour-Thomas, E. (2001). Mathematics teaching as problem solving: A framework for studying teacher metacognition underlying instructional practices in mathematics. In H. Hartman (Ed.), *Metacognition in learning and instruction: Theory, research and practice* (pp. 127–148). Norwell, MA: Kluwer.

Baker, L. (1984). Children's effective use of multiple standards for evaluating their comprehension. *Journal of Educational Psychology, 76,* 588–597.

Baker, L. (1985). How do we know when we don't understand? Standards for evaluating text comprehensions. In D. L. Forrest-Pressley, G. E. MacKinnon, & T. G. Waller (Eds.), *Metacognition, cognition, and human performance* (pp. 155–205). New York: Academic Press.

Baker, L. (1989). Metacognition, comprehension monitoring, and the adult reader. *Educational Psychology Review, 1,* 3–38.

Baker, L., & Brown, A. L. (1984). Metacognitive skills and reading. In D. P. Pearson, M. Kamil, R. Barr, & P. Mosenthal (Eds.), *Handbook of Reading Research* (pp. 353–394). New York: Longman.

Baumann, J. F., Seifert-Kessell, N., & Jones, L. A. (1992). Effect of think-aloud instruction on elementary students' comprehension monitoring abilities. *Journal of Reading Behavior, 24,* 143–172.

Beal, C. R. (1996). The role of comprehension monitoring in children's revision. *Educational Psychology Review, 8,* 219–238.

Beal, C. R., Garrod, A. C., & Bonitatibus, G. J. (1990). Fostering children's revision skills through training in comprehension monitoring. *Journal of Educational Psychology, 82,* 275–280.

Berardi-Coletta, B., Buyer, L. S., Dominowski, R. L., & Rellinger, E. R. (1995). Metacognition and problem solving: A process-oriented approach. *Journal of Experimental Psychology: Learning, Memory, and Cognition, 21,* 205–223.

Bereiter, C., & Scardamalia, M. (1987). *The psychology of written composition.* Hillsdale, NJ: Erlbaum.

Bialystok, E., & Ryan, E. B. (1985). A metacognitive framework for the development of first and second language skills. In D. L. Forrest-Pressley, G. E. MacKinnon, & T. G. Waller (Eds.), *Metacognition, cognition, and human performance* (pp. 207–252). New York: Academic Press.

Bonitatibus, G. J., & Beal, C. R. (1996). Finding new meanings: Children's recognition of interpretive ambiguity in text. *Journal of Experimental Child Psychology, 62,* 131–150.

Borkowski, J. G. (1996). Metacognition: Theory or chapter heading? *Learning and Individual Differences, 8,* 391–402.

Borkowski, J. G., & Muthukrishna, N. (1992). Moving metacognition into the classroom: "Working models" and effective strategy teaching. In M. Pressley, K. R. Harris, & J. T. Guthrie (Eds.), *Promoting academic competence and literacy in school* (pp. 477–501). San Diego, CA: Academic Press.

Bransford, J., Sherwood, R., Vye, N., & Rieser, J. (1986). Teaching thinking and problem solving: Research foundations. *American Psychologist, 41,* 1078–1089.

Brown, A. L., & Palincsar, A. S. (1989). Guided cooperative learning and individual knowledge acquisition. In L. B. Resnick (Ed.), *Knowing, learning, and instruction: Essays in honor of Robert Glaser* (pp. 393–451). Hillsdale, NJ: Erlbaum.

Carrell, P. L., Gajdusek, L., & Wise, T. (2001). Metacognition in EFL/ESL reading. In H. Hartman (Ed.), *Metacognition in learning and instruction: Theory, research and practice* (pp. 229–243). Norwell, MA: Kluwer.

Cassidy, J., & Cassidy, D. (2001/2002, December/January). What's hot, what's not for 2002? *Reading Today, 19*(3), 1, 18–19.

Cornoldi, C. (1998). The impact of metacognitive reflection on cognitive control. In G. Mazzoni & T. O. Nelson (Eds.), *Metacognition and cognitive neuropsychology: Monitoring and control processes* (pp. 139–159). Mahwah, NJ: Erlbaum.

Darling, S., Della Sala, S., Gray, C., & Trivelli, C. (1998). Putative functions of the prefrontal cortex: Historical perspectives and new horizons. In G. Mazzoni & T. O. Nelson (Eds.), *Metacognition and cognitive neuropsychology: Monitoring and control processes* (pp. 53–95). Mahwah, NJ: Erlbaum.

Davidson, J. E., Deuser, R., & Sternberg, R. J. (1994). The role of metacognition in problem solving. In J. Metcalfe & A. P. Shimamura (Eds.), *Metacognition: Knowing about knowing* (pp. 207–226). Cambridge, MA: MIT Press.

Davidson, J. E., & Sternberg, R. J. (1998). Smart problem solving: How metacognition helps. In D. J. Hacker, J. Dunlosky, & A. C. Graesser (Eds.), *Metacognition in educational theory and practice* (pp. 47–68). Mahwah, NJ: Erlbaum.

Delclos, V. R., & Harrington, C. (1991). Effects of strategy monitoring and proactive instruction on children's problem-solving performance. *Journal of Educational Psychology, 83,* 35–42.

Dewitz, P., Carr, E. M., & Patberg, J. P. (1987). Effects of inference training on comprehension and comprehension monitoring. *Reading Research Quarterly, 22,* 99–119.

Duffy, G. G., & Roehler, L. R. (1989). Why strategy instruction is so difficult and what we need to do about it. In C. B. McCormick,

G. Miller, & M. Pressley (Eds.), *Cognitive strategy research: From basic research to educational applications* (pp. 133–154). New York: Springer-Verlag.

Durst, R. K. (1989). Monitoring processes in analytic and summary writing. *Written Communication, 6,* 340–363.

El-Hindi, A. E. (1997). Connecting reading and writing: College learners' metacognitive awareness. *Journal of Developmental Education, 21,* 10–18.

Elliott-Faust, D. J., & Pressley, M. (1986). How to teach comparison processing to increase children's short- and long-term listening comprehension monitoring. *Journal of Educational Psychology, 78,* 27–33.

Ellis, D., & Zimmerman, B. J. (2001). Enhancing self-monitoring during self-regulated learning of speech. In H. Hartman (Ed.), *Metacognition in learning and instruction: Theory, research and practice* (pp. 205–228). Norwell, MA: Kluwer.

Englert, C. S., & Hiebert, E. H. (1984). Children's developing awareness of text structures in expository materials. *Journal of Educational Psychology, 76,* 65–74.

Englert, C. S., Raphael, T. E., Anderson, L. M., Anthony, H. M., & Stevens, D. D. (1991). Making strategies and self-talk visible: Writing instruction in regular and special education classrooms. *American Educational Research Journal, 28,* 337–372.

Englert, C. S., Raphael, T. E., Fear, K. L., & Anderson, L. M. (1988). Students' metacognitive knowledge about how to write informational texts. *Learning Disability Quarterly, 11,* 18–46.

Englert, C. S., Stewart, S. R., & Hiebert, E. H. (1988). Young writers' use of text structure in expository text generation. *Journal of Educational Psychology, 80,* 143–151.

Ertmer, P. A., & Newby, T. J. (1996). The expert learner: Strategic, self-regulated, and reflective. *Instructional Science, 24,* 1–24.

Everson, H. T., & Tobias, S. (2001). The ability to estimate knowledge and performance in college: A metacognitive analysis. In H. Hartman (Ed.), *Metacognition in learning and instruction: Theory, research and practice* (pp. 69–83). Norwell, MA: Kluwer.

Fitzgerald, J., & Teasley, A. B. (1986). Effects of instruction in narrative structure on children's writing. *Journal of Educational Psychology, 78,* 424–432.

Flavell, J. H. (1976). Metacognitive aspects of problem solving. In L. B. Resnick (Ed.), *The nature of intelligence* (pp. 231–235). Hillsdale, NJ: Erlbaum.

Flavell, J. H. (1979). Metacognition and cognitive monitoring: A new area of cognitive-developmental inquiry. *American Psychologist, 34,* 906–911.

Flavell, J. H. (1981). Cognitive monitoring. In W. P. Dickson (Ed.), *Children's oral communication skills* (pp. 35–60). New York: Academic Press.

Flower, L., & Hayes, J. R. (1981). A cognitive process theory of writing. *College Composition and Communication, 32,* 365–387.

Francis, W. S. (1999). Cognitive integration of language and memory in bilinguals: Semantic representation. *Psychological Bulletin, 125,* 193–222.

Fusco, E., & Fountain, G. (1992). Reflective teacher, reflective learner. In A. L. Costa, J. Bellanca, & R. Fogarty (Eds.), *If minds matter: A foreward to the future* (Vol. 1, pp. 239–255). Palatine, IL: Skylight.

Garcia, G. E., Jimenez, R. T., & Pearson, P. D. (1998). Metacognition, childhood bilingualism, and reading. In D. J. Hacker, J. Dunlosky, & A. C. Graesser (Eds.), *Metacognition in educational theory and practice* (pp. 193–219). Mahwah, NJ: Erlbaum.

Garner, R. (1980). Monitoring of understanding: An investigation of good and poor readers' awareness of induced miscomprehension of text. *Journal of Reading Behavior, 12,* 55–63.

Garner, R. (1987). *Metacognition and reading comprehension.* Norwood, NJ: Ablex.

Garner, R. (1988). Verbal-report data on cognitive and metacognitive strategies. In *Learning and study strategies: Issues in assessment, instruction, and evaluation* (pp. 63–76). San Diego, CA: Academic Press.

Garner, R., & Alexander, P. A. (1989). Metacognition: Answered and unanswered questions. *Educational Psychologist, 24,* 143–158.

Garner, R., & Kraus, C. (1981-1982). Good and poor comprehender differences in knowing and regulating reading behaviors. *Educational Research Quarterly, 6,* 5–12.

Garner, R., & Reis, R. (1981). Monitoring and resolving comprehension obstacles: An investigation of spontaneous text lookbacks among upper-grade good and poor readers. *Reading Research Quarterly, 16,* 569–582.

Ghatala, E. S., Levin, J. R., Foorman, B. R., & Pressley, M. (1989). Improving children's regulation of their reading PREP time. *Contemporary Educational Psychology, 14,* 49–66.

Glenberg, A. M., & Epstein, W. (1985). Calibration of comprehension. *Journal of Experimental Psychology: Learning, Memory, & Cognition, 11,* 702–718.

Glenberg, A. M., Wilkinson, A. C., & Epstein, W. (1982). The illusion of knowing: Failure in the self-assessment of comprehension. *Memory & Cognition, 10,* 597–602.

Goh, C. (1997). Metacognitive awareness and second language listeners. *ELT Journal, 51,* 361–369.

Gourgey, A. F. (2001). Metacognition in basic skills instruction. In H. Hartman (Ed.), *Metacognition in learning and instruction: Theory, research and practice* (pp. 17–32). Norwell, MA: Kluwer.

Graham, S., & Harris, K. R. (1989a). Componential analysis of cognitive strategy instruction: Effects on learning disabled students' composition and self-efficacy. *Journal of Educational Psychology, 81,* 353–361.

Graham, S., & Harris, K. R. (1989b). Improving learning disabled students' skills at composing essays: Self-instructional strategy training. *Exceptional Children, 56,* 201–214.

Graham, S., & Harris, K. R. (1994). The role and development of self-regulation in the writing process. In D. H. Schunk & B. J. Zimmerman (Eds.), *Self-regulation of learning and performance: Issues and educational applications* (pp. 203–228). Hillsdale, NJ: Erlbaum.

Grice, D. H. (1975). Logic and conversation. In P. Cole & J. L. Morgan (Eds.), *Syntax and semantics* (Vol. 3, pp. 41–58). New York: Academic Press.

Hacker, D. J. (1998a). Definitions and empirical foundations. In D. J. Hacker, J. Dunlosky, & A. C. Graesser (Eds.), *Metacognition in educational theory and practice* (pp. 1–23). Mahwah, NJ: Erlbaum.

Hacker, D. J. (1998b). Self-regulated comprehension during normal reading. In D. J. Hacker, J. Dunlosky, & A. C. Graesser (Eds.), *Metacognition in educational theory and practice* (pp. 165–191). Mahwah, NJ: Erlbaum.

Hacker, D. J., Dunlosky, J., & Graesser, A. C. (Eds.). (1998). *Metacognition in educational theory and practice*. Mahwah, NJ: Erlbaum.

Hadwin, A. F., Winne, P. H., Stockley, D. B., Nesbit, J. C., & Woszczyna, C. (2001). Context moderates students' self-reports about how they study. *Journal of Educational Psychology, 93,* 477–487.

Harris, P. L., Kruithof, A., Terwogt, M. M., & Visser, T. (1981). Children's detection and awareness of textual anomaly. *Journal of Experimental Child Psychology, 31,* 212–230.

Hartman, H. (Ed.). (2001a). *Metacognition in learning and instruction: Theory, research and practice*. Norwell, MA: Kluwer.

Hartman, H. (2001b). *Teaching metacognitively.* In H. Hartman (Ed.), *Metacognition in learning and instruction: Theory, research and practice* (149–172). Norwell, MA: Kluwer.

Jacobs, J. E., & Paris, S. G. (1987). Children's metacognition about reading: Issues in definition, measurement, and instruction. *Educational Psychologist, 22,* 255–278.

Kelemen, W. L., Frost, P. J., & Weaver, C. A. (2000). Individual differences in metacognition: Evidence against a general metacognitive ability. *Memory & Cognition, 28,* 92–107.

King, A. (1991). Effects of training in strategic questioning on children's problem-solving performance. *Journal of Educational Psychology, 83,* 307–317.

King, A. (1997). ASK to THINK—TEL WHY®©: A model of transactive peer tutoring for scaffolding higher level complex thinking. *Educational Psychologist, 32,* 221–235.

King, A. (1998). Transactive peer tutoring: Distributing cognition and metacognition. *Educational Psychology Review, 10,* 57–74.

King, A., Staffieri, A., & Adelgais, A. (1998). Mutual peer tutoring: Effects of structuring tutorial interaction to scaffold peer learning. *Journal of Educational Psychology, 90,* 134–152.

Klin, C. M., Guzman, A. E., & Levine, W. H. (1997). Knowing that you don't know: Metamemory and discourse processing. *Journal of Experimental Psychology: Learning, Memory, and Cognition, 23,* 1378–1393.

Kruger, J., & Dunning, D. (1999). Unskilled and unaware of it: How difficulties in recognizing one's own incompetence lead to inflated self-assessments. *Journal of Personality and Social Psychology, 77,* 1121–1134.

Kuhn, D. (1999). A developmental model of critical thinking. *Educational Researcher, 28*(2), 16–26, 46.

Kuhn, D. (2000). Metacognitive development. *Current Directions in Cognitive Science, 9,* 178–181.

Lambert, W. E. (1981). Bilingualism and language acquisition. *Annals of the New York Academy of Sciences, 379,* 9–22.

Loranger, A. L. (1994). The study strategies of successful and unsuccessful high school students. *Journal of Reading Behavior, 26,* 347–360.

Maki, R. H. (1998). Test predictions over text material. In D. J. Hacker, J. Dunlosky, & A. C. Graesser (Eds.), *Metacognition in educational theory and practice* (pp. 117–144). Mahwah, NJ: Erlbaum.

Maki, R. H., & Berry, S. (1984). Metacomprehension of text material. *Journal of Experimental Psychology: Learning, Memory, and Cognition, 10,* 663–679.

Markman, E. M. (1977). Realizing that you don't understand: A preliminary investigation. *Child Development, 48,* 986–992.

Markman, E. M. (1979). Realizing that you don't understand: Elementary school children's awareness of inconsistencies. *Child Development, 50,* 643–655.

Markman, E. M. (1985). Comprehension monitoring: Developmental and educational issues. In S. F. Chapman, J. W. Segal, & R. Glaser (Eds.), *Thinking and learning skills: Research and open questions* (pp. 275–291). Mahwah, NJ: Erlbaum.

Markman, E. M., & Gorin, L. (1981). Children's ability to adjust their standards for evaluating comprehension. *Journal of Educational Psychology, 73,* 320–325.

Matanzo, J. B., & Harris, D. L. (1999). Encouraging metacognitive awareness in preservice literacy courses. In J. R. Dugan (Ed.), *Advancing the world of literacy: Moving into the 21st century* (pp. 201–225). Carrollton, GA: College Reading Association.

Mayer, R. E. (2001). Cognitive, metacognitive, and motivational aspects of problem solving. In H. Hartman (Ed.), *Metacognition in learning and instruction: Theory, research and practice* (pp. 87–101). Norwell, MA: Kluwer.

McCormick, C. B., & Barnett, J. (1984). *Developmental differences in the effect of signalling upon students' ability to monitor prose comprehension.* Paper presented at the American Educational Research Association Meeting, New Orleans, LA.

McCormick, C. B., Busching, B. A., & Potter, E. F. (1992). Children's knowledge about writing: The development and use of evaluative criteria. In M. Pressley, K. R. Harris, & J. T. Guthrie

(Eds.), *Promoting academic competence and literacy in schools: Cognitive research and instructional innovation* (pp. 311–336). Orlando, FL: Academic Press.

McInerney, V., McInerney, D. M., & Marsh, H. W. (1997). Effects of metacognitive strategy training within a cooperative group learning context on computer achievement and anxiety: An aptitude-treatment interaction study. *Journal of Educational Psychology, 89,* 686–695.

Meichenbaum, D., & Biemiller, A. (1992). In search of student expertise in the classroom: A metacognitive analysis. In M. Pressley, K. R. Harris, & J. T. Guthrie (Eds.), *Promoting academic competence and literacy in school* (pp. 3–56). San Diego, CA: Academic Press.

Metcalfe, J. (1998). Insight and metacognition. In G. Mazzoni & T. O. Nelson (Eds.), *Metacognition and cognitive neuropsychology: Monitoring and control processes* (pp. 181–197). Mahwah, NJ: Erlbaum.

Miller, G. E. (1985). The effects of general and specific self-instruction training on children's comprehension monitoring performances during reading. *Reading Research Quarterly, 20,* 616–628.

Miller, G. E., Giovenco, A., & Rentiers, K. A. (1987). Fostering comprehension monitoring in below average readers through self-instruction training. *Journal of Reading Behavior, 14,* 379–393.

Myers, M., II, & Paris, S. G. (1978). Children's metacognitive knowledge about reading. *Journal of Educational Psychology, 70,* 680–690.

Nelson, T. O. (1996). Consciousness and metacognition. *American Psychologist, 51,* 102–116.

Nelson, T. O. (1999). Cognition versus metacognition. In R. J. Sternberg (Ed.), *The nature of cognition* (pp. 625–641). Cambridge, MA: MIT Press.

Nelson, T. O., & Dunlosky, J. (1991). When people's judgements of learning (JOLs) are extremely accurate at predicting subsequent recalls: The "delayed JOL effect." *Psychological Science, 2,* 267–270.

Nelson, T. O., & Narens, L. (1994). Why investigate metacognition? In J. Metcalfe & A. P. Shimamura (Eds.), *Metacognition: Knowing about knowing* (pp. 1–25). Cambridge, MA: MIT Press.

O'Donnell, A. M., Dansereau, D. F., Hall, R. H., & Rocklin, T. R. (1987). Cognitive, social/affective, and metacognitive outcomes of scripted cooperative learning. *Journal of Educational Psychology, 79,* 431–437.

Palincsar, A. S., & Brown, A. L. (1984). Reciprocal teaching of comprehension-fostering and monitoring activities. *Cognition and Instruction, 1,* 117–175.

Paris, S. G., & Lindauer, B. K. (1982). The development of cognitive skills during childhood. In B. Wolman (Ed.), *Handbook of developmental psychology* (pp. 333–349). Englewood Cliffs, NJ: Prentice-Hall.

Paris, S. G., & Myers, M., II. (1981). Comprehension monitoring, memory, and study strategies of good and poor readers. *Journal of Reading Behavior, 13,* 5–22.

Paris, S. G., & Winograd, P. (1990). How metacognition can promote academic learning and instruction. In B. Jones & L. Idol (Eds.), *Dimensions of thinking and cognitive instruction* (pp. 15–51). Hillsdale, NJ: Erlbaum.

Pearson, P. D., & Stephens, D. (1994). Learning about literacy: A 30-year journey. In R. B. Ruddell, M. R. Ruddell, & H. Singer (Eds.), *Theoretical models and processes of reading* (4th ed., pp. 22–42). Newark, DE: International Reading Association.

Pierce, B. H., & Smith, S. M. (2001). The postdiction superiority effect in metacomprehension of text. *Memory & Cognition, 29,* 62–67.

Pintrich, P. R., Smith, D. A. F., Garcia, T., & McKeachie, W. (1993). Reliability and predictive validity of the Motivated Strategies for Learning Questionnaire (MSLQ). *Educational and Psychological Measurement, 53,* 801–813.

Pratt, M. W., & Wickens, G. (1983). Checking it out: Cognitive style, context, and problem type in children's monitoring of text comprehension. *Journal of Educational Psychology, 75,* 716–726.

Pressley, M., Borkowski, J. G., & Schneider, W. (1987). Cognitive strategies: Good strategy users coordinate metacognition and knowledge. In R. Vasta & G. Whitehurst (Eds.), *Annals of child development* (Vol. 5, pp. 89–129). Greenwich, CT: JAI Press.

Pressley, M., & Ghatala, E. S. (1988). Delusions about performance on multiple-choice comprehension tests. *Reading Research Quarterly, 23,* 454–464.

Pressley, M., & Ghatala, E. S. (1989). Metacognitive benefits of taking a test for children and young adolescents. *Journal of Experimental Child Psychology, 47,* 430–450.

Pressley, M., & Ghatala, E. S. (1990). Self-regulated learning: Monitoring learning from text. *Educational Psychologist, 25,* 19–33.

Pressley, M., Ghatala, E. S., Woloshyn, V., & Pirie, J. (1990). Sometimes adults miss the main ideas and do not realize it: Confidence in responses to short-answer and multiple choice comprehension questions. *Reading Research Quarterly, 25,* 232–249.

Pressley, M., Snyder, B. L., Levin, J. R., Murray, H. G., & Ghatala, E. S. (1987). Perceived readiness for examination of performance (PREP) produced by initial reading of text and text containing adjunct questions. *Reading Research Quarterly, 22,* 219–236.

Pressley, M., Van Etten, S., Yokoi, L., Freebern, G., & Van Meter, P. (1998). The metacognition of college studentship: A grounded theory approach. In D. J. Hacker, J. Dunlosky, & A. C. Graesser (Eds.), *Metacognition in educational theory and practice* (pp. 347–366). Mahwah, NJ: Erlbaum.

Raphael, T. E., Englert, C. S., & Kirschner, B. W. (1989). Students' metacognitive knowledge about writing. *Research in the Teaching of English, 23,* 343–379.

Rawson, K. A., Dunlosky, J., & Thiede, K. W. (2000). The rereading effect: Metacomprehension accuracy improves across reading trials. *Memory & Cognition, 28,* 1004–1010.

Roehler, L. R., & Duffy, G. G. (1984). Direct explanation of comprehension processes. In G. G. Duffy, L. R. Roehler, & J. Mason (Eds.), *Comprehension instruction: Perspectives and suggestions* (pp. 265–280). New York: Longman.

Rosenshine, B., & Meister, C. (1994). Reciprocal teaching: A review of the research. *Review of Educational Research, 64,* 479–530.

Rubman, C. N., & Waters, H. S. (2000). A, B seeing: The role of constructive processes in children's comprehension monitoring. *Journal of Educational Psychology, 92,* 503–514.

Ruddell, R. B., Ruddell, M. R., & Singer, H. (Eds.). (1994). *Theoretical models and processes of reading* (4th ed.). Newark, DE: International Reading Association.

Salomon, G., Globerson, T., & Guterman, E. (1989). The computer as a zone of proximal development: Internalizing reading-related metacognitions from a reading partner. *Journal of Educational Psychology, 81,* 620–627.

Scardamalia, M., & Bereiter, C. (1986). Writing. In R. F. Dillon & R. J. Sternberg (Eds.), *Cognition and instruction* (pp. 59–81). Orlando, FL: Academic Press.

Schraw, G. (2001). Promoting general metacognitive awareness. In H. Hartman (Ed.), *Metacognition in learning and instruction: Theory, research and practice* (pp. 3–16). Norwell, MA: Kluwer.

Schraw, G., & Dennison, R. S. (1994). Assessing metacognitive awareness. *Contemporary Educational Psychology, 19,* 460–475.

Schraw, G., Dunkle, M. E., Bendixen, L. D., & Roedel, T. D. (1995). Does a general monitoring skill exist? *Journal of Educational Psychology, 87,* 433–444.

Schraw, G., & Impara, J. C. (Eds.). (2000). *Issues in the measurement of metacognition.* Lincoln, NE: Buros Institute of Mental Measurements and Department of Educational Psychology, University of Nebraska-Lincoln.

Schraw, G., & Moshman, D. (1995). Metacognitive theories. *Educational Psychology Review, 7,* 351–371.

Schraw, G., & Nietfeld, J. (1998). A further test of the general monitoring skill hypothesis. *Journal of Educational Psychology, 90,* 236–248.

Schwartz, B. L., & Metcalfe, J. (1994). Methodological problems and pitfalls in the study of human metacognition. In J. Metcalfe & A. P. Shimamura (Eds.), *Metacognition: Knowing about knowing* (pp. 93–113). Cambridge, MA: MIT Press.

Shimamura, A. (1994). The neuropsychology of metacognition. In J. Metcalfe & A. P. Shimamura (Eds.), *Metacognition: Knowing about knowing* (pp. 253–276). Cambridge, MA: MIT Press.

Sitko, B. (1998). Knowing how to write: Metacognition and writing instruction. In D. J. Hacker, J. Dunlosky, & A. C. Graesser (Eds.), *Metacognition in educational theory and practice* (pp. 93–115). Mahwah, NJ: Erlbaum.

Son, L. K., & Metcalfe, J. (2000). Metacognitive and control strategies in study-time allocation. *Journal of Experimental Psychology: Learning, Memory, and Cognition, 26,* 204–221.

Sternberg, R. J. (1985). *Beyond IQ: A triarchic theory of human intelligence.* Cambridge, England: Cambridge University Press.

Sternberg, R. J. (2001). Metacognition, abilities, and developing expertise: What makes an expert student? In H. Hartman (Ed.), *Metacognition in learning and instruction: Theory, research and practice* (pp. 247–260). Norwell, MA: Kluwer.

Stolarek, E. A. (1994). Prose modeling and metacognition: The effect of modeling on developing a metacognitive stance toward writing. *Research in the Teaching of English, 28,* 154–174.

Swanson, H. L. (1990). Influence of metacognitive knowledge and aptitude on problem solving. *Journal of Educational Psychology, 82,* 306–314.

Taylor, B. M., & Beach, R. W. (1984). The effects of text structure instruction on middle-grade students' comprehension and production of expository text. *Reading Research Quarterly, 19,* 134–146.

Vygotsky, L. S. (1986). *Thought and language.* Cambridge, MA: MIT Press.

Walczyk, J. J., & Hall, V. C. (1989a). Effects of examples and embedded questions on the accuracy of comprehension self-assessments. *Journal of Educational Psychology, 81,* 435–437.

Walczyk, J. J., & Hall, V. C. (1989b). Is the failure to monitor comprehension an instance of cognitive impulsivity? *Journal of Educational Psychology, 81,* 294–298.

Weaver, C. A., III. (1990). Constraining factors in calibration of comprehension. *Journal of Experimental Psychology: Learning, Memory, and Cognition, 16,* 214–222.

Weaver, C. A., III, & Bryant, D. S. (1995). Monitoring of comprehension: The role of text difficulty in metamemory for narrative and expository text. *Memory & Cognition, 23,* 12–22.

Weinstein, C. E., Zimmerman, S. A., & Palmer, D. R. (1988). Assessing learning strategies: The design and development of the LASSI. In C. Weinstein, E. T. Goetz, & P. A. Alexander (Eds.), *Learning and study strategies: Issues in assessment, instruction, and evaluation* (pp. 25–40). San Diego, CA: Academic Press.

Weir, C. (1998). Using embedded questions to jump-start metacognition in middle school remedial readers. *Journal of Adolescent & Adult Literacy, 41,* 458–467.

Winne, P. H., & Hadwin, A. F. (1998). Studying as self-regulated learning. In D. J. Hacker, J. Dunlosky, & A. C. Graesser (Eds.), *Metacognition in educational theory and practice* (pp. 277–304). Mahwah, NJ: Erlbaum.

Winograd, P., & Gaskins, R. W. (1992). Metacognition: Matters of the mind, matters of the heart. In A. L. Costa, J. Bellanca, & R. Fogarty (Eds.), *If minds matter: A foreward to the future* (Vol. 1, pp. 225–238). Palatine, IL: Skylight.

Winograd, P., & Johnston, P. (1982). Comprehension monitoring and the error detection paradigm. *Journal of Reading Behavior, 14,* 63–74.

Yussen, S. R. (1985). The role of metacognition in contemporary theories of cognitive development. In D. L. Forrest-Pressley, G. E. MacKinnon, & T. G. Waller (Eds.), *Metacognition, cognition, and human performance* (pp. 253–283). New York: Academic Press.

Zabrucky, K., & Ratner, H. H. (1986). Children's comprehension monitoring and recall of inconsistent stories. *Child Development, 57,* 1401–1418.

Zabrucky, K., & Ratner, H. H. (1989). Effects of reading ability on children's comprehension evaluation and regulation. *Journal of Reading Behavior, 21,* 69–83.

Zabrucky, K., & Ratner, H. H. (1992). Effects of passage type on comprehension monitoring and recall in good and poor readers. *Journal of Reading Behavior, 24,* 373–391.

Zimmerman, B. J. (1995). Self-regulation involves more than metacognition: A social cognitive perspective. *Educational Psychologist, 30,* 217–221.

Zimmerman, B. J., & Risemberg, R. (1997). Becoming a self-regulated writer: A social cognitive perspective. *Contemporary Educational Psychology, 22,* 73–101.

Zohar, A. (1999). Teachers' metacognitive knowledge and the instruction of higher order thinking. *Teaching and Teacher Education, 15,* 413–429.

CHAPTER 6

Motivation and Classroom Learning

PAUL R. PINTRICH

Classroom learning is often discussed solely in terms of cognition and the various cognitive and metacognitive processes that are involved when students learn in academic settings. In fact, in a key chapter on learning, remembering, and understanding in the *Handbook of Child Psychology,* Brown, Bransford, Ferrara, and Campione (1983) noted

> Bleak though it may sound, academic cognition is relatively effortful, isolated, and cold. . . . Academic cognition is cold, in that the principal concern is with the knowledge and strategies necessary for efficiency, with little emphasis placed on the emotional factors that might promote or impede that efficiency. (p. 78)

This quote in the most important and influential handbook on child development reflects the state of the field in the early 1980s. Most of the models and research on academic cognition did not address issues of motivation or emotion and how these factors might facilitate or constrain cognition and learning. Basically, motivation was irrelevant to these cold models of cognition as they concentrated on the role of prior knowledge and strategies in cognition and learning.

At the same time, most motivational research in general—and within educational psychology specifically—did not investigate the linkages between motivational beliefs and academic cognition. Motivational research was focused on examining performance, which often was operationalized in terms of experimental tasks such as performance on anagram tasks or other lab tasks that were knowledge-lean and did not really reflect school learning tasks. In addition, motivational research was concerned with the classroom factors that predicted student motivation and achievement, but achievement was usually operationalized as course grades, performance on classroom tests, or performance on standardized achievement tests. The research did not really examine learning on domain-specific academic tasks (e.g., math, science tasks), which is what the cognitive researchers were focused on in their research. Motivational models and constructs were cognitive—especially in social cognitive models of motivation—but the links between the motivational constructs and the cognitive tasks and models were not made explicit in the research or in the theoretical models of motivation.

Fortunately, this state of affairs has changed dramatically over the last 20 years of research. Cognitive researchers now recognize the importance of motivational constructs in shaping cognition and learning in academic settings (e.g., Bransford, Brown, & Cocking, 1999), and motivational researchers have become interested in how motivational beliefs relate to student cognition and classroom learning (e.g., Pintrich, 2000a, 2000c). This integrative work on academic cognition and motivation has provided a much more accurate and ecologically valid description of classroom learning. Given these advances in our scientific knowledge, our understanding of classroom learning is not only more robust and generalizable, but it is also more readily applicable to problems of instructional improvement.

The purpose of this chapter is to summarize this work and discuss how various motivational constructs are related to student cognition and learning in classrooms. Given space considerations, this chapter does not represent a comprehensive review of the extant research in this area; rather, it attempts to highlight the key features of the work and active areas of research interest and future directions for the field.

In addition, the chapter focuses on personal motivational beliefs and their role in cognition and learning. It does not consider the role of various classroom contextual features and how they shape the development of student motivation. Readers interested in the role of classroom context factors can consult other sources (e.g., Pintrich & Schunk, 2002; Stipek, 1996). This chapter first discusses four general outcomes of motivation; then it considers how different motivational constructs are related to these four outcomes. From this analysis, four generalizations are proposed for how motivational constructs can facilitate or constrain cognition and learning. The chapter concludes with a discussion of future research directions for integrating motivation and cognition.

MOTIVATIONAL THEORIES AND STUDENT OUTCOMES

There are many different motivational theories related to achievement and learning (see Pintrich & Schunk, 2002; Graham & Weiner, 1996). These theories make some different metatheoretical assumptions about human nature and have proposed a large number of different constructs to explain motivated human behavior. In fact, the large number of different motivational constructs with different labels often makes it difficult for novices to understand and use the different constructs in their own research (Murphy & Alexander, 2000). Nevertheless, these different theories have some important commonalities in outcomes and motivational constructs that allow for some synthesis across theories. In this chapter, the focus is on four general outcomes with which all motivational theories are concerned, as well as three macrolevel motivational components that are inherent in most models of motivation. Accordingly, this chapter does not focus on different theoretical models of motivation; rather, it discusses how the three different motivational components are related to the four outcomes. Within the discussion of the three general motivational components, different theoretical perspectives and constructs are highlighted.

The term *motivation* comes from the Latin verb *movere*, which means *to move*. Motivation is evoked to explain what gets people going, keeps them going, and helps them finish tasks (Pintrich & Schunk, 2002). Most important is that motivational constructs are used to explain the instigation of behavior, the direction of behavior (choice), the intensity of behavior (effort, persistence), and actual achievement or accomplishments. Motivational theories focus both on developing general laws of behavior that apply to all people (a nomothetic perspective) as well as seeking explanations for individual differences in behavior (an idiographic perspective). Historically,

cognitive researchers often ignored motivational research because it was assumed that motivational constructs were used to explain individual differences in behavior, which was not a useful perspective for general models of cognition. However, this classic distinction between nomothetic and idiographic perspectives has lessened over time as motivational researchers have developed general principles that apply to all individuals as well as constructs that can be used to explain individual differences.

Most motivational theories attempt to predict four general outcomes. First, motivational theories are concerned with why individuals choose one activity over another—whether it be the day-to-day decisions regarding the choice of working on a task or relaxing or the more momentous and serious choices regarding career, marriage, and family. In the academic domain, the main issues regarding choice concern why some students choose to do their schoolwork and others choose to watch TV, talk on the phone, play on the computer, play with friends, or any of the other activities that students can choose to do instead of their schoolwork. In addition, motivational theories have examined why students choose one major over another or choose to take certain classes over others when given a choice. For example, in high school, students are often allowed to choose some of their courses; motivational theories have examined why some students choose to take more academic math and science courses over less rigorous courses. Choice is an important motivational outcome, and choosing to do an academic task over a nonacademic task is important for classroom learning; however, it may not be as important to classroom learning as are some of the following outcomes.

A second aspect of motivated behavior that motivational research has examined is the students' level of activity or involvement in a task. It is assumed that students are motivated when they put forth a great deal of effort in courses—from not falling asleep to more active engagement in the course. Behavioral indicators of this involvement could include taking detailed notes, asking good questions in class, being willing to take risks in class by stating ideas or opinions, coming after class to discuss in more detail the ideas presented in class, discussing the ideas from the course with classmates or friends outside of class time, spending a reasonable amount of time studying and preparing for class or exams, spending more time on one course than on other activities, and seeking out additional or new information from the library or other sources that goes beyond what is presented in class. Motivational theories have developed constructs that help to predict these types of behavioral outcomes.

Besides these behavioral indicators, there are more covert or unobservable aspects of engagement that include cognitive engagement and processing, such as thinking deeply about the material, using various cognitive and self-regulatory strategies to learn the material in a more disciplined and thoughtful manner, seeking to understand the material (not just memorize it), and integrating the new material with previously held conceptions of the content. All of these cognitive processes are crucial for deeper understanding and learning. It is important to note that it is not enough for students to just be behaviorally engaged in the course; they also must be cognitively engaged in order for true learning and understanding to occur. In this sense, cognitive engagement refers to the quality of students' engagement, whereas sheer effort refers to the quantity of their engagement in the class. This outcome of cognitive engagement is the most important one for understanding classroom learning and is the main focus of this chapter.

The third general aspect of motivated behavior that has been examined in most motivational theories is persistence. If individuals persist at tasks even in the face of difficulty, boredom, or fatigue, it would be inferred that they are motivated to do that task. Persistence is easily observable in general because teachers do have opportunities to observe students actually working on course tasks during class time. It is common for teachers to comment on the students' willingness to persist and try hard on the classwork. In this sense, persistence and behavioral engagement are much easier for teachers and others to judge than is cognitive engagement.

The fourth general outcome that motivational theories have examined is actual achievement or performance; in the classroom setting, this involves predicting course grades, scores on classroom tests, or performance on standardized achievement tests. These are important outcomes of schooling, although they may not always reflect what students actually learned or the quality of their cognition and thinking. This mismatch between the quality of cognition and the performance on the academic tasks or tests that students actually confront in classrooms can lead to some different conclusions about the role of different motivational components. It may be that some motivational components predict general course achievement or performance on standardized tests, and others are better predictors of the quality of cognition or cognitive engagement in learning tasks. This general idea of differential links between different motivational components and different outcomes is an important contribution of current motivational research. The field has moved past the search for a single magic motivational bullet that will solve all learning and instructional problems to the consideration of how different motivational components can facilitate or constrain different outcomes.

The remainder of this chapter discusses how motivational components can shape and influence cognition, learning, and the other important outcomes of schooling. Of course, a key assumption is that motivation and cognition are related, and that contrary to Brown et al. (1983), there is a need to examine how motivational and emotional components can facilitate or constrain cognition and learning. Accordingly, the remainder of this chapter discusses how motivational components can predict the four outcomes, including cognition and learning. At the same time, it should be clear that most current models of motivation assume that there is a reciprocal relation between motivation and cognition such that cognitive outcomes like learning and thinking or general outcomes like achievement and performance do have feedback effects on motivation. For example, as a student learns more and becomes more successful in achieving in the classroom (as indexed by grades or test scores), these accomplishments have an influence on subsequent motivation. Nevertheless, the emphasis in the motivational research has been on how motivation influences cognition and learning; therefore, that is the general orientation taken in this chapter.

THE ROLE OF MOTIVATIONAL COMPONENTS IN CLASSROOM LEARNING

Although many models of motivation may be relevant to student learning (see Graham & Weiner, 1996; Heckhausen, 1991; Pintrich & Schunk, 2002; Weiner, 1992), a general expectancy-value model serves as a useful framework for analyzing the research on motivational components (Pintrich, 1988a, 1988b, 1989; Pintrich & Schunk, 2002). Three general components seem to be important in these different models: (a) beliefs about one's ability or skill to perform the task (expectancy components); (b) beliefs about the importance, interest, and utility of the task (value components); and (c) feelings about the self or emotional reactions to the task (affective components).

Expectancy Components

Expectancy components are students' answer to the question *Can I do this task?* If students believe that they have some control over their skills and the task environment and if they are confident in their ability to perform the necessary skills, they are more likely to choose to do the task, be cognitively involved, persist at the task, and achieve at higher levels. Different motivational theorists have proposed a variety of constructs that can be categorized as expectancy components. The main distinction is between how much control one believes one has over the situation and perceptions of efficacy to accomplish the task in that situation. Of course, these beliefs are correlated empirically, but most models do propose separate constructs for control beliefs and efficacy beliefs.

Control Beliefs

There have been a number of constructs and theories proposed about the role of control beliefs for motivational dynamics. For example, early work on locus of control (e.g., Lefcourt, 1976; Rotter, 1966) found that students who believed that they were in control of their behavior and could influence the environment (an internal locus of control) tended to achieve at higher levels. Deci (1975) and de Charms (1968) discussed perceptions of control in terms of students' belief in self-determination. This self-determination perspective is crucial in intrinsic motivation theories of motivation (e.g., Deci & Ryan, 1985; Ryan & Deci, 2000) in which students are only intrinsically motivated if they feel autonomous and their behavior is self-determined rather than controlled by others. De Charms (1968) coined the terms *origins* and *pawns* to describe students who believed they were able to control their actions and students who believed others controlled their behavior. Connell (1985) suggested that there are three aspects of control beliefs: an internal source, an external source or powerful others, and an unknown source. Students who believe in internal sources of control are assumed to perform better than do students who believe powerful others (e.g., faculty, parents) are responsible for their success or failure or those students who don't know who or what is responsible for the outcomes. In the college classroom, Perry and his colleagues (e.g., Perry, 1991; Perry & Dickens, 1988; Perry & Magnusson, 1989; Perry & Penner, 1990) have shown that students' beliefs about how their personal attributes influence the environment—what they label *perceived control*—are related to achievement and to aspects of the classroom environment (e.g., instructor feedback).

Skinner and her colleagues (e.g., Skinner, 1995, 1996; Skinner, Wellborn, & Connell, 1990) distinguish three types of beliefs that contribute to perceived control and that are important in school. These three beliefs can be organized around the relations between an agent, the means or strategies and agent might use, and the ends or goals that the agent is trying to attain through the means or strategies (Skinner, 1995). *Capacity beliefs* refer to an individual's beliefs about his or her personal capabilities with respect to ability, effort, others, and luck (e.g., *I can't seem to try very hard in school*). These beliefs reflect the person's beliefs that he or she has the means to accomplish something and are similar to efficacy

judgments (Bandura, 1997) or agency beliefs (Skinner, 1995, 1996; Skinner, Chapman, & Baltes, 1988). *Strategy beliefs* are expectations or perceptions about factors that influence success in school, such as ability, effort, others, luck, or unknown factors (e.g., *The best way for me to get good grades is to work hard.*). These beliefs refer to the perception that the means are linked to the ends—that if one uses the strategies, the goal will be attained. They also have been called outcome expectations (Bandura, 1997) and means-ends beliefs (Skinner, 1995, 1996). *Control beliefs* are expectations about an individual's likelihood of doing well in school without reference to specific means (e.g., *I can do well in school if I want to*). These beliefs refer to the relation between the agent and the ends or goals and also have been called control expectancy beliefs (Skinner, 1995, 1996). Skinner and colleagues (Skinner, 1995; Skinner et al., 1990) found that perceived control influenced academic performance by promoting or decreasing active engagement in learning and that teachers contributed to students' perceptions of control when they provided clear and consistent guidelines and feedback, stimulated students' interest in learning, and assisted students with resources.

In self-efficacy theory, outcome expectations refer to individuals' beliefs concerning their ability to influence outcomes—that is, their belief that the environment is responsive to their actions, which is different from self-efficacy (the belief that one can do the task; see Bandura, 1986; Schunk, 1985). This belief that outcomes are contingent on their behavior leads individuals to have higher expectations for success and should lead to more persistence. When individuals do not perceive a contingency between their behavior and outcomes, they may show passivity, anxiety, lack of effort, and lower achievement, often labeled *learned helplessness* (cf. Abramson, Seligman, & Teasdale, 1978). Learned helplessness is usually seen as a stable pattern of attributing many events to uncontrollable causes, which leaves the individual believing that there is no opportunity for change that is under their control. These individuals do not believe they can do anything that will make a difference and that the environment or situation is basically not responsive to their actions.

The overriding message of all these models is that a general pattern of perception of internal control results in positive outcomes (i.e., more cognitive engagement, higher achievement, higher self-esteem), whereas sustained perceptions of external or unknown control result in negative outcomes (lower achievement, lack of effort, passivity, anxiety). Reviews of research in this area are somewhat conflicting, however (cf. Findley & Cooper, 1983; Stipek & Weisz; 1981), and some have argued that it is better to accept responsibility for positive outcomes (an internal locus of control) and deny responsibility for negative or failure outcomes (an external locus of control; see Harter, 1985). Part of the difficulty in interpreting this literature lies in the use of different definitions of the construct of control, different instruments to measure the construct, different ages of the samples, and different outcomes measures used as a criterion in the numerous studies. In particular, the construct of internal locus of control confounds three dimensions of locus (internal vs. external), controllability (controllable vs. uncontrollable), and stability (stable vs. unstable). Attributional theory proposes that these three dimensions can be separated conceptually and empirically and that they have different influences on behavior (Weiner, 1986).

Attributional theory proposes that the causal attributions an individual makes for success or failure—not the actual success or failure event—mediates future expectancies. A large number of studies have shown that individuals who tend to attribute success to internal and stable causes like ability or aptitude will tend to expect to succeed in the future. In contrast, individuals who attribute their success to external or unstable causes (i.e., ease of the task, luck) will not expect to do well in the future. For failure situations, the positive motivational pattern consists of not an internal locus of control, but rather attribution of failure to external and unstable causes (difficult task, lack of effort, bad luck) and the negative motivational pattern consists of attributing failure to internal and stable causes (e.g., ability, skill). This general attributional approach has been applied to numerous situations and the motivational dynamics seem to be remarkably robust and similar (Weiner, 1986, 1995).

The key difference between attributional theory and intrinsic motivation theories of personal control (e.g., de Charms, 1968; Deci & Ryan, 1985; Skinner, 1995, 1996) is that attributions are post hoc explanations for performance after some feedback about success or failure has been provided to the student. The control beliefs that are of concern to intrinsic motivation theorists are prospective beliefs of the student before he or she begins a task. Both types of construct are important in predicting various outcomes, including cognitive engagement (see Pintrich & Schrauben, 1992), but the motivational dynamics are different, given the different temporal role of attributions and control beliefs in the theoretical models.

It also is important to note that from an attributional analysis, the important dimension that is linked to future expectancies (beliefs that one will do well in the future) is stability, not locus (Weiner, 1986)—that is, it is how stable you believe a cause is that is linked to future expectancies (i.e., the belief that your ability or effort to do the task is stable over time, not whether you believe it is internal or external to you). Attributional theory generally takes a situational view

of these attributions and beliefs, but some researchers have suggested that individuals have relatively consistent attributional patterns across domains and tasks that function somewhat like personality traits (e.g., Fincham & Cain, 1986; Peterson, Maier, & Seligman, 1993). These attributional patterns seem to predict individuals' performance over time. For example, if students consistently attributed their success to their own skill and ability as learners, then it would be predicted that they would continually expect success in future classes. In contrast, if students consistently attribute success to other causes (e.g., excellent instructors, easy material, luck), then their expectations might not be as high for future classes.

Individuals' beliefs about the causes of events can be changed through feedback and other environmental manipulations to facilitate the adoption of positive control and attributional beliefs. For example, some research on attributional retraining in achievement situations (e.g., Foersterling, 1985; Perry & Penner, 1990) suggests that teaching individuals to make appropriate attributions for failure on school tasks (e.g., effort attributions instead of ability attributions) can facilitate future achievement. Of course, there are a variety of issues to consider in attributional retraining, including the specification of which attributional patterns are actually dysfunctional, the relative accuracy of the new attributional pattern, and the issue of only attempting to change a motivational component instead of the cognitive skill that also may be important for performance (cf. Blumenfeld, Pintrich, Meece, & Wessels, 1982; Weiner, 1986).

In summary, individuals' beliefs about the contingency between their behaviors and their performance in a situation are linked to student learning and achievement. In a classroom context, this means that students' motivational beliefs about the link between their studying, self-regulated learning behavior, and achievement will influence their actual studying behavior. For example, if students believe that no matter how hard they study, they will not be able to do well on a chemistry test because they simply lack the aptitude to master the material, then they will be less likely to actually study for the test. In the same fashion, if students believe that their effort in studying can make a difference regardless of their actual aptitude for the material, then they will be more likely to study the material. Accordingly, these beliefs about control and contingency have motivational force because they influence future behavior.

Self-Efficacy Beliefs

In contrast to control beliefs, self-efficacy concerns students' beliefs about their ability to just do the task, not the linkage between their doing it and the outcome. Self-efficacy has been defined as individuals' beliefs about their performance capabilities in a particular domain (Bandura, 1982, 1986; Schunk, 1985). The construct of self-efficacy includes individuals' judgments about their ability to accomplish certain goals or tasks by their actions in specific situations (Schunk, 1985). This approach implies a relatively situational or domain-specific construct rather than a global personality trait or general perceptions of self-concept or self-competence. In an achievement context, it includes students' confidence in their cognitive skills to perform the academic task. Continuing the example from chemistry, a student might have confidence in his or her capability (a high self-efficacy belief) to learn the material for the chemistry test (i.e., *I can learn this material on stoichiometry*) and consequently exert more effort in studying. At the same time, if the student believes that the grading curve in the class is so difficult and that studying will not make much difference in his or her grade on the exam (a low control belief), that student might not study as much. Accordingly, self-efficacy and control beliefs are separate constructs, albeit they are usually positively correlated empirically. Moreover, they may combine and interact with each other to influence student self-regulation and outcomes.

An issue in most motivational theories regarding self-efficacy and control beliefs concerns the domain or situational specificity of the beliefs. As noted previously, self-efficacy theory generally assumes a situation-specific view—that is, individuals' judgment of their efficacy for a task is a function of the task and situational characteristics operating at the time (difficulty, feedback, norms, comparisons with others, etc.) as well as their past experience and prior beliefs about the task and their current beliefs and feelings as they work on the task. However, generalized efficacy beliefs that extend beyond the specific situation may influence motivated behavior. Accordingly, students could have efficacy beliefs not only for a specific exam in chemistry, but also for chemistry in general, natural science courses in contrast to social science or humanities courses, or learning and schoolwork in general. At these more global levels, self-efficacy beliefs would become very similar to perceived competence beliefs or self-concept, at least in terms of the motivational dynamics and functional relations to student outcomes (Eccles, Wigfield, & Schiefele, 1998; Harter, 1999; Pintrich & Schunk, 2002). An important direction for future research will be to examine the domain generality of both self-efficacy and control beliefs. Nevertheless, it has been shown in many studies in many different domains—including the achievement domain—that students' self-efficacy beliefs (or in more colloquial terms, their self-confidence in their capabilities to do a task) are strongly related to their choice of

activities, their level of cognitive engagement, and their willingness to persist at a task (Bandura, 1986; Pintrich, 1999; Pintrich & De Groot, 1990; Pintrich & Schrauben, 1992; Schunk, 1985).

In terms of self-efficacy beliefs, results from correlational research (Pintrich, 1999, 2000b; Pintrich & De Groot, 1990) are very consistent over time and in line with more experimental studies of self-efficacy (Bandura, 1997). Self-efficacy is one of the strongest positive predictors of actual achievement in the course, accounting for 9–25% of the variance in grades, depending on the study and the other predictors entered in the regression (see review by Pintrich, 1999). Students who believe they are able to do the course work and learn the material are much more likely to do well in the course. Moreover, in these studies, self-efficacy remains a significant predictor of final achievement, although it accounts for less total variance, even when previous knowledge (as indexed by performance on earlier tests) or general ability (as indexed by SAT scores) are entered into the equations in these studies.

Finally, in all of these studies (see review by Pintrich, 1999), self-efficacy is a significant positive predictor of student self-regulation and cognitive engagement in the course. Students who are confident of their capabilities to learn and do the course work are more likely to report using more elaboration and organizational cognitive strategies. These strategies involve deeper cognitive processing of the course material—students try to paraphrase the material, summarize it in their own words, or make outlines or concept maps of the concepts in comparison to just trying to memorize the material. In addition, students higher in their self-efficacy for learning also are much more likely to be metacognitive and try to regulate their learning by monitoring and controlling their cognition as they learn. In our studies (see review by Pintrich, 1999), we have measures of these cognitive and self-regulatory strategies at the start of the course and at the end of the course, and self-efficacy remains a significant predictor of cognitive and self-regulatory strategy use at the end of the course, even when the earlier measure of cognition is included as a predictor along with self-efficacy. Accordingly, positive self-efficacy beliefs can boost cognitive and self-regulatory strategy use over the course of a semester.

In summary, an important first generalization about the role of motivational beliefs in classroom learning emphasizes the importance of self-efficacy beliefs.

Generalization 1: Self-efficacy beliefs are positively related to adaptive cognitive and self-regulatory strategy use as well as actual achievement in the classroom.

Accordingly, students who feel capable and confident about their capabilities to do the course work are much more likely to be cognitively engaged, to try hard, to persist, and to do well in the course. In fact, the strength of the relations between self-efficacy and these different outcomes in our research as well as others (Bandura, 1997; Eccles et al., 1998; Pintrich & Schunk, 2002; Schunk, 1991) suggests that self-efficacy is one of the best and most powerful motivational predictors of learning and achievement. Given the strength of the relations, research on the motivational aspects of student learning and performance needs to include self-efficacy as an important mediator between classroom contextual factors and student outcomes.

Value Components

Value components of the model incorporate individuals' goals for engaging in a task as well as their beliefs about the importance, utility, or interest of a task. Essentially, these components concern the question *Why am I doing this task?* In more colloquial terms, value components concern whether students care about the task and the nature of that concern. These components should be related to cognitive and self-regulatory activities as well as outcomes such as the choice of activities, effort, and persistence (Eccles, 1983; Eccles et al., 1998; Pintrich, 1999). Although there are a variety of different conceptualizations of value, two basic components seem relevant: goal orientation and task value.

Goal Orientation

All motivational theories posit some type of goal, purpose, or intentionality to human behavior, although these goals may range from relatively accessible and conscious goals as in attribution theory to relatively inaccessible and unconscious goals as in psychodynamic theories (Zukier, 1986). In recent cognitive reformulations of achievement motivation theory, goals are assumed to be cognitive representations of the different purposes students may adopt in different achievement situations (Dweck & Elliott, 1983; Dweck & Leggett, 1988; Ford, 1992). In current achievement motivation research, there have been two general classes of goals that have been discussed under various names such as target and purpose goals (e.g., Harackiewicz, Barron, & Elliot, 1998; Harackiewicz & Sansone, 1991), or task-specific goals and goal orientations (e.g., Garcia & Pintrich, 1994; Pintrich & Schunk, 2002; Wolters, Yu, & Pintrich, 1996; Zimmerman & Kitsantas, 1997). The general distinction between these two classes of goals is that target and task-specific goals represent the specific outcome the individual is attempting to accomplish. In academic learning contexts, it would be represented by goals such as *wanting to get a 85% out of 100% correct on a quiz, trying to get an A on a midterm exam,* and so forth.

These goals are specific to a task and are most similar to the goals discussed by Locke and Latham (1990) for workers in an organizational context such as *wanting to make 10 more widgets an hour* or to *sell five more cars in the next week.*

In contrast, purpose goals or goal orientations reflect the more general reasons individuals do a task and are related more to the research on achievement motivation (Elliot, 1997; Urdan, 1997). It is an individual's general orientation (also called schema or theory) for approaching the task, doing the task, and evaluating his or her performance on the task (Ames, 1992; Dweck & Leggett, 1988; Pintrich, 2000a, 2000b, 2000c). In this case, purpose goals or goal orientations refer to why individuals want to get 85% out of 100%, why they want to get an A, or why they want to make more widgets or sell more cars as well as the standards or criteria (85%, an A) they will use to evaluate their progress towards the goal. Most of the research on classroom learning has focused on goal orientation—not specific target goals—so this chapter also focuses on the role of goal orientation in learning.

There are a number of different models of goal orientation that have been advanced by different achievement motivation researchers (cf. Ames, 1992; Dweck & Leggett, 1988; Harackiewicz et al., 1998; Maehr & Midgley, 1991; Nicholls, 1984; Pintrich, 1988a, 1988b, 1989; Wolters et al., 1996). These models vary somewhat in their definition of goal orientation and the use of different labels for similar constructs. They also differ on the proposed number of goal orientations and the role of approach and avoidance forms of the different goals. Finally, they also differ on the degree to which an individual's goal orientations are more personal and based in somewhat stable individual differences, or the degree to which an individual's goal orientations are more situated or sensitive to the context and a function of the contextual features of the environment. Most of the models assume that goal orientations are a function of both individual differences and contextual factors, but the relative emphasis along this continuum does vary between the different models. Much of this research also assumes that classrooms and other contexts (e.g., business or work settings, laboratory conditions in an experiment) can be characterized in terms of their goal orientations (see Ford, Smith, Weissbein, Gully, & Salas, 1998, for an application of goal orientation theory to a work setting), but for the purposes of this chapter the focus is on individuals' personal goal orientation.

Most models propose two general goal orientations that concern the reasons or purposes individuals are pursuing when approaching and engaging in a task. In Dweck's model, the two goal orientations are labeled *learning* and *performance goals* (Dweck & Leggett, 1988), with learning goals reflecting a focus on increasing competence and performance goals involving either the avoidance of negative judgments of competence or attainment of positive judgments of competence. Ames (1992) labels them *mastery* and *performance goals,* with mastery goals orienting learners to "developing new skills, trying to understand their work, improving their level of competence, or achieving a sense of mastery based on self-referenced standards" (Ames, 1992, p. 262). In contrast, performance goals orient learners to focus on their ability and self-worth, to determine their ability in reference to besting other students in competitions, surpassing others in achievements or grades, and receiving public recognition for their superior performance (Ames, 1992). Harackiewicz, Elliot, and their colleagues (e.g., Elliot, 1997; Elliot & Church, 1997; Elliot & Harackiewicz, 1996; Harackiewicz et al., 1998) have labeled them mastery and performance goals as well. Nicholls (1984) has used the terms task-involved and ego-involved for similar constructs (see Pintrich, 2000c, for a review). In this chapter we use the labels of mastery and performance goals.

In the literature on mastery and performance goals, the general theoretical assumption has been that mastery goals foster a host of adaptive motivational, cognitive, and achievement outcomes, whereas performance goals generate less adaptive or even maladaptive outcomes. Moreover, this assumption has been supported in a large number of empirical studies on goals and achievement processes (Ames, 1992; Dweck & Leggett, 1988; Pintrich, 2000c; Pintrich & Schunk, 2002)—in particular, the positive predictions for mastery goals. The logic of the argument is that when students are focused on trying to learn and understand the material and trying to improve their performance relative to their own past performance, this orientation will help them maintain their self-efficacy in the face of failure, ward off negative affect such as anxiety, lessen the probability that they will have distracting thoughts, and free up cognitive capacity and allow for more cognitive engagement and achievement. In contrast, when students are concerned about trying to be the best, get higher grades than do others, and do well compared to others under a performance goal, there is the possibility that this orientation will result in more negative affect or anxiety, increase the possibility of distracting and irrelevant thoughts (e.g., worrying about how others are doing rather than focusing on the task), and that this will diminish cognitive capacity, task engagement, and performance.

The research on the role of mastery and performance goals in learning and performance is fairly straightforward for mastery goals but not for performance goals. This research has included student use of strategies that promote deeper processing of the material as well as various metacognitive and self-regulatory strategies (Pintrich, 2000c). Much of this

research is based on self-report data from correlational classroom studies, although Dweck and Leggett (1988) summarize data from experimental studies. The classroom studies typically assess students' goal orientations and then measure students reported use of different strategies for learning either at the same time or longitudinally. Although there are some problems with the use of self-report instruments for measuring self-regulatory strategies (see Pintrich, Wolters, & Baxter, 2000), these instruments do display reasonable psychometric qualities. Moreover, the research results are overwhelmingly consistent—mastery goals account for between 10 and 30% of the variance in the cognitive outcomes. Studies have been done with almost all age groups from elementary to college students and have assessed students' goals for school in general as well as in the content areas of English, math, science, and social studies.

The studies have found that students who endorse a mastery goal are more likely to report attempts to self-monitor their cognition and to seek ways to become aware of their understanding and learning, such as checking for understanding and comprehension monitoring (e.g., Ames & Archer, 1988; Dweck & Leggett, 1988; Meece, Blumenfeld, & Hoyle, 1988; Meece & Holt, 1993; Middleton & Midgley, 1997; Nolen, 1988; Pintrich, 1999; Pintrich & De Groot, 1990; Pintrich & Garcia, 1991, 1993; Pintrich, Smith, Garcia, & McKeachie, 1993; Pintrich & Schrauben, 1992; Wolters et al., 1996). In addition, this research has consistently shown that students' use of various cognitive strategies for learning is positively related to mastery goals. In particular, this research has shown that students' reported use of deeper processing strategies such as the use of elaboration strategies (i.e., paraphrasing, summarizing) and organizational strategies (networking, outlining) is positively correlated with the endorsement of mastery goals (Ames & Archer, 1988; Bouffard, Boisvert, Vezeau, & Larouche, 1995; Graham & Golen, 1991; Kaplan & Midgley, 1997; Meece et al., 1988; Pintrich, 1999; Pintrich & De Groot, 1990; Pintrich & Garcia, 1991; Pintrich et al., 1993; Wolters et al., 1996). Finally, in some of this research, mastery goals have been negatively correlated with the use of less effective or surface processing strategies (i.e., rehearsal), especially in older students (Anderman & Young, 1994; Kaplan & Midgley, 1997; Pintrich & Garcia, 1991; Pintrich et al., 1993). In contrast to this research on the use of various self-regulatory and learning strategies, there has not been much research on how mastery goals are linked to the use of other problem-solving or thinking strategies. This is clearly an area that will be investigated in the future.

The research on performance goals and cognitive outcomes is not as easily summarized as are the results for mastery goals. The original goal theory research generally found negative relations between performance goals and various cognitive and behavioral outcomes (Ames, 1992; Dweck & Leggett, 1988), although it did not discriminate empirically between approach and avoidance performance goals. The more recent research that has made the distinction between approach and avoidance performance goals does show some differential relations between approaching a task focused on besting others and approaching a task focused on trying not to look stupid or incompetent. In particular, the general distinction between an approach and an avoidance orientation suggests that there could be some positive aspects of an approach performance orientation. If students are approaching a task trying to promote certain goals and strategies, it might lead them to be more involved in the task than are students who are trying to avoid certain goals, which could lead to more withdrawal and less engagement in the task (Harackiewicz et al., 1998; Higgins, 1997; Pintrich, 2000c).

Most of the research on performance goals that did *not* distinguish between approach and avoidance versions finds that performance goals are negatively related to students' use of deeper cognitive strategies (e.g., Meece et al., 1988; Nolen, 1988; cf., however, Bouffard, Boisvert, Vezeau, & Larouche, 1995). This finding would be expected, given that performance goals that include items about besting others as well as avoiding looking incompetent would guide students away from the use of deeper strategies. Students focused on besting others may be less likely to exert the time and effort needed to use deeper processing strategies because the effort needed to use these strategies could show to others that they lack the ability, given that the inverse relation between effort-ability is usually operative under performance goals, and trying hard in terms of strategy use may signify low ability. For students who want to avoid looking incompetent, the same self-worth protection mechanism (Covington, 1992) may be operating, whereby students do not exert effort in their strategy use in order to have an excuse for doing poorly—lack of effort or poor strategy use.

However, more recent research with measures that reflect only an approach or avoidance performance goal suggests that there may be differential relations between these two versions of performance goals. For example, Wolters et al. (1996) in a correlational study of junior high students found that—independent of the positive main effect of mastery goals—an approach performance goal focused on besting others was positively related to the use of deeper cognitive strategies and more regulatory strategy use. However, Kaplan and Midgley (1997) in a correlational study of junior high students found no relation between an approach performance goal and adaptive learning strategies, but approach performance goals were positively related to more surface processing or maladaptive

learning strategies. These two studies did not include separate measures of avoid performance goals. In contrast, Middleton and Midgley (1997) in a correlational study of junior high students, found no relation between either approach or avoidance performance goals and cognitive self-regulation. Some of the differences in the results of these studies stem from the use of different measures, classroom contexts, and participants, making it difficult to synthesize the results. Clearly, there is a need for more theoretical development in this area and empirical work that goes beyond correlational self-report survey studies to clarify these relations.

One factor that adds to the complexity of the results in discussing approach and avoidance performance goals is that in Dweck's original model (Dweck & Leggett, 1988), the links between performance goals and other cognitive and achievement outcomes were assumed to be moderated by efficacy beliefs—that is, if students had high perceptions of their competence to do the task, then performance goals should not be detrimental for cognition, motivation, and achievement, and these students should show the same basic pattern as mastery-oriented students. Performance goals were assumed to have negative effects only when efficacy was low. Students who believed they were unable and who were concerned with besting others or wanted to avoid looking incompetent did seem to show the maladaptive pattern of cognition, motivation, and behavior (Dweck & Leggett, 1988).

Other more correlational research that followed this work did not always explicitly test for the predicted interaction between performance goals and efficacy or did not replicate the predicted moderator effect. For example, both Kaplan and Midgley (1997) and Miller, Behrens, Greene, and Newman (1993) did not find an interaction between approach performance goals and efficacy on cognitive outcomes such as strategy use. Harackiewicz, Elliot, and their colleagues (Harackiewicz et al., 1998), using both experimental and correlational designs, did not find moderator or mediator effects of efficacy in relation to the effects of approach mastery or approach performance goals on other outcomes such as actual performance.

Nevertheless, it may be that approach performance goals could lead to deeper strategy use and cognitive self-regulation as suggested by Wolters et al. (1996) when students are confronted with overlearned classroom tasks that do not challenge them, interest them, or offer opportunities for much self-improvement (see also Pintrich, 2000b). In this case, the focus on an external criterion of besting others or being the best in the class could lead them to be more involved in these boring tasks and try to use more self-regulatory cognitive strategies to accomplish this goal. On the other hand, it may be that approach performance goals are not that strongly related to cognitive self-regulation in either a positive or negative way, as suggested by the results of Kaplan and Midgley (1997) and Middleton and Midgley (1997). Taken together, the conflicting results suggest that approach performance goals do not have to be negatively related to cognitive self-regulatory activities in comparison to avoidance performance goals. This conclusion suggests that there may be multiple pathways between approach and avoidance performance goals, cognitive strategy use and self-regulation, and eventual achievement. Future research should attempt to map out these multiple pathways and determine how approach and avoidance performance goals may differentially relate to cognitive self-regulation activities (Pintrich, 2000b, 2000c).

One of the most important behavioral outcomes is actual achievement or performance. Goals may promote different patterns of motivation, affect, and cognition, but they also should be linked to actual classroom achievement. The more experimental research on mastery goals has shown that students in mastery conditions usually achieve or perform at higher levels (Dweck & Leggett, 1988). In fact, given all the positive motivational, affective, and cognitive outcomes associated with mastery goals, it would be expected that mastery goals would also lead to higher levels of achievement. However, in some of the correlational classroom studies, this does not seem to be the case (e.g., Elliot, McGregor, & Gable, 1999; Harackiewicz et al., 1998; Harackiewicz, Barron, Carter, Lehto, & Elliot, 1997; Pintrich, 2000c; VanderStoep, Pintrich, & Fagerlin, 1996). The pattern that seems to emerge is that mastery goals are unrelated to performance or achievement in the classroom, usually indexed by grades or grade point average (GPA). In contrast, in some of these studies, approach performance goals (trying to be better than others) are associated with better grades or higher GPAs (Elliot et al., 1999; Harackiewicz et al., 1997, 1998).

This newer research on the role of performance goals has led some researchers to develop a revised goal theory perspective (e.g., Elliot, 1997; Harackiewicz et al., 1998; Pintrich, 2000c). They have suggested that there is a need to move beyond the simple dichotomy of mastery goals as good-adaptive versus performance goals as bad-maladaptive to a conceptualization of the different goals as being adaptive or maladaptive for different types of cognitive, motivational, affective, and behavioral outcomes. In other words, depending on what outcome is under consideration, goals may be adaptive or maladaptive—for example, mastery goals might lead to more interest and intrinsic motivation, but approach performance goals might lead to better performance (Harackiewicz et al., 1998). It is important to note that a revised perspective on goal theory and the normative perspective are in complete agreement about the detrimental

effects of avoid performance goals. The main revision proposed is that approach performance goals may be adaptive for some outcomes. In addition, the concept of equifinality, or the idea that there are multiple means to accomplish a goal, suggests that there may be multiple pathways or trajectories of development that are set in motion by different goals, and these different pathways can lead to similar outcomes overall (Pintrich, 2000c; Shah & Kruglanski, 2000). Finally, there may be interactions between multiple goals, and these interactions can lead to different patterns of outcomes that are more complex than the simple linear relations suggested by normative goal theory under the mastery-good and performance-bad generalization (Pintrich, 2000c).

In contrast, Midgley, Kaplan, and Middleton (2001) have argued that there is no need to revise goal theory and that the basic assumption that mastery goals are adaptive and performance goals are maladaptive is still the best overall generalization from goal theory. They suggest that most of the research on the positive effects of approach performance goals are for special cases, such as for students high in self-efficacy (Dweck & Leggett, 1988), for students high in mastery goals as well approach performance goals (Pintrich, 2000c), or in contexts such as competitive college classrooms (Harackiewicz et al., 1998) in which there may be an advantage to adopting performance goals. Moreover, they note that classrooms and schools are often inherently performance-oriented and competitive to begin with, and that any suggestion by researchers that approach performance goals are adaptive would encourage teachers and school personnel to continue to stress the competitive nature of schooling, with the continued many detrimental effects for many schoolchildren. This issue is currently a very active area of research and there will no doubt be continued research and clarification of these issues as the field progresses.

In summary, the research on goal orientation suggests that at this point in time only one stable generalization can be made, given the diversity in findings.

Generalization 2: Mastery goals are positively related to adaptive cognitive and self-regulatory strategy use in the classroom. Students who adopt a mastery goal and focus on learning, understanding, and self-improvement are much more likely to use adaptive cognitive and self-regulatory strategies and to be deeply engaged in learning. Accordingly, classroom contexts that foster the adoption of mastery goals by students should facilitate motivation and learning. For example, classrooms that encourage students to adopt goals of learning and understanding through the reward and evaluation structures (i.e., how grades are assigned, how tasks are graded and evaluated) rather than just getting good grades or competing with other students should foster a mastery goal orientation. At the same time, this generalization does not mention higher levels of actual achievement, as indexed by grades, because the research is still mixed on this outcome.

Task Value

Goal orientation can refer to students' goals for a specific task (a midterm exam) as well as a general orientation to a course or a field. In the same way, students' task value beliefs can be rather specific or more general. Three components of task value have been proposed by Eccles (1983) as important in achievement dynamics: the individual's perception of the importance of the task, his or her personal interest in the task (similar to intrinsic interest in intrinsic motivation theory), and his or her perception of the utility value of the task for future goals. These three value components may be rather parallel in children and college students but can vary significantly in adults (Wlodkowski, 1988).

The importance component of task value refers to individuals' perception of the task's importance or salience for them. The perceived importance of a task is related to a general goal orientation, but importance could vary by goal orientation. An individual's orientation may guide the general direction of behavior, whereas value may relate to the level of involvement. For example, a student may believe that success in a particular course is very important (or unimportant) regardless of his or her intrinsic or extrinsic goals—that is, the student may see success in the course as learning the material or getting a good grade, but he or she still may attach differential importance to these goals. Importance should be related to individuals' persistence at a task as well as choice of a task.

Student interest in the task is another aspect of task value. Interest is assumed to be individuals' general attitude or liking of the task that is somewhat stable over time and a function of personal characteristics. In an educational setting, this component includes the individual's interest in the course content and reactions to the other characteristics of the course such as the instructor (cf. Wlodkowski, 1988). Personal interest in the task is partially a function of individuals' preferences as well as aspects of the task (e.g., Malone & Lepper, 1987). However, personal interest should not be confused with situational interest, which can be generated by simple environmental features (e.g., an interesting lecture, a fascinating speaker, a dramatic film) but that are not long-lasting and do not necessarily inculcate stable personal interest (Hidi, 1990). Schiefele (1991) has shown that students' personal interest in the material being studied is related to their level of involvement in terms of the use of cognitive strategies as well as actual performance. There is a current revival in research on the role of interest in learning after a hiatus in research on this important

motivational belief (see Renninger, Hidi, & Krapp, 1992; Sansone & Harackiewicz, 2000).

In contrast to the means or process motivational dynamic of interest, utility value refers to the ends or instrumental motivation of the student (Eccles, 1983). Utility value is determined by the individual's perception of the usefulness of the task for him or her. For students, utility value may include beliefs that the course will be useful for them immediately in some way (e.g., help them cope with college), in their major (e.g., they need this information for upper-level courses), or their career and life in general (e.g., this will help them somehow in graduate school). At a task level, students may perceive different course assignments (e.g., essay and multiple-choice exams, term papers, lab activities, class discussion) as more or less useful and decide to become more or less cognitively engaged in the task.

Research on the value components has shown that they are consistently positively related to student engagement and cognition in the classroom setting (e.g., Pintrich, 1999). Not surprisingly, students who believe that schoolwork or course work is more important, interesting, and useful to them are more likely to be cognitively engaged in the learning activities. In this work, self-efficacy has been a stronger predictor of engagement, but task value beliefs also show positive relations (Pintrich, 1999). In longitudinal research on the role of expectancy and value components in academic settings, Eccles and her colleagues (Eccles et al., 1998) have found a similar pattern of results. Their work has shown that value beliefs are better predictors of choice behavior, whereas expectancy components (i.e., self-efficacy and perceived competence) are better predictors of actual achievement. In other words, task value beliefs help to predict what courses students might take (e.g., higher level math or science courses), but after students actually enroll in those courses, self-efficacy and perceived competence are better predictors of their performance. This differential prediction of outcomes for different motivational beliefs is an important finding in motivational research.

A related vein of research from an intrinsic motivation perspective (Deci & Ryan, 1985; Ryan & Deci, 2000) has suggested that interest (one of the components of task value) is an important associated process with being intrinsically motivated (enjoyment is another associated process). In this theoretical perspective, intrinsic motivation is represented by individuals choosing to do a task freely and feeling self-determined or autonomous in their behavior while doing the task. This form of intrinsic motivation should result in the most adaptive levels of motivation, cognition, and behavior. Students who are intrinsically motivated should be interested in the task, enjoy it, be more likely to be cognitively engaged, and also perform at high levels (Deci & Ryan, 1985). Although this perspective makes some different metatheoretical assumptions about human nature and human behavior, the functional role of intrinsic interest is similar to that of personal interest in an expectancy-value model.

In addition, in intrinsic motivation models, individuals can be motivated in more extrinsic ways as well, some of which are similar to the components of importance and utility from expectancy-value models. Deci and Ryan recognize that not all behavior is intrinsically motivated. They propose four levels of external regulation or extrinsic motivation (Ryan & Deci, 2000). The first level includes what they call *external regulation.* For example, students initially may not want to work on math but do so to obtain teacher rewards and avoid punishment. These students would react well to threats of punishment or the offer of extrinsic rewards and would tend to be compliant. They would not be intrinsically motivated or show high interest, but they would tend to behave well and do try to do the work to obtain rewards or avoid punishment. Obviously, the control is external in this case and there is no self-determination on the part of the students, but this level of motivation could result in good performance or achievement.

At the next level of extrinsic motivation, students may engage in a task because they think they should and may feel guilty if they don't do the task (e.g., study for an exam). Deci and Ryan call this *introjected regulation* because the source of motivation is internal (feelings of *should, ought,* guilt) to the person but not self-determined because these feelings seem to be controlling the person. The person is not doing the task solely for the rewards or to avoid punishment; the feelings of guilt or *should* are actually internal to the person, but the source is still somewhat external because he or she may be doing the task to please others (teacher, parents). Again, Deci and Ryan assume that this level of motivation also could have some beneficial outcomes for engagement, persistence, and achievement.

The third level or style is called *identified regulation.* Individuals engage in the activity because it is personally important to them. In this case, this style is similar to what Eccles and her colleagues (Eccles et al., 1998) call the importance and utility aspects of task value. For example, a student may study hours for tests in order to get good grades to be accepted into college. This behavior represents the student's own goal, although the goal has more utility value (Wigfield & Eccles, 1992) than it does intrinsic value such as learning. The goal is consciously chosen by the student; in this sense, the locus of causality is somewhat more internal to the person as the person feels it is very important to him- or herself, not just to others such as teachers or parents. In this case, students want to do the task because it is important to them, even if it is more for utilitarian reasons rather than intrinsic interest in the task.

The final level of extrinsic motivation is *integrated regulation,* whereby individuals integrate various internal and external sources of information into their own self-schema and engage in behavior because of its importance to their sense of self. This final level is still instrumental rather than autotelic (as in intrinsic motivation), but integrated regulation does represent a form of self-determination and autonomy. As such, both intrinsic motivation and integrated regulation will result in more cognitive engagement and learning than do external or introjected regulation (Rigby et al., 1992; Ryan & Deci, 2000).

These findings from both expectancy-value, interest, and intrinsic motivation research lead to a third generalization.

Generalization 3: Higher levels of task value (importance, interest, and utility) are associated with adaptive cognitive outcomes such as higher levels of self-regulatory strategy use as well as higher levels of achievement. This generalization may not be surprising, but it is important to formulate because constructs like value, utility, and interest are often considered to be unrelated to cognitive outcomes or achievement, and they are considered to be important noncognitive outcomes. It is of course important to foster value, utility, and interest as outcomes in their own right, but the generalization suggests that by facilitating the development of task value in the classroom, an important by-product will be more cognitive engagement, self-regulation, and achievement. For example, the use of materials (e.g., tasks, texts, articles, chapters) that are meaningful and interesting to students can foster increased levels of task value. In addition, class activities (demonstrations, small group activities) that are useful, interesting, and meaningful to students will facilitate the development of task value beliefs and classroom learning.

Affective Components

Affective components include students' emotional reactions to the task and their performance (i.e., anxiety, pride, shame) and their more emotional needs for self-worth or self-esteem, affiliation, and self-actualization (cf. Covington & Beery, 1976; Veroff & Veroff, 1980). Affective components address the basic question *How does the task make me feel?* In terms of the links between cognition and affect, there has been a long history of research on the causal ordering of cognition and affect (cf. Smith & Kirby, 2000; Weiner, 1986; Zajonc, 1980, 2000). Like many of these disagreements (i.e., the debate over the causal precedence of self-concept versus achievement; Wigfield & Karpathian, 1991), the current and most sensible perspective is that the influence is bidirectional. It is not clear that there is a need to continue to argue over whether cognition precedes affect or vice versa, but rather to develop models that help educational psychologists understand (a) how, why, and when (under what conditions) does cognition precede and influence affect and (b) how, why, and when affect precedes and influences cognition. Nevertheless, in this section we do focus on how affect might facilitate or constrain cognition and learning.

In terms of the relations between affect and subsequent cognition, learning, and performance, Pekrun (1992) has suggested that there are four general routes by which emotions or mood might influence various outcomes (see also Linnenbrink & Pintrich, 2000). Three of these routes are through cognitive mediators, and the fourth is through a motivational pathway. The different models and constructs discussed in this chapter illustrate all four of these routes quite well; here, we give a brief overview of the four pathways as an advance organizer.

The first route by which emotions or mood might influence learning and performance is through memory processes such as retrieval and storage of information (Pekrun, 1992). There is quite a bit of research on mood-dependent memory with the general idea being that affective states such as mood get encoded at the same time as other information and that the affect and information are intimately linked in an associative network (Bower, 1981; Forgas, 2000). This leads to findings such as affect-state dependent retrieval, in which retrieval of information is enhanced if the person's mood at the retrieval task matches the person's mood at the encoding phase (Forgas, 2000). Forgas (2000) also notes that some findings show that mood or affective state facilitates the recall of affectively congruent material, such that people in a good mood are more likely to recall positive information and people in a bad mood are more likely to recall negative information. In other work, Linnenbrink and Pintrich (2000) and Linnenbrink, Ryan, and Pintrich (1999) suggest that negative affect might influence working memory by mediating the effects of different goal orientations. In this work, it appears that negative affect might have a detrimental effect on working memory, but positive affect was unrelated to working memory. This general explanation for the integration of encoding, retrieval, and affective processes is one of the main thrusts of the personal and situational interest research that is discussed later in this chapter.

The second mediational pathway that Pekrun (1992) suggests is that affect influences the use of different cognitive, regulatory, and thinking strategies (cf. Forgas, 2000), which could then lead to different types of achievement of performance outcomes. For example, some of the original research suggested that positive mood produced more rapid, less detailed, and less systematic processing of information, whereas negative mood resulted in more systematic, analytical, or detailed

processing of information (Forgas, 2000; Pekrun, 1992). However, recent work suggests that this position is too simplistic, and more complex proposals have been made. For example, Fiedler (2000) has suggested that positive affect as a general approach orientation facilitates more assimilation processes including generative, top-down, and creative processes, including seeking out novelty. In contrast, he suggests that negative mood reflects a more aversive or avoidance orientation and can result in more accommodation including a focus more on external information and details, as well as being more stimulus bound and less willing to make mistakes.

Other research on the use of cognitive and self-regulatory strategies in school settings has not addressed the role of affect in great detail; the few studies that have, however, show that negative affect decreases the probability that students will use cognitive strategies that result in deeper, more elaborative processing of the information (Linnenbrink & Pintrich, 2000). For example, Turner, Thorpe, and Meyer (1998) found that negative affect was negatively related to elementary students' deeper strategy use. Moreover, negative affect mediated the negative relation between performance goals and strategy use. If negative affect or emotion is a generally aversive state, it makes sense that students who experience negative affect are less likely to use deeper processing strategies because such strategies require much more engagement and a positive approach to the academic task. In contrast, positive affect should result in more engagement and deeper strategy use. This latter argument is also consistent with some of the findings from the personal and situational interest research discussed later in this chapter.

The third cognitive pathway that Pekrun (1992) suggests is that affect can increase or decrease the attentional resources that are available to students. Linnenbrink and Pintrich (2000) make a similar argument. As Pekrun (1992) notes, emotions can take up space in working memory and increase the cognitive load for individuals. For example, if a student is trying to do an academic task and at the same time is having feelings of fear or anxiety, these feelings (and their accompanying cognitions about worry and self-doubt) can take up the limited working memory resources and can interfere with the cognitive processing needed to do the academic task (Hembree, 1988; Zeidner, 1998). In fact, this general interference or cognitive load explanation is a hallmark of work on test anxiety that is discussed in more detail later in this chapter. Under this general cognitive load hypothesis, it might be expected that any emotion—positive or negative— would take up attentional resources and result in reduced cognitive processing or performance. However, this does not seem to be the case, given the differential and asymmetrical findings for positive and negative affect (Forgas, 2000), so it is clear that there is a need for further exploration of how emotions and mood can influence attentional resources and ultimately performance.

The fourth and final general pathway that Pekrun (1992) suggests is that emotions can work through their effect on intrinsic and extrinsic motivational processes. Linnenbrink and Pintrich (2000) also have suggested that motivational and affective processes can interact to influence cognitive and behavioral outcomes. Under this general assumption, positive emotions such as the experience of enjoyment in doing a task or even anticipatory or outcome-related joy of a task may lead to intrinsic motivation for the task. Of course, negative emotions such as boredom, sadness, or fear should decrease intrinsic motivation for doing the task, albeit some of them (e.g., fear) might increase the extrinsic motivation for the task. It seems clear that affective and motivational processes can interact and through these interactions can influence cognition, learning, and performance (Linnenbrink & Pintrich, 2000). At the same time, there is a need for much more research on how to effectively integrate affective processes with the motivational and cognitive processes that have been examined in much more detail. This question is sure to be one of the major areas of future research in achievement motivation research. We now turn to some of the specific constructs and models that have integrated affective processes with motivational and cognitive processes to better explain learning and achievement.

Anxiety

There is a long history of research on test anxiety and its general negative relationship to academic performance (Covington, 1992; Zeidner, 1998). Test anxiety is one of the most consistent individual difference variables that can be linked to detrimental performance in achievement situations (Hill & Wigfield, 1984). The basic model assumes that test anxiety is a negative reaction to a testing situation that includes both a cognitive worry component and a more emotional response (Liebert & Morris, 1967). The worry component consists of negative thoughts about performance while taking the exam (e.g., *I can't do this problem. That means I'm going to flunk, what will I do then?*) that interfere with the students' ability to actually activate the appropriate knowledge and skills to do well on the test. These *self-perturbing ideations* (Bandura, 1986) can build up over the course of the exam and spiral out of control as time elapses, which then creates more anxiety about finishing in time. The emotional component involves more visceral reactions (e.g., sweaty palms, upset stomach) that also can interfere with performance.

Zeidner (1998) in his review of the research on test anxiety and information processing notes that anxiety generally has a detrimental effect on all phases of cognitive processing. In the planning and encoding phase, individuals with high levels of anxiety have difficulty attending to and encoding appropriate information about the task. In terms of actual cognitive processes while doing the task, high levels of anxiety lead to less concentration on the task, difficulties in the efficient use of working memory, more superficial processing and less in-depth processing, and problems in using metacognitive regulatory processes to control learning (Zeidner, 1998). Of course, these difficulties in cognitive processing and self-regulation usually result in less learning and lower levels of performance.

In summary, research on test anxiety leads to a fourth generalization.

Generalization 4: High levels of test anxiety are generally not adaptive and usually lead to less adaptive cognitive processing, less adaptive self-regulation, and lower levels of achievement. This generalization is based on a great deal of both experimental and correlational work as reviewed by Zeidner (1998). Of course, Zeidner (1998) notes that there may be occasions when some aspects of anxiety may lead to some facilitating effects for learning and performance. For example, Garcia and Pintrich (1994) have suggested that some students, called *defensive pessimists* (Norem & Cantor, 1986), can use their anxiety about doing poorly to motivate themselves to try harder and study more, leading to better achievement. The harnessing of anxiety for motivational purposes is one example of a self-regulating motivational strategy that students might use to regulate their learning. Nevertheless, in the case of test anxiety, which is specific to testing situations, the generalization still holds that students who are very anxious about doing well do have more difficulties in cognitive processing and do not learn or perform as well as might be expected. One implication is that teachers need to be aware of the role of test anxiety in reducing performance and try to reduce the potential debilitating effects in their own classrooms.

Other Affective Reactions

Besides anxiety, other affective reactions can influence choice and persistence behavior. Weiner (1986, 1995) in his attributional analysis of emotion has suggested that certain types of emotions (e.g., anger, pity, shame, pride, guilt) are dependent on the types of attributions individuals make for their successes and failures. For example, this research suggests that a instructor will tend to feel pity for a student who did poorly on an exam because of some uncontrollable reason (e.g., death in family) and would be more likely to help that student in the future. In contrast, a instructor is more likely to feel anger at a student who did poorly through a simple lack of effort and be less willing to help that student in the future. In general, an attributional analysis of motivation and emotion has been shown repeatedly to be helpful in understanding achievement dynamics (Weiner, 1986), and there is a need for much more research on these other affective reactions in the classroom.

Emotional Needs

The issue of an individual's emotional needs (e.g., need for affiliation, power, self-worth, self-esteem, self-actualization) is related to the motivational construct of goal orientation, although the needs component is assumed to be less cognitive, more affective, and perhaps less accessible to the individual. There have been a number of models of emotional needs suggested (e.g., Veroff & Veroff, 1980; Wlodkowski, 1988), but the need for self-worth or self-esteem seems particularly relevant. Research on student learning shows that self-esteem or sense of self-worth has often been implicated in models of school performance (e.g., Covington, 1992; Covington & Beery, 1976). Covington (1992) has suggested that individuals are always motivated to establish, maintain, and promote a positive self-image. Given that this hedonic bias is assumed to be operating at all times, individuals may develop a variety of coping strategies to maintain self-worth; at the same time, however, these coping strategies may actually be self-defeating. Covington and his colleagues (e.g., Covington, 1984; Covington & Berry, 1976; Covington & Omelich, 1979a, 1979b) have documented how several of these strategies can have debilitating effects on student performance. Many of these poor coping strategies hinge on the role of effort and the fact that effort can be a double-edged sword (Covington & Omelich, 1979a). Students who try harder will increase the probability of their success, but they also increase their risk of having to make an ability attribution for failure, followed by a drop in expectancy for success and self-worth (Covington, 1992).

There are several classic failure-avoiding tactics that demonstrate the power of the motive to maintain a sense of self-worth. One strategy is to choose easy tasks. As Covington (1992) notes, individuals may choose tasks that ensure success although the tasks do not really test the individuals' actual skill level. Students may choose this strategy by continually electing easy tasks, easy courses, or easy majors. A second failure-avoiding strategy involves procrastination. For example, a student who does not prepare for a, test because of lack of time, can—if successful—attribute it to superior aptitude. On the other hand, this type of procrastination maintains an individual's sense of self-worth

because if the student is not successful, he or she can attribute the failure to lack of study time, not poor skill. Of course, this type of effort-avoiding strategy increases the probability of failure over time, which will result in lowered perceptions of self-worth; it is thus ultimately self-defeating.

In summary, although less researched, affective components can influence students' motivated behavior. Moreover, as the analysis of the self-worth motive shows (Covington, 1992), the affective components can interact with other more cognitive motivational beliefs (i.e., attributions) as well as self-regulatory strategies (management of effort) to influence achievement. However, we do not offer any generalizations for these components, given that they have not been subject to the same level of empirical testing as the other motivational components.

CONCLUSION AND FUTURE DIRECTIONS FOR RESEARCH

The four generalizations about the relations between motivational constructs and classroom cognition and learning demonstrate the importance of considering how motivation can facilitate or constrain cognition. There is no longer any doubt that academic learning is hot, so to speak, and involves motivation and affect (Pintrich, Marx, & Boyle, 1993) and that contrary to Brown et al., academic cognition is not cold and concerned only with the efficiency of knowledge and strategy use. However, that being said, there is still much we still do not understand, and there are a number of directions for future research.

First, much of the work on motivation and classroom learning has been conducted from a motivational perspective and—following a motivational paradigm—has used self-report questionnaires to measure both motivation and strategy use and self-regulated learning in actual classrooms. This work has provided us with insight into how different motivational beliefs can facilitate or constrain cognition; it has also been ecologically valid, given its focus on classrooms. At the same time, due to the inherent limitations of self-reports (Pintrich et al., 2000), the work has not been able to delve deeply into the cognitive processes and mechanisms, at least not at the level at which most cognitive psychologists operate in their own research. Accordingly, there is a need for more detailed and fine-grained analysis of the linkages between motivation and cognition, more akin to what cognitive psychologists have undertaken in their laboratory studies of cognition. Of course, this will require more experimental and laboratory work, which of course immediately lowers the ecological validity and makes it difficult to assess the participants' motivation for doing a laboratory task. However, at this point in the development of our science, these trade-offs are reasonable because we need to build on these generalizations to really understand how motivation influences basic cognitive and learning processes.

Related to this first issue, much of the work reported on in this chapter has focused on use of general learning strategies and self-regulated learning. It has not examined in much detail how motivation relates to domain-specific knowledge activation and use, such as conceptual change (Pintrich, Marx, & Boyle, 1993), or to other types of cognition such as thinking, reasoning, and problem solving in general or in domains such as mathematics or science. Accordingly, there is a need both for correlational field studies and for more experimental work on how different motivational beliefs can facilitate and constrain these cognitive and learning processes.

A third issue relates to the general developmental progression of the relations between motivation and cognition. The four generalizations offered here have been derived from work that has focused on elementary school through college students but has not really been developmental in focus. There have not been many longitudinal studies of these relations and there may important changes in the nature of these relations over time. In addition, there has not been very much research on the development of expertise or on how the nature of the relations between motivation and cognition may change as a individual gains more experience and knowledge with a particular domain of tasks (Pintrich & Zusho, 2001). Accordingly, there is a need for microgenetic studies of how motivation and cognition unfold over the course of the development of expertise with a task, as well as more macrolevel longitudinal studies of motivation and self-regulation over the life course.

Besides developmental differences, there are of course other potential individual difference variables that may moderate the relations between motivation and cognition. Gender may be one, although there have not been many gender differences in the relations between motivation and cognition, albeit there can be gender differences in levels and quality of motivation (Eccles et al., 1998; Pintrich & Schunk, 2002). More important is that for building generalizable models of motivation and cognition, there is a need to understand whether these generalizations hold across different ethnic groups and cultures. Graham (1992, 1994) has already pointed out the lack of research on African American students' motivation, let alone research on motivation and cognition in diverse populations. If educational psychologists are able to propose generalizations about motivation and cognition, then these generalizations should apply to all ethnic groups. At this time, however, little empirical research has been conducted to support the

generalizations in different groups. In addition, there is a need to test these generalizations in different cultures to see whether the same relations obtain. There may be important differences in ethnic groups or in different cultures that moderate the relations between motivation and cognition. There is a clear need for more research on these possibilities.

Finally, although this chapter has not focused on the role of classroom factors in generating, shaping, and scaffolding student motivation and cognition, classrooms do have clear effects on motivation and cognition (Bransford et al., 1999; Pintrich & Schunk, 2002). However, following the general logic of potential moderator effects for different ethnic or cultural groups, we do not know whether different classroom cultures might also moderate these four generalizations about motivation and cognition. There may be classrooms in which self-efficacy, interest, goals, or anxiety play different roles in supporting or constraining different types of cognition than in traditional classrooms. A great deal of school and classroom reform is currently on-going, and classrooms are becoming quite different places because of the technology and curriculum changes that are being implemented. These new classroom environments might afford quite different opportunities for student motivation and cognition, and we have little empirical work on such possibilities.

Nevertheless, we do know more about how motivation and cognition relate to one another in classroom settings than we did even 20 years ago. The four generalizations presented here do represent our best knowledge at this time in the development of our scientific understanding. Much more remains to be done to be sure, but the theoretical foundation and empirical base are solid and should provide important guidance not only to researchers, but also to educators who wish to improve student motivation and learning in the classroom.

REFERENCES

Abramson, L., Seligman, M., & Teasdale, J. (1978). Learned helplessness in humans: A critique and reformulation. *Journal of Abnormal Psychology, 87,* 49–74.

Ames, C. (1992). Classrooms: Goals, structures, and student motivation. *Journal of Educational Psychology, 84,* 261–271.

Ames, C., & Archer, J. (1988). Achievement goals in the classroom: Students' learning strategies and motivation processes. *Journal of Educational Psychology, 80,* 260–267.

Anderman, E., & Young, A. (1994). Motivation and strategy use in science: Individual differences and classroom effects. *Journal of Research in Science Teaching, 31,* 811–831.

Bandura, A. (1982). Self-efficacy mechanisms in human agency. *American Psychologist, 37,* 122–147.

Bandura, A. (1986). *Social foundations of thought and action: A social cognitive theory.* Englewood Cliffs, NJ: Prentice Hall.

Bandura, A. (1997). *Self-efficacy: The exercise of control.* New York: W. H. Freeman.

Blumenfeld, P., Pintrich, P. R., Meece, J., & Wessels, K. (1982). The formation and role of self-perceptions of ability in the elementary classroom. *Elementary School Journal, 82,* 401–420.

Bouffard, T., Boisvert, J., Vezeau, C., & Larouche, C. (1995). The impact of goal orientation on self-regulation and performance among college students. *British Journal of Educational Psychology, 65,* 317–329.

Bower, G. (1981). Mood and memory. *American Psychologist, 36,* 129–148.

Bransford, J., Brown, A., & Cocking, R. (1999). *How people learn: Brain, mind, experience, and school.* Washington, DC: National Academy Press.

Brown, A. L., Bransford, J. D., Ferrara, R. A., & Campione, J. C. (1983). Learning, remembering, and understanding. In J. H. Flavell & E. M. Markman (Eds.), *Handbook of child psychology: Cognitive development* (Vol. 3, pp. 77–166). New York: Wiley.

Connell, J. P. (1985). A new multidimensional measure of children's perceptions of control. *Child Development, 56,* 1018–1041.

Covington, M. V. (1984). The motive for self-worth. In R. Ames & C. Ames (Eds.), *Research on motivation in education* (Vol. 1, pp. 77–113). New York: Academic Press.

Covington, M. V. (1992). *Making the grade: A self-worth perspective on motivation and school reform.* Cambridge: Cambridge University Press.

Covington, M. V., & Beery, R. (1976). *Self-worth and school learning.* New York: Holt, Rinehart and Winston.

Covington, M. V., & Omelich, C. L. (1979a). Are causal attributions causal? A path analysis of the cognitive model of achievement motivation. *Journal of Personality and Social Psychology, 37,* 1487–1504.

Covington, M. V., & Omelich, C. L. (1979b). Effort: The double-edged sword in school achievement. *Journal of Educational Psychology, 71,* 169–182.

Deci, E. L. (1975). *Intrinsic motivation.* New York: Plenum.

Deci, E. L., & Ryan, R. M. (1985). *Intrinsic motivation and self-determination in human behavior.* New York: Plenum.

de Charms, R. (1968). *Personal causation: The internal affective determinants of behavior.* New York: Academic Press.

Dweck, C. S., & Elliott, E. S. (1983). Achievement motivation. In P. H. Mussen (Series Ed.) & E. M. Hetherington (Vol. Ed.), *Handbook of child psychology: Vol 4. Socialization, personality, and social development* (4th ed., pp. 643–691). New York: Wiley.

Dweck, C. S., & Leggett, E. L. (1988). A social-cognitive approach to motivation and personality. *Psychological Review, 95,* 256–273.

Eccles, J. S. (1983). Expectancies, values, and academic behaviors. In J. T. Spence (Ed.), *Achievement and achievement motives* (pp. 75–146). San Francisco: Freeman.

Eccles, J. S., Wigfield, A., & Schiefele, U. (1998). Motivation to succeed. In W. Damon (Series Ed.) & N. Eisenberg (Vol. Ed.), *Handbook of child psychology: Vol. 3. Social, emotional, and personality development* (5th ed., pp. 1017–1095). New York: Wiley.

Elliot, A. J. (1997). Integrating the "classic" and "contemporary" approaches to achievement motivation: A hierarchical model of approach and avoidance achievement motivation. In M. L. Maehr & P. R. Pintrich (Eds.), *Advances in motivation and achievement* (Vol. 10, pp. 143–179). Greenwich, CT: JAI Press.

Elliot, A. J. (1999). Approach and avoidance motivation and achievement goals. *Educational Psychologist, 34,* 169–189.

Elliot, A. J., & Church, M. (1997). A hierarchical model of approach and avoidance achievement motivation. *Journal of Personality and Social Psychology, 72,* 218–232.

Elliot, A. J., & Harackiewicz, J. M. (1996). Approach and avoidance achievement goals and intrinsic motivation: A mediational analysis. *Journal of Personality and Social Psychology, 70,* 461–475.

Elliot, A. J., McGregor, H., & Gable, S. (1999). Achievement goals, study strategies, and exam performance: A mediational analysis. *Journal of Educational Psychology, 91,* 549–563.

Fiedler, K. (2000). Toward an integrative account of affect and cognition phenomena using the BIAS computer algorithm. In J. Forgas (Ed.), *Feeling and thinking: The role of affect in social cognition* (pp. 223–252). New York: Cambridge University Press.

Fincham, F. D., & Cain, K. M. (1986). Learned helplessness in humans: A developmental analysis. *Developmental Review, 6,* 301–333.

Findley, M., & Cooper, H. (1983). Locus of control and academic achievement: A review of the literature. *Journal of Personality and Social Psychology, 44,* 419–427.

Foersterling, F. (1985). Attributional retraining: A review. *Psychological Bulletin, 98,* 495–512.

Ford, J. K., Smith, E. M., Weissbein, D. A., Gully, S. M., & Salas, E. (1998). Relationships of goal orientation, metacognitive activity, and practice strategies with learning outcomes and transfer. *Journal of Applied Psychology, 83,* 218–233.

Ford, M. (1992). *Motivating humans: Goals, emotions, and personal agency beliefs.* Newbury Park, CA: Sage.

Forgas, J. (2000). Introduction: The role of affect in social cognition. In J. Forgas (Ed.), *Feeling and thinking: The role of affect in social cognition* (pp. 1–28). New York: Cambridge University Press.

Garcia, T., & Pintrich, P. R. (1994). Regulating motivation and cognition in the classroom: The role of self-schemas and self-regulatory strategies. In D. H. Schunk & B. J. Zimmerman

(Eds.), *Self-regulation of learning and performance: Issues and educational applications* (pp. 127–153). Hillsdale, NJ: Erlbaum.

Graham, S. (1992). "Most of the subjects were white and middle class". Trends in reported research on African Americans in selected APA journals, 1970–1989. *American Psychologist, 47,* 629–639.

Graham, S., (1994). Motivation in African Americans. *Review of Educational Research, 64,* 55–117.

Graham, S., & Golen, S. (1991). Motivational influences on cognition: Task involvement, ego involvement, and depth of information processing. *Journal of Educational Psychology, 83,* 187–194.

Graham, S., & Weiner, B. (1996). Theories and principles of motivation. In D. Berliner & R. Calfee (Eds.), *Handbook of educational psychology* (pp. 63–84). New York: Macmillan.

Harackiewicz, J., Barron, K., Carter, S., Lehto, A., & Elliot, A. J. (1997). Determinants and consequences of achievement goals in the college classroom: Maintaining interest and making the grade. *Journal of Personality and Social Psychology, 73,* 1284–1295.

Harackiewicz, J. M., Barron, K. E., & Elliot, A. J. (1998). Rethinking achievement goals: When are they adaptive for college students and why? *Educational Psychologist, 33,* 1–21.

Harackiewicz, J. M., & Sansone, C. (1991). Goals and intrinsic motivation: You can get there from here. In M. L. Maehr & P. R. Pintrich (Eds.), *Advances in motivation and achievement: Goals and self-regulation* (Vol. 7, pp. 21–49). Greenwich, CT: JAI Press.

Harter, S. (1985). Competence as a dimension of self-evaluation: Toward a comprehensive model of self-worth. In R. Leary (Ed.), *The development of the self* (pp. 95–121). New York: Academic Press.

Harter, S. (1999). *The construction of the self: A developmental perspective.* New York: Guilford Press.

Heckhausen, H. (1991). *Motivation and action.* New York: Springer-Verlag.

Hembree, R. (1988). Correlates, causes, effects and treatment of test anxiety. *Review of Educational Research, 58,* 47–77.

Hidi, S. (1990). Interest and its contribution as a mental resource for learning. *Review of Educational Research, 60,* 549–571.

Higgins, E. T. (1997). Beyond pleasure and pain. *American Psychologist, 52,* 1280–1300.

Hill, K., & Wigfield, A. (1984). Test anxiety: A major educational problem and what can be done about it. *Elementary School Journal, 85,* 105–126.

Kaplan, A., & Midgley, C. (1997). The effect of achievement goals: Does level of perceived academic competence make a difference? *Contemporary Educational Psychology, 22,* 415–435.

Lefcourt, H. (1976). *Locus of control: Current trends in theory research.* Hillsdale, NJ: Erlbaum.

Liebert, R., & Morris, L. (1967). Cognitive and emotional components of test anxiety: A distinction and some initial data. *Psychological Reports, 20,* 975–978.

Linnenbrink, E., & Pintrich, P. R. (2000). Multiple pathways to learning and achievement: The role of goal orientation in fostering adaptive motivation. Affect and cognition. In C. Sansone & J. Harackiewicz (Eds.), *Intrinsic and extrinsic motivation: The search for optimal motivation and performance* (pp. 195–227). San Diego, CA: Academic Press.

Linnenbrink, E., Ryan, A., & Pintrich, P. R. (1999). The role of goals and affect in working memory functioning. *Learning and Individual Differences, 11,* 213–230.

Locke, E. A., & Latham, G. P. (1990). *A theory of goal setting and task performance.* Englewood Cliffs, NJ: Prentice Hall.

Maehr, M. L., & Midgley, C. (1991). Enhancing student motivation: A school-wide approach. *Educational Psychologist, 26,* 399–427.

Malone, T., & Lepper, M. (1987). Making learning fun: A taxonomy of intrinsic motivations for learning. In R. Snow & M. Farr (Eds.), *Aptitude, learning, and instruction: Vol. 3. Cognitive and affective process analyses* (pp. 223–253). Hillsdale, NJ: Erlbaum.

Meece, J., Blumenfeld, P., & Hoyle, R. (1988). Students' goal orientation and cognitive engagement in classroom activities. *Journal of Educational Psychology, 80,* 514–523.

Meece, J., & Holt, K. (1993). A pattern analysis of students' achievement goals. *Journal of Educational Psychology, 85,* 582–590.

Midgley, C., Kaplan, A., & Middleton, M. (2001). Performance-approach goals: Good for what, for whom, under what circumstances, and at what costs? *Journal of Educational Psychology, 93,* 77–86.

Middleton, M., & Midgley, C. (1997). Avoiding the demonstration of lack of ability: An under explored aspect of goal theory. *Journal of Educational Psychology, 89,* 710–718.

Miller, R., Behrens, J., Greene, B., & Newman, D. (1993). Goals and perceived ability: Impact on student valuing, self-regulation, and persistence. *Contemporary Educational Psychology, 18,* 2–14.

Murphy, P., & Alexander, P. (2000). A motivated exploration of motivation terminology. *Contemporary Educational Psychology, 25,* 3–53.

Nicholls, J. (1984). Achievement motivation: Conceptions of ability, subjective experience, task choice, and performance. *Psychological Review, 91,* 328–346.

Nolen, S. B. (1988). Reasons for studying: Motivational orientations and study strategies. *Cognition and Instruction, 5,* 269–287.

Norem, J. K., & Cantor, N. (1986). Defensive pessimism: Harnessing anxiety as motivation. *Journal of Personality and Social Psychology, 51,* 1208–1217.

Pekrun, R. (1992). The impact of emotions on learning and achievement: Towards a theory of cognitive/motivational mediators. *Applied Psychology: An International Review, 41,* 359–376.

Perry, R. (1991). Perceived control in college students: Implications for instruction in higher education. In J. Smart (Ed.), *Higher education: Handbook of theory and research* (Vol. 7, pp. 1–56). New York: Agathon Press.

Perry, R., & Dickens, W. (1988). Perceived control and instruction in the college classroom: Some implications for student achievement. *Research in Higher Education, 27,* 291–310.

Perry, R., & Magnusson, J.-L. (1989). Causal attributions and perceived performance: Consequences for college students' achievement and perceived control in different instructional conditions. *Journal of Educational Psychology, 81,* 164–172.

Perry, P., & Penner, K. (1990). Enhancing academic achievement in college students through attributional retraining and instruction. *Journal of Educational Psychology, 82,* 262–271.

Peterson, C., Maier, S., & Seligman, M. (1993). *Learned helplessness: A theory for the age of personal control.* New York: Oxford University Press.

Pintrich, P. R. (1988a). A process-oriented view of student motivation and cognition. In J. S. Stark & L. Mets (Eds.), *Improving teaching and learning through research: Vol. 57. New directions for institutional research* (pp. 55–70). San Francisco: Jossey-Bass.

Pintrich, P. R. (1988b). Student learning and college teaching. In R. E. Young & K. E. Eble (Eds.), *College teaching and learning: Preparing for new commitments: Vol. 33. New directions for teaching and learning* (pp. 71–86). San Francisco: Jossey-Bass.

Pintrich, P. R. (1989). The dynamic interplay of student motivation and cognition in the college classroom. In C. Ames & M. L. Maehr (Eds.), *Advances in motivation and achievement: Motivation-enhancing environments* (Vol. 6, pp. 117–160). Greenwich, CT: JAI Press.

Pintrich, P. R. (1999). The role of motivation in promoting and sustaining self-regulated learning. *International Journal of Educational Research, 31,* 459–470.

Pintrich, P. R. (2000a). An achievement goal theory perspective on issues in motivation terminology, theory, and research. *Contemporary Educational Psychology, 25,* 92–104.

Pintrich, P. R. (2000b). Multiple goals, multiple pathways: The role of goal orientation in learning and achievement. *Journal of Educational Psychology, 92,* 544–555.

Pintrich, P. R. (2000c). The role of goal orientation in self-regulated learning. In M. Boekaerts, P. R. Pintrich, & M. Zeidner (Eds.), *Handbook of self-regulation: Theory, research, and applications* (pp. 451–502). San Diego, CA: Academic Press.

Pintrich, P. R., & De Groot, E. V. (1990). Motivational and self-regulated learning components of classroom academic performance. *Journal of Educational Psychology, 82,* 33–40.

Pintrich, P. R., & Garcia, T. (1991). Student goal orientation and self-regulation in the college classroom. In M. L. Maehr & P. R. Pintrich (Eds.), *Advances in motivation and achievement: Goals and self-regulatory processes* (Vol. 7, pp. 371–402). Greenwich, CT: JAI Press.

Pintrich, P. R., & Garcia, T. (1993). Intraindividual differences in students' motivation and self-regulated learning. *Zeitschrift fur Padagogische Psychologie, 7,* 99–187.

Pintrich, P. R., Marx, R., & Boyle, R. (1993). Beyond "cold" conceptual change: The role of motivational beliefs and classroom contextual factors in the process of conceptual change. *Review of Educational Research, 63,* 167–199.

Pintrich, P. R., & Schrauben, B. (1992). Students' motivational beliefs and their cognitive engagement in classroom tasks. In D. Schunk & J. Meece (Eds.), *Student perceptions in the classroom: Causes and consequences* (pp. 149–183). Hillsdale, NJ: Erlbaum.

Pintrich, P. R., & Schunk, D. H. (2002). *Motivation in education: Theory, research and applications* (2nd ed.). Englewood Cliffs, NJ: Prentice Hall Merrill.

Pintrich, P. R., Smith, D., Garcia, T., & McKeachie, W. (1993). Predictive validity and reliability of the Motivated Strategies for Learning Questionnaire (MSLQ). *Educational and Psychological Measurement, 53,* 801–813.

Pintrich, P. R., Wolters, C., & Baxter, G. (2000). Assessing metacognition and self-regulated learning. In G. Schraw & J. Impara (Eds.), *Issues in the measurement of metacognition* (pp. 43–97). Lincoln, NE: Buros Institute of Mental Measurements.

Pintrich, P. R., & Zusho, A. (2001). The development of academic self-regulation: The role of cognitive and motivational factors. In A. Wigfield & J. Eccles (Eds.), *Development of achievement motivation* (pp. 249–284). San Diego, CA: Academic Press.

Renninger, K. A., Hidi, S., & Krapp, A. (1992). *The role of interest in learning and development.* Hillsdale, NJ: Erlbaum.

Rigby, C., Deci, E., Patrick, B., & Ryan, R. (1992). Beyond the intrinsic-extrinsic dichotomy: Self-determination in motivation and learning. *Motivation and Emotion, 16,* 165–185.

Rotter, J. B. (1966). Generalized expectancies for internal versus external control reinforcement. *Psychological Monographs, 80,* 1–28.

Ryan, R., & Deci, E. (2000). Intrinsic and extrinsic motivation: Classic definitions and new directions. *Contemporary Educational Psychology, 25,* 54–67.

Sansone, C., & Harackiewicz, J. (2000). *Intrinsic and extrinsic motivation: The search for optimal motivation and performance.* San Diego, CA: Academic Press.

Schiefele, U. (1991). Interest, learning, and motivation. *Educational Psychologist, 26,* 299–323.

Schunk, D. H. (1985). Self-efficacy and school learning. *Psychology in the Schools, 22,* 208–223.

Schunk, D. H. (1991). Self-efficacy and academic motivation. *Educational Psychologist, 26,* 207–231.

Shah, J., & Kruglanski, A. (2000). Aspects of goal networks: Implications for self-regulation. In M. Boekaerts, P. R. Pintrich, & M. Zeidner (Eds.), *Handbook of self-regulation* (pp. 85–110). San Diego, CA: Academic Press.

Skinner, E. (1995). *Perceived control, motivation, and coping.* Thousand Oaks, CA: Sage.

Skinner, E. (1996). A guide to constructs of control. *Journal of Personality and Social Psychology, 71,* 540–570.

Skinner, E., Chapman, M., & Baltes, P. (1988). Control, means-ends, and agency beliefs: A new conceptualization and its measurement during childhood. *Journal of Personality and Social Psychology, 54,* 117–133.

Skinner, E., Wellborn, J., & Connell, J. (1990). What it takes to do well in school and whether I've got it: A process model of perceived control and children's engagement and achievement in school. *Journal of Educational Psychology, 82,* 22–32.

Smith, C., & Kirby, L. (2000). Consequences require antecedents: Toward a process model of emotion elicitation. In J. Forgas (Ed.), *Feeling and thinking: The role of affect in social cognition* (pp. 83–106). New York: Cambridge University Press.

Stipek, D. (1996). Motivation and instruction. In D. Berliner & R. Calfee (Eds.), *Handbook of Educational Psychology* (pp. 85–113). New York: Macmillan.

Stipek, D., & Weisz, J. (1981). Perceived personal control and academic achievement. *Review of Educational Research, 51,* 101–137.

Turner, J., Thorpe, P., & Meyer, D. (1998). Students' reports of motivation and negative affect: A theoretical and empirical analysis. *Journal of Educational Psychology, 90,* 758–771.

Urdan, T. (1997). Achievement goal theory: Past results, future directions. In M. L. Maehr & P. R. Pintrich (Eds.), *Advances in motivation and achievement* (Vol. 10, pp. 99–141). Greenwich, CT: JAI Press.

VanderStoep, S. W., Pintrich, P. R., & Fagerlin, A. (1996). Disciplinary differences in self-regulated learning in college students. *Contemporary Educational Psychology, 21,* 345–362.

Veroff, J., & Veroff, J. B. (1980). *Social incentives: A life-span developmental approach.* New York: Academic Press.

Weiner, B. (1986). *An attributional theory of motivation and emotion.* New York: Springer-Verlag.

Weiner, B. (1992). *Human motivation: Metaphors, theories, and research.* Newbury Park, CA: Sage.

Weiner, B. (1995). *Judgments of responsibility: A foundation for a theory of social conduct.* New York: Guilford Press.

Wigfield, A., & Eccles, J. (1992). The development of achievement task values: A theoretical analysis. *Developmental Review, 12,* 265–310.

Wigfield, A., & Karpathian, M. (1991). Who am I and what can I do? Childrens' self-concept and motivation in achievement situations. *Educational Psychologist, 26,* 233–262.

Wlodkowski, R. (1988). *Enhancing adult motivation to learn.* San Francisco: Jossey-Bass.

Wolters, C., Yu, S., & Pintrich, P. R. (1996). The relation between goal orientation and students' motivational beliefs and self-regulated learning. *Learning and Individual Differences, 8,* 211–238.

Zajonc, R. (1980). Feeling and thinking: Preferences need no inferences. *American Psychologist, 35,* 151–175.

Zajonc, R. (2000). Feeling and thinking: Closing the debate over the independence of affect. In J. Forgas (Ed.), *Feeling and thinking: The role of affect in social cognition* (pp. 31–58). New York: Cambridge University Press.

Zeidner, M. (1998). *Test anxiety: The state of the art.* New York: Plenum.

Zimmerman, B. J., & Kitsantas, A. (1997). Developmental phases in self-regulation: Shifting from process to outcome goals. *Journal of Educational Psychology, 89,* 29–36.

Zukier, H. (1986). The paradigmatic and narrative modes in goal-guided inference. In R. M. Sorrentino & E. T. Higgins (Eds.), *Handbook of motivation and cognition: Foundations of social behavior* (pp. 465–502). New York: Guilford Press.

PART THREE

SOCIOCULTURAL, INSTRUCTIONAL, AND RELATIONAL PROCESSES

CHAPTER 7

Sociocultural Contexts for Teaching and Learning

VERA JOHN-STEINER AND HOLBROOK MAHN

The increased recognition of the roles that cultural and social factors play in human development along with advances in neuroscience and cognition research present challenges to existing theories of learning and development. Creating new explanatory theories that address the complexities of human learning is a research priority in a number of different fields (National Research Council [NRC], 1999). This new agenda is especially important if education is going to meet the needs of all students, including the linguistically and culturally diverse. In this chapter, we explore the work of the Russian psychologist Lev Semyonovich Vygotsky, whose growing influence is shaping culturally relevant and dynamic theories of learning. In spite of increasing references to his work in the fields of education and educational psychology, his theoretical foundations and his methodological approach to the study of the mind remain relatively unknown to broader audiences in those fields.

We begin our discussion of Vygotsky's contributions to educational psychology with an overview of his life and work and then discuss ways in which sociocultural theorists have built on his legacy. Vygotsky emphasized the critical roles that individuals play in creating contexts and the ways in which they internalize interactions with the environment and other people. Humans' use and appropriation of socially created symbols were at the center of this investigation. We provide a brief overview of his theories on language acquisition, sign-symbol use, and concept formation in their relationships to learning and development. We use these concepts as the primary lenses for our examination of some salient issues in educational psychology and current educational reform efforts. To support our analyses we rely on an extensive and diverse literature reflecting what has been variously referred to as sociocultural or cultural-historical research.

Sociocultural Research

The central shared theme in this family of theories is the commitment to study the acquisition of human knowledge as a process of cognitive change and transformation. Sociocultural approaches use different disciplinary tools, including discourse analysis as developed by linguists, longitudinal methods familiar to developmental psychologists, and, most frequently, qualitative methods of observation, participation, and documentation as practiced by ethnographers and cultural psychologists. This research does not fit easily into the methodological framework most familiar to readers of psychology. Our colleagues (Cole, 1996; Rogoff, 1990; Scribner & Cole, 1981; Wells, 1999) found that they could not adapt large-scale, cross-sectional methods to their inquiries into psychological processes in culturally distinct contexts. Their research demanded an interdisciplinary methodological approach for which they chose Vygotsky's. Using his approach and theoretical framework, they examined the interrelationships of social and individual processes in the construction of knowledge and the ways in which culture shapes the "apprenticeships of thinking" and diverse ways of knowing.

In their cross-cultural study of literacy among the Vai of Liberia, Scribner and Cole (1981) at first applied traditional, experimental methods of research. However, those efforts failed because the researchers had not adequately identified the specific contexts and purposes for which that population used writing. To accomplish meaningful participation by their subjects, they used ethnographic inquiries and the development of culturally relevant problem-solving tasks. Scribner and Coles' resulting work, *The Psychology of Literacy,* has influenced many sociocultural theorists because their methodological approach provides complex documentation of existing conditions and subsequent change. The emphasis is on examining real-life problems in natural settings (frequently in classrooms) and analyzing the ways in which people appropriate new learning strategies, jointly develop artifacts, and practice newly acquired competencies.

Sociocultural Approaches and Educational Psychology

The experiences of sociocultural researchers using ethnographic approaches and the theoretical framework developed by Vygotsky have contributed to a view of teaching/learning (*obuchenie* in Russian) that places culture, context, and system at the center of inquiry. Our purpose, then, is to clarify the concepts that guide sociocultural interdisciplinary research and its relevance for educational psychology. We realize that the framework we describe is not easy to convey, as it relies on philosophical assumptions and psychological ideas at variance with a common understanding of educational psychology. What, then, is its relevance to this volume? A common ground, we believe, is a shared commitment to the improvement of all children's opportunities to learn in rapidly changing, complex societies. Sociocultural researchers have a contribution to make to this objective, as much of their

work—while situated at the interface of a number of disciplines—is aimed at educational reform. This contribution is especially important today with the increased presence of linguistically and culturally diverse learners. Vygotsky's theoretical framework, with its emphasis on language, culture, social interaction, and context as central to learning and development, is particularly relevant to teaching these learners. Our intent is to describe this broad framework and then apply it to a narrower focus—the obstacles these learners face when acquiring literacy in a second language.

A Vygotskian Framework

In developing his framework, Vygotsky studied and critiqued contemporary psychologists' theories of the mind and, in particular, focused on the ways that they addressed the development of higher psychological functions. Vygotsky's theoretical approach stressed the complex relationships between the cognitive functions that we share with much of the natural world and those mental functions that are distinct to humans. He emphasized the dialectical relationship between individual and social processes and viewed the different psychological functions as part of a dynamic system. His study of the interrelationships between language and thought, and his examination of the role of concept formation in the development of both, clearly illustrates a central component of his methodological approach: *functional systems analysis.* Alexander Luria (1973, 1979) further developed the concept of a dynamic system of functions in his neurological research on the ways in which brain trauma affects cognitive processing.

Vygotsky's use of functional systems analysis to study language acquisition, concept formation, and literacy provides insights into *synthesis* and *transformation* in learning and development. This synthesis is hard to conceptualize because we are used to methodological individualism—a single focus on behavior in isolation from culturally constituted forms of knowing, productive social interaction, and dynamic contexts. In contrast, the weaving together of individual and social processes through the use of mediational tools, such as language and other symbol systems, and the documentation of their synthesis and transformation is crucial for understanding sociocultural theories and, in particular, the role that they ascribe to context. In educational psychology, where the relationship between students and teachers has been of vital concern, the emphasis throughout the twentieth century has been on the developmental unfolding of the self-contained learner. In contrast, Vygotsky stressed the important role of interaction of the individual and the social in the teaching/learning process. He defined *social* in the broadest sense, including everything cultural as social: "Culture is both a product of social life and of the social activity of man and for this reason, the very formulation of the problem of cultural development of behavior already leads us directly to the social plane of development" (Vygotsky, 1997a, p. 106). His emphasis on the interdependence of individual and social processes is one reason why his work is so important today.

The transformation of social processes into individual ones is central in sociocultural theory and contributes to its interdisciplinary nature. Within a framework based on Vygotsky's theory, it is difficult to maintain the traditional distinctions between individual and social processes, between educational and developmental psychology, between teaching and learning, and between quantitative and qualitative methods. Sociocultural approaches thus draw on a variety of disciplines, including linguistics, anthropology, psychology, philosophy, and education. Their contemporary influence is most noticeable in interdisciplinary fields such as sociolinguistics and cultural psychology.

Overview of Vygotsky's Work

Dominant psychological theorists (such as Piaget and Freud) generally ignore the role of history and culture, and consequently, they base their analysis of teaching on universal models of human nature. In contrast, Vygotsky's sociocultural framework supports pedagogical methods that honor human diversity and emphasize social and historical contexts. Although some of Vygotsky's concepts, most notably the *zone of proximal development,* have been widely described in textbooks, the full range of his contributions has yet to be explored and applied. (For overviews of Vygotsky's work, see Daniels, 1996; John-Steiner & Mahn, 1996; Kozulin, 1990; Moll, 1990; Newman & Holzman, 1993; Van der Veer & Valsiner, 1991; Veresov, 1999; Wertsch, 1985a, 1991.) There was very little biographical material in the first works of Vygotsky to appear in English. James Wertsch (1985b), a sociocultural theorist who played an instrumental role in helping make Vygotsky's ideas available in English, interviewed people who knew Vygotsky to provide biographical material for his books. Although more biographical material has become available, including important information from his daughter, Gita Vygotskaya (1999), there is still one important unresolved question: At what point was Vygotsky able to synthesize his understanding of Marx and Engels's methodological approach with his increasingly empirical knowledge of psychology? When Vygotsky began his investigation of higher mental functions, he clearly had assimilated Marx and Engels's dialectical method and their analysis of the formation and the development of human society as foundations for his own work.

Vygotsky's Experimental Method

In this chapter we look at Vygotsky's application of the dialectical method to the study of the development of human cognitive processes and emphasize, in particular, his analysis of how language and other symbol systems affect the origins and development of higher mental functions. Vygotsky used the concept of *meaning* to analyze this relationship. He also looked at the ways in which other culturally constituted symbol systems such as mathematics and writing contributed to the development of human cognition.

Other topics of shared interest to educational psychologists and sociocultural scholars include the study of memory (Leontiev, 1959/1981); of concept formation (Panofsky, John-Steiner, & Blackwell, 1990; Van Oers, 1999; Vygotsky, 1986); of teaching and learning processes (Moll, 1990; Tharp & Gallimore, 1988; Vygotsky, 1926/1997, 1978; Wells, 1999; Wells & Claxton, 2002); of mathematical development (Davydov, 1988; Schmittau, 1993); of literacy (John-Steiner, Panofsky, & Smith, 1994; Lee & Samgorinsky, 2000). We recognize how little is known in the West of the research conducted by Vygotsky, his collaborators, and his students. The reasons for the limited attention their work has received may reside in linguistic and cultural differences and also in its differing methodological approach. The Soviet scholars in the 1920s and 1930s did not use sophisticated statistics and carefully chosen experimental controls; instead, their focus was on the short- and long-term consequences of theoretically motivated interventions. Their approach centered on provoking rather than controlling change. "Any psychological process, whether the development of thought or voluntary behavior, is a process undergoing changes right before one's eyes" (Vygotsky, 1978, p. 61). These experiments, though called *formative,* had no relationship to *formative evaluation* common in the West. Griffin, Belyaeca, Soldatova, & Velikhov-Hamburg Collection (1993) described formative experiments:

> The question of interest is not *if* a certain type of subject performs correctly on a criterion task under certain conditions, but, rather, *how* the participants, including the experimenter, accomplish *what* task, using cultural artifacts. The task and goal are purposefully vague; they are underspecified initially from the perspectives of both subject and experimenter. A formative experiment specifies task and goal as the participants experience "drafts" of it being constructed, deconstructed, and reconstructed. The coordinations and discoordinations of the participants in the experiment make public "what is going on here"—what the task is. In this way of working, goal formation and context creation are a part of the material taken as data, not given a priori. (p. 125)

Our focus in this chapter is to examine how Vygotsky explained context creation through his studies of language, thought, and concept formation. Drawing on sociocultural studies based on Vygotsky's work, including our research in two, often overlapping fields—second language learning and literacy—we describe how Vygotsky's theoretical framework and methodological approach influenced our own studies. We conclude by examining how the sociocultural tradition can help us meet the challenge of providing effective education for all students, including the culturally and linguistically diverse and those with special needs. We start with an examination of the origins of the sociocultural tradition established by Vygotsky over 70 years ago.

VYGOTSKY AND SOCIOCULTURAL THEORY

How is Vygotsky to be understood? As a hidden treasure who can now be revealed to the world? As an historical figure; part icon, part relic? As the construction of a historical figure used for contemporary purposes to ventriloquate contemporary arguments? As a lost contemporary, speaking to us across time? There is no exclusively correct choice among these alternatives, he is all of these. (Glick, 1997, p. v)

Historical and Biographical Background

Lev Semyonovich Vygotsky was born in 1896 in the small Russian town of Orsha and was raised in Gomel in Belorussia. His middle-class parents were able to afford private tutoring at a time when most Jewish students were excluded from regular public schooling. His mother's influence was profound, as she introduced Vygotsky to languages, literature, and the pleasures of daily conversation. In 1913 he was fortunate to be admitted as a result of a lottery to Moscow University, where he enrolled in the medical school. After a month he transferred to the law school, from which he earned a law degree in 1917. In 1914 he also enrolled in a free university, from which he also graduated in 1917 with majors in history and philosophy (Blanck, 1990). Literature remained a lifelong passion and furnished Vygotsky with important psychological insights. He was an avid reader of the work of European scholars, in particular, Spinoza, whose work was central to his theory of emotions. Vygotsky studied and translated many works of the leading psychological thinkers of his time (including Freud, Buhler, James, Piaget, and Pavlov). After graduating from the universities, Vygotsky returned to Gomel, where he spent the next 7 years teaching and continuing his intellectual pursuits: "He taught literature and Russian at the Labor School, at adult schools, at courses for the specialization of teachers, at Workers' Faculty, and at technical schools for pressmen and

metallurgists. At the same time, he taught courses in logic and psychology at the Pedagogical Institute, in aesthetics and art history at the Conservatory, and in theater at a studio. He edited and published articles in the theater section of a newspaper" (Blanck, 1990, p. 35). His interest in teaching/learning and in psychology resulted in one of his earliest books, *Pedagogical Psychology,* published in 1926 (the American edition of this volume was retitled *Educational Psychology;* Vygotsky, 1926/1997).

The aftermath of the Russian revolution of 1917 provided new opportunities to Vygotsky. He was able to teach and travel, to present papers at psychological congresses, and to start to address the challenge of the nature of consciousness from a Marxist point of view. In 1924 he spoke at the Second All-Russian Psychoneurological Congress in Leningrad. His brilliant presentation resulted in his joining the Psychological Institute in Moscow, where he and his wife lived in the basement. A year later, Vygotsky was supposed to defend his dissertation titled *The Psychology of Art,* but he was bedridden with a serious bout of tuberculosis, the disease that killed him in 1934.

Developing a New Psychology

Once in Moscow, surrounded with young colleagues and students, Vygotsky devoted himself to the construction of a new psychology using a Marxist approach. During the turbulent years in the Soviet Union spanning from the 1917 revolution through the Civil War in the Soviet Union to Stalin's purges in the 1930s, many psychologists took part in rethinking basic issues, such as "What is human nature?" or "How do we define consciousness?" Vygotsky sought to apply Marx's dialectical method to the study of the mind rather than patch together quotations from Marx, as became the practice after Stalin took power in 1924. Vygotsky's creative, nondogmatic approach ran afoul of the ruling Stalinist bureaucracy, but he died right before the political climate became so repressive that the very discipline of psychology was temporarily obliterated.

Luria (1979), one of Vygotsky's closest collaborators, wrote, "Vygotsky was the leading Marxist theoretician among us" (p. 43). After quoting a passage from Marx on the nature of human consciousness, Luria wrote, "This kind of general statement was not enough, of course, to provide a detailed set of procedures for creating an experimental psychology of higher psychological functions. But in Vygotsky's hands Marx's methods of analysis did serve a vital role in shaping our course" (p. 43).

In addition to developing a new course for psychology, another of Vygotsky's goals was "to develop concrete ways of dealing with some of the massive practical problems confronting the USSR—above all the psychology of education and remediation" (Wertsch, 1985a, p. 11). This was a huge undertaking in an underdeveloped, poor country that had borne the brunt of World War I in terms of loss of life and economic devastation, and then had gone through a profound social revolution and a prolonged civil war. The extraordinary challenge of developing literacy in a society where the population over the age of 9 years was largely illiterate made it difficult to use traditional approaches.

In their travels throughout the Soviet Union, Vygotsky and his collaborators were able to assess the population's needs and to set up laboratories and special education programs for children who had suffered trauma. This work contributed to Vygotsky's recognition of the crisis in psychology and led him to develop a new methodological approach for psychological research that included formative experiments rather than just laboratory experiments. "The central problems of human existence as it is experienced in school, at work, or in the clinic all served as the contexts within which Vygotsky struggled to formulate a new kind of psychology" (Luria, 1979, pp. 52–53).

Vygotsky's Methodological Approach

Elsewhere, we have written more extensively on Vygotsky's theoretical foundations and methodological approach (John-Steiner & Souberman, 1978; Mahn, 1999); here, we limit ourselves to examining the theoretical foundations for his functional systems analysis. An integral component of functional systems analysis is *genetic analysis*—the study of phenomena in their origins, their development, and eventual disintegration. Although Vygotsky's use of genetic analysis is perhaps better known, functional systems analysis constitutes the core of his scientific analysis and remains one of his most significant contributions to the study of the mind.

Use of Dialectics

Although Vygotsky's focus was on the development of the mind, of human consciousness, he situated that study in the historical development of society and in concrete contexts for human development. Vygotsky drew heavily from Marx and Engels's application of dialectical materialism to the study of human social development (historical materialism). He examined the origins and evolution of phenomena, such as higher mental functions, as dynamic, contextual, and complex entities in a constant state of change. His dialectical approach had the following as central tenets: (a) that phenomena should be examined as a part of a developmental process starting with

their origins; (b) that change occurs through qualitative transformations, not in a linear, evolutionary progression; and (c) that these transformations take place through the unification of contradictory, distinct processes. He used dialectics to examine the processes that brought the mind into existence and to study its historical development. "*To study something historically means to study it in the process of change; that is the dialectical method's basic demand*" (Vygotsky, 1978, pp. 64–65). Vygotsky saw change in mental functioning not as the result of a linear process, but rather as the result of quantitative changes leading to qualitative transformations. In these transformations, formerly distinct processes became unified. Vygotsky grounded this approach in the material world, starting his analysis with the changes that occurred when humans began to control and use nature to meet their needs.

The Search for Method

This approach revealed the need for psychology to develop a new methodology that surmounted the weaknesses of both behaviorism and subjective psychology. Vygotsky (1978) wrote, "The search for method becomes one of the most important problems of the entire enterprise of understanding the uniquely human forms of psychological activity. In this case, the method is simultaneously prerequisite and product, the tool and the result of the study" (p. 65). In one of his first major works, "The Historical Meaning of the Crisis in Psychology: A Methodological Investigation," Vygotsky (1997b) subjected the dominant theories of his time to a critical analysis starting with the methodology that they inherited from the natural sciences.

This methodology based on formal logic posits a static universe in which immutable laws determine categories with impenetrable boundaries. It dichotomizes reality and creates binary contradictions: mind versus matter, nature versus culture, individual versus social, internal versus external, process versus product. Reductionist approaches "depend on the separation of natural processes into isolable parts for individual study. They have provided a rich repertoire of information about the world, but they systematically ignore the aspects of reality that involve relations between the separated processes" (Bidell, 1988, p. 330). Rather than isolating phenomena, Vygotsky approached the study of the mind by examining its origins and development and then exploring its interconnections with biological, emotional, cultural, and social systems. Luria (1979) clearly articulated the dialectical approach that Vygotsky used to study the relationship between the higher mental and elementary functions:

Influenced by Marx, Vygotsky concluded that the origins of higher forms of conscious behavior were to be found in the individual's social relations with the external world. But man is not only a product of his environment, he is also an active agent in creating that environment. The chasm between natural scientific explanations of elementary processes and mentalist descriptions of complex processes could not be bridged until we could discover the way natural processes such as physical maturation and sensory mechanisms become intertwined with culturally determined processes to produce the psychological functions of adults. We needed, as it were, to step outside the organism to discover the sources of specifically human forms of psychological activity. (p. 43)

Ethnographic Research Methods

This stepping outside of the organism led sociocultural researchers to use ethnographic methods when they found that they could not adopt large-scale, cross-sectional methods to their inquiries into the apprenticeships of thinking in Guatemala (Rogoff, 1990) or the study of literacy in Liberia (Cole, 1996; Scribner & Cole, 1981). John-Steiner and Osterreich (1975) faced a similar dilemma in her work with Navajo children when she found that traditional vocabulary tests were inappropriate in assessing the language development of these bilingual children. She needed to develop culturally appropriate methods of observation and documentation to identify the learning activities in which traditionally raised Navajo children participated and to design new methods (e.g., story retelling) for evaluating their language learning. Her work among Native American populations played an important role in the development of her theory of cognitive pluralism (John-Steiner, 1991, 1995).

Cognitive Pluralism

Through her observations in Native American schools, John-Steiner noted that Navajo and Pueblo children conveyed knowledge not only through language, but also by dramatic play, by drawing, and by reenacting their experiences, as well as in spatial and kinesthetic ways. This caused a shift in her approach to the nature of thought and theories of thinking. To show the importance of varied semiotic means—sign-symbol systems used for understanding reality and appropriating knowledge—John-Steiner (1991, 1995) developed a pluralistic rather than a monistic theory of semiotic mediation based on her studies of these learners who were raised in culturally diverse contexts. Likewise, in her studies of apprenticeships, Rogoff (1990) found the importance of visual as well as verbal semiotic means in participatory learning. Although Vygotsky's (1981) focus was more on language's mediational role, he also recognized other semiotic means: "various systems of counting; mnemonic techniques; algebraic symbol systems; works of art; writing; schemes, diagrams, maps and mechanical drawings; all sorts of conventional signs and so on" (p. 137).

The concept of cognitive pluralism provided John-Steiner with a lens to examine the impact of external activities on the acquisition and representation of knowledge. Ecology, history, culture, and family organization play roles in the patterning of events and experience in the creation of knowledge (John-Steiner, 1995). In a culture where linguistic varieties of intelligence are dominant in the sharing of knowledge and information, verbal intelligence is likely to be widespread. In cultural contexts where visual symbols predominate, as is the case in many Southwestern communities, internal representations of knowledge reflect visual symbols and tools. John-Steiner's interpretation of the multiplicity of ways in which we represent knowledge does not have the strong biological base of Gardner's (1983) theory of multiple intelligences but shares the emphasis on the diversity of knowledge acquisition and representation. Her *Notebooks of the Mind* further illustrates the concept of cognitive pluralism by examining the varied ways in which experienced thinkers make and represent meaning through the use of words, drawings, musical notes, and scientific diagrams in their planning notes (John-Steiner, 1985a). She cites the work of Charles Darwin, who relied on tree diagrams in his notebooks to capture his developing evolutionary theories in a condensed visual form.

The Role of Culture

Cross-cultural studies such as Cole, Gay, Glick, and Sharp's work (1971) on adult memory illustrate the relevance of cognitive pluralism and contribute to our understanding of the impact of culture on cognition. In their work among the Kpelle and the Vai in Liberia, Cole and his collaborators found that categories organized in a narrative form were remembered very well by native participants whereas their performance on standard (Western) tasks compared poorly with that of North American and European participants. In *Cultural Psychology*, Cole (1996) proposed that the focus of difference among distinct groups is located in the ways they organize the activity of everyday life. Sociocultural researchers have increasingly made such activity a focus for study as described by Wertsch (1991):

When action is given analytic priority, human beings are viewed as coming into contact with, and creating, their surroundings as well as themselves through the actions in which they engage. Thus action provides the entry point into analysis. This contrasts on the one hand with approaches that treat the individual primarily as a passive recipient of information from the environment, and on the other with approaches that focus on the individual and treat the environment as secondary, serving merely as a device to trigger certain developmental processes. (p. 8)

Sociocultural studies, such as those just mentioned, explore the role played by culture in shaping both thinking and context. They illustrate Vygotsky's analyses of both the growth and change of higher psychological processes through cultural development and of the relationship between the elementary and the higher mental functions.

VYGOTSKY'S ANALYSIS OF ELEMENTARY AND HIGHER MENTAL FUNCTIONS

We will term the first structures primitive; this is a natural psychological whole that depends mainly on the biological features of the mind. The second, arising in the process of cultural development, we will term higher structures since they represent a genetically more complex and higher form of behavior. (Vygotsky, 1997a, p. 83)

When Vygotsky developed his analysis of higher mental functions, psychology was divided into two dominant and distinct camps: one that relied on stimulus-response to explain human behavior and the other that relied on introspection as an alternative to empirical research. Rather than trying to reconcile these two disparate approaches, Vygotsky argued that a whole new approach was necessary to study the mind—one that critically examined psychology's origins in the natural sciences. In developing his new approach, Vygotsky focused on the origins and the development of the higher mental processes. He distinguished between mental functions that reside in biology—the reflexes of the animal kingdom (involuntary attention, mechanical memory, flight)—and those that result from cultural development—voluntary attention, logical memory, formation of concepts.

Vygotsky studied prevailing psychological explanations of the development of higher mental functions and found that they addressed the origins, development, and purposes of the elementary mental functions but not the roles of language, human society, and culture in the genesis and development of the higher mental functions. His analysis of Freud was particularly intriguing in this regard. While he accepted the subconscious, Vygotsky also commented that "the subconscious is not separated from consciousness by an impassable wall" (quoted in Yaroshevsky, 1989, p. 169). Vygotsky (1997a) felt that clinical studies that isolated features or functions of human behavior resulted in "an enormous mosaic of mental life . . . comprised of separate pieces of experience, a

grandiose atomistic picture of the dismembered human mind" (p. 4). Vygotsky's (1997a) critique of this picture became the starting place for his research.

He drew the distinction between the higher and lower mental functions along four major criteria: origins, structure, function, and their interrelationships:

By origins, most lower mental functions are genetically inherited, by structure they are unmediated, by functioning they are involuntary, and with regard to their relation to other mental functions they are isolated individual mental units. In contrast, a higher mental function is socially acquired, mediated by social meanings, voluntarily controlled and exists as a link in a broad system of functions rather than as an individual unit. (Subbotsky, 2001, ¶ 4)

Functional Systems Analysis

To study higher mental functions, Vygotsky developed a *functional systems approach,* which analyzed cognitive change as both within and between individuals. In a previous paper we defined functional systems as "dynamic psychological systems in which diverse internal and external processes are coordinated and integrated" (John-Steiner & Mahn, 1996, p. 194). A functional systems approach captures change and provides a means for understanding and explaining qualitative transformations in mental functions. In their analysis of psychological processes as functional systems formed in the course of development, Vygotsky and Luria examined the ways biological, social, emotional, and educational experiences of learners contribute to and function within dynamic teaching/learning contexts.

Research Applications

In *The Construction Zone,* Newman, Griffin, and Cole (1989) described their application of Vygotsky's and Luria's functional systems analysis to education. They conceptualized a functional system as including "biological, culturally variable, and socially instantiated mechanisms in variable relations to the invariant tasks that we investigate" (p. 72). Invariant tasks here refers to specific memory and concept sorting tasks used in clinical evaluations and experimental studies in which participants are provided with mediating tools. This approach was also used in Vygotsky's well-known block test, which consisted of 22 wooden blocks of varying sizes, shapes, and colors, with nonsense syllables on the bottom of the blocks serving as guides to systematic sorting. These syllables are mediating tools because they help the subjects to construct consistent clusters of blocks. As children acquire increasingly more sophisticated ways of sorting blocks, their progress reveals changes and reorganizations in their functional systems and not just the simple addition of new strategies.

In his research with patients with frontal lobe injuries, Luria (1973) found that their injuries limited their use of external devices so that they needed assistance in using semiotic means. He found that patients improved when clinicians provided new tools and mechanisms to solve memory and sorting tasks. Wertsch (1991) described the *semiotic mediation* between individuals and cultural or mediational tools:

> The incorporation of mediational means does not simply facilitate actions that could have occurred without them; instead as Vygotsky (1981, p. 137) noted, "by being included in the process of behavior, the psychological tool alters the entire flow and structure of mental functions. It does this by determining the structure of a new instrumental act, just as a technical tool alters the process of a natural adaptation by determining the form of labor operations." (pp. 32–33)

Elsewhere, Wertsch (1985a) described multiplication as an example of mediation because of the ways in which semiotic rules provide a system, spatially arranged, to assist the individual who is engaged in mediated action.

Cultural Tools

Sociocultural researchers examine the use of mediational tools such as talk or charts in the evolution of cognitive constructs. These external tools reflect the crystallized experiences of learners from previous generations:

> Sociocultural theory . . . can be characterized by its central claim that children's minds develop as a result of constant interactions with the social world—the world of people who do things for and with each other, who learn from each other and use the experiences of previous generations to successfully meet the demands of life. These experiences are crystallized in "cultural tools" and children have to master these tools in order to develop specifically human ways of doing things and thus become competent members of a human community. These tools can be material objects (e.g., an item of kitchenware for one specifically human way of eating and cooking), or patterns of behavior specifically organized in space and time (for example, children's bedtime rituals). Most often however, such tools are combinations of elements of different order, and human language is the multi-level tool, par excellence, combining culturally evolved arrangements of meanings, sounds, melody, rules of communication, and so forth. (Stetsenko & Arievitch, 2002)

These symbolic tools and artifacts reveal information about the ways in which humans think, reason, and form concepts.

Vygotskian approaches that focus on symbolic representation and mastery of mathematical concepts are becoming more popular in mathematics education. In their research of high school mathematics, Tchoshanov and Fuentes (2001) explored the role of multiple representations and symbolic artifacts (numerical, visual, computer graphic symbols, and discourse). These multiple semiotic means constitute a functional system that, if used flexibly by different learners, effectively contributes to the development of abstract mathematical thinking.

In studies of literacy, a functional systems analysis highlights the integration of the semantic, syntactic, and pragmatic systems in reading and focuses on ways learners from diverse backgrounds use their past learning strategies to acquire new knowledge. In a study of Hmong women, Collignon (1994) illustrates a synthesis between traditional sewing practices and English as a Second Language (ESL) instruction. The method by which sewing was taught to young Hmong women became their preferred method for learning English as a second language. Here, developmental change goes beyond the addition of a new skill as represented in many traditional learning theories; it implies synthesis and transformation through the weaving together of individual and social processes.

INDIVIDUAL AND SOCIAL PROCESSES IN LEARNING

One of Vygotsky's major contributions to educational psychology—his analysis of the interweaving of individual and social processes—is also a major theme of a recent volume that reports on a 2-year project evaluating new developments in the science of learning (NRC, 1999). Two central aspects of learning presented in the findings of this project coincide with essential concepts of Vygotsky's analysis. First is the role of social interaction and culture in teaching/learning: "Work in social psychology, cognitive psychology, and anthropology is making clear that all learning takes place in settings that have particular sets of cultural and social norms and expectations and that these settings influence learning and transfer in powerful ways" (NRC, 1999, p. 4). The second aspect is the functional systems approach: "Neuroscience is beginning to provide evidence for many principles of learning that have emerged from laboratory research, and it is showing how learning changes the physical structure of the brain and, with it, the functional organization of the brain" (NRC, 1999, p. 4). The analysis presented in this volume also supports Vygotsky's position that learning leads development.

Learning and Development

"Learning and development are interrelated from the child's very first day of life," Vygotsky (1978, p. 84) wrote. In comparing his own approach to that of some of his influential contemporaries, including Thorndike, Koffka, and Piaget, Vygotsky argued against using maturation as the central explanatory principle in development. He also had a different view on the relationship of development and social processes. "In contrast to Piaget, we believe that development proceeds not toward socialization, but toward converting social relations into mental functions" (Vygotsky, 1997a, p. 106). He further opposed approaches that reduced learning to the acquisition of skills. In contrast to traditional "banking" concepts of learning, Vygotsky (1926/1997) introduced a different metaphor:

> Though the teacher is powerless to produce immediate effects on the student, he's all-powerful in producing direct effects on him through the social environment. The social environment is the true lever of the educational process, and the teacher's overall role is reduced to adjusting this lever. Just as a gardener would be acting foolishly if he were to affect the growth of a plant by directly tugging at its roots with his hands from underneath the plant, so the teacher is in contradiction with the essential nature of education if he bends all his efforts at directly influencing the student. But the gardener affects the germination of his flowers by increasing the temperature, regulating the moisture, varying the relative position of neighboring plants, and selecting and mixing soils and fertilizers. Once again, indirectly by making appropriate changes to the environment. Thus, the teacher educates the student by varying the environment. (p. 49)

This metaphor describes a process of scaffolded learning (Wood, Bruner, & Ross, 1976) in which someone who is more expert creates the foundation for the *zone of proximal development.* Vygotsky (1978) used this concept, for which he is best known, to differentiate between two levels of development: The first, the actual level of development, is achieved by independent problem solving. This is the level of development of a child's mental functions that has been established as a result of certain already-completed developmental cycles and is measured when students are given tests to complete on their own. The second level, designated by Vygotsky as the potential level of development, describes what a child or student can accomplish with the guidance or collaboration of an adult or more capable peer. Through the concept of the zone of proximal development, learning processes are analyzed by looking at their dynamic development and recognizing the immediate needs for students'

development. The issue, however, is not resolved once we find the actual level of development. "It is equally important to determine the upper threshold of instruction. Productive instruction can occur only within the limits of these two thresholds of instruction. . . . *The teacher must orient his work not on yesterday's development in the child but on tomorrow's*" (Vygotsky, 1987, p. 211). Vygotsky developed the concept of the zone of proximal development late in his life and did not have the opportunity to elaborate it fully. Therefore, it is important to situate this concept in his more developed theory of teaching and learning.

Teaching/Learning

Vygotsky's work is characterized by its emphasis on the dialectical relationship between teaching and learning. The Russian word *obuchenie,* which means teaching/learning, speaks of a unified process, rather than the paradigmatic separation of the two: "The Russian word obuchenie does not admit to a direct English translation. It means both teaching and learning, both sides of the two-way process, and is therefore well suited to a dialectical view of a phenomenon made up of mutually interpenetrating opposites" (Sutton, 1980, pp. 169–170). Among sociocultural theorists, teaching/learning is represented as a joint endeavor that encompasses learners, teachers, peers, and the use of socially constructed artifacts:

> The importance of material artifacts for the development of culture is by now well understood; the invention of the flint knife and later of the wheel are recognized to have radically changed the possibilities for action of the prehistoric societies which invented them. . . . In more recent times, the same sort of significance is attributed to the invention of the printing press, powered flying machines and the microchip. But Vygotsky's great contribution was to recognize that an even greater effect resulted from the development of semiotic tools based on signs, of which the most powerful and versatile is speech. For not only does speech function as a tool that mediates social action, it also provides one of the chief means—in what Vygotsky (1987) called "inner speech"—of mediating the individual mental activities of remembering, thinking, and reasoning. (Wells, 1999, p. 136)

In addition to his emphasis on socially constructed artifacts, Vygotsky also stressed the role of the environment as reflected in the gardening metaphor just quoted. In conceiving of environment more broadly than the physical context, Vygotsky attributed an important role to individuals' contributions to the environment, including their emotional appropriation of interactions taking place within specific contexts.

Affective Factors

In constructing a general trajectory of development and clarifying the role of context, Vygotsky (1994) underscored the specificity of human experience through his notion of *perezhivanija*—"how a child becomes aware of, interprets, [and] emotionally relates to a certain event" (p. 341); "the essential factors which explain the influence of environment on the psychological development of children and on the development of their conscious personalities, are made up of their emotional experiences [*perezhivanija*]" (p. 339). Vygotsky developed the concept of *perezhivanija* to describe an important component of the dynamic complex system that constitutes context—what the child or student brings to and appropriates from interactions in a specific context.

The translators of the article, "The Problem of the Environment," in which Vygotsky (1994) explained his notion of *perezhivanija,* noted that the "Russian term serves to express the idea that one and the same objective situation may be interpreted, perceived, experienced or lived through by different children in different ways" (Van der Veer & Valsiner, 1994, p. 354). This notion, often left out of discussions of context, was a central consideration for Vygotsky.

Sociocultural Approaches to Context

The word "context" is open to a multitude of interpretations. The etymology of "context" from the Latin *contextera* (to weave together) is closely related to that of "text," the Latin *textum* (that which is woven, a fabric; Skeat, 1995). This explanation of the word helps capture two central elements in Vygotsky's theoretical framework: the dialectical weaving together of individual and social processes in learning and development, and the recognition that human activity takes place in a social and historical context and is shaped by and helps shape that context. Vygotsky viewed humans as the creators and the creations of context and felt that their activity reflected the specificity of their lives rather than ahistorical, universal principles. In emphasizing the active role of learners, we see them, along with other sociocultural theorists (i.e., Rogoff, 1990; Tharp & Gallimore, 1988), as members of learning communities. Such an approach helps synthesize a frequently dichotomized view of teaching and learning in education where the works of learning theorists are isolated from the findings of developmentalists.

In studying learning communities, sociocultural theorists have made the cultural and social aspects of context a focus for their studies (Cole, 1996; Forman, Minick, & Stone, 1993; Lave, 1988; Lave & Wegner, 1991; Rogoff, 1990).

Tharp, Estrada, Dalton, and Yamuchi (2000) highlighted the educational importance of context in *Teaching Transformed:* "Effective teaching requires that teachers seek out and include the contexts of students' experiences and their local communities' points of view and situate new academic learning in that context" (p. 26). Tharp et al. illustrated a growing consensus among educational reformers of the significance of contextualized activities. They provided an example of contextualized activity consisting of sixth graders collecting height and weight data in the children's home communities and discussing the best way to represent the data while acquiring the relevant mathematical concepts. They further suggested that "the known is the bridge over which students cross to gain the to-be-known. This bridging or connecting is not a simple association between what is already known and what is new; it is an active process of sorting, analysis, and interpretation" (p. 29).

Assessment and Context

An important component in this bridging is accurate assessment of what the student brings to the classroom. Sociocultural approaches to assessment value the role that context plays and are concerned with the ways in which its influence can be described and measured. Wineburg (2001) contrasts Vygotskian approaches to traditional approaches that focus on the individual.

> [I]n contrast to traditional psychometric approaches, which seek to minimize variations in context to create uniform testing conditions, Vygotsky argued that human beings draw heavily on the specific features of their environment to structure and support mental activity. In other words, understanding how people think requires serious attention to the context in which their thought occurs. (Alternative Approach section, ¶ 5)

Language Use and Context

Lily Wong-Fillmore (1985) contributes to a broader understanding of context through her studies of teachers' language use in the classroom. In analyzing successful environments for learning a second language, she examines both the linguistic input of teachers as well as their ability to contextualize language. If teachers put their lessons in the context of previous ones, they

> anchor the new language in things that they have reason to believe the students already know. If the students remember what they did or learned on the earlier occasion, the prior experience becomes a context for interpreting the new experience. In lessons like this, prior experiences serve as the contexts within which the language being used is to be understood. (p. 31)

These studies illustrate that context is a widely shared concern among sociocultural theorists and one that virtually needs redefinition for different situations.

Culture and Context

The specific description of context is not separated from the process being studied and needs to include cultural considerations, as each context may call for distinct approaches. John-Steiner, for example, found that story retelling was an effective elicitation method for many children, but was not as effective with Navajo children until traditional winter tales were substituted for the generic stories she had used with mainstream students. Similarly, Tharp found that collaborative groupings that he used successfully with Hawaiian students did not work with Native American students where considerations of clan and gender had to be included in decisions about how to pair children. Griffin et al. (1993) include other elements that play a role in context: "the semantic significance of grammatical constructions, the media and mediation, communicative acts, social roles and classes, cultural (and ethnic) conventions and artifacts, institutional constraints, past history, and negotiated goals imaging the future" (pp. 122–123).

Sociocultural researchers whose studies focus on the workplace as a setting for learning also stress the importance of context. The Finnish researcher Yrjö Engeström (1994, 1999) and his collaborators (Engeström, Miettinen, & Punamäki, 1999) looked at school, hospital, outpatient, and industrial contexts. In their recent work they emphasized *knotworking,* which they define as "the notion of knot refers to a rapidly pulsating, distributed and partially improvised orchestration of collaborative performance between otherwise loosely connected actors and activity systems" (1999, p. 346). Among linguists, Michael Halliday (1978) is most emphatic in emphasizing the role of context, as seen in his influential book, *Language as Social Semiotic.* He succinctly summarized the relationship between language and context: "The context plays a part in what we say; and what we say plays a part in determining the context" (p. 3). This echoes Vygotsky's emphasis on the individual shaping context and language shaping the individual.

MEDIATION AND HIGHER PSYCHOLOGICAL PROCESSES

If language is as ancient as consciousness itself, if language is consciousness that exists in practice for other people, and therefore for myself, then it is not only the development of thought but the development of consciousness as a whole that is connected with the development of the word. (Vygotsky, 1987, p. 285)

The way that language and, in particular, *word meaning* developed was a central concern of Vygotsky's and is key to understanding the intricate dialectical relationship he described between language, thought, and consciousness. In this section we examine one of the most influential and most original aspects of Vygotsky's legacy: his analysis of language's mediational role in the development of higher mental functions. In his study of the higher mental functions, Vygotsky (1997a) described two distinct streams of development of higher forms of behavior, which were inseparably connected but never merged into one:

These are, first, the processes of mastering external materials of cultural development and thinking: language, writing, arithmetic, drawing; second the processes of development of special higher mental functions not delimited and not determined with any degree of precision and in traditional psychology termed voluntary attention, logical memory, formations of concepts, etc. (p. 14)

Vygotsky's analyses of the external materials—language, writing, and arithmetic—help us understand psychology's role in guiding educational approaches to teaching/learning. An important part of this analysis of the development of higher mental functions is his theory of concept formation and its relationship to language acquisition and verbal thinking.

Language Acquisition

Contemporary scholars have added to Vygotsky's theoretical claim that language is central to human mental development in a variety of ways, including showing "how symbolic thinking emerges from the culture and community of the learner" (NRC, 1999, p. 14). Vygotsky (1981) included important cultural and psychological tools in addition to language, such as mathematical symbols, maps, works of art, and mechanical drawings that serve to shape and enhance mental functioning. These socially constructed semiotic means are transmitted and modified from one generation to the next. Language, as the chief vehicle of this transmission, is a cultural tool (Wertsch, 1998).

Vygotsky examined semiotic mediation, including language, developmentally. In *Thinking and Speech* (1987) he wrote, "The first form of speech in the child is purely social" (p. 74). In this short statement he captures the fact that human survival requires the sustained attention to and care of others. In comparison to that of other species, the behavior of human infants is immature and indeterminate. Therefore, their earliest efforts at communication require careful, finely tuned interpretations provided by caregivers:

> From the moment of birth this adaptation places the infant into social relations with . . . adults and through them into a sociocultural system of meaning. Thus the requirements of care allow the infant's individuality to develop with cultural sources and also provide the communicative formats necessary for the development of language. (John-Steiner & Tatter, 1983, p. 87)

Socialization of Attention

In order to begin understanding adult references, the very young learner has to share an attentional focus with the adult through a process of *socialization of attention* (Zukow-Goldring & Ferko, 1994). While children are dependent on their caregivers, the windows of opportunity to create joint attention are short because their attention is intermittent with their gazes shifting from faces to objects:

> We have called this process in which caregivers specify culturally relevant and socially shared topics perceptually for the child's benefit *socializing attention*. In socializing attention caregivers use both gesture and speech. In these situations the occurrence of a linguistic device, say a name, is actually coincident *both* with the presence of some stable pattern in the environment, the labeled topic of attention, and with the action directing attention to that object. (p. 177)

Before infants appropriate linguistic meaning they have to follow the adult's gaze and have their modes of expression interpreted. The connection between objects and their referents is not easy to establish because it requires multiple cognitive processes and it proceeds by fits and starts. This connection is also linked to the development of practical thinking, to the toddlers' manipulation of objects, and to their practical activities as well as to emotional and expressive behavior. "Laughter, babbling, pointing, and gesture emerge as means of social contact in the first months of the child's life" (Vygotsky, 1987, p. 110).

Language and Thought

Vygotsky conceived of two distinct and originally separate processes: prelinguistic development of thought and preintellectual development of expressive and social communication. These two paths of development become interdependent when children shift from passively receiving words to actively seeking language from the people around them. The merger of the expressive verbal and intellectual lines of development gives rise to the earliest forms of verbal thinking

and communicative, intelligent speech. This change is manifested in children's constantly asking for names of things, leading to an extremely rapid increase in their vocabulary. In this process the "child makes what is the most significant discovery of his life" (Vygotsky, 1987, pp. 110–111), the discovery that each object has a *name,* a permanent symbol, a sound pattern that identifies it.

Since Vygotsky first described this qualitative change in young learners from learning words item by item to the 2-year-old's active search for names, the field of language acquisition has grown enormously. Research by Scaife and Bruner in 1975 highlighted the Vygotskian notion of shared attention and joint activity that starts at a very young age. They demonstrated that infants follow the gaze of adults and pay selective attention to those aspects of their environment that are also of interest to those around them. Katherine Nelson (1989) showed that the creation of scripts by the infant and adult, necessary for language acquisition, also supports shared attention. "Children like to talk and learn about familiar activities, scripts or schemes, the 'going to bed' script or the 'going to McDonald's' script" (NRC, 1999, p. 96). Bruner (1985) argued that sharing goes beyond the immediacy of gaze and reciprocal games—that it illustrates the principle of *intersubjectivity,* which is critical to the acquisition of language.

Intersubjectivity and Language Acquisition

Rommetveit (1985, p. 187) relates the intersubjectivity of the young child to an adult's as he described an inherent paradox in intersubjectivity. His description started by drawing on William James's (1962) quote, *"You accept my verification of one thing. I yours of another. We trade on each other's truth"* (p. 197):

> *Intersubjectivity must in some sense be taken for granted in order to be attained.* This semiparadox may indeed be conceived of as a basic pragmatic postulate of human discourse. It captures in a condensed form an insight arrived at by observers of early mother-child interaction and students of serious communication disorder. (p. 189)

Explanations of language acquisition that rely on biologically hardwired mechanisms tend to diminish the role of social interaction and intersubjectivity. The debates in the field between those who look to innate mechanisms and those who look to the sustaining impact of social interaction and finely tuned exchanges help highlight the distinction that Vygotsky drew between basic biological processes on the one hand and language as socially constructed by interactive processes on the other. These debates have important implications for education:

> The social interaction of early childhood becomes the mind of the child. Parent-child interactions are transformed into the ways the developing child thinks, as are interactions with siblings, teachers and friends. . . . In schools, then, dedicated to the transformation of minds through teaching and learning, the social processes by which minds are created must be understood as the very stuff of education. (Tharp et al., 2000, p. 45)

Individual and Social Processes

The interdependence between social and individual processes in language acquisition described by sociocultural researchers illustrates the unity of distinct processes—an essential tenet of Vygotsky's methodological approach. Vygotsky examined the contradictory aspects of this unity. Children are born into a culture and develop language through the communicative intent that adults bring to their child's utterances, but there is another process at play: the development of a child's individual personality: "Dependency and behavioral adaptability provide the contextual conditions for the correlative processes of individuation and enculturation, both of which are essential to the development of language" (John-Steiner & Tatter, 1983, p. 87).

In tracing the process of individuation in the development of the child, Piaget's early research, especially his concept of egocentric speech, a form of language in which the speaker uses speech for noncommunicative, personal needs influenced Vygotsky. Vygotsky described the separation and transformation of social (interpersonal) speech into private speech—utterances that are vocalized but not for communicative purposes (Diaz & Berk, 1992)—and of private speech into inner (intrapersonal) speech. Vygotsky's analysis of this internalization process provides an important example of the utility of a functional systems approach. For Vygotsky, developmental change unifies the usual polarity between those processes that occur among individuals (studied by sociologists and anthropologists) and those that occur within individuals (the domain of psychologists). In his well-known *genetic principle* he proposed that each psychological process occurs first between the child and a more experienced adult or peer, and then gradually becomes internalized by the child. Jerome Bruner (1962) captured this aspect of sociocultural theory when he wrote that "it is the internalization of overt action that makes thought, and particularly the internalization of external dialogue that brings the powerful tool of language to bear on the stream of thought" (p. vii).

Internalization of Speech

The process of internalization, however, is not accomplished through simple imitation; rather, it involves a complex interplay of social and individual processes that include transmission, construction, transaction, and transformation. The internalization process described by Vygotsky has had a number of interpretations and remains a topic of interest among sociocultural theorists (Chang-Wells & Wells, 1993; Galperin, 1966; John-Steiner & Mahn, 1996; Packer, 1993; Wertsch & Stone, 1985). The internalization of language and its interweaving with thought was a central focus of Vygotsky's analysis. An important concept in this examination was *semiotic mediation*.

Humans learn with others as well as via the help of historically created semiotic means such as tools, signs, and practices. Yaroshevsky and Gurgenidze (1997) described the centrality language held for Vygotsky in semiotic mediation and, therefore, in the development of thinking:

> Then the word, viewed as one of the main variants of the cultural sign, acquired the meaning of a psychological tool whose interference changes (along with other signs) the natural, involuntary mental process into a voluntarily guided process, or more exactly, a self-guided process. The attempt to understand the character of the interrelations between the different mental processes made Vygotsky think about the instrumental role of the word in the formation of the functional systems. (p. 351)

Vygotsky used a functional systems approach to examine the relationship between thought and word. His analysis revealed both word and thought as changing and dynamic instead of constant and eternal. Their relationship was part of a complex process at the center of which Vygotsky discovered *word meaning* and *verbal thinking*.

Word Meaning and Verbal Thinking

Instead of isolating language as an object for study (linguistics) and thinking as another object for study (psychology), Vygotsky studied their unity and sought an aspect of that unity that was irreducible and that maintained the essence of the whole. The concept of word meaning provided him with the foundation for examining children's use of inner speech and verbal thinking:

> Word meaning is a unity of both processes [thinking and speech] that cannot be further decomposed. That is, we cannot say that word meaning is a phenomenon of either speech or thinking. The word without meaning is not a word but an empty sound. Meaning is a necessary, constituting feature of the word

itself. It is the word viewed from the inside. This justifies the view that word meaning is a phenomenon of speech. In psychological terms, however, word meaning is nothing other than a generalization, that is a concept. In essence, generalization and word meaning are synonyms. Any generalization—any formation of a concept—is unquestionably a specific and true act of thought. Thus, word meaning is also a phenomenon of thinking. (Vygotsky, 1987, p. 244)

In his analysis of the relationships between thought and word, Vygotsky examined the origins of both and then traced their developments and interconnectedness, concluding that "these relationships emerge and are formed only with the historical development of human consciousness. They are not the precondition of man's formation but its product" (Vygotsky, 1987, p. 243).

Inner Speech

Using word meaning as a unit of analysis, Vygotsky (1987) studied the internalization of speech and its relationship to verbal thinking. He concluded that "inner speech is an internal plane of verbal thinking which mediates the dynamic relationship between thought and word" (p. 279). He investigated children's appropriation of socially elaborated symbol systems as a critical aspect of their learning-driven development. These investigations led to his most fully elaborated application of the concept of internalization—the transformation of communicative language into inner speech and further into verbal thinking:

> The movement from inner to external speech is not a simple unification of silent speech with sound, a simple vocalization of inner speech. This movement requires a complete restructuring of speech. It requires a transformation from one distinctive and unique syntax to another, a transformation of the sense and sound structure of inner speech into the structural forms of external speech. External speech is not inner speech plus sound any more than inner is external speech minus sound. The transition from inner to external speech is complex and dynamic. It is the transformation of a predicative, idiomatic speech into the syntax of differentiated speech which is comprehensible to others. (pp. 279–280)

As the condensed, telegraphic, predicative style of inner speech is hard to access overtly, it rarely occurs in ordinary conversation. Vygotsky relied on literary examples to illustrate inner speech. The most famous was the account from Tolstoy's *Anna Karenina* in which Kitty and Levin declare their love for each other by relying solely on the first letters of words. Vygotsky's interpretation of this conversation

of condensed exchanges was that the participants were so deeply involved with each other that there was minimal psychological distance between them. Their expressive means then became reduced to the smallest possible units as well.

Word Meaning and Word Sense

While looking for related forms that reveal the dynamics of inner speech, John-Steiner (1985a) examined the notebooks of writers. In several writers' diaries, she found condensed, jotted notes through which these writers, including Virginia Woolf, Henry Miller, and Dostoyevsky, planned their chapters and books. "Use of a telegraphic style makes it possible to gallop ahead, exploring new connections. . . . [O]ften when there is a transcribed record of the way in which writers plan their work, it takes the form of these very condensed thoughts" (p. 112). These planning notes that John-Steiner named *inner speech writing* reveal two aspects of verbal thinking, word *sense* and word *meaning*:

> A word's sense is the aggregate of all the psychological facts that arise in our consciousness as a result of the word. Sense as a dynamic, fluid, and complex formation has several zones that vary in their stability. Meaning is only one of these zones of the sense that the word acquires in the context of speech. It is the most stable, unified, and precise of these zones. In different contexts, a word's sense changes. In contrast, meaning is a comparatively fixed and stable point, one that remains constant with all the changes of the word's sense that are associated with its use in various contexts. (p. 276)

Vygotsky utilizes different genres of language use to distinguish between word *meaning* and word *sense*. Actors use "sense" to convey the specific, contextually bound ways in which a person acts and feels. Poets use meaning and sense to convey the general and specific possibilities of a poetic image or an unexpected phrase. Meaning and sense are transformed for children through development as they reflect the changing complexity of experience.

> Our desire to differentiate the external and sense aspects of speech, word, and thought has concluded with the attempt to illustrate the complex form and subtle connections of the unity that is verbal thinking. The complex structure of this unity, the complex fluid connections and transitions among the separate planes of verbal thinking, arise only in process of development. The isolation of meaning from sound, the isolation of word from thing, and the isolation of thought from word are all necessary stages in the history of the development of concepts. (Vygotsky, 1987, pp. 283–284)

It is to Vygotsky's developmental examination of concept formation that we turn next.

Language Acquisition and Concept Formation

Language depends on classification. In order to label two objects with the same word, the child needs to identify them as similar in some crucial way. However, to achieve effective categorizing, children traverse through a number of phases. At first, they tend to apply words to "a series of elements that are externally connected in the impression that they have had on the child but not unified internally among themselves" (Vygotsky, 1987, p. 134). While a child's word meaning is not complete and is diffuse in its application, it will at times externally coincide with the adult's word meaning. At those points of intersection the child will "establish social interaction through words that have meaning" (p. 134), even though the child's meanings differ from those of the adult.

At the beginning of the process of categorizing objects, children develop a syncretic image, a "heap" of "objects that are in one way or another combined in a single fused image in the child's representation and perception" (Vygotsky, 1987, pp. 134–135). Through a process of trial and error, children begin to refine the syncretic image but do so "guided not by the objective connections present in the things themselves, but by the subjective connections that are given in their own perception" (p. 135). Objects that are in close proximity with each other in everyday life, but do not share any common features, may be placed together in a heap. On the other hand, the child may just have a subjective feeling that certain things belong together. When children no longer mistake the connections in their impression of objects for connections between the objects themselves, Vygotsky says that they have passed to a mode of thinking in complexes.

Complexive Thinking

In complexive thinking, "the world of objects is united and organized for [children] by virtue of the fact that objects are grouped in separate though interconnected families" (Vygotsky, 1987, p. 136). In a concept-sorting task, developed for Head Start children, John and Goldstein (1967) found that first graders tended to group cards functionally. For instance, they placed a barn, a farmer, and a horse into a single group, rather than placing the farmer with other working people and the horse with other animals. Kozulin (1990) illustrated such concrete and functional grouping of objects that complement each other (e.g., saucers and spoons). At an early stage of language use "word meanings are best

characterized as family names of objects that are united in complexes or groups. What distinguishes the construction of the complex is that it is based on connections among the individual elements that constitute it as opposed to abstract logical connections" (Vygotsky, 1987, p. 136). In order to be included in a group or complex, any empirically present connection of an element is sufficient. Language plays a significant role in facilitating the connection of objects and events.

Double Stimulation and Concept Formation

Vygotsky developed a method with Lev Sakharov to study the different stages of concept formation. They referred to their approach as the *method of double simulation*—a method in which both objects and mediating artifacts such as signs are introduced. In this case, the researchers used nonsense syllables on the bottom of the blocks of different colors, shapes, heights, and surfaces. The task of the participants was to discover a systematic way of grouping these blocks. As mentioned earlier, the youngest children grouped blocks in syncretic ways, whereas the next-older children displayed thinking in complexes. The achievement of true concepts (that of a triangle, for instance) requires not only that the mature and developing learners have a joint understanding and a common referent when they point to a triangle, but also that the developing learner has mastered the processes of analysis, separation, and abstraction—all needed to achieve the mastery of true concepts. The research Vygotsky (1987) described in chapter 5 of *Thinking and Speech* is relevant to the study of categorization and to the study of language development. It documents how communication is linked to concept formation, and how concepts become more fully mastered by children and adolescents. As semantic mastery is achieved, *meaning* continues to develop further through social interaction and learning.

Everyday and Scientific Concepts

Vygotsky was not fully satisfied by these studies because he realized the artificiality of the tasks, particularly in their reliance on nonsense syllables in guiding the sorting process. He subsequently moved to another aspect of concept formation, drawing a basic distinction between everyday and scientific concepts—work partially informed by Piaget's work on spontaneous and nonspontaneous concepts. Everyday concepts are developed in the context of the child's experiences in noninstructional settings and are supported by the young learner's engagement in joint activities. Adults do not teach these concepts in a systematic fashion. A frequently used example of an everyday concept is that of *brother*. A child correctly identifies his own brother or those of his friends without being able to define it in a more systematic way as a "male sibling." Vygotsky (1987) defined scientific concepts as ones usually introduced to the child in school and ones that are part of systems: *"The system emerges only with the development of the scientific concept and it is this new system that transforms the child's everyday concepts"* (p. 223).

Vygotsky (1987) noted that before scientific concepts could emerge, higher mental functions such as "voluntary attention, logical memory, abstraction, comparison, and differentiation" (p. 170) needed to develop. When scientific concepts do emerge, there is a "complete restructuring of the child's spontaneous concepts" (p. 236), with scientific concepts providing "the gate through which conscious awareness enters the domain of the child's concepts" (p. 193). Vygotsky added, "The basic characteristic of [scientific concepts'] development is that they have their source in school instruction. Therefore, the general problem of instruction and development is fundamental to the analysis of the emergence and formation of scientific concepts" (p. 214).

Context and Concept Formation

In a study conducted in the upper Amazon region of Brazil, Elvira Lima (1998) examined concept formation in her work with Indian teachers from the Tikuna tribe. Over a period of three years, she learned about the ways in which members of this community as a part of their learning relied on drawing as culturally shaped mediation: "Tikuna culture uses body and nature dynamically as supports for graphic representation to convey meaning. Even orality in the school culture is functionally articulated with visual production" (Lima, 1998, p. 97). Drawing is thus a central mode of expression among this large tribe, whose members are committed to cultural continuity while embracing traditional schooling as a mode of survival. In her work with the lay teachers (individuals who were simultaneously teaching and obtaining their certification), Lima introduced two scientific concepts: the *developing child* and the *milieu* adopted from the French cultural-historical theorist, Henri Wallon.

Because drawing and graphic representations are central to the way in which the Tikuna deal with their world, this was the medium that Lima used to capture key features of the tribe's world, including the central role of the forest in which they live. She also relied on the notion of contrast for teaching the concept of *milieu* and showed a documentary on the Masai people from Africa. The words in the documentary were in English, but the teachers who did not know English captured the "meaning" of the film by relying on the visual elements and the music. They conveyed their own understandings of this unfamiliar milieu by drawings assembled into a mural and placed on the wall of the school. Verbal and written activities, including contrastive structures between the tribe's native language and Portuguese, further developed the concept. The study of the milieu led easily to exploring the lay teachers' concepts of how the Tikuna child develops through instruction designed to construct a scientific concept of the developing child.

Lima is an ethnographer and a cognitive psychologist who uses all possible resources to teach and gather information. Her intent in her work with the Tikuna teachers was to help them understand the developing Tikuna child. Lima had the lay teachers rely on their observations represented in drawings and stories to construct their understanding of the concept of the developing child. She and the teachers went through a systematic analysis of the themes in these drawings. They supplemented their representations with diagrams, verbal abstractions, and written language.

Lima also relied on other learning and planning experiences that had taken place in the Tikuna village. Her students, the lay teachers, participated in a mathematics course in which spatial concepts that the villagers needed to build a school and living quarters were used as the basis of teaching and learning. The development of the blueprints and the subsequent building of the school provided these teachers with an opportunity to weave everyday with scientific concepts. Lima helped them to reflect on these experiences through verbal and written means and provided them with grammatical constructions that captured concepts not immediately accessible in their native language by introducing the appropriate terminology in Portuguese.

This study also illustrates the concept of *formative experiments,* a notion mentioned earlier. Lima had the opportunity to evaluate how her students, the lay teachers, appropriated the concepts that she was teaching them over time. She alternated between intensive periods of teaching and travel in Brazil and abroad. After each of her trips she examined some of the new educational materials her students had developed during her absence. They reflected an increasingly sophisticated understanding of the environment, a development that reflected the mutual coconstruction of academic-scientific concepts through "drawings, written Tikuna and Portuguese, oral Tikuna, and diagrams as equally relevant mediation" (Lima, 1998, p. 103). She described the learning styles of her students as the dialectical weaving together of experiential and scientific knowledge where "success [is] defined as the learning of formal knowledge [that] depends on the creation of a pedagogy that is culturally appropriate but that does not restrict the student to what he or she already experiences culturally" (p. 103).

Lima's research illustrates the dynamic interweaving of various means of representation into a functional system. It also illustrates the way in which a native language and a second language may complement each other in expanding conceptual understanding while enriching the bilingual's sensitivity to the expanding possibilities of semantic understanding.

Concepts and First and Second Language Acquisition

In order to explain his theory of concept formation, Vygotsky related the differences between scientific and everyday concepts to the differences between acquiring one's native language and a second language. Children learn their native languages without conscious awareness or intention. In learning a second language in school, the approach "begins with the alphabet, with reading and writing, with the conscious and intentional construction of phrases, with the definition of words or with the study of grammar" (Vygotsky, 1987, p. 221). He added that with a second language the child first must master the complex characteristics of speech, as opposed to the spontaneous use of speech in acquiring the native language. In contrast to first language acquisition, where the young child focuses primarily on communicative intent, second-language learners are more conscious of the acquisition process. They are eager to approximate native use. As they listen to themselves while communicating, they refine and expand their conscious knowledge of both their first and second languages. Second-language speakers' conscious awareness of their syntax and vocabulary is well documented by researchers who focus on repairs in speech. These corrections of one's utterances during speech are common. An example of such self-repair is "I see much friends . . . a lot of friends" (Shonerd, 1994, p. 86). In suggesting that these corrections reflect the speakers' efforts to refine their linguistic knowledge, Shonerd quoted Wolfgang Klein: "The language learner must make his raincoat in the rain" (p. 82).

Vygotsky's (1987) examination of the relationships between first and second language acquisition shows how both "represent the development of two aspects of a single process, the development of two aspects of the process of verbal thinking. In foreign language learning, the external, sound and phasal aspects of verbal thinking [related to everyday concepts] are the most prominent. In the development of scientific concepts the semantic aspects of this process come to the fore" (pp. 222–223). He added another comparison between scientific concepts and learning a second language. The meanings a student is acquiring in a second language are mediated by meanings in the native language. Similarly, prior existing everyday concepts mediate relationships between scientific concepts and objects (Vygotsky, 1987). Vygotsky

cautions, however, that the examination of the profound differences in the acquisition processes of first and second language acquisition

> must not divert us from the fact that they are both aspects of speech development. The processes involved in the development of written speech are a third variant of this unified process of language development; it repeats neither of the two processes of speech development mentioned up to this point. All three of these processes, the learning of the native language, the learning of foreign languages, and the development of written speech interact with each other in complex ways. This reflects their mutual membership in a single class of genetic processes and the internal unity of these processes. (Vygotsky, 1987, p. 179)

This unity Vygotsky found in inner speech, verbal thinking, and meaning.

MAKING MEANING IN THE CLASSROOM

Using Vygotsky's theoretical approach and methodology, Mahn (1997) examined ways in which inner speech, verbal thinking, and meaning making unified the processes of first and second language acquisition and writing in English as a second language. We examine his study in some depth to illustrate how students' prior experiences and *perezhivanija* help constitute the teaching/learning contexts. Mahn (1997) also shows how Vygotsky's notions of inner speech and verbal thinking can help develop efficacious pedagogical approaches for culturally and linguistically diverse students.

A Study of Second Language Writers

In a three-year-long study, Mahn (1997) examined the role of inner speech, verbal thinking, culture, discourse, and affect in students learning to write in a second language. This study involving 74 students from 27 countries revealed ways in which second-language learners make meaning through written communication with their instructor. Mahn used Vygotsky's theoretical framework to analyze students' perceptions of the use of written dialogue journals with their instructor as a means to build their self-confidence and to help them with academic writing. Their perceptions, which were gathered through interviews, questionnaires, reflective quick writes, their journals, and in academic essays, helped illuminate the role played by inner speech and verbal thinking in their composing processes. Particularly revealing were their descriptions of obstacles in the movement to written speech, or as one student artfully phrased it, "blocks in the elbow" and the effect of these blockages on inner speech and verbal thinking. Mahn used a functional system analysis to examine the alternative systems or channels that students used when blockages occurred.

Although Mahn's study analyzed other aspects of the writing process, we focus here on his use of Vygotsky's theoretical framework in three areas: (a) the way bilingualism exemplifies the unification of diverse language processes; (b) the relationship between verbal thinking and the internalization and externalization of speech; and (c) the relationship between verbal thinking and writing. Mahn focused on the students' descriptions of the interruptions or blockages in both the internalization and externalization processes that students described when writing in a second language. Students reported that the main cause of interruption of these processes was an overemphasis on correctness in their previous instruction. They described the tension between having a thought or concept and becoming lost in their struggle to produce it correctly. This is similar to the tension Vygotsky described between the external manifestations of speech, an everyday concept, and the development of meanings in a system, a scientific concept.

Vygotsky and Bilingualism

The functional systems approach Vygotsky used to analyze this tension was also used in his analysis of bilingualism. He was particularly interested in the issue of bilingualism because of the many nationalities represented in Russia, which presented complicated challenges for educators. In his discussion of the psychological and educational implications of bilingualism, Vygotsky stressed an important aspect of a functional systems approach discussed previously: the unification of diverse processes. The achievement of balanced, successful bilingualism entails a lengthy process. On the one hand, it requires the separation of two or more languages at the production level, that is, the mastery of autonomous systems of sound and structure. At the same time, at the level of verbal meaning and thought, the two languages are increasingly unified. "These complex and opposing interrelationships were noted by Vygotsky, who had suggested a two-way interaction between a first and second language. . . . The effective mastery of two languages, Vygotsky argued, contributes to a more conscious understanding and use of linguistic phenomena in general" (John-Steiner, 1985b, p. 368). His concept of inner speech played an important role in the separation and combination of the two languages.

Writing and Inner Speech

In his analysis of verbal thinking, Vygotsky (1987) traced the internalization of word meaning from external speech to its innermost plane—the affective-volitional plane that lies behind

and motivates thought. He also examined the reverse process of externalization, which "moves from the motive that gives birth to thought, to the formation of thought itself, to its mediation in the internal word, to the meanings of external words, and finally, to words themselves. However, it would be a mistake to imagine that this single path from thought to word is always realized" (p. 283). The study of language has revealed the "extraordinary flexibility in the manifold transformations from external to inner speech" (John-Steiner, 1985a, p. 118) and from inner speech to thought. In Mahn's study (1997) students described using dialogue journals to overcome obstacles in both the internalization and externalization processes and to expedite inner speech's function of facilitating "intellectual orientation, conscious awareness, the overcoming of difficulties and impediments, and imagination and thinking" (Vygotsky, 1987, p. 259).

The differentiation of speech for oneself and speech for others, a process in which social interaction plays a crucial role, is an important part of this process. An interlocutor in oral speech helps achieve intersubjective understanding through intonation, gesture, and creation of a meaningful context centered on communicative intent. This recognition of speech for others leads to a differentiation between speech for others and speech for oneself. Until that realization, egocentric speech is the only mode a child uses. The differentiation of speech functions leads to the internalization of "speech for oneself" and then to inner speech. When the differentiation is extensive, we "know our own phrase before we pronounce it" (Vygotsky, 1987, p. 261). It is the struggle to "know the phrase" that can provide a stumbling block for the second-language learners. For them, the movement from thought to production is often problematic, especially if they have learned English through a grammar-based approach.

The way that a child or student acquires a second language has an impact on the development of inner speech and verbal thinking. Inner speech functions differently for children learning the second language simultaneously than it does for those learning the second language through traditional, grammar-based approaches in school. If awareness of correctness dominates, affective factors, including those that result from different cultural practices, may impede the internalization of English and disrupt verbal thinking. A number of students, who described this disruption in their thinking or composing processes, added that when they wrote in their dialogue journals without worrying about correctness, their ideas were both more accessible and easier to convey. They also reported that disruption was less likely to occur if they were able to describe an event that occurred in the context of their native language using their native language and one that occurred in an English context in English.

Writing and Verbal Thinking

John-Steiner (1985a) underlined the importance of drawing on the perspectives of writers when looking at aspects of verbal thinking: "A psychological description of the processes of separation and unification of diverse aspects of language is shallow without a reliance on the insights of writers, they who have charted the various ways in which ideas are woven into text" (p. 111). Because it is a more deliberate act, writing engenders a different awareness of language use. Rivers (1987) related Vygotsky's discussion of inner speech and language production to writing as discovery: "As the writer expands his inner speech, he becomes conscious of things of which he was not previously aware. In this way he can write more than he realizes" (p. 104). Zebroski (1994) noted that Luria looked at the reciprocal nature of writing and inner speech and described the functional and structural features of written speech, which "inevitably lead to a significant development of *inner speech*. Because it delays the direct appearance of speech connections, inhibits them, and increases requirements for the preliminary, internal preparation for the speech act, written speech produces a rich development for inner speech" (p. 166).

Obstacles in Writing

Problems arise for second language writers when the "rich development" becomes mired during the time of reflection, when they perform mental "grammar checks" on the sentences under construction. Students' descriptions of this process indicate that during this grammar check they lose the unity between inner speech and external speech and consequently lose their ideas. Vygotsky (1987) wrote that whereas "external speech involves the embodiment of thought in the word, in inner speech the word dies away and gives birth to thought" (p. 280). The problem for students who focus excessively on correctness is that the words do not become the embodiment of thought; nor do they "die." They remain until the student creates what they feel is a grammatically correct sentence. In the meantime, the thought dies, and the motivation for communication diminishes. When the students take the focus off correctness, words die as they enter the realm of thought. Vygotsky (1987) took the analysis of internalization beyond even this realm, locating the motivation for thought in the affective/volitional realm:

> Thought has its origins in the motivating sphere of consciousness, a sphere that includes our inclinations and needs, our interests and impulses and our affect and emotion. The affective and volitional tendency stands behind thought. Only here do we find the answer to the final "why" in the analysis of thinking. (p. 282)

When students used only those words or grammatical forms that they knew were correct, they felt that they could not clearly transmit ideas from thought to writing. If they did not focus on correctness, they took chances and drew on the word meanings in their native language as a stimulus to verbal thinking. This helped them develop their ideas (e.g., "Journals helped me to think first; to think about ideas of writing instead of thinking of the grammar errors that I might make"). They describe how verbal thinking helped in the move to written speech because it was initiated with the intent of communicating an idea rather than producing the correct form—be it vocabulary, spelling and usage, sentence structure, genre, or rhetoric. The fluency entailed with writing in dialogue journals depends on the simultaneous operation of inner speech and external speech and writing, an operation that is diminished when the focus of inner speech is on correctness.

Shaughnessey (1977) observed that the sentence unfolding on paper is a reminder to the basic writer of the lack of mechanical skill that makes writing down sentences edited in the head even more difficult. In more spontaneous writing, writers do not have a finely crafted sentence in their head; rather, as in oral speech, the writer, at the time of initiation, will not know where the sentence will end. For ESL students, the focus on form short-circuits the move to inner speech, and the thought process and writing are reduced to the manipulation of external speech forms. Students reported that with too much attention to correctness they would lose their ideas or not be able to convey them (e.g., "When I'm afraid of mistakes, I don't really write the ideas I have in mind"). Students related that through writing in their dialogue journals they decreased the attention to surface structure and experienced an increased flow of ideas inward and outward. With this increased flow, a number of students reported that they benefited from the generative aspect of verbal thinking (e.g., "With the journal you have one idea and start writing about it and everything else just comes up"; "They seemed to help me focus on what I was writing in the sense that I let the words just flow and form by themselves"; "The journals we did in our class were useful to me because it helped me form my thoughts"; "Journal helps me to have ideas flow and write them down instead of words sticking in my mind").

In written speech the absence of intersubjective understanding and meaningful communicative interaction makes production difficult and constrained. The traditional reaction to students' text with a focus on error provides interaction that diminishes the intersubjective understanding and the motivation to communicate. This not only makes production more difficult but also impairs the internalization of speech. In contrast, students reported that dialogue journals helped to promote intersubjective understanding and the creation of a context for meaningful communication. This helped them overcome blockages in both the internalization and externalization processes. Through the interaction in the journals and by shifting the focus from form and structure to meaning, students reflected that they could think better in English (i.e., that they could use inner speech more effectively). They also commented that their motivation to communicate ideas facilitated production of written speech. With the focus on meaning, the students could get their ideas on paper and then revise the form and structure rather than trying to work out the grammar in their heads before committing the thought to paper (e.g., "I wrote while thinking rather than formulating sentences in the mind"). Attention to mechanical correctness in verbal thinking caused the students' ideas to evanesce not into thought, but into thin air.

Vygotsky's Influence on Literacy Research

Mahn's study resonates with the findings of other writing researchers who focus on the processes of writing and not just on the final product. Writing theorists such as Emig (1971), Britton (1987), Langer and Applebee (1987), and Moffett (1981) constructed a new approach to literacy that relied on some of Vygotsky's key ideas. In a similar vein, Vygotsky's influence has been important in the development of reading theories by Clay (1991), Holdaway (1979), Goodman and Goodman (1990), and Taylor (1998). Among the topics explored by these literacy researchers are sociocultural considerations of the literacy socialization process (Panofsky, 1994).

Foundations for Literacy

In the "Prehistory of Written Language," Vygotsky (1978) examined the roles of gesture, play, and drawing in this socialization for literacy. He analyzed the developmental processes children go through before schooling as a foundation for literacy learning in school. He argued that gestures lay the groundwork for symbol use in writing: "The gesture is the initial visual sign that contains the child's future writing as an acorn contains a future oak. Gestures, it has been correctly said, are writing in the air, and written signs frequently are simply gestures that have been fixed" (Vygotsky, 1978, p. 107). In a study on parent-child book reading, Panofsky (1994) also emphasized the importance of connecting visual signs with verbal representations. She suggested that children need assistance in interpreting pictures in books, a process that contributes to the move from signs to representations. An example of such a move is a parent's saying, "See that tear?

He is crying" (Panofsky, 1994, p. 232). Anne Dyson (1989), who has shown the importance of dramatic play, drawing, and writing in the development of child writers, also emphasized the multidimensionality of literacy.

Vygotsky (1978) described the interweaving of diverse forms of representation such as scribbles accompanying dramatic play: "A child who has to depict running begins by depicting the motion with her fingers, and she regards the resultant marks and dots on paper as a representation of running" (p. 107). When children use symbols in drawing, writing development continues. As they begin to draw speech, writing begins to develop as a symbol system for children.

Implications for Teaching

The emphasis on the functions of writing for children is paramount among contemporary literacy scholars (Smith, 1982). Such an emphasis also characterizes Vygotsky's thoughts and predates some of the current, holistic approaches to reading and writing: "Teaching should be organized in such a way that reading and writing are necessary for something . . . writing must be 'relevant to life' . . . and must be taught naturally . . . so a child approaches writing as a natural moment in her development, and not as training from without. . . . In the same way as they learn to speak, they should be able to learn to read and write" (1978, pp. 117–119). The contributors to a recently published volume, *Vygotskian Perspectives on Literacy Research* (Lee & Smagorinsky, 2000), expand on the zone of proximal development (Lee, 2000), present cross-cultural studies of teachers' socialization and literacy instruction (Ball, 2000), and present different approaches to classroom literacy practices (Gutiérrez & Stone, 2000), among other topics. Literacy learning, from a sociocultural perspective, is situated in a social milieu and arises from learners' participation in a community's communicative practices. These studies highlight the relationships between context and individual and social processes and at the same time underscore the need to develop environments for literacy teaching/learning that honor linguistic and cultural diversity.

An underlying current in these studies is the need for social action, especially among those who rely on critical literacy, defined by Shor (2001, ¶ 4) as "language use that questions the social construction of the self." Harste (2001) drew the connection between critical literacy and social action:

> While critical literacy involves critical thinking, it also entails more. Part of that "more" is social action built upon an understanding that literacy positions individuals and in so doing, serves some more than others. As literate beings, it behooves us

not only to know how to decode and make meaning but also to understand how language works and to what ends, so that we can better see ourselves in light of the kind of world we wish to create and the kind of people we wish to become. (Introduction, ¶ 7)

In her article "Selected Traditions: Readings of Vygotsky in Writing Pedagogy," Courtney Cazden (1996) highlighted a current of critical theorists (Burgess, 1993; Kress, 1993) who rely on Vygotsky and address issues of power, conflict, and resistance. She also highlighted other researchers who use inner speech, verbal thinking, and literacy to relate social and cultural factors to the development of the cognitive processes involved in reading and writing (Britton, 1987; Moffet, 1981).

In this chapter we chose to examine the ways in which Vygotsky's ideas help to understand and redefine teaching/learning contexts by focusing on language acquisition, verbal thinking, concept formation, second language acquisition, and literacy. In the last section we briefly describe some of Vygotsky's work in other domains—special education, assessment, and collaboration—as they relate to efforts to reform education to meet the needs of all students.

VYGOTSKY'S CONTRIBUTIONS TO EDUCATIONAL REFORM

Two recent volumes—*Learning for Life in the 21st Century: Sociocultural Perspectives on the Future of Education* (Wells & Claxton, 2002) and *Vygotsky and Culture of Education: Sociocultural Theory and Practice in the 21st Century* (Ageev, Gindis, Kozulin, & Miller, in press)—add to the already considerable corpus of research that uses Vygotsky's theory to understand educational psychology and educational reform. As mentioned previously, Vygotsky played a significant role in shaping education in the Soviet Union following the 1917 revolution. One of the great challenges for educators then, as now, was providing appropriate education for students with special needs. These students had been severely neglected under the czar: "A tragic product of the years of war, revolution, civil strife, and famine was the creation of an army of homeless, orphaned, vagrant, abandoned, and neglected children—about seven million of them by 1921–1922" (Knox & Stevens, 1993, p. 3). Vygotsky's approach to educating these children speaks across time to educators today who are developing inclusive education environments that serve the needs of special learners and all students. His views on the social construction of concepts of "disability," "defect" (which was the common term in Vygotsky's time), or "exceptionality" also speak to us across the decades.

Special Needs

A child whose development is impeded by a defect is not simply a child less developed that his peers; rather he has developed differently . . . a child in each stage of his development in each of his phases, represents a qualitative uniqueness, i.e., a specific organic and psychological structure; in precisely the same way a handicapped child represents a qualitatively different, unique type of development. (Vygotsky, 1993, p. 30)

In a special issue of *Educational Psychologist* devoted to Vygotsky's ideas, Boris Gindis (1995) described the emphasis that Vygotsky placed on the variety of psychological tools that had been developed to help students with special needs: "Vygotsky pointed out that our civilization has already developed different means (e.g., Braille system, sign language, lip-reading, finger spelling, etc.) to accommodate a handicapped child's unique way of acculturation through acquiring various symbol systems" (p. 79). Signs, as used by the deaf, constitute a genuine language with a complex, ever-expanding lexicon capable of generating an infinite number of propositions. These signs, which are embedded in the rich culture of the deaf and represent abstract symbols, may appear pantomimic, but their meaning cannot be guessed by nonsigners. The "hypervisual cognitive style" (Sacks, 1989, p. 74) of the deaf, with a reliance on visual thought patterns, is of interest in this regard: "The whole scene is set up; you can see where everyone or everything is; it is all visualized with a detail that would be rare for the hearing" (p. 75). Sign language is but one example of the multiplicity of semiotic means in the representation and transformation of experience. The diversity of the semiotic means and psychological tools is of special interest to educators who work in multicultural settings and with children who have special needs.

In two special issues of *Remedial and Special Education* devoted to sociocultural theory (Torres-Velásquez, 1999, 2000), educators and researchers reported on studies using Vygotsky's theory as a framework and addressed two important considerations: the ways in which the needs of children are determined and the ways in which their performance is measured and assessed. Linguistic and cultural diversity among students with special needs adds a layer of complexity to this process:

The transitory nature of our populations and the existence of public laws mandating that all children be treated equally in schools have increased the diversity of learners in classrooms. Children gifted, average, and those with special needs are learning together in the same classroom. Understanding and recognizing who these children are is a prerequisite for guiding their ability to learn. Understanding the importance of students' perceptions of themselves as learners, and the effect of these perceptions on self-esteem is paramount. Since it is the obligation of all teachers to find a way for all children to learn, knowing how each child processes information is essential. (Glazer, 1998, p. 37)

The challenge is to develop assessment that is authentic and that is sensitive to the diversity in the ways students process and communicate information.

Assessment and Standardized Testing

Assessment is an integral part of the teaching/learning context and is becoming even more so with the emphasis from politicians and school administrators on the results of standardized testing. There are broad implications for pedagogy resulting from the push to make such testing more pervasive. Some of Vygotsky's earliest work critiqued the standardized intelligence tests being developed at that time:

Vygotsky is rightfully considered to be the "founding father" of what is now known as "dynamic assessment" (Minick, 1987; Guthke & Wingenfeld, 1992; Lidz, 1995). In the early 1930s, at the height of the enthusiasm for IQ testing, Vygotsky was one of the first (if not the only one in his time) who defined IQ tests' limitations based on his understanding of disability as a process, not a static condition, and on his understanding of development as a dialectical process of mastering cultural means. He noted that standardized IQ tests inappropriately equalize the natural and cultural processes, and therefore are unable to make the differentiation of impaired functioning that can be due to cultural deprivation or can be the result of organic damage. (Gindis, 1999, p. 337)

One of the most important considerations of dynamic assessment is making sure that there is not a bias against linguistically and culturally diverse students. Sybil Kline (2001), through the Center for Research on Education, Diversity, and Excellence, produced a report on the development of alternative assessment for such students. The Opportunity Model is based on cultural-historical theory and the research of Vygotsky and Luria. This nondiscriminatory approach to special education evaluation has as key features "a socioculturally-based alternative to the IQ test, and the introduction of the concepts of 'teachability,' 'opportunity niche,' and 'cognitive nurturance' into the special education eligibility and intervention process" (Kline, 2001, ¶ 3).

Sociocultural critics also argue that because knowledge construction is social, "a focus on individual achievement

actually distorts what individuals can do" (Wineberg, 1997). There is reluctance among those researchers who rely on traditional psychometrics to try to assess the role of collaboration, as they view even minimal collaboration as a threat:

If, on the other hand, we view teaching through the lens of Vygotsky and other sociocultural theorists, we will see collaboration in a different light. Instead of worrying that collaboration wreaks havoc on the meaning of the overall score, we may view the lack of collaboration as a more serious defect than its inclusion. (Wineburg, 1997, A different way section, ¶ 1)

Collaboration in Education

In describing Vygotsky's work, we have highlighted his emphasis on the collaboration involved in the coconstruction of thinking, meaning, and consciousness. Vygotsky described a synthesis that evolved from the sustained dynamic of individuals engaged in symbolic behavior both with other humans, present and past, and with material and nonmaterial culture captured in books, artifacts, and living memory. He achieved some of his most important insights by cultivating intellectual interdependence with his immediate collaborators, and with other psychologists whose writings he studied and translated into Russian (including Piaget, Freud, Claparede, Montessori, and Kohler). In this collaborative context sociocultural theory was born (John-Steiner, 2000).

The benefits of collaboration are numerous; they include the construction of novel solutions to demanding issues and questions. Through joint engagement and activity, participants in collaboration are able to lighten the burdens of their own past socialization while they coconstruct their new approaches. A fine example of this aspect of collaboration is provided by Rogoff, Goodman-Turkanis, and Bartlett (2001) in the students', returning student-tutors', teachers', and parents' descriptions of an innovative educational community. The multiple voices document participatory learning in the building of a democratic collaborative and also underscore the importance of dialogue in education.

Vygotsky's focus on dialogue was shared by his contemporaries Bakhtin and Voloshinov, and it remains a central focus for sociocultural theorists today (Wells, 1999). Dialogue and the social nature of learning guided the work of Paulo Freire (1970) and provided the theoretical foundation for collaborative/cooperative learning:

The critical role of dialogue, highlighted by both Freire and Vygotsky, can be put into effect by the conscious and productive reliance upon groups in which learners confront and work through—orally and in writing—issues of significance to their lives. (Elsasser & John-Steiner, 1977, p. 368)

It is only when participants are able to confront and negotiate their differences and, if necessary, to modify the patterns of their relationship that learning communities can be sustained. As Rogoff and her collaborators concluded: "Conflicts and their resolutions provide constant opportunities for learning and growth, but sometimes the learning is not easy" (2001, p. 239). In some cases, these conversations become so difficult that a facilitator from outside of the group is asked to assist. In spite of these difficulties, the experience of multiple perspectives in a dynamic context provides particularly rich opportunities for cognitive and emotional growth for learners of all ages.

Collaborative efforts to bring about transformative change require a prolonged period of committed activity. Issues of time, efficiency, sustained exchanges, and conflict resolution face schools that are building learning communities, but most schools are reluctant to undertake these issues. For some participants in school reform such a task is too time-consuming, and the results appear too slowly. When participants leave working, egalitarian communities, their abandonment highlights the ever-present tensions between negotiation and bureaucratic rule. Successful collaboration requires the careful cultivation of trust and dignified interdependence, which contrasts with a neat, efficient division of labor. These issues highlight the important role that affective factors play in the building of such learning communities and in creating safe, engaging, and effective teaching/learning contexts.

CONCLUSION

Faced with myriad concrete problems, teachers frequently question the need for abstract theories. Vygotsky suggested that practice challenges us to develop theory, as do the experiences of those confronted with daily problems needing urgent solutions. Practice inspires theory and is its ultimate test: "Practice pervades the deepest foundations of the scientific operation and reforms it from beginning to end. Practice sets the tasks and serves as the supreme judge of theory, as its truth criterion. It dictates how to construct the concepts and how to formulate the laws" (Vygotsky, 1997b, p. 305). To meet the challenges facing educators today, we need the influence of both theory and practice to answer the urgent questions facing us at the beginning of this new century: How should we deal with the increasing linguistic and cultural diversity of our students? How do we document learning-based gains in our classrooms? How do we balance skills, knowledge, and

creativity? How do teachers overcome their isolation? The theory we have presented here does not answer all these questions, but it provides tools for thinking about these questions, which differ from the ones posed to us in our schooling. We were taught to look for ways to simulate learning and memory tasks in controlled situations; in contrast, sociocultural researchers study these tasks in the classroom as they develop. Their observations are complex and hard to summarize. They point to funds of knowledge that children bring to the classroom, to resistance among learners who are marginalized, to children's development of concepts that reflect their families and their own daily experiences, to the importance of dialogue between learners, teachers, and texts, and to the multiplicity of semiotic means and the diversity of teaching/learning contexts both within and outside of schools. Sociocultural scholars and educators view school as a context and site for collaborative inquiry, which requires the practice of mutual respect and productive interdependence.

We have emphasized an approach that looks at human activities from the perspective of functional systems: the organization and reorganization of learners' problem-solving strategies, which integrate the social and individual experiences of learners with the culturally shaped artifacts available in their societies. In this chapter we examined *meaning making* in the acquisition of first and additional languages through a functional-systems lens.

The concept of meaning making, which was a central focus for Vygotsky at the end of his life, is one that we place at the center of discussions about educational reform. The ways in which we communicate through culturally developed means need to be valued in schools. By valuing all of the ways in which children represent and appropriate knowledge, we can begin to meet the challenges that face educational psychology in the twenty-first century: "The success of educational experiences depends on methods that foster cultural development, methods that have as a starting point the developmental processes of students and their accumulated knowledge, the developmental milieu, social practices, and the political meaning of education itself" (Lima, 1998, p. 103).

We began this chapter with a reference to the National Research Council's project on teaching and learning, and we conclude it with a quote from the book on that project that summarizes the challenge that lies ahead for educational reform:

There are great cultural variations in the ways in which adults and children communicate, and there are wide individual differences in communications styles within any cultural community. All cultural variations provide strong supports for children's development. However, some variations are more likely than others to encourage development of the specific kinds of knowledge and interaction styles that are expected in typical U.S. school environments. It is extremely important for educators—and parents—to take these differences into account. (NRC, 1999, pp. 96–97)

REFERENCES

Ageev, V., Gindis, B., Kozulin, A., & Miller, S. (Eds.). (in press). *Vygotsky's educational theory in cultural contexts.* New York: Cambridge University Press.

Ball, A. (2000). Teacher's developing philosophies on literacy and their use in urban schools: A Vygotskian perspective on internal activity and teacher change. In C. D. Lee & P. Smagorinsky (Eds.), *Vygotskian perspectives on literacy research: Constructing meaning through collaborative inquiry* (pp. 226–255). New York: Cambridge University Press.

Bidell, T. (1988). Vygotsky, Piaget and the dialectic of development. *Human Development, 31,* 329–348.

Blanck, G. (1990). The man and his cause. In L. C. Moll (Ed.), *Vygotsky and education: Instructional implications of sociohistorical psychology* (pp. 31–58). New York: Cambridge University Press.

Britton, J. (1987). Vygotsky's contribution to pedagogical theory. *English in Education* (UK), *21,* 22–26.

Bruner, J. (1962). Introduction. In E. Hanfmann & G. Vakar (Eds.), Vygotsky, *Thought and language* (pp. v–x). Cambridge, MA: MIT Press.

Bruner, J. (1985). *Child's talk: Learning to use language.* New York: W. W. Norton.

Burgess, T. (1993). Reading Vygotsky: Notes from within English teaching. In H. Daniels (Ed.), *Charting the agenda: Educational activity after Vygotsky* (pp. 1–29). New York: Routledge.

Cazden, C. (1996). Selective traditions: Readings of Vygotsky in writing. In D. Hicks (Ed.), *Discourse, learning, and schooling* (pp. 165–188). New York: Cambridge University Press.

Chang-Wells, G. L. M., & Wells, G. (1993). Dynamics of discourse: Literacy and the construction of knowledge. In E. A. Forman, N. Minick, & C. A. Stone (Eds.), *Contexts for learning: Sociocultural dynamics in children's development* (pp. 58–90). New York: Oxford University Press.

Clay, M. (1991). *Becoming literate: The construction of inner control.* Portsmouth, NH: Heinemann.

Cole, M. (1996). *Cultural psychology: A once and future discipline.* Cambridge, MA: Harvard University Press.

Cole, M., Gay, J., Glick, J., & Sharp, D. (1971). *The cultural context of learning and thinking: An exploration in experimental anthropology.* London: Tavistock, Methuen.

Collignon, F. F. (1994). From "Paj Ntaub" to paragraphs: Perspectives on Hmong processes of composing. In V. John-Steiner, C. P. Panofsky, & L. W. Smith (Eds.), *Sociocultural approaches to language and literacy: An interactionist perspective* (pp. 331–346). New York: Cambridge University Press.

Daniels, H. (1996). *An introduction to Vygotsky.* New York: Routledge.

Davidov, V. V. (1988). Problems of developmental teaching: The experience of theoretical and experimental psychological research. *Soviet Education,* Part 1: *30*(8), 15–97; Part II: *30*(9), 3–38; Part III: *30*(10), 3–77.

Diaz, R., & Berk, L. (1992). *Private speech: From social interaction to self-regulation.* Hillsdale, NJ: Erlbaum.

Dyson, A. (1989). *Multiple worlds of child writers.* New York: Teachers College Press.

Elsasser, N., & John-Steiner, V. (1977). An interactionist approach to advancing literacy. *Harvard Educational Review, 47*(3), 355–369.

Emig, J. (1971). *The composing processes of twelfth graders.* Urbana, IL: National Council of Teachers of English.

Engeström, Y. (1994). Teachers as collaborative thinkers: Activity-theoretical study of an innovative teacher team. In I. Carlgren, G. Handal, & S. Vaage (Eds.), *Teachers' minds and actions: Research on teachers' thinking and practice.* Bristol, PA: Falmer Press.

Engeström, Y. (1999). Innovative learning in work teams: Analyzing cycles of knowledge creation in practice. In Y. Engeström, R. Miettinen, & R. Punamäki, (Eds.), *Perspectives on activity theory* (pp. 377–404). New York: Cambridge University Press.

Engeström, Y., Miettinen, R., & Punamäki, R. (1999). *Perspectives on activity theory.* New York: Cambridge University Press.

Forman, E. A., Minick, N., & Stone, C. A. (Eds.). (1993). *Contexts for learning: Sociocultural dynamics in children's development.* New York: Oxford University Press.

Freire, P. (1970). *Pedagogy of the oppressed.* New York: Continuum.

Galperin, P. Y. (1966). On the notion of internalization. *Soviet Psychology, 12*(6), 25–32.

Gardner, H. (1983). *Frames of mind: The theory of multiple intelligences.* New York: Basic Books.

Gindis, B. (1995). The social/cultural implication of disability: Vygotsky's paradigm for special education. *Educational Psychologist, 30*(2), 77–82.

Gindis, B. (1999). Vygotsky's vision: Reshaping the practice of special education for the 21st Century. *Remedial and Special Education, 20*(6), 333–340.

Glazer, S. (1998). *Assessment is instruction: Reading, writing, spelling, and phonics for all learners.* Norwood, MA: Christopher-Gordon.

Glick, J. (1997). Prologue. In R. Reiber (Ed.), *The history of the development of higher mental functions. The collected works of L. S. Vygotsky: Vol. 4. Problems of the theory and history of psychology* (pp. v–xvi). New York: Plenum.

Goodman, K., & Goodman, Y. (1990). Vygotsky in a whole-language perspective. In L. C. Moll (Ed.), *Vygotsky and education: Instructional implications of sociohistorical psychology* (pp. 223–251). New York: Cambridge University Press.

Griffin, P., Belyaeca, A., Soldatova, G., & Velikhov-Hamburg Collective. (1993). Creating and reconstituting contexts for educational interactions, including a computer program. In E. A. Forman, N. Minick, & C. A. Stone (Eds.), *Contexts for learning: Sociocultural dynamics in children's development* (pp. 120–152). New York: Oxford University Press.

Guthke, J., & Wingenfeld, S. (1992). The learning test concept: Origins, state of the art, and trends. In H. C. Haywood & D. Tzuriel (Eds.), *Interactive Assessment.* New York: Springer-Verlag.

Gutiérrez, K. D., & Stone, L. D. (2000). Synchronic and diachronic dimensions of social practice: An emerging methodology for cultural-historical perspectives on literacy learning. In C. Lee & P. Smagorinsky (Eds.), *Vygotskian perspectives on literacy research: Constructing meaning through collaborative inquiry* (pp.150–164). New York: Cambridge University Press.

Halliday, M. A. K. (1978). *Language as social semiotic: The social interpretation of language and meaning.* Baltimore, MD: University Park Press.

Harste, J. (2001). *Supporting critical conversations in classrooms.* Retrieved August 2001, from http://www.indiana.edu/~langed/faculty/harste/paper.html

Holdaway, D. (1979). *The foundations of literacy.* New York: Ashton Scholastic.

James, W. (1962). Pragmatism's conception of truth. In W. Barrett & H. D. Aiken (Eds.), *Philosophy in the twentieth century* (Vol. 1). New York: Random House.

John, V., & Goldstein, L. S. (1967). Social context of language acquisition. In J. Hellmuth (Ed.), *Disadvantaged child* (Vol. 1, pp. 455–469). Seattle: Special Child Publications.

John-Steiner, V. (1985a). *Notebooks of the mind: Explorations in thinking.* New York: Harper & Row.

John-Steiner, V. (1985b). The road to competence in an alien land: A Vygotskian perspective on bilingualism. In J. V. Wertsch (Ed.), *Culture, communication, and cognition: Vygotskian perspectives* (pp. 348–371). New York: Cambridge University Press.

John-Steiner, V. (1991). Cognitive pluralism: A Whorfian analysis. In B. Spolsky & R. Cooper (Eds.), *Festschrift in honor of Joshua Fishman's 65th birthday* (pp. 61–74). The Hague, The Netherlands: Mouton.

John-Steiner, V. (1995). Cognitive pluralism: A sociocultural approach. *Mind, Culture, and Activity, 2*(1), 2–10.

John-Steiner, V. (2000). *Creative collaboration.* New York: Oxford University Press.

John-Steiner, V., & Mahn, H. (1996). Sociocultural approaches to learning and development: A Vygotskian framework. *Educational Psychologist, 31*(3/4), 191–206.

John-Steiner, V., & Osterreich, H. (1975). *Learning styles among Pueblo children.* NIE Research Grant, Final Report, Albuquerque. University of New Mexico, Department of Educational Foundations.

John-Steiner, V., Panofsky, C. P., & Smith, L. W. (Eds.). (1994). *Sociocultural approaches to language and literacy: An interactionist perspective.* New York: Cambridge University Press.

John-Steiner, V., & Souberman, E. (1978). Afterword. In M. Cole, V. John-Steiner, S. Scribner, & E. Souberman (Eds.), *Mind in society: The development of higher psychological processes* (pp. 121–133). Cambridge, MA: Harvard University Press.

John-Steiner, V., & Tatter, P. (1983). An interactionist model of language development. In B. Bain (Ed.), *The sociogenesis of language and human conduct* (pp. 79–97). New York: Plenum Press.

Kline, S. R. (2001). *Alternative assessment of exceptional culturally and linguistically diverse students.* Retrieved September 2001, from http://www.crede/ Reports/intsummain.html

Knox, J. E., & Stevens, C. (1993). Vygotsky and Soviet Russian defectology. In R. W. Rieber & A. S. Carton (Eds.), *The collected works of L. S. Vygotsky: Vol. 2. The fundamentals of defectology* (pp. 1–25). New York: Plenum Press.

Kozulin, A. (1990). *Vygotsky's psychology: A biography of ideas.* Brighton, UK: Harvester Wheatsheaf.

Kress, G. (1993). Genre as social process. In B. Cope & M. Kalautzis (Eds.), *The powers of literacy: A genre approach to teaching writing* (pp. 22–37). Philadelphia: Falmer.

Langer, J., & Applebee, A. (1987). *How writing shapes thinking: A study of writing and teaching.* Urbana, IL: National Council of Teachers of English.

Lave, J. (1988). *Cognition in practice: Mind, mathematics and culture in everyday life.* Cambridge, MA: Cambridge University Press.

Lave, J., & Wenger, E. (1991). *Situated learning: Legitimate peripheral participation.* New York: Cambridge University Press.

Lee, C. (2000). Signifying in the zone of proximal development. In C. Lee & P. Smagorinsky (Eds.), *Vygotskian perspectives on literacy research: Constructing meaning through collaborative inquiry* (pp. 191–225). New York: Cambridge University Press.

Lee, C., & Smagorinsky, P. (Eds.). (2000). *Vygotskian perspectives on literacy research: Constructing meaning through collaborative inquiry.* New York: Cambridge University Press.

Leontiev, A. N. (1981). *Problems of the development of mind.* Moscow: Progress. (Original work published 1959)

Lidz, C. (1995). Dynamic assessment and the legacy of L. S. Vygotsky. *School Psychology International, 16*(2), 143–153.

Lima, E. (1998). The educational experience with the Tikuna: A look into the complexity of concept construction. *Mind, Culture, and Activity, 5*(2), 95–104.

Luria, A. (1973). *The working brain: An introduction to neuropsychology.* New York: Basic Books.

Luria, A. (1979). *The making of mind.* Cambridge, MA: Harvard University Press.

Mahn, H. (1997). *Dialogue journals: Perspectives of second language learners in a Vygotskian theoretical framework.* Unpublished doctoral dissertation, University of New Mexico, Albuquerque, NM.

Mahn, H. (1999). Sociocultural theory: Vygotsky's methodological contribution. *Remedial and Special Education, 20*(6), 341–350.

Minick, N. (1987). The development of Vygotsky's thought: An introduction. In R. W. Rieber (Ed.), *The collected works of L. S. Vygotsky: Vol. 1. Problems of general psychology.* New York: Plenum.

Moffett, J. (1981). *Coming on center: English education in evolution.* Portsmouth, NH: Boynton/Cook.

Moll, L. C. (Ed.). (1990). *Vygotsky and education: Instructional implications of sociohistorical psychology.* New York: Cambridge University Press.

National Research Council. (1999). *How people learn: Brain, mind, experience, and school.* Washington, DC: National Academy Press.

Nelson, K. (1989). Monologue as representation of real-life experience. In K. Nelson (Ed.), *Narratives from the crib* (pp. 27–72). Cambridge, MA: Harvard University Press.

Newman, D., Griffin, P., & Cole, M. (1989). *The construction zone: Working for cognitive change in schools.* Cambridge, MA: Cambridge University Press.

Newman, F., & Holzman, L. (1993). *Lev Vygotsky: Revolutionary scientist.* New York: Routledge.

Packer, M. (1993). Away from internalization. In E. A. Forman, N. Minick, & C. A. Stone (Eds.), *Contexts for learning: Sociocultural dynamics in children's development* (pp. 254–265). New York: Oxford University Press.

Panofsky, C. (1994). Developing the representational functions of language: The role of parent-child book-reading activity. In V. John-Steiner, C. Panofsky, & L. Smith (Eds.), *Sociocultural approaches to language and literacy* (pp. 223–242). New York: Cambridge University Press.

Panofsky, C., John-Steiner, V., & Blackwell, P. (1990). The development of scientific concepts and discourse. In L. C. Moll (Ed.), *Vygotsky and education: Instructional implications of sociohistorical psychology* (pp. 251–267). New York: Cambridge University Press.

Rivers, W. J. (1987). *Problems in composition: A Vygotskian perspective.* Unpublished doctoral dissertation, University of Delaware, Newark, DE.

Rogoff, B. (1990). *Apprenticeship in thinking.* New York: Oxford University Press.

Rogoff, B., Goodman-Turkanis, C., & Bartlett, L. (Eds.). (2001). *Learning together: Children and adults in a school community.* New York: Oxford University Press.

Rommetveit, R. (1985). Language acquisition as increasing linguistic structuring of experience and symbolic behavior control. In J. V. Wertsch (Ed.), *Culture, communication, and cognition: Vygotskian perspectives* (pp. 183–204). New York: Cambridge University Press.

Sacks, O. (1989). *Seeing voices: A journey into the world of the deaf.* Los Angeles: University of California Press.

Scaife, M., & Bruner, J. (1975). The capacity for joint visual attention in the infant. *Nature, 253,* 265–266.

Schmittau, J. (1993). Vygotskian scientific concepts: Implications for mathematics education. *Focus on Learning Problems in Mathematics, 15,* (2&3), 29–39.

Scribner, S., & Cole, M. (1981). *The psychology of literacy.* Cambridge, MA: Harvard University Press.

Shaughnessy, M. P. (1977). *Errors & expectations: A guide for the teacher of basic writing.* New York: Oxford University Press.

Shonerd, H. (1994). Repair in spontaneous speech: A window on second language development. In V. John-Steiner, C. P. Panofsky, & L. W. Smith (Eds.), *Sociocultural approaches to language and literacy: An interactionist perspective* (pp. 82–108). New York: Cambridge University Press.

Shor, I. (2001). *What is critical literacy?* Retrieved September 2001, from http://www.lesley.edu/journals/jppp/4/shor.html

Skeat, W. W. (1995). *Etymological dictionary of the English language.* Oxford, UK: Clarendon Press.

Smith, F. (1982). *Writing and the writer.* Hillsdale, NJ: Erlbaum.

Stetsenko, A., & Arievitch, I. (2002). Learning and development: Post-Vygotskian perspectives. In G. Wells & G. Claxton (Eds.), *Learning for life in the 21st century: Sociocultural perspectives on the future of education* (pp. 84–96). Cambridge, MA: Blackwell.

Subbotsky, E. (2001). *Vygotsky's distinction between lower and higher mental functions and recent studies on infant cognitive development.* Retrieved October 5, 2001, from Hanover College, Psychology Department Web site: http://psych.hanover.edu/vygotsky/subbot.html

Sutton, A. (1980). Backward children in the USSR. In J. Brine, M. Perrie, & Andrew Sutton, (Eds.), *Home, school and leisure in the Soviet Union* (pp. 160–191). St. Leonards, Australia: Allen & Unwin.

Taylor, D. (1998). *Beginning to read and the spin doctors of science: The political campaign to change America's mind about how children learn to read.* Urbana, IL: National Council of Teachers of English.

Tchoshanov, M., & Fuentes, C. (2001, May–June). *Cognition, visualization, and technology: In-Depth learning of mathematics.* Paper presented at the Annual Meeting of the NMMATYC. Albuquerque, NM.

Tharp, R., Estrada, P., Dalton, S. S., & Yamuchi, L. A. (2000). *Teaching transformed: Achieving excellence, fairness, inclusion and harmony.* Boulder, CO: Westview Press.

Tharp, R. G., & Gallimore, R. (1988). *Rousing minds to life: Teaching and learning in social context.* New York: Cambridge University Press.

Torres-Velásquez, D. (Ed.). (1999). Sociocultural perspectives in special education. *Remedial and Special Education, 20*(6), 321–384.

Torres-Velásquez, D. (Ed.). (2000). Sociocultural perspectives in special education. Part 2. *Remedial and Special Education, 21*(2), 65–128.

Van der Veer, R., & Valsiner, J. (1991). *Understanding Vygotsky: A quest for synthesis.* Cambridge, MA: Blackwell.

Van der Veer, R., & Valsiner, J. (Eds.). (1994). *The Vygotsky reader.* Cambridge, MA: Blackwell.

Van Oers, B. (1998). The fallacy of decontextualization. *Mind, Culture, and Activity, 5*(2), 135–142.

Veresov, N. (1999). *Undiscovered Vygotsky.* New York: Peter Lang.

Vygotskaya, G. (1999). On Vygotsky's research and life. In S. Chaiklin, M. Hedegaard, & U. J. Jensen (Eds.), *Activity theory and social practice* (pp. 31–38). Oakville, CT: Aarhus University Press.

Vygotsky, L. S. (1978). *Mind in society: The development of higher psychological processes.* Cambridge, MA: Harvard University Press.

Vygotsky, L. S. (1981). The instrumental method in psychology. In J. V. Wertsch (Ed.), *The concept of activity in Soviet psychology.* Armonk, NY: M. E. Sharpe.

Vygotsky, L. S. (1986). *Thought and language* (A. Kozulin, Ed.). Cambridge, MA: MIT Press.

Vygotsky, L. S. (1987). *The collected works of L. S. Vygotsky: Vol. 1. Problems of general psychology* (R. W. Rieber & A. S. Carton, Eds.). New York: Plenum.

Vygotsky, L. S. (1993). *The collected works of L. S. Vygotsky: Vol. 2. The fundamentals of defectology (abnormal psychology and learning disabilities).* (R. W. Rieber & A. S. Carton, Eds.). New York: Plenum.

Vygotsky, L. S. (1994). The problem of the environment. In R. Van der Veer & J. Valsiner (Eds.), *The Vygotsky reader* (pp. 338–354). Cambridge, MA: Blackwell.

Vygotsky, L. S. (1997). *Educational psychology.* Jamaica Hills, NY: Saint Lucie Press. (Original work published 1926)

Vygotsky, L. S. (1997a). *The collected works of L. S. Vygotsky: Vol. 4. The history of the development of higher mental functions* (R. W. Rieber, Ed.). New York: Plenum.

Vygotsky, L. S. (1997b). The historical meaning of the crisis in psychology: A methodological investigation. In R. W. Rieber & J. Wollock (Eds.), *The collected works of L. S. Vygotsky: Vol. 3. Problems of the theory and history of psychology* (pp. 233–343). New York: Plenum.

Wells, G. (1999). *Dialogic inquiry: Toward a sociocultural practice and theory of education.* New York: Cambridge University Press.

Wells, G., & Claxton, G. (Eds.). (2002). *Learning for life in the 21st century: Sociocultural perspectives on the future of education.* Cambridge, MA: Blackwell.

Wertsch, J. V. (1985a). *Vygotsky and the social formation of mind.* Cambridge, MA: Harvard University Press.

Wertsch, J. V. (Ed.). (1985b). *Culture, communication, and cognition: Vygotskian perspectives.* New York: Cambridge University Press.

Wertsch, J. V. (1991). *Voices of the mind: A sociocultural approach to mediated action.* Cambridge, MA: Harvard University Press.

Wertsch, J. V. (1998). *Mind as action.* New York: Oxford University Press.

Wertsch, J. V., & Stone, C. A. (1985). The concept of internalization in Vygotsky's account of the genesis of higher mental functions. In J. V. Wertsch (Ed.), *Culture, communication, and cognition: Vygotskian perspectives* (pp. 162–179). New York: Cambridge University Press.

Wineburg, S. (2001, September). *T. S. Eliot, collaboration, and the quandaries of assessment in a rapidly changing world* [Electronic version]. *Phi Delta Kappan.* Retrieved http://www.pdkintl.org/kappan/kwin9709.htm

Wong-Fillmore, L. (1985). When does teacher talk work as input? In S. M. Gass & C. G. Madden (Eds.), *Input in second language acquisition: Series on issues in second language research* (pp. 17–50). Rowley, MA: Newbury House.

Wood, D. J., Bruner, J. S., & Ross, G. (1976). The role of tutoring in problem solving. *Journal of Child Psychology and Psychiatry, 17*(2), 89–100.

Yaroshevsky, M. (1989). *Lev Vygotsky.* Moscow: Progress.

Yaroshevsky, M. G., & Gurgenidze, G. S. (1997). Epilogue. In R. W. Reiber & J. Wollack (Eds.), *The collected works of L. S. Vygotsky: Vol. 3. Problems of theory and history of psychology* (pp. 345–369). New York: Plenum.

Zebroski, J. T. (1994). *Thinking through theory: Vygotskian perspectives on the teaching of writing.* Portsmouth, NH: Heinemann.

Zukow-Goldring, P., & Ferko, K. R. (1994). An ecological approach to the emergence of the lexicon: Socializing attention. In V. John-Steiner, C. P. Panofsky, & L. W. Smith (Eds.), *Sociocultural approaches to language and literacy: An interactionist perspective* (pp. 170–190). New York: Cambridge University Press.

CHAPTER 8

Teaching Processes in Elementary and Secondary Education

MICHAEL PRESSLEY, ALYSIA D. ROEHRIG, LISA RAPHAEL, SARA DOLEZAL, CATHERINE BOHN, LINDSEY MOHAN, RUTH WHARTON-McDONALD, KRISTEN BOGNER, AND KASS HOGAN

At the beginning of the twenty-first century, we know a great deal about the teaching processes that occur in classrooms, including the teaching processes that can improve achievement (e.g., Borko & Putnam, 1996; Brophy & Good, 1986; Calderhead, 1996; Cazden, 1986; Clark & Peterson, 1986; Doyle, 1986; Rosenshine & Stevens, 1986; Shuell, 1996). This chapter reviews the most important findings and emerging directions in the study of teaching in elementary and secondary schools.

Most work reviewed in the first section of this chapter was generated in quantitative research. Researchers spent a great deal of time observing in classrooms, looking for particular teaching behaviors and coding when they occurred. Often, these researchers also carried out analyses in which classroom teaching processes were correlated with achievement. Such observational and correlation work sometimes was complemented by experimentation to determine whether particular teaching processes could result in improved learning. The result of this work was a great deal of knowledge about naturalistically occurring teaching processes, including direct transmission and constructivist teaching processes.

In the second section, we take up an important part of teaching—motivating students. There has been a great deal of research focusing on stimulating student motivation through teaching, so as to increase academic efforts and accomplishments.

The third section covers teacher thinking about teaching. Such thinking presumably directs acts of teaching; hence, understanding teacher thinking is essential to understanding teaching.

The fourth section is about expert teaching; it summarizes what excellent teachers do as they teach well. Such teaching is exceptionally complicated. Excellent teachers masterfully orchestrate many of the most potent teaching approaches to create their expert teaching.

In the fifth section, we review the challenges teachers face. A realistic analysis of teaching processes must consider that when excellent teaching occurs, it happens largely because the teacher is a very good problem solver—very capable of negotiating the many demands on her or him.

CLASSROOM TEACHING PROCESSES AND THEIR EFFECTS ON ACHIEVEMENT

There was a great deal of research during the second half of the twentieth century about the nature of classroom teaching, what it is like, and when it is effective. Although many different teaching mechanisms were identified, two overarching approaches to teaching emerged—the direct transmission approach and constructivist teaching.

Direct Transmission Approach

One of the most famous analyses of classroom teaching processes was conducted by Mehan (1979), who observed that much of teaching involves a teacher's initiating a question, waiting for a student response, and then evaluating the response—what Mehan referred to as *IRE cycles* (i.e., initiate-respond-evaluate cycles). A hefty dose of such interactions reduces the teacher's classroom management burden (Cazden, 1988, chap. 3) because students know what is required of them during such cycles given their frequent involvement in them. The teacher can go through a lesson in an orderly fashion, covering what she or he considers to be essential points. Given that many teachers view their jobs as covering so much content, days and days of such interactions make much sense to many teachers (Alvermann & Hayes, 1989; Alvermann, O'Brien, & Dillon, 1990). Such teaching, however, has many downsides; one is that lower-level and literal questions are more likely than higher-level questions. Moreover, this approach to teaching and learning is very passive, with the discussions often boring and only one student at a time interacting with the teacher (Bowers & Flinders, 1990, chap. 5; Cazden, 1988, chap. 3); this is direct transmission teaching, in which the teacher decides what will be discussed and learned.

Mehan (1979) documented that direct transmission of information in school is more the norm than the exception. Much of teaching involves a teacher's explaining, demonstrating, and asking questions. The explanations and demonstrations tend to come first, followed by the teacher-led IREs, sometimes followed by more teacher explanation and demonstration if students struggle with the content. Such direct instruction of information is defensible in that there is substantial evidence that direct transmission of information from teachers to students produces student learning (Brophy & Good, 1986; Rosenshine & Stevens, 1986).

Collapsing across the process-product studies (i.e., investigations correlating teaching process differences with variations in student achievement), the following conclusions about effective direct instruction emerged (see Brophy & Good,

1986, for a review, with many of the conclusions that follow generated by those authors; also see Rosenshine & Stevens, 1986):

- In general, the more academically focused the classroom, the greater the learning—that is, the greater the proportion of class time spent on academics, the greater the learning. The less time spent on low-level management of the class (e.g., checking attendance, discipline), the greater the learning. The tasks assigned should neither be too hard, nor too easy, but rather challenging enough to require the students to engage in them—challenging enough so that effort produces success. The more time the teacher directly teaches, the greater the learning.

- Achievement increases to the extent that teachers structure learning. This can be done through provision of advance organizers, outlines, and summaries.

- Practicing newly-taught skills to the point of mastery, with the teacher providing support as needed, improves achievement.

- Teacher questioning improves student learning (Redfield & Rousseau, 1981). It helps when the teacher's questions are clear and when the teacher permits the student time to formulate answers (i.e., the teacher uses wait time). Questioning as part of guided practice permits the teacher to check understanding of concepts being practiced (e.g., a math skill). Such checking of understanding promotes student learning.

- Feedback improves achievement—that is, it helps students to know when they are correct. Praise should make clear what the student did well, providing information about the value of the student's accomplishment. It should emphasize that the student's success was due to effort expended (Brophy, 1981).

- Seatwork and homework should be engaging rather than busywork. The teacher should monitor whether and how well such work was completed.

- Having students work together cooperatively during seatwork usually improves achievement.

- Regular review of material improves achievement.

The direct transmission approach focuses on teaching behaviors—teacher explanations, questioning, feedback to students, and assignments. The more teacher behaviors stimulate students to attend to things academic—especially things academic that are within the student's grasp (i.e., neither too easy nor too difficult)—the greater the achievement is; positive associations have been found between direct teaching behaviors and student achievement, with a great strength of the direct transmission approach being an impressive data-base of support.

Constructivist Teaching

In contrast to direct transmission is the constructivist approach to teaching and learning. An extreme version is discovery learning (Ausubel, 1961; Wittrock, 1966), which entails placing children in environments and situations that are rich in discovery opportunities—that is, rather than explaining to students what they should do, they are left to discover both what to do and how to do it, consistent with theories such as Piaget's that assert learning is best and most complete (i.e., understanding is most certain) when children discover concepts for themselves (Brainerd, 1978; Piaget, 1970). Teacher input often boils down to answering questions that students might pose as they attempt to do a task.

To be certain, students sometimes can make powerful discoveries, for instance, of strategies during problem solving (e.g., Groen & Resnick, 1977; Svenson & Hedonborg, 1979; Woods, Resnick, & Groen, 1975). That said, many times students fail when left to discover how to carry out an academic task. Worse is that sometimes they make errant discoveries; for example, they may discover weak strategies for solving a problem or strategies that are just plain wrong (Shulman & Keislar, 1966; Wittrock, 1966)! For example, when students are left to discover how to subtract on their own, there are hundreds of errant approaches that they can and do invent (Valheln, 1990).

Short of pure discovery, however, is guided discovery, which involves the teacher posing questions to students as they attempt a task. The questions are intended to lead students to notice ways that a task could be approached—that is, the questions provide hints about the concepts the child is to discover, but the child has to make substantial effort to figure out the situation compared to when a teacher directly teaches how to do a task. In recent years, such guided discovery teaching has come to be known as *scaffolding* (Wood, Bruner, & Ross, 1976)—Like the scaffolding of a building, the teacher provides support when needed, with the scaffolding reduced as the child's mind, which is under construction, is increasingly able to handle the task. The teacher provides enough support (hints and prompts) for the child to continue to make progress understanding a situation but does not provide the student with answers or complete explanations about how to find answers. Such guided discovery takes more time than more direct teaching, however. Moreover, it requires teachers who know the concepts being taught so well that they can make up questions in response to student attempts and errors as they attempt tasks (Collins & Stevens, 1982).

Many science educators favor guided discovery. Tobin and Fraser (1990) documented that effective constructivist science teachers monitor their students well as they attempt academic tasks, quickly intervening with questions and prompts when students get off task. Excellent constructivist science teachers continue lessons until they are certain their students understand what is being taught. The goal of constructivist teaching is student understanding, not simply the student's getting through the task or getting a correct answer. Constructivist science educators require students to explain their thinking, and they work with students until the students do understand. In good science classes, all students are required to be active, for example, attempting to generate a solution to a problem and discuss alternative problem solutions with one another (Champagne & Bunce, 1991)—that is, students do not discover alone but work together to discover (e.g., doing chemistry or math problems together). Students learn how to think together (e.g., Newman, Griffin, & Cole, 1989), which mirrors much of the problem solving that occurs in the real world (e.g., problem solving by committees, which is the typical approach to many important problems in adult life).

Although guided discovery more certainly leads to learning than pure discovery, there is a cost. The students do explore less than they do during pure discovery. They tend to wait for teacher's guiding questions and prompts rather than explore the problem or topic on their own (Hogan, Nastasi, & Pressley, 1999). Even so, when students in Hogan et al.'s (1999) study were left on their own to solve a science problem through group discovery, they joked around more and often were distracted compared to when a teacher scaffolded their interactions; this finding is consistent with similar observations in other studies of students in discovery learning situations (e.g., Basili & Sanford, 1991; Bennett & Dunne, 1991; Roth & Roychoudhury, 1992). Bickering also is common during pure discovery and student small-group problem solving (e.g., Nastasi, Braunhardt, Young, & Margiano-Lyons, 1993). Frequently, only a subset of the students do most of the work and thinking during such interactions (e.g., Basili & Sanford, 1991; Gayford, 1989; Richmond & Striley, 1996). Communications between discovering learners are often unclear; conclusions are incomplete and sometimes illogical (e.g., Bennett & Dunne, 1991; Eichinger, Anderson, Palincsar, & David, 1991). Despite the problems with discovery and guided discovery approaches, supporters of these approaches are adamant that it is good for children's cognitive development to struggle to discover (e.g., Ferreiro, 1985; Petitto, 1985; Pontecorvo & Zucchermaglio, 1990) because conceptual disagreements between students can lead to much hard thinking by the students.

The case in favor of guided discovery has grown stronger in recent years, with many demonstrations that good teachers can scaffold students as they work on difficult academic tasks (Hogan & Pressley, 1997b), including learning to recognize words (e.g., Gaskins et al., 1997), use comprehension strategies to understand texts (e.g., Pressley, El-Dinary, et al., 1992), solve math problems (e.g., Lepper, Drake, & O'Donnell-Johnson, 1997), and figure out scientific concepts (Hogan & Pressley, 1997a). Student errors can be revealing about what students do not understand and be used by a teacher to shape questions and comments that cause students to think hard about misconceptions and sometimes come to better conceptions.

Direct Transmission Versus Constructivist Approaches to Teaching

Kohlberg and Mayer (1972) starkly contrasted direct transmission and constructivist views of instruction. Both require teachers to do more than do methods favored by romantic views of development and schooling inspired by Rousseau's (1979) *Emile*. Rousseau made the case there that education at its best left the child alone to explore the world. Perhaps the most famous school in modern times conceptualized along such romantic lines was A. S. Neill's (1960) Summerhill. Learning proved to be anything but certain at Summerhill, however (Hart, 1970; Hemmings, 1973; Popenoe, 1970; Snitzer, 1964). It is notable that there have been no serious, large-scale attempts to implement romantic education since Summerhill—reflecting (at least in part) an awareness growing out of that experience that, when Mother Nature is left in charge, children's intellectual development is not as certainly upward as Rousseau proposed.

Kohlberg and Mayer (1972) were very critical of transmission approaches, focusing on the behavioral underpinnings, which did not put any value on understanding—only on observable performances. Kohlberg and Mayer, who adopted a Piagetian perspective, believed that the centerpiece of education should put the child in situations that are just a bit perplexing to the child and just a bit beyond the child's current understanding. Hence, the child who has single-digit subtraction mastered is ready to try double-digit subtraction. The good teacher provides such a child with some double-digit subtraction problems and perhaps hints about how double-digit subtraction is like single-digit subtraction but does not teach the child how to do double-digit subtraction in a step-by-step fashion.

Constructivist-oriented educators in the Kohlberg tradition were particularly interested in how to increase students' ability to reason about difficult social and moral problems. Their hypothesis was that letting children discuss such problems to come up with solutions was the route to cognitive growth. During such discussions, many challenges would stimulate the participants to think hard about social and moral dilemma situations, with the result that students would develop and internalize more sophisticated reasoning skills. The teacher should play the role of one of the participants in the conversation, gently nudging the participants to think about some possibilities not yet offered in the conversation (e.g., *What about——?*). In fact, when students have opportunities to participate in such discussions about moral dilemmas, their social and moral reasoning skills do improve—consistent with Kohlberg's theory—although the effects are more pronounced among secondary than among elementary students (Enright, Lapsley, & Levy, 1983).

Since Kohlberg and Mayer (1972), the direct transmission versus constructivist debate has played out many times in American education. For example, in recent years, there has been a huge debate about how to teach beginning reading—one side favors direct instruction of word recognition competencies (i.e., phonics), and the other favors an approach known as *whole language,* which includes learning to recognize words through discovery as children experience great children's literature and write their own compositions (Pressley, 1998; see chapter by Pressley on literacy in this volume). Consistent with how those favoring direct transmission have made their case in the past, those favoring direct teaching of reading have amassed a great deal of scientific evidence that direct teaching of phonics and related skills produces more certain word recognition than less direct teaching. The National Reading Panel (2000) report was particularly systematic in reviewing all of the evidence favoring such a direct instruction perspective. Consistent with traditional constructivist arguments, whole language proponents feel that direct teaching of word recognition does not result in a complete understanding of reading; they have produced an impressive array of evidence that children's understandings are more developed in whole language contexts (e.g., Dahl & Freppon, 1995; Graham & Harris, 1994; Morrow, 1990, 1991; Neuman & Roskos, 1990). For example, experiences with literature increase children's understanding of the structure of stories (e.g., Feitelson, Kita, & Goldstein, 1986; Morrow, 1992; Rosenhouse, Feitelson, Kita, & Goldstein, 1997). Children's comprehension of ideas expressed in text increase when they have conversations about literature with peers and teachers (Van den Branden, 2000).

Direct Transmission and Constructivism

Kohlberg and Mayer (1972) believed that if students were taught, they could not then discover. Another possibility, however, does exist. Kohlberg and Mayer (1972) are correct in their assertion that when a teacher teaches directly (i.e., explains a concept), understanding is incomplete. Even so, understanding is complete enough so that the student can at least begin to apply the new knowledge or use the new skill that was just explained. To do so correctly, however, might require some help from the teacher (i.e., scaffolding), with understanding of the new idea or procedure increasing as the student, in fact, does use it—that is, by attempting to use what has been taught directly, the learner constructs a much more complete understanding. That direct transmission and constructivism are not completely incompatible has stimulated new thinking about how teaching can be done better.

For example, what has emerged in the beginning reading debate is a middle position calling for instructional balance of direct teaching of skills and whole language experiences (i.e., reading of literature, composition; see Pressley, 1998; also see chapter by Pressley in this volume). Advocates for balanced literacy instruction make the reasonable assumptions that learning how to sound out words is more certain if taught directly and that reading of real literature provides especially rich practice of word recognition. Writing also provides much opportunity to explore and experiment with words, with the knowledge of letter-sound combinations tried out and stretched in many ways as children try to figure out how to spell the words they want to put in their stories.

That direct transmission and constructivist literacy experiences can be coordinated was documented explicitly by Pressley, El-Dinary, et al. (1992) in their work on the teaching of comprehension strategies to elementary students. The teachers they studied first explained and modeled a small repertoire of comprehension strategies to their students, including predicting based on prior knowledge, asking questions during reading, constructing mental images during reading, seeking clarification when confused, and summarizing. Then, over a long period of time, the teachers scaffolded students' use of the strategies as they read in small reading groups. Brown, Pressley, Van Meter, and Schuder (1996) demonstrated that a year of such scaffolded practice at the second-grade level resulted in more active reading and greater comprehension of what was read. Collins (1991) and Anderson and Roit (1993) produced comparable outcomes in the later elementary grades and at the middle school level, respectively.

Learning of comprehension strategies as conceived by Pressley, El-Dinary, et al. (1992) was highly constructivist (Harris & Pressley, 1991; Pressley, Harris, & Marks, 1992). The students did not apply the strategies mechanically; rather, they worked at flexibly adjusting the strategies relative to the demands of reading tasks. Students discussed among

themselves their strategy attempts and alternative understandings of texts (e.g., how their summaries of a text differed). Teachers did not direct students to use particular strategies as they read text, but rather provided general prompts to be active and to experiment (e.g., *What might you do if you're not sure you understand?*). They also encouraged students to use what they were learning during reading in class across the day (e.g., *When you are reading for social studies, try some of the strategies.*).

As we offer these examples from reading that represent a balancing of direct instruction and constructivist experiences, we are also reminded that direct transmission versus constructivist battles continue to be fought. A prominent one is in mathematics education, with the National Council of Teachers of Mathematics (2000) arguing strongly for constructivist mathematics teaching and many traditionalists favoring direct teaching of skills (e.g., Dixon, Carnine, Lee, Wallin, & Chard, 1998).

Summary

Although both direct instruction and constructivist advocates can point to research supporting their favored teaching mechanisms, the alternative that enjoys increasing support is instruction that involves both direct transmission and constructivist elements. The invention of such teaching does inspire some extreme advocates both of direct instruction and of constructivist teaching to assert their positions even more adamantly, resulting in conflicting and sometimes confusing advice presented to teachers. Such recommendations must be sorted out in the teacher's own mind, which was one motivation for researchers interested in teaching processes to study teacher thinking.

MOTIVATIONAL PROCESSES

During the last quarter century there has been a revolution in thinking about how academic learning and achievement can be motivated in classrooms. There are now a number of specific motivating, instructional approaches that are defensible based on well-regarded educational research.

Rewarding Achievement

The behaviorists contended that to increase behavior, one should reward (reinforce) it. It is not quite that simple! If the behavior is one that the student does not like or is not doing, then providing reward for performing the behavior (or for performing the behavior well) is defensible. Alternatively, however, if it is a behavior that a student likes already (i.e., a behavior the student finds intrinsically rewarding), then providing an explicit reward can actually undermine the student's future motivation to do this activity (Lepper & Hoddell, 1989). This phenomenon is called the *overjustification effect* (Lepper, Greene, & Nisbett, 1973): There is a natural tendency when a person is rewarded for doing something to explain one's behavior as being caused by the reward. As an example, consider a child who really loves reading and reads plenty of books just for the fun of it. Suppose one day the teacher adds the explicit reward of a pizza certificate for reading so many books, an incentive system used in many schools. As long as the pizza certificates keep coming, the situation is fine; alas, however, in the spring, when the pizza certificates stop as the incentives program winds down, reading might actually decline: The child stops reading because she or he now believes that reading was occurring because of the reward for reading.

One common form of reward in classrooms is praise, which can be very effective. Praise works best when it is given contingent on desirable student behaviors, when the teacher makes clear what was praiseworthy, when the praise is sincere, when there is an implication that the student can be similarly successful in the future by exerting appropriate effort, and when the praise conveys the message that the student seemed to enjoy the task or value the competencies gained from the exertion of effort (Brophy, 1981).

Encourage Moderate Risk Taking

Many students fear failure and hence are afraid to take risks. Good teachers encourage such students to be reasonable risk takers. Such risk taking, however, often produces increased achievement (see Clifford, 1991). Why? Consider writing as an example. Students have no chance to improve their writing skills if they refuse to try to write, fearing that their efforts will be unsuccessful; improvement can occur only after students try to write.

Emphasizing Improvement Over Doing Better Than Others

Most American classrooms emphasize performance—in particular, doing better than other students on academic tasks. Only a few students receive As relative to most students, who are much less successful. Such an approach undermines the motivation of all students (Ames, 1984; Nicholls, 1989), however. Those who do not receive As feel as if they failed relative to the A students. If the A students could do better than they are doing, they have no incentive to do so, for they are already earning the top grade that is available.

There is an alternative to emphasizing competitive grades—to praise students for improving from where they are now rather than for performing better than do other students. Classrooms that emphasize improvement, in fact, are more likely to keep students interested in and committed to school (Nicholls, 1989; Nicholls & Thorkildsen, 1987).

Cooperative Learning

Beyond downplaying competition, students can be encouraged to cooperate with one another, with reliably positive effects on achievement. Students often learn more when they work together (e.g., Johnson & Johnson, 1975, 1979, 1985). The most motivating situation is one in which students actually receive reward based on how well their fellow group members perform, creating great incentive for students to work together to make certain that everyone in the cooperative group is making progress (Fantuzzo, King, & Heller, 1992; Slavin, 1985a, 1985b).

Cognitive Conflict

Providing students with tasks that are just a little bit beyond them or a little different from what they already know is very motivating. Thus, if a student has the single-digit addition facts down (e.g., $5 + 2 = 7$), single-digit subtraction problems might be intriguing and just a bit confusing. Thus, presenting a flash card with $5 - 2 = 3$ might give the student motivation to pause to figure out why the answer is not 7, raising curiosity about that $-$ and what that dash might signify. Similar curiosity would not be expected in a child who did not know the addition facts already, for there would be no reason for such a child to think that $5 - 2 = 3$ is a little strange. A variety of Piagetian-inspired educators (see Kohlberg, 1969) have made the case that students' curiosity can be stimulated by presenting new content that is just a little bit different from what the students already know.

Making Academic Tasks Interesting

People pay more attention to content that is interesting—a good reason to present students with content that will grab them (e.g., Hidi, 1990; Renninger, 1990; Renninger & Wozniak, 1985). That said, sometimes material grabs student attention but distracts from what is really important. For example, juicy anecdotes in a history piece can reduce the attention paid to the main points of the article (e.g., stories about Kennedy playing touch football with the family on the White House lawn can be remembered better than can the accomplishments of the Kennedy administration, which were the main focus; e.g., Garner, 1992). Similarly, educational computer games are often loaded with distractions that succeed in orienting student attention to lights and bells rather than to the content that the program is intended to teach (e.g., Lepper & Malone, 1987). On a more positive note, reading can be made more fun by having the students read books that they find interesting. Similarly, social studies and science content can be illustrated by examples that students find intriguing rather than boring—examples that illustrate well important points made in the text.

Encouraging Effort Attributions

Students can attribute successes and failures they have experienced to a number of factors. Unfortunately, most of these attributions are to factors out of their control. Thus, explaining one's success as due to high ability or one's failure to low ability is tantamount to attributing outcomes to something the student cannot control. Luck is also out of the student's control, so that to attribute a success to good luck or a failure to bad luck is to conclude that one's educational fates are not under personal control. Finally, explaining good and bad grades as due to easy and difficult tests is the same as believing that educational success is all in the hands of the test makers. Explaining successes and failures in terms of such uncontrollable factors undermines motivation. If success in school depends on ability, luck, or test difficulty, then there is no incentive to try because successes and failures will occur unpredictably.

Alternatively, students can explain their educational outcomes in terms of the one factor they can control—their effort. Explaining successes as reflecting hard work—and failures as due to not enough work—wields positive motivational power. The message is that doing well depends on personal effort, which the student can decide to expend. Encouraging students to make effort attributions increases their motivation to learn new skills that are taught (e.g., Carr & Borkowski, 1989).

Emphasizing the Changeable Nature of Intelligence

A related point is that students can believe their academic intelligence is fixed and out of their control, with this belief undermining motivation to work hard in school. Alternatively, students can believe their intelligence is modifiable—that by learning more, people really became smarter (e.g., Henderson & Dweck, 1990). In fact, when classrooms emphasize that school is about mastering what is being taught there and such mastery produces intellectual empowerment, achievement is greater (e.g., Ames, 1990; Ames & Archer, 1988; Nicholls, 1989).

Increasing Student Self-Efficacy

People with positive academic self-efficacy believe they can do academic tasks; academic self-efficacy is often quite specific (e.g., believing that one can achieve in mathematics—or more specific still, believing one can do even difficult word problems; Bandura, 1977, 1986). High self-efficacy motivates future effort (e.g., a student who perceives she or he can do math is more likely to try hard in math; Schunk, 1989, 1990, 1991). Self-efficacy is largely a product of success in a domain (e.g., success in mathematics produces math self-efficacy). Hence, it is important that students be successful in school and that assignments provide some challenge but not so much as to overwhelm.

Encouraging Healthy Possible Selves

It is academically motivating for a child to believe that she or he could go to college and eventually become a well-respected, well-rewarded professional. Such students have healthy possible selves, which motivates them to work hard in school as part of a long-term plan that will get them to a productive role in the world (Markus & Nurius, 1986). Many children do not have such understandings or such positive possible selves, believing that higher education is something that could never happen to them and that they could never achieve valued roles in society. For children who do not have healthy possible selves, it makes sense to encourage more positive views about possible long-range futures. For example, Day, Borkowski, Dietmeyer, Howsepian, and Saenz (1994) were able to shift the expectations of Mexican American children upward through participation in discussions emphasizing how education can result in desirable jobs.

Discussion

Educational researchers have identified many specific approaches to motivate academic effort and achievement. One reading of this section is that these mechanisms are in competition with one another—that there are so many of them that it would be impossible to carry them all out. Jere Brophy (1986, 1987), however, proposed just the opposite—that trying to do it all with respect to motivation is exactly the way to produce more motivating classrooms and more motivated students. Brophy urged teachers to model interest in learning and communicate to students high enthusiasm for what is going on in school and that what is being learned in school is important. Brophy urged keeping achievement anxiety low and emphasizing learning and improvement rather than outdoing other students. Teachers should induce curiosity and suspense, make abstract material more concrete, make learning objectives salient, and provide much informative feedback. According to Brophy, teachers also should adapt tasks to students' interest, offer students choices whenever possible, and encourage student autonomy and self-reliance. Learning by doing should be encouraged; tasks that produce a product are especially appealing (e.g., class-produced big books). Games should be part of learning. The case is made later in this chapter that Brophy's perspective that teachers should try to do much to motivate is enjoying support in the most recent research on classroom motivation, with exceptionally engaging teachers doing much to motivate their students—that is, excellent teachers know much about how to motivate their students, and they use what they know.

TEACHERS' KNOWLEDGE, BELIEFS, AND THINKING

The cognitive revolution heightened awareness that teachers actively think as they teach and that what they know and believe about teaching very much affects the classroom decisions they make. During the last two decades of the twentieth century, there were substantial analyses of what teachers know and believe (see Borko & Putnam, 1996; Calderhead, 1996; Carter & Doyle, 1996; Clark & Peterson, 1986; Reynolds, 1989; Richardson, 1996); what follows in this section is an amalgamation of conclusions from these previous reviews of the evidence.

Teachers think before they teach (i.e., they plan for the year, this unit, this week, what will be covered today, and what will be covered in this lesson; Clark & Yinger, 1979), and they think as teaching proceeds (e.g., they react to student needs). Teachers also can think after they teach, reflecting on what went on in their classroom, the effects of their teaching, and how their teaching might be improved in the future. All of this thinking is informed and affected by various types of knowledge possessed by teachers: Teachers know how to teach, having learned classroom management strategies, instructional strategies, motivational techniques, and a variety of theories of learning. They have beliefs about themselves as teachers. They have subject matter knowledge, including knowledge about how particular subjects can be taught (i.e., pedagogical content knowledge; Shulman, 1986).

With respect to every type of knowledge that teachers can possess, there are individual differences between teachers in what they know and believe. For example, some teachers know more than do others about cognitive strategies instruction. Among those knowledgeable about cognitive strategies, some believe that strategies should be taught directly, whereas others think that students should be helped to

discover powerful strategies but not be told explicitly how to carry them out. Some teachers even know about strategies instruction but choose not to teach strategies because they do not believe that reading comprehension really is a consciously strategic process (e.g., Pressley & El-Dinary, 1997). Teacher beliefs can powerfully affect teaching, including beliefs about self as teacher (e.g., *I'm not good at teaching math.*), the nature of students (e.g., *They don't want to learn. The students do not have much prior knowledge that can be related to science lessons.*), effective classroom management (e.g., *Students should be seen and not heard. A good teacher is clearly in charge of the classroom. In a good classroom, students are self-regulating.*), and the nature of effective teaching and learning (e.g., *Teachers should be coaches more than dictators. Students learn best through direct instruction. Students learn best when given opportunities to construct their own knowledge.*).

A teacher's knowledge is acquired over a long period of time, with some of it reflecting information garnered from experiencing kindergarten through college education as a student. Some was conveyed formally in courses in college—for example, education methods courses. Other knowledge was acquired on the job as a function of gaining experience in the classroom, observing other teachers, and experiencing professional development provided to teachers in the field. Teachers' practical knowledge of schools dramatically shifts with experience. Only through actually teaching in a working school can subtle knowledge of the teaching craft be acquired. Formal knowledge of teaching, however, can transform as teachers attempt to use modern conceptions of teaching and learning compared to conceptions of teaching and learning that predominated when they were taught. Thus, knowledge of writing can change as a function of experience as a writing workshop teacher of composition. The shift can be from a focus on writing as mastery of mechanics (which was the emphasis during schooling for many who are now teachers) to writing as a process of planning, drafting, and revising (which is the current focus of most curricular thinking about composition), with concerns about mechanics most prominent as the composition product is being polished. Knowledge of and beliefs about mathematics instruction can change when a school district decides to move away from curricula emphasizing procedural learning to curricula emphasizing student construction of mathematical understandings and real-world problem solving. To become an expert professional takes a while (5–10 years; e.g., Ericsson, Krampe, & Tesch-Römer, 1993)—both to learn how to teach and to believe one can teach well—despite the fact that while they are in teacher education programs, many are very confident (probably overconfident) that they will be good teachers (e.g., Book & Freeman, 1986; Weinstein, 1988, 1989).

EXPERT TEACHING

That teachers have much to learn themselves has stimulated much hard thinking about what experienced teachers know and need to know—especially what really good teachers know and believe. By analyzing the thinking and teaching of experienced and skilled teachers, an understanding of teaching at its best is emerging. A possible reading of the research summarized briefly in this section is that a teacher can possess many bits and pieces of knowledge that can mediate discrete teaching events. The research reviewed in the next section goes far in emphasizing that real teachers, however, connect their knowledge and their practices to create entire lessons, school days, content units, and years.

Cognitive psychologists have carried out many expert-novice comparisons, especially focusing on the thinking of experts compared to novices as they do important tasks (e.g., reading X rays, flying planes; e.g., Lesgold et al., 1988). Experts think about problems in a way very different from that of novices. Experts quickly size up a situation as roughly like others they have seen—that is, they have well-developed schemas in their domain of expertise (e.g., expert radiologists know what metastatic adenocarcinoma of the lung looks like, and this knowledge is quickly activated when they confront a specific X ray having some of the features of metastatic adenocarcinoma of the lung). After a candidate schema is generated, the expert then carefully searches for information confirming or disconfirming the schema (e.g., noticing whether the many tumors in this X ray of the lung are more round than spiculated, which would be consistent with metastatic adenocarcinoma; noticing whether there is a metastatic path from the primary tumor). The novice might not be so thorough and thus might rush to a conclusion (e.g., concluding quickly that the many tumors in the lung field must be adenocarcinoma, perhaps even explaining away the spiculated look of the tumors as due to the poor fidelity of X rays). Also, unlike the novice, the expert radiologist is not going to be distracted by irrelevancies (e.g., looking at sections of the X ray that do not contain telling information). Cognitive psychologists interested in expert-novice differences in cognition consistently were able to demonstrate that experts had better developed schematic knowledge in their domains of expertise; this knowledge was used more systematically and completely by experts compared to novices to accomplish tasks in the domain of expertise.

The most prominent expert-novice work done in the field of teaching was carried out by David Berliner and his associates (e.g., Berliner, 1986, 1988; Carter, Cushing, Sabers, Stein, & Berliner, 1988; Carter, Sabers, Cushing, Pinnegar, & Berliner, 1987). They studied both teachers identified by their schools as expert teachers and early-career teachers. For example, Sabers, Cushing, and Berliner (1991) had teachers watch a videotaped lesson, with the wide-screen image capturing everything that was happening in the room. The teachers were asked to talk aloud as they watched what was happening; the researchers also posed some specific questions about what was happening in the classroom, probing teachers' understanding of the classroom routines, the content being covered, motivational mechanisms being used by the teacher, and interactions between students and teachers.

The main result was that the expert teachers saw the room much differently from the way the novices saw it. Basically, the experts made better interpretations of what they saw and were more likely to recognize well-developed routines, to identify classroom structures the teacher had put in place, and to detect student interest and boredom. The experts also took in more of the room rather than overfocusing on one part to the exclusion of another. The experts listened more to what the students said, whereas the novice teachers were more likely to focus on the visual clues alone. Berliner and his associates concluded that expert teachers have well-developed knowledge of classroom schemas: They know what particular routines look like (e.g., entering the room and getting to work immediately), the important approaches to curriculum and instruction (e.g., a hands-on science activity), and prototypical ways in which students and teachers can interact (e.g., cooperative learning); this knowledge base permits them to interpret what can seem to be many disjointed activities to novices who lack such knowledge. Thus, novices are likely to focus on the many specific behaviors in a hands-on science activity rather than simply recognize it as a unified activity. Such schemas allow much more complete comprehension and memory of what is going on in a classroom (e.g., Peterson & Comeaux, 1987).

A criticism of these studies is that expert teaching is not just about teacher thinking. In fact, it is mostly about actual teaching, which was not captured at all in the expert-novice studies focusing on teacher cognition. In a series of studies conducted with our associates (Bogner, Raphael, & Pressley, 2002; Pressley, Allington, Wharton-McDonald, Block, & Morrow, 2001; Pressley, Wharton-McDonald, et al., 2001; Wharton-McDonald, Pressley, & Hampston, 1998), we captured the many ways in which the teaching of excellent elementary teachers differs from the teaching of more typical and weaker elementary teachers. In each of these studies, we identified teachers who were very engaging (i.e., most of their students were academically engaged most of the time) and those who were less engaging (i.e., students were often off task, or the tasks they were doing were not academically oriented). As we anticipated, when engagement was high, there were also indications of better achievement (i.e., students wrote longer, more coherent, and generally more impressive compositions; students read more advanced books; students performed better on achievement tests than students in classrooms where engagement was lower). This work was more decidedly qualitative and intended to develop a theory of effective elementary teaching rather than quantitatively hypothetico-deductive (see Strauss & Corbin, 1998). The theory that emerged was that excellent teachers do much well: (a) They develop a motivating classroom atmosphere, (b) classroom management is superb, and (c) their curriculum and instructional decisions sum to excellent teaching for all students.

A Motivating Classroom Atmosphere

Effective elementary teachers create a motivating classroom environment. Excellent teachers have both the physical environment and the psychological input to the students aligned to promote engagement and learning.

Physical Environment

The teacher has constructed a comfortable and inviting place for learning, with many educational materials readily accessible for students. For example, there are reading corners filled with great books, listening stations with tapes of favorite stories, and math labs with concrete manipulatives (e.g., play money, counting blocks) that appeal to students. Charts and maps that can support teaching and learning are hung so that they can be used during teaching and referenced easily by students. The classroom is decorated with fun and attractive items (e.g., brightly colored signs, posters that are appealing to the eye). Some of the decorations are student-produced work. The displays change frequently as the seasons change, new topics are covered in class, and students produce new products that can be showcased. Posters reflect some of the psychological virtues the teacher espouses for the classroom (e.g., exerting effort, making good choices, high expectations), making salient the interconnections between the physical and psychological classroom worlds.

Psychological Environment

Excellent teachers promote *community* in their classroom and it shows—beginning with their communications (e.g., *our class, we work together*). The teacher makes frequent connections to students, mentioning in passing a student's achievement, alluding to the birth of a sibling, and expressing empathy to a child who has a reason to feel blue (e.g., a grandparent is ill)—that is, excellent teachers send the message that they are interested in students' lives, which are valuable. The teacher's communications are filled with respect for students, and the students' communications mirror that respect—for example, with many *please* and *thank-you* comments. Teachers remind

students often about the virtues of being helpful, respectful, and truthful with one another. Excellent teachers have gentle, caring manners in the classroom, with positive interactions in abundance. The teacher is often playful with the kids (e.g., actually playing with them during recess, kidding around with them as they work). Excellent teachers typically have good senses of humor—for example, laughing at themselves when they make a mistake solving an arithmetic problem. Good teachers model inclusion and embrace diversity by including all of the children in the class and celebrating openly the various traditions and backgrounds represented by students (e.g., celebrating with genuine enthusiasm Columbus Day, St. Patrick's Day, and Martin Luther King Day). Cooperation is encouraged (e.g., much cooperative learning), as is altruism (students helping other students, making valentines for people in nursing homes, collecting soda cans to donate the proceeds to an adopted family in Guatemala).

The classroom is also a *democratic* place. There are serious discussions between students and teachers about classroom issues (e.g., how disobedience should be handled, how the needs of individuals can be balanced against the needs of the entire class). Sometimes these discussions take up matters of power and inequity (e.g., how kids don't always get the respect they deserve). Good teachers reduce such inequalities by permitting the students to make up classroom rules and to be involved in decision making (e.g., what novel to read next). When students disagree, respectful disagreement is encouraged and compromises are sought (e.g., if the vote between two novels is split, it might be resolved by a coin flip, with the decision to read the losing novel after the winning novel is completed).

The teacher does much to create an *interesting* classroom. He or she arouses curiosity (e.g., *Listen carefully. You'll find out some of the answers to the questions we've been asking.* or *Go ahead and open our new book—see anything interesting?*). The good teacher creates anticipation (e.g., *Tomorrow, I'm going to teach you how I figure out those percentages on tests, which will be cool.*).

Excellent teachers create classrooms *emphasizing effort*. The teacher lets students know that they can do the assigned tasks if they try, also making clear that the way smart people became smart was by trying hard and thus learning much. Good teachers send the message that school tasks deserve attention and serious effort and that much good comes from doing and reflecting on school work. When students have difficulties, the teacher encourages stick-to-itiveness, letting the students know that they can succeed by persevering. The teacher does not attribute either student successes or failures to luck, ability, or task difficulty—factors out of the students' control. The teacher downplays competition, emphasizing not who is doing better than others in the class but that students are improving. The teacher encourages effort in many ways—for example, often remarking *Who can tell me? Who remembers? Make your best guess if you are not sure.*

Excellent teachers create classrooms *downplaying performance outcomes*—that is, the teacher does not make salient who is doing well and who is not. Grades are not made publicly (e.g., by calling grades in or putting papers with the best grades on display). The teacher does not criticize student mistakes. There are no academic games with obvious losers (e.g., a spelling bee) but rather academic games in which everyone wins often (e.g., social studies Jeopardy in which students are made to feel they are winners when they get the answer in their heads).

Excellent teachers *foster self-regulation.* They give their students choice in their work (e.g., allowing students to select which books they will read). Students in excellent elementary classrooms are expected to move from task to task on their own rather than wait for teacher direction. Students are encouraged to set their own goals (e.g., how many books to read in a month). The teacher honors student ownership of their own work and control of it (e.g., *Would you mind if other children look at what you wrote?*). In short, the teacher wants students to be in charge of themselves.

The excellent teacher publicly *values learning.* The teacher frequently makes remarks about the value of education, using the mind, and achieving dreams through academic pursuits. The teacher is enthusiastic about academic pursuits, such as reading books and writing. The excellent teacher does not emphasize extrinsic rewards (e.g., stickers) for doing things academic but rather focuses on the intrinsic rewards (e.g., the excitement felt when one is reading a particular novel, the sense of accomplishment accompanying effective writing).

The excellent teacher also has *high expectations* about students, communicating frequently to students that they can learn at a high level (e.g., *Wow, third graders, this is stuff usually covered in fifth grade, and you are doing great with it.*). Moreover, excellent teachers are determined that students in their charge will learn. Even so, excellent teachers have realistic ambitions and goals for their students, encouraging their students to try tasks they can accomplish—ones that with effort are within their reach.

Excellent teachers create classrooms filled with *helpful feedback*—especially praising students when they do well and trying to do so immediately. Teachers do not give blanket praise, but rather are very explicit in their praise (e.g., *I really like this story—it is a page longer than your last story, with much better spelling and punctuation and a great ending.*).

In summary, excellent teachers go to great lengths to create a generally motivating classroom atmosphere. In fact, the classroom day is saturated with teacher actions that motivate. For example, Bogner et al. (2002) studied 7 first-grade teachers and found that two were much more motivating than were the others in the sample (e.g., their students were much more engaged in academic activities than were students in other classes). One of these two teachers used 43 different motivational mechanisms to encourage her students over the course of the school day, with many of these mechanisms used multiple times; the other used 47 different approaches—again, with many repeated multiple times. In both classrooms, the motivational attempts were always positively toned and never punitive or critical of students. In contrast, much more criticism and far fewer approaches to motivating students were observed in the other five classrooms.

Dolezal, Mohan, and Pressley (2002) conducted a similar study at the third-grade level. Their most engaging teacher used 45 different motivating mechanisms over the course of the school day, compared to far fewer motivational mechanisms in other third-grade classrooms, in which students were much less engaged. Excellent teachers create classroom environments that are massively motivating: It is impossible to be in their rooms for even a few minutes without several explicit teacher actions intended to motivate student engagement and learning.

Effective Classroom Management

The classroom management of effective teachers is so good that observers hardly notice it—there is little misbehavior in the classroom and rarely a noticeable disciplinary event. This result is due in part to a classroom management strategy that has at its core the development of self-regulated students.

Self-Regulation Routines

Effective teachers make clear from early in the year how students in the class are supposed to act. The teacher communicates to students that is important for them to learn and carry out the classroom routines and act responsibly. There are routines for many daily classroom tasks (e.g., a hot lunch counter can on the teacher's desk, with students depositing their token counter in the can)—tasks that can consume much time in ordinary classrooms (i.e., the lunch counter can eliminate the need for the teacher to do lunch count during the morning meeting). An especially important routine is for students to learn that they are to keep on working even if the teacher is not available; the internalization of this routine is obvious in effective classrooms because it does not matter whether the teacher is in the room—everyone works regardless of the teacher's absence. Early in the year, excellent teachers teach their students how to work cooperatively, and for the rest of the year, cooperative learning is the norm. In short, just as excellent teachers have high academic expectations of students, they also have high behavioral expectations.

Explanations and Rationales

Excellent teachers do not simply pronounce rules. Rather, they explain why the classroom community has the rules and regulations that are in place. Explanations are also given as the teacher makes important decisions (e.g., why the class is going to the library tomorrow rather than today, why the class is reading the current story and how it connects with the current social studies unit). The message is clear that the classroom is a reasonable world rather than an arbitrary one.

Monitoring

Excellent teachers monitor their classes and show high awareness of what everyone is doing. Excellent teachers act quickly when students experience frustrations or are getting off task (e.g., asking a student with wandering attention what he or she is doing and what he or she should be doing). When excellent teachers detect potential disruptions, they respond quickly and efficiently to eliminate such disruptions (e.g., giving paper towels to a student who just spilled, helping the student so that the spill is cleaned up quietly).

Discipline

There are few discipline events; the teacher does not have to use discipline or disciplinary threats to keep students on task. In fact, excellent teachers do not threaten their students. If punishment is necessary, it is done quietly and in a way that gets the student back on task very quickly. Thus, excellent teachers never send students to a time-out corner; rather, they swiftly move to correct the behavior and get the student back to the work assigned at the place where the work should be performed (e.g., whispering to the student *We'll talk at recess.*).

Excellent Use of Other Adults

Excellent teachers use parent volunteers and classroom aides well. Basically, these adults interact with the children much like the teacher: They provide support as needed, always in a positive way. Such good use happens because excellent teachers coach volunteers and aids well, making certain they know what to do to be consistent with the ongoing philosophy, instruction, and curriculum in the classroom. Excellent teachers often use such adults to provide additional help to weaker students—for example, listening to weaker readers read or helping weaker arithmetic students with challenging problems. (Often, during our visits, parents and aides told us how excellent the teacher was, reflecting that good teachers inspire great confidence in the other adults who work in their classrooms!)

In summary, excellent teachers orchestrate everyone in their classroom well—through persuasion rather than coercion. They are continuously aware of the state of their classroom and the students in it, and they do what is required to keep students engaged and productive. Their management style is consistent with the generally positive atmosphere in the classroom, with few reasons for punishment and few punishments dispensed.

Curriculum and Instruction

Excellent teachers make curriculum and instruction decisions that result in exciting teaching and interesting lessons. Students learn content that is exciting; the lessons are presented in interesting ways that match their abilities to deal with it.

Engaging Content and Activities

The books that are read and the lessons that are taught are interesting to the students, with the teacher consciously selecting materials that will intrigue the class (e.g., because it worked well last year). There are many demonstrations that make abstract content more concrete and do so in ways that connect academic content to the child's world and larger life (e.g., a lesson on biological adaptations that protect a species includes exploring the parts of a rose plant and reflecting on why it has thorns)—that is, students learn by doing. When new content is covered, the teacher highlights for students how it connects to ideas covered previously in the class (e.g., when an information book is read about how the colors of bears are matched to their habitats, the teacher reminds students about the previous lesson on biological adaptations). Such opportunities to connect across lessons are not accidental; the teacher plans extensively—both individual lessons and the sequence of lessons across the year.

Lessons do not merely scratch the surface; rather, the teacher explanations and class discussions have some depth. In general, depth is favored over breadth in excellent classrooms.

Play and games are incorporated into instruction. Thus, the class might play social studies Jeopardy to review for an upcoming test or math baseball. The emphasis in these games is decidedly on the content, however—the teacher takes advantage of misses to provide reinstruction (i.e., the misses inform the teacher about ideas that need additional coverage and reexplanation).

The students make products as part of instruction. Thus, it is common in very good primary classrooms to see big books on display that the class has written and produced. A science unit on plants can result in a small forest in the corner of the room. A sex education unit can include a class-made incubator in which chicks are hatched by the end of the lessons. Such products are a source of pride for students and do much to motivate their interest in what is going on in the classroom.

The message is salient that what goes on in school has clear relevance to the world. One way this occurs is through use of current events to stimulate classroom activities. Hence, a presidential election can be used to stimulate literacy and social studies activities related to the presidency. Space shuttle launches can be prime motivation for thinking about topics in astronomy, exploration, or technology. The annual dogsled races in Alaska can be used to heighten interest in the study of Alaska, the character issue of perseverance, or use of the Internet (i.e., the race can be followed on the Internet, which has many resources about the race available for students to explore).

There is no doubt that interest is high in classrooms staffed by excellent teachers. One indicator is that students are all doing activities connected to lessons (e.g., self-selecting library books related to current content coverage). Another is that the students are excited about any possibility of doing more or participating more extensively (e.g., student hands are always up to volunteer; students will stay in at recess to finish composition of a big book or help distribute the concrete manipulatives for the next activity). When a student is asked about what she or he is doing the student will often give a long and enthusiastic response. The teacher's selection of interesting and exciting content goes far in creating an interesting and exciting classroom.

Instructional Density

Excellent teachers are constantly teaching and providing instruction. Whole-group, small-group, and individual mini-lessons intermingle across the day, and the teacher often takes advantage of teachable moments (e.g., moments that provide the opportunity to teach), such as when students pose questions. The teachers sometimes prompt students how to find answers themselves and sometimes use the question as an opportunity to provide an in-depth explanation. Students also do much reading and writing because excellent teachers do not permit students simply to sit and do nothing. Excellent teachers teach in multiple ways—explaining, demonstrating, and scaffolding student learning. Teacher-led lessons and activities are sometimes complemented by film or Internet experiences. Although many lessons involve multiple activities, the academically demanding parts of the lesson get the most time and attention. For example, if students write in response to a reading, they might be asked to illustrate what they wrote. The illustration activity will never be the focus; rather, the teacher makes it clear that the illustrating comes after reading and writing and should be accomplished quickly. The dense articulation of instruction and activities in excellent classrooms requires great teacher organization and planning.

Balanced Instruction

Rather than embracing instructional extremes, excellent teachers use a range of methods. Admittedly, because the focus of our work is primary-level education, we know more about this issue with respect to literacy. Engaging teachers clearly balance skills instruction and holistic reading and writing experiences, rather than embracing either a skills-first or whole language approach exclusively.

Excellent teachers are not dependent on worksheets or workbooks; they favor much more authentic tasks, such as reading real books, writing letters that will be mailed, and composing stories that end up in big books on display in the classroom. Moreover, the real books that the students read are great books—Newberry Award winners and enduring classics—great stories that are well told and that inspire the students. Such books are read aloud, read in small groups, and then reread by students to one another and by students with their parents at home. Practicing a book until it can be read to proficiency is more successful when the books being read and reread are so very appealing. Moreover, students never just read one book at a time; typically, they are reading several. Good books contain important vocabulary, which the teacher covers before reading.

The excellent illustrations in good books provide much to be seen and talked about by students—for example, when the teacher does a picture walk through a book before reading it. Part of instruction is that the teacher always encourages students to read books that are a little bit challenging—ones that can be grasped with effort. Much of reading instruction is such matching of students to books, providing students with opportunities to learn to read by doing reading.

Writing provides opportunity to teach higher-order composing skills (i.e., planning, drafting, and revising as a recursive cycle) as well as lower-order skills (e.g., mechanics and grammar). Writing also reinforces reading skills. Thus, just as students are encouraged to stretch words to sound them out during reading, they are encouraged to stretch them to spell them during writing. Instructional activities in excellent classrooms provide complementary learning experiences and orderly articulation of experiences, rather than a jumbled mix of disconnected experiences that never comes together.

Cross-Curricular Connections

Reading, writing, and content learning often connect in excellent classrooms. Thus, science and social studies lessons require reading and writing in response to what is read and experienced as part of content lessons. In general, excellent teachers do much to make connections across the curriculum. Often, they accomplish this task by emphasizing a particular theme for a week or so (e.g., a social studies unit about the post office in which students read books about the post office or read books in which postal letters play a prominent role, with the reading and social studies lessons complemented by the writing of postal letters). Connections occur across the entire year of instruction in excellent classrooms; the teachers remind students of how ideas encountered in today's lesson connect to ideas in previous lessons (e.g., during a story about polar bears, the teacher reminds students about the unit earlier in the year about animal biological adaptations). Connections, of course, do not stop at the classroom door. For example, the excellent teacher makes certain that students know about books in the library connecting with current instructional themes and is effective in getting students interested in such books.

Thinking Processes

Excellent teachers send the message that students can learn to think better, explicitly teaching the students problem-solving processes and strategies for a variety of academic tasks. The excellent teacher encourages students to reflect critically about ideas and to be creative in their thinking. As part of stimulating their students' thinking, excellent teachers model problem-solving skills, often thinking aloud as they do so. For example, when writing directions on the board, the excellent teacher might reread what was written, asking aloud whether it makes sense or whether there might be some errors that could be corrected. Similarly, when reading a passage aloud, the teacher might model rereading in order to understand the passage better. Perhaps when confronting a new vocabulary word in a text, the teacher might sound out the word for the students.

Provides Appropriate Challenges

Excellent teachers appropriately challenge their students, consistently presenting content that is not already known by their students but not so advanced that students cannot understand it even if they exert effort. For example, elementary classrooms often have many leveled books, with students encouraged to read books at a level slightly beyond their current one. Also, when excellent teachers ask questions during lessons, they are difficult enough to require some thinking by students but not so difficult that there are only a few bidders to answer them. The pace of questioning—and the pace of all instruction—is not so slow as to bore students. During question-and-answer sessions and all of instruction, excellent teachers

encourage risk taking (e.g., encouraging students to give their answers to a question even if the expressions on their faces suggest that they are not certain about it).

Different students get challenged in different ways in good classrooms: Excellent teachers embrace the diversity of talents and abilities in their classes. The need to personalize challenges often means that one-on-one teaching is required, with the teacher monitoring carefully what the student can handle and then providing input well matched to the student.

Scaffolding

Excellent teachers scaffold student learning, providing just enough support so that students can continue to make progress with learning tasks and withdrawing help as students can do tasks autonomously. As part of scaffolding, excellent teachers ask questions as students attempt tasks—questions that can be revealing about what students know and do not know. Scaffolding also includes hints to students to check work, especially when the teacher detects shortcomings in student work (e.g., encouraging students to reread their own writing to detect potential problems). Scaffolding also involves urging students to help one another—for example, by encouraging students to read their compositions in progress to others in order to obtain suggestions about how to continue the writing. Scaffolding teachers also encourage students to apply the problem solving, reading, and writing strategies that have been taught in class (e.g., prompting use of the word wall to find some of the words they want to include in their stories).

Monitoring

Excellent teachers walk around their classrooms a great deal, monitoring how their students are doing and asking questions to check for understanding. As they do so, excellent teachers note who needs additional help and which ideas should be covered additionally with the whole class.

Clear Presentations

Excellent teachers give clear directions, which are easy to follow. The expectations are always clear for students as are the learning objectives.

Home-School Connections

Excellent teachers communicate to parents their expectations about parental involvement in student learning (e.g., reading with their children, helping with homework rather than doing it). Such teachers also ask students to have parents assist them with test preparation and sign selected assignments. Excellent teachers make certain through conferences, newsletters, and take-home assignment folders that parents know what is happening in class as well as what their students know and what help they need in order to achieve at higher levels.

Summary

What we have found in our work is that excellent teachers do much to make certain that the curriculum and instruction in their classrooms is excellent. Many different approaches to instruction are used, and many resources are organized to support student learning (e.g., classroom aides, students helping students, parental involvement with homework). The teacher models and encourages active thinking, not only with respect to today's lesson but also in connecting the ideas encountered today with those encountered earlier in the year. The content and teaching challenge students but do not overwhelm them, which requires much planning because students are at different levels of ability. Although excellent teachers encourage student self-regulation, they always provide a safety net of support when students falter—teacher scaffolding, reinstruction, and reexplanations are prominent in excellent classrooms.

Discussion

Our work has been qualitative—intended to generate hypotheses about excellent teaching. The megahypothesis emerging from this work is that excellent teachers do not do simply one or a few things differently from more typical teachers. Rather, their teaching is massively different. They do much to motivate students. Their classroom management is masterful. Their classroom instruction is complex and coherent, meeting the needs of the whole class while matching to the abilities and interests of individual students.

This hypothesis contrasts with the perspectives of many educational researchers. Those who claim that achievement is largely a function of motivation are like blind persons touching part of the elephant. Those who argue that classroom management is the key to classroom success are similarly blind, similarly touching only a different part of the elephant. Those who contend that one particular type of instruction or curriculum material will do the trick with respect to improving classroom functioning join the ranks of the blind persons from this perspective, simply tugging at yet another section of the elephant. The elephants that are excellent classrooms, however, are complex, articulated animals, with many parts spun together by their teacher leaders. The resulting elephant

coherently walks and proceeds through a long life (i.e., for any particular cohort of students, usually at least a school year with the same teacher). The hypothesis we have generated is that to understand the elephants that are classrooms, it is necessary to understand the parts as well as the functioning whole, aware that masterful teachers develop classroom elephants with every individual part better—and every part articulating better—than do less masterful teachers who develop less impressive classroom elephants. That is to say, as anyone who has visited a zoo knows, although all elephants are complex creatures, some are more magnificent than others. We love watching the most magnificent of these beasts when we visit the zoo, preferring them to their less imposing cage mates, just as we love watching the classrooms created by excellent teachers much more than we love watching the classrooms created by more typical teachers down the hall.

CHALLENGES OF TEACHING

Teaching is a challenging activity. Thus, beginning teachers are challenged during their first year or two of teaching (Veenman, 1984); analyses of beginning teaching challenges appear throughout the twentieth century, from Dewey (1913) to U.S. Department of Education reports at the end of the century (Lewis et al., 1999). There were many studies in between (Barr & Rudisell, 1930; Broadbent & Cruickshank, 1965; Dropkin & Taylor, 1963; Hermanowicz, 1966; Johnson & Ryan, 1980; Lambert, 1956; Lortie, 1975; Martin, 1991; Olson & Osborne, 1991; Ryan, 1974; Thompson, 1991; Wey, 1951). Although the challenges seem to decrease with experience, teaching remains a very challenging profession even for veterans (Adams, Hutchinson, & Martray, 1980; Dunn, 1972; Echternacht, 1981; Koontz, 1963; Lieter, 1995; Litt & Turk, 1985; Olander & Farrell, 1970; Pharr, 1974; Rudd & Wiseman, 1962; Thomas & Kiley, 1994). A complete analysis of teaching processes appreciates that teaching always occurs amidst contextual challenges.

Roehrig, Pressley, and Talotta (2002) summarized all of the types of challenges that elementary and secondary teachers can face. Their starting point was the many published case studies of beginning teaching (e.g., Dollase, 1992; Kane, 1991; Kowalski, Weaver, & Henson, 1994; Ryan et al., 1980; Shapiro, 1993). Then they had a sample of first-year teachers and experienced teachers indicate which of the potential challenges occurred in their school lives during the past school year. The result was nearly 500 separate challenges, all of which were reported as experienced by one or more teachers. The challenges clustered into 22 categories, summarized in Table 8.1.

TABLE 8.1 Categories of Challenges of Teaching

Category	Examples
Classroom discipline	Spending too much time on discipline. Not disciplining enough. Not knowing when and how to punish students.
Student misbehavior	Students cutting class. Student inattention. Student violence and weapons violations.
Motivating students	Undermotivated students. Students under too much pressure to do well. Students who do not believe they can do well.
Dealing with individual differences between students	Immature students. Angry and depressed students. Students living in poverty.
Assessing students' work	Concerns about how to do assessment. Lack of confidence in ability to judge student work. Keeping up with volume of assessment (grading).
Relations with parents	Alcoholic parents, divorced parents, or parents with other characteristics adversely affecting student. Lack of support of teacher by parents. Getting parents to come to conferences.
Classroom management	Challenges of organizing classroom environment, especially if moving from room to room across the day. Difficulties in teaching and monitoring students at same time. Special education teachers sometimes do not show up on time.
Resource issues	Insufficient supplies and materials. Dated textbooks. Classroom in disrepair.
Teacher-student communications and interactions	Learning names of so many students. Hard to relate to students who want to be left alone. Handling students with rage.
School-based demands on time	Too much paperwork. Committee work. Coaching can be draining.
Relations with colleagues	Cliques among teachers. Disagreements between teachers about fundamental goals of the school. Other teachers suspicious of your methods of teaching.
Planning lessons and school days	Not receiving enough information before school starts to plan well. Not having enough time to plan. Stressed by staying one chapter ahead.
Classroom instruction	Balancing direct instruction and constructivism. Meetings needs of individual students and needs of whole class. Providing challenge to the brightest students.
Induction, mentoring, and inadequate guidance	Receiving little mentoring. Being observed by mentor is stressful. Receiving little information about the folkways and norms of the school.
Relations with principals and administrators	Principals being critical or disrespectful. Principal directives that are vague. Worrying about being rehired the next year.
Diversity issues	Teaching students with different backgrounds from own background. Teacher can be victim of racial resentment. Students claiming teacher discriminates.
Personal life issues	Having little spare time. Difficulties getting continuing education credits. Physical illness or injuries interfering with teaching.
Having unconstructive attitudes and perceptions	Feeling anxious, overwhelmed, or incompetent. Feeling the rewards of teaching are not great enough. Not believing that the material being taught is important or useful for students.
Gender and sexual issues	Sexual harassment by another teacher. Student flirting with the teacher. Teacher finding a student attractive.
Concerns about the greater community	If community is deteriorating, often negatively affects life in school. Some communities are boring. Some communities are hard to get around.

Note. From Roehrig, Pressley, and Talotta (2002).

Some challenges are caused by characteristics of teachers themselves—by what they do not know (e.g., curriculum, rules of the school), teacher attitudes (e.g., not liking teaching), or physical illness. Some are caused by the students (e.g., their diversity, individual differences in abilities). Some are caused by the many responsibilities of the job (e.g., curriculum planner, disciplinarian, assessor). Some are caused by other adults in the school (e.g., other teachers, administrators, parents). Furthermore, there are the challenges outside the school (e.g., the teacher's family or lack of family, challenges of inner city life). In short, challenges are coming from many directions.

That said, for both beginning and experienced teachers, Roehrig et al. (2002) found that the most frequent source of challenge that teachers report is the students—student misbehavior, lack of motivation, and individual differences were rated as frequent sources of challenge. There are many different types of student folks, all of whom need different strokes.

Roehrig et al. (2002) also found that both beginning and experienced teachers reported facing multiple challenges every day, with some teachers reporting many, many challenges daily (i.e., 20 or more) and across the year (200 or more different challenges during the year). More positively, most challenges can be handled. There are some very serious challenges (i.e., serious in the sense that they cannot be solved easily), however that occur often in the lives of teachers. Beginning teachers often have serious problems with disruptive or uncontrollable students, rude and disrespectful students, students who do not do homework, and students who are mean, living in dysfunctional families, or have special education needs. Beginning teachers also are frequently hassled by not having enough time to help each student as much as needed and by not having any spare time for themselves. The picture is not much different for experienced teachers; they report frequent challenges with angry and hard-to-reach students as well as with students living in dysfunctional families. Hyperactive and tardy students cause many difficulties for experienced teachers, as do students who do not do assignments or who do sloppy work. In short, again, the message is clear that students are the source of many of the challenges in teaching.

In summary, to teach well, it is necessary to surmount many and diverse challenges, many of which persist throughout one's teaching career. The most serious source of challenge is the students, who challenge by what they do (e.g., misbehave), by what they do not do (e.g., homework), and by who they are (e.g., people with different talents and needs). That student motivation can be problematic makes clear the importance of the work on academic motivation of the past quarter century. That student behavior is a challenge validates that the emphasis on classroom management in the teaching literature is well founded. That there are students with varying abilities and needs justifies the emphasis on instruction—much needs to be known about the many different ways of teaching if all students are to be reached. Educational researchers have been pursuing the right issues in constructing a science of teaching. That educational researchers and excellent teachers converge in their emphases on motivating instruction, classroom management, and curriculum and instruction provides strongly convergent support for a framework of teaching that focuses on increasing student achievement motivation, crafting effective classroom management, and developing complexly coherent curricula and instruction.

CONCLUDING REMARKS

We know a great deal about how teaching can be excellent. Excellent teachers do much to motivate their students, excel at classroom organization and management, and engage in a complex orchestration of teaching processes—sometimes directly teaching with modeling and explanations, sometimes providing experiences that permit students to construct understandings, and sometimes scaffolding instruction (i.e., guiding discovery or assisting students to apply skills that were taught directly). Excellent teaching is a complex balancing act, which is all the more impressive because there are many challenges to doing it well. The greatest challenge is students—some of whom do not want to learn, some of whom have difficulties learning, and all of whom must be affected positively if the teacher is to be considered really successful. One of the great joys in studying expert teachers is spending time in classrooms in which absolutely every student is engaged, happy, and making progress. It can and does happen.

One of the sad outcomes of studying expert teaching is the awareness that far too few classrooms are really excellent classrooms. To find the classrooms that were showcased as excellent in our research, we spent much time in many more classrooms that were far from excellent. In many classrooms, motivation is low, management is weak, and instruction falls far short of the complex balancing of direct teaching, scaffolded practice, and discovery that occurs in excellent classrooms.

How can weaker classrooms become better classrooms? Based on our analyses of excellent classrooms, we believe it requires a commitment on the part of the teacher to make the classroom completely motivating by using the many motivational mechanisms that have been validated in the research literature. It also requires getting so good at classroom management that it becomes unnoticeable—that is, classroom management needs to be mastered to the point at which there are very few discipline problems. To some extent, management will become less of an issue if instruction becomes excellent—if the material and lessons taught are interesting and clear to students; so much instruction is going on that students have no time to be distracted; powerful connections are drawn across the curriculum and to the world, which make what is being learned meaningful and understandable; and the instruction is at such a level that kids can get something out of it, at least with assistance that is available in the form of scaffolding. In short, to become excellent teachers, teachers must work on improving many competencies at once—being motivators, managers, and curriculum and instruction experts who can tailor to the many individual needs of their students.

Essential to improvement is the head of the teacher. Excellent teachers know a great deal about motivation, management, and teaching—from extensive knowledge of the curriculum to detailed knowledge about the lives of the children in their classrooms. We have been struck again and again that the excellent teachers we have studied are absolutely certain they can change their students for the better—that their students can and will learn in their classrooms. Such teachers have internalized a set of beliefs about themselves and their students that empowers them. Although it seems likely that some of what teachers know is learned through formal education (i.e., college courses, professional development, professional reading), much more of it is probably learned on the job. Formal education and on-the-job experience are clearly not enough for the teacher to mature to the point of being an excellent teacher, however, for there are many, many experienced teachers who are far from excellent. How is it that some develop magnificently as teachers and others do not? This is a huge next question for the educational researcher community to tackle. It will not be an easy question to answer because development of high teaching proficiency probably requires much in the way of experiences and personal motivation. Such development is probably at least as complex as excellent teaching itself.

There continue to be simple conceptions of teaching improvement in the marketplace of ideas about education. This review is being written at the start of a new school year when the media is filled with ideas about education; thus, claims abound that if schools simply turn to direct instruction models, problems will be solved. At the other extreme, constructivist educators argue that direct instruction is the problem and that the cure is constructivism. Some educators continue to peddle classroom management schemes that also promise to solve the achievement ills of the nation. The simplicity of the proposed approaches to improved teaching,

however, contrasts with the complexity of the excellent teaching documented in the past quarter century. Moreover, the many challenges that must be confronted to be an excellent teacher make it seem unlikely that anyone ever became a great teacher by simply changing one or two elements of teaching—ones that would work well with all students.

Finally, in closing this chapter, we recognize that much more seems to be known about teaching in elementary classrooms than in secondary classrooms. More positively, some analyses tapping both elementary and secondary teaching suggest greater similarities than differences—for example, in the challenges facing elementary and secondary teachers (Roehrig et al., 2002). Even so, we are also aware of analyses such as Stodolsky (1988), which made the case that secondary teaching and learning vary greatly depending on the content area. Still, as we have surveyed the literatures pertaining to secondary content teaching, we have been struck by the presence of discussions about direct transmission, constructivist teaching, motivating instruction, and teacher thinking—the themes overviewed in this chapter. Moreover, the major hypothesis emerging from our own work—that excellent teachers create complex classroom worlds flooded with motivating input, which are well managed and elegantly balance instructional approaches—seems a hypothesis worth evaluating across the entire elementary and secondary range. Another way of stating this hypothesis is that there are no quick fixes—just the great big fix of educators working very hard for years to acquire the knowledge, beliefs, and skills necessary to put together motivating, orderly, instructionally rich environments.

REFERENCES

Adams, R., Hutchinson, S., & Martray, C. (1980, April). *A developmental study of teacher challenges across time.* Paper presented at the annual meeting of the American Educational Research Association, Boston.

Alvermann, D. E., & Hayes, D. A. (1989). Classroom discussions of content area reading assignments: An intervention study. *Reading Research Quarterly, 24,* 305–335.

Alvermann, D. E., O'Brien, D. G., & Dillon, D. R. (1990). What teachers do when they say they're having discussions of content area reading assignments: A qualitative analysis. *Reading Research Quarterly, 25,* 296–322.

Ames, C. (1984). Competitive, cooperative, and individualistic goal structures: A motivational analysis. In R. Ames & C. Ames (Eds.), *Research on motivation in education* (Vol. 1, pp. 117–207). New York: Academic Press.

Ames, C. (1990). Motivation: What teachers need to know. *Teachers College Record, 91,* 409–421.

Ames, C., & Archer, J. (1988). Achievement goals in the classroom: Students' learning strategies and motivation processes. *Journal of Educational Psychology, 80,* 260–270.

Anderson, V., & Roit, M. (1993). Planning and implementing collaborative strategy instruction for delayed readers in grades 6–10. *Elementary School Journal, 94,* 121–137.

Ausubel, D. P. (1961). Learning by discovery: Rationale and mystique. *Bulletin of the National Association of Secondary School Principles, 45,* 18–58.

Bandura, A. (1977). Self-efficacy: Toward a unifying theory of behavioral change. *Psychological Review, 84,* 191–215.

Bandura, A. (1986). *Social foundations of thought and action: A social cognitive theory.* Englewood Cliffs, NJ: Prentice-Hall.

Barr, A. S., & Rudisell, M. (1930). Inexperienced teachers who fail—and why. *The Nations Schools, 5,* 30–34.

Basili, P. A., & Sanford, J. P. (1991). Conceptual change strategies and cooperative group work in chemistry. *Journal of Research in Science Teaching, 28,* 293–304.

Bennett, N., & Dunne, E. (1991). The nature and quality of talk in cooperative classroom groups. *Learning and Instruction, 1,* 103–118.

Berliner, D. (1986). In pursuit of the expert pedagogue. *Educational Researcher, 15*(7), 5–13.

Berliner, D. C. (1988). *The development of expertise in pedagogy.* Washington, DC: American Association of College for Teacher Education.

Bogner, K., Raphael, L. M., & Pressley, M. (2002). How grade-1 teachers motivate literate activity by their students. *Scientific Studies of Reading, 6,* 135–165.

Book, C., & Freeman, D. (1986). Differences in entry characteristics of elementary and secondary teacher candidates. *Journal of Teacher Education, 37,* 47–51.

Borko, H., & Putnam, R. T. (1996). Learning to teach. In D. C. Berliner & R. C. Calfee (Eds.), *Handbook of educational psychology* (pp. 673–708). New York: Macmillan.

Bowers, C. A., & Flinders, D. J. (1990). *Responsive teaching: An ecological approach to classroom patterns of language, culture, and thought.* New York: Teachers College Press.

Brainerd, C. J. (1978). Learning research and Piagetian theory. In L. S. Siegel & C. J. Brainerd (Eds.), *Alternatives to Piaget: Critical essays on the theory* (pp. 69–109). New York: Academic Press.

Broadbent, F., & Cruickshank, D. (1965). *The identification and analysis of problems of first year teachers.* Brockport, NY: The State University of New York. (ERIC Document Reproduction Service No. ED012786)

Brophy, J. (1981). Teacher praise: A functional analysis. *Review of Educational Research, 51,* 5–32.

Brophy, J. (1986, October). *On motivating students* (Occasional Paper No. 101). East Lansing, MI: Michigan State University, Institute for Research on Teaching.

Brophy, J. (1987). Socializing students' motivation to learning. In M. L. Maehr & D. A. Kleiber (Eds.), *Advances in motivation and achievement: Enhancing motivation* (Vol. 5, pp. 181–210).

Brophy, J., & Good, T. L. (1986). Teacher behavior and student achievement. In M. C. Wittrock (Ed.), *Handbook of research on teaching* (3rd ed., pp. 328–375). New York: Macmillan.

Brown, R., Pressley, M., Van Meter, P., & Schuder, T. (1996). A quasi-experimental validation of transactional strategies instruction with low-achieving second grade readers. *Journal of Educational Psychology, 88,* 18–37.

Calderhead, J. (1996). Teachers: Beliefs and knowledge. In D. C. Berliner & R. C. Calfee (Eds.), *Handbook of educational psychology* (pp. 709–725). New York: Macmillan.

Carr, M., & Borkowski, J. G. (1989). Attributional training and the generalization of reading strategies with underachieving children. *Learning and Individual Differences, 1,* 327–341.

Carter, K., Cushing, K., Sabers, D., Stein, P., & Berliner, D. (1988). Expert-novice differences in perceiving and processing visual classroom information. *Journal of Teacher Education, 39,* 25–31.

Carter, K., & Doyle, W. (1996). Personal narrative and life history in learning to teach. In J. Sikula, T. J. Buttery, & E. Guyton (Eds.), *Handbook of research on teacher education* (2nd ed., pp. 120–142). New York: Macmillan.

Carter, K., Sabers, D., Cushing, K., Pinnegar, S., & Berliner, D. C. (1987). Processing and using information about students: A study of expert, novice, and postulant teachers. *Teaching & Teacher Education, 3,* 147–157.

Cazden, C. B. (1986). Classroom discourse. In M. C. Wittrock (Ed.), *Handbook of research on teaching* (3rd ed., pp. 432–463). New York: Macmillan.

Cazden, C. B. (1988). *Classroom discourse: The language of teaching and learning.* Portsmouth, NH: Heinemann.

Champagne, A. B., & Bunce, D. M. (1991). Learning-theory-based science teaching. In S. M. Glynn, R. H. Yeany, & B. K. Britton (Eds.), *The psychology of learning science* (pp. 21–41). Hillsdale, NJ: Erlbaum.

Clark, C. M., & Peterson, P. L. (1986). Teachers' thought processes. In M. C. Wittrock (Ed.), *Handbook of research on teaching* (3rd ed., pp. 255–296). New York: Macmillan.

Clark, C. M., & Yinger, R. J. (1979). Teachers' thinking. In P. L. Peterson & H. J. Walberg (Eds.), *Research on teaching* (pp. 231–263). Berkeley, CA: McCutchan.

Clifford, M. M. (1991). Risk taking: Theoretical, empirical, and educational considerations. *Educational Psychologist, 26,* 263–297.

Collins, A., & Stevens, A. L. (1982). Goals and strategies of inquiry teachers. In R. Glaser (Ed.), *Advances in instructional psychology* (Vol. 2, pp. 65–119). Hillsdale, NJ: Erlbaum.

Collins, C. (1991). Reading instruction that increases thinking abilities. *Journal of Reading, 34,* 510–516.

Dahl, K. L., & Freppon, P. A. (1995). A comparison of innercity children's interpretations of reading and writing instruction in the early grades in skills-based and whole language classrooms. *Reading Research Quarterly, 30,* 50–74.

Day, J. D., Borkowski, J. G., Dietmeyer, D. L., Howsepian, B. A., & Saenz, D. S. (1992). Possible selves and academic achievement. In L. Winegar & J. Valsiner (Eds.), *Children's development within social context* (Vol. 2, pp. 181–201). Hillsdale, NJ: Erlbaum.

Dewey, J. (1913). *Interest and effort in education.* Boston: Riverside.

Dixon, R. C., Carnine, D. W., Lee, D.-S., Wallin, J., & Chard, D. (1998). *Report to the California State Board of Education and addendum to principal report: Review of high quality experimental mathematics research.* Retrieved October 3, 2001, from the World Wide Web: http://idea.uoregon.edu/~ncite/documents/math/math.html

Dolezal, S., Mohan, L., & Pressley, M. (2002). *How grade-3 teachers motivate students.* Notre Dame, IN: Institute for Educational Initiatives. Manuscript in preparation.

Dollase, R. H. (1992). *Voices of beginning teachers: Visions and realities.* New York: Teachers College Press.

Doyle, W. (1986). Classroom organization and management. In M. C. Wittrock (Ed.), *Handbook of research on teaching* (3rd ed., pp. 392–431). New York: Macmillan.

Dropkin, S., & Taylor, M. (1963). Perceived problems of beginning teachers and related factors. *The Journal of Teacher Education, 14*(4), 384–390.

Dunn, L. E. (1972). Problems encountered by the Northwest State University secondary education graduates: A comparative study of problems of beginning and experienced teachers (Doctoral dissertation, Northwestern State University of Louisiana, 1972). *Dissertation Abstracts International, 33.*

Echternacht, L. (1981). Instructional problems of business teachers perceived by first-year teachers and experienced teachers. *College Student Journal, 15,* 352–358.

Eichinger, D. C., Anderson, C. W., Palincsar, A. S., & David, Y. M. (1991, April). *An illustration of the roles of content knowledge, scientific argument, and social norms in collaborative problem solving.* Paper presented at the annual meeting of the American Educational Research Association, Chicago.

Enright, R. D., Lapsley, D. K., & Levy, V. M. (1983). Moral education strategies. In M. Pressley & J. R. Levin (Eds.), *Cognitive strategy research: Educational applications* (pp. 43–83). New York: Springer-Verlag.

Ericsson, K. A., Krampe, R. T., & Tesch-Römer, C. (1993). The role of deliberate practice in the acquisition of expert performance. *Psychological Review, 100,* 363–406.

Fantuzzo, J., King, J., & Heller, L. R. (1992). Effects of reciprocal peer tutoring on mathematics and school adjustment: A component analysis. *Journal of Educational Psychology, 84,* 331–339.

Feitelson, D., Kita, B., & Goldstein, Z. (1986). Effects of listening to series stories on first graders' comprehension and use of language. *Research in the Teaching of English, 20,* 339–356.

Ferreiro, E. (1985). Literacy development: A psychogenetic approach. In D. R. Olsen, N. Torrance, & A. Hildyard (Eds.), *Literacy, language, and learning: The nature and consequences of reading and writing* (pp. 217–228). Cambridge, England: Cambridge University Press.

Garner, R. (1992). Learning from school texts. *Educational Psychologist, 27,* 53–63.

Gaskins, I. W., Rauch, S., Gensemer, E., Cunicelli, E., O'Hara, C., Six, L., & Scott, T. (1997). Scaffolding the development of intelligence among children who are delayed in learning to read. In K. Hogan & M. Pressley (Eds.), *Scaffolding student instruction* (pp. 43–73). Cambridge, MA: Brookline Books.

Gayford, C. (1989). A contribution to a methodology for teaching and assessment of group problem-solving in biology among 15 year old pupils. *Journal of Biological Education, 23,* 193–198.

Graham, S., & Harris, K. R. (1994). The effects of whole language on children's writing: A review of literature. *Educational Psychologist, 29,* 187–192.

Groen, G., & Resnick, L. (1977). Can preschool children invent addition algorithms? *Journal of Educational Psychology, 69,* 645–652.

Harris, K. R., & Pressley, M. (1991). The nature of cognitive strategy instruction: Interactive strategy construction. *Exceptional Children, 57,* 392–404.

Hart, H. H. (Ed.). (1970). *Summerhill: For and against.* New York: Hart.

Hemmings, R. (1973). *Children's freedom: A. S. Neill and the evolution of the Summerhill idea.* New York: Schocken Books.

Henderson, V. L., & Dweck, C. S. (1990). Motivation and achievement. In S. S. Feldman & G. R. Elliott (Eds.), *At the threshold: The developing adolescent* (pp. 308–329). Cambridge, MA: Harvard University Press.

Hermanowicz, H. J. (1966). *The real world of the beginning teacher: The pluralistic world of beginning teachers.* Washington, DC: National Education Association. (ERIC Document Reproduction Service No. ED030616)

Hidi, S. (1990). Interest and its contribution as a mental resource for learning. *Review of Educational Research, 60,* 549–571.

Hogan, K., Nastasi, B. K., & Pressley, M. (1999). Discourse patterns and collaborative scientific reasoning in peer and teacher-guided discussions. *Cognition and Instruction, 17,* 379–432.

Hogan, K., & Pressley, M. (1997a). Scaffolding scientific competencies within classroom communities of inquiry. In K. Hogan & M. Pressley (Eds.), *Scaffolding student instruction* (pp. 74–107). Cambridge, MA: Brookline Books.

Hogan, K., & Pressley, M. (Eds.) (1997b). *Scaffolding student instruction.* Cambridge, MA: Brookline Books.

Johnson, D. W., & Johnson, R. (1975). *Learning together and alone: Cooperation, competition, and individualization.* Englewood Cliffs, NJ: Prentice-Hall.

Johnson, D. W., & Johnson, R. (1979). Conflict in the classroom: Controversy and learning. *Review of Educational Research, 49,* 51–70.

Johnson, D. W., & Johnson, R. (1985). Classroom conflict: Controversy over debate in learning groups. *American Educational Research Journal, 22,* 237–256.

Johnson, J. M., & Ryan, K. (1980). *Research on the beginning teacher: Implications for teacher education.* Washington, DC: Department of Education, National Institute of Education. (ERIC Document Reproduction Service No. ED 209 188)

Kane, P. R. (1991). *The first year of teaching: Real world stories from America's teachers.* New York: Walker.

Kohlberg, L. (1969). Stage and sequence: The cognitive-developmental approach to socialization. In D. Goslin (Ed.), *Handbook of socialization theory and research* (pp. 347–480). New York: Rand McNally.

Kohlberg, L., & Mayer, R. (1972). Development as the aim of education: The Dewey view. *Harvard Educational Review, 42,* 449–496.

Koontz, J. E. (1963). Problems of Arkansas secondary school teachers in certain selected schools (Doctoral dissertation, University of Arkansas, 1963). *Dissertation Abstracts International, 24A,* 1493.

Kowalski, T. J., Weaver, R. A., & Henson, K. T. (1994). *Case studies of beginning teachers.* New York: Longman.

Lambert, S. (1956). Beginning teachers and their education. *The Journal of Teacher Education, 7*(4), 347–351.

Lepper, M. R., Drake, M. F., & O'Donnell-Johnson, T. (1997). Scaffolding techniques of expert human tutors. In K. Hogan & M. Pressley (Eds.), *Scaffolding student instruction* (pp. 108–144). Cambridge, MA: Brookline Books.

Lepper, M. R., Greene, D., & Nisbett, R. E. (1973). Undermining children's intrinsic interest with extrinsic rewards: A test of the "over-justification" hypothesis. *Journal of Personality and Social Psychology, 28,* 129–137.

Lepper, M. R., & Hodell, M. (1989). Intrinsic motivation in the classroom. In C. Ames & R. Ames (Eds.), *Research on motivation in education: Vol. 3. Goals and cognitions* (pp. 73–105). San Diego, CA: Academic Press.

Lepper, M. R., & Malone, T. W. (1987). Intrinsic motivation and instructional effectiveness in computer-based education. In R. E. Snow & M. J. Farr (Eds.), *Aptitude, learning, and instruction: Vol. 3. Conative and affective process analyses* (pp. 255–286). Hillsdale, NJ: Erlbaum.

Lesgold, A., Glaser, R., Rubinson, H., Klopfer, D., Feltovich, P., & Wang, Y. (1988). Expertise in a complex skill: Diagnosing x-ray pictures. In M. T. H. Chi, R. Glaser, & M. J. Farr (Eds.), *The nature of expertise* (pp. 311–342). Hillsdale, NJ: Erlbaum.

Lewis, L., Parsad, B., Carey, N., Bartfai, N., Farris, E., Smerdon, B., & Greene, B. (1999). *Teacher quality: A report on teacher preparation and qualifications of public school teachers.* (NCES Publication No. 1999080). Washington, DC: U.S. Department of Education.

Lieter, M. P. (1995, June). *Burnout in the 1990s: Research agenda and theory.* Invited symposium, Canadian Society for Industrial/Organization Psychology, Annual Convention of the Canadian Psychological Association, Charlottetown, Prince Edward Island.

Litt, M. D., & Turk, D. C. (1985). Sources of stress and dissatisfaction in experienced high school teachers. *Journal of Educational Research, 78*(3), 178–185.

Lortie, D. C. (1975). *Schoolteacher: A sociological study.* Chicago: University of Chicago Press.

Markus, H., & Nurius, P. (1986). Possible selves. *American Psychologist, 41,* 954–969.

Martin, G. J. (1991). *Teachers' perceptions of their first year of teaching.* (Doctoral dissertation, Claremont Graduate School, 1991). *Dissertation Abstracts International, 52-03A,* 885.

Mehan, H. (1979). *Social organization in the classroom.* Cambridge, MA: Harvard University Press.

Morrow, L. M. (1990). Preparing the classroom environment to promote literacy during play. *Early Childhood Research Quarterly, 5,* 537–554.

Morrow, L. M. (1991). Relationships among physical designs of play centers, teachers' emphasis on literacy in play, and children's literacy behaviors during play. In J. Zutell & S. McCormick (Eds.), *Learner factors/teacher factors: Issues in literacy research and instruction* (pp. 127–140). Chicago: National Reading Conference.

Morrow, L. M. (1992). The impact of a literature-based program on literacy achievement, use of literature, and attitudes of children from minority backgrounds. *Reading Research Quarterly, 27,* 251–275.

Nastasi, B. K., Braunhardt, L., Young, M., & Margiano-Lyons, S. (1993, October). *Cooperative and mathematical problem solving in the Jasper context.* Paper presented at the Northeastern Educational Research Association, Ellenville, NY.

National Council of Teachers of Mathematics. (2000). *Principles and standards for school mathematics.* Reston, VA: Author.

National Reading Panel. (2000). *Teaching children to read: An evidence-based assessment of the scientific research literature on reading and its implications for reading instruction: Reports of the subgroups.* Washington, DC: National Institute of Child Health and Development.

Neill, A. S. (1960). *Summerhill: A radical approach to child rearing.* New York: Hart.

Neuman, S. B., & Roskos, K. (1990). The influence of literacy-enriched play settings on preschoolers' engagement with written language. In J. Zutell & S. McCormick (Eds.), *Literacy theory and research: Analyses from multiple paradigms* (pp. 179–188). Chicago: National Reading Conference.

Newman, D., Griffin, P., & Cole, M. (1989). *The construction zone: Working for cognitive change in school.* Cambridge, England: Cambridge University Press.

Nicholls, J. G. (1989). *The competitive ethos and democratic education.* Cambridge, MA: Harvard University Press.

Nicholls, J. G., & Thorkildsen, T. A. (1987, October). *Achievement goals and beliefs: Individual and classroom differences.* Paper presented at the meeting of the Society for Experimental Social Psychology, Charlottesville, VA.

Olander, H. T., & Farrell, M. E. (1970). Professional problems of elementary teachers. *Journal of Teacher Education, 21,* 276–280.

Olson, M. R., & Osborne, J. W. (1991). Learning to teach: The first year. *Teaching & Teacher Education, 7,* 331–343.

Peterson, P. L., & Comeaux, M. A. (1987). Teachers' schemata for classroom events: The mental scaffolding of teachers' thinking during classroom instruction. *Teaching & Teacher Education, 3,* 319–331.

Petitto, A. L. (1985). Division of labor: Procedural learning in teacher-led small groups. *Cognition and Instruction, 2,* 233–270.

Pharr, H. J. (1974). *A study of skills and competencies identified as problem areas for beginning and experienced teachers.* (Doctoral dissertation, University of Northern Colorado, University Microfilms International 74-24503).

Piaget, J. (1970). Piaget's theory. In P. H. Mussen (Ed.), Carmichael's *Manual of child psychology* (3rd ed., Vol. 1, pp. 703–732). New York: Wiley.

Pontecorvo, C., & Zucchermaglio, C. (1990). A passage to literacy: Learning in social context. In Y. M. Goodman (Ed.), *How children construct literacy: Piagetian perspectives* (pp. 59–98). Newark, DE: International Reading Association.

Popenoe, J. (1970). *Inside Summerhill.* New York: Hart.

Pressley, M. (1998). *Reading instruction that works: The case for balanced teaching.* New York: Guilford.

Pressley, M. (2002). *Reading instruction that works: The case for balanced teaching* (2nd ed.). New York: Guilford.

Pressley, M., Allington, R., Wharton-McDonald, R., Block, C. C., & Morrow, L. M. (2001). *Learning to read: Lessons from exemplary first grades.* New York: Guilford.

Pressley, M., & El-Dinary, P. B. (1997). What we know about translating comprehension strategies instruction research into practice. *Journal of Learning Disabilities, 30,* 486–488.

Pressley, M., El-Dinary, P. B., Gaskins, I., Schuder, T., & Bergman, J. L., Almasi, J., & Brown, R. (1992). Beyond direct explanation: Transactional instruction of reading comprehension strategies. *Elementary School Journal, 92,* 513–556.

Pressley, M., Harris, K. R., & Marks, M. B. (1992). But good strategy instructors are constructivists! *Educational Psychology Review, 4,* 3–31.

Pressley, M., Wharton-McDonald, R., Allington, R., Block, C. C., Morrow, L., Tracey, D., Baker, K., Brooks, G., Cronin, J., Nelson, E., & Woo, D. (2001). A study of effective grade-1 literacy instruction. *Scientific Studies of Reading, 5,* 35–58.

Redfield, D. L., & Rousseau, E. W. (1981). A meta-analysis of experimental research on teacher questioning behavior. *Review of Educational Research, 51,* 237–246.

Renninger, K. A. (1990). Children's play interests, representation, and activity. In R. Fivush & J. Hudson (Eds.), *Knowing and remembering in young children* (pp. 127–165). Cambridge, MA: Cambridge University Press.

Renninger, K. A., & Wozniak, R. H. (1985). Effect of interest on attentional shift, recognition, and recall in young children. *Developmental Psychology, 21,* 624–632.

Reynolds, M. C. (Ed.). (1989). *Knowledge base for the beginning teacher.* Oxford, England: Pergamon.

Richardson, V. (1996). The role of attitudes and beliefs in learning to teach. In J. Sikula, T. J. Buttery, & E. Guyton (Eds.), *Handbook of research on teacher education* (2nd ed., pp. 102–119). New York: Macmillan.

Richmond, G., & Striley, J. (1996). Making meaning in classrooms: Social processes in small-group discourse and scientific knowledge building. *Journal of Research in Science Teaching, 33,* 839–858.

Roehrig, A. D., Pressley, M., & Talotta, D. (2002). *Stories of beginning teachers: First year challenges and beyond.* Notre Dame, IN: University of Notre Dame Press.

Rosenhouse, J., Feitelson, D., Kita, B., & Goldstein, Z. (1997). Interactive reading aloud to Israeli first graders: Its contribution to literacy development. *Reading Research Quarterly, 32,* 168–183.

Rosenshine, B., & Stevens, R. (1986). Teaching functions. In M. C. Wittrock (Ed.), *Handbook of research on teaching* (3rd ed., pp. 376–391). New York: Macmillan.

Roth, W. M., & Roychoudhury, A. (1992). The social construction of scientific concepts or the concept map as conscription device and tool for social thinking in high school science. *Science Education, 76,* 531–557.

Rousseau, J.-J. (1979). *Emile or On education.* New York: Basic Books.

Rudd, W. G. A., & Wiseman, S. (1962). Sources of dissatisfaction among a group of teachers. *British Journal of Educational Psychology, 32,* 275–291.

Ryan, K. (1974). *Survival is not good enough: Overcoming the problems of beginning teachers* (Report No. AFT-Pop-15). Washington, DC: American Federation of Teachers. (ERIC Document Reproduction Service No. ED090200)

Ryan, K., Newman, K., Mager, G., Applegate, J., Lasley, T., Flora, R., & Johnston, J. (1980). *Biting the apple: Accounts of first year teachers.* New York: Longman.

Sabers, D. S., Cushing, K. S., & Berliner, D. C. (1991). Differences among teachers in a task characterized by simultaneity, multidimensionality, and immediacy. *American Educational Research Journal, 28,* 63–88.

Schunk, D. H. (1989). Social cognitive theory and self-regulated learning. In B. J. Zimmerman & D. H. Schunk (Eds.), *Self-regulated learning and academic achievement* (pp. 83–110). New York: Springer-Verlag.

Schunk, D. H. (1990). Goal setting and self-efficacy during self-regulated learning. *Educational Psychologist, 25,* 71–86.

Schunk, D. H. (1991). Self-efficacy and academic motivation. *Educational Psychologist, 26,* 207–232.

Shapiro, M. (1993). *Who will teach for America?* Washington, DC: Farragut.

Shuell, T. J. (1996). Teaching and learning in a classroom context. In D. C. Berliner & R. C. Calfee (Eds.), *Handbook of educational psychology* (pp. 726–764). New York: Macmillan.

Shulman, L. (1986). Paradigms and research programs in the study of teaching: A contemporary perspective. In M. C. Wittorck (Ed.), *Handbook of research on teaching* (3rd ed., pp. 3–36). New York: Macmillan.

Shulman, L. S., & Keislar, E. R. (Eds.). (1966). *Learning by discovery: A critical appraisal.* Chicago: Rand McNally.

Slavin, R. (1985a). An introduction to cooperative learning research. In R. Slavin, S. Sharan, S. Kagan, R. H. Lazarowitz, C. Webb, & R. Schmuck (Eds.), *Learning to cooperate, cooperating to learn* (pp. 5–15). New York: Plenum.

Slavin, R. (1985b). Team-assisted individualization: Combining cooperative learning and individualized instruction in mathematics. In R. Slavin, S. Sharan, S. Kagan, R. H. Lazarowitz, C. Webb, & R. Schmuck (Eds.), *Learning to cooperate, cooperating to learn* (pp. 177–209). New York: Plenum.

Snitzer, H. (1964). *Living at Summerhill.* New York: Macmillan.

Stodolsky, S. S. (1988). The subject matters: Classroom activity in math and social studies. Chicago: University of Chicago Press.

Strauss, A., & Corbin, J. (1998). *Basics of qualitative research: Grounded theory procedures and techniques* (2nd ed.). Newbury Park, CA: Sage.

Svenson, O., & Hedonborg, M.-L. (1979). Strategies used by children when solving simple subtractions. *Acta Psychologica, 43,* 477–489.

Thomas, B., & Kiley, M. A. (1994, February). *Concerns of beginning, middle, and secondary school teachers.* Paper presented at the annual meeting of the Eastern Educational Research Association, Sarasota, FL.

Thompson, M. H. (1991). *A classroom of one's own: An ethnographic account of the induction process focusing on problems experienced by first-year, secondary English teachers.* (Doctoral dissertation, University of California, Los Angeles, 1991). *Dissertation Abstracts International, 53-01A,* 59.

Tobin, K., & Fraser, B. J. (1990). What does it mean to be an exemplary science teacher? *Journal of Research in Science Teaching, 27,* 3–25.

Van den Branden, K. (2000). Does negotiation of meaning promote reading comprehension? A study of multilingual primary school classes. *Reading Research Quarterly, 35,* 426–443.

Valheln, K. (1990). *Mind bugs: The origins of procedural misconceptions.* Cambridge, MA: MIT Press.

Veenman, S. (1984). Perceived problems of beginning teachers. *Review of Educational Research, 54,* 143–178.

Weinstein, C. (1988). Preservice teachers' expectations about the first year of teaching. *Teaching and Teacher Education, 4,* 31–41.

Weinstein, C. (1989). Teacher education students' preconceptions of teaching. *Journal of Teacher Education, 40,* 53–60.

Wey, H. W. (1951). Difficulties of beginning teachers. *The School Review, 59*(1), 32–37.

Wharton-McDonald, R., Pressley, M., & Hampston, J. M. (1998). Outstanding literacy instruction in first grade: Teacher practices and student achievement. *Elementary School Journal, 99,* 101–128.

Wittrock, M. C. (1966). The learning by discovery hypothesis. In L. S. Shulman & E. R. Keislar (Eds.), *Learning by discovery: A critical appraisal* (pp. 33–75). Chicago: Rand-McNally.

Wood, S. S., Bruner, J. S., & Ross, G. (1976). The role of tutoring in problem solving. *Journal of Child Psychology and Psychiatry, 17,* 89–100.

Woods, S. S., Resnick, L. B., & Groen, G. J. (1975). Experimental test of five process models for subtraction. *Journal of Educational Psychology, 67,* 17–21.

CHAPTER 9

Cooperative Learning and Achievement:
Theory and Research

ROBERT E. SLAVIN, ERIC A. HURLEY, AND ANNE CHAMBERLAIN

Research on cooperative learning is one of the greatest success stories in the history of educational research. Although there is some research on this topic from the early days of the last century, the amount and quality of that research greatly accelerated in the early 1970s and continues today, more than a quarter-century later. Hundreds of studies have compared cooperative learning to various control methods on a broad range of outcome measures, but by far the most frequent objective of this research is to determine the effects of cooperative learning on student achievement. Studies of the achievement effects of cooperative learning have taken place in every major subject, at all grade levels, and in all types of educational settings in many countries. Both field studies and laboratory studies have produced a great deal of knowledge about the effects of many types of cooperative interventions and about the mechanisms responsible for these effects. Further, cooperative learning is not only a subject of research and theory; it is used at some level by millions

of teachers. One national survey (Puma, Jones, Rock, & Fernandez, 1993) found that 79% of elementary teachers and 62% of middle school teachers reported making some sustained use of cooperative learning. By 1998, a study by Antil, Jenkins, Wayne, and Vadasy found that 93% of teachers sampled reported using cooperative learning, with 81% reporting daily use.

Given the substantial body of research on cooperative learning and the widespread use of cooperative learning techniques, it might be assumed that there is little further research to be done. Yet this is not the case. There are many important unresolved research questions on this topic, and a great deal of development and evaluation is still needed. In its fullest conception, cooperative learning provides a radically different approach to instruction, whose possibilities have been tapped only on a limited basis.

According to David Johnson and Roger Johnson (1999), two of the leading authorities in the field, "cooperative learning exists when students work together to accomplish shared learning goals" (p. 1). Though conceptually straightforward, the functional definition of cooperative learning is the subject of considerable discussion and will be at issue throughout this chapter.

Although there is a fair consensus among researchers about the positive effects of cooperative learning on student

This article was written under funding from the Office of Educational Research and Improvement (OERI), U.S. Department of Education (No. R-117-40005). However, any opinions expressed are those of the authors and do not necessarily represent Department of Education positions or policies.

achievement, as well as a rapidly growing number of educators using cooperative learning in all levels of schooling and many subject areas, there remains much confusion, even controversy, about why and how cooperative learning methods affect achievement and, most important, under what conditions cooperative learning has these effects. Different groups of researchers investigating cooperative learning effects on achievement begin with different assumptions and conclude by explaining the achievement effects of cooperative learning in terms that are substantially unrelated or contradictory. In earlier work, Slavin (1989, 1992, 1995) identified motivationalist, social cohesion, cognitive-developmental, and cognitive-elaboration as the four major theoretical perspectives on the achievement effects of cooperative learning.

The motivationalist perspective presumes that task motivation is the single most impactive part of the learning process, asserting that the other processes such as planning and helping are driven by individuals' motivated self-interest. Motivationalist-oriented scholars focus more on the reward or goal structure under which students operate, even going so far as to suggest that under some circumstances interaction may not be necessary for the benefits of cooperative goal structures to manifest (Slavin, 1995). By contrast, the social cohesion perspective (also called social interdependence theory) suggests that the effects of cooperative learning are largely dependent on the cohesiveness of the group. This perspective holds that students help each other learn because they care about the group and its members and come to derive self-identity benefits from group membership (Hogg, 1987; Johnson & Johnson, 1989, 1999; Turner, 1987). The two cognitive perspectives focus on the interactions among groups of students, holding that in themselves these interactions lead to better learning and thus better achievement. Within the general cognitive heading, developmentalists attribute these effects to processes outlined by scholars such as Piaget and Vygotsky. Work from the cognitive elaboration perspective asserts that learners must engage in some manner of cognitive restructuring (elaboration) of new materials in order to learn them. Cooperative learning is said to facilitate that process. One reason for the continued lack of consensus among cooperative learning scholars is that each perspective tends to approach the topic without deference to the body of similar work from other perspectives and without attending to the larger picture.

Historically, it has been useful that divergent paths of research have developed around this topic. First, the sheer amount of interest and energy that has been directed toward understanding this complex set of processes reflects a general consensus concerning the enormous implications of cooperative learning for education practice. Second, as a result, a great many possible explanations and scenarios have been explored. It should be little surprise, however, that no single explanation has been sufficient to describe fully the functioning of cooperative learning. Depending on the nature of the tasks, objectives, and students involved, any of the major perspectives can rightfully claim some explanatory power in relating students' learning to the functioning of cooperative learning.

Although disagreement among cooperative learning perspectives may have served to accelerate advancement in the field from an academic view, this disagreement has resulted in problems of confusion, skepticism, and divergent expectations among policy makers, administrators, practitioners, and the general public. Already there are a few voices advising caution. There is, for example, growing frustration among practitioners with the many different cooperative approaches that have passed through their campuses but that have inconsistently yielded the promised results (Battisch, Solomon, & Delucci, 1993). There is also pressure at the policy level. Lawmakers have begun to demand increasingly rigorous evidence of effectiveness in the reform models that receive federal and other funding. In order not to jeopardize the tremendous opportunity that is currently available in the form of public, professional, and political trust, it has become imperative that cooperative learning scholarship move beyond competitive attempts to resolve the individual terms of what we now know is a complex equation. We must move toward a unified theory, which in bringing together dissident theoretical perspectives may teach us how best to configure cooperative learning for large-scale classroom implementation under common sets of conditions.

In 30 years of intense activity in cooperative learning scholarship, there has never been an accepted cohesive model of the relationships among the important variables involved in cooperative learning. This chapter offers as a framework for discussion and continued debate a theoretical model of cooperative learning processes that intends to acknowledge the contributions of work from each of the major theoretical perspectives. It places them in a model that depicts the likely role that each plays in cooperative learning processes. This work further explores conditions under which each may operate and suggests research and development needed to advance cooperative learning scholarship so that educational practice may truly benefit from the lessons of 30 years of research.

The alternative perspectives on cooperative learning may be seen as complementary, not contradictory. For example, motivational theorists would not argue that the cognitive

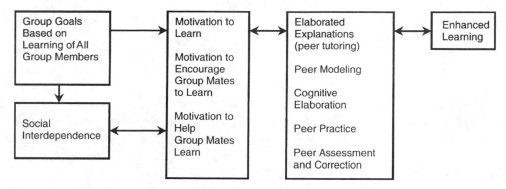

Figure 9.1 Functional relationships among the major interaction components of group learning.

theories are unnecessary. Instead, they assert that motivation drives cognitive process, which in turn produces learning. They would argue that it is unlikely that over the long haul students would engage in the kind of elaborated explanations found by Webb (1989) to be essential to profiting from cooperative activity, without a goal structure designed to enhance motivation. Similarly, social cohesion theorists might hold that the utility of extrinsic incentives must lie in their contribution to group cohesiveness, caring, and prosocial norms among group members, which could in turn affect cognitive processes.

A simple path model of cooperative learning processes, adapted from Slavin (1995), is diagrammed in Figure 9.1. It depicts the main components of a group-learning interaction and represents the functional relationships among the major theoretical approaches to cooperative learning.

This diagram of the interdependent relationships among each of the components begins with a focus on group goals or incentives based on the individual learning of all group members. That is, the model assumes that motivation to learn and to encourage and help others to learn activates cooperative behaviors that will result in learning. This would include both task motivation and motivation to interact in the group. In this model, motivation to succeed leads to learning directly and also drives the behaviors and attitudes that lead to group cohesion, which in turn facilitates the types of group interactions—peer modeling, equilibration, and cognitive elaboration—that yield enhanced learning and academic achievement. The relationships are conceived to be reciprocal, such that as task motivation leads to the development of group cohesion, that development may reinforce and enhance task motivation. By the same token, the cognitive processes may become intrinsically rewarding and lead to increased task motivation and group cohesion.

Each aspect of the diagrammed model is well represented in the literature on theoretical and empirical cooperative

learning. All have well-established rationales and some supporting evidence. What follows is a review of the basic theoretical orientation of each perspective, a description of the cooperative-learning mode that each prescribes, and a discussion of the empirical evidence supporting each.

FOUR MAJOR THEORETICAL PERSPECTIVES

Motivational Perspectives

Motivational perspectives on cooperative learning presume that task motivation is the most important part of the process and hold that the other processes are driven by motivation. Therefore, scholars with this perspective focus primarily on the reward or goal structures under which students operate (see Slavin, 1977, 1983a, 1995). From a motivationalist perspective (e.g., Johnson & Johnson, 1992; Slavin, 1983a, 1983b, 1995), cooperative incentive structures create a situation in which the only way group members can attain their own personal goals is if the group is successful. Therefore, to meet their personal goals, group members must both help their group mates to do whatever enables the group to succeed, and, perhaps even more important, to encourage their group mates to exert maximum efforts. In other words, rewarding groups based on group performance (or the sum of individual performances) creates an interpersonal reward structure in which group members will give or withhold social reinforcers (e.g., praise, encouragement) in response to group mates' task-related efforts (see Slavin, 1983a). One intervention that uses cooperative goal structures is group contingencies (see Slavin, 1987), in which group rewards are given based on group members' behaviors.

The theory underlying group contingencies does not require that group members actually be able to help one another or work together. That their outcomes are dependent on one another's behavior is expected to be sufficient to motivate students to engage in behaviors that help the group to be rewarded, because the group incentive induces students to encourage goal-directed behaviors among their group mates (Slavin, 1983a, 1983b, 1995). A substantial literature in the behavior modification tradition has found that group contingencies can be very effective at improving students' appropriate behaviors and achievement (Hayes, 1976; Litow & Pumroy, 1975).

The motivationalist critique of traditional classroom organization holds that the competitive grading and informal reward systems of the classroom create peer norms opposing academic efforts (see Coleman, 1961). Because one student's success decreases the chances that others will succeed, students are likely to express norms that high achievement is for "nerds" or "teachers' pets." However, when students work together toward a common goal, they may be motivated to express norms favoring academic achievement, to reinforce one another for academic efforts.

Not surprisingly, motivational theorists build group rewards into their cooperative learning methods. In methods developed at Johns Hopkins University (Slavin, 1994, 1995), students can earn certificates or other recognition if their team's average scores on quizzes or other individual assignments exceed a preestablished criterion (see also Kagan, 1992). Methods developed by David Johnson and Roger Johnson (1994) and their colleagues at the University of Minnesota often give students grades based on group performance, which is defined in several different ways. The theoretical rationale for these group rewards is that if students value the success of the group, they will encourage and help one another to achieve.

Empirical Support for the Motivational Perspective

Considerable evidence from practical applications of cooperative learning in elementary and secondary schools supports the motivationalist position that group rewards are essential to the effectiveness of cooperative learning—with one critical qualification. Use of group goals or group rewards enhances the achievement outcomes of cooperative learning if and only if the group rewards are based on the individual learning of all group members (Slavin, 1995). Most often, this means that team scores are computed based on average scores on quizzes that all teammates take individually, without teammate help. For example, in Student Teams-Achievement Divisions (STAD; Slavin, 1994) students work in mixed-ability teams to master material initially presented by the teacher. Following this, students take individual quizzes on the material, and the teams may earn certificates based on the degree

to which team members have improved over their own past records. The only way the team can succeed is to ensure that all team members have learned, so the team members' activities focus on explaining concepts to one another, helping one another practice, and encouraging one another to achieve. In contrast, if group rewards are given based on a single group product (e.g., the team completes one worksheet or solves one problem), there is little incentive for group members to explain concepts to one another, and one or two group members may do all the work (see Slavin, 1995).

In assessing the empirical evidence supporting cooperative learning strategies, the greatest weight must be given to studies of longer duration. Well executed, these are bound to be more realistically generalizable to the day-to-day functioning of classroom practices. A review of 99 studies of cooperative learning in elementary and secondary schools that involved durations of at least 4 weeks compared achievement gains in cooperative learning and control groups. Of 64 studies of cooperative learning methods that provided group rewards based on the sum of group members' individual learning, 50 (78%) found significantly positive effects on achievement, and none found negative effects (Slavin, 1995). The median effect size for the studies from which effect sizes could be computed was +.32 (32% of a standard deviation separated cooperative learning and control treatments). In contrast, studies of methods that used group goals based on a single group product or provided no group rewards found few positive effects, with a median effect size of only +.07. Comparisons of alternative treatments within the same studies found similar patterns; group goals based on the sum of individual learning performances were necessary to the instructional effectiveness of the cooperative learning models (e.g., Fantuzzo, Polite, & Grayson, 1990; Fantuzzo, Riggio, Connelly, & Dimeff, 1989; Huber, Bogatzki, & Winter, 1982). The significance and implications of group goals and individual accountability is discussed in detail later in this chapter.

Social Cohesion Perspective

A theoretical perspective somewhat related to the motivational viewpoint holds that the effects of cooperative learning on achievement are strongly mediated by the cohesiveness of the group. The quality of the group's interactions is thought to be largely determined by group cohesion. In essence, students will engage in the task and help one another learn because they identify with the group and want one another to succeed. This perspective is similar to the motivational perspective in that it emphasizes primarily motivational rather than cognitive explanations for the instructional effectiveness of cooperative learning. However, motivational theorists hold that students help their group mates learn primarily because it is in their own interests to do so.

Social cohesion theorists, in contrast, emphasize the idea that students help their group mates learn because they care about the group. A hallmark of the social cohesion perspective is an emphasis on team-building activities in preparation for cooperative learning, and processing or group self-evaluation during and after group activities. Social cohesion theorists have historically tended to downplay or reject the group incentives and individual accountability held by motivationalist researchers to be essential. They emphasize, instead, that the effects of cooperative learning on students and on student achievement depend substantially on the quality of the group's interaction (Battisch et al., 1993). For example, Cohen (1986, pp. 69–70) stated that "if the task is challenging and interesting, and if students are sufficiently prepared for skills in group process, students will experience the process of groupwork itself as highly rewarding. . . . [N]ever grade or evaluate students on their individual contributions to the group product."

Cohen's (1994a) work, as well as that of Shlomo Sharan and Yael Sharan (1992) and Elliot Aronson and his colleagues (e.g., Aronson, Blaney, Stephan, Sikes, & Snapp, 1978), may be described as social cohesiveness theories. Cohen, Aronson, and the Sharans all use forms of cooperative learning in which students take on individual roles within the group, which Slavin (1983a) called *task specialization* methods. In Aronson's Jigsaw method, students study material on one of four or five topics distributed among the group members. They meet in expert groups to share information on their topics with members of other teams who had the same topic, and then take turns presenting their topics to the team. In the Sharans' Group Investigation (GI) method groups take on topics within a unit studied by the class as a whole, and then further subdivide the topic into tasks within the group. The students investigate the topic together and ultimately present their findings to the class as a whole. Cohen's adaptation of De Avila and Duncan's (1980) Finding Out/Descubrimiento program has students play different roles in discovery-oriented science activities.

One main purpose of the task specialization used in Jigsaw, GI, and Finding Out/Descubrimiento is to create interdependence among group members. In the Johnsons' methods a somewhat similar form of interdependence is created by having students take on roles as "checker," "recorder," "observer," and so on. The idea is that if students value their group mates (as a result of team building and other cohesiveness-building activities) and are dependent on one another, they are likely to encourage and help one another succeed. Johnson and Johnson's (1989, 1994, 1999) work straddles the social cohesion and motivationalist perspectives described in this paper; while their models do use group goals and individual accountability, their theoretical writings emphasize these as means to the development of social interdependence (group cohesion). Their prescriptive writings also emphasize team building, group self-evaluation, and other means more characteristic of social cohesion theorists. In addition, although in most cooperative learning theory and scholarship individual accountability is typically conceived as accountability to the teacher, social cohesion, it seems, would make individual accountability to the group highly salient because group members would have the best information about member efforts, even in the absence of explicit task accountability.

Empirical Support for the Social Cohesion Perspective

There is some evidence that the achievement effects of cooperative learning depend on social cohesion and the quality of group interactions (Ashman & Gillies, 1997; Battisch et al., 1993). The achievement outcomes of cooperative learning methods that emphasize task specialization are less clear. Research on the original form of Jigsaw has not generally found positive effects of this method on student achievement (Slavin, 1995). One problem with this method is that students have limited exposure to material other than that which they studied themselves, so learning gains on their own topics may be offset by losses on their group mates' topics. In contrast, there is evidence that when it is well implemented, GI can significantly increase student achievement (Sharan & Shachar, 1988). In studies of at least 4 weeks' duration, the Johnsons' (1994) methods have not been found to increase achievement more than individualistic methods unless they incorporate group rewards (in this case, group grades) based on the average of group members' individual quiz scores (see Slavin, 1995). Studies of forms of Jigsaw that have added group rewards to the original model have found positive achievement outcomes (Mattingly & Van Sickle, 1991).

Research on practical classroom applications of methods based on social cohesion theories provides inconsistent support for the proposition that building cohesiveness among students through team building alone (i.e., without group incentives) will enhance student achievement. There is some evidence that group processing activities, such as reflection at the end of each class period on the group's activities, can enhance the achievement effects of cooperative learning (Yager, Johnson, Johnson, & Snider, 1986). On the other hand, an Israeli study found that team-building activities had no effect on the achievement outcomes of Jigsaw (Rich, Amir, & Slavin, 1986).

In general, methods that emphasize team building and group process but do not provide specific group rewards based on the learning of all group members are no more effective than traditional instruction in increasing achievement (Slavin, 1995), although there is evidence that these methods can be effective if group rewards are added to them.

Chapman (2001) reported on three studies that assessed the impact of social cohesion in cooperative learning under three different incentive structures. In two of these studies students selected from their classmates those with whom they would and would not like to work. Students were then assigned to one of two types of groups. Low-cohesion groups were composed of no preferred students and some rejected students. High-cohesion groups were composed of no rejected students and some selected students. Students then studied in groups that included group goals and individual accountability, group incentives only, or no incentives. The researcher's hypothesis that results would vary according to group cohesion was not supported. The third of these studies is clearer. It examined high and low group cohesion based on task-related cohesiveness (via group processing) as opposed to social cohesiveness as in the first two studies reported. This study found a marginal advantage of high task cohesion and group goals with individual accountability combined over all of the other conditions. This finding is congruent with the body of evidence concerning group cohesion and group goals and individual accountability. One major exception is GI (Sharan & Hertz-Lazarowitz, 1980; Sharan & Shachar, 1988; Sharan & Sharan, 1992). However, in this method groups are evaluated based on their group products, which are composed of unique contributions made by each group member. Thus, this method may be using a form of the group goals and individual accountability held by motivationalist theories to be essential to the instructional effectiveness of cooperative learning.

Cognitive Perspectives

The major alternative to the motivationalist and social cohesiveness perspectives on cooperative learning, both of which focus primarily on group norms and interpersonal influence, is the cognitive perspective. The cognitive perspective holds that interactions among students will in themselves increase student achievement for reasons that have to do with mental processing of information rather than with motivations. Cooperative methods developed by cognitive theorists involve neither the group goals that are the cornerstone of the motivationalist methods nor the emphasis on building group cohesiveness characteristic of the social cohesion methods. However, there are several quite different cognitive perspectives, as well as some that are similar in theoretical perspec-

tive but have developed on largely parallel tracks. The two most notable of these are described in the following sections.

Developmental Perspective

One widely researched set of cognitive theories is the developmental perspective (e.g., Damon, 1984; Murray, 1982). The fundamental assumption of the developmental perspective on cooperative learning is that interaction among children around appropriate tasks increases their mastery of critical concepts. Vygotsky (1978, p. 86) defined the zone of proximal development as "the distance between the actual developmental level as determined by independent problem solving and the level of potential development as determined through problem solving under adult guidance or in *collaboration with more capable peers* [italics added]." In his view, collaborative activity among children promotes growth because children of similar ages are likely to be operating within one another's proximal zones of development, modeling in the collaborative group behaviors that are more advanced than those that they could perform as individuals. Vygotsky (1978, p. 17) described the influence of collaborative activity on learning as follows: "Functions are first formed in the collective in the form of relations among children and then become mental functions for the individual. . . . Research shows that reflection is spawned from argument."

Similarly, Piaget (1926) held that social-arbitrary knowledge—language, values, rules, morality, and symbol systems—can be learned only in interactions with others. Peer interaction is also important in logical-mathematical thought in disequilibrating the child's egocentric conceptualizations and in providing feedback to the child about the validity of logical constructions.

There is a great deal of empirical support for the idea that peer interaction can help nonconservers become conservers. Many studies have shown that when conservers and nonconservers of about the same age work collaboratively on tasks requiring conservation, the nonconservers generally develop and maintain conservation concepts (see Bell, Grossen, & Perret-Clermont, 1985; Murray, 1982; Perret-Clermont, 1980). In fact, a few studies (e.g., Ames & Murray, 1982; Mugny & Doise, 1978) have found that both individuals in pairs of disagreeing nonconservers who had to come to consensus on conservation problems gained in conservation. The importance of peers' operating in one another's proximal zones of development was demonstrated by Kuhn (1972), who found that a small difference in cognitive level between a child and a social model was more conducive to cognitive growth than was a larger difference.

On the basis of these and other findings, many Piagetians (e.g., Damon, 1984; Murray, 1982; Wadsworth, 1984) have called for an increased use of cooperative activities in schools. They argue that interaction among students on learning tasks will lead in itself to improved student achievement. Students will learn from one another because in their discussions of the content, cognitive conflicts will arise, inadequate reasoning will be exposed, disequilibration will occur, and higher quality understandings will emerge.

From the developmental perspective, the effects of cooperative learning on student achievement would be largely or entirely due to the use of cooperative tasks. Damon (1984, p. 337) explicitly rejected the use of "extrinsic incentives as part of the group learning situation," arguing that "there is no compelling reason to believe that such inducements are an important ingredient in peer learning." In this view, opportunities for students to discuss, to argue, and to present and hear one another's viewpoints are the critical element of cooperative learning with respect to student achievement.

For example, Damon (1984, p. 335) integrated Piagetian, Vygotskian, and Sullivanian perspectives on peer collaboration to propose a "conceptual foundation for a peer-based plan of education":

1. Through mutual feedback and debate, peers motivate one another to abandon misconceptions and search for better solutions.
2. The experience of peer communication can help a child master social processes, such as participation and argumentation, and cognitive processes, such as verification and criticism.
3. Collaboration between peers can provide a forum for discovery learning and can encourage creative thinking.
4. Peer interaction can introduce children to the process of generating ideas.

One category of practical cooperative methods closely related to the developmental perspective is group discovery methods in mathematics, such as Marilyn Burns's (1981) Groups of Four method. In these techniques students work in small groups to solve complex problems with relatively little teacher guidance. They are expected to discover mathematical principles by working with unit blocks, manipulatives, diagrams, and other concrete aids. The theory underlying the presumed contribution of the group format is that in the exploration of opposing perceptions and ideas, higher order understandings will emerge; also, students operating within one another's proximal zones of development will model higher quality solutions for one another.

Empirical Evidence for the Developmental Perspective. Although considerable theoretical work and laboratory research points to the potential utility of developmentally based methods to cooperative learning, there is almost no research explicitly linking this conceptual work to classroom practice. It seems likely, however, that the cognitive processes described by developmental theorists are important mediating variables that can help explain the positive outcomes of effective cooperative learning methods (Slavin, 1987, 1995).

Cognitive Elaboration Perspective

A cognitive perspective on cooperative learning quite different from the developmental viewpoint is one that might be called the cognitive elaboration perspective. Research in cognitive psychology has long held that if information is to be retained in memory and related to information already in memory, the learner must engage in some sort of cognitive restructuring, or elaboration, of the material (Wittrock, 1986). One of the most effective means of elaboration is explaining the material to someone else. Research on peer tutoring has long found achievement benefits for the tutor as well as the tutee (Devin-Sheehan, Feldman, & Allen, 1976). In this method students take roles as recaller and listener. They read a section of text, and then the recaller summarizes the information while the listener corrects any errors, fills in any omitted material, and helps think of ways that both students can remember the main ideas. The students switch roles on the next section.

One practical use of the cognitive elaboration potential of cooperative learning is in writing process models (Graves, 1983), in which students work in peer response groups or form partnerships to help one another draft, revise, and edit compositions. Such models have been found to be effective in improving creative writing (Hillocks, 1984), and a writing process model emphasizing use of peer response groups is part of the Cooperative Integrated Reading and Composition Writing/Language Arts program (Stevens, Madden, Slavin, & Farnish, 1987), a program that has also been used to increase student writing achievement. Part of the theory behind the use of peer response groups is that if students learn to evaluate others' writing, they will become better writers themselves, a variant of the cognitive elaboration explanation. However, it is unclear at present how much of the effectiveness of writing process models can be ascribed to the use of cooperative peer response groups as opposed to other elements (such as the revision process itself).

Other teaching models based on the cognitive elaboration perspective on cooperative learning include transactional teaching and reciprocal teaching (see chapter by Pressley in this volume for a discussion of transactional teaching). Reciprocal teaching (Palincsar & Brown, 1984) is a method for teaching reading comprehension skills. In this technique students are taught to formulate questions for one another around narrative or expository texts. In doing so, they must process the material themselves and learn how to focus in on the essential elements of the reading passages.

Empirical Evidence for the Cognitive Elaboration Perspective.   Donald Dansereau and his colleagues at Texas Christian University have found in a series of brief studies that college students working on structured "cooperative scripts" can learn technical material or procedures far better than can students working alone (Dansereau, 1988; O'Donnell, 1996; O'Donnell & Dansereau, 1992; Newbern, Dansereau, Patterson, & Wallace, 1994). In one of those studies, Dansereau and his colleagues found that whereas both the recaller and the listener learned more than did students working alone, the recaller learned more (O'Donnell & Dansereau, 1992). This mirrors both the peer tutoring findings and the findings of Noreen Webb (1989, 1992), who discovered that the students who gained the most from cooperative activities were those who provided elaborated explanations to others. In this research as well as in Dansereau's, students who received elaborated explanations learned more than did those who worked alone, but not as much as those who served as explainers.

Studies of reciprocal teaching have generally supported its positive effects on student achievement (O'Donell, 2000; Palincsar, 1987; Rosenshine & Meister, 1994). However, studies of group discovery methods such as Groups of Four (Burns, 1981) find few achievement benefits for students in comparison to traditional expository teaching (Davidson, 1985; Johnson, 1985; Johnson & Waxman, 1985).

WHAT FACTORS CONTRIBUTE TO THE ACHIEVEMENT EFFECTS OF COOPERATIVE LEARNING?

Although the four perspectives discussed in this chapter can rightfully be considered complementary as they relate functionally to cooperative learning, real philosophical differences underlie the differing conceptions on how best to proceed. They differ in large part in where they locate motivation for learning behaviors. There is particular disagreement between researchers who emphasize the changes in incentive structure brought about by certain forms of cooperative learning and those who hold that changes in task structure are all that is required to enhance learning. The difficulty in settling these differences lies in the fact that research in each of the four traditions tends to establish settings and

conditions favorable to that perspective. For example, most research on cooperative learning models from the motivational and social cohesiveness perspectives takes place in real classrooms over extended periods, as both extrinsic motivation and social cohesion may be assumed to take time to show their effects.

In contrast, studies undertaken from the developmental and cognitive elaboration perspectives tend to be very short, making issues of motivation moot. These latter paradigms also tend to use pairs rather than groups of four. Pairs involve a much simpler social process than groups of four, whose members may need time to develop ways of working well together. Developmental research almost exclusively uses young children trying to master conservation tasks, which bear little resemblance to the social-arbitrary learning that characterizes most school subjects; most cognitive elaboration research involves college students. Disentangling the effects is further complicated by the fact that empirical investigation and classroom applications of cooperative learning typically change aspects of both incentive and task structures, making it difficult to determine which factors are responsible for which outcomes.

Nonetheless, research on cooperative learning has moved beyond the question of whether cooperative learning is effective in accelerating student achievement to focus on the conditions under which it is optimally effective. The preceding discussion described alternative overarching theories to explain cooperative learning effects, as well as an impressive set of empirical findings associated with each. It is useful to examine the empirical cooperative learning research across the boundaries of theoretical perspective in order to determine which factors consistently contribute to or detract from the effectiveness of cooperative learning.

There are two primary ways to learn about factors that contribute to the effectiveness of cooperative learning. One is to compare the outcomes of studies of alternative methods. For example, if programs that incorporated group rewards produced stronger or more consistent positive effects (in comparison to control groups) than programs that did not, this would provide one kind of evidence that group rewards enhance the outcomes of cooperative learning. The problem with such comparisons is that the studies being compared usually differ in measures, durations, subjects, and many other factors that could explain differing outcomes. Better evidence is provided by studies that compared alternative forms of cooperative learning in a single investigation or series of investigations, such as the important series of studies reported by Chapman (2001). In these 10 studies conducted in Australian schools, Chapman and her colleagues set out to examine systematically and under a common methodological framework several of the major mediating factors that have been identified in cooperative learning research and practice. In such studies, most factors other than those being studied can be held constant. The following sections discuss both types of studies to further explore factors that contribute to the effectiveness of cooperative learning for increasing achievement.

Structuring Group Interactions

There is some evidence that carefully structuring the interactions among students in cooperative groups can be effective even in the absence of group rewards. For example, Meloth and Deering (1992) compared students working in two cooperative conditions. In one, students were taught specific reading comprehension strategies and were given "think sheets" to remind them to use these strategies (e.g., prediction, summarization, character mapping). In the other group students earned team scores if their members improved each week on quizzes. A comparison of the two groups on a reading comprehension test found greater gains for the strategy group (also see Meloth & Deering, 1994); Berg (1993) and Newbern et al. (1994) found positive effects of scripted dyadic methods that did not use group rewards; and Van Oudenhoven, Wiersma, and Van Yperen (1987) found positive effects of structured pair learning whether feedback was given to the pairs or only to individuals. Ashman and Gillies (1997) found better performance among students trained in specific cooperative learning skills and strategies than among untrained students. They also found that children trained in cooperative learning skills were consistently more helpful and inclusive of their peers and that the differences were maintained over the 12 weeks of the study. Webb and Farvier (1994) also found better achievement and helping behaviors among Latino and African American students but not among White or Asian students who received training in academic helping skills.

Research on reciprocal teaching (Palincsar & Brown, 1984) also shows how direct strategy instruction can enhance the effects of a technique related to cooperative learning. In this method the teacher works with small groups of students and models such cognitive strategies as question generation and summarization. The teacher then gradually turns over responsibility to the students to carry on these activities with each other. Studies of reciprocal teaching have generally found positive effects of this method on reading comprehension (Palincsar & Brown, 1984; Palincsar, Brown, & Martin, 1987; Rosenshine & Meister, 1994). Chapman (2001) compared structured group interaction (resource interdependence) to individual learning and to structured group interaction with group-interdependent reward. She reported that structuring group interactions was superior to individual learning and that the addition of group goals and individual accountability did

not further enhance these effects. Such findings make it clear that the effects of group rewards based on the individual efforts of all group members in cooperative learning are largely indirect. They serve to motivate students to engage in the types of behaviors, such as providing group mates with elaborated explanations, that enhance learning outcomes. The research by Meloth and Deering (1992, 1994), Berg (1993), and others suggests that students can be directly taught to engage in cognitive and interpersonal behaviors that lead to higher achievement, without the need for group rewards.

However, there is also evidence to suggest that a combination of group rewards and strategy training produces much better outcomes than does either alone. Fantuzzo, King, and Heller (1992) study, cited earlier, directly made a direct comparison between rewards alone, strategy alone, and a combination and found the combination to be by far the most effective. Further, the outcomes of dyadic learning methods, which use group rewards as well as strategy instruction, produced some of the largest positive effects of any cooperative methods, much larger than those found in the Berg (1993) study that provided groups with structure but not rewards. As noted earlier, studies of scripted dyads also find that adding incentives adds to the effects of these strategies (O'Donnell, 1996). The consistent positive findings for Cooperative Integrated Reading and Composition (CIRC; Stevens et al., 1987), which uses both group rewards and strategy instruction, also argue for this combination.

Group Goals and Individual Accountability

As noted earlier, several reviews of the cooperative learning literature have concluded that cooperative learning is most consistently effective when groups are recognized or rewarded based on individual learning of their members (Davidson, 1985; Ellis & Fouts, 1993; Manning & Lucking, 1991; Mergendoller & Packer, 1989; Newmann & Thompson, 1987; Slavin, 1983a, 1983b, 1989, 1992, 1995). The specific form of group goals implemented ranges from simple recognition to classroom privileges to material rewards, such as certificates. Individual accountability may be achieved by averaging students' individual quiz scores to derive the group score or by using the performance of a randomly selected individual to represent the group. In contrast, methods lacking group goals give students only individual grades or other individual feedback, with no group consequence for doing well as a group. Methods lacking individual accountability might reward groups for doing well, but the basis for this reward would be a single project, worksheet, quiz, or other product that could theoretically have been done by only one group member.

If we presume that students act solely out of self-interest, the importance of group goals and individual accountability is in providing students with an incentive to help each other and to encourage each other to put forth maximum effort (Slavin, 1995). If students can only do as well as the group and the group can succeed only by ensuring that all group members have learned the material, then group members will be motivated to teach each other. Studies of behaviors within groups that relate most to achievement gains consistently show that students who give each other explanations (and less consistently, those who receive such explanations) are the students who learn the most in cooperative learning. Giving or receiving answers without explanation has generally been found to reduce achievement (Webb, 1989, 1992). At least in theory, group goals and individual accountability should motivate students to engage in the behaviors that increase achievement and avoid those that reduce it. If a group member wants her group to be successful, she must teach her group mates (and learn the material herself). If she simply tells her group mates the answers, they will fail the quiz that they must take individually. If she ignores a group mate who does not understand the material, the group mate will fail, and the group will fail as well.

In groups lacking individual accountability, one or two students may do the group's work, while others engage in "free riding" or "social loafing" (Latane, Williams, & Harkins, 1979; Williams & Karau, 1991). For example, in a group asked to complete a single project or solve a single problem, some students may be discouraged from participating. A group trying to complete a common problem may not want to stop and explain what is going on to a group mate who does not understand or may feel that it is useless or counterproductive to try to involve certain group mates.

The importance of group goals that can be achieved only by ensuring the learning of all group members is supported by empirical evidence that emphasizes both degree and consistency. Recall that 25 studies of methods that incorporated group goals and individual accountability produced a much higher median effect size (+.32) than did studies of other methods (+.07). Recall also that 78% of studies assessing the effectiveness of methods using group goals and individual accountability found significantly positive effects and that there were no significantly negative effects. This is compared with only 37% significantly positive effects and 14% significantly negative effects in studies of methods lacking group goals and individual accountability.

A comparison among the Johnson's methods studies (Johnson & Johnson, 1989) supports the same conclusions. Across eight studies of learning together methods in which students were rewarded based on a single worksheet or product, the median effect size was near zero (+.04). However, among four studies that evaluated forms of the program in which students were graded based on the average performance of all group members on individual assessments, three found significantly positive effects.

Finally, comparisons within the same studies consistently support the importance of group goals and individual accountability. For example, Chapman (2001) reported on five studies that compared group goals and individual accountability to other incentive formats. In two of those, cooperative learning with group goals and individual accountability resulted in better performance than did individualized incentives on a math task. Two more of the studies found similar results using a reading task. In the fifth study, mentioned earlier, resource interdependence with and without group-interdependent incentives yielded similar performance. That is, students who simply shared materials performed similarly to others who shared materials and were assigned interdependent goals. It is also noteworthy that an additional study by the same researchers compared group goals and individual accountability with and without cooperative interaction and found that the combination of group goals and individual accountability and cooperative interaction was superior to incentive alone. In four of the five comparisons made by Chapman and her associates, cooperative learning with group goals and individual accountability resulted in superior student performance in comparison to cooperation without such elements.

Fantuzzo et al. (1992) conducted a component analysis of Reciprocal Peer Tutoring (RPT). They compared four conditions in which students worked in dyads to learn math. In one, students were rewarded with opportunities to engage in special activities of their choice if the sum of the dyad's scores on daily quizzes exceeded a set criterion. In another, students were taught a structured method of tutoring each other, correcting efforts, and alternating tutor-tutee roles. A third condition involved a combination of rewards and structure, and a fourth was a control condition in which students worked in pairs but were given neither rewards nor structure. The results showed that the reward + structure condition had by far the largest effects on math achievement (+1.42) and that reward alone had much larger effects than structure alone. The reward + structure condition exceeded the structure-only condition by an effect size of +1.88, and the reward-only group exceeded control by an effect size of +.21 (the structure-only group performed less well than did the control group).

Other studies also found greater achievement for cooperative methods using group goals and individual accountability than for those that did not. Huber et al. (1982) compared a form of STAD to traditional group work lacking group goals and individual accountability. The STAD group scored significantly better on a math test (+.23). In a study of Team Assisted Individualization (TAI), Cavanaugh (1984) found that students who received group recognition based on the number of units accurately completed by all group members both learned more (+.24) and completed more units (+.25) than did students who received individual recognition only. O'Donnell (1996) compared dyads working with and without incentives. In three experimental studies students who received explicit incentives based on their learning learned significantly more than those who did not. Okebukola (1985), studying science in Nigeria, found substantially greater achievement in STAD and teams games tournaments (TGT) methods using group goals and individual accountability than in forms of Jigsaw and Johnsons' methods that did not. In another study Okebukola (1986) found much higher achievement in classes that used a method combining cooperation and group competition (one form of group reward) than in a cooperative method that did not use group rewards of any kind (+1.28).

IS THERE ANY ALTERNATIVE TO GROUP GOALS AND INDIVIDUAL ACCOUNTABILITY?

Many educators express discomfort with using group goals and individual accountability to manipulate motivation to achieve. Teachers often complain of the record keeping involved, and some voice philosophical objections to the idea of using extrinsic rewards to motivate learning. Such concerns raise the question of whether group goals and individual accountability are always necessary and, indeed, whether such goal structures are detrimental to continued learning.

Before exploring this question, it is important to make clear the theoretical rationale for the importance of group goals and individual accountability. This combination is designed principally to motivate students not only to work together but also to be concerned about the learning of their group mates. The assumption is that although group mates may readily interact with and help each other, without appropriate structuring this interaction and help may take the form of sharing answers or doing each other's work, rather than making certain that group mates understand the material and can independently solve problems. In cooperative learning techniques in which groups are rewarded based on the individual learning of each member, the group members want to succeed. The only way that they can make this happen is to teach and assess one another and to make certain that every group member can independently show mastery of whatever the group is studying.

Those opposed to using group goals and individual accountability in cooperative learning warn of possible costs of using rewards in classrooms. A few reviewers (e.g., Damon, 1984; Kohn, 1986) have recommended against the use of group rewards, fearing that they may undermine long-term motivation. There is little empirical evidence of undermining effects resulting from the use of group goals and individual accountability. Chapman (2001), noting that it would be "difficult to justify the use of a procedure that impacted positively on student achievement but negatively on their affective response to the subject matter" (p. 3), measured students' affective reactions to the lesson content and subject matter used in 10 studies that compared group goals and individual accountability to other incentive structures and found no evidence that the use of group goals and individual accountability had negative effects on student self-reports of subject-related attitudes. In some cases, students' attitudes were significantly more positive. This goal structure certainly does not undermine long-term achievement. Among multiyear studies, methods that incorporate group rewards based on individual learning performance have consistently shown continued or enhanced achievement gains over time (Calderón, Hertz-Lazarowitz, & Slavin, 1998; Greenwood, Delquadri, & Hall, 1989; Stevens & Slavin, 1995a, 1995b). In contrast, multiyear studies of methods lacking group rewards found few achievement effects in the short or long term (Solomon, Watson, Schaps, Battistich, & Solomon, 1990; Talmage, Pascarella, & Ford, 1984).

The rationale that assumes a cost to be incurred for using group goals and individual accountability is not well articulated in the literature but seems to derive from the ongoing debate over the relationship among reinforcement, reward, and students' intrinsic motivation. A 1994 meta-analysis (Cameron & Pierce, 1994), which supported earlier assertions that, overall, reward does not decrease students' intrinsic motivation, sparked considerable debate (Cameron & Pierce, 1996; Deci, Koestner, & Ryan, 1999; Lepper, Henderlong, & Gingras, 1999; Lepper, Keavney, & Drake, 1996). However, insofar as the use of the specific goal structure that combines group goals and individual accountability is concerned, there is little empirical evidence of these undermining effects. Moreover, the pervasive use of extrinsic incentives in elementary and secondary schools with or without cooperative learning makes the question largely moot. A more pertinent question is whether extrinsic incentives should be given at the group *and* individual level or only at the individual level (as is current practice in virtually all classrooms in existence). It remains incumbent on theorists who oppose these methods to develop and demonstrate consistent, substantial, and enduring achievement benefits of cooperative learning or other learning models that do not use this goal structure. For now, the preponderance of evidence indicates that the combination of cooperative learning strategies with group goals and individual accountability is a practical, feasible, and effective method of enhancing students' academic achievement.

However, there do appear to be a few instances in which this structure of group goals and individual accountability may not be necessary. These are cases in which achievement gains, in comparison to control groups, have been found for cooperative learning treatments that lack group goals, individual accountability, or both of these elements. Whereas theoretical and empirical support for the centrality of group goals and individual accountability is strong for a broad range of school tasks, the following paragraphs summarize the evidence that some kinds of learning may not require these elements.

Higher Level Cognitive Tasks

Cohen (1994b) raised the possibility that whereas group rewards and individual accountability may be necessary for lower level skills, they may not be for higher level ones. As evidence of this she cited a study by Sharan et al. (1984) that compared STAD and GI. In this study STAD and GI students performed equally well (and better than controls) on a test of English as a foreign language, and STAD students did significantly better than GI on "lower level" (knowledge) items (+.38). On "higher level" items, GI students performed nonsignificantly higher than STAD students, with a difference of less than half of a point on a 15-point test. Otherwise, there is no evidence that group rewards are less important for higher order skills, although the possibility is intriguing.

Controversial Tasks Without Single Answers

One category of tasks that may not require group goals and individual accountability consists of tasks in which it is likely that students will benefit from hearing others thinking aloud—the classic Vygotskian paradigm. Students in collaborating groups make overt their private speech, giving peers operating at a slightly lower cognitive level on a given task a stepping stone to understanding and incorporating higher quality solutions in their own private speech (see Bershon, 1992). Tasks of this kind would be at a very high level of cognitive complexity but without a well-defined path to a solution or a single correct answer, especially tasks on which there are likely to be differences of opinion. For such tasks, the process of participating in arguments or even of listening to others argue and justify their opinions or solutions may be enough to enhance learning, even without in-group teaching, explanation, or assessment. Perhaps the best classroom evidence on this type of task is from Johnson and Johnson's (1979) studies of structured controversy, in which students argue both sides of a controversial issue using a structured method of argumentation. Other examples of such tasks might include group projects without a single right answer (e.g., planning a city) and solving complex problems (e.g., nonroutine problems in mathematics) or finding the main idea of paragraphs. In each of these cases, it may be that hearing the thinking processes of others is beneficial even in the absence of coteaching.

At the same time, is still important to note that use of group goals and individual accountability is unlikely to interfere with modeling of higher level thinking but is likely to add teaching and elaborated explanation (Webb, 1992). For example, Stevens, Slavin, and Farnish (1991) evaluated a method of teaching students to find the main ideas of paragraphs in which four-member groups first came to consensus on a set of paragraphs and then worked to make certain that every group member could find the main idea. Groups received certificates based on the performance of their members on individual quizzes. The consensus procedure evokes arguments and explanations, modeling higher quality thinking, but the teaching procedure ensures that students can each apply their new understandings.

Voluntary Study Groups

A second category of cooperative tasks that may not require group goals and individual accountability consists of situations in which students are strongly motivated to perform well on an external assessment and can clearly see the benefits of working together. The classic instance of this is voluntary study groups common in postsecondary education, especially in medical and law schools. Medical and law students must master an enormous common body of information, and it is obvious to many students that participating in a study group will be beneficial. Although there is little extrinsic reason for students to be concerned about the success of other study group members, there is typically a norm within study groups that each member must do a good job of presenting to the group. Because study group membership is typically voluntary, study group members who do not participate effectively may be concerned about being invited back the next term.

There is little research on voluntary study groups in postsecondary institutions, and it is unclear how well this idea would apply at the elementary or secondary levels. In the United States it would seem that only college-bound high school seniors are likely to care enough about their grades to participate actively in study groups like those seen at the postsecondary level, yet it may be that similar structures could be set up by teachers and that norms of reciprocal responsibility to the group could be developed. Another problem, however, is that voluntary study groups can and do reject (or fail to select) members who are felt to have little to contribute to the group. This could not be allowed to happen in study groups sponsored by the school.

Structured Dyadic Tasks

A third category of cooperative tasks that may not require group goals and individual accountability consists of tasks that are so structured that learning is likely to result if students engage in them, regardless of their motivation to help their partners learn. Examples of this were discussed earlier. One is the series of studies by Dansereau (1988) and his colleagues in which pairs of college students proceeded through a structured sequence of activities to help each other learn complex technical information or procedures (see O'Donnell & Dansereau, 1992). Other examples are the two Dutch studies of spelling that also involved dyads and in which the study behavior (quizzing each other in turn) was structured and obviously beneficial (Van Oudenhoven, Van Berkum, & Swen-Koopmans, 1987; Van Oudenhoven, Wiersma, et al., 1987). In contrast to cooperative methods using group goals and individual accountability indirectly to motivate students to teach each other, these methods allow the teacher directly to motivate students to engage in structured turn-taking behaviors known to increase learning. The successful use of structured dyadic tasks in elementary schools seems largely limited to lower level rote skills such as memorizing multiplication tables, spelling lists, or place names.

As in the case of controversial tasks without single correct answers, there is evidence that adding group rewards to structured dyadic tasks enhances the effects of these strategies. Fantuzzo et al. (1990) evaluated the dyadic study strategy called Reciprocal Peer Tutoring (RPT). A simple pair study format did not increase student arithmetic achievement, but when successful dyads were awarded stickers and classroom privileges, their achievement increased markedly. A similar comparison of dyadic tutoring with and without group rewards at the college level also found that group rewards greatly enhanced the achievement effects of a structured dyadic study model (Fantuzzo et al., 1989), and a series of studies showed positive effects of the RPT model in many subjects and at many grade levels (e.g., Fantuzzo et al., 1990). A similar program combining structured reciprocal tutoring with group rewards called Classwide Peer Tutoring has also been successful in increasing student achievement in a variety of subjects and grade levels (Greenwood et al., 1989; Maheady, Harper, & Mallette, 1991).

Communal Study Groups

Building on scholarship and research that are focused on the relationship between culture and cognitive development (Boykin, 1986, 1994; Jordan, 1992; Rogoff & Chavajay, 1995; Rogoff & Wadell, 1982; Serpell, 1979, 1993; Tharp & Gallimore, 1988; Vygotsky, 1978), researchers at Howard University have conducted a series of studies of African American children's performance after studying in communal learning groups without extrinsic group goals. Boykin (1994)

and others have long maintained that there is a distinct group orientation in the culture of African American communities, which he terms *communalism*. Communal learning groups are defined for the research as groups that share materials and are administered a *communal prompt* (Hurley, 1999). The communal prompt is a set of instructions designed to make salient the common bonds of school and community shared by group members and to draw out communal tendencies that may otherwise be subdued at school. These investigations have consistently found that African American students who studied in communal groups performed better on individually administered quizzes than did similar students who studied individually (Coleman, 1998, 2001; Dill & Boykin, 2000; Hurley, 1997, 1999; Lilja, 2001) and as well (Hurley, 2000) or better (Albury, 1993; Dill & Boykin, 2000) than African American students who studied in cooperative learning groups with group goals and individual accountability.

Hurley (2000) suggested that this is due to the particularly strong group orientation in African American culture, which "insulates or exempts African-American children from some of the motivation and coordination hindrances typically associated with [cooperative learning groups]" (p. 38). Stated in the terms of this discussion, this work seems to argue that group interdependence (cohesion), as described earlier, is more readily attainable and motivating for African American students. This body of research is promising as a case where group goals and individual accountability are not essential elements of cooperative learning. By the same token, these studies found no evidence that group goals and individual accountability undermine student motivation or achievement. Moreover, though two of these studies (Coleman, 2001; Lilja, 2001) demonstrated the generalizability of these findings to longer time periods (three weeks), most of these studies have been very brief. Additional research is needed to clarify the relationship of these findings to the present discussion.

RECONCILING THE FOUR PERSPECTIVES

The process model discussed earlier describes how group goals might operate to enhance the learning outcomes of cooperative learning. Provision of group goals based on the individual learning of all group members might affect cognitive processes directly, by motivating students to engage in peer modeling, cognitive elaboration, and practice with one another. Group goals may also lead to group cohesiveness, increasing caring and concern among group members and making them feel responsible for one another's achievement, thereby motivating students to engage in cognitive processes that enhance learning. Finally, group goals may motivate students to take responsibility for one another independently of the teacher, thereby solving important classroom organization problems and providing increased opportunities for cognitively appropriate learning activities.

Scholars whose theoretical orientations deemphasize the utility of extrinsic rewards attempt to intervene directly on mechanisms identified as mediating variables in the model offered here. For example, social cohesion theorists intervene directly on group cohesiveness by engaging in elaborate team building and group processing training. The Sharan and Shachar (1988) GI study suggests that this can be successfully done, but it takes a great deal of time and effort. In this study, teachers were trained over the course of a full year, and then teachers and students used cooperative learning for 3 months before the study began. Earlier research on GI failed to provide a comparable level of preparation of teachers and students, and the achievement results of these studies were less consistently positive (Sharan et al., 1984).

Cognitive theorists would hold that the cognitive processes that are essential to any theory relating cooperative learning to achievement can be created directly, without the motivational or affective changes discussed by the motivationalist and social cohesion theorists. This may turn out to be accurate. For example, research on reciprocal teaching in reading comprehension (Palincsar & Brown, 1984; Rosenshine & Meister, 1994) shows promise as a means of intervening directly in peer cognitive processes. Reciprocal teaching strategies can be effective in a variety of subject areas, with students of various ages and in both controlled experiments and classroom practice (Alfassi, 1998; Carter, 1997; Hart & Speese, 1998; King & Johnson-Parent, 1999; Lederer, 2000). Long-term applications of Dansereau's (1988) cooperative scripts for comprehension of technical material and procedural instructions also seem likely to be successful.

From the perspective of the model diagrammed in Figure 9.1, starting with group goals and individual accountability permits students in cooperative learning groups to benefit from the full range of factors that are known to affect cooperative learning outcomes. Although group goals and individual accountability may not always be absolutely necessary, to ignore them would be to ignore the tool with the most consistent evidence of positive effects on student achievement.

WHICH STUDENTS GAIN MOST?
(IMPORTANT SUBPOPULATIONS)

Several studies have focused on the question of which students gain the most from cooperative learning. One particularly important question relates to whether cooperative learning is beneficial to students at all levels of prior achievement. It would be possible to argue (see, e.g., Allan, 1991; Robinson, 1990) that high achievers could be held back by having to explain material to their low-achieving group mates. However, it would be equally possible to argue that because students who give elaborated explanations typically learn more than do those who receive them (Webb, 1992), high achievers should be the students who benefit most from cooperative learning because they most frequently give elaborated explanations.

Slavin (1995) concluded that the evidence from experimental studies that met the inclusion criteria for his review supported neither position. A few studies found better outcomes for high achievers than for low, and a few found that low achievers gained the most. Most, however, found equal benefits for high, average, and low achievers in comparison with their counterparts in control groups. One 2-year study of schools using cooperative learning during most of their instructional days found that high, average, and low achievers all achieved better than did controls at similar achievement levels. However, a separate analysis of the very highest achievers, those in the top 10% and top 5% of their classes at pretest, found particularly large positive effects of cooperative learning on these students (Slavin, 1991; Stevens & Slavin, 1995b).

A number of studies have looked for possible differences in the effects of cooperative learning on students of different ethnicities. As mentioned earlier, several have found different, often more pronounced effects for African American students (Albury, 1993; Boykin, 1994; Coleman, 1998; Garibaldi, 1979; Haynes & Gebreyesus, 1992; Hurley, 1999; Johnson & Johnson, 1985; Jordan, 1992; Slavin, 1983b; Slavin & Oickle, 1981; Tharp & Galimore, 1988). However, other studies have found equal effects of cooperative learning for students of different backgrounds (see Slavin, 1995). These differing findings are likely due to differences in experimental methodologies and to differences in the forms of cooperation employed in the research. The second of these distinctions may be particularly important to educational practice. Because African American and other minority students are overrepresented among underachievers (U.S. Department of Education, 2000), it will be important to understand how students' backgrounds may mediate the effects of particular cooperative learning strategies. The communalism studies mentioned earlier and a few others have begun to explore these issues, and the evidence to date is encouraging. Despite some significant variation in methodology and in empirical findings, cooperative techniques have proven to have generally positive effects for African American, European American (Hurley, 1999; Slavin, 1985), Israeli (Rich et al., 1986), Hispanic (Calderón et al., 1998), Nigerian (Okebukola, 1986), and other cultural and ethnic groups. Still, much additional information will be needed to ensure that cooperative learning practices are implemented in ways that meet the needs of the children being served.

Other studies have examined a variety of factors that might interact with achievement gain in cooperative learning. Okebukola (1986) and Wheeler and Ryan (1973) found that students who preferred cooperative learning learned more in cooperative methods than did those who preferred competition. Chambers and Abrami (1991) found that students on successful teams learned more than did those on less successful teams.

Finally, a small number of studies have compared variations in cooperative procedures. Moody and Gifford (1990) found that although there was no difference in achievement gains, homogeneous groups performed better than did mixed groups. Foyle, Lyman, Tompkins, Perne, and Foyle (1993) found that individuals assigned daily homework in cooperative learning classes achieved more than did those not assigned homework. Kaminski (1991) and Rich et al. (1986) found that explicit teaching of collaborative skills had no effect on student achievement. Hurley (1999) found that African American students performed best in cooperative learning groups with shared goals, whereas European American students performed best in cooperative learning groups with explicit individual accountability. Jones (1990) compared cooperative learning using group competition to an otherwise identical method that compared groups to a set standard (as in STAD). There were no achievement differences, but a few attitude differences favored the group competition.

OUTCOMES OTHER THAN ACHIEVEMENT

Another important justification for the widespread use of cooperative learning techniques in education is that they have been associated with a host of affective, nonachievement effects. These include increases in all of the following areas: willingness to take on difficult tasks, intrinsic motivation, long-term retention, higher order thinking, metacognition, creative problem solving, ability to generalize concepts across content areas, positive attitudes toward schooling and towards curriculum content, time on task, on-task verbalization, positive cross-group relations (ethnicity, ability), fewer disruptions, psychological health, self-esteem, and emotional intelligence (Albury, 1993; Ellison & Boykin, 1994; Johnson & Johnson, 1983; Leikin & Zaslavsky, 1997; Nelson, Johnson, & Marchand-Martella, 1996; Sharan, 1980; Slavin, 1995; Yost & Tucker, 2000; Zahn, Kagan & Widaman, 1986; see Johnson & Johnson, 1999, for a detailed discussion of nonachievement benefits of cooperative learning). Thus, aside from the compelling, if somewhat pragmatic,

goal of enhancing simple academic achievement, cooperative learning techniques have shown enormous potential to facilitate children's psychological health and development while preparing them for the intellectual demands of an information-dependent society.

DIRECTIONS FOR ADDITIONAL RESEARCH

The four theoretical perspectives explaining the achievement effects of cooperative learning described in this paper are all useful in expanding our understanding of the conditions under which various forms of cooperative learning may affect student achievement. Figure 9.1, which links these theoretical perspectives in a causal model, provides a framework for predicting different causal paths by which cooperative learning might affect achievement.

In particular, the model shows the importance of group goals and individual accountability but also suggests ways that achievement might be affected more directly by introducing peer activities that may not require extrinsic motivation. This paper explores three types of tasks or situations in which group goals and individual accountability may not be necessary: controversial tasks lacking single right answers, voluntary study groups, and structured dyadic tasks. There is little research on voluntary study groups (such as those in medical or law schools), but research does find instances in which certain types of cooperative tasks are effective without group goals and individual accountability. However, there is also evidence that adding group goals and individual accountability to these tasks further enhances their instructional effectiveness.

Clearly, there is a need for further research on conditions under which group goals and individual accountability may not be necessary. As a practical matter, it is probably the case that most teachers using cooperative learning do not provide group rewards based on the individual learning of all group members and that most teachers feel that it is unnecessary and cumbersome to do so. Widespread reluctance to use extrinsic incentives, based in part on a misreading of research on the "undermining" effects of rewards on long-term motivation (Cameron & Pierce, 1994), has contributed to many educators' reluctance to use group rewards. For both theoretical and practical reasons it would be important to know how to make reward-free cooperative learning methods effective.

A related need for research concerns documenting the functional mechanisms that account for cooperative learning benefits. Too often, descriptions of the processes by which any of the important components contribute to learning reside in the domain of theory. Given recent advances in video and behavior coding methodologies, it should be possible to identify the specific behavioral manifestations of things like social cohesion and cognitive elaboration and to quantify their relationship to performance outcomes. Such work was not a focus of this review; however, by way of example, Hurley (2000) found that the reward structure of learning groups did affect the incidence of process-loss behaviors (behaviors that detract from group functioning) among fifth-grade students studying a math task. Moreover, the incidence of such behaviors during study was negatively correlated with subsequent performance on the task. More of this sort of research will go a long way toward helping scholars to understand the facilitating effects of cooperative learning while providing guidance in the development of cooperative learning methods that have a meaningful positive impact on children's learning.

There is as yet much to learn about the effective uses of project-based learning. Most research on cooperative learning has involved the use of cooperative methods to help children master fairly well-defined skills or information. The key exceptions to this are studies by the Sharans (e.g., Sharan & Sharan, 1992) and by Elizabeth Cohen (1994b). Cooperative learning practice has shifted increasingly toward project-based or active learning (Stern, 1996), in which students work together to produce reports, projects, experiments, and so on. It is possible to make inferences to optimal conditions for project-based learning from research on more cut-and-dried content (see Slavin, 1996), and the work of Cohen and the Sharans does imply that well-implemented, project-based learning can be more effective than traditional instruction (Sharan & Shachar, 1988, is by far the best evidence of this). However, there is a great deal of work yet to be done to identify effective, replicable methods, to understand the conditions necessary for success in project-based learning, and to develop a more powerful theory and rationale to support project-based learning.

There is a need for both development and research at the intersection of cooperative learning and curriculum. Work at Johns Hopkins University and at the Success for All Foundation has for many years focused on development and evaluation of cooperative learning methods that are tied to particular subjects and grade levels, such as CIRC (Stevens et al., 1987), WorldLab (social studies and science; Slavin & Madden, 2000), and MathWings (Madden, Slavin, & Simons, 2000). Elizabeth Cohen's (1994a) Complex Instruction program and Eric Schaps's (Soloman et al., 1990) Child Development Project have also developed specific, broadly applicable curriculum materials to be used in a cooperative learning format. These contrast with most cooperative learning models, which typically provide some general guidance for how to adapt cooperative learning to different subjects and grade levels but rarely provide actual student materials. How is cooperative learning affected by the existence of specific materials? Does use of these materials improve the learning outcomes of cooperative learning? Does it make cooperative learning more likely to be implemented well in the first place and maintained over time? Or does the use of prepared materials lead to less thoughtful use of cooperative learning or less ability to adapt in situations lacking materials? These questions are more important for practice than for theory, but they are very important for practice. Not incidentally, there is a need for development of high-quality, well-developed, and well-researched cooperative curricula in many subjects and grade levels, especially at the secondary level.

Related to the need for research on curriculum-based methods is the need for research on effective strategies for professional development and follow-up to support cooperative learning. Nearly all training programs for cooperative learning make extensive use of simulations. It is at least worth documenting the effectiveness of this practice. There has been some research on the effectiveness of peer coaching to support implementations of cooperative learning (e.g., Joyce, Hersh, & McKibbin, 1983). Yet there is much more work to be done to identify strategies for professional development likely to lead to high-quality, thoughtful, and sustained implementation. A few factors worth studying might include contrasts between school-wide and teacher-by-teacher implementations, expert versus peer coaches, inservice focusing on generic principles versus specific strategies, and use of teacher learning communities (Calderón, 1994), that is, groups of teachers who meet on a regular basis to support each other's innovative efforts.

Perhaps the only determined opposition to cooperative learning within the community of professional educators has come from advocates for gifted students. There is some research on the effects of cooperative learning on gifted students both within heterogeneous classes (Stevens & Slavin, 1995b) and within separate programs for the gifted (Gallagher, 1995), and so far there is little evidence to support fears that gifted students are shortchanged by cooperative learning. One study did find that while low-ability students achieved most in heterogeneous-ability groups, high-ability students achieved most in homogeneous groups (Hooper & Hannafin, 1991). However, much more research is needed in this area to expand our understanding of the effects of different cooperative methods with gifted students and of how the effects of cooperative learning might be different in homogeneous and heterogeneous settings. On this last question, there is a broader need to study cooperative learning in the context of attempts to replace homogeneous with heterogeneous grouping, especially in middle and high schools, and to use cooperative learning instead of homogeneous reading groups in elementary schools.

This chapter focused on the achievement outcomes of cooperative learning, but of course many of the other outcomes mentioned earlier are in need of further research. In particular, further research is needed on the effects of cooperative learning on intergroup relations, self-esteem, attitudes toward schooling, acceptance of mainstreamed classmates, prosocial norms, and other outcomes (see Hawley & Jackson, 1995; Slavin, 1995).

In general, there is a need for more research on all outcomes for older students (seniors in high school and students in postsecondary institutions), as well as a need for development and evaluations of cooperative methods for young children, especially those in prekindergarten, kindergarten, and first grade.

In summary, although cooperative learning has been studied in an extraordinary number of field experiments of high methodological quality, there is still much more to be done. Cooperative learning has the potential to become a primary format used by teachers to achieve both traditional and innovative goals. Research must continue to provide the practical, theoretical, and intellectual underpinnings to enable educators to achieve this potential. This chapter has advanced a cohesive model of the relationships among the important variables involved in the functioning of cooperative learning. It offered a framework for discussion and continued debate while calling for a move away from competitive attempts to explain this complex phenomenon toward a unified theoretical model that can guide future research efforts and inform education practice.

REFERENCES

Albury, A. (1993). *Social orientations, learning conditions and learning outcomes among low-income Black and White grade school children.* Unpublished doctoral dissertation, Howard University, Washington, DC.

Alfassi, M. (1998). Reading for meaning: the efficacy of reciprocal teaching in fostering reading comprehension in high school students in remedial reading classes. *American Educational Research Journal, 35*(2), 309–332.

Allen, S. D. (1991). Ability grouping research reviews: What do they say about grouping and the gifted? *Educational Leadership, 48*(6), 60–65.

Ames, G. J., & Murray, F. B. (1982). When two wrongs make a right: Promoting cognitive change by social conflict. *Developmental Psychology, 18,* 894–897.

Antil, L. R., Jenkins, J. R., Wayne, S., & Vadasy, P. F. (1998). Cooperative learning: Prevalence, conceptualizations, and the relation between research and practice. *American Educational Research Journal, 35*(3), 419–454.

Aronson, E., Blaney, N., Stephan, C., Sikes, J., & Snapp, M. (1978). *The Jigsaw classroom.* Beverly Hills, CA: Sage.

Ashman, A. F., & Gillies, R. M. (1997). Children's cooperative behavior and interactions in trained and untrained workgroups in regular classrooms. *Journal of School Psychology, 7*(1), 261–279.

Battisch, V., Solomon, D., & Delucci, K. (1993). Interaction process and student outcomes in cooperative learning groups. *The Elementary School Journal, 94*(1), 19–32.

Bell, N., Grossen, M., & Perret-Clermont, A.-N. (1985). Socio-cognitive conflict and intellectual growth. In M. Berkowitz (Ed.), *Peer conflict and psychological growth.* San Francisco: Jossey-Bass.

Berg, K. F. (1993, April). *Structured cooperative learning and achievement in a high school mathematics class.* Paper presented at the annual meeting of the American Educational Research Association, Atlanta, GA.

Bershon, B. L. (1992). Cooperative problem solving: A link to inner speech. In R. Hertz-Lazarowitz & N. Miller (Eds.), *Interaction in cooperative groups* (pp. 36–48). New York: Cambridge University Press.

Boykin, A. W. (1986). The triple quandary and the schooling of Afro-American children. In U. Neisser (Ed.), *The school achievement of minority children* (pp. 57–92). Hillsdale, NJ: Erlbaum.

Boykin, A. W. (1994). Afrocultural expression and its implications for schooling. In E. Hollins, J. King, & W. Hayman (Eds.), *Teaching diverse populations: Formulating a knowledge base* (pp. 243–257). New York: Albany State University of New York Press.

Burns, M. (1981, September). Groups of four: Solving the management problem. *Learning, 24*(2), 46–51.

Calderón, M. (1994). Mentoring and coaching minority teachers. In J. DeVillar & J. Cummins (Eds.), *Successful cultural diversity: Classroom practices for the 21st century.* Albany, NY: SUNY Press.

Calderón, M., Hertz-Lazarowitz, R., & Slavin, R. E. (1998). Effects of Bilingual Cooperative Integrated Reading and Composition on students making the transition from Spanish to English reading. *Elementary School Journal, 99*(2), 153–165.

Cameron, J., & Pierce, W. D. (1994). Reinforcement, reward, and intrinsic motivation: A meta-analysis. *Review of Educational Research, 64*(3), 363–423.

Cameron, J., & Pierce, W. D. (1996). The debate about rewards and intrinsic motivation: Protests and accusations do not alter the results. *Review of Educational Research, 66*(1), 39–51.

Carter, C. J. (1997). Why reciprocal teaching? *Educational Leadership, 54,* 64–68.

Cavanagh, B. R. (1984). Effects of interdependent group contingencies on the achievement of elementary school children. *Dissertation Abstracts, 46,* 1558.

Chambers, B., & Abrami, P. C. (1991). The relationship between Student Team Learning outcomes and achievement, causal attributions, and affect. *Journal of Educational Psychology, 83,* 140–146.

Chapman, E. (2001, April). *More on moderators in cooperative learning outcomes.* Paper presented at the annual meeting of the American Educational Research Association, Seattle, WA.

Cohen, E. (1986). *Designing groupwork: Strategies for the heterogeneous classroom.* New York: Teachers College Press.

Cohen, E. G. (1994a). *Designing groupwork: Strategies for the heterogeneous classroom* (2nd ed.). New York: Teachers College Press.

Cohen, E. G. (1994b). Restructuring the classroom: Conditions for productive small groups. *Review of Educational Research, 64*(1), 1–35.

Coleman, J. (1961). *The adolescent society.* New York: Free Press.

Coleman, K. (1998). *The influence of communal learning contexts on Black and White third and sixth grade students' utilization of meta-cognitive strategies and behaviors.* Unpublished doctoral dissertation, Howard University, Washington, DC.

Coleman, S. (2001, April). *Communal versus individualistic learning context as they relate to mathematical task performance under simulated classroom conditions.* Paper presented at the annual meeting of the American Educational Research Association, Seattle, WA.

Damon, W. (1984). Peer education: The untapped potential. *Journal of Applied Developmental Psychology, 5,* 331–343.

Dansereau, D. F. (1988). Cooperative learning strategies. In C. E. Weinstein, E. T. Goetz, & P. A. Alexander (Eds.), *Learning and study strategies: Issues in assessment, instruction, and evaluation* (pp. 103–120). Orlando, FL: Academic Press.

Davidson, N. (1985). Small-group learning and teaching in mathematics: A selective review of the research. In R. E. Slavin, S. Sharan, S. Kagan, R. Hertz-Lazarowitz, C. Webb, & R. Schmuck (Eds.), *Learning to cooperating to learn* (pp. 211–230). New York: Plenum.

De Avila, E., & Duncan, S. (1980). *Finding Out/Descubrimiento.* Corte Madera, CA: Linguametrics Group.

Deci, E. L., Koestner, R., & Ryan, R. M. (1999). The undermining effect is a reality after all—Extrinsic rewards, task interest, and self-determination: Reply to Eisenberger, Pierce, and Cameron. *Psychological Bulletin, 125*(6), 692–700.

Devin-Sheehan, L., Feldman, R., and Allen, V. (1976). Research on children tutoring children: A critical review. *Review of Educational Research, 46*(3), 355–385.

Dill, E., & Boykin, A. W. (2000). The comparative influence of individual, peer-tutoring and communal learning contexts on the text-recall learning of African-American children. *Journal of Black Psychology, 26*(1), 65–78.

Ellis, A. K., & Fouts, J. T. (1993). *Research on educational innovations.* Princeton Junction, NJ: Eye on Education.

Ellison, B. N. & Boykin, A. W. (1994). Comparing outcomes from differential cooperative and individualistic learning methods. *Social Behavior and Personality, 22,* 91–103.

Fantuzzo, J. W., King, J. A., & Heller, L. R. (1992). Effects of reciprocal peer tutoring on mathematics and school adjustment: A component analysis. *Journal of Educational Psychology, 84,* 33–339.

Fantuzzo, J. W., Polite, K., & Grayson, N. (1990). An evaluation of reciprocal peer tutoring across elementary school settings. *Journal of School Psychology, 28,* 309–323.

Fantuzzo, J. W., Riggio, R. E., Connelly, S., & Dimeff, L. A. (1989). Effects of reciprocal peer tutoring on academic achievement and psychological adjustment: A component analysis. *Journal of Educational Psychology, 81,* 173–177.

Foyle, H. C., Lyman, L. R., Tompkins, L., Perne, S., & Foyle, D. (1993). Homework and cooperative learning: A classroom field experiment. *Illinois School Research and Development, 29*(3), 25–27.

Gallagher, J. J. (1995). Educational of gifted students: A civil rights issue? *Phi Delta Kappan, 76*(5), 408–410.

Garibaldi, A. (1979). Affective contributions of cooperative and group goal structures. *Journal of Educational Psychology, 71,* 788–794.

Graves, D. (1983). *Writing: Teachers and children at work.* Exeter, NH: Heinemann.

Greenwood, C. R., Delquadri, J. C., & Hall, R. V. (1989). Longitudinal effects of classwide peer tutoring. *Journal of Educational Psychology, 81,* 371–383.

Hart, E. R., & Speece, D. L. (1998). Reciprocal teaching goes to college: Effects for post-secondary students at risk for academic failure. *Journal of Educational Psychology, 90*(4), 670–681.

Hawley, W. D., & Jackson, A. W. (Eds.). (1995). *Toward a common destiny: Improving race and ethnic relations in America.* San Francisco: Jossey-Bass.

Hayes, L. (1976). The use of group contingencies for behavioral control: A review. *Psychological Bulletin, 83,* 628–648.

Haynes, N. M., & Gebreyesus, S. (1992). Cooperative learning: A case for African-American students. *School Psychology Review, 21*(4), 577–585.

Hillocks, G. (1984). What works in teaching composition: A meta-analysis of experimental treatment studies. *American Journal of Education, 93,* 133–170.

Hogg, M. A. (1987). Social identity and group cohesiveness. In J. C. Turner (Ed.), *Rediscovering the social group: A self-categorization theory* (pp. 89–116). New York: Basil Blackwell.

Hooper, S., & Hannafin, M. J. (1991). The effects of group composition on achievement, interaction and learning efficiency during computer-based cooperative instruction. *Educational Techniques, Research and Development, 39*(3), 27–40.

Huber, G. L., Bogatzki, W., & Winter, M. (1982). *Kooperation als Ziel schulischen Lehrens und Lernens.* (Cooperative learning: Condition and goal of teaching and learning in Classrooms).

Tubingen, Germany: Arbeitsbereich Padagogische Psychologie der Universitat Tubingen.

Hurley, E. A. (1997, April). *The interaction of communal orientation in African-American children with group processes in cooperative learning: Pedagogical and theoretical implications.* Paper presented at the annual meeting of the American Educational Research Association, Chicago.

Hurley, E. A. (1999, April). *The cultural significance of communal group learning to the mathematics achievement and motivation of African-American children.* Paper presented at the annual meeting of the American Educational Research Association, Montreal, Quebec, Canada.

Hurley, E: A. (2000, April). *The interaction of culture with math achievement and group processes among African-American and European-American students.* Paper presented at the annual meeting of the American Educational Research Association, New Orleans, LA.

Johnson, D. W., & Johnson, R. T. (1983). Social interdependence and perceived academic and personal support in the classroom. *Journal of Social Psychology, 120,* 77–82.

Johnson, D. W., & Johnson, R. T. (1985). The internal dynamics of cooperative learning groups. In R. Slavin, S. S. Sharan, S. Kagan, R. H. Lazarowitz, C. Webb, & R. Schmuck (Eds.), *Learning to cooperate: Cooperating to learn* (pp. 103–123). New York: Plenum Press.

Johnson, D. W., & Johnson, R. T. (1979). Conflict in the classroom: Controversy and learning. *Review of Educational Research, 49,* 51–70.

Johnson, D. W., & Johnson, R. T. (1989). *Cooperation and competition: Theory and research.* Edina, MN: Interaction.

Johnson, D. W., & Johnson, R. T. (1992). Positive interdependence: Key to effective cooperation. In R. Hertz-Lazarowitz & N. Miller (Eds.), *Interaction in cooperative groups: The theoretical anatomy of group learning* (pp. 174–199). New York: Cambridge University Press.

Johnson, D. W., & Johnson, R. T. (1994). *Learning together and alone: Cooperative, competitive, and individualistic learning* (4th ed.). Boston: Allyn & Bacon.

Johnson, D. W., & Johnson, R. T. (1999). *The impact of cooperative learning.* Retrieved December 1, 2000, from http://www.clcrc.com/pages/SIT.html

Johnson, L. C. (1985). *The effects of the groups of four cooperative learning model on student problem-solving achievement in mathematics.* Unpublished doctoral dissertation, University of Houston, TX.

Johnson, L. C., & Waxman, H. C. (1985, March). *Evaluating the effects of the "groups of four" program.* Paper presented at the annual convention of the American Educational Research Association, Chicago.

Jones, D. S. P. (1990). *The effects of contingency based and competitive reward systems on achievement and attitudes in cooperative*

learning situations. Unpublished doctoral dissertation, Temple University, Philadelphia.

Jordan, C. (1992). The role of culture in minority school achievement. *The Kamehameha Journal of Education, 2,* 16–18.

Joyce, B. R., Hersh, R. H., & McKibbin, M. (1983). *The structure of school improvement,* New York: Longman.

Kagan, S. (1992). *Cooperative learning* (8th ed.). San Juan Capistrano, CA: Kagan Cooperative Learning.

Kaminski, L. B. (1991). *The effect of formal group skill instruction and role development on achievement of high school students taught with cooperative learning.* Unpublished doctoral dissertation, East Lansing: Michigan State University.

King, C. M., & Johnson-Parent, L. M. (1999). Constructing meaning via reciprocal teaching. *Reading Research and Instruction, 38*(3) 169–186.

Kohn, A. (1986). *No contest: The case against competition.* Boston: Houghton-Mifflin.

Kuhn, D. (1972). Mechanism of change in the development of cognitive structures. *Child Development, 43,* 833–844.

Latane, B., Williams, K., & Harkins, S. (1979). Many hands make light the work: The causes and consequences of social loafing. *Journal of Personality and Social Psychology, 37,* 822–832.

Lederer, J. M. (2000). Reciprocal teaching of social studies in inclusive elementary classrooms. *Journal of Learning Disabilities, 33*(1), 91–106.

Leikin, R., & Zaslavsky, O. (1997). Facilitating student interactions in mathematics in a cooperative learning setting. *Journal for Research in Mathematics Education, 28*(3), 331–354.

Lepper, M. R., Henderlong, J., & Gingras, I. (1999). Understanding the effects of extrinsic rewards on intrinsic motivation: Uses and abuses of meta-analysis: Comment on Deci, Koestner, & Ryan (1999). *Psychological Bulletin, 124*(6), 669–676.

Lepper, M. R., Keavney, M., & Drake, J. (1996). Intrinsic motivation and extrinsic Rewards: A commentary on Cameron and Pierce's meta-analysis. *Review of Educational Research, 66*(1), 5–32.

Lilja, A. (2001). *An investigation into the influence of communal versus individual learning context on the academically relevant task performance of African-American children.* Unpublished master's thesis, Washington, DC. Howard University.

Litow, L., & Pumroy, D. (1975). A brief review of classroom group-oriented contingencies. *Journal of Applied Behavior Analysis, 8,* 341–347.

Madden, N. A., Slavin, R. E., & Simons, K. (2000). *MathWings: Effects on student Mathematics performance.* Baltimore: Johns Hopkins University Center for Research on the Education of Students Placed at Risk.

Maheady, L., Harper, G. F., & Mallette, B. (1991). Peer-mediated instruction: Review of potential applications for special education. *Reading, Writing, and Learning Disabilities, 7,* 75–102.

Manning, M. L., & Lucking, R. (1991, May/June). The what, why, and how of cooperative learning. *The Social Studies, 12,* 120–124.

Mattingly, R. M., & Van Sickle, R. L. (1991). Cooperative learning and achievement in social studies: Jigsaw II. *Social Education, 55*(6), 392–395.

Meloth, M. S., & Deering, P. D. (1992). The effects of two co-operative conditions on peer group discussions, reading comprehension, and metacognition. *Contemporary Educational Psychology, 17,* 175–193.

Meloth, M. S., & Deering, P. D. (1994). Task talk and task awareness under different cooperative learning conditions. *American Educational Research Journal, 31*(1), 138–166.

Mergendoller, J., & Packer, M. J. (1989). *Cooperative learning in the classroom: A knowledge brief on effective teaching.* San Francisco: Far West Laboratory.

Moody, J. D., & Gifford, V. D. (1990, November). *The effect of grouping by formal reasoning ability levels, group size, and gender on achievement in laboratory chemistry.* Paper presented at the annual meeting of the Mid-South Educational Research Association, New Orleans, LA.

Mugny, B., & Doise, W. (1978). Socio-cognitive conflict and structuration of individual and collective performances. *European Journal of Social Psychology, 8,* 181–192.

Murray, F. B. (1982). Teaching through social conflict. *Contemporary Educational Psychology, 7,* 257–271.

Nelson, J. R., Johnson, A., & Marchand-Martella, N. (1996). Effects of direct instruction, cooperative learning, and independent learning practices on the classroom behavior of students with disorders: A comparative analysis. *Journal of Emotional and Behavioral Disorders, 4*(1) 53–62.

Newbern, D., Dansereau, D. F., Patterson, M. E., & Wallace, D. S. (1994, April). *Toward a science of cooperation.* Paper presented at the annual meeting of the American Educational Research Association, New Orleans, LA.

Newmann, F. M., & Thompson, J. (1987). *Effects of cooperative learning on achievement in secondary schools: A summary of research.* Madison: University of Wisconsin, National Center on Effective Secondary Schools.

O'Donnell, A. M. (1996). The effects of explicit incentives on scripted and unscripted cooperation. *Journal of Educational Psychology, 88*(1), 74–76.

O'Donnell, A. M. (2000). Interactive effects of prior knowledge and material format on cooperative teaching. *Journal of Experimental Education, 68*(2), 101–108.

O'Donnell, A. M., & Dansereau, D. F. (1992). Scripted cooperation in student dyads: A method for analyzing and enhancing academic learning and performance. In R. Hertz-Lazarowitz & N. Miller (Eds.), *Interaction in cooperative groups: The theoretical anatomy of group learning* (pp. 120–144). New York: Cambridge University Press.

Okebukola, P. A. (1985). The relative effectiveness of cooperative and competitive interaction techniques in strengthening students' performance in science classes. *Science Education, 69,* 501–509.

Okebukola, P. A. (1986). The influence of preferred learning styles on cooperative learning in science. *Science Education, 70,* 509–517.

Palincsar, A. S. (1987, April). *Reciprocal teaching: Field evaluations in remedial and content area reading.* Paper presented at the annual convention of the American Educational Research Association, Washington, DC.

Palincsar, A. S., & Brown, A. L. (1984). Reciprocal teaching of comprehension monitoring activities. *Cognition and Instruction, 2,* 117–175.

Palincsar, A. S., Brown, A. L., & Martin, S. M. (1987). Peer interaction in reading comprehension instruction. *Educational Psychologist, 22,* 231–253.

Perret-Clermont, A.-N. (1980). *Social interaction and cognitive development in children.* London: Academic Press.

Piaget, J. (1926). *The language and thought of the child.* New York: Harcourt Brace.

Puma, M. J., Jones, C. C., Rock, D., & Fernandez, R. (1993). *Prospects: The congressionally mandated study of educational growth and opportunity. Interim Report.* Bethesda, MD: Abt.

Rich, Y., Amir, Y., & Slavin, R. E. (1986). *Instructional strategies for improving children's cross-ethnic relations.* Ramat Gan, Israel: Bar Ilan University, Institute for the Advancement of Social Integration in the Schools.

Robinson, G. E. (1990). Synthesis of research on class size. *Educational Leadership, 47*(7), 80–90.

Rogoff, B., & Chavajay, P. (1995). What's become of research on the cultural basis of cognitive development? *American Psychologist, 50*(10), 859–877.

Rogoff, B., & Wadell, K. (1982). Memory for information organized in a scene by children from two cultures. *Child Development, 53,* 1224–1228.

Rosenshine, B., & Meister, C. (1994). Reciprocal teaching: A review of research. *Review of Educational Research, 64,* 479–530.

Serpell, R. (1979). How specific are perceptual skills? A cross-cultural study of the pattern reproduction. *British Journal of Psychology, 70,* 365–380.

Serpell, R. (1993). *The significance of schooling: Life journeys in an African society.* Cambridge, England: Cambridge University Press.

Sharan, S. (1980). Cooperative learning in small groups: Recent methods and effects on achievement, attitudes and ethnic relations. *Review of Educational Research, 50,* 241–271.

Sharan, S., & Hertz-Lazarowitz, R. (1980). A group-investigation method of cooperative learning in the classroom. In S. Sharan, P. Hare, C. Webb, & R. Hertz-Lazarowitz (Eds.), *Cooperation in education* (pp. 125–129). Provo, UT: Brigham Young University Press.

Sharan, S., Kussell, P., Hertz-Lazarowitz, R., Bejarano, Y., Raviv, S., & Sharan, Y. (1984). *Cooperative learning in the classroom: Research in desegregated schools.* Hillsdale, NJ: Erlbaum.

Sharan, S., & Shachar, C. (1988). *Language and learning in the cooperative classroom.* New York: Springer-Verlag.

Sharan, Y., & Sharan, S. (1992). *Expanding cooperative learning through group investigation.* New York: Teachers College Press.

Slavin, R. E. (1977). Classroom reward structure: An analytic and practical review. *Review of Educational Research, 47,* 633–650.

Slavin, R. E. (1983a). *Cooperative learning.* New York: Longman.

Slavin, R. E. (1983b). When does cooperative learning increase student achievement? *Psychological Bulletin, 94,* 429–445.

Slavin, R. E. (1987). Cooperative learning: Where behavioral and humanistic approaches to classroom motivation meet. *Elementary School Journal, 88,* 9–37.

Slavin, R. E. (1989). Cooperative learning and achievement: Six theoretical perspectives. In C. Ames & M. L. Maehr (Eds.), *Advances in motivation and achievement* (pp. 136–164). Greenwich, CT: JAI Press.

Slavin, R. E. (1991). Are cooperative learning and untracking harmful to the gifted? *Educational Leadership, 48*(6), 68–71.

Slavin, R. E. (1992). When and why does cooperative learning increase achievement? Theoretical and empirical perspectives. In R. Hertz-Lazarowitz & N. Miller (Eds.), *Interaction in cooperative groups: The theoretical anatomy of group learning* (pp. 145–173). New York: Cambridge University Press.

Slavin, R. E. (1994). *Using Student Team Learning* (2nd ed.). Baltimore: Johns Hopkins University, Center for Social Organization of Schools.

Slavin, R. E. (1995). *Cooperative learning: Theory, research, and practice* (2nd ed.). Boston: Allyn & Bacon.

Slavin, R. E. (1996). Cooperative learning: Theory, research, and implications for active learning. In D. Stern (Ed.), *Active Learning* (pp. 88–101). Paris: Organisation for Economic Co-operation and Development.

Slavin, R. E., & Madden, N. A. (2000). Roots & Wings: Effects of whole-school reform on student achievement. *Journal of Education for Students Placed at Risk, 5*(1 & 2), 109–136.

Slavin, R. E., & Oickle, E. (1981). Effects of cooperative learning teams on student achievement and race relations: Treatment by race interaction. *Sociology of Education, 54,* 174–180.

Solomon, D., Watson, M., Schaps, E., Battistich, V., & Solomon, J. (1990). Cooperative learning as part of a comprehensive classroom program designed to promote prosocial development. In S. Sharan (Ed.), *Cooperative learning: Theory and research.* (pp. 19–31). New York: Praeger.

Stern, D. (Ed.). (1996). *Active learning.* Paris: Organization for Economic Co-Operation and Development.

Stevens, R. J., Madden, N. A., Slavin, R. E., & Farnish, A. M. (1987). Cooperative Integrated Reading and Composition: Two field experiments. *Reading Research Quarterly, 22,* 433–454.

Stevens, R. J., & Slavin, R. E. (1995a). Effects of a cooperative learning approach in reading and writing on academically handicapped and nonhandicapped students. *The Elementary School Journal, 95*(3), 241–262.

Stevens, R. J., & Slavin, R. E. (1995b). The cooperative elementary school: Effects on students' achievement, attitudes, and social relations. *American Educational Research Journal, 32,* 321–351.

Stevens, R. J., Slavin, R. E., & Farnish, A. M. (1991). The effects of cooperative learning and direct instruction in reading comprehension strategies on main idea identification. *Journal of Educational Psychology, 83,* 8–16.

Tajfel, H., & Turner, J. C. (1985). The social identity theory of intergroup behavior. In S. Worchel & W. C. Austin (Eds.), *Psychology of intergroup relations* (pp. 7–24). Chicago: Nelson Hall.

Talmage, H., Pascarella, E. T., & Ford, S. (1984). The influence of cooperative learning strategies on teacher practices, student perceptions of the learning environment, and academic achievement. *American Educational Research Journal, 21,* 163–179.

Tharp, R., & Gallimore, R. (1988). *Rousing minds to life.* New York: Cambridge University Press.

Turner, J. C. (1987). *Rediscovering the social group: A self-categorization theory.* New York: Basil Blackwell.

U.S. Department of Education, National Center for Education Statistics. (2000). *The condition of Education 2000* (Report No. NCES 2000-602). Washington, DC: U.S. Government Printing Office.

Van Oudenhoven, J. P., Van Berkum, G., & Swen-Koopmans, T. (1987). Effect of cooperation and shared feedback on spelling achievement. *Journal of Educational Psychology, 79,* 92–94.

Van Oudenhoven, J. P., Wiersma, B., & Van Yperen, N. (1987). Effects of cooperation and feedback by fellow pupils on spelling achievement. *European Journal of Psychology of Education, 2,* 83–91.

Vygotsky, L. S. (1978). *Mind in society* (M. Cole, V. John-Steiner, S. Scribner, & E. Souberman, Eds.). Cambridge, MA: Harvard University Press.

Wadsworth, B. J. (1984). *Piaget's theory of cognitive and affective development* (3rd ed.). New York: Longman.

Webb, N. M. (1989). Peer interaction and learning in small groups. *International Journal of Educational Research, 13,* 21–39.

Webb, N. M. (1992). Testing a theoretical model of student interaction and learning in small groups. In R. Hertz-Lazarowitz & N. Miller (Eds.), *Interaction in cooperative groups: The theoretical anatomy of group learning* (pp. 102–119). New York: Cambridge University Press.

Webb, N. M., & Farvier, S. (1994). Promoting helping behavior in cooperative small groups in middle school mathematics. *American Educational Research Journal, 31*(2), 369–395.

Wheeler, R., & Ryan, F. L. (1973). Effects of cooperative and competitive classroom environments on the attitudes and achievement of elementary school students engaged in social studies inquiry activities. *Journal of Educational Psychology, 65*, 402–407.

Williams, K., & Karau, S. (1991). Social loafing and social compensation: The effects of expectations of co-worker performance. *Journal of Personality and Social Psychology, 61*(4), 570–581.

Wittrock, M. C. (1986). Students' thought processes. In M. C. Wittrock (Ed.), *Handbook of research on teaching* (3rd ed.) (pp. 297–314). New York: Macmillan.

Yager, S., Johnson, R. T., Johnson, D. W., & Snider, B. (1986). The impact of group processing on achievement in cooperative learning. *Journal of Social Psychology, 126*, 389–397.

Yost, C. A., & Tucker, M. L. (2000). Are effective teams more emotionally intelligent? Confirming the importance of effective communication in teams. *Delta Pi Epsilon Journal, 42*(2), 101–109.

Zahn, G., Kagan, S., & Widaman, K. (1986). Cooperative learning and classroom climate. *Journal of Social Psychology, 24*, 351–362.

CHAPTER 10

Relationships Between Teachers and Children

ROBERT C. PIANTA, BRIDGET HAMRE, AND MEGAN STUHLMAN

Relationships between teachers and children have been a focus of educators' concerns for decades, although this attention had taken different forms and had been expressed using a wide range of constructs and paradigms. Over many years, diverse literatures attended to teachers' and students' expectations of one another, discipline and class management, teaching and learning as socially mediated, teachers' own self- and efficacy-related feelings and beliefs, school belonging and caring, teacher-student interactions, and the more recent attention to teacher support as a source of resilience for children at risk (e.g., Battistich, Solomon, Watson, & Schaps, 1997; Brophy & Good, 1986; Eccles & Roeser, 1998). In many ways, these literatures provided the conceptual and scientific grounding for the present focus on child-teacher relationships, and in turn, a focus on relationships provides a mechanism for integrating these diverse literatures into a more common language and focus. In fact, one of the goals of this chapter is to advance theory and research in these many areas by changing the unit of analysis and focus to *relationships* between teachers and children. This new framework has potential for integrating what, up to this point, has been a large array

of findings involving how teachers and students relate to one another that has been spread among sources and outlets that often have little contact and overlap. This integrative, cross-cutting perspective, utilizing the more holistic, molar unit of analysis of relationship, is consistent with modern views of human development in which the developmental process is viewed as a function of dynamic, multilevel, reciprocal interactions involving person and contexts (Bronfenbrenner & Morris, 1998; Lerner, 1998; Magnusson & Stattin, 1998).

Including a chapter of child-teacher relationships in this volume marks, to some degree, the coming of age of this research and conceptual focus. Over the course of the last 10 years there has been an accelerating trend for increased attention to the role of relationships between children and teachers in influencing child outcomes (Pianta, 1999).

It is the broad aim of this chapter to summarize historic trends in the emergence of research on child-teacher relationships and to further advance theoretical and applied efforts by organizing the available work on child-teacher relationships currently residing across diverse areas of psychology and education.

Child-Teacher Relationships: Historical Perspectives and Intersections

Relationships, detailed in a subsequent section, involve many component entities and processes integrated within a dynamic system (Hinde, 1987; Magnusson & Stattin, 1998). Components include expectations, beliefs about the self or other, affects, and interactions, to identify a few (Eccles & Roeser, 1998; Pianta, 1999; Sroufe, 1989a; Stern, 1989). In a school or classroom setting, each of these components has its own extensive literature, for example, on teacher expectations or the role of social processes as mediators of instruction (see Eccles & Roeser, 1998). Therefore, the study of child-teacher relationships traces its roots to many sources in psychology and education.

Educational psychology, curriculum and instruction, and teacher education each provide rich sources of intellectual nourishment for the study of relationships between teachers and children. From a historical perspective, early in Dewey's writing (Dewey, 1902/1990) and in texts by Vygotsky (e.g., 1978), there are frequent references to relationships between teachers and children. Social relations, particularly a sense of being cared for, were considered an important component in Dewey's conceptualization of the school as a context, and certainly Vygotsky's emphasis on support provided to the child in the context of performing and learning challenging tasks was a central feature of his concept of the *zone of proximal development.*

Based on the exceptionally detailed descriptions of human activity and interaction undertaken by Barker and colleagues (see Barker, 1968), extensive observational research on classroom interactions involving teachers and children was conducted, with refinement and further development of methods and concepts culminating in the foundation studies on child-teacher interactions by Brophy and Good (1974).

Somewhat parallel to the focus of Brophy and Good on classroom interactions was the emergence of the broad literatures on interpersonal perception that took form in research on attribution and expectation, notably studies by Rosenthal (1969) on the influence of expectations on student performance. These studies strongly indicated that instruction is something more than simply demonstration, modeling, and reinforcement, but instead a complex, socially and psychologically mediated process. Work on student motivation, self-perceptions, and goal attainment has documented strong associations between these child outcomes and school contexts, including teachers' attitudes and behaviors toward the child (see Eccles & Roeser, 1998). More recently, research and theory on the concept of students' help-seeking behavior (Nelson-Le Gall & Resnick, 1998; Newman, 2000) actively addresses the integration of emotions, perceptions, and motivations in the context of instructional interactions, pointing again to the importance of the relational context created for the child.

At the same time, there has always been anecdotal and case study evidence for child-teacher relationships in the clinical psychology and teacher training literatures. These anecdotes typically describe how a child's relationship with a particular teacher was instrumental in somehow rescuing or saving that child and placing the child on the path to success and competence in life (e.g., Pederson, Faucher, & Eaton, 1978; Werner & Smith, 1980). Such stories often provide compelling evidence for attempts to harness the potential of these relationships as resources for children.

Developmental psychology and its applied branches related to prevention provide considerable conceptual and methodological underpinnings to the study of child-teacher relationships (see Pianta, 1999). The study of human development has contributed a scientific paradigm for studying relationships, conceptual models that advance ideas about how contexts and human development are linked with one another, and scores of studies demonstrating the value of relationships for human development in other arenas (see Bronfenbrenner & Morris, 1998).

In part because of the extensive and long-standing empirical and theoretical work on marital and parent-child relationships, core conceptual and methodological frameworks and concepts for understanding and studying interpersonal relationships have emerged (Bakeman & Gottman, 1986; Bornstein, 1995). These scientific tools form a foundation, or infrastructure, that can be applied to the study of children and teachers (e.g., Howes, Hamilton, & Matheson, 1994; Pianta & Nimetz, 1991). Clearly, the work of Bowlby (1969), Ainsworth (e.g., Ainsworth, Blehar, Waters, & Wall, 1978), and Sroufe (1983; Sroufe & Fleeson, 1988) on attachment between children and parents provides some of the strongest theoretical and empirical support for the influence of relationships between children and adults on child development. It was largely the concentrated focus on understanding child-mother attachment that helped to advance the idea of child-adult relationships as systems and to identify the component processes and mechanisms.

In addition to work on child-parent attachment, developmental psychologists were involved in research on early intervention and day care experiences as they contribute to child development, which identified relational or interactional aspects of those settings (e.g., quality of care and caregiver sensitivity) that were related to child outcomes (Howes, 1999, 2000a). Furthermore, this line of inquiry also described how structural aspects of settings (e.g., child-teacher ratios and teacher training and education) contributed to the social and emotional quality of interactions between child and teacher (see NICHD Early Child Care Research Network [NICHD ECCRN], 2002). Developmental methodologists interested in child-parent interactions, peer, and marital interactions as well as those working from a comparative or ethological framework contributed substantially to the study of child-teacher relationships by describing the functions and processes of relationships (Bakeman & Gottman, 1986; Hinde, 1987). Finally, recent work on motivation and the development of the child's sense of self and identity provides compelling evidence that teachers are an important source of information and input to these processes (Eccles & Roeser, 1998).

Over the last two decades, as developmental psychology, school psychology, and clinical psychology have formed convergent interests (Pianta, 1999) and as the more integrative paradigm of developmental psychopathology emerged (Cicchetti & Cohen, 1995), relationships between children and adults have received much attention as a resource that can be targeted and harnessed in prevention efforts. Paradigms for prevention and early intervention in the home environment, as well as intervention approaches focusing on parent-child dyads in which the child demonstrates serious levels of problem behavior (e.g., Barkley, 1987; Eyberg & Boggs, 1998), have focused on improving the quality of child-parent relationships. That work has resulted in a fairly large body of knowledge concerning how relationships can be changed through intentional focus on interactions, perceptions, and interactive skills (Eyberg & Boggs, 1998). These studies have provided a strong basis for extensions into school settings (McIntosh, Rizza, & Bliss, 2000; Pianta, 1999).

In more recent years the focus on prevention that has arisen from this nexus of overlapping interests among scientists, policy makers, and practitioners has viewed school settings as a primary locus for the delivery and infusion of resources that have a preventive or competence-enhancing effect (Battistich et al., 1997; Cowen, 1999; Durlak & Wells, 1997). School-based mental health services, delivery of a range of associated services in full-service schools, reforms aimed at curriculum and school management, and issues related to school design and construction frequently identify child-teacher relationships as a target of their efforts under the premise that improving and strengthening this school-based relational resource can have a dramatic influence on children's outcomes (see Adelman, 1996; Battistich et al., 1997; Durlak & Wells, 1997; Haynes, 1998). Finally, it has also been suggested that one by-product of such efforts to enhance relationships between teachers and children is an improvement in teachers' own mental health, job satisfaction, and sense of efficacy (e.g., Battsitich et al., 1997; Pianta, 1999).

Although diverse areas of psychology address issues related to relationships between teachers and children, extending back in time nearly 80 years, the study of child-teacher relationships has not, until the last decade, been an area of inquiry unto itself. This lack of focus has been due to the widely scattered nature of its intellectual roots and a tendency toward insularity among disciplines, problems with the use of different terminology and languages, seams between research and practice and between psychology in education and psychology in the family or laboratory, and the lack of theoretical models that adequately emphasize the role of multiple contexts in the development of children over the life span (Lerner, 1998). Perhaps one of the strongest conceptual advances contributing to the last decade of work on child-teacher relationships has been the developmental psychopathology paradigm, with its emphasis on integration across diverse theoretical frameworks and its embrace of a developmental systems model of contexts and persons in time (see Cicchetti & Cohen, 1995).

The present focus on child-teacher relationships reflects this integration and interweaving of theoretical traditions, methodologies, and applications across diverse fields. This area of inquiry, understanding, and application is inherently interdisciplinary. Yet the organizing frame for such work—although different areas have evolved from different traditions—is best found in current models of child development (Bronfenbrenner & Morris, 1998; Cairns & Cairns, 1994; Lerner, 1998; Magnusson & Stattin 1998; Sameroff, 1995). In these models, development of the person in context is depicted as a function of dynamic processes embedded in multilevel interactions between person and contexts over time. Developmental systems theory (Lerner, 1998) forms the core of an analysis of child-teacher relationships.

DEVELOPMENTAL SYSTEMS THEORY

In the last two decades, views that embrace the perspective that the study of development is in large part the study of living *systems* and is therefore informed by the study of systems have been adopted as the primary conceptual paradigm in human development (see Lerner, 1998, for example). As noted by Lerner (1998), "a developmental systems perspective is an overarching conceptual framework associated with contemporary theoretical models in the field of human development" (p. 2). General systems theory has a long history in the understanding of biological, ecological, and other complex living systems (e.g., Ford & Ford, 1987; Ford & Lerner, 1992) and has been applied to child development by Ford and Lerner (1992) and Sameroff (1995) in what is called developmental systems theory (DST). DST can be applied to the broad array of systems involved in the practice of psychology with children and adolescents (Pianta, 1999). The principles of DST help integrate analysis of the multiple factors that influence young children, such as families, communities, social processes, cognitive development, schools, teachers, peers, or conditions such as poverty. This analysis of child-teacher relationships draws heavily on developmental systems perspectives for principles and constructs that guide inquiry, understanding, and integration of diverse knowledge sources.

For the purposes of this discussion, *systems* are defined as units composed of sets of interrelated parts that act in organized, interdependent ways to promote the adaptation and survival of the whole. Families, classrooms, child-parent and child-teacher relationships, self-regulatory behaviors, and peer groups are systems of one form or another, as are various biologic systems within the organism. These systems function at a range of levels in relation to the child—some distal and some more proximal (Bronfenbrenner & Morris, 1998). They are involved in multiple forms of activity involving interactions within levels and across levels (Gottlieb, 1991) that form a pattern, or matrix, of reciprocal, bidirectional interactions that varies with time. In the case of child-teacher relationships, this perspective is reflected in analysis of the ways that school policies about child-teacher ratios affect student-teacher interactions that in turn are related to students' and teachers' perceptions and affects toward one another. It is important to note that one must recognize the vertical as well as lateral interactions across and within levels and associated systems. The concept of within- and across-level interactions among systems is a key aspect of DST as applied to child-teacher relationships; for example, just as these relationships are influenced by the interactions of two individuals, they are in turn affected (and affect) classroom organization and climate.

Principles Influencing the Behavior and Analysis of Developmental Systems

The behavior of developmental systems is best understood in the context of a number of general principles. These principles apply across all forms of living systems (Magnusson & Stattin, 1998).

Holism and Units of Analysis

Because of the preponderance of rich, cross-level interactions, interpretation and study of the behavior of systems at any level must take place in the context of activity at these other levels. Behavior of a "smaller" system (e.g., children's self-regulation in a classroom) should be understood in relation to its function in the context of systems at more distal levels (e.g., child-teacher relationships) as well as more proximal or micro levels (e.g., biological systems regulating temperament) and vice versa. The rich, reciprocal interconnections among these units promote the idea that a relational unit of analysis is required for analysis of development (Lerner, 1998). From this perspective, noted Lerner (1998), the *causes* of development are *relationships* among systems and their components, not actions in isolation. This is highly similar to the perspective advanced by Bronfenbrenner and Morris (1998), who argued that the primary engine of development is *proximal process*—interactions that take place between the child and contexts over extended periods of time. Bronfenbrenner and Morris cited interactions with teachers as one course of proximal process. For several developmental theorists, acknowledging the existence of multilevel interactions leads directly to the need for research that has these interactions and relationships as their foci.

Magnusson and Stattin (1998) approached the issue of holism from a somewhat different perspective. They noted that most psychological (and educational) research and theory are variable-focused—that is, a construct of interest is the sole focus of measurement and inquiry, inasmuch as variation in that construct relates to other sources of variation. This approach, argued Magnusson and Stattin, yields a science that examines selective aspects of the person but misses large sectors of experience that may hold descriptive and explanatory power. Behavior is better viewed in terms of higher order organized patterns of relations across different components of the system.

The developing child is also a system. From this point of view, motor, cognitive, social, and emotional development are *not* independent entities on parallel paths but are integrated within organized, dynamic processes. Psychological practices (assessment or intervention) that focus solely on one of these domains (e.g., cognition, personality, attention span, aggression, or reading achievement) can reinforce the notion that developmental domains can be isolated from one another and from the context in which they are embedded. Taking a developmental systems perspective, many argue that child assessment should focus on broad indexes reflecting *integrated* functions across a number of behavioral domains as they are observed in context (e.g., Greenspan & Greenspan, 1991; Sroufe, 1989b). Terms such as *adaptation* have been used to capture these broad qualities of behavioral organization, and although fairly abstract, they call attention to a focus on how children use the range of resources available to them (including their own skills and the resources of peers, adults, and material resources) to respond to internal and external demands.

In terms of this analysis of child-teacher relationships, holism means that to understand the discipline-related behavior of a teachers in their classrooms, one must know something about the school, school system, and community in which the teachers are embedded, their experiences, and their own internal systems of cognition and affect regulation in relation to behavioral expectations in the classroom. From the perspective of holism, the whole (i.e., the pattern or organization of interconnections) gives meaning to the activity of the parts (Sameroff, 1995).

Reciprocal, Functional Relations Between Parts and Wholes

Systems and their component entities are embedded within other systems. Interactions take place within levels (e.g., beliefs about children affect a teachers' beliefs about a particular child; Brophy, 1985) and across levels (e.g., teachers' beliefs about children are related to their training as well as to the school in which they work; Battstitch et al., 1997) over time. It is a fundamental tenet of developmental systems theories that these interactions are reciprocal and bidirectional. Gottlieb (1991) refered to these interactions as *coactivity* in part to call attention to the mutuality and reciprocity of these relations. Similarly, Magnusson and Stattin (1998) and Sameroff (1995) emphasized that in multilevel, dynamic, active, moving systems, it is largely fictional to conceptualize "cause" or "source" of interactions and activity. Again, this view has consequences for considerations of child-teacher relationships when examining the large number of components of these relationships as well as the multilevel systems in which they are embedded (Eccles & Roeser, 1998).

Motivation and Change

Systems theory offers alternative views of the locus of motivation and change. Within behavioral perspectives, change and motivation to change are often viewed as derived extrinsically—from being acted on by positive (or negative) reinforcement, or reinforcement history. Maturationist or biological views of change posit that the locus of change resides in the unfolding of genetic programs, or chronological age. From both perspectives the child is a somewhat passive participant in change—change is something that happens to the child, whether from within or without.

In developmental systems theory the motivation to change is an intrinsic property of a system, inherent in that system's activity. Developmental change follows naturally as a consequence of the activity of interacting systems. That children are active can be seen in the ways they continually construct meaning, seek novelty and challenges, or practice emergent capacities. Furthermore, the child acts within contexts that are dynamic and fluid. Motivation, or the desire to change, is derived from the coaction of systems—of child and context (Bronfenbrenner & Morris, 1998). That relationships play a fundamental role as contexts for coaction between child and the world is supported by Csikszentmihalyi and Rathunde's (1998) proposition that relationships with parents are foundational for establishing the rhythm of interaction between the child and the external world.

Maturationist or biological views of the motivation for developmental change tend to rely on characteristics of the child as triggers for developmental experience and can result in practices and policies that neglect individual variation or notions of adaptation. Strongly behavioral views of motivation focus solely on contingencies while failing to acknowledge the meaning of target behaviors and contextual responses to the child's goals, leading to a disjunction between how the child perceives his or her fit in the world and how helpers may be attempting to facilitate change. Views of motivation informed by systems theory lead to a *developmental interactionism* (Magnusson & Stattin, 1998) that focuses attention on issues of goodness of fit, relationships, and related relational constructs. As Lerner (1998) acknowledged, because of relationism, an attribute of the organism has meaning for psychological development only by virtue of its timing of interaction with contexts or levels.

Developmental change occurs when systems reorganize and transform under pressure to adapt. Development takes place, according to Bronfenbrenner and Morris (1998), through progressively more complex reciprocal interactions. Change is not simply a function of acquiring skills but a reorganization of skills and competencies in response to internal and external challenges and demands that yields novelty in emergent structures and processes (Magnusson & Stattin, 1998).

Competence as a Distributed Property

Children, as active systems, interact with contexts, exchanging information, material, energy, and activity (Ford & Ford, 1987). Within schools, teacher and children engage within a context of multilevel interactions involving culture, policy, and biological processes (Pianta & Walsh, 1996). The dynamic, multilevel interactionism embodied in the principle of holism also suggests that children's competence is so intertwined with properties of contexts that properties residing in the child (e.g., cognition, attention, social competence, problem behaviors) are actually *distributed* across the child and contexts (e.g., Campbell, 1994; Hofer, 1994; Resnick, 1994). Cognitive processes related to attending, comprehending, and reasoning (Resnick, 1994); emotion-related processes such as emotion regulation and self-control; help-seeking; and social processes such as cooperation are all properties not of the child but of relations and interactions of the child in the context of the classroom: They reflect a certain level of organization and function (Magnusson & Stattin, 1998).

The concept of *affordance* (see Pianta, 1999, for an explanation of this construct as applied to classrooms) embodies the idea that contexts contain resources for the child that can be activated to sustain the child's adaptation to the demands of that setting. It is important to note that the affordance of a context must be accessed by interactions with the child. From the perspective of developmental systems theory, competence (and problems) in a classroom setting cannot be conceptualized or assessed separately from attributes of the setting and the interactions that features of the child have with those setting attributes (and in turn how these interactions are embedded in larger loops of interaction). At the level of social and instructional behavior between teachers and children, understanding these interactions may require a moment-by-moment analysis of behavioral loops, whereas understanding how the teacher's behavior in these loops is a function of her education and training may require a much wider time frame (Pianta, La Paro, Payne, Cox, & Bradley, 2002). The coordination of these temporal cycles of interaction within and across levels is critical to understanding behavior within the specific setting of interest.

Centrality of Relationships in Human Development

In the context of all these multilevel and multisystem interactions, enduring patterns of interaction between children and adults (i.e., relationships) are the primary conduit through which the child gains access to developmental resources. These interactions, as noted earlier, are the primary engine of developmental change. Relationships with adults are like the keystone or linchpin of development; they are in large part responsible for developmental success under conditions of risk and—more often than not—transmit those risk conditions to the child (Pianta, 1999).

Our focus here is primarily on school-age children and their relationships with teachers in classroom settings. There is virtually no question that relationships between children and adults (both teachers and parents) play a prominent role in the development of competencies in the preschool, elementary, and middle-school years (Birch & Ladd, 1996; Pianta &

Walsh, 1996; Wentzel, 1996). They form the developmental infrastructure on which later school experiences build. Child-adult relationships also play an important role in adaptation of the child within the context in which that relationship resides—home or classroom (e.g., Howes, 2000b; Howes, Hamilton, et al., 1994; Howes, Matheson, & Hamilton, 1994). The key qualities of these relationships appear to be related to the ability or skill of the adult to read the child's emotional and social signals accurately, respond contingently based on these signals (e.g., to follow the child's lead), convey acceptance and emotional warmth, offer assistance as necessary, model regulated behavior, and enact appropriate structures and limits for the child's behavior. These qualities determine that relationship's affordance value.

Relationships with parents influence a range of competencies in classroom contexts (Belsky & MacKinnon, 1994; Elicker, Egeland, & Sroufe, 1992; LaFreniere & Sroufe, 1985; Pianta & Harbers, 1996; Sroufe, 1983). Research has established the importance of child-parent (often child-mother) relationships in the prediction and development of behavior problems (Campbell, 1990; Egeland, Pianta, & O'Brien, 1993), peer competencies (Elicker et al., 1992; Howes, Hamilton, et al., 1994), academic achievement, and classroom adjustment (Pianta & Harbers, 1996; Pianta, Smith, & Reeve, 1991). Consistent with the developmental systems model, various forms of adaptation in childhood are in part a function of the quality of child-parent relationships.

For example, a large number of studies demonstrate the importance of various parameters of child-parent interaction in the prediction of a range of academic competencies in the early school years (e.g., de Ruiter & van IJzendoorn, 1993; Pianta & Harbers, 1996; Pianta et al., 1991; Rogoff, 1990). These relations between mother-child interaction and children's competence in mastering classroom academic tasks reflect the extent to which basic task-related skills such as attention, conceptual development, communication skills, and reasoning emerge from, and remain embedded within, a matrix of interactions with caregivers and other adults. Furthermore, in the context of these interactions children acquire the capacity to approach tasks in an organized, confident manner, to seek help when needed, and to use help appropriately.

Qualities of the mother-child relationship also affect the quality of the relationship that a child forms with a teacher. In one study, teachers characterized children with ambivalent attachments as needy and displayed high levels of nurturance and tolerance for immaturity toward them, whereas their anger was directed almost exclusively at children with histories of avoidant attachment (Motti, 1986). These findings are consistent with results in which maltreated and nonmaltreated children's perceptions of their relationships with mothers were related to their need for closeness with their teacher (Lynch & Cicchetti, 1992), as well as to the teachers' ratings of child adjustment (Toth & Cicchetti, 1996). Cohn (1990) found that boys classified as insecurely attached to their mothers were rated by teachers as less competent and more of a behavior problem than were boys classified as securely attached. In addition, teachers reported that they liked these boys less. This link between the quality of child-parent relationships and the relationship that a child forms with a teacher confirms Bowlby's (1969) contention that the mother-child relationship establishes for the child a set of internal guides for interacting with adults that may be carried forward into subsequent relationships and affect behavior in those relationships (Sroufe, 1983). These representations can affect the child's perceptions of the teacher (Lynch & Cicchetti, 1992), the child's behavior toward the teacher and the teacher's behavior toward the child (Motti, 1986), and the teacher's perceptions of the child (Pianta, 1992; Toth & Cicchetti, 1996). On the other hand, there are limits to concordance and stability in mother-child and teacher-child relationships as children move from preschool to school (Howes, Hamilton, & Phillipsen, 1998).

In sum, there is no shortage of evidence to support the view that—particularly for younger children, but also for children in the middle and high school years—relationships with adults are indeed involved centrally in the development of increasingly complex levels of organizing one's interactions and relationships with the world. In this view, adult-child relationships are a cornerstone of development, and from a systems perspective intervention involves the intentional structuring or harnessing of developmental resources (such as adult-child relationships) or the skilled use of this context to developmental advantage (Lieberman, 1992). This is inherently a prevention-oriented view (Henggeler, 1994; Roberts, 1996) that depends on professionals' understanding the mechanisms responsible for altering developmental pathways and emulating (or enhancing) these influences in preventive interventions (e.g., Hughes, 1992; Lieberman, 1992).

In conclusion, a developmental systems perspective draws attention to this child as an active, self-motivated organism whose developmental progress depends in large part on qualities of interactions established and maintained over time with key adult figures. Such interactions, and their effects, are best understood using child-adult relationships as the unit of analysis and then embedding this focus on relationships within the multilevel interactions that impinge on and are affected by this relationship from various directions.

CONCEPTUAL-THEORETICAL ISSUES IN RESEARCH ON CHILD-TEACHER RELATIONSHIPS

This section updates and extends Pianta's (1999) model of relationships between children and teachers and reviews research related to components of this model. The model is offered as an integrative heuristic. It draws heavily on principles and concepts of systems theory, positing that by focusing at the *level of relationships as the unit of analysis,* significant advances can be made in understanding the development of child-teacher relationships and in their significance in relation to child outcomes. Considering the wide-ranging and diverse literatures that currently address, in some form or another, the multiple systems that interact with and comprise child-teacher relationships, a model of such relationships needs to be integrative. As suggested by the examples used in the previous discussion of developmental systems theory, this model must incorporate aspects of children (e.g., age or gender), teachers (experience, efficacy), teacher-child interactions (discipline, instruction), activity settings, children's and teachers' perceptions and beliefs about one another, and school policy (ratios) and climate (Battistich et al., 1997; Brophy, 1985; Brophy & Good, 1974; Eccles & Roeser, 1998).

It is our firm belief that greater understanding of the developmental significance of school settings can be achieved by this focus on child-teacher relationships as a central, core system involved in transmitting the influence of those settings to children. Narrow-focused examinations of one or two of the factors just noted, as they relate in bivariate fashion to one another, are unlikely to yield a comprehensive understanding of the dynamic, multilevel interactions that take place in schools, the complexities of which have frustrated educational researchers and policy makers for years (Haynes, 1998). In many ways, a focus on the system of child-teacher relationships as a key unit of analysis may provide the kind of integrative conceptual tool for understanding development in school settings that a similar focus on parent-child relationships provided in the understanding of development in family settings (Bronfenbrenner & Morris, 1998; Pianta, 1999).

Hinde (1987) and others (e.g., Sameroff, 1995) describe relationships as dyadic systems. As such, relationships are subject to the principles of systems behavior described earlier; they are dynamic, multicomponent entities involved in reciprocal interactions across and within multiple levels of organization and influence (Lerner, 1998). They are best considered as abstractions that represent a level or form of organization within a much larger matrix of systems and interactions. The utility of a focus at this level of analysis is borne out by ample evidence from the parent-child literature as well as studies examining children and teachers using this relational focus (Howes, 2000a). For example, when the focus of teachers' reports about children is *relational* rather than simply a focus on the child's behavior, it is the relational aspects of teachers' views that are more predictive of long-term educational outcomes compared with their reports about children's classroom behavior (Hamre & Pianta, 2001). Evidence also suggests that teachers' reflections on their own relational histories, as well as current relationships with children, relate to their behavior with and attitudes toward the child more than do teacher attributes such as training or education (Stuhlman & Pianta, in press). Coming to view the disparate and multiple foci of most research on teachers and children using the lens or unit of child-teacher relationships appears to provide considerable gain in understanding the complex phenomenon of classroom adjustment.

A relationship between a teacher and child is not equivalent to only their interactions with one another, or to their characteristics as individuals. A relationship between a teacher and a child is not wholly determined by that child's temperament, intelligence, or communication skills. Nor can their relationship be reduced to the pattern of reinforcement between them. Relationships have their own identities apart from the features of interactions or individuals (Sroufe, 1989a).

A Conceptual Model of Child-Teacher Relationships

A conceptual model of child-teacher relationships is presented in Figure 10.1. As depicted in Figure 10.1, the primary components of relationships between teachers and children are (a) features of the two individuals themselves, (b) each individual's representation of the relationship, (c) processes by which information is exchanged between the relational partners, and (d) external influences of the systems in which the relationship is embedded. Relationships embody features of the individuals involved. These features include biologically predisposed characteristics (e.g., temperament), personality, self-perceptions and beliefs, developmental history, and attributes such as gender or age. Relationships also involve each participant's views of the relationship and the roles of each in the relationship—what Bowlby (1969) and Sroufe and Fleeson (1988) called the members' representation of the relationship. Consistent with evidence from the literature on parent-child relationships (Main, Kaplan, & Cassidy, 1985; Sroufe & Fleeson; 1986), representational models are conceptualized not as features of individuals but as a higher order construct that embodies properties of the relationship

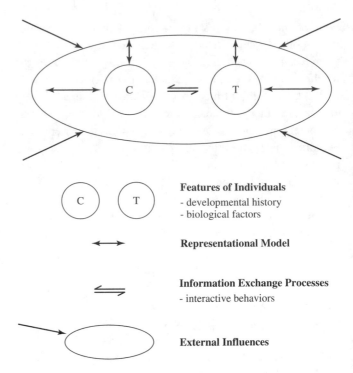

Figure 10.1   A conceptual model of teacher-child relationships.

that are accessed through the participants. Note that this is an advance from the model presented by Pianta (1999) in that the current model places more emphasis on the partners' representations of the relationship as distinct from characteristics of the individuals.

Relationships also include processes that exchange information between the two individuals and serve a feedback function in the relationship system (Lerner, 1998). These processes include behavioral interactions, language, and communication. These feedback, or information exchange, processes are critical to the smooth functioning of the relationship. It is important to recognize that these relationship components (individual characteristics, representational models, information exchange processes) are themselves in dynamic, reciprocal interactions, such that behaviors of teacher and child toward one another influence representations (Stuhlman & Pianta, in press), and attributes of the child or teacher are related to teachers' perceptions of the relationship (Saft & Pianta, 2001) or interactive behaviors (Pianta et al., 2002).

In turn, these relationship systems are embedded in many other systems (schools, classrooms, communities) and interact with systems at similar levels (e.g., families and peer groups). Finally, it is important to emphasize that adult-child relationships embody certain asymmetries. That is, there are differential levels of responsibility for interaction and quality that are a function of the discrepancy in roles and maturity of the adult and child, the balance of which changes across the school-age years (Eccles & Roeser, 1998).

Features of Individuals in Relationships

At the most basic level, relationships incorporate features of individuals. These include biological facts (e.g., gender) and biological processes (e.g., temperament, genetics, responsivity to stressors) as well as developed features such as personality, self-esteem, or intelligence. In this way developmental history affects the interactions with others and, in turn, influences relationships (Fonagy, Steele, & Steele, 1991; Zeanah et al., 1993). For example, a teacher's history of being cared for can be related to how he or she understands the goals of teaching and, in turn, can relate to the way he or she interprets and attends to a child's emotional behavior and cues (Zeanah et al., 1993).

Characteristics of Teachers

In contrast to what is known about parents in relation to their interactions with children, virtually nothing is known about teachers. Despite a general recognition that teacher characteristics and perceptions influence the practice of teaching, little is known about how individual teacher characteristics and perceptions impact the formation of their relationships with children. Some have suggested that due to the importance of the social climate of the classroom, teaching may require more personal involvement than most other professions:

> The act of teaching requires teachers to use their personality to project themselves in particular roles and to establish relationships within the classroom so that children's interest is maintained and a productive working environment is developed. The teacher relies on his personality and his ability to form relationships in order to manage the class and ensure smooth running. (Calderhead, 1996, p. 720)

When questioned about their relationships with teachers, children acknowledge that teachers' abilities to access this more personal part of themselves is an important component of creating a feeling of caring between teachers and children (Baker, 1999). By providing emotional support and asking children about their lives, teachers may enable children to feel more comfortable and supported in the school environment.

Teachers, like all adults, vary in their ability and desire to become personally involved in their work. In a series of case studies logging the thoughts of several student teachers over the course of training, Calderhead and Robson (1991)

discussed teachers' images of themselves as educators and provided examples of several very different perspectives on what it means to be a teacher. Some student teachers emphasized their role as emotional supporters of children, whereas others tended to speak more about the importance of efficiency and organization of the classroom. It is likely that these different orientations and associated styles of behavioral interaction are related in important ways to the types of relationships that teachers tend to form with students. Brophy (1985) suggested that teachers view themselves primarily as *instructors* or *socializers* and that these different perceptions impact the way in which they interact with students. Instructors tend to respond more negatively to students who are underachievers, unmotivated, or disruptive during learning tasks, whereas socializer teachers tended to act more negatively toward students they viewed as hostile, aggressive, or those who pushed away as teachers attempted to form relationships (Brophy, 1985). Although there is some preliminary evidence that teachers do vary in the pattern of relationships they form with children (Pianta, 1994), connections between these patterns and other teacher characteristics have yet to be elucidated.

How do teachers form this image of themselves as teachers? Several of the teachers in Calderhead and Robson's (1991) study consistently referred to experiences with previous teachers as essential to their own ideas about teaching. The student teachers' perceptions of past teachers ranged from very negative (intolerant, impatient, unsympathetic) to very positive (caring, attentive, friendly), and the students linked these perceptions to their thoughts about what it means to be a good or bad teacher. For example, one student teacher vividly recalled being ridiculed and embarrassed as a child by teachers who failed to take the time to explain things to her. She also remembered one teacher who took the time to help her understand. This student teacher described having patience with children as being extremely important to her own work as a teacher. Teachers' images of their roles as teachers develop in part from their own experiences in school.

Additionally, teachers may rely on past experiences with other important people in their lives to help form their image of themselves as a teacher. Kesner (2000) gathered data on student teachers' representations of attachment relationships with their own parents and showed that beginning teachers who viewed their relationships with their parents as secure were also those who formed relationships with students characterized as secure. In a related study, Horppu and Ikonen-Varila (2001) showed that beginning teachers' representations of attachment with their parents related to their stated motives for their work and their beliefs about a kindergarten teacher's work and goals in the classroom. Beginning teachers classified as having a secure-autonomous relationship with their parent(s) were more likely than those classified as insecure to express motives that were child-centered as well as centered on goals for the self. Teachers classified as secure also described more complex conceptions of a teacher's work (involving social, emotional, and instructional components) and were more likely to view relationships with students as mutually satisfying (Horppu & Ikonen-Varila, 2001). Teachers' own personal histories of relationship experiences with parents and their representations of those experiences were associated with their current views about teaching, the degree to which they viewed teaching as involving a relational component, and their comfort with that relational component, demonstrating the extent to which multiple aspects of the teacher's own representational system and belief system are interrelated and related to other components of the child-teacher dyadic system.

In a case-based extension of these ideas, Case (1997) suggested that one instance in which teachers' early relationships may be particularly important to their own classroom philosophy is in the case of *othermothering* in urban elementary schools. She described othermothering as "African American women's maternal assistance offered to the children . . . within the African American community" (p. 25). Othermothering constitutes a culturally held belief in women's responsibility for the raising of other mothers' children, which for some women is enacted through the role of a teacher. Case (1997) described two African American teachers working in urban districts in Connecticut. Both of these women related the connections they made with children in the classroom to the experiences that they had with their own mothers as children. Describing her early experiences in rural North Carolina, one of the teachers stated,

> At an early age, it was all self-esteem, believing in yourself. But one of the things that we valued most as a family was the way that we must treat other people. We must look to the values from within and realize that everybody's human: They're going to make mistakes, they're going to fall flat on their faces sometimes, but you pick yourself up and say, "Well, I've learned from this." (p. 33)

As this teacher describes her first day of teaching, the connection between these early experiences and her view of her role as a teacher becomes apparent:

> When I first had this class, their faces were hanging down to the floor. . . . I had never seen such unhappy children. I felt as if they had no self-worth. I just couldn't believe the first couple of days. They were at each other's throats. I found that many of them thought that school was a place to come and act out, and now they are in cooperative groups, they share. It's just that you start

where they are. . . . I think it's about empathy. You look at them and say, "It's going to be a better day" and they say, "How did you know?" (pp. 34–35)

These findings (Case, 1997; Kesner, 2000; Horppu & Ikonen-Verida, 2001) suggest mechanisms by which teachers develop styles of relating to all of the children in their classrooms. Beyond a global relational style, teachers bring with them experiences, thoughts, and feelings that lead to specific styles of relating to certain types of children. Research in this area is scant, but there is a general recognition that the match or mismatch between teachers and students can be important to children's development as well as to teachers' job satisfaction (Goodlad, 1991).

Teachers also hold beliefs about their efficacy in the classroom and associated expectations for children that are related to experiences with children and their own success and satisfaction. Teachers who believe that they have an influence on children can enhance student investment and achievement (Midgley, Feldlaufer, & Eccles, 1989). When teachers hold high generalized expectations for student achievement, students tend to achieve more, experience a greater sense of self-esteem and competence as learners, and resist involvement in problem behaviors during both childhood and adolescence (Eccles, 1983, 1993; Roeser, Eccles, & Sameroff, 1998; Rutter, 1987; Weinstein, 1989). Furthermore, teachers who view self improvement and effort as more important than innate ability are more likely to have children who not only are more motivated but also report more positive and less negative affective states (Ames, 1992).

These studies, just a selective part of a much larger literature on teacher beliefs and student motivation (see Eccles & Roeser, 1998), call attention to the extent to which teacher beliefs, experiences, and expectations are involved within a model of child-teacher relationships. These beliefs, experiences, and expectations are closely intertwined with teachers' and students' behaviors toward one another. They change with developmental time and with experiences with specific children and stimulate loops of interaction in which changes in student motivation and achievement feedback on teacher beliefs in confirming or disconfirming ways.

In addition to psychological aspects of teachers as individuals as described earlier, other attributes of teachers warrant discussion in terms of their roles in a model of child-teacher relationships. These include teacher gender, experience and education, and ethnicity. Although the teacher workforce is overwhelmingly female, particularly at the younger grades (Goodlad, 1991), there is sufficient variability in teacher gender to examine its consequences for child-teacher relationships. By and large, this evidence is sparse, and the topic has not been a focus of dedicated study. However, anecdotal and survey data do suggest that teacher gender plays a role in the extent of children's use of the teacher as a role model; not surprisingly, this is particularly true for male children and teachers (Goodlad, 1991; Holland, 1996). Male teachers, who are found more frequently in the older grades, are reported by children to provide role models and are described as important sources of support.

Holland (1996) suggested that, particularly for African American boys, an African American male teacher plays a key role in organizing male students' adoption of educational goals and behaviors. The extent to which this finding—as well as others involving the match between African American male students and teachers—is related to gender or race is at this time unknown and unexamined. In a related finding, teacher ethnicity appears to play a role in teachers' perceptions of their relationships with students, particularly as their ethnicities interact with student ethnicities (Saft & Pianta, 2001). African American teachers (nearly all female) report more positive relationships (less conflict) with their students (of all ethnicities) than do Caucasian teachers, and they are particularly more positive (than White teachers) about their relationships with African American children.

Teacher experience, in and of itself, has shown little relation to teachers' own reports about the qualities of their relationships with children in the elementary grades (Beady & Hansell, 1981; Stuhlman & Pianta, in press). Battistich et al. (1997) reported that in a large sample of upper elementary school students there were no significant associations between child-reported or teacher-reported perceptions of the school as a caring community (which included an index of teacher emotional support) and teacher age, number of years teaching, education, or ethnic status. However, these data were aggregated within schools and related to each other at the school level, so they may mask significant associations for individual teachers and children.

In a study that elicited teachers' representations of their relationships with specific students using an interview procedure (Stuhlman & Pianta, in press), the extent to which teachers' reported negative emotional qualities in the relationship were related to their negative behaviors toward the children varied as a function of teacher experience. Teachers who were more experienced were more likely to have their represented negativity reflected in their behavior than were teachers with fewer than 7 years of experience. The extent to which the less experienced teachers held negative beliefs and experienced negative emotions in their relationship with a specific child was not related to their negative behavior with that child. These data suggest some type of emotional buffering mechanism that may wane with more years in the profession.

Characteristics of Children

From the moment students enter a classroom, they begin to make impressions on a teacher, impressions that are important in the formation of the relationships that develop over the course of the school year. Though it is likely that a wide variety of child characteristics, behaviors, and perceptions are associated with the development of their relationships with teachers, our understanding of these associations is limited and derived in part due from inferences about how these characteristics function in relationships. Some characteristics, such as gender, are both static and readily apparent to teachers, whereas others are more psychological or behavioral in nature.

Young girls tend to form closer and less conflictual relationships with their teachers, as noted in studies using teacher (Hamre & Pianta, 2001) and child (Bracken & Crain, 1994; Ryan, Stiller, & Lynch, 1994) reports on the quality of the relationship as well as in studies in which trained observers rated relationship quality (Ladd, Birch, & Buhs, 1999). Even as late as middle school, girls report higher levels of felt security and emulation of teachers than do boys (Ryan et al., 1994).

These gender differences may be related in part to the fact that boys typically show more frequent antisocial behaviors, such as verbal and physical aggression. These behaviors are, in turn, associated with the formation of poorer child-teacher relationships, as rated by trained observers (Ladd et al., 1999). It is important to note, however, that the majority of teachers in primary grades are females and that there are no existing data to suggest how male teachers may relate differentially to boys and girls in the primary grades. There is some evidence that as children mature, gender matching may be important in the formation of closeness with teachers. In one study, 12th-grade girls reported that they perceived greater positive regard from female teachers whereas the boys in the study perceived more positive regard from male teachers (Drevets, Benton, & Bradley, 1996). However, this gender specificity in children's perceptions was not reported by the 10th- and 11th-grade students in this study.

Another child characteristic that is apparent to teachers is ethnicity. As with the findings on gender, there are preliminary indications that the ethnic match between teacher and child is associated with more positive relationships (Saft & Pianta, 2001). Caucasian children tend to have closer relationships with teachers, as indicated in studies using reports by teachers (Ladd et al., 1999) and students (Hall & Bracken, 1996). Unfortunately, teachers in most of these studies are Caucasian, so it is difficult to make any clear inference about the impact of a child's ethnicity on his or her ability to form a strong relationship with teachers and other school personnel.

Other child characteristics that may be linked to the relationship that children develop with teachers include their own social and academic competencies and problems (Ladd et al., 1999; Murray & Greenberg, 2000). In a large sample of elementary school children, Murray and Greenberg reported that children's own reports of feeling a close emotional bond with their teacher were related to their own and their teachers' reports of problem behavior and competence in the classroom. Similarly, Pianta (1992) reported that teachers' descriptions of their relationships with students in kindergarten were related to their reports of the child's classroom adjustment and, in turn, related to first-grade teacher reports. A cycle of child behavior and interactions with the teacher appeared to influence (in part) the teachers' relationship with the child, which in turn was independently related (along with reports of classroom behavior) to teacher reports of classroom adjustment in the next grade. Ladd et al. (1999) suggested that relational style of the child is a prominent feature of classroom behavior.

Also important to the formation of the child-teacher relationship, though less visible to teachers, are the thoughts and feelings of their students, including their general feelings about the school environment and about using adults as a source of support. Third through fifth graders from urban, at-risk schools who reported the highest levels of dissatisfaction with the school environment reported less social support at school and a more negative classroom social environment than did their more satisfied peers (Baker, 1999). Similarly, elementary school children who report an emotionally close and warm relationship with their teacher view the school environment and climate more positively (Murray & Greenberg, 2000). Clearly, one issue in sorting out associations (or lack thereof) of children's judgments of school climate and the quality of child-teacher relationships is the experiential source of these judgments. Given the much greater weight on classroom experience in young children's judgment of school climate, it is likely that these findings demonstrate the influence of child-teacher relationships on children's judgments of climate and social support in the broader school environment. Whether and how this relation changes with development, such that school climate plays a relatively greater role in judgments of the relational quality of classroom experiences over time, is at this time unknown.

Just as teachers make judgments about when to invest or not invest in a relationship, children, especially as they grow older, calculate their relational investment based on the expected returns (Muller, Katz, & Dance, 1999). Urban youths (largely African American males) enrolled in two supplemental programs near Boston reported investing more with teachers who show that they care yet are also able to provide structure and have high expectations for students progress.

Clearly, these child characteristics, behaviors, and perceptions are not independent of one another. As suggested earlier, boys tend to act out more in primary grades, and this behavior, rather than simply gender itself, may account for the conflict they have with teachers. Similarly, there is evidence linking child factors such as socioeconomic status, ethnicity, and disability classification, and the associations between these factors and the quality of the child-teacher relationship are likely to be complex. Nevertheless, what the child brings into the classroom each day is an important piece of the child-teacher relationship.

Representational Models

An individual's representational model of relationships (Bowlby, 1969; Zeanah et al., 1993) is the set of feelings and beliefs that has been stored about a relationship that guides feelings, perceptions, and behavior in that relationship. These models are open systems: The information stored in them, while fairly stable, is open to change based on new experience. Also, representational models reflect two sides of a relationship (Sroufe & Fleeson, 1988). A teacher's representational model of how children relate to teachers is both the teacher's experience of being taught (and parented) and his or her own experience as a teacher.

Representational models can have an effect on the formation and quality of a relationship through brief, often subtle qualities of moment-to-moment interaction with children such as the adult's tone of voice, eye contact, or emotional cues (Katz, Cohn, & Moore, 1996), and in terms of the tolerances that individuals have for certain kinds of interactive behaviors. Therefore, adults with a history of avoidant attachment, who tend to dismiss or diminish the negative emotional aspects of interactions, will behave differently in a situation that calls for a response to an emotionally needy child than will adults whose history of secure attachment provides support for perceiving such needs as legitimate and responding to them sensitively.

In Pedersen et al.'s (1978) case study, adults were asked to recall experiences with a particular teacher who had a reputation as exceptional. This was an attempt to examine (retrospectively) the features of experience associated with an influential teacher. These recollections describe the impact of a teacher who formed relationships with students that, according to their reports, made them feel worthwhile, supported their independence, motivated them to achieve, and provided them with support to interpret and cope with environmental demands. Students' representations of their relationships with a specific teacher appeared to be a key feature of their experience in relationship with that teacher.

Teachers' representations have been examined only recently. Based on interview techniques developed for assessment of child-parent relationships, Stuhlman and Pianta (in press) gathered information from 50 teachers of kindergarten and first-grade children. Teachers of first graders had relatively higher levels of negative emotion represented in relationships with students than did the kindergarten teachers. For both groups of teachers, representations of negative emotion were related to their discipline and negative affect in interactions with the children about whom they were interviewed. Teachers' representations were only somewhat related to the child's competence in the classroom, and teachers' representations were related to their behavior with the child independent of the child's competence. The Stuhlman and Pianta (in press) study suggests that teacher representations, while related in predicted directions to their ratings of child competence and to their behavior with the child, are not redundant with them, with indications that representations are unique features of the child-teacher relationship.

Muller et al. (1999) argued that teachers' expectations for students are essential components of the development of positive or negative relationships with children. They suggested that teachers calculate expected payoffs from investing in their relationships with students. The authors provided an example of one teacher's differential expectations for two students with very similar backgrounds. Both were Latino students with excellent elementary school records who were getting poor grades in middle school. Although both boys were involved with a peer group that encouraged cutting class, one student broke away from his friends to attend the teacher's class. Interviews with the teacher suggested that she invested much more time and energy into this student, who she thought was less susceptible to peer pressure, because she believed she could have a greater influence on him than on the other.

Further work on representational aspects of child-teacher relationships is needed to distinguish these processes from general expectations and beliefs held by the child or teacher. At present, there is sufficient evidence from research on child-parent relationships to posit that representational models, although assessed via individuals' reports and behaviors, may in fact reflect properties of the relationship (Main, 1996) and therefore be better understood not as features of individuals but as relational entities at a different level of organization.

Information Exchange Processes: Feedback Loops Between Child and Teacher

Like any system, the components of the child-teacher relationship system interact in reciprocal exchanges, or loops in which feedback is provided across components, allowing

calibration and integration of component function by way of the information provided in these feedback loops. In one way, dyadic relationships can be characterized by these feedback processes. For example, the ways that mother and child negotiate anxiety and physical proximity under conditions of separation characterize the attachment qualities of that mother-child relationship (Ainsworth et al., 1978). As in the attachment assessment paradigm, feedback processes are most easily observed in interactive behaviors but also include other means by which information is conveyed from one person to another. What people do with, say or gesture to, and perceive about one another can serve important roles in these feedback mechanisms.

Furthermore, the qualities of information exchange, or how it is exchanged (e.g., tone of voice, posture and proximity, timing of behavior, contingency or reciprocity of behavior), may be even more important than what is actually performed behaviorally, as it has been suggested that these qualities convey more information in the context of a relationship that does actual behavioral content (Cohn, Campbell, Matias, & Hopkins, 1990; Greenspan, 1989).

Teacher-Child Interactions

Although there is a large literature on interactions between teachers and children (e.g., Brophy & Good, 1986; Zeichner, 1995), it is focused almost entirely on instruction. Recent work has integrated a social component to understanding instructional interactions (e.g., Rogoff, 1990), but in the majority of studies of teachers' behaviors toward children in classrooms, the social, emotional, and relational quality of these interactions is almost always neglected.

Teachers and children come together at the beginning of the year, each with their own personality and beliefs, and from the moment the children enter the classroom, they begin interacting with one another. It is through these daily interactions, from the teacher welcoming students in the morning to the moment the children run out the door to catch the bus, that relationships develop. Recently, investigators have gained a better understanding of the specific types of interactions that lead to the formation of relationships between students and teachers. As with studies on individual characteristics and perceptions, these relational interaction studies are imbedded within a much larger field of research on classroom interactions.

It is not surprising that teachers' interactions with children are related to characteristics of the children themselves. Peer-rejected children tend to be more frequent targets of corrective teacher feedback than nonrejected classmates (e.g., Dodge, Coie, & Brakke, 1982; Rubin & Clarke, 1983), and it has been repeatedly demonstrated that teachers direct more of their attention to children with behavior or learning problems and to boys (e.g., Brophy & Good, 1974). Similarly, children rated as more competent in the classroom are more frequent recipients of sensitive child-teacher interactions and teachers' positive affect (Pianta et al., 2002). Once again, when considering child-teacher interactions in the context of this dyadic relationship system, it is important to recognize that there are strong bidirectional relations between child characteristics and teacher behavior.

Research on teacher-child interactions as they relate to student motivation provides some insight into associations between interactions and relationships. Skinner and Belmont (1993) suggested that although motivation is internal to a child, it requires the social surrounding of the classroom to flourish. They suggested three major components to this social environment: involvement, autonomy support, and structure. Involvement is defined as "the quality of interpersonal relationships with teachers and peers. . . . [T]eachers are involved to the extent that they take time for, express affection toward, enjoy interaction with, are attuned to, and dedicate resources to their students" (p. 573). This definition closely resembles definitions of a positive child-teacher relationship.

Skinner and Belmont (1993) found that upper elementary teachers' reports of greater involvement with students were the feature of the social environment most closely associated with children's positive perceptions of the teacher. Furthermore, they found a reciprocal association between teacher and student behavior such that teacher involvement facilitated children's classroom engagement and that this engagement, in turn, led teachers to become more involved. Students who are able to form strong relationships with teachers are at an advantage that may grow exponentially as the year progresses. Similar research conducted with adolescents suggests that student engagement with teachers is dependent not only on their feelings of personal competence and relevance of course material but also on students' perceptions of feelings of safety and caring in the school environment (Roeser, Eccles, & Sameroff, 2000).

Teachers' Interactions With Other Students as Observed by Peers

An interesting line of recent research has focused on teachers as social agents of information and the role that their interactions with a given student serve as sources of information about child-teacher relationships for the other students in the classroom (Hughes, Cavell, & Willson, in press; White & Kistner, 1992). Hughes et al. (in press) reported that classmates'

perceptions of the quality of the relationship between their teacher and a selected child in the classroom were related to their own perceptions of the quality of their relationship with the teacher. It is important to note that these relations were observed independent of the characteristics of the child, suggesting that this is a unique source of social information in the classroom setting that has consequences for the impressions that children form of their teacher (and vice versa), which in turn could relate to help seeking and other motivational and learning behaviors (Newman, 2000). In a related study, White and Kistner (1992) examined relations between teacher feedback and children's peer preferences in early elementary students, finding that teachers' negatively toned feedback toward selected children was related negatively to classmates' preferences for these children.

With regard to understanding the role that interactive behaviors play in the context of the entire teacher-child relationship, patterns of behavior appear to be more important indicators of the quality of a relationship than do single instances of behavior. It is not the single one-time instance of child defiance (or compliance) or adult rejection (or affection) that defines a relationship. Rather, it is the pattern of child and adult responses to one another—and the quality of these responses. Pianta (1994) argued that these qualities can be captured in the combination of degree of interactive involvement between the adult and child and the emotional tone (positive or negative) of those interactions. Birch and Ladd (1996) pointed out that relationship patterns can be observed in global tendencies of the child in relation to the adult—a tendency to move toward, move away, or move against.

Also involved in the exchange of information between adult and child are processes related to communication, perception, and attention (Pianta, 1999). For example, how a child communicates about needs and desires (whiny and petulant or direct and calm), how the teacher selectively attends to different cues, or how these two individuals interpret one another's behavior toward each other (e.g. "This child is needy and demanding" vs. "This child seems vulnerable and needs my support") are all aspects of how information is shaped and exchanged between child and teacher. Perceptions and selective attending (often related to the individuals' representations of the relationship; see Zeanah et al., 1993) act as filters for information about the other's behavior. These filters can place constraints on the nature and form of information present in feedback loops and can be influential in guiding interactive behavior because they tend to be self-fulfilling (Pianta, 1999). Over time, these feedback and information exchange processes form a structure for the interactions between the adult and child.

In sum, processes involving transmission of information via behavioral, verbal, and nonverbal channels play a central role in the functioning of the dyadic system of the child-teacher relationship. For the most part, research has focused on descriptions of instructional behaviors of teachers, on teachers' differential attentiveness to children, and on children's engagement and attention in learning situations (see Brophy & Good, 1974). There is much less information available on social and affective dimensions of child-teacher interactions, nonverbal components of interaction, and the dynamics of multiple components of interaction in classroom time or developmental time. Furthermore, how these interactive processes are shaped by and shape school- and system-level parameters (e.g. school climate, policies on productive use of instructional time) is even less well described. Nonetheless the available data provide support for the developmental systems perspective of child-teacher relationships and the complex ways in which information is transmitted through multiple channels between child and teacher and the fact that this information plays an important role in children's and teachers' perceptions and representations of one another.

External Influences

Systems external to the child-teacher relationship also exert influence. Cultures can prescribe timetables for expectations about students' performance or the organization of schools (Sameroff, 1995) that can shape how students and teacher relate to one another. What other external influences shape student-teacher relationships? State regulations mandate standards for student performance that affect what teachers must teach, and at times how they must teach it. School systems have codes for discipline and behavior, sometimes mandating how discipline will be conducted. States and localities prescribe policies and regulations regarding student-teacher ratios, the placement of children in classrooms, at what grade students move to middle school, or the number of teachers a child comes into contact with in a given day. Teachers also have a family and personal lives of their own.

Structural Aspects of the School Environment

Structural variables in classrooms and schools play an important role in constraining child-teacher relationships through direct effects on the nature of interaction and indirectly via attributes of the people involved. For example, observations of child-teacher interactions in kindergarten and first grade are observed to vary as a function of the ratio of children to adults in the room, the activity setting (small or large group), and the characteristics of the children in the classroom. In large

samples of students in kindergarten (Pianta et al., 2002) and first grade (NICHD Early Child Care Research Network [ECCRN], 2001), children in classrooms with a low ratio of children to adults receive more frequent contacts with their teacher and contacts that are more positive emotionally. Teachers in these classrooms are observed to be more sensitive. Similarly, in both of these samples, when the activity setting was large-group or whole-class instruction, children had many fewer contacts with the teacher than when in small groups. In a sample of more than 900 first-grade classrooms, children, on average, were engaged in individual contact with their teachers on approximately 4 occasions during a 2-hr morning observation (NICHD ECCRN, 2001).

It appears that attributes of the class as a whole are related to the quality of interactions that teachers have with an individual child (NICHD ECCRN, 2001). Therefore, when the classroom is composed of a higher percentage of African American children or children receiving free-reduced lunch, teachers were observed to show less emotional sensitivity and support and lower instructional quality in their intersections with an individual (unselected) student. These findings suggest perhaps that the racial and poverty composition of the classroom may represent demand features of the children, which can result in a teacher's behaving more negatively with children (with attendant consequences for their relationships) when high as a function of the concentration of children with these characteristics in classroom. This suggestion is supported by survey data demonstrating that teachers with high concentrations of ethnic minority or poor children in their classrooms experience a greater degree of burden (Rimm-Kaufman, Pianta, Cox, & Early 1999).

Finally, the level or organization of the school also affects how child and teacher relationships form and function. Eccles and Roeser (1998) summarized findings suggesting that as children move through elementary school and into middle school, there is an increasing mismatch between their continuing needs for emotional support and the school's increasing departmentalization and impersonal climate.

School Climate and Culture

How the school values and supports the emotional-social component of teacher-child interactions involves its view of the role and importance of child-teacher relationships (e.g., Battstich et al., 1997; Haynes, 1998). As noted earlier, it is difficult to disentangle the extent to which teacher-child relationships and school climate influence one another and the extent to which the balance of influence shifts as children grow older and their experiences are more widely distributed within a school. Nonetheless, there is ample evidence that school climate and the quality of child-teacher relationships share a mutually reciprocal association (Solomon, Watson, Battistich, Schaps, & Delucci, 1992; 1996). In fact, definitions of climate frequently refer to the role of child-teacher relationships as a key component of climate:

> School climate refers to the quality and consistency of interpersonal interactions within the school community that influence children's cognitive, social, and psychological development. (Haynes, Emmons, & Ben-Avie, 1997, p. 322)
>
> The teacher plays the critical role in creating a classroom that students experience as a caring community . . . by sharing concern for all students and being sincerely interested in their ideas, experiences, and products. (Solomon et al., 1992, p. 384)

One source of information about school climate comes from interventions aimed at changing climate. These interventions are often aimed at changing relationships in the school and creating a sense of community (Baker, Terry, Bridger, & Winsor, 1997). For example, the goals of the Caring Communities approach are to help children "feel psychologically safe, responsibly connected to others, [and] practice ethical decision making and self-governance in the microcosm of the classroom" (Baker et al., 1997, p. 598). These are similar to those of the Comer School Development Program (Haynes, 1998), which includes an emphasis on caring and sensitivity of school personnel and access to the school's resources (personal and social as well as material and instructional). Furthermore, the Child Development Project (CDP; e.g., Battistich et al., 1997) places a great emphasis on students' feeling emotionally supported by teachers and on cultivating a school climate in which emotional resources are available and flow readily as needed. Kasen, Johnson, and Cohen (1990), in their review of the school climate literature, described student-teacher relationships as a central facet of school climate and proposed that the various dimensions of school climate described in the literature can be organized into three domains: task orientation, relationships, and order. School climate and classroom climate have a relational component that is fundamental to their description and influence.

When considering the role that school climate plays in relation to child-teacher relationships, the pathways by which this association might occur is likely to be somewhat circuitous. Most of the evidence available suggests that climate alters the behavior and expectations of students and teachers—it creates standards that shape these components of the child-teacher relationship. As reported by Battistich et al. (1997), in classrooms with improved climate children had a greater sense of community, exhibited more prosocial

interactions, were better at social problem solving and conflict resolution, and scored higher on reading comprehension tests. They also liked school better, were more empathetic and motivated, and had higher self-esteem as compared with children in schools that did not receive the intervention. Clearly, based on the perspective described in earlier sections, one would expect relational behaviors and perceptions between teachers and children to be more positive and less conflictual under these conditions.

Yet relations between school climate and the components of the child-teacher relationship system are complex. It appears that climate interacts with child variables such as child age, sex, and socioeconomic status (Kasen et al., 1990) such that child-teacher conflict and academic focus declined and autonomy increased in schools attended by older students. Schools characterized by higher socioeconomic status were described as having lower conflict and greater autonomy. An interaction of dimensions of climate on child symptoms was also informative. In schools with high conflict, social facilitation led to greater symptoms of externalizing behavior problems, whereas in schools with low conflict, social facilitation led to decreased symptoms of externalizing behavior problems (Kasen et al., 1990).

Middle school children's positive perceptions of school are related to their motivation, achievement, and emotional functioning (Roeser et al., 1998). Middle school students who had higher levels of motivation and emotional well-being also felt their schools were more developmentally appropriate in the teacher-student interactions, practices, and norms (this is especially important because many middle schools are less supportive of the developmental needs of students than are elementary schools). Middle schools can be developmentally appropriate by encouraging positive teacher-child interactions; by espousing instructional techniques that emphasize progress or improvement, effort, and mastery as goals; and by not emphasizing competition and comparisons among students (Roeser et al., 1998). Teacher-student interactions that lead students to feel supported by their teachers, as well as smaller communities of teachers and students, are also important in enhancing young adolescents' motivation and emotional well-being (Roeser et al., 1998). As a result, it appears that climate and teacher-child relationship quality have reciprocal influences in the middle school years.

This point about the bidirectionality of climate and child-teacher relationships is underscored in work related to school violence and antisocial behavior (Farmer, 2000). When looking at problems with antisocial behavior in the school context, not only does antisocial behavior influence the climate of the school, but the school social context influences the expression of antisocial behaviors (Farmer, 2000). Research and intervention paradigms must be multilevel and attendant to the bidirectional influences that transact across and within levels over time.

Summary

As a final note, it is important to recognize that child-adult relationships are *asymmetric* and that the relative degree of asymmetry is subject to considerable variation across age, grade, or schools. These changes in asymmetry are not well understood, and the lack of coordination or calibration between the child's emergent developmental capacities for relationship and the school system's provision of support for those capacities (Magnusson & Stattin, 1998) is considered to be a primary locus of concern related to children's competencies (Eccles & Roeser, 1998).

In sum, available evidence from diverse literatures on child and teacher attributes, representations of relationships, child-teacher interactions and communication, and school and classroom climate can be integrated within a systems conceptualization of the child-teacher relationship. In so doing these diverse literatures provide complementary and converging information about the unique role of each of these components and the importance of a focus on them in their own right, as well as confirming the view that because of the bidirectional intertwining of their relations with one another, each component is best viewed within a systems perspective.

DIMENSIONS, TYPOLOGIES, AND DEVELOPMENTAL CHANGE IN CHILD-TEACHER RELATIONSHIPS

Because relationships are systems, a relationship is more than simply the sum of interactions, representations, and characteristics of the two individuals involved. Instead, relationships are a product of the dynamic, reciprocal interactions of these components over time and over hundreds of occasions. When it comes to describing the quality of relationships— the dimensions along which relationships vary—one must approach the task from multiple points of view using multiple assessments of relational components. Relationships can be described from the inside and from the outside, with data on perceptions, behaviors, and beliefs of the child and of the teacher. Any one source of this knowledge about relationships is almost always an indirect and incomplete assessment. Because they are systems (e.g., Lerner, 1998; Magnusson &

Stattin, 1998), for Sroufe (1989a, 1996) relationships are a form of organization; they follow rule structures in their actions; and their components are rule-governed as well. The patterns and rules in relationships suggest that their activity is nonrandom; they can be studied formally and can be reliably described. Description of relationships is then, by necessity, best when informed by multiple perspectives, by multiple methods, across multiple occasions, and in multiple contexts.

One concern when reviewing the available data on child-teacher relationships is the extent to which conclusions concerning these dimensions are driven by the use of a particular method or form of assessment. Caution is in order, particularly because this literature is fairly new, because large-scale, multimethod, multiinformant studies are rare, and because longitudinal or even cross-sectional data at different ages are uncommon. The following discussion is organized according to descriptions of relationships using data sources that emanate from the child, the teacher, or observations.

The Child's View

Children have often been asked about qualities of their relationships with teachers, usually using questionnaire methods, in terms of constructs such as teacher support and liking, classroom climate, relatedness, and so on.

Wellborn and Connell's (1987) Relatedness Scale has been used in several studies with children who range in age and risk level (Lynch & Cicchetti, 1992, 1997; Toth & Cicchetti, 1996), reliably describing variations in children's perceptions on two dimensions of relationship experience: emotional quality and psychological proximity seeking. *Emotional quality* refers to the range of emotions (positive and negative) that a child experiences with the teacher in an attempt to capture the overall emotional tone of the relationship from the child's perspective. *Psychological proximity seeking* assesses the degree to which children desire to be psychologically closer to the adult. These two dimensions differentially relate (in predictable directions) to teachers' descriptions of the children as well as the children's relational histories (Lynch & Cicchetti, 1992, 1997; Toth & Cicchetti, 1996).

From a person-centered perspective, Lynch and Cicchetti (1992) have described procedures for deriving five patterns of relatedness between children and teachers: optimal, adequate, deprived, disengaged, and confused. Children with optimal patterns report higher-than-average positive emotion and lower-than-average psychological proximity seeking. Deprived patterns are associated with lower-than-average emotional quality and higher-than-average proximity seeking. These children do not experience positive emotion and want to be closer to the teacher. Children with disengaged patterns report low emotional quality and low psychological proximity seeking. They are insecure and dissatisfied but do not want to be closer to their teachers. Children with confused patterns report high emotional quality and extremely high proximity seeking. They seem very needy despite reporting feeling secure. Finally, children with average patterns are in the midrange on both dimensions.

Wentzel (1996) reported on a similar construct describing the child-teacher relationship from the child's perspective in a sample of middle schoolers. Perceived Caring is a dimension assessed using the Classroom Life Measure (Johnson, Johnson, Buckman, & Richards, 1985) and reflects the degree to which the child experiences social support and concern from teachers. These perceptions are related to a range of teacher behaviors as well as student outcomes (Wentzel, 1996).

Perceived support as a key dimension of relationships between children and teachers even at older ages is confirmed in a national survey of adolescents. When asked to identify relationships that were *emotionally* supportive—someone the youth could count on to understand and offer advice—teachers were often listed in relation to this construct. In fact, a factor associated with healthy outcomes was whether youth reported having a relationship with an adult that they identified in this way, many of whom were teachers (Resnick et al., 1997).

Aspects of teacher behavior that map onto feedback processes in the model of teacher-child relationships can also be assessed from the student's perspective (Weinstein & Marshall, 1984) by examining student ratings of the teacher behavior, expectations, individual attention to the student, and nurturance. Students' evaluations of the degree to which they perceive teacher expectations as fair, consistent, and accurate; the degree to which they feel the teacher attends and responds to their individual needs; and how caring or concerned the teacher behaves toward them are related to motivational and behavioral aspects of classroom adjustment (Wentzel, 1996).

Ryan et al. (1994) presented reports of more than 600 early adolescents (seventh and eighth graders) using the Inventory of Adolescent Attachments (assessing felt security and emotional utilization; Greenberg, 1982) as well as self-report measures of emulation of the teacher and motivation. Results indicate that emotional quality of the child-teacher relationship, as described by the felt security construct, was particularly salient for these middle schoolers. Similarly, Bracken and Crain (1994) presented findings from self-reported child-teacher relationship qualities for 2,501 children between the ages of 9 and 19, suggesting that dimensions of companionship, emotional support, and trust can be reliably assessed and used to describe these relationships.

Teachers' Views

Teachers' ratings or judgments of children's problem behavior, social competence, work habits, and even temperament all provide indications of relational quality or factors that influence relational quality. However, the focus of most of these assessments is not relational in nature. As stated by Lerner (1998), if one adopts the developmental systems point of view, then the focus or nature of the key units of analysis must be relational (Lerner, 1998). Drawing from this postulate, then, the items rated by informants and behaviors observed in settings should have a relational nature or be of relational form in order to provide information about the type of organization (relationships) that could be most informative about developmental processes (Lerner, 1998).

For this reason, Pianta and Nimetz (1991) began the study of teachers' views of their relationship with a specific child with a focus on teacher perceptions of warmth, openness of communication, and dependency, in their relationship with a child using items reflecting teachers' feelings about and perceptions of the child's *relational behavior* toward them— not ratings of the child's skills or abilities in general or in other contexts. Analysis revealed that warmth and open communication were highly correlated and formed a closeness dimension, whereas kindergarten teachers viewed dependency as a somewhat negative dimension. These constructs were moderately related to concurrent measures of classroom adjustment in kindergarten, teacher ratings of adjustment in first grade, and retention decisions (Pianta & Nimetz, 1991).

Further conceptualization of child-teacher relationships led to a focus on more overtly negative aspects of the relationship involving anger, conflict, and confusion. Initial analyses reported that five correlated dimensions accounted for kindergarten teachers' perceptions of their relationships with students: Conflict/Anger, Warmth/Closeness, Open Communication, Dependency, and Troubled Feelings (Pianta & Steinberg, 1992). The Conflict dimension indicates that the teacher and child are frequently at odds with each other ("This child and I are always struggling"). The Warmth dimension assesses positive affect ("I share a warm affectionate relationship with this student"), and Open Communication measures the degree to which the child and teacher communicate about personal items ("This student shares information about him- or herself with me"). The Dependent dimension measures the child's degree of developmentally inappropriate dependency ("This child is always seeking my help when its not necessary"), and the Troubled Feelings dimension indicates the teacher's being worried about his or her inability to relate to the child.

From a person-centered perspective, cluster analysis was used to describe patterns of relationships with students (Pianta, 1994). Six clusters of relationships were derived: Dependent, Positively Involved, Dysfunctional, Functional/Average, Angry/Dependent, and Uninvolved. Children whose child-teacher relationships fell in different clusters differed significantly in their adjustment in first-grade classrooms, with the Dysfunctional and Angry/Dependent relationship clusters showing the most problems. Relationships classified as Angry were very high on the conflict dimension and very low on warmth. Teachers experienced very high amounts of negative emotion and very little amounts of emotional warmth or personal contact with students in these relationships. Uninvolved relationships were marked by the child's strong tendency to be uncommunicative about personal information and not to rely on the teacher for help. In these relationships children made very few emotional demands on their teacher. Positively Involved relationships were characterized by children's showing behaviors toward their teachers that were indicative of a secure relationship; they shared personal information, appeared comfortable with dependency, but were not too dependent, and they displayed positive affect in response to the teachers' interactions or in regard to their relationship with the teacher. In the context of these relationships, teachers felt warm and close to the child. In first grade, they were clearly the most competent of the cluster groups. Children with histories of Positively Involved relationships in kindergarten showed the fewest behavior problems and the highest levels of competence behaviors in both the social and instructional areas. Dysfunctional child-teacher relationships represent a group with needs for intervention. Teachers characterized these relationships as filled with conflict and anger, with little warmth and communication. These relationships were emotionally very negative and also disconnected. Teachers felt troubled by their inability to reach these children and thought about them when not at work. Children for whom these relationships were reported were also the least competent in first grade, indicating that they were on a path toward continued school problems in the social and academic arenas and that some form of intervention was likely to be needed in order to change the direction of their school trajectories.

Recent cross-sample validations suggest that child-teacher relationships assessed from teachers' perspectives can be reliably described by three dimensions: Conflict, Closeness, and Dependency (Pianta, Steinberg, & Rollins, 1995; Saft & Pianta, 2001). These dimensions have been replicated with early elementary school samples from Illinois (Birch & Ladd, 1997) and in a multistate study of children in child care (Cost, Quality and Child Outcomes Study Team,

1995). Furthermore, these dimensions appear relatively stable from preschool into second grade (Howes, 2000b; Pianta et al., 1995).

Teachers' representations of their relationship with a target child have been assessed with respect to three broad areas: (a) content or themes represented, (b) how the teacher views him- or herself in relation to the child, and (c) the affective tone of representations (Stuhlman & Pianta, in press). Together, these three areas provide a fairly comprehensive view of representations with respect to a given teacher-child relationship, from the teacher's perspective. The Content area includes scales such as Compliance, Achievement, and Secure Base and reflects the degree to which these themes are present in the teacher's responses. The Process area includes scales such as Perspective Taking and Neutralizing/Avoidance of Negative Emotion, reflecting the stance the teacher takes vis-à-vis the child's expressed or perceived needs. The Affect area includes scales such as Positive and Negative Affect. These constructs can be reliably detected in teachers' narratives about their relationship with a specific child and in turn are related to their behavior toward the child in the classroom. It is important to note that the constructs that reflect negativity in the teacher's representations (e.g., compliance, neutralizing, negative affect) are more strongly related to observed behavior than are the other dimensions (Stuhlman & Pianta, in press).

Observed Interactions Between Teachers and Children

Many classroom observation systems contain codes for teacher-child interaction (e.g., Ladd & Price, 1987; Pianta et al., 2002), and these systems can be used to glean information from the classroom environment that is relevant for interpretation of teacher-child relationships. Ladd et al. (1999) reported using a Likert rating scale for capturing observed emotional tone of child-teacher relationships as well as closeness and conflict. These investigators reported good reliability for these constructs as well as relations of these dimensions to other aspects of observed and reported behavior.

The Teacher Attachment Q-Set (Howes, Hamilton, & Matheson, 1994; Pianta, Nimetz, & Bennett, 1997) is an adaptation of the Attachment Q-Set (Waters, 1987; Waters & Deane, 1985), which was designed to assess attachment organization in young children with their mothers. The Teacher Attachment Q-Set consists of 90 descriptions of child behaviors derived from attachment theory and research and thought to reflect different aspects of the child's attachment (e.g., "When upset the child seeks physical contact from the parent"). These 90 items were derived from extensive observations in home environments.

Q-set methods utilize *criterion sorts* in order to derive scores for subjects on relevant constructs. Experts knowledgeable regarding a particular construct (e.g., child-teacher security) are asked to sort Q descriptions according to their view of what an ideal child would receive as a sort, in the case of the aforementioned example, a child who was ideally secure in relationship to the teacher.

In several studies (e.g., Howes, Matheson, et al., 1994; Pianta et al., 1997) criterion sorts were developed to describe children in specific types of relationships with teachers—for example, a child in a secure relationship, a child in a conflicted relationship, and a child in a dependent relationship. Interrater reliability for these sorts tends to be high, suggesting that two observers' impressions of characteristic behaviors can agree for individual children. Also, correlations between sorts of teacher-child relationships are strongly related to similar sorts of parent-child relationships for constructs such as security, indicating a high level of consensus among various reporters on the behaviors reflective of a secure child-adult relationship.

Summary

Teachers' reports of child-teacher relationships reflect dimensions of conflict and closeness. These dimensions replicate across samples that vary by age, ethnicity, and economic status (see Pianta, 1999), are fairly stable, and correlate with concurrent and future teacher-reported measures of adjustment, school achievement, and student motivation (Birch & Ladd, 1997; Howes, 2000b; Pianta et al., 1995). Children's reports of relationships with teachers reflect dimensions of emotional closeness and support, communication and involvement, and negativity, suggesting parallels with teachers' reports (Bracken & Crain, 1994; Ryan et al., 1994; Wentzel, 1996). It appears that in relation to student or teacher outcomes, negativity is the most salient feature of teachers' reports, whereas a sense of closeness and support appears most salient from the child's point of view.

It is critical to note that these conclusions are qualified by the fact that the literature is limited in terms of multimethod, multi-informant longitudinal studies. Missing from this literature is description of the same child-teacher relationship from its two participants, as well as the extent to which use of these two perceptions of the same relationship yields dimensions similar to those reported earlier for single-participant reports and whether two participants' perceptions converge or are concordant with one another.

CORRELATES OF RELATIONAL DIMENSIONS

In this section we review studies that link the aforementioned child-teacher relationship dimensions to child outcomes and other correlates. Studies cited in the review assess child-teacher relationships at the relational unit of analysis. These findings attempt to address the extent to which a focus on this unit of analysis is helpful in advancing understanding of development in school settings.

Over the last 10 years research on child-teacher relationships focused around several lines of inquiry, each resulting in support for these relationships as salient features of development. These lines of inquiry involve child-teacher relationships and peer relations, parent-child relationships, academic competence, and features of social and emotional adjustment (see Pianta, 1999). Teacher-child relationships are related to children's competencies with peers in the classroom (e.g., Birch & Ladd, 1998; Howes, 2000b; Howes, Hamilton, et al., 1994) and trajectories toward academic success or failure (Birch & Ladd, 1996; Hamre & Pianta, 2001; Pianta et al., 1995; van IJzendoorn, Sagi, & Lambermon, 1992), as well as with patterns of child-mother relationships (Lynch & Cicchetti, 1992) and disruptive behavior (Hamre & Pianta, 2001).

Howes and colleagues (see Howes, 2000a, 2000b) conducted a series of studies relating child-parent and child-teacher relationships to each other and to early childhood social outcomes (Hamilton & Howes, 1992; Howes, Hamilton, et al., 1994; Howes et al., 1998; Howes, Matheson, et al., 1994). They established a low to moderate degree of continuity in the quality of relationships that children have with mothers and form with teachers (Howes & Matheson, 1992). They further found that both of these relationships play a role in children's peer competencies, although relationships with teachers are stronger predictors of behavior with peers in the classroom than are relationships with parents (Howes, Matheson, et al., 1994). Also, child-teacher relationships show low to moderate levels of continuity in the early grades of school—at least through second grade (Howes, Phillipsen, & Peisner-Feinberg, 2000), echoing Birch and Ladd's (1998) contention that children's relationships demonstrate a coherence across relational figures and across time.

Pianta and colleagues reported links between teachers' reports of relationships with children and a range of school outcomes in the early grades. In one such study (Pianta et al., 1995), kindergarten teachers' reports of the degree to which children displayed security toward them was related to first-grade teachers' reports of the children's competence. In a series of descriptive studies, Pianta and Steinberg (1992) and Pianta (1994) showed that teacher-child relationships are also fairly stable across the period from kindergarten to second grade and correlate with concurrent and future teacher-reported measures of adjustment, grade retention, and special education referrals (Birch & Ladd, 1997; Pianta et al., 1995). Furthermore, changes in student adjustment from year to year were correlated in expected directions with these dimensions (Pianta et al., 1995): Downward deflections are correlated with child-teacher conflict, whereas upward deflections are related to child-teacher closeness. Finally, there is evidence that child-teacher relationships operate as a protective factor against risk: Children at high risk for retention or referral for special education who are not referred or retained are reported to be more close to their teachers, whereas their retained/referred counterparts are in greater conflict with teachers (Pianta et al., 1995).

Within a group of children designated on the basis of low kindergarten screening scores as high risk for referral for special education or retention, those who ultimately did get retained or referred were compared with those who, despite being high risk, were promoted or not referred (Pianta et al., 1995). The children who, despite predictions of retention or referral, were ultimately promoted or not referred had far more positive relationships with their teachers than did their high-risk peers who were retained or referred. Significantly, this successful high-risk group was notable for its lack of conflict and high degree of open communication. In short, it appeared that there was a buffering effect of the relationship between the child and teacher (Pianta et al., 1995).

Hamre and Pianta (2001) extended analysis of the longitudinal relations between early child-teacher relationships (in kindergarten) and child school outcomes through eighth grade. Controlling for kindergarten-entry cognitive ability and problem behavior, negativity in the child-teacher relationship reported by the child's kindergarten teacher predicted achievement test scores, disciplinary infractions, and school suspensions through either grade. The effects on eighth-grade achievement scores appeared largely mediated by effects of the kindergarten child-teacher relationship on achievement in early elementary school. Furthermore, effects on disciplinary infractions were most pronounced for children who had problems in kindergarten adjustment. This was the first study to report longitudinal findings for early child-teacher relationships extending into middle and junior high school, and in addition the study supports the conclusion of other investigations that the quality of these relationships appears particularly important for children who might otherwise have adjustment problems.

The work of several other investigators also supports the child-teacher relationship as a key context in which early school outcomes are developed. Van IJzendoorn et al. (1992) demonstrated that child-caregiver security added unique variance over and above that contributed by the child-mother relationship in the prediction of a range of developmental status and school readiness variables. Studies have also used children's reports of their relationship with teachers, with findings similar to those using teacher perceptions. Wentzel (1996) reported that middle school students benefited from relationships with teachers characterized by open communication and a sense of closeness, suggesting that this is a relational context with salience for children beyond the early grades and preschool years. Similarly, Lynch and Cicchetti (1992) established that maltreated children, as a result of experiences with parents, are sensitized to seek certain relational experiences with teachers; they are less likely to form optimal relational patterns and seek psychological proximity and support from teachers.

Birch and Ladd (1996) studied teacher-child relationships extensively in early elementary classrooms and suggested that children have a generalized interpersonal style (moving toward, moving against, moving away) that characterizes their interactions with peers and teachers. Presumably, this style is a product of interactions with parents. This relational style of the child is related in predictable ways to the quality of relationships that children form with teachers and peers in the classroom (Birch & Ladd, 1998; Ladd & Burgess, 1999). Those children who displayed moving against behaviors in kindergarten, such as verbal and physical aggression toward teacher and peers, were more likely to form negative relationships with teachers in first and second grade (Ladd & Burgess, 1999). Children who tended to move away from others in kindergarten were more likely to be rated as overly dependent by first-grade teachers, although there was less stability in these behaviors than in aggressive behaviors (Birch & Ladd, 1998). Observed conflict in the child-teacher relationship is related to less classroom participation and lower achievement over the first half of kindergarten (Ladd et al., 1999). Children's moving toward, or prosocial, behavior in kindergarten was not related to aspects of children's relationships with first-grade teachers. However, kindergarten teachers' reports of the quality of relationships with students accounted for significant variance in children's social behavior in first grade after controlling for gender and kindergarten social behavior (Birch & Ladd, 1998).

Research on teachers' and classmates' effects on adolescents' motivation, self-esteem, and ability to express their opinion are reviewed in Harter (1996). Harter discussed how relationships with teachers change from elementary to junior high school (relationships between teachers and students become less personal, more formal, more evaluative, and more competitive). These changes can lead to more negative self-evaluations and attitudes toward learning because the impersonal and evaluative nature of the relational context in junior high does not match well with the children's relational needs at that age. Harter (1996) found that this model applies particularly to students who have lower levels of intrinsic motivation. In this way, teacher-child relationships (which are typically viewed as potential resources for amelioration of risk) can actually exacerbate risk if they either are not positive or do not match with the developmental needs of the child. Harter (1996) also reported that classmate support and teacher approval are associated with self-esteem in middle-school-aged populations. Teacher support can be particularly salient in students who have low levels of parent support (i.e., teacher and parent support may have additive effects on student self-esteem).

Consistent with this view of middle schoolers' ongoing needs for support from adult figures, teacher support has been found to be related to sixth-grade children's school- and class-related interests and to their pursuit of social goals (Wentzel, 1998). These self-beliefs and motivations in sixth grade in turn predicted pursuit of social goals and grades in seventh grade (Wentzel, 1998). It is important to note that the support that youth receive from their parents, peers, and teachers seemed to have additive, and thus fairly independent, effects. Support from teachers was uniquely related to classroom functioning (Wentzel, 1998). Wentzel (1998) suggested the possibility that support in teacher-child relationships may be particularly salient at transition points, such as the transition from elementary to middle school.

In young children (kindergarten, first, and second grade), a teacher's feedback about a child's behavior also has a significant impact on how peers perceive that child (Hughes, Cavell, & Willson, in press; White & Kistner, 1992). When a teacher characterizes a child's behavior as positive, other children report increased preferences for that child and are more likely to characterize the child's behavior as positive. When a teacher characterizes a child's behavior as negative, an impact on peer preferences was not found; but if the teacher was derogatory toward the child, peers demonstrated more negative views of that child (White & Kistner, 1992). Implications of these findings include the possibility that teachers can play an active role in changing peers' perceptions of rejected children by sensitizing the class to the positive behaviors that the child engages in (Hughes et al., in press; White & Kistner, 1992).

Summary

There is ample evidence to demonstrate that the qualities of child-teacher relationships are related in expected ways to child

outcomes throughout the school-age years. Although there are expected developmental transformations in the extent to which these qualities are manifest in highly proximal or concrete forms with age, the degree and form of child-teacher engagement or involvement and the affective quality of that involvement describe a wide range of variation in individual and group differences in child-teacher relationships. Variable-focused or individual-focused analyses of these dimensions consistently show that various parameterizations of these two dimensions relate to children's engagement in learning, motivation and self-esteem, attitudes and engagement with the goals of school, and behavior toward one another and the teacher. As characterized by Hamre and Pianta (2001), these findings reveal that the quality of child-teacher relationships is an indicator of the extent to which the child is benefiting from the resources of schooling. This general conclusion is consistent with the theoretical framework of developmental systems theory outlined earlier, in which the qualities of child-adult relationships are key developmental resources for children.

It is critical to emphasize that in several of the investigations described earlier (e.g., Birch & Ladd, 1998; Hamre & Pianta, 2001; Howes, 2000b; Stuhlman & Pianta, in press), relations were reported between child outcomes and qualities of the child-teacher relationship controlling for aspects of child behavior considered principle predictors of the outcomes assessed. For example, Hamre and Pianta (2001) controlled for kindergarten teachers' reports of children's problem behavior when predicting problem behavior outcomes in later elementary and middle school using kindergarten child-teacher relational negativity as a predictor. Similarly, Stuhlman and Pianta (in press) controlled for observed child competence when examining relations between teachers' representations and observed sensitivity. Relational dimensions provide unique prediction of child outcomes independent of attributes of the child (e.g., Birch & Ladd, 1998) and teacher (Stuhlman & Pianta, in press). This focus on this *relational* unit of analysis, rather than on discrete characteristics of the individuals themselves, provides considerably more conceptual power for the purposes of understanding behaviors in settings and the influence that such settings have on developmental processes.

EDUCATIONAL AND PSYCHOLOGICAL APPLICATIONS RELATED TO CHILD-TEACHER RELATIONSHIPS

Evidence that qualities of child-teacher relationships predict child outcomes and are related to features of school climate, teacher characteristics, child attributes, and classroom variables provides ample support for examining how this information can be used to create more developmentally supportive school environments (see Battistich et al., 1997; Hughes & Cavell 1999; Pianta, 1999). Consistent with the prevention-oriented bias in applications informed by developmental systems theory (Magnusson & Stattin, 1998), a comprehensive approach to prevention suggests that applications should have long-term implementation and be aimed at changing institutions as well as people (Weissberg & Bell, 1997). More specifically, Weissberg and Bell (1997) outlined four different foci for application of techniques or resources, including a focus on changing the child, changing the immediate environment, changing multiple components of the environment that affect adults who are working with children, and changing structure or policy, each of which intersects with the research base available on child-teacher relationships.

Issues in Prevention-Oriented Applications Involving Child-Teacher Relationships

In thinking about applications of knowledge about child-teacher relationships across the many levels of organization and processes in schools, we approach the task with a bias toward the deployment of resources (or applications of techniques) prior to emergence of problems, with the distinct goal of enhancing wellness and strengthening developmental competencies (Cowen, 1999). Several principles inform this analyses: an emphasis on application in context, the extent to which an application embraces conceptualizations of developmental pathways in its design and execution (Loeber, 1990), emphasis on standardized protocols and theoretically driven decision making, and focus on risk reduction or wellness promotion.

Applications in Context

Intervention in educational and psychological processes with children and teachers most often involves rearranging contextual inputs to achieve a desired outcome (Nastasi, 1998). Interventions applied in the contexts in which the concern arises and is manifest can be more effective agents of change than efforts at change that take place in a context remote to the problem at hand (e.g., Henggeler, 1994; Henggeler, Schoenwald, Borduin, Rowland, & Cunningham, 1998; Nastasi, 1998). The design of treatment plans for child and adolescent problem behavior ideally recognizes distributed competence and the related concept of contextual affordance and produces change as a function of manipulating contextual properties (Adelman, 1996; Henggeler et al., 1998; Roberts, 1996). Unfortunately, due to the inherent asymmetries in

child and adult relationships, it is usually the case that problem identification and remediation focus on the child as a locus of the "problem" (Adelman, 1996; Henggeler et al., 1998; Johnson, Malone, & Hightower, 1996; Nastasi, 1998). A specific, dedicated focus on the *relational* unit of analysis inherent in child-teacher relationships supports a view of bidirectionality and reciprocity, which can enhance the extent to which contextualized, comprehensive approaches to intervention can be designed.

Developmental Time: Pathways

One lesson learned from developmental research is that there is no single, linear, one-to-one mapping of early risk (or non-risk) status onto problem (or competent) outcomes. Instead, many possible outcomes are possible from a given starting point (Egeland, Pianta, & O'Gawa, 1996). The success of risk reduction and competence enhancement efforts depends on understanding the processes that shape developmental pathways. Targeting these processes for intervention could be key to interrupting the relation between risk and later problems (Loeber, 1990) by creating alternate routes along developmental pathways to positive outcomes.

Intentional efforts to reduce risk and enhance competence through the application of psychological and educational interventions vary widely in the extent to which they embody principles of developmental pathways and a longitudinal focus in their design and execution (Durlak & Wells, 1997; McConaughy, Kay, & Fitzgerald, 1999). It is in fact the norm that resources are deployed to children in short-term bursts of six-week groups, semester-long mentoring, or placements that last a school year (Durlak & Wells, 1997). Most efforts are short-term in focus, with pressure increasing to deliver positive effects in shorter and shorter time frames. In addition to the problem of a short-term focus, interventions rarely conceptualize their effects or efforts in terms of developmental pathways that link subordinate outcomes or processes to the goals that the interventions embrace. For example, a large number of children are enrolled in programs designed to reduce antisocial behavior and teach social skills (Durlak & Wells, 1997). It is a laudable goal to accomplish such significant developmental changes in patterns of maladaptation and skill deficit in (usually) the short time frame of 6 weeks, particularly for children for whom these have a long-standing history and status as concerns. However, rather than conceptualizing intervention success as a return to health or normative functioning, interventionists might examine intermediate or subordinate outcomes or processes that signal developmental change in increments that, although smaller than ultimately desired, may be more realistic indicators of true developmental achievement. Attention to developmental pathways rather than a narrower focus on specific outcomes of concern may be of use to intervention design and application.

Standardized Protocols and Local Politics

Psychological and educational interventions vary widely on their embrace of standardization in application of ideas and resources. School reform efforts, for example, can vary from locally controlled efforts to achieve standardized targets to implementation of regimented standardization of curriculum and school management (e.g., Felner, Favazza, Shim, & Brand, 2001). In other areas of educational innovation, for the most part, local control and local politics overwhelm efforts at standardization, to the extent that prominent federal officials suggest that the lack of research and evaluation on innovations using standard protocols is a fundamental flaw impeding the development, implementation, and dissemination of promising educational practices (Lyon, 2000). In addition, educational research over the last decade has increasingly been dominated by qualitative methodology and theoretical paradigms that embrace the uniqueness of nearly every subject of inquiry (e.g., child, teacher, school). It is fair to conclude that in educational practice, standardization of practice (not to be equated with the use of standardized assessment or achievement standards) is the exception, not the rule.

On the other hand, psychological interventions, such as those used in clinical and school psychology practice, are increasingly coming under scrutiny for the use of standardized, empirically supported protocols, most often those that have been described in manualized form. This movement reflects a growing body of information on the effectiveness of protocols that have been implemented in standard fashion and a movement toward accountability in mental health services and care (see Henggeler et al., 1998; Weissberg & Bell, 1997). By and large, the available evidence suggests that manualized treatment protocols, particularly those that focus on specific behavioral targets, demonstrate significant gains and improvements in targeted outcomes.

Yet most efforts at educational innovation and application of psychological theory in school settings must also recognize the realities of local constraints and local pressures while at the same time embracing a validated knowledge base that can inform choices about intervention strategies and techniques. Theory about the processes that produce the problem under consideration—particularly the role of contexts in shaping behavioral patterns—can provide a useful guide for local-level applications of treatment protocols.

Theory-based knowledge used in this way should be well validated and can serve as a means for practitioners to make the many important local decisions that they face. Developmental systems theory provides child and adolescent psychologists with a set of principles by which behavior change in context can be understood, an asset to local decision-making processes.

Wellness Enhancement and Risk Reduction

Although the widespread interest in preventive intervention (often through applications in schools) has been embraced by nearly all educational and psychological researchers and policy makers, Cowen (1999) pointed out that such a perspective differs from a focus on competence enhancement. As Cowen noted, prevention approaches or risk-reduction approaches nearly always have as their primary goal or desired outcome the elimination of pathology. Risk-reduction approaches are therefore biased by this singular focus on negative outcomes, a phenomenon that in Cowen's view could mislead and reduce efforts to promote health in the population. For example, in dental health a focus on eliminating cavities and tooth decay led to the widespread use of fluoride in the water supply, by all estimations a success. However, the limitations of this intervention for children who did not brush their teeth, receive regular teeth cleanings, or have adequate nutrition have been well documented. The narrow focus on preventing negative outcomes neglected the larger needs to promote and maintain adequate dental health practices. Prevention and health promotion are not one and the same.

On the contrary, wellness or competence enhancement approaches utilize an understanding of the resources and practices that promote healthy human development and focus efforts on developing and deploying such resources to all individuals. In education we see an emphasis on providing high-quality literacy instruction to all children in an effort to see that all children become literate, in contrast to identification of disabilities in children who fail to learn to read. Wellness enhancement is different from, and complementary to, risk reduction, and Cowen argued that it is not sufficient to focus solely on disease prevention. What is needed is a multilevel, proactive approach that includes strong wellness and competence enhancement as well as provisions for children who are not likely to benefit fully from those efforts (Cowen, 1997, 1999). Because only one third of clinically distressed children or adolescents will receive mental health treatment (Durlak & Wells, 1997), approaches that promote health and reduce risk preventively will be prominent among the considerations of policy makers for the near future.

Influencing Relationship Resources in Schools

Schools, as public institutions in which nearly the entire population participates, are often a very frequent focus of efforts to promote health and reduce risk (Cowen, 1999). Along with families, schools are the single most frequently mentioned context as a site for intervention (Nastasi, 1998). Risk reduction efforts that attempt to make either environmental changes or person-level changes often do it in a school setting. For example, Durlak and Wells (1997) found that 72.9% of all preventive intervention studies for children took place in schools, and 20% of change agents were teachers. In fact, one might argue that public education is a very large competence-enhancement policy and strategy.

Within schools, efforts can be person or environment focused (Durlak & Wells, 1997), and environmentally focused interventions can target person-environment interaction patterns. Felner et al. (2001) argued that because developmental outcomes are based on transactions between individuals and environments, prevention-intervention should be aimed at *both* individuals and environments. When promoting health for all children, alterations in the environment are preferable to alterations in individuals (Felner et al., 2001)—yet another reason to view competence enhancement and risk reduction as distinct (Cowen, 1999).

It is in this context that improved relationships between teachers and children are either (a) a focus of intervention efforts or (b) a by-product of other efforts directed at children, teachers, classrooms, or schools. Using Eccles and Roeser's (1998) model of school processes and structure, it is possible to discuss an assortment of educational and psychological applications that either focus on improving child-teacher relationships or, as a function of improvement in other aspects of the larger network of systems in which this relationship is embedded, have consequences for the quality of child-teacher relationships. Eccles and Roeser's (1998) model of the context of schooling is a helpful organizing framework because of its focus on understanding the multiple layers of school organization and process. In particular, we discuss applications related to (a) organizational ethos of the school, its structure, and resources; (b) classroom ethos, structure, and characteristics of the teacher; and (c) social interactions between teachers and children. In addition, we review applications that focus on altering aspects of the child that have, as a by-product, consequences for how the child and teacher interact and relate.

As noted by Eccles and Roeser (1998), the multiple levels of regulatory processes within school organizations are dynamic and interrelated, sometimes characterized by moment-by-moment change and other times appearing immovably entrenched and stable. On this basis, attempts to deploy resources directed at altering any aspect of this complex web of activity must attend to the need to implement and evaluate such efforts over time and to the direct and indirect effects of the effort on the targeted focus as well as at other levels and locations. Furthermore, interventions that target critical processes across multiple levels and processes over time are likely to result in a greater likelihood of change, although the change may be more diffuse and less easy to evaluate.

Organizational Ethos, Structure, and Resources of Schools

There is widespread acknowledgement that schools function somewhat like communities in that they vary in terms of climate, ethos, values, and generalized expectations regarding the behavior of students and teachers. Furthermore, there are very marked differences in schools across the developmental span—thus, middle schools are quite different from elementary schools, and both in turn vary considerably from high schools (e.g., Harter, 1996). Climate influences children's' confidence in their abilities (Cauce, Comer, & Schwartz, 1987) and teachers' efficacy beliefs (Bandura, 1994) and can influence teaching practices that affect children's motivation and self-views (MacIver, Reuman, & Main, 1995). Interventions at this level are complex and often diffuse, involving restructuring of time and scheduling, allocation of space and teaching resources, and placement policies (e.g., practices such as looping), as well as work related to school values, staff support and involvement in decision-making, and cultural issues (Felner et al., 2001; Haynes, 1998). With a few exceptions (e.g., looping), interventions at this level are not directly focused on improving relationships between teachers and children, yet these relationships can be profoundly affected.

In a comprehensive review of whole-school restructuring projects and their consequences for student mental health, Felner et al. (2001) concluded that there is often a "mismatch between the conditions and practices students encounter in grades k-12 and the developmental needs, readiness, and capacities of students" (p. 3). One of these needs, as argued by many scholars and practitioners, is to form functional, effective, supportive relationships with peers and adults in the school setting (Connell & Wellborn, 1991; Eccles & Roeser, 1998).

With regard to specific interventions that focus on the entire school, a range of such approaches shows promise with regard to positive influences on child-teacher relationships. Next we briefly describe a few approaches and then discuss their relevance for relationships between teachers and children.

Durlak and Wells's (1997) meta-analysis of primary prevention efforts supports the effectiveness of programs that modify the school environment and help children negotiate transitions. School Transitional Environments Project (STEP) focuses on promoting health in the transition from elementary school to junior high or from junior to senior high school; this focus on transition is warranted because of evidence suggesting that these transitions both heighten risk time and create opportunity for growth (Felner et al., 2001). Because risk during transition is driven by heightened complexity and developmental demands as well as the school's inability to provide needed supports, this project increases the school's ability to respond to children's needs by essentially creating schools within schools. In this approach (which is widely used in large schools), teams of 60 to 100 students have classes together and have consistent homeroom advisors and counselors. Time is allotted for all teachers to meet and discuss students, to integrate curriculum, and to increase coherence and support available to students. These efforts reduce complexity for students and build a sense of continuity and community. Critically, these school restructuring efforts result in an increase in and stabilization of contact between children and a teacher or teachers (Felner et al., 2001).

Consistent with conclusions that relations between high-quality child-teacher relationships and child outcomes indicate a process of engagement between the child and schooling, results of STEP have been promising for children's school adjustment. Felner et al. (2001) reported 40% to 50% declines in school dropout, maintenance of achievement levels, and fewer child- and teacher-reported behavioral-emotional problems. It is not surprising that teachers also reported higher job satisfaction and less burnout (see Felner et al., 2001). Felner's group also examined features of the school that interacted with the intervention and concluded that the riskier the school, the more complete the intervention must be to see positive results in school adjustment. Common dimensions of successful schools, according to Felner et al. (2001) include the following: a sense of belongingness and agency; engagement of families; an integrated, quality curriculum; ongoing professional development (both in curriculum content and in child development); high expectations for students; and opportunities for success (see Felner et al., 2001).

For nearly two decades, the CDP (Battistich et al., 1997; Solomon et al., 1996) has been involved intensively with schools to promote social and moral development, a sense of community, and active caring for children within the school. The need for schools to become caring communities (Battistich et al., 1997) is most commonly identified at the middle and high school levels, where preadolescent and adolescent disengagement and lack of connection to school values and social ethos are most marked; however, the CDP has been primarily involved with elementary schools. Although the actual implementation and end product of the CDP intervention involve mostly a set of changes taking place at the classroom level, CDP involves extensive analysis and reshaping of the school environment as a prerequisite for changes sought at the classroom level (Battistich et al., 1997). In the view of CDP, interventions to address concerns such as caring, relationships, student autonomy, and values need to engage both at the classroom and school levels, with primary focus in their most recent work at the school level.

Prominent among the outcomes sought at the classroom level are opportunities for (a) collaboration among students in pursuit of common goals, (b) providing help and receiving help when needed, (c) reflection and discussion of one's own and other's perspectives and goals, and (d) practice of social competencies and exercise of autonomy and decision making. Battistich et al. (1997) stated that "students in such classrooms should feel strong affective ties to one another and to the teacher" (p. 138). In the San Ramon Project (Battistich, Solomon, Watson, Solomon, & Schaps, 1989), CDP focused on changing the whole school level by drawing on parent, child, and teacher involvement and investment to maximize children's autonomy, relatedness, and competence. This approach involved changing discipline practices, teaching style (i.e., emphasizing cooperative learning, making curriculum meaningful), and broadening the focus of schools such that goals include facilitating social and ethical dispositions, attitudes and motivations, and metacognitive skills in addition to facilitating academic development (Battistich, Watson, Solomon, Lewis, & Schaps, 1999). To promote these skills, Battistich et al. suggested that schools emphasize building and maintaining supportive, caring relationship between teachers and students (as well as among teachers and among peers). More specifically, to build these relationships, they suggested activities such as having teachers and students share appropriate aspects of their personal lives, eat lunch together in small groups, and engage in other activities that communicate to students that teachers are genuinely interested and concerned about the range of their experiences and not only about their academic work. They also suggest that teacher-parent communication should be a priority so that teachers can have a greater awareness of what is going on in their students' lives. When schools prioritize these activities, it should allow teachers to know enough about their students to be able to adapt the curriculum so that it is relevant and interesting to students and so that students will know that their teachers care for them and want to be in a collaborative partnership with them to help them attain their goals.

Several studies have evaluated the approach used by the CDP at both the school and classroom levels (see Battistich et al., 1997; Strachota, 1996). Battistich et al. (1997) summarized the evaluation of two years of implementation data in 24 (12 comparison) highly diverse schools. By and large the findings indicate positive changes in desired outcomes for the 12 CDP schools (and associated teachers and children). It is significant that the CDP was able to demonstrate that the targets of its approach at both the school and classroom level changed as a function of implementation and that changes in classroom practice were in turn responsible for changes in student achievement, attitude, and behavior as well as attitudes and behaviors of teachers. With regard to student-teacher relationships, the CDP produced changes in teachers' observed warmth and supportiveness to students and low use of extrinsic control measures, both of which were in part responsible for children's increased engagement, influence in the classroom setting, and positive behavior toward peers and adults. Students reported an increase in the enjoyment of the classroom and motivation to learn, both of which are perceptions related to the child's sense of relatedness within the classroom environment (Connell & Wellborn, 1991).

Nelson (1996) addressed the need for schools to change teacher-child interactions around children's disruptive behavior so that children improve and teachers feel more effective. The goal of this elementary school intervention effort was to identify and change school and classroom practices that fostered disruptive behavior. Adults' management of disruptive behavior through school-, classroom-, and individually focused strategies was the goal of this approach, premised on the notion that adult-child relationships can enhance child social development when the adults make it clear to children which behaviors are acceptable and which are not (Nelson, 1996). The space and scheduling of the school were changed to make it easier for adults to supervise children in less crowded settings. Behavioral guidelines for all common areas were taught, and enforced inappropriate behavior was responded to quickly and effectively. Also, the interactions between teachers and children in the classroom were changed. There was a school-wide classroom management system for disruptive behavior that reduced patterns of escalating negativity between classroom teachers and students. The results were that disciplinary actions decreased notably, teachers felt more supported, and their sense of confidence increased. The target children's social adjustment fell within normal range, and their work habits improved after the intervention. This behaviorally focused approach to reduction of disruption is consistent with Pianta's (1999)

view that such approaches enhance the feedback and information exchange processes in child-teacher relationships by making information clear to both children and teachers, thereby creating a sense of predictability and safety that enhances the affective and interactive quality of the relationship system.

Classroom Ethos and Practices

It can be difficult to distinguish between school- and classroom-level interventions, particularly those that involve social and attitudinal processes and mechanisms. Often, attempts to alter teachers' classroom behavior occur as a function of meetings involving groups of teachers within a school (e.g., Nelson, 1996), in which school leaders also participate. As noted earlier, even though interventions may target classroom practices and behaviors, to the extent that they are delivered through or otherwise involve groups of teachers or all teachers in the school, these interventions may best be considered as whole-school in their focus, although they differ from interventions that target only whole-school issues (such as Felner et al., 2001). In this section we focus on intervention approaches that involve, to a greater extent than those reviewed earlier, within-classroom practices of specific teachers.

Project Fast Track (Conduct Problems Prevention Research Group [CPPRG], 1999) has a specific focus on enhancing children's social and emotional competencies and reducing negative, aggressive social behavior, starting with children as they enter school. Although the intervention is multifaceted, involving academic tutoring and social skills groups among others, a core component of the intervention is the classroom teachers' use of the Promoting Alternative Thinking Strategies (PATHS) curriculum (Greenberg, Kusche, Cook, & Quamma, 1995). PATHS is designed to help children identify and label feelings and social interactions, reflect on those feelings and interactions, generate solutions and alternatives for interpretation and behavior, and test such alternatives. For example, teachers are trained to add lessons to their first-grade curriculum that teach children emotional understanding, communication skills, self-control, and social participation.

Evaluation indicates that PATHS can be effective in altering the quality of the classroom climate and relationships within the classroom (CPPRG, 1999). Specifically, teachers who had a better understanding of the importance of teaching PATHS skills, generalized the lessons taught in the PATHS curriculum to their interactions with students throughout the day, and had effective management skills reported more decreases in aggressive behavior in their classrooms. The authors concluded that perhaps the greatest effects of the PATHS curriculum are not linked to the number of discrete lessons that are presented didactically to children; rather, effects are linked to the degree to which teachers accept the PATHS model and generalize it to the way that they run their classroom (CPPRG, 1999), consistent with the bidirectionality of relation between teachers' beliefs and their behavior with children.

McConaughy et al. (1999) found that Parent-Teacher Research Teams (P-TAR teams), in which parents and teacher communicated about elementary-aged children considered at risk for emotional disturbance to identify the child's strengths and potential goals, were effective at preventing at-risk children from becoming identified with the label of "emotionally disturbed" over and above teachers teaching whole-group social skills. The mechanism of this intervention may have been to change teacher attitudes and behavior toward children before the children developed low self-esteem and poor social interactions that would lead them farther toward behavior problems, a process that altered perceptions of the child-teacher relationship.

Shaftel and Fine (1997) emphasized the role that teachers' subjective beliefs play in determining how child behaviors are interpreted and responded to by teachers. Shaftel and Fine targeted aspects of teaching style such as the amount of feedback children receive, how long teachers present material in a single modality and expect children to attend, or structural issues such as how seating is arranged. They also suggest that another important area to consider when planning interventions is whether teachers manage their classrooms in ways that deal appropriately with child behaviors and are perceived by the children as fair and reasonable. These ideas are applied within a consultation method that focuses on the classroom as a system, when designing interventions for problem behaviors.

Dyad-Focused Approaches

Based on the success of fairly structured programs of parent consultation and training (see Barkley, 1987; Eyberg & Boggs, 1998), Pianta (1999) and Pianta and Hamre (2002) developed the Students, Teachers, and Relationship Support (STARS) system for consultation with teachers to enhance their relationship with a specific child (or children) with whom the teacher reports a problem in their relationship. STARS is a multifaceted program targeting a teacher's representation of his or her relationship with a child and his or her interactive behavior toward the child in the context of a supportive relationship with a consultant.

The specific technique directed at improving child-teacher interactions (and indirectly their beliefs about each other and

their relationship) is *Banking Time*. In Banking Time (Pianta, 1999; Pianta & Hamre, 2002) the teacher works with a consultant and implements a regular regimen of between 5 and 15 min of individual time with a target child. The intervention is called Banking Time because of the metaphor of saving up positive experiences so that the relationship between teacher and child can withstand conflict, tension, and disagreement without deteriorating and returning to a negative state. The child and teacher can draw on their accrued relationship capital and withdraw from the relationship resources that enable them to interact effectively in times of stress. The teacher's behavior in these sessions is highly constrained in order to produce changes in interaction and beliefs.

There is an emphasis in Banking Time sessions on the child's choice of activities and the regular occurrence of sessions. Sessions are not contingent on the child's good behavior and neutral verbalizations from the teacher that do not focus on the child's performance of skills convey relational messages of safety, support for exploration, or predictability that help the child and teacher define their relationship. Behavioral standards are implemented consistent with classroom standards. These principles of Banking Time sessions are very similar to Teacher Child Interaction Therapy (as described by McIntosh et al., 2000), in which teachers engage in nondirective sessions with children designed to enhance the quality of their relationship.

The Banking Time technique acts on nearly every component of a relationship between a child and adult; thus it is a powerful source of pressure on the relationship system. First and foremost it constrains the behavior of the adult. In so doing, a variant of interaction is created between child and adult that typically is viewed as different, novel, and better by most child and adult participants. This constraining of adult behavior in turn frees up the child to display behaviors (and competencies) that are typically not seen in routine interactions between teacher and child. The child often explores at a higher level and shows interest in the teacher and the teacher's attention; in turn, the teacher's perceptions (representational beliefs) may change or at least be subject to reexamination. Feedback and exchange processes between teacher and child are altered as well—especially if the teacher utilized Banking Time sessions to impart a particular message to the child. Banking Time sessions allow the teacher to build credibility that supports these messages so that their words have meaning for the child. In this way, new pathways or dimensions of feedback and communication between teacher and child become possible as Banking Time is implemented.

The STARS approach also involves a set of other procedures that act on teachers' representations and beliefs. These include videotaping interactions with children in the classroom for review with the consultant, engaging in reflection on relationships with children through directed interviews, and analyzing classroom practices related to instruction and discipline. In combination with Banking Time sessions, these techniques are a comprehensive approach to intervention with child-teacher relationships.

PATHS (Greenberg et al., 1995), just described as a classroom-level intervention, also has a focus on teacher-child interactions and relationships. In one study teachers implemented PATHS with specific regular and special education children in the second and third grades (Greenberg et al., 1995). This was designed to promote these children's emotional understanding as assessed through emotional vocabulary, ability to recognize emotional cues, and ability to connect emotions to personal experiences. Teachers were trained to teach 60 30-min lessons on self-control, emotions, and problem solving to their classes. Participating teachers were observed and received consultation weekly in addition to an initial training workshop. Children who received the intervention had a larger emotional vocabulary, a more advanced ability to connect basic emotions to personal experiences, and a more advanced understanding of recognizing emotional cues in others, and they believed that they could manage their feelings more than the children who did not receive the intervention (Greenberg et al., 1995). Children with lower initial symptom levels (as measured by teacher reports) were more likely to improve their emotional vocabulary as a result of the intervention than were children with highly elevated initial symptoms.

Finally, Hughes and Cavell (1999) described an intervention called *Primetime* for aggressive children that includes enhancing the teacher-child relationship (in addition to other relationship components and problem-solving skills training). The Primetime intervention espouses a relationship-based perspective on competence and attempts to reduce aggressive behavior by reorganizing the child's relational skills with parents, peers, and teachers. Primetime focuses on building a mentoring relationship as a support and source of skill training. Evaluations suggest that positive relationships between the children and the mentors were related to reduced levels of teacher-reported externalizing behavior.

Summary

In sum, child-teacher relationships have been the focus of a number of applications directed at improving child outcomes. In some applications relationships are affected as a by-product of interventions targeted at children's skills or at school organizations, whereas in other applications improvements in child-teacher relationships are the specific focus of

the intervention. Results indicate that child-teacher relationships can be improved as a consequence of direct and indirect effects and that improvements in relational quality are correlated with improved child outcomes, particularly in the domain of social adjustment.

CONCLUSIONS AND FUTURE DIRECTIONS: DEVELOPMENTAL ANALYSIS OF CHILD-TEACHER RELATIONSHIPS

Throughout this chapter we have emphasized the advantages to be gained—conceptually, empirically, and practically—from a developmental system analysis of child-teacher relationships. The arguments, review, and positions advanced as a result of this analysis have confirmed this view and lead to the following conclusions concerning these relationships.

1. In analysis of the complex assortment of child-, teacher-, classroom-, school-, and community-level influences on children's adjustment in school settings, it is helpful to focus on child-teacher relationships as a key unit of analysis. A relational focus is an important conceptual advance and may provide a means for understanding processes that have been difficult to study.

2. Child-teacher relationships are themselves best characterized as multicomponent systems involving attributes of the individuals involved, reciprocal, bidirectional processes related to representation and exchange of information, and embedded in ongoing interactions with school and community factors. These factors interrelate in complex ways, and understanding the unit as a system provides importance conceptual and methodological leverage on this complexity.

3. Across samples of children of diverse age, ethnicity, geographical region, and school profiles—and using multiple methods of informant-based or observational assessment—relationships between children and teachers are marked by variation in the extent of emotional and interactional engagement or involvement and in qualities of the emotional experience of that involvement. Negativity appears to be a particularly salient aspect of teachers' relationship experience whereas emotional closeness, involvement, and support appear salient from the child's perspective.

4. Across similarly diverse samples, variation in the quality of child-teacher relationships is related in expected directions to a number of concurrent and future indicators of child outcomes in the domains of classroom adjustment, motivation, and self-esteem; to beliefs about school and schooling; to academic success; and to teachers'

perceptions and emotional-well being. Child-teacher relationships are also associated with indicators of the broader school climate and organizational ethos. It is important to note that there is converging evidence that these relations between child-teacher relationships and child outcomes are independent of other commonly used predictors of those outcomes, providing support for the view that the child-teacher relationship is a unique source of variation in children's experience.

5. Applications that focus on improving children's' experiences in school—particularly applications that emphasize social, emotional, or motivational aspects of school experience or that build on findings from naturalistic studies of child-teacher relationships—demonstrate that child-teacher relationships can be enhanced and that such enhancements are related to improvements in child competencies and perceptions as well as teacher confidence and beliefs.

These conclusions establish fairly clearly that a decade of research with a specific focus on child-teacher relationships has been productive and fruitful. Clearly, a well-defined and identifiable literature has developed and yielded information of conceptual and applied benefit to educators and psychologists. Yet the literature is fairly new, and if its potential is to be realized, several challenges lie ahead in terms of issues that require attention in the next decade:

1. There is a need to examine domain-specificity in the associations of child-teacher relationships with child outcomes, teacher outcomes, and school climate variations. For example, teacher-child conflict and emotional negativity appear to be more predictive of child outcomes in elementary school than is teacher-child closeness (Hamre & Pianta, 2001; Ladd et al., 1999), whereas emotional support experienced from teachers seems quite important in middle school (see Eccles & Roeser, 1998). It is important to establish, in either multi-age cross-sectional studies or longitudinal studies, the extent to which different qualities of child-teacher relationships are related to different outcome domains for children and teachers, at different ages or grades.

2. The extent to which associations between child outcomes and child-teacher relationships are context specific (e.g., stronger for behavior in school vs. home settings) is another area for analysis. Questions concerning whether these relations are localized or specific to a given classroom setting and whether they extend to other settings and the extent to which context-specific or disperses associations extend longitudinally are of great interest.

3. For years there has been interest in the coherence in the quality and form of relationships that children develop with parents, teachers, and peers. From the view of *relationships* as the focal unit of analysis, examination of the key relationships in which children are involved, with a focus on the extent of similarity and dissimilarity (and the personal and contextual correlates of similarity and dissimilarity), will yield insights into the development of personality and social relationships.

4. With regard to naturalistic and intervention research, there is much to be learned from further understanding of the degree to which child-teacher relationships can compensate for the negative effects of earlier experiences. The relative power of the child-teacher relationship to alter or affect developmental trajectories in relation to established and ongoing influence of the parents or peers can provide insight into the plasticity of developmental processes as well as fuel advances in school policy and programming.

5. There is a dire need for further integration among the constituencies involved in research and theory on child-teacher relationships and for this integration to lead to productive use and application of information for the purposes of teacher training (pre and in-service), teacher evaluation, and school design. Continuation of the relative isolation of teacher education from this emergent knowledge base will constrain both the advancement and application of that knowledge. In particular, we believe that a focused effort to study the development and training of teachers from a relational perspective (Goodlad, 1991) is imperative to improving teacher and child outcomes.

In sum, this chapter marks the emergence and consolidation of a relatively new area of inquiry and understanding: relationships between teachers and children. The insights and improvements gained from the last decade of research in this area bode well for the future.

REFERENCES

Adelman, H. S. (1996). Restructuring education support services and integrating community resources: Beyond the full service school model. *School Psychology Review, 25,* 431–445.

Ainsworth, M. D., Blehar, M. C., Waters, E., & Wall, D. (1978). *Patterns of attachment: A psychological study of the strange situation.* Hillsdale, NJ: Erlbaum.

Ames, C. (1992). Classrooms: Goals, structures, and student motivation. *Journal of Educational Psychology, 84,* 261–271.

Bakeman, R., & Gottman, J. M. (1986). *Observing interaction: An introduction to sequential analysis.* Cambridge, MA: Cambridge University Press.

Baker, J. A. (1999). Teacher-student interaction in urban at-risk classrooms: Differential behavior, relationship quality, and student satisfaction with school. *The Elementary School Journal, 100,* 57–70.

Baker, J., Terry, T., Bridger, R., & Winsor, A. (1997). Schools as caring communities: A relational approach to school reform. *School Psychology Review, 26*(4), 586–602.

Bandura, A. (1994). *Self-efficacy: The exercise of control.* New York: W. H. Freeman.

Barker, R. G. (1968). *Ecological psychology: Concepts and methods for studying the environment of human behavior.* Stanford, CA: Stanford University Press.

Barkley, R. (1987). *Defiant children: A clinician's manual for parent training.* New York: Guilford.

Battistich, V., Solomon, D., Watson, M., & Schaps, E. (1997). Caring school communities. *Educational Psychologist, 32*(3), 137–151.

Battistich, V., Solomon, D., Watson, M., Solomon, J., & Schaps, E. (1989). Effects of an elementary school program to enhance prosocial behavior on children's cognitive-social problem-solving skills and strategies. *Journal of Applied Developmental Psychology, 10,* 147–169.

Battistich, V., Watson, M., Solomon, D., Lewis, C., & Schaps, E. (1999). Beyond the three R's: A broader agenda for school reform. *The Elementary School Journal, 99*(5), 415–429.

Beady, C. H., & Hansell, S. (1981). Teacher race and expectations for student achievement. *American Educational Research Journal, 18*(2), 191–206.

Belsky, J., & MacKinnon, C. (1994). Transition to school: Developmental trajectories and school experiences. *Early Education and Development, 5,* 106–119.

Birch, S., & Ladd, G. W. (1996). Interpersonal relationships in the school environment and children's early school adjustment. In K. Wentzel & J. Juvonen (Eds.), *Social motivation: Understanding children's school adjustment* (pp. 199–225). Cambridge, MA: Cambridge University Press.

Birch, S. H., & Ladd, G. W. (1997). The teacher-child relationship and children's early school adjustment. *Journal of School Psychology, 35,* 61–79.

Birch, S. H., & Ladd, G. W. (1998). Children's interpersonal behaviors and the teacher-child relationship. *Developmental Psychology, 34,* 934–946.

Bornstein, M. H. (1995). *Handbook of Parenting.* Mahwah, NJ: Erlbaum.

Bowlby, J. (1969). *Attachment and loss: Vol. 1. Attachment.* New York: Basic Books.

Bracken, B. A., & Craine, R. M. (1994). Children's and adolescents' interpersonal relations: Do age, race, and gender define normalcy? *Journal of Psychoeducational Assessment, 12,* 14–32.

Bronfenbrenner, U., & Morris, P. A. (1998). The ecology of developmental processes. In W. Damon & R. M. Lerner (Eds.), *Handbook of child psychology: Vol. 1. Theoretical models of human development* (5th ed., pp. 993–1028). New York: Wiley.

Brophy, J. (1985). Teachers' expectations, motives, and goals for working with problem students. In C. Ames & R. Ames (Eds.), *Research on motivation in education: Vol. 2. The classroom milieu* (pp. 175–213). New York: Academic Press.

Brophy, J., & Good, J. L. (1974). *Teacher-student relationships.* New York: Holt, Rinehart & Winston.

Brophy, J., & Good, J. L. (1986). Teacher behavior and student achievement. In M. Wittrock (Ed.), *Handbook of research on teaching* (pp. 328–375). New York: Macmillan.

Cairns, R. B., & Cairns, B. D. (1994). *Lifelines and risks. Pathways of youth in our time.* Hempstead, NY: Harvester Wheatsheaf.

Calderhead, J. (1996). Teachers, beliefs, and knowledge. In D. C. Berliner & R. C. Calfee (Eds.), *Handbook of educational psychology* (pp. 709–725). New York: Simon & Schuster.

Calderhead, J., & Robson, M. (1991). Images of teaching: Student teachers' early conceptions of classroom practice. *Teaching and Teacher Education, 7,* 1–8.

Campbell, S. B. (1990). *Behavior problems in preschool children.* New York: Guilford.

Campbell, S. B. (1994). Hard-to-manage preschool boys: Externalizing behavior, social competence, and family context at two-year follow-up. *Journal of Abnormal Child Psychology, 22,* 147–166.

Case, K. I. (1997). African-American othermothering in the urban elementary school. *The Urban Review, 29,* 25–39.

Cauce, A. M., Comer, J. P., & Schwartz, D. (1987). Long term effects of a systems oriented school prevention program. *American Journal of Orthopsychiatric Association, 57,* 127–131.

Cicchetti, D., & Cohen, D. J. (1995). *Developmental psychopathology.* New York: Wiley.

Cohn, D. A. (1990). Child-mother attachment of six-year-olds and social competence at school. *Child Development, 61,* 152–162.

Cohn, J., Campbell, S., Matias, R., & Hopkins, J. (1990). Face-to-face interactions of pastpartum depressed and non-depressed mother-infant pairs. *Developmental Psychology, 26,* 15–23.

Conduct Problems Prevention Research Group. (1999). Initial impact of the fast track prevention trial for conduct problems: II. Classroom effects. *Journal of Consulting and Clinical Psychology, 67*(5), 648–657.

Connell, J. P., & Wellborn, J. G. (1991). Competence, autonomy, and relatedness: A motivational analysis of self-system processes. In R. Gunnar & L. A. Sroufe (Eds.), *Minnesota symposia on child psychology* (Vol. 23, pp. 43–77). Hillsdale, NJ: Erlbaum.

Cost, Quality and Child Outcomes Study Team. (1995). *Cost, quality and child outcomes in child care centers: Public report.* Denver: University of Colorado at Denver, Economics Department.

Cowen, E. (1997). On the semantics and operations of primary prevention and wellness enhancement. *American Journal of Community Psychology, 25*(3), 245–256.

Cowen, E. (1999). In sickness and in health: Primary prevention's vows revisited. In D. Cicchetti & S. L. Toth (Eds.), *Rochester Symposium on developmental psychopathology: Vol. 9. Developmental approaches to prevention and intervention* (pp. 1–24). Rochester, NY: University of Rochester Press.

Csikszentmihalyi, M., & Rathunde, K. (1998). The development of the person: An experiential perspective on the ontogenesis of psychological complexity. In W. Damon & R. M. Lerner (Eds.), *Handbook of child psychology: Vol. 1. Theoretical models of human development* (5th ed., pp. 635–684). New York: Wiley.

de Ruiter, C., & van IJzendoorn, M. (1993). Attachment and cognition: A review of the literature. *International Journal of Educational Research, 19,* 5–20.

Dewey, J. (1990). *The child and the curriculum.* Chicago: University of Chicago Press. (Original work published 1902)

Dodge, K. A., Coie, J. D., & Brakke, N. P. (1982). Behavior patterns of socially rejected and neglected preadolescents: The roles of social approach and aggression. *Journal of Abnormal Child Psychology, 10,* 389–410.

Drevets, R. K., Benton, S. L., & Bradley, F. O. (1996). Students' perceptions of parents' and teachers' qualities of interpersonal relations. *Journal of Youth and Adolescents, 25,* 787–802.

Durlak, J., & Wells, A. (1997). Primary prevention mental health programs for children and adolescents: A meta-analytic review. *American Journal of Community Psychology, 25*(2), 115–152.

Eccles, J. S. (1983). Expectancies, values, and academic behaviors. In J. T. Spence (Ed.), *Achievement and achievement motives: Psychological and sociological approaches* (pp. 75–146). San Francisco: Freeman.

Eccles, J. S. (1993). School and family effects on the ontogeny of children's interests, self-perceptions, and activity choices. In J. Jacobs (Ed.), *Nebraska Symposium on Motivation: Vol. 40. Developmental perspectives on notivation* (pp. 145–208). Lincoln: University of Nebraska Press.

Eccles, J., & Roeser, R. (1998). School and community influences on human development. In M. H. Bornstein & M. E. Lamb (Eds.), *Developmental psychology: An advanced textbook* (4th ed., pp. 503–554). Mahwah, NJ: Erlbaum.

Egeland, B., Pianta, R. C., & O'Brien, M. (1993). Maternal intrusiveness in infancy and child maladaptation in early school years. *Development and Psychopathology, 5,* 359–370.

Egeland, B., Pianta, R. C., & O'Gawa, J. (1996). Early behavior problems: Pathways to mental disorders in adolescence. *Development and Psychopathology, 8,* 735–750.

Elicker, J., Egeland, B., & Sroufe, L. A. (1992). Predicting peer competence and peer relationships in childhood from early parent-child relationships. In R. Parke & G. Ladd (Eds.), *Family-peers relationships: Modes of linkage* (pp. 77–106). Hillsdale, NJ: Erlbaum.

Eyberg, S. M., & Boggs, S. R. (1998). Parent-child interaction therapy: A psychosocial intervention for the treatment of young conduct-disordered children. In C. E. Schaefer & J. M. Briesmeister (Eds.), *Handbook of parent training: Parents as co-therapists for children's behavior problems* (2nd ed.) (pp. 61–97). New York: Wiley.

Farmer, T. (2000). The social dynamics of aggressive and disruptive behavior in school: Implications for behavior consultation. *Journal of Educational and Psychological Consultation, 11*(3 & 4), 299–321.

Felner, R., Favazza, A., Shim, M., & Brand, S. (2001). Whole school improvement and restructuring as prevention and promotion: Lessons from project STEP and the project on high performance learning communities. *Journal of School Psychology, 39,* 177–202.

Fonagy, P., Steele, H., & Steele, M. (1991). Maternal representations of attachment during pregnancy predict the organization of mother-infant attachment at one year of age. *Child Development, 62,* 891–905.

Ford, D. H., & Ford, M. E. (1987). *Humans as self-constructing living systems.* Hillsdale, NJ: Erlbaum.

Ford, D. H., & Lerner, R. M. (1992). *Developmental systems theory: An integrative approach.* Newbury Park, CA: Sage.

Goodlad, J. I. (1991). *Teachers for our nation's schools.* San Francisco: Jossey-Bass.

Gottlieb, G. (1991). Experimental canalization of behavioral development: Theory. *Developmental Psychology, 27,* 4–13.

Greenberg, M. T. (1982). *Reliability and validity of the Inventory of Adolescent Attachments.* Unpublished manuscript, University of Washington, Seattle.

Greenberg, M., Kusche, C., Cook, E., & Quamma, J. (1995). Promoting emotional competence in school-aged children: The effects of the PATHS curriculum. *Development and Psycholopathology, 7,* 117–136.

Greenspan, S. I. (1989). *Development of the ego.* Madison, CT: International Universities.

Greenspan, S. I., & Greenspan, N. (1991). *Clinical interview of the child* (2nd ed.). Madison, CT: International Universities Press.

Hall, W. N., & Bracken, B. A. (1996). Relationship between maternal parenting syles and African Americna and white adolescents' interpersonal relationships. *School Psychology International, 17*(3), 253–267.

Hamilton, C. E., & Howes, C. (1992). A comparison of young children's relationships with mothers and teachers. In R. C. Pianta (Ed.), *Relationships between children and non-parental adults: New directions in child development* (pp. 41–60). San Francisco: Jossey-Bass.

Hamre, B., & Pianta, R. (2001). Early teacher-child relationships and the trajectory of children's school outcomes through eighth grade. *Child Development, 72*(2), 625–638.

Harter, S. (1996). Teacher and classmate influences on scholastic motivation, self-esteem, and level of voice in adolescents. In J. Juvonen & K. Wentzel (Eds.), *Social motivation: Understanding children's school adjustment* (pp. 11–42). New York: Cambridge University Press.

Haynes, N. (1998). Creating safe and caring school communities: Comer school development program schools. *Journal of Negro Education, 65*(3), 308–314.

Haynes, N., Emmons, C., & Ben-Avie, M. (1997). School climate as a factor in student adjustment and achievement. *Journal of Educational and Psychological Consultation, 8*(3), 321–329.

Henggeler, S. W. (1994). A consensus: Conclusions of the APA Task Force Report on innovative models of mental health services for children, adolescents and their families. *Journal of Clinical Child Psychology, 23,* 3–6.

Henggeler, S. W., Schoenwald, S. K., Borduin, C. M., Rowland, M. D., & Cunningham, P. B. (1998). *Multisystemic treatment of antisocial behavior in children and adolescents.* New York: Guilford Press.

Hinde, R. (1987). *Individuals, relationships, and culture.* New York: Cambridge University.

Hofer, M. A. (1994). Hidden regulators in attachment, separation, and loss. In N. A. Fox (Ed.), *The development of emotion regulation: Biological and behavioral considerations. Monographs of the Society for Research in Child Development, 59*(240), 192–207.

Holland, S. H. (1996). PROJECT 2000: An educational mentoring and academic support model for inner-city African-American boys. *Journal of Negro Education, 65*(3), 315–323.

Horppu, R., & Ikonen-Varila, M. (2001). Adult attachment representations, motives for working with children, and conceptions of a kindergarten teacher's work in first-year kindergarten teacher students. *Journal of School Psychology.* Manuscript submitted for publication.

Howes, C. (1999). Attachment relationships in the context of multiple caregivers. In J. Cassidy & P. R. Shaver (Eds.), *Handbook of attachment theory and research* (pp. 671–687).New York: Guilford.

Howes, C. (2000a). Social development, the family and attachment relationships of infants and toddlers: Research into practice. In D. Cryer & T. Harms (Eds.), *Infants and toddlers in out-of-home care* (pp. 87–113). Baltimore: Brooks.

Howes, C. (2000b). Social-emotional classroom climate in child care, child-teacher relationships and children's second grade peer relations. *Social Development, 9,* 191–204.

Howes, C., Hamilton, C. E., & Matheson, C. C. (1994). Children's relationships with peers: Differential associations with aspects of the teacher-child relationship. *Child Development, 65,* 253–263.

Howes, C., Hamilton, C. E., & Phillipsen, L. (1998). Stability and continuity of child-caregiver and child-peer relationships. *Child Development, 69,* 418–426.

Howes, C., & Matheson, C. C. (1992). Contextual constraints on the concordance of mother-child and teacher-child relationships. In R. C. Pianta (Ed.), *Relationships between children and nonparental adults: New directions in child development.* San Francisco: Jossey-Bass.

Howes, C., Matheson, C. C., & Hamilton, C. E. (1994). Maternal, teacher, and child-care history correlates of children's relationships with peers. *Child Development, 65,* 264–273.

Howes, C., Phillipsen, L., & Peisner-Feinberg, E. (2000). The consistency and predictability of teacher-child relationships during the transition to kindergarten. *Journal of School Psychology, 38*(2), 113–132.

Hughes, J. N. (1992). Social psychology of consultation. In F. J. Medway & T. P. Cafferty (Eds.), *School psychology: A social psychological perspective* (pp. 269–303). Hillsdale, NJ: Erlbaum.

Hughes, J., & Cavell, T. (1999). School-based interventions for aggressive children: Primetime as a case in point. In S. Russ & T. Ollendick (Eds.), *Handbook of psychotherapies with children and families.* New York: Kluver Academic/Plenum.

Hughes, J., Cavell, T., & Jackson, T. (1999). Influence of teacher-student relationship on childhood aggression: A prospective study. *Journal of Clinical Child Psychology, 28,* 173–184.

Hughes, J. N., Cavell, T. A., & Willson, V. (in press). Further support for the developmental significance of the quality of the teacher-student relationship. *Journal of School Psychology.*

Johnson, D. B., Malone, P. J., & Hightower, A. D. (1997). Barriers to primary prevention efforts in the schools: Are we the biggest obstacle to the transfer of knowledge? *Applied and Preventive Psychology, 6,* 81–90.

Johnson, D. W., Johnson, R. T., Buckman, L. A., & Richards, P. S. (1985). The effect of prolonged implementation of cooperative learning on social support within the classroom. *Journal of Psychology, 119,* 405–411.

Kasen, S., Johnson, J., & Cohen, P. (1990). The impact of school emotional climate on student psychopathology. *Journal of Abnormal Child Psychology, 18*(2), 165–177.

Katz, G. S., Cohn, J. F., & Moore, C. (1996). A combination of vocal, dynamic and summary features discriminates between three pragmatic categories of infant-directed speech. *Child Development, 67,* 205–217.

Kesner, J. E. (2000). Teacher characteristics and the quality of child-teacher relationships. *Journal of School Psychology, 38*(2), 133–150.

Ladd, G. W., Birch, S. H., & Buhs, E. S. (1999). Children's social and scholastic lives in kindergarten: Related spheres of influence? *Child Development, 70,* 1373–1400.

Ladd, G. W., & Burgess, K. B. (1999). Charting the relationship trajectories of aggressive, withdrawn, and aggressive/withdrawn children during early grade school. *Child Development, 70,* 910–929.

Ladd, G. W., & Price, J. M. (1987). Predicting children's social and school adjustment following the transition from preschool to kindergarten. *Child Development, 58,* 1168–1189.

LaFreniere, P. J., & Sroufe, L. A. (1985). Profiles of peer competence in the preschool: Interrelations among measures, influence of social ecology, and relation to attachment history. *Developmental Psychology, 21,* 56–69.

Lerner, R. M. (1998). Theories of human development: Contemporary perspectives. In W. Damon & R. M. Lerner (Eds.),

Handbook of child psychology: Vol. 1. Theoretical models of human development (5th ed., pp. 1–24). New York: Wiley.

Lieberman, A. F. (1992). Infant-parent psychotherapy with toddlers. *Development and Psychopathology, 4,* 559–574.

Loeber, R. (1990). Development and risk factors of juvenile antisocial behavior and delinquency. *Clinical Psychology Review, 10,* 1–41.

Lynch, M., & Cicchetti, D. (1992). Maltreated children's reports of relatedness to their teachers. In R. C. Pianta (Ed.), *Relationships between children and non-parental adults: New directions in child development* (pp. 81–108). San Francisco: Jossey-Bass.

Lynch, M., & Cicchetti, D. (1997). Children's relationships with adults and peers: An examination of elementary and junior high school students. *Journal of School Psychology, 35,* 81–100.

Lyon, G. R. (2000). *Overview of reading and literacy initiatives.* Statement delivered to Committee on Labor and Human Resources, Washington, DC.

Mac Iver, D. J., Reuman, D. A., & Main, S. R. (1995). Social structuring of school: Studying what is, illuminating what could be. In M. R. Rosenzweig & L. W. Porter (Eds.), *Annual Review of Psychology, 46,* 375–400.

Magnusson, D., & Stattin, H. (1998). Person-context interaction theory. In W. Damon & R. M. Lerner (Eds.), *Handbook of child psychology: Vol. 1. Theoretical models of human development* (5th ed., pp. 685–760). New York: Wiley.

Main, M. (1996). Introduction to the special section on attachment and psychopathology: 2. Overview of the field of attachment. *Journal of Consulting and Clinical Psychology, 64,* 237–243.

Main, M., Kaplan, N., & Cassidy, J. (1985). Security in infancy, childhood, & adulthood: A move to the level of the representation. In I. Bretherton & E. Waters (Eds.), *Growing points in attachment theory and research. Monographs of the Society for Research in Child Development, 50*(1-2, Serial No. 209), 66–104.

McConaughy, S., Kay, P., & Fitzgerald, M. (1999). The achieving, behaving, caring project for preventing ED: Two year outcomes. *Journal of Emotional and Behaivoral Disorders, 7*(4), 224–239.

McIntosh, D. E., Rizza, M. G., & Bliss, L. (2000). Implementing empirically supported interventions: Teacher-child interaction therapy. *Psychology in the School, 37*(5), 453–462.

Midgley, C., Feldlaufer, H., & Eccles, J. S. (1989). Student/teacher relations and attitudes toward mathematics before and after the transition to junior high school. *Child Development, 60,* 981–992.

Motti, F. (1986). *Relationships of preschool teachers with children of varying developmental histories.* Unpublished doctoral dissertation, University of Minnesota, Minneapolis.

Muller, C., Katz, S. R., & Dance, L. J. (1999). Investing in teaching and learning: Dynamics of the teacher-student relationship from each actor's perspective. *Urban Education, 34,* 292–337.

Murray, C., & Greenberg, M. T. (2000). Children's relationship with teachers and bonds with school: An investigation of patterns and correlates in middle childhood. *Psychology in the Schools, 38*(5), 425–446.

Nastasi, B. K. (1998). A model for mental health programming in schools and communities: Introduction to the Mini-Series. *School Psychology Review, 27,* 165–174.

Nelson, J. R. (1996). Designing schools to meet the needs of students who exhibit disruptive behavior. *Journal of Emotional and Behaivoral Disorders, 4*(3), 147–161.

Nelson-Le Gall, S., & Resnick, L. (1998). Help seeking, achievement motivation, and the social practice of intelligence in school. In S. A. Karabenick (Ed.), *Strategic help seeking: Implications for learning and teaching* (pp. 39–60). Hillsdale, NJ: Erlbaum.

Newman, R. S. (2000). Social influences on the development of children's adaptive help seeking: The role of parents, teachers, and peers. *Developmental Review, 20,* 350–404.

NICHD Early Child Care Research Network. (2001, April). *Observations in first grade classrooms: The other side of school readiness.* Paper presented at the Biennial Meeting of the Society for Research in Child Development, Minneapolis, MN.

NICHD Early Child Care Research Network. (2002). Structure → Process → Outcome: Direct and indirect effects of caregiving quality on young children's development. *Psychological Science.* Manuscript submitted for publication.

Pederson, E., Faucher, T. A., & Eaton, W. W. (1978). A new perspective on the effects of first grade teachers on children's subsequent adult status. *Harvard Educational Review, 48,* 1–31.

Pianta, R. C. (1992). *New directions in child development: Vol. 57. Beyond the parent: The role of other adults in children's lives.* San Franciso: Jossey-Bass.

Pianta, R. C. (1994). Patterns of relationships between children and kindergarten teachers. *Journal of School Psychology, 32,* 15–32.

Pianta, R. C. (1999). *Enhancing relationships between children and teachers.* Washington, DC: American Psychological Association.

Pianta, R. C., & Harbers, K. (1996). Observing mother and child behavior in a problem solving situation at school entry: Relations with academic achievement. *Journal of School Psychology, 34,* 307–322.

Pianta, R. C., & Heave, B. (2002). *Students, Teachers, and Relationship Support: STARS.* Odessa, FL: PAR, Inc.

Pianta, R., La Paro, K., Payne, C., Cox, M., & Bradley, R. (2002). Observed quality of the kindergarten classroom environment: Description and relations with teacher, family, and school characteristics and child outcomes. *Elementary School Journal, 102,* 225–238.

Pianta, R. C., & Nimetz, S. (1991). Relationships between children and teachers: Associations with classroom and home behavior. *Journal of Applied Developmental Psychology, 12,* 379–393.

Pianta, R. C., Nimetz, S. L., & Bennett, E. (1997). Mother-child relationships, teacher-child relationships and adjustment in preschool and kindergarten. *Early Childhood Research Quarterly, 12,* 263–280.

Pianta, R. C., Smith, N., & Reeve, R. (1991). Observing mother and child behavior in a problem-solving situation at school entry: Relations with classroom adjustment. *School Psychology Quarterly, 6,* 1–16.

Pianta, R. C., & Steinberg, M. (1992). Relationships between children and kindergarten teachers from the teachers' perspective. In R. Pianta (Ed.), *Beyond the parent: The role of other adults in children's lives* (pp. 61–80). San Francisco: Jossey-Bass.

Pianta, R. C., Steinberg, M., & Rollins, K. (1995). The first two years of school: Teacher-child relationships and deflections in children's classroom adjustment. *Development and Psychopathology, 7,* 295–312.

Pianta, R. C., & Walsh, D. (1996). *High-risk children in the schools: Creating sustaining relationships.* New York: Routledge.

Resnick, L. B. (1994). Situated rationalism: Biological and social preparation for learning. In L. Hirschfield & S. Gelman (Eds.), *Mapping the mind: Domain specificity in cognition and culture* (pp. 474–493). Cambridge, England: Cambridge University Press.

Resnick, M. D., Bearman, P. S., Blum, R. W., Bauman, K., Harris, K. M., Jones, J., Tabor, J., Beuhring, T., Sieving, R. E., Shew, M., Ireland, M., Behringer, L. H., & Udry, J. R. (1997). Protecting adolescents from harm: Findings from the national longitudinal study of adolescent health. *JAMA, 278,* 823–832.

Rimm-Kaufman, S., Pianta, R., Cox, M., & Early, D. (2000). Teachers' judgments of problems in the transition to kindergarten. *Early Childhood Research Quarterly, 15*(2), 147–166.

Roberts, M. C. (1996). *Model programs in child and family mental health.* Hillsdale, NJ: Erlbaum.

Roeser, R., Eccles, J. S., & Sameroff, A. J. (1998). Academic and emotional functioning in early adolescence: Longitudinal relations, patterns, and prediction by experience in middle school. *Development and Psychopathology, 10,* 321–352.

Roeser, R. W., Eccles, J. S., & Sameroff, A. J. (2000). School as a context of early adolescents' academic and social-emotional development: A summary of research findings. *The Elementary School Journal, 100,* 443–471.

Rogoff, B. (1990). *Apprenticeship in thinking: Cognitive development in social context.* New York: Oxford University Press.

Rosenthal, R. (1969). Interpersonal expectations effects of the experimenter's hypothesis. In R. Rosenthal & R. L. Rosnow (Eds.), *Artifact in behavioral research* (pp. 182–279). New York: Academic Press.

Rubin, K. H., & Clark, M. L. (1983). Preschool teacher's ratings of behavioral problems: Observational, sociometric, and social-cognitive correlates. *Journal of Abnormal Child Psychology, 11,* 273–286.

Rutter, M. (1987). Psychosocial resilience and protective mechanisms. *American Journal of Orthopsychiatry, 57,* 316–331.

Ryan, R. M., Stiller, J. D., & Lynch, J. H. (1994). Representations of relationships to teachers, parents, and friends as predictors of academic motivation and self-esteem. *Journal of Early Adolescence, 14*(2), 226–249.

Saft, E. W., & Pianta, R. C. (2001). Teachers' perceptions of their relationships with students: Relations with child and teacher characteristics. *School Psychology Quarterly, 16,* 125–141.

Sameroff, A. J. (1995). General system theory and developmental psychopathology. In D. Cicchetti & D. J. Cohen (Eds.), *Developmental psychopathology: Vol. 1. Risk, disorder, and adaptation* (pp. 659–695). New York: Wiley.

Shaftel, J., & Fine, M. (1997). Ecosystem intervention with teachers: A collaborative approach. In J. Swartz & W. Martin (Eds.), *Applied ecological psychology for schools within communities* (pp. 95–114). New York: Erlbaum.

Skinner, E. A., & Belmont, M. J. (1993). Motivation in the classroom: Reciprocal effects of teacher behavior and student engagement across the school year. *Journal of Educational Psychology, 85,* 571–581.

Solomon, D., Watson, M., Battistich, V., Schaps, E., & Delucci, K. (1992). Creating a caring community: Educational practices that promote children's prosocial development. In C. F. Oser, A. Dick, & J. Patry (Eds.), *Effective and responsible teaching: The new synthesis.* (pp. 386–396), San Francisco: Jossey-Bass.

Solomon, D., Watson, M., Battistich, V., Schaps, E., & Delucci, K. (1996). Creating classrooms that students experience as communities. *American Journal of Community Psychology, 24*(6), 719–748.

Sroufe, L. A. (1983). Infant-caregiver attachment and patterns of adaptation in preschool: The roots of maladaptation and competence. In M. Perlmutter (Ed.), *Minnesota symposium in child psychology* (Vol. 16, pp. 41–81). Hillsdale, NJ: Erlbaum.

Sroufe, L. A. (1989a). Pathways to adaptation and maladaptation: Psychopathology as developmental deviation. In D. Cicchetti (Ed.), *Emergence of a discipline: Rochester Symposium on Developmental Psychopathology* (pp. 13–40). Hillsdale, NJ: Erlbaum.

Sroufe, L. A. (1989b). Relationships and relationship disturbances. In A. Sameroff & R. Emde (Eds.), *Relationship disturbances in early childhood* (pp. 97–124). New York: Basic Books.

Sroufe, L. A. (1996). *Emotional development.* New York: Cambridge University Press.

Sroufe, L. A., & Fleeson, J. (1988). Attachment and the construction of relationships. In W. Hartup & Z. Rubin (Eds.), *Relationships and development.* Hillsdale, NJ: Erlbaum.

Stern, D. (1989). The representation of relationship patterns: Developmental considerations. In A. J. Sameroff & R. Emde (Eds.), *Relationship disturbances in early childhood* (pp. 52–69). New York: Basic Books.

Strachota, B. (1996). On their side: Helping children take charge of their learning. Greenfield, MA: Northeast Foundation for Children.

Stuhlman, M., & Pianta, R. (in press). A narrative approach to assessing teacher-child relationships: Associations with behavior in classrooms. *School Psychology Review.*

Toth, S., & Cicchetti, D. (1996). The impact of relatedness with mother on school functioning. *Journal of School Psychology, 34,* 247–266.

van IJzendoorn, M. H., Sagi, A., & Lambermon, M. W. E. (1992). The multiple caretaker paradox: Some data from Holland and Israel. In R.C. Pianta (Ed.), *Relationships between children and non-parental adults: New directions in child development* (pp. 5–24). San Francisco: Jossey-Bass.

Vygotsky, L. S. (1978). *Mind in society: The development of higher psychological processes* (M. Cole, V. John-Steiner, S. Scribner, & E. Souberman, Eds.). Cambridge, MA: Harvard University Press.

Waters, E. (1987). *Attachment Behavior Q-Set, Revision, 3.0.* SUNY Stony Brook.

Waters, E., & Deane, K. E. (1985). Defining and assessing individual differences in attachment relationships: Q-methodology and the organization of behavior in infancy and early childhood. In I. Bretherton & E. Waters (Eds.), *Growing points of attachment theory and research. Monographs of the Society for Research in Child Development, 50*(1, Serial No. 209).

Weinstein, R. (1989). Perceptions of classroom processes and student motivation: Children's views of self-fulfilling prophecies. In C. Ames & R. Ames (Eds.), *Research on motivation in education: Vol. 3. Goals and cognitions* (pp. 13–44). New York: Academic Press.

Weinstein, R. S., & Marshall, H. H. (1984). *Ecology of students' achievement expectations.* Final report to the National Institute of Education. Washington, DC: U.S. Govt. Printing Office.

Weissberg, R., & Bell, D. (1997). A meta-analytic review of primary prevention programs for children and adolescents: Contributions and caveats. *American Journal of Community Psychology, 25*(2), 207–215.

Wellborn, J. G., & Connell, J. P. (1987). *Rochester Assessment Package for Children.* Rochester, NY: University of Rochester.

Wentzel, K. (1996). *Effective teachers are like good parents: Understanding motivation and classroom behavior.* Paper presented at the annual meeting of the American Educational Research Association, New York.

Wentzel, K. (1998). Social relationships and motivation in middle school: The role of parents, teachers, and peers. *Journal of Educational Psychology, 90*(2), 202–209.

Werner, E., & Smith, R. (1980). *Vulnerable but invincible.* New York: Wiley.

White, K., & Kistner, J. (1992). The influence of teacher feedback on young children's peer preferences and perceptions. *Developmental Psychology, 28*(5), 933–940.

Zeanah, C. H., Benoit, D., Barton, M., Regan, C., Hirschberg, L., & Lipsitt, L. (1993). Representations of attachment in mothers and their one-year old infants. *Journal of the American Academy of Child and Adolescent Psychiatry, 32,* 278–286.

Zeichner, K. (1995). Educating teachers to close the achievement gap: Issues of pedagogy, knowledge and teacher preparation. In *Closing the achievement gap: A vision to guide change in beliefs and practice* (pp. 39–52). U.S. Department of Education Regional Educational Laboratory Network, Washington, DC.

CHAPTER 11

School Adjustment

KATHRYN R. WENTZEL

SCHOOL ADJUSTMENT

Being successful at school requires children to perform a range of social as well as academic competencies. In addition to mastering subject matter, developing effective learning strategies, and performing well on tests, children also must work to maintain and establish interpersonal relationships, strive to develop social identities and a sense of belongingness, observe and model standards for performance displayed by others, and behave in ways that are valued by teachers and peers. Quite often, children who succeed in these social endeavors are also the most academically successful students. Although these social activities might vary somewhat as a function of a child's age or the subject being taught, they reflect the fact that positive forms of social behavior can create a classroom environment that is conducive to learning and cognitive development; similarly, positive interpersonal relationships with teachers and peers can motivate and support the development of intellectual competencies.

In the present chapter, children's adjustment to school is discussed with respect to those social competencies that facilitate achievement of school-related objectives. Specifically, the focus is on school adjustment as defined by social motivation, behavioral competence, and positive interpersonal relationships. Research on each aspect of school adjustment is reviewed, with a particular focus on how these aspects form a profile of competencies that are related to each other as well as to academic achievement. The implications of this

literature for future work on school adjustment are discussed. In addition, research on socialization processes that promote healthy adjustment at school are reviewed.

DEFINING SCHOOL ADJUSTMENT

School adjustment is often used as a fairly generic term that refers to any school-related outcome under investigation. Quite often, adjustment is defined with respect to the absence of negative or maladaptive student outcomes (e.g., aggressive, inattentive, or disruptive behavior) in addition to the presence of normative or positive competencies (e.g., cooperative, compliant, or self-regulated behavior). In most cases, however, formal models have not been proposed to guide our thinking about what healthy adjustment to school entails or how it develops and can be supported within the classroom environment (cf. Ladd, 1989).

To guide the present discussion, therefore, an ecological approach is proposed in which adjustment is defined as the achievement of goals that result in social integration, as well as those resulting in positive developmental outcomes for the self. Socially integrative goals are desired outcomes that promote the smooth functioning of the social group, social approval, and social acceptance, whereas self-related goals are those that promote the achievement of personal competence, feelings of self-determination, and feelings of social and emotional well-being (Bronfenbrenner, 1989; Ford, 1992). This goal-based definition implies that classroom competence is a highly context-specific outcome reflecting the degree to which students are able to meet the demands of the classroom environment as well as achieve their own personal goals.

Several perspectives on the nature of competence provide support for this approach. Bronfenbrenner (1989) argues that competence can only be understood in terms of context-specific effectiveness, as reflected in mastery of culturally and socially defined tasks. Therefore, competence is a product not only of personal attributes such as goals, values, self-regulatory skills, and cognitive abilities, but also of ways in which these attributes contribute to meeting situational requirements and demands. Moreover, Bronfenbrenner argues that competence is achieved in part when contexts provide opportunities for the growth and development of personal attributes as well as scaffolding for learning what is expected by the social group.

A similar perspective developed specifically to understand adjustment at school is found in the work of Connell and his colleagues (Connell & Wellborn, 1991; Deci & Ryan, 1991). According to Connell and Wellborn, students will engage in positive intellectual and social activities as well as experience a positive sense of self and emotional well-being when teachers provide structure (e.g., articulation of clear and consistent expectations), autonomy support (e.g., opportunities for personal choice and decision making), and involvement (e.g., individual attention). These conditions are believed to contribute to adjustment by enhancing students' sense of competence, self-determination, and social relatedness—that is, feeling that one is an integral and valued part of the social group.

Ford (1992) also expands on Bronfenbrenner's notion of person-environment fit by specifying four dimensions of competence: the achievement of personal goals, the achievement of goals that are situationally relevant, the use of appropriate means to achieve these goals, and accomplishing goals that result in positive developmental outcomes for the individual. Applying Bronfenbrenner's and Ford's perspectives to classroom functioning suggests that students are competent and well-adjusted if several criteria are met. First, students must be able to achieve goals that are valued by themselves as well as by teachers and peers. Second, they must do so in ways that are sanctioned by the group. Third, goals must be accomplished in ways that set the stage for other positive outcomes such as healthy self-concept or increased interest in academics. Finally, the classroom context must provide the structure and support for students to accomplish these goals.

Little direct evidence exists to support the notion that levels of person-environment fit can influence classroom functioning and school adjustment. However, Hall and Cairns (1984) demonstrated that children are aggressive depending in part on the degree to which aggression is condoned in their setting at the time. Phelan, Davidson, and Cao (1991) documented that adolescents can be categorized with respect to goodness of fit—that is, according to the degree to which they feel comfortable with and can easily adapt to the multiple demands of parents, peers, and school. In Phelan et al.'s research, students who reported the best fit also demonstrated successful adaptation to the academic and social demands of school, whereas those who reported the least amount of comfort and belongingness felt disenfranchised and alienated, often dropping out of school altogether.

This ability to coordinate and achieve a balance between personal and socially valued goals is especially relevant for understanding school adjustment when one considers the potentially negative motivational effects of competing, incongruent goals across family, peer, and classroom contexts often experienced by minority students (Phelan et al., 1991). Children from minority cultures often are expected to adapt to normative expectations for behavior that are inconsistent with those espoused by their families and communities. Ogbu (1985; Fordham & Ogbu, 1986) describes how failing to achieve academically can be interpreted by some minority children as an accomplishment rather than a failure. In such cases, noncompliance with the majority culture's institutional norms and standards for achievement can lead to acceptance within the minority community but to social rejection and academic failure at school.

In summary, a full appreciation of how and why students thrive or fail to thrive at school requires an understanding of a student's personal interests and goals, as well as the degree to which these are valued by teachers and peers, and contribute to the stability and smooth functioning of the classroom. Implicit in this perspective is that personal attributes such as the ability to coordinate multiple goals, motivation to behave in prosocial and responsible ways, and concomitant social-cognitive skills make critical contributions to school adjustment. In addition, the *developmentally instigating* properties (Bronfenbrenner, 1989) of the classroom that support and promote the expression and development of these personal attributes as well as goal attainment must also be in place. In the following section, research on student adjustment as defined by social motivation, behavioral competence, and relationships with teachers and peers is reviewed. Next, ways in which positive interpersonal relationships at school might support healthy adjustment are discussed.

RESEARCH ON SOCIAL ASPECTS OF SCHOOL ADJUSTMENT

Social Motivation: Social Goal Pursuit

A basic tenet of motivational theories is that people do set goals for themselves and that these goals can be powerful motivators of behavior (Austin & Vancouver, 1996; Bandura,

1986; Dweck, 1991). Although definitions vary slightly as a function of theoretical perspective, *goals* are generally referred to as cognitive representations of desired future outcomes. As noted at the beginning of this chapter, work in the area of social competence and social development suggests that competence in social settings often requires the achievement of goals that result in approval and acceptance by the social group, as well as those resulting in the achievement of personal competence and feelings of self-determination (see Bronfenbrenner, 1989; Ford, 1992). Examples of school-related goals that reflect these outcomes are social relationship goals such as to gain approval from others, to establish personal relationships with teachers or peers, or to cooperate with classmates; task-related goals such as to master subject matter or to meet as a specific standard of achievement; or more cognitive goals such as to engage in creative thinking or to satisfy intellectual curiosity or challenge (see Ford, 1992, for a comprehensive list of goals).

Research on classroom motivation is typically focused on the latter set of task-related and cognitive goals. However, the pursuit of socially integrative goals such as to be cooperative and compliant or to establish interpersonal relationships is equally important for understanding school success. Researchers have studied social goals from three fairly distinct perspectives (see Wentzel, 2002b). First, researchers have investigated children's knowledge about and choice of social goals as a social cognitive skill. Based on models of social information processing (e.g., Crick & Dodge, 1994; Dodge, 1986; Ford, 1984), this perspective highlights children's interpretations of social situations and their knowledge of which goals are appropriate or inappropriate to pursue under which conditions. Second, social goals have been construed as motivational or personality orientations that guide children's behavioral responses to social opportunities and challenges (Dweck & Legget, 1988; McClelland, 1987). For the most part, these more global social goals or needs are believed to function independently of context.

Finally, the pursuit of social goals has been studied as a motivational process that provides direction to behavior and is related to situation-specific competence. In this case, the extent to which children try to achieve certain prescribed goals is examined as a predictor of social competence and person-environment fit (Ford, 1992; Wentzel, 1991b, 1991c). Based on this perspective, I have explored the degree to which school-related success can be predicted by children's pursuit of specific social goals to behave in prosocial and socially responsible ways. I define personal goals with respect to their content—that is, as a cognitive representation of what it is that an individual is trying to achieve in a given situation

(see also Ford, 1992). This perspective is the focus of the present discussion.

Goals For Education

What are the goals for education that are pursued by teachers and their students? Goals for classroom life reflect a wide range of social as well as intellectual outcomes. At the policy level, educational objectives have included the development of social competencies as well as scholastic achievements—for producing model citizens as well as scholars. In general, character development and social responsibility have been stated as explicit objectives for public schools in almost every educational policy statement since 1848; they are promoted with the same frequency as the development of academic skills (see Wentzel, 1991c, for a review). Specifically, social behavior in the form of moral character, conformity to social rules and norms, cooperation, and positive styles of social interaction have been promoted consistently as goals for students to achieve.

Teachers' and students' goals for school reflect the concerns for social development articulated in federal mandates. For instance, Krumboltz, Ford, Nichols, and Wentzel (1987) evaluated goals for students to achieve by age 18 in a sample of several hundred parents, teachers, and students. Goal statements reflected five academic domains (verbal, math, science, social studies, and fine arts), and five nonacademic domains (motivation, interpersonal competence, moral development, health, and career development). These statements were chosen based on school district curriculum guides from around the country and in consultation with local teachers and other experts in each domain. The most notable aspect of this study is that for each set of respondents, the social domains were regarded as more important than were any of the academic domains. In particular, students rated positive motivational outcomes (e.g., valuing education, being intrinsically motivated) as most important, whereas teachers and parents rated the moral domain as most important with motivation being ranked second. Interpersonal competence was ranked either second or third by all three groups. In short, motivation and social competence in the form of cooperation, respect for others, and positive interpersonal relationships were nominated consistently as critical outcomes for students to achieve, over and above academic accomplishments.

Although other researchers rarely have asked teachers about their specific goals for students, teachers have expressed their ideas concerning what well-adjusted and successful students are like. When describing ideal students, middle school teachers mentioned three types of desirable outcomes: social outcomes reflecting socially integrative characteristics such as sharing, being helpful to others, and being responsive to rules; learning outcomes reflecting motivational qualities related to learning such as being persistent, hardworking, inquisitive, and intrinsically interested; and performance outcomes reflecting task-related outcomes such as getting good grades, being informed, and completing assignments (Wentzel, 2000). In other research, teachers identified elementary-aged students toward whom they felt attachment, concern, indifference, or rejection (Brophy & Good, 1974). Of interest is that students placed in these categories displayed distinct behavioral profiles in the classroom, with characteristics of well-liked students matching those described in Wentzel's (2000) study. *Attachment* students were typically bright, hardworking, and model students; *concern* students made excessive but appropriate demands for teachers' attention; *indifference* students had few contacts with teachers; and *rejection* students typically displayed problem behaviors and made illegitimate demands for attention. Similarly, elementary-school teachers have consistently reported preferences for students who are cooperative, conforming, cautious, and responsible rather than independent and assertive or argumentative and disruptive (Brophy & Good, 1974; Feshbach, 1969; Helton & Oakland, 1977; Kedar-Voivodas, 1983). Teachers tend to report antisocial and aggressive behavior as most detrimental to classroom order (Safran & Safran, 1985).

Research on school-related goals that students value has not been frequent (cf. Wigfield & Eccles, 1992). However, students do report trying to achieve positive social as well as academic outcomes. In an ethnographic study, Allen (1986) interviewed ninth-grade students about their school-related goals and found that two major goals were mentioned by almost all students—goals to socialize with peers and to pass the course. Students believed these goals could be accomplished by trying to figure out the teacher, having fun, giving the teacher what he or she wants, minimizing work, reducing boredom, and staying out of trouble. When given a list of possible social and academic goals to pursue at school, high school students have indicated trying to achieve social goals to have fun and to be dependable and responsible, in addition to task-related goals to learn new things and to get good grades (Wentzel, 1989). Finally, middle school students also have reported trying to achieve social goals to behave appropriately more frequently than they have reported goals to learn or to socialize with peers (Wentzel, 1991b, 1992).

Specific student characteristics also have been related to personal goals. High school students identified as being at risk due to problem behavior tend to attach greater importance to goals concerning self-determination and rule breaking than do not-at-risk students, who tend to value achievement of positive academic outcomes and responsible, interpersonal

behavior (Carrol, Durkin, Hattie, & Houghton, 1997). Although research on ethnic minorities is rare, Graham, Taylor, and Hudley (1998) reported that African-American students value high levels of achievement less than do Caucasian students.

Students' Goals in Relation to Other Forms of Adjustment

The literature just reviewed clearly indicates that students as well as teachers value goals to be prosocial and socially responsible. In addition, findings provide support for the notion that social goal pursuit represents a basic psychological process underlying social behavior and interpersonal competence. For instance, pursuit of goals to be prosocial and socially responsible have been related consistently and positively to displays of prosocial and responsible behavior (Wentzel, 1991a, 1994). Similarly, pursuit of goals to be sociable has been related positively to acceptance by peers as well as by teachers (Wentzel, 1991a, 1991b, 1994). Moreover, there is ample evidence that students who pursue certain social goals at school also succeed academically; pursuit of goals to be prosocial and socially responsible is related to classroom grades as well as to IQ (Wentzel, 1989, 1991a, 1993a, 1996, 1997, 1998).

Social goals also have been examined as part of a coordinated effort to achieve multiple classroom goals. As predicted by an ecological perspective, high- and low-achieving high school students can be distinguished on the basis of the sets of social and academic goals they pursue or do not pursue at school (Wentzel, 1989). Specifically, 84% of the highest achieving students reported always trying to be a successful student, to be dependable and responsible, and to get things done on time; only 13% of the lowest achieving students reported always trying to achieve these three goals. Moreover, although the highest achieving students reported frequent pursuit of academic goals (i.e., to learn new things, to understand things), less frequent pursuit of these goals did not distinguish the lowest achieving from average achieving students. Rather, an unwillingness to try to conform to the social and normative standards of the classroom uniquely characterized the lowest achieving students. These low-achieving students also reported frequent pursuit of other types of social goals such as to have fun and to make and keep friendships. In a follow-up study of middle school students (Wentzel, 1993a), two academic goals (reflecting efforts to master new and challenging tasks and to earn positive evaluations) and two social goals (reflecting efforts to be prosocial and to be socially responsible) were investigated. Pursuits of these social and academic goals were significant, independent predictors of classroom effort over time, even when other motivational variables such as self-efficacy and values were taken into account (Wentzel, 1996).

Implications for Future Research

Several themes emerge from the literature on educational goals and objectives that are relevant for understanding school adjustment from an ecological perspective. First, an examination of which goals a student is trying to achieve and the degree to which these goals are compatible with the expectations and requirements of the classroom can explain in part students' overall success and adjustment at school. Of concern, however, is that explanations of competence based on students' pursuit of socially valued goals assumes that students understand how they are supposed to behave and what it is they are supposed to accomplish while at school. For some students these expectations are not always immediately obvious. In particular, young children who are just beginning school and students who are raised in cultures with goals and values dissimilar to those espoused by educational institutions might also need explicit guidance with respect to the goals they are expected to achieve (Ogbu, 1985).

In addition, teachers do not always communicate clearly their own goals for their students. In two recent studies of young adolescents, almost half the students reported that their current teachers did not have clear classroom rules for them to follow, nor did they think their teachers had explained what would happen if rules were broken (Wentzel, 2000; Wentzel, Battle, & Cusick, 2000). Therefore, the more explicit and clearly defined teachers can make the social expectations for classroom conduct, the more likely it is that students will at least understand the goals they are expected to achieve. The identification of contextual factors as well as student attributes that make these expectations more or less salient to students is an important challenge for researchers of classroom goal pursuit.

It also is worth noting that only a limited number of social goals have been studied in relation to academic outcomes. However, a broad array of goals that reflect social concerns and influences are potentially relevant for understanding students' academic motivation and general adjustment to school. Ford (1992) has identified three general categories of goals that require input from or interaction with the social environment: integrative social relationship goals, self-assertive social relationship goals, and task goals. The social relationship goals identified by Ford are perhaps most relevant to the social motivational issues raised thus far, with goals to benefit the welfare of others and the social group (integrative social relationship goals) having been studied most frequently (e.g., Ford, 1996; Wentzel, 1991a, 1993a, 1994). In addition, a focus on self-

assertive social relationship goals (e.g., obtaining help or resources from others) reminds us of the potential benefits of social relationships to the individual. An inclusion of these goals in studies of academic motivation (e.g., Ryan & Pintrich, 1997) would provide added insight into issues of how individuals derive personal benefits from working and learning with others.

In addition, development and testing of theoretical models that explain links between social motivation and academic achievement are needed. At the simplest level, positive relations between social and academic variables might reflect that students are rewarded for their social efforts with good grades. Goals to achieve social and academic outcomes might also be related in more complex fashion, functioning in an interdependent, hierarchical manner. For instance, goal hierarchies can develop over time as individuals are taught to prioritize goals and to associate goals with each other in causal fashion (Pervin, 1983). With respect to students' goals, children might come to school with a basic goal to establish positive relationships with others. Over time, this goal might become linked causally to more specific goals such as to establish a positive relationship with teachers. This relationship goal might be accomplished by pursuing even more specific goals such as to behave appropriately, to pay attention, or to complete assignments. Similarly, children might learn that in order to achieve a rather global goal of demonstrating competence, they first must achieve subordinate goals such as learning subject matter, outperforming others, or supporting group efforts (see Ames, 1992). Therefore, students learn which goals are most important to achieve and how the attainment of one set of goals can lead to the attainment of others.

The concept of goal hierarchies also is helpful for understanding ways in which beliefs about relations among social and task-related goals might have an impact on efforts to achieve academically. For instance, students might pursue goals to do well at academic tasks in order to achieve a social goal to please one's parents or teachers; students might try to engage in academic tasks because they see this as a way to achieve goals to cooperate or to comply with classroom rules; or students might believe that pleasing a teacher by behaving in socially appropriate ways will ultimately result in accomplishing academic goals. For the most part, students who believe that achieving at learning tasks can be accomplished solely by social means (e.g., pleasing a teacher) are setting themselves up for failure. However, cooperative learning activities provide contexts wherein students who pursue this kind of goal hierarchy might experience positive academic gains (e.g., Damon & Phelps, 1989). Similarly, students who believe that adhering to socially derived rules and conventions will lead to task-related accomplishments also are more likely to be successful than are those who do not. Most academic activities are governed by procedures and behavioral conventions that facilitate successful completion of tasks.

Furthermore, students might have multiple reasons for trying to achieve academically, some of which are social. Therefore, in situations in which a learning activity is less than stimulating or interesting to students, reasons other than an intrinsic interest in the task might be needed to motivate performance. In such cases, multiple social as well as task-related reasons for engaging in the task, such as *I'll probably learn something, it's what I'm supposed to do, it will get me a job someday, it will please mom and dad,* or *it will impress my friends* can provide a powerful motivational foundation for promoting continued engagement.

Finally, an identification of specific self-regulatory strategies that enable students to accomplish multiple goals simultaneously seems essential for helping students coordinate demands to achieve multiple and often conflicting goals at school. For instance, some students who try to pursue multiple goals might be unable to coordinate the pursuit of their goals into an organized system of behavior, and as a consequence they become distracted or overwhelmed when facing particularly demanding aspects of tasks that require focused concentration and attention. Students who are unable to coordinate social goals and academically related goals might opt to pursue social relationship goals with peers (e.g., to have fun) in lieu of task-related goals such as to complete class assignments. Students with effective goal coordination skills would likely find a way to achieve both goals—for instance, by doing homework with friends.

Behavioral Competence: Prosocial and Socially Responsible Behavior

Behavioral competence at school has been studied most often with respect to adherence to social rules and expectations reflecting cooperation, respect for others, and positive forms of group participation that govern social interaction in the classroom. Most generally, positive aspects of behavioral outcomes are studied in terms of prosocial and responsible behavior, with behavioral incompetence taking the form of aggressive and antisocial behavior (Wentzel, 1991c). Interpersonal competence—especially establishing positive relationships with peers—also has been a focus of empirical investigations.

Of interest for the present discussion is the degree to which these social competencies contribute to academic accomplishments. Correlational studies indicate that tendencies to be prosocial and empathic (Feshbach & Feshbach, 1987), prosocial interactions with peers (Cobb, 1972; Green, Forehand, Beck, & Vosk, 1980), appropriate classroom conduct (Entwisle, Alexander, Pallas, & Cadigan, 1987;

Lambert & Nicoll, 1977), and compliance have been related positively to intellectual outcomes in the elementary years. Positive social interactions of preschool children also predict engagement and positive motivational orientations in the classroom (Coolahan, Fantuzzo, Mendez, & McDermott, 2000). In a meta-analysis of factors related to early learning problems, social-emotional factors explained as much or more variance in achievement as intellectual abilities, sensory deficits, or neurological factors explained (Horn & Packard, 1985). Similarly, socially responsible decision making in adolescents has been related positively to academic outcomes (Ford, 1982; Wentzel, Wood, Seisfeld, Stevens, & Ford, 1987). Young adolescents' prosocial behavior also has been related positively to classroom grades and standardized test scores (Wentzel, 1991a, 1993b).

Longitudinal studies also have linked behavioral competence to academic achievements. Safer (1986) found that elementary grade retention is related to conduct as well as to academic problems, whereas recurring nonpromotion at the junior high level is related primarily to classroom misconduct and other behavioral problems. Adaptive classroom behavior in elementary school predicts later grades and test scores in elementary school (Alexander, Entwisle, & Dauber, 1993) as well as in high school (Lambert, 1972), over and above early achievement and IQ. Similarly, Feldhusen, Thurston, and Benning (1970) found that aggressive and disruptive behavior in the third and sixth grades is a strong negative predictor of classroom grades in middle school and high school after taking into account IQ, sex, grade level, and other demographic factors. Based on a comprehensive review of both follow-up and follow-back studies, Parker and Asher (1987) concluded that antisocial and aggressive behavior in the early grades places children at risk for dropping out of high school. Interventions that teach children appropriate social responses to instruction—such as paying attention and volunteering answers—have led to significant and stable gains in academic achievement (Cobb & Hopps, 1973; Hopps & Cobb, 1974).

Finally, behaving in prosocial and responsible ways is related to positive relationships with teachers and peers. Indeed, teachers' preferences for students are based in large part on students' social behavior in the classroom (e.g., Brophy & Good, 1974; Wentzel, 2000). Likewise, acceptance by peers is related to prosocial and responsible behavior, whereas rejection is related to a lack of behavioral competence (Coie, Dodge, & Kupersmidt, 1990; Newcomb, Bukowski, & Pattee, 1993).

Implications for Future Research

Clear and consistent relations between students' prosocial and responsible classroom behavior and their academic accomplishments have been documented. However, researchers have not focused consistently on why these relations exist despite ongoing and serious concerns about students' classroom behavior and how to manage it (see Doyle, 1986). Nevertheless, there are several ways in which social behavior can contribute to achievement at school. First, prosocial and responsible behavior can contribute to academic achievement by creating a context conducive to learning. Quite simply, students' adherence to classroom rules and displays of socially competent behavior allows teachers to focus their efforts on teaching rather than classroom management. Presumably, all students will learn more when this occurs. In addition, being socially responsible also means conforming to rules and conventions for completing learning activities; teachers provide students with procedures for accomplishing academic tasks and dictate specific criteria and standards for performance. Students who follow these rules are more likely to excel academically than those who do not. Finally, constructivist theories of development (Piaget, 1965; Youniss & Smollar, 1989) propose that positive social interactions (e.g., cooperative and collaborative problem solving) can create cognitive conflict that hastens the development of higher-order thinking skills and cognitive structures. Empirical research supports this notion in that cooperative learning results in greatest gains when interactive questioning and explanation are an explicit part of the learning task (e.g., Damon & Phelps, 1989; Slavin, 1987).

An important issue with respect to these models, however, concerns the direction of effects. Assuming that causal relations do exist, is it that behavioral competence influences learning and achievement or that academic success promotes behavioral competence? It is clear that bidirectional influences exist. For instance, negative academic feedback can lead to acting out, noncompliance, and other forms of irresponsible behavior. From a developmental perspective, however, antisocial behavior and a lack of prosocial skills appear to begin with poor family relationships (e.g., Patterson & Bank, 1989). Therefore, how children are taught to behave before they enter school should have at least an initial impact on how they behave and subsequently learn at school. In addition, interventions designed to increase academic skills do not necessarily lead to decreases in antisocial behavior (Patterson, Bank, & Stoolmiller, 1990), nor do they enhance social skills typically associated with academic achievement (Hopps & Cobb, 1974). Therefore, it is reasonable to assume that at least to some degree, behavioral competence precedes academic competence at school.

Relations between behavioral and academic competence, however, might not be as straightforward as this literature suggests. For instance, Hinshaw (1992) concludes that aggressive and delinquent behavior are stronger correlates of underachievement for adolescents than for elementary-aged children. Moreover, whereas aggressive, externalizing behavior in young children appears to be the result of academic difficulties, the reverse seems to be true for older children. At both stages of development, however, Hinshaw argues that associations are fairly weak, especially when other factors such as family influences or developmental delays are taken into account.

Interpersonal Relationships With Peers and Teachers

A final aspect of social competence that appears to be a valued educational objective is the formation of positive interpersonal relationships with peers and teachers. As with behavioral competence, positive interpersonal relationships are necessary for successful group functioning. In addition, it is likely that having positive and supportive relationships with teachers and peers contributes to feelings of relatedness and belongingness that in turn motivate the adoption of other socially valued goals (Connell & Wellborn, 1991). In the following sections, research on school adjustment as defined by peer relationships is discussed first, followed by research on teacher-student relationships.

Relationships With Peers

Although children are interested in and even emotionally attached to their peers at all ages, they exhibit increased interest in their peers and a growing psychological and emotional dependence on them for support and guidance as they make the transition into adolescence (Steinberg, 1990; Youniss & Smollar, 1989). One reason for this growing interest is that many young adolescents enter new middle school structures that necessitate interacting with larger numbers of peers on a daily basis. In contrast to the greater predictability of self-contained classroom environments in elementary school, the relative uncertainty and ambiguity of multiple classroom environments, new instructional styles, and more complex class schedules often result in middle school students turning to each other for information, social support, and ways to cope. Therefore, the quality of peer relationships is of special interest as an indicator of school adjustment in middle school and high school. At all ages, however, peer relationships have been studied in relation to a range of academic accomplishments.

Peer relationships have typically been defined in three ways: levels of peer acceptance or rejection, dyadic friendships, and peer groups. Peer acceptance and rejection are often assessed along a continuum of social preference (e.g., *How much do you like this person?*) or in terms of sociometric status groups (i.e., popular-, rejected-, neglected-, controversial-, and average-status children). Sociometrically rejected children are those who are infrequently nominated as someone's best friend and are actively disliked by their peers, whereas neglected children are those who are infrequently nominated as a best friend but are not strongly disliked by their peers. Controversial children are frequently nominated as someone's best friend and as being actively disliked, whereas popular children are frequently nominated as a best friend and rarely disliked by their peers. In general, when compared to average-status peers (i.e., students with scores that do not fall into these statistically defined groups), popular students tend to be more prosocial and sociable and less aggressive; rejected students tend to be less compliant, less self-assured, less sociable, and more aggressive and withdrawn; neglected students tend to be more motivated and compliant and less aggressive and sociable; and controversial students tend to be less compliant and more aggressive and sociable (Newcomb et al., 1993; Parkhurst & Asher, 1992; Wentzel, 1991a; Wentzel & Asher, 1995).

Most researchers interested in peer relationships and academic achievement have studied sociometric status or peer acceptance. Their work has yielded consistent findings relating popular status and acceptance to successful academic performance, and rejected status and low levels of acceptance to academic difficulties (e.g., Austin & Draper, 1984; DeRosier, Kupersmidt, & Patterson, 1994; Wentzel, 1991a). Findings are most consistent with respect to classroom grades (Hatzichristou & Hopf, 1996; Wentzel, 1991a), although peer acceptance has been related positively to standardized test scores (Austin & Draper, 1984) as well as IQ (Wentzel, 1991a). Moreover, results are robust for elementary-aged children as well as adolescents, and longitudinal studies document the stability of these relations over time (e.g., Wentzel & Caldwell, 1997).

In addition to measures of cognitive and academic ability, being accepted by peers also has been related positively to motivational outcomes, including satisfaction with school, pursuit of goals to learn and to behave in socially appropriate ways (Wentzel, 1994; Wentzel & Asher, 1995), and perceived academic competence (Hymel, Bowker, & Woody, 1993). In contrast, being rejected by peers has been related to low levels of interest in school (Wentzel & Asher, 1995) and disengaging altogether by dropping out (Hymel, Comfort, Schonert-Reichl, & McDougall, 1996; Parker & Asher, 1987). Peer status also has been related to prosocial and socially responsible goal pursuit during middle school (Wentzel, 1991b). When compared with average-status children, popular children reported more frequent pursuit of prosocial goals, neglected students reported more frequent pursuit of prosocial and social responsibility goals, and controversial students reported less frequent pursuit of responsibility goals.

Peers also exert influence at the level of dyadic relationships, or friendships, and within smaller cliques and groups (Brown, 1989). In general, when children are with friends, they engage in more positive interactions, resolve more conflicts, and accomplish tasks with greater proficiency than they do when they are with nonfriends (Newcomb & Bagwell, 1995). Research linking friendships to academic achievement is sparse. However, having friends has been related positively to grades and test scores in elementary school and middle school (Berndt & Keefe, 1995; Wentzel & Caldwell, 1997). During adolescence, stable, reciprocal friendships also appear to have a greater impact on educational outcomes than do unreciprocated and unstable friendships (Epstein, 1989; Kandel, 1978). Although almost all of these findings have been correlational, a recent longitudinal study suggests that the relation of having a friend to positive academic achievements is stable over 2 years of middle school (Wentzel & Caldwell, 1997).

Having friends also has been related to other aspects of school adjustment. For instance, children entering kindergarten with existing friends and those who are able to make new friends appear to make better social and academic adjustments to school than do those who do not (Ladd, 1990; Ladd & Price, 1987). Having friends at school also appears to support other motivational outcomes such as involvement and engagement in school-related activities (Berndt & Keefe, 1995; Berndt, Laychak, & Park, 1990; Ladd, 1990; Ladd & Price, 1987; Wentzel & Caldwell, 1997). In kindergarten, friendships characterized by nurturance predict positive motivational outcomes such as liking school and engaging in classroom activities, whereas those characterized by conflict predict less than optimal outcomes (Ladd, Kochenderfer, & Coleman, 1996). For the most part, dyadic friendships in adolescence appear to exert only minimal overt influence on student motivation (see Berndt & Keefe, 1996). However, Berndt and Keefe argue that when influence in adolescence does occur, it is likely to support positive behavior such as academic studying, making plans for college, and avoiding antisocial, self-destructive actions (e.g., Berndt et al., 1990; Epstein, 1983).

A final aspect of peer relationships that has been studied in relation to academic achievement is group membership. A distinction between friendship and peer group influence is important given that friendships reflect relatively private, egalitarian relationships, whereas peer groups, although they are often self-selected, are likely to have publicly acknowledged hierarchical relationships based on personal characteristics valued by the group (Brown, 1989; McAuliffe & Dembo, 1994). In contrast to peer status, which is measured by unilateral assessments of a child's relative standing or reputation within the peer group, group membership is typically assessed by asking students who actually hangs out in groups with each other or by identifying clusters of friends who form a group.

Adolescent peer groups seem to play several important roles in the social and emotional development of young people. Peer crowds are believed to serve two primary functions: to facilitate the formation of identity and self-concept and to structure ongoing social interactions with each other (Brown, Mory, & Kinney, 1994). With respect to identity formation, crowds are believed to provide adolescents with values, norms, and interaction styles that are sanctioned and commonly displayed. Behaviors and interaction styles that are characteristic of a crowd are modeled frequently so that they can be easily learned and adopted by individuals. In this manner, crowds provide prototypical examples of various identities for those who wish to try out different lifestyles, and crowds can easily affirm an adolescents' sense of self. As adolescents enter high school and the number of crowds increases (Brown et al., 1994), identities associated with crowds are more easily recognized and afford the opportunity to try on various social identities with relatively little risk.

The power of crowd influence is reflected in relations between crowd membership and adolescents' attitudes toward academic achievement. Clasen and Brown (1985) found that adolescent peer groups differ in the degree to which they pressure members to become involved in academic activities; so-called jocks and popular groups provided significantly more pressure for academic involvement than did other groups. Although peer group membership has rarely been linked to objective indexes of achievement, group membership has been related to motivational orientations toward learning and achievement as well as academic effort (Brown, 1989; Kindermann, 1993; Wentzel & Caldwell, 1997). Kindermann (1993; Kindermann, McCollam, & Gibson, 1996) reports that elementary-aged students tend to self-select into groups of peers that have motivational orientations to school similar to their own. Over the course of the school year, these orientations appear to become stronger and more similar within groups (see also Berndt et al., 1990; Hall & Cairns, 1984).

Relationships With Teachers

Teacher-student relationships have not been studied extensively in relation to children's achievement; however, children who are well-liked by teachers tend to get better grades than do those who are not as well liked (e.g., Hadley, 1954; Kelley, 1958; Wentzel & Asher, 1995; see also the chapter by Pianta, Hamre, & Stuhlman in this volume). The reasons for these significant relations are not clear, although there is some indication that student characteristics can influence the nature of teacher-student interactions and therefore can influence the quality of instruction received. For instance, the teachers observed in Brophy's research (Brophy & Good, 1974; Brophy & Evertson, 1978) reported that they were

more appreciative and positive toward students who were cooperative and persistent (i.e., behaviorally competent) than they were toward students who were less cooperative but displayed high levels of creativity and achievement. Teachers responded to students about whom they were concerned with help and encouragement when these students sought them out for help. In contrast, students toward whom they felt rejection were treated most often with criticism and typically were refused help. In short, these latter students were most likely to receive less one-on-one instruction than were other students.

Teachers' preference for students also appears to be related to the goals that students pursue (Wentzel, 1991b). Teacher preference (i.e., how much they would like to have each of their students in their class again next year) was related significantly and positively to students' reports of efforts to be socially responsible as well as to achieve positive evaluations of performance. Of particular interest is that teacher preference was not related to student pursuit of prosocial goals or goals to learn. Moreover, in a study of children without friends at school, Wentzel and Asher (1995) concluded that being liked by teachers might offset whatever the negative effects of peer rejection might be on children's adjustment to school. In particular, being liked by teachers was more important for the adoption of school-related goals than was a high level of acceptance among peers. Indeed, the most highly motivated group of students was comprised of young adolescents who had very few friends. However, these students were also those most preferred by teachers.

Implications for Future Research

Although establishing positive interpersonal relationships at school is an important aspect of school adjustment in and of itself, children's relationships with teachers and peers take on added significance when considered in relation to other aspects of school adjustment. On the one hand, it is likely that interpersonal relationships and other aspects of adjustment are interrelated. For instance, behavioral competence appears to mediate positive relationships between multiple aspects of peer relationships and academic achievement (Wentzel, 1991a, 1997). In addition, however, the extant literature indicates that these relations are likely reciprocal and complex. For instance, social rejection by peers can result in antisocial as well as other maladaptive forms of behavior. However, aggressive and antisocial forms of behavior also appear to be part of a maladaptive cycle of peer rejection, inappropriate behavior, and peer rejection, with behavioral incompetence often instigating initial peer rejection (Dodge, 1986). In some cases this is true of academic achievement as well, with peer rejection appearing after academic difficulties are experienced

(Dishion, 1990). Although similar work has not been conducted on teachers, children's relationships with parents can result in similar cycles of inappropriate behavior followed by harsh parenting, escalated child aggression, and finally maladaptive outcomes at school (Patterson & Bank, 1989). It is reasonable to expect that similar patterns of interaction might also develop with teachers.

Of central importance to a discussion of school adjustment, however, is how these behavioral competencies develop in the first place and how educators might intervene to facilitate positive adjustment when it has not occurred. One common explanation for how social influence takes place focuses on the motivational significance of children's social relationships. In general, it is hypothesized that children are more likely to adopt and internalize goals that are valued by others when their relationships are nurturing and supportive than they are when their relationships are harsh and critical (see Grusec & Goodnow, 1994). In turn, if goals for socially desirable outcomes have been internalized, efforts to achieve these goals and corresponding displays of appropriate behavior are likely to follow (Wentzel, 1991a, 1994). Given the centrality of goal pursuit for understanding multiple aspects of school adjustment, the role of interpersonal relationships with teachers and peers in explanations of why students pursue social goals is the focus of the following section.

SOCIAL INFLUENCES ON SCHOOL ADJUSTMENT

There are two general mechanisms whereby the aspects of school adjustment discussed in this chapter might be influenced by interpersonal interactions and relationships. First, interactions with adults and peers can provide children directly with resources that promote the development of specific competencies. These resources can take the form of information and advice, modeled behavior, or specific experiences that facilitate learning. In the classroom, students provide each other with valuable resources necessary to accomplish academic tasks (Sieber, 1979). Students frequently clarify and interpret their teacher's instructions concerning what they should be doing and how they should do it, provide mutual assistance in the form of volunteering substantive information and answering questions (Cooper, Ayers-Lopez, & Marquis, 1982), and share various supplies such as pencils and paper. Classmates provide each other with information by modeling both academic and social competencies (Schunk, 1987) and with normative standards for performance by comparing work and grades (Butler, 1995; Guay, Boivin, & Hodges, 1999).

Second, social interactions can facilitate the development of intrapersonal outcomes related to the development of

social and academic skills. Theoretical models of these latter indirect influences describe the socialization process as one of communicating goals and expectations for specific behavioral outcomes and then providing a context wherein these goals are learned and subsequently internalized (see Darling & Steinberg, 1993; Grusec & Goodnow, 1994). Therefore, the challenge is to identify the socialization processes that lead children to pursue certain goals and not others, and to develop generalized social orientations that direct behavior across multiple settings.

The present discussion focuses on children's motivation to achieve valued social goals as a central target of socialization influences from adults and peers. A thorough review of work on parental influence and children's school adjustment is beyond the scope of this chapter. However, models of parental socialization are relevant for understanding ways in which teachers might influence their students' adjustment. Therefore, I discuss work on parents as socializers of children's motivation first, followed by a description of ways in which effective teachers are similar to effective parents. Next, literature on peers as socializers of student motivation is discussed.

Adult Socialization of Children's Goal Pursuit

Although children pursue goals for many reasons, the question of what leads them to pursue goals for their own sake without the need for external prompts or rewards lies at the heart of research on socialization (e.g., Grusec & Goodnow, 1994; Maccoby, 1992). One way to understand this phenomenon with respect to schooling is to consider goals to be internalized when a student pursues them consistently across many learning situations. These goals could represent outcomes in which a student is intrinsically interested or those for which he or she has acquired personal value (e.g., Ryan, 1993). If specific socialization experiences promote the development of these internalized goals, how then does this influence occur? For the most part, mechanisms that link parenting styles to children's internalization of specific goals have not been the target of empirical investigations. However, many researchers have identified general types of parental behavior that relate to their children's motivational and behavioral adjustment to school. Their work is reviewed in the following section.

Parents as Socializers

Much research on parental influence on children's school functioning has focused on links between particular types of parenting styles and child outcomes (Ryan, Adams,

Gullotta, Weissberg, & Hampton, 1995). Based on extensive observations of parents and children, Diana Baumrind concluded that specific dimensions of parent-child interactions could predict reliably children's social, emotional, and cognitive competence (Baumrind, 1971, 1991). In general, these dimensions reflect consistent enforcement of rules, expectations for self-reliance and self-control, solicitation of children's opinions and feelings, and expressions of warmth and approval. Of interest for the present discussion is that parenting behavior reflecting these dimensions has been associated with children's academic motivation, including intrinsic interest (Ginsberg & Bronstein, 1993; Rathunde, 1996) and goal orientations toward learning (Hokoda & Fincham, 1995). Although studies provide little evidence that specific parenting practices promote the consistent pursuit of specific social goals, they do indicate that motivational processes might be a critical outcome of socialization experiences that can partly explain school adjustment outcomes.

A more specific model of influence proposed by Ryan (1993) recognizes the importance of parenting styles similar to those identified by Baumrind and speaks directly to the issue of why children adopt and internalize socially valued goals (for similar arguments, see Deci & Ryan, 1991; Connell & Wellborn, 1991; Grolnick, Kurowski, & Gurland, 1999; Lepper, 1983). Ryan argues that within the context of a secure parent-child relationship in which caregivers provide contingent feedback, nurturing, and developmentally appropriate structure and guidance, young children develop a generalized positive sense of social relatedness, personal competence, and autonomy when presented with new experiences and challenges. These positive aspects of self-development then support the internalization of socially prescribed goals and values—that is, "the transformation of external controls and regulations into internal ones" (Ryan, 1993, p. 29). In contrast, children who do not experience secure relationships tend to enter situations with detachment or high levels of emotional distress.

This perspective on parent socialization implies that students' orientations toward achieving socially valued outcomes in the classroom, including academic success, might be part of an overarching or more global motivational system derived from early socialization experiences. Although it is limited, research supports this notion. For instance, young children's initial orientations toward achievement of academic tasks appears to be grounded in children's fundamental view of themselves as morally and socially acceptable human beings (Burhans & Dweck, 1995; Dweck, 1991; Heyman, Dweck, & Cain, 1992). Further, Heyman et al. (1992) report that these beliefs are related to children's reports of how they think their parents will react to their successes and failures;

children who express relatively maladaptive orientations toward failure also report high levels of parental criticism, and those who express positive orientations report caring and supportive parental responses. At a more general level, researchers have related aspects of parenting to young children's sense of relatedness, personal competence, and autonomy (Grolnick & Slowiaczek, 1994).

Although Ryan's (1993) model of internalization poses the intriguing hypothesis that the foundations for internalization can only be laid within the context of early socialization experiences, it is likely that teachers can influence which classroom-specific goals children choose to pursue. First, teachers define appropriate types of classroom behavior and standards for social as well as academic competence. In doing so, they provide students with information concerning which goals they should and should not pursue. Second, teachers appear to establish contexts that reflect those provided by effective parents (e.g., Grolnick & Ryan, 1989; Skinner & Belmont, 1993; Wentzel, 2002a). In doing so, they likely promote directly the adoption and pursuit (if not internalization) of classroom-specific goals.

Teachers as Socializers of Classroom Rules and Norms

Like parents, teachers communicate socially valued goals and expectations to their students. Teachers are sensitive to individual differences in classroom conduct, value socially competent behavior, and spend an enormous amount of time teaching their students how to behave and act responsibly (see Doyle, 1986). In fact, teachers tend to have a core set of behavioral expectations for their students reflecting appropriate responses to academic requests and tasks, impulse control, mature problem solving, cooperative and courteous interaction with peers, involvement in class activities, and recognition of appropriate contexts for different types of behavior (LeCompte, 1978a, 1978b; Trenholm & Rose, 1981). Moreover, teachers actively communicate these expectations to their students—regardless of their instructional goals, teaching styles, and ethnicity (Hargreaves, Hester, & Mellor, 1975). Teachers also communicate expectations for students' interactions with each other. High school teachers promote adherence to interpersonal rules concerning aggression, manners, stealing, and loyalty (Hargreaves et al., 1975), and elementary school teachers tend to focus on peer norms for sharing resources, being nice to each other, working well with others, and harmonious problem solving (Sieber, 1979). Teachers also communicate directly to students when students need to pay attention as a function of which contexts they are in (Shultz & Florio, 1979) and when and where it is appropriate to interact with peers (Sieber, 1979).

Teachers tend to promote prosocial and socially responsible behavior in several ways. For instance, various classroom management practices can be used to establish group order and control (see Doyle, 1986). Blumenfeld and her colleagues (Blumenfeld, Hamilton, Bossert, Wessels, & Meece, 1983; Blumenfeld, Hamilton, Wessels, & Faulkner, 1979) have documented specific ways in which social responsibility is taught at school. In particular, they have studied teacher communications to students that relay why students ought to behave in certain ways—that ascribe causal attributions for students' behavior and suggest sanctions for classroom conduct. These researchers found that teachers' communications reflect specific issues concerning academic performance, academic procedures (i.e., proper ways to do work), social procedures (e.g., talking, adhering to social conventions), and social-moral norms (e.g., cheating, fighting). Within the procedural and social-moral domain, 46% of the academic procedure statements concerned staying on task, 51% of the social procedure statements concerned talking, and 57% of the social-moral statements concerned respect for others. The power of these communications was reflected in that they were related to students' ratings of how important classroom procedures and norms were to them personally.

Developmental issues also are important with respect to the influence of teachers' communications on students' beliefs about behavior at school. For example, Smetana and Bitz (1996) reported that almost all adolescents believe that teachers have authority over issues such as stealing and fighting, somewhat less authority over issues such as misbehaving in class, breaking school rules, and smoking or substance abuse, and least authority over issues involving peer interactions, friendships, and personal appearance. Moreover, when compared to beliefs about the authority of their parents and friends to dictate their school behavior, adolescents reported that teachers have more authority with respect to moral issues such as stealing and fighting and conventional rules involving school and classroom conduct. Adolescent students also believed that teachers have as much authority as do parents with respect to smoking or substance abuse. These beliefs, however, tended to change as children got older; younger adolescents in middle school reported that teachers have legitimate authority in all areas of school conduct, and older adolescents in high school believed that teachers have little authority over most aspects of students' lives at school.

Teachers as Providers of Appropriate Contexts

In addition to communicating to students what they should be trying to achieve, teachers also can provide students with contexts that have the potential to either support or discourage the adoption of these goals. For instance, in studies of elementary school-aged students, teacher provisions of structure, guidance, and autonomy have been related to a range of positive, motivational outcomes (e.g., Grolnick & Ryan, 1989; Skinner & Belmont, 1993). Birch and Ladd (1996) report that young children's healthy adjustment to school is related to teacher-student relationships characterized by warmth and the absence of conflict as well as open communication. In contrast, kindergartners' relationships with teachers marked by conflict and dependency predict less than adaptive academic and behavioral outcomes through eighth grade—especially for boys (Hamre & Pianta, 2001). When teachers are taught to provide students with warmth and support, clear expectations for behavior, and developmentally appropriate autonomy, their students develop a stronger sense of community, increase displays of socially competent behavior, and show academic gains (Schaps, Battistich, & Solomon, 1997; Watson, Solomon, Battistich, Schaps, & Solomon, 1989).

Teachers also structure learning environments in ways that make certain goals more salient than other goals to students. For example, cooperative learning structures can be designed to promote the pursuit of social goals to be responsible to the group and to achieve common objectives (Ames & Ames, 1984; Cohen, 1986; Solomon, Schaps, Watson, & Battistich, 1992). Teachers also provide students with evaluation criteria and design tasks in ways that can focus attention on goals to learn and develop skills (task-related and intellectual goals) or to demonstrate ability to others (performance goals; see Ames, 1992; Blumenfeld, 1992). Teachers who provide students with a diverse set of tasks that are challenging, have personal relevance, and promote skill development are likely to foster pursuit of mastery goals; teachers who use normative and comparative evaluation criteria and who provide students with controlling, noncontingent extrinsic rewards are likely to promote pursuit of performance goals (see Ames, 1992; Lepper & Hodell, 1989).

It is interesting that theoretical models developed to explain how teachers promote positive student outcomes are quite similar to family socialization models (Baumrind, 1971; Ryan, 1993). For instance, Noddings (1992) suggested that four aspects of teacher behavior are critical for understanding the establishment of an ethic of caring in classrooms: modeling caring relationships with others, establishing dialogues characterized by a search for common understanding, providing confirmation to students that their behavior is perceived and interpreted in a positive light, and providing practice and opportunities for students to care for others. Noddings' notions of dialogue and confirmation correspond closely with Baumrind's parenting dimensions of democratic communication styles and maturity demands. Moreover, empirical findings provide some support for these models. When asked to characterize teachers who care (Wentzel, 1997), middle school students described teachers who demonstrate democratic and egalitarian communication styles designed to elicit student participation and input, who develop expectations for student behavior and performance in light of individual differences and abilities, who model a caring attitude and interest in their instruction and interpersonal dealings with students, and who provide constructive rather than harsh and critical feedback. Moreover, students who perceive their teachers to display high levels of these characteristics also tend to pursue appropriate social and academic classroom goals more frequently than do students who do not (Wentzel, 2002a).

Little is known about how teachers define their roles as socialization agents. In a recent interview study, however, middle school teachers offered a variety of important things that they did in the classroom—ranging from instruction to promoting students' social and emotional development (Wentzel, 2000). For instance, half of the 20 teachers mentioned promoting social-emotional development as an important part of their job, 40% mentioned instruction and establishing positive teacher-student relationships, and 33% mentioned classroom management and the teaching of learning skills. In addition, a good day for teachers was typically described as one in which students are motivated and on task, whereas bad days were those in which classroom management issues and problems with instruction were prevalent.

Peers as Socializers of School Adjustment

Models of socialization by adults have not been used to understand ways in which children influence each other's development. In fact, interactions with peers have been viewed most often as having a potentially negative impact on the pursuit and achievement of educational goals (Berndt, 1999). Group work is often seen as antithetical to individual achievement, and peer norms are generally believed to be antagonistic to those of the school. However, peer acceptance among school-aged children is based in large part on cooperative, prosocial, and nonaggressive types of behavior (Coie et al., 1990), and positive peer interactions tend to promote the development of perspective-taking and empathic skills that serve as bases for prosocial interactions (e.g., Youniss, 1994; Youniss & Smollar, 1985). Moreover, as noted earlier, positive relationships with peers have been consistently related to positive academic outcomes.

Can parenting or teacher models of socialization be used to understand peer influence? Although empirical evidence is generally lacking, children—like adults—articulate sets of goals that they would like and expect each other to achieve.

Specific aspects of peer contexts and interactions that lead children to pursue these goals are not well understood. However, peer group membership has been associated with the development of classroom goals in several ways. For example, the larger peer group can be the source for behavioral standards, as well as the mechanism whereby classroom rules are monitored and enforced; this is especially the case when students as a group are held accountable for the behavior of the group's members or when teachers use peer group leaders to monitor the class when they must leave their classrooms (Sieber, 1979). Students also have been observed to monitor each other by ignoring noninstructional behavior and responses during group instruction and by private sanctioning of inappropriate conduct (Eder & Felmlee, 1984; Sieber, 1979).

Cooperative learning activities can also provide contexts in which peers hold each other accountable to certain standards of conduct. Indeed, socially responsible behavior in the form of helping and sharing knowledge and expertise is an integral part of the cooperative learning process (Ames & Ames, 1984; Slavin, 1987). With respect to goal pursuit, the group enforces individual efforts to achieve common goals that represent both social and task-related outcomes (see also Sherif, Harvey, White, Hood, & Sherif, 1988). It should be noted, however, that peer monitoring of behavior is a useful motivational tool only insofar as the peer group has adopted adult standards for achievement and norms for conduct. As children enter middle school and establishing independence from adult influence becomes a developmental task, it is less likely that students will automatically enforce their teachers' classroom rules (Eccles & Midgley, 1989).

Students' Beliefs as Mediating Processes

Of final interest for a discussion of socialization influences is that differences in the degree to which a student believes that teachers and peers accept and care about him or her might account in large part for significant links between the nature of interpersonal relationships at school and aspects of school adjustment. Indeed, individuals construct beliefs about themselves and their social worlds as they experience and interact with others. Subjective beliefs concerning acceptance and support from classmates and teachers represent an important aspect of social cognitive functioning that might influence behavior to a greater degree than actual levels of acceptance and support (see Harter, 1996; Harter, Stocker, & Robinson, 1996; Parker & Asher, 1987). The role of these beliefs in explaining ways in which teachers and peers exert influence is explored next.

Research on perceived social support underscores the important role that students' perceptions and interpretations of their peers' and teachers' behavior plays in their active pursuit of appropriate classroom goals. Few studies have examined sociometric status in relation to students' own perceptions of their peer relationships (cf. Zakriski & Coie, 1996). However, students who believe that their peers support and care about them tend to be more engaged in positive aspects of classroom life than do students who do not perceive such support. In particular, perceived social and emotional support from peers has been associated positively with prosocial outcomes such as helping, sharing, and cooperating, and it has been related negatively to antisocial forms of behavior (Wentzel, 1994). Young adolescents who do not perceive their relationships with peers as positive and supportive also tend to be at risk for academic problems (e.g., Goodenow, 1993; Midgley, Feldlaufer, & Eccles, 1989; Phelan et al., 1991). In addition, perceived social and emotional support from peers has been associated with pursuit of academic and prosocial goals (DuBois, Felner, Brand, Adan, & Evans, 1992; Felner, Aber, Primavera, & Cauce, 1985; Harter, 1996; Wentzel, 1994, 1997, 1998). It is interesting that perceived support from peers appears to be more strongly related to pursuit of goals to be prosocial than is perceived support from parents and teachers (Wentzel, 1998).

Perceived support from teachers also has been related to positive motivational outcomes, including the pursuit of goals to learn and to behave prosocially and responsibly, educational aspirations and values, and self-concept (Felner et al., 1985; Goodenow, 1993; Harter, 1996; Marjoribanks, 1985; Midgley et al., 1989; Wentzel, 1994). In middle school, students' perceptions that teachers care about them have been related to positive aspects of student motivation such as pursuit of social and academic goals, mastery orientations toward learning, and academic interest (Wentzel, 1997). In a recent study of perceived support from teachers, parents, and peers (Wentzel, 1998), perceived support from teachers was unique in its relation to students' interest in class and pursuit of goals to adhere to classroom rules and norms. Finally, Eccles and her colleagues (Feldlaufer, Midgley, & Eccles, 1988; Midgley et al., 1989) found that young adolescents report declines in the nurturing qualities of teacher-student relationships after the transition to middle school; these declines correspond to declines in academic motivation and achievement. As students proceed through middle school, they also report that teachers become more focused on students' earning high grades, competition between students, and maintaining adult control, with a decrease in personal interest in students (Harter, 1990, 1996). Students who report these changes also tend to report less intrinsic motivation to achieve than do students who do not report such changes (Harter, 1996).

Implications for Future Research

A growing body of evidence suggests that models of socialization might be well suited for understanding which goals children pursue at school and the degree to which these goals have been internalized and represent personal values. Socialization models are especially important to consider with respect to the content of students' goals, given that successful students must achieve social and academic objectives that are imposed externally by adults. In this regard, it is important to note that some students reject these goals outright. It is likely that other students merely comply with these expectations and present the impression that they are interested in achieving what is required when in fact they are not (see Juvonen, 1996; Sivan, 1986). Some students, however, are likely to have internalized adult-valued goals and are committed to achieving them regardless of competing expectations. Therefore, identifying the precise socialization experiences that lead to these fundamentally different orientations toward learning remains a significant challenge to the field.

Several issues remain unresolved with respect to teacher influences on student goal setting. First, teachers tend to focus on different issues depending on the age of their students. For instance, teachers of early elementary and junior high school students tend to spend more of their time on issues related to social conduct than do teachers at other grade levels (Brophy & Evertson, 1978). In addition, the contribution of various socialization agents to the development and internalization of goals and values might also change with age. Whereas parents and teachers might facilitate the learning and adoption of goals in young children, peers might play an increasingly important role as children reach adolescence.

The reward structures that teachers establish in their classrooms also might have differential impact depending on students' age and family environment. Ames (1984, 1992) has identified several classroom reward structures that communicate the value of goals to compete with others, to improve one's own personal performance, and to cooperate with group efforts. However, middle school and high school students might be more attuned than are elementary-aged children to evaluation practices that are competitive and normative (see Harter, 1996; Ruble, 1983). Students from families who stress mastery over performance might also be less susceptible to teacher practices that focus on performance and ability (Ames & Archer, 1987). In addition, teachers are likely to differ in their promotion of specific classroom goals as well as beliefs concerning what it means to be a successful student. For example, a student who pursues social needs for relatedness and therefore chooses to adopt classroom goals valued by her or his teacher might learn that being better than others (pursuing competitive goals) defines success, whereas this same student might learn from another teacher that progressively mastering subject matter (achieving individualistic goals) or perhaps even behaving cooperatively (achieving prosocial goals) defines success (see Ames, 1984, 1992). Therefore, it is difficult to predict which students will be most successful without knowing the content of goals and belief systems being communicated by individual teachers.

Perhaps one of the more interesting questions with respect to socialization within peer contexts is the strength of peer influence compared to that of parents and other adults. Studies of parents and peers provide evidence that parents can influence their children to a much greater extent than can peers (Youniss & Smollar, 1989). Moreover, it appears that the existence or quality of peer relationships is not destined to influence motivation negatively *or* positively if supportive relationships with parents or teachers exist. With respect to practice, these findings imply that although peer influence might be strong, it can be superseded. In fact, interventions to offset the often negative influence of peer groups and gangs might be especially successful if children are exposed to interactions with adults who can instill a sense of autonomy, mutuality, warmth, and guidance into their relationships with these children (see Heath & McLaughlin, 1993). Moreover, peer group membership tends to change frequently, suggesting that influence by a particular group might also be fairly transient. Therefore, having access to adult relationships that are stable and predictable also should contribute positively to intervention efforts.

With respect to the issue of social support and student pursuit of socially valued goals, it is possible that students who perceive low levels of social support experience psychological distress that in turn will increase focus on the self and decrease the likelihood of positive orientations toward learning and social interactions. In support of this specific focus on emotion regulation are findings that perceived support from families is related negatively to depression and depressive affect in young adolescents (Cumsille & Epstein, 1994; Feldman, Rubenstein & Rubin, 1988; Kaplan, Robins, & Martin, 1983; Wenz-Gross, Siperstein, Untch & Widaman, 1997). Other studies have linked psychological distress and depression to interest in school (Wentzel, Weinberger, Ford, & Feldman, 1990) as well as to academic performance (Harter, 1990; Wentzel et al., 1990). Negative emotional states have been related to negative attitudes, poor adjustment to school (Dubow & Tisak, 1989), and ineffective cognitive functioning (Jacobsen, Edelstein, & Hofmann, 1994). The relevance of this literature for understanding the impact of social relationships on student

outcomes is demonstrated in recent work documenting that emotional distress can explain (in part) significant relations between perceived support from peers and young adolescents' interest in school (Wentzel, 1998), as well as between peer acceptance and adolescents' prosocial behavior (Wentzel & McNamara, 1999). Actual levels of peer rejection as well as peer harassment have also been linked to perceived academic competence and achievement by way of negative affect (Guay et al., 1999; Juvonen, Nishina, & Graham, 2000).

Future research also might focus on identifying additional student characteristics that predispose students to perceive relationships with adults and peers in either positive or negative ways. The literature on peer relationships suggests that children who are socially rejected tend to believe that others are out to harm them when in fact they are not, and such children choose to pursue inappropriate and often antisocial goals in social situations (see Dodge & Feldman, 1990; Erdley, 1996). Over time, these children develop peer relationships marked by mistrust and hostility. Similar research has not been conducted on student-teacher relationships. However, it is possible that students who believe that teachers do not like them might also be perceiving and interpreting these adult relationships in ways that are biased and unfounded. Therefore, efforts to promote perceptions that peers and teachers are caring and supportive are likely to be most successful if students themselves are targets of intervention.

It also is important to extend our understanding of the underlying belief systems that are reflected in a general perception of social support. In this regard, Ford (1992) has described a set of context beliefs about social relationships and settings that have the potential to link generalized perceptions of social support and belongingness to classroom functioning. Specifically, Ford argues that within specific situations, individuals formulate beliefs concerning the correspondence between their personal goals and those of others, the degree to which others will provide access to information and resources necessary to achieve one's goals, and the extent to which social relationships will provide an emotionally supportive environment. This implies that students will engage in positive social and academic activities when they perceive the classroom as a place that provides opportunities to achieve social and academic goals; as a safe and responsive environment; as a place that facilitates the achievement of goals by providing help, advice, and instruction; and as a place that is emotionally supportive and nurturing. Recent research (Wentzel et al., 2000) demonstrates that students can define their classroom relationships along these dimensions, with respect to teachers as well as to peers. Moreover, these dimensions appear to predict students' classroom behavior, their motivation to behave appropriately, and their interest in subject matter.

These context beliefs most likely reflect the outcome of students' history of interacting with specific teachers and peers at school. For instance, students who come to school with strong motives to behave prosocially rather than competitively (e.g., Knight & Kagan, 1977) might develop a generalized belief that classroom goals are antagonistic to their personal goals if they have a history of interacting with teachers who have rewarded demonstrations of superiority rather than equality. Similarly, students might have experienced teachers who have not taken the time to give them extra help (Brophy & Evertson, 1978) or who have failed to provide opportunities for students to model skills for each other in interactive settings (Schunk, 1987). These students also are likely to perceive the classroom as an unsupportive if not hostile learning environment. Research that examines the degree to which negative context beliefs can be changed to reflect a more positive outlook might provide valuable insights into ways that the social context of the classroom can be engineered to have a maximum impact on students' adoption and pursuit of appropriate classroom goals.

CONCLUSIONS AND PROVOCATIONS FOR THE FIELD

Throughout this chapter, I have highlighted the importance of defining school adjustment within an ecological, systemic framework. In doing so, I have documented the importance of social motivational processes, behavioral competence, and interpersonal relationships not only as critical aspects of school adjustment, but also as a complex and interrelated set of outcomes that contribute to academic accomplishments. In addition, work that underscores the importance of students' interpersonal relationships with teachers and peers in promoting healthy and adaptive functioning at school has been described. Although definitions of school adjustment and the relative importance of various outcomes are likely to vary depending on context-specific values and norms of a classroom, the literature provides strong support for the notion that general levels of adjustment require personal attributes such as the ability to coordinate multiple goals, motivation to behave in socially desirable ways, and the social skills necessary to behave in socially competent ways. In turn, it appears that the development of these personal attributes can be supported by developmentally appropriate expectations for behavior, as well as provisions of emotional and social support, autonomy, and consistency and structure on the part of teachers and peers.

Beyond these basic observations, however, many interesting and provocative questions remain. In conclusion, therefore,

I would like to raise several general issues in need of additional consideration and empirical investigation if educational psychologists are to make progress in understanding children's adjustment to school. These issues concern the expectations and goals we hold for our students, the role of developmental processes in choosing these goals (and therefore in how we view healthy adjustment), the development of more sophisticated models to guide research on school adjustment, and research methods and designs.

Defining School Adjustment

Perhaps our most important task as researchers and educators is to come to terms with the questions raised at the beginning of this chapter: What are our educational goals for our children? Do we want to teach simply to the test or nurture our children in ways that will help them become productive and healthy adults and citizens? By the same token, what are the goals that children bring with them to school? Do they strive to excel in relation to their peers, satisfy their curiosities, get along with others, or simply feel safe? In order to understand fully children's adjustment to school, it is imperative that we continue to seek answers to these questions and identify ways to coordinate these often antagonistic goals to achieve a healthy balance of multiple objectives. Indeed, the process of achieving more adaptive levels of adjustment will always include negotiations and coordination of the multiple and often conflicting goals of teachers, peers, students themselves, and their parents.

Although we as educational psychology researchers are beginning to understand the basic goals that most teachers and students wish to achieve, we know little about how and why students come to learn about and to adopt these goals as their own. For instance, how do teachers communicate their expectations and goals to students, and which factors predispose students to accept or reject these communications? We know that parental messages are more likely to be perceived accurately by children if they are clear and consistent, are framed in ways that are relevant and meaningful to the child, require decoding and processing by the child, and are perceived by the child as being of clear importance to the parent and as being conveyed with positive intentions (Grusec & Goodnow, 1994). Do these same factors reflect effective forms of teacher-student communication—and if so, can we teach teachers to communicate goals and expectations to their students in similar ways?

Similarly, we need to focus on understanding student characteristics that facilitate their acceptance of teachers' communications. Motivational factors such as perceived autonomy, competence, and belongingness (e.g., Connell & Wellborn,

1991) and social-emotional competencies such as the ability to experience empathy and interpersonal trust (see Grusec & Goodnow, 1994) are well-documented correlates of compliance with—if not internalization of—socially valued goals. Other factors such as students' beliefs regarding the fairness, relevance, and developmental appropriateness of teachers' goals and expectations also need to be investigated in this regard (e.g., Smetana & Bitz, 1996). Finally, social information processing skills that determine which social messages and cues are attended to, how they are interpreted, and how they are responded to are a critical component of socially competent behavior (Crick & Dodge, 1994). These skills have been widely researched in the area of peer relationships; extending our knowledge of their influence to the realm of teacher-student relationships and adaptation to classroom contexts is a necessary next step in research on school adjustment.

Developmental Processes

If the achievement of socially valued goals is accepted as a critical component of school adjustment, investigations of appropriate goals and expectations also must be conducted within a developmental framework, taking into account the age-related capabilities of the child. Issues of developmentally appropriate practices have been addressed primarily at the level of preschool education. However, a consideration of developmental issues is critically important for students of all ages. To illustrate, Grolnick (Grolnick et al., 1999) argues that children face normative motivational challenges as they make their way through school; issues of social integration define the transition to school, the development self-regulatory skills and positive perceptions of autonomy and competence define the elementary years, and flexible coping and adaptation to new environments mark the transitions into middle and high school. The undertaking and mastery of these developmental tasks as they relate to school activities need to be incorporated into definitions and models of school adjustment and recognized as core competencies that children need to achieve as they progress through their school-aged years.

A developmental focus also is necessary for understanding the demands on teachers of students of different ages. Researchers (e.g., Brophy & Good, 1974; Eccles & Midgley, 1989) have observed that teachers treat students differently and focus on different tasks and goals depending on the age of their students. At this point, we do not know if changing developmental needs of students or normative and societal expectations for children at different ages drive these differences. However, if we are to understand the nature and requirements of school adjustment, a critical look at the abilities of children at different ages as well as the normative

requirements for competent classroom functioning is necessary. Systematic longitudinal and experimental research is needed to tease apart the relative contributions of children and teachers to patterns of classroom behavior and student-teacher interactions that appear to change across the elementary, middle school, and high school years.

Theory Building

As noted throughout this chapter, theoretically based models of school adjustment are not well developed. In particular, the role of context as it interacts with individual differences and psychological processes needs careful and systematic consideration. First, models need to address the possible ways in which children and the various social systems in which they develop—including home, peer groups, and schools—interact to create definitions of school-related competence (see Bronfenbrenner, 1989). In this regard, models that incorporate lay theories of what it means to be successful and beliefs concerning how success is achieved are essential (see Ogbu, 1985; Sternberg & Kolligian, 1990). How these beliefs change as children develop and ways in which they contribute to children's developing school-related goal hierarchies should be a primary target of researchers' efforts. Models of socialization also need to be developed with specific types of social relationship configurations in mind (e.g., dyads vs. groups, friendships vs. acquaintanceships) and perhaps modified depending on whether the relationships are with parents, peers, or teachers, and whether the target student is in elementary, middle, or high school. Similarly, the impact of other social context factors such as gender, race, and culture need to be incorporated into the model. Continued research on classroom reward structures (Ames, 1984), organizational culture and climate (Maehr & Midgley, 1991), and person-environment fit (Eccles & Midgley, 1989) also can inform our understanding of how the social institutions and contexts within which learning takes place can motivate children to learn and behave in very specific ways.

Theoretical considerations of school adjustment also must continue to focus on underlying psychological processes and skills that promote the development and display of adjustment outcomes. For example, researchers have clearly established significant and powerful links between prosocial and socially responsible behaviors and academic accomplishments. What have not been identified, however, are the psychological underpinnings of these behaviors. Research on skills and strategies involved in emotion regulation (Eisenberg & Fabes, 1992), self-regulated learning (see the chapter by Schunk & Zimmerman in this volume), social information processing (Crick & Dodge, 1994), and goal coordination (Wentzel,

1991b, 2002b) might be particularly fruitful in determining the degree to which multiple aspects of school adjustment (e.g., prosocial behavior, academic performance) reflect a core set of psychological and emotional competencies as well as the degree to which social behaviors themselves contribute directly to learning outcomes.

Research Methods and Designs

Our current understanding of school adjustment is based primarily on correlational studies of white middle-class children. Correlational strategies have resulted in a wealth of data that can serve as a strong foundation for further theory building and research. However, continued investigations in this area would profit from extending these simple correlational designs to incorporate ethnographic as well as experimental components. For instance, understanding what constitutes school adjustment in a classroom or broader school setting requires in-depth conversations with and extensive observations of students and teachers as they carry out their day-to-day lives at school. In addition, identifying ways to promote school adjustment requires careful, systematic long-term intervention studies. Although such projects are rare (cf. Schaps et al., 1997; Solomon et al., 1992), ongoing research involving experimentation and evaluation of progress is essential if we are to identify strategies and experiences that will improve the lives of students in significant ways.

In addition to design considerations, researchers also need to focus on more diverse samples. Although it is likely that the underlying psychological processes that contribute to school adjustment are similar for all students regardless of race, ethnicity, gender, or other contextual and demographic variables, the degree to which these latter factors interact with psychological processes to influence adjustment outcomes is not known. For instance, goal coordination skills might be more important for the adjustment of children from minority backgrounds than for children who come from families and communities whose goals and expectations are similar to those of the educational establishment (e.g., Fordham & Ogbu, 1986; Phelan et al., 1991). Peer relationship skills might be especially important for adjustment in schools where peer cultures are particularly strong or where collaborative and cooperative learning is emphasized. Achieving a better understanding of such interactions deserves our full attention. Similarly, definitions of competence and adjustment are likely to vary as a function of race, gender, neighborhood, or family background. Expanding our database to include the voices of underrepresented populations can only enrich our understanding of how and why children make successful adaptations to school.

REFERENCES

Alexander, K. L., Entwisle, D. R., & Dauber, S. L. (1993). First-grade classroom behavior: Its short- and long-term consequences for school performance. *Child Development, 64,* 801–814.

Allen, J. D. (1986). Classroom management: Students' perspectives, goals, and strategies. *American Educational Research Journal, 23,* 437–459.

Ames, C. (1984). Competitive, cooperative, and individualistic goal structures: A cognitive-motivational analysis. In R. Ames & C. Ames (Eds.), *Research in motivation in education* (Vol. 1, pp. 177–208). New York: Academic Press.

Ames, C. (1992). Classrooms: Goals, structures, and student motivation. *Journal of Educational Psychology, 84,* 261–271.

Ames, C., & Ames, R. (1984). Systems of student and teacher motivation: Toward a qualitative definition. *Journal of Educational Psychology, 76,* 535–556.

Ames, C., & Archer, J. (1987). Mothers' beliefs about the role of ability and effort in school learning. *Journal of Educational Psychology, 79,* 409–414.

Austin, A. B., & Draper, D. C. (1984). The relationship among peer acceptance, social impact, and academic achievement in middle school. *American Educational Research Journal, 21,* 597–604.

Austin, J. T., & Vancouver, J. B. (1996). Goal constructs in psychology: Structure, process, and content. *Psychological Bulletin, 120,* 338–375.

Bandura, A. (1986). *Social foundations of thought and action: A social cognitive theory.* Englewood Cliffs, NJ: Prentice-Hall.

Baumrind, D. (1971). Current patterns of parental authority. *Developmental Psychology Monograph, 4*(1, Pt. 2).

Baumrind, D. (1991). Effective parenting during the early adolescent transition. In P. A Cowan & M. Hetherington (Eds.), *Family transitions* (pp. 111–164). Hillsdale, NJ: Erlbaum.

Berndt, T. J. (1999). Friends' influence on students' adjustment to school. *Educational Psychologist, 34,* 15–28.

Berndt, T. J., & Keefe, K. (1995). Friends' influence on adolescents' adjustment to school. *Child Development, 66,* 1312–1329.

Berndt, T. J., & Keefe, K. (1996). Friends' influence on school adjustment: A motivational analysis. In J. Juvonen & K. Wentzel (Eds.), *Social motivation: Understanding children's school adjustment* (pp. 248–278). New York: Cambridge.

Berndt, T. J., Laychak, A. E., & Park, K. (1990). Friends' influence on adolescents' academic achievement motivation: An experimental study. *Journal of Educational Psychology, 82,* 664–670.

Birch, S. H., & Ladd, G. W. (1996). Interpersonal relationships in the school environment and children's early school adjustment: The role of teachers and peers. In J. Juvonen & K. Wentzel (Eds.), *Social motivation: Understanding children's school adjustment* (pp. 199–225). New York: Cambridge University Press.

Blumenfeld, P. C. (1992). Classroom learning and motivation: Clarifying and expanding goal theory. *Journal of Educational Psychology, 84,* 272–281.

Blumenfeld, P. C., Hamilton, V. L., Bossert, S. T., Wessels, K., & Meece, J. (1983). Teacher talk and student thought: Socialization into the student role. In J. M. Levine & M. C. Wang (Eds.), *Teacher and student perceptions: Implications for learning* (pp. 143–192). Hillsdale, NJ: Erlbaum.

Blumenfeld, P. C., Hamilton, V. L., Wessels, K., & Faulkner, D. (1979). Teaching responsibility to first graders. *Theory Into Practice, 18,* 174–180.

Bronfenbrenner, U. (1989). Ecological systems theory. In R. Vasta (Ed.), *Annals of child development* (Vol. 6, pp. 187–250). Greenwich, CT: JAI.

Brophy, J. E., & Evertson, C. M. (1978). Context variables in teaching. *Educational Psychologist, 12,* 310–316.

Brophy, J. E., & Good, T. L. (1974). *Teacher-student relationships: Causes and consequences.* New York: Holt, Rinehart & Winston.

Brown, B. B. (1989). The role of peer groups in adolescents' adjustment to secondary school. In T. J. Berndt & G. W. Ladd (Eds.), *Peer relationships in child development* (pp. 188–215). New York: Wiley.

Brown, B. B., Mory, M. S., & Kinney, D. (1994). Casting adolescent crowds in a relational perspective: Caricature, channel, and context. In R. Montemayor, G. R. Adams, & T. P. Gullotta (Eds.), *Personal relationships during adolescence* (pp. 123–167). Newbury Park, CA: Sage.

Burhans, K. K., & Dweck, C. S. (1995). Helplessness in early childhood: The role of contingent worth. *Child Development, 66,* 1719–1738.

Butler, R. (1995). Motivational and informational functions and consequences of children's attention to peers' work. *Journal of Educational Psychology, 87,* 347–360.

Carroll, A., Durkin, K., Hattie, J., & Houghton, S. (1997). Goal setting among adolescents: A comparison of delinquent, at-risk, and not-at-risk youth. *Journal of Educational Psychology, 89,* 441–450.

Clasen, D. R., & Brown, B. B. (1985). The multidimensionality of peer pressure in adolescence. *Journal of Youth and Adolescence, 14,* 451–468.

Cobb, J. A. (1972). Relationship of discrete classroom behaviors to fourth-grade academic achievement. *Journal of Educational Psychology, 63,* 74–80.

Cobb, J. A., & Hopps, H. (1973). Effects of academic survival skills training on low achieving first graders. *The Journal of Educational Research, 67,* 108–113.

Cohen, E. G. (1986). *Designing group work: Strategies for the heterogeneous classroom.* New York: Teachers College Press.

Coie, J. D., Dodge, K. A., & Kupersmidt, J. B. (1990). Peer group behavior and social status. In S. R. Asher & J. D. Coie (Eds.), *Peer rejection in childhood* (pp. 17–59). New York: Cambridge University Press.

Connell, J. P., & Wellborn, J. G. (1991). Competence, autonomy, and relatedness: A motivational analysis of self-system processes. In M. R. Gunnar & L. A. Sroufe (Eds.), *Self processes and development: The Minnesota symposia on child development* (Vol. 23, pp. 43–78). Hillsdale, NJ: Erlbaum.

Coolahan, K., Fantuzzo, J., Mendez, J., & McDermott, P. (2000). Preschool peer interactions and readiness to learn: Relationships between classroom peer play and learning behaviors and conduct. *Journal of Educational Psychology, 92,* 458–465.

Cooper, C. R., Ayers-Lopez, S., & Marquis, A. (1982). Children's discourse during peer learning in experimental and naturalistic situations. *Discourse Processes, 5,* 177–191.

Crick, N., & Dodge, K. A. (1994). A review and reformulation of social information-processing mechanisms in children's social adjustment. *Psychological Bulletin, 115,* 74–101.

Cumsille, P. E., & Epstein, N. (1994). Family cohesion, family adaptability, social support, and adolescent depressive symptoms in outpatient clinic families. *Journal of Family Psychology, 8,* 202–214.

Damon, W., & Phelps, E. (1989). Strategic uses of peer learning in children's education. In T. J. Berndt & G. W. Ladd (Eds.), *Peer relationships in child development* (pp. 133–157). New York: Wiley.

Darling, N., & Steinberg, L. (1993). Parenting style as context: An integrative model. *Psychological Bulletin, 113,* 487–496.

Deci, E. L., & Ryan, R. M. (1991). A motivational approach to self: Integration in personality. *Nebraska symposium on motivation 1990* (pp. 237–288). Lincoln: University of Nebraska Press.

DeRosier, M. E., Kupersmidt, J. B., & Patterson, C. J. (1994). Children's academic and behavioral adjustment as a function of the chronicity and proximity of peer rejection. *Child Development, 65,* 1799–1813.

Dishion, T. (1990). The family ecology of boys' peer relations in middle childhood. *Child Development, 61,* 874–892.

Dodge, K. A. (1986). A social information processing model of social competence in children. In M. Perlmutter (Ed.), *Minnesota symposium on child psychology* (Vol. 18, pp. 77–126). Hillsdale, NJ: Erlbaum.

Dodge, K. A., & Feldman, E. (1990). Issues in social cognition and sociometric status. In S. R. Asher & J. D. Coie (Eds.), *Peer rejection in childhood* (pp. 119–155). New York: Cambridge University Press.

Doyle, W. (1986). Classroom organization and management. In M. C. Witrock (Ed.), *Handbook of research on teaching* (pp. 392–431). New York: Macmillan.

DuBois, D. L., Felner, R. D., Brand, S., Adan, A. M., & Evans, E. G. (1992). A prospective study of life stress, social support, and adaptation in early adolescence. *Child Development, 63,* 542–557.

Dubow, E. F., & Tisak, J. (1989). The relation between stressful life events and adjustment in elementary school children: The role of social support and social problem-solving skills. *Child Development, 60,* 1412–1423.

Dweck, C. S. (1991). Self-theories and goals: Their role in motivation, personality, and development. In R. Dienstbier (Ed.),

Nebraska symposium on motivation (Vol. 38, pp. 199–236). Lincoln: University of Nebraska Press.

Dweck, C. S., & Leggett, E. L. (1988). A social-cognitive approach to motivation and personality. *Psychological Review, 95,* 256–272.

Eccles, J. S., & Midgley, C. (1989). Stage-environment fit: Developmentally appropriate classrooms for young adolescents. In C. Ames & R. Ames (Eds.), *Research on motivation in education* (Vol. 3, pp. 139–186). New York: Academic Press.

Eder, D. E., & Felmlee, D. (1984). The development of attention norms in ability groups. In P. L. Peterson, L. C. Wilkinson, & M. Hallinan (Eds.), *The social context of instruction: Group organization and group processes* (pp. 189–225). New York: Academic Press.

Eisenberg, N., & Fabes, R. A. (1992). Emotion, regulation, and the development of social competence. In M. S. Clark (Ed.), *Review of personality and social psychology: Vol. 14. Emotional and social behavior* (pp. 119–150). Newbury Park, CA: Sage.

Entwisle, D. R., Alexander, K. L., Pallas, A. M., & Cadigan, D. (1987). The emergent academic self-image of first graders: Its response to social structure. *Child Development, 58,* 1190–1206.

Epstein, J. L. (1983). The influence of friends on achievement and affective outcomes. In J. L. Epstein & N. Karweit (Eds.), *Friends in school* (pp. 177–200). New York: Academic Press.

Epstein, J. L. (1989). The selection of friends: Changes across the grades and in different school environments. In T. J. Berndt & G. W. Ladd (Eds.), *Peer relationships in child development* (pp. 158–187). New York: Wiley.

Erdley, C. A. (1996). Motivational approaches to aggression within the context of peer relationships. In J. Juvonen & K. Wentzel (Eds.), *Social motivation: Understanding children's school adjustment* (pp. 98–125). New York: Cambridge University Press.

Feldhusen, J. F., Thurston, J. R., & Benning, J. J. (1970). Longitudinal analyses of classroom behavior and school achievement. *Journal of Experimental Education, 38,* 4–10.

Feldlaufer, H., Midgley, C., & Eccles, J. S. (1988). Student, teacher, and observer perceptions of the classroom before and after the transition to junior high school. *Journal of Early Adolescence, 8,* 133–156.

Feldman, S. S., Rubenstein, J. L., & Rubin, C. (1989). Depressive affect and restraint in early adolescents: Relationships with family structure, family process and friendship support. *Journal of Early Adolescence, 8,* 279–296.

Felner, R. D., Aber, M. S., Primavera, J., & Cauce, A. M. (1985). Adaptation and vulnerability in high-risk adolescents: An examination of environmental mediators. *American Journal of Community Psychology, 13,* 365–379.

Feshbach, N. D. (1969). Student teacher preferences for elementary school pupils varying in personality characteristics. *Journal of Educational Psychology, 60,* 126–132.

Feshbach, N. D., & Feshbach, S. (1987). Affective processes and academic achievement. *Child Development, 58,* 1335–1347.

Ford, M. E. (1982). Social cognition and social competence in adolescence. *Developmental Psychology, 18,* 323–340.

Ford, M. E. (1984). Linking social-cognitive processes with effective social behavior: A living systems approach. In P. C. Kendall (Ed.), *Advances in cognitive-behavioral research and therapy* (Vol. 3, pp. 167–211). New York: Academic Press.

Ford, M. E. (1992). *Motivating humans: Goals, emotions, and personal agency beliefs.* Newbury Park, CA: Sage.

Ford, M. E. (1996). Motivational opportunities and obstacles associated with social responsibility and caring behavior in school contexts. In J. Juvonen & K. Wentzel (Eds.), *Social motivation: Understanding children's school adjustment* (pp. 126–153). New York: Cambridge University Press.

Fordham, S., & Ogbu, J. U. (1986). Black students' school success: Coping with "the burden of 'acting white.'" *The Urban Review, 18,* 176–206.

Ginsberg, G. S., & Bronstein, P. (1993). Family factors related to children's intrinsic/extrinsic motivational orientations and academic performance. *Child Development, 64,* 1461–1474.

Goodenow, C. (1993). Classroom belonging among early adolescent students: Relationships to motivation and achievement. *Journal of Early Adolescence, 13,* 21–43.

Graham, S., Taylor, A., & Hudley, C. (1998). Exploring achievement values among ethnic minority early adolescents. *Journal of Educational Psychology, 90,* 606–620.

Green, K. D., Forehand, R., Beck, S. J., & Vosk, B. (1980). An assessment of the relationships among measures of children's social competence and children's academic achievement. *Child Development, 51,* 1149–1156.

Grolnick, W. S., Kurowski, C. O., & Gurland, S. T. (1999). Family processes and the development of children's self-regulation. *Educational Psychologist, 34,* 3–14.

Grolnick, W. S., & Ryan, R. M. (1989). Parent styles associated with children's self-regulation and competence in school. *Journal of Educational Psychology, 81,* 143–154.

Grolnick, W. S., & Slowiaczek, M. L. (1994). Parents' involvement in children's schooling: A multidimensional conceptualization and motivational model. *Child Development, 65,* 237–252.

Grusec, J. E., & Goodnow, J. J. (1994). Impact of parental discipline methods on the child's internalization of values: A reconceptualization of current points of view. *Developmental Psychology, 30,* 4–19.

Guay, F., Boivin, M., & Hodges, E. V. E. (1999). Predicting change in academic achievement: A model of peer experiences and self-system processes. *Journal of Educational Psychology, 91,* 105–115.

Hadley, S. (1954). A school mark—fact or fancy? *Educational Administration and Supervision, 40,* 305–312.

Hall, W. M., & Cairns, R. B. (1984). Aggressive behavior in children: An outcome of modeling or social reciprocity? *Developmental Psychology, 20,* 739–745.

Hamre, B. K., & Pianta, R. C. (2001). Early teacher-child relationships and the trajectory of children's school outcomes through eighth grade. *Child Development, 72,* 625–638.

Hargreaves, D. H., Hester, S. K., & Mellor, F. J. (1975). *Deviance in classrooms.* London: Routledge & Kegan Paul.

Harter, S. (1990). Self and identity development. In S. S. Feldman & G. R. Elliott (Eds.), *At the threshold: The developing adolescent* (pp. 352–387). Cambridge, MA: Harvard University Press.

Harter, S. (1996). Teacher and classmate influences on scholastic motivation, self-esteem, and level of voice in adolescents. In J. Juvonen & K. Wentzel (Eds.), *Social motivation: Understanding children's school adjustment* (pp. 11–42). New York: Cambridge University Press.

Harter, S., Stocker, C., & Robinson, N. S. (1996). The perceived directionality of the link between approval and self-worth: The liabilities of a looking glass self-orientation among young adolescents. *Journal of Research on Adolescence, 6,* 285–308.

Hatzichristou, C., & Hopf, D. (1966). A multiperspective comparison of peer sociometric status groups in childhood and adolescence. *Child Development, 67,* 1085–1102.

Heath, S. B., & McLaughlin, M. W. (1993). *Identity and inner-city youth.* New York: Teachers College Press.

Helton, G. B., & Oakland, T. D. (1977). Teachers' attitudinal responses to differing characteristics of elementary school students. *Journal of Educational Psychology, 69,* 261–265.

Heyman, G. D., Dweck, C. S., & Cain, K. M. (1992). Young children's vulnerability to self-blame and helplessness: Relationship to beliefs about goodness. *Child Development, 63,* 401–415.

Hinshaw, S. P. (1992). Externalizing behavior problems and academic underachievement in childhood and adolescence: Causal relationships and underlying mechanisms. *Psychological Bulletin, 111,* 127–155.

Hokoda, A., & Fincham, F. D. (1995). Origins of children's helpless and mastery achievement patterns in the family. *Journal of Educational Psychology, 87,* 375–385.

Hopps, H., & Cobb, J. A. (1974). Initial investigations into academic survival-skill training, direct instruction, and first-grade achievement. *Journal of Educational Psychology, 66,* 548–553.

Horn, W. F., & Packard, T. (1985). Early identification of learning problems: A meta-analysis. *Journal of Educational Psychology, 77,* 597–607.

Hymel, S., Bowker, A., & Woody, E. (1993). Aggressive versus withdrawn unpopular children: Variations in peer and self-perceptions in multiple domains. *Child Development, 64,* 879–896.

Hymel, S., Comfort, C., Schonert-Reichl, K., & McDougall, P. (1996). Academic failure and school dropout: The influence of peers. In J. Juvonen & K. R. Wentzel (Eds.), *Social motivation: Understanding children's school adjustment* (pp. 313–345). New York: Cambridge University Press.

Jacobsen, T., Edelstein, W., & Hofmann, V. (1994). A longitudinal study of the relation between representations of attachment in childhood and cognitive functioning in childhood and adolescence. *Developmental Psychology, 30,* 112–124.

Juvonen, J. (1996). Self-presentation tactics promoting teacher and peer approval: The function of excuses and other clever explanations. In J. Juvonen & K. R. Wentzel (Eds.), *Social motivation: Understanding children's school adjustment* (pp. 43–65). New York: Cambridge University Press.

Juvonon, J., Nishina, A., & Graham, S. (2000). Peer harassment, psychological adjustment, and school functioning in early adolescence. *Journal of Educational Psychology, 92,* 349–359.

Kandell, D. B. (1978). Homophily, selection, and socialization. *American Journal of Sociology, 84,* 427–438.

Kaplan, H. B., Robins, C., & Martin, S. S. (1983). Antecedents of psychological distress in young adults: Self-rejection, deprivation of social support, and life events. *Journal of Health and Social Behavior, 24,* 230–244.

Kedar-Voivodas, G. (1983). The impact of elementary children's school roles and sex roles on teacher attitudes: An interactionist analysis. *Review of Educational Research, 53,* 415–437.

Kelly, E. A. (1958). A study of consistent discrepancies between instructors grades and term-end examination grades. *Journal of Educational Psychology, 49,* 328–334.

Kindermann, T. A. (1993). Natural peer groups as contexts for individual development: The case of children's motivation in school. *Developmental Psychology, 29,* 970–977.

Kindermann, T. A., McCollam, T. L., & Gibson, E. (1996). Peer networks and students' classroom engagement during childhood and adolescence. In J. Juvonen & K. R. Wentzel (Eds.), *Social motivation: Understanding children's school adjustment* (pp. 279–312). New York: Cambridge University Press.

Knight, G. P., & Kagan, S. (1977). Development of prosocial and competitive behaviors in Anglo-American and Mexican-American children. *Child Development, 48,* 1385–1394.

Krumboltz, J., Ford, M. E., Nichols, C., & Wentzel, K. (1987). The goals of education. In R. C. Calfee (Ed.), *The study of Stanford and the schools: Views from the inside: Part II.* Stanford, CA: School of Education.

Ladd, G. W. (1989). Children's social competence and social supports: Precursors of early school adjustment? In B. H. Schneider, G. Atilli, J. Nadel, & R. P. Weissberg (Eds.), *Social competence in developmental perspective* (pp. 277–291). Amsterdam, The Netherlands: Kluwer.

Ladd, G. W. (1990). Having friends, keeping friends, making friends, and being liked by peers in the classroom: Predictors of children's early school adjustment. *Child Development, 61,* 1081–1100.

Ladd, G. W., Kochenderfer, B. J., & Coleman, C. (1996). Friendship quality as a predictor of young children's early school adjustment. *Child Development, 58,* 1168–1189.

Ladd, G. W., & Price, J. M. (1987). Predicting children's social and school adjustment following the transition from preschool to kindergarten. *Child Development, 58,* 1168–1189.

Lambert, N. M. (1972). Intellectual and non-intellectual predictors of high school status. *Journal of Special Education, 6,* 247–259.

Lambert, N. M., & Nicoll, R. C. (1977). Conceptual model for nonintellectual behavior and its relationship to early reading achievement. *Journal of Educational Psychology, 69,* 481–490.

LeCompte, M. (1978a). Establishing a workplace: Teacher control in the classroom. *Education and Urban Society, 11,* 87–106.

LeCompte, M. (1978b). Learning to work: The hidden curriculum of the classroom. *Anthropology and Education Quarterly, 9,* 22–37.

Lepper, M. (1983). Social control processes, attributions of motivation, and the internalization of social values. In E. T. Higgins, D. Ruble, & W. Hartup (Eds.), *Social cognition and social development: A sociocultural perspective* (pp. 294–330). Cambridge, England: Cambridge University Press.

Lepper, M. R., & Hodell, M. (1989). Intrinsic motivation in the classroom. In C. Ames & R. Ames (Eds.), *Research on motivation in education* (Vol. 3, pp. 73–106). New York: Academic Press.

Maccoby, E. E. (1992). Trends in the study of socialization: Is there a Lewinian heritage? *Journal of Social Issues, 48,* 171–185.

Maehr, M. L., & Midgley, C. (1991). Enhancing motivation: A schoolwide approach. *Educational Psychologist, 26,* 399–427.

Marjoribanks, K. (1985). Ecological correlates of adolescents' aspirations: Gender-related differences. *Contemporary Educational Psychology, 10,* 329–341.

McAuliffe, T. J., & Dembo, M. H. (1994). Status rules of behavior in scenarios of peer learning. *Journal of Educational Psychology, 86,* 163–172.

McClelland, D. C. (1987). *Human motivation.* New York: Cambridge University Press.

Midgley, C., Feldlaufer, H., & Eccles, J. (1989). Student/teacher relations and attitudes toward mathematics before and after the transition to junior high school. *Child Development, 60,* 981–992.

Newcomb, A. F., & Bagwell, C. L. (1995). Children's friendship relations: A meta-analytic review. *Psychological Bulletin, 117,* 306–347.

Newcomb, A. F., Bukowski, W. M., & Pattee, L. (1993). Children's peer relations: A metaanalytic review of popular, rejected, neglected, and controversial sociometric status. *Psychological Bulletin, 113,* 99–128.

Noddings, N. (1992). *The challenge to care in schools: An alternative approach to education.* New York: Teachers College Press.

Ogbu, J. U. (1985). Origins of human competence: A cultural-ecological perspective. *Child Development, 52,* 413–429.

Parker, J. G., & Asher, S. R. (1987). Peer relations and later personal adjustment: Are low-accepted children at risk? *Psychological Bulletin, 102,* 357–389.

Parkhurst, J. T., & Asher, S. R. (1992). Peer rejection in middle school: Subgroup differences in behavior, loneliness, and interpersonal concerns. *Developmental Psychology, 28,* 231–241.

Patterson, G. R., & Bank, C. L. (1989). Some amplifying mechanisms for pathologic processes in families. In M. R. Gunnar & E. Thelan (Eds.) *Systems and development: The Minnesota symposia on child psychology* (Vol. 22, pp. 167–210). Hillsdale, NJ: Erlbaum.

Patterson, G. R., Bank, C. L., & Stoolmiller, M. (1990). The preadolescent's contributions to disrupted family process. In R. Montemayor, G. R. Adams, & T. P. Gullota (Eds.), *From childhood to adolescence: A transitional period?* (Vol. 2, pp. 107–133). Newbury Park, CA: Sage.

Pervin, L. A. (1983). The stasis and flow of behavior: Toward a theory of goals. In M. M. Page (Ed.), *Personality-Current theory and research* (pp. 1–53). Lincoln: University of Nebraska Press.

Phelan, P., Davidson, A. L., & Cao, H. T. (1991). Students' multiple worlds: Negotiating the boundaries of family, peer, and school cultures. *Anthropology and Education Quarterly, 22,* 224–250.

Piaget, J. (1965). *The moral judgment of the child.* New York: Free Press.

Rathunde, K. (1996). Family context and talented adolescents' optimal experience in school-related activities. *Journal of Research on Adolescence, 6,* 605–628.

Ruble, D. N. (1983). The development of social comparison processes and their role in achievement-related self-socialization. In E. T. Higgins, D. Ruble, & W. Hartup (Eds.), *Social cognition and social development: A sociocultural perspective* (pp. 134–157). Cambridge, England: Cambridge University Press.

Ryan, A. M., & Pintrich, P. R. (1997). Should I ask for help? The role of motivation and attitudes in adolescents' help seeking in math class. *Journal of Educational Psychology, 89,* 329–341.

Ryan, B. A., Adams, G. R., Gullotta, T. P., Weissberg, R. P., & Hampton, R. L. (1995). *The family-school connection: Theory, research, and practice.* Thousand Oaks, CA: Sage.

Ryan, R. M. (1993). Agency and organization: Intrinsic motivation, autonomy, and the self in psychological development. In J. Jacobs (Ed.), *Nebraska symposium on motivation* (Vol. 40, pp. 1–56). Lincoln: University of Nebraska Press.

Safer, D. J. (1986). Nonpromotion correlates and outcomes at different grade levels. *Journal of Learning Disabilities, 19,* 500–503.

Safran, S. P., & Safran, J. S. (1985). Classroom context and teachers' perceptions of problem behaviors. *Journal of Educational Psychology, 77,* 20–28.

Schaps, E., Battistich, V., & Solomon, D. (1997). School as a caring community: A key to character education. In A. Molnar (Ed.), *Ninety-sixth yearbook of the National Society for the Study of Education* (pp. 127–139). Chicago: University of Chicago Press.

Schunk, D. H. (1987). Peer models and children's behavioral change. *Review of Educational Research, 57,* 149–174.

Sherif, M., Harvey, O. J., White, B. J., Hood, W. R., & Sherif, C. W. (1988). *The robber's cave experiment: Intergroup conflict and cooperation.* Middletown, CT: Wesleyan Press.

Shultz, J., & Florio, S. (1979). Stop and freeze: The negotiation of social and physical space in a kindergarten/first grade classroom. *Anthropology and Education Quarterly, 10,* 166–181.

Sieber, R. T. (1979). Classmates as workmates: Informal peer activity in the elementary school. *Anthropology and Education Quarterly, 10,* 207–235.

Sivan, E. (1986). Motivation in social constructivist theory. *Educational Psychologist, 21,* 209–233.

Skinner, E. A., & Belmont, M. J. (1993). Motivation in the classroom: Reciprocal effects of teacher behavior and student engagement across the school year. *Journal of Educational Psychology, 85,* 571–581.

Slavin, R. E. (1987). Developmental and motivational perspectives on cooperative learning: A reconciliation. *Child Development, 58,* 1161–1167.

Solomon, D., Schaps, E., Watson, M., & Battistich, V. (1992). Creating caring school and classroom communities for all students. In R. Villa, J. Thousand, W. Stainback, & S. Stainback (Eds.), *Restructuring for caring and effective education: An administrative guide to creating heterogeneous schools* (pp. 41–60). Baltimore: Brookes.

Smetana, J., & Bitz, B. (1996). Adolescents' conceptions of teachers' authority and their relations to rule violations in school. *Child Development, 67,* 1153–1172.

Steinberg, L. (1990). Autonomy, conflict, and harmony in the family relationship. In S. S. Feldman & G. R. Elliott (Eds.), *At the threshold: The developing adolescent* (pp. 255–276). Cambridge, MA: Harvard University Press.

Sternberg, R. J., & Kolligian, J. (1990). *Competence considered.* New Haven, CT: Yale University Press.

Trenholm, S., & Rose, T. (1981). The compliant communicator: Teacher perceptions of appropriate classroom behavior. *The Western Journal of Speech Communication, 45,* 13–26.

Watson, M., Solomon, D., Battistich, V., Schaps, E., & Solomon, J. (1989). The child development project: Combining traditional and developmental approaches to values education. In L. Nucci (Ed.), *Moral development and character education: A dialogue* (pp. 51–92). Berkeley, CA: McCutchan.

Wentzel, K. R. (1989). Adolescent classroom goals, standards for performance, and academic achievement: An interactionist perspective. *Journal of Educational Psychology, 81,* 131–142.

Wentzel, K. R. (1991a). Relations between social competence and academic achievement in early adolescence. *Child Development, 62,* 1066–1078.

Wentzel, K. R. (1991b). Social and academic goals at school: Achievement motivation in context. In M. Maehr & P. Pintrich (Eds.), *Advances in motivation and achievement* (Vol. 7, pp. 185–212). Greenwich, CT: JAI.

Wentzel, K. R. (1991c). Social competence at school: Relations between social responsibility and academic achievement. *Review of Educational Research, 61,* 1–24.

Wentzel, K. R. (1992). Motivation and achievement in adolescence: A multiple goals perspective. In D. Schunk & J. Meece (Eds.), *Student perceptions in the classroom: Causes and consequences* (pp. 287–306). Hillsdale, NJ: Erlbaum.

Wentzel, K. R. (1993a). Social and academic goals at school: Motivation and achievement in early adolescence. *Journal of Early Adolescence, 13,* 4–20.

Wentzel, K. R. (1993b). Does being good make the grade? Relations between academic and social competence in early adolescence. *Journal of Educational Psychology, 85,* 357–364.

Wentzel, K. R. (1994). Relations of social goal pursuit to social acceptance, classroom behavior, and perceived social support. *Journal of Educational Psychology, 86,* 173–182.

Wentzel, K. R. (1996). Social and academic motivation in middle school: Concurrent and longterm relations to academic effort. *Journal of Early Adolescence, 16,* 390–406.

Wentzel, K. R. (1997). Student motivation in middle school: The role of perceived pedagogical caring. *Journal of Educational Psychology, 89,* 411–419.

Wentzel, K. R. (1998). Social support and adjustment in middle school: The role of parents, teachers, and peers. *Journal of Educational Psychology, 90,* 202–209.

Wentzel, K. R. (2000). *Teachers' beliefs about pedagogical caring.* Unpublished manuscript, University of Maryland, College Park.

Wentzel, K. R. (2002a). Are effective teachers like good parents? Interpersonal predictors of school adjustment in early adolescence. *Child Development, 73,* 287–301.

Wentzel, K. R. (2002b). The contribution of social goal setting to children's school adjustment. In A. Wigfield & J. Eccles (Ed.), *Development of motivation.* (pp. 221–246). New York: Academic Press.

Wentzel, K. R., & Asher, S. R. (1995). Academic lives of neglected, rejected, popular, and controversial children. *Child Development, 66,* 754–763.

Wentzel, K. R., Battle, A., & Cusick, L. (March, 2000). *Teacher and peer contributions to classroom climate in middle school: Relations to school adjustment.* Paper presented at the annual meeting of the American Educational Research Association, Seattle, WA.

Wentzel, K. R., & Caldwell, K. (1997). Friendships, peer acceptance, and group membership: Relations to academic achievement in middle school. *Child Development, 68,* 1198–1209.

Wentzel, K. R., & McNamara, C. (1999). Interpersonal relationships, emotional distress, and prosocial behavior in middle school. *Journal of Early Adolescence, 19,* 114–125.

Wentzel, K. R., Weinberger, D. A., Ford, M. E., & Feldman, S. S. (1990). Academic achievement in preadolescence: The role of motivational, affective, and self-regulatory processes. *Journal of Applied Developmental Psychology, 11,* 179–193.

Wentzel, K. R., Wood, D., Siesfeld, G., Stevens, E., & Ford, M. (1987, April). *Does being good make the grade? A study of adolescent social responsibility and academic achievement.* Paper presented at the annual meeting of the American Educational Research Association, Washington, DC.

Wenz-Gross, M., Siperstein, G. N., Untch, A. S., & Widaman, K. F. (1997). Stress, social support, and adjustment of adolescents in middle school. *Journal of Early Adolescence, 17,* 129–151.

Wigfield, A., & Eccles, J. S. (1992). The development of achievement task values: A theoretical analysis. *Developmental Review, 12,* 265–310.

Youniss, J. (1994). Children's friendship and peer culture: Implications for theories of networks and support. In F. Nestmann & K. Hurrelmann (Eds.), *Social networks and social support in childhood and adolescence* (pp. 75–88). Berlin, Germany: Degrader.

Youniss, J., & Smollar, J. (1985). *Adolescent relations with mothers, fathers, and friends.* Chicago: University of Chicago Press.

Youniss, J., & Smollar, J. (1989). Adolescents' interpersonal relationships in social context. In T. J. Berndt & G. Ladd (Eds.), *Peer relationships in child development* (pp. 300–316). New York: Wiley.

Zakriski, A. L., & Coie, J. D. (1996). A comparison of aggressive-rejected and nonaggressive-rejected children's interpretations of self-directed and other-directed rejection. *Child Development, 67,* 1048–1070.

CHAPTER 12

Gender Issues in the Classroom

JANICE KOCH

This chapter examines the research literature on the gendered socialization of students as they participate in the social and academic culture of the classroom. The term *gendered socialization* refers to how female and male students receive different messages about appropriate classroom behaviors. It explores the attributes of classrooms where the academic and social experiences for both female and male students are not limited by their gender, and it reveals recommendations, strategies, and insights into fostering equitable learning environments for females and males in early childhood, middle grades, and high school environments. For all of our students, coming to understand what they know and are able to do in the world is our central goal. This chapter emphasizes the importance for educators of understanding the role of gender in their expectations of the academic and social behaviors of their female and male students.

The central questions addressed by this chapter are (a) *To what extent do schools and teachers' expectations of males and females influence their development, behavior, and academic success in school?* and (b) *How do classroom interactions and school curriculum socially construct what it means to be female and male and in what ways does that limit possibilities for girls and boys in schools?* This chapter seeks to guide individuals to a heightened awareness of the impact of gender issues in the classroom on student learning and self-concept and on the social relations within the classroom. Furthermore, it explores the ways in which sexual

harassment in schools and school programs interferes with the equal access to education—afforded all students under Title IX of the Education Amendments of 1972. Beyond the classroom climate, this chapter seeks to expose the embedded gender messages in formal precollege curriculum and suggest possibilities for examining curriculum through the lens of gender. Gender issues in the classroom are examined from a developmental perspective as well as from a sociocultural perspective, exploring the interactive nature of student socialization and achievement and the role of school curriculum in fostering a sense of competence in all students. It concludes with a guide for establishing gender-equitable learning environments that contribute to the well-being of all the students.

DEFINING GENDER ISSUES AND EQUITY IN EDUCATION

A *gender issue* refers to a classroom practice or policy that differentiates the learning experience in ways that limit opportunities for females and males in the classroom. Each gender issue or gender-related issue addresses educationally relevant processes and skills. The field of gender equity in education refers to educational practices that are fair and just toward both males and females, are free from bias or favoritism, show preference toward neither gender, and show concern for both genders (adapted from Klein, Ortman, &

Friedman, 2002). The topic of gender issues in the classroom addresses the following questions: What are the attributes of gender equitable classroom environments? How does the socialization of girls and boys promote gender stereotypes in the classroom? How are gender stereotypes supported by the classroom teacher? In what ways do classroom gender issues limit opportunities for social and academic advancement for girls and boys? Amidst an array of widely varied responses to these questions is the understanding that an awareness of the role of gender in learning and behavior can help educators to avoid the trap of limiting children's growth by making and acting upon stereotypical assumptions about individual students' abilities and development.

Furthermore, it is understood that a study of gender-equitable classroom practices addresses the content of the formal curriculum and the curriculum of classroom interactions that give tacit messages to females and males about their roles in the classroom community and the larger formal curriculum. Hence, gender issues move researchers to explore the study of the formal curriculum, the content of curricular materials, classroom interactions as curriculum (also called the hidden curriculum), the ways in which the materials are taught, and the evaded curriculum, the things that are not taught in our nation's schools (American Association of University Women Educational Foundation, 1992).

Informing the field of gender equity in education and consequently the areas relating to classroom gender issues is the understanding that classroom communities create social and academic climates that are diversified by socioeconomic class, ethnicity, and geographic region. Because social interactions in classrooms emerge from dominant cultural constructs in specific communities, attention to diversity is imperative for the understanding of the full range of gender issues in the classroom. Profound changes in school demographics have demanded that the field of gender equity in education examine the impacts of changing communities on gender relations and gender equity in classrooms. Studies relating to diverse environments and considering schools and communities of learners that differ from the dominant White middle-class model are emerging in the research literature and are addressed in this chapter.

Gender Equity in Education and the Law

Key United States civil rights laws focus on prohibiting discrimination on the basis of sex, race, and national origin as well as age, religion, and disability. Title IX of the Education Amendments of 1972 prohibits discrimination on the basis of sex in education programs or activities receiving federal financial assistance; this key civil rights statute makes it

illegal to treat students differently or separately on the basis of sex. Modeled on Title VI of the Civil Rights Act of 1964 that prohibits discrimination based on race, color, and national origin, it differs from Title VI, which applied to all federal financial assistance, by being limited to *education* programs that receive federal financial assistance (Klein et al., 2002). Also included in the Civil Rights Act of 1964 was Title VII, which prohibits employment discrimination in education on the basis of sex, race, and national origin.

At the United Nations Fourth World Conference on Women held in Beijing in 1995, the Platform for Action to raise the status of women around the world was adopted by representatives from 189 countries, including the United States. Included in this platform were provisions for the advancement of gender equity in education, with an entire section devoted to resolutions on that topic. The declaration specifically states

> Education is a human right and an essential tool for achieving the goals of equality, development and peace. Non-discriminatory education benefits both girls and boys and thus ultimately contributes to more equal relationships between women and men. Equality of access to and attainment of educational qualifications is necessary if more women are to become agents of change. (United Nations, 1995, summary, p. 1.)

Sexual Harassment and the Law

Under the guidelines established by the Office for Civil Rights (OCR), sexual harassment is a form of sex discrimination prohibited by Title IX of the Education Amendments of 1972. The regulation implementing Title IX, Section 106.31 outlaws sexual harassment as a form of disparate treatment that impedes access to an equitable education. OCR identifies two types of sexual harassment in schools—quid pro quo and hostile environment. *Quid pro quo sexual harassment* occurs when a school employee causes a student to believe that he or she must submit to unwelcome sexual conduct to participate in a school program or activity. It can also occur when a teacher suggests to a student that an educational decision such as grades will be based on whether the student submits to unwelcome sexual conduct. *Hostile environment harassment* occurs when unwelcome verbal or physical conduct is sufficiently severe, persistent, or pervasive that it creates an abusive or hostile environment for the affected student (U.S. Department of Education, 1997). On May, 24, 1999, the Supreme Court ruled that school districts can be liable for damages under federal law for failing to stop a student from subjecting another to severe and pervasive sexual harassment, hence denying its victim of equal access to education guaranteed under Title IX of the Education Amendments of 1972 (as reported in Greenhouse, 1999).

Gender-Equitable Learning Environments

While implying quality education and equal opportunities and access for all students, gender equity differs from gender *equality*. Equality sets up a comparison between males and females and asks the question *Are they receiving the same education?* (AAUW, 1998). Gender equity poses a different question for the classroom dynamic: Do students receive the *right* education to achieve a shared standard of excellence? Gender equity asserts that males and females do *not* need the same things to achieve shared outcomes. Gender equity is *not* sameness or equality; it is equity of outcomes—equal access to achievement and opportunity. Hence, equitable education addresses the needs of girls and boys rather than questions whether each receives the same thing (AAUW, 1998).

The field of gender equity in the classroom began as an outgrowth of the women's movement of the 1970s and focused on the damaging effects of holding male achievement and accomplishment as the norm against which females are measured. This led to a deficit model that emphasized girls' inabilities to perform as well as boys on various standardized tests throughout the precollege experience. Early work in gender equity challenged this deficit model because it suggested that there was something wrong with the girls that needed to be fixed or remedied. This situation prompted researchers to explore learning environments for girls and boys while they were participating in the same classroom with the same teacher (Klein, 1985; Sadker & Sadker, 1982). What they found (in predominantly White middle-class classrooms) was that the problems were not internal to the girls; rather, they were situated in the external learning environment. Early studies then revealed that classroom practices routinely favor the academic development of boys (discussed later in this chapter), and interventions were developed to provide more equitable learning environments for girls (Clewell, Anderson, & Thorpe, 1992; Greenberg, 1985; Logan, 1997; Saker & Sadker, 1984; Sanders et al., 1997). Although these interventions helped individual girls to achieve in areas in which they were lagging, this deficit model inferred that girls would be successful if they just acquired the same strengths as the boys. This view has shifted to conceptualize equitable learning environments as those that capitalize on the strengths of all individuals—both boys and girls—and invite each to adopt behaviors that help each gender cultivate strengths not usually developed due to socialization practices and stereotyping.

The field of gender equity in education generally acknowledges that equitable classroom environments have the following attributes in common (AAUW, 1992, 1995, 1998; McIntosh, 2000):

- Classrooms are caring communities where individuals feel safe and where understanding is promoted among peers.
- Classrooms are free from violence and peer or adult harassment.
- Classrooms have routines and procedures that ensure equal access to instructional materials and extracurricular activities.
- Classrooms have a *gender agenda* referring to the deconstruction of gendered expectations for students and encouraging full participation of each student including the expression of nonstereotyped behaviors.
- Classrooms address the evaded curriculum by exploring those who have been omitted and by integrating evaded topics such as sexuality, violence, abuse, and gender politics.
- Classrooms address the lived experience of students by providing assignments or projects that develop all students' capacities to see their life experience as part of knowledge, wherein students are authorities of their own experience and contribute to the classroom textbooks by creating "textbooks of their lives" (McIntosh & Style, 1999).

GENDER ISSUES FACING EDUCATORS

Gender equity research beginning in the 1970s and continuing through the early 1990s consistently reported a series of behaviors that characterized coeducational classrooms in predominantly White middle-class communities (AAUW, 1992; Becker, 1981; Brophy, 1981; Klein, 1985; Lockheed, 1984, 1985; Sadker & Sadker, 1982, 1994). These behaviors revealed differential treatment of girls and boys in the same classrooms, with the same teacher, and experiencing the same curriculum. Categories of analysis included student-teacher interactions (both teacher- and student-initiated), peer interactions, and gender segregation (Lockheed, 1985). Educational researchers sought to gain insight into coeducational environments by spending time, observing in classrooms at precollege grade levels, and documenting teacher-student interactions and peer interactions in classrooms, hallways, cafeterias, and school grounds. These studies compiled data about the nature of teacher-student and student-student interactions in both the classroom and more informal school environments. Field researchers took notes and made extensive ethnographic reports about the experience of being in these classrooms. The researchers recorded and coded interactions by gender and interviewed teachers and students. Some studies used survey data whereby students' hobbies, attitudes, and preferences were recorded on open-ended and quantitative surveys. One such study of an independent school in an urban area yielded valuable data for faculty and administrators about the ways in which their male and female students were experiencing school and their lives outside the classroom (Koch, 1996).

When looking at classroom interactions through the lens of gender, one repeatedly sees similar gendered patterns of student-teacher interactions, which are elucidated later in this chapter in detail. However, the repetition of these patterns in research studies from the 1970s as well as those documented by the end of the 1990s reveals the consistent pervasiveness of gender bias in the classroom (Marshall & Reinhartz, 1997); this situation has persisted because classrooms continue to be microcosms of society, mirroring the gender roles that teachers and students develop through their socialization patterns. Both ingrained in our individual identities and mediated by social class and ethnicity, gender roles inform much of the behavior we observe in classrooms. In the following discussion are common classroom interactions between teachers and students as they communicate with each other in formal and informal ways. Instances of gender bias in teacher-student interactions are often subtle, well intended, and not designed to limit opportunities for either gender. Several researchers have noted, however, that consistent gender-biased practices can contribute to lowered self-esteem for girls in ways that can be remedied by intervention strategies (Chapman, 1997; Sadker & Sadker, 1994).

Changing teachers' gender-stereotyped behavior requires prior knowledge of gender issues in the classroom. Teachers who participate in gender workshops designed to create an awareness of and an agenda for gender issues in the classroom tend to promote more equitable classroom settings than do their peers who have had little or no exposure to the topic. This participation is differentiated from simple awareness of the role of gender equity in the classroom. Studies have found that awareness is not sufficient to change behavior because well-intended teacher behaviors have been ingrained and practiced for so many years that teachers automatically respond in certain ways to boys and girls (Levine & Orenstein, 1994). Because many teachers have been socialized over their lifetimes to believe certain stereotypes about genders and have also had some of the same experiences that their students have had, it is difficult for them to acquire teaching strategies that call these belief systems into question.

Gender research results are often described by attributing behaviors to aggregate groups and disregarding individual differences within groups (i.e., active girls, silent boys). This trend toward describing female groups and male groups as a whole—disregarding individual differences—is changing as

education researchers explore differences within groups and build an understanding of how race and class mediate gender socialization. Studies addressing gender issues in the classroom, however, described differences between populations of girls and boys in the same classroom settings. The results indicated different patterns of classroom interactions and performance for precollege boys and girls. These patterns were not random; they reflect differing social and academic expectations and opportunities for male and female students. Many of the differentiated experiences reflect the ways in which teachers in classrooms reinforce group stereotypes about student skills and opportunities (AAUW, 1998).

The Hidden, Formal, and Null Curriculums

These teacher behaviors are components of what researchers have termed the *hidden curriculum*—the tacit messages students receive from the daily practices, routines, and behaviors that occur in the classroom. The hidden curriculum of the school's climate are "things not deliberately taught or instituted, but which are the cumulative result of many unconscious or unexamined behaviors that add to a palpable style or atmosphere" (Chapman, 1997). An example of these types of behaviors can be seen in elementary school environments— for example, when teachers assign girls the task of recording on the board during a demonstration lesson in science while boys are required to set up or assemble the accompanying materials. This fine-motor/gross-motor distinction is one of many types of gendered expectations that can lead to differentiated outcomes.

In middle school, extracurricular computer clubs are often dominated by middle-grades boys. No one questions the absence of girls. This lack of taking notice is another example of the ways schools communicate a hidden curriculum. The high schools often offer advanced placement (AP) science courses in chemistry and physics that have more males than females enrolled. When school administrators or teachers are not asking *Where are the girls?*, the message is that they are not expected. Similarly, when advanced placement language arts courses are underenrolled by boys, their absence needs to signal that the school needs to examine the issue. When teachers tend to focus the microscope for the female students who seek help, but the same teachers encourage the male students to figure it out for themselves, they show another example of the implementation of the hidden curriculum (Koch, 1996; Sanders et al., 1997). In short, the hidden curriculum comprises the unstated lessons that students learn in school: It is the running subtext through which teachers communicate behavioral norms and individual status in the school culture—the process of socialization that cues children into their place in the hierarchy of larger society (Orenstein, 1994).

The hidden curriculum is distinguished from the *formal curriculum,* which consists of subject-matter disciplines and the ways they are taught and tested. The importance of the formal curriculum cannot be overstated: "I think the main message any school delivers about what counts is delivered through its curriculum" (McIntosh, 1984, p. 8). The *informal curriculum* is comprised of activities that include athletics, school government, and extracurricular activities. The informal curriculum includes the social messages that males and females receive as they participate in school activities beyond the formal classroom environment. The *null curriculum—* also referred to as the *evaded curriculum*—refers to what is missing from all other curricula—not as a result of a conscious decision to include it, but merely because it never occurred to anyone to consider whether it should be there (Chapman, 1997). The evaded curriculum, examined later in this chapter, refers to absences in the curriculum that often include social topics and subject matter content that explores the experiences of females.

Gender Issues in the Classroom: The Gaps

The last decade witnessed the publication of several research reports that examined the lives of girls and boys in precollege environments. These reports were commissioned by the American Association of University Women (AAUW) Educational Foundation and contribute to an important fund of data on gender issues in the classroom and beyond. In 1998, the foundation assessed developments in Grades K–12 education through the lens of gender and noted gaps that persist despite educators' increased awareness of the problem of gender stereotyping in schools. To assess the achievement and risk factors, several of the glaring gender gaps in education are summarized in the following discussion; underlying issues and causes are revealed in subsequent sections of this chapter.

Risks for Girls

Girls are more vulnerable to widespread sexual violence and harassment that interferes with their ability to learn. One out of every five girls says that she has been sexually or physically abused; one in four girls shows signs of depression. The teen birth rate dropped by 17% percent among African Americans between 1991 and 1996 and by more than 9% among non-Hispanic Whites. There was no similar decline in birth rate for Hispanic teens.

Dropout Rates

Boys repeat grades and drop out of school at a higher rate than do girls; however, girls who repeat a grade are more likely to drop out than are boys who are held back. Not only is being held back more harmful to girls, but dropping out also is: Girls who drop out are less likely to return and complete school, and dropout rates among females are also correlated strongly with lower-income families and higher rates of pregnancy. Dropout rates are especially high among Hispanic girls. In 1995, 30% of Hispanic females age 16–24 had dropped out of school and not yet passed a high school equivalency test. In contrast, dropout rates for White students and Black males have remained stable. Dropout rates for Hispanic males and Black females have declined.

Risks for Boys

Boys are more likely than are girls to be labeled problems in need of assistance, to fail a course, or to repeat a grade. Boys are more likely to be identified for special education programs and are more likely than are girls to be labeled for their entire school career. Boys are more likely to gain social status through disruptive classroom behavior, which leads to school failure. Boys are more likely than are girls to engage in high-risk behavior (experimenting with drugs and alcohol), and they are more prone to accidents caused by violence. In school, boys' misbehavior is more frequently punished than is that of girls. More than 70% of students suspended from school are boys.

Sports and Physical Activity

Girls are twice as likely to be inactive as boys, and male high school graduates are more likely than are females to have taken at least 1 year of physical education. Research links physical activity for girls to higher self-esteem, better body image, and lifelong health. Classroom teachers are urged to recognize the importance of encouraging both girls and boys to participate in organized physical activity.

Boys outnumber girls in team sports, whereas girls outnumber boys in performing arts, school government, and literary activities. Poverty is the largest barrier to participation in sports or extracurricular activities, which are linked to better school performance.

Course Taking and Testing

Girls take English courses in greater numbers than do boys— except in remedial English, where boys outnumber girls. Furthermore, girls outnumber boys in crucial subjects like sociology, psychology, foreign languages, and fine arts. Girls take more AP courses in English, biology, and foreign languages. More girls than boys take voluntary AP tests to earn college credit; in fact, African American girls are far more likely to take AP exams than are African American boys (by a factor of almost two to one). Girls, however, receive fewer scores of 3 or higher, the score needed to receive college credit. This is true even in subjects like English in which girls traditionally earn top grades. Girls lag behind boys in participation in AP physical science classes and in computer science and computer design classes. Girls make up only a small percentage of students in computer science and computer design classes. In 1996, girls comprised only 17% of AP test takers in computer science.

In the college-bound population, males of all racial and ethnic backgrounds score higher than do females on the math section and on the verbal section of the Scholastic Achievement Test (SAT) (AAUW, 1998a). The gender gaps are widest among high-achieving students. On the verbal section of the American College Testing Program (ACT), girls outscore boys on the verbal section.

THE CLASSROOM CLIMATE

The research on gender issues in the classrooms describes differential treatment of males and females who sit the same classroom, use the same materials, and work with the same teacher. The central questions remains *To what extent do classroom teachers, school administrators, counselors, and peers limit the development of females and males through promoting gender stereotyping and gender-biased classroom practices and school policies?*

Gender Bias in Student-Teacher Interactions

Gender bias in student-teacher interactions has been documented in classrooms from kindergarten through the end of high school. Areas of gender-differentiated instruction include:

- Teacher questions and student responses.
- Types of teacher questions and sanctions.
- Student voice or air time, so to speak.
- Teacher attention to student appearance.
- Amount of wait time.
- Teacher-student coaching.
- Teacher assigned jobs.

A significant finding has been that classroom teachers engage boys in question-and-answer periods more frequently than they engage girls. Involving boys more actively in the classroom dialogue has been seen as a way to control male behavior in the classroom and has often been a response to male aggressiveness. Studies found that in classroom discourse, boys frequently raised their hands—sometimes impulsively and sometimes without even knowing the answer. Conversely, studies found that girls tended not to raise their hands as often; when they did, they were overlooked frequently and male students were chosen instead. Teachers, when asked to monitor their interactions with students, consciously changed this pattern, but only after active participation in a gender workshop or related intervention. Several teacher education institutions offer courses addressing gender issues in the classroom, and pre- and postcourse assessments indicate that teachers make adjustments to their own student interactions after learning the ways in which their unintentionally biased behaviors affect girls and boys' self-concepts in classrooms. For example, in teacher training courses on gender and schooling, teachers are asked to examine their classroom interactions and to tape themselves. Often, they notice that they call on boys more frequently for responses and coach boys for correct responses more frequently than they do with girls. Teachers tend to change their interactions when they are made aware of their practices. For example, some elementary school teachers tend to praise girls for how they dress and wear their hair. In courses and workshops, however, teachers are encouraged to extend more praise to girls' problem-solving skills and performance in class. Similarly, teachers are encouraged to acknowledge boys' skills in working well in cooperative groups and to praise their capacity to work in a team within the classroom context. Teachers report that they change those behaviors when made aware of them (Koch, 1998a).

A related finding revealed that teachers tended to ask boys more open-ended, thought-provoking questions than they asked girls, demonstrating the expectation that boys were capable of greater abstract thinking. As noted later in this chapter, these findings become exaggerated in different subject area classes in middle and high school, especially mathematics, science, and technology.

Several studies revealed that although the classroom helpers selected by teachers are carefully selected girls, the boys are more likely to demonstrate and use technical equipment and actively engage with materials during experiments.

When girls exhibited boisterous behavior and impulsively called out a response, they were reprimanded in ways in which boys who routinely exhibited the same behaviors were not. One study described third-grade elementary school girls as suffering from *overcontrol,* a term used to indicate the silence of girls and their reluctance to ask questions even when they did not understand a concept (Harvard Education Newsletter, 1989).

Research studies affirm repeatedly that males receive more of all types of the teacher's attention in classrooms and are given more time to talk in class from preschool through high school. Teachers tend to offer more praise, criticism, remediation, and acceptance to boys than to girls. Although males receive harsher punishment than do females for the same offense, females are often unduly punished when they exhibit male social behavior. Teachers are often invested in the silence of the girls. Girls tend not to call attention to themselves and to be quiet, social, and well behaved in classrooms. Even when they are sure of an answer, they are not apt to volunteer. Teachers often sanction so-called good girl behavior in elementary classrooms as a way of maintaining their vision of proper classroom management. Teachers tend to offer different types of praise—rewarding girls for their appearance or the appearance of their work and praising boys for the ways in which they solve a problem or accomplish a task. Girls learn early on that their appearance matters in ways that are not valid for the boys. Being pretty, cute, thin, charming, alluring, well-dressed, and sexy are attributes to which girls aspire because such attributes are valued by adults and media messages. Classrooms reinforce those values when girls are praised for appearance and dress on a consistent basis.

When asking the class questions, teachers tend to exhibit longer wait times for boys than for girls. *Wait time* refers to the period of time between asking a question and calling on a student for a response. Research has found that wait time is an important teacher technique for encouraging full participation of all students and promoting higher order thinking rather than simple recall (Rowe, 1987). Whereas some researchers assert that teachers give males longer wait time than they give females to keep males' interest and manage classroom behavior, other researchers believe that teachers expect more abstract or higher order thinking from the males and that those expectations are manifested in longer wait times. Studies reveal that teachers tend to coach boys for the correct answers through prodding and cajoling, but they go on to the next student when a girl has an incorrect response (Sadker & Sadker, 1994; Sandler, Silverberg, & Hall, 1996).

Most teachers believe that they treat girls and boys the same; research reveals that they frequently do not. The teacher's gender has little bearing on the outcome; it is the gender of the student that determines the differential behavior (Sadker & Sadker, 1994).

GENDER EQUITY IN EARLY CHILDHOOD ENVIRONMENTS

The classroom is a place where students are socialized into behaving in certain ways. Children arrive at school with early gender socialization patterns that often influence the life of the classroom. The structure and climate created in the classroom need to mitigate these social differences in order to capitalize on strengths of each gender and build skills that may be lacking due to stereotyping. One study explored the lives of girls and boys in kindergarten classrooms (Greenberg, 1985). Observations of early childhood teachers reveal that girls are praised in kindergarten for arriving to school willing and able to conform to classroom structures and rules. Teachers spend more time socializing boys into classroom life, and the result is that girls get less teacher attention. Boys receive what they need—additional work on obeying rules, following classroom protocols, controlling unruly impulses, and establishing the preconditions for learning.

Girls' needs are more subtle and tend to be overlooked. For example, most girls arrive into kindergarten with better development of fine motor skills than most boys have. They often do not have as well-developed gross motor skills, although that steadily improved in the 1990s with the institutionalization of organized sports for girls. Early childhood environments would serve little girls well by exposing them purposefully to activities requiring large motor skills, ranging from block corner activities to climbing and running during recess. Instead, researchers noted that the activities girls needed most in early childhood were relegated to free play or recess time. The needs of boys, however, were met during the instructional class time (Klein, 1985).

Segregated play in early educational environments does not meet the needs of both genders. For example, one study revealed that boys wanted to enter the doll corner but only got there by invading as superheroes (Paley, 1993). For boys, this type of aggressive behavior can be lessened—not accentuated—by doll corner play. Other studies explore the affect on playtime of setting up the early childhood classroom in ways that encourage cooperative play between girls and boys (Gallas, 1998; Greenberg, 1985; Schlank & Metzger, 1997). One study followed a group of kindergarten boys whose boys-only club exclusively limited enrollment to athletic boys (Best, 1983). Belonging to the boys' club was directly correlated with higher achievement. This type of all-boys group adversely affects those who do not belong.

Furthermore, segregated play activities are encouraged by heavy media promotion of so-called girls' toys and boys' toys; this further differentiates interactions and communication styles of girls and boys. This differentiation disadvantages girls and boys as they participate in learning communities because it limits the range of behaviors, skills, speech patterns, communication styles, and ways of knowing to same gender groupings. Early childhood classrooms that are structured to maximize boy-girl interaction during free time as well as instructional time help both girls and boys to develop with fewer restrictions.

In one kindergarten classroom, a girls' group was building a tall tower in the block corner when it suddenly fell over; they left the task in dismay. A group of boys had built a tower and knocked it down purposely for the sheer joy of building it back up again. Risk taking and building confidence are important attributes for all students to acquire. Testing ideas and risking error are significant components of learning. Similarly, the kind of family-like communication that occurs in the doll corner provides important experiences for little boys who are not traditionally socialized to develop their verbal expression skills in ways in which girls are (Best, 1983; Greenberg, 1985; Paley, 1993).

Boys need to recognize the value and importance of attitudes and competencies stereotypically associated with the feminine. Girls need to acquire many of the attitudes and competencies associated with the masculine. Classrooms are places where mixed-gender grouping can foster an appreciation for qualities each gender has been socialized to acquire from birth. Instead, gender teachings (McIntosh, 2000) are full of inherited ideas that comprise a set of rules each biological sex must follow. These rules are invented, differ across cultures, and can change over time. As the years go on, girls and boys come to see their gender teachings (e.g., *boys don't cry*) as a part of their sex and hence natural for their sex. To the extent that early childhood classrooms can begin to deconstruct restricted notions about how to be a boy or how to be a girl, it is possible to achieve gender-equitable learning communities. Although progress was made in the last decade of the twentieth century, the White Western societal belief persists that the sexes are somehow opposite. Classroom communities that reflect this belief tacitly encourage separate gender play, with boys persisting in the block corner and girls remaining in the dramatic play or house corner. This chapter is informed by the belief that classroom communities can challenge existing beliefs of what is natural for girls and boys and hence broaden opportunities for children.

Gender and Identity in the Primary Grades

"Girls are usually sitting in a tree when they are told, 'Girls don't climb trees'. . . Women who do not climb, literally or figuratively, come to feel it is natural to the female sex that women do not 'climb'" (McIntosh, 2000, p. 1). This quote represents an important connection between the messages girls and boys receive about what they can and cannot do and the abilities they refine as they mature. How do teachers and the classroom climates they create encourage girls and boys to move beyond gender-stereotyped expectations and expand their abilities? This section explores the effects of sex-role stereotyping and social roles on the behavior of girls and boys in classrooms.

Bad Boys and Silent Girls

Social stereotyping and bias influence children's self-concepts and attitudes toward others. Although sweeping generalizations currently categorize the lives of little boys and little girls, this chapter seeks to highlight the tendency toward oversimplification that the field of gender equity—well-intentioned and significant—has wrought upon classroom contexts.

At age 30 months, children are learning to use gender labels (boy-girl) and by 3–5 years of age, children try to figure out if they will remain a boy or a girl or if that is subject to change. They possess internalized gender roles (Derman-Sparks, 1989) and arrive at school having already acquired a set of values, attitudes, and expectations of what girls and boys can do. Research findings reveal that teacher attitudes and interactions and the ways in which the classroom community is established can reinforce prevailing gender norms, positing masculine as opposite to feminine, or they can expand the boundaries of sex role stereotyping by providing all children with a wide range of experiences and possibilities. We know that the differences among boys and among girls are far greater than the actual differences between the sexes (Golumbok & Fivusch, 1996). Much of what we know as gender teachings may be unnatural for individual children of either sex. For example, a very artistic boy may be discouraged from refining his talents by adults whose expectations are that as a young boy, he should be playing ball rather than drawing pictures.

Consequently, a gender agenda becomes crucial to the primary teacher as he or she sets out to actively listen to the voices of girls and boys and empower them with new possibilities. Children differentiate between appropriate behaviors for girls and boys in the areas of physical appearance, toy choices, play activities, and peer preferences (AAUW, 1993; Sadker & Sadker, 1986). Consequently, children are placed in a suboptimal position—wanting to participate in activities that they perceive they should not want because of their sex. These conflicts between personal likes and doing what they are led to think they *should* do need to be made visible in the primary grades and throughout schooling.

Unfortunately, much of the gender equity research has revealed that boys dominate and silence girls and that teachers collude with this agenda. This teacher collusion—allowing boys to dominate—ignores the complexities of small children's behaviors, conflicts, and needs for acceptance. A gender agenda in a primary classroom would include using gender-inclusive language, arranging the primary classroom in a way that encourages mixed-gender play, and providing children with classroom rules that disallow exclusions by gender. For example, explicitly stating that all children can play with all toys in all activity areas and that no children may be kept from playing because of something they cannot change—such as gender, skin color, or disability are two rules that provide children with the freedom to explore all areas and try out many different roles (Schlank & Metzger, 1997).

Karen Gallas (1998), however, in her extended classroom research work with her own first and second graders, reminds us that the construction of a gender-balanced classroom is a goal that reflects incomplete understandings of classroom life and denies the cultural dynamic of today's classrooms (p. 3). Although proactive methods of instruction to promote gender consciousness and employ gender-neutral materials are tools that can help teachers, Gallas asserts that in fact the social climate of the classroom is highly complex and that teachers are well served by exploring the conditions within their own classrooms that promote certain social relations over others. In other words, to be gender equitable, primary teachers need to know how the dynamics of gender identity and power relations plays out in their specific classroom contexts. There are no simple formulas for creating equitable classroom environments.

Gallas's research presents a more complex response to creating equitable climates; she describes the underlying causes of boy dominance in her 7- and 8-year-olds and the purposes they serve for attaining power in the classroom (Gallas, 1994, 1998). Boys appear to suffer more from their early indoctrination into school structures than do girls. Sitting and listening for long periods of time is seen as possible—even easy—for girls and torture for boys. Working quietly on a project and taking turns almost seems to satisfy the girls, whereas it becomes an occasion for shouting out, pushing, or running for the boys. Gallas describes the so-called bad boys in her first- and second-grade classes as those outspoken boys who use physical and verbal intrusions in the classroom to rebel against prevailing power. She notes, as others have (Best, 1983; Paley, 1993; Sadker & Sadker, 1994), that while signaling their power, these boys are also lost to the community of learning. Boys who are more physical and verbal also tend to spend more time attempting to garner adulation from the less aggressive boys and popular girls; consequently, they pay the price of isolation from the community of the classroom.

> As they [bad boys] develop and refine their ability to use language to critique, judge, and embarrass, they also disrupt instruction, intimidate classmates, and force a code of detachment

on themselves that denies their potential as learners and thinkers. (Gallas, 1998, p. 35)

Silence can be another way to negotiate power in the gender relations of the first-grade classroom. The gender stereotype pervading elementary school classrooms provides images of silent girls and bad boys. Boys may be quiet and shy, but they are rarely silent, whereas girls who are silent or whose voices are so low they are barely audible are not uncommon. One oversimplification of this phenomenon includes the belief that girls are silenced by the boys and somehow—if the teacher only intervenes—the girls will no longer be so quiet. Another oversimplification describes the gendered dichotomies of classroom discourse as originating in the classroom, as though the gender relations suppress the girls' voices. There is a lack of research on girls' silence, and an acceptance of their silence in the early grades remains. As a result, early childhood teachers see the need to manage the boys while the girls remain compliant and quiet. Teachers do not attempt to examine the possible causes of the girls' silences because the silences are not seen as problematic.

In fact, girls' silences serve to isolate them from a learning community and leave them out of the loop in the same way that boys' aggression isolates boys. Some classroom researchers have observed that for girls, the shrinking from the limelight of the classroom is connected to many complex factors—not just the reluctance to call attention to themselves. For some girls, remaining silent in the face of a classroom dynamic that includes outspoken and judgmental boys can be the only way they feel psychologically safe.

> Bad boys, like most children, are not naturally mean-spirited; they are experimental. They are small social scientists studying the effects of their behavior on others. (Gallas, 1998, p. 44)

Hence, the status of dominance among the children often determines who gets to have public voice in the classroom. Understanding how a child's classroom status can determine how that child gets to dominate the public voice in the classroom allows teachers the opportunity to reflect on those who are most frequently heard in the classroom—not only as a taken-for-granted gender issue, but also through the lens of social relations within and between genders in the classrooms. Because having a public voice is important to the development of all children, studying the classroom contexts that provide or discourage opportunities for voice is a necessary prerequisite to exploring the inner lives of silent girls and mediating the behaviors of outspoken boys.

Although researchers have observed *patterns* of girl and boy behaviors in early childhood environments that conform to gender stereotypes (i.e., boys in the block corner, girls in the doll corner), it is necessary for the classroom teacher to interrogate those separations and actively research the underlying subtexts of the classroom environment in order to provide greater possibilities for girls and boys. Equitable environments seek to uncover the needs and social issues behind these gendered behaviors, and—rather than provide equal treatment—seek ways to encourage all children to see themselves as contributors to the classroom community. This task often requires offering different experiences to girls and boys in the effort to level the playing field for all students.

Because each classroom is unique, the social relations that inform the dynamic give rise to what Gallas (1998) calls an *evolving consciousness*. Understanding this consciousness through the lens of gender is one way for a teacher to be an active facilitator of equitable classroom environments.

Gender Equity in Early Childhood Pedagogy and Curriculum

As part of the formal curriculum of the primary grades, researchers have explored ways in which teachers can introduce gender-equitable activities into the formal structure of the classroom curriculum. Peer discovery learning at activity centers is commonplace in early educational environments. Exploring the structure and content of the activity centers through the lens of gender reveals possibilities for organizing the classroom for more cross-gender play ideas. For example, placing the teacher's desk in close proximity to the block corner to encourage girls' participation in block building is a strategy informed by the finding that many girls like to stay around the teacher in the early grades (Greenberg, 1985). Further block-playing incentives include an *everybody plays with blocks* day every 2 weeks or a *girls' only* or *boys only* day with the block corner, the science center, or any other area that appears underutilized by girls or boys. To provide a variety of experiences for both girls and boys, teachers are encouraged to be vigilant that both girls and boys experience the sand table, water table, computer, crafts, and math centers. Further, renaming the center for playing house or dolls as the drama center and equipping it with boys' and girls' clothing, construction hats and tools, puppets, and anatomically correct dolls removes the gender stereotype and encourages boys as well as girls to participate in creative role-playing. It is useful to avoid action figures and glamour dolls that reinforce anatomical stereotypes and extremes (Mullen, 1994). Vivian Gussin Paley (1993) describes the ways in which framing the early childhood context around these types of interventions enables girls and boys to broaden their experiences.

In girls-only science talks, Gallas (1994) drew out primary girls' thinking about natural phenomena in ways that would go unexpressed in a mixed gender discussion. However, some studies reveal that when gender segregation happens without the teacher's sanction, it can be detrimental to student learning. In a study of first graders engaged in writers' workshop processes, conferencing about written work became divided by gender; boys excluded the girls by refusing to conference with them and girls conferenced only with girls as a way to avoid rejection (Henkin, 1995). The boys' literacy club was the dominant feature of this classroom, and the unspoken rule of the boys' club was that any member had to be a boy of who the leader approved. The girls and two boys in the class were excluded. Interviews with the boys revealed that they believed the girls were simply not adequate partners, but none of the girls challenged the boys' statements about why girls made poor conference partners. Boys deemed girls as inadequate because the girls' interests were not in sports, inventors, or science—they only wanted to write about babies, a prince, and a princess.

These girls were only in first grade, yet they had already experienced bigotry and rejection. Henkin concludes that discrimination among students in elementary classrooms merits a closer look. Educators need to be aware of who is being included, who is being excluded, and how exclusion affects the self-concepts and literacy development of their students. In this first-grade class, little boys felt better than and superior to the girls, deeming girls' interests as less valuable. The girls were puzzled and hurt. However, excluded boys also suffered academically and socially. The classroom dynamic that went on was unnoticed at first by the teacher; that boys conferenced only with boys and girls only with other girls was not immediately salient to the teacher-researcher. Of significance is that the initiative of single-sex writers' workshop conferencing was begun by the boys in this study because the girls were "simply not adequate partners" (Henkin, 1995, p. 430). At this early age, writing about babies and other so-called female writing interests was not valued by the boys, whose stories included adventure and sports. Even when girls wrote about sports, however, they were not deemed good conferencing partners.

Curriculum research in the early years points to the development of reading skills. Selection criteria for appropriate literature for young children has undergone great change as the field of gender equity in education evolved from the 1980s to the present. The advent of literature-based reading programs called into question what the children were reading. The gender roles of literary characters have great impact on small children. Hence, gender-neutral and nonstereotyped literature choices for young children have emerged, with significant implications. Curriculum transformation work explored later in this chapter examines the importance of providing children with windows into the worlds of those different from themselves and mirrors in which students can see themselves reflected in the school curriculum while exploring the lives of others (Style, 1998).

The metaphor of curriculum as window and mirror is applicable to all disciplines and has particular significance for early childhood education, in which stories, acting, and reading aloud play central roles in the classroom discourse. How are the protagonists presented in each story and in what ways do they reinforce or depart from gender stereotypes? The National Council of Teachers of English (NCTE) maintains ongoing lists of appropriate children's literature that posits both girls and boys as capable of strengths conventionally associated with the other gender (NCTE, 1995).

The importance of attending to gender-equitable early educational environments cannot be overstated. In the daily classroom interactions, teachers can challenge stereotypes about what girls and boys can and cannot do. Simple gross-motor tasks like moving a pile of books from one place in the classroom to another can be attended to by a boy, a girl, or both. Comforting a child in distress can be encouraged for the boys as well as for the girls (Chapman, 1997). What evolves as acceptable behavior for boys and girls in early years of schooling can be reinforced in later grades.

In early childhood environments, academic researchers and teacher-researchers describe gender separations that influence performance in many academic areas. The implications are often hierarchical—male interests and classroom behaviors often dominate the classroom contexts. The formal curriculum taught in the classroom comprises the guts of any school. It is the most important of the messages that we as educators send to students, parents, and ourselves about what reality is like and about what is truly worth teaching and learning (Chapman, 1997, p. 47). As we examine gender equity issues in middle and high school, the formal curriculum becomes more critical, revealing to students and their teachers what it is that is supposedly worth knowing while signaling less value to what is omitted. The omissions, called the null curriculum or the evaded curriculum, deliver powerful messages by their absences.

GENDER EQUITY IN THE MIDDLE GRADES AND HIGH SCHOOL YEARS

For many years, early adolescence has been identified as a time of heightened psychological risk for girls (Brown & Gilligan, 1992). At this stage in their development, girls

have been observed to lose their vitality, their voice, their resilience, their apparent immunity to depression, their self-confidence, and often their spunkiness (Gilligan, 1982; Orenstein, 1994; Pipher, 1994). These events are often invisible in middle grades classrooms as teachers and students alike see this passage as normal behavior for girls at this time and not influenced by culture, the hidden curriculum, or gender socialization, underscoring the importance of defining and redefining a gender issue in the classroom (Koch & Irby, 2002). How does understanding the psychology behind this passage help teachers to create more equitable middle grades and then high school classroom environments?

In analyzing women's development, Brown and Gilligan (1992) and others (Belenky, Clinchy, & Tarule, 1986; Gilligan, 1982; Miller, 1986) found that an inner sense of connection with others is a central organizing feature of women's development and that psychological crises in women's lives stem from disconnections. Women often silence themselves in relationships rather than risk open conflict or disagreement that might lead to isolation. In tracing this process backwards through adolescence, researchers learned that the desire for authentic connection, the experience of disconnection, the difficulties speaking out, and the feeling of not being heard or being able to convey one's own experience even to oneself accompany the preadolescent girl's passage (Brown & Gilligan, 1992).

Girls at this middle grades stage begin to question themselves as they struggle to remain in connection with others and see themselves in relation to the larger culture of women. Adolescent girls' inner conflicts about their abilities to belong, to achieve, to look right, to be popular, and to hear and validate their own voices while maintaining relationships are manifested in classrooms and often result in silences. Schools and specifically classrooms become places where early adolescent girls become reluctant to confront and publicly engage with others (Orenstein, 1994). Even girls with strong self-concepts will silence their inner voices for the sake of securing relationships. In a course for teachers that addressed gender issues in the classroom, one female teacher identified with the experiences described in the course readings by Brown and Gilligan (1992) about the psychological development of girls at puberty. What follows is an excerpt from a prolonged exchange about girls at puberty. The teachers' reflections were posted to a shared Web site. This woman's contribution to a discussion of the reading was supported by many of her female peers. It is included here to illustrate a shared understanding among White middle-class women as they reflected on their own early adolescent experiences.

Speaking as a white, middle class Caucasian woman who went through puberty, I was not at all surprised by reading that girls becoming quieter and more passive within the classroom after puberty because I remember what they are going through. It does not mean that the girls withdrew from life and social activity. In actuality, they were still vocal and showing confidence within their social groups and around females, but not inside the classroom. Basically, when puberty starts the awareness between the sexes greatly increases and the females especially become self-conscious about the changes. Around this time boys and girls start going on dates and hanging out in mixed groups. Middle school was a time of fitting-in and wanting to be popular. Students dressed the same and acted the same because being different was not socially accepted. Girls were unsure about themselves and the changes they experienced and wanted to fit-in. Being vocal inside the classroom would leave them open to criticism. They wanted to be asked out by the 'cool' boys and being too involved in school or showing how smart/'stupid' they were could deter the boys from liking you. The boys also wanted to fit-in and did not want girlfriends who were outspoken or smarter than them because they would end up feeling peer pressure or being ousted from their own group. Plus, since we are all socialized from the time we are born about the proper behaviors for males and females, when puberty hits these notions are magnified because we just came into our womanhood and manhood. Girls act more feminine and play up the 'girlie role,' and boys act more manly so that the opposite sex will notice and like them. No way would a girl take on what is considered a masculine quality in the classroom and risk rejection. Not until later on in high school when the females felt established within the school and their friends did many of us show our other sides and how we were unique and confident. Well, that was what it was like for many of the people I grew up with. There were exceptions and outspoken girls, but I don't think they were as outspoken as their personalities really were. . . . It is up to us, the teachers, to show the students that it is acceptable for everyone to show who they are and act in both masculine and feminine ways without fear of being rejected for their differences. (Web-based discourse, excerpted from Koch, 2001)

Brown and Gilligan (1992) conclude that authentic relationships with women are important to help adolescent girls hold onto their authentic inner voices. They refer to "resonant relationships between girls and women" as crucial for girls' development and for bringing women's voices fully into the world so that the "social construction of reality—the construction of the human world that is institutionalized by society and carried across generations by culture—will be built by and acoustically resonant for both women and men" (p. 7). Examples of girl-women pairings include big-sister/little-sister connections between middle and high school girls and young women in college and graduate school. Further pairings are cited between women scientists and aspiring girls in science at the middle and high school grades (Clewell et al., 1992).

One classroom researcher used these findings to actively listen to and for the voices of her seventh-grade girls in English class at an all-girls school (Barbieri, 1995). By providing venues for their private communications with her, Barbieri was able to delve more deeply into their authentic beliefs about themselves, writing, poetry, and the literature they would grow to love and critique. Barbieri used dialogic journals that were maintained with her all-female classes. The student journals, in which she wrote responses, became a way to make personal connections with each of her female students, providing her middle grades girls with an adult female connection. Barbieri explored the lives and work of important women writers, thus providing women's voices for the newly subverted adolescent voices of her students and once again providing women with whom her students could connect. In coeducational classes, the importance of these teaching strategies signals that both males and females are heard at deeply important levels. Not allowing the young adolescent girls to remain silent means more than coaxing their participation. It means finding ways to authentically include their voices without risking their withdrawal by promoting open confrontation in the classroom. It means seeking inclusive curriculum and pedagogy that honors all students' lived experiences. In short, listening for girls' voices at the middle and high school levels provides a richer educational experience for all students.

In a fifth-year language arts class in Britain, the teacher-researcher studied the experiences of students reading a story of a boy who was transformed for the day into a girl (Wing, 1997). This examination of the story *Bill's New Frock* (Fine, 1991) promoted extensive study of gender stereotypes and adult expectations of different genders' behaviors. The findings revealed that unraveling socially constructed systems of opportunities for males and females can be quite complex. This classroom teacher learned that the classroom environment she created provided a safe space in which the students could discuss their reactions to the story. They revealed their attitudes about gender stereotyping, and by identifying with the main character Bill, they expressed unhappiness with their own treatment in school. For example, the fictitious Bill encountered boundaries on the playground when he was a girl that were absent for him as a boy. Girls in the class felt aggrieved by the amount of space they were allowed on the playground and by their exclusion from football on the grounds because of their gender. Both girls and boys were surprised by the extent to which adult treatment differed for Bill when he became a girl for the day. This analysis revealed the depth of discourse that emerges when the hidden curriculum and the evaded curriculum become part of the formal curriculum.

In a 2-year exploratory study of risk taking in middle school mathematics, a girls-only seventh- and eighth-grade math class in a coeducational middle school was studied (Streitmatter, 1997). Through observations and interviews, this study found that girls were more likely to ask and answer questions about subject matter in the girls-only math class than they were in their other, coeducational classes. The girls reported that their ability to learn math and view themselves as mathematicians was enhanced by the girls-only setting. The girls in this setting took academic risks repeatedly during their work with the teacher and each other. They experienced more personal freedom and were less fearful of participating or of having the wrong answer than they were in coeducational classes. The girls expressed examples of peer behavior in their other classes that was belittling of them. The girls in this study expressed their perceptions of boys' expert status in math, which ultimately had the effect of silencing them. In their single-gender class, there were no self-proclaimed experts and there was much collaboration. Although it is not a prescription for single-gender schooling, this study poses questions for the classroom teacher about climate and pedagogy in mixed-gender classrooms. If math class lends itself to encouraging stereotyped male expertise to the exclusion of females, teachers must develop strategies to ensure cooperation and collaboration in the coeducational setting. Furthermore, the classroom teacher in this study became aware that her pedagogy differed in the mixed-gender seventh- and eighth-grade math class. This teacher acknowledged working differently with the girls-only group, allowing herself to delve more deeply into the processes of mathematics; no reason was determined for why this was so.

Unmasking the Hidden Curriculum

Using case studies and a gender-equity CD-ROM, researchers discovered ways to make students more aware of gender-equity issues and to give them tools to resolve these situations (Matthews, Brinkley, Crisp, & Gregg, 1998). Although this study took place with fifth graders, it has implications for upper middle school grades. Students examined gender-equity materials over the course of a year; the materials included specific scenarios depicting stereotypical classroom behavior—that is, boys shouting out answers and not getting reprimanded and boys taking charge in a group science experiment. Open-ended discussions and structured questions followed the case study examples. Furthermore, the students took pretest and posttest questionnaires exploring

the interactions in their classrooms and their beliefs about jobs and abilities. One question asked the fifth graders to name the best students in their class in math, science, social studies, and English. Boys named only boys to math and science, while naming girls and boys to the other subjects. Girls indicated girls or boys equally in math, science, and social studies, and they named girls only in English. This finding is consistent with many other findings (Sadker & Sadker, 1994); this study also suggests the importance of gender equity as a shared agenda in the classroom. Those classrooms in which a gender agenda is overt and in which curriculum interventions are explored on behalf of males and females learning more about themselves, their own interactions, and those who have been omitted from curriculum have an excellent track record for fairness and equity (Logan, 1997; Orenstein, 1994).

Logan's middle school interventions promote awareness of self and other through a myriad of experiences, stories, role-modeling, and even quilt-making exercises that allow students to explore the realities of their gendered lives. In one exercise, she asks her students to imagine that they wake up the next day as a member of the opposite sex. "Now make a list of how your life would be different" (Logan, 1997, p. 35). Through a carefully structured discussion, students come to see that they are more similar than different; this is a step toward mutual respect and an understanding of the power of communication.

One middle school classroom researcher approaches gender issues in a language arts classroom by using sentence starters such as *Being a female means* or *Being a male means* according to their gender. Then students respond in terms of the opposite sex. This method begins the discussion, which quickly uncovers the expectations each gender has for its own and for the other gender (Mitchell, 1996, p. 77). Additionally, inviting middle school students to analyze picture books through the lens of gender proves powerful as students research the images and draw conclusions about the messages.

Girls are not the only ones harmed by gender-role effects in language arts (McCracken, Evans, & Wilson, 1996). Some areas of the language arts curriculum—notably, journal writing—pose problems for boys in ways that they do not for girls. For example, boys have difficulty getting started and sounding fluent. Language arts students are often asked to be reflective and responsive in their writing, and boys often need support to find facility in this type of reflective writing.

In middle school science classrooms, boys traditionally monopolize the teachers' time as well as the lab equipment, and girls encourage them to do so (Orenstein, 1994; Sadker & Sadker, 1986, 1994). The costs of this behavior are high—both for a society that ultimately loses potential scientists and for the girls themselves, who find they are rewarded when they deny their intelligence and individuality (McCracken et al., 1996). Referred to as *gender-binding,* these practices require resistance on the part of teachers and middle school girls. Creating cooperative settings in middle school science in which mixed-gender groups have assigned tasks that rotate with each lab activity is one structure that helps. Authentic expectations for everyone's active participation are shown to promote participation. Bringing real-life conflicts and stories into the middle school science curriculum is good science education and encourages girls' participation (Koch, 1998c). Furthermore, posters of men and women and curriculum material that make connections between science and daily life encourage female participation and enhance the quality of instruction (see Linn, 2000).

Research demonstrates a decline in middle school girls' ability or willingness to express individual opinions that pose even the slightest possibility of creating real conflict with their peers. Research also demonstrates that some middle school teachers scold girls for speaking in a disagreeable or strident manner (Brown & Gilligan, 1992). An implication of this finding is that middle school teachers need to encourage their female middle school students to risk making their peers angry; these teachers also need to teach their female students how to be assertive and articulate without being or feeling hostile. This task is not simple; it requires research into successful strategies on behalf of listening to all students. Barbieri (1995) and Logan (1997) offer important suggestions for voice and identity.

Furthermore, studies have shown that even when teachers reflect knowledge of gender-equity issues in the classroom, they are not always able to translate the knowledge of the issue into changes in their behavior (Levine & Orenstein, 1994). Teachers themselves have been socialized to believe certain stereotypes about genders and have also had some of the same experiences that their students are having; gender equity in the classroom should therefore be a shared goal for teachers with their students.

Body Image and the Secondary School Student

In the United States, magazines, billboards, movies, television shows, commercials, and MTV send a message that being thin is the central attribute of beauty for women and will eventually lead to success and happiness. Although this obsession with weight loss and being very thin is associated with middle grades social behavior for girls, there is evidence that discussions about weight begin in earlier grades. A second- and third-grade teacher reports the following excerpt.

'I need to lose weight,' Kayla was saying. Another second grade girl chimed in 'So do I. I'm way too fat.' My students' conversation shocked me . . . Linda, a third grade girl who is thin to the point of looking unhealthy, grabbed a piece of paper from Kayla. 'I'm the one who needs this.' 'No, I need it!' insisted Rhonda. The hotly contested paper turned out to contain the name of an exercise video that my second- and third-grade class had seen in gym. Although the video was for health and fitness, not weight loss, the girls were convinced that the video would help them lose weight and were frantic to get hold of it. (Lyman, 2000)

By middle grades the thinness crisis often reaches out-of-control proportions, as mostly White middle-class girls strive to be beautiful in the way that beauty is socially constructed to mean acute thinness. Teenagers are under a lot of pressure to succeed and fit in. Many spend a lot of time worrying about what others think, and they desperately try to conform to society's unattainable so-called ideal body image. Young teenage girls are led to believe that if they are thin, they will be accepted. Because many teenagers buy teen or fashion magazines regularly, the images of emaciated models appearing in those magazines only reinforces their belief that in order to be happy, successful, and accepted, they must be thin. As recently as 5 years ago, African American girls were immune to such pressures; however, as young Black models increasingly adopt White images for beauty, more middle-class teenage Black girls are aspiring to what was formerly a White middle-class image of beauty.

Many teenagers believe that dieting is a normal way to eat. Teenagers with eating disorders such as anorexia nervosa have distorted perceptions of their body weight and shape—they persist in believing they need to lose weight even when they are seriously underweight. More than one third of all middle grades girls believe they are overweight (Giarratano, 1997).

The classroom teacher needs to be aware of the complexity of anorexia nervosa and bulimia. The underlying causes that promote excessive weight loss are complex issues found in the personal, peer, family, and societal influences on a particular teen. Most teens with eating disorders try to avoid conflicts at all costs, so they usually do not express negative feelings and try to wear a happy face all the time to try to please people. They end up using food as a way to stuff down all those negative feelings, and purging usually gives them a sense of relief—almost as though they are releasing all those built-up emotions (Thompson, 2001).

There are at least 8 million individuals with eating disorders in the Unites States; the most common disorders are *anorexia nervosa,* characterized by starving oneself, and *bulimia,* characterized by binging and purging. These disorders affect 10–15% of adolescents, and 90% of those affected are girls. Anorexia nervosa can and does cause serious medical problems; it is estimated that 5–18% of those who become anorexic will die because of medical problems associated with malnutrition. Signs associated with anorexia nervosa include a sickly and emaciated overall appearance, lack of energy, loss of ability to concentrate, and loss of hair. Binge-purging results in damage to the esophagus, internal bleeding, and severe electrolyte imbalance; it also can lead to heart failure. The young woman who is bulimic is often of normal weight and uses gorging and vomiting or excess laxatives to maintain her weight. Hence, bulimic teens are less visible at first glance unless they also have anorexia. Forty percent of individuals with anorexia are also bulimic.

Eating disorders pose a significant gender issue for secondary school teachers and students. It is not often addressed in school curriculum; hence, as a result of the evaded or null curriculum, girls with eating disorders go unnoticed, or it is perceived as normal for girls to be abnormally thin or constantly dieting. Teachers need to take an active role in preventing eating disorders by educating their students about the dangers of excess dieting and binging and purging. Teachers and school counselors should also be made aware of the signs to look for. Researchers have established protocols for addressing the problem in the context of the classroom.

If a teacher believes a student to have anorexia nervosa or bulimia, the student should be approached. Teachers need to talk to her or him, state their concern, and suggest a chat with a counselor or parent. Educators should be prepared to offer local resources for treatment and avoid making any comments about the student's eating behavior or subsequent weight gain. Most important is that research indicates the value of letting the student know that the teacher cares (Michigan Model, 2000).

Sexual Harassment and the Middle and High School Grades

Understanding the impact of body image on adolescent development is related to learning about another increasingly common phenomenon in schools—the occurrence of sexually harassing behavior in classrooms, hallways, on school grounds, and in school buses. Ignoring this phenomenon or worse—coding the occurrence as normal for girls and boys—gives tacit approval to disturbing behaviors that limit the educational possibilities for girls and many boys.

> School is a harassing and unkind place for students . . . [they] tell us they feel powerless and are looking to the adults in schools to behave like adults and to enforce a climate that is healthy and supportive. (Shakeshaft et al., 1995, p. 42.)

Sexual harassment was defined for a recent survey as "unwanted and unwelcome sexual behavior that interferes with your life. Sexual harassment is not behaviors that you like or want (for example, wanted kissing, touching or flirting)" (AAUW, 2001, p. 2). School sexual harassment has a negative effect on the emotional and educational lives of students. Sexually harassing behaviors happen in hallways, stairwells, and classrooms. The importance to educators of knowing and understanding the risks of coding sexist behavior as normal cannot be understated. Although boys are increasingly becoming more victimized by sexually harassing classroom and school incidents, they remain less likely than are girls to have this experience.

According to a recent Harris Poll (AAUW, 2001), 8 in 10 students experience some form of sexual harassment during their school lives. Slightly more than half the students polled say they have sexually harassed someone during their school lives; this is significant in view of the finding that 9 in 10 students report that students sexually harass other students at their school. Moreover, a sizable number of students surveyed (38%) report that teachers and other school employees sexually harass students. In the last 8 years this percentage has declined (from 44% in 1993).

According to the students surveyed, sexual harassment—words and actions—in school happens often, occurs under teachers' noses, can begin in elementary school, and is very upsetting to both girls and boys. This report (AAUW, 2001) is a follow-up to the first nationwide survey on sexual harassment in schools, also commissioned by the AAUW Educational Foundation and researched by Harris Interactive (then known as Louis Harris & Associates, 1993). Eighty-three percent of girls and 79% of boys report having experienced harassment. The number of boys reporting experiences with harassment often or occasionally has increased since 1993 (56% vs. 49%), although girls are still somewhat more likely to experience it. Seventy-six percent of students have experienced nonphysical harassment, whereas 58% have experienced physical harassment. Nonphysical harassment includes taunting, rumors, graffiti, jokes, or gestures. One third of all students report experiencing physical harassment often or occasionally. Although large groups of both boys and girls report experiencing harassment, girls are more likely to report being negatively affected by it. Girls are far more likely than are boys to feel self-conscious, embarrassed, and less confident because of an incident of harassment. Girls are more likely than are boys to change behaviors in school and at home because of the experience—including not talking as much in class and avoiding the person who harassed them. Nearly all students (96%) say they know what harassment is, and boys' and girls' definitions do not differ substantially.

Most harassment occurs under teachers' noses in the classroom and in the halls. Students are perpetrators, too. Slightly more than half of students say that they have sexually harassed someone during their school lives; this represents a decrease from 1993, when 59% admitted as much. In particular, boys are less likely than in 1993 to report being a perpetrator (adapted from www.aauw.org and AAUW, 2001).

Findings from the Harris Poll survey studies have led to more stringent legal guidelines for sexual harassment cases. The Supreme Court ruling of May 1999 held school districts liable for damages under federal law for failing to stop a student from subjecting another to severe and pervasive sexual harassment. As a result of this ruling, school districts are developing policies to address sexual harassment events promptly and to protect targets of harassment from abusers' continuing torment. These policies are made known to all school personnel, students, and parents. Classroom teachers must seek curriculum materials to address harassment issues—formerly a part of the hidden and evaded curriculums. Noted researcher in the study of school sexual harassment, Nan Stein, working with classroom teachers, has developed useful curriculum guides that provide teachers and students with activities and role-playing scenarios that can help students to address harassing behavior when it occurs. They are also useful guides for helping students to distinguish between acceptable and unacceptable behaviors. *Bullyproof: A Teacher's Guide on Teasing and Bullying for Use With Fourth and Fifth Grade Students* by Sjostrum and Stein (1996) and *Flirting or Hurting: A Teacher's Guide on Student-to-Student Sexual Harassment in Schools (Grades 6 Through 12)* by Stein and Sjostrum (1994) help students to acquire strategies for coping with unwanted attention.

Gender Equity and the Formal Curriculum

Curriculum considerations inform all of precollege schooling, but influences become more pronounced in the segue from middle school to high school as students prepare for college, the workplace, or both. What are they studying? Whose lives are worth knowing about? How do they learn? How is knowledge viewed in the context of the classroom? In what ways does the curriculum reflect the human condition and provide windows and mirrors? "More than half of our culture's population (all girls, and boys from minority groups) are trained and expected to look through windows at others who are viewed as the valid participants [on life's stage as well as the playing field] . . . at the same time those whose (white male) experience is repeatedly mirrored are narrowly and provincially educated to see themselves (and their own kind) as the only real players on life's stage" (Style,

1998, p. 155). A balanced education should be for all of us—"knowledge of both self and other, and clarification of the known and illumination of the unknown" (p. 155).

If educators are to fully represent the scope of the human condition through the topics addressed in the academic disciplines, then the very nature of and content of those disciplines needs to be explored though the lens of gender. In her seminal work, *Interactive Phases of Curricular and Personal Re-Vision: A Feminist Perspective,* Peggy McIntosh (1983) examines curriculum transformation as an interactive and iterative process that weaves forward and backward at the same time. McIntosh's theory suggests new ways of seeing and coming to terms with what counts for history, language arts, science, mathematics, and more—in terms of whose voices are being validated and for whom are there mirrors. To begin her work, McIntosh (1983) asked, "what is the content, scope and methodology of the discipline?" Furthermore, "how would that discipline need to change to reflect the fact that women are half the world's population and have had, in one sense, half the world's experience?" (p. 2). In describing types of curriculum corresponding to five phases of curriculum transformation, McIntosh asserts their fluidity with the educator's understanding that we should teach and learn between the phases in an attempt to address not only the absences in the formal curriculum, but also its very structure.

The following description is an overview of this theory of curriculum revision; it takes the reader through McIntosh's five phases of curriculum development, moving further toward an inclusive body of knowledge with each phase. Using history as an example, these phases are seen as Phase 1: Womanless History; Phase 2: Women in History; Phase 3: Women as a Problem, Anomaly, or Absence in History; Phase 4: Women as History; and Phase 5: History Redefined or Reconstructed to Include Us All.

Hence, looking though the lens of gender, much of formal curriculum is seen as womanless. Students neither learn about women nor notice their absence. Students learn about laws, wars, and events in which power and politics appear to have been the only experience the world has had. This phase, referred to as Phase 1 curriculum, says that women and people of color do not matter; it is not important to learn about them. Phase 2 is reminiscent of the early textbook transformations that emerged after the women's movement of the 1970s. There are images of women, but only those few who could reach this pinnacle of importance on White male terms. Are they valuable enough to include? Did they accomplish visibly significant tasks as defined by White men? This phase can be problematic for curriculum development because it overwhelmingly tells girls and women that only if they are good enough on criteria external to them and their experience will they be important enough to be studied.

Phase 3 curriculum addresses women in the curriculum by exploring the barriers they faced and historical discrimination against women. Phase 3 curriculum describes the ways in which women were denied access and discriminated against. The image of women as victims dominates Phase 3 curriculum; instead of being seen as the norm, women are viewed as a problem or anomaly. An example would be a curriculum that only addressed the women's suffrage movement as a way to include women in the formal curriculum.

When we examine Phase 4 curriculum, we can begin to see women as history and explore the real work in the life of civilization. This phase addresses questions like *What was life like in America during the War of 1812 and what were people doing?* Students' stories and their interviews with others are part of the curriculum. For example, immigration is taught by reading about or having interviews with immigrants. The curriculum is viewed as the study of people—not solely the study of power, relationships, or rewards. Stories are integrated with personal knowledge so that reality is constructed from the ground up. "One key element of phase four curriculum is that the 'other' stops being considered something lesser to be dissected, deplored, devalued or corrected" (McIntosh, 1983, p. 19). When well done, McIntosh asserts, "phase four work honors particularity. . . . it stresses diversity and plurality" (McIntosh, 1983, p. 20). In Phase 4, curriculum relies on women's experience by "developing ourselves through the development of others" (Miller, 1986).

Phase 5 curriculum revision is the hardest to conceive. "Human collaborative potential is explored and competitive potential subjected to a sustained critique" (McIntosh, 1983, p. 21). Phase 5 curriculum has promise for meshing private-sphere values with the public sphere. History can be explored through stories of ancestors' experiences; knowledge of the world is constructed through personal experience, and curriculum honors all peoples' contributions to the human condition. In this phase of curriculum transformation, the hierarchical distinctions between who is valuable to know about and who is not are deconstructed. McIntosh quotes Ruth Schmidt as remarking, "If you claim to teach about the human race and you don't know anything about half the human race, you really can't claim to know or teach much about the human race" (McIntosh, 1983, p. 23).

The formal curriculum is as much a classroom gender issue as teacher-student interactions and peer socialization. The topic of gender issues in the classroom cannot be oversimplified by critiquing prevailing stereotypes. The depth of the issues tells us more about the multilayered effects of curriculum and pedagogy on perpetuating belief systems that render females as lesser and male accomplishment and voice as dominant. For men and women, curriculum and pedagogical transformations to honor contributions—formal and informal—of females and males holds promise for excellent education, nonexistent without opportunities for equity. The following sections address curriculum and pedagogical revisions in science and mathematics classrooms that provide insight into making science and mathematics education more equitable.

Mathematics, Science, and Technology: Equity and Access

Traditionally, science, mathematics, and technology classrooms have been male domains. Although there have been great gains for females in mathematics and the life sciences in the past 15 years, physical sciences, computer science, and engineering fields still lag behind in encouraging the participation of girls and women (AAUW, 1998). Girls' participation in Algebra I, Algebra II, geometry, precalculus, trigonometry, and calculus increased markedly from the early to mid-1990s; enrollments increased from 10% to 20% in the first half of the last decade (U.S. Dept of Education, 2000). However, data suggest a disturbing gap in the participation of female students in computer science and computer design classes. The gender gap widens from 8th to 11th grade. In 1996, girls comprised only 17% of the AP test takers in computer science. Girls of all ethnicities consistently rate themselves lower than do boys on computer ability (AAUW, 1998). Computer science has become the new boys' club, so to speak; this is a red flag for educators and must signal that schools and teachers are ignoring a rich, necessary, and vital resource—both for the computer science field and for the high school girls themselves. In this century, the educational question that persists is *What is wrong with the school when few girls participate in computer science?* (Koch, 2001). Some of the persistent interventions reviewed in the following discussion to encourage more female participation in mathematics and science need to be applied to the computer science field. When teachers transform curriculum and pedagogy to encourage female participation, they improve the quality of instruction and the diversity of the curriculum. Many standards-based interventions in science have been suggested previously by equity educators as encouraging female participation (Campbell & Storo, 1994; Sanders et al., 1997). Equitable educational environments are apt to meet standards-based interventions on behalf of student learning.

A marked gender gap persists in physics, in which girls' enrollments lag behind boys. In math and science, a more boys than girls receive top scores on the National Assessment of Education Progress (NAEP), a nationally representative test of specific subject matter given to students in 4th, 8th, and 12th grades. The gender gap increases with grade level. African American girls, however, outscore African American boys at every assessment point (AAUW, 1998; http://nces.ed.gov).

A review of research within science and mathematics classes provides insight and hope for creating a more equitable climate of participation and a more engaging curriculum. Research demonstrates that when high school physics teachers give appropriate attention to gender issues in their classrooms, achievement and participation improve for all their students—especially for their female students (Rop, 1998). Creating a classroom culture that is emotionally safe for females and males alike and sanctioning risks and mistakes as vital to learning requires that teachers model ways to take individual risks (Kasov, as quoted by Rop, 1998). In high school chemistry and physics, assigning students research articles by women, taking a direct approach with females to actively encourage their participation in advanced science courses, and providing female mentoring are interventions that have proven successful. One such intervention for chemistry students includes creating electronic or face-to-face mentoring relationships with women chemists who have successful careers. High school chemistry teachers have reported that this intervention has resulted in encouraging young women to consider science as a career (Campbell & Storo, 1994; Kahle & Meece, 1994; Rop, 1998; Sanders et al., 1997). High school science teachers have learned that—in coeducational environments—often single-sex science lab groups are more effective for encouraging young women than are the mixed-gender groups (Rop, 1998). This and other studies revealed that in mixed gender groups, the girls are often the scribes or the recorders for the lab experience and the males are more often the doers; this situation is eliminated in single-sex lab groups.

Restructuring curriculum to provide a holistic view of the subject area encourages scientific study for both males and females. Integrating the history, social context, and social implications of scientific study by making connections to contemporary issues in the scientific field brings the physical sciences to life in important and meaningful ways. Making connections to lived experience is both an agenda for the National Science Education Standards (National Research Council, 1996) and for encouraging participation in the sciences.

Meyer (1998) found that feeling included is a necessary prerequisite to participation in school science. As a science education professor, she was engaged in teaching physical science to future elementary school science teachers. Renaming her university course Creative Expression in Science, she encouraged participation of her females in the physical

science course. Engaging her students in deep and lengthy discussion and experimentation in a safe and inclusive environment has led to female students' pursuing science in ways that the students previously had not imagined. In one intervention, Meyer (1998) studied motion with her female students by swimming in the university pool, ice skating at the local rink, and doing simple gymnastics in the university gym: "In-class discussions were richly based on the movements we shared" (p. 469).

In studies, adult women reflect on their science experiences through personal narratives. These stories reveal both a sense of estrangement from the scientific disciplines as well as fear of making a mistake (Koch, 1998b; Meyer, 1998). Incompetent pedagogy and an inability to make connections to students' lived experiences can result in feelings of incompetence in science and—for women—a sense of feeling that "this is not your space" (Larkin, 1994, p. 109). In these studies, surveys, personal interviews, and analysis of personal narratives, sometimes called science autobiographies, reveal that the distance that many women feel from affiliations toward natural science is frequently a result of feeling like a deficient female. Although males may feel deficient in science, the images of scientific heroes and their stories create a culture of entitlement to success that allows males' feelings of incompetence to be separated from issues of gender. Many females feel that they are part of an aggregate group whose members are not supposedly good in science.

The rigor of natural science is not seen as a deterrent to female participation; rather, the method of teaching has emphasized a false disconnection between studying the sciences and understanding their contributions to society. In a recent study (Linn, 2000), researchers and teachers created important curriculum contexts for making science relevant to students' lives. By integrating scientific controversies into the secondary science curriculum, students gained the opportunity to connect to a contemporary scientific controversy and began to see that scientists regularly revisit their ideas and rethink their views, empowering students to do the same.

> I challenge all concerned about science education to remedy the serious declines in science interest, the disparities in male and female persistence in science, and the public resistance to scientific understandings by forming partnerships to bring to life the excitement and controversy in scientific research. (Linn, 2000, p. 16)

In one study, students were engaged in exploring a contemporary controversy about deformed frogs. By using selected Internet materials to construct their own arguments, students prepared for a classroom debate around two main hypotheses: the parasite hypothesis stating that the trematode parasite explains the increase in frog deformities or the environmental hypothesis suggesting that an increase in specific chemicals used to spray adjacent fields to the frog pond caused the frog deformities. In order to construct an argument, students examined evidence from research laboratories, discussed their ideas with peers, and searched for additional information. Using a Web-based environment, middle school students partnered with graduate students working in a laboratory at Berkeley as well as with technology and assessment experts (see http://wise.berkeley.edu).

In the study of this project, researchers interviewed and surveyed teachers and students prior to their participation in this partnership. They designed pre- and posttests, inquiry activities, and curriculum materials that ensured that curriculum and assessment were aligned. The classroom research continued to help teachers to refine the materials used for instruction. Prior to this scientific controversy unit, the students often reported that science had no relevance to their lives and that science was best learned by memorizing (Linn & Hsi, 1999). In the deformed frogs study, pre- and posttest assessments revealed that more than two thirds of the students were able to use the mechanism for the parasite hypothesis that they learned from the Internet evidence. The answers often revealed the complex use of language and showed that the students learned from reviewing and integrating Web resources. On all assessment measures for content, females and males were equally successful.

This scientific controversy unit about deformed frogs was carried out with diverse middle school students—half the students qualified for free or reduced-price lunches, and one in four students spoke English at home. As a result of this scientific controversy unit of study, more students participated in science, more students gained scientific understanding, and students became more aware of the excitement that motivates scientists to pursue careers in science (Linn, 2000, p. 25).

The skills that students acquired by working in these partnerships and critically evaluating and interpreting scientific data were contextualized and situated within the real world of science—ponds and frogs. Using McIntosh's theory (1983), this Phase 4 curriculum brought science, scientists, and research to life in ways that allowed students to be participants and contributors, seeing themselves as valuable and capable of working collaboratively. This type of curriculum transformation works on behalf of all students by stating overtly that they and their thinking do matter. School science has been too removed from real-life experiences, and thus it has suffered from not attracting females; this type of curriculum transformation will potentially attract those who have seen themselves as other to the study of science.

Classroom researchers describe pedagogy and practices that are employed to encourage girls' participation in physics that reveal the importance of gender-sensitive classrooms for promoting girls' interest in physics (Martin, 1996). The learning environments that are most effective include respecting girls as central players—researchers refer to honoring their experiences and their within-group diversity by encouraging participation strategies, providing a safe classroom, highlighting the accomplishments as well as the barriers to women and science, and becoming involved in making connections between the physics and girls' lived experience (Martin, 1996; Meyer, 1998). Requiring that students maintain reflective journals in the physics class has been seen as a useful strategy to engage all students in their thinking. Maintaining reflective journals in the physics classroom helps males and females integrate communication skills into the understanding of the physics concepts (Sanders et al., 1997). Results from gender-sensitive classes reveal that attitudes and achievement increase and speak to the importance of institutionalizing gender-equitable practices.

Mathematics educators have identified pedagogy and curriculum interventions that result in attracting more females to higher order mathematics while improving the quality of teaching and learning in mathematics (Fennema & Leder, 1990; Noddings, 1990; Reynolds, 1995). In fact, strategies advocated by the National Council of Teachers of Mathematics (NCTM, 2000), affirm the that gender-equitable teaching is a prerequisite to excellent practice. Such practices are similar for science educators—namely, making connections between mathematics and lived experience, working in cooperative learning groups, providing mentors and images of women in mathematics, coaching females for deeper responses to higher order questions, and holding out the expectation that females as well as males will be successful in mathematics.

Addressing cognitive research, Reynolds (1995) includes pointers for teaching mathematics to all students; suggestions include using a constructivist approach to teaching (Brooks & Brooks, 1999). The following behaviors are examples of those advocated on behalf of all students' learning in mathematics:

- Considering problems of emerging interest to the students.
- Studying the big picture and situating major concepts.
- Seeking and valuing students' points of view.
- Communicating both verbally and in writing.
- Giving nonjudgmental feedback.
- Reflecting and caring.
- Interacting in groups.
- Listening to each other.
- Honoring creativity (Reynolds, 1995, p. 26).

By making connections between previously documented gender-equity strategies for mathematics teaching and learning, Reynolds (1995) notes the overlap with constructivist practice. Furthermore, in addition to teachers' monitoring their interactions with students to ensure that both genders receive comparable treatment with respect to student voice, extending wait time, and placing students at the center of learning, Reynolds notes that constructivist teachers are constantly monitoring student understanding, which is at the core of more gender-equitable settings. It is hoped that technology instruction will follow the lead of science and mathematics instruction by designing curriculum and pedagogical practices that increase possibilities for females' participation.

With each generation, gender images and gendered systems of privilege get revisited in schools and colleges. The impulse to repeat offenses because they appear invisible is pervasive in all schooling. As the new century begins, educators look anew at ways to improve the learning environments for girls and boys—for men and women.

In an intensive study (Hopkins, 1999) of working conditions for women academic scientists and engineers at MIT, it was revealed that women scientists experienced many inequities in their working conditions, allocation of resources, and salaries. The data were collected over several years and the analysis was intense. Women at several other institutions joined ranks with their colleagues in documenting differential research environments for men and women at their universities. In response to these data, the Ford Foundation has awarded a $1 million grant to MIT to promote similar efforts for equity at other campuses.

CONCLUSIONS

Creating a Gender-Equitable Culture in the Classroom

In all academic disciplines, research has shown that girls and boys as well as young men and women sitting in the same classroom and experiencing the same curriculum often receive differential treatment—usually unwittingly—based on their gender. Most teachers, both men and women, elementary and secondary, interact more with boys than with girls. In addition, both male and female teachers view girls as more independent, creative, and academically persistent, whereas boys are seen as more aggressive. Teachers who are successful in addressing classroom interaction strategies that further the growth and development of both females and males are ones who are aware of the research findings about gender and equity and who employ conscious strategies on behalf of creating equitable environments. These strategies include using nonsexist, inclusive language and avoiding sexist humor. Gender-equitable teachers encourage all students to

participate in class discussions by employing specific strategies for calling on students. They tend to value creativity and multiple ways of solving problems, honoring differences.

In teacher sanctions, equitable teachers praise and affirm both girls and boys for performance and do not overpraise girls for their appearance. In their interactions, they coach all students to search for deeper meanings and provide role models for both males and females from all socioeconomic strata. Teachers can employ wait time to encourage risk taking when students are answering questions. By consciously addressing gender issues, teachers adapt instructional strategies to account for gender (i.e., girls-only science talks; mixed-gender writing groups).

Gender-equitable teaching involves monitoring the classroom discourse, understanding the context-specific complexities of dominance in classroom environments, and integrating cooperative learning into regular teacher-directed environments. It is necessary for teachers to hold out the expectation that both females and males can accomplish a task or solve a problem. It is important not to perform a task for a female student while expecting a male student to do it on his own. This practice leads to learned helplessness (Eccles Parsons, Meece, Adler, & Kaczala, 1982).

Gender-equitable teaching uncovers the hidden curriculum and enables teachers to identify bias and confront sexism in the classroom. Teachers must avoid comparisons of boys and girls regarding behavior, achievement, and attitudes. They need to ask students whether teachers are treating persons differently because of gender. Additionally, teachers should ask students to tell them when teachers are treating either group differently. Finally, teachers need to accept and encourage emotional expression from both girls and boys (adapted from Greenberg, 1985; Pratchler, 1996; Sadker & Sadker, 1994; Sanders et al., 1997).

The formal curriculum must be explored through the lens of race, class, and gender: Who is included and who is significant to learn about? Formal curriculum must reflect the lived experience of all students so that knowledge construction is a shared endeavor. Schools limit possibilities for gender equity when they fail to confront or discuss risk factors for students. Risk factors for students must be addressed through the formal curriculum. Deconstructing gender teachings means asking what programs, pedagogies, and curricula will best serve the needs of female and male students.

In teacher education schools, colleges, and departments, equity must be viewed as essential to professional education programs; gender-equity issues must be integrated into preservice training. Colleges and universities must confront the risks for girls and boys in school and develop programs to stem high dropout rates and address the underrepresentation of girls in computer science and physics. Understanding the importance of extracurricular activities for girls, schools should strive to recruit and retain more females in those activities. Researchers need to explore the overrepresentation of males in remedial reading programs and seek to learn the causes. "Research should analyze educational data by sex, race, ethnicity, and social class to provide a more detailed picture of all students" (AAUW, 1998, p. 10).

Examining school violence gives clues to the gender socialization of boys that alienates them from the dominant school culture. Examining risk factors for boys and exploring interventions on behalf of their healthy development must become a priority.

Studies of girls and schooling need to explore single-sex public schools for minority females, such as the Young Women's Leadership School in New York City. What are the attributes of these environments that can be institutionalized in coeducational schools? In coeducational classrooms, researchers needs to explore girls' silences and how entitlement to voice differs across ethnicity and socioeconomic class.

Studies need to examine how the computer science gender gap is affecting the educational gap, and they should identify useful interventions on behalf of girls and computer science. Female participation in physics and engineering requires further study because it lags seriously behind their participation in the life sciences. Nancy Hopkins, a noted biologist who led the MIT study on women scientists mentioned previously, stated, "It's a different world now for women scientists, but the question is, 'How do you institutionalize it so it will last for the next generation?'" (Zernike, 2001, p. A11). That, indeed, is the question that underlies gender issues in the classroom—what would institutionalizing this agenda look like? It is hoped this chapter gives some glimpses.

REFERENCES

American Association of University Women Educational Foundation. (1992). *How schools shortchange girls: A study of major findings on girls and education.* Washington, DC: Author.

American Association of University Women Educational Foundation. (1993). *Hostile hallways: The AAUW survey on sexual harassment in America's schools.* Washington, DC: Author.

American Association of University Women Educational Foundation. (1995). *How schools shortchange girls: The AAUW report.* Washington, DC: Author.

American Association of University Women Educational Foundation. (1998a). *Gender gaps executive summary.* Washington, DC: Author.

American Association of University Women Educational Foundation. (1998b). *Gender gaps: Where schools still fail on children.* Washington, DC: Author.

American Association of University Women Educational Foundation. (2000). *A license for bias: Sex discrimination, schools, and Title IX.* Washington, DC: Author.

American Association of University Women Educational Foundation. (2001). *Hostile hallways: Bullying, teasing, and sexual harassment in schools.* Washington, DC: Author.

American Association of University Women. (n.d.). Retrieved May 3, 2002, from http://www.aauw.org

Barbieri, M. (1995). *Sounds from the heart: Learning to listen to girls.* Portsmouth, NH: Heinemann.

Belenky, M., Clinchy, B., & Tarule, J. (1996). *Women's ways of knowing.* New York: Basic Books.

Best, R. (1983). *We've all got scars: What boys and girls learn in elementary school.* Indianapolis: University of Indiana Press.

Brooks, J. G., & Brooks, M. (1999). *In search of understanding: The case for constructivist classrooms.* Alexandria, VA: Association for Supervision and Curriculum Development.

Brophy, J. (1981). Teacher praise: A functional analysis. *Review of Educational Research, 51,* 5–32.

Brown, L. M., & Gilligan, C. (1992). *Meeting at the crossroads: Women's psychology and girls' development.* Cambridge, MA: Harvard University Press.

Campbell, P., & Storo, J. (1994). *Why me? Why my classroom? The need for equity in coed math and science classes.* Groton, MA: Campbell-Kibler.

Chapman, A. (1997). *A great balancing act: Equitable education for girls and boys.* Washington, DC: National Association of Independent Schools.

Clewell, B. C., Anderson, B. T., & Thorpe, M. E. (1992). *Breaking the barriers: Helping female and minority students succeed in mathematics and science.* San Francisco: Jossey-Bass.

Derman-Sparks, L. (1989). *Anti-bias curriculum: Tools for empowering your children.* Washington, DC: National Association for the Education of Young Children.

Eccles-Parsons, J., Meece, J., Adler, T. F., & Kaczala, C. M. (1982). Sex differences in attributions and learned helplessness. *Sex Roles, 8,* 421–432.

Fennema, E., & Leder, G. (Eds.). (1990). *Mathematics and gender: Influences on teachers and students.* New York: Teachers College Press.

Fine, A. (1991). *Bill's new frock.* London: Mammoth.

Gallas, K. (1994). *Talking their way into science.* New York: Teachers College Press.

Gallas, K. (1998). *"Sometimes I can be anything.": Power, gender, and identity in a primary classroom. The practitioner inquiry series.* New York: Teachers College Press.

Giarratano, S. (1997). *Body images and eating disorders.* Santa Cruz, CA: ETR.

Gilligan, C. (1982). *In a different voice: Psychological theory and women's development.* Cambridge, MA: Harvard University Press.

Golumbok, S., & Fivusch, R. (1996). *Gender development.* London: Cambridge University Press.

Greenberg, S. (1985). Educational equity in early education environments. In S. Klein (Ed.), *Handbook for achieving sexual equity through education* (pp. 457–469). Baltimore: Johns Hopkins University Press.

Greenhouse, L. (1999, May 25). Sex harassment in class is ruled schools' liability. *New York Times,* pp. A1–A26.

Harvard Educational Newsletter. (1989). Girls: Drawbacks of early success? *Harvard Educational Newsletter, 5*(6), 8.

Henkin, R. (1995). Insiders and outsiders in first-grade writing workshops: Gender and equity issues. *Language Arts, 72*(6), 429–434.

Hopkins, N. (1999). A study on the status of women faculty in science at MIT. *The MIT Faculty Newsletter,* 11(4). Retrieved May 3, 2002, from Massachusetts Institute of Technology Web site: http://web.mit.edu/fnl/women/women.html

Kahle, J. B., & Meece, J. (1994). Research on girls and science: Lessons and applications. In D. Gabel (Ed.), *Handbook of research in science teaching and learning.* Washington, DC: National Science Teachers Association.

Klein, S. (Ed). (1985). *Handbook for achieving sexual equity through education.* Baltimore: Johns Hopkins University Press.

Klein, S., Ortman, P., & Friedman, B. (2002). What is the field of gender equity in education? Questions & answers. In J. Koch & B. Irby (Eds.), *Defining and redefining gender equity in education* (pp. 2–23). Greenwich, CT: Infoage.

Koch, J. (1996, April). *A gender study of private school students' attitudes and beliefs about school life.* Paper presented at the annual conference of the American Educational Research Association, New York, NY.

Koch, J. (1998a, April). *Insitutionalizing the discourse: The long term experience of facilitating a graduate course on gender issues in the classroom.* Paper presented at the annual conference of the American Educational Research Association, San Diego, CA.

Koch, J. (1998b). Lab coats and little girls: The science experiences of women majoring in biology and women majoring in education. In L. Longmire & L. Merrill (Eds.), *Untying the tongue: Gender, power and the word* (pp. 175–191). Boston: Houghton Mifflin.

Koch, J. (1998c). Response to Karen Meyer: Reflections on being female in school science. *Journal of Research in Science Teaching, 35*(4), 473–474.

Koch, J. (2001). *Gender issues in the classroom.* Graduate seminar with a web-based discussion. Board. Retrieved September 6, 2001, from www.Blackboard.com/courses/CT250

Koch, J., & Irby, B. (Eds.). (2002). *Defining and redefining gender equity in education.* Greenwich, CT: Infoage.

Larkin, J. (1994). *Sexual harassment: High school girls speak out.* Toronto, Ontario, Canada: Second Story Press.

Levine, E. Z., & Orenstein, F. M. (1994). *Sugar and spice and puppy dog tails: Gender equity among middle school children.* Clearinghouse number PS023836 (ERIC Document Reproduction Service No. ED389457). New York, NY.

Linn, M. (1992). Gender differences in educational achievement. *Sex equity in educational opportunity, achievement and testing* (pp. 11–50). Educational Testing Service Proceedings of the 1991 Invitational Conference, Joanne Pfleiderer: Proceedings editor. Princeton, NJ: Educational Testing Service.

Linn, M. (2000). Controversy, the internet, and deformed frogs: Making science accessible. *Who will do the science of the future?* (pp. 16–27). National Academy of Sciences, Committee on Women in Science and Engineering. Washington, DC: National Academy Press.

Linn, M. (2002). *WISE: The Web-based inquiry science environment.* Retrieved May 3, 2002, from University of California, Berkeley, Web site: http://wise.berkeley.edu

Linn, M., & Hsi, S. (1999). *Computers, teachers, peers: Science learning partners.* Hillsdale, NJ: Erlbaum.

Lockheed, M. (1984). *Final report: A study of sex equity in classroom interaction.* Washington, DC: National Institute of Education.

Lockheed, M. (1985). Sex equity in classroom organization and climate. In S. Klein (Ed.), *Handbook for achieving sexual equity through education* (pp. 189–217). Baltimore: Johns Hopkins University Press.

Logan, J. (1997). *Teaching stories.* New York: Kodansha Press.

Lyman, K. (2000). Girls, worms, and body image: A teacher deals with gender stereotypes among her second- and third-graders. *Rethinking Schools, 14*(3), 1–6.

Marshall, C. S., & Reinhartz, J. (1997). Gender issues in the classroom. *Clearing House, 70*(6), 333–337.

Martin, M. V. (1996). *Inside a gender-sensitive classroom: An all girls physics class.* Clearinghouse number SE058317 (ERIC Document Reproduction Service No. ED398053). Paper presented at the Annual Meeting of the National Association of Research in Science Teaching, St. Louis, MO. April, 1996.

Matthews, C. E., Brinkley, W., Crisp, A., & Gregg, K. (1998). Challenging gender bias in fifth grade. *Educational Leadership, 55*(4), 54–57.

McCracken, N. M., Evans, D. H., & Wilson, K. (1996). Resisting gender-binding in the middle school. *Voices from the Middle, 3*(1), 4–10.

McIntosh, P. (1983). *Interactive phases of curricular re-vision: A feminist perspective.* Wellesley College Center for Research on Women, Working Paper No. 124, Wellesley, MA.

McIntosh, P. (1984). Gender issues for the schools: An interview with Peggy McIntosh. *Independent School, 44*(2), 6–14.

McIntosh, P. (2000, May). *A learning community with feminist values.* Address at Ewha Womans University, Seoul, Korea.

McIntosh, P., & Style, E. (1999). Social, emotional and political learning. In. J. Cohen (Ed.). *Educations minds and hearts* (pp. 137–157). New York: Teachers College Press.

Meyer, K. (1998). Reflections on being female in school science: Toward a praxis of teaching science. *Journal of Research in Science Teaching, 35*(4), 463–471.

Michigan Model. (2000). *The Michigan Model for comprehensive school health education grade 8 module 2 lesson 8.* Ann Arbor, MI: Center for Eating Disorders.

Miller, J. B. (1986). *Toward a new psychology of women.* Boston: Beacon Press.

Mitchell, D. (1996). Approaching race and gender issues in the context of the language arts classroom. *English Journal, 85*(8), 77–81.

Mullen, J. K. (1994). *Count me in: Gender equity in the primary classroom.* Toronto, Ontario, Canada: Green Dragon Press.

National Council of Teachers of English. (1995). *Women in Literature and Life Assembly (WILLA) of NCTE* (Report No. 19727–1450). Urbana, IL: Author.

National Council of Teachers of Mathematics. (2000). *Principles and Standards for School Mathematics.* Reston, VA: Author.

National Research Council. (1996). *The National Science Education Standards.* Washington, DC: National Academy Press.

Noddings, N. (1990). Constructivism in mathematics education. *Journal for Research in Mathematics Education.* Monograph No. 4, pp. 7–29.

Orenstein, P. (1994). *School girls: Young women, self-esteem and the confidence gap.* New York: Doubleday.

Paley, V. G. (1993). *You can't say that you can't play.* Cambridge, MA: Harvard University Press.

Pipher, M. (1994). *Reviving Ophelia: Saving the selves of adolescent girls.* New York: Putnam.

Pratchler, J. (1996). *A voice for all students: Realizing gender equity in schools. Diversity in the classroom series, Number six.* Clearinghouse number SP038826 (ERIC Document Reproduction Service No. ED434891) Regina, SK, Canada: Saskatchewan Instructional Development and Research Unit.

Reynolds, T. H. (1995). *Addressing gender and cognitive issues in the mathematics classroom: A constructivist approach.* Clearinghouse number SE059726 (ERIC Document Reproduction Service No. ED404183). New York, NY: Columbia University Klingenstein Center for Independent Schools.

Rop, C. (1998). Breaking the gender barrier in the physical sciences. *Educational Leadership, 56*(4), 58–60.

Rowe, M. B. (1987). Wait-time: Slowing down may be a way of speeding up. *American Educator, 11*(1), 38–47.

Sadker, M., & Sadker, D. (1982). *Sex equity handbook for schools.* New York: Longman.

Sadker, M., & Sadker, D. (1984). *Year 3: Final report: Promoting effectiveness in classroom instruction.* Washington, DC: National Institute of Education.

Sadker, M., & Sadker, D. (1986). Sexism in the classroom: From grade school to graduate school. *Phi Delta Kappan, 67*(7), 512–515.

Sadker, M., & Sadker, D. (1994). *Failing at fairness: How America's schools cheat girls.* New York: Scribner.

Sanders, J., Koch, J., & Urso, J. (1997). *Right from the start: Instructional activities for teacher educators in mathematics, science and technology.* Hillsdale, NJ: Erlbaum.

Sandler, B. R., Silverberg, L. A., & Hall, R. M. S. (1996). *The chilly classroom climate: A guide to improve the education of women.* Washington, DC: National Association for Women in Education.

Schlank, C. H., & Metzger, B. (1997). *Together and equal: Fostering cooperative play and promoting gender equity in early childhood programs.* Needham Heights, MA: Allyn & Bacon.

Shakeshaft, C., Barber, E., Hergenrother, M., Johnson, Y. M., Mandel, L., & Sawyer, J. (1995). Peer harassment in schools. *Journal for a Just and Caring Education, 1*(1), 30–43.

Sjostrum, L., & Stein, N. (1996). *Bullyproof: A teacher's guide on teasing and bullying for use with fourth and fifth grade students.* Wellesley, MA: Center for Research on Women.

Sjostrum, L., & Stein, N. (1994). *Flirting or hurting: A teacher's guide on student-to-student sexual harassment in schools (grades 6 through 12).* Washington, DC: National Education Association.

Streitmatter, J. (1997). An exploratory study of risk-taking and attitudes in a girls-only middle school math class. *Elementary School Journal, 98*(1), 15–26.

Style, E. (1998). Curriculum as a window and mirror? In C. L. Nelson & K. A. Wilson (Eds.), *Seeding the process of multicultural education* (pp. 149–156). Plymouth: Minnesota Inclusiveness Program.

Thompson, C. (2001). *Children and eating disorders. Teenagers and eating disorders.* Retrieved June 6, 2001, from www.mirror-mirror.org/child.htm

United Nations. (1995). *Summary of the Beijing declaration and platform for action adopted by the United Nations Fourth World Conference on Women.* New York: Author.

United States Department of Education, National Center for Education, Office for Civil Rights. (1997). *Sexual harassment guidance: Harassment of students by school employees, other students, or third parties.* Washington, DC: Author.

United States Department of Education, National Center for Education Statistics. (2000). *Trends in educational equity of girls & women.* Washington, DC: Author.

United States Department of Education. (n.d.). *National Center for Education Statistics (NCES).* Retrieved May 3, 2002, from http://nces.ed.gov

Wing, A. (1997). How can children be taught to read differently? "Bill's new frock" and the "hidden curriculum." *Gender and Education, 9*(4), 491–504.

Zernike, K. (2001, Jan. 31). Nine universities will address sex inequities. *New York Times,* p. A11.

PART FOUR

CURRICULUM APPLICATIONS

CHAPTER 13

Early Childhood Education

HILLEL GOELMAN, CATHERINE J. ANDERSEN, JIM ANDERSON, PETER GOUZOUASIS, MAUREEN KENDRICK, ANNA M. KINDLER, MARION PORATH, AND JINYOUNG KOH

AN OVERVIEW OF THE FIELD OF EARLY CHILDHOOD EDUCATION

As perhaps one of the first discussions of early childhood education (ECE) to appear in a comprehensive handbook of psychology in the twenty-first century, this chapter begins with a glance in the rearview mirror to consider what parallel chapters had to say in the first half of the twentieth century. In 1929 the National Society for the Study of Education (NSSE) published its annual yearbook on the topic of preschool and parental education, in which editors referred to a

> new and different conception of the educational significance of the first half-dozen years of life. This new conception of the significance of the preschool period has led to the development of several new educational activities, more especially to the development of nursery schools and of new organizations and methods for the better training of parents. (NSSE, 1929, p. iv)

From the 1920s to the 1950s preschool or nursery school education were considered by most educators, researchers, and parents to be the only legitimate manifestation of what was referred to as early childhood education. The 1929 yearbook refers to full-day child care programs as "day nurseries," which were part of the parallel and very different

world of child welfare, clearly distinct in purpose, orientation, and content from the early childhood *education* programs of nursery schools. When the 1939–1940 yearbook titled *Intelligence: Its Nature and Nurture* was published (NSSE, 1939), the primary focus was, again, on one kind of setting (half-day nursery school programs) and on one specific outcome (IQ scores). Titles of chapters in the 1939–1940 yearbook included the following:

- "A Longitudinal Study of the Effects of Nursery-School Training on Successive Intelligence-Test Ratings,"
- "The Effect of Nursery-School Attendance Upon Mental Growth of Children,"
- "Influence of the Nursery School on Mental Growth,"
- "The Mental Development of Nursery School Children Compared With That of Non-Nursery-School Children,"
- "Mental Growth as Related to Nursery School Attendance,"
- "A Follow-Up Study of a Group of Nursery School Children," and
- "Subsequent Growth of Children With and Without Nursery School Experience."

Early childhood education—as a discipline, a discourse of inquiry, and a body of educational practices and approaches—has changed dramatically since those early chapters written by the leading scholars of the day. The current chapter does not attempt to be either "definitive" or "comprehensive," but it does attempt to provide an accurate reflection of the diversity of philosophies, theories, and practices into which the field of early childhood education has matured. We no longer identify one specific program as "typical" or model, and the once-firm line between "child welfare" and "educational" programs has all but disappeared. In this chapter we consider the wide range of settings in which young children participate from birth to approximately age 8 years. The chapter is designed to provide an understanding of both the breadth and depth of early childhood education and, in so doing, to give the reader the opportunity to become acquainted with what we consider to be some of the major themes in this field. It is our intention that the reader will gain this level of understanding and will be able to use the chapter to identify further sources of information and knowledge based on what we present here.

This chapter on early childhood education draws on Bronfenbrenner's ecological model of child development in order to share our understandings of the most recent developments in early childhood education and research at the different nested systemic levels of analysis (Bronfenbrenner, 1979; Bronfenbrenner & Morris, 1998). At the center of these nested concentric levels is the *microsystem,* which is seen as the immediate and naturalistic ecological niche within which the child develops. Examples of microsystems are home environments, child care settings, and classrooms. The *mesosystem* is the network of relationships among the various microsystem environments. For example, the degree of continuity or conflict between the home environments and school environments is a mesosystem dynamic. Embedding both of these inner systems is what Bronfenbrenner refers to as the *exosystem,* which includes broader societal influences that impact on the meso- and microsystems. Exosystem factors include legislation and social policy, labor force participation rates, neighborhood characteristics, teacher training programs, and the like. The overarching *macrosystem* refers to the societal and cultural values, beliefs, and attitudes that shape and influence the creation of policies and programs that ultimately impact on the lives of young children and their families.

In the first section, titled "Learning and Teaching in Early Childhood Education: Art, Literacy, Music, and Play," we focus on child growth and activity as it is observed within the early childhood microsystem environments in which young children play, learn, and develop. In this section we explore what is known about the abilities and interests that young children bring to early childhood settings, and how the early

childhood environment can challenge, engage, and interact with their abilities and interests. Within and across the areas of art, play, literacy, and music this section explores the dynamic tension between more endogenous and maturational views of early education and development at one end of the continuum and an approach that advocates for more direct instruction at the other.

The second section, "Diversity in Early Childhood Education: Individual Exceptionality and Cultural Pluralism," considers the importance and impact of diversity in early childhood education. Although much of the work in early childhood education in the early twentieth century represented an attempt to define a set of universal norms, our understanding today is that early childhood education includes a very wide continuum of children with diverse abilities and disabilities who come from an ever increasing range of cultural and linguistic backgrounds. Rather than attempting to reduce the field to a few narrow common denominators, we wish to reflect the diversity that enlivens this field and challenges practitioners, researchers, and policy analysts. In this section we maintain our focus on the microsystems of early childhood education but broaden our perspective to include the mesosystem relationships among the various microsystems, and we begin to explore the exosystem levels of the social, legal, and regulatory contexts of early childhood education.

In the third section, "Programs and Quality in Early Childhood Education," we attempt to integrate theory, research, and practice in early childhood education as we consider the impact of ECE programs on the children and families who participate in them. Specifically, we examine two of the most dominant forms of ECE programming: compensatory education programs for at-risk children and nonparental child care programs. The issue of quality relates directly to the notion of an ecology of early childhood care, education, and development. Within this complex ecology there are dynamic interactions between the endogenous, biological factors of individual children and the environmental influences of classrooms, curricula, and the social, economic, and demographic realities that frame the development and education of young children. This framework, in turn, is informed by societal values and beliefs that contribute to the very definition of "quality" in ECE programs. In this third section we present a model of program quality that draws on empirical data from the different systemic levels of early childhood education and child care programs, across the curricular areas discussed in the first section of this chapter and in recognition of the individual differences and cultural diversity that are presented in the second section.

LEARNING AND TEACHING IN EARLY CHILDHOOD EDUCATION: ART, LITERACY, MUSIC, AND PLAY

Many textbooks on early childhood education are organized by curriculum subject areas with discrete how-to chapters on teaching literacy, music, art, science, social studies, movement, and mathematics to young children. The lives and abilities of young children are not so easily compartmentalized. For this reason we take a different tack when considering what children learn and how children learn in their early childhood years. We consider the ways in which children comprehend and represent their own lived realities across subject areas and domains of development. We open this discussion with an exploration of the nature and significance of art in early childhood education and artistic development in children. This discussion of the representational and semiotic functions of children's art is followed by a consideration of children's representations of thoughts, scripts, and inner realities in their spontaneous play. We then turn to children's early encounters with the world of literacy in which the written word is seen as yet another powerful representation of both thought and language. The section concludes with an exploration of the significance of music, yet one additional form of representation and meaning in the child's world that develops throughout the early childhood years

Art and Aesthetics in Early Childhood Education

The artistic production of young children has been a source of delight and enjoyment for many parents and early childhood educators. It is difficult to resist the simplicity of early forms that depict with enthusiasm and energy the worlds of childhood. It is hard not to be seduced by the directness and expressive quality of images that in their apparent inaccuracies, approximations, and technical deficiencies capture the element of youthful innocence that is but a memory in the adult universe. The aesthetic appeal of young children's pictorial imagery seems to be closely bound to the emotional response that they evoke that allows for a nostalgic journey back to one's early years. Fineberg (1997) highlighted the significance of these sentiments in Picasso's fascination with the "visual inventiveness of children" by pointing to its connection with the artist's "own extraordinary access to the memories and urges of childhood that most of us have buried beyond the reach of our adult consciousness" (p. 137).

The value of early childhood as a period of uncontaminated purity where one has the benefit of perceiving the world through what Vasily Kandinsky (1912) called "unaccustomed eyes" and thus has the ability to attend to the "pure inner tone" of the objects in the world has been strongly reflected in the work of many artists of the modern area and has created a powerful legacy. Jean Dubuffet, who "turned in the 1940s to children's drawings as a means of cutting to the truth of the ordinary experience" (Franciscono, 1998, p. 116); Joan Miro, whose work associated with the phenomenon of primitivism in French art of the 1920s and 1930s; and Paul Klee are among the icons of modernism who elevated children's art to an unprecedented height. Consider Picasso's famous remark made to Sir Herbert Read in 1956: "It took me years to learn to draw like . . . children." This one sentence captures the respect and admiration for young children's artistic production shared by the most influential artists of the modern era (quoted by Fineberg, 1997, p. 133).

The sentiment expressed by Klee (1957) that "the more helpless they [children] are, the more instructive their examples and already at an early stage one has to save them from corruption" (translation by Hofmann, 1998, p. 13) echoes in the works of one of the most influential Western art educators of the twentieth century, Victor Lowenfeld. In his most acclaimed work *Creative and Mental Growth,* Lowenfeld and Brittain (1964) argued that if "children developed without any interference from the outside world no special stimulation for their creative work would be necessary. Every child would use his deeply rooted creative impulse without inhibition" (p. 20). Needless to say, these assertions have never been empirically tested; nor have any scientific grounds been provided to offer them validity. Furthermore, it is impossible to conceive of circumstances in which children would grow up in environments devoid of visual manifestations of culture.

Yet, contemporary early childhood art education has been greatly affected by what had earlier been referred to as "a myth of natural unfolding" (Kindler, 1996). This is the notion that artistic abilities are contained within the child at birth and that a nonintrusive social environment is what is needed to bring them to the surface. This sentiment often echoes in early childhood texts and is well exemplified by Morgan (1988), who stated that we should consider "children's symbolic activity to be sacrosanct in early years . . . and therefore teacher intervention is inappropriate" (p. 37). The nonintervention approach relies on the assumption that children are happy explorers who have an innate ability to satisfy their creative desires.

Art educators and researchers in day care, preschool, and primary classrooms have frequently witnessed children's frustrating struggles with producing art rather than the happy explorations of young children trying to negotiate solutions to pictorial problems. Regretfully, many children emerge from these struggles with a loss of confidence that eventually leads to the abandonment of pictorial efforts. A question can then be asked about the merits of theoretical frameworks and pedagogical approaches that sacrifice on the altar of "natural development" opportunities of young children to grow into individuals who can use with confidence and competence pictorial means for expression and communication throughout their lives. This question is particularly valid in the light of alternative theories that stipulate that development in pictorial representation is in fact a process of learning from cultural models and that these models are absolutely essential in artistic development (Wilson & Wilson, 1977, 1981). Wilson and Wilson's research clearly contradicts the idea that "creative expression comes from within the child" (Edwards, 1990, p. 66) or that "talent doesn't need any experience of life" (Klee, quoted by Franciscono, 1998, p. 98). Instead, this work points to the significance of socialization and cultural exposure in the development of pictorial vocabulary that can be used for expressive purposes.

The very concept of artistic development and some long-standing models developed to describe it (e.g., Gaitskell, Hurwitz, & Day, 1982; Lowenfeld & Brittain, 1964; Luquet, 1977) have in fact become a subject of criticism in recent years. Four particular issues have been identified in this collective body of criticism. First, questions have been raised about the appropriateness of unilinear conceptions of development in explaining a wide range of pictorial imagery produced by children, adolescents, and adults. Second, a disparity has been noted between the breadth of the world of art and the narrowness of the focus on visual realism that has served as the endpoint in these developmental models. Third, cultural biases that mark these models have been identified theoretically and empirically. Fourth, insufficient recognition has been paid to the role of other modalities of expression in some forms of pictorial representation (e.g., Duncum, 1986; Golomb, 1994; Kindler & Darras, 1997b, 1998; Korzenik, 1995; Wolf, 1994; Wolf & Perry, 1998). Critics of the traditional stage models of development argued that alternative explanations are necessary to account for the range of pictorial systems that children begin to develop early in life and to engage in research relating to the reasons for selecting specific pictorial solutions. It has been pointed out that even very young children have at their disposal more than one pictorial system and that they choose among them as a function of their representational intentions and purposes (Bremmer & Moore, 1984). The notion of the significance of purpose—or teleology—of pictorial behavior in the discourse about development of graphic abilities has been at the center of a map-like model of development that has emerged as an alternative to the traditional stage models (Darras & Kindler, 1996; Kindler & Darras, 1997a, 1997b, 1998).

This model regards emergence and development of pictorial imagery as a semiotic process occurring in an interactive social environment that leads to pictorial behaviors that may engage single or multiple modalities of expression. This framework acknowledges psychobiological factors that found development of pictorial activity while emphasizing the role of culture in validating or deselecting specific pictorial systems. It constitutes an attempt to decolonize discourse about artistic development by pointing to the usefulness and value of pictorial repertoires that have remained outside of the acclaim of the Western art world and yet play a significant role in children's lives (Kindler, 1999). In addition to highlighting the dimension of pictorial choices and their relationship to specific purposes of pictorial behavior, the model proposed by Darras and Kindler recognizes frequent interplay of the gestural, vocal-verbal, and graphic actions in the emergence and development of pictorial systems. This is consistent with Parsons's (1998) notion about the nature of cognition in the arts. Parsons argues that the prevailing systems approach to cognition identifies the different arts as each being a different symbol system and "requires thought to stay within the boundaries of a single medium it is dealing with on the assumption that, if it moves from one system to another, it looses its coherence" (p. 106). He expresses concern that such understanding of cognition in the arts "transforms a dimension of difference into a principle of separation" (p. 106). The repertoire model of development in pictorial imagery moves beyond this principle and accommodates cognitive processes that result in pictorial systems contained within a graphic medium as well as those that cross traditional boundaries of music, drama, and visual arts. This broader conception of development is also more accommodating of cultural factors that define artistic growth than some of the earlier proposed models. The issue of a cultural bias in these earlier theories has vividly surfaced in recent studies that revisited the long-standing notion of the U-shaped curve of artistic development (Davis, 1991, 1997a, 1997b; Gardner, 1980; Gardner & Winner, 1982). The proponents of the U-shaped model argued that while young children exhibit very high levels of creativity in their pictorial work, older children and adolescents suffer from a serious decline in their artistic abilities, which are regained in adulthood only by artistically gifted individuals. The empirical data that confirmed the U-shaped developmental pattern were collected in North America and relied on aesthetic assessments of artistic merit executed by North American and other Western judges.

When this study was recently replicated in settings involving Chinese populations, the U-shaped pattern failed to be confirmed (Kindler, 2001; Pariser & van den Berg, 1997). In none of these recent studies was young children's work considered to be artistically superior to the work of their older peers or nonartistic adults. This suggests that the cultural criteria of artistic merit indeed played a powerful role in defining the very concept of artistic development in research that led to the universality claims of the U-shaped developmental progression. It is important to note that the repertoire model of development does not disprove the U-shape model. In pictorial repertoires that emphasize modernist values, this prediction quite possibly continues to hold true. However, the repertoire model provides also for alternative developmental trajectories in other areas of pictorial pursuits, where technical mastery and preciseness of line, for example, may be of more interest and significance than the image's overall expressive quality.

The revised understanding of development in pictorial representation presents an exciting challenge to the field of early childhood art education. It defines a teacher's role in much more complex terms and places more responsibility on his or her shoulders for ensuring that children's development in this domain does not become unduly constrained by a narrow set of cultural biases and preferences. Valuing and encouraging what we see as children's spontaneous self-directed explorations need to remain an important consideration in structuring learning environments of young children. However, in order to solve pictorial problems, children also require active assistance in (a) pursuing their own intuitive interests in the visual culture that surrounds them, (b) helping them achieve success in meeting their own pictorial expectations, and (c) exploring their emerging metacognitive abilities in relation to their pictorial production and strategies that can enhance this production. It draws on the use of peer- as well as adult-generated examples and readiness to discuss ways in which different systems of pictorial representation can be further mastered and extended to suit children's specific needs and ambitions.

While advocating a much greater sensitivity to and use of cultural models in early childhood education, it is important to clarify that the intention is not to train young children into able performers within a particular system of representation. The answer to early childhood art education will never be presenting children with coloring books or insisting that they copy a particular pictorial schema as *the way* to learn how to draw. However, a sensitive introduction of activities that help children understand the nature, value, and place of iconic representation and introduce them to a wider range of pictorial systems that function within their culture, supported by conversations and modeling of how different effects can be achieved, will provide children with freedom to choose whatever systems may best serve their purposes and needs in different times in their lives.

It is important to note that especially in the early childhood years children's pictorial intentions may have little to do with creating a picture meeting the modernist standards of "child art." Their graphic activity is often just one component of a semiotic process in which sounds, gestures, and words carry a significant portion of meaning. In this context, a teacher's ability to accept these images as active happenings rather than as objects to be posted on day care or primary classroom walls may help children understand the value of this unique multimodal system of representation and see it as an alternative to other pictorial efforts where, in conformity with the deep-rooted tradition of Western art, images are supposed to stand on their own. Similarly, understanding that telling of a dynamic story may require a child to use different pictorial devices than in the case of a descriptive effort, a greater range of imagery can become socially encouraged and validated (Kindler, 1999). Activities that combine musical, dramatic, and visual art dimensions can further help children grow in pictorial repertoires that rely on multiple modalities of expression and that are often a natural choice of young children who spontaneously combine the gestural, the vocal, and the visual in their everyday play.

The importance of teachers' assistance in a child's growing understanding of the technical possibilities and limitations of specific artistic media can perhaps be best demonstrated by looking at young children's clay productions. Children as young as 3 years of age who perform in nonintrusive self-exploration environments tend to be much more limited in subject matter, scale, detail, and stylistic diversity in their clay productions than are those who benefit from appropriate instruction (Kindler, 1997). But perhaps most important, sensitive teaching that relies on constructivist approaches and actively guides children toward important discoveries that support their pictorial efforts translates into a sense of accomplishment and pride that sustains children's interest in creative endeavors and encourages them to continue to use and further master this medium of representation. These recommended forms of adult intervention and teaching can be easily integrated into the play format, and skillful and sensitive teachers can make a tremendous difference in children's artistic growth without compromising the child-centered emphasis and the relaxed and playful atmosphere in their early childhood classrooms.

What is needed, however, is a paradigm shift from understanding the concept of developmentally appropriate art education in terms of curricula targeting children's actual levels of attainment to that of creating environments that allow children to perform within their "zones of proximal development" (Vygotsky, 1978). This shift can take place only if we free ourselves from the cultural baggage of romanticized notions of child art and accept that while it certainly can appeal to our aesthetic sensitivities and emotions, there are other territories of pictorial worlds that children should be free to explore, encouraged to learn about, and provided with assistance to master. Our love of children's natural creative efforts should not become detrimental to their artistic growth in the broadest sense of the term.

This revised conception of human development in the area of the pictorial extends the discourse to a new territory inclusive of a wide range of manifestations of visual culture. It still accounts for repertoires that conform to the modernist expectations or give prominence to visual realism, but it also embraces pictorial worlds that rely on different rules, salient attributes, and criteria of excellence. In pluralistic, diversified societies it is especially important to plan early childhood education in ways that do not define artistic growth in hegemonic terms laden by a strong cultural bias. Recent research on artistic development has provided a platform for accommodating this diversity not by proposing a tight universal developmental sequence, but rather by suggesting a range of pictorial repertoires along which children's growth in art can be witnessed and encouraged. The work needs to continue with mapping of the different repertoires and exploration of them in regard to the nature and modes of acquisition of these pictorial systems. Some of them may rely on self-directed discovery; others may require guidance and teaching starting early on in one's life. Because the concept of art is constantly broadening and multicultural awareness is leading to a more inclusive dialogue about aesthetic merit and value of different kinds of pictorial imagery, the need to explore diverse avenues of growth and pedagogies that will support it along these multiple dimensions will continue to be an important area of concern and research for the years to come.

Literacy in Early Childhood Education

From Reading Readiness to Emergent Literacy

There were considerable changes in our understanding of early literacy development in the last decades of the twentieth century. Prior to the late 1970s, a *reading readiness* paradigm dominated thinking about early literacy development. Central to the concept of reading readiness was the notion that children need to acquire certain prerequisite perceptual and motor skills and to attain a certain mental age before they could begin learning to read (Teale & Sulzby, 1986). Also implicit in reading readiness was the notion that children could not write (i.e., compose) until they had learned to read.

However, in the 1960s researchers began to conduct research on literacy development in children prior to their introduction to formal literacy instruction in school (i.e., Clark, 1976; Durkin, 1966). This groundbreaking body of research revealed that for many children literacy development begins long before their formal schooling and that, indeed, some children entered school as competent and independent readers. This early work precipitated a flurry of research in a number of aspects of literacy. Clay (1979) and Holdaway (1979) showed that young children's reading behaviors developed along a continuum from initial, rough approximations of reenacting texts to accurate decoding of print. Research on emergent literacy included work on children's writing as well their reading. For example, Bissex (1980), Chomsky (1977), and Read (1975) investigated young children's writing development and were able to show that children's early attempts at spelling were not random but were quite systematic and demonstrated a sophisticated and developmental understanding of phoneme-grapheme relationships. Working from within a Piagetian tradition, Ferreiro and Teberosky (1982) demonstrated that young children formed hypotheses about representing speech through writing that they modified as they refined their knowledge. From this collective body of work with young children sprung the theory of *emergent literacy* (Clay, 1966). Sulzby and Teale (1991) defined emergent literacy thus:

> [A]n emergent literacy perspective ascribes to the child the role of constructor of his or her own literacy. Unlike previous work, the central issues now being addressed are the nature of the child's contributions (i.e., individual construction), the role of the social environment in the process (i.e., social construction), and the interface between the two. (p. 729)

The research in emergent literacy had a profound impact on our understanding of both how literacy is learned and how it could be taught. For example, many of the tenets of whole language, a movement that flourished in the 1980s and 1990s, could be traced to this work. As this body of research on emergent literacy grew, so did the number of questions in four specific areas: the generalizability of the research, the presumed similarity between oral language learning and the development of literacy, the impact of culture on literacy development, and the importance of storybook reading.

Questions about the generalizability were focused on both the methodologies that were used as well as on the target populations under study. As Adams (1990) pointed out, much of the research in emergent literacy has been limited to "case studies, chronologies and descriptions" (p. 336). Heath and Thomas (1984) pointed to the fact that in many of these studies the children on whom the research was conducted were the children of "parent-academics" (Heath & Thomas, 1984, p. 51) with their own children.

Questions were also raised about the presumed similarity between oral language development and literacy learning. For many researchers (i.e., Holdaway, 1979), literacy development was portrayed as a natural process that paralleled the development of language acquisition. A number of critiques attempted to refute this notion by pointing out the ways in which literacy acquisition was fundamentally different from first-language acquisition (i.e., Luke, Baty, & Stehbens, 1989); in particular, other research showed that in contrast to natural language development, some children did benefit from direct instruction in literacy (e.g., Adams, 1990).

Increasingly, researchers have begun to address questions of social, cultural, and linguistic diversity. When many of the original studies on emergent literacy were replicated with diverse populations, the initial positive findings on the effects of whole language–emergent literacy approaches were not replicated. For example, Anderson and Matthews (1999) and Elster (1994) found that children from working-class homes did not always follow the developmental trajectory of storybook reading that Sulzby (1985) found with the children from middle-class homes in her study. Other researchers have found that parents from diverse cultural groups support their young children's literacy development differently (i.e., Anderson, 1995; Reyes, 1992). For example, many of the Chinese-Canadian parents in Anderson's study expressed very strong opposition to many of the literacy practices considered sacrosanct within an emergent literacy paradigm. These practices included accepting the use of invented spelling and children's pretend reading behaviors. The initial position paper by the National Association for the Education of Young Children on developmentally appropriate practices in literacy reflected a more or less homogenous prescription for a universal application of the principles of emergent literacy; it was later revised in recognition of cultural diversity in literacy learning (Bredekamp, 1997).

Related to questions of culture, researchers and practitioners have also raised questions about the relative importance of storybook reading in the early years. Because some of the earlier research with precocious readers (i.e., Clark, 1976; Durkin, 1966; Wells, 1985) found that storybook reading was often a part of their daily literacy routine, the general assumption was drawn that this activity was a necessary prerequisite that applied to all children (Pellegrini, 1991). This sweeping assumption tended to prevail even though in some cultures where storybook reading to children is practically nonexistent, most children in that culture still can achieve literate competence (Mason, 1992). Further, a major meta-analysis has suggested that storybook reading accounts for only about 8% of the variance in reading (Scarborough & Dobrich, 1994).

Despite these issues and concerns, the concept of emergent literacy has fundamentally altered the way that literacy learning in early childhood is conceived (Adams, 1990). Consistent with the basic premises of emergent literacy, for example, it is now widely acknowledged that literacy learning should be meaningful, functional, and contextualized and that a great deal of literacy learning occurs before children enter school. Research on literacy continues to focus both on some traditional areas of debate (e.g., the relative importance of phonics instruction) as well as on some emerging areas of interest (e.g., family literacy). It is to these two perspectives on literacy in early childhood education that we now turn.

The Role of Phonological Awareness

Perhaps no other single issue in early literacy has received as much attention over the decades than has phonological awareness or the ability to segment the speech stream into its constituent parts (e.g., phonemes). For example, many literacy researchers and educators see phonemic awareness as a prerequisite to learning to read and write (Bradley & Bryant, 1983; Stanovich, 1986). In contrast, other researchers (Malicky & Norman, 1999) acknowledge that while a certain level of phonemic awareness is needed to learn to decode print, children can become more phonemically aware through the process of learning to read and write. Mustafa (1997) and others argue that phonemic awareness is but one component of a more general competency in language and that it relates, for example, to vocabulary size. The debate continues whether phonological development is best achieved through direct instruction or through more informal, meaningful, and contextualized activities such as word play, rhymes, games, and songs.

Perhaps the most contentious issue in early literacy over the past half century has been the role of systematic instruction in the alphabetic code, commonly known as phonics (Chall, 1967). Although the debate still rages, especially in the United States, a more moderate position or middle ground is evolving. Recent reports have called for direct instruction in the phonics code but in contextualized ways with ample opportunity for children to apply the skill being learned in meaningful situations (Pressley et al., 1998; Snow, Burns, & Griffin, 1998).

The relationship between phonemic awareness in writing as well as in reading has been the focus of much research in recent decades. For example, whereas proponents of whole language once argued that children learned to spell through writing and "invented" spelling, researchers have shown that structured word study could also help young children become more proficient spellers (Templeton & Morris, 1999). These researchers have also shown that although it was once thought that learning to spell essentially consisted of memorizing lists of isolated words, efficient spellers use layers of information to help them learn the orthography. During the heyday of the process writing movement (e.g., Graves, 1983), personal writing such as journals, diaries, and so forth was heavily promoted. An underlying assumption of the writing process movement was that writing skills are generic and transferable from one context to another. However, researchers are now beginning to find that such is not the case and that each particular genre requires specialized knowledge and forms. Chapman's (1995) research has shown that children who are exposed to a variety of genres in their daily experiences will also incorporate the specific features of different genres into their writing at a young age.

The debate on the relative importance of phonemic awareness in children and of phonics instruction with young children manifests itself in a variety of curriculum debates as well. There has been a general trend away from the use of programs based on behavioristic psychology (e.g., DISTAR) and toward approaches that are based more on principles of cognitive psychology. One widely known and widely applied curriculum program, Reading Recovery, was developed by Marie Clay in New Zealand. In Reading Recovery the children who have the most difficulty in reading and writing receive one half hour of individualized tutoring per day with teachers specially trained in Reading Recovery techniques. Despite the ubiquity of this program and even though generally favorable research reports on its effectiveness, it has received criticism on a number of points, including the following: The program is overly structured and inflexible (Dudley-Marling & Murphy, 1997); it does include a specific phonological awareness component (Chapman, Tumner, & Prochnow, 1998); it does not remediate the needs of those children most in need of support (Santa & Hoien, 1999); its initial gains wash out after children have attained expected grade-level proficiency in reading and, in the terminology of the program, are discontinued (Chapman et al., 1998); it does not lead to the staff development that its originator and proponents argue would happen (Center, Whedall, Freeman, Outhred, & McNaught, 1995); and it expends scarce resources without being any more effective than alternate, small-group tutoring (Santa & Hoien, 1999). Whereas the concept of multiple literacies (the notion that meaning is encoded in myriad ways other than print) has been around for some time, Luke and Luke (2001) argued that mainstream thinking in the early literacy field still privileges print literacy. That is, despite the advances in technology that allow for new ways of constructing and communicating meaning, the focus in early literacy still seems to be on decoding print. This fact is evidenced by recent trends in some parts of the United States to prescribe decodable texts for early reading instruction and to emphasize basic reading and writing skills. Decodable texts are texts written specifically for beginning reading instruction. They have a very high level of grapheme-phoneme agreement, which proponents argue helps children learn to crack the code. Critics argue that such texts use contrived, unnatural language that will not engender a desire to read in children. Thus, at this point in time it appears unlikely that curricula and instruction in early literacy will begin to reflect in any significant way a multiple-literacies perspective in the near future.

Family Literacy

Another trend that will deserve increasing attention in the coming years is the proliferation of family literacy programs. Taylor (1983) initially coined the term *family literacy* to describe the myriad ways in which the middle-class families with whom she worked embedded literacy in their daily lives. Taylor's portrayal of the family as a site where considerable literacy learning takes place generated substantial interest in this phenomenon. Educators have subsequently been involved in developing family literacy programs that are intended to help parents support their young children's literacy development. Critics of family literacy programs contend that underlying many such programs are some very troubling deficit assumptions about families that are poor where relatively little literacy is observed. There appears to be some kind of causal or predictive relationship between a family's poverty and their lower levels of literacy practices in the home. Further, the argument has been that the literacy that does occur in these homes is not the "right" kind of literacy that will adequately prepare the children for school. The criticism has also been raised that many of these programs are gender-biased in that they are targeted specifically at children's mothers. Mace (1998) has argued that

> [t]he evidence of a literacy "problem" in industrialized countries with mass schooling systems has revealed that schools alone cannot meet this need. Families must be recruited to do their bit too. This is where the spotlight falls on the mother. She it is who must ensure that the young child arrives at school ready for school literacy and preferably already literate. (p. 5)

Whereas play has traditionally been seen within the early childhood community as the medium through which children learn (see also the section on the role of play in early childhood education), it is only recently that researchers have begun to investigate the role of play in young children's literacy learning. For example, using an ethnographic research approach, Anderson (1995) documented the many ways in which one child incorporated various forms of workplace literacy into her play. In their work in day care settings, Neuman and Roskos (1993) found that children's interest in literacy and their interaction with literacy materials were enhanced when appropriate literacy materials were placed in different play centers. They also suggested that "more challenging and complex language use may be produced in play environments that are literacy based" (p. 221). These authors cautioned that the literacy knowledge that children develop through play may not be sufficient for literacy acquisition. However, they argue that children's "comprehension of the act of literacy" is developed through play (p. 221). Purcell-Gates (1996) proposed that this comprehension is crucial to children's literacy development. She commented, "Grasping the signifying nature of print and the many ways it can function in peoples lives has been called the big picture . . . and is basic to any further knowledge about the forms and conventions of written language" (p. 422). However, the importance of play in literacy development is not universally embraced, as the pendulum appears to be swinging back—at least in some quarters in the United States—toward formal instruction in phonics. Thus, the zeitgeist of literacy theory continues to include simultaneously both advocates of child-centered, emergent literacy approaches and those who focus on the importance of phonemic segmentation and code breaking that can only be acquired through direct formal instruction.

Concluding Thoughts on Literacy in Early Childhood Education

Increasing trends of globalization are beginning to raise important policy issues in the area of early literacy. For example, in Vancouver, Canada, over 50% of the children entering kindergarten speak English as a second language, and there are over 50 different foreign languages that these children collectively bring to school. In a landmark report, Snow et al. (1998) proposed that initial literacy instruction should be in the child's first language. Although this might be possible where there are concentrations of families and children with a common language, it would not be possible for the 50% of children entering Vancouver kindergartens every year who speak English as a second language as well as for countless others such as those in the schools in Canada alluded to earlier. The issue of literacy in one's own first language in addition to literacy in English will continue

to grow in complexity as society becomes increasingly diverse.

Music in Early Childhood Education

All children are born with some degree of music ability. A major challenge that confronts ECE music educators and researchers alike is to determine the relative importance of (a) a child's innate music aptitude, (b) the music environments that contextualize the child's life, and (c) the roles of indirect and direct instruction in music in the early years. This discussion briefly addresses each of these issues from theoretical, empirical, and applied perspectives.

It is widely understood that a child's music aptitude has an ideal chance for optimal development if parents, caregivers, and teachers provide a varied and rich music environment for a child early in life (Brand, 1982, 1985, 1986; Gordon, 1990; Pond, 1981; Simons, 1986). In fact, some researchers have hypothesized that children can suffer severe music developmental delays when music is not a frequent part of their home and school environments. Beyond enhancing the development of a child's music abilities, Doxey and Wright (1990) also reported significant positive relationships between music and mathematics abilities in their study of music cognition and general intelligence. Subsequent research conducted over the past decade has also reported findings of enhanced cognitive development and spatial-temporal reasoning as the result of rich, stimulating preschool music activities (Rauscher et al., 1997; Shaw, 1999). The research evidence strongly suggests that an enriched music environment—a combination of quality, quantity, and a variety of music experiences—in the first several years of a child's life can impact strongly on a child's success in and enjoyment of music, as well as in other areas of cognitive development.

Innate Audiation and Learned Music Skill Development

Although environmental factors can contribute to a child's success in music, the most important factor for potential growth in music is the child's innate music aptitude, an ability that can now be evaluated by a reliable, standardized test (Gordon, 1978, 1979, 1986a, 1986b, 1989). In contemporary terms, standardized music aptitude tests measure a child's ability to *audiate* music. Audiation is the innate human ability to create and recreate music, to conceptualize and comprehend and to compare music that has been heard in the past with music being heard in the present, and to music that may be heard in the future (Gouzouasis, 1992). Humans sing, chant, move, play instruments, and respond to music that they audiate. Humans audiate when they listen to music, recall music, read music, improvise music, and compose music (Gordon, 1986b).

In all of these ways and more, children, adolescents, and adults *play* music and *play with* music. Music play may occur consciously or unconsciously, spontaneously or planned, in unstructured or structured environments, and in informal or formal contexts, and may either be child initiated or adult initiated. Fundamental to all of these forms of music comprehension, production, and enjoyment is the child's ability to audiate. A child's ability to audiate may greatly influence the way in which he or she organizes the physical aspect of music (i.e., sound) in terms of melody, harmony, form, texture, and timbre and may greatly influence the way a child produces music through singing, chanting, moving, and performing on instruments. Of the many different elements of music, the tonal and rhythmic aspects can be most reliably measured in young children (Gordon, 1979).

Research has shown that children's audiation abilities fluctuate during the early childhood years (Flohr, 1981; Gouzouasis, 1987, 1991; Jessup, 1984; Levinowitz, 1985; Zimmerman, 1986). It is widely accepted that children by the age of 9 years can learn to play an instrument, to dance, to sing, to read, to improvise, and to compose music. Although music achievement can certainly continue to develop in and beyond middle childhood, after age 9 the *degree* of music achievement a child may attain is seriously attenuated by his or her stabilized level of audiation ability. Indeed, there is ample evidence to support the notion that even young adults can be taught music listening strategies and instrumental performance that enable them to maximize their basic audiation ability in a variety of music contexts (Gouzouasis, 2000). Ultimately, however, their success in those music activities will be restricted by their ability to make connections between a broad range of acquired music skills and their innate audiation ability.

Central to developing a child's music ability is the importance of objectively assessing each child's music aptitude level. This allows the child's teacher to teach to the child's music strengths, thereby facilitating the child's level of music achievement. In the early 1980s a number of researchers began to scrutinize traditional music-teaching practices in an attempt to observe how very young children acquire music in natural and noninstructional settings. This research represented a sharp departure from earlier top-down curriculum approaches that had been generated primarily by Western European composers and practitioners (Andress, 1986, 1989; Boswell, 1986; Goetze, Cooper, & Brown, 1990). This was in stark contrast to traditional, historical recapitulation models of music teaching and learning. Within this body of work four

specific areas of focus (discussed later) are (a) the development of a child's singing voice, (b) the relationship between music and movement, (c) the implications of "hot" and "cool" music media on children, and (d) children's singing songs with and without words.

The research on singing voice has revealed that two- and three-pitch diatonic stepwise patterns are easier to sing than are arpeggiated patterns (Gordon, 1990; Gouzouasis, 1991; Guilmartin & Levinowitz, 1989–2000; Jersild & Bienstock, 1931, 1934). Because pitched vocal glides are easily produced by children as young as 1 month of age, stepwise patterns are a natural feature in the developmental sequence of pitched vocalization. In contrast, arpeggiated patterns require more vocal precision. The research demonstrated that when young children move their bodies to music, it is important that they experience the free exploration of weight, flow, space, and time with the whole body and various body parts without the expectation that they attempt to coordinate their movements with an externally imposed steady beat (Gouzoausis, 1991). Because singing is in many ways a movement activity, the acquisition of a sense of steady beat is fundamental to all aspects of music learning, and it needs to be nurtured in a variety of play activities, with and without music accompaniment.

Gouzouasis (1987) drew metaphoric allusions between McLuhan's idea of "cool" and "hot" media and the effects of two types of music accompaniment and nonaccompaniment on the singing achievement of 5-year-old children. There is evidence that nonaccompaniment facilitates the learning of songs, especially for children who possess low tonal audiation ability. Ironically, because of the prevalence of heavily textured, hot music learning contexts in contemporary music, twenty-first-century culture may be depriving young children of informal exposure to music experiences presented in developmentally appropriate learning contexts, or cool music media. Further, children who possess high tonal audiation ability can be expected to acquire a singing voice and sing songs consistently better than children who possess low tonal audiation ability, regardless of style and accompaniment texture. Thus, children who have inherently lower levels of audiation may have their music potential additionally compromised by the intensity and texture of much of the hot music media to which they are exposed.

A related application of that line of research led to the practice of singing songs without words with very young children (Gordon, 1990; Gouzouasis, 1987; Levinowitz, 1987). Very young children who possess few linguistic skills tend to respond very positively to singing activities with a neutral syllable such as "bah" or "too" than to songs with many words, sentences, and lyrics. Many young children sing the songs with which they are most familiar in tune, and they sing less familiar songs out of tune. That may be because they are better able to concentrate their listening, audiation, and vocal-production abilities on the music aspects of the song rather than the text, a characteristic that seems to be true of children who possess low to average music aptitude (Gouzouasis, 1987). Children seem to benefit most from singing songs without words because an emphasis on learning the words of the song can distract and detract from their attention to the music content. As a child's language skills develop, song texts (i.e., lyrics) seem to interfere less with vocal development. A mixture of songs with and without words should be of benefit to older children (Levinowitz, 1987). Parents, caregivers, and teachers may still teach their favorite songs, but they can teach them using a neutral syllable instead of text. The ability of a child to sing one or more short phrases of a song, with or without text and in tune, is evidence that he or she has emerged from the tonal babble stage.

Music Acquisition and Language Acquisition

Although music is not a language, it is acquired in a manner and context similar to those in which language is learned (Gouzouasis & Taggart, 1995). The mechanisms that a young child uses to produce sounds are the same for both music and language. The throat, mouth, nose, lungs, and diaphragm are used in a variety of ways to produce meaningful music and linguistic sounds. For both music and language, sounds may vary in loudness, pitch, duration, and stress. When sound (or, technically, *phones*) in the form of vowels and consonants (*segmentals*), is organized into morphemes—the smallest meaning-based unit in language—the sound is expressed as a linguistic medium (Jakobson, 1968). Similarly, when sound in the form of pitches and durations is organized into tonal and rhythm patterns, it may be considered a music medium (Gouzouasis, 1987). Young children are encouraged to produce linguistic sounds from the time they enter our world through what psycholinguists have described as *motherese,* a reciprocal and contingent interaction between parent and infant (Broen, 1972; Cross, 1977; Newport, Gleitman, & Glietman, 1977; Phillips, 1970; Snow, 1977). Motherese is characterized by language that is simplified and limited in vocabulary, with words pronounced slowly with careful and exaggerated enunciation and in a repetitive manner. Motherese makes use of three different components of language: semantics (vocabulary), syntax (the predictability of sentence patterns), and pragmatics (the social and instrumental uses of language). Although there appears to be a similar babbling and mimicking stage in music, most young children are not exposed to a corresponding music variant of motherese

(Holohan, 1984), perhaps because a shared system of semantics, syntax, and pragmatics has not yet been worked out between parent and infant.

Research has shown, however, that the music babble stage has at least two parts, rhythm and tonality, which seem to operate independently of each other (Gordon, 1990). Although the music babble stage can last essentially from birth until the child is 6 or 7 years old, some children have been observed to leave the babble stage completely as early as 24 months, depending on their music aptitude and environmental influences. A child can still be engaged in tonal babble after he or she is out of rhythm babble, and vice versa. On their own, children may babble by singing short patterns and experimenting (i.e., playing) with their voices. Children who babble on a tonal level seem to be singing in a monotone; that is, it centers in a narrow range around one pitch. The songs that such children sing are often unrecognizable to an adult, and the children may be unaware that their singing is different from that produced by adults. Although tonal babble may sound amusical to an adult, it should be encouraged through parental play and imitation that can begin as soon as an infant begins to produce pitched sounds (Stark, 1977; Stark, Rose, & McClagen, 1975). Many children who babble early and often tend be identified as those who learn to sing with the music syntax of an adult earlier than children who babble considerably less.

When a child is at the stage of using tonal babble, rhythm babble, or both, all music instruction should be informal (Gordon, 1990). Children who emerge from the tonal babble stage are able to audiate music with tonal syntax and are able to audiate and sing music with a sense of tonality—with a sense of how patterns are organized. They learn to sing what they audiate and to audiate what they sing (Gordon, 1990). In essence, they learn to coordinate their listening (perception) of music, their audiation (conception), and their vocal production of music (through their breathing, diaphragm, and vocal chords) in order to sing with a sense of tonality.

Play and Music Play

In many ways babble is an elemental form of play in music. Play, imagination, and creativity are naturally rooted in music activities in early childhood. In fact, one may consider music itself as a form of play. Humans *play* music. Young children play in a variety of activities while listening to music, and they play musically in a variety of contexts—with their voices, with their bodies, with props, and with music instruments. Observational research reveals that children spontaneously accompany their play with music. It is a simple form of multitasking, in that young children possess the abilities to attend to more than one activity while engaged in conscious and unconscious music making. Music play may be child initiated or caregiver initiated. Both forms are equally as diverse, rich, and valuable in learning. Moreover, music play may occur in both structured and unstructured and formal and informal settings (Gouzouasis, 1991, 1994). An understanding of the multifaceted relationships between play and music is central to both theories of music acquisition and learning. Moorehead and Pond (1981), Pond (1978), and Littleton (1999) provided brilliant insight to this topic, which sadly has been neglected by education researchers and psychologists.

Concluding Thoughts on Music in Early Childhood Education

A child who is developmentally delayed in music learning deserves the same type of specialized instruction that a child receives who is developmentally delayed in some other aspect of learning. Although it seems that various forms of media made positive contributions to the proliferation of music in the twentieth century, the developmentally detrimental aspects and negative influences of electronic and digital media are too numerous to mention in this chapter (Gouzouasis, 2000). One may begin by scrutinizing the use of music in children's television programming and the lack of quality music for young children on radio, recordings, and new forms of digital media (e.g., the Internet). Much of what is marketed as music for young children is actually developmentally appropriate for older children and is composed to appeal to parents and caregivers. Those factors are compounded by the gross commercialization of early childhood music instruction by corporate early childhood music trainers. From a perspective informed by both research and praxis, it is arguable that any music instruction is better than none at all.

Play in Early Childhood Education

"The play of children may strike us at times as fragile and charming, rowdy and boisterous, ingenuous, just plain silly, or disturbingly perceptive in its portrayals of adult actions and attitudes" (Garvey, 1977, p. 1). A plethora of scholars have focused on these and other aspects of play's characteristic forms, which has led to a proliferation of theories to account for the origins, properties, and functions of these forms. Thus, to begin to understand play, in all of its ambiguities, requires multiple perspectives. This section provides a brief review of selected theories and research on children's play, highlighting the paradoxical nature of the phenomenon.

Defining Play

Given the protean nature of play, defining it has proven problematic in the literature. In Western cultures, our understanding of play has been influenced most significantly by shared attitudes about what play is *not;* for example, "play is not work, play is not serious, play is not productive—therefore, play is not important" (Schwartzman, 1991, p. 214). Caillois (1961) argued that "in effect, play is essentially a separate occupation, carefully isolated from the rest of life and generally, is engaged in within precise limits of time and place" (p. 6). Denzin (1980a), on the other hand, proposed that the world of play is not distinct from everyday taken-for-granted reality, but that it occurs in the immediately experienced here and now. He also stressed that on an a priori basis play cannot be distinguished from other everyday interactions, including conversation and other activities of habit. Other definitions of play include that play is pleasurable and enjoyable, has no extrinsic goals, and is spontaneous and voluntary (Garvey, 1977); that play is free, separate, uncertain, unproductive, governed by rules, and full of make-believe (Caillois, 1961); and that play is a story that children tell themselves about themselves (Geertz, 1973). The ambiguity of these definitions reflects Western society's struggle over how to conceptualize and value play.

Perspectives on Play

The diversity and ambiguity inherent in definitions of play have resulted in broad conceptualizations of the forms and functions of the phenomenon. These conceptualizations include play and cognition, psychoanalytic theory, educational perspectives, play and literacy, and play as communication, among others.

Traditional Theories of Play and Cognition. Child development theorists and researchers have attempted to explain the relationship between play and children's cognitive development. Two major theorists, Jean Piaget and Leo Vygotsky, are perhaps the most noted for furthering our understanding of this relationship. Piaget (1962) believed that children gain knowledge through the dual processes of assimilation and accommodation. In assimilation, children take in information from their experiences in the external world, which is then integrated—*assimilated*—into existing mental structures. Because children's cognitive structures are often inadequate to incorporate new information, they must learn to change or *accommodate* their mental structures to better accept information that is inconsistent with what they already know. Typically, the opposing forces of assimilation and accommodation must work in tandem to reach a state of equilibrium. The activity of play, however, is unique because children are able to suspend reality and make the world adapt to them; thus, assimilation assumes primacy over accommodation (Saracho & Spodek, 1995). Piaget (1962) offered an account of children's unfolding cognitive process by identifying three stages of play: sensorimotor, symbolic, and games with rules. According to Piaget, each stage is part of a sequential order in a child's development. The first stage involves repetitive actions that focus on physical activity. In the second stage children use their symbolic abilities to create and act out stories. The final stage involves the social conventions of rules in games. The cross-cultural applicability of Piaget's theory, however, has been widely questioned because his data are based primarily on observations of White, middle-class children in Western society (see, e.g., Denzin, 1980b).

Vygotsky's view of the relationship between play and development differs significantly from Piaget's. Vygotsky (1976) argued that children's play *extends* their cognitive development. Specifically, children have a "zone of proximal development," a range of tasks between those that can be completed independently and those that can be mastered only through the mediation of adults or more competent peers. Vygotsky believed that social interaction with more competent others is critical to a child's cognitive development because it is the social context of socialization experiences that shapes the thought processes of the young child. The emphasis on social interaction renders Vygotsky's theory of play and cognition applicable across social and cultural contexts.

Psychoanalytic Theories of Play.   Freud (1909) used the pretend play of children as the medium for understanding their conscious and unconscious wishes and fears. His theory of play was based on the idea of internal conflict, and he postulated that play is cathartic for children because it allows them to resolve negative feelings that may result from traumatic experiences. For instance, a child who has experienced the trauma of an accident and must be taken to the hospital, away from the safety and familiarity of home, may later play and replay various hospital scenes in order to cope with feelings of fear and pain. Other theorists have modified Freud's psychoanalytic theory and have related play to wish fulfillment, anxiety, and ego processes (see Takhvar, 1988, for a review). Erikson, in contrast, believed that children use play to dramatize the past, present, and future, and to resolve conflicts that they experience in each stage of their development. Peller (1952) thought that children's imitations of life in their play were caused by feelings of love, admiration, fear, and aggression.

Educational Perspectives on Play.   Since the early nineteetn century, educators have observed the transition from play to learning as children struggle to leave the world of play at home to enter the world of learning at school. The idea that play could be used as an articulation of teaching practices and curricula was first put into practice by Pestalozzi (1827), who believed that young children could be educated to develop an inquiring approach to things and words. He developed a pedagogy that encouraged the development of children's activity that was built on their potential for moral and aesthetic discernment through reflection.

It was Froebel's modification of Pestalozzi's theory, however, that became a medium for learning within the context of schooling. Froebel proposed that "play is the purest, most spiritual activity, and at the same time, typical of human life as a whole—of the inner hidden natural life of [human beings]" (Froebel, 1885, pp. 86–87). Froebel also suggested that children attempt to maintain continuity in their lives by bringing playful activity to their formalized learning experiences. For example, he argued that play allows children to achieve mastery over many aspects of themselves and their environment through symbolic enactment of roles, exploration of feelings, and interaction with others (Garvey, 1977). Such themes are typically repeated during several play episodes, which suggests that play is also cathartic for children because it allows them to reexperience and thereby resolve or master a difficult situation.

Froebel observed that the way in which children play often reveals their inner struggles (Adelman, 1990) and that play is often the primary means for children to learn social expectations, attempt to understand culturally appropriate behaviors, struggle to learn to manage emotions, and gain access to the techniques and skills of the world in which they live (Michelet, 1986). According to Froebel, it is essentially the child's whole personality that can be seen to be involved in play. He in fact contended that to understand the whole child, it is crucial to understand that the inextricable link between the inner and the outer parts of children's play have a visible and metaphysical aspect (Adelman, 1990). All of Froebel's activities and materials symbolized spiritual meanings that he wanted children to gain (Saracho & Spodek, 1995), and the activities he developed were based on observations he made of German peasant children.

Maria Montessori (1965) also conceptualized her teaching methods from the natural play activities of children. She developed her methods by bringing into the classroom materials she was designing. She watched children play freely with them and then abstracted what she considered the essential elements of the play. Free play, however, was discouraged after she decided how the materials could be used best

(Montessori, 1965). Montessori contended that by using her materials, "children could sharpen their abilities to gather and organize their sensory impressions in order to better absorb knowledge" (Saracho & Spodek, 1995, p. 130).

It was the advent of the progressive kindergarten movement, however, that provided the basis for contemporary educational uses of play (Saracho & Spodek, 1995). The movement was spearheaded by Dewey, who broke from the colonial view that children should avoid play to become more work oriented as they matured (Hartley & Goldenson, 1963). Dewey argued that play could be used to help children construct their understanding of the world, and that through play, children would learn to function at higher levels of consciousness and action (Saracho & Spodek, 1995). Play in Dewey's terms, however, was still not a free activity. Instead, teachers were to use play to create an environment to nurture and enhance children's mental and moral growth (Dewey, 1916).

Play and Literacy

Understanding the connection between children's knowledge and use of literacy and their play behavior is a focus of current research. Research in the area of play and literacy is grounded in the theoretical work of Piaget (1962) and Vygotsky (1976). Both theorists compare the use of symbols in symbolic play and literacy. Piaget described play as being largely assimilative and viewed it as a reflection of the child's cognitive development. He maintained that during play children demonstrate a mental distancing from what is real in the here and now through their symbolic representations of people, places, things, and actions. Moreover, he suggested that play may serve as a catalyst for the child's emerging literacy skills. Vygotsky (1976) described how children represent literacy—from the gesture to the written word—as a unified process. He also believed that the social meaning of marks on a piece of paper is rooted in how a child's indicatory gestures are responded to during play. Unlike Piaget, however, Vygotsky proposed that play is the primary factor in fostering children's development, liberating their thoughts from specific contexts and from the literal meanings of concrete actions and uses of objects. He also theorized that the ability to engage in symbolic play enables children to develop a variety of represented (symbolic) meanings that serve as the basis for later success in literacy.

Other theorists have also hypothesized about the relationship between play and literacy. Bruner (1983), for example, advised that children's early literacy development should be an integral aspect of play-based experiences that support children's ideas, purposes, and social interpretations. He

cautioned, however, that structuring and organizing play for educational purposes often results in "taking the action away from the child" (p. 62). Others, such as Donaldson (1978) and Heath (1983), pointed out that engaging in play and learning to read and write demand similar cognitive abilities; that is, through interacting with print, the learner moves from episodes of the here and now to settings that are decontexualized within text.

Theoretical studies on the play-literacy connection have provided the impetus for a number of empirical studies. There are two main strands of research in this area, both of which focus on the parallel representational processes involved in literacy and play. One strand of research examines how to enhance literacy use and knowledge through symbolic play (see, e.g., Jacob, 1984; Miller, Fernie, & Kantor, 1992; Neuman & Roskos, 1992, 1993; Roskos, 1988). Schrader (1991) and others (see, e.g., Roskos & Neuman, 1993) have been interested in the ways that children pretend to write as part of their dramatic play. Michaels (1981) examined children's sharing-time narrative styles and differential access to literacy. Dyson (1997) studied the reciprocal relationship between children's writing and the superhero dramas and discussions that followed in the classroom and on the playground.

A second strand of research has emphasized children's use of language in symbolic play. Much of the research in this area has demonstrated that when teachers and parents become involved with children's pretend play, there are positive increases in children's literacy, language, reading, and writing (Bloch & Pellegrini, 1989; Christie, 1991; Galda & Pellegrini, 1985; Goelman & Jacobs, 1994; Pellegrini, 1984; Pellegrini & Galda, 1998).

Play as Communication

It was Bateson (1955, 1972) who first suggested that play was a paradoxical form of communication. He argued that play is socially situated and characterized by the production and exchange of paradoxical statements about people, objects, activities, situations, and the relationships among these. Bateson (1972) saw play as an ancient form of communication, which was based on his notion about animals' play fighting. He argued that because animals have no negatives (i.e., they cannot say "no"), negative behaviors such as "biting must be illustrated positively by *not really* biting" (Kelly-Byrne, 1989, p. 246). Playful nipping must be communicated as not really biting, even though it stands for biting. Thus, play is not merely play, but is also a message about itself. In Bateson's words, "these actions in which we now engage do not denote what these actions for which they stand denote. . . . The playful nip denotes the bite but it does not denote what would be denoted by the bite" (1955, p. 41). Play is therefore paradoxical because the behavior engaged in by the players is at once real and not real. Thus, the child playing mother is both a mother and yet not a mother. Other players' awareness of this paradox is, according to Bateson (1955), a form of metacommunication.

Both Garvey (1977) and Schwartzman (1978) have expanded Bateson's perceptions of play. Their body of work has concentrated on how children organize and communicate about make-believe, how the message "this is play" is signaled, and how play is initiated, sustained, and concluded. Schwartzman (1978) extended Garvey's work by focusing on the meanings children attached to the texts they generated in play. Following the work of Geertz (1972) and Ehrmann (1968), Schwartzman (1978) argued that children's pretend play could be analyzed "as a text in which players act as both subjects and the objects of their created play event" (p. 232). In her interpretations of play texts, she emphasized the importance of social and cultural contexts and suggested that play was very much about dominance and manipulation. Schwartzman's understanding of hierarchical relationships in play "illustrates the weaving of the children's social histories with the texts of their play and the relationship of both elements to the wider sociocultural context of the place of children and their hierarchical ranking in a variety of institutions such as the family and school" (Kelly-Byrne, 1989, p. 12). As children weave their social histories into their play texts, they fashion their relationships with others and express in subtle—and sometimes not so subtle—ways their individual perceptions of the world around them (Bakhtin, 1981). In other words, play is a medium through which children communicate and make sense of who they are in relation to others.

Closing Thoughts on Play in Early Childhood Education

Play has been defined and examined across a number of disciplines including biology, psychology, linguistics, sociology, anthropology, art, literature, and leisure studies. It has provide the means to delve into children's inner thoughts and feelings, extend their cognitive growth and development, enhance their language and literacy development, and understand how they communicate their perceptions of the world. Such diversity in the interpretation of play both augments and constrains our understanding of the phenomenon, making reconciliation among play scholars difficult. Perhaps the best point of convergence is for both researchers and teachers to adopt an interdisciplinary approach focusing on the meanings that children themselves attach to play. Children are, after all, the ultimate authorities on the subject.

DIVERSITY IN EARLY CHILDHOOD EDUCATION: INDIVIDUAL EXCEPTIONALITY AND CULTURAL PLURALISM

Giftedness and Early Childhood Education

Gifted children are found in every community. These very able youngsters reason, create, speak, write, read, interact, feel, make music, or move in ways that distinguish them from their age peers. They are developmentally advanced in one or more areas of human accomplishment and often demonstrate early indicators of their gifts as infants. As they enter ECE settings, they may encounter mixed reactions to their abilities that have consequences for the educational programs they are offered. Appropriate educational experiences for young gifted children are impacted by different macrosystem factors: the ideologies of parents, teachers, and society as a whole; the education system; and psychology, the discipline that provides a knowledge base for understanding and educating young gifted children and important directions for research. This discussion on giftedness presents some of the issues relevant to ensuring appropriate early childhood education for gifted children within the context of contemporary psychological knowledge. It also summarizes directions for research that will have implications for gifted children in ECE classrooms, for although the early years are acknowledged as critically formative, a significant body of research focused on gifted young children has yet to accrue (Robinson, 1993, 2000).

Prevalent Ideologies and the Education System

A number of powerful ideological factors may influence how young gifted children are educated. In some cases, ideology is combined with systemic factors, resulting in school administrative structures that are not responsive to individual children's needs. First, an age-grade mindset may prevail, resulting in the belief that, for example, all 6-year-olds belong in first grade for both academic and social reasons (Robinson & Robinson, 1982). Second, a prevalent ideology is that special programming should begin in middle childhood. Underlying this ideology are several beliefs: (a) Ability will have stabilized by the time children are about 8 or 9 years old; (b) psychoeducational testing is unreliable before middle childhood; and (c) early childhood and primary school educators are well equipped to meet individual needs within their classrooms.

Another powerful ideology is that matching advanced developmental characteristics with appropriate curricula puts unnecessary stress on young children. Parents and teachers who respond to children's advanced capabilities by offering them opportunities to develop these abilities often are viewed with suspicion as being "pushy." Advocacy for accelerated school placements may also be viewed as a desire to speed up development in an unhealthy fashion, with negative social-emotional consequences (Southern & Jones, 1991). Also influencing the availability of educational opportunity is the belief that gifted young children have the intellectual and social-emotional resources to get what they need from the educational system; in other words, they will "make it on their own."

There is little research support for the ideologies and systemic perspectives just described. Most of these powerful beliefs stem from anecdotal data. This is not to say that there may not be some children for whom one or more of the issues may be salient. There is always the imperative to consider each child individually, taking into account family, school, and community contexts. However, there also is a compelling imperative to examine these ideologies in light of relevant research.

Psychological Perspectives and the Nature of Advanced Development

Psychology offers important perspectives on the nature of advanced development, including explanations and descriptions of conceptual understanding and skills, different developmental pathways to giftedness, asynchrony in development, motivation, and social and emotional development. Precocity in development may be evident in infancy. Retrospective parental reports of unusually advanced development in infancy (e.g., Feldman, 1986) may be questioned for their reliability; however, observations and behavioral ratings of infants have been linked prospectively to intellectual and academic precocity (e.g., Gottfried, Gottfried, Bathurst, & Guerin, 1994; Louis & Lewis, 1992). Domain-specific abilities (e.g., linguistic or mathematical precocity) are apparent in very young children, and these abilities tend to be stable over time (Dale, Robinson, & Crain-Thoresen, 1995; Robinson, Abbott, Berninger, & Busse, 1996).

In addition to the strikingly advanced capabilities of young gifted children, some age-typical or even below-average capabilities may be evident. Gifted young children demonstrate considerable inter- and intra-individual variance, a phenomenon described as *asynchronous development* (Morelock, 1996). One of the ways in which their development may be more closely related to chronological than mental age is in their conceptual understanding of a domain. Gifted young children may bump up against a conceptual ceiling that is related to maturation (Fischer & Canfield, 1986; Porath, 1992).

For example, in coordinating plot elements in narrative or rendering perspective, abilities that are related to stage and structure of thought (Porath, 1996a, 1997), gifted children may be distinguished more by the complex use of the thought available to them than by exceptional developmental stage advancement. Gifted young children also may differ from each other in their developmental pathways.

Multiple Expressions of Giftedness

Each young gifted child has a distinct profile of abilities. In addition, there are multiple pathways to, and demonstrations of, giftedness in any one domain (Fischer, Knight, & Van Parys, 1993; Golomb, 1992; Porath, 1993, 2000; Robinson, 1993). Perhaps the best way to illustrate this is to introduce some young gifted children: Jessica, Holly, Sara, Sam, and Jill, five of the gifted children who participated in a series of studies on giftedness.

Six-year-old Jessica arrived to participate in a research project on narrative full of enthusiasm about her abilities to read and write: "I can read. Do you want me to read? I can write stories. Can I write a story for you?" (Porath, 1986, p. 1). Jessica and the researcher settled on tape-recording a story to allow for production to keep pace with thinking. Jessica told "The Leprechaun's Gold," a story richly representative of the fairy tale genre (see Porath, 1996, for the story's text). Jessica had a strong sense of story and a remarkable feel for language. Her vocabulary and syntax were mature, and she incorporated appropriate dialogue into her story. All of the aforementioned are advanced capabilities in a child of 6 years. Other 6-year-olds with whom Porath has worked have demonstrated their advanced verbal abilities in different ways: by playing with words (a story featuring a cat named Nip); through understanding the power of language (using rhymed couplets as humorous additions to a story); and by wanting to know all they can about words and their derivations.

Holly, aged 4.5 years, drew pictures in an enthusiastic, confident way with obvious mastery of different media. Her drawings of human figures were detailed and well proportioned. Most striking was her feel for composition, described by an art educator as entailing "some rather sophisticated propositions regarding spatial organization" (p. 31). The simple formal harmony of the composition also was noted. Sara, age 6, showed her talent in a somewhat different way, producing elaborate drawings with colors chosen for contrast and detail (Porath, 1993). Sam, age 2, showed advanced social role-taking ability. While playing with the toy telephone in his preschool, Sam initiated a conversation with, "Hello! I fine!" followed by adult-like speech inflections and twirling of the telephone cord. He engaged both a peer and his teacher by offering them the telephone and saying, "Talk to you?" (Porath, 2000, p. 203).

Jill, age 4, demonstrated social capability through her advanced interpersonal understanding, as elicited through responses to a picture story of a little girl who has lost her favorite book. Jill showed remarkable abilities to incorporate multiple emotions into her responses and empathize with the protagonist. Part of the discussion with Jill is reproduced below:

Researcher: How was the little girl feeling?

Jill: Surprised, mad, and sad—all three.

Researcher: Why?

Jill: Because her friends were near. That's why she's mad; and she was sad and surprised because her book was lost.

[Upon being asked what another character in the story would do, Jill replied that he would help].

Researcher: Why?

Jill: Because he didn't want her to be sad and lost it again. You know why? Cause I lost my kitty . . . my favorite kitty, I would be feeling like that. (Porath, 2001, p. 20)

Motivation, Social-Emotional Development, and Giftedness

Young gifted children are notable for their motivation to learn (Gottfried et al., 1994; Robinson, 1993). Winner (1996) characterized this high intrinsic motivation as "a rage to master" (p. 3). Claire Golomb (1992) powerfully illustrated this rage to master in her research on an artistically gifted boy who, from the age of 2, explored topics by drawing numerous variations on a theme from every possible point of view. Similarly, at age 4 Wang Yani, an artistic prodigy, painted monkeys until she had exhausted the subject, often sustaining interest for incredibly long periods of time (Wang, 1987). Young gifted children may play an important role in creating environments that sustain them (Robinson, 1987).

In general, young gifted children are well adjusted socially and emotionally (Robinson & Noble, 1991). They tend to be socially mature, preferring older children's company. However, young gifted children's social-emotional development, while mature, still can be discrepant from their cognitive development. This asynchrony can interact with parental and teacher expectations of across-the-board maturity, with the possible result of denial of appropriate programming until the child "improves" socially. Another conundrum is that young gifted children, faced with an insufficiently challenging curriculum, will "act their age," again with the possible

result that social behavior becomes the focus of educational efforts rather than appropriate curriculum (Keating, 1991).

Very highly gifted children are the exception to the general finding of healthy social-emotional adjustment among gifted children. Because these children's capabilities are so unusual, they find it very difficult to find their place in the world (Hollingworth, 1942; Winner, 1996). When asked how he was the same as and different from other children, a highly gifted 6-year-old replied, "I like Raphael and Michelangelo, but as artists not as Ninja Turtles" (Porath, 1996b, p. 15). This child struggled to find his place, both academically and socially, from the time he entered school.

Educational Implications

Psychological perspectives on the development of gifted children have important implications for early childhood education. The findings on the early emergence and stability of exceptional capabilities strongly suggest that the provision of an optimal curricular match to these advanced abilities in early childhood settings is essential to nurture young children's curiosity, motivation, and accomplishment (Keating, 1991; Robinson et al., 1996). Well-designed programs that honor the constructive nature of understanding sustain children's excitement in learning and extend their achievements (Freeman, 2000; Robinson, Abbott, Berninger, Busse, & Mukhopadhyay, 1997). These programs also have the potential to support different developmental pathways.

The importance of considering the nature and structure of conceptual understanding in planning educational programs is underscored by work on expertise. The knowledge structures of experts are complex; instruction that has as its objective the nurturance of expertise incorporates meaningful conceptual material (Bereiter & Scardamalia, 1986). Instruction that fails to incorporate conceptual material can lead to cumulative deficits in achievement (Meichenbaum & Biemiller, 1998). This outcome was illustrated powerfully by Jeanne Bamberger (1982) in her study of gifted adolescent musicians. These young musicians went through a sort of midlife crisis when called on to learn formal theoretical musical concepts. Having experienced a largely skills-based approach to musical instruction since early childhood, they were unprepared for the demands to think more deeply about music and became frustrated and unmotivated.

Well-planned academic programs also support social and emotional development (Keating, 1991). Creative and flexible options are needed to address the diversity of development among young gifted children. Most particularly, highly gifted children need options that are sensitively matched to the needs implicit in development that includes abilities far ahead of even other gifted young children. A "nurturant resourceful environment" (Meichenbaum & Biemiller, 1998, p. 13) is necessary to support high motivation. Children need to be helped and supported to be interested (Bereiter & Scardamalia, 1986), even when they are highly intrinsically motivated. Intensive early support and education result in high levels of competence and satisfaction (Bloom, 1985).

Giftedness is apparent in early childhood. Its presence signals a need to step outside the confines of a lockstep approach to education in which age and grade seem inextricably joined. When faced with compelling advanced developmental needs, the predictive question of subsequent performance is not relevant; however, an optimal match between school program and abilities is. Keating (1991) suggested that the following question be posed: "Is there an appropriate match between the child and the program?" If the answer is negative, then we must ask what needs to be done to make the program appropriate.

Directions for Future Research

Important guiding principles for early educational experiences for gifted children are apparent in psychological research. These principles need to be translated into an applied research program to guide practice. We need richly descriptive classroom-based and system-based examples of exemplary practice and studies of intervention effects. Coupled with a need to expand how we conceive of intelligent behavior (see, e.g., Ceci, 1996; Gardner, 1983) is the need for valid and reliable assessment tools that go beyond IQ. Basic research into cognitive processes and the nature of abilities across domains needs to continue. Longitudinal research that includes an applied dimension would strengthen our understanding of the nature and development of giftedness. The complexities of gifted abilities and achievements are recognized (Freeman, 2000), as is the dynamic relationship between young children and their environments (Smitsman, 2000). This intensive and challenging research agenda is essential to ensuring appropriate early childhood education opportunities for children who demonstrate exceptional potential.

Linguistic and Cultural Diversity in Early Childhood Education

Recent decades have witnessed an increasing number of immigrants to many, if not most, Western industrialized countries. This continuing upswing in immigration and demographic changes has resulted in a dramatic increase of students with diverse ethnic, cultural, and linguistic backgrounds in the school system and in ECE programs of many industrial societies,

especially in North America. Within existing societal contexts where family values, education equity, and human rights are discussed, contemporary education faces new understandings and challenges to meet the needs of culturally and linguistically diverse students who had been historically placed in contexts of social, economical, and educational vulnerability.

An important challenge in educating minority students has been how best to help them learn the majority language and culture without precluding them from developing and maintaining their native languages and cultures. In fact, decades of literature addressing best educational practices for minority children continue to stress the importance of developing home languages and cultural identity (Campos, 1995; Cummins, 1979, 1992; Hakuta, 1986; Paul & Jarvis, 1992). Such findings, however, have not exerted much influence on the practices in early childhood education (Bernhard, Lefebvre, Chud, & Lange, 1995; Kagan & Garcia, 1991; LaGrange, Clark, & Munroe, 1995; Soto, 1997). Research in this area has indicated that large numbers of early childhood settings have adopted at best superficial or token expressions of cultural diversity, such as presenting diverse holidays, foods, or customs. The issue of how to balance the competing interest between developing native and second languages during the early years has still relied ultimately on parental and individual struggles. A lack of responsiveness and efficacy for the diverse populations in many early childhood programs may be due partly to the limited understanding of cultural and language issues in the process of transition from the home culture to that of the school in minority children (Bernhard et al., 1991).

This brief discussion is an attempt to introduce some of the language and cultural issues raised regarding young immigrant children with a focus on the role and importance of the children's home languages and cultures in ECE settings.

Second-Language Learning in the Preschool Years

Historically, researchers who have explored issues of second-language learning and language maintenance in immigrant populations have been more concerned with school-age children than with preschool-aged children (Cummins, 1986; Lyon, 1996). In the past decade, however, researchers have become increasingly concerned about language learning of 2- to 6-year-old immigrant children due to the general increase in early education enrollment and growing minority populations, resulting in more and more immigrant children becoming exposed to a majority language during this early period. In addition, because younger children are presumed to be better language learners than older children, there has been a strong emphasis on immigrant children's being fluent in the majority language prior to school entry. As a result, the goal of preparing immigrant children in the majority language has been pushed down to the preschool level (Kagan & Garcia, 1991; Prince & Lawrence, 1994; Wong Fillmore, 1991).

Within this context, researchers have become increasingly concerned about the consequences of emphasizing English to language-minority children during the preschool years. The major concern is that this could result in a subtractive bilingual experience; that is, the addition of the majority (second) language can cause a deterioration or erosion of the native (first) language. Thus, instead of English serving as enhancement to the child's linguistic repertoire, it often serves as a replacement (Lambert & Taylor, 1983; Wong Fillmore, 1991; Wright, Taylor, & Macarthur, 2000). Such subtractive processes can be associated with considerable cognitive, emotional, and developmental risks (Cummins, 1991; Skutnabb-Kangas, 1981; Wong Fillmore, 1991; Wright & Taylor, 1995). The extent to which such language loss or subtractive bilingualism takes place during the preschool years and the role that early educational institutions play in language development of these children, however, have been matters of significant debate. We turn now to this debate.

The Debate on Early Schooling of Language Minority Children

Perhaps the two important and interrelated questions raised in this debate are these: When should children be exposed to the majority language in a school-like setting? Is there a threshold of native language skills that children should reach *before* the majority language is introduced? In which language should children be instructed in their early years?

A rapid acquisition of English in a school-like setting before competence in the native language has been achieved, combined with a corresponding lack of incentive to develop the native language, not only slow the native language development but also adversely lead to difficulties in acquisition of a second language (Cummins, 1986; Schiff-Myers, 1992). To explain this bilingual language delay, many have cited Cummins's (1984, 1986) hypotheses of threshold and developmental interdependence, which would suggest that a child's second language competence is partly a function of the competence previously developed in the first language. The child must acquire and maintain a threshold level of proficiency, which include literacy skills as well as aural and oral skills, to avoid the subtractive effects of second language instruction. Therefore, if the first language proficiency is at a lower stage before the second language is introduced, it is more difficult to develop the second (Cummins, 1986; Lambert & Taylor, 1983; Skutnabb-Kangas, 1981; Soto, 1993).

The acquisition of a second language at the preschool stage can also lead to the loss of the home language (Cummins, 1991; Faulstich Orellana, 1994; Siren, 1991), which can, in turn, cause serious problems with communication and socialization within the families (Wong Fillmore, 1991). This does not mean that learning English, even in a limited way, should be a taboo for young minority children; however, as Wong Fillmore (1991, p. 345) stressed, "The problem is timing, not English. The children have to learn English, but they should not be required to do so until their native languages are stable enough to handle the inevitable encounter with English and all it means."

However, other researchers have recommended that language-minority children take advantage of an early start in introducing both languages (Baker & deKanter, 1983; Porter, 1991). Language skills require up to 7 years of practice to reach the levels necessary for academic learning, and learning English in an ECE program can support the natural and easy acquisition of a second language. Porter (1991), for example, argued that early immersion in a second language, preferably between ages 3 and 5, offers the greatest opportunity to learn native pronunciation and the highest level of literacy in that language. The earlier the children learn a second language, the more easily they appear to achieve high levels of fluency.

The matter then rests as a problem of deciding the appropriate time and manner of exposing preschool-aged children to a second-language setting to promote the children's bilingual competence, academic success, and family relations. A missing component in this discussion is how this issue can affect parents, who have the ultimate decisions of when and how to balance the competing interest between the two languages. How, exactly, are immigrant parents of young children dealing with these issues?

In a study of immigrant parents in Sweden, Siren (1991) reported that although most parents supported the goal of bilingual development, there were differences of opinion among parents regarding *when* this goal of bilingualism should be achieved. According to Soto (1993), parents of academically high-achieving Puerto Rican immigrant children in kindergarten through second grade strongly believed in developing a foundation in Spanish first while gradually introducing English to their children. Parents of children who were lower achievers also valued Spanish, but they expressed a preference for simultaneous learning in both languages and were much more ambivalent about the developmental progression of first- and second-language learning. In her study of Korean immigrant families in Canada, Koh (2000) similarly found that parents who enrolled their children in bilingual preschools expressed a strong preference for their children building a strong foundation in Korean before learning English. Accordingly, they tended to provide exclusive Korean language environments at home. In contrast, Korean immigrants who enrolled their children in English-speaking preschools believed that children at an early age could acquire two languages naturally and actively supported this scenario by their choice of preschool setting and the nature of home literacy activities. Thus, a major question among immigrant parents of young children concerns the most appropriate balance between developing fluency in both their native language and the majority language. Parental attitudes influence language practices and interaction patterns at home and parents' selection of a particular preschool program.

There is general agreement among researchers that a child's success in learning both the native language and the majority-culture language is more dependent on the nature of the home and preschool learning environments and less dependent on the child's age per se (Arnberg, 1987; Schiff-Myers, 1992). In other words, minority children's second-language learning in the early years is not always a problem if the home languages and literacy are valued and encouraged in the home, preschool, and community. Nevertheless, the appropriate balance between developing the native language and the majority language during the early school years is a critical issue about which language minority parents and ECE practitioners need to have more solid theoretical and empirical bases.

Another hotly debated issue surrounds the instructional use of the two languages in minority children's early schooling (Garcia, 1993). At one end of this debate are proponents of native or bilingual language instruction who recommend learning of the native language prior to the introduction of an English curriculum (transitional or maintenance bilingual education). In this approach it is suggested that "competencies in the native language, particularly as related to academic learning, provide important cognitive and social bases for second-language and academic learning" (Garcia, 1973, p. 379). The other end of this debate recommends immersion to the English curriculum from the very start of the students' schooling experience with the minimal use of the native language (English immersion education). Perhaps the most familiar examples of this debate are results on bilingual or native-language ECE classrooms for Spanish speakers in the United States (see Bilingual Research Journal, 1992). However, this issue could extend to a wide variety of language-minority groups who have a choice of native or bilingual language instruction in their early years. Evaluation of immersion, native, or bilingual programs includes political and ideological as well as methodological and technical debates.

However, a number of researchers have increasingly noted a positive outcome in the language and cognitive development for the children attending effective bilingual or native language classrooms (Campos, 1995; Paul & Jarvis, 1992; Rodriguez, Diaz, Duran, & Espinosa, 1995).

The language of instruction is but one of many factors that can determine the outcomes of learning in a specific early education program. These other factors could include teacher training, classroom interactions, the nature of peer relations, the curriculum that is used, parent involvement, or program philosophies that contextualize the teaching and learning in the programs. Further study of language practices in the early schooling of language-minority children should focus on more than the language of instruction alone and should include such ecological factors of the programs. The issue of minority students' early education should also be understood not only in the classroom or school but also in a broader societal context where the children are learning the native and majority language (Garcia, 1993; Wong Fillmore, 1991).

The Role of Home Culture in Early Childhood Education

In the past, the language and culture that minority families and children brought from their home into new environment were considered to be deficiencies (Collins, 1988). Deficiency theory attributed the academic failure of children from certain ethnic groups to culturally determined socialization practices in the home. Much recent and current research has helped to refute this cultural deficiency model and has begun to contribute to our understanding of cultural differences between the school and the minority students. The cultural differences—or discontinuities—position, supported by a number of well-documented ethnographic studies, suggests that a major source of children's education failure lies in the culture clash between home and school (e.g., Delgado-Gaitan & Trueba, 1991; Garcia, 1988; Heath, 1983).

Others have pointed out that deficit-difference models have oversimplified the problem of minority achievement by generalizing and perhaps overemphasizing home-school discontinuities (Goldenberg, Reese, & Gallmore, 1992; Weisner, Gallimore, & Jordan, 1993). Although home-school discontinuities must be recognized and accommodated appropriately in the school, not all cultural discontinuities between minority families and school are negative (Delgado-Gaitan & Truba, 1991; Schmidt, 1998; Volk, 1997; Weisner et al., 1993). Thus, it is necessary to look at some new and emerging data that suggest certain positive outcomes of some discontinuities. Weisner et al. (1993) gave an example of how educators identified cultural differences between school and Hawaiian families and then incorporated the family's teaching-learning style from the home culture into their classroom practices:

> Sibcare is a ubiquitous aspect of Hawaiian child life; it reinforces habits of attending and orienting to siblings and other children rather than to adults. These habits can be generalized to the classroom by providing opportunities for peer teaching and learning. In a traditional classroom, these culture-based habits lead to problems; in classrooms using peer teaching, they produce better achievement. (p. 62)

Similarly, the Kamelahama Early Education Program (KEEP) in Hawaii showed that incorporating features of the home culture into reading lessons in primary classrooms resulted in an increase of the children's reading achievement scores (Grant, 1995). Instead of mainstream classroom discussions of stories, discussions were adjusted to incorporate the Hawaiian storytelling tradition, which involves a high proportion of turn taking and cooperative production of responses (Au, 1997; Au & Carroll, 1997). Studies such as these showed that minority home cultures and values must be factored into children's educational plans. Modifying old approaches and developing new conceptual insights and educational practices can help minority language children succeed in school.

The Socialization and Resocialization of Young Minority Children

Socialization is a means by which patterns of behavior, attitudes, values, and beliefs are transmitted to children from families, schools, peers, the media, and other influences (Garcia, 1993). During the early childhood years, family is essentially the major socialization source for a child. After the child enters early education programs, both the family and the school are primary socialization sources. The transition from home to early schooling marks a critical socialization period for all children, and perhaps more so for culturally and linguistically diverse children whose languages and ways of life are different from those of the mainstream (Kagan & Garcia, 1991; Villarruel, Imig, Kostelnik, 1995).

Families from diverse ethnic backgrounds may have different values, goals, and practices concerning what they consider important early experiences for children. These variations can reflect differences in their cultural belief systems about the status and role of children in society and their perceptions of how children learn (Goodnow, 1988). As an example, the traditional culture and socialization of northeast Asian countries are deeply rooted in Confucian philosophy,

which strongly emphasizes interdependence from parents, group harmony, close family ties, and respect to adults. Children raised in this kind of cultural consciousness are not encouraged to initiate conversations with adults or to compete verbally with others publicly. These precise characteristics of socialization, however, are inconsistent with those of Western culture, which tend to emphasize the development of self-expression, autonomous choice, and independent individuals (Choi, Kim, & Choi, 1993). When the cultural climate of the home differs significantly from that of school and society at large, the child may be caught in the middle of home-school value conflict.

What happens if ECE programs of these children do not understand the values and child developmental goals behind cultural differences and seek to resocialize the children to a new set of values? Clearly, an appropriate function of education is socialization, and it is not unrealistic to expect that older children will accommodate such norms. However, asking very young children to be resocialized, just as formative socialization is taking place, unduly burdens them (Kagan & Garcia, 1991). The attempt to fit in to the socialization-resocialization conundrum can result in confusion within the child and the rejection of the home culture and language. This in turn often creates a deep emotional gap between the child and the family and in some cases could lead to emotional or learning problems for the child (Delgado-Gaitan & Trueba, 1991; Kagan & Garcia, 1991). In fact, reports of Asian immigrants in North America have indicated a significant challenge in their children's socialization and serious communication problems with their children at home (Kim & Choi, 1994; Lee & Lehmann, 1986; "There is no Utopia," 1999). Pettingill and Rohner (1985), who compared children's perception of parenting among Korean, Korean Canadian, and Korean American samples, found that perceived parental control was correlated with high parental warmth and low neglect, and slightly with parental hostility and rejection in the Korean sample. On the other hand, for the Korean Canadian and Korean American children, parental control was perceived as low warmth and high hostility, neglect, and rejection. This study showed that parental control—a positive feature of the parent-child relationship in Korea—was transformed into a negative feature for the children of Korean immigrants in North America.

Although there are always individual variations within the cultural groups, it is important to understand that the socialization characteristics of one cultural group are governed by its cultural values and beliefs and can be significantly different from those of another. Schools need to understand that minority families' cross-cultural adjustments can be a difficult and complex process, so schools should provide learning environments that can mediate the adjustment and develop a healthy sense of self.

Closing Thoughts on Language, Culture, and Immigration

With so many children from diverse language and cultural groups in early childhood programs, it has become an increasingly important challenge to appreciate the significance of the family's language and culture and to move from appreciation to action on the part of early childhood professionals. A number of key issues regarding language, culture, and the education of young immigrant children must remain high priorities for both early childhood educators and researchers.

First, there is concern with the possibility of subtractive bilingualism, that is, losing proficiency in the child's first language. Supporting the child's native language at an early age has been strongly encouraged for the children's academic success, bilingual proficiency, family relations, and a healthy sense of self. ECE programs for minority children must encourage and appreciate the language skills and cultural values that these children bring from their home, so that they neither directly nor indirectly stop the children's native language and cultural development.

Parents of minority preschoolers are challenged to decide when and how to provide the relative balance between the native and second languages for their children, and they need more information and support. Studies of the impact of family culture on children's learning have showed that identifying cultural differences between the school and the families, and incorporating the information into classroom practices, resulted in better academic achievement.

For the children of minority groups, parenting values and practices at home may be very different from what educators expect, and socialization experiences may be unique and complex as children often interact in multiple linguistic and cultural groups. Thus, ECE professionals are expected to look at children within the context of their family and culture. The potential conflicts and confusion that these families and their children might experience in their cross-cultural adjustment must be acknowledged, understood, and overcome.

Child Temperament and Early Childhood Education

> I didn't get any information about temperament in my training. That community talk was when I first learned about Thomas and Chess's study, you know, and about temperament. I didn't learn that in my early childhood training. That's terrible, right? ("Corinne," cited in Andersen & McDevitt, 2000, p. 14)

The early childhood special educator just quoted reported that she had to remove her 3-year-old son from a day care

setting in which he was in constant conflict with teachers and peers. She was on a desperate search for caregivers who were knowledgeable and skilled in working with challenging behavior. She was also seeking emotional support and practical suggestions for herself from early intervention professionals. This parent had learned from medical and mental health specialists that her child was neurologically intact but that his intensity, slowness to adapt, negative mood, high activity level, and short attention span were aspects of his temperament that were colliding with the expectations of his parents and teachers. However, her attempts to impart this well-informed assessment of the basis of her son's behavior fell on deaf ears in her neighborhood day care center. The skepticism she encountered left her feeling judged and blamed, and her son was labeled "disturbed" and "troublesome." Yet she herself could not blame the teachers, whose training, like her own, had included so little attention to the extensive research that now exists on child temperament (Andersen & McDevitt, 2000). Although her experience in encountering ignorance of temperament is tragically commonly reported (Andersen, 1994), it is also true that ECE professionals have been among the most enthusiastic supporters of the concept. Many have acknowledged that the topic needs more attention in personnel preparation and as a variable that affects the functioning of children in group settings (Andersen, 1990; Soderman, 1985).

The History of Temperament Research

The idea of temperament has a long history, dating back at least as far Hippocrates (Rutter, 1982). However, after the hereditarian views of personality that held sway in the nineteenth century were rejected, by the middle of the twentieth century children's traits were considered either to be all learned or to be projections of their parents' often-distorted perceptions. These psychodynamic and social-learning theories of children's individual differences were first systematically challenged by the formulation and investigation of the construct of temperament by the American psychiatrists Stella Chess and Alexander Thomas. The attribution of all differences in children, including infants, to differences in parental (usually maternal) handling or to the projection of parental personality characteristics, ran counter to their own personal and professional experiences (Chess & Thomas, 1987). They knew that they could not refute these ideas on the basis of their opinions alone. The task called for a major research enterprise. Their New York Longitudinal Study (NYLS) was initiated in 1956 and followed 133 children from early infancy to adult life. This turned out to be a landmark study, and these two American psychiatrists paved the way for a veritable revolution in our understanding of children's individuality and development. Their work was soon followed, and expanded upon, by other leading thinkers. The topic of temperament has consequently played a central role in the development of new interactionist theories of child development and in the formulation of etiological theories in child and adolescent psychiatry. It has been accompanied by intensive discussion of basic research and clinical questions, many of which continue to arise as children's individuality is investigated today. It is therefore useful to consider first the central themes that have recurred as the concept of temperament has been put to the empirical test and as new conceptual issues have emerged. Following this, the implications and empirical investigation of temperament in early childhood education and day care will be discussed.

The Definition of Temperament and Temperament Traits

Chess and Thomas defined temperament as the behavioral style of a person, distinguishing this aspect from the person's abilities and motivations (Chess & Thomas, 1987). They have also characterized it as "a non-motivational factor in the determination of behavioral patterns" (Chess & Thomas, in Carey & McDevitt, 1989, p. 26). They clarified this idea by explaining that an individual responds to an internal or external stimulus through the mediating effects of temperament, along with other factors, such as past events, cognitive level, subjective feelings, and ideals. Others have characterized temperament as a mediating variable, representing an individual's response patterns and manner of coping with stress and adversity (Rutter, 1994). Carey and McDevitt (1995) stated that although there is still no universal agreement on a definition, the general usage is in accord with the view of Thomas and Chess's original concept of behavioral style. They noted an important distinction between temperament and cognitive factors:

> Thomas and Chess explain it as the "how" of behavior as contrasted with the "what" (abilities or developmental level) and the "why" (motivations and behavioral adjustment). This conceptual and empirical separation of temperament and cognitive function has been demonstrated at various times in childhood including infancy (Plomin et al., 1990, 1993) and the elementary school years (Keogh, 1986; Martin, 1989, 1989b). (p. 10)

Although new methods are now available to investigators, particularly in molecular genetics and in direct studies of brain function, no new findings have overturned earlier views that temperament represents an innate attribute of a child and arises from a combination of genetic, biological, and environmental contributors.

TABLE 13.1   The Nine Temperament Traits Identified by Chess and Thomas

Trait	Definition
Activity level	Motor activity and the proportion of active and inactive periods.
Rhythmicity	The predictability or unpredictability of the timing in biological functions, such as hunger, sleep-wake cycle, and bowel elimination.
Approach/withdrawal	The nature of the initial response to a new situation or stimulus—a new food, toy, person, or place.
Adaptability	Long-term responses to new or altered situations. Here the concern is not the nature of the initial responses but the ease with which they are modified in desired directions.
Sensory threshold	The intensity level of stimulation necessary to evoke a discernible response, irrespective of the specific form the response may take.
Quality of mood	The amount of pleasant, friendly, and joyful behavior and mood expression, as contrasted with unpleasant crying and unfriendly behavior and mood expression.
Intensity of reactions	The energy level of response, positive or negative.
Distractibility	The effectiveness of an outside stimulus in interfering or changing the direction of the child's ongoing behavior.
Persistence and attention span	These two categories are usually related. Persistence refers to the continuation of an activity in the face of obstacle or difficulties. Attention span concerns the length of time a particular activity is pursued without interruption.

Source: Based on Chess & Thomas (1984, pp. 42–43).

Chess and Thomas identified the nine temperament traits listed in Table 13.1. Although the traits developed by Chess and Thomas have formed the basis of several temperament scales, which in turn have been utilized clinically as well as in vast numbers of individual studies, others have developed different formulations of the construct. Drawing on Carey and McDevitt's (1995) discussion of these alternatives, a brief summary is presented in Table 13.2.

The Measurement and the Functional Significance of Temperament

Although temperament is manifested in behavioral styles, researchers, clinicians, and parents are aware that similar behavior can have any number of nontemperamental causes. It is not surprising, then, that the assessment of specific behavior as related to temperament and the measurement of an individual's temperamental profile have posed especially difficult problems for researchers and clinicians alike. Although some investigators have used psychophysiological

TABLE 13.2   Six Alternative Definitions of Temperament

Theorist	Definition of Temperament
Buss and Plomin	The EASI formulation: The four traits of emotionality, activity, sociability, and impulsivity, although impulsivity was later withdrawn when it was not found to be heritable.
Eysenck	Features of personality: Extraversion-introversion, neuroticism, and psychoticism.
Goldsmith and Campos	Temperament is limited to the emotional sphere.
Rothbart and Derryberry	Dimensions of reactivity and self-regulation.
Strelau	Regulative theory of temperament, including components of energy and temporal traits.
Zuckerman's	Description of sensation seeking.

Source: Based on Carey & McDevitt (1995, pp. 15–18).

instruments to support their claims about biological factors, most contemporary research has been conducted using paper-and-pencil checklists of children's behavioral tendencies as observed by parents, teachers, investigators, and clinicians. These scales are usually based on the nine dimensions developed by Chess and Thomas. These instruments are designed to tap children's behavioral dispositions by asking parents and other observers questions about the child's typical behavior in day-to-day situations. These scales, and modifications of them, have been validated on large numbers of children internationally (Carey & McDevitt, 1995). Currently, several scales are available that are appropriate for use by ECE personnel, often in combination with parent ratings and observations (McDevitt, in Andersen & McDevitt, 2000). These include a new questionnaire for caregivers and preschool teachers, the Teacher and Caregiver Temperament Inventory for Children (TACTIC), which measures temperament, attention, emotions, and conduct in 2- to 7-year-old children, and the Basic Behavioral Assessment Scale (BBAS) by Carey and McDevitt, which measures behavioral adjustment in 4- to 14-year-old children in the areas of behavior, achievement, self-relations, internal state, and coping (S. C. McDevitt, personal communication, November 2001).

Although there appears to be a growing consensus on many issues raised in the earlier years, more recent discussions of temperament continue to reflect earlier concerns about measurement. In response to Clarke-Stewart, Fitzpatrick, Allhausen & Goldberg (2000) presentation of a short and easy measure of infant temperament, Carey (2000) has argued for caution when hoping that there could be a brief and simple way to capture a complex phenomenon.

Although the work of Chess and Thomas and their followers was published as early as the mid-1960s, the findings on the predictive validity of children's individual differences in emotional disposition and behavioral style did not win acceptance until the early 1980s. This was in spite of the fact that several independent lines of research had essentially replicated the early findings (Graham, Rutter, & George, 1973; Barron & Earls, 1984; Maziade, Caron, Cote, Boutin, & Thivierige, 1990). Fears of a deterministic view of human behavior may have played a role in the reluctance of developmentalists to accept the notion that biologically based differences exist in children's emotional and behavioral dispositions. Carey and McDevitt (1995) suggested that in clinical circles another central reason for the slow acceptance of temperament concepts may lie in the fact that the risks associated with temperament are seen to lie not in the temperament itself but in the lack of goodness of fit between the child's temperament and the expectations and values of the environment. Clinicians may have found it difficult to consider the question of fit because this notion is not in keeping with the habit of looking for problems within either the child or the environment. However, such a contextual approach has become not only acceptable, but fully in keeping with current theoretical understandings of the interplay between children's dispositions, abilities, and interests and the complex factors that interact with their individuality at all levels of the ecology.

Despite the early resistance to the concept and despite the clinical world's slowness to adopt complex etiological models, accumulating evidence has left little room for doubt about the reality and importance of temperament. Research in temperament has now involved the efforts of hundreds of scientists in numerous areas, and the second wave of temperament research has adopted stringent methodological standards and extended its reach across cultures and into the genome, utilizing research methods ranging from ethnographic studies to the most recent technology such as brain scans and electrophysiological measurement. Clinician-researchers have been appraising the role of temperament across culture and socioeconomic differences, exploring the interaction between temperament and physical status, and behavioral-geneticists and neuroscientists continue to study the relative contribution of genes and the environment, including the environment of the womb. Twin and adoption studies have revealed that there is a substantial genetic contribution to temperament—about 50% on average. (Contrary to previous views, there is compelling evidence that temperament in infancy is not highly under genetic control and that genetic influences are stronger in the postinfancy years. In addition, temperament is not as stable or continuous as was once proposed.) Investigation of the role of maternal hormones, stress, prenatal infections, and perinatal stress has reminded developmentalists that environmental contributors to temperament can be biological (Carey &

McDevitt, 1995, pp. 18–24). At the same time, interactions of parenting style, family stress factors, and social pressures continue to be seen as important contributors to outcome.

In the past two decades temperament has been shown to affect a wide range of areas of children's functioning, no less so in the preschool and school years than in infancy. Current knowledge about the functional significance of temperament was recently summarized by Carey (1998, pp. 27) as cited by Andersen and McDevitt (2000) as

fundamental part of the parent-child relationship;

significant factor in patterns of growth and feeding;

predisposition to prolonged crying in infancy;

possible contributor to sleep problems;

reason some children are hard to discipline;

major risk factor for social behavior problems;

substantial component of school performance;

factor in physical conditions;

one factor in recurrent pain;

partial determinant of response to crises.

Although temperament has been shown to play an important role in many areas of development, perhaps the most significant area for application in early childhood education is the role of temperament in children's psychological adjustment and educational achievement. It is useful, therefore, to review the major findings about this relationship. One of the most important and replicated findings of the early temperament research was the identification of specific clusters of traits that differentiated parents' experiences with children. Forty percent of the sample of children who were rated by their parents as adaptable, approaching, mildly active, mildly intense, and regular in biological rhythms were described by their middle-class North American parents as "easy." These children fitted well with the demands of family life and cultural expectations and were found to be at low risk for (but not immune to) the development of psychological and educational problems (Chess & Thomas, 1987). Ten percent of the sample were, by contrast, described as "difficult." These children were low in adaptability, predominantly negative in mood, irregular, withdrawn in new situations, and intense in reactivity. A third group of children, comprising 15% of the sample, were mildly intense in response, mildly negative in mood, and slow to adapt to new situations. This group was described as "slow-to-warm-up."

The most important finding of the NYLS was the discovery that "difficult" children were at significantly higher risk of developing problems in behavioral and emotional adjustment. However, adjustment problems were not inevitable.

Chess and Thomas invoked the concept of goodness of fit to describe a compatible relationship between parental expectations and a child's temperament; when the fit was poor, the child experienced excessive stress and developed reactive behavioral and emotional problems. The finding that temperamentally difficult children were at higher risk of developing psychological problems has been replicated in subsequent research (Earls & Jung, 1987; Graham et al., 1973; Maziade, Cote, Bernier, Boutin, & Thivierge, 1989; Maziade et al., 1990). However, fit has been shown to be context dependent. Consequently, Carey and McDevitt (1989) proposed the term *temperament risk factors:*

Temperament risk factors are any temperament characteristic predisposing a child to a poor fit (incompatible relationship) with his or her environment, to excessive interactional stress and conflict with his or her caretakers, and to secondary problems in the child's physical health, development and behavior. These characteristics are usually perceived as hard to manage, but may not be. The outcome depends on the strength and durability of the characteristics and the environmental stresses and supports. (p. 195)

Temperament Research in Early Childhood Education

Despite the consensus that now exists about the importance of the role of children's individual differences in temperament as a significant risk factor in specific contexts, applications of this knowledge in all levels of early childhood education have been few (Andersen, 1990). In 1995 Carey and McDevitt published an extensive review of the extant studies of temperament. In their chapter on day care, they decried the failure of the prevention, intervention, and caregiving communities to apply this important knowledge. In their chapters on infants and young children, they noted that "behavioral investigation in the area [of child day care] has almost completely ignored the impact of children's temperament on the experience" (p. 83). They summarized the little research there was at the time. However, what little research there is suggests that further investigation is likely to be fruitful (Anderson-Goetz & Worobey, 1984; Field & Greenberg, 1982; Keogh & Burstein, 1988; Palison, 1986).

Among the most important preliminary findings cited by Carey and McDevitt (1995) was the (counterintuitive to some) discovery that mothers of children with difficult temperaments were less likely to go back to work and to place their children in day care, although the authors commented that this study was conducted in the late 1950s and early 1960s, when "the pressure to seek employment outside the home might not have been felt quite as strongly by middle-class mothers as it is today" (p. 85). More recently, Canadian researchers McKim, Cramer, Stuart, and O'Connor (1999) examined the family and child factors associated with child care decisions and found that mothers who preferred to stay home were more depressed and that their children were more likely to experience unstable care than were those who were working and wanted to work. The age at which the child entered day care and aspects of the care such as quality were not related to attachment measures. However, infants with difficult temperaments were at higher risk of being rated as insecurely attached. Attending day care appeared to reduce the strength of this relationship. This study, though preliminary, lends some support to the notion that enrolling a difficult infant in day care might have beneficial effects for the infant and possibly also for depressed mothers.

Another important question is how children's individual temperaments affect their socioemotional adjustment to, and functioning in, early childhood group environments. In an early study of 2.5- to 3.5-year-old children entering day care, Billman and McDevitt (1980) obtained mothers' and observers' temperament ratings on a sample of 78 predominantly White middle-class children ranging in age from 34 to 64 months and attending two nursery schools in a small Midwestern American community. There were 40 girls and 38 boys in the study. The researchers set out to clarify the relationship between home-rated temperament and social behavior at nursery school, to investigate any relationship between difficult temperament and peer interaction, and to assess the consistency of temperament ratings made by different raters in different settings. Parental ratings of the temperament characteristic of low approach predicted teacher evaluations of slower adjustment. It is interesting to note that the "difficult child" cluster of traits emerged as a significant predictor of peer interactions. Although convergence between the two temperament ratings was moderate (.18–.46), correlations were statistically significant for all dimensions except mood. Activity level, approach-withdrawal, and sensory threshold were significantly related to peer interaction. Very active children were both more sociable than inactive children and more often involved in conflictual interactions. More rhythmic children spoke more to peers and got on with their tasks more effectively. When the children were assigned to the temperament clusters identified by Chess and Thomas, the difficult child was found to engage in more wrestling, hitting, jumping, pushing, and beating.

More recently, Harden et al. (2000) used Bronfenbrenner's ecological framework to explore externalizing behavior problems among children enrolled in a suburban Head Start program and compared them with a subgroup of children with behavior problems in the clinical or borderline range. Children's externalizing behavior was positively associated with internalizing behavior, parent psychological adjustment, child temperament, family environment, and exposure to community violence.

Yen and Ispa (2000) tested the hypothesis that curriculum type (Montessori and constructivist) moderates the impact of temperament (specifically, activity level and attention span and persistence) on the classroom behavior of 3- to 5-year-old children. A near-significant trend suggested that temperamentally active boys were more likely to be perceived by their teachers as having behavior problems if they were enrolled in Montessori programs than if they were enrolled in constructivist programs. An interesting finding was that attention span and persistence did not have any effect on the impact of the type of curriculum on children's behavior. This is one of the few studies that explores the important question of the goodness of fit between specific types of curriculum and children's temperament.

Stansbury and Harris (2000) conducted a study to ascertain whether standardized peer entry paradigm would produce stress responses in 38 3-year-olds and 25 4-year-olds and how such stress responses might correlate with temperament, approaches to peers, and peer competence as perceived by the children themselves. Four-year-olds were significantly less avoidant and were rated higher on the temperament trait of "approach." They showed larger Hypothalamic-Pituitary-Adrenal Cortical Axis (HPA) stress responses to new peers, and the disparity between self-reported peer competence and behavior in the peer-entry situation was associated with greater stress responses on a physiological measure. The researchers stressed the importance of examining discrepancies between self-perception and action in research on stress.

The need for the education of early childhood professionals about temperament was acknowledged in a study by Franyo and Hyson (1999) of the effectiveness of temperament training of early childhood caregivers. This study provided information about caregivers' preexisting knowledge of temperament concepts and investigated the effect of educational workshops about temperament concepts. The findings were that without training, caregivers had heard about temperament but knew little about the specifics of the empirical findings. Without training, caregivers did not appear to have many ideas about how to achieve a goodness of fit by using behavioral management techniques, although this was an area in which they showed special interest. Encouragingly, caregivers were very accepting of the concept of temperament, and training sessions were effective in increasing their knowledge about temperament concepts. However, the investigators reported that there was no statistically significant evidence that the training was effective in improving the caregivers' acceptance of children's behaviors and feelings.

Implications for Further Research

Although these new efforts are encouraging, there continues to be a dearth of empirical research on the role of child temperament in early childhood group settings. Much more work remains to be done. There are many areas of child temperament research that have direct implications for early childhood education. The first of these is the direct education of caregivers and teachers about the origins and significance of individual differences in children's behavioral styles so as to avoid misattributing all these differences to central nervous system dysfunction or parenting. Second, research is demonstrating that temperament has an impact on the way children experience, and affect, their environments. Active children are often criticized by staff for their restlessness when a programmatic modification may be in their interests. Children who need time to adapt to new situations require teachers who have the patience to help them overcome their period of hesitation (Soderman, 1985). There is particular concern about children whose temperaments challenge and frustrate caregivers and about peers who may be the recipients of rejection or neglect, leading to the development of secondary problems. More work is needed in formulating effective training programs that will bring about both significant attitudinal and behavior management changes in caregivers. This is particularly important in view of the fact that families of children with challenging temperament-related issues may seek assistance from ECE staff. Because there is often an overlap between this group of children and those diagnosed at school age with attention-deficit/hyperactivity disorder or oppositional defiant disorder, early intervention agencies should recognize that these children are at very high risk when the fit is poor and should be eligible for services under such circumstances (Andersen & McDevitt, 2000).

No less important than applying research about temperament risk factors is an appreciation of the fact that temperament traits can serve also as assets (Carey & McDevitt, 1995). Researchers would do well to explore how specific temperament traits may benefit children in their interactions with adult caregivers, with peers, and with the curriculum of ECE programs, and practitioners need to avoid automatically associating the word "temperament" with risk factors. Carey and McDevitt stated the key questions for the conduct of research on temperament in day care this way:

> What kinds of children do better in what kinds of care arrangements? Does a child's temperament influence his or her behavior with peers and child care professionals in the day care situation in the same ways as in the home? How can we deliver day care that best meets the needs of parents and children? What happens

when there is a poor fit between the child's characteristics and the handling provided by the day care facility? How is this dissonance best detected? Will the management principles that seem to work for parents in the home also prove effective in the day care setting? What do day care workers generally know about important mental health matters, including temperament differences? Where do they get such information, and how successfully do they apply it? What is the best way to augment such knowledge? What benefits can be demonstrated for its use? What are the consequences of day care workers not having this knowledge? For aggressive or non-compliant behavior, what management strategies beside time-out are suitable? How can parents and day care workers best collaborate for the well-being of the child? (Carey & McDevitt, 1995, p. 90)

Closing Thoughts on Child Temperament

The field of early childhood education has made great strides and, indeed, has demonstrated leadership in showing respect to cultural diversity among young children and their families and in serving as teachers of, and advocates for, young children with disabilities and social risk factors. A burgeoning body of empirical studies in a wide range of fields has led to a consensus that child temperament exists, can be reliably measured, and is an important and universal individual difference among infants and young children that can serve as an asset or create risk. Respecting diversity among young children must now be extended to respecting this diversity in behavioral style. Early childhood researchers and practitioners will undoubtedly rise to the challenge of the new millennium by absorbing and applying the substantial knowledge that has been accumulated about temperament in the past four decades. We can look forward to seeing further attention to this important variable in empirical studies, in personnel preparation, and in curricula and programming.

PROGRAMS AND QUALITY IN EARLY CHILDHOOD EDUCATION

Compensatory Programs and Early Childhood Special Education

The title of "father of the kindergarten" was given to Friedrich Froebel. If Froebel is granted this acknowledgement, then the title of mother of early childhood special education (ECSE) should be granted to Maria Montessori (1870–1952). Indeed, Montessori anticipated the broad sweep that the field would make across the spectrum of childhood experiences and needs. In 1901 she became the director of the "orthophrenic" school associated with the University of Rome, a former asylum for city children, most of whom were likely intellectually disabled or autistic. She mounted a campaign to reform the system that had previously confined these children to a life of isolation and neglect. Montessori understood the need they had for purpose in life, for stimulation and for achieving a sense of self-worth. Anticipating the modern ethos, Montessori emphasized the importance of showing respect to all children and of teaching them self-care skills as well as to observe and respect the world around them. Also foreshadowing current trends, Montessori took an interest in children who were at risk because they were poor.

An Overview of the History of Early Childhood Special Education

In 1907 Montessori began an experimental school in the poorest part of Rome to demonstrate that her educational methods could be effective with inner-city preschoolers who were not disabled. She also anticipated the contemporary approach to the field of ECSE by applying herself to a rigorous analysis of research on the education of the mentally handicapped, focusing on the work of two French doctors, Jean Itard and Edouard Seguin. Itard's work with the *Wild Boy of Aveyron* brought into focus another constant theme in contemporary ECSE, the long-standing question of the relative weights of nature and nurture in children's development. Seguin's influence was to encourage Montessori in her already-strong belief in making education systematic and specific. Although many consider Seguin to be the father of special education, it is an irony of history that in North America Montessori's influence was not felt in the education of young children with special needs as much as it was in the development of Montessori nursery schools for normal children of middle- and upper-middle-class parents.

Indeed, in most Western countries the early education of young children at risk for compromised development was a neglected field until shortly after World War II. Although each modern state has followed its own path in developing and expanding services for children at risk, the United States is unique in mandating these services—a mandate that has driven academic research as much as it has program delivery. As a result, much research on the education of young children at risk has been conducted in the United States, and it is therefore the American experience in the field that followed federal legislation that will be reflected, for the most part, in this section.

As was described in the opening section of this chapter, the theme of nature versus nurture was present in the earliest years of the field of early childhood education. The 1961 publication of McVicker Hunt's *Intelligence and Experience* fueled a renewed emphasis on the role of environmental experience in cognitive development. In 1965 the U.S. federal government initiated the first Head Start program, a summer initiative to bring America's poorest children into programs in which they would receive stimulation and nutrition and that would involve their parents in a broad-sweeping and early attempt to provide compensation for the known detrimental effects of poverty and social disadvantage on children's development. These early short-term programs were followed by programs that were more intensive and broader in conceptualization. Consequently, by 1972 a mandated quota of 10% of children with disabilities in Head Start programs was established. And although the Education for All Handicapped Children Act (PL 94-142), passed in 1972, did not cover children from birth to 3 years of age, in time services for preschool-aged children were mandated, and standards and incentives for providing services to infants and toddlers were included. One outcome of international significance in the American legislation and experience has been the emergence of a unified discipline that subsumed all the early childhood risk factors under its umbrella: ECSE. This new field was heralded by the formation of the Division for Early Childhood as a subsection of the Council for Exceptional Children in 1973 (McCollum, 2000).

Early childhood special education is the branch of the field of early childhood education that addresses the diverse educational needs of children with disabilities and developmental delays. The field has also come to include children whose developmental risk was at first seen to arise from the disadvantage of being raised in certain family and sociocultural contexts. Although the term *compensatory education* has been used to describe the aim of programs attempting to make up for presumed deficits in children's environments, many theorists now regard it as unreasonable to think in terms of a dichotomy between children with endogenous difficulties and those with problems arising from environmental factors. It has been known for some time now that many risk factors arising from social conditions, such as maternal ingestion of alcohol, are translated into biological problems in children. In addition, many genetic risk factors are triggered only in the presence of certain environmental conditions. Recent neurobiological research has confirmed the potentially devastating impact of social stresses on young children's neurodevelopment. Recent medical research has also shown that the technologies that are used to sustain survival of very high risk infants may create additional disabilities in those children.

Multidisciplinary Perspectives on Early Childhood Special Education

The complexity of the difficulties that face contemporary young children is matched by the need for multidisciplinary academic inquiry informed by many specialties and with a knowledge base of evidence-based practices that are reproducible in a field that continues to be marginalized and underfunded. One consequence of the scope and diversity of needs in the field of ECSE has been a major effort, in past decades, in the development of a professional identity. McCollum (2000) discussed how, between 1976 and 1985, several related movements were influential in shaping the nature of ECSE. The development of empirically based systematic instruction, furthered by academic investigation based on current learning theories, came first. Second, attention to preventing school failure became a mandate of the states, and the beginnings of a relationship between early childhood education and ECSE were forged as attempts were made to identify those young children who might be in need of early intervention. Third, increasing attention was paid to the noninstructional roles of teachers as ecological theory began to influence the way that interventionists understood the importance of the social context of development. Finally, younger and younger children began to receive attention and intervention programs because infants and toddlers grew rapidly.

The impact of these diverse influences challenged the assumption that this new field was a branch of special education alone. As the influence of other specialties was brought to bear on the questions of how best to help young children whose development might not proceed well, the new field was increasingly being referred to not only in educational terms. In keeping with paradigm shifts that occurred in early childhood education in general, ecological perspectives transformed the way in which relationships between culture, society, family, and the individual child were construed. In addition, the vocabulary of health and human services became recognizable in the discourse of the field, which became more broadly known as *early intervention*. This term, which was formerly used exclusively to refer to a point of time in a clinical intervention, had now become a separate area of study and of practice. As Bailey (2000) has commented, in the past three decades the field of early intervention has grown rapidly from its inception to its current state of maturity.

As diverse as its origins were, it is to the credit of its leading thinkers that the field of early intervention has reached a remarkable consensus about its goals, methods, values, and achievements. This consensus, sharpened by the presence of self-critical dialogue within its ranks, is well demonstrated by the publication of two recent special issues of Topics in Early Childhood Special Education (TECSE) that present a compelling picture of the field as it stands today: *Early Childhood Special Education in a New Century: Voices from the Past, Visions for Our Future, Parts 1 and 2*. These papers provide rich and often personal historical accounts of issues as far-ranging as personnel preparation, remedial teaching, inclusion, new theoretical understandings, child care, social conditions, the role of governments in mandating services, methodological issues, interdisciplinary relations, and interventions for specific disabilities. Only some of the major themes of these special issues will receive attention here: (a) inclusion; (b) new theoretical and empirical influences, including a clearer conceptualization by Dunst of family-centered intervention as evidence-based practice; (c) lessons learned from the past; (d) current issues in personnel preparation; and (e) the impact of legislation on services.

The Principle and Practice of Inclusion

Zigler and Styfco (2000) pointed out that Head Start programs were deliberately segregationist at their conception. The idea was to provide special and separate programs for young children from disadvantaged environments. Although this practice effectively cut them off from opportunities to learn in the company of peers from wealthier backgrounds, at the time it was considered that these children would not otherwise attend community nursery schools. Rather, the motivation was to offer them enriching opportunities, including nutritional and health care, that could not be provided by their homes. Likewise, programming for young children with disabilities was equally separate because it was thought that community preschool teachers did not know how to teach them. The inclusion of young children with disabilities in regular preschool and day care programs began slowly, and with much resistance. It is of interest that inclusion is less often justified on empirical grounds than defended in terms of a philosophical position regarding the rights of children with disabilities to experience the same privileges as those without. The emergence of day care into the field of early childhood education added a new dimension to these issues as educational questions became intertwined with questions about custodial care and the needs of working parents.

Although there have been many separate rationales invoked from time to time as policy makers and trainers have sought to persuade communities to move toward the adoption of inclusive practices, Bricker (2000) reminded us that the movement was originally driven by a clearly formulated developmental integration approach, which emerged from examining the detrimental effects of institutionalization on young children. She commented that this was by no means a well-accepted notion at the time. Her account of the gradual acceptance of the principle of inclusion demonstrates how quickly a questioned idea becomes its opposite: "Perhaps the biggest change has been the shift in perspective of inclusion from an idea about how to improve services to young children with disabilities to a human 'right' that has become closely tied to important movements focused on social equality" (p. 17). She acknowledged that inclusion is still hotly debated despite an apparent consensus about its desirability, as evidenced by position papers put forth by organizations such as the Division of Early Childhood of the Council for Exceptional Children. Bricker herself stated that

> the continuing debate over inclusion will do well to focus on the reality of current parental choices when facing placement options for their children. For many parents, the debate raging at the philosophical level may be very different from the realities they face when deciding on a placement for their child. (p. 17)

On a more optimistic note, Odom (2000) argued that

> thirty years of research and practice have produced a knowledge base that informs policy and practice. . . . [N]ow, more than any time in the past, we have a greater awareness of the type of support professionals can provide to create productive learning environments for children with and without disabilities and inclusive settings. With political will, local leadership, willing parents, and committed teachers, most young children with disabilities can benefit from inclusive settings. (p. 25)

It is noteworthy that Odom did not use the rather absolute statements—that inclusion benefits all children—that have entered the position papers put out by both professional and advocacy organizations.

The issues that surround the implementation of inclusion and the emergence in the next decades of large-scale research projects bring us to consider the strengths and struggles of the endeavor to subject early intervention programs to rigorous inquiry. The Head Start experience demonstrates how essential it is to consider how laudable programs can fail in the details of their implementation when errors are made early in their planning. Zigler and Styfco (2000) acknowledged the extent of the problems that surrounded Head Start from its inception: First was an exclusionary ethos, in which economically disadvantaged children were served separately from their peers

from wealthier homes. This segregation extended to excluding those who were disabled until recent times. Second, the lack of a broad unitary goal in favor of a set of discrete objectives led to a misconception of Head Start as a cognitive enrichment program and a decreased emphasis on its original interest in social competence. The third problem was that programming was based on the questionable construct of school readiness. Finally, and perhaps most seriously, was lack of attention to quality. The first of these problems and the difficulties surrounding solutions to it were discussed earlier. The likelihood that topics of school readiness, social competence outcomes, and quality of programming will continue to be pressing issues in the field is acknowledged briefly here.

As researchers look at outcomes in diverse populations, they will be challenged to define common goals that should receive emphasis in the education of all at-risk young children. It is therefore of significance that the special issues of TECSE that were published in the summer of 2000 highlighted two interrelated themes: social competence and language development. In examining the question of social competence, Strain and Hoyson (2000) used research on social-skills intervention with children with autism to illustrate how increasingly sophisticated theoretical formulations of essential research-to-practice questions have produced gains in our ability to engender "rapid, occasionally sustainable, and socially meaningful changes in children's social behavior" (p. 116). They identified four basic assumptions that historically have been used to determine the targets of intervention: (a) the notion that the difficulty with communication is intrinsic to the individual; (b) the notion that the individual has acquired the difficulty as a result of a long-standing interactional history; (c) the notion that dyadic interactions between children sustain the problem; and (d) the notion that the entire ecology of the child with special needs is responsible for altering its norms and the manner in which it structures opportunities for social interaction.

Arguing that none of these assumptions is sufficient to produce effective intervention, they described how a fifth assumption has led to a comprehensive research-to-practice model for children with autism in the past two decades: the LEAP program. The positive results of LEAP are presented to illustrate the potential of both short- and long-term positive benefits of interventions that are individualized and data-driven, have a generalization (transfer of skills) focus, maximize learning opportunities, and add a focus on family skills to the preschool intervention. These results identify the intensity of the intervention as a critical variable in yielding sustainable, long-term outcomes. One of their conclusions will likely be absorbed as the next generation of researchers attempts to achieve similar gains with other populations of children at risk:

> The social interaction challenges presented by young children with special needs represent a complex, multivariate universe. That multivariate universe demands complex, longitudinal, intensive approaches—approaches holding greater promise for children and families but also greater challenges to our ways of designing, executing, and describing credible studies and longitudinal data sets. These are challenges worthy of all eager pioneers with a visionary spirit. (Strain & Hoyson, 2000, p. 121)

A complementary theme that emerges from Hart's (2000) review of studies observing young children is the nature of the language interactions between children and their parents. As the field shifts from theory to data and back again, there is a constant return to children's ecologies as the source of new understanding about how they learn. In reflecting on how much has been learned from observing the way children learn to express themselves in their conversations with their parents, Hart commented on the need for more information on the nature and extent of conversation between teachers and young children and between children and their peers in group environments. She discussed the challenges of group education in enhancing the ability of young children to express themselves:

> Some teachers, like some parents, need more information concerning what children should be learning through play and how to arrange environments, materials, and activities that prompt and facilitate talking. Research is needed to add to interventions the power of engagement (Risley, 1977) and to design low-demand environments (Wasik, 1970) that encourage children to talk when the only object is conversation. (p. 31)

New Theoretical Influences and Their Implications

The themes of social skills and communicative competence are not new to the field, but many argue that they still remain underemphasized in programming. Perhaps two of the most central, truly revolutionary theoretical and empirical influences facing the field in the next millennium are those emerging from brain research and those supporting the use of family-centered practices. New brain research is currently the political driving force behind many fresh initiatives for young children in North America (Greenspan, 1997; Shore 1997). It is of interest that despite its great press appeal, this paradigm is not widely heralded in the summer 2000 issues of TECSE as either the rationale for or the solution to the most pressing problems facing young children today. In fact, it is telling that Zigler and Styfco (2000) appear to be urging some caution in this regard as they reflect on the wildly exaggerated hopes that fueled the original Head Start programs:

"Indeed, the current bandwagon that infant brains need constant stimulation for superior neural wiring and growth is the environmental mystique with a biological twist. . . . [T]he moral is that there is no quick fix for poverty and no magical treatment that will turn us all into Nobel laureates or Rhodes scholars" (p. 68).

Models stressing the importance of social processes as conceptualized by Vygotsky (1978) and of social contexts as conceptualized by Bronfenbrenner (1979) and his followers continue to hold sway. In his review and in anticipation of the "third generation" of research in the field, Dunst (2000) pointed to the intersection between children's learning opportunities and parental supports as the pathway to instructional practices that are most likely to be development enhancing and reminded us that the influence of social support variables on parents' contingent responses to children continues to draw empirical support. He calls for further research on natural learning opportunities provided by family and community life, reminding us that interventionists often have to more learn from families than they have to teach them.

Dunst's (2000) social support paradigm links child developmental outcomes clearly to family-centered interventions. He pointed out that evidence-based, family-centered help giving is becoming more highly specified and can be divided into two central elements: relational and participatory. "Relational practices are a necessary condition for effective practitioner/ family transactions. . . . [T]hey are not sufficient for either strengthening family competence or promoting new capabilities. The latter has been found to be the case only when the family is an active participant in achieving desired outcomes" (pp. 100–101). Dunst acknowledged that his own interest in family-centered practices has become increasingly conceptual and empirical rather than philosophical: "I believe that a philosophically-based, family-centered approach is likely to run its course as a fad and is open to all kinds of criticism, as has recently occurred" (p. 97). He anticipated the continuance of third-generation research that establishes and describes the evidence that supports specific early family-centered intervention practices shaped by an evidence-based social support paradigm. As the field absorbs the impact of the hard data, practitioners will be increasingly asked to demonstrate, rather than discuss, the specific skills that emerge from this knowledge.

Current Issues in Personnel Preparation

McCollum (2000) stated that "between the late 1960s and the present, personnel standards and preparation opportunities have grown from no state certification in ECSE and no targeted preparation programs to widespread certification and many pre-service programs" (p. 80). By 1996 a set of published personnel standards were adopted by the Division of Early Childhood (DEC) and the NAEYC, and most states had some sort of certification for teachers of young children with disabilities. Credentialing programs had been set in place in many states, and ECSE programs at the university level became widely available. It is noteworthy that these events appear to be related directly to the United States legislated mandate described earlier, as there has not been a parallel growth in personnel preparation in countries such as Canada, where university-based ECSE courses are still something of a rarity (Andersen, 1999). However, even in the United States, personnel preparation has not kept pace with the expansion of services. This situation has led contemporary commentators to call for a renewed emphasis on this topic and for new training models that take account of important systemic changes. McConnell (2000) highlighted two such changes that she believed should receive special attention: The first is how both the content and the context of personnel preparation for those working at the preschool and primary levels should be altered given the inclusion of young children with disabilities in community settings. This new context calls for a revised understanding of the relationship of the early childhood educator to the early childhood special educator. The second change regards the delivery of services to infants and toddlers in the United States: The fee-for-service structure is driving a fragmented approach that is not in the interests of children and families. Regarding the latter, McConnell stated that few parents or practitioners are fully aware of the danger that this practice poses to the ability to provide integrated, family-centered interventions. In turn, this may lead to the loss of ECSE generalists and to their replacement by a service coordinator who lacks a solid foundation in child development. She called upon the field to protect children by more clearly defining its own identity and importance for their development.

Winton (2000) argued that the field has currently failed to implement what research has demonstrated needs to be done to improve the outcomes for all young children. She posits that the development of learning communities of multiple partners at multiple levels will help to create the shared vision and commitment from the community that will help to bridge this research-practice gap. She claims that this in itself is an empirically supported approach to personnel preparation, in spite of the very real barriers to its implementation. She suggested a series of small stepping-stones and identified some successful models as the pathway to this important destination.

The Impact of Legislation

Bailey (2000) stated that the field of ECSE in the United States would never have arisen in this fashion without the commitment of the U.S. government. He anticipated that the role of the federal government will now shift from its emphasis on legislated mandates to a more facilitative role, with more decision-making power being left in the hands of the states. He asserted that a strong federal presence will continue to be needed and anticipated the funding of large research projects of nationally representative populations.

Most contributors to these special summer 2000 issues of TECSE see legislated mandates as a positive measure but not without problems. Bruder (2000), in arguing that the field has not successfully fulfilled a commitment to the family-centered practices it espouses, suggested that the programmatic requirements under some sections of the legislation are complex and require more skills and knowledge of the theory than are currently held by state and local administrators. (This problem is complicated by the use of finance models made up of billable services created on a child-centered rehabilitation model rather than a family-centered approach.) She also saw categorical and discipline-specific funding streams as creating barriers to the implementation of truly family-centered services. Odom (2000), too, saw similar bureaucratic barriers to the effective implementation of inclusive practices, some of which arise from administrators' misconception that inclusive programs cost more than traditional special education programs. Other barriers include policies over the manner in which funds are used: In some states money can be spent on tuition to permit a child with disabilities to spend some of his or her day in a community-based program; in other states this is not permissible. The allocation of special education teachers to nonspecialized settings is prohibited in some programs because the specialized teachers are paid out of special education funds. He regarded the flexibility with which administrators handle budgets as a key factor in overcoming these bureaucratic obstacles.

Although her discussion of the impact of federal legislation on personnel preparation is largely positive, McCollum (2000) stated that "the different paths taken by those interested in birth to 2 and in ages 3 to 8 after the passage of PL 99-457 was an unfortunate outcome of the new legislation" (p. 85). When states were permitted to use different agencies and different personnel requirements for the two age groups, a dual system of service and personnel preparation was enabled that created identity problems in the field. The field of ECSE was redefining its identity in relation to early childhood education and special education, with services delivered in educational settings; but with the younger group of infants and toddlers, professional identity was being reconceptualized through comparisons to noneducation disciplines. Indeed, the publications or organizations such as Zero to Three clearly demonstrate the influence of fields such as social work. As well some infant-parent intervention programs have adopted psychotherapeutic models from infant psychiatry. Corresponding with this divergence from the main discipline of ECSE, a number of systemic changes were occurring, complicating the question of personnel roles even further. In the same series, Smith (2000) discussed the need to shift efforts from the federal to the local level so that widespread community support, including fiscal support, will sustain and enhance the achievements begun with federal initiatives and legislation. Smith (2000) argues that communities need to be willing to invest tax dollars and to rethink social policy so that parents can spend more time at home. She also calls for greater respect for early childhood professionals and enhancement of the work environment and salaries so that the field will attract better qualified individuals.

Bailey (2000) noted that the role of the U.S. federal government was shifting from its emphasis on legislated mandates to a more facilitative role, with more decision-making power being left in the hands of the states. He asserted that a strong federal presence will continue to be needed and anticipated the funding of large research projects of nationally representative populations. Perhaps this is where the international field of early childhood education will feel the impact the most—as new research projects of sufficient scale and quality emerge that further our understanding of the impact of specific educational practices with targeted but representative groups of young children.

If the next decade will bring new large-scale studies with results that convince policy makers, there will continue to be a major challenge in bringing that knowledge to the field. Several authors of the special issue decried the research-practice gap in ECSE. Bruder (2000), in particular, focused on the failure of trainers and agencies to adopt truly family-centered approaches, in spite of the substantial amount of evidence of its desirability and effectiveness. She also called for learning communities that can reform current efforts at personnel preparation "in which the norm is the use of ineffective training models (episodic, short-term workshops)" (p. 111). The learning communities that Bruder envisioned are ongoing, make use of technology such as Web sites and e-mail, and are founded on mentorship and distance education models. What is at stake when personnel are inadequately prepared is poignantly demonstrated by her use of three case studies of young children (one of whom is her own nephew) served dismally by intervention staff. About him, she stated, "I am as responsible as any for the shortcomings in our field that are currently impacting his life" (p. 108).

Bruder's (2000) injection of a personal confession into the academic discourse is an appropriate note on which to end this section. It is to the credit of leading early intervention theorists

that in being invited to reflect on the state of the art of early intervention, they do not rest on their laurels. They stand united in recognizing that in spite of the very significant achievements of this fledging field, a great deal of work remains to be done to serve the growing numbers of young children in need of specialized and compensatory early childhood education.

Child Care and Early Childhood Education

The Ecology of Child Care

Beginning in the mid to late 1970s, a number of major changes in North America and other parts of the developed world began to have an impact on the provision of child care services and the nature of research that was conducted on child care. One major change was the sharp increase in the number and percentage of mothers of young children who worked in the paid labor force outside the home. For much of the century until this point, day nurseries were largely provided to low-income families either as part of governmental child welfare programs or by private philanthropists or religious organizations. Child care was now changing from its previous status as a welfare service for poor parents (who, it should be noted, were assumed to provide poor parenting to their children) to its emerging status as a family-support program for working parents in all income levels. Further, the programs were seen less as providing custodial baby-sitting and more as a setting in which young children's early development could be stimulated and facilitated through appropriate kinds of learning activities and materials.

As pointed out in Belsky and Steinberg's (1979) seminal literature review, another major change was the growing interest by researchers in what they referred to as *modal* child care programs as opposed to *model* programs. The model programs to which they referred tended to be situated in or affiliated with university settings. These programs tended to be well funded and staffed by well-educated professionals and to serve the children of university faculty, staff, and students. Questions began to be raised around the generalizability of findings drawn from these model programs to the more frequently used—or modal—community-based programs that tended to suffer from low and unstable funding and lower levels of staff training and that were not restricted to university-affiliated families.

Another shift was that researchers were increasingly critical of earlier studies that had reported that enrollment in child care programs could have a negative impact on mother-infant attachment patterns. Based largely on Ainsworth's *strange situation* paradigm, these studies tended to focus on one-time observations of mother-infant interaction patterns in laboratory settings and typically included very little contextual data on the participants in these studies. Cross-cultural comparisons began to identify different patterns of mother-child attachment even within Western, developed countries (Lamb, 2001), calling into question the notion of a universal construct of attachment. Researchers began to examine attachment patterns within a broader range of child, maternal, family, and child care variables. The largest study of this kind was conducted by the National Institute of Child Health and Development (NICHD), a multisite study of 576 infant-mother dyads. While different patterns of attachment were found in this sample, none of the differences were attributable to the different kinds of child care arrangements in which the children participated (NICHD, 1994, 1996, 1998). In other words, there were no differences in the attachment patterns of children who were cared for by a parent in their own home or by a nonparent in a group care setting outside the home.

This shift in the attachment-related research reflected a significant shift in the nature of the research questions being posed by child care researchers. Much of the previous research on child care tended to focus on such main-effects questions such as, "Is child care good or bad for children?" This research tended to examine specific domains of child development with the child's enrollment in a child care program as the only major independent variable. The emerging consensus was that it was not simply a child's attendance in child care that impacted on that child's development, but also the *quality* of the child care program in which the child was enrolled. Questions regarding the *definition, measurement,* and *impact* of quality child care have framed and guided much of the recent and current research. These programs of research have been guided very much by Bronfenbrenner's (1979; Bronfenbrenner & Morris, 1998) work on the ecology of childhood. Bronfenbrenner argued that a child's development is influenced by a number of concentric systems within which the child lives and grows. The *microsystem* includes the immediate setting in which the child is found and the nature of the experiences and activities in those settings. The *mesosystem* is the network and relationships among the various microsystems in which the child participates (i.e., home, child care, swim lessons, etc.). The *exosystem* includes these two primary systems, but its impact on the child is mediated through other individuals and institutions. Exosystem variables include legislative and policy factors that determine licensing requirements, staff education requirements, funding mechanisms, and so on. All of these systems are embedded within what Bronfenbrenner called the *macrosystem,* which is the virtual space in which societies and communities articulate their beliefs, attitudes, and values toward public policy regarding children and families.

Structure and Process Variables in Child Care Quality

In short, then, instead of the main-effects question ("Is child care good or bad?"), researchers began to explore the ways in which different factors from different systemic levels interacted and to determine how that interaction of factors contributed to child care quality. A number of small-scale, local studies conducted in different parts of North America in the same time frame reported a consistent and complementary set of findings regarding both the *structural* and the *process* variables that impacted on child care quality. Structural variables are those standardized, quantifiable, and regulatable variables such as group size, the adult-child ratio, licensing auspice (nonprofit or commercial), and levels of staff education. These variables were found to be significant predictors of child care quality in different sociocultural contexts using similar instruments: Los Angeles (Howes, 1987); Victoria, British Columbia (Goelman & Pence, 1987); Bermuda (Phillips, McCartney, & Scarr, 1987); and Chicago (Clarke-Stewart, 1987).

These structural factors frame the child care experience for the children and the staff and provide actors a basic foundation on which process quality could then be constructed. The term *process* refers to the kinds of caregiving, facilitating, educating, and playing that go on within the structural framework.

Measures of process quality extended far beyond the strange situation laboratory procedures and examined the nature of adult-child and child-child interactions in the child care setting. Goelman and Pence (1987) observed the frequency with which children engaged in activities that promote positive developmental outcomes (i.e., emergent literacy, dramatic play, fine motor play) and activities that do not (i.e., excessive television watching). Adult-child interactions were observed by Howes (1987), Phillips et al. (1987), Clarke-Stewart (1987), and others who focused on such adult characteristics as sensitivity, receptivity, detachment, and punitiveness (see Table 13.3).

Thus, in contrast to the earlier generations of child care research, which treated child care as a uniform and universal treatment variable, researchers became much more keenly aware of the tremendous diversity that exists in the daily lives of adults and children in child care settings and of how the dynamics of those settings impact both the children and the adults. Perhaps the most consistent conclusion drawn from studies of quality in child is that the concept of *quality* is dynamic and does not rest on any one measure, scale, or quantifiable variable.

Toward a Predictive Model of Child Care Quality

The drawback to these smaller scale local studies was that while they represented careful analyses of child care in different communities, the small numbers of children and child care programs included in these studies put serious limitations on their interpretation and generalizability. In the 1990s, therefore, a new trend in child care research was to mount research studies that included larger numbers of children from larger numbers of communities in very distinct policy and jurisdictional contexts. For example, the U.S. National Staffing Study collected data from 643 child care rooms in urban and suburban communities in Arizona, Georgia, Massachusetts, Michigan, and Washington (Howes, Phillips, & Whitebook, 1992). The U.S. Cost Quality and Outcomes Study examined quality in 604 rooms in California, Colorado, Connecticut, and North Carolina (Hellburn, 1995). The Canadian You Bet I Care! Project examined quality in 308 rooms in nonprofit and commercial infant-toddler and preschool centers in the provinces of New Brunswick, Quebec, Ontario, Saskatchewan, Alberta, and British Columbia and in the Yukon Territory (Goelman, Doherty, Lero, LaGrange, & Tougas, 2000). Although the different studies used somewhat different sampling and instrumentation techniques, there is a strong and

consistent pattern across all of these findings that both confirms and extends the findings from the earlier, smaller scale studies.

The quality of child care centers was found to be strongly linked to a combination of variables at the center, classroom, and teacher levels. Higher quality programs were found in centers that were operated as nonprofit organizations (as opposed to a commercial centers), with well trained staff both in terms of their overall levels of education and their levels of ECE-specific training. Group size and ratio provided the conditions for higher quality care, but the quality of care itself was found in distinct patterns of adult-child interaction. These patterns were characterized by heightened levels of sensitivity, responsiveness, and contingency on the part of child care staff and lower levels of punitive or detached patterns of interaction. Although it was important that the child care setting be well supplied and well stocked with developmentally appropriate materials, it was the training and education of the staff that determined whether these materials were used in the most appropriate

TABLE 13.3   An Overview of Studies That Identify the Predictors of Child Care Quality and the Predictors of Positive Child Outcomes

Studies	Structure Variables						Process Variables		
	Overall Level of Education	ECE-Specific Education	Group Size	Adult-Child Ratio	Auspice[a]	Other Structure Variables	Adult-Child Interactions[b]	Learning Environment[c]	Other Process Predictors
Arnett, 1989	X	X					X		
Berk, 1985	X	X					X		
Burchinal et al., 1996		X	X	X		Staff experience.			
Goelman et al., 1992	X	X			NP > C		X	X	
Goelman et al., 2000	X	X	X	X	NP > C	Staff wages. Subsidized rent. Practicum students. Parent fees.	X	X	Staff satisfaction
Hellburn, 1995	X	X	X	X	NP > C	Staff wages. Subsidized rent.	X	X	
Holloway & Reichhart-Erikson, 1988			X	X	NP > C		X		
Howes, 1983	X	X	X	X		Staff experience.	X		
Howes, 1997	X	X	X	X			X		
Howes & Smith, 1995	X	X	X	X					
Howes et al., 1992	X	X	X	X		Staff experience.	X	X	
Kontos et al., 1996		X	X	X					
Lyon & Canning, 1995	X	X	X	X	NP > C	Director's ECE education. Staff experience.	X	X	
NICHD, 1994, 1996, 1998	X	X	X	X		Staff experience.	X		Staff beliefs about caregiving
Scarr et al., 1994	X	X	X	X	NP > C	Low staff turnover.	X	X	
Vandell & Corasaniti, 1990	X				X	Staff wages.	X	X	
Whitebook et al., 1990	X	X	X	X	NP > C	Subsidized rent.	X	X	

[a]NP = Nonprofit; C = Commerical.
[b]Tools used include the Caregiver Interaction Scale (CIS); ORCE,
[c]ECERS; FDCHERS; ITERS.

manner. Michael Lamb (1998) summed up this body of research in this way:

> Quality day care from infancy clearly has positive effects on children's intellectual, verbal, and cognitive development, especially when children would otherwise experience impoverished and relatively unstimulating home environments. Care of unknown quality may have deleterious effects. (p. 104)

The identification of specific child care predictors can provide guidance and assistance to legislators, policy makers, and educators who deal with child care programs and the preparation of child care professionals. A closer look at the Canadian study (Goelman et al., 2000) suggests that whereas all of these are critical factors in child care quality, the responsibility for achieving these different quality criteria would fall to different groups of stakeholders. The quality criteria appear to fall into four distinct groups. The first group would be factors that are *regulatable* by local authorities: staff education levels, group size, and the adult-child ratio. Elsewhere we have argued at length for the primacy of training of staff both in terms of their overall education levels and their ECE-specific education levels (Goelman et al., 2000). Because the data from all of the studies just cited report that higher quality tends to be found in nonprofit centers than in commercial centers, there appears to be an implicit endorsement for regulatory statutes that encourage the creation of child care programs in the nonprofit rather than in the commercial sector. The establishment, implementation, and monitoring of these regulatable variables would help to provide the structural framework for quality.

A second set of variables consists of those that are related to the *financial* operation of the child care center. The critical financial factors were found to be staff wages, parent fees, and whether the center receives free or subsidized rent. All of these factors point to the financial vulnerability within which child care centers operate and the positive impact that is created when staff are well-compensated for their time. Subsidized or free rent helps to create additional funds that can be directed into salaries, in turn leading to lower levels of turnover. There appears also to be a set of *administrative* factors that can contribute significantly to child care quality. For example, the presence of student teachers from early childhood training programs has a number of positive effects on the life of the center. It assists with the adult-child ratios and brings highly motivated individuals into the center. The presence of student-teachers also helps to create a culture of inquiry and discourse among the student teachers, their supervising teachers, and their supervisors from the ECE training programs.

Finally, and as reported elsewhere, the Canadian study also found that specific *attitudinal* factors among the staff contributed to child care quality. Attitudes are difficult but important factors that cannot be regulated, factored into financial spreadsheets, or implemented as part of a novel administrative framework. Yet it appears that all of the three preceding categories of variables can contribute to the positive attitudes and levels of staff satisfaction that are so critical to the creation of a positive child care environment. A much-cited (but unsourced) quotation attributed to Albert Einstein claims that, "Not everything that can be counted counts. And not everything that counts can be counted." Positive attitude may or may not be able to be assessed accurately, with validity and reliability, but the data suggest that when it can be identified, it provides a vital piece in the puzzle of quality child care.

What then, precisely, does this child care puzzle look like? Most studies of child care have relied on traditional analyses of variance, covariance, or multiple regression to bring statistical rigor to their arguments for including different and discrete pieces of the child care puzzle. Lamb (2001) and others have pointed out that in many of the child care studies the effect sizes tend to be very modest and the amount of variance accounted for is not overly impressive. Another challenge to data analyses is the determination of precisely how the variables interact. It is not clear, for example, whether the cumulative effect of these various predictors is additive, multiplicative, or exponential. For these reasons researchers are turning increasingly to more sophisticated and more powerful hierarchical linear modeling (HLM) techniques. In addition to identifying the discrete pieces of the child care puzzle, techniques such as path analysis can suggest the directionality of the paths. The metaphor of the puzzle, then, should be replaced with the image of an engine that has different parts, working together to move the vehicle forward.

Path analyses were applied to the data generated in the Canadian study (Goelman et al., 2000), and the resulting analyses identified a set of direct and indirect predictors of child care quality in rooms for infants and toddlers (0–35 months) and in rooms for 3- to 5-year-old children. Table 13.4 shows the seven direct predictors of quality in the preschool room, four staff predictors (staff wages, staff satisfaction, staff education, number of staff in the observed room), and three center predictors (whether the center receives free or subsidized rent, whether the center uses student-teachers, and the adult-child ratio in the observed room). These paths are shown graphically in Figure 13.1. The path analysis strongly suggests, however, a more complex interaction among these and other predictor variables. For example, although the auspice of the center and the parent fees were not found to be significant direct predictors of quality, their *indirect* impact on quality was found to be mediated through the direct predictors (see Figure 13.2). Auspice was a significant predictor of

TABLE 13.4   Summary of Path Analyses of Quality of Child Care Programs

Type of Predictors	Infant-Toddler Rooms	Preschool Rooms
Direct predictors	The observed staff member's wages. The center received subsidized rent and/or utilities. The center was used as a student practicurn placement setting.	The observed staff member's wages. The observed staff member's level of satisfaction with the working climate and his/her colleagues. The center was used as a student practicum placement setting. The center received subsidized rent and/or utilities. The adult-child ratio at the time of the observation.
Direct and indirect	The observed staff member's level of ECE-specific education. The number of adults in the observed room.	The observed staff member's level of ECE-specific education. The number of adults in the observed room.
Indirect predictors	Auspice of the center. Parent fees.	Auspice of the center. Parent fees.

Source: Goelman et al. (2000). Reprinted courtesy of University of Guelph: Centre for Families, Work and Well-Being.

both staff wages and centers that received free or subsidized rent, both of which were found to be significant direct predictors. Parent fees were a significant predictor of wages and staff education levels, both of which, in turn, were direct predictors of quality. Finally, we note that two of the variables (staff education levels and number of staff in the observed room) served as both direct and indirect predictors of quality.

Conclusion

The role of child care in early childhood education continues to grow and evolve both as part of broader social and cultural changes in which the field is embedded and in terms of the practices and policies that determine the shape and content of child care programs. The demand for quality, licensed child care programs will continue to increase with the rising numbers of families with two working parents in the labor force and of single-parent families. We can expect the demand for infant child care to grow as part of this general trend. In addition, we are already witnessing an increasing demand for child care services and professionals who can respond appropriately to children with a wide range of special needs. This demand represents a challenge to create more spaces—and more appropriate spaces—for children with special needs, and a challenge to train more early childhood educators who have the skill set and knowledge base to work with young children who have special needs. At the policy level, schools, school boards, and training institutions will have to recognize that child care is no longer remedial service for poor children or a child-minding service for the children of working parents. Child care represents a major environmental niche for the majority of young children in industrialized societies, and it is in child care settings that children's development can be facilitated and supported given the right combination of predictors of quality.

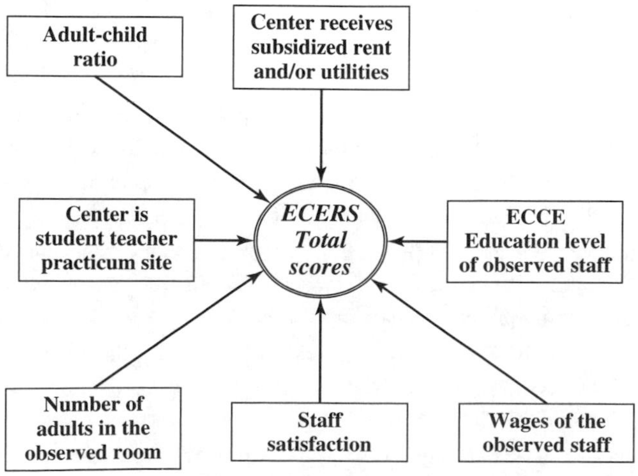

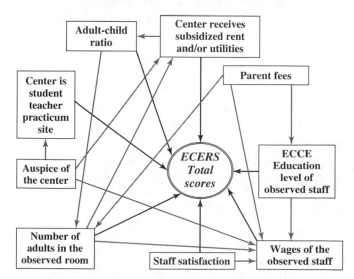

Figure 13.1 Path analyses of direct predictors of child care quality. *Source:* Goelman et al. (2000). Reprinted courtesy of University of Guelph: Centre for Families, Work and Well-Being.

Figure 13.2 Path analyses of direct and indirect predictors of child care quality. *Source:* Goelman et al. (2000). Reprinted courtesy of University of Guelph: Centre for Families, Work and Well-Being.

CLOSING THOUGHTS ON EARLY CHILDHOOD EDUCATION AT THE BEGINNING OF THE TWENTY-FIRST CENTURY

This chapter began with a brief reflection on how early childhood education was seen at the beginning of the twentieth century and then proceeded to discuss recent, current, and emerging areas of research and practice. The field continues both to deepen and to broaden its perspectives on the innate learning and developmental abilities of the young child and the ways in which those abilities are acknowledged and facilitated in the wide range of early childhood settings in which young children participate. The developing child represents his or her world through a variety of media, modalities, and disciplines including art, reading, writing, and music. Whereas the adult world divides the world of early childhood education into content or subject areas, it seems increasingly clear that it is that complex set of behaviors, insights, expectations, and explorations known collectively as *play* that is the major and overarching phenomenon that infuses, guides, and largely determines what and how children learn in their early years.

What currently captures the imagination and what drives the disciplined inquiry of ECE researchers are questions about how adults and learning environments facilitate the development of a more diverse population of children than had been the focus in earlier periods. This diversity includes, but is not limited to, children at both the highest and the lowest ends of the continuum of cognitive development, the social and linguistic needs of an increasingly multicultural and immigrant early childhood population, poor children, and children whose special needs are seen as problematic but more harder to diagnose and harder still to respond to.

Early childhood theorists, researchers, and practitioners have made significant strides by acknowledging the relevance of Bronfenbrenner's ecological systems approach to the field of early childhood. It allows for the consideration of child actions and interactions in the microsystems where the children play, learn, and grow within the broader contexts of the legislative, regulatory, and societal values in which those immediate early childhood programs are embedded. The continuing challenge to the field is to find ways of operationalizing the ecological model in ways that inform and guide emerging areas of interest, research, and practice in early childhood education.

REFERENCES

Adams, M. (1990). *Beginning to read: Thinking and learning about print.* Cambridge, MA: MIT Press.

Adelman, R. D. (1990). What will I become? Play helps with the answer. *Play & Culture, 3,* 193–205.

Andersen, C. J. (1990). *Temperament and the child in family day care.* Unpublished master's thesis. Vancouver, British Columbia, Canada: University of British Columbia.

Andersen, C. J. (1994). Parent support groups. In W. B. Carey & S. C. McDevitt (Eds.), *Prevention and early intervention: Individual differences as risk factors for the mental health of children* (pp. 267–275). New York: Brunner/Mazel.

Andersen, C. J. (1999). *A review of formal educational opportunities in British Columbia for infant development and supported child care consultants.* Victoria, British Columbia, Canada: Ministry of Advanced Education, Training and Technology.

Andersen, C. J., & McDevitt, S. C. (2000). *The temperament guides: Resources for early intervention professionals.* Scottsdale, AZ: Behavioral Developmental Initiatives.

Anderson, J. (1995). Listening to parents' voices: Cross cultural perceptions of learning to read and to write. *Reading Horizons, 35*(5), 394–413.

Anderson, J., & Matthews, R. (1999). Emergent storybook reading revisited. *Journal of Research in Reading, 22,* 293–298.

Anderson-Goetz, D., & Worobey, J. (1984). The young child's temperament: Implications for child care. *Childhood Education, 61*(2), 134–140.

Andress, B. (1986). Toward an integrated developmental theory for early childhood music education. *Bulletin of the Council for Research in Music Education, 86,* 10–17.

Andress, B. (Ed.). (1989). *Promising practices: Prekindergarten music education.* Reston, VA: Music Educators National Conference.

Andress, B. (1998). *Music for young children.* Fort Worth, TX: Harcourt Brace.

Arnberg, L. (1987). *Raising children bilingually: The preschool years.* Clevedon, UK: Multilingual Matters.

Arnett, J. (1989). Caregivers in day care centers: Does training matter? *Journal of Applied Developmental Psychology, 10,* 541–552.

Au, K. H. (1997). A sociocultural model of reading instruction: The Kamehameha Elementary Education Program. In S. A. Stahl & D. A. Hayes (Eds.), *Instructional models in reading* (pp. 181–202). Mahwah, NJ: Erlbaum.

Au, K. H., & Carroll, J. H. (1997). Improving literacy achievement through a constructivist approach: The KEEP demonstration classroom project. *Elementary School Journal, 97*(3), 203–221.

Bailey, D. B. (2000). The federal role in early intervention: Prospects for the future. *Topics in Early Childhood Special Education, 20*(2), 71–78.

Baker, K. A., & deKanter, A. A. (1983). An answer from research on bilingual education. *American Education, 19*(6), 40–48.

Bakhtin, M. (1981). *The dialogic imagination.* Austin: University of Texas.

Bamberger, J. (1982). Growing up prodigies: The midlife crisis. *New Directions for Child Development, 17*, 61–77.

Barron, A., & Earls, F. (1984). The relation of temperament and social factors to behavior problems in three-year-old children. *Journal of Child Psychology and Psychiatry, 25*, 23–33.

Bateson, G. (1955, December). A theory of play and fantasy. *Psychiatric Research Reports, 2*, 39–51.

Bateson, G. (1972). *Steps to an ecology of mind*. New York: Ballantine.

Belsky, J., & Steinberg, L. (1979). What does research tell us about day care? A follow-up report. *Children Today, 8*, 21–26.

Bereiter, C., & Scardamalia, M. (1986). Educational relevance of the study of expertise. *Interchange, 17*(2), 10–19.

Berk, L. (1985). Relationship of educational attainment, child oriented attitude, job satisfaction, and career commitment to caregiver behavior toward children. *Child Care Quarterly, 14*, 103–129.

Bernhard, J. K., Lefebvre, M. L., Chud, G., & Lange, R. (1995). *Paths to equity: Cultural, linguistic and racial diversity in Canadian early childhood education*. Toronto, Ontario, Canada: York Lanes Press.

Bilingual Research Journal. (1992). Washington, DC: National Association for Bilingual Education.

Billman, J., & McDevitt, S. C. (1980). Convergence of parent and observer ratings of temperament with observations of peer interaction in nursery school. *Child Development, 51*, 395–400.

Bissex, G. (1980). *GYNS AT WRK: A child learns to read and write*. Cambridge, MA: Harvard University Press.

Bloch, M. N., & Pellegrini, A. D. (1989). *The ecological context of children's play*. New York: Academic Press.

Bloom, B. S. (1985). *Developing talent in young people*. New York: Ballantine.

Boswell, J. (Ed.). (1986). *The young child and music: Contemporary principles in child development and* music *education*. Reston, VA: Music Educators National Conference.

Bradley, L., & Bryant, P. E. (1983). Categorising sounds and learning to read: A causal connection. *Nature, 301*, 419–521.

Brand, M. (1982). Relationship between musical environment and musical aptitude among sixth-grade children. *(PMEA) Bulletin of Research in Music Education, 13*, 13–19.

Brand, M. (1985). Development and validation of the *Home Musical Environment Scale* for use at the early elementary level. *Psychology of Music, 13*, 40–48.

Brand, M. (1986). Relationship between home music environment and selected musical attributes of second-grade children. *Journal of Research in Music Education, 34*, 111–120.

Bredekamp, S. (1997). NAEYC issues revised position statement on Developmentally Appropriate Practices in early childhood programs. *Young Children, 52*, 34–40.

Bremmer, J., & Moore, S. (1984). Prior visual inspection and object naming: Two factors that enhance hidden feature inclusion in young children's drawings. *British Journal of Developmental Psychology, 2*, 371–376.

Bricker, D. (2000). Inclusion: How the scene has changed. *Topics in Early Childhood Special Education, 20*, 14–19.

Broen, P. A. (1972). The verbal environment of the language learning child. *Monograph of American Speech and Hearing Association, 17*.

Bronfenbrenner, U. (1979). *The ecology of human development: Experiments by nature and design*. Cambridge, MA: Harvard University Press.

Bronfenbrenner, U., & Morris, P. A. (1998). The ecology of developmental processes. In R. M. Lerner (Ed.), *Handbook of child psychology: Vol. 1. Theory* (5th ed., pp. 993–1028). New York: Wiley.

Bruder, M. B. (2000). Family-centered early intervention: Clarifying our values for the new millennium. *Topics in Early Childhood Special Education, 20*(2), 105–116.

Bruner, J. (1983). Play, thought, and language. *Peabody Journal of Education, 60*, 60–69.

Burchinal, M. R., Roberts, J. E., Nabors, L. A., & Bryant, D. M. (1996). Quality of center child care and infant cognitive and language development. *Child Development, 67*, 606–620.

Caillois, R. (1961). *Man, play, and games*. New York: Free Press.

Campos, S. J. (1995). The Carpinteria preschool program: A longterm effects study. In E. Garcia & B. McLaughlin (Eds.), *Meeting the challenge of linguistic and cultural diversity in early childhood education* (pp. 34–48). New York: Teachers College Press.

Carey, W. B. (1998). Let's give temperament its due. *Contemporary Pediatrics*, 91–113.

Carey, W. B. (2000). Estimates of temperament are easy; accurate measurements take a little longer. *Journal of Developmental and Behavioral Pediatrics, 21*, 221–223.

Carey, W. B., & McDevitt, S. C. (1989). *Clinical and educational applications of temperament research*. Amsterdam: Swets & Zweitlinger.

Carey, W. B., & McDevitt, S. C. (1995). *Coping with children's temperament: A guide for professionals*. New York: Basic.

Ceci, S. J. (1996). *On intelligence. A bioecological treatise on intellectual development*. Cambridge, MA: Harvard University Press.

Center, Y., Wheldall, K., Freeman, L., Outhred, L., & McNaught, M. (1995). An evaluation of Reading Recovery. *Reading Research Quarterly, 30*, 240–263.

Chall, J. S. (1967). *Learning to read: The great debate*. New York: McGraw-Hill.

Chapman, J. W., Tunmer, W. E., & Prochnow, J. E. (1998). *Success in reading recovery depends on the development of phonological processing skills: A report prepared for the Ministry of Education*. Auckland, New Zealand: Massey University.

Chapman, M. L. (1995). Designing literacy learning experiences in a multi-age classroom. *Language Arts, 72*(6), 416–428.

Chess, S., & Thomas, A. (1987). *Origins and evolutions of behavior disorders: From infancy to early adult life.* Cambridge, MA: Harvard University Press.

Choi, S. C., Kim, U., & Choi, S. H. (1993). Indigenous analysis of collective representations: A Korean perspective. In U. Kim & J. W. Berry (Eds.), *Indigenous psychology* (pp. 193–210). Newbury Park, CA: Sage.

Chomsky, C. (1977). Approaching reading through invented spelling. In L. Resnick & P. Weaver (Eds.), *Theory and practice of early reading* (pp. 43–65). Hillsdale, NJ: Erlbaum.

Christie, J. F. (1991). Play and early literacy development: Summary and discussion. In J. F. Christie (Ed.), *Play and early literacy development* (pp. 233–246). Albany: State University of New York Press.

Clark, M. (1976). *Young fluent readers: What can they teach us?* London: Heinemann.

Clarke-Stewart, K. A. (1987). Predicting child development from child care forms and features: The Chicago study. In D. Phillips (Ed.), *Quality in child care: What does research tell us* (pp. 21–42). Washington, DC: National Association for the Education of Young Children.

Clarke-Stewart, K. A., Fitzpatrick, M. J., Allhusen, V. D., & Goldberg, W. A. (2000). Measuring difficult temperament the easy way. *Journal of Developmental and Behavioral Pediatrics, 21,* 207–220.

Clay, M. (1966). *Emergent reading behavior.* Unpublished doctoral dissertation, University of Auckland, New Zealand.

Clay, M. (1979). *Reading: The patterning of complex behavior* (2nd ed.). Auckland, New Zealand: Heinemann Educational.

Collins, J. (1988). Language and class in minority education. *Anthropology and Education Quarterly, 19,* 299–326.

Cross, T. G. (1977). Mothers' speech adjustments: The contribution of selected listener variables. In C. E. Snow & C. A. Ferguson (Eds.), *Talking to children: Language input and acquisition.* New York: Cambridge University Press.

Cummins, J. (1979). Linguistic interdependence and the educational development of bilingual children. *Review of Educational Research, 49*(2), 222–251.

Cummins, J. (1984). *Bilingualism and special education: Issues in assessment and pedagogy.* Austin, TX: PRO-ED.

Cummins, J. (1986). Empowering minority students: A framework for intervention. *Harvard Education Review, 56*(1), 18–36.

Cummins, J. (1991). The development of bilingual proficiency from home to school: A longitudinal study of Portuguese-speaking children. *Journal of Education, 173*(2), 85–98.

Cummins, J. (1992). Heritage language teaching in Canadian schools. *Journal of Curriculum Studies, 24*(3), 281–286.

Dale, P. S., Robinson, N. M., & Crain-Thoreson, C. (1995). Linguistic precocity and the development of reading: The role of extralinguistic factors. *Applied Psycholinguistics, 16,* 173–187.

Darras, B., & Kindler, A. M. (1996). Morphogenese et teleology des images et de l'imagerie initiale. In B. Darras, *Au commencement etait l'image: Du dessin de l'enfant a la communication de l'adulte* (pp. 73–94). Paris: ESF.

Davis, J. H. (1991). *Artistry lost: U-shaped development in graphic symbolization.* Unpublished doctoral dissertation. Harvard Graduate School of Education, Cambridge, MA.

Davis, J. H. (1997a). Drawing's demise: U-shaped development in graphic symbolization. *Studies in Art Education, 38*(3), 132–157.

Davis, J. H. (1997b). The "U" and the wheel of "C": Development and devaluation of graphic symbolization and the cognitive approach at the Harvard Project Zero. In A. M. Kindler (Ed.), *Child development in art* (pp. 45–58). Reston, VA: NAEA.

Delgado-Gaitan, C., & Trueba, H. (1991). *Crossing cultural borders: Education for immigrant families in America.* London: Falmer Press.

Denzin, N. K. (1980a). Play, games, and interaction: The contexts of childhood socialization. *The Sociological Quarterly, 16,* 458–478.

Denzin, N. K. (1980b). The paradoxes of play. In J. W. Joy (Ed.), *The paradoxes of play* (pp. 13–24). West Point, NY: Leisure Press.

Dewey, J. (1916). *Democracy and education.* New York: Macmillan.

Donaldson, M. (1978). *Children's minds.* New York: Norton Press.

Doxey, C., & Wright, C. (1990). An exploratory study of children's music ability. *Early Childhood Research Quarterly, 5*(3), 425–440.

Dudley-Marling, C., & Murphy, S. (1997). A political critique of remedial reading programs: The example of Reading Recovery. *The Reading Teacher, 50,* 460–468.

Duncum, P. (1986). Breaking down the U-curve of artistic development. *Visual Arts Research, 12*(1), 43–54.

Dunst, C. J. (2000). Revisiting "Rethinking Early Intervention." *Topics in Early Childhood Special Education, 20*(2), 95–104.

Durkin, D. (1966). *Children who read early.* New York: Teachers College Press.

Dyson, A. H. (1997). *Writing superheroes: Contemporary childhood, popular culture, and classroom literacy.* New York: Teachers College Press.

Earls, F., & Jung, K. G. (1987). Temperament and home environment as causal factors in the development of childhood psychopathology. *Journal of the American Academy of Child and Adolescent Psychiatry, 26,* 491–498.

Edwards, L. C. (1990). *Affective development and creative arts.* Toronto, Ontario, Canada: Merrill.

Elster, C. (1994). Patterns within preschoolers emergent reading. *Reading Research Quarterly, 29,* 409–425.

Erhmann, J. (Ed.). (1968). *Game, play, literature.* Boston: Beacon Press.

Faulstich Orellana, M. (1994). Appropriating the voice of the super-heroes: Three preschoolers' bilingual language uses in play. *Early Childhood Research Quarterly, 9,* 171–193.

Feldman, D. H. (1986). *Nature's gambit: Child prodigies and the development of human potential.* New York: Basic Books.

Ferreiro, E., & Teberosky, A. (1982). *Literacy before schooling.* Exeter, NH: Heinemann.

Field, T., & Greenberg, R. (1982). Temperament ratings by parents and teachers of infants, toddlers, and preschool children. *Child Development, 53,* 160–163.

Fineberg, J. (1997). *The innocent eye: Children's art and the modern artist.* Princeton, NJ: Princeton University Press.

Fischer, K. W., & Canfield, R. L. (1986). The ambiguity of stage and structure of behavior: Person and environment in the development of psychological structure. In I. Levin (Ed.), *Stage and structure: Reopening the debate* (pp. 246–367). Norwood, NJ: Ablex.

Fischer, K. W., Knight, C. C., & Van Parys, M. (1993). Analyzing diversity in developmental pathways: Methods and concepts. In R. Case & W. Edelstein (Eds.), *The new structuralism in cognitive development: Theory and research on individual pathways* (pp. 33–56). Basel, Switzerland: Karger.

Flohr, J. W. (1981). Short-term music instruction and young children's developmental music aptitude. *Journal of Research in Music Education, 29,* 219–223.

Franciscono, M. (1998). Paul Klee and children's art. In J. Fineberg (Ed.), *Discovering child art* (pp. 95–121). Princeton, NJ: Princeton University Press.

Franyo, G., & Hyson, M. (1999). Temperament training for early childhood caregivers: A study of the effectiveness of training. *Child and Youth Care Forum, 28,* 329–349.

Freeman, J. (2000). Teaching for talent: Lessons from the research. In C. F. M. van Lieshout & P. G. Heymans (Eds.), *Developing talent across the life span* (pp. 231–248). Hove, UK: Psychology Press.

Freud, S. (1909). *The complete psychological works of Sigmund Freud: Vol. 10. Analysis of a phobia in a five-year-old boy.* London: Hogarth Press.

Froebel, F. (1885). *The education of man* (J. Jarvis, Trans.). New York: Lovell.

Gaitskell, C. D., Hurwitz, A., & Day, M. (1982). *Children and their art* (4th ed.). New York: Harcourt, Brace, Jovanovich.

Galda, L., & Pellegrini, A. D. (1985). *Play, language, and stories.* Norwood, NJ: Ablex.

Garcia, E. E. (1988). *Effective schooling for language minority students.* Arlington, VA: National Clearing House for Bilingual Education.

Garcia, E. E. (1993). The education of linguistically and culturally diverse children. In B. Spodek (Ed.), *Handbook of research on the education of young children* (pp. 372–384). New York: Macmillan.

Gardner, H. (1980). *Artful scribbles: The significance of children's drawings.* New York: Basic Books.

Gardner, H. (1983). *Frames of mind. The theory of multiple intelligences.* New York: Basic Books.

Gardner, H., & Winner, E. (1982). First intimations of artistry. In S. Strauss (Ed.), *U-shaped behavioral growth.* New York: Academic Press.

Garvey, C. (1977). *Play.* Cambridge, MA: Harvard University Press.

Geertz. C. (1972). *The interpretation of cultures.* New York: Basic Books.

Goelman, H., Doherty, G., Lero, D., LaGrange, & Tougas, J. (2000). *Caring and learning in child care centres across Canada.* Guelph, Ontario, Canada: University of Guelph Centre for Families, Work and Well-Being.

Goelman, H., & Jacobs, E. V. (1994). *Children's play in childcare settings.* Albany: State University of New York Press.

Goelman, H., & Pence, A. R. (1987). Effects of child care, family and individual characteristics on children's language development: The Victoria Day Care Research Project. In D. A. Phillips (Ed.), *What does research tell us?* (pp. 89–104). Washington, DC: National Association of the Education of Young Children.

Goelman, H., Shapiro, E. & Pence, A. R. (1992). Family environment and family day care. *Family Relations, 4*(19), 251–270.

Goetze, M., Cooper, N., & Brown, C. J. (1990). Recent research on singing in the general music classroom. *Bulletin of the Council for Research in Music Education, 104,* 16–37.

Goldenberg, C., Reese, L., & Gallimore, R. (1992). Effects of school literacy materials on Latino children's home experiences and early reading achievement. *American Journal of Education, 100*(4), 497–536.

Golomb, C. (1992). *The child's creation of a pictorial world.* Berkeley: University of California Press.

Golomb, C. (1994). Drawing as representation: The child's acquisition of a meaningful graphic language. *Visual Arts Research, 20*(2), 14–28.

Goodnow, J. J. (1988). Parents' ideas, actions, and feelings: Models and methods from developmental and social psychology. *Child Development, 59,* 286–320.

Gordon, E. E. (1978). *Primary measures of music audiation.* Chicago: G.I.A.

Gordon, E. E. (1979). Developmental aptitude as measured by the Primary Measures of Music Audiation. *Psychology of Music, 7,* 42–49.

Gordon, E. E. (1986a). *Intermediate measures of music audiation.* Chicago: G.I.A.

Gordon, E. E. (1986b). *The nature, description, measurement, and evaluation of music aptitudes.* Chicago: G.I.A.

Gordon, E. E. (1989). *Advanced measures of music audiation.* Chicago: G.I.A.

Gordon, E. E. (1990). *A music learning theory for newborn and young children.* Chicago: G.I.A.

Gordon, E. E. (1993). *Learning sequences in music: Skill, content, and patterns.* Chicago: G.I.A.

Gottfried, A. W., Gottfried, A. E., Bathurst, K., & Guerin, D. W. (1994). *Gifted IQ: Early developmental aspects. The Fullerton longitudinal study.* New York: Plenum Press.

Gouzouasis, P. J. (1987). *The comparative effects of three types of accompaniment on the singing achievement and developmental tonal aptitude of young children.* Unpublished master's thesis, Temple University, Philadelphia.

Gouzouasis, P. J. (1991). A progressive developmental approach to the music education of preschool children. *Canadian Music Educator, 32*(3), 45–53.

Gouzouasis, P. J. (1992). An organismic model of music learning for young children. *Update: Applications of Research in Music Education, 11*(1), 13–18.

Gouzouasis, P. J. (1993). Music aptitude: A comparison of the music abilities of kindergarten children of various ethnic backgrounds. *The Quarterly Journal of Music Teaching and Learning, 4*(2), 70–76.

Gouzouasis, P. J. (1994). A developmental model of music literacy. *Research Forum, 12*(spring), 21–24.

Gouzouasis, P. J. (2000). Understanding music media: Digital (re)genesis or cultural meltdown in the 21st century. In B. Hanley & B. A. Roberts (Eds.), *Looking forward: Challenges to Canadian music education.* Toronto, Ontario, Canada: Hushin House.

Gouzouasis, P. J., & Taggart, C. (1995). The music learning and language learning metaphor: An organismic perspective. *Update: Applications of Research in Music Education, 13*(2), 9–13.

Graham, P., Rutter, M., & George, S. (1973). Temperamental characteristics as predictors of behavior disorders in children. *American Journal of Orthopsychiatry, 43*, 328–339.

Grant, R. (1995). Meeting the needs of young second language learners. In E. Garcia & B. McLaughlin (Eds.), *Meeting the challenge of linguistic and cultural diversity in early childhood education* (pp. 1–17). New York: Teachers College Press.

Graves, D. (1983). *Writing: Teachers and children at work.* Exeter, NH: Heinemann.

Greenspan, S. (1997). *Growth of the mind.* New York: Addison Wesley.

Guilmartin, K., & Levinowitz, L. M. (1989–2000). *Music Together Curriculum.* Princeton, NJ: Birch Tree Group.

Hakuta, K. (1986). *Mirror of language: The debate of bilingualism.* New York: Basic Books.

Harden, B., Winslow, M., Kendziora, K., Shahinfar, A., Rubin, K., Fox, N., Crowley, M., and Zahn-Waxler, C. (2000). Externalizing problems in Head Start children: An ecological exploration. *Early Education and Development, 11*, 357–385.

Hart, B. (2000). A natural history of early language experience. *Topics in Early Childhood Special Education, 20*(1), 28–35.

Hartley, R. E., & Goldenson, R. M. (1963). *The complete book of children's play* (Rev. ed.). New York: Crowell.

Heath, S. B. (1983). *Ways with words: Language, life, and work in communities and classroom.* Cambridge, UK: Cambridge University Press.

Heath, S. B., & Thomas, C. (1984). The achievement of preschool literacy for mother and child. In H. Goelman, A. Oberg, & F. Smith (Eds.), *Awakening to literacy* (pp. 51–72). Portsmouth, NH: Heinman.

Helburn, S. W. (Ed). (1995). *Cost, quality and child outcomes in child care centers.* Denver: University of Colorado at Denver, Department of Economics, Center for Research and Social Policy.

Hofmann, W. (1998). The art of unlearning. In J. Fineberg (Ed.), *Discovering child art* (pp. 3–14). Princeton, NJ: Princeton University Press.

Holdaway, D. (1979). *The foundations of literacy.* Sydney, Australia: Ashton Scholastic.

Hollingworth, L. S. (1942). *Children above 180 IQ.* Yonkers, NY: World Book.

Holloway, S. D., & Reichhart-Erickson, M. (1988). The relationship of day care quality to children's free play behavior and social problem-solving skills. *Early Childhood Research Quarterly, 3*, 39–53.

Holohan, J. M. (1984, June). *The development of music syntax: Some observations of music babble of young children.* Paper delivered at the Music in Early Childhood Conference, Brigham Young University, Provo, UT.

Howes, C. (1983). Caregiver behavior in center and family day care. *Journal of Applied Developmental Psychology, 4*, 99–107.

Howes, C. (1987) Quality indicators in infant and toddler child care: The Los Angeles Study. In D. A. Phillips (Ed.), *Quality in child care: What does research tell us?* (pp. 81–88). Washington, DC: National Association for the Education of Young Children.

Howes, C. (1997). Children's experiences in center-based child care as a function of teacher background and adult:child ratio. *Merrill-Palmer Quarterly, 43*, 404–425.

Howes, C., Phillips, D. A., & Whitebook, M. (1992). Thresholds of quality: Implications for the social development of children in center-based child care. *Child Development, 63*, 449–460.

Howes, C., & Smith, E. W. (1995). Relations among child care quality, teacher behavior, children's play activities, emotional security, and cognitive activity in child care. *Early Childhood Research Quarterly, 10*, 381–404.

Hunt, J. M. (1961). *Intelligence and experience.* New York: Ronald Press.

Jacob, E. J. (1984). Learning literacy through play: Puerto Rican kindergarten children. In H. Goelman, A. Oberg, & F. Smith (Eds.), *Awakening to literacy.* Exeter, NH: Heinemann.

Jakobson, R. (1968). *Child language, aphasia, and phonological universals* (A. R. Keiler, Trans.). The Hague, The Netherlands: Mouton.

Jersild, A. T., & Bienstock, S. F. (1931). The influence of training on the vocal ability of three-year-old children. *Child Development, 2*, 272–291.

Jersild, A. T., & Bienstock, S. F. (1934). A study of the development of children's ability to sing. *Journal of Educational Psychology, 25,* 481–503.

Jessup, L. L. (1984). The comparative effects of indirect and direct music teaching upon the developmental music aptitude and music achievement of early primary children (Doctoral dissertation, Temple University, 1984). *Dissertation Abstracts International, 45,* 1678A.

Kagan, S. L., & Garcia, E. E. (1991). Educating culturally and linguistically diverse preschoolers: Moving the agenda. *Early Childhood Research Quarterly, 6,* 427–443.

Kandinsky, V. (1912). Über die Formfrage. *Der Blaue Reiter, 168,* 10.

Keating, D. P. (1991). Curriculum options for the developmentally advanced: A developmental alternative to gifted education. *Exceptionality Education Canada, 1,* 53–84.

Kelly-Byrne, K. (1989). *A child's play life: An ethnographic study.* New York: Teachers College Press.

Keogh, B. K., & Burstein, N. D. (1988). Relationship of temperament to preschoolers' interactions with peers and teachers. *Exceptional Children 54*(5), 456–461.

Kim, U., & Choi, S. H. (1994). Individualism, collectivism, and child development: A Korean perspective. In P. M. Greenfield & R. R. Cocking (Eds.), *Cross-cultural roots of minority child development* (pp. 227–257). Hillsdale, NJ: Erlbaum.

Kindler, A. M. (1996). Myths, habits, research and policy: The four pillars of early childhood art education. *Arts Education Policy Review, 97*(4), 24–30.

Kindler, A. M. (1997). Directions in primary and intermediate art education. *BCATA Journal for Art Teacher, 37*(1), 30–37.

Kindler, A. M. (1998). Artistic development and art education. *Translations, 7*(2), 1–6.

Kindler, A. M. (1999). "From endpoints to repertoires": A challenge to art education. *Studies in Art Education, 40*(4), 330–349.

Kindler, A. M. (2001). From the u-curve to dragons: Culture and understanding of artistic development. *Visual Arts Research, 26*(2), 15–29.

Kindler, A. M., & Darras, B. (1997a). Development of pictorial representation: A teleology-based model. *Journal of Art and Design Education, 16*(3), 217–222.

Kindler A. M., & Darras, B. (1997b). Map of artistic development. In A. M. Kindler (Ed.), *Child development in art* (pp. 17–24). Reston, VA: NAEA.

Kindler, A. M., & Darras, B. (1998). Culture and development of pictorial repertoires. *Studies in Art Education, 39*(2), 147–166.

Klee, P. (1957). *Tagebucher von Paul Klee 1898–1918.* Cologne: Verlag M. DuMont Schauberg.

Koh, J. (2000). *Korean immigrant parents' attitudes and practices regarding Korean and English development in preschool-aged children: A comparison of bilingual and English-speaking programs.* Unpublished master's thesis, University of British Columbia, Vancouver, British Columbia, Canada.

Kontos, S., Howes, C., & Galinsky, E. (1996). Does training make a difference to quality in family child care? *Early Childhood Research Quarterly, 11,* 427–445.

Korzenik, D. (1995). The changing concept of artistic giftedness. In C. Golomb (Ed.), *The development of artistically gifted children* (pp. 1–30). Hillsdale, NJ: Erlbaum.

LaGrange, A., Clark, D., & Munroe, E. (1995). *Culturally sensitive child care: The Alberta study.* Edmonton, Alberta, Canada: Alberta Association for Young Children.

Lamb, M. E. (2001, March 5). *Developmental theory and public policy: A cross-national perspective.* Lecture given as part of the Green College Distinguished Lecture Series on, "Multiple lenses, multiple images: Perspectives on the child across time, space and disciplines." Vancouver, British Columbia, Canada.

Lamb, M. E. (1998). Nonparental child care: Context, quality, correlates, and consequences. In W. Damon, I. E. Sigel, & K. A. Renninger (Eds.), *Handbook of child psychology: Vol. 4. Child psychology in practice* (pp. 73–133). New York: Wiley.

Lambert, W. E., & Taylor, D. M. (1983). Language in the education of ethnic minority immigrants. In R. J. Samuda & S. L. Woods (Eds.), *Perspectives in immigrant and minority education* (pp. 267–280). Washington, DC: University Press of America.

Lee, R., & Lehmann, F. (1986). Korean immigrants in British Columbia. In K. V. Ujimoto & J. Naidoo (Eds.), *Asian Canadian Symposium: Vol. 7. Asian Canadian: Contemporary issues* (pp. 49–68). Winnipeg, Manitoba, Canada: University of Manitoba Press.

Levinowitz, L. M. (1985). *The comparative effects of two types of song instruction on the development of a sense of tonality in four-year-old children.* Unpublished master's thesis, Temple University, Philadelphia.

Levinowitz, L. M. (1987). An experimental study of the comparative effects of singing songs with words and without words on children in kindergarten and first grade (Doctoral dissertation, Temple University, 1987). *Dissertation Abstracts International, 48,* 863A.

Littleton, D. (1998). Music learning and child's play. *General Music Today, 12*(1), 8–15.

Louis, B., & Lewis, M. (1992). Parental beliefs about giftedness in young children and their relation to actual ability level. *Gifted Child Quarterly, 36,* 27–31.

Lowenfeld, V., & Brittain, W. L. (1964). *Creative and mental growth* (4th ed.). New York: Macmillan.

Luke, A., Baty, A., & Stehbens, C. (1989). Natural conditions for language learning: A critique. *English in Australia, 89,* 36–49.

Luke, A., & Luke, C. (2001). Adolescence lost/childhood regained: On early intervention and the emergence of the techno-subject. *Journal of Early Childhood Literacy, 1,* 91–120.

Luquet, G. H. (1977). *Le dessin enfantin.* Paris: Delachaux et Niestle.

Lyon, J. (1996). *Becoming bilingual: Language acquisition in a bilingual community.* Clevedon, UK: Multilingual Matters.

Lyon, M., & Canning, P. (1995). *The Atlantic Day Care Study.* St John's, Newfoundland: Memorial University of Newfoundland.

Mace, J. (1998). *Playing with time: Mothers and the meaning of literacy.* London: UCL Press.

Malicky, G. V., & Norman, C. A. (1999). Phonological awareness and reading: An alternative interpretation of the literature from a clinical perspective. *Alberta Journal of Educational Research, 45*(1), 18–34.

Mason, J. (1992). Reading stories to preliterate children: A proposed connection to reading. In P. Gough, L. Ehri, & R. Truman (Eds.), *Reading Acquisition* (pp. 215–239). Hillsdale, NJ: Erlbaum.

Mason, J., & Kerr, B. (1992). Literacy transfer from parents to children in the preschool years. In T. Sticht, M. Beeler, & B. McDonald (Eds.), *The intergenerational transfer of cognitive skills: Vol. 2. Theory and research in cognitive science.* Norwood, NJ: ABLEX.

Maziade, M., Caron, C., Cote, R., Boutin, P., & Thivierge, J. (1990). Extreme temperament and diagnosis: A study in a psychiatric sample of consecutive children. *Archives of General Psychiatry, 47,* 477–484.

Maziade, M., Cote, R., Bernier, H., Boutin, P., & Thivierge, J. (1989). Significance of extreme temperament in infancy for clinical status in pre-school years. *British Journal of Psychiatry, 154,* 544–551.

McCollum, J. A. (2000). Taking the past along: Reflecting on our identity as a discipline. *Topics in Early Childhood Special Education, 20*(2), 79–86.

McKim, M. K., Cramer, K. M., Stuart, B., & O'Connor, D. L. (1999). Infant care decisions and attachment security: The Canadian "Transition to Child Care" Study. *Canadian Journal of Behavioural Science, 31*(2), 92–106.

Meichenbaum, D., & Biemiller, A. (1998). *Nurturing independent learners. Helping students take charge of their learning.* Cambridge, MA: Brookline Books.

Michaels, S. (1981). "Sharing time": Children's narrative styles and differential access to literacy. *Language in Society, 10,* 423–442.

Michelet, A. (1986). Teachers and play. *Prospects, 16,* 113–122.

Miller, S. M., Fernie, D., & Kantor, K. (1992). Distinctive literacies in different preschool play contexts. *Play and Culture, 5,* 107–119.

Montessori, M. (1965). *Dr. Montessori's own handbook.* New York: Schoken. (Original work published 1914)

Moorhead, G., & Pond, D. (1978). *Music of young children.* Santa Barbara, CA: Pillsbury Foundation for the Advancement of Music Education.

Morelock, M. J. (1996). On the nature of giftedness and talent: Imposing order on chaos. *Roeper Review, 19,* 4–12.

Morgan, M. (1988). *Art 4-11: Art in early years of schooling.* Oxford, UK: Basil Blackwell.

Music Educators National Conference. (1986). *The school music program. Descriptions and standards.* Reston, VA: Author.

Music Educators National Conference. (1991). *Issues in music education: An advisory from the Music Educators National Conference.* Reston, VA. Author.

Mustafa, M. (1997). *Beyond traditional phonics.* Portsmouth, NH: Heinemann.

National Institute of Child Health and Development, Early Child Care Network. (1994). Child care and child development: The NICHD study of early child care. In S. L. Friedman & H. C. Haywood (Eds.), *Developmental follow-up: Concepts, domains, and methods* (pp. 378–396). New York: Academic Press.

National Institute of Child Health and Development, Early Child Care Research Network. (1996). Characteristics of infant child care: Factors contributing to positive caregiving. *Early Childhood Research Quarterly, 11,* 269–306.

National Institute of Child Health and Development, Early Child Care Research Network. (1998). Early child care and self-control, compliance, and problem behaviors at twenty-four and thirty-six months. *Child Development, 69*(4), 1145–1170.

National Society for the Study of Education. (1929). *Preschool and parental education.* Bloomington, IL: Public School.

National Society for the Study of Education. (1939). *Intelligence: Its nature and nurture.* Bloomington, IL.: Public School Company.

Neuman, S. B., & Roskos, K. (1992). Literacy objects as cultural tools: Effects on children's literacy behaviours in play. *Reading Research Quarterly, 27,* 202–225.

Neuman, S. B., & Roskos, K. (1993). Access to print for children of poverty: Differential effects of adult mediation and literacy-enriched play settings on environmental and functional print tasks. *American Educational Research Journal, 30,* 95–122.

Newport, E. L., Gleitman, H., & Gleitman, L. R. (1977). Mother, I'd rather do it myself: Some effects and noneffects of maternal speech style. In C. E. Snow & C. A. Ferguson (Eds.), *Talking to children: Language input and acquisition* (pp. 109–150). New York: Cambridge University Press.

Odom, S. (2000). Preschool inclusion: What we know and where we go from here. *Topics in Early Childhood Special Education, 20*(1), 20–29.

Palison, H. (1986). Preschool temperament and performance on achievement tests. *Developmental Psychology, 22,* 766–770.

Pariser, D., & van den Berg, A. (1997). The mind of the beholder: Some provisional doubts about the u-curve aesthetic development thesis. *Studies in Art Education, 38*(3), 158–178.

Parsons, M. J. (1998). Intergrated curriculum and our paradigm of cognition in the arts. *Studies in Art Education, 39*(2), 103–116.

Paul, B., & Jarvis, C. (1992). *The effects of native language use in New York city pre-kindergarten classes.* Paper presented at the 1992 Annual meeting of the American Educational Research Association, San Francisco.

Pellegrini, A. D. (1991). A critique of the concept of at risk as applied to emergent literacy. *Language Arts, 68,* 380–385.

Pellegrini, A. D. (1984). The effect of dramatic play on children's generation of cohesive text. *Discourse Processes, 7,* 57–67.

Pellegrini, A. D., & Galda, L. (1998). *The development of school-based literacies: A social ecological perspective.* New York: Routledge.

Pellegrini, A. D., Galda, L., Dresden, J., & Cox, S. (1991). A longitudinal study of the predictive relations among symbolic play, linguistic verbs, and early literacy. *Research in the Teaching of English, 25,* 219–235.

Peller, L. E. (1952). Models of children's play. *Mental Hygiene, 36,* 66–83.

Pestalozzi, H. (1827). *Letters on early education.* London: Charles Gilpin.

Pettengill, S. M., & Rohner, R. P. (1985). Korean-American adolescents' perceptions of parental control, parental acceptance-rejection and parent-adolescent conflict. In I. R. Lanunes & Y. H. Poortinga (Eds.), *From different perspectives: Studies of behavior across cultures* (pp. 241–249). Lisse, The Netherlands: Swets & Zeitlinger.

Phillips, D. A., & Howes, C. (1987). Indicators of quality child care: Review of research. In D. A. Phillips (Ed.), *Quality in child care: What does research tell us?* Washington, DC: National Association of the Education of Young Children.

Phillips, D. A., McCartney, K., & Scarr, S. (1987). Child-care quality and children's social development. *Developmental Psychology, 23,* 537–544.

Phillips, J. R. (1970). Formal characteristics of speech which mothers address to their young children. (Doctoral dissertation, Johns Hopkins University, 1970). *Dissertation Abstracts International, 31,* 4369B.

Piaget, J. (1962). *Play, dreams, and imitation in childhood.* New York: Norton.

Pond, D. (1981). A composer's study of young children's innate musicality. *Bulletin of the Council for Research in Music Education, 68,* 1–12.

Porath, M. (1986). Gifted children's responses to research participation. Unpublished raw data.

Porath, M. (1992). Stage and structure in the development of children with various types of "giftedness." In R. Case (Ed.), *The mind's staircase: Exploring the conceptual underpinnings of children's thought and knowledge* (pp. 303–317). Hillsdale, NJ: Lawrence Erlbaum.

Porath, M. (1993). Gifted young artists: Developmental and individual differences. *Roeper Review, 16,* 29–33.

Porath, M. (1996). Affective and motivational consideration in the assessment of gifted learners. *Roeper Review, 19,* 13–17.

Porath, M. (1996). Narrative performance in verbally gifted children. *Journal for the Education of the Gifted, 19,* 276–292.

Porath, M. (1997). A developmental model of artistic giftedness in middle childhood. *Journal for the Education of the Gifted, 20,* 201–223.

Porath, M. (2000). Social giftedness in childhood: A developmental perspective. In R. C. Friedman & B. M. Shore (Eds.), *Talents unfolding: Cognitive and developmental frameworks* (pp. 195–215). Washington, DC: American Psychological Association.

Porath, M. (2001). Young girls' social understanding: Emergent interpersonal expertise. *High Ability Studies, 12,* 113–126.

Porter, R. P. (1991). Language choice for Latino students. *The Public Interest, 105,* 48–60.

Pressley, M., El-Dinary, P. B., Marks, M. B., Brown, R., & Stein, S. (1992). Good strategy instruction is motivating and interesting. In K. A. Renninger, S. Hidi, & A. Krapp (Eds.), *The role of interest in learning and development* (pp. 333–358). Hillsdale, NJ: Erlbaum.

Pressley, M., Wharton-McDonald, R., Allington, R., Block, C. C., Morrow, L., Tracy, D., Baker, K., Brooks, G., Cronin, J., Nelson, E., & Woo, D. (1998). *The nature of effective first-grade literacy instruction.* (Research Rep. No. 11007). Albany, NY: University of New York at Albany, National Research Center on English Learning & Achievement.

Pressley, M., & Woloshyn, V. (1995). *Cognitive strategy instruction that really improves children's academic performance* (2nd ed.). Cambridge, MA: Brookline Books.

Prince, C., & Lawrence, L. (1994). *School readiness and language minority students: Implications of the first national education goal.* Washington, DC: NCBE.

Purcell-Gates, V. (1996). Stories, coupons, and the "TV Guide": Relationships between home literacy experiences and emergent literacy knowledge. *Reading Research Quarterly, 31*(4), 406–428.

Rauscher, F. H., Shaw, G. L., Levine, L. J., Wright, E. L., Dennis, W. R., & Newcomb, R. (1997). Music training causes long-term enhancement of preschool children's spatial-temporal reasoning abilities. *Neurological Research, 19,* 1–8.

Read, C. (1975). *Children's categorization of speech sounds in English.* Urbana, IL: National Council of Teachers of English.

Reyes, M. de la Luz. (1992). Challenging venerable assumptions: Literacy instruction for linguistically different students. *Harvard Educational Review, 62,* 427–445.

Robinson, N. M. (1987). The early development of precocity. *Gifted Child Quarterly, 31,* 161–164.

Robinson, N. M. (1993). Identifying and nurturing gifted, very young children. In K. A. Heller, F. J. Monks, & A. H. Passow (Eds.), *Research and development of giftedness and talent* (pp. 507–524). Tarrytown, NY: Pergamon.

Robinson, N. M. (2000). Giftedness in very young children: How seriously should it be taken? In R. C. Friedman & B. M. Shore (Eds.), *Talents unfolding: Cognition and development* (pp. 7–26). Washington, DC: American Psychological Association.

Robinson, N. M., Abbott, R. D., Berninger, V. W., & Busse, J. (1996). The structure of abilities in math-precocious young children: Gender similarities and differences. *Journal of Educational Psychology, 88,* 341–352.

Robinson, N. M., Abbott, R. D., Berninger, V. W., Busse, J., & Mukhopadhyay, S. (1997). Developmental changes in mathematically precocious young children: Longitudinal and gender effects. *Gifted Child Quarterly, 41,* 145–158.

Robinson, N. M., & Noble, K. D. (1991). Social-emotional development and adjustment of gifted children. In M. G. Wang, M. C. Reynolds, & H. J. Walberg (Eds.), *Handbook of special education: Vol. 4. Research and practice* (pp. 23–36). New York: Pergamon.

Robinson, N. M., & Robinson, H. B. (1982). The optimal match: Devising the best compromise for the highly gifted student. In D. Feldman (Ed.), *New directions for child development: Vol. 17. Developmental approaches to giftedness and creativity* (pp. 79–94). San Francisco: Jossey-Bass.

Rodriguez, J., Diaz, R., Duran, D., & Espinosa, L. (1995). The impact of bilingual preschool education on the language development of Spanish-speaking children. *Early Childhood Research Quarterly, 10,* 475–490.

Roskos, K. (1988). Literacy at work in play. *The Reading Teacher, 41,* 562–566.

Roskos, K., & Neuman, S. B. (1993). A typology of young children's literacy activity in play. *Journal of Play Theory and Research, 1*(1), 17–25.

Rutter, M. (1982). Temperament: Concepts, issues and problems. In R. Porter & G. M. Collins (Eds.), *Temperamental differences in infants and young children, Ciba Foundation Symposium 89* (pp. 1–16). London: Pitman.

Rutter, M. (1994). Temperament: Changing concepts and implications. In W. B. Carey & S. C. McDevitt (Eds.), *Prevention and early intervention: Individual differences as risk factors for the mental health of children* (pp. 23–34). New York: Brunner/Mazel.

Santa, C., & Hoien, T. (1999). An assessment of early steps: A program for early intervention of reading problems. *Reading Research Quarterly, 34,* 54–79.

Saracho, O. N., & Spodek, B. (1995). Children's play and early childhood education: Insights from history and theory. *Journal of Education, 177*(3), 129–49.

Scarborough, H. S., & Dobrich, W. (1994). On the efficacy of reading to preschoolers. *Developmental Review, 14,* 245–302.

Scarr, S., Eisenberg, M., & Deater-Deckard, K. (1994). Measurement of quality in child care centers. *Early Childhood Research Quarterly, 9,* 131–151.

Schiff-Myers, N. B. (1992). Considering arrested language development and language loss in the assessment of second language learners. *Language, Speech, and Hearing Services in Schools, 23,* 28–33.

Schmidt, P. R. (1998). *Cultural conflict and struggle: Literacy learning in a kindergarten program.* New York: P. Lang.

Schrader, C. T. (1991). Symbolic play: A source of meaningful engagements with writing and reading. In J. F. Christie (Ed.), *Play and early literacy development* (pp. 189–213). Albany: State University of New York Press.

Schwartzman, H. B. (1978). *Transformations: The anthropology of children's play.* New York: Plenum.

Schwartzman, H. B. (1991). Imagining play. *Play and Culture, 4*(3), 214–222.

Shaw, G. L. (1999). *Keeping Mozart in mind.* New York: Academic Press.

Shore, R. (1997). *Rethinking the brain: New insights into early development.* New York: Families and Work Institute.

Simons, G. (1986). Early childhood music development: A survey of selected research. *Bulletin of the Council for Research in Music Education, 86,* 36–52.

Siren, U. (1991). *Minority language transmission in early childhood: Parental intention and language use.* Stockholm, Sweden: Stockholm University Press.

Skutnabb-Kangas, T. (1981). *Bilingualism or not: The education of minorities.* Clevedon, UK: Multilingual Matters.

Smith, B. J. (2000). The federal role in early childhood special education policy in the next century: The responsibility of the individual. *Topics in Early Childhood Special Education, 20*(1), 7–11.

Smitsman, A. W. (2000). Slumbering talents: Where do they reside? In C. F. M. van Lieshout & P. G. Heymans (Eds.), *Developing talent across the life span* (pp. 17–40). Hove, UK: Psychology Press.

Snow, C. E. (1977). Mothers' speech research: From input to interaction. In C. E. Snow & C. A. Ferguson (Eds.), *Talking to children: Language input and acquisition.* New York: Cambridge University Press.

Snow, C. E., Burns, M. S., & Griffin, P. (Eds.). (1998). *Preventing reading difficulties in young children.* Washington, DC: National Academy Press.

Soderman, A. K. (1985, July). Dealing with difficult young children: Strategies for teachers and parents. *Young Children, 41,* 15–20.

Soto, L. D. (1993). Native language for school success. *Bilingual Research Journal, 17,* 83–97.

Soto, L. D. (1997). *Language, culture, and power: Bilingual families and the struggle for quality education.* New York: SUNY Press.

Southern, W. T., & Jones, E. D. (1991). *The academic acceleration of gifted children.* New York: Teachers College Press.

Stanovich, K. E. (1986). Matthew effects in reading: Some consequences of individual differences in the acquisition of literacy. *Reading Research Quarterly, 21,* 360–406.

Stansbury, K., & Harris, M. L. (2000). Individual differences in stress reactions during a peer entry episode: Effects of age, temperament, approach behavior, and self-perceived peer competence. *Journal of Experimental Child Psychology, 76*(1), 50–63.

Stark, R. E. (1977). Features of infant sounds: The emergence of cooing. *Journal of Child Language, 5,* 379–390.

Stark, R. E., Rose, S. N., & McClagen, A. (1975). Features of infant sounds: The first eight weeks of life. *Journal of Child Language, 2,* 205–222.

Strain, P. S., & Hoyson, M. (2000). The need for longitudinal, intensive social skills intervention: LEAP follow-up outcomes for children with autism. *Topics in Early Childhood Special Education, 20*(2), 116–122.

Sulzby, E. (1985). Children's emergent reading of favourite storybooks: A developmental study. *Reading Research Quarterly, 20,* 427–446.

Sulzby, E., & Teale, W. (1991). Emergent literacy. In R. Barr, M. Kamil, P. Mosenthall, & P. D. Pearson (Eds.), *Handbook of reading research: Vol. 2* (pp. 727–757). New York: Longman.

Takhvar, M. (1988). Play and theories of play: A review of the literature. *Early Child Development and Care, 39,* 221–244.

Taylor, D. (1983). *Family literacy.* Exeter, NH: Heinemann.

Teale, W., & Sulzby, E. (1986). Emergent literacy as a perspective for examining how young children become readers and writers. In W. Teale & E. Sulzby (Eds.), *Emergent literacy: Writing and reading* (pp. vii–xxv). Norwood, MA: Ablex.

Templeton, S., & Morris, D. (1999). Questions teachers ask about spelling. *Reading Research Quarterly, 34,* 102–112.

There is no Utopia: The story of returning immigrants. (1999, December 23). The Hangyurea Newsletter, Issue No. 288. Retrieved from *http://www.hani.co.kr/h21/data/l991213/1pascd 01 .html.*

Vandell, D. L., &. Corasaniti, M. A. (1990). Variations in early child care: Do they predict subsequent social, emotional, and cognitive differences? *Early Childhood Research Quarterly, 5,* 55–72.

Villarruel, F. A., Imig, D. R., & Kostelnik, M. J. (1995). Diverse families. In E. Garcia & B. McLaughlin (Eds.), *Meeting the challenge of linguistic and cultural diversity in early childhood education* (pp. 103–124). New York: Teachers College Press.

Volk, D. (1997). Questions in lessons: Activity settings in the homes and school of two Puerto Rican kindergarteners. *Anthropology and Education Quarterly, 28*(1), 22–49.

Vygotsky, L. S. (1976). Play and its role in the mental development of the child. In J. Bruner, J. Jolly, & K. Sylva (Eds.), *Play: Its role in development and evolution* (pp. 537–554). New York: Basic Books.

Vygotsky, L. S. (1978). *Mind in a society.* Cambridge, MA: Harvard University Press.

Wang, S. (1987). Yani as I see her. In *Wang Yani: Pictures by a young Chinese girl* (pp. 15–23). Munich: Prestel.

Weisner, T. S., Gallimore, R., & Jordan, C. (1993). Unpacking cultural effects of classroom learning: Hawaiian peer assistance and child-generated activity. In R. N. Roberts (Ed.), *Coming home to preschool: The sociocultural context of early education* (pp. 59–87). Norwood, NJ: Ablex.

Wells, G. (1985). Preschool literacy-related activities and success in school. In D. R. Olson, N. Torrence, & A. Hildyard (Eds.), *Literacy language and learning: The nature and consequences of reading and writing* (pp. 229–255). Cambridge, England: Cambridge University Press.

Whitebook, M., Howes, C., & Phillips, D. (1990). *Who cares? Child care teachers and the quality of care in America.* Final Report, National Child Care Staffing Study. Oakland, CA: Child Care Employee Project.

Wilson, B., & Wilson, M. (1977). An iconoclastic view of the imagery sources in the drawings of young people. *Art Education, 30*(1), 5–11.

Wilson, B., & Wilson, M. (1981). Review of *Artful scribbles: The significance of children's drawings,* by H. Gardner. *Studies in Visual Communication, 7*(1), 86–89.

Winner, E. (1996). *Gifted children: Myths and realities.* New York: Basic Books.

Winton, P. J. (2000). Early childhood intervention personnel preparation: Backward mapping for future planning. *Topics in Early Childhood Special Education, 20*(2), 87–94.

Wolf, D. (1994). Development as growth of repertoires. In M. F. Franklin & B. Kaplan (Eds.), *Development and the arts* (pp. 59–78). Hillsdale: Erlbaum.

Wolf, D., & Perry, M. (1988). From endpoints to repertoires: New conclusions about drawing development. *Journal of Aesthetic Education, 22*(1), 17–35.

Wong Fillmore, L. (1991). When learning a second language means losing the first? *Early Childhood Research Quarterly, 6,* 323–346.

Wright, S. C., & Taylor, D. M. (1995). Identity and the language of the classroom: Investing the impact of heritage versus second language instruction on personal and collective self-esteem. *Journal of Educational Psychology, 87,* 241–252.

Wright, S. C., Taylor, D. M., & Macarthur, J. (2000). Subtractive bilingualism and the survival of the Inuit language: Heritage-versus second-language education. *Journal of Educational Psychology, 92*(1), 63–84.

Yen, C. C., & Ispa, J. M. (2000). Children's temperament and behavior in Montessori and constructivist early childhood programs. *Early Education and Development, 11*(2), 171–186.

Zigler, E., & Styfco, S. J. (2000). Pioneering steps (and fumbles) in developing a federal preschool intervention. *Topics in Early Childhood Special Education, 20*(2), 67–70.

Zimmerman, M. P. (1986). Music development in middle childhood: A summary of selected research studies. *Bulletin of the Council for Research in Music Education, 86,* 18–35.

CHAPTER 14

Psychology of Literacy and Literacy Instruction

MICHAEL PRESSLEY

When first asked whether I could prepare a chapter summarizing literacy research, my initial response was that the request was impossible. What came to mind immediately were the three volumes of the *Handbook of Reading Research* (Barr, Kamil, Mosenthal, & Pearson, 1991; Kamil, Mosenthal, Pearson, & Barr, 2000; Pearson, Barr, Kamil, & Mosenthal, 1984), the most prominent compendiums of reading research, which collectively include 3,000 pages to summarize just reading research (although some writing research found its way into those volumes).

Even more daunting than just the volume of research, however, is its diversity. From a methodological perspective, there are experimental and correlational traditions in literacy studies. In recent years, however, such traditional and quantitative approaches have been supplanted largely by more qualitative methods, including ethnographies (Florio-Ruane & McVee, 2000), verbal protocol analyses (Afflerbach, 2000; Pressley & Afflerbach, 1995), narrative approaches (Alvermann, 2000), and single-subject designs (Neuman & McCormick, 2000).

Conceptually, literacy at one time was primarily seen from a behavioral perspective, with such behaviorism yielding to cognitivism in the 1970s and 1980s. Although there is still much cognitive study of reading, sociocultural emphasis in the field has been increasing, beginning in the 1990s and moving into the twenty-first century (Gaffney & Anderson, 2000).

Literacy is also a decidedly international field of study; exciting ideas have come from Australia and New Zealand (Wilkinson, Freebody, & Elkins, 2000), the United Kingdom (Harrison, 2000), Latin America (Santana, 2000), and increasingly from former Iron Curtain countries (Meredith & Steele, 2000). Although much of literacy instruction has been and remains focused on kindergarten through Grade 12 instruction, in recent decades a great deal of work has been done on literacy development during the preschool years (Yaden, Rowe, & McGillivray, 2000) as well as research extending into the college years (Flippo & Caverly, 2000) and beyond (Kirsch, Jungeblut, Jenkins, & Kolstad, 1993). Also, there has been a clear shift away from thinking about literacy as a development that occurs purely in the schools; it is now conceived as more an acquisition that occurs in families, (Purcell-Gates, 2000) in the workplace, and in the larger, increasingly technological community (Reinking, McKenna, Labbo, & Kieffer, 1998).

Of course, one way to deal with this enormous and multidimensionally expanding literature would be to focus only on the parts that are decidedly psychological because much of literacy research was not carried out by psychologists and seems rather far afield from psychological issues; in fact, that is a tactic taken in this chapter. The downside of this approach is that some of the most interesting and cutting-edge directions are neglected. Some ideas that might start psychologists thinking about new directions they might pursue are not put before readers' eyes. The serious scholar in literacy—or anyone who wants to have a broadly informed opinion—will (at a minimum) spend much time with the 3,000 *Handbook* pages now available at the beginning of this millennium.

Another tactic that I employ here is to focus on primary and significant issues and questions—ones that have been of concern for a very long time. This approach in particular makes sense because it does lead to some answers—that is, a number of important issues in reading and writing have been studied long enough that replicable findings have emerged. This emphasis on replicable findings—on the surface at least—makes this chapter consistent with the approach of the National Reading Panel (2000). I am inconsistent with the National Reading Panel, however, in that I am willing to consider a greater diversity of methods than that group was. That group generally limited itself to experimental studies; it admitted only the occasional quasi-experimental study and distanced itself from qualitative approaches entirely. This chapter certainly does present much coverage of outcomes produced in true experiments and approximations to experiments, but these outcomes are complemented by other scientific findings as well. In particular, descriptive methods, including ethnographies, have provided rich understandings about the complexities of some important instructional approaches—understandings that never would be produced in true experiments or represented in the write-ups of experimental studies.

This chapter could have been organized in a number of different ways; I have decided to organize this one along developmental lines. In fact, there have been studies of literacy development beginning in late infancy and proceeding through adulthood. Of course, what develops varies with each developmental period; the development of general language competencies is particularly critical during the preschool years. Although beginning reading instruction during the early elementary school years focuses on the development of letter- and word-level competencies in reading and writing, this focus eventually gives way to the development of fluent reading as a goal and increasing concerns with comprehension and composition in the later elementary and middle school grades. By high school and college, much of the emphasis is on honing literacy skills in the service of the learning demands of secondary and postsecondary education. Researchers interested in adult literacy have often focused on adults who did not develop literacy competencies during the schooling years; such research generally attempts to develop interventions to promote literacy in these populations, whose members often suffer socioeconomic and personal disadvantages directly attributable to their reading problems.

EMERGENT LITERACY DURING THE PRESCHOOL YEARS

What happens to children during the preschool years relates to later literacy development. Many developmentalists interested in literacy have focused on what is known as *emergent literacy,* which is the development of the language skills underlying literacy through interactions with the social world. Other developmentalists who have been interested in children's beginning letter-level and word-recognition skills have focused more on a competency known as *phonemic awareness,* which is the awareness that words are composed of sounds blended together.

Emergent Literacy

One of the more heavily researched topics by developmental psychologists is the nature of mother-infant attachment. When interactions between the principal caregiver and an infant are constructive and caring, the attachment that develops can be described as *secure* (Bowlby, 1969). In particular, when parents are responsive to the child and provide for its needs, secure attachment is more likely. The securely attached baby interacts with the world comfortably in the caregiver's presence and responds favorably to the caregiver after a period of caregiver absence.

Matas, Arend, and Sroufe (1978) made a fundamentally important discovery. Children who experience secure attachment during infancy engage in more effective problem solving with their parents during the preschool years. When parents are securely attached to their children, they are more likely to provide appropriate degrees of support as their children attempt to solve problems (Frankel & Bates, 1990; Matas et al., 1978).

A related finding is that when parents and preschoolers are securely attached, they interact more productively in situations involving literacy. Bus and van IJzendoorn (1988) observed both securely attached and insecurely attached mother-child pairs as they watched *Sesame Street* together, read a picture book, and went through an alphabet book. The interactions involving securely attached parents and children were much more positive than were the interactions between insecurely attached parents and children. Securely attached preschoolers were more attentive and less easily distracted during interactions, and much more literate activity was observed in the interactions of securely attached pairs compared to those of insecurely attached pairs. Storybook reading was more intense with the secure pairs than with the insecure pairs; the secure parent-child pairs talked more about the story than did the insecure pairs. An especially interesting finding was that securely attached parents and their 3-year-old children reported doing more reading together (Bus & van IJzendoorn, 1995).

That storybook reading brings greater rewards when attachment security is greater is an important finding because high-quality storybook reading during the preschool years clearly promotes literacy development. There are clear correlations between the amount of storybook reading during the preschool years and subsequent language development, children's interest in reading, and their success as beginning readers (Sulzby & Teale, 1991); this is sensible because storybook reading at its best is a rich verbal experience, with much questioning and answering by both reader and child. Storybook reading permits practice at working out meaning from words in text and pictures, as well as opportunities for the child to practice relating ideas in stories to their own lives and the world as they understand it (Applebee & Langer, 1983; Cochran-Smith, 1984; Flood, 1977; Pelligrini, Perlmutter, Galda, & Brody, 1990; Roser & Martinez, 1985; Taylor & Strickland, 1986). As a child matures and gains experience with storybook reading, the conversations between reader and child increase in complexity (Snow, 1983; Sulzby & Teale, 1987). Older preschoolers who have had much storybook reading experience are much more attentive during such reading than are same-age peers who have had relatively little opportunity to experience books with their parents or other adults (Bus & van IJzendoorn, 1988). Many correlational data support the hypothesis that storybook reading is beneficial for children's cognitive development—that it stimulates language development and sets the stage for beginning reading.

This body of evidence in the context of storybook reading is complemented by other data substantiating striking connections between the richness of preschoolers' verbal worlds and subsequent language development. One of the most ambitious and most cited analyses was made by University of Kansas psychologists Hart and Risley (1995). They observed 42 families for 2.5 years, beginning in the second semester of a child's life. During these observations, they recorded all actions and interactions. The first important finding was that there were significant differences between families in both the quality and the extensiveness of verbal interactions. The quality of interactions in terms of completeness and complexity of language was greater in professional homes than in working-class homes, and language complexity in working-class homes was greater than in welfare homes—that is, in homes of higher socioeconomic status, parents listened more to their children, they asked their children to elaborate their comments more, and they taught their children how to cope verbally when confronted with ideas that were challenging for the children to

communicate. Quantitatively, the differences in verbal interactions were really striking: Whereas a child in a professional home might experience 4 million verbalizations a year, a child in a welfare family could be exposed to only 250,000 utterances. Did these vast differences in experience translate into later performance differences? There was no doubt about it; superior language was detected by age 3 in the children raised in professional families compared to children in working-class and welfare families.

Of course, the problem with correlational data is that causality is never clear. Yes, it could be that the richer experiences promoted language development, or it could be that more verbal children stimulated richer language interactions during storybook reading and throughout their days. Fortunately, complementary experimental studies establish more definitively that high-quality verbal interactions result in linguistic advances in children.

Grover Whitehurst and his colleagues (Whitehurst et al., 1988) hypothesized that if parents were coached in order to improve their verbal interactions with their children during storybook reading, the language functioning of the children would improve. Whitehurst et al. worked for a month with the parents of 14 children between the ages of 1.5–3 years. In particular, the parents were taught to use more open-ended questions as they read storybooks with their children; they were also taught to ask more questions about the functions and attributes of objects in stories. Whitehurst et al. (1988) also taught the parents to elaborate and expand on comments made by their children during reading. In short, the parents were taught the tricks of the trade for stimulating productive and verbally rich conversations with young children. In contrast, parents and children in a control condition simply continued to read together for the month corresponding to treatment for the experimental participants.

First, the intervention worked in that it did increase the verbal complexity and extensiveness of communications between parents and children. Although experimental and control parent-child interactions were similar before the study, the experimental group conversations during book reading were much richer following the intervention. Moreover, clear differences appeared in the language functioning of the experimental group children following the intervention, reflected by performance on standardized tests of psycholinguistic ability and vocabulary. These effects have been replicated several times, both by Whitehurst's associates (Valdez-Menchaca & Whitehurst, 1992; Whitehurst et al., 1994) and by others (Crain-Thoresen & Dale, 1995; Dickinson & Smith, 1994; Lonigan, Anthony, & Burgess, 1995).

In short, evidence suggests that preschool verbal experiences promote language development, potentially in ways promoting subsequent development of reading. Whether these effects are great enough to inspire enthusiasm, however, depends on the eye of the observing scientist; some scientists see large and important effects (Bus, van IJzendoorn, & Pelligrini, 1995; Dunning, Mason, & Stewart, 1994; Lonigan, 1994), whereas others who examine the same outcomes see small effects that might be explained away as due to factors other than verbal stimulation (Scarborough & Dobrich, 1994). I tend to favor the former rather than the latter conclusion; the experimental work of Whitehurst and his colleagues especially affects my thinking on this matter. In general, my optimism is consistent with the general optimism of the field that rich early language experiences affect language development in ways that should affect later reading development (Sulzby & Teale, 1991; Yaden et al., 2000).

Phonemic Awareness

In recent years, no prereading competency has received as much attention from researchers and practitioners as phonemic awareness has. Understanding that words are composed of blended sounds seems essential for rapid progress in learning letter-sound associations and learning to use those associations to sound out words (Adams, 1990; Pennington, Groisser, & Welsh, 1993; Stanovich, 1986, 1988). This is not an all-or-none acquisition, however; Adams (1990) provides a conceptualization of phonemic awareness subcompetencies, listed as follows from most rudimentary to most advanced: (a) sensitivity to rhymes in words, (b) being able to spot words that do not rhyme (e.g., picking the odd word out if given *can, dan, sod*), (c) being able to blend sounds to form words (e.g., blending the sounds for *M*, short *A*, and *T* to produce *mat*), (d) being able to break words down into sound components (e.g., sounding out *mat* to indicate awareness of *M*, short *A*, and *T* sounds), and (e) being able to split off sounds from words (e.g., dropping the *M* sound from *mat* to say *at;* dropping the *T* sound from *mat,* producing *ma*).

Why is there such great interest in phonemic awareness? When phonemic awareness is low at ages 4–5, there is increased risk of difficulties in learning to read and spell (Bowey, 1995; Griffith, 1991; Näsland & Schneider, 1996; Pratt & Brady, 1988; Shaywitz, 1996; Stuart & Masterson, 1992). Perhaps the best-known study establishing linkage between phonemic awareness at the end of the preschool years and later reading achievement was Juel (1988). She studied a sample of children as they progressed from first through fourth grade. Problems in reading during Grade 1 predicted problems in reading at Grade 4—that is, problem readers in first grade do not just learn to read when they are ready! Rather, they never

seem to learn to read as well as do children who were strong readers in Grade 1. More important to this discussion is that low phonemic awareness in Grade 1 predicted poor reading performance in Grade 4, a result generally consistent with other demonstrations that low phonemic awareness between 4 and 6 years of age predict later reading problems (Bowey, 1995; Griffith, 1991; Näsland & Schneider, 1996; Pratt & Brady, 1988; Shaywitz, 1966; Stuart & Masterson, 1992).

Given that phonological awareness is so critical in learning to read, it is fortunate that phonological awareness has proven teachable; when taught, it influences reading performance positively. Perhaps the best known demonstration of the potency of phonemic awareness instruction is that provided by Bradley and Bryant (1983). They provided 5- and 6-year-olds with 2 years of experience categorizing words on the basis of their sounds, including practice doing so with beginning, middle, and ending sounds. Thus, given the words *hen, men,* and *hat* with the request to categorize on the basis of initial sound, *hen* and *hat* went together; in contrast, *hen* and *men* was the correct answer when the children were asked to categorize on the basis of middle or ending sound. The students in the study first read pictures and made their choices on the basis of sounds alone; then they were transferred to words and could make their choices on the basis of letter and orthographic features as well as sounds.

The training made a substantial impact on reading measured immediately after training, relative to a control condition in which students made judgments about the conceptual category membership of words (e.g., identifying that *cat, rat,* and *bat* go together as animals). Even more impressive was that the trained participants outperformed control participants in reading 5 years after the training study took place (Bradley, 1989; Bradley & Bryant, 1991).

Bradley and Bryant's work was the first of a number of studies establishing that phonemic awareness could be developed through instruction and influence reading performance (Ball & Blachman, 1988, 1991; Barker & Torgesen, 1995; Blachman, 1991; Byrne & Fielding-Barnsley, 1991, 1993, 1995; Cunningham, 1990; Foster, Erickson, Foster, Brinkman, & Torgesen, 1994; Lie, 1991; Lundberg, Frost, & Peterson, 1988; O'Connor, Jenkins, & Slocum, 1995; Tangel & Blachman, 1992, 1995; Vellutino & Scanlon, 1987; Williams, 1980; Wise & Olson, 1995). Although the instructional procedures varied somewhat from study to study, in general, phonemic awareness training has included at least several months of exercises requiring young children to attend to the component sounds of words, categorizing and discriminating words on the basis of sound features. Thus, sometimes children were asked to tap out the syllables of words, sometimes asked to say the word with the last sound deleted, and sometimes requested to identify the odd word out when one does not share some sound with other words in a group.

Bus and van IJzendoorn (1999) provided especially complete and analytical review of the phonemic awareness instructional data. Collapsing data over 32 research reports, all of which were generated by U.S. investigators, Bus and van IJzendoorn (1999) concluded that there was a moderate relationship between phonemic awareness instruction and later reading. When long-term effects (i.e., 6 months or more following training) were considered, however, the phonemic awareness instruction had less of an impact on reading—a small impact at best. Thus, although delayed effects of phonemic awareness training can be detected, they are not huge.

All scientifically oriented reviewers of the early reading literature have concluded that phonemic awareness is important as part of learning to read (e.g., Adams, 1990; Adams, Treiman, & Pressley, 1998; Goswami, 2000; National Reading Panel, 2000; Snow, Burns, & Griffin, 1998). The available correlational and experimental data converge on the conclusion that phonemic awareness is probably an important prerequisite for learning to read words. After all, if a child does not understand that words are composed of sounds blended together, why would reading instruction emphasizing the component sounds of words make any sense to the child? Of course, the answer is that it would not, which explains why phonemic awareness is so critical for a child to learn to read (e.g., Fox & Routh, 1975). Acquiring phonemic awareness is just a start on word recognition competence, which is a critical task during the primary grades.

In summary, much progress in literacy development can and does occur before Grade 1, which has traditionally been viewed as the point of schooling for beginning reading instruction. Much of it is informal—the learning of language in a language-rich environment that can include activities such as storybook reading with adults. Increasingly, high-quality kindergarten programs include activities explicitly intended to develop phonemic awareness.

FIRST GRADE AND THE PRIMARY YEARS

There has been tremendous debate in the past quarter century about the best approach to primary-grades reading education. This debate somewhat reflects a much longer debate (i.e., one occurring over centuries to millennia) about the nature of beginning reading instruction (see Pressley, Allington, Wharton-McDonald, Block, & Morrow, 2001). In recent years, at one extreme have been those who have advocated an

approach known as *whole language,* which posits that children should be immersed in holistic reading and writing tasks from the very start of schooling—that is, reading trade books and composing their own stories. At the other extreme are those who argue that skills should be developed first. The skills-first advocates particularly favor phonics as an approach to developing word-recognition abilities; they argue that if students learn letter-sound associations and how to blend the component sounds in words to recognize words, their word recognition will be more accurate and more certain.

Word Recognition

Even preschoolers can read some words, such as *McDonald's* when in the context of the company's logo, *Coca-Cola* when encountered on a bottle or aluminum can, and *Yankees* when scripted across a ballplayer's chest. Young children learn to recognize such logographs from their day-to-day experiences. When presented the words *McDonald's, Coca-Cola,* and *Yankees* out of their familiar contexts, preliterate children cannot read them. Even so, encountering words as logographs somehow seems to make it easier for preschoolers to learn words out of context. When Cronin, Farrell, and Delaney (1995) taught preschoolers words as sight words, previously encountered logographs were learned more easily than were control words never encountered as logographs. At best, however, logographic reading is just a start on word-recognition skills and is very different from most of word recognition.

Well before children can sound out words using all the letters of a word, they sometimes can read words based on a few letters, a process Ehri (1991) referred to as *phonetic cue reading.* Thus, as a little boy, I learned the very long word *elementary* because I encountered it often during first grade. As a consequence, I could read *elementary* wherever I encountered the word. The problem was that I was reading the word based on a couple of cues (probably the beginning *e* and the fact that it was a long word) shared by other words. Thus, for quite a while, I thought that label on the escape hatch in the school bus was labeled *elementary door,* when in fact it was an *emergency door!* Such mistakes are common in children who are 5–6 years old (Ehri & Wilce, 1987a, 1987b; Gilbert, Spring, & Sassenrath, 1977; Seymour & Elder, 1986).

Many children do reach the kindergarten doors knowing the alphabet. One reason is that as a society, we decided to teach the alphabet to preschoolers—for example, through efforts such as those in *Sesame Street;* it is clear from the earliest evaluations that such environmental enrichment did affect acquisition of alphabetic knowledge (e.g., Anderson & Collins, 1988; Ball & Bogatz, 1970; Bogatz & Ball, 1971). It is now known that *Sesame Street* contributes to alphabetic learning over and above the contributions made by family and others (Rice, Huston, Truglio, & Wright, 1990).

Knowing letter names and letter-sound associations alone does not result in word recognition competence, however. Children must also learn the common blends (e.g., *dr, bl*) and digraphs (e.g., *sh, ch*). In general, primary education includes lots of repetition of the common letter-sound associations, blends, and digraphs—for example, through repeated reading of stories filled with high-frequency words. Walk into any Grade 1 classroom: It will be filled with many single-syllable words, including lists of words featuring the common digraphs and blends. Word families also will be prominent (e.g., *beak, peak, leak*). Grade 1 teachers spend a lot of time modeling for their students how to sound out words by blending the component sounds in words and using common chunks; they also spend a lot of time encouraging students to sound out words on their own, including doing so to write words in their compositions (Wharton-McDonald, Pressley, & Hampston, 1998).

The students most likely to make rapid progress in learning to sound out words are those who already have phonemic awareness and know their letter-sound associations (Tunmer, Herriman, & Nesdale, 1988). Even so, a large body of evidence indicates that teaching students to sound out words by blending components' sounds is better than alternative approaches with respect to development of word-recognition skills.

Teaching Primary-Level Students to Sound Out Words

One of the most important twentieth-century contributions to reading research was Jeanne Chall's (1967) *Learning to Read: The Great Debate.* After reviewing all of the evidence then available, Chall concluded that the best way to teach beginning reading was to teach students explicitly to sound out words—that is, she felt that early reading instruction should focus on teaching letter-sound associations and the blending of letter sounds to recognize words, an approach she referred to as *synthetic phonics.* Based on the available research, Chall concluded that synthetic phonics was superior to other approaches regardless of the ability level of the child, although synthetic phonics seemed to be especially beneficial to lower-ability children. After the publication of the first edition of the Chall book, there was a flurry of laboratory studies of phonics instruction, and most researchers found synthetic phonics to be better than alternatives (Chall, 1983, Table I-2, pp. 18–20).

The next book-length treatment of the scientific foundations of beginning reading instruction was Marilyn Adams' (1990) *Beginning to Read.* By the time of that publication, a great deal of conceptualization and analysis of beginning reading had occurred. Adams reviewed for her readers the evidence permitting the conclusion that phonemic awareness is a critical prerequisite to word recognition. So was acquisition of the *alphabetic principle,* which is the understanding that the sounds in words are represented by letters. Researchers interested in visual perceptual development had made the case that children gradually acquire understanding of the distinctive visual features of words, gradually learning to discriminate *R*s from *B*s and *V*s from *W*s (Gibson, Gibson, Pick, & Osser, 1962; Gibson & Levin, 1975). Consistent with Chall (1967, 1983), Adams also concluded that instruction in synthetic phonics promoted beginning word-recognition skills.

Since Adams' (1990) book, a number of demonstrations have shown that intensive instruction in synthetic phonics helps beginning struggling readers. For example, Foorman, Francis, Novy, and Liberman (1991) studied urban first-grade students who were enrolled either in a program emphasizing synthetic phonics or in a program downplaying phonics in word recognition in favor of whole language. By the end of the year, the students in the synthetic phonics program were reading and spelling words better than were students in the other program. Foorman, Francis, Fletcher, Schatschneider, and Mehta (1998) reported a similar outcome; a program emphasizing synthetic phonics produced better reading after a year of instruction than did three alternatives that did not provide systematic phonics instruction. Maureen Lovett treats 9- to 13-year-olds who are experiencing severe reading problems; she and her colleagues have presented considerable evidence that systematic teaching of synthetic phonics improves the reading of such children (Lovett, Ransby, Hardwick, Johns, & Donaldson, 1989; Lovett et al., 1994). Similar results have been produced in a number of well-controlled studies (Alexander, Anderson, Heilman, Voeller, & Torgesen, 1991; Manis, Custodio, & Szeszulski, 1993; Olson, Wise, Johnson, & Ring, 1997; Torgesen et al., 1996; Vellutino et al., 1996), permitting the clear conclusion that intensive (i.e., one-on-one or one teacher to a few students) synthetic phonics instruction can help struggling beginning readers.

In recent years, a popular alternative to synthetic phonics has been teaching students to decode words by recognizing common chunks (or rimes) in them (e.g., *tight, light,* and *sight* include the *-ight* chunk). Use of such chunks to decode, however, requires that students know something about letters and sounds and about blending (Ehri & Robbins, 1992; Peterson & Haines, 1992) because word recognition requires blending the sounds produced by individual letters with the sounds produced by a chunk (e.g., *tight* involves blending the *t* and *ight* sounds; Bruck & Treiman, 1992). In evaluations to date, when struggling readers have been taught to use common word chunks to decode words they have not seen before, this approach has been successful relative to controls who receive conventional instruction not emphasizing word recognition (e.g., Lovett et al., 2000). Students taught to use word chunks have fared as well after several months of such instruction as students taught to use synthetic phonics (Walton, Walton, & Felton, 2001). Thus, available data indicate that young children can learn to use both chunks and the sounding out of individual sounds as they learn to recognize words (Goswami, 2000). Perhaps most striking in the Walton et al. (2001) report was that weak first-grade readers tutored either to use chunks to decode or to sound out words using phonics caught up with good first-grade readers who continued to receive conventional reading instruction that emphasized neither use of chunks during reading nor synthetic phonics. These are powerful procedures for remediating the most salient problem in beginning reading, which is difficulty in recognizing words. Even so, they have not been the most popular procedures in recent years for remediating troubled beginning readers.

Reading Recovery

Reading Recovery™ is a widely disseminated approach to beginning reading remediation (Lyons, Pinnell, & DeFord, 1993). Typically, students in Reading Recovery are in Grade 1 and making slow progress in learning to read in the regular classroom. The intervention supplements classroom instruction and involves daily one-teacher-to-one-child lessons; each lesson lasts about a half hour, and lessons continue for as long as a semester.

A typical Reading Recovery lesson involves a series of literacy tasks (Clay, 1993; Lyons et al., 1993). First, the child reads a familiar book aloud to the teacher. Often, this task is followed by reading of another book that is not quite as familiar—one introduced to the child the day before. During this reading of yesterday's new book, the teacher makes a running record, noting what the child does well during reading and recording errors. Information gleaned by the teacher as the child reads is used to make instructional decisions, and the teacher attempts to determine the processes being used by the child during reading.

For example, when the child makes an error during reading, the teacher notes whether the child relied on meaning clues to guess the word, syntactic cues, or visual cues; this analysis of processing informs instructional decision making. Thus, if the child misreads *bit* as *sit,* the teacher might focus the child's attention on the *it* chunk in the word and prompt the child

to blend the *s* sound and the sound made by *it.* After the reading, the teacher continues the lesson by asking the student to identify plastic letters or by having the child make and break words with plastic letters. For example, the teacher might focus on words with the *it* chunk, prompting the child to form new words with the *it* chunk, using magnetic letters to construct the words (e.g., *bit, fit, mit, pit,* etc.). Then the child might break these words to see that *bit* is *b* plus *it, fit* is *f* plus *it,* and so on. Then the child might do some writing in response to the story, with the teacher providing assistance as the child works on writing (e.g., writing a sentence about the story, such as *The dog sits down*). During writing, the teacher encourages the child to listen for the sounds in words in order to spell out the word in writing. Then, the teacher writes the sentence constructed by the student on a paper strip, using conventional spelling to do so, then cutting up the strip into individual words. The child reassembles the sentence and reads it for the teacher. The Reading Recovery lesson concludes with the teacher's introducing a new book to the student, who attempts to read the book for the teacher. Homework involves taking home the books read during the lesson and reading them to a parent.

Reading Recovery is all about children's reading strategies and the teaching of strategies to struggling readers (Clay, 1993; Lyons et al., 1993). Throughout a Reading Recovery lesson, the teacher attempts to determine how the child is processing during reading and writing and the what reading and writing strategies are used by the child. Specifically, the teacher attempts to determine the reader's directions of processing (i.e., whether reading is left to right, from the top of the page down; whether writing is left to right, from the top to bottom of the page). The teacher also attempts to discern whether the child is processing individual words in a sequence—for example, whether the child is noticing the spaces between words read and putting spaces between words written. The teacher notes whether the child is monitoring reading and writing—for example, going back and attempting to reread a misread word or asking for help during writing regarding spelling an unknown word. The Reading Recovery teacher focuses on the nature of reading errors—whether they reflect attempts to sound out a word, a reliance on meaning or syntactic cues, or dependence on visual similarity of the attempted word with a word known by the child. In short, the assumption in Reading Recovery is that the struggling reader is attempting to problem-solve when reading and writing, and that the child's errors are particularly revealing about her or his reading and writing strategies.

The teacher's knowledge of the child's strategies is used to guide teaching, and the teacher's role is to stimulate use of strategies during reading and writing that are more effective than the ones currently being used by the young reader (Clay, 1993; Lyons et al., 1993). For example, to encourage the development of directionality, the teacher prompts the child to *Read it with your finger,* pointing to each word as it is encountered in text. At first, this can require the teacher actually holding and directing the child's hand, but eventually the child internalizes the left-to-right and top-to-bottom movements during reading. In order to increase the child's understanding of the concept of individual words, the teacher prompts the child to write words with spaces between them, using the strategy of putting a finger space between written words. The teacher teaches the child to sound out words by saying them slowly, breaking words into discrete sounds (e.g., *cat* into the *C*, short *A*, and *T* sounds). Consistent with the demonstration by Iversen and Tunmer (1993) that Reading Recovery is more effective when it includes systematic teaching of chunks and how they can be blended with letter sounds as part of reading, Reading Recovery now includes more making and breaking of words that share chunks (e.g., *bake, cake, lake, make, take,* etc.) to highlight blending of individual sounds and spelling patterns. The Reading Recovery teacher also teaches the young reader to check decodings by determining whether the reading of a word makes sense in that semantic context. In short, the Reading Recovery teacher instructs the struggling readers in the strategies that effective young readers use; the ultimate goal of Reading Recovery is the development of readers who use effective reading processes in a self-regulated fashion (Clay, 1991).

As is the case for many forms of strategy instruction (Duffy et al., 1987; Palincsar & Brown, 1984; Pearson & Gallagher, 1983; Pressley, El-Dinary, et al., 1992), there is a gradual release of responsibility during Reading Recovery; the teacher is more directive and explicit at first, and the child takes over as lessons proceed and competence develops—that is, the strategy instruction is *scaffolded* (Wood, Bruner, & Ross, 1976). The teacher provides just enough support so that the child can complete the task; then the teacher reduces the support as the child becomes more competent and able to assume greater responsibility for reading. Of course, the intent of such an instructional approach is to develop self-regulation in the child—first by permitting the child to tackle a task that is beyond her or him and then by allowing self-controlled functioning as the child becomes equal to the task.

Also, as is the case with many forms of strategy instruction, evidence indicates that scaffolded teaching of processes well matched to the target task is effective—that is, a large proportion of children who experience Reading Recovery improve as readers, and improvement is greater than that occurring when comparable children do not receive Reading Recovery, at least when reading achievement is measured immediately after Reading Recovery occurs (see Pinnell, 1997). An important

distinction is between Reading Recovery students who graduate and those who do not make enough progress in the program to graduate—that is, Reading Recovery does not always work; when it does work, however, it seems to produce substantial improvement (Elbaum, Vaughn, Hughes, & Moody, 2000). As is the case with many early childhood interventions, if students are simply returned to the classroom without additional support, however, the advantages of Reading Recovery fade, and such Reading Recovery students are often not discernibly different in reading achievement measured several years after the completion of the treatment (Hiebert, 1994).

Studies of Exceptional Primary-Level Teachers

Phonemic awareness instruction, phonics, and Reading Recovery are theory-driven educational interventions—that is, based on theory, researchers devised instruction they felt would promote beginning reading, and their instructional studies served as tests of the theories that inspired the interventions. There is another way to discover effective instruction, however, which is to find very good reading teachers and not-so-good ones and document what occurs in effective versus ineffective classrooms. Pressley and his colleagues have done exactly that with respect to Grade 1 in particular.

In both Wharton-McDonald et al. (1998) and Pressley et al. (2001), the researchers observed first-grade classrooms over the course of an academic year. In some classrooms, engagement and achievement was better than in other classrooms. For example, in some classrooms, a higher proportion of students were reading more advanced books than was observed in more typical classrooms; in some classrooms, students were writing longer, more coherent, and more mechanically impressive stories (i.e., stories with sentences capitalized, punctuation, correctly spelled high-frequency words, sensible invented spellings of lower-frequency words) than were students in other classrooms. Most striking was that the more engaged classrooms also tended to be the ones with more advanced reading and better writing.

What went on in the really impressive classrooms?

- There was a lot of teaching of skills, and this instruction was very consistent. Much of this instruction was in response to student needs, however, with many minilessons on skills.
- Fine literature was emphasized; students read excellent literature and heard it during teacher read-alouds.
- The students did a lot of reading and writing.
- Assignments were matched to students' abilities, and the demands were gradually increased as students improved. Such matching requires different assignments for different students (e.g., one student being urged to write a

two-page story and another a two-sentence story, with the demand in each case for a little more than the child produced previously).

- Self-regulation was encouraged; the message was consistent that students were to make choices for themselves and were to keep themselves on task.

- Strong connections were made across the curriculum; science and social studies occurred in the context of reading and writing, and science and social studies units were filled with good literature and composing.

- The class was positive and very reinforcing, with much cooperation between students and between teachers, other adults, and students.

- The teacher's classroom management was so good that it was hardly noticeable at all, with little apparent need for disciplining of students.

How different the effective classrooms were really became apparent in analyses that contrasted the effective and ineffective classrooms explicitly—analyses designed to identify what was very different in the excellent compared to the not-so-excellent classrooms:

- Many more skills were covered during every hour of instruction in the most effective compared to the least effective classrooms.

- Word-recognition instruction involved teaching multiple strategies (i.e., using phonics, noting word parts, looking at the whole word, using picture clues, using semantic context information provided earlier in the sentence or story, using syntactic cues).

- Comprehension strategies (e.g., making predictions, mental imagery, summarizing) were explicitly taught.

- Students were taught to self-regulate.

- Students were taught to plan, draft, and revise as part of writing.

- Extensive scaffolding (i.e., coaching) took place during writing—for example, with respect to spelling and elaborating on meanings in text.

- Printed prompts for the writing process (e.g., a card about what needs to be checked as part of revision) were available.

- By the end of the year, high demands to use writing conventions (e.g., capitalizing, using punctuation marks, spelling of high frequency words) were placed on students.

- Tasks were designed so that students spend more time doing academically rich processing (i.e., reading and writing) and relatively little time on nonacademic processing (e.g., illustrating a story).

- The class wrote big books, which were on display.

In short, excellent first-grade classrooms are very busy—filled with teaching of skills and demands but also filled with support and opportunities for rich intellectual experiences. Although phonics is taught as skills advocates would have it be taught, it is only part of an enormously complex curriculum enterprise that includes many holistic experiences—that is, systematic skills instruction does not happen first before getting to literature and writing in effective first-grade classrooms; rather, skills are learned largely in the context of reading literature and writing. Although literature and writing are emphasized as the whole language theorists would have it, holistic experiences are constantly intermixed with the systematic and opportunistic instruction of specific skills, and skills were much more an emphasis than many whole language theorists would consider appropriate. Excellent primary-level classrooms—ones in which growth in reading and writing is high—cannot be reduced to a very few instructional practices; rather, they are a complex, articulated mix of practices and activities.

The most recent work of Pressley and colleagues (Raphael, Bogner, Pressley, Masters, & Steinhofer, 2000) has taken a decided psychological turn. They observed first-grade classrooms with the goal of determining how excellent first-grade teachers motivate their students to participate in literacy-promoting activities. In part, this research was stimulated by the engagement perspective, which posits that literacy achievement depends on instruction that motivates literacy engagement (e.g., Guthrie & Alvermann, 1999). Such engagement is promoted when classrooms emphasize learning rather than student competition, meaningful interactions between students and ideas, student autonomy and self-regulation, interesting content, teaching of useful strategies, praise contingent on literacy engagement and progress, teacher involvement with students, and evaluations that make sense to students (Guthrie & Wigfield, 2000). From this perspective, it was expected that classrooms loaded with mechanisms promoting literacy engagement in fact would be classrooms high in student literacy engagement.

What Raphael et al. (2000) found was that first-grade teachers who had students who were highly engaged in reading and writing constructed classrooms filled with positive motivational mechanisms compared to teachers overseeing classrooms in which engagement was not as certain. Thus, in classrooms where engagement was high, the following motivational mechanisms were observed:

- Much cooperative learning took place.

- Individual accountability (i.e., students were rewarded for doing well and held accountable when they did not) was demonstrated.

- As they worked, students received much coaching.

- Strong library connections were maintained.
- Students were encouraged to be autonomous and given choices.
- The teacher was gentle, caring, and inviting.
- Much one-to-one interaction took place between teachers and students.
- Strong home-school connections were maintained.
- Many opportunistic minilessons were taught.
- Deep connections with students were maintained.
- Appropriate risk taking was supported.
- The classroom was fun.
- Strong connections to other classes in the school were maintained.
- The teacher encouraged creative and independent thinking.
- The teacher encouraged rich and detailed learning.
- The class took a clear positive tone.
- Assignments were appropriately challenging.
- Students produced meaningful products (e.g., stories).
- Depth in coverage was favored over breadth in coverage.
- Assignments and units matched student interests.
- Abstract content was made more personal and concrete.
- The teacher encouraged curiosity and suspense.
- Learning objectives were clear.
- Praise and feedback were effective.
- The teacher modeled interest and enthusiasm.
- The teacher modeled thinking and problem–solving.
- The teacher communicated that academic tasks deserve intense attention.
- The teacher inserted novel material into instruction.
- The teacher provided clear directions.
- The teacher made apparent the relevance of learning to real life.
- The teacher encouraged persistence.
- The teacher encouraged cognitive conflict.
- The teacher communicated a wide range of strategies for accomplishing academic tasks.
- The teacher encouraged self-reinforcement by students when they did well.
- The teacher provided immediate feedback.
- The teacher urged students to try hard.
- The teacher expressed confidence in students.
- The teacher encouraged students to attribute their successes to hard work and their failures to a need to work harder.
- The teacher had realistic ambitions and goals for students.

- The teacher encouraged students to think they can get smarter by working hard on school work.
- Classroom management was good.
- The teacher provided rewards that stimulate students positively (e.g., gift book).
- The teacher monitored the whole class.
- The teacher monitored individual students carefully.

In short, consistent with the engagement perspective, engaging classrooms were filled with positive motivational mechanisms; less engaging classrooms showed many fewer of these mechanisms.

That is not to say that the teachers in the less engaging classrooms did not try to motivate their students. In fact, they did. In less engaging classrooms, however, teachers were much more likely than were those in the more engaging classrooms to use negative approaches to motivations—emphasizing competition between students; giving students tasks that were very easy, boring, or both; providing negative feedback; making students aware of their failures; scapegoating students; threatening students; and punishing students. Such negative approaches to motivation were almost never observed in the most engaged classrooms.

Summary

Many psychologists have been at the forefront of efforts to develop effective beginning reading instruction. One reason is that learning to read is a salient event in the life of the developing child—an event that is decidedly psychological in nature. There are huge cognitive conceptions to acquire, such as phonemic awareness and the alphabetic principle, which develop in the context of much associative learning (i.e., learning letter-sound associations and chunk-sound associations) and development of subtle perceptual discriminations (e.g., the visual identity of each letter, both upper- and lowercase versions). An important hypothesis among psychologists is that beginning reading skills can be taught directly. In fact, quite a bit of evidence has accumulated making clear that direct teaching of synthetic phonics does in fact make development of word-recognition skills more certain. In recent years, there have also been validations of teaching involving emphasis on word chunks and blending of word parts in sounding out of words; this approach is now part of the prominent remedial approach to beginning reading known as Reading Recovery. Although Reading Recovery teachers are highly trained for their work, it is auspicious that even college students can tutor beginning struggling readers with substantial gains (Elbaum et al., 2000) because the need in the nation for tutoring primary-level readers in beginning reading skills is very, very great. This work on primary-level reading is an excellent example of how psychological theory and research can inform meaningful educational practice.

That said, the psychological theory related to beginning word recognition seems simple relative to the complexity of excellent first-grade instruction that can be observed in many (although certainly not all) classrooms. Although instruction to promote phonemic awareness, phonics, and word recognition in general is prominent in such classrooms, it occurs in a context that attends to student motivation and excellent holistic experiences, including the reading of much good literature and extensive writing.

COMPREHENSION

Developing students who can understand what they read is a primary goal of reading instruction. This goal should be prominent beginning with the introduction to stories and books in the preschool years. Even so, it definitely becomes a more prominent purpose for literacy instruction during the middle and upper elementary grades, with a number of aspects of reading that can be stimulated to improve comprehension (Pressley, 2000).

Fluent Word Recognition

When a reader cannot decode a word, it is impossible for the reader to understand it (Adams, 1990; Metsala & Ehri, 1998; Pressley, 1998, chap. 6). When young readers are first learning to recognize words—either by blending individual sounds or blending sounds and chunks—such decoding takes a lot of effort, and hence it consumes much of the reader's attention. This situation is a problem because human beings can only attend to a limited number of tasks at once (Miller, 1956). If that attention is totally devoted to word recognition, nothing is left over for comprehending the word, let alone the higher-order ideas encoded in sentences, paragraphs, and whole texts (LaBerge & Samuels, 1974). Thus, for comprehension to be high, not only must young readers learn how to recognize words, but they also must become fluent in word recognition (National Reading Panel, 2000). Although not every analysis has confirmed that comprehension improves as word recognition fluency improves (Fleisher, Jenkins, & Pany, 1979; Samuels, Dahl, & Archwamety, 1974; Yuill & Oakhill, 1988, 1991), some recent and especially well-done analyses have produced data in which fluency and comprehension have covaried (Breznitz, 1997a, 1997b; Tan & Nicholson, 1997). Unfortunately, little is known about how to develop fluency

beyond the fact that fluency generally increases with additional practice in reading (National Reading Panel, 2000).

Vocabulary

People with more extensive vocabularies understand text better than do individuals with less well-developed vocabularies (Anderson & Freebody, 1981; Nagy, Anderson, & Herman, 1987). In fact, some experimental studies have even suggested that the development of vocabulary knowledge resulted in improved comprehension (Beck, Perfetti, & McKeown, 1982; McKeown, Beck, Omanson, & Perfetti, 1983; McKeown, Beck, Omanson, & Pople, 1985). Although vocabulary is often taught extensively in school, for the most part, vocabulary is acquired incidentally as a by-product of encountering words in text and in real-world interactions (Sternberg, 1987). There have been a number of demonstrations that vocabulary knowledge increases with how much a reader reads (Dickinson & Smith, 1994; Elley, 1989; Fleisher et al., 1979; Pellegrini, Galda, Perlmutter, & Jones, 1994; Robbins & Ehri, 1994; Rosenhouse, Feitelson, Kita, & Goldstein, 1997; Valdez-Menchaca & Whitehurst, 1992; Whitehurst et al., 1988).

Comprehension Strategies

When mature readers are asked to think aloud as they read, they report using many strategies before, during, and after they read as part of processing the text. These processes include predicting what will be in the text based on prior knowledge and ideas encountered in the text already, constructing mental images of ideas expressed in the text, seeking clarification when confused, summarizing the text, and thinking about how ideas in the text might be used later (Pressley & Afflerbach, 1995). Because good readers consciously use such strategies, it was sensible to teach such strategies to young readers, with the hypothesis that the reading comprehension of young readers would improve following such instruction; that is exactly what happens.

There were many studies in the 1970s and 1980s in which a particular strategic process was taught to students in the elementary grades with comprehension and memory of texts that were read and then tested. These studies included those in which students were encouraged to activate prior knowledge (Levin & Pressley, 1981), generate questions as they read (Rosenshine & Trapman, 1992), construct mental images (Gambrell & Bales, 1986; Gambrell & Jawitz, 1993; Pressley, 1976), summarize (Armbruster, Anderson, & Ostertag, 1987; Bean & Steenwyk, 1984; Berkowitz, 1986; Brown & Day, 1983; Brown, Day, & Jones, 1983; Taylor, 1982; Taylor &

Beach, 1984), and analyze stories into component parts (Idol, 1987; Idol & Croll, 1987; Short & Ryan, 1984). In general, all of these strategies proved to improve comprehension and memory of texts when taught to elementary readers who did not use such approaches on their own.

The problem with single-strategy instruction, however, is that good readers do not use single strategies to understand text; rather, they use a repertoire of strategies (Pressley & Afflerbach, 1995). Thus, in the early to middle 1980s, researchers began experimenting with teaching repertoires of strategies to elementary-level readers. Perhaps the best known of these efforts was reciprocal teaching, developed by Palincsar and Brown (1984). Small groups of students met together to practice four strategies to read text: They predicted what would be in the text, asked questions about the content of the text, sought clarification when confused, and summarized the text. Although at first the teacher modeled the strategies and led the group in applying them to text, control of the strategies was quickly transferred to the members of the group; the members took turns leading the group as they read. The leader made predictions, asked questions, and attempted summaries; the leader also asked for clarification questions from group members and for predictions about what might be coming next in the text. The assumption was that by participating approximately 20 sessions of reciprocal teaching, students would internalize the reciprocal teaching strategies and come to use them when they read on their own.

Reciprocal teaching did increase use of the cognitive processes that were taught (i.e., prediction, questioning, seeking clarification, summarization). With respect to performance on standardized tests, the approach produced more modest benefits. In general, reciprocal teaching was more successful when there was more up-front teaching of the four component strategies by the teacher (Rosenshine & Meister, 1994).

In general, when researchers directly taught elementary students to use repertoires of comprehension strategies, students have shown increases in comprehension. Teachers who teach comprehension strategies effectively begin by explaining and modeling the strategies for their students (Roehler & Duffy, 1984)—typically by introducing a repertoire of strategies over the course of several months or a semester (e.g., introducing previewing, then connecting to prior knowledge, generating mental images about text meaning, asking questions, seeking clarification when confused, and summarizing). Often, these strategies are practiced in small groups of readers, and the students choose which strategies to carry out and when to do so. Thus, as students read a story aloud, they also think aloud about which strategies they are employing to understand the text. Sometimes other students in the group

react—perhaps coming up with a different mental image from that reported by the reader or perhaps using a different strategy altogether. Such discussions result in readers' getting a great deal out of a reading; they learn the literal meaning of the story but also have a chance to reflect on alternative interpretations of the story (Brown, Pressley, Van Meter, & Schuder, 1996). By practicing such strategies together, the individual members of the reading group gradually internalize the comprehension processes that are modeled and discussed (Pressley, El-Dinary, et al., 1992). In general, reading comprehension improves as a function of such teaching (Anderson, 1992; Brown et al., 1996; Collins, 1991). This form of teaching has become known as *transactional strategies instruction* (Pressley, El-Dinary, et al., 1992) because it encourages reader transactions with text (Rosenblatt, 1978), interpretations constructed by several readers interacting (transacting) together (Hutchins, 1991), and teachers and group members reacting to each others' perspectives (i.e., interactions were transactional; Bell, 1968).

Summary

High comprehension involves both word-level processes and processes above the word level. Fluent reading of words and extensive vocabulary are critical for readers to be able to understand demanding texts. Good readers, however, do much more than read words. They predict what will be in text, relate information in text to their prior knowledge, ask questions, summarize the big ideas in a text, and monitor whether they are understanding text. In short, good readers are very active as they make sense of text. The way to develop good comprehension in students is to encourage a great deal of reading to increase fluency, develop the readers' vocabulary, and teach them to use the comprehension strategies that good readers use. All of these competencies can be developed beginning in the early to middle elementary years.

WRITING

In recent decades, writing instruction in school has become commonplace, stimulated in large part by a language arts curriculum reform movement that argued for a broader view of literacy than simply reading (e.g., Atwell, 1987; Calkins, 1986; Graves, 1983). Yes, elements of writing such as grammar and spelling have been taught in school since the beginning of the institution; the thrust in recent decades, however, has been to encourage students, beginning in kindergarten, to develop and write whole pieces—both stories and expositions. One assumption is that a lot of learning of lower-level mechanics can occur in the context of writing real stories and essays.

Young children have much to learn about writing as composing. Many K–12 writers do not formulate a clear writing goal before they begin writing (i.e., they do not know what they want to say; Langer, 1986, chap. 3). Also, young writers often do not take into consideration the perspective of potential readers (e.g., Bereiter, 1980). These failures in planning are compounded by failures to revise first drafts; a K–12 student's first draft of a story or essay is often the final draft as well (Bereiter & Scardamalia, 1987; Fitzgerald, 1987). The coherence of writing does indeed improve with age during the K–12 years (Langer, 1986; Stahl, 1977); still, much so-called knowledge telling at the end of the elementary years continues into the secondary school years, with young writers simply adding ideas to essays willy-nilly as the ideas come to mind (Bereiter & Scardamalia, 1987; Emig, 1971; Pianko, 1979; Scardamalia & Bereiter, 1986). Even the best of high school writers tend to produce essays with a simple structure: Often, high school essays consist of a thesis statement, followed by several paragraphs, each of which makes one point. The writer then closes with a single-paragraph summary and conclusion (Applebee, 1984; Durst, 1984; Marshall, 1984).

Scholars interested in the development of composition skills reasoned that it was the attention to mechanics rather than to holistic composition that was the culprit behind the unimpressive writing typically occurring in school—that is, holistic composition skills were typically not taught before the 1980s. Moreover, the most frequent type of writing assignment in school did not demand much in the way of planning or revision; rather, it encourages students simply to dump knowledge—that is, the most typical writing assignment in school is to write a few sentences in reaction to short-answer questions on study guides or tests, with the evaluation of answers based on content rather than form (Applebee, 1984; Langer & Applebee, 1984, 1987; Marshall, 1984). When form does matter, typically spelling and punctuation count more than does overall organization of the writing, which does not encourage students to be attentive to the higher-order organizational aspects of writing (Langer, 1986).

An important analysis of composition was carried out by Flower and Hayes (1980, 1981). They directed college-level writing teachers and college freshmen to think aloud as they wrote. The most striking and important finding in the study was that excellent writers viewed writing as problem-solving; planning, drafting, and revision were the three processes required to solve the problem of creating a composition. Moreover, Flower and Hayes observed that good writers did not simply cycle through these processes in a linear fashion; rather, they used the processes recursively—some planning, then some drafting, followed by more planning, some drafting, and then some revision, which makes it clear that still more

planning and drafting are required, and so on until the writer is satisfied with the product. In contrast to the college writing teachers, freshmen were much less likely to have clear goals before beginning to write; they did less planning and revision than did the teachers; knowledge telling was more prominent in the student writing than in the teachers' writing. Attention to mechanics was prominent throughout writing for the students; in contrast, college writing teachers only worried about mechanics as they were nearing the end of writing, seeing it as part of the polishing process. The Flower and Hayes work provided both a clear vision of the nature of excellent writing and a vivid understanding about how the writing of beginning college students falls far short of the expert ideal.

Curriculum developers took notice of the Flower and Hayes' work. In particular, scholars identifying with the whole language approach to beginning language arts began to encourage much writing every day (Atwell, 1987; Calkins, 1986; Graves, 1983). The role of the teacher in this effort was largely to coach students during revision—providing prompts to student writers to revise spelling, grammar, and capitalization, and of course minilessons on these topics when they were required. Even so, instruction to plan, draft, and revise was less prominent in the whole language efforts than it was in other approaches to teaching of writing.

One notable approach was dubbed *cognitive strategy instruction in writing* (CSIW) by its creators (Englert, Raphael, Anderson, Anthony, & Stevens, 1991). Englert et al. particularly focused on expository writing. There was a great deal of teacher explanation about writing structures for conveying ideas (e.g., teaching of compare-and-contrast essay structures). Teachers often would share examples of good and poor essays with students, thinking aloud as they worked on revising such essays. Such thinking aloud was central as the teachers modeled the construction and revision of expositions. Thus, during planning, the teacher modeled the use of a series of questions that should be on the mind of anyone preparing to write an essay: Students saw the teacher reflecting on the questions *Who am I writing for?, Why am I writing this?, What do I know?, How can I group my ideas?,* and *How will I organize my ideas?* If such direct explanation and modeling of strategies seems familiar, it should, since Englert et al. (1991) were very much influenced by their Michigan State colleague Gerry Duffy, who developed the direct explanation and modeling approach to comprehension instruction covered earlier in this chapter. Just as such direct explanation of strategies improved comprehension, it also improved essay writing in Englert et al. (1991) relative to students not receiving such instruction, with the study taking place over an entire school year. In particular, the essays of students (both regular-education students and those with reading disabilities) taught to plan, draft, and revise were judged to convey their messages better overall. In recent years, a number of replications have supported the general finding that teaching elementary students to plan, draft, and revise improves writing (Harris & Graham, 1996).

Most striking, effective writing instruction for elementary students provides detailed guidance and support about how to plan, draft, and revise (e.g., De La Paz & Graham, 1997; Graham, 1997). Thus, one effective instruction for stimulating story writing involved providing prompts for each part of a story. Thus, young writers were taught to respond to the following questions as they wrote (Harris & Graham, 1996): Who is the main character? Who else is in the story? When does the story take place? Where does the story take place? What does the main character do or want to do? What do other characters do? What happens when the main character does or tries to do it? What happens with the other characters? How does the story end? How does the main character feel? How do other characters feel?

In summary, psychological research has greatly informed the teaching of writing in elementary schools; a substantial body of research validates the plan, draft, and revise model. Most impressively, writing researchers have been able to demonstrate consistent benefits for children experiencing great problems with writing, including those classified as reading and writing disabled (Harris & Graham, 1996).

ENCOURAGING ADULT LITERACY

Adults in need of literacy instruction vary greatly. Some require basic, word-level instruction, whereas others can read words but do not understand very well what they read. Many adults have not learned to compose well enough to express themselves well in writing.

Basic, Word-Level Difficulties

Many adults cannot read at all. Although the problem is especially acute in many developing countries, adult illiteracy in the industrialized world is common as well; persons who are illiterate suffer economically and psychologically because of their condition. A number of countries and their political leaders view literacy development as a key to their economic development and general betterment; hence, national literacy campaigns have been common in developing countries (Bhola, 1999; Wagner, 1999; Windham, 1999). Some who particularly identify with the masses in developing countries conceive of literacy development as a powerful political tool—one with the potential to empower the masses (Freire & Macedo, 1987).

Religious groups have also been interested in developing literacy in many underdeveloped regions as part of their evangelization efforts, recognizing that people who can read religious texts are more likely to become converts than are people who cannot (Venezky, 1999).

In some U.S. locales, for example, as much as 10–20% of the population lacks the most basic literacy skills (National Institute for Literacy, 1998). In recent years, the negative economic impact of these illiterate citizens has been emphasized as a motivation for addressing problems of adult literacy in America (Hull & Grubb, 1999). Most conspicuously, illiterate adults are much less employable than are people who can read and write, and they are also certainly less able to meet the demands of an ever more technological world.

Unfortunately, many adults who are illiterate have low psychometric intelligence, and no dramatic advances have been made in understanding how to develop reading and writing skills in illiterate adults who have low intelligence. What is offered to most adult illiterates—ones who cannot read at all—is very basic instruction in word recognition skills; groups such as Literacy Volunteers of America (LVA) and Laubach have been prominent in these efforts. This approach makes conceptual sense: The core problem for most illiterate adults—if they have at least average intelligence—is their ability to recognize words, and they have great difficulties in mapping the letters in words to component sounds and blending them (Bell & Perfetti, 1994; Elbro, Nielsen, & Petersen, 1994; Greenberg, Ehri, & Perin, 1997). Thus, there is good reason to believe that most normally intelligent adults who cannot read words could learn to do so with systematic instruction in the sounding out of words (e.g., Vellutino et al., 1996), if only these nonreaders would be willing to stay the course of basic letter- and word-level instruction—that is, many adult education programs focusing on basic reading have difficulty keeping students enrolled because the instruction is not very motivating (i.e., letter-sound drills and drilling on sight vocabulary bores many adults). Recent efforts to make such instruction attractive to adult learners have focused on use of technology in instruction, although much of the technology now available is running skill and drill routines much like the human skill and drill instruction that has failed previously to hold adults in basic reading education (Askov & Bixler, 1998).

Comprehension Difficulties

Although adults who cannot read words at all are saliently illiterate, many other adults can read words but do not comprehend or remember very well what they read. Other adults have great difficulty expressing themselves in writing. Adults who have difficulties with comprehension and writing are especially challenged by the demands of higher education; hence, it is during higher education that their problems are being addressed. Most contemporary institutions of higher education offer remedial reading, writing, and study skills courses. Although such efforts have more than a century of precedence in higher education, their prevalence increased throughout the twentieth century (Stahl & King, 2000), so that even the most elite of colleges and universities now offer such instruction. Such instruction early in the college career is important for many students because college requires reading of textbooks that are more demanding than are those encountered in high school, reading of genres never encountered before (e.g., journal articles), and—increasingly—interaction with electronic sources of information (Pugh, Pawan, & Antommarchi, 2000).

College reading, writing, and study skills courses—at their best—are informed by a substantial research literature on the improvement of reading, writing, and study skills in adults. Much of college-level remedial reading involves teaching students classic comprehension strategies (Nist & Holschuh, 2000). Thus, because most students are confronted with textbooks containing many related ideas, study skills courses typically teach students how to construct concept maps or outlines (Caverly, Orlando, & Mullen, 2000; Nist & Holschuh, 2000). The students are taught to devise maps or outlines that indicate relationships between ideas in the text, including hierarchical ideas as well as cause-and-effect relationships, sequences, and simple listings of ideas. Although such mapping has the benefit of forcing students to attend to relationships specified in text (Lipson, 1995), it can be very challenging to some students to identify the relationships that need to be mapped (Hadwin & Winne, 1996)—that is, concept mapping can make ideas clearer and more memorable, but if a student has real problems with text comprehension, she or he may not be able to produce much of a concept map. Students in study skills courses are also taught to underline, highlight, and annotate text selectively; again, however, doing so effectively requires understanding the material (e.g., Caverly et al., 2000; Nist & Kirby, 1989).

There are also a variety of strategies that require readers to work actively with text. Thus, elaborative rehearsal requires the reader to restate the text as she or he would if teaching a class (Simpson, 1994). Readers can be taught to self-test themselves on material they have read (Weinstein, 1994), which requires both rehearsal of material and confronting ideas that are not yet known (see Pressley, Borkowski, & O'Sullivan, 1984, 1985, for coverage of how testing increases awareness of what is known and unknown). Readers can also be taught to figure out why ideas and relationships in text make sense, rather than passively accepting facts and relationships as stated—an approach known as *elaborative interrogation* (see Menke & Pressley, 1994; Pressley, Wood, et al., 1992). Perhaps the most widely disseminated study skills approach is SQ3R (Robinson, 1946), which stands for *survey the text, ask questions about what might be in the text, read the text, recite it, and review it.*

Do such reading strategies work? Each of the strategies works under some circumstances, with some types of readers, and with some types of texts. Some require extensive instruction in order for students to learn them, such as the complex SQ3R (Caverly et al., 2000; Nist & Kirby, 1989). Most studies skills experts recommend teaching such strategies not alone, but rather in conjunction with other procedures intended to keep students on task, such as time management techniques. In addition, many studies skills programs also include teaching of vocabulary to increase comprehension, recognizing that many struggling college readers do not know the words they need to know in order to comprehend readings encountered in college (Simpson & Randall, 2000). For example, students are often taught the important Latin and Greek root words as an aid to understanding new vocabulary; also, they can be taught how to make use of context clues in sentences and paragraphs (Simpson & Randall, 2000).

Of course, a key ingredient in any program to enhance comprehension has to be reading itself. Like all skills, reading improves with practice. So do component competencies of reading. Thus, a great deal of incidental learning of vocabulary occurs during reading (Nagy, 1988; Sternberg, 1987), and this incidental learning makes future comprehension easier.

Writing Difficulties

With respect to writing, many college-age writers do not plan, draft, and revise (Flower et al., 1990). More positively, at least at selective universities, such as Carnegie-Mellon (i.e., where Flower et al.'s 1990 work was carried out), a sizable portion—perhaps 40% of students—do at least some planning before they write; they think about the goal of writing and how that goal can be accomplished as well as the information they need to accomplish the goal. That the majority of students at elite schools and a much higher proportion at less selective universities (see Rose, 1989, chap. 7) need instruction in all aspects of the composing process has stimulated the development of college writing programs that teach students how to plan, draft, and revise as part of composition, and one of the best developed of these was devised at Carnegie-Mellon (Flower, 1997). A variety of alternative approaches to teaching of college writing are available to students in need of assistance (Valeri-Gold & Deming, 2000), although few well-controlled evaluations of these programs are currently available.

Summary

Although some research has examined how to improve word-level problems in adults as well as their comprehension and writing difficulties, much remains left to learn. With the expansion of instructional opportunities for adults in need of literacy instruction, the need is greater than ever for research on adult literacy and how it can be enhanced. Society is willing to provide the resources for adult literacy instruction; research must provide interventions worth delivering to adults who need to improve their reading and writing skills.

CLOSING COMMENTS

Much has been learned about reading and writing and how it can be enhanced, beginning with infancy and extending into adulthood. That said, enormous gaps still remain in understanding literacy. For example, more is known about teaching word recognition skills to struggling young readers than is known about how such instruction affects normal and gifted readers. Finding out what difference word recognition instruction makes to such populations is important because society and the institution of schooling increasingly favors extensive, explicit decoding instruction for all primary-level students. Similarly, although much has been learned about how to increase comprehension in elementary students, we still do not know how to develop teachers who can deliver such instruction well and who will deliver it faithfully. What we do know is that such instruction is very challenging for many teachers (Pressley & El-Dinary, 1997). The many research successes in the area of literacy research and instruction should go far in stimulating a great deal of additional research in the next quarter century; such work is necessary because the research of the twentieth century permitted much progress in understanding literacy without providing definitive understanding about how to prevent literacy difficulties and failures. Many children and adults continue to struggle to be readers and writers, which is an increasingly serious situation because our technologically driven society demands greater literacy competencies in every new generation.

REFERENCES

Adams, M. J. (1990). *Beginning to read.* Cambridge, MA: Harvard University Press.

Adams, M. J., Treiman, R., & Pressley, M. (1998). Reading, writing, and literacy. In I. Sigel & A. Renninger (Eds.), *Handbook of child psychology: Vol. 4. Child psychology in practice* (pp. 275–355). New York: Wiley.

Afflerbach, P. (2000). Verbal reports and verbal protocol analysis. In M. L. Kamil, P. B. Mosenthal, P. D. Pearson, & R. Barr (Eds.), *Handbook of reading research* (Vol. 3, pp. 163–179). Mahwah, NJ: Erlbaum.

Alexander, A., Anderson, H., Heilman, P. C., Voeller, K. S., & Torgesen, J. K. (1991). Phonological awareness training and remediation of analytic decoding deficits in a group of severe dyslexics. *Annals of Dyslexia, 41,* 193–206.

Alvermann, D. E. (2000). Narrative approaches. In M. L. Kamil, P. B. Mosenthal, P. D. Pearson, & R. Barr (Eds.), *Handbook of reading research* (Vol. 3, pp. 123–139). Mahwah, NJ: Erlbaum.

Anderson, D. R., & Collins, P. A. (1988). *The impact on children's education: Television's influence on cognitive development* (Office of Research Working Paper No. 2). Washington, DC: U.S. Department of Education, Office of Educational Research and Improvement.

Anderson, R. C., & Freebody, P. (1981). Vocabulary knowledge. In J. T. Guthrie (Ed.), *Comprehension and teaching: Research reviews* (pp. 77–117). Newark, DE: International Reading Association.

Anderson, V. (1992). A teacher development project in transactional strategy instruction for teachers of severely reading-disabled adolescents. *Teaching and Teacher Education, 8,* 391–403.

Applebee, A. N. (1984). *Contexts for learning to write.* Norwood, NJ: Ablex.

Applebee, A. N., & Langer, J. A. (1983). Instructional scaffolding: Reading and writing as natural language activities. *Language Arts, 60,* 168–175.

Armbruster, B. B., Anderson, T. H., & Ostertag, J. (1987). Does text structure/summarization instruction facilitate learning from expository text? *Reading Research Quarterly, 22,* 331–346.

Askov, E. N., & Bixler, B. (1998). Transforming adult literacy instruction through computer-assisted instruction. In D. Reinking, M. C. McKenna, L. D. Labbo, & R. D. Kieffer (Eds.), *Handbook of literacy and technology* (pp. 167–184). Mahwah, NJ: Erlbaum.

Atwell, N. (1987). *In the middle: Reading, writing, and learning from adolescents.* Portsmouth, NH: Heinemann.

Ball, E. W., & Blachman, B. A. (1988). Phoneme segmentation training: Effect on reading readiness. *Annals of Dyslexia, 38,* 203–225.

Ball, E. W., & Blachman, B. A. (1991). Does phoneme segmentation training in kindergarten make a difference in early word recognition and developmental spelling? *Reading Research Quarterly, 26,* 49–66.

Ball, S., & Bogatz, G. A. (1970). *The first year of "Sesame Street": An evaluation.* Princeton, NJ: Educational Testing Service.

Barker, T. A., & Torgesen, J. K. (1995). The evaluation of computer-assisted instruction in phonological awareness with below average readers. *Journal of Educational Computing Research, 13,* 89–103.

Barr, R., Kamil, M. L., Mosenthal, P. B., & Pearson, P. D. (Eds.). (1991). *Handbook of reading research* (Vol. 2). New York: Longman.

Bean, T. W., & Steenwyk, F. L. (1984). The effect of three forms of summarization instruction on sixth graders' summary writing and comprehension. *Journal of Reading Behavior, 16,* 297–306.

Beck, I. L., Perfetti, C. A., & McKeown, M. G. (1982). Effects of long-term vocabulary instruction on lexical access and reading comprehension. *Journal of Educational Psychology, 74,* 506–521.

Bell, L. C., & Perfetti, C. A. (1994). Reading skill: Some adult comparisons. *Journal of Educational Psychology, 86,* 344–355.

Bell, R. Q. (1968). A reinterpretation of the direction of effects in studies of socialization. *Psychological Review, 75,* 81–95.

Bereiter, C. (1980). Development in writing. In L. W. Gregg & E. R. Steinberg (Eds.), *Cognitive processes in writing* (pp. 73–93). Hillsdale, NJ: Erlbaum.

Bereiter, C., & Scardamalia, M. (1987). *The psychology of written communication.* Hillsdale, NJ: Erlbaum.

Berkowitz, S. J. (1986). Effects of instruction in text organization on sixth-grade students' memory for expository reading. *Reading Research Quarterly, 21,* 161–178.

Bhola, H. S. (1999). Literacy campaigns: A policy perspective. In D. A. Wagner, R. L. Venezky, & B. V. Street (Eds.), *Literacy: An international handbook* (pp. 288–293). Boulder, CO: Westview Press.

Blachman, B. A. (1991). Phonological awareness: Implications for prereading and early reading instruction. In S. A. Brady & D. P. Shankweiler (Eds.), *Phonological processes in literacy: A tribute to Isabelle Y. Liberman* (pp. 29–36). Hillsdale, NJ: Erlbaum.

Bogatz, G. A., & Ball, S. (1971). *The second year of "Sesame Street": A continuing evaluation.* Princeton, NJ: Educational Testing Service.

Bowey, J. A. (1995). Socioeconomic status differences in preschool phonological sensitivity and first-grade reading achievement. *Journal of Educational Psychology, 87,* 476–487.

Bowlby, J. (1969). *Attachment and loss: Vol. 1. Attachment.* New York: Basic.

Bradley, L. (1989). Predicting learning disabilities. In J. Dumont & H. Nakken (Eds.), *Learning disabilities: Vol. 2. Cognitive, social, and remedial aspects* (pp. 1–18). Amsterdam: Swets.

Bradley, L., & Bryant, P. E. (1983). Categorizing sounds and learning to read—a causal connection. *Nature, 301,* 419–421.

Bradley, L., & Bryant, P. E. (1991). Phonological skills before and after learning to read. In S. A. Brady & D. P. Shankweiler (Eds.), *Phonological processes in literacy: A tribute to Isabelle Y. Liberman* (pp. 37–45). Hillsdale, NJ: Erlbaum.

Breznitz, Z. (1997a). Effects of accelerated reading rate on memory for text among dyslexic readers. *Journal of Educational Psychology, 89,* 289–297.

Breznitz, Z. (1997b). Enhancing the reading of dyslexic children by reading acceleration and auditory masking. *Journal of Educational Psychology, 89,* 103–113.

Brown, A. L., & Day, J. D. (1983). Macrorules for summarizing texts: The development of expertise. *Journal of Verbal Learning and Verbal Behavior, 22,* 1–14.

Brown, A. L., Day, J. D., & Jones, R. S. (1983). The development of plans for summarizing texts. *Child Development, 54,* 968–979.

Brown, R., Pressley, M., Van Meter, P., & Schuder, T. (1996). A quasi-experimental validation of transactional strategies instruction with low-achieving second grade readers. *Journal of Educational Psychology, 88,* 18–37.

Bruck, M., & Treiman, R. (1992). Learning to pronounce words: The limits of analogies. *Reading Research Quarterly, 27,* 374–398.

Bus, A. G., & van IJendoorn, M. H. (1988). Mother-child interactions, attachment, and emergent literacy: A cross-sectional study. *Child Development, 59,* 1262–1272.

Bus, A. G., & van IJzendoorn, M. H. (1995). Mothers reading to their 3-year-olds: The role of mother-child attachement security in becoming literate. *Reading Research Quarterly, 30,* 998–1015.

Bus, A. G., & van IJzendoorn, M. H. (1999). Phonological awareness and early reading: A meta-analysis of experimental training studies. *Journal of Educational Psychology, 91,* 403–414.

Bus, A. G., van IJzendoorn, M. H., & Pellegrini, A. D. (1995). Joint book reading makes for success in learning to read: A meta-analysis on intergenerational transmission of literacy. *Review of Educational Research, 65,* 1–21.

Byrne, B., & Fielding-Barnsley, R. (1991). Evaluation of a program to teach phonemic awareness to young children. *Journal of Educational Psychology, 83,* 451–455.

Byrne, B., & Fielding-Barnsley, R. (1993). Evaluation of a program to teach phonemic awareness to young children: A 1-year followup. *Journal of Educational Psychology, 85,* 104–111.

Byrne, B., & Fielding-Barnsley, R. (1995). Evaluation of a program to teach phonemic awareness to young children: A 2- and 3-year followup and a new preschool trial. *Journal of Educational Psychology, 87,* 488–503.

Calkins, L. M. (1986). *The art of teaching writing.* Portsmouth, NH: Heinemann.

Caverly, D. C., Orlando, V. P., & Mullen, J.-A. L. (2000). Textbook study reading. In R. F. Flippo & D. C. Caverly (Eds.), *Handbook of college reading and study strategy research* (pp. 105–147). Mahwah, NJ: Erlbaum.

Chall, J. S. (1967). *Learning to read: The great debate.* New York: McGraw-Hill.

Chall, J. S. (1983). *Learning to read: The great debate* (Rev. ed.). New York: McGraw-Hill.

Clay, M. M. (1991). *Becoming literate: The construction of inner control.* Portsmouth, NH: Heinemann.

Clay, M. M. (1993). *Reading recovery: A guidebook for teachers in training.* Portsmouth, NH: Heinemann.

Cochran-Smith, M. (1984). *The making of a reader.* Norwood, NJ: Ablex.

Collins, C. (1991). Reading instruction that increases thinking abilities. *Journal of Reading, 34,* 510–516.

Crain-Thoresen, C., & Dale, P. S. (1995, April). *Parent vs. staff storybook reading as an intervention for language delay.* Paper presented at the biennial meeting of the Society for Research in Child Development, Indianapolis, IN.

Cronin, V., Farrell, D., & Delaney, M. (1995, April). *Environmental print facilitates word reading.* Paper presented at the biennial meeting of the Society for Research in Child Development, Indianapolis, IN.

Cunningham, A. E. (1990). Explicit versus implicit instruction in phonemic awareness. *Journal of Experimental Child Psychology, 50,* 429–444.

De La Paz, S., & Graham, S. (1997). Effects of dictation and advanced planning instruction on the composing of students with writing and learning problems. *Journal of Educational Psychology, 89,* 203–222.

Dickinson, D. K., & Smith, M. W. (1994). Long-term effects of preschool teachers' book readings on low-income children's vocabulary and story comprehension. *Reading Research Quarterly, 29,* 104–122.

Duffy, G. G., Roehler, L. R., Sivan, E., Rackliffe, G., Book, C., Meloth, M., Vavrus, L. G., Wesselman, R., Putnam, J., & Bassiri, D. (1987). Effects of explaining the reasoning associated with using reading strategies. *Reading Research Quarterly, 22,* 347–368.

Dunning, D. B., Mason, J. M., & Stewart, J. P. (1994). Reading to preschoolers: A response to Scarborough & Dobrich (1994) and recommendations for future research. *Developmental Review, 14,* 424–339.

Durst, R. K. (1984). The development of analytic writing. In A. N. Applebee (Ed.), *Contexts for learning to write: Studies of secondary school instruction* (pp. 79–102). Norwood, NJ: Ablex.

Ehri, L. C. (1991). Development of the ability to read words. In R. Barr, M. L. Kamil, P. B. Mosenthal, & P. D. Pearson (Eds.), *Handbook of reading research* (Vol. 2, pp. 383–417). New York: Longman.

Ehri, L. C., & Robbins, C. (1992). Beginners need some decoding skill to read words by analogy. *Reading Research Quarterly, 27,* 12–27.

Ehri, L. C., & Wilce, L. S. (1987a). Does learning to spell help beginners learn to read words? *Reading Research Quarterly, 18,* 47–65.

Ehri, L. C., & Wilce, L. S. (1987b). Cipher versus cue reading: An experiment in decoding acquisition. *Journal of Educational Psychology, 79,* 3–13.

Elbaum, B., Vaughn, S., Hughes, M. T., & Moody, S. W. (2000). How effective are one-to-one tutoring programs in reading for elementary students at risk for reading failure? A meta-analysis of the intervention research. *Journal of Educational Psychology, 92,* 605–619.

Elbro, C., Nielsen, I., & Petersen, D. K. (1994). Dyslexia in adults: Evidence for deficits in non-word reading and in the phonological representation of lexical items. *Annals of Dyslexia, 44,* 205–226.

Elley, W. B. (1989). Vocabulary acquisition from listening to stories. *Reading Research Quarterly, 24,* 174–187.

Emig, J. (1971). *The composition process of twelfth graders.* Urbana, IL: National Council of Teachers of English.

Englert, C. S., Raphael, T. E., Anderson, L. M., Anthony, H. M., & Stevens, D. D. (1991). Making strategies and self-talk visible: Writing instruction in regular and special education classrooms. *American Educational Research Journal, 28,* 337–372.

Fitzgerald, J. (1987). Research on revision in writing. *Review of Educational Research, 57,* 481–506.

Fleisher, L., Jenkins, J., & Pany, D. (1979). Effects on poor readers' comprehension of training in rapid decoding. *Reading Research Quarterly, 15,* 30–48.

Flippo, R. F., & Caverly, D. C. (2000). *Handbook of college reading and study strategy research.* Mahwah, NJ: Erlbaum.

Flood, J. (1977). Parental styles in reading episodes with young children. *Reading Teacher, 30,* 864–867.

Florio-Ruane, S., & McVee, M. (2000). Ethnographic approaches to literacy research. In M. L. Kamil, P. B. Mosenthal, P. D. Pearson, & R. Barr (Eds.), *Handbook of reading research* (Vol. 3, pp. 153–162). Mahwah, NJ: Erlbaum.

Flower, L. (1997). *Problem-solving strategies for writing in college and community.* New York: Harcourt, Brace, Jovanovich College & School Division.

Flower, L., & Hayes, J. (1980). The dynamics of composing: Making plans and juggling constraints. In L. Gregg & E. Steinberg (Eds.), *Cognitive processes in writing* (pp. 31–50). Hillsdale, NJ: Erlbaum.

Flower, L., & Hayes, J. (1981). A cognitive process theory of writing. *College Composition and Communication, 32,* 365–387.

Flower, L., Stein, V., Ackerman, J., Kantz, M. J., McCormick, K., & Peck, W. C. (1990). *Reading to write: Exploring a cognitive and social process.* New York: Oxford University Press.

Foorman, B. R., Francis, D. J., Fletcher, J. M., Schatschneider, C., & Mehta, P. (1998). The role of instruction in learning to read: Preventing reading failure in at-risk children. *Journal of Educational Psychology, 90,* 37–55.

Foorman, B., Francis, D., Novy, D., & Liberman, D. (1991). How letter-sound instruction mediates progress in first-grade reading and spelling. *Journal of Educational Psychology, 83,* 456–469.

Foster, K. C., Erickson, G. C., Foster, D. F., Brinkman, D., & Torgesen, J. K. (1994). Computer administered instruction in phonological awareness: Evaluation of the *DaisyQuest* program. *Journal of Research and Development in Education, 27,* 126–137.

Fox, B., & Routh, D. K. (1975). Analyzing spoken language into words, syllables, and phonemes: A developmental study. *Journal of Psycholinguistic Research, 4,* 331–342.

Frankel, K. A., & Bates, J. E. (1990). Mother-toddler problem-solving: Antecedents in attachment, home behavior, and temperament. *Child Development, 61,* 810–819.

Freire, P., & Macedo, D. (1987). *Literacy: Reading the word and the world.* Granby MA: Bergin & Garvey.

Gaffney, J. S., & Anderson, R. C. (2000). Trends in reading research in the United States: Changing intellectual currents over three decades. In M. L. Kamil, P. B. Mosenthal, P. D. Pearson, & R. Barr (Eds.), *Handbook of reading research* (Vol. 3, pp. 53–74). Mahwah, NJ: Erlbaum.

Gambrell, L. B., & Bales, R. J. (1986). Mental imagery and the comprehension-monitoring performance of fourth- and fifth-grade poor readers. *Reading Research Quarterly, 21,* 454–464.

Gambrell, L. B., & Jawitz, P. B. (1993). Mental imagery, text illustrations, and children's comprehension and recall. *Reading Research Quarterly, 28,* 264–273.

Gibson, E. J., Gibson, J. J., Pick, A. D., & Osser, H. A. (1962). A developmental study of the discrimination of letter-like forms. *Journal of Comparative and Physiological Psychology, 55,* 897–906.

Gibson, E. J., & Levin, H. (1975). *The psychology of reading.* Cambridge, MA: MIT Press.

Gilbert, N., Spring, C., & Sassenrath, J. (1977). Effects of over-learning and similarity on transfer in word recognition. *Perceptual and Motor Skills, 44,* 591–598.

Goswami, U. (2000). Phonological and lexical processes. In M. L. Kamil, P. B. Mosenthal, P. D. Pearson, & R. Barr (Eds.), *Handbook of reading research* (Vol. 3, pp. 251–267). Mahwah, NJ: Erlbaum.

Graham, S. (1997). Executive control in the revising of students with learning and writing difficulties. *Journal of Educational Psychology, 89,* 223–234.

Graves, D. (1983). *Writing: Teachers and children at work.* Portsmouth, NH: Heinemann.

Greenberg, D., Ehri, L. C., & Perin, D. (1997). Are word reading processes the same or different in adult literacy students and 3rd-5th graders matched for reading level? *Journal of Educational Psychology, 89,* 262–275.

Griffith, P. L. (1991). Phonemic awareness helps first graders invent spellings and third graders remember correct spellings. *Journal of Reading Behavior, 23,* 215–233.

Guthrie, J. T., & Alvermann, D. A. (1999). *Engaged reading: Processes, practices, and policy implications.* New York: Teachers College Press.

Guthrie, J. T., & Wigfield, A. (2000). Motivation and reading. In M. L. Kamil, P. B. Mosenthal, P. D. Pearson, & R. Barr (Eds.), *Handbook of reading research* (Vol. 3, pp. 403–422). Mahwah, NJ: Erlbaum.

Hadwin, A. F., & Winne, P. H. (1996). Study strategies have meager support. *Journal of Higher Education, 67,* 692–715.

Harris, K. R., & Graham, S. (1996). *Making the writing process work: Strategies for composition and self-regulation.* Cambridge, MA: Brookline Books.

Harrison, C. (2000). Reading research in the United Kingdom. In M. L. Kamil, P. B. Mosenthal, P. D. Pearson, & R. Barr (Eds.), *Handbook of reading research* (Vol. 3, pp. 11–28). Mahwah, NJ: Erlbaum.

Hart, B., & Risley, T. R. (1995). *Meaningful differences in the everyday experience of young American children.* Baltimore: Brookes.

Hiebert, E. H. (1994). Reading Recovery in the United States: What difference does it make to an age cohort? *Educational Researcher, 23*(9), 15–25.

Hull, G., & Grubb, W. N. (1999). Literacy, skills, and work. In D. A. Wagner, R. L. Venezky, & B. V. Street (Eds.), *Literacy: An international handbook* (pp. 311–317). Boulder, CO: Westview Press.

Hutchins, E. (1991). The social organization of distributed cognition. In L. Resnick, J. M. Levine, & S. D. Teasley (Eds.), *Perspectives on socially shared cognition* (pp. 283–307). Washington, DC: American Psychological Association.

Idol, L. (1987). Group story mapping: A comprehension strategy for both skilled and unskilled readers. *Journal of Learning Disabilities, 20,* 196–205.

Idol, L., & Croll, V. J. (1987). Story-mapping training as a means of improving reading comprehension. *Learning Disability Quarterly, 10,* 214–229.

Iversen, S., & Tunmer, W. E. (1993). Phonological processing skills and the reading recovery program. *Journal of Educational Psychology, 85,* 112–120.

Juel, C. (1988). Learning to read and write: A longitudinal study of 54 children from first through fourth grades. *Journal of Educational Psychology, 80,* 417–447.

Kamil, M. L., Mosenthal, P. B., Pearson, P. D., & Barr, R. (Eds.). (2000). *Handbook of reading research* (Vol. 3). Mahwah, NJ: Erlbaum.

Kirsch, I., Jungeblut, A., Jenkins, L., & Kolstad, A. (Eds.). (1993). *Adult literacy in America: A first look at results of the National Adult Literacy Survey.* Washington, DC: National Center for Educational Statistics.

Langer, J. A. (1986). *Children reading and writing: Structures and strategies.* Norwood, NJ: Ablex.

Langer, J. A., & Applebee, A. N. (1984). Language, learning, and interaction: A framework for improving the teaching of writing. In A. N. Applebee (Ed.), *Contexts for learning to write: Studies of secondary school instruction* (pp. 169–181). Norwood, NJ: Ablex.

Langer, J. A., & Applebee, A. N. (1987). *How writing shapes thinking: A study of teaching and learning.* Champaign, IL: National Council of Teachers of English.

LaBerge, D., & Samuels, S. J. (1974). Toward a theory of automatic information processing in reading. *Cognitive Psychology, 6,* 293–323.

Levin, J. R., & Pressley, M. (1981). Improving childrens' prose comprehension: Selected strategies that seem to succeed. In C. M. Santa & B. L. Hayes (Eds.), *Children's prose comprehension: Research and practice* (pp. 44–71). Newark, DE: International Reading Association.

Lie, A. (1991). Effects of a training program for stimulating skills in word analysis in first-grade children. *Reading Research Quarterly, 26,* 234–250.

Lipson, M. (1995). The effect of semantic mapping instruction on prose comprehension of below-level college readers. *Reading Research and Instruction, 34,* 367–378.

Lonigan, C. J. (1994). Reading to preschoolers exposed: Is the emperor really naked? *Developmental Review, 14,* 303–323.

Lonigan, C. J., Anthony, J. L., & Burgess, S. R. (1995, April). *Exposure to print and preschool-age children's interest in literacy.* Paper presented at the biennial meeting of the Society for Research in Child Development, Indianapolis, IN.

Lovett, M. W., Borden, S. L., DeLuca, T., Lacerenza, L., Benson, N. J., & Brackstone, D. (1994). Treating the core deficits of developmental dyslexia: Evidence of transfer of learning after phonologically- and strategy-based reading training programs. *Developmental Psychology, 30,* 805–822.

Lovett, M. W., Lacerenza, L., Borden, S. L., Frijters, J. C., Steinbach, K. A., & DePalma, M. (2000). Components of effective remediation for developmental reading disabilities: Combing phonological and strategy based instruction to improve outcomes. *Journal of Educational Psychology, 92,* 263–283.

Lovett, M. W., Ransby, M. J., Hardwick, N., Johns, M. S., & Donaldson, S. A. (1989). Can dyslexia be treated? Treatment-specific and generalized treatment effects in dyslexic children's response to remediation. *Brain and Language, 37,* 90–121.

Lundberg, I., Frost, J., & Peterson, O. (1988). Effects of an extensive program for stimulating phonological awareness in preschool children. *Reading Research Quarterly, 23,* 263–284.

Lyons, C. A., Pinnell, G. S., & DeFord, D. E. (1993). *Partners in learning: Teachers and children in reading recovery.* New York: Teachers College Press.

Maclean, M., Bryant, P., & Bryant, L. (1987). Rhymes, nursery rhymes, and reading in early childhood. *Merrill-Palmer Quarterly, 33,* 255–281.

Main, M., Kaplan, N., & Cassidy, J. (1985). Security in infancy, childhood, and adulthood: A move to the level of representation. In I. Bretherton & E. Waters (Eds.), Growing points of attachment theory and research. *Monographs of the Society for Research in Child Development, 50*(1-2, Serial No. 209), 66–104.

Manis, F. R., Custodio, R., & Szeszulski, P. A. (1993). Development of phonological and orthographic skill: A 2-year longitudinal study of dyslexic children. *Journal of Experimental Child Psychology, 56,* 64–86.

Marshall, J. D. (1984). Process and product: Case studies of writing in two content areas. In A. N. Applebee (Ed.), *Contexts for learning to write: Studies of secondary school instruction* (pp. 149–168). Norwood, NJ: Ablex.

Matas, L., Arend, R. A., & Sroufe, L. A. (1978). Continuity of adaptation in the second year: The relationship between quality of attachment and later competence. *Child Development, 49,* 547–556.

McKeown, M. G., Beck, I. L., Omanson, R. C., & Perfetti, C. A. (1983). The effects of long-term vocabulary instruction on reading comprehension: A replication. *Journal of Reading Behavior, 15,* 3–18.

McKeown, M. G., Beck, I. L., Omanson, R. C., & Pople, M. T. (1985). Some effects of the nature and frequency of vocabulary instruction on the knowledge and use of words. *Reading Research Quarterly, 20,* 522–535.

Menke, D., & Pressley, M. (1994). Elaborative interrogation: Using "why" questions to enhance the learning from text. *Journal of Reading, 37,* 642–645.

Meredith, K. S., & Steele, J. L. (2000). Education in transition: Trends in central and eastern Europe. In M. L. Kamil, P. B. Mosenthal, P. D. Pearson, & R. Barr (Eds.), *Handbook of reading research* (Vol. 3, pp. 29–39). Mahwah, NJ: Erlbaum.

Metsala, J., & Ehri, L. (Eds.). (1998). *Word recognition in beginning reading.* Mahwah, NJ: Erlbaum.

Miller, G. A. (1956). The magical number seven, plus-or-minus two: Some limits on our capacity for processing information. *Psychological Review, 63,* 81–97.

Nagy, W. (1988). *Teaching vocabulary to improve reading comprehension.* Newark, DE: International Reading Association.

Nagy, W., Anderson, R., & Herman, P. (1987). Learning word meanings from context during normal reading. *American Educational Research Journal, 24,* 237–270.

Näsland, J. C., & Schneider, W. (1996). Kindergarten letter knowledge, phonological skills, and memory processes: Relative effects on early literacy. *Journal of Experimental Child Psychology, 62,* 30–59.

National Institute for Literacy. (1998). *The state of literacy in America: Estimates at the local, state, and national levels.* Washington, DC: Author.

National Reading Panel. (2000). *Final report of the National Reading Panel.* Washington, DC: National Institute of Child Health and Development.

Neuman, S. B., & McCormick, S. (2000). A case for single-subject experiments in literacy research. In M. L. Kamil, P. B. Mosenthal, P. D. Pearson, & R. Barr (Eds.), *Handbook of reading research* (Vol. 3, pp. 181–194). Mahwah, NJ: Erlbaum.

Nist, S. L., & Holschuh, J. L. (2000). Comprehension strategies at the college level. In R. F. Flippo & D. C. Caverly (Eds.), *Handbook of college reading and study strategy research* (pp. 75–104). Mahwah, NJ: Erlbaum.

Nist, S. L., & Kirby, K. (1989). The text marking patterns of college students. *Reading Psychology, 10,* 321–338.

O'Connor, R. E., Jenkins, J. R., & Slocum, T. A. (1995). Transfer among phonological tasks in kindergarten: Essential instructional content. *Journal of Educational Psychology, 87,* 202–217.

Olson, R. K., Wise, B., Johnson, M., & Ring, J. (1997). The etiology and remediation of phonologically based word recognition and spelling disabilities: Are phonological deficits the "hole" story? In B. Blachman (Ed.), *Foundations of reading acquisition* (pp. 305–326). Mahwah, NJ: Erlbaum.

Palincsar, A. S., & Brown, A. L. (1984). Reciprocal teaching of comprehension-fostering and monitoring activities. *Cognition and Instruction, 1,* 117–175.

Pearson, P. D., Barr, R., Kamil, M. L., & Mosenthal, P. B. (Eds.). (1984). *Handbook of reading research.* New York: Longman.

Pearson, P. D., & Gallagher, M. (1983). The instruction of reading comprehension. *Contemporary Educational Psychology, 8,* 317–344.

Pellegrini, A. D., Galda, L., Perlmutter, J., & Jones, I. (1994). *Joint reading between mothers and their head start children: Vocabulary development in two text formats* (Reading Research Report No. 13). Athens, GA: National Reading Research Center.

Pellegrini, A. D., Perlmutter, J. C., Galda, L., & Brody, G. H. (1990). Joint reading between black head start children and their mothers. *Child Development, 61,* 443–453.

Pennington, B. F., Groisser, D., & Welsh, M. C. (1993). Contrasting cognitive deficits in attention deficit hyperactivity disorder versus reading disability. *Developmental Psychology, 29,* 511–523.

Peterson, M. E., & Haines, L. P. (1992). Orthographic analogy training with kindergarten children: Effects of analogy use, phonemic segmentation, and letter-sound knowledge. *Journal of Reading Behavior, 24,* 109–127.

Pianko, S. (1979). A description of the composing processes of college freshmen writers. *Research in the Teaching of English, 13,* 5–22.

Pinnell, G. S. (1997). Reading Recovery: A summary of research. In J. Flood, S. B. Heath, & D. Lapp (Eds.), *Handbook of research on teaching literacy through the communicative and visual arts* (pp. 638–654). New York: Macmillan.

Pratt, A. C., & Brady, S. (1988). Relation of phonological awareness to reading disability in children and adults. *Journal of Educational Psychology, 80,* 319–323.

Pressley, G. M. (1976). Mental imagery helps eight-year-olds remember what they read. *Journal of Educational Psychology, 68,* 355–359.

Pressley, M. (1998). *Reading instruction that works: The case for balanced teaching.* New York: Guilford.

Pressley, M. (2000). What should comprehension instruction be the instruction of? In M. L. Kamil, P. B. Mosenthal, P. D. Pearson, & R. Barr (Eds.), *Handbook of reading research* (Vol. 3, pp. 545–561). Mahwah, NJ: Erlbaum.

Pressley, M., & Afflerbach, P. (1995). *Verbal protocols of reading: The nature of constructively responsive reading.* Hillsdale, NJ: Erlbaum.

Pressley, M., Allington, R., Wharton-McDonald, R., Block, C. C., & Morrow, L. M. (2001). *The good first grade.* New York: Guilford.

Pressley, M., Borkowski, J. G., & O'Sullivan, J. T. (1984). Memory strategy instruction is made of this: Metamemory and durable strategy use. *Educational Psychologist, 19,* 94–107.

Pressley, M., Borkowski, J. G., & O'Sullivan, J. T. (1985). Children's metamemory and the teaching of strategies. In D. L. Forrest-Pressley, G. E. MacKinnon, & T. G. Waller (Eds.), *Metacognition, cognition, and human performance* (pp. 111–153). Orlando, FL: Academic Press.

Pressley, M., & El-Dinary, P. B. (1997). What we know about translating comprehension strategies instruction research into practice. *Journal of Learning Disabilities, 30,* 486–488.

Pressley, M., El-Dinary, P. B., Gaskins, I., Schuder, T., Bergman, J., Almasi, L., & Brown, R. (1992). Beyond direct explanation: Transactional instruction of reading comprehension strategies. *Elementary School Journal, 92,* 511–554.

Pressley, M., Wood, E., Woloshyn, V. E., Martin, V., King, A., & Menke, D. (1992). Encouraging mindful use of prior knowledge: Attempting to construct explanatory answers facilitates learning. *Educational Psychologist, 27,* 91–110.

Pugh, S. L., Pawan, F., & Antommarchi, C. (2000). Academic literacy and the new college learner. In R. F. Flippo & D. C. Caverly (Eds.), *Handbook of college reading and study strategy research* (pp. 25–42). Mahwah, NJ: Erlbaum.

Purcell-Gates, V. (2000). Family literacy. In M. L. Kamil, P. B. Mosenthal, P. D. Pearson, & R. Barr (Eds.), *Handbook of reading research* (Vol. 3, pp. 853–870). Mahwah, NJ: Erlbaum.

Raphael, L., Bogner, K., Pressley, M., Masters, N., & Steinhofer, A. (2000). *Motivating literacy in first-grade classrooms.* Institute for Educational Initiatives, University of Notre Dame, Notre Dame, IN. Manuscript in preparation.

Reinking, D., McKenna, M. C., Labbo, L. D., & Kieffer, R. D. (1998). *Handbook of literacy and technology: Transformations in a post-typographic world.* Mahwah, NJ: Erlbaum.

Rice, M. L., Huston, A. C., Truglio, R., & Wright, J. (1990). Words from "Sesame Street." Learning vocabulary from viewing. *Developmental Psychology, 26,* 421–428.

Robbins, C., & Ehri, L. C. (1994). Reading storybooks to kindergartners helps them learn new vocabulary words. *Journal of Educational Psychology, 86,* 54–64.

Robinson, F. P. (1946). *Effective study* (2nd ed.). New York: Harper & Row.

Roehler, L. R., & Duffy, G. G. (1984). Direct explanation of comprehension processes. In G. G. Duffy, L. R. Roehler, & J. Mason (Eds.), *Comprehension instruction: Perspectives and suggestions* (pp. 265–280). New York: Longmans.

Rose, M. (1989). *Lives on the boundary: The struggle and achievements of America's underprepared.* New York: Free Press.

Rosenblatt, L. M. (1978). *The reader, the text, the poem: The transactional theory of the literary work.* Carbondale: Southern Illinois University Press.

Rosenhouse, J., Feitelson, D., Kita, B., & Goldstein, Z. (1997). Interactive reading aloud to Israeli first graders: Its contribution to literacy development. *Reading Research Quarterly, 32,* 168–183.

Rosenshine, B., & Meister, C. (1994). Reciprocal teaching: A review of nineteen experimental studies. *Review of Educational Research, 64,* 479–530.

Rosenshine, B., & Trapman, S. (1992, April). *Teaching students to generate questions: A review of research.* Paper presented at the annual meeting of the American Educational Research Association, San Francisco.

Roser, N., & Martinez, M. (1985). Roles adults play in preschool responses to literature. *Language Arts, 62,* 485–490.

Samuels, S. J., Dahl, P., & Archwamety, T. (1974). Effect of hypothesis/test training on reading skill. *Journal of Educational Psychology, 66,* 835–844.

Santana, I. S. (2000). Literacy research in Latin America. In M. L. Kamil, P. B. Mosenthal, P. D. Pearson, & R. Barr (Eds.), *Handbook of reading research* (Vol. 3, pp. 41–52). Mahwah, NJ: Erlbaum.

Scarborough, H. S., & Dobrich, W. (1994). On the efficiency of reading to preschoolers. *Developmental Review, 14,* 245–302.

Scardamalia, M., & Bereiter, C. (1986). Research on written composition. In M. C. Wittrock (Ed.), *Handbook of research on teaching* (3rd ed., pp. 778–803). New York: Macmillan.

Seymour, P. H. K., & Elder, L. (1986). Beginning reading without phonology. *Cognitive Neuropsychology, 3,* 1–36.

Shaywitz, S. E. (1996). Dyslexia. *Scientific American, 275*(5), 98–104.

Short, E. J., & Ryan, E. B. (1984). Metacognitive differences between skilled and less-skilled readers: Remediating deficits through story grammar and attribution training. *Journal of Educational Psychology, 76,* 225–235.

Simpson, M. L. (1994). Talk throughs: A strategy for encouraging active learning across the content areas. *Journal of Reading, 38,* 296–304.

Simpson, M. L., & Randall, S. N. (2000). Vocabulary development at the college level. In R. F. Flippo & D. C. Caverly (Eds.), *Handbook of college reading and study strategy research* (pp. 43–73). Mahwah, NJ: Erlbaum.

Snow, C. E. (1983). Literacy and language: Relationships during the preschool years. *Harvard Educational Review, 53,* 165–189.

Snow, C. E., Burns, M. S., & Griffin, P. (1998). *Preventing reading difficulties in young children.* Washington, DC: National Academy Press.

Stahl, A. (1977). The structure of children's compositions: Developmental and ethnic differences. *Research in the Teaching of English, 11,* 156–163.

Stahl, N. A., & King, J. R. (2000). A history of college reading. In R. F. Flippo & D. C. Caverly (Eds.), *Handbook of college reading and study strategy research* (pp. 1–23). Mahwah, NJ: Erlbaum.

Stanovich, K. E. (1986). Matthew effects in reading: Some consequences of individual differences in the acquisition of literacy. *Reading Research Quarterly, 21,* 360–407.

Stanovich, K. E. (1988). Explaining the differences between the dyslexic and the garden-variety poor reader: The phonological-core variable-difference model. *Journal of Learning Disabilities, 21,* 590–604.

Sternberg, R. J. (1987). Most vocabulary is learned from context. In M. G. McKeown & M. E. Curtis (Eds.), *The nature of vocabulary acquisition* (pp. 89–105). Hillsdale, NJ: Erlbaum.

Stuart, M., & Masterson, J. (1992). Patterns of reading and spelling in 10-year-old children related to prereading phonological abilities. *Journal of Experimental Child Psychology, 54,* 168–187.

Sulzby, E., & Teale, W. (1987). *Young children's storybook reading: Longitudinal study of parent-child instruction and children's independent functioning* (Final Report to the Spencer Foundation). Ann Arbor, MI: University of Michigan Press.

Sulzby, E., & Teale, W. (1991). Emergent literacy. In R. Barr, M. L. Kamil, P. B. Mosenthal, & P. D. Pearson (Eds.), *Handbook of reading research* (Vol. 2, pp. 727–758). New York: Longman.

Tan, A., & Nicholson, T. (1997). Flashcards revisited: Training poor readers to read words faster improves their comprehension of text. *Journal of Educational Psychology, 89,* 276–288.

Tangel, D. M., & Blachman, B. A. (1992). Effect of phoneme awareness instruction on kindergarten children's invented spellings. *Journal of Reading Behavior, 24,* 233–261.

Tangel, D. M., & Blachman, B. A. (1995). Effect of phoneme awareness instruction on the invented spelling of first-grade children: A one-year follow-up. *Journal of Reading Behavior, 27,* 153–185.

Taylor, B. M. (1982). Text structure and children's comprehension and memory for expository material. *Journal of Educational Psychology, 74,* 323–340.

Taylor, B. M., & Beach, R. W. (1984). The effects of text structure instruction on middle-grade students' comprehension and production of expository text. *Reading Research Quarterly, 19,* 134–146.

Taylor, D., & Strickland, D. (1986). *Family storybook reading.* Exeter, NH: Heinemann Educational Books.

Torgesen, J. K., Wagner, R. K., Rashotte, C. A., Alexander, A., Lindamood, P. C., Rose, E., & Conway, T. (1996). *Prevention and remediation of phonologically based reading disabilities.* Paper presented at the Spectrum of Developmental Disabilities XVIII: Dyslexia, Johns Hopkins Medical Institutions, Baltimore.

Tunmer, W. E., Herriman, M. L., Nesdale, A. R. (1988). Meta-linguistic abilities and beginning reading. *Reading Research Quarterly, 23,* 134–158.

Valdez-Menchaca, M. C., & Whitehurst, G. J. (1992). Accelerating language development through picture book reading: A systematic extension to Mexican day care. *Developmental Psychology, 28,* 1106–1114.

Valeri-Gold, M., & Deming, M. P. (2000). Reading, writing, and the college developmental student. In R. F. Flippo & D. C. Caverly (Eds.), *Handbook of college reading and study strategy research* (pp. 149–173). Mahwah, NJ: Erlbaum.

Vellutino, F. R., & Scanlon, D. W. (1987). Phonological coding, phonological awareness, and reading ability: Evidence from a longitudinal, experimental study. *Merrill-Palmer Quarterly, 33,* 321–363.

Vellutino, F. R., Scanlon, D. M., Sipay, E. R., Small, S. G., Pratt, A., Chen, R., & Denckla, M. B. (1996). Cognitive profiles of difficult-to-remediate and readily remediated poor readers: Early intervention as a vehicle for distinguishing between cognitive and experiential deficits as a basic cause of specific reading disability. *Journal of Educational Psychology, 88,* 601–638.

Venezky, R. L. (1999). Reading, writing, and salvation: The impact of Christian missionaries on literacy. In D. A. Wagner, R. L. Venezky, & B. V. Street (Eds.), *Literacy: An international handbook* (pp. 119–124). Boulder, CO: Westview Press.

Wagner, D. A. (1999). Rationales, debates, and new directions: An introduction. In D. A. Wagner, R. L. Venezky, & B. V. Street (Eds.), *Literacy: An international handbook* (pp. 1–8). Boulder, CO: Westview Press.

Walton, P. D., Walton, L. M., & Felton, K. (2001). Teaching rime analogy or letter recoding reading strategies to prereaders: Effects on prereading skills and word reading. *Journal of Educational Psychology, 93,* 160–180.

Weinstein, C. E. (1994). A look to the future: What we might learn from research on beliefs. In R. Garner & P. A. Alexander (Eds.), *Beliefs about text and instruction with text* (pp. 294–302). Hillsdale, NJ: Erlbaum.

Wharton-McDonald, R., Pressley, M., & Hampston, J. M. (1998). Outstanding literacy instruction in first grade: Teacher practices and student achievement. *Elementary School Journal, 99,* 101–128.

Whitehurst, G. J., Epstein, J. N., Angell, A. L., Payne, A. C., Crone, D. A., & Fischel, J. E. (1994). Outcomes of an emergent literacy intervention in Head Start. *Journal of Educational Psychology, 86,* 542–555.

Whitehurst, G. J., Falco, F. L., Lonigan, C. J., Fischel, J. E., DeBaryshe, B. D., Valdez-Menchaca, M. C., & Caulfield, M. (1988). Accelerating language development through picturebook reading. *Developmental Psychology, 24,* 552–559.

Wilkinson, I. A. G., Freebody, P., & Elkins, J. (2000). Reading research in Australia and Aotearoa/New Zealand. In M. L. Kamil, P. B. Mosenthal, P. D. Pearson, & R. Barr (Eds.), *Handbook of reading research* (Vol. 3, pp. 3–16). Mahwah, NJ: Erlbaum.

Williams, J. P. (1980). Teaching decoding with an emphasis on phoneme analysis and phoneme blending. *Journal of Educational Psychology, 72,* 1–15.

Windham, D. M. (1999). Literacy and economic development. In D. A. Wagner, R. L. Venezky, & B. V. Street (Eds.), *Literacy: An international handbook* (pp. 342–347). Boulder, CO: Westview Press.

Wise, B. W., & Olson, R. K. (1995). Computer-based phonological awareness and reading instruction. *Annals of Dyslexia, 45,* 99–122.

Wood, D., Bruner, J., & Ross, G. (1976). The role of tutoring in problem solving. *Journal of Child Psychology and Psychiatry, 17,* 89–100.

Yaden, D. B., Jr., Row, D. W., & MacGillivray, L. (2000). Emergent literacy: A matter (polyphony) of perspectives. In M. L. Kamil, P. B. Mosenthal, P. D. Pearson, & R. Barr (Eds.), *Handbook of reading research* (Vol. 3, pp. 425–454). Mahwah, NJ: Erlbaum.

Yuill, N., & Oakhill, J. V. (1988). Effects of inference awareness training on poor comprehension. *Applied Cognitive Psychology, 2,* 23–45.

Yuill, N. M., & Oakhill, J. V. (1991). *Children's problems in text comprehension: An experimental investigation.* Cambridge, England: Cambridge University Press.

CHAPTER 15

Mathematical Learning

RICHARD LEHRER AND RICHARD LESH

MATHEMATICAL LEARNING

Does beauty have structure? How does a hinge work? What happens if zero divides a number? Do the symmetries of a triangle and the set of integers under addition have any structure in common? How many distinct patterns of wallpaper design are possible? What are Nature's numbers? How do nurses determine the dosage of drugs (e.g., Pozzi, Noss, & Hoyles, 1998) or entomologists quantify relations among termites (e.g., Hall, Stevens, & Torralba, in press)? What forms of mathematical activity are found in automotive production (Smith, 1999)? Questions like these suggest the enormous imaginative scope and practical reach of mathematics and demonstrate that mathematicians are jugglers not of numbers, but of concepts (e.g., Stewart, 1975). Mathematical practice spans a universe of human endeavor, ranging from

art and craft to engineering design, and its products extend over much of recorded history. Despite this long history of mathematics, systematic study of mathematical learning occupies only a brief slice in time. Nevertheless, research in mathematics education and in the psychology of mathematical learning continues to grow, so that any review of this research is necessarily incomplete and highly selective.

Our choices for this review stem from a genetic view of knowledge (Piaget, 1970), a "commitment that the structures, forms, and possibly the content of knowledge is determined in major respects by its developmental history" (diSessa, 1995, p. 23). Mathematics develops within a collective history of *argument* and *inscription* (Davis & Hersh, 1981; Devlin, 2000; Kline, 1980; Lakatos, 1976; Nunes, 1999; Polya, 1945), so a genetic account of mathematical learning describes potential origins and developmental landscapes of these modes of thought. Accordingly, we first examine the nature of mathematical argument, tracing a path between everyday forms of argument and those that are widely recognized as distinctly mathematical. In this first section we focus on the epistemology (the grounds for knowing) and skills of argument, rather than on the more familiar heuristics and processes of mathematical reasoning (see, e.g., Haverty,

The authors appreciate the thoughtful comments and suggestions of Leona Schauble, David Williamson Shaffer, Kathy Metz, Ellice Forman, and the editors, William Reynolds and Gloria Miller. This work was supported by the National Science Foundation (REC 9903409). The opinions expressed do not necessarily reflect the position, policy, or endorsement of the NSF.

Koedinger, Klahr, & Alibali, 2000; Leinhardt & Schwarz, 1997; Schoenfeld, 1992). We suggest that developmental roots of mathematical argument reside in the structure of narrative and pretend play but note how these roots must be nurtured to promote epistemic appreciation of proof and related forms of mathematical argument.

We next turn to the role that inscriptions (e.g., markings in a medium such as paper) and notations play in the growth and development of mathematical ideas. Our intention once again is to illuminate the developmental relationship between informal scratches on paper and the kinds of symbol systems employed in mathematical practice. In concert with the core role assigned to argument, we suggest that mathematical thinking emerges as refinement of everyday claims about pattern and possibility yet departs from these everyday roots as these claims are progressively inscribed and otherwise symbolized. Inscription and mathematical thinking co-originate (Rotman, 1993), so that mathematics emerges as a distinct form of literacy, much in the manner in which writing distinguishes itself from speech.

From these starting points we examine how these general qualities of mathematical thinking play out in two realms: geometry measurement and mathematical modeling. We chose the former because spatial mathematics typically receives short shrift in reviews of this kind, yet it encompasses a tradition that spans two millennia. Furthermore, spatial visualization is increasingly relevant to scientific inquiry and is undergoing a renaissance in contemporary computational mathematics. Modeling was selected as the second strand because modeling emphasizes the need for a broad mathematical education that includes several forms of mathematical inquiry. Moreover, modeling underscores the need to develop accounts of mathematical learning at the boundaries of professional practices and conventionally recognized mathematical activity (e.g., Moschkovich, 2002).

The studies selected for this review reflect both cognitive (e.g., Anderson & Schunn, 2000) and sociocultural perspectives (e.g., Forman, in press; Greeno, 1998) on learning. Studies of cognitive development typically shed light on individual cognitive processes, for example, how young students might think about units of measure and how their understandings might evolve. In contrast, sociocultural perspectives typically underscore thinking as mediated activity (e.g., Mead, 1910; Wertsch, 1998). For example, one might consider the history of cultural artifacts, such as rulers, in children's developing conceptions of units. We believe that both forms of analysis are indispensable and that, in fact, these perspectives are interwoven for learners, regardless of researchers' proclivities to consider them as distinct enterprises. Consider, for example, the idea of learning to construct a

geometric proof. On the one hand, a cognitive analysis characterizes the kinds of skills required to develop a proof and describes how those skills must be orchestrated (e.g., Koedinger & Anderson, 1990). These forms of characterization seem indispensable to instructional design (Anderson & Schunn, 2000). On the other hand, the need for proof is cultural, arising from an epistemology that values proof as explanation (Harel & Sowder, 1998; Hersh, 1993). Accordingly, this perspective poses the challenge not just of accounting for the understanding of proof, but also of how one might inculcate a classroom culture that values proof. In the sections that follow, we attempt to strike a balance between these two levels of explanation because both supply important accounts of mathematical learning. Because we assume that readers are familiar with the general nature of these two kinds of analysis, we will not flesh out the assumptions of each perspective in this chapter.

THE GROWTH OF ARGUMENT

Arguments in mathematics aim to provide explanations of mathematical structures. Proof is often taken as emblematic of mathematical argument because it both explains and provides grounds for certainty that are hard to match or even imagine in other disciplines, such as science or history. Although everyday folk psychology often associates proof with drudgery, for mathematicians proof is a form of discovery (e.g., de Villiers, 1998), and even "epiphany" (e.g., Benson, 1999). Yet conviction does not start with proof, so in this section we trace the ontogeny of forms of reasoning that seem to ground proof and proof-like forms of explanation. Our approach here is necessarily speculative because there is no compelling study of the long-term development of an epistemic appreciation for mathematical argument. Moreover, the emblem of mathematical argument, proof, is often misunderstood as a series of conventional procedures for arriving at the empirically obvious, rather than as a form of explanation (Schoenfeld, 1988). International comparisons of students (e.g., Healy & Hoyles, 2000) confirm this impression, and apparently many teachers hold similar views (Knuth, 2002; Martin & Harel, 1989).

Nonetheless, several lines of research suggest fruitful avenues for generating an epistemology of mathematical argument that is more aligned with mathematical practice and more likely to expose progenitors from which this epistemology can be developed. (We are not discounting the growth of experimental knowledge in mathematics but are focusing on grounds for certainty here. We return to this point later.) In the sections that follow, we suggest that mathematical argument evolves from everyday argument and represents an epistemic refinement of everyday reasoning. We propose that the evolution is grounded in the structure of everyday conversation, is sustained by the growth and development of an appreciation of pretense and possibility, and is honed through participation in communities of mathematical inquiry that promote generalization and certainty.

Conversational Structure as a Resource for Argument

Contested claims are commonplace, of course, and perhaps there is no more common arena for resolving differing perspectives than conversation. Although we may well more readily recall debates and other specialized formats as sparring grounds, everyday conversation also provides many opportunities for developing "substantial" arguments (Toulmin, 1958). By substantial, Toulmin referred to arguments that expand and modify claims and propositions but that lead to conclusions not contained in the premises (unlike those of formal logic). For example, Ochs, Taylor, Rudolph, and Smith (1992) examined family conversations with young children (e.g., 4–6 years of age) around such mundane events as recall of "the time when" (e.g., mistaking chili peppers for pickles) or a daily episode, such as an employee's reaction to time off. They suggested that dinnertime narratives engender many of the elements of sound argument in a manner that parallels scientific debate. First, narratives implicate a problematic event, a tension in need of resolution, so that narratives often embody some form of contest, or at least contrast. Second, the problematic event often invites causal explanation during the course of the conversation. Moreover, these explanations may be challenged by conarrators or listeners, thus establishing a tacit anticipation of the need to ground claims. Challenges in everyday conversations can range from matters of fact (e.g., disputing what a character said) to matters of ideology (e.g., disputing the intentions of one of the characters in the account). Finally, conarrators often respond to challenges by redrafting narratives to provide alternative explanations or to align outcomes more in keeping with a family's worldview. By means of explicit parallels like these, Ochs et al. (1992) argued that theories and stories may be generated, critiqued, and revised in ways that are essentially similar (see Hall, 1999; Warren, Ballanger, Ogonowski, Rosebery, & Hudicourt-Barnes, 2001, regarding continuities between everyday and scientific discourses).

Studies like those of Ochs et al. (1992) are emblematic of much of the work in conversation analysis, which suggests that the structure of everyday talk in many settings is an important resource for creating meaning (Drew & Heritage, 1992). For example, Rips (1998; Rips, Brem, & Bailenson,

1999) noted that everyday conversationalists typically make claims, ask for justification of others' claims, attack claims, and attack the justifications offered in defense of a claim. The arrangement of these moves gives argumentation its characteristic shape. Judgments of the informal arguments so crafted depend not only on the logical structure of the argument but also on consideration of possible alternative states of the claims and warrants suggested. Rips and Marcus (1976) suggested that reasoning about such suppositions, or possible states, requires bracketing uncertain states in memory in order to segregate hypothetical states from what is currently believed to be true. In the next section we review evidence about the origins and constraints on this cognitive capacity to reason about the hypothetical.

From Pretense to Proof

Reasoning about hypothetical states implicates the development of a number of related skills that culminate in the capacity to reason about relations between possible states of the world, to treat aspects of them as if they were in the world, to objectify possibilities, and to coordinate these objects (e.g., conjectures, theories, etc.) with evidence. Both theory and evidence are socially sanctioned and thus cannot be properly regarded apart from participation in communities that encourage, support, and otherwise value these forms of reasoning. We focus first on the development of representational competence, which appears to originate in pretend play, and then on corresponding competencies in conditional reasoning. We turn then from competence to dispositions to construct sound arguments that coordinate theory and evidence and, in mathematics, to prove. Because these dispositions do not seem to arise as readily as the competencies that underlie them, we conclude with an examination of the characteristics of classroom practices that seem to support the development of generalization and grounds for certainty in early mathematics education.

Development of Representational Competence

One of the features of mathematical argument is that one must often reason about possible states of affairs, sometimes even in light of counterfactual evidence. As we have seen, this capacity is supported by everyday conversational structure. However, such reasoning about possibility begins with representation. This representational capacity generally emerges towards the end of the second year and is evident in children's pretend play. Leslie (1987) clarified the representational demands of pretending that a banana is a telephone, while knowing very well that whatever the transformation, the banana remains a banana, after all. He suggested that pretense is founded in metarepresentational capacity to constitute (and distinguish) a secondary representation of one's primary representation of objects and events.

Metarepresentation expands dramatically during the preschool years. Consider, for example, DeLoache's (1987, 1989, 1995) work on children's understanding of scale models of space. DeLoache encouraged preschoolers to observe while she hid small objects in a scale model of a living room. Then she brought them into the full-scale room and asked them to find similar objects in the analogous locations. DeLoache observed a dramatic increase in representational mapping between the model and the world between 2.5 and 3 years of age. Younger children did not seem to appreciate, for example, that an object hidden under the couch in the model could be used to find its correspondent in the room, even though they readily described these correspondences verbally. Yet slightly older children could readily employ the model as a representation, rather than as a world unto itself, suggesting that they could sustain a clear distinction between representation and world.

Gentner's (Gentner & Loewenstein, 2002; Gentner & Toupin, 1986) work on analogy also focuses on early developing capacities to represent relational structures, so that one set of relations can stand in for another. For example, Kotovsky and Gentner (1996) presented triads of patterns to children ranging from 4 to 8 years of age. One of the patterns was relationally similar to an initially presented pattern (e.g., small circle, large circle, small circle matched to small square, large square, small square), and the third was not (e.g., large square, small square, small square). Although the 4-year-olds responded at chance levels, 6- and 8-year-olds preferred relational matches. These findings are consistent with a relational shift from early reliance on object-matching similarity to later capacity and preference for reasoning relationally (Gentner, 1983). This kind of relational capacity undergirds conceptual metaphors important to mathematics, like those between collections of objects and sets in arithmetic, and forms the basis for the construction of mathematical objects (Lakoff & Nunez, 2000). Moreover, Sfard (2000) pointed out that although discourse about everyday events and objects is a kind of first language game (in Wittgenstein's sense), the playing field in mathematics is virtual, so that mathematical discourse is often about objects that have no counterpart in the world.

Knitting Possibilities: Counterfactual Reasoning

Collectively, research on the emergence of representational competence illuminates the impressive cognitive achievement of creating and deploying representational structures of actual, potential, and pretend states of the world. However, it is yet another cognitive milestone to act on these representations to knit relations among them, a capacity that relies on reasoning about relations among these hypothetical states. Children's ability to engage in such hypothetical reasoning is often discounted, perhaps because the seminal work of Inhelder and Piaget (1958) stressed children's, and even adults', difficulties with the (mental) structures of logical entailment. However, these difficulties do not rule out the possibility that children may engage in forms of mental logic that provide resources for dealing with possible worlds, even though they may fall short of an appreciation of the interconnectedness of mental operators dictated by formal logic. Studies of child logic document impressive accomplishments even among young children. For the current purpose of considering routes to mathematical argument, we focus on findings related to counterfactual reasoning—reasoning about possible states that run counter to knowledge or perception, yet are considered for the sake of the argument (Levi, 1996; Roese, 1997). This capacity is at the heart of deductive modes of thought that do not rely exclusively on empirical knowledge, yet can be traced to children's capacity to coordinate separate representations of true and false states of affairs in pretend play (Amsel & Smalley, 2001).

In one of the early studies of young children's hypothetical reasoning, Hawkins, Pea, Glick, and Scribner (1984) asked preschool children (4 and 5 years) to respond to syllogistic problems with three different types of initial premises: (a) congruent with children's empirical experience (e.g., "Bears have big teeth"), (b) incongruent with children's empirical experience (e.g., "Everything that can fly has wheels"), and (c) a fantasy statement outside of their experience (e.g., "Every banga is purple"). Children responded to questions posed in the syllogistic form of modus ponens ("Pogs wear blue boots. Tom is a pog. Does Tom wear blue boots?"). They usually answered the congruent problems correctly and the incongruent problems incorrectly. Furthermore, children's responses to incongruent problems were consistent with their experience, rather than the premises of the problem. This *empirical bias* was a consistent and strong trend. However, unexpectedly, when the fantasy expressions were presented first, children reasoned from premises, even if these premises contradicted their experiences. This finding suggested that the fantasy form supported children in orienting to the logical structure of the argument, rather than being distracted by its content.

Subsequently, Dias and Harris (1988, 1990) presented young children (4-, 5- and 6-year olds) with syllogisms, some counterfactual, such as, "All cats bark. Rex is a cat. Does Rex bark?" When they were cued to treat statements as make-believe, or when they were encouraged to imagine the states depicted in the premises, children at all ages tended to reason from the premises as stated, rather than from their knowledge of the world. Scott, Baron-Cohen, and Leslie (1999) found similar advantages of pretense and imagination with another group of 5-year-old children as well as with older children who had learning disabilities. Harris and Leevers (2001) suggested that extraordinary conditions of pretense need *not* be invoked. They obtained clear evidence of counterfactual reasoning with preschool children who were simply prompted to think about the content of counterfactual premises or, as they put it, to adopt an analytic perspective.

Further research of children's understandings of the entailments of conditional clauses suggests that at or around age 8, many children interpret these clauses biconditionally. That is, they treat the relationship symmetrically (Kuhn, 1977; Taplin, Staudenmayer, & Taddonio, 1974), rather than treating the first clause as a sufficient but not necessary condition for the consequent (e.g., treating "if anthrax, then bacteria" as symmetric). However, Jorgenson and Falmagne (1992) assessed 6-year-old children's understanding of entailment in story formats and found that this form of narrative support produced comprehension of entailment more like that typically shown by adults. O'Brien, Dias, Roazzi, and Braine (1998) suggested that the conflicting conclusions like these about conditional reasoning can be traced to the model of material implication (if P, then Q) based on formal logic. O'Brien and colleagues argued that it may be a mistake to evaluate conditional reasoning via the truth table of formal logic (especially the requirement that a conditional is true whenever its antecedent is false). This perspective, they think, obscures the role of conditionals in ordinary reasoning. They proposed instead that a set of logic inference schemas governs conditional reasoning. Collectively, these schemas rely on supposing that the antecedent is true and then generating the truth of the consequent. They found that second- and fifth-grade children in both the United States and Brazil could judge the entailments of the premises of a variety of conditionals (e.g., P or Q, Not-P or Not-Q) in ways consistent with these schemas, rather than strict material implication. Even preschool children judged a series of counterfactual events, for example, those that would follow from a character pretending to be a dog, as consistent with a story. An interesting result was that they also excluded events that were suppositionally inconsistent with the story, for example, the same character talking on the phone even though those events were presumably more consistent with their experience (i.e., people, not dogs, use phones).

Collectively, these studies of hypothetical reasoning point to an early developing competence for representing and comparing possible and actual states of the world, as well as for comparing possible states with other possible states. Moreover, these comparisons can be reasoned about in ways that generate sound deductions that share much, but do not overlap completely, with formal logic. These impressive competencies apparently arise from the early development of representational competence, especially in pretend play (Amsel & Smalley, 2001), as well as the structure of everyday conversation. However, despite these displays of early competence, other work suggests that the skills of argument are not well honed at any age, and are especially underdeveloped in early childhood.

The Skills of Argument

Kuhn (1991) suggested that an argument demands not only generation of possibilities but also comparison and evaluation of them. These skills of argument demand a clear separation between beliefs and evidence, as well as development of the means for establishing systematic relations between them (Kuhn, 1989). Kuhn (2001) viewed this development as one of *disposition* to use competencies like those noted, a development related to people's epistemologies: "what they take it to mean to know something" (Kuhn, 2001, p. 1). In studies with adults and adolescents (ninth graders) who attempted to develop sound arguments for the causes of unemployment, school failure, and criminal recidivism, most of those interviewed did not seem aware of the inherent uncertainty of their arguments in these ill-structured domains (Kuhn, 1991, 1992). Only 16% of participants generated evidence that would shed light on their theories, and only about one third were consistently able to generate counterarguments to their positions. Kuhn, Amsel, and O'Loughlin (1988) found similar trends with people ranging in age from childhood (age 8) to adulthood who also attempted to generate theories about everyday topics like the role of diet in catching colds. Participants again had difficulty generating and evaluating evidence and considering counterarguments.

Apparently, these difficulties are not confined to comparatively ill-structured problems. For example, in a study of the generality and specificity of expertise in scientific reasoning, Schunn and Anderson (1999) found that nearly a third of college undergraduate participants never supported their conjectures about a scientific theory with any mention of empirical evidence. Kuhn (2001) further suggested that arguments constructed in contexts ranging from science to social justice tend to overemphasize explanation and cause at the expense of evidence and, more important, that it is difficult for people at all ages to understand the complementary epistemic virtues of each (understanding vs. truth).

Proof

The difficulties that most people have in developing epistemic appreciations of fundamental components of formal or scientific argument suggest that comprehension and production of more specialized epistemic forms of argument, such as proof, might be somewhat difficult to learn. A number of studies confirm this anticipation. For example, Edwards (1999) invited 10 first-year high school students to generate convincing arguments about the truth of simple statements in arithmetic, such as, "Even x odd makes even." The modal justification was, "I tried it and it works" (Edwards, p. 494). When pressed for further justification, students resorted to additional examples. In a study of 60 high school students who were invited to generate and test conjectures about kites, Koedinger (1998) noted that "almost all students seemed satisfied to stop after making one or a few conjectures from the example(s) they had drawn" (p. 327). Findings like these have prompted suggestions that "it is safer to assume little in the way of proof understanding of entering college students" (Sowder, 1994, p. 5).

What makes proof hard? One source of difficulty seems to be instruction that emphasizes formalisms, such as two-column proofs, at the expense of explanation (Coe & Ruthven, 1994; Schoenfeld, 1988). Herbst (2002) went so far as to suggest that classroom practices like two-column proofs often bind students and their instructors in a pedagogical paradox because the inscription into columns embodies two contradictory demands. The format scripts students' responses so that a valid proof is generated. Yet this very emphasis on form obscures the rationale for the choice of the proposition to be proved: Why is it important to prove the proposition so carefully? What does the proof explain? Hoyles (1997; Healy & Hoyles, 2000) added that curricula are often organized in ways that de-emphasize deductive reasoning and scatter the elements of proof across the school year (see also Schoenfeld, 1988, 1994).

In their analysis of university students' conceptions of proof, Harel and Sowder (1998) found that many students seem to embrace ritual and symbolic forms that share surface characteristics with the symbolism of deductive logic. For example, many students, even those entering the university, appear to confuse demonstration and proof and therefore value a single case as definitive. Martin and Harel (1989) examined the judgments of a sample of preservice elementary teachers enrolled in a second-year university mathematics course. Over half judged a single example as providing a valid proof. Many did not accept a single countercase as invalidating a generalization, perhaps because they thought of mathematical generalization as a variation of the generalizations typical of prototypes of classes (e.g., Rosch, 1973).

Outcomes like these are not confined to prospective teachers: Segal (2000) noted that 40% of entry-level university mathematics students also judged examples as valid proofs.

Although many studies emphasize the logic of proof, others examine proof as a social practice, one in which acceptability of proof is grounded in the norms of a community (e.g., Hanna, 1991, 1995). These social aspects of proof suggest a form of rationality governed by artifacts and conventions about evidence, rigor, and plausibility that interact with logic (Lakatos, 1976; Thurston, 1995). Segal (2000) pointed out that conviction (one's personal belief) and validity (the acceptance of this belief by others) may not always be consistent. She found that for first-year mathematics students, these aspects of proof were often decoupled. This finding accords well with Hanna's (1990) distinction between proofs that prove and those that explain, a distinction reminiscent of Kuhn's (2001) contrast between explanation and evidence. Chazan (1993) explored the proof conceptions of 17 high school students from geometry classes that emphasized empirical investigation as well as deductive proof. Students had many opportunities during instruction to compare deduction and induction over examples. One component of instruction emphasized that measurement of examples may suffer from accuracy and precision limitations of measurement devices (such as the sum of the angles of triangles drawn on paper). A second component of instruction highlighted the risks of specific examples because one does not know if one's example is special or general. Nevertheless, students did not readily appreciate the virtues of proof. One objection was that examples constituted a kind of proof by evidence, if one was careful to generate a wide range of them. Other students believed that deductive proofs did not provide safety from counterexamples, perhaps because proof was usually constructed within a particular diagram.

Harel (1998) suggested that many of these difficulties can be traced to fundamental epistemic distinctions that arose during the history of mathematics. In his view, students' understanding of proof is often akin to that of the Greeks, who regarded axioms as corresponding to ideal states of the world (see also Kline, 1980). Hence, mathematical objects determine axioms, but in a more modern view, objects are determined by axioms. Moreover, in modern mathematics, axioms yield a structure that may be realized in different forms. Hence, students' efforts to prove are governed by epistemologies that have little in common with those of the mathematicians teaching them, a difficulty that is both cultural and cognitive. Of course, the cultural-epistemic obstacles to proof are not intended to downplay cognitive skills that students might need to generate sound proofs (e.g., Koedinger, 1998). Nevertheless, it is difficult to conceive of why students might acquire the skills of proof if they do not see its epistemic point.

Reprise of Pretense to Proof

The literature paints a somewhat paradoxical portrait of the development of mathematical argument, especially the epistemology of proof. On the one hand, mathematical argument utilizes everyday competencies, like those involved in resolving contested claims in conversation and those underlying the generation and management of relations among possible states of the world. On the other hand, mathematical argument invokes a disposition to separate conjectures from evidence and to establish rigorous relations between them—all propensities that appear problematic for people at any age. Moreover, the emphasis on structure and certainty in mathematics appears to demand an epistemological shift away from things in the world to structures governed by axioms that may not correspond directly to any personal experience, except perhaps by metaphoric extension (e.g., Lakoff & Nunes, 1997). To these cognitive burdens we can also safely assume that the practices from which this specialized form of argument springs are hidden, both from students and even (within subfields of mathematics) from mathematicians themselves (e.g., Thurstone, 1995). Despite this paradox, or perhaps because of it, emerging research suggests a synthesis where the everyday and the mathematical can meet, so that mathematical argument can be supported by—yet differentiated from—everyday reasoning. In the next section we explore these possibilities.

Mathematical Argument Emerges in Classrooms That Support It

As the previous summary illustrates, research generally paints a dim portrait of dispositions to create sound arguments, even in realms less specialized than mathematics. Nonetheless an emerging body of research suggests a conversational pathway toward developing mathematical argument in classrooms. The premise is that classroom discourse can be formatted and orchestrated in ways that make the grounds of mathematical argument visible and explicit even to young children, partly because everyday discourse offers a structure for negotiating and making explicit contested claims and potential resolutions (e.g., Wells, 1999), and partly because classrooms can be designed so that "norms" (e.g., Barker & Wright, 1954) of participant interaction can include mathematically fruitful ideas such as the value of generalization. Rather than treating acceptance or disagreement solely as internal states of mind, these are externalized

as discursive activities (van Eemeren et al., 1996). A related claim is that classrooms can be designed as venues for initiating students in the "register" (Halliday, 1978; Pimm, 1987) or "Discourse" (Gee, 1997, in press) of a discipline like mathematics.

Dialogue, then, is a potential foundation for supporting argument, and studies outside of mathematics suggest that sound arguments can be developed in dialogic interaction. For example, Kuhn, Shaw, and Felton (1997) asked adolescents and young adults to create arguments for or against capital punishment. Compared to a control condition limited to repeated (twice) elicitation of their views, a group engaged in dyadic interactions (one session per week for five weeks) was much more likely to create arguments that addressed the desirability of capital punishment within a framework of alternatives. Students in this dyadic group also were more likely to develop a personal stance about their arguments. The development of argument in the engaged group was not primarily related to hearing about the positions of others, but rather to the need to articulate one's own position, which apparently instigated voicing of new forms of argument. Moreover, criteria by which one might judge the desirability of capital punishment were elaborated and made more explicit by those participating in the dyadic conversations.

Studies of argument in classrooms where it is explicitly promoted are also encouraging. For example, Anderson, Chinn, Chang, Waggoner, and Yi (1997) examined the logical integrity of the arguments developed by fourth-grade children who participated in discussions about dilemmas faced by characters in a story. The discussions were regulated by norms of turn taking (students spoke one at a time and avoided interrupting each other), attentive listening, and the expectation of respectful challenge. The teacher's role was to facilitate student interaction but not to evaluate contributions. Anderson et al. (1997) analyzed the microstructure of the resulting classroom talk. They found that children's arguments generally conformed to modus ponens (if p, then q) if unstated but shared premises of children were taken into account. This context of shared understandings, generated from collective experiences and everyday knowledge, resolved referential ambiguities and thus constituted a kind of sound, conversational logic. However, "only a handful of children were consistently sensitive to the possibility of backing arguments with appeals to general principles" (Anderson et al., 1997, p. 162). Yet, such an emphasis on the general is an important epistemic component of argument in mathematics, which suggests that mathematics classrooms may need to be more than incubators of dialogue and the general norms that support conversational exchange.

Mathematical Norms

Cobb and his colleagues have conducted a series of teaching experiments in elementary school classrooms that examine the role of conversational norms more explicitly attuned to mathematical justification, such as those governing what counts as an acceptable mathematical explanation (e.g., Cobb, Wood, Yackel, & McNeal, 1992; Cobb, Yackel, & Wood, 1988; Yackel & Cobb, 1996). Cobb and his colleagues suggested that mathematical norms constitute an encapsulation of what counts as evidence, and a proliferation of norms suggests that students in a class are undertaking a progressive refinement and elaboration of mathematical meaning.

In this research several conversational gambits appear reliably to frame the emergence of mathematically fruitful norms. One is discussion of what constitutes a mathematical difference, prompted by teachers who ask if anyone has solved a problem in a different way. Yackel and Cobb (1996) described interactions among students and teachers solving number sentences like $78 - 53 = \underline{\qquad}$. During the course of this interaction the teacher accepted strategies that involved recomposition or decomposition of numbers as different, but simple restatements of a particular strategy were not accepted as different (e.g., similar counts with fingers vs. teddy bears). The need to contribute to this kind of collective activity prompted students to reflect about how their strategy was similar to or different from those described by classmates, a step toward generalization. Moreover, McClain and Cobb (2001) found that negotiation of norms such as what counted as a mathematical difference among first-graders also spawned other norms such as what counted as a sophisticated solution. This cascade of norms appeared to have more general epistemological consequences, orienting children toward mathematics as pattern as they discovered relationships among numbers.

Hershkowitz and Schwarz (1999) tracked the arguments made by sixth-grade students in small group and collective discussions of solution strategies and also noted steps toward mathematics as pattern via discussion of mathematical difference. They observed that pedagogy in the sixth-grade class they studied was oriented toward "purifying" students' invented strategies by suppressing surface-level differences among those proposed. The resulting distillation focused student attention on meaningful differences in mathematical structures. Here again a negotiation of what counted as a mathematical difference inspired the growth of mathematical thinking.

Krummheuer (1998) suggested that mathematical norms such as difference operate by formatting mathematical conversation, meaning that they frame the interactions among participants. Krummheuer (1995) proposed that formatting is consequential for learning because similarly formatted arguments invite cognitive recognition of similarity between approaches taken in these arguments, thus setting the stage for the distillation or purification noted previously. For example, Krummheuer (1995) documented how two second-grade boys initially disagreed about the similarity of their solution methods to the problem of 8×4, but later found that although one subtracted four from a previous result (9×4) and another eight from a previous result (10×4), they were really talking about the "same way." This realization initiated discovery of what made them the same—a quality that, in turn, was staged by the norm of what counted as different.

Teacher Orchestration of Mathematical Conversation

The work of the teacher to establish norms is by no means clear-cut because privileging certain forms of explanation may compete with other goals, such as including all students. Hence, part of the work of the teacher is to find ways to orchestrate discussions that make norms explicit while also developing means to make a norm work collectively (McClain & Cobb, 2001). In her study of argumentation in a second-grade classroom, Wood (1999) illustrated the important role played by teachers in formatting participation itself. She traced how a second-grade teacher apprenticed students to the discourse of mathematical disagreement, differentiating this kind of disagreement from everyday, personal contest. Children apprenticed in problem-solving contexts well within their grasp, so that when they later disagreed about the meaning of place value (one student counted by tens from 49 and another disagreed, contending that counts had to start at decades, as in 50, 60, etc.), the resulting argument centered around mathematical, not personal, claims. Wood cautioned that what might seem like fairly effortless ability to orchestrate arguments about mathematical difference relies instead on prior spadework by the teacher. In this instance, much of that spadework revolved around formatting disagreement. Other classroom studies indicate that teachers assist mathematical argument by explicit support of suppositional reasoning. For example, Lehrer, Jacobson, et al. (1998) conducted a longitudinal study of second-grade mathematics teachers who increasingly encouraged students to investigate the implications of counterfactual propositions (e.g., "What would happen if it were true?").

The work of the teacher to develop norms and format argument is part of a more general endeavor to understand how teachers assist student thinking about mathematics dialogically. Henningsen and Stein (1997) found that student engagement in classroom mathematics was associated with a sustained press for justification, explanations, or meaning through teacher questioning, comments, and feedback.

Spillane and Zeuli (1999) noted that despite endorsing mathematics reform, teachers nevertheless had difficulty orienting conversation in the classroom toward significant mathematical principles and concepts.

O'Connor and Michaels (1996) suggested that teacher orchestration of classroom conversations "provides a site for aligning students with each other and with the content of the academic work while simultaneously socializing them into particular ways of speaking and thinking" (p. 65). The conversational mechanisms by which teachers orchestrate mathematically productive arguments include "revoicing" student utterances so that teachers repeat, expand, rephrase, or animate these parts of conversation in ways that increase their scope or precision or that juxtapose temporally discrete claims for consideration (O'Connor & Michaels, 1993, 1996). For example, a student may explain how she solved a perimeter problem by saying that she counted all around the hexagonal shape. In response, her teacher might rephrase the student's utterance by substituting "perimeter" for her expression "all around." In this instance, the teacher is substituting a mathematical term, "perimeter," for a more familiar, but imprecise construction, "all around," thereby transforming the student's utterance spoken in everyday language into mathematical reference (Forman, Larreamendy-Joerns, Stein, & Brown, 1998).

Revoicing encompasses more complex goals than substitution of mathematical vocabulary for everyday words or even expanding the range of a mathematical concept. Some revoicing appears to be aimed at communicating respect for ideas and at the larger epistemic agenda of helping students identify aspects of mathematical activity, such as the need to "know for sure" or the idea that a case might be a window to a more general pattern (Strom, Kemeny, Lehrer, & Forman, 2001). For example, in a study of second graders who were learning about geometric transformations by designing quilts, Jacobson and Lehrer (2000) examined differences in how teachers revoiced children's comments about an instructional video that depicted various kinds of geometric transformations in the context of designing a quilt. They found an association between teacher revoicing and student achievement. In classes where teachers revoiced student comments in ways that invited conjectures about the causes of observed patterns or that drew attention to central concepts, students' knowledge of transformational geometry exceeded that of counterparts whose teachers merely paraphrased or repeated student utterances.

Pathways to Proof

In classroom cultures characterized by cycles of conjecture and revision in light of evidence, student reasoning can become quite sophisticated and can form an important underlying foundation for the development of proof (Reid, 2002). For example, Lampert (2001; Lampert, Rittenhouse, & Crumbaugh, 1996) described a classroom argument about a claim made by one student that 13.3 was one fourth of 55. Other students claimed, and the class accepted, 27.5 as one half of 55. Another student noted that $13.3 + 13.3 = 26.6$, with the tacit premise that one fourth and one fourth is one half, and hence refuted the first claim. Lampert (2001) noted that the logical form of this proof also served to generate an orientation toward student authority and justification, so that the teacher (Lampert) was not the sole or even chief authority on mathematical truth. Ball and Bass (2000) documented a similar process with third-grade students who worked from contested claims to commonly accepted knowledge by processes of conjecturing, generating cases, and "confronting the very nature and challenge of mathematical proof" (p. 196).

Although generating conjectures and exploring their ramifications is an important precursor to proof, ironically it is grasping the limitations of this form of argument that motivates an important development toward proof as necessity. In classrooms like those taught by Lampert and by Ball, the need for proof emerges as an adjunct to sound argument. For example, a pair of third graders working on a conjecture that an odd number plus an odd number is an even number generated many cases consistent with the conjecture. Yet they were not satisfied because, as one of them said: "You can't prove that Betsy's conjecture always works. Because um, there's, um like, numbers go on and on forever and that means odd numbers and even numbers go on forever, so you couldn't prove that all of them aren't" (Ball & Bass, 2000, p. 196).

Children's recognition of the limits of case-based induction has also been observed in other classrooms where teachers orchestrate discussions and develop classroom cultures consistent with mathematical practices. For example, Lehrer, Jacobson, et al. (1998) observed a class of second-grade students exploring transformational geometry who developed the conjecture that there would always be some transformation or composition of transformations that could be applied to an asymmetric cell (a core unit) that would result in a symmetric design. The class searched vigorously for a single countercase among all the asymmetric core units designed by the children in this class and could not generate any refutation. Nevertheless, a subset of the class remained unconvinced and continued to insist that that they could *not* "be really sure." Their rationale, like that of the third grader described earlier, focused on the need to exhaustively test all possible cases, a need that could not be met because "we'd have to test all the core squares in the world that are asymmetric" (Lehrer, Jacobson, et al., 1998, p. 183). They went on to note that this criterion could not possibly be met due to its infinite size

366 Mathematical Learning

and also because "people are probably making some right now" (p. 183). Hence, in classrooms like these, the need for proof arises as children recognize the limitations of the generalization of their argument. Of course, such need arises only when norms valuing generalization and its rationale are established.

When children have the opportunity to participate regularly in these kinds of classroom cultures, there is good evidence that their appreciation of mathematical generalization and the epistemology of proof take root (e.g., Kaput, 1999). For example, Maher and Martino (1996) traced the development of one child's reasoning over a five-year span (Grade 1 through 5) as she participated in classrooms of literate mathematical practice. A trace of conceptual change was obtained by asking Stephanie to figure out how many different towers four or five cubes tall can be made if one selects among red and blue cubes. In the third grade Stephanie attempted to generate cases of combination and eliminate duplicates. Her justification for claiming that she had found all possible towers was that she could not generate any new ones. By the spring of the fourth grade, Stephanie was no longer content with mere generation and instead constituted an empirical proof by developing a means for exhaustively searching all possibilities.

In another longitudinal study (Grades 2–3), Lehrer and his colleagues followed students in the same second-grade class that had discovered the limits of case-based generalization into and over the course of the third grade. These students' mathematical experiences continued in a classroom emphasizing conjecture, justification, and generalization. Over the course of the third-grade year, researchers recorded many instances of student-generated proof in the context of classroom discussion. At the end of the third grade, all children in the class were interviewed about their preferences for justifications of mathematical conjectures to determine whether proof genres sustained in classroom dialogues would guide the thinking of individual students (Strom & Lehrer, 1999).

Four conjectures were presented in the interview, two of which were false and two of which were true. Justifications for true conjectures included single cases, multiple cases, simple restatement of the conjecture in symbolic notation, abstraction of single cases (notation without generalization, as in using an abstract pattern of dots to represent the commutative property of a case), and valid generalizations, in the form of visual proofs (e.g., the rotational invariance of an arbitrary rectangle for commutative property of multiplication). The range of justification types was designed to distinguish between case-based and deductive generalizations on the one hand and the form of proof (the restatement of the conjecture in symbolic notation) from its substance on the other. A similar

format of justifications was employed for false conjectures, such as, "When you take half of an even number, you get an even number." Here, however, we also included a single counterexample. Students rank-ordered their preferences. For the false conjecture, over half (55%) of the students selected the counterexample as the best justification and the single case as the worst. For the true conjectures, the majority chose the visual proof as best and either the single case or simple translation of the statement into symbolic notation as worst.

Strom and Lehrer (1999) also observed processes of proof generation for these 21 students, asking students to prove that two times any number is an even number. Two of the 21 students rejected the claim immediately, citing counterexamples with fractions (we had intended whole numbers as a tacit premise). Three other students cited the problem of proof by induction, generated several cases, noted that they were "pretty sure" that the conjecture was true, and then decided that they could not prove it because, as one put it, "because the numbers never stop. . . . I couldn't ever really prove that" (p. 31). Other students ($n = 3$) followed a similar line of reasoning, suggesting that they had "proved it to myself, but not for others" (p. 32). Five students solved the problem of induction, either by drawing on definition to deduce the truth of the conjecture or by describing how the patterns they noticed from exploring several cases constituted a pattern that could be applied to all numbers. For example, two of these five students verified the conjecture for the numbers 1 through 10 and then stated that for numbers greater than 10 "any number that ends in an even number is even" (p. 32). Then each student showed how this implied that the pattern of even numbers they had verified for 1 through 10 extended to all numbers— "The rest of the numbers just have a different number at the beginning" (p. 32). The remaining students generated several cases, searched for and failed to find counterexamples, and then declared that they saw the pattern and so believed the conjecture true. In summary, students who had repeated opportunity to construct generalizations and proofs during the course of classroom instruction were sensitive to the role of counterexamples in refutation, and nearly all appreciated the limitations of relying on cases (unless one could exhaustively search the set). Generation of proof without dialogic assistance was considerably more difficult, but in fact, many were capable of constructing valid proofs, albeit with methods considerably more limited than those at the disposal of participants well versed in the discipline.

In well-constituted classrooms, young students can succeed at these forms of reasoning with appropriate assistance. However, work with adults illustrates how difficult it can be to acculturate students to proof-based argument. Simon and Blume (1996) conducted a study of prospective mathematics teachers who were schooled traditionally. At first, students were satisfied by induction over several cases to "prove" that the area of a rectangle could be constituted by multiplication of its width and length. Rather than challenging something that the students all knew to be true, the teacher (Simon) directed the conversation toward explanation, subtly reorienting the grounds of argument from the particular to the general (e.g., whether this would work all the time). Simon's emphasis on the general was further illustrated in another episode in which students attempted to determine the area of an irregular blob by transforming its contour to a more familiar form. Although students could see in a case that their strategy in fact also transformed the area, they were not bothered by this refutation (see also Schauble, 1996), a manifestation of an everyday sense of the general, rather than a mathematical sense. Simon and Blume (1996) also encountered the limits of persuasion when students considered justifications of their predictions about the taste of mixtures that were in different ratios. Here students talked past one another, apparently because some thought of the situation as additive and others as multiplicative. Such studies of teaching and learning again emphasize both the role of the teacher in establishing formats of argument consistent with the discipline and the need for enculturation so that students can see the functions of proof, not simple exposure to proof practices.

Reprise of Mathematical Argument

Mathematical argument emphasizes generality and certainty about patterns and is supported by cognitive capacities to represent possibility and to reason counterfactually about possible patterns. These capacities seem to be robustly supported by cultural practices such as pretense and storytelling. Nevertheless, dispositions to construct mathematically sound arguments apparently do not arise spontaneously in traditional schooling or in everyday cultural practices. Mathematical forms such as proof have their genesis in mathematics classrooms that emphasize conjecture, justification, and explanation. These forms of thinking demand high standards of teaching practice because the evidence suggests that although students may be the primary authors of these arguments, it is the teachers who orchestrate them. Classroom dialogue can spawn overlapping epistemologies, as students are oriented toward mathematics as structure and pattern while they simultaneously examine the grounds of knowledge. Ideally, pattern and proof epistemologies co-originate in classrooms because pattern provides the grounds for proof and proof the rationale for pattern. Thus, classroom conversation and dialogue constitute one possible genetic pathway toward the development of proof reasoning skills and an appreciation

of the epistemology of generalization. Yet even as we emphasize proposition and language, we are struck with the role played by symbolization and tools in the development of arguments in classrooms and in various guises of mathematical practice. This is not surprising when one considers the central historical role of such symbolizations in the development of mathematics. We turn next to considering a complementary genetic pathway to mathematical knowledge, that of students as writers of mathematics.

INSCRIPTIONS TRANSFORM MATHEMATICAL THINKING AND LEARNING

In this section we explore the invention and appropriation of inscriptions (literal marks on paper or other media, following Latour, 1990) as mediational tools that can transform mathematical activity. This view follows from our emphasis in the previous section on mathematics as a discursive practice in which everyday resources, such as conversation and pretense, provide a genetic pathway for the development of an epistemology of mathematical argument, of literally talking mathematics into being (Sfard, 2000; Sfard & Kieran, 2001). Here we focus on the flip side of the coin, portraying mathematics as a particular kind of written discourse— "a business of making and remaking permanent inscriptions . . . operated upon, transformed, indexed, amalgamated" (Rotman, 1993, p. 25). Rotman distinguished this view from a dualist view of symbol and referent as having independent existence, proposing instead that signifier (inscription) and signified (mathematical idea) are "co-creative and mutually originative" (p. 33). Accordingly, we first describe perspectives that frame inscriptions as mediators of mathematical and scientific activity, with attention to sociocultural accounts of inscription and argument. These accounts of inscription buttress the semiotic approach taken by Rotman (1988, 1993) and set the stage for cognitive studies of inscription. We go on to describe children's efforts to invent or appropriate inscriptions in everyday contexts such as drawing or problem solving. Collectively, these studies suggest that the growth of representational competence, as reviewed in the previous section, is mirrored by a corresponding competence in the uses of inscription and notation. In other words, the having of ideas and the inscribing of ideas coevolve. Studies of inscriptionally mediated thinking in mathematics indicate that mathematical objects are created as they are inscribed. This perspective calls into question typical accounts in cognitive science, where inscriptions are regarded as simply referring to mathematical objects, rather than constituting them. We conclude this section with the implications of these findings for an emerging arena of dynamic inscriptions, namely, computational media.

Disciplinary Practices of Inscription and Notation

Studies in the sociology of science demonstrate that scientists invent and appropriate inscriptions as part of their everyday practice (Latour, 1987, 1990; Lynch, 1990). Historically, systems of inscription and notation have played important roles in the quantification of natural reality (Crosby, 1997) and are tools for modeling the world on paper (Olson, 1994). DiSessa (2000, p. 19) noted,

> Not only can new inscription systems and literacies ease learning, as algebra simplified the proofs of Galileo's theorems, but they may also rearrange the entire terrain. New principles become fundamental and old ones become obvious. Entirely new terrain becomes accessible, and some old terrain becomes boring.

Visualizing Nature

One implication of this view of scientific practice as the invention and manipulation of the world on paper (or electronic screen) is that even apparently individual acts of perceiving the world, such as classifying colors or trees, are mediated by layers of inscription and anchored to the practices of disciplinary communities (Goodwin, 1994, 1996; Latour, 1986). Goodwin (1994) suggested that inscriptions do not mirror discourse in a discipline but complement it, so that professional practices in mathematics and science use "the distinctive characteristics of the material world to organize phenomena in ways that spoken language cannot—for example, by collecting records of a range of disparate events onto a single visible surface" (p. 611). For example, archaeologists classify a soil sample by layering inscriptions, field practices, and particular forms of talk to render a professional judgment (Goodwin, 2000). Instead of merely looking, archaeologists juxtapose the soil sample with an inscription (the Munsell color chart) that arranges color gradations into an ordered grid, and they spray water on the soil to create a consistent viewing environment. These practices format discussion of the appropriate classification and illustrate the moment-to-moment embedding of inscription within particular practices.

Repurposing Inscription

Inscriptions in scientific practice are not necessarily stable. Kaiser (2000) examined the long-term history of physicists' use of Feynman diagrams. Initially, these diagrams were invented to streamline, and make visible, computationally intensive components of quantum field theory. They drew heavily on a previous inscription, Minkowski's space-time diagrams, which lent an interpretation of Feynman diagrams as literal trajectories of particles through space and time. Of course, physicists knew perfectly well that the trajectories so described did not correspond to reality, but that interpretation was a convenient fiction, much in the manner in which physicists often talk about subatomic particles as if they were macroscopic objects (e.g., Ochs, Jacoby, & Gonzales, 1994; Ochs, Gonzales, & Jacoby, 1996). Over time, the theory for which Feynman developed his diagrams was displaced, and a competing inscription tuned to the new theory, *dual diagrams*, was introduced. Yet despite its computational advantages, the new inscription (dual diagrams) never replaced the Feynman diagram. Kaiser (2000) suggested that the reason was that the Fenyman diagrams had visual elements in common with the inscriptions of paths in bubble chambers, and this correspondence again had an appeal to realism:

> Unlike the dual diagrams, Feynman diagrams could evoke, in an unspoken way, the scatterings and propagation of real particles, with "realist" associations for those physicists already awash in a steady stream of bubble chamber photographs, in ways that the dual diagrams simply did not encourage. (Kaiser, 2000, pp. 76–77)

Hence, scientific practices of inscription are saturated in some ways with epistemic stances toward the world and thus cannot be understood outside of these views.

Inscription and Argument

Nevertheless, Latour (1990) suggested that systems of inscription, whether they are about archaeology or particle physics, share properties that make them especially well suited for mobilizing cognitive and social resources in service of argument. His candidates include (a) the literal mobility and immutability of inscriptions, which tend to obliterate barriers of space and time and fix change, effectively freezing and preserving it so that it can serve as the object of reflection; (b) the scalability and reproducibility of inscriptions, which guarantee economy even as they preserve the configuration of relations among elements of the system represented by the inscription; and (c) the potential for recombination and superimposition of inscriptions, which generate structures and patterns that might not otherwise be visible or even conceivable. Lynch (1990) reminded us, too, that inscriptions not only preserve change, but edit it as well: Inscriptions reduce and enhance information. In the next section we turn toward studies of the development of children as inscribers, with an eye toward continuities (and some discontinuities) between inscriptions in scientific and everyday activity.

The Development of Inscriptions as Tools for Thought

Children's inscriptions range from commonplace drawings (e.g., Goodnow, 1977) to symbolic relations among maps, scale models, and pictures and their referents (e.g., DeLoache, 1987) to notational systems for music (e.g., Cohen, 1985), number (e.g., Munn, 1998), and the shape of space (Newcombe & Huttenlocher, 2000). These inscriptional skills influence each other so that collectively children develop an ensemble of inscriptional forms (Lee & Karmiloff-Smith, 1996). As a consequence, by the age of 4 years children typically appreciate distinctions among alphabetical, numerical, and other forms of inscription (Karmiloff-Smith, 1992).

Somewhat surprisingly, children invent inscriptions as tools for a comparatively wide range of circumstances and goals. Cohen (1985) examined how children ranging in age from 5 to 11 years created inscriptions of musical tunes they first heard, and then attempted to play with their invented scores. She found that children produced a remarkable diversity of inscriptions that did the job. Moreover, a substantial majority of the 8- to 11-year-olds created the same inscriptions for encoding and decoding. Their inscriptions adhered to one-to-one mapping rules so that, for example, symbols consistently had one meaning (e.g., a triangle might denote a brief duration) and each meaning (e.g., a particular note) was represented by only one symbol. Both of these properties are hallmarks of conventional systems of notation (e.g., Goodman, 1976). Other studies of cognitive development focus on children's developing understandings and uses of inscription for solving puzzle-like problems.

Karmiloff-Smith (1979) had children (7–12 years) create an inscriptional system that could be used as an external memory for driving (with a toy ambulance) a route with a series of bifurcations. Children invented a wide range of adequate mnemonic marks, including maps, routes (e.g., R and L to indicate directions), arrows, weighted lines, and the like. Often, children changed their inscriptions during the course of the task, suggesting that children transform inscriptions in response to local variation in problem solving. All of their revisions in this task involved making information that was implicit, albeit economically rendered, explicit (e.g., adding an additional mark to indicate an acceptable or unacceptable branch), even though the less redundant systems appeared adequate to the task. Karmiloff-Smith (1992) suggested that these inscriptional changes reflected change in internal representations of the task. An alternative interpretation is that children became increasingly aware of the functions of

inscription, so that in this task with large memory demands, changes to a more redundant system of encoding provided multiple cues and so lightened the burden of decoding—a tradeoff between encoding and decoding demands.

Communicative considerations are paramount in other studies of children's revisions of inscriptions. For example, both younger (8–9 years) and older (10–11 years) children adjusted inscriptions designed as aides for others (a peer or a younger child) to solve a puzzle problem in light of the age of the addressee (Lee, Karmiloff-Smith, Cameron, & Dodsworth, 1998). Compared with adults, younger children were more likely to choose minimal over redundant inscriptions for the younger addressee, whereas the older children were equally likely to chose either inscription. Overall, there was a trend for older children to assume that younger addressees might benefit from redundancy.

In a series of studies with older children (sixth grade through high school), diSessa and his colleagues (diSessa, in press; diSessa, Hammer, Sherin, & Kolpakowski, 1991) investigated what students know about inscriptions in a general sense. They found that like younger children, older children and adolescents invented rich arrays of inscriptions tuned to particular goals and purposes. Furthermore, participants' inventions were guided by criteria such as parsimony, economy, compactness (spatially compact inscriptions were preferred), and objectivity (inscriptions sensitive to audience, so that personal and idiosyncratic features were often suppressed).

Collectively, studies of children's development suggest an emerging sense of the uses and skills of inscription across a comparatively wide range of phenomena. Invented inscriptions are generative and responsive to aspects of situation. They are also effective: They work to achieve the goal at hand. Both younger and older children adapt features of inscriptions in light of the intended audience, suggesting an early distinction between idiosyncratic and public functions of inscription. Children's invention and use of inscriptions are increasingly governed by an emerging meta-knowledge about inscriptions, which diSessa et al. (1991) termed *metarepresentational competence*. Such capacities ground the deployment of inscriptions for mathematical activity, although we shall suggest (much as we did for argument) that if mathematics and inscription are to emerge in coordination, careful attention must be paid to the design of mathematics education.

Inscriptions as Mediators of Mathematical Activity and Reasoning

Mathematical inscriptions mediate mathematical activity and reasoning. This position contrasts with inscriptions as mere records of previous thought or as simple conveniences for syntactic manipulation. In this section we trace the ontogenesis of this form of mediated activity, beginning with children's early experiences with parents and culminating with classrooms where inscriptions are recruited to create and sustain mathematical arguments.

Early Development

Van Oers (2000, in press) claimed that early parent-child interactions and play in preschool with counting games set the stage for fixing and selecting portions of counting via inscription. In his account, when a child counts, parents have the opportunity to interpret that activity as referring to cardinality instead of mere succession. For example, as a child completes his or her count, perhaps a parent holds up fingers to signify the quantity and repeats the last word in the counting sequence (e.g., 3 of 1, 2, 3). This act of inscription, although perhaps crudely expressed as finger tallies, curtails the activity of counting and signifies its cardinality. As suggested by Latour (1990), the word or tally (or numeral) can be transported across different situations, such as three candies or three cars, so number becomes mobile as it is recruited to situations of "how many."

Pursuing the role of inscription in developing early number sense, Munn (1998) investigated how preschool children's use of numeric notation might transform their understanding of number. She asked young children to participate in a "secret addition" task. First children saw blocks in containers, and then they wrote a label for the quantity (e.g., with tallies) on the cover of each of four containers. The quantity in one container was covertly increased, and children were asked to discover which of the containers had been incremented. The critical behavior was the child's search strategy. Some children guessed, and others thought that they had to look in each container and try to recall its previous state. However, many used the numerical labels they had written to check the quantity of a container against its previous state. Munn found that over time, preschoolers were more likely to use their numeric inscriptions in their search for the added block, using inscriptions of quantity to compare past and current quantities. In her view, children's notations transformed the nature of their activity, signaling an early integration of inscriptions and conceptions of number.

Coconstitution of conceptions of number and inscription may also rely on children's capacity for analogy. Brizuela (1997) described how a child in kindergarten came to understand positional notation of number by analogy to the use of capital letters in writing. For this child, the 3 in 34 was a "capital number," signifying by position in a manner

reminiscent of signaling the beginning of a sentence with a capital letter.

Microgenetic Studies of Appropriation of Inscription

The cocreation of mathematical thought and inscription is elaborated by microgenetic examination of mathematical activity of individuals in a diverse range of settings. Hall (1990, 1996) investigated the inscriptions generated by algebra problem solvers (ranging from middle school to adult participants, including teachers) during the course of solution. He suggested that the quantitative inferences made by solvers were obtained within representational niches defined by interaction among varied forms of inscription (e.g., algebraic expressions, diagrams, tables) and narratives, not as a simple result of parsing strings of expressions. These niches or material designs helped participants visualize relations among quantities and stabilized otherwise shifting frames of reference.

Coevolution of inscription and thinking was also prominent in Meira's (1995, in press) investigations of (middle school) student thinking about linear functions that describe physical devices, such as winches or springs. His analysis focused on student construction and use of a table of values to describe relations among variables such as the turns of a winch and the distance an object travels. As pairs of students solved problems, Meira (1995) noted shifting signification, reminiscent of the role of the Feynman diagrams, in that marks initially representing weight shifted to represent distance. He also observed several different representational niches (e.g., transforming a group of inscriptions into a single unit and then using that unit in subsequent calculation), a clear dependence of problem-solving strategies on qualities of the number tables, and a lifting away from the physical devices to operations in the world of the inscriptions—a way of learning to see the world through inscriptions.

Izsak (2000) found that pairs of eighth-grade students experimented with different possibilities for algebraic expressions as they explored the alignment between computations on paper and the behavior of the winch featured in the Meira (1995) study. Pairs also negotiated shifting signification between symbols and aspects of device behavior, suggesting that interplay between mathematical expression and qualities of the world may constitute one genetic pathway for mediating mathematical thinking via inscriptions. (We pick this theme up again in the section on mathematical modeling.)

In their studies of student appropriation of graphical displays, Nemirovsky and his colleagues (Nemirovsky & Monk, 2000; Nemirovsky, Tierney, & Wright, 1998) suggested that learning to see the world through systems of inscription is more accurately described as a fusion between signifiers and signified. In their view, coming to interpret an inscription mathematically often involves treating the signifiers and the signified as undifferentiated, even though one knows very well that they can be treated distinctly (the roots of these capabilities are likely found in pretense and possibility, as we described previously). In their studies of students' attempts to interpret graphical displays of physical motion, they recounted an instance of teacher scaffolding by using "these" to refer simultaneously to lines on a graph, objects (toy bears), and a narrative in which the bears were nearing the finish of a race. This referential ambiguity helped the student create an interpretation of the inscription that was more consistent with disciplinary practice as she sorted out the relations among inscription, object, and the ongoing narrative that anchored use of the inscription to a time course of events.

According to Stevens and Hall (1998), mathematical learning mediated by inscription is tantamount to disciplining one's perception: coming to see the inscription as a mathematical marking consistent with disciplinary interpretations, rather than as a material object consistent with everyday interpretations. That such a specialized form of perception is required is evident in the confusions that even older students have about forms of notation like the graph of a linear function. For example, a student's interpretation of slope in a case study conducted by Schoenfeld, Smith, and Arcavi (1993) included a conception of the line as varying with slope, y-intercept, and x-intercept. The result was that the student's conception of slope was not stable across contexts of use.

Stevens and Hall (1998) traced the interventions of a tutor who helped an eighth-grade student working on similar problems of interpretation of graphical displays. Their analysis focused on the tutoring moves that helped reduce the student's dependence on a literal grid representing Cartesian coordinates. Some of the teacher's assistance included literal occlusion of grid, a move designed to promote disciplinary understanding by literally short-circuiting the student's reliance on the grid in order to promote a disciplinary focus on ratio of change to describe the line. Moschkovich (1996) examined how pairs of ninth-grade students came to discipline their own perceptions by coordinating talk, gestures, and inscriptions of slope and intercept. Inscriptions helped orient students toward a shared object of reference, and the use of everyday metaphors such as hills and steepness grounded this joint focus of conversation. Ultimately, however, the relative ambiguity of these everyday metaphors instigated (for some pairs) a more disciplined interpretation because meanings for these terms proved ambiguous in the context of conversation. However, not all pairs of students

evolved toward disciplinary-centered interpretation, again suggesting the need for instructional support.

Studies of Inscription in Classrooms Designed to Support Invention and Appropriation

Some research provides glimpses of invention and use of inscription in classrooms where the design of instruction supports students' invention and appropriation of varying forms of mathematical inscription. These studies are oriented toward a collective level of analysis (i.e., treating the class as a unit of analysis) because the premise is that, following Latour (1990), inscriptions mobilize arguments in particular communities. In these studies the community is the mathematics culture of the classroom. Moreover, "a focus on inscriptions requires traditional learning environments to be redesigned in such a way that students can appropriate inscription-related practices and discourses" (Roth & McGinn, 1998, p. 52).

Cobb, Gravemeijer, Yackel, McClain, and Whitenack (1997) traced children's coordination of units of 10 and 1 in a first grade class. Instruction was designed to situate investigation of these units and unit collections in a context of packaging candies. Arithmetic reasoning was constituted as a "chain of signification" (Walkerdine, 1988) in which unifix cubes first signified a quantity of candies packed in the shop and then this sign (the unifix cubes–candies relation) was incorporated as a signified of various partitions of candies inscribed as pictured collections. At this point the structure of the collection, rather than the original packaging of candy, became the object of thinking. The structure of the collection, in turn, served as the signified of yet another signifier, a notational rendering of collections as, for instance, 3r13c (3 rolls, 13 candies). Cobb et al. (1997) noted that this rendering served as the vehicle by means of which the pictured collections became models of arithmetic reasoning (also see Gravemeijer, Cobb, Bowers, & Whitenack, 2000).

Kemeny (2001) examined the collective dialogic processes during a lesson in which a third-grade teacher helped students construct the mathematical object referred to by the inscription of the Cartesian system. Her analysis underscores the interplay between collective argument and inscription. It also highlights the role of the teacher's orchestration of conversation and inscription. First, the teacher introduced a new signifier, drawing the axes of the coordinate system on the blackboard, and invited students to consider whether it might be a good tool for thinking about relationships between the sides of similar rectangles. Because these students had a prior history of investigating concepts of ratio via the study of geometric similarity (Lehrer, Strom, & Confrey, in press), the introduction of the signifier (the inscription) created an opportunity for students to create the signified—the Cartesian grid (see Sfard, 2000). Children's first attempts to generate a signified were based on projecting metaphors of measure. They decided, for example, that the lengths of the axes should be subdivided into equal measures and that this subdivision implied an origin labeled numerically as zero because movement along the axis was a distance, not a count. They debated where this origin should be placed and generated several valid alternatives. At this point, the teacher stepped in to introduce a convention, which students accepted as sensible.

Some students then transported a practice they had generated in previous investigations, superimposing paper models of similar rectangles to observe their growth, to the axes on the blackboard, drawing rectangles that mimicked the paper material. This invited consideration of the axes as a literal support (and raised questions about what to label them), but it also inspired one student to notice a stunning possibility—a rectangle might be represented by one of its vertices. Perhaps there was no need to draw the whole thing! Their teacher promptly seized upon this suggestion, and the students went on to explore its implications. Eventually, they concluded that there could be as many rectangles as they liked, not just the cases initially considered, and that all similar rectangles could be represented and generated as a line through the origin.

Inscription (Cartesian coordinates) and argument (a generalization about similar figures) were co-originated. The inscription did not spring out of thin air, but it became a target of metaphoric projection and extension and was ultimately treated as an object in its own right. The construction of this object invited a format for generalization, the line representing all rectangles, and also an epistemology of pattern. What was true for three or four cases was accepted as true for infinitely many. Over the course of several lessons, students' inscriptions of similarity as numeric ratio, as algebraic pattern (e.g., the class of similar rectangles described by $LS = 3 \times SS$, where LS and SS refer to "long side" and "short side," respectively), and as a line in the Cartesian system introduced a resonance among inscriptional forms. For example, the sense of pattern generalization could be expressed in three distinctive forms of inscription, yet the equivalence of these forms invited construction of a signified that spanned all three (Lehrer et al., in press).

The lesson analyzed by Kemeny (2001) was anchored in a history of inscription in the classroom (Lehrer, Jacobson, Kemeny, & Strom, 1999; Lehrer & Pritchard, in press). The norms in the classroom included a stance toward adopting inscriptions as tools for thinking and, further, toward assuming that no inscription would be wasted; that is, if students developed a stable (and public) system of mathematical inscription, they could reasonably expect to use it again. One such opportunity was presented to students later in the year when they conducted investigations about the growth of plants. Lehrer, Schauble, Carpenter, and Penner (2000) tracked students' inscriptions of plant growth during successive phases of inquiry over the course of approximately three months. The investigators found a reflexive relationship between children's inscriptions of growth and their ideas about growth. Over time, children either invented or appropriated inscriptions that increasingly drew things together by increasing the dimensionality of their models of growth. For example, initial inscriptions were one-dimensional records of height, but these were later supplanted by models of plant volume that incorporated variables of height, width, and depth and that were sequenced chronologically to facilitate test of the conjecture that plant growth was an analogue of geometric growth (which it was not). Inscription and conception of growth were co-originated in Rotman's (1993) sense.

Notation: A Privileged Inscription

Developmental studies of children's symbolization, microgenetic studies of individuals' efforts to appropriate inscription, and collective studies of classrooms where inscriptions are recruited to argument describe a complementary genetic pathway for the development of mathematical reasoning: the interactive constitution of inscription and mathematical objects. These studies also reveal the cognitive and social virtues of privileging notations among inscriptions.

Goodman (1976) suggested heuristic principles to distinguish notational systems from other systems of inscription. The principles govern relations among inscriptions (signifiers—literal markings), objects (signified), character classes (equivalent inscriptions, such as different renderings of the numeral 7), and compliance classes (equivalent objects, such as dense materials or emotional people). Two principles govern qualities of inscriptions that qualify as notation: (a) syntactic disjointedness, meaning that each inscription belongs to only one character class (e.g., the marking 7 is recognized as a member of a class of numeral 7s, but not numeral 1s), and (b) syntactic differentiation, meaning that one can readily determine the intended referent of each mark (e.g., if one marked quantity with length, then the differences in length corresponding to differences in quantity should be perceived readily).

Two other principles regulate mappings between character classes and compliance classes. The first is that all inscriptions of a character class should have the same compliance class, which Goodman (1976) referred to as a principle of unambiguity. For example, all numeral 7s should refer to the same quantity, even though the quantity might be comprised of seven dogs or seven cats. It follows, then, that character classes should not have overlapping fields of compliance classes—the principle of semantic disjointedness. For example, the numeral 7 and the numeral 8 should refer to different quantities. This requirement rules out natural language's intersecting categories, such as whale and mammal. Finally, a principle of semantic differentiation indicates that every object represented in the notational scheme should be able to be classified discretely (assigned to a compliance class)—a principle of digitalization of even analog qualities. For example, the quantities 6.999 and 7.001 might be assigned to the quantity 7, either as a matter of practicality or as a matter of necessity before the advent of a decimal notation.

These features of notational systems afford the capacity to treat symbolic expressions as things in themselves, and thus to perform operations on the symbols without regarding what they might refer to. This capacity for symbolically mediated generalization creates a new faculty for mathematical reasoning and argument (Kaput, 1991, 1992; Kaput & Schaffer, in press). For example, the well-formedness of notations makes algorithms possible, transforming ideas into computations (Berlinski, 2000). Notational systems simultaneously provide systematic opportunity for student expression of mathematical ideas, but the same systematicity places fruitful constraints on that expression (Thompson, 1992).

We have seen, too, how notations transform mathematical experiences genetically, both over the life span (from early childhood to adulthood) and over the span of growing expertise (from novices to professional practitioners of mathematics and science). Consider, for example, the van Oers (2000, in press) account of parental scaffolding to notate children's counting. This marking objectifies counting activity so that it becomes more visible and entity-like. The use of a symbolic system for number foregrounds the quantity that results from the activity of counting and backgrounds the counting act itself. This separation of activity (counting) from its product (quantity) sets the stage for making quantity a substrate for further mathematical activities, such as counts of quantities as exemplified in the Cobb et al. (1997) study of first graders. Microgenetic studies like those of Hall (1990) and Meira (1995) suggest that inscriptions tend to drift over time and use toward notations that stabilize interactions among participants. The classroom studies by Kemeny (2001) and Lehrer et al. (2000) also suggest a press toward notation as a means of fixing, selecting, and composing mathematical objects as tools for argument. These studies, however, concentrate largely on the world on paper, so in the next section we address the implications of electronic technologies for bootstrapping the reflexive relation between conception and inscription.

Dynamic Notations

The chief effect of electronic technologies is the corresponding development of new kinds of notational systems, often described as *dynamic* (Kaput, 1992). The manifestations of electronically mediated notations are diverse, but what they share in common is an expression of mathematics as computation (Noss & Hoyles, 1996). DiSessa (2000) suggested that computation is a new form of mathematical literacy, concluding that computation, especially programming, "turns analysis into experience and allows a connection between analytic forms and their experiential implications" (p. 34). Moreover, simulating experience is a pathway for building students' understanding, yet it is also integral to the professional practices of scientists and engineers.

Sherin (2001) explored the implications of replacing algebraic notation with programming for physics instruction. Here again, notations did not simply describe experience for students, but rather reflexively constituted it. Programming expressions of motion afforded more ready expression of time-varying situations. This instigated a corresponding shift in conception from an algebraically guided physics of balance and equilibrium to a physics of process and cause.

Resnick (1994) pointed out that introducing students to parallel programming (e.g., multiple screen "turtles") provides an opportunity to develop mathematical descriptions at multiple levels and to understand how levels interact. The programming language provides an avenue for decentralized thinking. Wilensky and Resnick (1999) noted the difficulties that people have in comprehending levels of phenomena such as traffic jams. At one level, traffic jams result from cars moving forward, but the interactions among cars create jams that proliferate backward. This effect seems at first glance to violate common sense, so it is hard for people to comprehend, but dynamic notations such as parallel programming place new tools in the hands of students for thinking about relations between local agents and aggregate levels of description. Our (much) abbreviated tour of dynamic notations clearly indicates that this form of inscription affords new opportunities to coconstitute mathematical thought and writing. In the sections that follow, we revisit this theme in the realms of geometry measurement and mathematical modeling.

GEOMETRY AND MEASUREMENT

Geometry is a spatial mathematics that has its roots in antiquity yet continues to evolve in the present, as witnessed by continuing concern with computer-generated experiments in visualization. Although common school experiences of geometry emphasize the construction and proof schemes

Figure 15.1   Symmetries of design produced by varying transformations.

of the ancient Greeks, the scope of geometry is far wider, ranging from consideration of fundamental qualities of space such as shape and dimension (e.g., Banchoff, 1990; Senechal, 1990) to the very fabric of artistic design, commercial craft, and models of natural processes (e.g., Stewart, 1998). Consider, for example, the designs displayed in Figure 15.1. Both were created from the same primary cell (unit) but with different symmetries (the left by a translation, the right by a rotation). Systematic analyses of symmetries of design stimulate both mathematical inquiry (e.g., Schattschneider, 1997; Washburn & Crowe, 1988) and the ongoing practice of crafts such as quilting (e.g. Beyer, 1999).

Geometry's versatility and scope have oriented us to survey a range of studies that demonstrate the potential role of geometry in a general mathematics education (Goldenberg, Cuoco, & Mark, 1998; Gravemeijer, 1998). Our chief emphasis is on studies of the growth and development of spatial reasoning in contexts designed to support development (principally, schools). We first consider studies of children's unfolding understanding of the measure of space. Although measurement is (now) traditionally separated from geometry education, we argue for its reinstatement on two grounds. First, measuring a quality of a space invokes consideration of its nature. For example, although measure of dimension seems transparent, the dimension of fractal images in not obvious, and consideration of their measure leads one toward more fundamental ideas about their construction (e.g., Devaney, 1998). Second, measurement is inherently approximate so that it constitutes a bridge to related forms of mathematics, such as distribution and reasoning about variation. Third, practices of measurement span multiple realms of endeavor, especially the quantification of physical reality (Crosby, 1997). Even apparently simple acts, such as matching the color of a sample of dirt to an existing classification scheme, are in fact embedded within systems of inscription and practice, so that measurement is a window to the interplay between imagined qualities of the world and the practical grasp of these qualities (Goodwin, 2000). Consequently, our review focuses on research that helps us understand the

kinds of thinking at the heart of the interplay between this imaginative leap (i.e., an imagined quality of space) and practical grasp (e.g., its measure).

After completing our review of measure, we consider how inquiry about shape and form frames developing types of arguments, especially proof and related "habits of mind" (Goldenberg et al., 1998). Here we focus on the role of dynamic notational systems, embodied (currently) as software tools such as Logo (Papert, 1980) and the Geometer's Sketchpad (Jackiw, 1995), because these spotlight the role of dynamic notation in the development of mathematical reasoning and argument about space.

THE MEASURE OF SPACE

In the sections that follow, we review investigations of children's reasoning about measure. We focus primarily on studies of linear measure to illuminate the interactive roles of inscription and developing conceptions of space because these studies encapsulate many of the findings, issues, and approaches that emerge in investigations of other dimensions and qualities of space, such as area, volume, and angle (see Lehrer, 2002; Lehrer, Jaslow & Curtis, in press, for more extensive review of the latter). We include studies from multiple perspectives. Studies of *cognitive development* typically compare children at different ages (cross-sectional) or follow the same children for a period of time (longitudinal) to observe transitions in thinking, typically about units of measure. These studies provide glimpses of children's thinking under conditions of activity and learning that are typically found in the culture. They follow from the tradition first established by Piaget and his colleagues (e.g., Piaget, Inhelder, & Szeminska, 1960). In contrast, *design studies* modify the learning environment and then investigate the effects of these modifications (Brown, 1992; Cobb, 2001). These studies are often conducted from sociocultural perspectives with attendant attention to forms of inscription and notation and to forms of classroom talk that seem important to help learning to push development in the manner first articulated by Vygotsky (1978).

Mental Representation of Distance

Piaget et al. (1960) proposed that to obtain a measure of length, one must subdivide a distance and translate the subdivision. Thus, *n* iterations of a unit represent a distance of *n* units. Because distance is not a topological feature, Piaget et al. (1960) proposed that children may fail to understand that translation does not affect distance (i.e., that simple motion of a length does not change its measure), a symptom in Piaget's view of *topological primacy* in children's representations of space. For example, preschool children often assert that objects become closer together when they are occluded. Piaget et al. (1960) believed that this assertion revealed children's use of a topological representation that would preserve features such as continuity between points but not (necessarily) distance because occlusion disrupts the topological property of continuity.

A series of experiments conducted by Miller and Baillargeon (1990) suggested instead that children's assertions reflected their relative perceptions of occluded and unoccluded distances. Children from 3 to 6 years of age proposed wooden lengths that would span a distance between two endpoints of a bridge. The distance was then partially occluded. Although children often reported that the occluded endpoints were closer together, they also asserted that the length of the stick that "just fit" between them was unaffected. This lack of correspondence between what children said and what they did refuted the topological hypothesis, indicating instead that children's responses were guided by appearances, not mental representations of distance governed by continuity of points. Research solidly refutes Piaget's equating of the historic structuring of geometries (e.g., progressing from Euclidean to topological) to changes over the life span in ways of mentally representing space (e.g., Darke, 1982). For example, more contemporary research demonstrates that infants (and rats) encode (Euclidean) metric information (see Newcombe & Huttenlocher, 2000). Although it then seems reasonable to assume an implicit metric representation of distance, Piaget's core agenda of documenting transitions in children's constructions of invariants about units of measure has proven fruitful.

Developing Conceptions of Unit

Children's first understandings of length measure often involve direct comparison of objects (Lindquist, 1989; Piaget et al., 1960). Congruent objects have equal lengths, and congruency is readily tested when objects can be superimposed or juxtaposed. Young children (first grade) also typically understand that the length of two objects can be compared by representing them with a string or paper strip (Hiebert, 1981a, 1981b). This use of representational means likely draws on experiences of objects "standing for" others in early childhood, as we described previously. First graders (6- and 7-year-olds) can use *given* units to find the length of different objects, and they associate higher counts with longer objects (Hiebert, 1981a, 1981b; 1984). Most young children (first and second graders) even understand that, given the same length to measure, counts of smaller units will be larger than counts of larger units (Carpenter & Lewis, 1976).

Lehrer, Jenkins, and Osana (1998) conducted a longitudinal investigation of children's conceptions of measurement in the primary grades (a mixed age cohort of first-, second-, and third-grade children were followed for three years). They found that children in the primary grades (Grades 1–3, ages 6–8) may understand qualities of measure like the inverse relation between counts and size of units yet fail to appreciate other constituents of length measure, like the function of identical units or the operation of iteration of unit. Children in this longitudinal investigation often did not create units of equal size for length measure (Miller, 1984), and even when provided equal units, first and second graders typically did not understand their purposes, so they freely mixed, for example, inches and centimeters, counting all to measure a length.

For these students, measure was not significantly differentiated from counting (Hatano & Ito, 1965). Thus, younger students in the Lehrer, Jenkins, et al. (1998) study often imposed their thumbs, pencil erasers, or other invented units on a length, counting each but failing to attend to inconsistencies among these invented units (and often mixing their inventions with other units). Even given identical units, significant minorities of young children failed to iterate spontaneously units of measure when they ran out of units, despite demonstrating procedural competence with rulers (Hatano & Ito, 1965). For example, given 8 units and a 12-unit length, some primary-grade children in the longitudinal study sequenced all 8 units end to end and then decided that they could not proceed further. They could not conceive of how one could reuse any of the eight units, indicating that they had not mentally subdivided the remaining space into unit partitions.

Children often coordinate some of the components of iteration (e.g., use of units of constant size, repeated application) but not others, such as tiling (filling the distance with units). Hence, children in the primary grades occasionally leave spaces between identical units even as they repeatedly use a single unit to measure a length (Lehrer, 2002). The components of unit iterations that children employ appear highly idiosyncratic, most likely reflecting individual differences in histories of learning (Lehrer, Jenkins, et al., 1998).

Developing Conceptions of Scale

Measure of length involves not only the construction of unit but also the coordination of these units into scales. Scales reduce measurement to perception so that the measure of length can be read as a point on that scale. However, only a minority of young children understand that any point on a scale of length can serve as the starting point, and even a significant minority of older children (e.g., fifth graders) respond to nonzero origins by simply reading off whatever number on a ruler aligns with the end of the object (Lehrer, Jenkins, et al., 1998).

Many children throughout schooling begin measuring with one rather than with zero (Ellis, Siegler, & Van Voorhis, 2000). Starting a measure with one rather than zero may reflect what Lakoff and Nunez (2000) referred to as *metaphoric blend*. One everyday metaphor for measure is that of the measuring stick, where physical segments such as body parts (e.g., hands) are iterated and the basic unit is one stick. Another everyday metaphor is that of motion along a path, corresponding to children's experiences of walking (Lakoff & Nunez, 2000). Measure of a distance is then a blend of motion and measuring-stick metaphors, which may lead to mismappings between the 1 count of unit sticks and 0 as the origin of the path distance (Lehrer et al., in press). The difficulties entailed by this metaphoric blend are often most evident when children need to develop measures that involve partitions of units. For example, Lehrer, Jacobson, Kemeny, and Strom (1999) noted that some second-grade children (7–8 years of age) measured a 2 1/2-unit strip of paper as 3 1/2 units by counting, "1, 2, [pause], 3 [pause], 3 1/2." They explained that the 3 referred to the third unit counted, but "there's only a 1/2," so in effect the last unit was represented twice, first as a count of unit and then as a partition of a unit. Yet these same children could readily coordinate different starting and ending points for integers (e.g., starting at 3 and ending at 7 was understood to yield the same measure as starting at 1 and ending at 5).

Design Studies

Design studies focus on establishing developmental trajectories for children's conceptions of linear measure in contexts designed to promote children's use of inscription and tools. These tools and inscriptions are typically objects of conversation in classrooms, recruited to resolve contested claims about comparative lengths of objects or about reasonable estimates of an object's length. Hence, these studies are representative of contexts in which conversation, inscription, and tool use are typically interwoven.

Inscriptions and Tools Mediate Development of Conceptions of Measure

Choices of tools often have consequences for children's conceptions of length (Nunes, Light, & Mason, 1993). Clements, Battista, and Sarama (1998) reported that using computer tools that mediated children's experience of unit and iteration helped children mentally restructure lengths into units. Third graders (9-year-olds) created paths on a computer screen with the Logo programming language. Many activities focused on composing and decomposing lengths, which, in combination with the tool, encouraged students to privilege some segments and their associated command (e.g., forward 10) as units. Subsequently, children found unknown distances by iterations of these units. For example, one student found a length of 40 turtle units by iterating 10 turtle units. Students in this and related investigations apparently developed conceptual rulers to project onto unmarked segments (Clements, Battista, Sarama, Swaminathan, & McMillen, 1997). In an investigation conducted by Watt (1998), fifth-grade students employed a children's computer-aided design tool, kidCAD, to create blueprints of their classroom. At the outset of the investigation, students displayed many of the hallmarks of conceptions of measure that one might expect from the studies of cognitive development. That is, students evidenced tenuous grasp of the zero point of the measurement scale and mixed units of length measure. Here, students' efforts to create consistency between their kidCAD models and their classroom helped make evident the rationale for measurement conventions. These recognitions led to changes in measurement practices and conceptions.

Other studies place a premium on children's constructions of tools and inscriptions for practical measurements. This form of practical activity facilitates transition from embodied activity of length measure, such as pacing, to symbolizing these activities as "foot strips" and related measurement tools (Lehrer et al., 1999; McClain, Cobb, Gravemeijer, & Estes, 1999). By constructing tools and inscribing units of measure, children have the opportunity to discover, with guidance, how scales are constructed. For example, children often puzzle about the meaning of the marks on rulers, and the functions of these marks become evident to children as they attempt to inscribe units and parts of units on their foot strips (Lehrer et al., 1999). Moreover, when all students do not

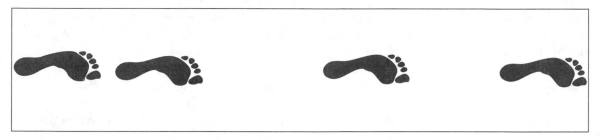

Figure 15.2 A foot-strip measure designed by a third grader.

employ the same unit of measure, the resulting mismatches in the measure of any object's length spurs the need for a conventional unit (Lehrer et al., in press). These mismatches highlight that measurement is not purely a cognitive act. It also relies on perceiving the social utility of conventional units and the communicative function served by common methods of measure.

Tools Enhance the Visibility of Children's Thinking for Teachers

The construction of tools also makes children's thinking more visible to teachers, who can then transform instruction as needed (Lehrer et al., in press). For example, Figure 15.2 displays a facsimile of a foot-strip tape measure designed by a third-grade student, Ike, who indicated that the measure of the ruler's length was 4 because 4 footprint units fit on the tape. Some components of iteration of unit are salient; the units are all alike, and they are sequenced. On the other hand, the process to be repeated appears to be a count, rather than a measure, as indicated by the lack of tiling (space filling) of the units. Construction of this tool mediated this student's understanding of unit, helping make salient some qualities of unit. As we noted previously, these qualities of selection and lifting away from the plane of activity are commonplace features of notational systems. Other qualities that were evident in this student's paces (when he walked a distance, he placed his feet heel to toe) remained submerged in activity. Hence, in this classroom, creation of the tool provided a discursive opening for the teacher and for other students who disagreed with Ike's production and who suggested that perhaps the "spaces mattered."

Splitting and Rational Number

Measurement can serve as a base metaphor for number. Confrey (1995; Confrey & Smith, 1995) suggested an interpenetration between measure and conceptions of number via splitting. *Splitting* refers to repeated partitions of a unit to produce multiple similar forms in direct ratio to the splitting factor. For example, halving produces ratios of 1 : 2. Rather than simply split paper strips as an activity for its own sake, measurement provides a rationale for splitting. Consequently, in a classroom study Lehrer et al. (1999) observed second-grade children repeatedly halving unit lengths as they designed rulers. The need for these partitions of unit arose as children attempted to measure lengths of objects that could not be expressed as whole numbers.

Most children folded their unit (represented as a length of paper strip) in half and then repeated this process to create fourths, eighths, and even sixty fourths. These partitions were then employed in children's rulers, and children noticed that they could increase the precision of measure. Eventually, these actions helped children develop operator conceptions of rational numbers, such as $1/2 \times 1/2 \times 1/2 = 1/8$, and so on. Similarly, division concepts of rational numbers were promoted by classroom attention to problems involving exchanges among units of measure for a fixed length. For example, if one Stephanie (unit) is one-half of a Carmen (unit) and a board is 4 Carmens long, what is its measure in Stephanies? The visual relations among paper-strip models of these units helped children differentiate between "one half of" and "divided by one half." Moss and Case (1999) also featured splitting of linear measurement units as a means to help students develop concepts of rational numbers. Their work with fourth-grade students indicated that measure and splitting, coupled with an emphasis on equivalence among different notations of rational number, helped students develop understanding of proportionality and, correlatively, of rational numbers.

Measure and Modeling as a Gateway to Form

Classroom studies point to ways of melding linear measure and the study of form in the elementary grades in ways that recall their historical codevelopment. Children in Elizabeth Penner's first- and second-grade classes searched for forms (e.g., lines, triangles, squares) that would model the configuration of players in a fair game of tag (Penner & Lehrer, 2000). Attempts to inscribe the shape of fairness initiated cycles of exploration involving length measure and properties related to length in each form (e.g., distances from the sides of a square to the center). Eventually, children decided that circles were the fairest of all forms because the locus of points defining a circle was equidistant from its center. This insight was achieved by emerging conceptions of units of linear measure (e.g., children created foot strips and other tools to represent their paces) and by employing these understandings to explore properties of shape and form. For example, children were surprised to find that the distance between the center of a square and a side varied with the path chosen. Diagonal paths were longer than those that were perpendicular to a side, so they concluded that square configurations were not fair, despite the congruence of their sides.

Children in Carmen Curtis's third-grade class investigated plant growth and modeled changes in their canopy as a series of cylinders. Developing the model posed a new challenge in mathematics, namely, grasping the correspondence between a measure of "width" (the diameter of the base of the cylinder) and its circumference. In other words, children could readily measure the width but then had to figure out how diameter could be used to find circumference. This challenge instigated mathematical investigation, one that culminated in an approximation of the relation between circumference and diameter as "about 3 1/5." So, in the course of modeling nature, children developed a conjecture about the relationship between properties of a circle. Of course, their investigations did not end here, because having convinced themselves and others about the validity of their model of the canopy of the plant, they next had to concern themselves with how to measure its volume (Lehrer et al., in press). In sum, tight couplings between space and measure in these modeling applications are reminiscent of Piaget's investigations but acknowledge that these linkages are the object of instructional design, instead of regarding them as preexisting qualities of mind.

Measure and Argument

In some classrooms measures are recruited in service of argument. For example, in one of the second-grade classrooms referred to previously (Lehrer et al., 1999), children saw paper models of three different rectangles and were asked to consider which covered the most space on the blackboard. The rectangles all had the same area but were of different dimension (1×12, 2×6, 3×4 units). The rectangles were not marked in any way, nor were any tools provided. Children's initial claims were based on mere appearance. Some thought that the "fat" rectangles (i.e., the 3×4) must cover the most space, others that the "long" (i.e., 1×12) rectangles must. These contested claims set the stage for the

teacher's orchestration of argument: How could these claims be resolved? Strom et al. (2001) analyzed the semantic structure of the resulting classroom conversation and rendered its topology as a directed graph. The nodes of the graph consisted of various senses of area as children conceived it (e.g., as space covered, as composed of units), as enacted (e.g., procedures to partition and reallot areas, procedures that privileged certain partitions as units), and as historically situated (e.g., children's senses of this situation as related to others that they had previously encountered). The analysis highlighted the interplay among these forms of knowledge—an interplay characteristic also of professional practice (e.g., Rotman, 1988)—and illustrated that the genetic trajectories of conceptual, procedural, and historical knowledge were firmly bound, not distinct. Moreover, a pivotal role was played by notating the unit-of-area measure, a process that afforded mobility and consequent widespread deployment of unit in service of argument. That is, once the unit-of-area measure assumed consensual status as a legitimate tool in the classroom, it was used literally to mark off segments of area on the three rectangles, eventually establishing that regardless of appearance, each covered 12 square units of space: All three rectangles covered the same space. Of course, the argument constructed by children was orchestrated by the teacher, who animated certain students' arguments, juxtaposed temporally distant forms of reasoning, and reminded students of norms of argument and justification throughout the lesson.

Estimation and Error

Much of the research about measurement explores precision and error of measure in relation to mental estimation (Hildreth, 1983; Joram, Subrahmanyam, & Gelman, 1998). To estimate a length, students at all ages typically employ the strategy of mentally iterating standard units (e.g., imagining lining up a ruler with an object). In their review of a number of instructional studies, Joram et al. (1998) suggested that students often develop brittle strategies closely tied to the original context of estimation. Joram et al. recommended that instruction should focus on children's development of reference points (e.g., landmarks) and on helping children establish reference points and units along a mental number line. It is likely that mental estimation would also be improved with more attention to the nature of unit, as suggested by many of the classroom studies reviewed previously. However, Forrester and Pike (1998) indicated that in some classrooms, estimation is treated dialogically as distinct from measurement. Employing conversation analysis, they examined the discursive status of measurement and estimation in two fifth-grade classrooms. Teachers formatted estimation as an activity that preceded measure and as one characterized by a lack of precision. In contrast, measurement was associated with real length (i.e., perimeter) and the use of a ruler. The consequence of this formatting was that students who employed nonstandard units to estimate, such as their fingers, could not conceive of any way in which the use of such units might be considered as measure. In short, treating estimation and measurement as discursively distinct resulted in a corresponding conceptual division between them.

In contrast, Kerr and Lester (1986) underscored a fusion between measurement and estimation. They suggested that instruction in measure should routinely encompass considerations of sources of error, especially (a) the assumptions (e.g., the model) about the object to be measured, (b) choice of measuring instrument, and (c) how the instrument is used (e.g., method variation). Historically, the recognition of error was troubling to scientists. For example, Porter (1986) documented the struggles in astronomy to come to grips with variability in the measures of interstellar distances. Varelas (1997) examined how third- and fourth-grade students made sense of the variability of repeated trials. Many children apparently did not conceptualize the differences among repeated observations as error and often suggested that fewer trials might be preferable to more. In other words, their solution was to sidestep the problem by avoiding the production of troubling variability. Their conceptions seemed bound with relatively diffuse conceptions of representative values of a set of repeated trials. In a related study, Lehrer et al. (2000) found that with explicit attention to ways of ordering and structuring trial-to-trial variability, second-grade children made sense of trial-to-trial variation by suggesting representative ("typical") values of sets of trials. Choices of typical values included "middle numbers" (i.e., medians) and modes, with a distinct preference for the latter. In contexts where the distinction between signal and noise was more evident, as in repeated measures of mass and volume of objects, fifth-grade students readily proposed variations of trimmed means as estimates of "real" weights and volumes (Lehrer, Schauble, Strom, & Pligge, 2001).

Petrosino, Lehrer, and Schauble (in press) further investigated children's ideas about sources and representations of measurement error. In a classroom study with fourth graders, children's conceptions of error were mediated by the introduction of concepts of distribution. Students readily conceptualized the center of a distribution of measures of the height of the school's flagpole as an estimate of its real height. Furthermore, indicators of variability were related to sources of error, such as individual differences and differences in tools used to measure height. Hence, students in this fourth-grade

classroom came to understand that errors in measure might be random, yet still evidence a structure that could be predicted by information about sources of error, such as instrumentation. Konold and Pollatsek (in press) suggested that contexts of repeated measures like those just described offer significant advantages for assisting students to come to see samples of measures as outcomes of processes, and statistics like center and spread as indicators of signal and noise in these processes, respectively.

Collectively, design studies and research in cognitive development suggest several trends. First, children's initial understandings of the measurement of length are likely grounded in commonplace experiences like walking and commonplace artifacts, like measuring sticks (e.g., rulers). Accordingly, engaging students in inscribing motion and designing tools leads to significant transitions in conceptual development. These transitions exceed those that one might expect from everyday activity and suggest some of the ways in which instructional design and learning can lead children's development. Second, understanding of length measure emerges as children coordinate conceptual constituents of the underpinnings of unit, such as subdivision of a length and iteration of these subdivisions, with the underpinnings of scale, such as origin and its numeric representation as zero. These coordinations appear to emerge in pieces, with procedural manipulation of given units to measure a length often preceding fuller understanding of the entailments of these procedures. Constructs of unit are intertwined with those of scale, so that, for example, the correspondence of zero and the origin of a scale likely undergo several transitions.

Third, length measure can serve as a springboard to related forms of mathematics. The continuity of linear measure, coupled with procedures of splitting, appears to offer important resources for the development of rational number concepts. Measure and modeling can also serve as a foundation for children's conceptions of shape, especially properties of shape. Fourth, measure can be recruited in service of mathematical argument. Such recruitment leads to conceptual change as students grapple with ways of resolving contesting claims by developing and refining their conceptions of unit. Fifth, considering measure as inherently imprecise provides a lead-in to the mathematics of distribution, especially when students are asked to develop accounts (and measures) of the contributions of different sources of error. Measurement processes are a good entry point for distribution because they clarify the contributions both of signal and error to the resulting shape of distribution. Consequently, children can come to see the structure inherent in a random process.

Finally, the need to promote conceptual development about measurement explicitly is acute when one considers that typical beginning university students often exhibit a relatively tenuous grasp of the measure of space. For example, Baturo and Nason (1996) noted that for the majority of a sample of preservice teachers, area measure was tightly bound to recall of formulas, like that used to find the area of a rectangle. Yet none had any idea about the basis of any formula. Most asserted that 128 cm^2 were larger than 1 m^2 because there were 100 cm in a meter. Many thought that area measure applied only to polygons and confused area with volume when presented with three-dimensional shapes. These fragile conceptions of measure appear similar to those of other preservice teachers as well (e.g., Simon & Blume, 1996, as we described earlier).

STRUCTURING SPACE

In the preceding section we described how children come to structure space through its measure, assisted by efforts to model and inscribe length. We reprise these themes by turning to studies that describe how children come to structure space through its construction. We focus on dynamic notations afforded by electronic technologies. These electronic technologies loosen the tether of geometry to its euclidean foundation by introducing motion to form, in contrast to the static geometry of the Greeks (Chazan & Yerushalmy, 1998). Motion is inscribed from either local or global perspectives. The former is represented by tools like Logo (Papert, 1980), which approach the tracing of a locus of points through the action of an agent. The agent's perspective is local because a pattern like a circle or square emerges from a series of movements of the agent, often called a turtle, such as the line segment that results from FD 40 (which traces a path 40 units from the current orientation of the turtle). In contrast, tools like the Geometer's Sketchpad (Jackiw, 1995) introduce motion from the perspective of the plane so that movement is defined globally by stretching line segments (or entire figures). For example, a construction of a square can be resized by dragging one of its vertices or sides. The resulting dynamic geometry is a new mathematical entity (Goldenberg, Cuoco, & Mark, 1998). So, too, is the geometry afforded by Logo, albeit in a different voice (Abelson & diSessa, 1980).

Potential Affordances of Motion Geometries

Like other innovations in notational systems, agent-based and dynamic geometries afford new ways of thinking about shape and form. Logo (representing agent-based geometries) affords a path perspective to shape and form—one comes to

see a figure as a trace of an agent's (e.g., the turtle's) motions. It allows procedural specification of figures, thus creating grounds for linking properties of a figure with operations necessary to generate those properties. For example, the three sides and three angles of a triangle correspond to three linear motions (e.g., Forward 70) and three turns (e.g., Right 120) of a turtle. Procedural specification, in turn, affords a distinction between the particular and the general. For instance, any polygon can be defined by the same procedure simply by varying the inputs to that procedure (e.g., the number of sides). Thus, a procedure can simultaneously represent a specific drawn polygon or any polygon. Dynamic geometries (e.g., the Geometer's Sketchpad) create a clear distinction between the particular and the general in a different way. Drawing allows the creation of particular figures, but construction allows the creation of general figures. The distinction between the two has a practical consequence in dynamic geometry. When dragged (e.g., continuously deforming a shape by pulling on a vertex), the relationships among constituents of drawings change, but the relationships among constituents of constructions do not. The result is that "the diagrams created with geometry construction programs seem poised between the particular and the general. They appear in front of us in all their particularity, but, at the same time, they can be manipulated in ways that indicate the generalities lurking behind the particular" (Chazan & Yerushalmy, 1998, p. 82). So, like Logo, geometry construction environments relax the notational constraint of semantic disjointedness, moving notation in the direction of natural language. The drag mode of dynamic geometries creates multiple examples, and the measurement capabilities of dynamic geometry tools provide a fertile ground for conjecture and experiment. Both Logo and dynamic geometry tools also provide means for individual expression—especially when they are harnessed to design (Harel & Papert, 1991; Lehrer, Guckenberg & Lee, 1988; Shaffer, 1998).

Learning in Motion

What, then, of learning? Do motion geometries create consequential opportunities for pedagogical improvement, or are they simply different? Such questions are fraught with difficulty because media are not neutral, yet their effects are usually bound with the kinds of pedagogical practices that they afford. When these tools for dynamic notation are used in ways that preserve the forms of teaching practice articulated by Schoenfeld (1988; e.g., separating construction and deduction), there seems to be little evidence of any substantive change in student conceptions or epistemologies (Chazan & Yerushalmy, 1998). However, when these tools are coupled with forms of instruction that emphasize conjecture, explanation, and individual expression, the research clearly indicates substantive conceptual change.

Logo Geometry

Perhaps because Logo and its descendants have a longer history, the evidence for learning with Logo spans multiple decades and forms of inquiry. Early studies of learning with Logo were conducted by its founders and featured carefully articulated cases of student investigation of, among other things, conjectures about the invariant sum of the turns (i.e., 360) in the paths of polygons and explorations of the relationships among constituents of shape, such as sides and angles (e.g., Papert, Watt, diSessa, & Weir, 1979). Follow-up studies attempted to articulate relations between teaching and learning with and without Logo tools, and again a subset of this work focused on children's learning about shape and form.

When students use Logo in environments crafted to invite student investigation and reflection, students (most research was conducted with elementary students) tended to analyze properties of shape and form, such as angle and side, and to develop concepts of definition of classes of forms, as well as relations among classes, such as squares and rectangles (e.g., Clements & Battista, 1989, 1990; Lehrer et al., 1988a; Lehrer, Guckenberg, & Sancilio, 1988b; Noss, 1987; Olive, 1991). Collectively, these studies painted portraits of children's learning of shape and form that (at the time) appeared unobtainable with conventional tools and instruction. Moreover, children's responses suggested that their learning followed from their use of Logo tools. For instance, third-grade children often compared forms such as triangles and squares by considering the programs they used to make them: "Well, it's . . . 3 times 120 here and 4 times 90 here equal 360 and that's once around" (Lehrer et al., 1988a, p. 548). Moreover, in the Lehrer et al. (1988a) study, independent measures of children's knowledge of Logo's turn and move commands and their ability to implement variables (tools for generalization in Logo) correlated substantially with measures of children's knowledge of angles and of relations among polygons, respectively. Not surprisingly, these effects were stronger when instruction was designed to help students develop knowledge of geometry, rather than simply good programming skills. Lehrer, Randle, and Sancilio (1989) suggested that some of what children were learning with Logo could be attributed to formats of instruction and argument because researchers were often serving as teachers, and most tended to promote conjecture and explanation in their teaching.

Lehrer et al. (1989) worked with groups of fourth-grade children with similar instructional goals and similar emphases on conjecture and explanation, but only some of the students used Logo as a tool. They found no differences between the groups on measures of simple attributes of shape and form, like angle measure or identification of properties like parallelism. However, students using Logo tools learned more about class inclusion relationships among quadrilaterals and were far better at distinguishing necessary and sufficient conditions in the definition of polygons. Moreover, these differences between groups endured beyond the cycle of instruction. Protocol analysis suggested that one likely source of these differences was children's use of variables to define shapes in ways that allowed them to coconstitute the general (the procedure defined with one or more variables) and the particular (the figure drawn on the screen). Related research with Logo-based microworlds expanded the scope of geometry to transformation and symmetry and to ratio and proportion (Edwards, 1991; see Edwards, 1998; Miller, Lehman, & Koedinger, 1999, for general perspectives on microworlds and learning).

A contemporary cycle of research featuring Logo as a tool for teaching and learning geometry significantly extends its reach and is best exemplified by the work of Clements, Battista, and Samara (2001), who documented a program of research conducted over the last decade. Teachers in Grades 1 through 6 used a Logo-based curriculum of ambitious scope in which study of shape and form featured cycles of conjecture and explanation. Their results replicated the major findings of previous research but also significantly expanded them to include broader portraits of student learning and development with diverse samples of students (See also Clements, Sarama, Yelland, & Glass, in press). In summary, although the path of research with Logo has hit its share of snags and setbacks, investigations of Logo as a tool for teaching and learning geometry in carefully crafted environments suggest clear support for the claim that it provides a new form of mathematical literacy.

Dynamic Geometries

Research with dynamic geometries, again conducted in environments crafted to support learning, also suggested productive means by which these tools can be harnessed to inform conceptual change. However, our tour of this literature is abbreviated due both to its relative novelty and to the practical limitations of space. Several studies indicate that the distinction between drawings and constructed diagrams exemplified in dynamic geometry tools constitutes a form of instructional capital. Constructions that can be subjected to motion afford systematic experimentation, and this capacity for experimentation can be instructionally focused to a search for an explanation of the invariants observed (Arcavi & Hadas, 2000; de Villiers, 1998; Olive, 1998). Koedinger (1998) proposed an explicit model of instructional support for encouraging generation and refinement of student conjectures, thus changing the grounds of deduction. For example, his model develops a tutoring architecture that supports students' constructions of diagrams and associated experiments. Arcavi and Hadas (2000) described instructional support for use of dynamic geometry tools to model situations, with particular attention to how symbolic expression of function is informed by systematic experimentation. Chazan (1993) found that the use of construction-geometry tools in concert with instruction that supported student conjecturing helped high school students become more aware of distinctions between empirical and deductive forms of argument.

Technologically Assisted Design Tools

Although dynamic geometry tools are most often employed to solve mathematical problems posed by teachers, Shaffer (1997) designed a dynamic geometry construction microworld, Escher's World, that high school students used for creating artistic designs by generating systems of mathematical constraints and searching for solutions to mathematical problems with particular design properties and, consequently, aesthetic appeal. Shaffer's instructional design deliberately incorporated practices of architectural design studios so that student design practices also included public displays (e.g., pinups) and conversations with critics about their evolving designs. This coupling of mathematics and design resulted in increased knowledge about transformational design as well as an appreciation of mathematics as a vehicle for expressive intent.

Studies with younger designers and related electronic technologies also indicate the fruitfulness of design contexts that intersect worlds of artistic expression and mathematical intent. Watt and Shanahan (1994) developed a computer microworld and curriculum materials to support design of quilts via transformational geometry. Research conducted with these tools and materials, together with professional development efforts to help teachers understand children's thinking, promoted primary grade students' understanding of transformational geometry, as well as their exploration of algebraic structure, qualities of symmetry, and the limits of induction (Jacobson & Lehrer, 2000; Kaput, 1999; Lehrer, Jacobson, et al., 1998). As with the designers described by Shaffer (1997), children's conversations often reflected their appreciation of an interaction between mathematics and expressive intent. For example, students debated the qualities of "interesting" design; one student, for example, suggested that

some units would be "boring" no matter what transformations or sequences of transformations were applied to make a quilt. He argued that multiple lines of symmetry would restrict the quilt design to simple translation of units (Hartmann & Lehrer, 2000). That is, units with four lines of symmetry restricted the space of possible design. In contrast, asymmetric units allowed for the greatest number of potential designs. Zech et al. (1998) developed dynamic design tools for children's (Grade 5) expression of architectural designs, such as those of swing sets on playground. Designing blueprints for these architectural challenges served as a forum for exploration of measure, shape, and their relations.

In summary, the development of motion geometry tools and related technologies affords new forms of mathematical expression. The dual expression of the particular and the general, together with experimentation about their relation, creates pedagogical opportunities to orient students toward mathematical argument as explanation, not just verification. Moreover, because these tools create conditions for construction and experimentation about shape and form, students at all ages tend to develop analytic capabilities that have long proven difficult to achieve. Perhaps most exciting is the potential for pedagogy at the boundaries of mathematics and design that capitalizes on the expression of mathematical intent. Of course, mathematical intent, in turn, is supported and shaped by these tools.

MODELING PERSPECTIVES

In this section we conclude with an abbreviated tour of some of the emerging work in mathematical modeling in K–12 education. Model-based reasoning is erected on foundations of analogy, representation, and inscription. Analogies, of course, are at the heart of modeling (Hesse, 1965). One system stands in for another. Models are sustained by mappings between the representing and represented worlds, and the nature of these mappings is governed by systems of inscription and notation (Hestenes, 1992). Consider that maps highlight and preserve some aspects of the world while sacrificing others. The familiar Mercator projection facilitates navigation but distorts area of landmasses, often with devastating political consequences.

Bridging Epistemologies

The separation of world and model constitutes a bridge between the epistemologies of mathematics and science. On the one hand, modeling provides opportunities to create coherent and valid mathematical structures. These invite proof so that one can better understand the edifice one is erecting for purposes of representation (Hodgson & Riley, 2001). On the other hand, because models and their referents are distinct, their relation is not one of copy, but rather of fit. Fits between models and worlds are never congruent (the separation between model and world just mentioned), so residuals between them can be determined only in light of other potential models (Grosslight, Unger, & Smith, 1991; Lesh & Doerr, 1998). These qualities of models and modeling practices are at the heart of professional practice in science and in some branches of mathematics (Giere, 1992; Stewart & Golubitsky, 1992).

Research studies of student modeling have generally followed two somewhat overlapping paradigms. The first line of inquiry focuses on *model-eliciting problems* (Lesh, Hoover, Hole, Kelly, & Post, 2000), in which students invent, revise, and share models as solutions to single problems that typically are solved during one lesson. Problems are often drawn from realms of professional practice, especially engineering, business, and the social sciences. Consequently, they often require students to integrate multiple forms of mathematics, not simply the application of a single solution procedure (see the volume by Doerr & Lesh, in press). The second line of inquiry complements the first by engaging students in the progressive mathematization of nature. For example, students pose questions about motion or biological growth and develop models as explanations (diSessa, 2000; Kaput, Roschelle, & Stroup, 2000; Lehrer & Schauble, 2002). This second strand of research focuses on long-term development of student reasoning because acquiring capabilities and propensities to adopt a modeling stance toward the world is an epistemology with slow evolution. Consequently, research typically spans months or even years of student learning. Both strands of work emphasize the development of model-based reasoning in contexts designed to support these practices, so they typically require substantial programs of teacher professional development (e.g., Clark & Lesh, 2002; Lehrer & Schauble, 2000; Schorr & Clark, in press). We focus on model-eliciting problems in the remainder of this section to represent this broader spectrum of research.

Cycles of Modeling

At the heart of a modeling perspective is the belief that some of the most important "big ideas" in elementary mathematics are models (or conceptual systems) for making sense of mathematically significant types of situations (Doerr & Lesh, 2002). Model-eliciting problems are designed to evoke mathematical systems, not single procedures, as solutions (Lesh et al., 2000). Students make sense of these situations not all at once, but rather in a cycle of invention and revision (Lesh & Doerr, 1998; Doerr, Post, & Zawojewski, 2002; Lesh & Harel, in press). Figure 15.3 displays one such

---

Statement of the Big Footprint Problem

Early this morning, the police discovered that, sometime late last night, some nice people rebuilt the old brick drinking fountain in the park. The mayor would like to thank the people who did it. But, nobody saw who it was. All the police could find were lots of footprints. ... You've been given a box (shown below) showing one of the footprints. The person who made this footprint seems to be very big. But, to find this person and his or her friends, it would help if we could figure out how big the person really is?

Your job is to make a "HOW TO" TOOL KIT that the police can use to figure out how big people are - just by looking at their footprints. Your tool kit should work for footprints like the one that is shown here. But it also should work for other footprints.

A Brief Summary of a Big Foot Transcript

<u>Interpretation #1</u>– based on <u>qualitative reasoning</u>: For the first 8 minutes of the session, the students used only global qualitative judgements about the size of footprints for people of different size and sex – or for people wearing different types of shoes. e.g., ... *Wow! This guy's huge. ... You know any girls that big?!! ... Those're Nike's. - The tread's just like mine.*

<u>Interpretation #2</u> – based on <u>additive reasoning</u>: One student put his foot next to the footprint. Then, he used two fingers to mark the distance between the toe of his shoe and the toe of the footprint. Finally, he moved his hand to imagine moving the distance between his fingers to the top of his head. This allowed him to estimate that the height of the person who made the footprint. But, instead of thinking in terms of multiplicative proportions (A/B=C/D), using this approach, the students were using additive differences. That is, if one footprint is 6" longer than another one, then the heights also were guessed to be 6" different.

Note: At this point in the session, the students' thinking was quite unstable. For example, nobody noticed that one student's estimate was quite different than another's; and, predictions that didn't make sense were simply ignored. ... Gradually, as predictions become more precise, differences among predictions began to be noticed; and, attention began to focus on answers that didn't make sense. Nonetheless, "errors" generally were assumed to result from not doing procedure carefully – rather than from not thinking in productive ways.

<u>Interpretation #3</u> – based on <u>primitive multiplicative reasoning</u>: Here, reasoning was based on the notion of being "twice as big". That is, if my shoe is twice as big as yours, then I'd be predicted to be twice as tall as you."

<u>Interpretation #4</u> – based on <u>pattern recognition</u>: Here, the students used a kind of concrete graphing approach to focus on <u>trends</u> across a sequence of measurements. That is, they lined up against a wall and used footprint-to-footprint comparisons to make estimates about height-to-height relationships as illustrated in the diagram shown here. ... This way of thinking was based on the implicit assumption that the trends should be LINEAR - which meant that the relevant relationships were unconsciously treated as being multiplicative. The students said: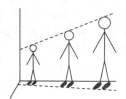

Here, try this... Line up at the wall... Put your heels here against the wall.... Ben, stand here. Frank, stand here.... I'll stand here 'cause I'm about the same (size) as Ben. {She points to a point between Ben and Frank that's somewhat closer to Ben}... {pause} ... Now, where should this guy be? - Hmmm. {She sweeps her arm to trace a line passing just in front of their toes.}... {pause} ... Over there, I think. - {long pause}... Ok. So, where's this guy stand? ... About here. {She points to a position where the toes of everyone's shoes would line up in a straight line.}

Note: At this point in the session, all three students were working together to measure heights, and the measurements were getting to be much more precise and accurate than earlier in the session.

<u>Interpretation #5</u>: By the end of the session, the students were being VERY explicit about comparing footprints-to-height. That is, they estimated that: Height is about six times the size of the footprint. For example, they say: *Everybody's a six footer! (referring to six of their own feet.)*

Figure 15.3   A modeling cycle is characterized by waves of invention and revision.

model-eliciting problem and a case of one group of seventh-grade students' progressive efforts to make sense of this situation. This case illuminates several features of modeling that have been replicated across widely diverse populations of students and problem types (see Doerr & Lesh, 2002, for a compendium of studies).

First, student modeling generally occurs through a series of develop-test-revise cycles. Each cycle involves somewhat different ways of thinking about the nature of givens, goals, and possible solution steps (Lesh & Harel, in press). Refinement typically occurs as students attempt to create coherent and consistent mappings between the representing and represented worlds, often by noticing the implications of a particular choice of representation for the world or by noticing how a feature of the world remains unaccounted for in a model system. These observations resulted in several different interpretations across time. Second, recalling our earlier descriptions of inscriptional mediation of mathematical thinking, modeling nearly always involves multiple and interacting systems of inscription and notation as students grapple with potential correspondences between the world and the emerging mathematical description. Third, there nearly always seem to be multiple and often uncoordinated ideas "in the air" during early phases of modeling, and these are reconciled and stabilized as students attempt to fit models to what they consider data. Thus, data and models often codevelop. Fourth, initial efforts to establish fit are nearly always local, and it is the need to consider others' models and data that often prompts testing for more general structures (Lesh & Doerr, 2002). In the case outlined in Figure 15.3, the group's model was tested further in light of data gathered and models proposed by other student-modelers. This underscores an expanded sense of mathematical argument as conviction and experiment.

Although this chapter is aimed primarily at student learning, modeling research has prompted the development of new forms of research practices and research design methodologies (Kelly & Lesh, 2000). These arose to enable multiple researchers at distant research sites to coordinate work that employed distinct theoretical perspectives focused on multiple levels of interacting participants (students, teachers, curriculum designers, and researchers; Lesh, in press). Cross-site collaborations were accomplished by using shared tasks and research tools (Lesh, Hoover, Hole, Kelly, & Post, 2001) and by recognizing that all of the relevant participants (researchers, teachers, students, and others) can all be thought of as being in the business of designing models and accompanying conceptual tools to make sense of their experiences. Thus, multiple tiers of analysis were required for the conduct of these studies (Lesh, 2002), a prospect that augments the design study perspective described previously.

IMPLICATIONS

Mathematical thinking is a specialized form of argument and inscription, but it has its genesis in the development of everyday capacities of pretense, possibility, conversation, and inscription. Development of mathematical literacy relies on the design of learning niches that support its continued evolution. Schooling provides an unparalleled opportunity to nurture mathematical thinking because it is one of the few arenas where histories of learning can be systematically supported. Of course, this opportunity is founded on the material support of curriculum, the commitment of teachers as professionals, and the development of knowledge about student thinking and learning in contexts where argument and inscription take center stage. With this in mind, we suggest a few plausible directions for research in mathematics education.

First, we urge consideration of a broader scope of mathematics as worthy of research. Most studies focus on analysis (in later grades) and number concepts (in earlier grades). Although we believe this research has proven productive and valuable, it ignores realms of mathematics that may well prove foundational for a mathematics education. For example, the Elkonin-Davydov approach to elementary mathematics education in Russia takes measurement, not "natural" numbers, as foundational. Hence, in this program children's early mathematical experiences are oriented toward measure, not count. Other possibilities suggest themselves, such as early and prolonged emphasis on space and geometry and consideration of the roles of modeling and design in the formation of mathematical expression and epistemology.

Second, and following from a broader scope of inquiry, the nature and grounds of professional practice in the community of researchers require fundamental change. Study of the development of mathematical thinking, rather than piecemeal attention to relatively small components, requires considerate crafting of mathematical experience so that learners consistently participate in mathematical argument and expression. In addition, it requires research designs that are coordinated with this craftsmanship to come to understand long-term development. The complexity of this problem suggests a reorganization of professional practices so that design of learning environments and study of development can be systematically examined and become coconstituted. This form of research is practiced currently in engineering professions, with their emphasis on design prototypes and iterative design. However, to our knowledge, only embryonic forms of this way of working currently exist in mathematics education research.

Third, and in concert with the previous two suggestions, the focus on a mathematics education needs to be coordinated with other realms of endeavor, recalling that the same child who is learning to participate in mathematical argument is also learning to participate in scientific argument, historical argument, and so on. Each of these forms of literacy has implications for the development of identities and interests, and these should be more systematically scrutinized. Dewey (1938) suggested that identities and interests emerge from personal experience and expression. Hence, if we aim to promote students as authors of mathematical expression, then we need to understand more about how these experiences (which are the objects of instructional design) are coordinated and differentiated during the course of education.

REFERENCES

Amsel, E., & Smalley, J. D. (2001). Beyond really and truly: Children's counterfactual thinking about pretend and possible worlds. In P. Mitchell & K. J. Riggs (Eds.), *Children's reasoning and the mind* (pp. 121–147). Hove, UK: Taylor and Francis.

Anderson, J. R., & Schunn, C. D. (2000). Implications of the ACT-R learning theory: No magic bullets. In R. Glaser (Ed.), *Advances in instructional psychology. Educational design and cognitive science* (Vol. 5, pp. 1–33). Mahwah, NJ: Erlbaum.

Anderson, R. C., Chinn, C., Chang, J., Waggoner, M., & Yi, H. (1997). On the logical integrity of children's arguments. *Cognition and Instruction, 15*(2), 135–167.

Arcavi, A., & Hadas, N. (2000). Computer mediated learning: An example of an approach. *International Journal of Computers for Mathematical Learning, 5*, 25–45.

Ball, D. L., & Bass, H. (2000). Making believe: The collective construction of public mathematical knowledge in the elementary classroom. In D. Phillips (Ed.), *Yearbook of the national society for the study of education, Constructivism in education* (pp. 193–224). Chicago: University of Chicago Press.

Banchoff, T. F. (1990). Dimension. In L. A. Steen (Ed.), *On the shoulders of giants. New approaches to numeracy* (pp. 11–59). Washington, DC: National Academy Press.

Barker, R. G., & Wright, H. F. (1954). *Midwest and its children: The psychological ecology of an American town.* Evanston, IL: Row, Peterson.

Baturo, A., & Nason, R. (1996). Student teachers' subject matter knowledge within the domain of area measurement. *Educational Studies in Mathematics, 31*, 235–268.

Benson, D. C. (1999). *The moment of proof.* Oxford, UK: Oxford University Press.

Berlinski, D. (2000). *The advent of the algorithm.* New York: Harcourt.

Brizuela, B. (1997). Inventions and conventions: A story about capital numbers. *For the Learning of Mathematics, 17*, 2–6.

Brown, A. L. (1992). Design experiments: Theoretical and methodological challenges in creating complex interventions in classroom settings. *Journal of the Learning Sciences, 2*, 141–178.

Carpenter, T. P., & Lewis, R. (1976). The development of the concept of a standard unit of measure in young children. *Journal for Research in Mathematics Education, 7*, 53–64.

Chazan, D. (1993). High school geometry students' justification for their views of empirical evidence and mathematical proof. *Educational Studies in Mathematics, 24*, 359–387.

Chazan, D., & Yerushalmy, M. (1998). Charting a course for secondary geometry. In R. Lehrer & D. Chazan (Eds.), *Designing learning environments for developing understanding of geometry and space* (pp. 67–90). Mahwah, NJ: Erlbaum.

Clements, D. H., & Battista, M. A. (1989). Learning of geometric concepts in a LOGO environment. *Journal for Research in Mathematics Education, 20*, 450–467.

Clements, D. H., & Battista, M. A. (1990). The effects of LOGO on children's conceptualizations of angle and polygons. *Journal for Research in Mathematics Education, 21*, 356–371.

Clements, D. H., Battista, M. T., & Sarama, J. (1998). Development of geometric and measurement ideas. In R. Lehrer & D. Chazan (Eds.), *Designing learning environments for developing understanding of geometry and space* (pp. 201–225). Mahwah, NJ: Erlbaum.

Clements, D. H., Battista, M. T., & Sarama, J. (2001). *Logo and geometry.* Reston, VA: National Council of Teachers of Mathematics.

Clements, D. H., Battista, M. T., Sarama, J., Swaminathan, S., & McMillen, S. (1997). Students' development of length concepts in a Logo-based unit on geometric paths. *Journal for Research in Mathematics Education, 28*(1), 70–95.

Clements, D. H., Sarama, J., Yelland, N., & Glass, B. (in press). Learning and teaching geometry with computers in the elementary and middle school. In K. Heid & G. Blume (Eds.), *Research on Technology in the Learning and Teaching of Mathematics: Syntheses and Perspectives.* New York: Information Age Publishing, Inc.

Cobb, P. (2001). Supporting the improvement of learning and teaching in social and institutional context. In S. Carver & D. Klahr (Eds.), *Cognition and instruction: Twenty-five years of progress* (pp. 455–478). Mahwah, NJ: Erlbaum.

Cobb, P., Gravemeijer, K., Yackel, E., McClain, K., & Whitenack, J. (1997). Mathematizing and symbolizing: The emergence of chains of signification in one first-grade classroom. In D. Kirshner & J. A. Whitson (Eds.), *Situated cognition: Social, semiotic, and psychological perspectives* (pp. 151–233). Mahwah, NJ: Erlbaum.

Cobb, P., Wood, T., Yackel, E., & McNeal, B. (1992). Characteristics of classroom mathematics traditions: An interactional analysis. *American Education Research Journal, 29*(3), 573–604.

Cobb, P., Yackel, E., & Wood, T. (1988). Curriculum and teacher development: Psychological and anthropological perspectives. In E. Fennema, T. P. Carpenter, & S. J. Lamon (Eds.), *Integrating research on teaching and learning mathematics* (pp. 92–121). Madison: University of Wisconsin.

Coe, R., & Ruthven, K. (1994). Proof practices and constructs of advanced mathematics students. *British Educational Research Journal, 20*, 41–53.

Cohen, S. (1985). The development of constraints on symbol-meaning structure in notation: Evidence from production, interpretation, and forced-choice judgments. *Child Development, 56,* 177–195.

Confrey, J. (1995). *Student voice in examining "splitting" as an approach to ratio, proportions, and fractions.* Paper presented at the 19th International Conference for the Psychology of Mathematics Education, Universidade Federal de Permanbuco, Recife, Brazil.

Confrey, J., & Smith, E. (1995). Splitting, covariation and their role in the development of exponential functions. *Journal for Research in Mathematics Education, 26,* 66–86.

Crosby, A. W. (1997). *The measure of reality.* Cambridge, UK: Cambridge University Press.

Darke, I. (1982). A review of research related to the topological primacy hypothesis. *Educational Studies in Mathematics, 13,* 119–142.

Davis, P. J., & Hersh, R. (1981). *The mathematical experience.* Boston: Houghton Mifflin.

DeLoache, J. S. (1987). Rapid change in symbolic functioning of young children. *Science, 238,* 1556–1557.

DeLoache, J. S. (1989). Young children's understanding of the correspondence between a scale model and a larger space. *Cognitive Development, 4,* 121–139.

DeLoache, J. S. (1995). Current understanding and use of symbols: The model model. *Current Directions in Psychological Science, 4,* 109–113.

Devaney, R. L. (1998). Chaos in the classroom. In R. Lehrer & D. Chazan (Eds.), *Designing learning environments for developing understanding of geometry and space* (pp. 91–107). Mahwah, NJ: Erlbaum.

de Villiers, M. (1998). An alternative approach to proof in dynamic geometry. In R. Lehrer & D. Chazan (Eds.), *Designing learning environments for developing understanding of geometry and space* (pp. 369–393). Mahwah, NJ: Erlbaum.

Devlin, K. (2000). *The math gene. How mathematical thinking evolved and why numbers are like gossip.* New York: Basic Books.

Dewey, J. (1938). *Experience and education.* New York: Collier Books.

Dias, M. G., & Harris, P. L. (1988). The effect of make-believe play on deductive reasoning. *British Journal of Developmental Psychology, 6,* 207–221.

Dias, M. G., & Harris, P. L. (1990). The influence of the imagination on reasoning by young children. *British Journal of Developmental Psychology, 8,* 305–318.

diSessa, A. (1995). Epistemology and systems design. In A. diSessa, C. Hoyles, R. Noss, & L. D. Edwards (Eds.), *Computers and exploratory learning* (pp. 15–29). Berlin, Germany: Springer-Verlag.

diSessa, A. (2000). *Changing minds: Computers, learning, and literacy.* Carmbridge, MA: MIT Press.

diSessa, A. A. (in press). Students' criteria for representational adequacy. In K. Gravemeijer, R. Lehrer, B. van Oers, & L. Verschaffel (Eds.), *Symbolizing, modeling and tool use in mathematics education.* Dortrecht, The Netherlands: Kluwer.

diSessa, A., Hammer, D., Sherin, B., & Kolpakowski, T. (1991). Inventing graphing: Metarepresentational expertise in children. *Journal of Mathematical Behavior, 10,* 117–160.

Doerr, H., & Lesh, R. (Eds.). (2002). *Beyond constructivism: A models and modeling perspective on mathematics teaching, learning, and problem solving.* Mahwah, NJ: Erlbaum.

Drew, P., & Heritage, J. E. (1992). *Talk at work.* Cambridge, UK: Cambridge University Press.

Edwards, L. D. (1991). Children's learning in a computer microworld for transformation geometry. *Journal for Research in Mathematics Education, 22,* 122–137.

Edwards, L. D. (1998). Embodying mathematics and science: Microworlds as representations. *Journal of Mathematical Behavior, 17,* 53–78.

Edwards, L. D. (1999). Odds and evens: Mathematical reasoning and informal proof. *Journal of Mathematical Behavior, 17,* 489–504.

Ellis, S., Siegler, R. S., & Van Voorhis, F. E. (2000). *Developmental changes in children's understanding of measurement procedures and principles.* Unpublished manuscript.

Forman, E. A. (in press). A sociocultural approach to mathematics reform: Speaking, inscribing, and doing mathematics within communities of practice. In J. Kilpatrick, G. Martin, & D. Shifter (Eds.), *A research companion to the Standards and Principles.* Reston, VA: National Council of Teachers of Mathematics.

Forman, E. A., Larreamendy-Joerns, J., Stein, M. K., & Brown, C. A. (1998). "You're going to want to find out which and prove it": Collective argumentation in a mathematics classroom. *Learning and Instruction, 8,* 527–548.

Forrester, M. A., & Pike, C. D. (1998). Learning to estimate in the mathematics classroom: A conversation-analytic approach. *Journal for Research in Mathematics Education, 29,* 334–356.

Gee, J. P. (1997). Thinking, learning, and reading: The situated sociocultural mind. In D. Kirshner & J. A. Whitson (Eds.), *Situated cognition: Social, semiotic, and psychological perspectives* (pp. 235–259). Mahwah, NJ: Erlbaum.

Gee, J. P. (in press). Critical discourse analysis. In R. Beach, J. Green, M. Kamil, & T. Shanahan (Eds.), *Multidisciplinary perspectives on literacy research.* Cresskill, NJ: Hampton Press.

Gentner, D. (1983). Structure-mapping: A theoretical framework for analogy. *Cognitive Science, 7,* 155–170.

Gentner, D., & Loewenstein, J. (2002). Relational language and relational thought. In E. Amsel & J. P. Byrnes (Eds.), *Language, literacy, and cognitive development. The development and consequences of symbolic communication* (pp. 87–120). Mahwah, NJ: Erlbaum.

Gentner, D., & Toupin, C. (1986). Systematicity and surface similarity in the development of analogy. *Cognitive Science, 10,* 277–300.

Giere, R. N. (1992). *Cognitive models of science*. Minneapolis: University of Minnesota Press.

Goldenberg, E. P., Cuoco, A. A., & Mark, J. (1998). A role for geometry in general education. In R. Lehrer & D. Chazan (Eds.), *Designing learning environments for developing understanding of geometry and space* (pp. 3–44). Mahwah, NJ: Erlbaum.

Goodman, N. (1976). *Languages of art*. Indianapolis, IN: Hackett.

Goodnow, J. (1977). *Children's drawings*. Cambridge, MA: Harvard University Press.

Goodwin, C. (1994). Professional vision. *American Anthropologist, 96*(3), 606–633.

Goodwin, C. (2000). Practices of color classification. *Mind, culture, and activity, 7*(1 & 2), 19–36.

Greeno, J. G. (1998). The situativity of knowing, learning, and research. *American Psychologist, 53*, 5–26.

Hall, R. (1990). *Making mathematics on paper: Constructing representations of stories about related linear functions*. Unpublished doctoral dissertation, University of California at Irvine.

Hall, R. (1996). Representation as shared activity: Situated cognition and Dewey's cartography of experience. *The Journal of the Learning Sciences, 5*(3), 209–238.

Hall, R. (1999). The organization and development of discursive practices for "having a theory." *Discourse Processes, 27*, 187–218.

Hall, R., Stevens, R., & Torralba, T. (in press). Disrupting representational infrastructure in conversations across disciplines. *Mind, Culture, and Activity, 9*(3).

Halliday, M. A. K. (1978). Sociolinguistics aspects of mathematical education. In M. Halliday (Ed.), *Language as social semiotic: The social interpretation of language and meaning* (pp. 195–204). London: University Park Press.

Hanna, G. (1991). Mathematical proof. In D. Tall (Ed.), *Advanced mathematical thinking* (pp. 54–61). Dordrecht, The Netherlands: Kluwer Academic Publishers.

Hanna, G. (1995). Challenges to the importance of proof. *For the Learning of Mathematics, 15*, 42–49.

Harel, G. (1998). *Greek versus modern mathematical thought and the role of Aristotelian causality in the mathematics of the Renaissance: Sources for understanding epistemological obstacles in college students' conceptions of proof*. Plenary talk given at the International Linear Algebra Society Conference, Madison, WI.

Harel, G., & Sowder, L. (1998). Students' proof schemes. In E. Dubinsky, A. Schoenfeld, & J. Kaput (Eds.), *Research on collegiate mathematics education* (Vol. 3, pp. 234–283). American Mathematical Society.

Harel, I., & Papert, S. (1991). *Constructionism*. Norwood, NJ: Ablex.

Harris, P. J., & Leevers, H. J. (2001). Reasoning from false premises. In P. Mitchell & K. J. Riggs (Eds.), *Children's reasoning and the mind* (pp. 67–86). UK: Psychology Press, Taylor and Francis.

Hartmann, C., & Lehrer, R. (2000). *Quilt design as incubator for geometric ideas and mathematical habits of mind*. Proceedings of the 22nd annual meeting of the North American Chapter of the International Group for the Psychology of Mathematics Education, Tucson, AZ.

Hatano, G., & Ito, Y. (1965). Development of length measuring behavior. *Japanese Journal of Psychology, 36*, 184–196.

Haverty, L. A., Koedinger, K. R., Klahr, D., & Alibali, M. W. (2000). Solving inductive reasoning problems in mathematics: Not-so-trivial pursuit. *Cognitive Science, 24*, 249–298.

Hawkins, J., Pea, R. D., Glick, J., & Scribner, S. (1984). "Merds that laugh don't like mushrooms." *Developmental Psychology, 20*, 584–594.

Healy, L., & Hoyles, C. (2000). A study of proof conceptions in algebra. *Journal for Research in Mathematics Education, 31*, 396–428.

Henningsen, M., & Stein, M. K. (1997). Mathematical tasks and student cognition: Classroom-based factors that support and inhibit high-level mathematical thinking and reasoning. *Journal for Research in Mathematics Education, 28*(5), 524–549.

Herbst, P. (2002). Understanding the work of the teacher getting students to prove. *Journal of Research in Mathematics Education, 33*, 176–203.

Hersh, R. (1993). Proving is convincing and explaining. *Educational Studies in Mathematics, 24*(4), 389–399.

Hershkowitz, R., & Schwarz, B. B. (1999). Reflective processes in a mathematics classroom with a rich learning environment. *Cognition and Instruction, 17*, 65–91.

Hesse, M. B. (1965). *Forces and fields*. Totowa, NJ: Littlefield, Adams.

Hestenes, D. (1992). Modeling games in the Newtonian world. *American Journal of Physics, 60*, 440–454.

Hiebert, J. (1981a). Cognitive development and learning linear measurement. *Journal for Research in Mathematics Education, 12*, 197–211.

Hiebert, J. (1981b). Units of measure: Results and implications from national assessment. *Arithmetic Teacher, 28*, 38–43.

Hiebert, J. (1984). Why do some children have trouble learning measurement concepts? *Arithmetic Teacher, 31*, 19–24.

Hildreth, D. J. (1983). The use of strategies in estimating measurements. *Arithmetic Teacher, 30*, 50–54.

Hodgson, T., & Riley, K. J. (2001). Real-world problems as contexts for proof. *Mathematics Teacher, 94*(9), 724–728.

Hoyles, C. (1997). The curricular shaping of students' approaches to proof. *For the Learning of Mathematics, 17*, 7–16.

Izsak, A. (2000). Inscribing the winch: Mechanisms by which students develop knowledge structures for representing the physical world with algebra. *The Journal of the Learning Sciences, 9*(1), 31–74.

Jackiw, N. (1995). *The geometer's sketchpad*. Berkeley, CA: Key Curriculum Press.

Jacobson, C., & Lehrer, R. (2000). Teacher appropriation and student learning of geometry through design. *Journal for Research in Mathematics Education, 31,* 71–88.

Joram, E., Subrahmanyam, K., & Gelman, R. (1998). Measurement estimation: Learning to map the route from number to quantity and back. *Review of Educational Research, 68,* 413–449.

Jorgensen, J. C., & Falmagne, R. J. (1992). Aspects of the meaning of if . . . then for older preschoolers: Hypotheticality, entailment, and suppositional processes. *Cognitive Development, 7,* 189–212.

Kaiser, D. (2000). Stick-figure realism: Conventions, reification, and the persistence of Feynman diagrams, 1948–1964. *Representations, 70,* 49–86.

Kaput, J. (1992). Technology and mathematics education. In D. A. Grouws (Ed.), *Research on mathematics teaching and learning* (pp. 515–556). New York: Macmillan.

Kaput, J. (1999). Teaching and learning a new algebra. In E. Fennema & T. A. Romberg (Eds.), *Mathematics classrooms that promote understanding* (pp. 133–155). Mahwah, NJ: Erlbaum.

Kaput, J., & Shaffer, D. (in press). On the development of human representational competence from an evolutionary point of view. In K. Gravemeijer, R. Lehrer, B. Van Oers, & L. Verschaffel (Eds.), *Symbolizing, modeling, and tool use in mathematics education* (pp. 269–286). Dordrecht, The Netherlands: Kluwer Academic.

Karmiloff-Smith, A. (1992). *Beyond modularity.* Cambridge, MA: MIT Press.

Kelly, A. E., & Lesh, R. A. (Eds.). (2000). *Handbook of research design in mathematics and science education.* Mahwah, NJ: Erlbaum.

Kemeny, V. (2001). *Discursive construction of mathematical meaning: A study of teaching mathematics through conversation in the primary grades.* Unpublished doctoral dissertation, University of Wisconsin, Madison.

Kerr, D. R., & Lester, S. K. (1976). An error analysis model for measurement. In D. Nelson & R. E. Reys (Eds.), *Measurement in school mathematics* (pp. 105–122). Reston, VA: National Council of Teachers of Mathematics.

Kline, M. (1980). *Mathematics: The loss of certainty.* Oxford, UK: Oxford University Press.

Koedinger, K. R. (1998). Conjecturing and argumentation in high-school geometry students. In R. Lehrer & D. Chazan (Eds.), *Designing learning environments for developing understanding of geometry and space* (pp. 319–347). Mahwah, NJ: Erlbaum.

Koedinger, K. R., & Anderson, J. R. (1990). Abstract planning and perceptual chunks: Elements of expertise in geometry. *Cognitive Science, 14,* 511–550.

Konold, C., & Pollatsek, A. (in press). Data analysis as the search for signals in noisy processes. *Journal for Research in Mathematics Education.*

Kotovsky, L., & Gentner, D. (1996). Comparison and categorization in the development of relational similarity. *Child Development, 67,* 2797–2822.

Krummerheuer, G. (1995). The ethnography of argumentation. In P. Cobb & H. Bauersfeld (Eds.), *The emergence of mathematical meaning* (pp. 229–269). Mahwah, NJ: Erlbaum.

Krummerheuer, G. (1998). Formats of argumentation in the mathematics classroom. In H. Steinbring, M. G. Bartolini Bussi, & A. Sierpinska (Eds.), *Language and communication in the mathematics classroom* (pp. 223–234). Reston, VA: National Council of Teachers of Mathematics.

Kuhn, D. (1977). Conditional reasoning in children. *Developmental Psychology, 13,* 342–353.

Kuhn, D. (1989). Children and adults as intuitive scientists. *Psychological Review, 96,* 674–689.

Kuhn, D. (1991). *The skills of argument.* Cambridge, UK: Cambridge University Press.

Kuhn, D. (1992). Thinking as argument. *Harvard Educational Review, 62,* 155–178.

Kuhn, D. (2001). How do people know? *Psychological Science, 12*(1), 1–8.

Kuhn, D., Amsel, E., & O'Loughlin, M. (1988). *The development of scientific thinking skills.* New York: Academic Press.

Kuhn, D., Shaw, V., & Felton, M. (1997). Effects of dyadic instruction on argumentative reasoning. *Cognition and Instruction, 15,* 287–315.

Lakatos, I. (1976). *Proofs and refutations.* Cambridge, UK: Cambridge University Press.

Lakoff, G., & Nunez, R. E. (1997). The metaphorical structure of mathematics: Sketching out cognitive foundations for a mind-based mathematics. In L. D. English (Ed.), *Mathematical reasoning. Analogies, metaphors, and images* (pp. 21–89). Mahwah, NJ: Erlbaum.

Lakoff, G., & Nunez, R. E. (2000). *Where mathematics comes from.* New York: Basic Books.

Lampert, M. (2001). *Teaching problems and the problems of teaching.* New Haven, CT: Yale University Press.

Lampert, M., Rittenhouse, P., & Crumbaugh, C. (1996). Agreeing to disagree: Developing sociable mathematical discourse. In D. Olson & N. Torrance (Eds.), *The handbook of education and human development* (pp. 731–764). Cambridge, MA: Blackwell.

Latour, B. (1986). Visualization and cognition: Thinking with eyes and hands. *Knowledge and Society: Studies in the Sociology of Culture Past and Present, 6,* 1–40.

Latour, B. (1987). *Science in action: How to follow scientists and engineers through society.* Cambridge, MA: Harvard University Press.

Lee, K., Karmiloff-Smith, A., Cameron, C. A., & Dodsworth, P. (1998). Notational adaptation in children. *Canadian Journal of Behavioural Science, 30,* 159–171.

Lehrer, R. (2002). Developing understanding of measurement. In J. Kilpatrick, G. Martin, & D. Schifter (Eds.), *A research companion to the Standards and Principles.* Reston, VA: National Council of Teachers of Mathematics.

Lehrer, R., Guckenberg, T., & Lee, O. (1988a). Comparative study of the cognitive consequences of inquiry-based Logo instruction. *Journal of Educational Psychology, 80*(4), 543–553.

Lehrer, R., Jacobson, C., Kemeny, V., & Strom, D. (1999). Building on children's intuitions to develop mathematical understanding of space. In E. Fennema & T. A. Romberg (Eds.), *Classrooms that promote mathematical understanding* (pp. 63–87). Mahwah, NJ: Erlbaum.

Lehrer, R., Jacobson, C., Thoyre, G., Kemeny, V., Strom, D., Horvath, J., Gance, S., & Koehler, M. (1998). Developing understanding of geometry and space in the primary grades. In R. Lehrer & D. Chazan (Eds.), *Designing learning environment for developing understanding of geometry and space* (pp. 169–200). Mahwah, NJ: Erlbaum.

Lehrer, R., Jenkins, M., & Osana, H. (1998). Longitudinal study of children's reasoning about space and geometry. In R. Lehrer & D. Chazan (Eds.), *Designing learning environment for developing understanding of geometry and space* (pp. 137–167). Mahwah, NJ: Erlbaum.

Lehrer, R., & Pritchard, C. (in press). Symbolizing space into being. In K. Gravemeijer, R. Lehrer, B. Van Oers, & L. Verschaffel (Eds.), *Symbolizing, modeling, and tool use in mathematics education*. Dordrecht, The Netherlands: Kluwer Academic Press.

Lehrer, R., Randle, L., & Sancilio, L. (1989). Learning pre-proof geometry with LOGO. *Cognition and Instruction, 6,* 159–184.

Lehrer, R., & Schauble, L. (2000). Modeling in mathematics and science. In R. Glaser (Ed.), *Advances in Instructional Psychology* (pp. 101–159). Mahwah, NJ: Erlbaum.

Lehrer, R., & Schauble, L. (2002). Symbolic communication in mathematics and science: Co-constituting inscription and thought. In E. Amsel & J. Byrnes (Eds.), *The development of symbolic communication* (pp. 167–192). Mahwah, NJ: Erlbaum.

Lehrer, R., Schauble, L., Carpenter, S., & Penner, D. E. (2000). The inter-related development of inscriptions and conceptual understanding. In P. Cobb, E. Yackel, & K. McClain (Eds.), *Symbolizing and communicating in mathematics classrooms: Perspectives on discourse, tools, and instructional design* (pp. 325–360). Mahwah, NJ: Erlbaum.

Lehrer, R., Strom, D., & Confrey, J. (in press). Grounding metaphors and inscriptional resonance: Children's emerging understanding of mathematical similarity. *Cognition and Instruction.*

Leinhardt, G., & Schwarz, B. B. (1997). Seeing the problem: An explanation from Polya. *Cognition and Instruction, 15,* 395–434.

Lesh, R. (2002). Research design in mathematics education: Focusing on design experiments. In L. English (Ed.), *The international handbook of research design in mathematics education* (pp. 241–287). Hillsdale, N.J.: Erlbaum.

Lesh, R., & Doerr, H. (1998). Symbolizing, communicating, and mathematizing: Key components of models and modeling. In P. Cobb & E. Yackel (Eds.), *Symbolizing and communicating in mathematics classrooms* (pp. 361–383). Mahwah, NJ: Erlbaum.

Lesh, R., & Harel, G. (in press). Problem solving, modeling and local conceptual development. Models and modeling in mathematics education [Monograph for *International Journal for Mathematical Thinking and Learning*]. Hillsdale, NJ: Erlbaum.

Lesh, R., Hoover, M., Hole, B., Kelly, A., & Post, T. (2000). Principles for developing thought revealing activities for students and teachers. In A. Kelly & R. Lesh (Eds.), *The handbook of research design in mathematics and science education* (pp. 591–646). Hillsdale, NJ: Erlbaum.

Leslie, A. M. (1987). Pretense and representation: The origins of "theory of mind." *Psychological Review, 94,* 412–426.

Levi, I. (1996). *For the sake of the argument.* Cambridge, England: Cambridge University Press.

Lindquist, M. (1989). The measurement standards. *Arithmetic Teacher, 37,* 22–26.

Lynch, M. (1990). The externalized retina: Selection and mathematization in the visual documentation of objects in the life sciences. In M. Lynch & S. Woolgar (Eds.), *Representation in scientific practice* (pp. 153–186). Cambridge, MA: MIT Press.

Martin, W. G., & Harel, G. (1989). Proof frames of preservice elementary teachers. *Journal for Research in Mathematics Education, 20,* 41–51.

McClain, K., & Cobb, P. (2001). An analysis of development of sociomathematical norms in one first-grade classroom. *Journal for Research in Mathematics Education, 32,* 236–266.

McClain, K., Cobb, P., Gravemeijer, K., & Estes, B. (1999). Developing mathematical reasoning within the context of measurement. In L. V. Stiff & F. R. Curcio (Eds.), *Developing mathematical reasoning in grades K-12* (pp. 93–106). Reston, VA: National Council of Teachers of Mathematics.

Meira, L. (1995). The microevolution of mathematical representations in children's activity. *Cognition and Instruction, 13,* 269–313.

Meira, L. (in press). Mathematical representations as systems of notations-in-use. In K. Gravemeijer, R. Lehrer, B. Van Oers, & L. Verschaffel (Eds.), *Symbolizing, modeling, and tool use in mathematics education* (pp. 89–106). Dordrecht, The Netherlands: Kluwer.

Miller, C. S., Lehman, J. F., & Koedinger, K. R. (1999). Goals and learning in microworlds. *Cognitive Science, 23,* 305–336.

Miller, K. F. (1984). Child as the measurer of all things: Measurement procedures and the development of quantitative concepts. In C. Sophian (Ed.), *Origins of cognitive skills* (pp. 193–228). Hillsdale, NJ: Erlbaum.

Miller, K. F., & Baillargeon, R. (1990). Length and distance: Do preschoolers think that occlusion bring things together? *Developmental Psychology, 26,* 103–114.

Moschkovich, J. N. (1996). Moving up and getting steeper: Negotiating shared descriptions of linear graphs. *The Journal of the Learning Sciences, 5,* 239–277.

Moss, J., & Case, R. (1999). Developing children's understanding of the rational numbers: A new model and an experimental curriculum. *Journal for Research in Mathematics Education, 30,* 122–147.

Munn, P. (1998). Symbolic function in pre-schoolers. In C. Donlan (Ed.), *The development of mathematical skills* (pp. 47–71). Hove, UK: Psychology Press, Taylor & Francis.

Nemirovsky, R., & Monk, S. (2000). "If you look at it the other way . . .": An exploration into the nature of symbolizing. In P. Cobb, E. Yackel, & K. McClain (Eds.), *Symbolizing and communicating in mathematics classrooms. Perspectives on discourse, tools, and instructional design* (pp. 177–221). Mahwah, NJ: Erlbaum.

Nemirovsky, R., Tierney, C., & Wright, T. (1998). Body motion and graphing. *Cognition and Instruction, 16,* 119–172.

Newcombe, N. S., & Huttenlocher, J. (2000). *Making space.* Cambridge, MA: MIT Press.

Noss, R., & Hoyles, C. (1996). *Windows on mathematical meaning.* Amsterdam: Kluwer Academic.

Nunes, T. (1999). Mathematics learning as the socialization of the mind. *Mind, Culture, and Activity, 6,* 33–52.

Nunes, T., Light, P., & Mason, J. (1993). Tools for thought: The measurement of length and area. *Learning and Instruction, 3,* 39–54.

O'Brien, D., Dias, M., Roazzi, A., & Braine, M. (1998). Conditional reasoning: The logic of supposition and children's understanding of pretense. In M. D. S. Braine & D. P. O'Brien (Eds.), *Mental logic* (pp. 245–272). Mahwah, NJ: Erlbaum.

Ochs, E., Jacoby, S., & Gonzales, P. (1994). Interpretive journeys: How physicists talk and travel through graphic space. *Configurations, 2,* 151–171.

Ochs, E., Taylor, C., Rudolph, D., & Smith, R. (1992). Storytelling as a theory-building activity. *Discourse Processes, 15,* 37–72.

O'Connor, M. C., & Michaels, S. (1993). Aligning academic task and participation status through revoicing: Analysis of a classroom discourse. *Anthropology and Education Quarterly, 24,* 318–335.

O'Connor, M. C., & Michaels, S. (1996). Shifting participant frameworks: Orchestrating thinking practices in group discussion. In D. Hicks (Ed.), *Discourse, learning, and schooling* (pp. 63–103). Cambridge, UK: Cambridge University Press.

Olson, D. R. (1994). *The world on paper.* Cambridge, UK: Cambridge University Press.

Papert, S. (1980). *Mindstorms: Children, computers, and powerful ideas.* New York: Basic Books.

Papert, S., Watt, D., diSessa, A., & Weir, S. (1979). *Final report of the Brookline Logo Project: Pt. II. Project summary and data analysis* (Logo Memo No. 53). Cambridge, MA: MIT, Artificial Intelligence Laboratory.

Penner, E., & Lehrer, R. (2000). The shape of fairness. *Teaching Children Mathematics, 7,* 210–214.

Petrosino, A., Lehrer, R., & Schauble, L. (in press). Structuring error and experimental variation as distribution in the fourth grade. *Mathematical Thinking and Learning.*

Piaget, J., Inhelder, B., & Szeminska, A. (1960). *The child's conception of geometry.* New York: Harper and Row.

Pimm, D. (1987). *Speaking mathematically: Communication in mathematics classrooms.* London: Routledge & Kegan Paul.

Polya, G. (1945). *How to solve it.* Princeton, NJ: Princeton University Press.

Porter, T. M. (1986). *The rise of statistical thinking 1820–1900.* Princeton, NJ: Princeton University Press.

Pozzi, S., Noss, R., & Hoyles, C. (1998). Tools in practice, mathematics in use. *Educational Studies in Mathematics, 36,* 105–122.

Resnick, M. (1994). *Turtles, termites, and traffic jams.* Cambridge, MA: MIT Press.

Rips, L. J. (1998). Reasoning and conversation. *Psychological Review, 105,* 411–441.

Rips, L. J., Brem, S. K., & Bailenson, J. N. (1999). Reasoning dialogues. *Current Directions in Psychological Science, 8,* 172–177.

Roese, N. (1997). Counterfactual thinking. *Psychological Bulletin, 121,* 133–148.

Roth, W. M., & McGinn, M. K. (1998). Inscriptions: Toward a theory of representing as social practice. *Review of Educational Research, 68,* 35–59.

Rotman, B. (1988). Toward a theory of semiotics of mathematics. *Semiotica, 72,* 1–35.

Rotman, B. (1993). *Ad Infinitum.* Stanford, CA: Stanford University Press.

Schauble, L. (1996). The development of scientific reasoning in knowledge-rich contexts. *Developmental Psychology, 32,* 102–119.

Schoenfeld, A. H. (1988). When good teaching leads to bad results: The disasters of "well taught" mathematics courses. *Educational Psychologist, 23,* 145–166.

Schoenfeld, A. H. (1992). Learning to think mathematically: Problem solving, metacognition, and sense making in mathematics. In D. A. Grouws (Ed.), *Handbook of research on mathematics teaching and learning* (pp. 334–370). New York: Macmillan.

Schoenfeld, A. H. (1994). What do we know about mathematics curricula? *Journal of Mathematical Behavior, 13,* 55–80.

Schoenfeld, A. H., Smith, J. P., III, & Arcavi, A. (1993). Learning: The microgenetic analysis of one student's evolving understanding of a complex subject matter domain. In R. Glaser (Ed.), *Advances in instructional psychology* (pp. 55–175). Hillsdale, NJ: Erlbaum.

Schorr, R., & Clark, K. (in press). Using a modeling approach to analyze the ways in which teachers consider new ways to teach mathematics: Models and modeling in mathematics education [Monograph for *International Journal for Mathematical Thinking and Learning*]. Hillsdale, NJ: Erlbaum.

Schunn, C. D., & Anderson, J. R. (1999). The generality/specificity of expertise in scientific reasoning. *Cognitive Science, 23,* 337–370.

Scott, F. J., Baron-Cohen, S., & Leslie, A. (1999). "If pigs could fly": A test of counterfactual reasoning and pretense in children with autism. *British Journal of Developmental Psychology, 17*, 349–362.

Segal, J. (2000). Learning about mathematical proof: Conviction and validity. *Journal of Mathematical Behavior, 18*, 191–210.

Senechal, M. (1990). Shape. In L. A. Steen (Ed.), *On the shoulders of giants. New approaches to numeracy* (pp. 139–181). Washington, DC: National Academy Press.

Sfard, A. (2000). Symbolizing mathematical reality into being—Or how mathematical discourse and mathematical objects create each other. In P. Cobb, E. Yackel, & K. McClain (Eds.), *Symbolizing and communicating in mathematics classrooms. Perspectives on discourse, tools, and instructional design* (pp. 37–98). Mahwah, NJ: Erlbaum.

Sfard, A., & Kieran, C. (2001). Cognition as communication: Rethinking learning-by-talking through multi-faceted analysis of students' mathematical interactions. *Mind, Culture, and Activity, 8*, 42–76.

Shaffer, D. W. (1997). Learning mathematics through design: The anatomy of Escher's world. *Journal of Mathematical Behavior, 16*, 95–112.

Shaffer, D. W. (1998). *Expressive mathematics: Learning by design.* Unpublished doctoral dissertation, MIT, Cambridge, MA.

Sherin, B. L. (2001). A comparison of programming languages and algebraic notation as expressive languages for physics. *International Journal of Computers for Mathematical Learning, 6*, 1–61.

Simon, M. A., & Blume, G. W. (1996). Justification in the mathematics classroom: A study of prospective elementary teachers. *Journal for Research in Mathematics Education, 15*, 3–31.

Stevens, R., & Hall, R. (1998). Disciplined perception: Learning to see in technoscience. In M. Lampert & M. L. Blunk (Eds.), *Talking mathematics* (pp. 107–149). Cambridge, UK: Cambridge University Press.

Stewart, I. (1975). *Concepts of modern mathematics.* New York: Dover.

Stewart, I. (1998). *Life's other secret.* New York: Wiley.

Stewart, I., & Golubitsky, M. (1992). *Fearful symmetry: Is God a geometer?* London: Penguin Books.

Strom, D., Kemeny, V., Lehrer, R., & Forman, E. (2001). Visualizing the emergent structure of children's mathematical argument. *Cognitive Science, 25*, 733–773.

Strom, D., & Lehrer, R. (1999). *The epistemology of generalization.* Paper presented at the Annual Meeting of the American Educational Research Association, Montreal, Quebec, Canada.

Taplin, J. E., Staudenmayer, H., & Taddonio, J. L. (1974). Developmental changes in conditional reasoning: Linguistic or logical? *Experimental Child Psychology, 17*, 360–373.

Thompson, P. W. (1992). Notations, conventions, and constraints: Contributions to effective use of concrete materials in elementary mathematics education. *Journal for Research in Mathematics Education, 23*(2), 123–147.

Thurston, W. P. (1995). On proof and progress in mathematics. *For the Learning of Mathematics, 15*(1), 29–37.

Toulmin, S. E. (1958). *The uses of argument.* Cambridge, England: Cambridge University Press.

van Eemeren, F. H., Grootendorst, R., Henekemans, F. S., Blair, J. A., Johnson, R. H., Krabbe, E. C., Walton, D. N., Willard, C. A., Woods, J., & Zarefsky, D. (1996). *Fundamentals of argumentation theory.* Mahwah, NJ: Erlbaum.

van Oers, B. (2000). The appropriation of mathematical symbols: A psychosemiotic approach to mathematics learning. In E. Y. P. Cobb & K. McClain (Ed.), *Symbolizing and communicating in mathematics classrooms: Perspectives on discourse, tools, and instructional design* (pp. 133–176). Mahwah, NJ: Erlbaum.

van Oers, B. (in press). The mathematization of young children's language. In K. Gravemeijer, R. Lehrer, B. van Oers, & L. Verschaffel (Eds.), *Symbolizing, modeling, and tool use in mathematics education.* Dortrecht, The Netherlands: Kluwer Academic.

Varelas, M. (1997). Third and fourth graders' conceptions of repeated trials and best representatives in science experiments. *Journal of Research in Science Teaching, 34*, 853–872.

Vygotsky, L. (1978). *Mind in society. The development of higher psychological processes.* Cambridge, MA: Harvard University Press.

Warren, B., Ballenger, C., Ogonowski, M., Rosebery, A. S., & Hudicourt-Barnes, J. (2001). Rethinking diversity in learning science: The logic of everyday sense-making. *Journal of Research in Science Teaching, 38*, 529–552.

Watt, D. L. (1998). Mapping the classroom using a CAD program: Geometry as applied mathematics. In R. Lehrer & D. Chazan (Eds.), *Designing learning environments for developing understanding of geometry and space* (pp. 419–438). Mahwah, NJ: Erlbaum.

Watt, D., & Shanahan, S. (1994). *Math and More 2—Teacher Guide.* Atlanta, GA: International Business Machines.

Wells, G. (1999). *Dialogic inquiry.* Cambridge, UK: Cambridge University Press.

Wertsch, J. V. (1998). *Mind as action.* New York: Oxford University Press.

Wilensky, U., & Resnick, M. (1999). Thinking in levels: A dynamic systems approach to making sense of the world. *Journal of Science Education and Technology, 8*, 3–18.

Wood, T. (1999). Creating a context for argument in mathematics class. *Journal for Research in Mathematics Education, 30*(2), 171–191.

Yackel, E., & Cobb, P. (1996). Sociomath norms, argumentation, and autonomy in mathematics. *Journal for Research in Mathematics Education, 27*, 458–477.

CHAPTER 16

Computers, the Internet, and New Media for Learning

RICKI GOLDMAN-SEGALL AND JOHN W. MAXWELL

The Points of Viewing (POV) theory is the foundation upon which this chapter is based. In the POV theory viewers and readers actively layer their viewpoints and interpretations to create emergent patterns and themes (Goldman-Segall, 1996b, 1998b). The purpose of understanding this theory is to enable learners, educators, and designers to broaden their scope and to enable them to learn from one another. The POV theory has been used for more than a decade in ethnographic studies to interpret video research data, but here we apply this theory to interpret and make meaning of a variety of theories of learning and technology, expecting that readers will reinterpret and resituate the theoretical positions in new configurations as they read the text.

We explore how leading theorists have understood learning and teaching in relation to the use of computers, the Internet, and new media technologies. Our goal is to envision the directions in which the field is going and, simultaneously, to tease out some of the sticky webs that have confused decision makers and academics in their search for a singular best practice. The underlying theme running through this chapter is that many routes combining a vast array of perspectives are needed to shape an educationally sound approach to learning and teaching with new media technology. We call this new approach to design and application *perspectivity technologies*.

CONTEXTS AND INTELLECTUAL HISTORY

The legacy of the Enlightenment magnified the age-old debate between empiricism and idealism. In the early twentieth century the debate shifted: Science could be used not only to observe the external world with microscopes and telescopes but also to change, condition, and control behavior. Russian physiologist Ivan Pavlov, most renowned for his experiments with dogs, called his theory *conditioning*. Dogs "learned" to salivate to the sound of a bell that had previously accompanied their eating, even when they received no food. Pavlov's theory of conditioning played a central role in inspiring John B. Watson, who is often cited as the founder of behaviorist psychology. As early as 1913, Watson, while continuing to work with animals, also applied Pavlov's theories to children, believing that people act according to the stimulation of their nervous system and can be conditioned to learn just as easily as dogs can. A turbulent personal turn of events—leading to his dismissal from Johns Hopkins University—extended Watson's behaviorist approach into the domain of marketing. He landed a job as vice president of J. Walter Thompson, one of the largest U.S. advertising companies, and helped changed the course of advertising forever (Daniels, 2000). As media, education, and business enter a convergent course in the twenty-first century and new tools for learning are being designed, behaviorist theories are still a strong, silent partner in the new knowledge economy.

The most noted behaviorist in the educational domain, Burrhus Frederic (B. F.) Skinner, contributed the idea of *operant conditioning*—how positive and negative reinforcement (reward and punishment) can be used as stimuli to shape how humans respond. With this variation, the theory of behavior modification was born. All human actions are seen to be shaped (caused) by the stimulus of the external world on the body. In short, there is no *mind* creating reality, merely a hardwired system that responds to what it experiences from external sources. Infamous for designing the glass Air Crib, which his daughter—observed, measured, and "taught" how to behave—spent time living in, Skinner not only practiced what he preached but led the way for even more elaborate experiments to prove how educators could shape, reinforce, and manipulate humans through repeated drills.

With the advent of the computer and man-machine studies in the postwar period, intrepid behavioral scientists designed and used drill-and-practice methods to improve memorization tasks (e.g., Suppes, 1966). They turned to an examination of the role and efficacy of computers and technology in education, a subject understood in a behaviorist research agenda that valued measurable results and formal experimental methods, as Koschmann (1996, pp. 5–6) noted in his erudite critique of the period. Accordingly, a large amount of learning research in the 1960s, 1970s, and 1980s asked how the computer (an external stimulus) affects (modifies) the individual (a hardwired learning system). Research questions focused on how the process of learning could be improved by using the computer, applied as enhancement or supplement to an otherwise unchanged learning environment.

The approach one takes to using technologies in the learning setting is surely rooted in one's concept of the mind. The mind as a site of research (and not just idealization or speculation) has its modern roots in the work of Jean Piaget (b. 1896), a natural scientist trained in zoology but most renowned for his work as a developmental psychologist and epistemologist. After becoming disillusioned with standardized testing methodology at the Sorbonne in France, Piaget returned to Geneva in 1921 to dedicate the rest of his academic life to studying the child's conception of time (Piaget, 1969), space (Piaget & Inhelder, 1956), number (Piaget, 1952), and the world (Piaget, 1930). Although the idea that children could do things at one age that they could not do at another was not new, Piaget was able to lay out a blueprint for children's conceptual development at different stages of their lives. For example, the classic theory of *conservation* eludes the young child: A tall glass contains more water than a short one even if the young child pours the same water from one glass into the other. Until Piaget, no one had conducted a body of experiments asking children to think about these phenomena and then mapped into categories the diverse views that children use to solve problems. By closely observing, recording his observations, and applying these to an emerging developmental theory of mind, Piaget and his team of researchers in Geneva developed the famous hierarchy of thinking stages: sensorimotor, preoperational, concrete, and formal. Piaget did not limit all thinking into these four rigid categories but rather used them as a way to deepen discussion on how children learn.

What is fundamentally different in Piaget's conception of mind is that unlike the behaviorist view that the external world affects the individual—a unidirectional approach with no input from the individual—the process of *constructivist* learning occurs in the mind of the child encountering, exploring, and theorizing about the world as the child encounters the world while moving through preset stages of life. The child's mind *assimilates* new events into existing cognitive structures, and the cognitive structures *accommodate* the new event, changing the existing structures in a continually interactive process. *Schemata* are formed as the child assimilates new events and moves from a state of disequilibrium to equilibrium, a state only to be put back into disequilibrium every time the child meets new experiences that cannot fit the existing schema. In this way, as Beers (2001) suggests, assimilation and accommodation become part of a dialectical interaction.

We propose that learners, their tools and creations, and the technology-rich *learning habitat* are continually affecting and influencing each other, adding diverse points of viewing to the topic under investigation. This wider range of viewpoints sets the stage for a third state called *acculturation*—the acceptance of diverse points of viewing—that occurs simultaneously with both the assimilation and accommodation processes. Learning becomes an evolving social event in which ideas are diffused among the elements within a culture, as Kroeber argued in 1948 (p. 25), and also are changed by the participation of the elements.

Piaget believed that learning is a spontaneous, individual, cognitive process, distinct from the sort of socialized and nonspontaneous instruction one might find in formal education, and that these two are in a somewhat antagonistic relationship. Critiquing Piaget's constructivism, the Soviet psychologist L. S. Vygotsky (1962) wrote,

> We believe that the two processes—the development of spontaneous and of nonspontaneous concepts—are related and constantly influence each other. They are parts of a single process: the development of concept formation, which is affected by varying external and internal conditions but is essentially a unitary process, not a conflict of antagonistic, mutually exclusive forms of mentation. (p. 85)

Vygotsky heralded a departure from individual mind to social mind, and under his influence educational theorizing moved away from its individual-focused origins and toward more socially or culturally situated perspectives. The paradigmatic approaches of key theorists in learning technology reflect this change as contributions from anthropology and social psychology gained momentum throughout the social sciences. The works of Vygotsky and the Soviet cultural-historical school (notably A. R. Luria and A. N. Leontiev), when translated into English, began to have a major influence, especially through the interpretations and stewardship of educational psychologists such as Jerome Bruner, Michael Cole, and Sylvia Scribner (Bruner, 1990; Cole & Engeström, 1993; Cole & Wertsch, 1996; Scribner & Cole, 1981). Vygotsky focused on the role of social context and mediating tools (language, writing, and culture) in the development of the individual and argued that one cannot study the mind of a child without examining the "social milieu, both institutional and interpersonal" in which she finds herself (Katz & Lesgold, 1993, p. 295). Vygotsky's influence, along with that of pragmatist philosopher John Dewey (1916/1961), opened up the study of technology in learning beyond individual cognition. The ground in the last decade of the twentieth century thus became fertile for growing a range of new media and computational environments for learning, teaching, and research based on a socially mediated conceptualization of how people learn. But the path to social constructionism at the end of the twentieth century first took a circuitous route through what was known as computer-aided instruction (CAI).

Instructional Technology: Beginnings of Computer-Aided Instruction

An examination of the theoretical roots of computers in education exposes its behaviorist beginnings: The computer could reinforce activities that would bring about more efficient learning. For some, this meant "cheaper," for others, "faster," and for yet others, it meant without needing a teacher (see Bromley, 1998, for a discussion). The oldest such tradition of computing in education is CAI. This approach dates back to the early 1960s, notably in two research projects: at Stanford under Patrick Suppes (1966), and the Programmed Logic for Automated Teaching Operations (PLATO) project at the University of Illinois at Urbana-Champaign (UIUC) under Donald Bitzer and Dan Alpert (Alpert & Bitzer, 1970). Both projects utilized the then-new time-sharing computer systems to create learning opportunities for individual students. The potential existed for a time-sharing system to serve hundreds or even thousands of students simultaneously, and this economy of scale was one

of the main drivers of early CAI research. A learner could sit at a terminal and engage in a textual dialogue with the computer system: question and answer. As such, CAI can be situated mostly within the behavioral paradigm (Koschmann, 1996, p. 6), although its research is also informed by cognitive science.

The Stanford CAI project explored elementary school mathematics and science education, and the researchers worked with local schools to produce a remarkable quantity of research data (Suppes, Jerman, & Brian, 1968; Suppes & Morningstar, 1972). Suppes began with tutorial instruction as the key model and saw that the computer could provide individualized tutoring on a far greater scale than was economically possible before. Suppes envisioned computer tutoring on three levels, the simplest of which is drill-and-practice work, in which the computer administers a question and answer session with the student, judging responses correct or incorrect and keeping track of data from the sessions. The second level was a more direct instructional approach: The computer would give information to the student and then quiz the student on the information, possibly allowing for different constructions or expressions of the same information. In this sense, the computer acts much like a textbook. The third level involved more sophisticated dialogic systems in which a more traditional tutor-tutee relationship could be emulated (Suppes, 1966). Clearly, the simple drill-and-practice model is the easiest to implement, and as such the bulk of the early Stanford research uses this model, especially in the context of elementary school arithmetic (Suppes et al., 1968).

The research results from the Stanford experiments are hardly surprising: Students improve over time and with practice. For the time (the 1960s), however, to be able to automate the process was a significant achievement. More interesting from our perspective are the reflections that Suppes (1966) offered regarding the design of the human-computer interface: How and when should feedback be given? How can the system be tailored to different cognitive styles? What is the best way to leverage the unprecedented amount of quantitative data the system collects about each student's performance and progress? These questions still form the cornerstone of much educational technology research.

The PLATO project at UIUC had a somewhat different focus (Alpert & Bitzer, 1970). Over several incarnations of the PLATO system through the 1960s, Bitzer, Alpert, and their team worked at the problems of integrating CAI into university teaching on a large scale, as indeed it began to be from the late 1960s. The task of taking what was then enormously expensive equipment and systems and making them economically viable in order to have individualized tutoring for students drove the development of the systems and led

PLATO to a very long career in CAI—in fact, the direct descendants of the original PLATO system are still being used and developed. The PLATO project introduced some of the first instances of computer-based manipulables, student-to-student conferencing, and computer-based distance education (Woolley, 1994).

From these beginnings CAI and the models it provides for educational technology are now the oldest tradition in educational computing. Although only partly integrated in the school system, CAI is widely used in corporate training environments and in remedial programs and has had something of a resurgence with the advent of the World Wide Web as online training has become popular. It is worth noting that Computer Curriculum Corporation, the company that Suppes started with Richard Atkinson at Stanford in 1967, and NovaNet, a PLATO descendant spun off from UIUC in 1993, were both recently acquired by Pearson Education, the world's largest educational publisher (Pearson Education, 2000).

Cognitive Science and Research on Artificial Intelligence

In order to situate the historical development of learning technology, it is also important to appreciate the impact of what Howard Gardner (1985) refers to as the "cognitive revolution" on both education and technology. For our purposes, the contribution of cognitive science is twofold. First, the advent of the digital computer in the 1940s led quickly to research on artificial intelligence (AI). By the 1950s AI was already a substantial research program at universities such as Harvard, MIT, and Stanford. And although AI research has not yet produced an artificial mind, and we believe it is not likely to do so, the legacy of AI research has had an enormous influence on our present-day computing paradigms, from information management to feedback and control systems, and from personal computing to the notion of programming languages. All derive in large part from a full half-century of research in AI.

Second, cognitive science—specifically the contributions of Piagetian developmental psychology and AI research—gave the world the first practical models of mind, thinking, and learning. Prior to the cognitive revolution, our understanding of the mind was oriented either psychoanalytically and philosophically out of the Western traditions of metaphysics and epistemology or empirically via behaviorism. In the latter case, cognition was regarded as a black box between stimulus and response. Because no empirical study of the contents of this box was thought possible, speculation as to what went on inside was both discouraged and ignored.

Cognitive science, especially by way of AI research, opened the box. For the first time researchers could work from a model of mind and mental processes. In 1957 AI pioneer Herbert Simon went so far as to predict that AI would soon provide the substantive model for psychological theory, in the same way that Newton's calculus had once done for physics (Turkle, 1984, p. 244). Despite the subsequent humbling of AI's early enthusiasm, the effect that this thinking has had on research in psychology and education and even the popular imagination (consider the commonplace notion of one's short-term memory) is vast.

The most significant thread of early AI research was Allen Newell and Herbert Simon's information-processing model at Carnegie-Mellon University. This research sought to develop a generalized problem-solving mechanism, based on the idea that problems in the world could be represented as internal states in a machine and operated on algorithmically. Newell and Simon saw the mind as a "physical symbol system" or "information processing system" (Simon, 1969/1981, p. 27) and believed that such a system is the "necessary and sufficient means" for intelligence (p. 28). One of the venerable traditions of this model is the chess-playing computer, long bandied as exemplary of intelligence. Ironically, world chess master Gary Kasparov's historic defeat by IBM's supercomputer Deep Blue in 1997 had far less rhetorical punch than did AI critic (and chess novice) Hubert Dreyfus's defeat in 1965, but the legacy of the information-processing approach cannot be underestimated.

Yet it would be unfair to equate all of classical AI research with Newell and Simon's approach. Significantly, research programs at Stanford and MIT, though perhaps lower profile, made significant contributions to the field. Two threads in particular are worthy of comment here. One was the development of expert systems concerned with the problem of knowledge representation—for example, Edward Feigenbaum's DENDRAL, which contained large amounts of domain-specific information in biology. Another was Terry Winograd's 1970 program SHRDLU, which first tackled the issue of indexicality and reference in an artificial microworld (Gardner, 1985). As Gardner (1985) pointed out, these developments demonstrated that Newell and Simon's generalized problem-solving approach would give way to more situated, domain-specific approaches.

At MIT in the 1980s, Marvin Minsky's (1986) work led to a theory of the society of minds—that rather than intelligence being constituted in a straightforward representational and algorithmic way, intelligence is seen as the emergent property of a complex of subsystems working independently. The notion of *emergent AI,* more recently explored through massively parallel computers, has with the availability of greater computing power in the 1980s and 1990s become the mainstream of AI research (Turkle, 1995, pp. 126–127).

Interestingly, Gardner (1985) pointed out that the majority of computing—and therefore AI—research has been located within the paradigm defined by Charles Babbage, Lady Ada Lovelace, and George Boole in the nineteenth century. Babbage and Lovelace are commonly credited with the basic idea of the programmable computer; Lady Ada Lovelace's famous quote neatly sums it up: "The analytical engine has no pretensions whatever to originate anything. It can do whatever we know how to order it to perform" (quoted in Turing, 1950). George Boole's contribution was the notion that a system of binary states (0 and 1) could suffice for the representation and transformation of logical propositions. But computing research began to find and transcend the limits of this approach. The rise of emergent AI was characterized as "waking up from the Boolean dream" (Douglas Hofstadter, quoted in Turkle, 1995, p. 135). In this model intelligence is seen as a property emergent from, or at least observable in, systems of sufficient complexity. Intelligence is thus not defined by programmed rules, but by adaptive behavior within an environment.

From Internal Representation to Situated Action

The idea of taking contextual factors seriously became important outside of pure AI research as well. A notable example was the reception given to Joseph Weizenbaum's famous program, Eliza. When it first appeared in 1966, Eliza was not intended as serious AI; it was an experiment in creating a simple conversational interface to the computer—outputting canned statements in response to certain "trigger" phrases inputted by a user. But Eliza, with *her* reflective responses sounding a bit like a Rogerian psychologist, became something of a celebrity—much to Weizenbaum's horror (Turkle, 1995, p. 105). The popular press and even some psychiatrists took Eliza quite seriously. Weizenbaum argued against Eliza's use as a psychiatric tool and against mixing up human beings and computers in general, but Eliza's fame has endured. The interface and relationship that Eliza demonstrates has proved significant in and of itself, regardless of what computational sophistication may or may not lie behind it.

Another contextualist effort took place at Xerox's Palo Alto Research Center (PARC) in the 1970s, where a team led by Alan Kay developed the foundation for the personal computing paradigm that we know today. Kay's team is most famous for developing the mouse-and-windows interface—which Brenda Laurel (Laurel & Mountford, 1990) later called the *direct manipulation interface*. However, at a more fundamental level, the Xerox PARC researchers defined a model of computing that branched away from a formalist,

rules-driven approach and moved toward a notion of the computer as curriculum: an environment for designing, creating, and using digital tools. This approach came partly from explicitly thinking of children as the designers of computing technology. Kay (1996) wrote,

> We were thinking about learning as being one of the main effects we wanted to have happen. Early on, this led to a 90-degree rotation of the purpose of the user interface from "access to functionality" to "environment in which users learn by doing." This new stance could now respond to the echoes of Montessori and Dewey, particularly the former, and got me, on rereading Jerome Bruner, to think beyond the children's curriculum to a "curriculum of user interface." (p. 552)

In the mid-1980s Terry Winograd and Fernando Flores's *Understanding Computers and Cognition: A New Foundation for Design* (1986) heralded a new direction in AI and intelligent systems design. Instead of a rationalist, computational model of mind, Winograd and Flores described the emergence of a decentered and situated approach. The book drew on the phenomenological thinking of Martin Heidegger, the biology of perception work of Humberto Maturana and Francisco Varela, and the speech-act theory of John Austin and John Searle to call for a situated model of mind in the world, capable of (or dependent on) commitment and intentionality in real relationships. Winograd and Flores's work raised significant questions about the assumptions of a functionalist, representational model of cognition, arguing that such a view is based on highly questionable assumptions about the nature of human thought and action.

In short, the question of how these AI and cognitive science developments have affected the role of technology in the educational arena can be summed up in the ongoing debate between instructionist tutoring systems and constructivist toolkits. Whereas the earliest applications of AI to instructional systems attempted to operate by creating a model of knowledge or a problem domain and then managing a student's progress in terms of deviation from that model (Suppes, 1966; Wenger, 1987), later and arguably more sophisticated construction systems looked more like toolkits for exploring and reflecting on one's thinking in a particular realm (Brown & Burton, 1978; Papert, 1980).

THE ROLE OF TECHNOLOGY IN LEARNING

When theorizing about the role of technology in learning, the tendency is often to use an instrumentalist and instructionist approach—the computer, for example, is a useful tool for gathering or presenting information (which is often and incorrectly equated with knowledge). Even within the constructionist paradigm, the social dimension of the learning experience is forgotten, focusing only on the individual child. And even when we remember the Vygotskian *zone of proximal development* (ZPD) with its emphasis on the socially mediated context of learning, we tend to overlook the differences that individuals themselves have in their learning styles when they approach the learning experience. And even when we consider group and individual differences, we fail to examine that individuals themselves try out many styles depending on the knowledge domain being studied and the context within which they are participating. Most important, even when the idea that individuals have diverse points of viewing the world is acknowledged, technologists and new media designers often do little to construct learning environments that truly encourage social construction and knowledge creation.

Designing and building tools as *perspectivity technologies,* we argue, enables learners to participate as members of communities experiencing and creating new worlds from the points of viewing of their diverse personal identities while contributing to the public good of the digital commons. Perspectivity technologies are technologies that enable learners—like stars in a constellation—to be connected to each other and to change their positions and viewpoints yet stay linked within the larger and movable construct of the total configuration of many constellations, galaxies, and universes. It is within the elastic tension among all the players in the community—the learner, the teacher, the content, the artifacts created, and most important, the context of the forces within which they communicate—that new knowledge in, around, and about the world is created.

This next section is organized less chronologically and more functionally and examines technologies from a variety of perspectives: as information sources, curricular areas, communications media, tools, environments, partners, scaffolds, and perspectivity toolkits. In the latter, we return to the importance of using the Points of Viewing theory as a framework for designing new media technological devices.

Technology as Information Source

When we investigate how meaning is made, we can no longer assume that actual social meanings, materially made, consist only in the verbal-semantic and linguistic contextualizations (paradigmatic, syntagmatic, intertextual) by which we have previously defined them. We must now consider that meaning-in-use organizes, orients, and presents, directly or implicitly, through the resources of multiple semiotic systems. (Lemke, 1998)

Access to information has been the dominant mythology of computers in education for many educators. Not taking the time to consider how new media texts bring with them new ways of understanding them, educators and educational technologists have often tried to add computers to learning as one would add salt to a meal. The idea of technology as information source has captured the imagination of school administrators, teachers, and parents hoping that problems of education could be solved by providing each student with access to the most current knowledge (Graves, 1999). In fact, legislators and policy makers trying to bridge the digital divide see an Internet-connected computer on every desktop as a burning issue in education, ranking closely behind public versus charter schools, class size, and teacher expertise as hot-button topics.

Although a growing number of postmodern theorists and semioticians see computers and new media technologies as *texts* to deconstruct (Landow, 1992; Lemke, 1998), it is more common to see computers viewed as *textbooks.* Despite Lemke's reminder that these new media texts require translation and not only digestion, the computer is commonly seen as merely a more efficient method of providing instruction and training, with *information* equated with *knowledge.* Learners working with courseware are presented with information and then tested or questioned on it, much as they would using traditional textbooks. The computer can automatically mark student responses to questions and govern whether the student moves on to the next section, freeing the teacher from this task—an economic advantage noted by many educational technology thinkers. In the late 1980s multimedia—audio, graphics, and video—dominated the educational landscape. Curriculum and learning resources, first distributed as textbook and accompanying floppy disks, began to be distributed on videodisc or CD-ROM, media formats able to handle large amounts of multiple media information. In the best cases, multimedia resources employed hypertext or hypermedia (Landow, 1992; Swan, 1994) navigation schemes, encouraging nonlinear traversal of content. Hypermedia, as such, represented a significant break with traditional, linear instructional design models, encouraging users to explore resources by following links between discrete chunks of information rather than simply following a programmed course. One of the best early exemplars was Apple Computer's Visual Almanac: An Interactive Multimedia Kit (Apple Multimedia Lab, 1989), that enabled students to explore rich multimedia vignettes about interesting natural phenomena as well as events from history and the arts.

More recently, the rise of the Internet and the World Wide Web has stimulated the production of computer-based curriculum resources once again. As a sort of universal multimedia platform, the Web's ability to reach a huge audience very inexpensively has led to its widespread adoption in schools, training centers, corporations, and, significantly, the home. More than packaged curriculum, however, the use of the Internet and the World Wide Web as an open-ended research tool has had an enormous impact on classrooms. Because the software for browsing the web is free (or nearly free) and the technology and skills required to use it are so widespread, the costs of using the Web as a research tool are largely limited to the costs of hardware and connectivity. This makes it an obvious choice for teachers and administrators often unsure of how best to allocate technology funds. The popular reputation of the Web as a universal library or as access to the world's information (much more so than its reputation as a den of pornographers and pedophiles) has led to a mythology of children reaching beyond the classroom walls to tap directly into rich information sources, communicate with scientists and experts, and expand their horizons to a global view. Of course, such discourse needs to be examined in the light of day: The Web is a source of bad information as well as good, and we must also remember that downloading is not equivalent to learning. Roger Schank observed,

> Access to the Web is often cited as being very important to education, for example, but is it? The problem in the schools is not that the libraries are insufficient. The Web is, at its best, an improvement on information access. It provides a better library for kids, but the library wasn't what was broken. (Schank, 2000)

In a similar vein, correspondence schools—both University-based and private businesses dating back to the nineteenth century—are mirrored in today's crop of online distance learning providers (Noble, 1999). In the classic distance education model, a student enrolls, receives curriculum materials in the mail, works through the material, and submits assignments to an instructor or tutor by mail. It is hoped that the student completes everything successfully and receives accreditation. Adding computers and networks to this model changes very little, except for lowering the costs of delivery and management substantially (consider the cost savings of replacing human tutors and markers with an AI system).

If this economic reality has given correspondence schools a boost, it has also, significantly, made it almost imperative that traditional education providers such as schools, colleges, and universities offer some amount of distance access. Despite this groundswell, however, the basic pedagogical questions about distance education remain: To what extent do learners in isolation actually *learn?* Or is distance education better considered a business model for selling accreditation (Noble,

1999)? The introduction of electronic communication and conferencing systems into distance education environments has no doubt improved students' experiences (Hiltz, 1994), and this development has certainly been widespread, but the economic and educational challenges driving distance education still make it an ambivalent choice for both students and educators concerned with the learning process.

Technology as Curriculum Area

Driven by economic urgency—a chronic labor shortage in IT professions (Meares & Sargent, 1999), the extensive impact of computers and networks in the workplace, and the promise of commercial success in the new economy—learning *about* computers is a curriculum area in itself, and it has a major impact on how computers and technology are viewed in educational settings.

The field of technology studies, as a curriculum area, has existed in high schools since the 1970s. But it is interesting to note how much variation there is in the curriculum, across grade levels, from region to region, and from school to school—perhaps increasingly so as years go by. Apart from the U.S. College Board's Advanced Placement (AP) Computer Science Curriculum, which is very narrowly focused on professional computer programming, what one school or teacher implements as the "computer science" or "information technology" curriculum is highly varied, and probably very dependent on individual teachers' notions and attitudes toward what is important. The range includes straightforward computer programming (as in the AP curriculum), multimedia production (Roschelle, Kaput, Stroup, & Kahn, 1998), technology management (Wolfson & Willinsky, 1998), exploratory learning (Harel & Papert, 1991), textbook learning about bits and bytes, and so on. Standards are hard to come by, of course, because the field is so varied and changing.

A most straightforward conclusion that one may draw from looking at our economy, workplace, and prospects for the future is that computer-based technologies are increasingly part of how we work. It follows that simply knowing how to use computers is a requirement for many jobs or careers. This basic idea drives the job skills approach to computers in education. In this model computer hardware and software, particularly office productivity and data processing software, are the cornerstone of technology curriculum because skill with these applications is what employers are looking for. One can find this model at work in most high schools, and it is dominant in retraining and economic development programs. And whereas its simple logic is easy to grasp, this model may be a reminder that simple ideas can be limiting. MIT professor Seymour Papert (1992), invoking curriculum theorist Paolo Freire, wrote,

> If "computer skill" is interpreted in the narrow sense of technical knowledge about computers, there is nothing the children can learn now that is worth banking. By the time they grow up, the computer skills required in the workplace will have evolved into something fundamentally different. But what makes the argument truly ridiculous is that the very idea of banking computer knowledge for use one day in the workplace undermines the only really important "computer skill": the skill and habit of using the computer in doing whatever one is doing. (p. 51)

Papert's critique of computer skills leads to a discussion of *computer literacy,* a term almost as old as computers themselves, and one that is notoriously elusive. Critic Douglas Noble (1985, p. 64) noted that no one is sure what exactly computer literacy is, but everyone seems to agree that it is good for us. Early attempts to define it come from such influential figures as J. C. R. Licklider, one of the founders of what is now the Internet, whose notion of computer literacy drew much on Dewey's ideas about a democratic populous of informed citizens.

As computers became more widespread in the 1980s and 1990s, popular notions of computer literacy grew up around people struggling to understand the role of these new technologies in their lives. The inevitable reduction of computer literacy to a laundry list of knowledge and skills (compare with E. D. Hirsch's controversial 1987 book *Cultural Literacy*) prompted Papert to respond with appeals to the richness of what literacy means:

> When we say "X is a very literate person," we do not mean that X is highly skilled at deciphering phonics. At the least, we imply that X knows literature, but beyond this we mean that X has certain ways of understanding the world that derive from an acquaintance with literary culture. In the same way, the term computer literacy should refer to the kinds of knowing that derive from computer culture. (Papert, 1992, p. 52)

Papert's description broadens what computer literacy might include, but it still leaves the question open. Various contributions to the notion of literacy remain rooted in the particular perspectives of their contributors. Alan Kay (1996) wrote of an "authoring literacy." Journalist Paul Gilster (2000) talked about "digital literacy." Most recently, Andrea diSessa (2000), creator of the Boxer computer program, has written extensively on "computational literacy," a notion that he hopes will rise above the banality of earlier conceptions: "Clearly, by computational literacy I do not mean a casual familiarity with a machine that computes. In retrospect, I find it remarkable that society has allowed such a shameful debasing of the term *literacy* in its conventional use in connection with computers" (p. 5).

The difficulty of coming to terms with computer or digital literacy in any straightforward way has led Mary Bryson to identify the "miracle worker" discourse that results, in which experts are called on to step in to a situation and implement the wonders that technology promises:

> [W]e hear that what is essential for the implementation and integration of technology in the classroom is that teachers should become "comfortable" using it. . . . [W]e have a master code capable of utilizing in one platform what for the entire history of our species thus far has been irreducibly different kinds of things. . . . [E]very conceivable form of information can now be combined with every other kind to create a different form of communication, and what we seek is comfort and familiarity? (deCastell, Bryson, & Jenson, 2000)

However difficult to define, some sense of literacy is going to be an inescapable part of thinking about digital technology and learning. If we move beyond a simple instrumental view of the computer and what it can do, and take seriously how it changes the ways in which we relate to our world, then the issue of how we relate to such technologies, in the complex sense of a *literacy,* will remain crucial.

Technology as Communications Media

The notion of computer as communications medium (or media) began to take hold as early as the 1970s, a time when computing technology gradually became associated with telecommunications. The beginnings of this research are often traced to the work of Douglas Engelbart at the Stanford Research Institute (now SRI International) in the 1960s (Bootstrap Institute, 1994). Englebart's work centered around the oNLine System (NLS), a combination of hardware and software that facilitated the first networked collaborative computing, setting the stage for workgroup computing, document management systems, electronic mail, and the field of *computer-supported collaborative work* (CSCW). The first computer conference management information system, EMISARI, was created by Murray Turoff while working in the U.S. Office of Emergency Preparedness in the late 1960s and was used for monitoring disruptions and managing crises. Working with Starr Roxanne Hiltz, Turoff continued developing networked, collaborative computing at the New Jersey Institute of Technology (NJIT) in the 1970s. Hiltz and Turoff (1978/1993) founded the field of *computer-mediated communication* (CMC) with their landmark book, *The Network Nation.* The book describes a new world of computer conferencing and communications and is to this day impressive in its insightfulness. Hiltz and Turoff's work inspired a generation of CMC researchers, notably including technology theorist Andrew Feenberg (1989) at San

Diego State University and Virtual-U founder Linda Harasim (1990, 1993) at Simon Fraser University.

Although Hiltz and Turoff's *Network Nation* is concerned mostly with business communications and management science, it explores teaching and learning with network technologies as well, applying their insights to practical problems of teaching and learning online:

> In general, the more the course is oriented to teaching basic skills (such as deriving mathematical proofs), the more the lecture is needed in some form as an efficient means of delivering illustrations of skills. However, the more the course involves pragmatics, such as interpretations of case studies, the more valuable is the CMC mode of delivery. (Hiltz & Turoff, 1978/1993, p. 471)

Later, Hiltz wrote extensively about CMC and education. Her 1994 book, *The Virtual Classroom,* elaborates a methodology for conducting education in computer-mediated environments and emphasizes the importance of assignments using group collaboration to improve motivation. Hiltz hoped that students would share their assignments with the community rather simply mail them to the instructor. Hiltz was surely on the mark in the early 1990s as researchers around the world began to realize the promise of "anyplace, anytime" learning (Harasim, 1993) and to study the dynamics of teachers and learners in online, asynchronous conferencing systems.

Parallel to the early development of CMC, research in CAI began to take seriously the possibilities of connecting students over networks. As mentioned earlier, the PLATO system at UIUC was probably the first large-scale distributed CAI system. PLATO was a large time-sharing system, designed (and indeed economically required) to support thousands of users connecting from networked terminals. In the 1970s PLATO began to offer peer-to-peer conferencing features, making it one of the first online educational communities (Woolley, 1994).

Distance education researchers were interested in CMC as an adjunct to or replacement for more traditional modes of communication, such as audio teleconferencing and the postal service. The British Open University was an early test-bed of online conferencing. Researchers such as A. W. Bates (1988) and Alexander Romiszowski and Johan de Haas (1989) were looking into the opportunities presented by computer conferencing and the challenges of conducting groups in these text-only environments. More recently, Bates has written extensively about the management and planning of technology-based distance education, drawing on two decades of experience building "open learning" systems in the United Kingdom and Canada (Bates, 1995). In a 1996 article, Timothy Koschmann suggested that the major educational technology paradigm of the late 1990s would be

computer-supported collaborative learning (CSCL), a close relative of the emerging field of CSCW. Educational technology, Koschmann pointed out, was now concerned with collaborative activities, largely using networks and computer conferencing facilities. Whether CSCL constitutes a paradigm shift is a question we will leave unanswered, but Koschmann's identification of the trend is well noted. Two of the most oft-cited research projects of the 1990s fall into this category. The work of Margaret Riel, James Levin, and colleagues on teleprenticeship (Levin, Riel, Miyake, & Cohen, 1987) and on learning circles (Riel, 1993, 1996) connected many students at great distances—classroom to classroom as much as student to student—in large-scale collaborative learning.

In the early 1990s students, teachers, and researchers around the world engaged in networked collaborative projects. At the Institute for the Learning Sciences (ILS) at Northwestern University, the Collaborative Visualization (Co-Vis) project involved groups of young people in different schools conducting experiments and gathering scientific data on weather patterns (Edelson, Pea, & Gomez, 1996). At the Multimedia Ethnographic Research Lab (MERLin) at the University of British Columbia, young people, teachers, and researchers conducted ethnographic investigations on a complex environmental crisis at Clayoquot Sound on the west coast of Vancouver Island (Goldman-Segall, 1994), with the aim of communicating with other young people in diverse locations. The Global Forest project resulted in a CD-ROM database of video and was designed to link to the World Wide Web to allow participants from around the world to share diverse points of viewing and interpretation of the video data.

At Boston's TERC research center, large-scale collaborative projects were designed in conjunction with the National Geographic Kids Network (Feldman, Konold, & Coulter, 2000; Tinker, 1996). The TERC project was concerned with network science, and as with Riel's learning circles, multiple classrooms collaborated together, in this case gathering environmental science data and sharing in its analysis:

> For example, in the NG Kids Network Acid Rain unit, students collect data about acid rain in their own communities, submit these data to the central database, and retrieve the full set of data collected by hundreds of schools. When examined by students, the full set of data may reveal patterns of acidity in rainfall that no individual class is able discover by itself based on its own data. Over time, the grid of student measurements would have the potential to be much more finely grained than anything available to scientists, and this would become a potential resource for scientists to use. (Feldman et al., 2000, p. 7)

But in the early 1990s, despite much written about the great emerging advances in telecommunications technology, no one could have predicted the sheer cultural impact that the Internet would have. It is difficult to imagine, from the standpoint of the early twenty-first century, any educational technology project that does not in some way involve the Internet. The result is that all education computing is in some way a communications system, involving distributed systems, peer-to-peer communication, telementoring, or some similar construct—quite as Hiltz and Turoff predicted. What is still to be realized is how to design perspectivity technologies that enable, encourage, and expand users' POVs to create more democratic, interactive, convivial, and contextual communication.

One of the most interesting developments in CMC since the advent of the Internet is immersive virtual reality environments—particularly multiuser dungeons (MUDs) and MOOs—within which learners can meet, interact, and collaboratively work on research or constructed artifacts (Bruckman, 1998; Dede, 1994; Haynes & Holmevik, 1998). Virtual environments, along with the popular but less-interesting chat systems on the Internet, add synchronous communications to the asynchronous modes so extensively researched and written about since Hiltz and Turoff's early work. One could position these immersive, virtual environments as perspectivity technologies as they create spaces for participants to create and share their worlds.

The Internet has clearly opened up enormous possibilities for shared learning. The emergence of broad standards for Internet software has lent a stability and relative simplicity to learning software. Moreover, the current widespread availability and use of Internet technologies could be said to mark the end of CMC as a research field unto itself, as it practically merges CMC with all manner of other conceptualizations of new media technological devices: CAI, intelligent tutoring systems, simulations, robotics, smart boards, wireless communications, wearable technologies, pervasive technologies, and even smart appliances.

Technology as Thinking Tool

David Jonassen (1996) is perhaps best known in the educational technology domain as the educator connected with bringing to prominence the idea of computer as *mindtool*. Breaking rank with his previous instructionist approach detailing what he termed *frames for instruction* (Duffy & Jonassen, 1992), Jonassen's later work reflects the inspiration of leading constructionist thinkers such as Papert. In a classic quotation on the use of the computer as a tool from the landmark book, *Mindstorms: Children, Computers, and Powerful Ideas,* Papert (1980) stated, "For me, the phrase 'computer as pencil' evokes the kind of uses I imagine children of the future making of computers. Pencils are used for scribbling as well as writing, doodling as well as drawing, for illicit notes as well as for official assignments" (p. 210).

Although it is easy to think of the computer as a simple tool—a technological device that we use to accomplish a certain task as we use a pen, abacus, canvas, ledger book, file cabinet, and so on—a tool can be much more than just a better pencil. It can be a vehicle for interacting with our intelligence—a thinking tool and a creative tool. For example, a popular notion is that learning mathematics facilitates abstract and analytic thinking. This does not mean that mathematics can be equated with abstract thinking. The computer as a tool enables learners of mathematics to play with the elements that create the structures of the discipline. To employ Papert's (1980) example, children using the Logo programming language explore mathematics and geometry by manipulating a virtual turtle on the screen to act out movements that form geometric entities. Children programming in Logo think differently about their thinking and become epistemologists. As Papert would say, Logo is not just a better pencil for doing mathematics but a tool for thinking more deeply about mathematics, by creating procedures and programs, structures within structures, constructed, deconstructed, and reconstructed into larger wholes. At the MIT Media Lab in the 1970s and 1980s, Papert and his research team led a groundbreaking series of research projects that brought computing technology to schoolchildren using Logo. In *Mindstorms,* Papert explained that Logo puts children in charge of creating computational objects—originally, by programming a mechanical turtle (a 1.5-ft round object that could be programmed to move on the floor and could draw a line on paper as it moved around), and then later a virtual turtle that moved on the computer screen. Papert, a protégé of Jean Piaget, was concerned with the difficult transition from concrete to formal thinking. Papert (1980) saw the computer as the tool that could make the abstract concrete:

> Stated most simply, my conjecture is that the computer can concretize (and personalize) the formal. Seen in this light, it is not just another powerful educational tool. It is unique in providing us with the means for addressing what Piaget and many others see as the obstacle which is overcome in the passage from child to adult thinking. (p. 21)

Beyond Piaget's notion of constructivism, the theory of *constructionism* focused its lens less on the stages of thought production and more on the artifacts that learners build as creative expressions of their understanding. Papert (1991) understood the computer as not merely a tool (in the sense of a hammer) but as an *object-to-think-with* that facilitates novel ways of thinking:

> Constructionism—the N word as opposed to the V word—shares constructivism's connotation of learning as building knowledge structures irrespective of the circumstances of the learning. It then adds the idea that this happens especially felicitously in a context where the learner is consciously engaged in constructing a public entity, whether it's a sand castle on the beach or a theory of the universe. (p. 1)

By the late 1980s, and continuing up to today, the research conducted by Papert's Learning and Epistemology Research Group at MIT had become one of the most influential forces in learning technology. A large-scale intensive research project called Project Headlight was conducted at the Hennigan School in Boston and studied all manner of phenomena around the experience of schoolchildren and Logo-equipped computers. A snapshot of this research is found in the edited volume titled *Constructionism* (Harel & Papert, 1991), which covers the perspectives of 16 researchers.

Goldman-Segall and Aaron Falbel explored Ivan Illich's (1973) theory of conviviality—a theory that, in its simplest form, recommends that tools be simple to use, accessible to all, and beneficial for humankind—in relation to new technologies in learning. Goldman-Segall (2000) conducted a 3-year video ethnography of children's thinking styles at Project Headlight and created a computer-based video analysis tool called Learning Constellations to analyze her video cases. Falbel worked with children to create animation from original drawings and to think of themselves as convivial learners. In Judy Sachter's (1990) research, children explored their understanding of three-dimensional rotation and computer graphics, leading the way for comprehending how children understand gaming. At the same time, Mitchell Resnick, Steve Ocko, and Fred Martin designed smart LEGO bricks controlled by Logo. These LEGO objects could be programmed to move according to Logo commands (Martin & Resnick, 1993; Resnick & Ocko, 1991). Nira Granott asked adult learners to deconstruct how and why these robotic LEGO creatures moved in the way they did. Her goal was to understand the construction of internal cognitive structures that allow an interactive relationship between creator and user (Granott, 1991). Granott's theory of how diverse individuals understand the complex movements of LEGO/Logo creatures was later woven into a new fabric that Resnick—working with many turtles on a screen—called *distributed constructionism* (Resnick, 1991, 1994). Uri Wilensky, with Resnick, deepened the theoretical framework around the behavior of complex systems (Resnick & Wilensky, 1998). To model, describe, and predict emergent phenomena in complex system, Resnick designed LEGO/Logo and Wilensky

and Resnick designed StarLogo. Wilensky more recently designed NetLogo. Wilensky (2000, 2001), a mathematician concerned with probability, is often cited for his asking a simple question to young people: How do geese fly in formation? The answers that young people give reveal how interesting yet difficult emergent phenomena are to describe.

Given Papert's background as a mathematician, mathematics was an important frame for much of the research conducted in Project Headlight. Idit Harel introduced Alan Collin's theory of apprenticeship learning into the intellectual climate involving elementary students becoming software designers. Harel worked with groups of children creating games in Logo for other children to use in learning about fractions. This idea that children could be designers of their learning environments was developed further by Yasmin Kafai, who introduced computer design as an environment to understand how girls and boys think when playing and designing games—a topic of great interest to video game designers (Kafai, 1993, 1996). Kafai has spent more than a decade creating a range of video game environments for girls and boys to design environments for learning. In short, Kafai connected the world of playing and designing to the life of the classroom in a number of studies in the 1990s.

Continuing to expand Papert's legacy with a new generation of graduate students, Kafai at UCLA, Resnick at the MIT Media Lab, Goldman-Segall at the MERLin Lab at the University of British Columbia, Granott at the University of Texas in Dallas, and Wilensky at the Institute of the Learning Sciences at Northwestern continue to explore the notion of computer device as a thinking tool from the constructionist perspective. Over the last decade the focus on understanding the individual mind of a child has shifted to understanding how groups of people collaborate to make sense of the world and participate as actors in shared constructions. Constructionism, in its more social, distributed, and complex versions, is now being reinterpreted through a more situated and ecological point of view.

Technology as Environment

The line between technology as tool and technology as environment is thus a thin one and in fact becomes even more permeable when one considers tools and artifacts as part of a cultural ecology (Cole, 1996; Vygotsky, 1978). As Alan Kay (1996) noted, "Tools provide a path, a context, and almost an excuse for developing enlightenment. But no tool ever contained it, or can provide it. Cesare Pavese observed: *to know the world, we must make it* [italics added]" (p. 547).

Historically, constructivist learning theories were rooted in the epistemologies of social constructivist philosopher

Dewey, social psychologist Vygotsky, and developmental and cognitive psychologist Bruner. Knowledge of the world is seen to be constructed through experience; the role of education is to guide the learner through experiences that provide opportunities to construct knowledge about the world. In Piaget's version, this process is structured by the sequence of developmental stages. In Vygotsky's cultural-historical version, the process is mediated by the tools and contexts of the child's sociocultural environment. As a result of the influence of Vygotsky's work in the 1980s and 1990s across North America, researchers in a variety of institutions began to view the computer and new media technologies as environments, drawing on the notion that learning happens best for children when they are engaged in creating personally meaningful digital media artifacts and sharing them publicly. The MIT Media Lab's Learning and Epistemology Group under the direction of Papert, the Center for Children and Technology under Jan Hawkins and Margaret Honey, Vanderbilt's Cognition and Technology Group under the leadership of John Bransford and Susan Goldman, TERC and the Concord Consortium in Boston under Bob Tinker, Marcia Linn at Berkeley, Georgia Tech under Janet Kolodner, the Multimedia Ethnographic Research Lab (MERLin) under Goldman-Segall, and SRI under Roy Pea are just a few of the exemplary research settings involved in the exploration of learning and teaching using technologies as learning environments during the 1990s. Several of these communities (SRI, Berkeley, Vanderbilt, and the Concord Consortium) formed an association called CILT, the Center for Innovation in Learning and Teaching, which became a hub for researchers from many institutions.

The range of theoretical perspectives employed in conducting research about learning environments in these various research centers has been as diverse as might be expected. Most of these centers have asked what constitutes good research in educational technology and designed research methods that best address the issues under investigations. At the University of Wisconsin–Madison, Richard Lehrer and Leona Schauble (2001) have asked what constitutes *real data* in the classroom. As Mary Bryson from the University of British Columbia and Suzanne de Castell from Simon Fraser University have reminded us for over a decade now, studying technology-based classrooms is at best a complex narrative told by both students and researchers (Bryon & de Castell, 1998).

One might ask what constitutes scientific investigation of the learning environment and for whom. Sharon Derry, another learning scientist from University of Wisconsin–Madison who previously assessed knowledge building in

computer-rich learning environments with colleague Suzanne Lajoie (Lajoie & Derry, 1993) using quantitative measures, has begun to investigate the role of rich video cases in online learning communities with colleagues Constance Steinkuehler, Cindy Hmelo-Silver, and Matt DelMarcelle (Steinkuehler, Derry, Hmelo-Silver, & DelMarcelle, in press). Derry established the Secondary Teacher Education Project (STEP) as an online preservice teacher education learning environment. In collaboration with Goldman-Segall at the New Jersey Institute of Technology's emerging eARTh Lab, Derry is currently exploring how to integrate elements of Goldman-Segall's conceptual framework of conducting digital video ethnographic methods and her software ORION for digital video analysis (shown later in Figure 16.5), as well as use tools designed at the University of Wisconsin for teacher analysis of video cases.

These qualitative research tools and methods, with their emphasis on case studies and in-depth analyses, best describe the conclusions of a study that is constructionist by design. In short, they are methods and tools to study the technology learning environment and to enter into the fabric of the environment as part of the learning experience. Employing perspectivity technologies and using a theoretical framework that encourages collaborative theory building are basic foundations of rich learning environments. When individuals and groups create digital media artifacts for learning or conducting research on learning, the artifacts inhabit the learning environment, creating an ecology that we share with one another and with our media constructions. Perspectivity technologies become expressive tools that allow learners to manipulate *objects-to-think-with* as *subjects-to-think-with*. Technology is thus not just an instrument we use within an environment, but is part of the environment itself.

Technology as Partner

Somewhere amid conceiving of computing technology as artificial mind and conceiving of it as communications medium is the notion of computer as partner. This somewhat more romanticized version of "technology as tool" puts more emphasis on the communicative and interactive aspects of computing. A computer is more than a tool like the pencil that one writes with because, in some sense, it writes back. And although this idea has surely existed since early AI and intelligent tutoring systems (ITS) research, it was not until an important article in the early 1990s (Salomon, Perkins, & Globerson, 1991) that the idea of computers as partners in cognition was truly elaborated.

As early as the 1970s, Gavriel Salomon (1979) had been exploring the use of media (television in particular) and its effect on childhood cognition. Well-versed in Marshall McLuhan's adage, "The medium is the message," Salomon built a bridge between those who propose an instrumentalist view of media (media effects theory) and those who understand media to be a cultural artifact in and of itself. Along these lines, in 1991 Salomon et al. drew a very important distinction: "effects *with* technology obtained during partnership with it, and effects *of* it in terms of the transferable cognitive residue that this partnership leaves behind in the form of better mastery of skills and strategies" (p. 2).

Their article came at a time when the effects of computers on learners were being roundly criticized (Pea & Kurland, 1987), and it helped break new ground toward a more distributed view of knowledge and learning (Brown, Collins, & Duguid, 1996; Pea, 1993). To conceive of the computer as a partner in cognition—or learning, or work—is to admit it into the cultural milieu, to foreground the idea that the machine in some way has *agency* or at least influence in our thinking.

If we ascribe agency to the machine, we are going some way toward anthropomorphizing it, a topic Sherry Turkle has written about extensively (Turkle, 1984, 1995). Goldman-Segall wrote of her partnership with digital research tools as "a partnership of intimacy and immediacy" (Goldman-Segall, 1998b, p. 33). MIT interface theorist Andrew Lippman defined interactivity as mutual activity and interruptibility (Brand, 1987), and Alluquere Rosanne Stone went further, referring to the partnership with machines as a prosthetic device for constructing desire (Stone, 1995). Computers are, as Alan Kay envisioned in the early 1970s, *personal* machines.

The notion of computers as cognitive partners is further exemplified in research conducted by anthropologist Lucy Suchman at Xerox PARC. Suchman's (1987) *Plans and Situated Actions: The Problem of Human-Machine Communication* explored the difference between rational, purposive plans, and circumstantial, negotiated, situated actions. Rather than actions being imperfect copies of rational plans, Suchman showed how plans are idealized representations of real-world actions. With this in mind, Suchman argued that rather than working toward more and more elaborate computational models of purposive action, researchers give priority to the contextual situatedness of practice: "A basic research goal for studies of situated action, therefore, is to explicate the relationship between structures of action and the resources and constraints afforded by physical and social circumstances" (p. 179).

Suchman's colleagues at Xerox PARC in the 1980s designed tools as structures within working contexts; innovative technologies such as collaborative design boards, real-time virtual meeting spaces, and video conferencing between coworkers were a few of the environments at Xerox PARC where people could scaffold their existing practices.

Technology as Scaffold

The computer as scaffold is yet another alternative to tool, environment, or partner. This version makes reference to Vygotsky's construct of the ZPD, defined as "the distance between the actual developmental level as determined by independent problem solving and the level of potential development as determined through problem solving under adult guidance or in collaboration with more capable peers" (Vygotsky, 1978, p. 86). The scaffold metaphor originally referred to the role of the teacher, embodying the characteristics of providing support, providing a supportive tool, extending the learner's range, allowing the learner to accomplish tasks not otherwise possible, and being selectively usable (Greenfield, 1984, p. 118).

Vygotsky's construct has been picked up by designers of educational software, in particular the Computer Supported Intentional Learning Environment (CSILE) project at the Ontario Institute for Studies in Education (OISE). At OISE, Marlene Scardamalia and Carl Bereiter (1991) worked toward developing a collaborative knowledge-building environment and asked how learners (children) could be given relatively more control over the ZPD by directing the kinds of questions that drive educational inquiry. The CSILE environment provided a scaffolded conferencing and note-taking environment in which learners themselves could be in charge of the questioning and inquiry of collaborative work—something more traditionally controlled by the teacher—in such a way that kept the endeavor from degenerating into chaos.

Another example of technological scaffolding comes from George Landow's research into using hypertext and hypermedia—nonlinear, reader-driven text and media, as mentioned earlier—in the study of English literature (Landow & Delany, 1993). In Landow's research, a student could gain more information about some aspect of Shakespeare, for example, by following any number of links presented in an electronic document. A major component of Landow's work was his belief in providing students with the context of the subject matter. The technological scaffolding provides a way of managing that context—so that it is not so large, complicated, or daunting that it prevents learners from exploring, but is flexible and inviting enough to encourage exploration beyond the original text. The question facing future researchers of these nonlinear and alternately structured technologies may be this: Can the computer environment create a place in which the context or the culture is felt, understood, and can be communicated to others? More controversially, perhaps, can these technologies be designed and guided by the learners themselves without losing the richness that direct engagement with experts and teachers can offer them?

Technology as Perspectivity Toolkit

The Perspectivity Toolkit model we are introducing in this chapter (a derivative of the Points of Viewing theory) proposes that the next step in understanding new media technologies for learning is to define them as *lenses* to explore both self and world through layering viewpoints and looking for underlying patterns that lead to agreement, disagreement, and understanding. Perspectivity technologies provide a platform for sharing (not always shared) values and for building (not only participating in) cultures or communities of practice. Because we live in a complex global society, this new model is critical if we are to communicate with each other. Illich (1972) called this form of communication, *conviviality* and Geertz (1973) called it *commensurability.* Goldman-Segall (1995) referred to the use of new media, especially digital video technologies, to layer views and perspectives into new theories as *configurational validity*—a form of *thick communication.*

One can trace the first glimmer of perspectivity technologies to Xerox PARC in the 1970s. There, Alan Kay was inventing what we now recognize as the personal computer—a small, customizable device with substantial computing power, mass storage, and the ability to handle multiple media formats. Though simply pedestrian today, Kay's advances were at the time revolutionary. Kay's vision of small, self-contained personal computers was without precedent, as was his vision of how they would be used: as personalized media construction toolkits that would usher in a new kind of literacy. With this literacy would start the discourse between technology as scientific tool and technology as personal expression: "The particular aim of [Xerox's Learning Research Group] was to find the equivalent of writing—that is, learning and thinking by doing in a medium—our new 'pocket universe'" (Kay, 1996, p. 552).

At Bank Street College in the 1980s, a video and videodisc project called *The Voyage of the Mimi* immersed learners in scientific exploration of whales and Mayan cultures. Learners identified strongly with the student characters in the video stories. Similarly, the Cognition and Technology Group at Vanderbilt (CTGV) was working on video-based units in an attempt to involve students in scientific inquiry (Martin, 1987). *The Adventures of Jasper Woodbury* is a series of videodisc-based adventures that provide students with engaging content and contexts for solving mysteries and

mathematical problems (http://peabody.vanderbilt.edu/ctrs/ltc/Research/jasper.html). While both of these environments were outstanding exemplars of students using various media forms to get to know the people and the culture within the story structures, the lasting contribution is not only one of enhanced mathematical or social studies understanding, but also a connection to people who are engaged in real-life inquiry and in expanding on perspective in the process.

With an AI orientation, computer scientist, inventor, and educator Elliot Soloway at the University of Michigan built tools to enable learners to create personal hypermedia documents, reminiscent of Kay's personalized media construction toolkits. In his more current work with Joe Krajcik, Phyllis Blumenfeld, and Ron Marx, Soloway participated with communities of students and teachers as they explored project-based science through the design of sophisticated technologies developed for distributed knowledge construction (Soloway, Krajcik, Blumenfeld, & Marx, 1996). Similarly, at Berkeley, Marcia Linn analyzed the cognition of students who wrote programs in the computer language LISP, and Andrea diSessa worked with students who were learning physics using his program called Boxer. For diSessa, physics deals with

> a rather large number of fragments rather than one or even any small number of integrated structures one might call "theories." Many of these fragments can be understood as simple abstractions from common experiences that are taken as relatively primitive in the sense that they generally need no explanation; they simply happen. (diSessa, 1988, p. 52)

Andrea diSessa's theory of physics resonates strongly with the notion of *bricolage,* a term first used by the French structural anthropologist Claude Lévi-Strauss (1968) to describe a person who builds from pieces and does not have a specific plan at the onset of the project. Lévi-Strauss was often used as a point of departure for cognitive scientists interested in the analysis of fragments rather than in building broad generalizations from top-down rationalist structures. By the 1990s French social theory has indeed infiltrated the cognitive paradigm, legitimizing cultural analysis.

Influenced by the notion of bricolage, however, one might ask whether these technology researchers were aware that they had designed perspectivity platforms for interactions between individuals and communities. Perhaps not, yet we propose that these environments should be reviewed through the perspectivity lens to understand how learners come to build consensual theories around complex human-technology interactions. Goldman-Segall's digital ethnographies of children's thinking (1990, 1991, 1998b) are exemplars in perspectivity theory. She established unique partnerships among viewer, author, and media texts—a set of partnerships that revolves around, and is revolved around, the constant recognition of cultural connections as core factors in using new-media technologies. Goldman-Segall explored the tenuous, slippery, and often permeable relations between creator, user, and media artifact through an online environment for video analysis. A video chunk, for example, became the representation of a moment in the making of cultures. This video chunk became both cultural object and personal subject, something to turn around and reshape. And just as we, as users and creators (readers and writers) of these artifacts, change them through our manipulation, so they change us and our cultural possibilities. Two examples of Goldman-Segall's video case studies and interactive software that illustrate the implementation of perspectivity technologies for culture making and collaborative interpretation can be found on the Web at http://www.pointsofviewing.com.

Another good example of perspectivity technology is described in the doctoral work of Maggie Beers who, working with Goldman-Segall in the MERLin Research Lab, explored how preservice teachers learning modern languages build and critique digital artifacts connecting self and other (Beers, 2001; Beers & Goldman-Segall, 2001). Beers showed how groups of preservice teachers create video artifacts as representations of their various cultures in order to share and understand each other's perspectives as an integral part of learning a foreign language. The self becomes a strong reference point for understanding others while engaged in many contexts with media tools and artifacts.

Another exemplary application of perspectivity theory is demonstrated by Gerry Stahl. Stahl has been working on the idea of perspective and technology at the University of Colorado for several years. Stahl's *Web Guide* forms the technical foundation into an investigation of the role of artifacts in collaborative knowledge building for deepening perspective. Drawing on Vygotsky's theories of cultural mediation, Stahl's work develops models of collaborative knowledge building and the role of shared cultural artifacts—and particularly digital media artifacts—in that process (Stahl, 1999).

In sum, perspectivity technologies enhance, motivate, and provide new opportunities for learning, teaching, and research because they address how the personal point of view connects with evolving discourse communities. Perspectivity thinking tools enable knowledge-based cultures to grow, creating both real and virtual communities within the learning environment to share information, to alter the self-other relationship, and to open the door to a deeper, richer partnership with our technologies and one another. Just as a language

changes as speakers alter the original form, so will the nature of discourse communities change as cultures spread and variations are constructed.

EXEMPLARY LEARNING SYSTEMS

The following is a collage of technological systems designed to aid, enhance, or inspire learning.

Logo

Logo (see Figure 16.1), one of the oldest and most influential educational technology endeavors, dates back to 1967. Logo is a dialect of the AI research language LISP and was developed by Wally Feurzig's team at Bolt, Beranek, and Newman (BBN), working with Papert. Papert's work made computer programming accessible to children, not through dumbing down computer science, but by carefully managing the relationship between abstract and concrete. Logo gave children the means to concretize mathematics and geometry via the computer, which made them explorers in the field of math. As mentioned earlier, Papert believed that because the best way to learn French is not to go to French class, but to France, the best way to learn mathematics would be in some sort of "Mathland" (Papert, 1980, p. 6). Logo provided a microworld operating in terms of mathematical and geometric ideas. By experimenting with controlling a programmable turtle, children had direct, concrete experience of how mathematical and geometric constructs work. Through reflection on their experiments, they would then come to more formalized understandings of these constructs. Papert saw children as epistemologists thinking about their thinking about mathematics by living in and creating computer cultures.

With the growing availability of personal computers in the late 1970s and 1980s, the Logo turtle was moved onscreen. The notion of the turtle in its abstract world was called a microworld, a notion that has been the lasting legacy of the Logo research (Papert, 1980). The Logo movement was very popular in schools in the 1980s, and many, many versions of the language were developed for different computer systems. Some implementations of Logo departed from Papert's geometry microworlds and were designed to address other goals, such as the teaching of computer programming (Harvey, 1997). Some implementations of Logo are freely distributed on the Internet. See http://www.cs.berkeley.edu/~bh/logo.html. The Logo Foundation, at http://el.www.media.mit.edu/groups/logo-foundation/, has continued to expand the culture of Logo over the years.

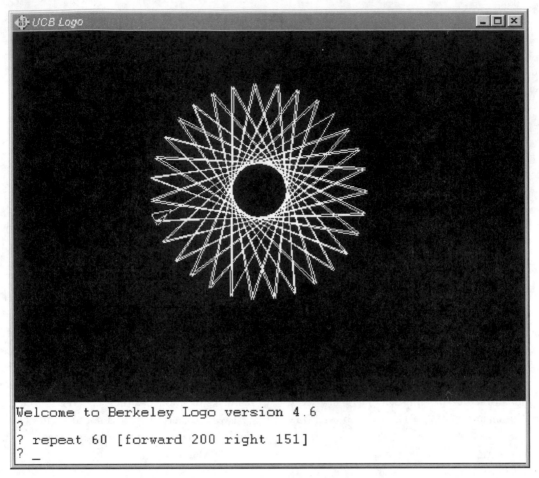

Figure 16.1   UBCLogo in action.

Squeak

Squeak (see Figure 16.2) is the direct descendant of Alan Kay's Dynabook research at Xerox PARC in the 1970s. It is a multimedia personal computing environment based on the SmallTalk, the object-oriented programming language that formed the basis of Kay's investigations into personal computing (Kay, 1996). Squeak is notable in that it is freely distributed on the Internet, runs on almost every conceivable computing platform, and is entirely decomposable: Although one can create new media tools and presentations as with other environments, one can also tinker with the underlying operation of the system—how windows appear or how networking protocols are implemented. A small but enthusiastic user community supports and extends the Squeak environment, creating such tools as web browsers, music synthesizers, three-dimensional graphic toolkits, and so on—entirely within Squeak. See http://www.squeak.org.

Boxer

Boxer (see Figure 16.3) is a computational medium—a combination of a programming language, a microworld

environment, and a set of libraries and tools for building tools for exploring problem solving with computers. Developed by Andrea diSessa, Boxer blends the Logo work of Seymour Papert (1980) and the mutable medium notion of Alan Kay (1996) in a flexible computing toolkit. diSessa's work has been ongoing since the 1980s, when he conceived of an environment to extend the Logo research into a more robust and flexible environment in which to explore physics concepts (diSessa, 2000). Boxer is freely distributed on the Internet. See http://www.soe.berkeley.edu/boxer.html/.

HyperCard

In 1987 Apple Computer was exploring multimedia as the fundamental rationale for people wanting Macintosh computers. However, as there was very little multimedia software available in the late 1980s, Apple decided to bundle a multimedia-authoring toolkit with every Macintosh computer. This toolkit was HyperCard, and it proved to be enormously popular with a wide variety of users, and especially in schools. HyperCard emulates a sort of magical stack of index cards, and its multimedia documents were thus called stacks. An

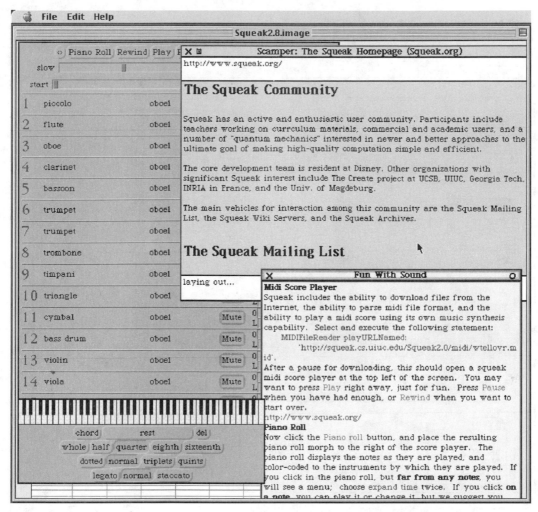

Figure 16.2   The Squeak environment showing Midi score player (audio), web browser, and documentation.

author could add text, images, audio, and even video components to cards and then use a simple and elegant scripting language to tie these cards together or perform certain behaviors. Two broad categories of use emerged in HyperCard: The first was collecting and enjoying predesigned stacks; the second was authoring one's own. In the online bulletin board systems of the early 1990s, HyperCard authors exchanged great volumes of "stackware." Educators were some of the most enthusiastic users, either creating content for students (a stellar example of this is Apple's *Visual Almanac,* which married videodisc-based content with a HyperCard control interface) or encouraging students to create their own. Others used HyperCard to create scaffolds and tools for learners to use in their own media construction. A good snapshot of this Hyper-Card authoring culture is described in Ambron and Hooper's (1990) *Learning with Interactive Multimedia.* Unfortunately, HyperCard development at Apple languished in the mid-1990s, and the World Wide Web eclipsed this elegant, powerful software. A HyperCard derivative called HyperStudio is

still popular in schools but lacks the widespread popularity outside of schools that the original claimed.

Constellations/ORION

Constellations (see Figure 16.4) is a collaborative video annotation tool that works with the metaphor of stars and constellations. An individual data chunk (e.g., a video clip) is a star. Stars can be combined to make constellations, but different users may place the same star in different contexts, depending on their understanding by viewing data from various perspectives. Constellations is thus a data-sharing system, promoting Goldman-Segall's notion of configurational validity by allowing different users to compare and exchange views on how they contextualize the same information differently in order to reach valid conclusions about the data. It also features collaborative ranking and annotation of data nodes. Although other video analysis tools have been developed and continue to be developed (Harrison & Baecker, 1992; Kennedy, 1989;

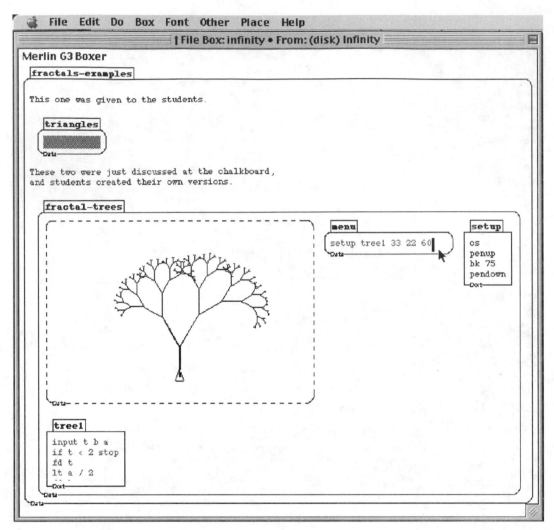

Figure 16.3 The Boxer environment showing interactive programming of fractals.

Mackay, 1989; Roschelle, Pea, & Trigg, 1990), Constellations (also called Learning Constellations) was the first video data-analysis tool to analyze a robust set of video ethnographic data (Goldman-Segall, 1989, 1990). Constellations was originally developed as a stand-alone application using the HyperCard platform with a significance measure to layer descriptions and attributes (Goldman-Segall, 1993). However, in 1998 the tool went online as a Web-based collaborative video analysis tool called WebConstellations (see http://www.webconstellations .com) and focused more on data management and integration (Goldman-Segall, 1999; Goldman-Segall & Rao, 1998). The most recent version, ORION, provides more functionality for the administrator to designate access to users (see Figure 16.5). Unlike WebConstellations, ORION has returned to its original functionality of being a tool for video chunking, sorting, analysis, ethnographic theory building and story making. See http://www.pointsofviewing.com for a version of how video data can be analyzed.

Adventures of Jasper Woodbury

Jasper Woodbury is the name of a character in a series of adventure stories that CTGV uses as the basis for anchored instruction. The stories, presented on videodisc or CD-ROM, are carefully crafted mysteries that present problems to be solved by groups of learners. Since the video can be randomly accessed, learners are encouraged to re-explore parts of the story in order to gather clues and develop theories about the problem to be solved. The Jasper series first appeared in the 1980s, and there are now 12 stories (CTGV, 1997). See http://peabody.vanderbilt.edu/ctrs/ltc/Research/jasper.html.

KidPix

KidPix was the first kid-friendly, generic graphics studio program. It includes a wealth of design tools and features that make it easy and fun to create images, and it has been widely adopted in schools. KidPix was originally developed by

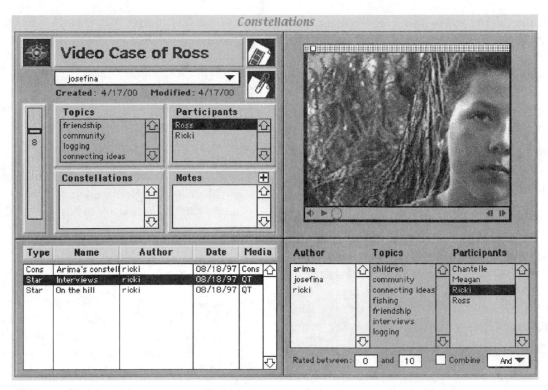

Figure 16.4   Constellations 2.6 showing Star video node and collaborative ranking-annotation interface for analysis.

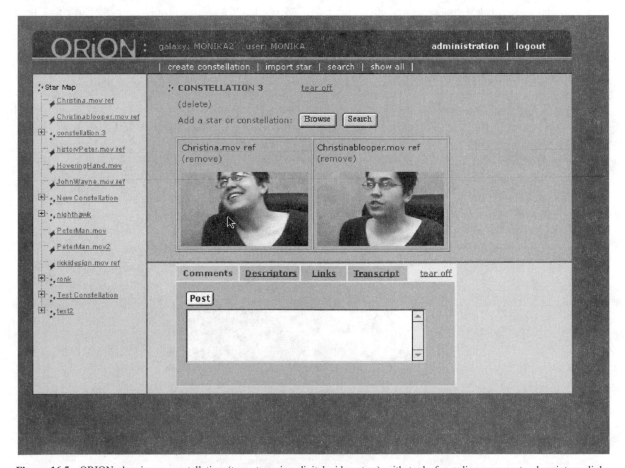

Figure 16.5   ORION showing a constellation (two streaming digital video stars) with tools for online comments, descriptors, links, and transcripts.

Craig Hickman in the late 1980s for his own son and was subsequently marketed by Broderbund software (now owned by The Learning Company). See the official site at http://www.kidpix.com/ and Craig Hickman's unofficial site at http://www.pixelpoppin.com/kidpix.

CSILE

Marlene Scardamalia and Carl Bereiter at OISE developed CSILE. CSILE is a collaborative, problem-based, knowledge-building environment. Learners can collaborate on data collection, analysis of findings, constructing and presenting conclusions by exchanging structured notes and attaching further questions, contributions, and so on to preexisting notes. CSILE was originally conceived to provide a dynamic scaffold for knowledge construction—one that would let the learners themselves direct the inquiry process (Scardamalia & Bereiter, 1991). CSILE is now commercially developed and licensed as Knowledge Forum. See http://www.learn.motion.com/lim/kf/KF0.html.

StarLogo

StarLogo (see Figure 16.6) is a parallel-computing version of Logo. By manipulating multiple (thousands) of distributed turtles, learners can work with interactive models of complex interactions, population dynamics, and other decentralized systems. Developed by Resnick, Wilensky, and a team of researchers at MIT, StarLogo was conceived as a tool to move learners' thinking beyond a centralized mindset and to study how people make sense of complex systems (Resnick, 1991; Resnick & Wilensky, 1993; Wilensky & Resnick, 1999). StarLogo is available for free on the Internet, as is NetLogo—a next generation multiagent environment developed by Wilensky at the Center for Connected Learning and Computer-Based Modeling at Northwestern University. See http://www.media.mit.edu/starlogo and http://ccl.northwestern.edu/netlogo/.

MOOSE Crossing

Georgia Tech researcher Amy Bruckman created MOOSE Crossing (see Figure 16.7) as part of her doctoral work while at the MIT Media Lab. MOOSE Crossing can be characterized as something of a combination of the Logo/microworlds work of Papert (1980), the mutable media notions of Kay (1996), and a MOO (Haynes & Holmevik, 1998)—a real-time, collaborative, immersive, virtual environment. MOOSE Crossing is a thus a microworld that learners can

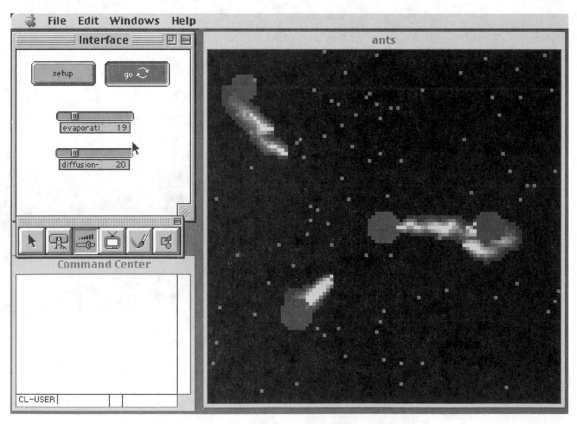

Figure 16.6   StarLogo's interactive "Ants" simulation in action.

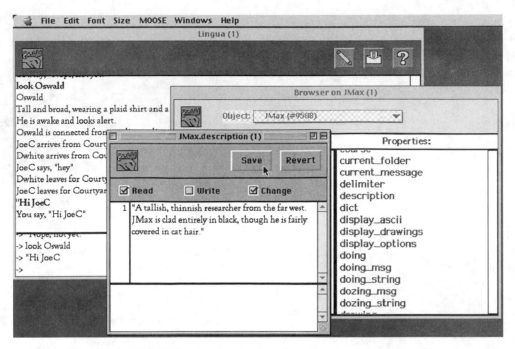

Figure 16.7   The MacMOOSE client interface showing editing, browsing, and main interaction windows.

themselves enter, designing and programming the virtual environment from within. It becomes a sort of lived-in text that one shares with other readers, writers, and designers. Bruckman (1998) calls MOOSE Crossing "community support for constructionist learning":

> Calling a software system a place gives users a radically different set of expectations. People are familiar with a wide variety of types of places, and have a sense of what to do there. . . . Instead of asking What do I do with this software?, people ask themselves, What do I do in this place? The second question has a very different set of answers than the first. (p. 49)

Bruckman's (1998) thesis is that community and constructionist learning go hand in hand. Her ethnographic accounts of learners inside the environment reveals very close, very personal bonds emerging between children in the process of designing and building their worlds in MOOSE Crossing. "The emotional support," she writes, "is inseparable from the technical support. Receiving help from someone you would tell your secret nickname to is clearly very different from receiving help from a computer program or a schoolteacher" (p. 128). The MacMOOSE and WinMOOSE software is available for free on the Internet. See http://www.cc.gatech .edu/elc/moose-crossing/.

SimCalc

SimCalc's tag line is "Democratizing Access to the Mathematics of Change," and the goal is to make the understanding of change accessible to more learners than the small minority who take calculus classes (see Figure 16.8). SimCalc, a project at the University of Massachusetts under James Kaput working with Jeremy Roschelle and Ricardo Nemirovky, is a simulation and visualization system for learners to explore calculus concepts in a problem-based model, one that avoids traditional problems with mathematical representation (Kaput, Roschelle, & Stroup, 1998). The core software, called MathWorlds (echoing Papert's Mathland idea), allows learners to manipulate variables and see results via real-time visualizations with both animated characters and more traditional graphs. SimCalc is freely available on the Internet. See http://www.simcalc.umassd .edu/.

Participatory Simulations

Participatory Simulations, a project overseen by Uri Wilensky and Walter Stroup at Northwestern University, is a distributed computing environment built on the foundations of Logo and NetLogo that encourages learners collaboratively to explore complex simulations (Wilensky & Stroup, 1999). This project centers around HubNet, a classroom-based network of handheld devices that enables learners to participate in and collaboratively control simulations of dynamic systems. The emergent behavior of the system becomes the object of collective discussion and collaborative analysis.

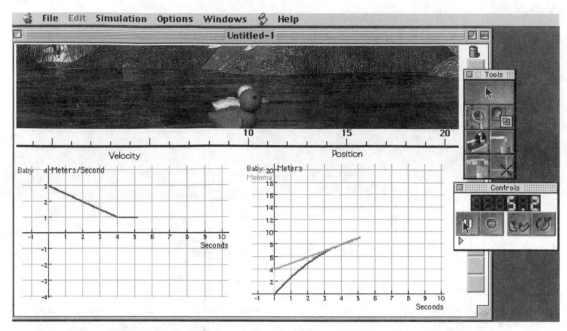

Figure 16.8   SimCalc's interactive velocity lab, with animation and real-time graphs.

CoVis

CoVis (Collaborative Visualization), a project developed at Northwestern University in the 1990s, focuses on science learning through projects using a telecommunications infrastructure, scientific visualization tools, and software to support collaboration between diverse schools in distributed locations (Edelson et al., 1996). Much of learners' investigation centered on atmospheric and environmental studies, allowing wide-scale data sharing across the United States. Learners could then use sophisticated data analysis tools to visualize and draw conclusions. CoVis made use of a variety of networked software: collaborative "notebooks," distributed databases, and system visualization tools, as well as the Web and e-mail. The goal in the CoVis project was for young people to study topics in much the same way as professional scientists do. See http://www.covis.nwu.edu/.

Network Science

In the late 1980s and 1990s a number of large-scale research projects explored the possibilities of connecting multiple classrooms across the United States for data sharing and collaborative inquiry (Feldman et al., 2000). Programs like National Geographic Kids Network (NGKNet), a National Science Foundation–funded collaboration between the National Geographic Society and TERC, reached thousands of classrooms and tens of thousands of students. TERC's NGKNet provided curriculum plans and resources around

issues such as acid rain and tools that facilitated large-scale data collection, sharing, and analysis of results. Other projects, such as Classroom BirdWatch and EnergyNet, focused on issues with comparable global significance and local implications, turning large numbers of learners into a community of practice doing distributed scientific investigation. Feldman, Konold, and Coulter noted that these large-scale projects question the notion of the individual child as scientist, pointing instead toward interesting models of collaborative engagement in science, technology, and society issues (pp. 142–143).

Virtual-U

Developed by Linda Harasim and Tom Calvert at Simon Fraser University and the Canadian Telelearning National Centres of Excellence, Virtual-U is a Web-based course-delivery platform (Harasim, Calvert, & Groeneboer, 1996). Virtual-U aims to provide a rich, full-featured campus environment for learners, featuring a cafe and library as well as course materials and course-management functionality. See http://virtual-u.cs.sfu.ca/ and http://www.telelearn.ca/.

Tapped In

Tapped In (see Figure 16.9) is a multiuser online educational workspace for teachers and education professionals. The Tapped In project, led by Mark Schlager at SRI International,

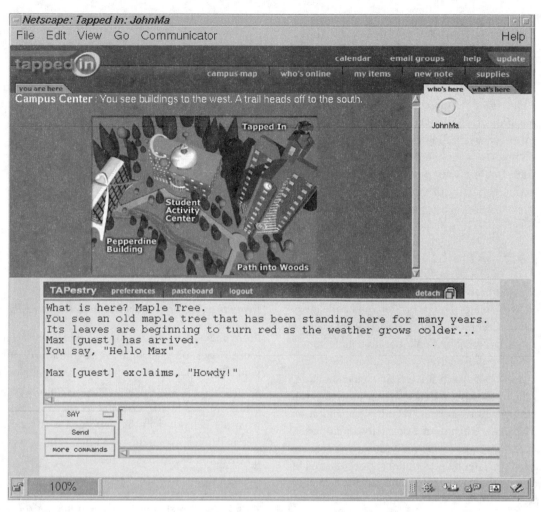

Figure 16.9   The TAPestry interface to the Tapped In environment.

began in the late 1990s as a MOO (textual virtual reality) environment for synchronous collaboration and has since grown into a sophisticated (Web plus MOO) multimedia environment for both synchronous and asynchronous work, with a large and very active user population (Schlager & Schank, 1997). Tapped In uses a technological infrastructure similar to that of MOOSE Crossing but has a different kind of community of practice at work within it; Tapped In functions more like an ongoing teaching conference, with many weekly or monthly events, workshops, and happenings. Tapped In is an exemplary model of a multimode collaborative environment. See http://www.tappedin.sri.com/.

CoWeb

At Georgia Tech Mark Guzdial and colleagues at the Collaborative Software Laboratory (CSL) have created a variety of software environments building on the original educational computing vision of Alan Kay in the 1970s (Kay 1996); the

computer can be a tool for composing and experiencing dynamic media. Growing from Guzdial's (1997) previous work on the CaMILE project—a Web-based anchored collaboration environment, CSL's CoWeb project explores possibilities in designing and using collaborative media tools online (Guzdial, 1999). CoWeb and other CSL work are largely based on the Squeak environment, a direct descendant of Alan Kay's research at Xerox PARC in the 1970s. See http://coweb.cc.gatech.edu/csl.

MaMaMedia

The rationale of MaMaMedia, a company founded by MIT Media Lab graduate Idit Harel, is to enable young learners and their parents to participate in web experiences that are safe, constructionist by nature, and educational. MaMaMedia maintains a filtered collection of dynamic Web sites aimed at challenging young children to explore, express, and exchange (Harel's three Xs) ideas. Harel's (1991) book

Children Designers, lays the foundation for MaMaMedia and for research in understanding how children in rich online environments construct and design representations of their thinking. In Harel's doctoral work, one young girl named Debbie was part of the experimental group at the Hennigan School, working with fractions in Logo. After several months of working on her project, she looked around the room and said, "Fractions are everywhere." MaMaMedia enables thousands of girls and boys to be online playing games, learning how to think like Debbie, and participating in the vast MaMaMedia community. To join this constructionist community for kids and parents, go to http://www.mamamedia .com/.

WebGuide

WebGuide, a web-based, collaborative knowledge-construction tool, was created by Gerry Stahl and colleagues at the University of Colorado (Stahl, 1999). WebGuide is designed to facilitate personal and collaborative understanding through mediating perspectivity via cultural artifacts. WebGuide acts as a scaffold for group understanding. WebGuide is a structured conferencing system supporting rich interlinking and information reuse and recontextualization, as well as multiple views on the structure of the information set. Learners contribute information from individual perspectives, but this information can later be negotiated and recollected in multiple contexts construct. See http://www.cs.colorado.edu/ ~gerry/webguide/.

Affective Computing and Wearables

A series of research projects under Rosalind Picard at the MIT Media Lab are aimed at investigating affective computing (Picard 1997)—the emotional and environmental aspects of digital technologies. Research areas include computer recognition of human affect, computer synthesis of affect, wearable computers, and affective interaction with computers. Jocelyn Schreirer conducted several experiments with advisors Picard, Turkle, and Goldman-Segall to explore how affective wearable technologies become expressive devices for augmenting communication. This relatively new area for research will undoubtedly prove very significant for education as well as other applications because the affective component of computing has been overlooked until recently. See http://www.media.mit.edu/affect/.

WebCT

Originally developed in the late 1990s by Murray Goldberg at the University of British Columbia, WebCT has grown to be an enormously popular example of a course management system. What began as an easy-to-use Web-based courseware environment is now in use by more than 1,500 institutions. Indeed, it is so widespread among postsecondary institutions that WebCT, now a company, is almost a de facto standard for online course delivery. See http://www.webct.com.

CHALLENGING PARADIGMS AND LEARNING THEORIES

Cognition: Models of Mind or Creating Culture?

In this section, two challenging cognitive paradigms will be discussed. The overriding discussion focuses on whether cognition is best understood as a model of the mind or rather as a creation of culture.

From the Cognitive Revolution to Cultural Psychology

From the vantage point of the mid-1990s, Jerome Bruner looked back on the cognitive revolution of the late 1950s, which he helped to shape, and reflected on a lost opportunity. Bruner had imagined that the new cognitive paradigm would bring the search for meaning to the fore, distinguishing it from the behaviorism that preceded it (Bruner, 1990, p. 2). Yet as Bruner wrote, the revolution went awry—not because it failed, but because it succeeded:

> Very early on, for example, emphasis began shifting from "meaning" to "information," from the *construction* of meaning to the *processing* of information. These are profoundly different matters. The key factor in the shift was the introduction of computation as the ruling metaphor and computability as a necessary criterion of a good theoretical model. (p. 4)

The information-processing model of cognition became so dominant, Bruner argued, and the roles of meaning and meaning making ended up as much in disfavor as they had been in behaviorism. "In place of stimuli and responses, there was input and output," and hard empiricism ruled again, with a new vocabulary, but with the same disdain for mentalism (Bruner, 1990, p. 7).

Bruner's career as a theorist is itself instructive. Heralded by Gardner and others as one of the leading lights of 1950s cognitivism, Bruner has been one of a small but vocal group calling for a return to the role of culture in understanding the mind. This movement has been tangled up closely with the evolution of educational technology over the same period, perhaps illuminated in a pair of titles that serve as bookends for one researcher's decade-long trajectory: Etienne Wenger's (1987) *Artificial Intelligence and Tutoring*

Systems: Computational and Cognitive Approaches to the Communication of Knowledge and his (1998) *Communities of Practice: Learning, Meaning, and Identity.*

Cognitive Effects, Transfer, and the Culture of Technology: A Brief Narrative

In his 1996 article, "Paradigm Shifts and Instructional Technology: An Introduction," Timothy Koschmann began by identifying four defining paradigms of technology in education. In roughly chronological (but certainly overlapping) order, these are CAI, characterized by drill-and-practice and programmed instruction systems; ITS, which drew on AI research to create automated systems that could evaluate a learner's progress and tailor instruction accordingly; the Logo-as-Latin paradigm, led by Papert's microworld and children-as-programmers efforts; and CSCL, a socially-oriented, constructivist approach that focuses on learners in practice in groups. Koschmann invoked Thomas Kuhn's (1996) controversial notion of the *incommensurability* of competing paradigms:

> Kuhn held that the effect of a paradigm shift is to produce a divided community of researchers no longer able to debate their respective positions, owing to fundamental differences in terminology, conceptual frameworks, and views on what constitutes the legitimate questions of science. (Koschmann, 1996, p. 2)

Koschmann's analysis may well be accurate. The literature surrounding the effects that learning technology produces certainly displays examples of this incommensurability, even within the writings of individual theorists.

As mentioned earlier, Papert's work with teaching children to program in Logo was originally concerned with bridging the gap between Piaget's concrete and formal thinking stages, particularly with respect to mathematics and geometry. Over time, however, Papert's work with children and Logo began to be talked about as "computer cultures" (Papert, 1980, pp. 22–23): Logo gave its practitioners a vocabulary, a framework, and a set of tools for a particular kind of learning through exploration. Papert envisaged a computer culture in which children could express themselves as epistemologists, challenging the nature of established knowledge. But although Papert's ideas and the practice of Logo learning in classrooms contributed significantly to the *esprit de temps* of the 1980s, it was difficult for many mainstream educational researchers and practitioners to join the mindset that he believed would revolutionize learning.

A large-scale research project to evaluate the claims of Logo in classrooms was undertaken by Bank Street College

in the mid-1980s. The Bank Street studies came to some critical conclusions about the work that Papert and his colleagues were doing (Pea & Kurland, 1987; Pea, Kurland, & Hawkins, 1987). Basically, the Bank Street studies concluded with a cautious note—that no significant effects on cognitive development could be confirmed—and called for much more extensive and rigorous research amid the excitement and hype. The wider effect of the Bank Street publications fed into something of a popular backlash against Logo in the schools. A 1984 article in the magazine *Popular Psychology* summarized the Bank Street studies and suggested bluntly that Logo had not delivered on Papert's promises.

Papert responded to this critique (Papert, 1985) by arguing that the framing of research questions was overly simplistic. Papert chided his critics for looking for cognitive effects by isolating variables as if classrooms were treatment studies. Rather than asking "technocentric" questions such as "What is THE effect of THE computer?" (p. 23), Papert called for an examination of the culture-building implications of Logo practice, and for something he called "computer criticism," which he proposed as akin to literary criticism.

Pea (1987) responded, claiming that Papert had unfairly characterized the Bank Street research (Papert had responded only to the *Psychology Today* article, not to the original literature) and arguing that as researchers they had a responsibility to adhere to accepted scientific methods for evaluating the claims of new technology. The effect of this exchange was to illuminate the vastly different perspectives of these researchers. Where Papert was talking about the open-ended promise of computer cultures, Pea and his colleagues, developmental psychologists, were evaluating the work from the standpoint of demonstrable changes in cognition (Pea & Kurland, 1987). Whereas Papert accused his critics of reductionism, Davy (1985) likened Papert to the proverbial man who looks for his keys under the streetlight because the light is better there.

Gavriel Salomon and Howard Gardner responded to this debate with an article that searched for middle ground (Salomon & Gardner, 1986): An analogy, they pointed out, could be drawn from research into television and mass media, a much older pursuit than educational computing, and one in which Salomon was an acclaimed scholar. Salomon and Gardner argued that one could not search for independent variables in such a complex area; instead, they called for a more holistic, exploratory research program, and one that took more than the overt effects of the technology into account.

Indeed, in 1991 Salomon and colleagues David Perkins and Tamar Globerson published a groundbreaking article that shed more light on the issue (Salomon et al., 1991). To consider the *effects of* a technology, one had to consider what was changed after a learner had used a technology—but in the absence of it. The questions that arise from this are whether there is any cognitive residue from the prior experience and whether there is transfer between tasks. This is a different set of questions than those that arise from investigating the *effects with* technology, which demand a more decentered, system-wide approach, looking at the learner in *partnership* with technology.

Although it contributed important new constructs and vocabulary to the issue, the Salomon et al. (1991) article is still deeply rooted in a traditional cognitive science perspective, like much of Pea's research, taking first and foremost the individual mind as the site of cognition. Salomon, Perkins, and Globerson, all trained in cognitive psychology, warn against taking the "effects with" approach too far, noting that computers in education are still far from ubiquitous, and that the search for the "effects of" is still key.

In a 1993 article Pea responded to Salomon et al. (1991) from yet a different angle. Pea, then at Northwestern and working closely with his Learning Sciences colleagues, wrote on "distributed intelligence" and argued against taking the individual mind as the locus of cognition, criticizing Salomon and colleagues' individualist notions of cognitive residue: "The language used by Salomon et al. (1991) to characterize the concepts involved in how they think about distributed intelligence is, by contrast, entity-oriented—a language of containers holding things" (Pea, 1993, p. 79).

Pea, reviewing recent literature on situated learning and distributed cognition (Brown et al., 1996; Lave, 1988; Winograd & Flores, 1986), had changed his individualist framework of cognitive science for a more "situative perspective" (Greeno, 1997, p. 6), while Salomon (1993) argued that cognition still must reside in the individual mind. It is interesting to note that neither Salomon nor Pea in this exchange seemed completely comfortable at this point with the notion of culture making beyond its influence as a contributing factor to mind, artifacts, and such empirically identifiable constructs.

Bricolage and Meaning Making at MIT

Scholarship at MIT's Media Lab was also changing in the early 1990s. The shift played out amid discussions of bricolage, computer cultures, relational approaches, the construction and sharing of public artifacts, and so on (Papert, 1980, 1991; Turkle, 1984, 1995), as well as amid the centered, developmental cognitive science perspective from which their work historically derives. Theorizing on epistemological pluralism, Turkle and Papert (1991) clearly revealed the tension between the cognitivist and situative perspective: Papert and Turkle desired to understand the mind and simultaneously

to reconcile how knowledge and meaning are constituted in community, culture, and technology. The cognitivist stance might well have been limiting for constructionist theory in the 1980s. Pea (1993) offered a critique of Papert's constructionism from the standpoint of distributed intelligence:

> Papert described what marvelous machines the students had built, with very little interference from teachers. On the surface, the argument was persuasive, and the children were discovering important things on their own. But on reflection, I felt this argument missed the key point about the invisible human intervention in this example—what the designers of LEGO and Logo crafted in creating just the interlockable component parts of LEGO machines or just the Logo primitive commands for controlling these machines. (p. 65)

Pea's critique draws attention to the fact that what is going on in the Logo project exists partly in the minds of the children, and partly in the Logo system itself—that they are inseparable. Pea's later work pointed to distributed cognition, whereas the Media Lab's legacy—even in the distributed constructionism of Mitchel Resnick and Uri Wilensky and in the social constructionism of Goldman-Segall—is deeply rooted in unraveling the mystery of the mind and its ability to understand complexity and complex systems. For example, whereas Resnick's work explores ecologies of Logo turtles, it does not so much address ecologies of learners. Not until the late 1990s did the research at the Media Lab move toward distributed environments and the cultures and practices within them (Bruckman, 1998; Picard, 1997).

Learning, Thinking Attitudes, and Distributed Cognition

Understanding the nature of technology-based learning systems greatly depends on one's conceptualization of how learning occurs. Is learning linear and developmental, or a more fluid, flexible (Spiro, Feltovich, Jacobson, & Coulson, 1991) and even random "system" of making meaning of experience? Proponents of stage theory have tried to show how maturation takes place in logical causal sequences or stages according to observable stages in growth patterns—the final stage being the highest and most coveted. Developmental theories, such as Freud's oral, anal, and genital stages (Freud, 1952), Erikson's eight stages of psychological growth from basic trust to generativity (Erikson, 1950), or Piaget's stages from sensorimotor to formal operational thinking (see Grubner & Voneche, 1977), are based on the belief that the human organism must pass through these stages at critical periods in its development in order to reach full healthy integrated maturation, be it psychological, physical, spiritual, or intellectual.

Strict adherence to developmentalism, and particularly to its unidirectional conception, has been significantly challenged by Gilligan (1982), Gardner (1985), Fox Keller (1983), Papert (1991), and Illich and Sanders (1989)—not to mention a wave of postmodern theorists—proposing theories that address the fundamental issues underlying how we come to terms with understanding our thinking. One such challenge, raised by Illich and Sanders (1989), reflects on the prehistorical significance of the narrative voice. Thinking about thinking as essentially evolving stages of development requires the kind of calibration possible only in a world of static rules and universal truths. Illich and Sanders pointed out that narrative thinking is rather a weaving of different layers or versions of stories that are never fixed in time or place. Before the written word and

[p]rior to history . . . there is a narrative that unfolds, not in accordance with the rules of art and knowledge, but out of divine enthusiasm and deep emotion. Corresponding to this prior time is a different truth—namely, myth. In this truly oral culture, before phonetic writing, there can be no words and therefore no text, no original, to which tradition can refer, no subject matter that can be passed on. A new rendering is never just a new version, but always a new song. (Illich & Sanders, 1984, p. 4)

Illich and Sanders (1984) contended that the prehistoric mode of thinking was a relativistic experience—that what was expressed at any given moment in time changed from the previous time it was expressed. Thus there could be neither fixed recall nor truth as we define it today. This concept of knowledge as a continually changing truth, dependent on both communal interpretation and storytellers' innovation, dramatically changed with the introduction of writing. The moment a story could be written down, it could be referred to. Memory changed from being an image of a former indivisible time to being a method of retrieving a fixed, repeatable piece or section of an experience.

A parallel notion emerges in Carol Gilligan's (1982) research on gender and moral development. Gilligan made the case that in the "different voice" of women lies an ethic of care, a tie between relationship and responsibility, and the origins of aggression in the failure of connection (p. 173). Gilligan set the stage for a new mode of research that includes intimacy and relation rather than the separation and objectivity of traditional developmental theory.

Evelyn Fox Keller, a leading critic of the masculinization of science, heralded the relational model as a legitimate alternative for doing science. She pointed out that science is a deeply personal as well as a social activity (1983) historically preferential to a male and objectivist manner of thinking.

Combining Thomas Kuhn's ideas about the nature of scientific thinking with Freud's analysis of the different relationship between young boys and their mothers and between girls and their mothers, Fox Keller analyzed underlying reasons for scientific objectivism. She claimed that boys are encouraged to separate from their mothers and girls to maintain attachments, influencing the manner in which the two genders relate to physical objects. The young boy, in competition with his father for his mother's attentions, learns to compete in order to succeed. Girls, not having to separate from their mothers, find that becoming personally involved—getting a feeling for the organism, as Barbara McClintock (Fox Keller, 1983) would say—is a preferred mode of making sense of their relationship with the physical world. As a result, girls may do science in a more connected style, seeking relationships with, rather than dissecting, what they investigate. Girls seek to understand meaning through these personal attachments: "Just as science is not the purely cognitive endeavor we once thought it, neither is it as impersonal as we thought: science is a deeply personal as well as a social activity" (Fox Keller, 1983, p. 7).

Obviously, we will never know if a scientific discipline would really be different if it had been driven by more relational or narrative influences. Yet we may want to ask how people with a tendency toward relational or narrative thinking can be both invited into the study of the sciences and be encouraged to contribute to its theoretical foundations. In addition, we may want to ask how new media and technologies expand how we study what we study, thereby inviting a range of epistemologically diverse thinkers into the mainstream of intellectual pursuits.

Epistemological Pluralism

The emphasis on pluralism in constructionist practice was also a major theme to emerge from the MIT Media Lab in the 1980s. In Sherry Turkle's (1984) book *The Second Self: Computers and the Human Spirit,* she explored the different styles of mastery that she observed in boys and girls in Logo classrooms. In a 1991 article with Papert, "Epistemological Pluralism and the Revaluation of the Concrete," Turkle outlined two poles of technological mastery: hard and soft. Hard mastery, identified with top-down, rationalist thinking, was observed in a majority of boys. Soft mastery, identified with relational thinking and Claude Lévi-Strauss's notion of bricolage, was observed in a majority of girls (Turkle & Papert, 1991, pp. 167–168).

The identification of soft mastery and bricolage in programming was very important for Papert and Turkle for a number of reasons. This relational, negotiated approach to understanding systems has much in common with Piaget's constructivist theory and is also very much in line with how Papert saw children tinkering while programming in Logo, exploring the features of a microworld, and in doing so building an intimate connection with their own thinking. Papert and Turkle led MIT's Media Lab Epistemology and Learning Group to a revaluation of the concrete, which they saw as woefully undervalued in contemporary life, and especially in math and science education.

Although Turkle and Papert used the terms *hard* and *soft* to explain different approaches to computation, their contribution reaches out to broader domains. They cited feminism and ethnography of science and computation (Turkle & Papert, 1991, p. 372) as three of several movements that promote concrete thinking to an object of science in its own right. They proposed accepting diverse styles of creating knowledge and understanding systems as equally significant to the world of thought, such that the personal relational perspective that Papert identifies with concrete thinking will gain respectability in the scientific community:

> The development of a new computer culture would require more than technological progress and more than environments where there is permission to work with highly personal approaches. It would require a new and softer construction of the technological, with a new set of intellectual and emotional values more like those we apply to harpsichords than hammers. (Turkle & Papert, 1991, p. 184)

Multiple Perspectives and Thinking Attitudes

Goldman-Segall proposed a more dynamic conceptualization using the terms *frames* and *attitudes*. Her framing is rooted in several diverse but interwoven contexts: Marvin Minsky's (1986) artificial intelligence, Howard Gardner's (1983) theory of multiple intelligences, Erving Goffman's (1986) everyday sociology, and Trinh Minh T. Ha's (1992) cinematography. The important thing about frames—in contrast to the more essentialist notion of styles—is that they implicate both the framer and that which is left out of the frame:

> I have become less comfortable with the notion of styles . . . The kinds of frames I now choose open the possibility for both those who are being portrayed and those who view them to become partners in framing [their stories]. (Goldman-Segall, 1998b, pp. 244–245)

In Goldman-Segall's notion of *thinking attitudes* (instead of thinking or learning styles) imply positionality and orienta-

tion, and are situated in time and place:

> I define attitudes, not as psychologists have used the word in any number of studies that start with the phrase, "children's attitudes *toward* . . . ," but as indicator of a fluid state of mind. Attitude is a ballet pose in which the dancer, standing on one leg, places the other behind it, resting on the calf. Attitude, as a pose, leads to the next movement. (Goldman-Segall, 1998b, p. 245)

The idea that dynamic epistemological attitudes may run at odds with the gender breakdown of hard and soft mastery led Goldman-Segall (1996a, 1998a, 1998b) to suggest that *genderflexing* may occur: Boys may take on attitudes that are traditionally associated with those of girls, and vice versa. The underlying theme here is the primacy of situated points of viewing, rather than essential qualities. She sees learners as ethnographers, observing and engaging with the cultural environments in which they participate. Cognitive attitudes, being dynamic, are transitional personae, taken on to make a moment of transition from one conceptual framing to the next as learners layer their points of viewing. Video excerpts are available on the Web at http://www.pointsofviewing.com.

The focus had clearly changed from understanding the mind of a child to understanding the situated minds of collaborative teams. Simultaneously, learning moved from learning modules, to open-ended constructionism, to problem-based learning (PBL) environments and rich-media cases of teaching practices.

Distributed Cognition and Situated Learning

> Our memories are in families and libraries as well as inside our skins; our perceptions are extended and fragmented by technologies of every sort. (Brown et al., 1996, p. 19)

The 1989 article by John Seely Brown, Alan Collins, and Paul Duguid (1996) titled "Situated Cognition and the Culture of Learning" is generally credited with introducing the concepts and vocabulary of situated cognition to the educational community. This influential article, drawing on research at Xerox PARC and at the Institute for Research on Learning (IRL), expressed the authors' concern with the limits to which conceptual knowledge can be abstracted from the situations in which it is situated and learned (p. 19), as is common practice in classrooms. Building on the experiential emphasis of pragmatist thinkers like Dewey and on the social contexts of learning of Russian activity theorists like Vygotsky and Leontiev, Brown et al. proposed the notion of *cognitive apprenticeship*. In a cognitive apprenticeship model, knowledge and learning are seen as situated in practice: "Situations might be said to co-produce knowledge through activity. Learning and cognition, it is now possible to argue, are fundamentally situated" (p. 20). This idea is carried forward to an examination of tools and the way in which they are learned and used:

> Learning how to use a tool involves far more than can be accounted for in any set of explicit rules. The occasions and conditions for use arise directly out of the context of activities of each community that uses the tool, framed by the way members of each community see the world. The community and its viewpoint, quite as much as the tool itself, determine how a tool is used. (p. 23)

The work that brings the situated perspective firmly home to the learning environment is Jean Lave and Etienne Wenger's (1991) *Situated Learning: Legitimate Peripheral Participation,* which goes significantly beyond Brown's cognitive apprenticeship model. Core to Lave and Wenger's work is the idea of knowledge as distributed or stretched across a community of practice—what Salomon later called the radical situated perspective (Salomon, 1993):

> In our view, learning is not merely situated in practice—as if it were some independently reifiable process that just happened to be located somewhere; learning is an integral part of generative social practice in the lived-in world. . . . Legitimate peripheral participation is proposed as a descriptor of engagement in social practice that entails learning as an integral constituent. (Lave & Wenger, 1991, p. 35)

This perspective flips the argument over: It is not that learning happens best when it is situated (as if there were learning settings that are not situated), but rather, learning is an integral part of all situated practice. So, instead of asking—as Bransford and colleagues at Vanderbilt had—"How can we create authentic learning situations?" they ask "What is the nature of communities of practice?" and "How do newcomers and oldtimers relate and interact within communities of practice?" Lave and Wenger answer these questions through elaborating the nature of communities of practice in what they term *legitimate peripheral participation:*

> By this we mean to draw attention to the point that learners inevitably participate in communities of practitioners and that mastery of knowledge and skill requires newcomers to move toward full participation in the sociocultural practices of a community. (p. 29)

Lave and Wenger (1991) also elaborated on the involvement of cultural artifacts and technologies within communities of practice. As knowledge is stretched over a community of practice, it is also embodied in the material culture of that community, both in the mechanisms of practice and in the shared history of the community:

> Participation involving technology is especially significant because the artifacts used within a cultural practice carry a substantial portion of that practice's heritage. . . . Thus, understanding the technology of practice is more than learning to use tools; it is a way to connect with the history of the practice and to participate more directly in cultural life. (p. 101)

Artifacts and technology are not just instrumental in embodying practice; they also help constitute the structure of the community. As Goldman-Segall (1998b) reminded us, "They are not just tools used by our culture; they are tools used for making culture. They are partners that have their own contribution to make with regard to how we build a cultural understanding of the world around us" (pp. 268–269). Situated cognition, then, becomes perspectival knowledge, and the tools and artifacts we create become perspectivity technologies: viewpoints, frames, lenses, and filters—reflections of selves with others.

CONCLUSION

In this chapter the Points of Viewing theory was applied to an already rich understanding of the use of computer, the Internet, and new media technologies. We have called this new approach to designing new learning technology environments for engaging in perspectival knowledge construction Perspectivity Technologies. We provided an in-depth analysis of the historical and epistemological development of computer technologies for learning over the past century. Yet, we realize that the range of possible contributors was so broad that we would have to focus only on those theories and tools that were directly connected with the notion of perspectival knowledge construction and perspectivity technologies. We regret that we did not find the opportunity to include the work of all researchers in this field.

Perspectivity technologies represent the next phase of thinking with our technologies partners. Not only will we build them, shape them, and use them. They will also affect, influence, and shape us. They will become, if some researchers have their way, part of our bodies, not only augmenting our relationships but also becoming members in their own right. As robotic objects become robotic subjects, we will have to consider how Steven Spielberg's robot boy in the movie *A.I.* felt when interacting with humans—and we hope that we will be kinder to ourselves and to our robots.

A perspectivity technology is not only a technology that enables us to see each other's viewpoints better and make decisions based on multiple points of viewing. It is also concerned with the creation and design of technologies that add perspectives. Technologies have built-in filters. Recording an event with pen and paper, an audiotape recorder, and a camcorder each provides different perspectives of the same event. The technology provides an important filter or lens—a viewpoint, one could say. And while that viewpoint is deeply influenced by who the filmmaker is, or who the reporter is, the technology also contributes a new perspective. A camera tells a story different from that of the audio or text tool. Designing perspectivity technologies for learning will enable multiple filters to be applied, easily understood, and felt. Learners will be able to observe the many layers that create the curricular story. Moreover, they will be able to use new media as communication devices. They will have the capability to shape the story being told. Beyond the "media is the message" theme of theorists Marshall McLuhan and Harold Innis, we are now deeply entrenched in a participatory relationship with content knowledge because technologies have become part of our perspective, our consciousness, and our way of life. The level of interaction with our virtual creatures (technologies) transforms our relationships. We are never completely alone. We are connected through media devices even if we cannot see them. They see us. For better and for worse.

Yet what has changed in learning? It seems that we have moved a long way from believing that learning is putting certain curriculum inside of students' heads and then testing them for how well they have learned that material. Yet, instructionism is still alive and well. From kindergarten to higher education, students are still being trained to pass tests that will provide them with entrance into higher education. In spite of learning theories moving from behaviorism to cognitivism to distributed and situated cognition, educators are caught in the quagmire of preparing students for their future education instead of trying to make the present educational, engaging, and challenging fun. Teachers are caught in a web of uncertainty as they scramble to learn the new tools of the trade (the Internet, distance learning environments, etc.), to learn the content that they must teach, and then to organize the learning into modules that will fit into the next set of learning modules.

The irony is that when we think of who our best teachers were, they invariably were those who were able to elicit something within us and help us connect our lives to the lives of others—the lives of poets, mathematicians, physicists, and the fisher down at the docks. These teachers created a sense of community in the classroom. We became part of a discovery process that had no end. It was not knowledge that was already known that we craved. It was putting ideas together that had not yet been put together—at least in our own minds. We

felt we invented something new. And, indeed, we and others within these learning environments did invent new ideas. Yet people say that this cannot happen to most students in most classes and that the best we can do is to teach the curriculum, provide a safe learning environment, and test people for what we wanted them to learn. This is not good enough. And if students do not become partners in their learning now, technologies will create islands of despair as more and more students stop learning how to be creative citizens interested in each other, in differences, and in understanding complexity.

Technologies have become many things for many people. But technologies that are designed for the creative sharing of perspectives and viewpoints will lead to building better communities of practice in our schools and in our societies. Since the tragedy of September 11, 2001, we have come to realize that the world is not what we thought it was. We know so little about each other. We know so little about the world. Our educational lenses have focused too long on curricular goals that were blinders to what was happening around us. We thought we did not need multiple perspectives—that one view of knowledge was enough. Yet what we know and what we make is always a reflection of our beliefs and assumptions about the world. And we need to build new bridges now.

Perspectival knowledge—the ability to stand up and view unknown territory—enables students, educators, and the public at large to take a second and third look at the many lenses that make up the human experience. The purpose is not to always like what we see, but to learn how to put different worldviews into a new configuration and uncover paths that we might yet not see. We might, if we are brave enough, respect students not for what has been taught them after they have taken prescribed courses and completed assignments, but respect them as they walk through the door—or through the online portal as they enter the *learning habitat*—on the first day of class.

REFERENCES

Alpert, D., & Bitzer, D. L. (1970). Advances in computer-based education. *Science, 167,* 1582–1590.

Ambron, S., & Hooper, K. (1990). *Learning with interactive multimedia*. Redmond, WA: Microsoft Press.

Apple Multimedia Lab. (1989). *The visual almanac: An interactive multimedia kit.*

Bates, A. W. (1988). Technology for distance education: A 10-year prospective. *Open Learning, 3*(3), 3–12.

Bates, A. W. (1995). *Technology: Open learning and distance education*. London: Routledge.

Beers, M. (2001). *Subjects-in interaction version 3.0: An intellectual system for modern language student teachers to appropriate multiliteracies as designers and interpreters of digital media texts.* Unpublished doctoral dissertation, University of British Columbia, Vancouver, British Columbia, Canada.

Beers, M., & Goldman-Segall, R. (2001). *New roles for student teachers becoming experts: Creating, viewing, and critiquing digital video texts.* Paper presented at the American Educational Research Association Annual Meeting, Seattle, WA.

Bootstrap Institute. (1994). *Biographical sketch: Douglas C. Engelbart.* Retrieved October 12, 2001, from http://www.bootstrap.org/dce-bio.htm

Brand, S. (1987). *The Media Lab: Inventing the future at MIT.* New York: Viking.

Bromley, H. (1998). Introduction: Data-driven democracy? Social assessment of educational computing. In H. Bromley & M. W. Apple (Eds.), *Education, technology, power: Educational computing as a social practice* (pp. 1–27). Albany: State University of New York.

Brown, J. S., & Burton, R. R. (1978). A paradigmatic example of an artificially intelligent instructional system. *International Journal of Man-Machine Studies, 10*(3), 323–339.

Brown, J. S., Collins, A., & Duguid, P. (1996). Situated cognition and the culture of learning. In H. McLellan (Ed.), *Situated learning perspectives* (pp. 32–42). Englewood Cliffs, NJ: Educational Technology. (Original work published 1989)

Bruckman, A. S. (1997). *Moose Crossing: Construction, community, and learning in a networked virtual world for kids.* Unpublished doctoral dissertation, MIT, Cambridge, MA. Retrieved October 10, 2001, from http://www.cc.gatech.edu/~asb/thesis

Bruckman, A. S. (1998). Community support for constructionist learning. *CSCW, 7,* 47–86. Retrieved September 17, 2001, from http://www.cc.gatech.edu/elc/papers/bruckman/cscw-bruckman.pdf

Bruner, J. (1990). *Acts of meaning.* Cambridge, MA: Harvard University Press.

Bryson, M., & deCastell, S. (1998). Telling tales out of school: Modernist, critical, and "true stories" about educational computing. In H. Bromley & M. W. Apple (Eds.), *Education, technology, power: Educational computing as a social practice* (pp. 65–84). Albany: State University of New York.

Cognition and Technology Group at Vanderbilt. (1997). *The Jasper project: Lessons in curriculum, instruction, assessment and professional development.* Mahwah, NJ: Erlbaum.

Cole, M. (1996). *Cultural psychology: A once and future discipline.* Cambridge, MA: Harvard University Press.

Cole, M., & Engeström, Y. (1993). A cultural-historical approach to distributed cognition. In G. Salomon (Ed.), *Distributed cognitions: Psychological and educational considerations.* Cambridge, UK: Cambridge University Press.

Cole, M., & Wertsch, J. V. (1996). Beyond the individual-social antinomy in discussions of Piaget and Vygotsky. *Human Development, 39*(5), 250–256.

Daniels, V. (2000). *Lecture on John B. Watson.* Retrieved October 15, 001, from http://www.sonoma.edu/people/daniels/Wason.html

Davy, J. (1985). Mindstorms in the lamplight. In D. Sloan (Ed.), *The computer in education: A critical perspective* (pp. 11–20). New York: Teachers College Press.

deCastell, S., Bryson, M., & Jenson, J. (2000). *Object lessons: Critical visions of educational technology.* Paper presented at American Educational Research Association Annual Meeting, New Orleans, LA.

Dede, C. (1994). The evolution of constructivist learning environments: Immersion in distributed, virtual worlds. *Educational Technology, 35*(5), 46–52.

Dewey, J. (1961). *Democracy and education: An introduction to the philosophy of education.* New York: Macmillan. (Original work published 1916)

diSessa, A. A. (1988). Knowledge in pieces. In G. Forman & P. B. Pufall (Eds.), *Constructivism in the computer age* (pp. 49–70). Hillsdale, NJ: Erlbaum.

diSessa, A. A. (2000). *Changing minds: Computers, learning, and literacy.* Cambridge, MA: MIT Press.

Duffy, T. M., & Jonassen, D. (1992). *Constructivism and the technology of instruction: A conversation.* Hillsdale, NJ: LEA.

Edelson, D., Pea, R., & Gomez, L. (1996). Constructivism in the collaboratory. In B. G. Wilson (Ed.), *Constructivist learning environments: Case studies in instructional design* (pp. 151–164). Englewood Cliffs, NJ: Educational Technology.

Erikson, E. (1950). *Childhood and society.* New York: Norton.

Feenberg, A. (1989). The written world: On the theory and practice of computer conferencing. In R. Mason & A. Kaye (Eds.), *Mindweave: Communication, computers and distance education* (pp. 22–39). Oxford: Pergamon Press.

Feldman, A., Konold, C., & Coulter, B. (2000). *Network science, a decade later: The Internet and classroom learning.* Mahwah, NJ: Erlbaum.

Fox Keller, E. (1983). *A feeling for the organism: The life and work of Barbara McClintock.* San Francisco: W. H. Freeman.

Freud, S. (1975). *The standard edition of the complete psychological works of Sigmund Freud.* New York: W. W. Norton.

Gardner, H. (1983). *Frames of mind: The theory of multiple intelligences.* New York: Basic Books.

Gardner, H. (1985). *The mind's new science: A history of the cognitive revolution.* New York: Basic Books.

Geertz, C. (1973). *The interpretation of cultures.* New York: Basic Books.

Gilligan, C. (1982). *In a different voice: Psychological theory and women's development.* Cambridge, MA: Harvard University Press.

Gilster, P. (2000). *Digital literacy, The Jossey-Bass reader on technology and learning.* San Francisco: Jossey-Bass.

Goffman, E. (1986). *Frame analysis: An essay on the organization of experience.* Boston: Northeastern University Press.

Goldman-Segall, R. (1989). Thick description: A tool for designing ethnographic interactive videodisks. *SIGCHI Bulletin, 21*(2), 118–122.

Goldman-Segall, R. (1990). *Learning Constellations: A multimedia ethnographic research environment using video technology to explore children's thinking.* Unpublished doctoral dissertation, MIT, Cambridge, MA.

Goldman-Segall, R. (1991). Three children, three styles: A call for opening the curriculum. In I. Harel & S. Papert (Eds.), *Constructionism* (pp. 235–268). Cambridge, MA: MIT Press.

Goldman-Segall, R. (1993). Interpreting video data: Introducing a "significance measure" to layer descriptions. *Journal for Educational Multimedia and Hypermedia, 2*(3), 261–282.

Goldman-Segall, R. (1994). *Virtual Clayoquot: The Bayside Middle School implements a multimedia study of a Canadian rain forest.* Proceedings of Ed-Media '94, World Conference on Educational Multimedia and Hypermedia, AACE, 603–609.

Goldman-Segall, R. (1995). Configurational validity: A proposal for analyzing ethnographic multimedia narratives. *Journal of Educational Multimedia and Hypermedia, 4*(2/3), 163–182.

Goldman-Segall, R. (1996a). *Genderflexing: A theory of gender and socio-scientific thinking.* Proceedings of the International Conference on the Learning Sciences, Chicago, IL.

Goldman-Segall, R. (1996b). Looking through layers: Reflecting upon digital ethnography. *JCT: An Interdisciplinary Journal for Curriculum Studies, 13*(1), 23–29.

Goldman-Segall, R. (1998a). *Gender and digital media in the context of a middle school science project. MERIDIAN, A Middle School Gender and Technology Electronic Journal 1*(1). Retrieved October 5, 2001, from http://www.ncsu.edu/meridian/jan98/feat_3/gender.html

Goldman-Segall, R. (1998b). *Points of viewing children's thinking: A digital ethnographer's journey.* Mahwah, NJ: Erlbaum. Accompanying video cases retrieved from http://www.pointsofviewing.com.

Goldman-Segall, R. (1999). *Using video to support professional development and improve practice.* White Paper presented to the Board on International Comparative Studies in Education (BICSE) Invitational Consortium on Uses of Video in International Studies, National Academy of Education, Washington, DC.

Goldman-Segall, R. (2000). Video cases: Designing Constellations, a perspectivity digital video data analysis tool. Paper presented at *CILT 2000.* Retrieved October 10, 2001, from http://kn.cilt.org/cilt2000/abstracts/2053.html

Goldman-Segall, R., & Rao, C. (1998). *WebConstellations: A collaborative online digital data tool for creating living narratives in organizational knowledge systems.* Proceedings for the 31st Hawaii International Conference for Systems Sciences, IEEE, 194–200.

Granott, N. (1991). Puzzled minds and weird creatures: The spontaneous process of knowledge construction. In I. Harel & S. Papert (Eds.), *Constructionism* (pp. 295–310). Cambridge, MA: MIT Press.

Graves, W. H. (1999). The instructional management systems cooperative: Converting random acts of progress into global progress. *Educom Review, 34*(6). Retrieved October 12, 2001, from http://www.educause.edu/ir/library/html/erm9966.html

Greenfield, P. M. (1984). A theory of the teacher in the learning activities of everyday life. In B. Rogoff & J. Lave (Eds.), *Everyday cognition: Its development in social context* (pp. 117–138). Cambridge, MA: Harvard University Press.

Greeno, J. G. (1997). On claims that answer the wrong questions. *Educational Researcher, 26*(1), 5–17.

Gruber, H. E., & Voneche, J. J. (Eds.). (1977). *The essential Piaget.* New York: Basic Books.

Guzdial, M. (1997). Information ecology of collaborations in educational settings: Influence of tool. Paper presented at the Computer-Supported Collaborative Learning. Retrieved October 9, 2001, from http://guzdial.cc.gatech.edu/papers/infoecol/

Guzdial, M. (1999). *Teacher and student authoring on the web for shifting agency.* Paper presented at the American Educational Research Association Annual Meeting, Montreal, CA. Retrieved October 15, 2001, from http://guzdial.cc.gatech.edu/papers/aera99/

Harasim, L. M. (1990). *Online education: Perspectives on a new environment.* New York: Praeger.

Harasim, L. M. (1993). Networlds: Networks as social space. In L. M. Harasim (Ed.), *Global networks: Computers and international communication* (pp. 15–36). Cambridge, MA: MIT Press.

Harasim, L. M., Calvert, T., & Groeneboer, C. (1996). *Virtual-U: A web-based environment customized to support collaborative learning and knowledge building in post secondary courses.* Paper presented at the International Conference of the Learning Sciences, Northwestern University, Evanston, IL.

Harel, I. (1991). *Children designers: Interdisciplinary constructions for learning and knowing mathematics in a computer-rich school.* Westport, CT: Ablex.

Harel, I., & Papert, S. (Eds.). (1991). *Constructionism.* Norwood, NJ: Ablex.

Harrison, B., & Baecker, R. (1992). *Designing video annotation and analysis systems.* Paper presented at the Proceedings of Computer Human Interface (CHI) 1992, Monterey, CA.

Harvey, B. (1997). *Computer science Logo style* (2nd ed.). Cambridge, MA: MIT Press.

Haynes, C., & Holmevik, J. R. (Eds.). (1998). *High-wired: On the design, use, and theory of educational MOOs.* Ann Arbor: University of Michigan Press.

Hirsch, E. D., Jr. (1987). *Cultural literacy.* Boston: Houghton Mifflin.

Hiltz, S. R. (1994). *The virtual classroom: Learning without limits via computer networks.* Norwood, NJ: Ablex.

Hiltz, S. R., & Turoff, M. (1993). *The network nation: Human communication via computer* (Rev. ed.). Cambridge, MA: MIT Press. (Original work published 1978)

Illich, I. (1972). *Deschooling society.* New York: Harrow Books.

Illich, I. (1973). *Tools for conviviality.* New York: Marion Boyars.

Illich, I., & Sanders, B. (1989). *ABC: Alphabetization of the popular mind.* Vintage Books.

Jonassen, D. (1996). *Computers in the classroom: Mindtools for critical thinking.* Englewood Cliffs, NJ: Merrill.

Kafai, Y. (1993). *Minds in play: Computer game design as a context for children's learning.* Unpublished doctoral dissertation, Graduate School of Education of Harvard, Cambridge, MA.

Kafai, Y. (1996). Software by kids for kids. *Communications of the ACM, 39*(4), 38–39.

Kaput, J., Roschelle, J., & Stroup, W. (1998). SimCalc: Accelerating students' engagement with the mathematics of change. In M. Jacobson & R. Kozma (Eds.), *Educational technology and mathematics and science for the 21st century* (pp. 47–75). Hillsdale, NJ: Erlbaum.

Katz, S., & Lesgold, A. (1993). The role of the tutor in computer-based collaborative learning situations. In S. P. Lajoie & S. J. Derry (Eds.), *Computers as cognitive tools* (pp. 289–317). Hillsdale, NJ: Erlbaum.

Kay, A. C. (1996). The early history of SmallTalk. In J. Thomas, J. Bergin, J. Richard, & G. Gibson (Eds.), *History of programming languages—II* (pp. 511–578). New York: ACM Press.

Kennedy, S. (1989). Using video in the BNR utility lab. *SIGCHI Bulletin, 21*(2), 92–95.

Koschmann, T. (1996). Paradigm shifts and instructional technology: An introduction. In T. Koschmann (Ed.), *CSCL: Theory and practice of an emerging paradigm* (pp. 1–23). Mahwah, NJ: Erlbaum.

Kroeber, A. L. (1948). *Anthropology: Race, language, culture, psychology, prehistory.* New York: Harcourt, Brace & World.

Kuhn, T. (1996). *The structure of scientific revolutions* (3rd ed.). Chicago: University of Chicago Press.

Lajoie, S. P., & Derry, S. J. (1993). *Computers as cognitive tools.* Hillsdale, NJ: Erlbaum.

Landow, G. P. (1992). *Hypertext: The convergence of contemporary critical theory and technology.* Baltimore: Johns Hopkins University Press.

Landow, G. P., & Delany, P. (1993). *The digital word: Text-based computing in the humanities.* Cambridge, MA: MIT Press.

Laurel, B., & Mountford, S. J. (Eds.). (1990). *The art of human-computer interface design.* Reading, MA: Addison-Wesley.

Lave, J. (1988). *Cognition in practice: Mind, mathematics, and culture in everyday life.* Cambridge, UK: Cambridge University Press.

Lave, J., & Wenger, E. (1991). *Situated learning: Legitimate peripheral participation.* Cambridge, UK: Cambridge University Press.

Lehrer, R., & Schauble, L. (Eds.). (2001). *Real data in the classroom: Expanding children's understanding of mathematics and science.* New York: Teachers College Press.

Lemke, J. (1998). Multiplying meaning: Visual and verbal semiotics in scientific text. In J. R. Martin & R. Veel (Eds.), *Reading science* (pp. 87–113). London: Routledge.

Levin, J., Riel, M., Miyake, N., & Cohen, E. (1987). Education on the electronic frontier. *Contemporary Educational Psychology, 12,* 254–260.

Lévi-Strauss, C. (1968). *The savage mind.* Chicago: University of Chicago Press.

Lifter, M., & Adams, M. (1999). *Multimedia projects for Kid Pix.* Bloomington, IL: FTC.

Mackay, W. (1989). Eva: An experimental video annotator for symbolic analysis of video data. *SIGCHI Bulletin, 21*(2), 68–71.

Martin, F., & Resnick, M. (1993). Lego/Logo and electronic bricks: Creating a scienceland for children. In D. L. Ferguson (Ed.), *Advanced educational technologies for mathematics and science.* Berlin: Springer-Verlag.

Martin, L. M. W. (1987). Teachers' adoption of multimedia technologies for science and mathematics instruction. In R. D. Pea & K. Sheingold (Eds.), *Mirrors of minds: Patterns of experience in educational computing* (pp. 35–56). Norwood, NJ: Ablex.

Meares, C. A., & John F. Sargent, J. (1999). *The digital work force: Building infotech skills at the speed of innovation.* Retrieved September 25, 2001, from U.S. Department of Commerce, http://www.ta.doc.gov/reports/itsw/Digital.pdf

Minsky, M. (1986). *The society of mind.* New York: Simon and Schuster.

Noble, D. (1985). Computer literacy and ideology. In D. Sloan (Ed.), *The computer in education: A critical perspective* (pp. 64–76). New York: Teachers College Press.

Noble, D. (1999). *Digital diploma mills part IV: Rehearsal for the revolution.* Retrieved October 15, 2001, from http://communication.ucsd.edu/dl/ddm4.html

Papert, S. (1980). *Mindstorms: Children, computers, and powerful ideas.* New York: Basic Books.

Papert, S. (1985). Information technology and education: Computer criticism vs technocentric thinking. *Educational Researcher, 16*(1), 22–30.

Papert, S. (1991). Situating constructionism. In I. Harel & S. Papert (Eds.), *Constructionism* (pp. 1–12). Norwood, NJ: Ablex.

Papert, S. (1992). *The children's machine.* New York: Basic Books.

Pea, R. D. (1987). The aims of software criticism: Reply to Professor Papert. *Educational Researcher, 20*(3), 4–8.

Pea, R. D. (1993). Practices of distributed intelligence and designs for education. In G. Salomon (Ed.), *Distributed cognitions: Psychological and educational considerations* (pp. 47–87). Cambridge, UK: Cambridge University Press.

Pea, R. D., & Kurland, D. M. (1987). On the cognitive effects of learning computer programming. In R. Pea & K. Sheingold (Eds.), *Mirrors of minds* (pp. 147–177). Norwood, NJ: Ablex. (Original work published 1984)

Pea, R. D., Kurland, D. M., & Hawkins, J. (1987). Logo and the development of thinking skills. In R. Pea & K. Sheingold (Eds.), *Mirrors of minds* (pp. 178–197). Norwood, NJ: Ablex.

Pearson Education. (2000). Pearson Education History. Retrieved October 25, 2001, from http://www.pearsoned.com/history.htm

Piaget, J. (1930). *The child's conception of the world.* London: Harcourt, Brace, and World.

Piaget, J. (1952). *The child's conception of number.* London: Routledge & Kegan Paul.

Piaget, J. (1969). *The child's conception of time.* London: Rutledge & Kegan Paul.

Piaget, J., & Inhelder, B. (1956). *The child's conception of space.* London: Routledge & Kegan Paul.

Picard, R. (1997). *Affective computing.* Cambridge, MA: MIT Press.

Resnick, M. (1991). Overcoming the centralized mindset: Towards an understanding of emergent phenomena. In I. Harel & S. Papert (Eds.), *Constructionism* (pp. 205–214). Norwood, NJ: Ablex.

Resnick, M. (1994). *Turtles, termites, traffic jams: Explorations in massively parallel microworlds.* Cambridge, MA: MIT Press.

Resnick, M., & Ocko, S. (1991). Lego/Logo: Learning through and about design. In I. Harel & S. Papert (Eds.), *Constructionism* (pp. 141–150). Norwood, NJ: Ablex.

Resnick, M., & Wilensky, U. (1993). *Beyond the deterministic, centralized mindsets: New thinking for new sciences.* Paper presented at the American Educational Research Association Annual Meeting, Atlanta, GA.

Resnick, M., & Wilensky, U. (1998). Diving into complexity: Developing probabilistic decentralized thinking through role-playing activities. *Journal of Learning Sciences, 7*(2). Retrieved November 9, 2001, from http://ccl.sesp.northwestern.edu/cm/papers/starpeople

Riel, M. (1993). Global education through learning circles. In L. M. Harasim (Ed.), Global networks: Computers and international communication. Cambridge, MA: MIT Press, 221–236.

Riel, M. (1996). Cross-classroom collaboration: Communication and education. In T. Koschmann (Ed.), *CSCL: Theory and practice of an emerging paradigm* (pp. 187–207). Mahwah, NJ: Erlbaum.

Romiszowski, A. J., & de Haas, J. A. (1989). Computer mediated communication for instruction: Using e-mail as a seminar. *Educational Technology, 29*(10), 7–14.

Roschelle, J., Kaput, J., Stroup, W., & Kahn, T. M. (1998). Scaleable integration of educational software: Exploring the promise of component architectures. *Journal of Interactive Media in Education, 98*(6). Retrieved October 10, 2001, from http://www-jime.open.ac.uk/98/6

Roschelle, J., Pea, R., & Trigg, R. (1990). Video Noter: A tool for exploratory video analysis. *IRL Technical Report No. IRL 90-002,* Menlo Park, CA.

Sachter, J. E. (1990). *Kids in space: Exploration into spatial cognition of children's learning 3-D computer graphics.* Unpublished doctoral dissertation, MIT, Cambridge, MA.

Salomon, G. (1979). *Interaction of media, cognition, and learning.* San Francisco: Jossey-Bass.

Salomon, G. (1993). No distribution without individuals' cognition: A dynamic interactional view. In G. Salomon (Ed.), *Distributed cognitions: Psychological and educational considerations.* Cambridge, UK: Cambridge University Press.

Salomon, G., & Gardner, H. (1986). The computer as educator: Lessons from television research. *Educational Researcher, 15*(1), 13–19.

Salomon, G., Perkins, D. N., & Globerson, T. (1991). Partners in cognition: Extending human intelligence with intelligent technologies. *Educational Researcher, 20*(3), 2–9.

Scardamalia, M., & Bereiter, C. (1991). Higher levels of agency for children in knowledge building: A challenge for the design of new knowledge media. *Journal of the Learning Sciences, 1*(1), 37–68.

Schank, R. C. (2000). *Educational outrage: Are computers the bad guys in education?* Retrieved July 11, 2000, from http://movietone.ils.nwu.edu/edoutrage/edoutrage11.html

Schlager, M., & Schank, P. (1997). *Tapped In: A new on-line teacher community concept for the next generation of Internet technology.* Paper presented at the Computer-Supported Collaborative Learning 1997. Retrieved July, 27, 2000, from http://www.tappedin.sri.com/info/papers/cscl97

Scribner, S., & Cole, M. (1981). *The psychology of literacy.* Cambridge: Harvard University Press.

Simon, H. A. (1981). *The sciences of the artificial.* Cambridge, MA: MIT Press. (Original work published 1969)

Soloway, E., Krajcik, J. S., Blumenfeld, P., & Marx, R. (1996). Technological support for teachers transitioning to project-based science projects. In T. Koschmann (Ed.), *CSCL: Theory and practice of an emerging paradigm* (pp. 269–305). Mahwah, NJ: Erlbaum.

Spiro, R. J., Feltovich, P. J., Jacobson, M. J., & Coulson, R. L. (1991). Cognitive flexibility, constructivism, and hypertext: Random access instruction for advanced knowledge acquisition in ill-structured domains. *Educational Technology, 31*(5), 24–33.

Stahl, G. (1999). *WebGuide: Guiding collaborative learning on the web with perspectives.* Paper presented at the American Educational Research Association Annual Meeting, Montreal, Quebec, Canada. Retrieved November 15, 2000 from http://www.cs.colorado.edu/~gerry/publications/conferences/1999/aera99/

Steinkuehler, C. A., Derry, S. J., Hmelo-Silver, C. E., & DelMarcelle, M. (in press). Cracking the resource nut with distributed problem-based learning in secondary teacher education. *Journal of Distance Education.* Retrieved June 26, 2002, from http://www.wcer.wisc.edu/step/

Stone, A. R. (1995). *The war between desire and technology at the end of the mechanical age.* Cambridge, MA: MIT Press.

Suchman, L. A. (1987). *Plans and situated actions: The problem of human-machine communication.* Cambridge, UK: Cambridge University Press.

Suppes, P. (1966). The uses of computers in education. *Scientific American, 215*(3), 206–220.

Suppes, P., Jerman, M., & Brian, D. (1968). *Computer-assisted instruction: Stanford's 1965–66 arithmetic program.* New York: Academic Press.

Suppes, P., & Morningstar, M. (1972). *Computer-assisted instruction at Stanford, 1966–68: Data, models, and evaluation of the arithmetic programs.* New York: Academic Press.

Swan, K. (1994). History, hypermedia, and criss-crossed conceptual landscapes. *Journal of Educational Multimedia and Hypermedia, 3*(2), 120–139.

Tinker, R. F. (1996). Telecomputing as a progressive force in education. *The Concord Consortium.* Retrieved October 15, 2000, from http://www.concord.org/library/pdf/telecomputing.pdf

Trinh, M. H. (1992). *Framer-framed.* New York: Routledge.

Turing, A. M. (1950). Computing machinery and intelligence. *Mind, 59,* 433–460. Retrieved June 19, 2002, from http://www.loebner.net/Prizef/TuringArticle.html

Turkle, S. (1984). *The second self: Computers and the human spirit.* New York: Simon and Schuster.

Turkle, S. (1991). Romantic reactions: Paradoxical responses to the computer presence. In J. J. Sheehan & M. Sosna (Eds.), *The boundaries of humanity: Humans, machines, animals* (pp. 224–252). Berkeley: University of California Press.

Turkle, S. (1995). *Life on the screen: Identity in the age of the Internet.* New York: Simon and Schuster.

Turkle, S., & Papert, S. (1991). Epistemological pluralism: Styles and voices within the computer culture. In I. Harel & S. Papert (Eds.), *Constructionism* (pp. 161–192). Cambridge, MA: MIT Press.

Vygotsky, L. S. (1962). *Thought and language* (E. Hanfmann & G. Vakar, Trans.). Cambridge, MA: MIT Press.

Vygotsky, L. S. (1978). *Mind in society: The development of higher psychological processes.* Cambridge, MA: Harvard University Press.

Wenger, E. (1987). *Artificial intelligence and tutoring systems: Computational and cognitive approaches to the communication of knowledge.* Los Altos, CA: Morgan Kaufmann.

Wenger, E. (1998). Communities of practice: Learning, meaning, and identity. Cambridge, UK: Cambridge University Press.

Wilensky, U. (2000). *Modeling emergent phenomena with StarLogo.* Retrieved May 31, 2001, from http://concord.org/library/2000winter/starlogo.html

Wilensky, U. (2001). *Emergent entities and emergent processes: Constructing emergence through multiagent programming.* Paper presented at the American Educational Research Association Annual Meeting, Seattle, WA.

Wilensky, U., & Resnick, M. (1999). Thinking in levels: A dynamic systems perspective to making sense of the world. *Journal of Science Education and Technology, 8*(1), 3–18.

Wilensky, U., & Stroup, W. (1999). *Learning through participatory simulations: Network-based design for systems learning in classrooms.* Proceedings of the Computer-Supported Collaborative Learning Conference, Stanford, CA. Retrieved May 31, 2001, from http://www.ccl.sesp.northwestern.edu/cm/papers/partsims/cscl/

Winograd, T., & Flores, F. (1986). *Understanding computers and cognition: A new foundation for design.* Norwood, NJ: Ablex.

Wolfson, L., & Willinsky, J. (1998). Situated learning of information technology management. *Journal of Research on Computing in Education, 31*(1), 96–110.

Woolley, D. R. (1994). PLATO: The emergence of online community. *Computer-Mediated Communication Magazine, 1*(3). Retrieved November 15, 2001, from http://www.december.com/cmc/mag/1994/jul/plato.html

PART FIVE

EXCEPTIONAL LEARNER PROGRAMS AND STUDENTS

CHAPTER 17

School Psychology

DANIEL J. RESCHLY

The school psychology profession that exists today was shaped over the last century by multiple factors that continue to influence current thought and practice. These foundational influences are discussed in the initial section of this chapter and are followed by a review of the current status of school psychology in terms of roles and services, legal requirements, employment conditions, credentialing, infrastructure (professional associations, standards, journals), demographics, and supply-demand issues. The concluding section addresses probable future developments in light of current trends.

Although much has changed over the last century in psychology and education, the *core* features of school psychology practice have remained remarkably stable. School psychology's earliest practitioners were concerned with identification and interventions for students with atypical patterns of learning and development, a core mission that dominates practice today. The principal basis for initiating services was then—and continues to be—referral of children due to learning problems, behavior problems, or both, most often by classroom teachers who are frustrated because the usual classroom strategies are not working. Moreover, then as now the vast majority of school psychologists' professional

practice involved a close association with educational services to students with disabilities such as mental retardation (MR), emotional disturbance (ED) and, recently, specific learning disability (SLD).

Throughout school psychology's history there has been a parallel concern with enhancing the educational and developmental opportunities of all children through the implementation of sound mental health practices in schools, homes, neighborhoods, and communities. Current programs to establish schools as full-service educational and health agencies are one of the contemporary reflections of the latter trend. The broader positive mental health mission has always been, however, secondary to the core role of identification and interventions with students with learning and behavior problems.

HISTORICAL TRENDS

The early roots, the disciplinary foundations, and the societal trends that produced modern school psychology are discussed in this section. The early roots of school psychology emerged in the late 1890s in urban settings where school attendance was increasingly expected of all children and youth. Concerns for children with low achievement soon emerged, and efforts to identify the causes and solutions to low achievement were undertaken in several urban centers at about the same time (Fagan, 1992). It is interesting to note that the same concerns dominate most of school psychology practice today.

Disciplinary Foundations of School Psychology

Multiple disciplinary foundations exist for graduate education and school psychology practice. School psychology originated in the very early practice of what became clinical psychology involving the application of psychological methods to the understanding of learning and behavior problems of school-age children and youth (Fagan, 2000). Understanding and intervening with these problems always has involved multiple disciplines, including educational psychology (especially, the learning, measurement, and child development components), psychopathology and psychology of exceptional individuals, developmental psychology, counseling, clinical psychology, applied behavior analysis, and special education. These disciplinary foundations are clearly present in the authoritative statements of the crucial features of school psychology graduate education and practice (National Association of School Psychologists, 2000; Ysseldyke et al., 1997).

Societal Trends and School Psychology

School psychology always has been responsive to societal trends. In fact, whatever the current major issue is, it will be represented prominently in contemporary exhortations regarding what school psychologists should be doing. Two examples of this pattern should suffice. During the 1980s enormous emphasis was placed on drug abuse among youth and the school's role in preventing drug abuse. The outcome was that awareness was increased and a few really good preventive programs were developed; however, although drug abuse continues to be a huge problem, relatively little attention is paid to this problem in the current school psychology literature.

A contemporary trend involves prevention of violence in schools, undoubtedly prompted by a few highly publicized horrific incidents in American schools resulting in the loss of approximately 60 students' lives. The emphasis on violence prevention is important but perhaps a bit disproportionate in comparison to other more common problems. For example, overall, schools are overall, safer in the early 2000s than in the 1980s in terms of the number of lives lost in schools due

to violence; however, youth violence remains a serious and often-discussed issue (U.S. Department of Health and Human Services, 2001).

The persistence and impact of school psychology's attention to immediate societal problems depends on how well interventions become embedded in typical practice and implemented successfully in schools. For example, the use of group counseling and other peer group support procedures was expanded in the 1980s and then embedded in the practice of many school psychologists working in secondary schools. These methods are now applied to many different problems, including decision making about sexual behavior, social skills training, and, of course, drug abuse.

Similarly, the current emphasis on violence prevention will have a lasting influence in school psychology to the degree that the intervention methods developed are generally useful in preventing or ameliorating a range of problems. For example, the schoolwide interventions currently being implemented in schools as part of violence prevention efforts have positive influences on overall school and classroom climate, on preventing violent incidents, and on the reduction of other problems such as disciplinary referrals and dropout rates (Horner & Sugai, 2000; Sugai et al., 2000; Walker et al., 1996). If these interventions are incorporated into standard practice, then the current attention to school violence will have a lasting and positive effect.

Compulsory Education and Educational Outcomes

Fagan (1992) documented the impact of compulsory schooling on the development of school psychology in the twentieth century. Compulsory schooling and (increasingly) the expectation of high educational achievement for all children and youth continue to influence school psychology. Exceptional patterns of development and differences in achievement became much more problematic with compulsory school attendance beginning in the early 1900s and expanding through the rest of the century. A contemporary expression of the expansion of compulsory schooling is the strong emphasis on improving school attendance and preventing school withdrawal prior to the completion of high school. School dropout after a certain age (age 14, 15, or 16) was tolerated more readily in the 1960s, 1970s, and 1980s. Today, dropout prevention is a major goal of school reform along with expectations for high achievement for all children and youth (McDonnell, McLaughlin, & Morison, 1997).

Compulsory school attendance and expectations for high achievement for all students influenced early and contemporary school psychology in many ways. More children were in public schools. Moreover, through the century it was progressively less likely that students with serious achievement and behavior problems were excluded from schools, increasing the need for school psychological services and educational accommodations for students who varied on important dimensions related to education (learning rate, cognitive functioning, behavior, etc.). Today the demand for high achievement for all students, including those with disabilities, places more emphasis on effective general and special education interventions and school psychology services that are directly related to producing better outcomes.

Exceptional Individuals and Special Education

School psychology always emphasized recognition of individual differences in learning and development. The association with special education also occurred early in the history of school psychology, and (as discussed later) the existence of school psychology has closely paralleled the development of special education funding in the states. In most states, school psychologists have had mandated roles with the development of special education eligibility and placement. Part of that role always has been measurement of individual differences, often through comparing individual performance to national normative standards, and the development of educational programs to accommodate those differences.

Child Study and Mental Health

The early child study movement in the 1890 to 1910 period was another foundation for school psychology (Fagan, 1992). Child study methods later merged with school and clinical psychology and formed the basis for the increasingly close ties of school psychology to special education. The mental health movement that emerged in the 1920s is the basis for contemporary efforts to prevent academic, social-behavioral, and emotional problems through positive parenting and responsive school programs. The mental health movement has fostered many different approaches to prevention and intervention, varying from the psychoanalytic and psychodynamic roots in the early period to contemporary, behaviorally based schoolwide positive discipline programs. The effectiveness of mental health programs always has been controversial (e.g., Bickman, 1997).

Individual Rights and Legal Guarantees

The expansion of individual rights and legal guarantees to educational services for all children and youth exerted vast influences on school psychology. The U.S. Supreme Court decision in *Brown v. Board of Education* (1954) that outlawed

segregation of students by race in public schools initiated a movement that continues to grow and develop. *Brown* and subsequent litigation and legislation established strong sanctions against differential treatment of individuals on the basis of race, sex, age, and disability status (Reschly & Bersoff, 1999). Perhaps the most pervasive effect of this movement was to change the relationship of parents and students to schools. The discretion of schools to limit access or to segregate students was changed forever. Moreover, parents and students increasingly acquired the rights to challenge the decisions of educators and to seek redress in the courts.

The greatest current influences on school psychology are the court cases and legislation guaranteeing educational rights to students with disabilities (SWD). As noted later, the expanded rights changed the practice of school psychology in significant ways and markedly expanded special education and school psychology.

DEMOGRAPHICS AND CURRENT PRACTICE CONDITIONS

The current status of school psychology is discussed in this section, including roles and practices, employment conditions, personnel needs, and demographics. The characteristics of school psychology practice and practitioners have changed rapidly in a few areas while many other factors have remained stable over the last quarter century.

Employment

Numbers and Salaries

The number of school psychologists working in public school positions in the United States is impossible to know with certainty. Two methods have been used to estimate the total employed in schools—surveys of state department of education personnel and state school psychology leadership officials and the annual state reports to the Federal Office for Special Education Programs (OSEP) of personnel employed working with SWD. The results of the two methods are generally very similar in overall numbers and correlated at $r = .9$ or above (Lund, Reschly, & Martin, 1998). The OSEP results may be a very slight undercount because they do not include practitioners in schools *not* counted as working with special education programs.

According to the most recent OSEP count, over 25,000 school psychologists are employed in school settings. There are perhaps another 3,000 school psychology practitioners working in other roles in schools, such as director of special education, or in other settings, such as medical clinics, community mental health, and private practice. Other career settings for school psychologists include college and university teaching and research as well as state department of education staff. Of course, some persons with graduate education and experience in school psychology are in a very wide variety of roles such as university president, college provost and dean, school superintendent or principal, test publishing, and private consultation. The exact number of persons with school psychology graduate education and experience in the schools working in related careers or settings is impossible to determine; however, it is likely that the there are at least 30,000 such persons.

School psychology employment has grown rapidly since the enactment of the Education of the Handicapped Act (EHA; 1975, 1977), now the Individuals with Disabilities Education Act (IDEA; 1991, 1997, 1999). Prior to about 1975, the number of school psychologists and the ratio of students to psychologists in a state depended very heavily on whether the state had strong special education legislation and—as a part of that legislation—funding for school psychological services. Kicklighter (1976) reported an average ratio of about 22,000 students to one psychologist and a median of about 9,000 students per psychologist. The large differences between the median and mean indicate that there were enormous differences between states and regions and generally high (by present standards; see later discussion) ratios in nearly all localities (Fagan, 1988).

School psychology's growth over the last 25 years is documented through OSEP annual reports on the implementation of EHA and IDEA since 1976 (see Figure 17.3 later in this chapter; U.S. Department of Education, 1978–2001). The number of school psychologists over that time period increased from about 10,000 in 1977–1978 to more than 26,000 in 1998–1999—an increase of more than 150%. Approximately 750 school psychologists have been added annually to the profession, severely challenging the ability of graduate programs to provide an adequate supply of fully credentialed persons (see later discussion). For example, in the most recent year for which data are available, 1998–1999 (U.S. Department of Education, 2001), 1,025 of the 26,266 psychologists reported by the states to OSEP were not fully certified as school psychologists. Moreover, the growth of school psychology is tied to school budgets. Increased growth has occurred in good economic times (Lund et al., 1998), and it is likely that less growth or perhaps even a slight contraction is currently underway. Figure 17.3 (later in this chapter) summarizes the growth of school psychology by year since 1977–1978.

Employers and Salary

The vast majority of school psychologists (85% or more) work for publicly supported educational agencies such as school districts or regional education units. Most practitioners work very closely with special education programs in which they have particularly demanding responsibilities with disability diagnosis and special education program placement (see later discussion of roles and legal influences). Most are employed on 190- to 200-day contracts. The salaries for school psychologists nearly always are determined by years of professional experience, degree level, length of contract, and—occasionally—increased by supervisory responsibilities, specialized roles, or unique strengths such as bilingual capabilities. The average beginning salary is in the low $30,000s, but the variations among districts, states, and regions are substantial. The average salary for a school psychologist with a 190-day contract, 15 years of experience, and the equivalent of specialist-level graduate education (see later section) is in the mid-$50,000s, although again, there are large regional variations (Hosp & Reschly, 2002).

Job Satisfaction

Overall, the job satisfaction of school psychologists has been positive and stable over the last two decades. Reschly and colleagues began studies of job satisfaction in the mid-1980s in response to anecdotal reports that many school psychologists were unhappy with their work and planned to leave the profession in the near future (Vensel, 1981). Contrary to the anecdotal observations that received a good deal of attention in the early 1980s, job satisfaction is generally positive. The vast majority of practitioners plan to continue in school psychology for many years or until retirement and are satisfied with their career choice (Hosp & Reschly, 2002; Reschly, Genshaft, & Binder, 1987; Reschly & Wilson, 1995).

The picture becomes more nuanced when different aspects of job satisfaction are considered. Using a five-area job satisfaction scale in a Likert scale format patterned after the five-factor content of the Job Descriptive Index (JDI; Smith, Kendall, & Hulin, 1969), Reschly and Wilson's (1995) national survey results indicated high and positive satisfaction with colleagues and work, moderate satisfaction with supervision, and neutral perceptions of pay, but they also reported low satisfaction with promotion opportunities—a pattern also reported by Hosp and Reschly (2002) in a more recent survey (see Figure 17.1). For many practitioners—especially those at the specialist level of graduate preparation—advancement opportunities are seen as rather limited. One of

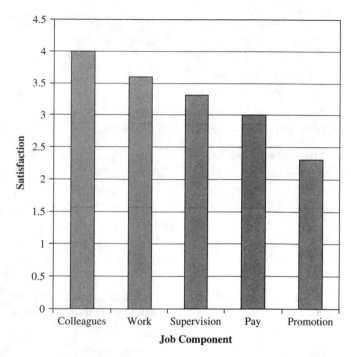

Figure 17.1   Job satisfaction of school psychologists.

the advantages associated with doctoral-level graduate education for practitioners is greater opportunity to pursue alternative career settings or to augment the usual role with other professional activities such as teaching in a local college, private practice, or consulting. Persons engaged in these activities generally see the job advancement and promotion opportunities more positively.

Demographics

Gender

School psychology demographics have changed significantly over the last 40 years (Reschly, 2000). The greatest changes occurred in gender; the practitioner work force has changed from 40% to 70% female. This gender trend is likely to continue because today slightly more than 80% of all school psychology graduate students are women. The composition of school psychology faculty, which started at a lower proportion of women (20%) also reflects the same trend; about 50% of all faculty are female currently. The gender trends in school psychology are consistent with the increasing feminization of psychology generally—a strong trend that is apparent among undergraduate majors and graduate students in all areas of psychology (Pion et al., 1996). The proportion of women in graduate programs in many areas of psychology—including clinical and counseling—are close to the 80% figure cited previously for school psychology.

Age

The average age of school psychology practitioners has increased from about 38–47 since 1985 (Curtis, Hunley, Walker, & Baker, 1999; Hosp & Reschly, 2002; Reschly et al., 1987). Similar age trends likely exist with school psychology faculty who were about 6 years older than practitioners in a 1992 survey (Reschly & Wilson, 1995). The advancing age of practitioners and faculty creates opportunities for greater gender representation among faculty, a trend that appears to be well underway and (perhaps) increasing diversity among all types of school psychologists. Moreover, the likely high rate of retirements over the next decade will contribute to the already healthy demand for school psychologists in both practitioner and faculty positions.

Diversity

Greater diversity in school psychology is an intense need and challenge. Curtis et al. (1999) reported that approximately 5.5% of practitioners identified themselves as being in a non-Caucasian group; however, only 1% reported being African American and 1.7% were self-identified as Hispanic. Graduate program enrollments and faculty have become slightly more diverse over the last decade; minority faculty membership has increased from 11% to 15%, and minority graduate students have increased from 13% to 17% (McMaster, Reschly, & Peters, 1989; Thomas, 1998). The latter statistics on minority representation were not reported by group; hence, there is no way to determine whether the most underrepresented groups (African American and Hispanic) are increasing. Regardless of this last point, the composition of the school psychology profession is markedly different from the current U.S. public school population, which is approximately 1% American Indian, 4% Asian or Pacific Islander, 15% Hispanic, 17% African American, and 63% White. It is likely that the racial-ethnic compositions of school psychologists and students will continue to be very different far into the future.

Degree Level

One of the most controversial issues is the appropriate level of graduate education for the independent, nonsupervised practice of school psychology in schools and other settings. Degree level is the principal issue that divides the American Psychological Association (APA) and its Division 16 (School Psychology) from the National Association of School Psychologists (NASP; see this chapter's later section on infrastructure). The degree composition of the current practitioner force is heavily at the specialist level—that is, 60 hours of graduate work in an organized program of study in school psychology with a 1-year internship. Although surveys differ slightly, about 75% of the current practitioners are at the specialist level and about 25% are at the doctoral level. Over the past 25 years there has been an enormous shift from the masters to the specialist level, and over the same period, the proportion of doctoral-level practitioners has only slightly increased. The current pattern is highly likely to continue because the vast majority of current school psychology graduate students are in specialist-level programs (75–80%), and the majority of school psychology graduate programs are located in institutions that are not authorized by their governing authorities to offer doctoral degrees in any area (Reschly & Wilson, 1997; Thomas, 1998).

The data on degree level of current practitioners and graduate students destroy the credibility of assertions in the mid-1980s that school psychology was rapidly changing to the doctoral level (Brown, 1987, 1989a, 1989b; Brown & Minke, 1986). Brown predicted that ". . . by 1990 over half of the students in training will be at the doctoral level" and that ". . . a majority of graduates in the near future will be doctoral" (1987, p. 755). Others suggested a slightly less rapid progression toward the doctoral level—for example, Fagan predicted that half of all practitioners in 2010 would be doctoral (Fagan, 1986). Past and current trends make those predictions impossible to achieve. In fact, school psychology is a largely nondoctoral profession and is likely to remain so for several decades into the new century.

Roles and Services

Based on the traditional literature (Cutts, 1955; Fagan & Wise, 2000; Magary, 1967; Phye & Reschly, 1979; White & Harris, 1961), the following summary reflects the research of Reschly and colleagues on the roles of school psychologists (Reschly & Wilson, 1995, p. 69).

- *Psychoeducational assessment* is "evaluations for diagnosis of handicapping conditions, testing, scoring and interpretation, report writing, eligibility or placement conferences with teachers and parents, re-evaluations."
- *Interventions* refer to "direct work with students, teachers, and parents to improve competencies or to solve problems, counseling, social skills groups, parent or teacher training, crisis intervention."
- *Problem-solving consultation* refers to "working with consultees (teachers or parents) with students as clients, problem identification, problem analysis, treatment design and implementation, and treatment evaluation."

- *Systems-organizational consultation* refers to "working toward system level changes, improved organizational functioning, school policy, prevention of problems, general curriculum issues."
- *Research-evaluation* refers to "program evaluation, grant writing, needs assessment, determining correlates of performance, evaluating effects of programs."

Using this scheme, several surveys (Hosp & Reschly, 2002; Reschly et al., 1987; Reschly & Wilson, 1995) have yielded generally consistent results regarding practitioners' perceptions of their current and preferred roles (see Figure 17.2). The current services of school psychologists involve a heavy emphasis on psychoeducational assessment, which accounts for over half of the role (Hosp & Reschly, 2002). Approximately 35% of the time is devoted to direct interventions and problem-solving consultation, with less than 10% devoted to systems-organizational consultation and research-evaluation. Preferred roles involve significantly less time in assessment (32%) and slightly more time in each of the other four roles.

Further information on the character of school psychology services is revealed by responses to the following item: *How much of your time is spent in determining special education*

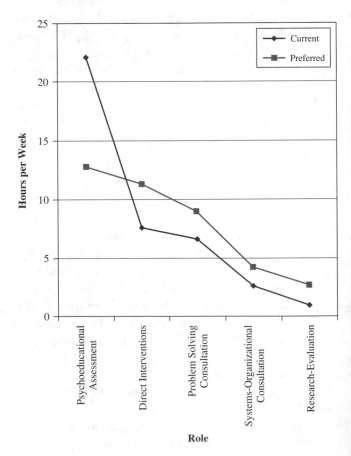

Figure 17.2   Current and preferred hours per week in different roles.

eligibility, staffings, follow-up on placements, and reevaluations? The average amount of time in services strongly connected to special education eligibility, and placement in 1997 was 60%. Moreover, the results of a survey on the use of different assessment instruments or approaches further supported the strong tie to eligibility determination in special education. School psychology assessment is dominated by assessment of intellectual ability and the use of other measures related to determining eligibility for special education such as behavior rating scales and projective assessment devices. The behavior rating scales are nearly always completed by teachers or parents and the projective devices used typically were the less complex variety, such as figure drawings and sentence completion tasks. A good case can be made that IQ testing for the purpose of determining special education eligibility still dominates much of school psychology practice.

Ratios and Regional Differences

The content thus far on demographics, roles, and services has been based on averages derived from national surveys of school psychologists that mask large variations between regions, states, and districts within states. Regional differences are a significant influence on the interpretation of some of these results. A good example of the large variations among regions is the ratio of students to psychologists. The national ratio is about 1900:1. That overall average masks significant regional variations that differ from 3800:1 in the East-South-Central states to 1000:1 in the New England states (Hosp & Reschly, 2002). Even greater variations exist among states and in some cases between districts within the same state. It is therefore difficult to generalize about school psychology practice across all districts, states, and regions. The variables discussed thus far that are most affected by regional factors are—in addition to ratio—salary (higher in the eastern and western coasts and lower in the southern and West-South-Central states), assessment practices (more IQ testing in the southern states and less in the Northeast; less use of projective measures in the central and mountain states), and nonassessment roles (more time devoted to them in the East and less in the Pacific states). Job satisfaction, age, gender composition, and time devoted to special education services did not vary substantially across the regions.

LEGAL REQUIREMENTS

Legal requirements influence every facet of school psychology practice in schools and in many other settings. Public schools are creations of federal, state, and local governments. School psychology employment depends heavily on public funding—a generally secure foundation that expands or contracts at a moderate rates with economic circumstances. Varied sources of legal requirements and legal mechanisms influence the practice of school psychology (Prasse, 2002; Reschly & Bersoff, 1999).

The sources of legal requirements influencing school psychology vary from the U.S. Constitution's 5th and 14th Amendments used in the *Diana* (1970), *Guadalupe* (1972)—both cases regarding minority overrepresentation in special education—and *Pennsylvania Association of Retarded Children v. Commonwealth of Pennsylvania* (1972)—a landmark right of students with mental retardation to appropriate educational services, due process protections, and participation in normal educational environments to the greatest extent feasible—to regulations developed by state education agencies. Litigation beginning in the late 1960s continues to markedly influence school psychology practice (Reschly & Bersoff, 1999). Although litigation and constitutional protections continue to be important, the greatest contemporary legal influences come from federal statutes and regulations and state statutes and rules governing the provision of educational services to students with disabilities (Reschly, 2000).

Legislation

The previously cited litigation was instrumental in the development of state and federal legislation regarding the educational rights of children and youth with disabilities. The EHA (1975, 1977) was the touchstone federal legislation that appears in an updated form today as IDEA (1991, 1997, 1999). All of the major principles of IDEA—that is, free appropriate education at public expense, least restrictive environment, individualized educational programs, procedural safeguards, and nondiscrimination and appropriate assessment—appeared earlier in the EHA. These principles and their implications for school psychology practice are summarized in Table 17.1. For example, the state and federal guarantees of a free and appropriate education for *all* SWD greatly increased the number of such students in the public school setting (from about 2.2 million students age 6–17 to over 5 million today), markedly increasing the number of eligibility evaluations and reevaluations.

Psychological services are defined in the IDEA regulations, but the terms *school psychology* or *school psychologist* do not appear in the IDEA statute or regulations. A broad conception of psychological services appears in the following IDEA (1999) regulations:

(9) Psychological *services* includes—
   (i) Administering psychological and educational tests, and other assessment procedures;
   (ii) Interpreting assessment results;

TABLE 17.1 EHA-IDEA Principles: Effects on Schools and Impact on School Psychology

Right to a free appropriate education at public expense (FAPE)

Effects: All students with disabilities (SWD) are guaranteed educational rights leading to (a) more students in the existing population of students classified as having mild disabilities such as specific learning disabilities and (b) students with complex multiple disabilities and severe disabilities gain access to public schools for the first time. Litigation interpreting FAPE makes EHA-IDEA a zero-reject guarantee of access to the publicly supported education.

Impact: More psychologists are needed to conduct evaluations and provide other services to SWD; some psychologists are needed with highly specialized skills in working with students with low incidence and severe disabilities such as autism and severe and profound levels of MR.

Least restrictive environment (LRE)

Effects: More SWD are served in general education environments or in part-time resource teaching programs. Special education is increasingly becoming a range of services brought to children and youth in natural environments rather than in places where educational services are provided. Pressure is being put on states to reduce the use of restrictive placements in settings such as residential institutions or self-contained special education classes.

Impact: More emphasis is on psychologists' conducting assessments in natural environments and on developing interventions and support services that assist students in general education environments. More emphasis is on positive behavior supports and functional behavior analysis to teach appropriate and eliminate inappropriate behaviors so that LRE can be achieved.

Individualized educational program (IEP)

Effects: Detailed plans have been developed to guide the provision of special education and related services, including general goals and specific objectives, assessment of progress, and annual review of the IEP.

Impact: More emphasis is on identifying specific educational needs during evaluations, monitoring progress toward goals, assessing performance in terms of general education settings with direct measures, and development of testing accommodations.

Procedural safeguards (due process)

Effects: Formal procedures protect rights and involve parents in decision-making through requirements of informed consent and rights to appeal decisions, to present additional information, to submit an independent evaluation, to acquire legal representation, to obtain impartial hearings to adjudicate disputes, and to appeal to state or federal courts.

Impact: School psychologists' work is more open to parental scrutiny, parents can access records and challenge findings, more emphasis is placed on communicating with parents as partners in decision making, and the likelihood has increased that psychologists will be asked testify under oath in due process hearings or in courts when decisions are challenged by parents.

Procedures for evaluation and determination of eligibility (PEDE)

Effects: Nondiscrimination became more important in evaluation and decision making, multifactored assessment, and decision making by a team that includes various professionals and parents, valid assessment that focuses on educational need, primary language, and triennial reevaluation.

Impact: Some traditional prerogatives of school psychologists were curtailed through placing less emphasis on IQ and greater emphasis on achievement and adaptive behavior, consideration of language differences and sociocultural status, determining educational need, and team decision making. More assessment in natural settings such as classrooms using direct measures has been fostered.

Confidentiality of records and parental access to records

Effects: Access to records is controlled by the client-parent. Access is restricted to school officials with a need to know. Parents or youth of legal age are guaranteed access to records. Content of records can be challenged and adjudicated.

Impact: Psychologists' work and records are open to parental inspection, including test protocols and treatment notes (unless excluded under state law)—raising legal issues about violation of copyright laws and professional ethical issues regarding disclosure of sensitive information. In some instances schools are required to make copies of copyrighted test protocols for parental inspection. Scrutiny and review of psychologists' work is increasing.

(iii) Obtaining, integrating, and interpreting information about child behavior and conditions relating to learning;

(iv) Consulting with other staff members in planning school programs to meet the special needs of children as indicated by psychological tests, interviews, and behavioral evaluations;

(v) Planning and managing a program of psychological services, including psychological counseling for children and parents; and

(vi) Assisting in developing positive behavioral intervention strategies.

Although the conception of psychological services in the IDEA regulations is broad and progressive, the actual effects of the close association with special education constitute a two-edged sword for school psychology. One side is that the legislation has prompted the enormous growth in school psychology over the last 25 years and provides a secure funding base in nearly all states. Strong special education funding nearly always has meant strong funding for school psychology, and vice versa. The other side is that the top service priority for the vast majority of school psychologists is to conduct eligibility evaluations and to participate in other special education placement activities, thus limiting the amount of time available for preventive mental health, direct interventions, and problem-solving consultation.

Assessment and Eligibility Determination Regulations

In addition to greater demand, the nature of school psychological services changed dramatically after 1975 and continues to change with statutes and regulations that require eligibility evaluations to meet certain standards. The regulations that have the most influence on school psychology practice appear as the Procedures for Evaluation and Determination of Eligibility section of the federal IDEA regulations (34 C. F. R. 300-530 through 543). Comparable state education agency rules exist at the state level. The key regulations that have the most impact on school psychology practice are:

- A full and individual evaluation that meets certain standards must be conducted prior to determining eligibility for disability status and placement in special education.

- The evaluation must not be racially or culturally discriminatory, and it must be administered in the child's native language unless to do so is clearly not feasible.

- Disability classification shall not occur if the tests or other evaluation procedures are unduly affected by language differences.

- The evaluation results must be relevant to determining disability eligibility and to the development of the child's individualized educational program.

- Standardized tests must be validated for the purpose for which they are used and must be administered by knowledgeable and trained personnel in accordance with test publishers' requirements.

- Tests and other evaluation procedures must focus on specific educational needs, not merely on a single construct such as general intellectual functioning.

- The evaluation accounts for the effects of other limitations such as sensory loss or psychomotor disabilities and does not merely reflect those limitations.

- No single procedure is used; a multifactored assessment must be provided that includes areas related to the suspected disability, including (if appropriate) health, vision, hearing, social and emotional status, general intelligence, academic performance, communicative status, and motor abilities. All of the child's special education and related services needs must be identified regardless of whether those needs are commonly associated with a specific disability.

- A review of existing information pertaining to the child's disability eligibility and special education program placement must be conducted every 3 years or more often if requested by a parent or teacher. A comprehensive reevaluation may be conducted as part of the review.

- An evaluation report shared with parents must be developed.

- Eligibility and placement decisions must be based on a wide variety of information and be made by a team that includes evaluation personnel, teachers, special educators, and parents.

- In the area of SLD, a severe discrepancy must be established between achievement and intellectual ability; furthermore, cause of the SLD cannot be sensory impairment; mental retardation; emotional disturbance; or environmental, economic, or cultural disadvantage.

The discerning reader will notice almost immediately the inherent ambiguity in many regulations. For example, what does *nondiscrimination* or *validated for a specific purpose* mean? Does nondiscrimination mean equal average scores for all groups on relevant measures? Equal predictive accuracy? Equal classification and placement outcomes? Similarly, how valid is sufficiently valid to meet the legal requirement? Is a validity coefficient of $r = .5$ sufficient, or does it have to be higher? No answers are given in the regulations, and for the most part, these questions have not been answered in litigation. Some of the regulations regarding eligibility evaluation might be regarded best as aspirational because—given the current state of knowledge—achieving nondiscrimination in an absolute sense or attaining perfect or near-perfect validity are nearly impossible. Clearly, the regulations give notice that high-quality evaluations are required and that special sensitivity to sociocultural differences is expected.

In addition to the regulations governing the processes and procedures for eligibility evaluations, the actual disability classification criteria also exert a strong influence on the kinds of evaluations conducted by school psychologists. The IDEA regulations provide conceptual definitions for 13 disabilities. The federal conceptual definitions generally indicate the fundamental bases for each of the disability categories—for example, MR is defined in terms of intellectual functioning and adaptive behavior, but classification criteria are not provided in the federal regulations (e.g., the IQ and adaptive behavior cutoff scores to define eligibility in MR). The state education agency rules generally are the most important influences on classification criteria.

States have wide discretion in the use of disability categories and disability names and—most especially—in the classification criteria used to define disabilities. The frequent use of standardized tests of intellectual functioning and achievement by school psychologists is closely tied to the nature of these state eligibility criteria. The disability with the highest prevalence, SLD (accounting for over half of all

SWD), is operationalized by classification criteria that require a severe discrepancy between intellectual ability and achievement. The exact criterion or criteria for the discrepancy varies by state with some establishing relatively less (e.g., 1 SD) and some relatively more (1.5 or 2.0 SD) stringent standards. The use of an IQ test, however, is nearly always required to implement the SLD classification criteria—a practice that may be changing. Likewise, in MR an IQ test nearly always is required by states to determine the child's status on the intellectual functioning dimension of the MR disability category.

IQ testing often is done routinely as part of a comprehensive evaluation for other suspected disabilities such as emotional disturbance or autism, although the classification criteria for these disabilities rarely mention intellectual functioning specifically. For many school and child psychologists, an IQ test is an essential part of an overall evaluation (Sattler, 2001). This view appears to be changing as more emphasis is placed on accountability for child outcomes in special education legislation and practice (see this chapter's section on future trends).

Trends in Legal Requirements

The EHA-IDEA legal requirements and their state counterparts have evolved gradually over the last 25 years, with changes primarily in the realm of further specification of requirements or inclusion of broader age ranges in the mandate to serve SWD. IDEA (1991, 1997, 1999) represented a modest break with the prior trends; the greater emphasis was on accountability for academic and social outcomes for SWD and the use of regulatory powers to focus greater attention on positive outcomes. Prior to 1997, IDEA-EHA legal requirements focused on process, inclusion, and extending services to all eligible children and youth. Compliance monitoring prior to 1997 involved checking on whether the mandated services were provided without cost to parents in the least restrictive environment feasible and were guided by an individualized educational program and an evaluation that included essential features; procedural safeguards followed rigorously. The missing element in this array of legal requirements was outcomes—that is, what tangible benefits were derived by children and youth from participating in special education and related services programs?

The greater emphasis on outcomes in special education legal requirements follows the national trends in the late 1980s and 1990s toward greater accountability through systematic assessment of student achievement (McDonnell et al., 1997). Several additions were made by Congress to the IDEA regulations (1991, 1997, 1999) to ensure greater accountability in special education. Among these requirements are the strong preference for SWD to remain in the general education curriculum, to participate in local and state assessment programs (including the standardized achievement testing that is done at least annually in nearly all states), and to have individualized educational programs that are developed around general education curriculum standards.

The effects of this legislation on SWD are not clear yet, but the accountability demands influence school psychology in a number of ways. First, evaluations must include content from the general education classroom and curriculum in order to provide the information needed for planning the special education program. More emphasis on curriculum-based measurement is highly likely (Shapiro, 1996; Shinn, 1998) along with other direct measures of classroom performance. Second, the portions of reevaluations involving progress in achieving goals must in most cases include a general education context as well as the results of the child's performance in the school's accountability program. These areas are becoming essential components of annual reviews of progress and triennial reevaluations of disability eligibility and special education program placement. Third, school psychologists are involved frequently in judgments about the alterations in standardized testing procedures that are needed in order for SWD to participate, without undermining the essential purpose of the assessment. Finally—and most important—the work of school psychologists is increasingly examined in relation to outcomes for children, leading to scrutiny of the value of standardized tests and other assessment procedures in facilitating positive outcomes for SWD (discussed later in this chapter; Reschly & Tilly, 1999).

IDEA (1991, 1997, 1999) also placed more emphasis on the delivery of effective interventions for social and emotional behaviors that might interfere with academic performance or that lead to placement in more restrictive education settings for SWD. A positive behavior support plan is required in every IEP if social or emotional behavior interferes with learning—a frequent occurrence for SWD. Moreover, before disciplinary action can be taken against SWD, a functional behavior analysis must be conducted with interventions implemented (Tilly, Knoster, & Ikeda, 2000), a requirement that focuses more attention on outcomes and draws heavily on the expertise that some school psychologists have with applied behavior analysis.

Summary of Legal Requirements

It is this author's thesis that legal requirements are the greatest influence on the existence and work of school psychologists. The close association of school psychology with special education emerged in the early twentieth century, developed rapidly over the last 25 years, and continues to evolve. The legal requirements themselves are, of course, the outgrowth of societal trends that placed great value on the rights of each individual—including persons with disabilities—to educational services. Further changes in legal requirements should be expected with concomitant further influences on school psychology.

SCHOOL PSYCHOLOGY INFRASTRUCTURE

The infrastructure for school psychology includes the body of knowledge claimed by the profession, graduate programs, standards, professional associations, and credentialing mechanisms (including licensing and state education agency certification). The school psychology infrastructure grew rapidly over the last 25 years in parallel with the legal requirements necessitating the employment of school psychologists and the rapid increase in the numbers of school psychologists.

Professional Associations

School psychology professional associations exist in the United States, Canada, most nations of the European Community, and selected other nations throughout the world. There is an International Association of School Psychologists that holds an annual summer seminar, usually in Europe or North America. In addition, all states have school psychology associations, as do most Canadian provinces. The two major national school psychology organizations in the United States are discussed in this chapter. Readers interested in the international association are encouraged to consult their Web site (http://www.ispaweb.org/en/index.html).

Division 16 of the APA

The oldest national school psychology organization in the United States is Division 16 (School Psychology) of the APA (http://education.indiana.edu/~div16/). Division 16 was founded in the late 1940s when the APA was reorganized and the divisional structure was established. Many of the other divisions such as Educational Psychology (Division 15) and Clinical Psychology (Division 12) were established at the same time. Full membership in the APA requires a doctoral degree, rendering ineligible for full membership the vast majority of practicing school psychologists who have specialist-level graduate education. For that and perhaps other reasons the membership of Division 16 is a relatively small percentage of the overall school psychology community,

dominated principally by university faculty. The membership of Division 16 is composed of 174 fellows, 1,392 members, and 226 associates (associates generally are graduate students or nondoctoral affiliates of the APA).

Division 16 plays a vital role in representing school psychology in the broader realm of American psychology and professional psychology. Division 16 is very powerful when it can align its interests with those of the much larger APA (over 84,000 members). Major activities of this Division are publishing a journal (*School Psychology Quarterly*) and a newsletter (*The School Psychologist*), the developing of standards documents, advocating for school psychology services, and maintaining school psychology as one of the four officially recognized areas of professional psychology in APA (along with clinical, counseling, and industrial-organizational). Division 16 organizes a program at the annual APA conventions that includes awards to outstanding members, symposia, invited addresses, and poster sessions.

National Association of School Psychologists

The NASP (http://www.nasponline.org/index2.html) was established in 1969 to represent the interests of all school psychologists, with special attention to the interests and needs of most practitioners who were at that time primarily at the master's level of graduate preparation. The NASP admitted all persons certified or licensed to practice in a state as a school psychologist as well as graduate students in school psychology to full membership. Today NASP is the largest school psychology organization in the world with approximately 22,000 members, of whom about 5,000 have doctoral-level graduate preparation. Although it might have been accurate to characterize Division 16 and NASP in the 1970s and 1980s as representing the interests of doctoral- and nondoctoral-level school psychologists, respectively, it now is clear that about four times as many school psychologists with doctoral degrees are in NASP as in APA. NASP maintains a headquarters in the Washington, DC area and has an executive director and a growing staff that conducts the organization's business, provides membership services, and advocates for school psychological services.

NASP publishes a journal (*The School Psychology Review*), a newsletter (*NASP Communique*), and a variety of monographs such as *Best Practices* (now in a fourth edition), a graduate training directory, and reports of innovative practices in such areas as intervention techniques and models (Shinn, Walker, & Stoner, 2002). NASP also publishes graduate program standards and provides a program approval service through an affiliation with the National Council on Accreditation of Teacher Education (NCATE). NASP program approval is especially influential at the specialist level, whereas APA accreditation dominates at the doctoral level. A national credential with increasing recognition by the states was established by NASP in the early 1990s, the National Certificate in School Psychology (NCSP). Close relationships are maintained with nearly all of the state associations of school psychologists through a variety of cooperative and service-oriented programs. Over the past decade, NASP has become increasingly active and influential in shaping federal policies that affect school psychologists—especially the IDEA (1991, 1997, 1999) legislation.

The principal disagreement between APA Division 16 and NASP is the appropriate entry level for the independent, unsupervised practice of school psychology in public and private settings. NASP advocates the specialist level, and Division 16—in line with APA policy—promotes the doctoral level. The dispute over entry level has been intense and divisive at different times in the history of school psychology (Bardon, 1979; Brown, 1979; Coulter, 1989; Hyman, 1979; Trachtman, 1981), although (with a few exceptions) it has not been a prominent issue at the national level for the two organizations in recent years. Intense struggles over this issue sometimes still occur at the state level drawing in the national leadership, but these events have been rare in the 1990s.

The outcome of the debate over entry level is relatively clear in most states. The entry level for practice in the schools is the specialist level, whereas the entry level for the private, independent practice of school psychology generally is the doctoral level. When school psychologists at the specialist level do attain the authority to practice privately without supervision by a doctoral-level professional, that practice typically is limited to a narrow range of services.

Increased cooperation on the many common interests that exist between NASP and APA has been the prevailing pattern during the 1990s, although the official policies of the organizations continue to differ sharply on the graduate preparation required to use the title *school psychologist*. For reasons discussed in the next section, it is highly unlikely that school psychology practitioners will reach the doctoral level for several decades into the future. The APA and NASP cooperation is in the best interests of both organizations and consistent with both organizations' commitment to expanding and improving psychological services for children and youth (Fagan, 1986a).

Graduate Programs

Graduate programs in school psychology have been studied with increasing intensity over the last 35 years (Bardon,

Costanza, & Walker, 1971; Bardon & Walker, 1972; Bardon & Wenger, 1974, 1976; Bluestein, 1967; Brown & Lindstrom, 1977; Brown & Minke, 1984, 1986; Cardon & French, 1968–1969; Fagan, 1985, 1986b; French & McCloskey, 1979, 1980; Goh, 1977; McMaster et al., 1989; Pfeiffer & Marmo, 1981; Reschly & McMaster-Beyer, 1991; Reschly & Wilson, 1997; Smith & Fagan, 1995; Thomas, 1998; White, 1963–1964). The early studies were restricted to a listing of the available programs with meager analyses of the characteristics or the nature of the programs. Beginning with the NASP-sponsored graduate programs directories led by Brown and colleagues (Brown & Lindstrom, 1977; Brown & Minke, 1984) and then continued by others (McMaster et al., 1989; Thomas, 1998), a more complete picture of school psychology graduate education has emerged.

Two levels of graduate education are prominent in school psychology. The specialist level typically involves 2 years of full-time study in an organized school psychology program, the accumulation of 60 semester hours at the graduate level in approved courses, and a full-time internship during a third year, usually with remuneration at about a half-time rate for a beginning school psychologist. Specialist-level programs typically are designed around NASP standards for graduate programs in school psychology (NASP, 2000). Most specialist-program students complete their programs in 3 years. The overwhelming majority of specialist-program graduates are employed in public school settings as school psychologists.

Doctoral programs involve at least 3 years of full-time study on campus, followed by a full-time internship that usually is paid but at a level well below beginning salaries for psychologists, and a year for dissertation completion. Students occasionally complete doctoral degrees in 4 years, but 5–6 years is much more common in school psychology programs. Doctoral requirements typically follow APA accreditation standards (APA, 1996). Career paths of doctoral program graduates are highly variable. Many work in non-school settings such as medical clinics or community mental health, whereas others go into teaching and research roles in universities. Perhaps 40% of doctoral graduates work in public school settings as school psychologists or as program administrators.

The specialist level dominates school psychology graduate education and practice, and it is likely to continue to do so. Specialist-level graduate students constitute about 70% of all graduate students and 80% of all graduates of programs. The latter is, of course, the most accurate predictor of the future composition of the school psychology workforce. For many reasons that are well known to students and faculty, doctoral programs require a longer period of study (5–6 years) compared to specialist programs (3 years), not to mention the all-too-common occurrence of doctoral degree candidates' delaying or failing to complete the degree because of the dissertation. For these and other reasons, there always will be a higher proportion of doctoral students than program graduates.

The number of institutions *actively* engaged in school psychology graduate education has remained stable for a decade, at about 195. Surveys sometimes list as many as 210–220 institutions, but closer examination indicates that about 195 institutions have active programs that admit and graduate students each year. Approximately 90% of the institutions offer specialist-level degrees; however, only 40% offer doctoral degrees (Thomas, 1998; Reschly & Wilson, 1997). A limitation in the movement to the doctoral level is that about 60% of the institutions that offer school psychology graduate programs are *not* authorized by their governing boards or state legislatures to offer doctoral degrees (Reschly & Wilson, 1997). The Carnegie Foundation classifies most of these institutions as comprehensive institutions, meaning that they offer undergraduate degree programs in a wide variety of areas and master's or specialist degrees in selected areas. They are not authorized to offer doctoral degrees, and—in the current higher education climate—it is highly unlikely that very many of them will acquire the authority to offer doctoral degrees in the future.

In a development that most professional psychologists did not anticipate, master's-level practice of counseling and clinical psychology has strengthened over the last decade due at least in part to the influences of managed care and other factors. The strong pressure that existed from APA Division 16 in the 1970s and 1980s appears to have diminished as a result of the dominance of managed care in the private-practice market and other developments (Benedict & Phelps, 1998; Phelps, Eisman, & Kohout, 1998).

The actual graduate education of specialist- and doctoral-level school psychologists overlaps significantly—especially in terms of preparation for practice in the school setting (Reschly & Wilson, 1997). Doctoral training is different primarily in (a) domains of supervised practice in nonschool settings; (b) specialization with a particular population, kind of problem, or treatment approach; and (c) advanced preparation in measurement, statistics, research design, and evaluation. These findings suggest that doctoral-level graduates are better prepared for broader practice roles, including evaluation of treatment and program effects and provision of services in nonschool settings. It is crucial to presenting an accurate picture to emphasize a high degree of overlap between specialist and doctoral graduate education as well as the large amount of variation across specialist programs and doctoral programs.

The only development on the horizon that might lead to a change in the largely specialist-level character of school psychology practice is the recent emergence of school psychology PsyD programs at the freestanding schools of professional psychology (SPP). There are approximately 25 SPPs in the United States today that have been devoted almost exclusively to training clinical psychologists. The SPPs are noted for being expensive, for offering little student financial aid other than loans, and for graduating large numbers of students compared to more traditional university-based programs. Today these 25 schools of professional psychology graduate twice as many clinical psychologists as do the approximately 185 university-based clinical programs (How Do Professional Schools' Graduates Compare with Traditional Graduates?, 1997; Maher, 1999; Yu et al., 1997). Clearly the SPPs have shown the capacity to train and graduate large numbers of persons. Due to changes in managed care as well as the rapid increase in the numbers of clinical psychologists—especially those from the SPPs—the market demand for doctoral-level clinical and counseling psychologists has diminished, as have the number of applications for admission to clinical and counseling graduate programs.

The SPPs are tuition driven—that is, they depend directly and primarily on student-paid tuition and fees to support the institution. They also are entrepreneurial. The weakening demand for clinical psychologists has led some of the SPPs to enter new areas of training. One of the California SPPs has initiated a teacher education program, and the SPPs in Fresno, CA and Chicago have announced plans to initiate PsyD programs in school psychology. Clearly, these announcements represent entrepreneurial efforts to maintain financial viability rather than a long-standing commitment to these new areas. If the other SPPs enter school psychology training and graduate large numbers of persons, the current supply-demand picture and the dominance of the specialist level could change over the next decade.

I am very skeptical about the SPPs' role in school psychology training as well as their attractiveness to prospective school psychologists. An SPP graduate education is enormously expensive in view of realistic expectations for postgraduate salary levels; moreover, the typical SPP graduate acquires enormous debt. Recent conversations with training directors at several of the SPPs suggest that the average *graduate school* debt of 1999 graduates was in the $80,000–$100,000 range. I doubt that very many students will choose SPPs in view of the current average beginning school psychology salaries of $30,000 to $40,000.

Graduate Program Standards and Accreditation-Approval

APA and NASP provide graduate program standards and program accreditation or approval services (Fagan & Wells, 2000). The NASP standards are preeminent for specialist-level programs, whereas the APA standards clearly dominate at the doctoral level. The NASP Standards for Training and Field Placement Programs in School Psychology (hereafter NASP Standards) first appeared in 1972, and the most recent revision was published in 2000. Copies are available at http://www.nasponline.org/index2.html. The NASP Standards are applicable to both doctoral and specialist programs; however, the main influence is at the specialist level. The specialist-level standards require a minimum of 60 semester hours, 2 years of full-time study in an organized program, coverage of essential content, a supervised practicum, and a full-year supervised internship in the 3rd year. The domains of graduate training in the NASP Standards, based on the *Blueprint* (Ysseldyke et al., 1997), are data-based decision making and accountability, consultation and collaboration, effective instruction and development of cognitive-academic skills, socialization and development of life skills, student diversity in development and learning, school and system organization, policy development, and climate, prevention, crisis intervention, and mental health, home-school-community collaboration, research and program evaluation, school psychology practice and development, and information technology.

Standards also are published for practicum experiences during the on-campus part of the program and for the full-time internship (NASP, 2000). NASP Standards are implemented through a folio review process involving submission of an extensive array of documents (course syllabi, practicum and internship contracts, etc.). There is no on-site component of the program approval process, weakening the evaluation of a program's implementation of the standards. NASP publishes a list of approved programs biannually in the *NASP Communique*. According to the NASP Web site cited previously, 125 institutions are approved at the specialist level of graduate education in school psychology. Overall, the NASP Standards and the program approval process have stimulated improved graduate education at the specialist level—leading to more faculty in programs, more coherent training, and improved supervised experiences. The NASP approval process could be strengthened with an on-campus site visit component.

The APA Guidelines and Principles for Accreditation of Programs in Professional Psychology (hereafter APA Standards; APA, 1996; http://www.apa.org/) are the most recent iteration of APA program accreditation services that can be traced to 1945. APA accredits doctoral-level programs only, in three of the four areas of professional psychology—clinical, counseling, and school. The fourth area of professional psychology, industrial-organizational, has never sought program accreditation. Recent APA policies permit the expansion of accreditation to new areas of professional psychology (e.g., developmental psychology), but so far no institutions with programs in the nontraditional areas have been accredited. Unlike the NASP Standards, the APA Standards are generic in the sense that they are designed to apply to all areas of professional psychology—not a single area such as school psychology.

The APA Standards require the institution to specify a training model and then organize experiences that produce the outcomes consistent with that model. Despite the appearance of a system that allows maximum freedom in the design of graduate education, the APA Standards specify essential domains in which "all students can acquire and demonstrate understanding of and competence . . ." The domains listed are biological bases of behavior, cognitive and affective aspects of behavior, social aspects of behavior, history and systems of psychology, psychological measurement, research methodology, techniques of data analysis, individual differences in behavior, human development, dysfunctional behavior or psychopathology, professional standards and ethics, theories and methods of assessment and diagnosis, effective interventions, consultation and supervision, evaluation of the efficacy of interventions, cultural and individual diversity, and attitudes essential to lifelong learning and problem solving as psychologists. Obvious overlap exists in the NASP and APA Standards; however, the NASP Standards are more specific to the training of school psychologists, whereas the APA Standards are more generic and pertain to the graduate education across areas of professional psychology.

APA has accredited graduate programs in school psychology since 1971 (Fagan & Wells, 2000). Currently there are 66 institutions with accredited programs in school psychology or school psychology and another area (combined accreditation in either school and clinical or school and counseling). The institutional location of about 80% of the APA-accredited school psychology programs is a college of education, often a department of educational psychology or a department of counseling and school psychology. The college and department profile of counseling and school psychology is almost identical. In contrast, APA-accredited clinical programs are usually located in departments of psychology in arts and sciences colleges (about 80%; Reschly & Wilson, 1997) or in freestanding SPPs. A significant proportion of the graduate education in professional psychology occurs in colleges of education, usually within a broader context of educational psychology or a context that is significantly influenced by educational psychology.

APA accreditation processes involve a self-study, submission of documents to APA, and a site visit by a three-person team over a 2- to 3-day period. The site visit is rigorous, and most programs seeking initial accreditation receive either conditional accreditation or are rejected. Most apply again and eventually gain full accreditation. It is extremely rare for a program that is fully accredited to lose its accreditation, although a few programs have managed to do so.

Summary

Clearly, APA accreditation is the oldest and most prestigious of the mechanisms whereby a school psychology graduate program is endorsed by an authoritative body. APA accreditation is, however, available only to doctoral programs that account for less than half of all school psychology graduate programs. The recent development of the NASP approval process is a significant milestone in improving specialist-level graduate education. It is highly likely that dual accreditation-approval mechanisms in school psychology will be needed far into the future unless an unlikely breakthrough occurs in the current APA and NASP disagreement on the appropriate level of graduate education required for independent school psychology practice.

School Psychology Scholarship

Improvements in school psychology scholarship are apparent in a number of developments over the last three decades. Over that period a significant number of books and monographs have been devoted to school psychology thought and

practice. The references for some of the most prominent contemporary resources are Fagan and Wise (2000); Reschly, Tilly, and Grimes (1999); Reynolds and Gutkin (1999); Shinn et al. (2002); and Thomas and Grimes (2002). NASP publishes monographs relevant to school psychology and cooperates with other publishers in marketing books and other materials that are relevant to school psychology. Some of the books developed by APA publications also are relevant to school psychology (e.g., Phelps, 1998).

The major U.S. refereed journals in school psychology that publish content directly or closely related to school practice are *School Psychology Review (SPR)*, *Journal of School Psychology, Psychology in the Schools, Journal of Psychoeducational Assessment,* and *School Psychology Quarterly.* Information on these journals appears in Table 17.2. *SPR,* published by NASP, is the leading journal in the discipline based on its circulation (approximately 22,000) and on the number of citations to articles published in the journal—that is, the number of times a particular article is cited by other scholars. The other school psychology journals have much lower circulation (< 2,500) and lower citation rates. It is important to note, however, that valuable content is published by each of the school psychology journals, and conscientious scholars need to examine the contents of each.

The Federal Department of Education, especially the Office of Special Education Programs, is the major source of funding for school psychology research and personnel preparation. Other important sources of support are the Federal Department of Education Office of Educational Research and Innovation, the National Institute of Health (particularly the National Institute of Child Health and Human Development), and private foundations. Research awards are provided by the Society for the Study of School Psychology (SSSPS), Division 16 of APA, and NASP. SSSPS provides approximately $65,000–$90,000 in small grants to school psychology investigators annually.

TABLE 17.2   Citation Rates and Circulation of the Major School Psychology Journals

Title[a]	First Volume[b]	Issues/Page Size per Year[c]	Estimated Circulation[e]	Number of Articles in 1998	1998 Total Citations[f]
PITS	1964	6	1,300	35	370
JPA	1983	4	500	15	190
JSP	1963	6[d]	1,500	25	338
SPQ	1986	4	2,500	21	220
SPR	1972	4	22,000	31	739

Notes. From Journal Citation Reports (http://www.isinet.com/isi/products/citation/jcr/)
[a]*PITS = Psychology in the Schools; JPA = Journal of Psychoeducational Assessment; JSP = Journal of School Psychology; SPQ = School Psychology Quarterly;* and *SPR = School Psychology Review.* [b]*First volume* refers to the first year the journal was published. [c]*PITS* increased the number of issues per year from 4 to 6 with the 1999 volume. [d]*JSP* increased the number of issues per volume from 4 to 6 with the 2001 volume. [e]*Estimated circulation* is based on the *total paid and/or requested circulation* item in the U.S. Post Office form Statement of Ownership, Management, and Circulation published typically in either the first or last issue of each volume. Personal correspondence with the current editor was used to confirm this information. [f]1998 total citations is the total number of times that an article from the journal was cited in 1998 in the journals included in the comprehensive *Social Sciences Citation Index* (1999).

CONTEMPORARY AND FUTURE CHALLENGES

School psychology has grown at a rapid pace over the last three decades (see Figure 17.3). The rapid growth was tied directly to the expansion of special education legal mandates. These mandates have the most influence on the existence of school psychologists and the services they provide, and it is highly likely that the legal influences will be crucial to school psychology in the future. There are, however, a number of problems in this relationship and with contemporary practice that likely will prompt significant changes in school psychology practice in the future.

Disability Determination and Special Education Placement

As noted previously, the practice of school psychology today is closely tied to special education eligibility determination and placement. The tie to special education is supported by special education legal requirements, the federal and state requirements for the legally mandated full and individual evaluation, and current conceptual definitions and classification criteria for educationally related disabilities. The disabilities that consume the most time for school psychologists are SLD, MR, and ED. Changes in the conceptual definitions or

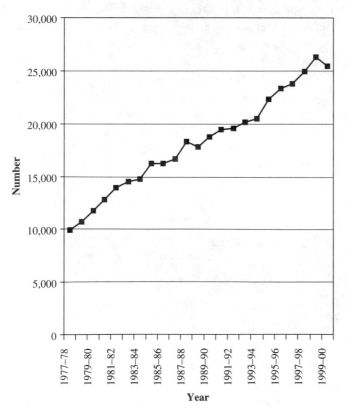

Figure 17.3 Growth of school psychology, 1977–1978 to 1998–1999. From the U.S. Department of Education (2001).

classification criteria for any of these disabilities—especially for SLD due to the large numbers in that category—could have a significant impact on school psychology. It is likely that such changes will occur.

What happens to school psychology if the intellectual functioning requirement is removed from the SLD classification criteria? What if states and the federal government adopt noncategorical conceptions of high-incidence disabilities (SLD, MR, ED) with disability classification based on low achievement and insufficient response to high-quality interventions, as recommended by a recent National Academy of Sciences Report (Donovan & Cross, 2002)?

> Recommendation SE.1: The committee recommends that federal guidelines for special education eligibility be changed in order to encourage better integrated general and special education services. We propose that eligibility ensue when a student exhibits large differences from typical levels of performance in one or more domain(s) *and* with evidence of insufficient response to high-quality interventions in the relevant domain(s) of functioning in school settings. These domains include achievement (e.g., reading, writing, mathematics), social behavior, and emotional regulation. As is currently the case, eligibility determination would also require a judgment by a multidisciplinary team, including parents, that special education is needed. (Donovan & Cross, 2002, p. ES-6)

> While an IQ test may provide supplemental information, no IQ test would be required, and the results of an IQ test would not be a primary criterion on which eligibility rests. Because of the irreducible importance of context in the recognition and nurturance of achievement, the committee regards the effort to assess students' decontextualized potential or ability as inappropriate and scientifically invalid. (Donovan & Cross, 2002, pp. 8–23)

These changes have occurred in some states (e.g., Iowa) and in some school districts across the United States in which functional assessment—emphasizing direct measures of skills in relevant domains such as academic skills, social behaviors, and emotional regulation—are used instead of standardized tests (Reschly et al., 1999). School psychologists have flourished in the few places that have changed disability classification significantly, but large continuing education efforts were required to support those changes (Ikeda, Tilly, Stumme, Volmer, & Allison, 1996; Reschly & Grimes, 1991).

In discussing the issues related to disability determination and the likely future challenges for school psychologists it is crucial first to understand that enormous variations exist across the states in disability definitions, classification criteria, and prevalence. Table 17.3, constructed from the most recent federal child-count data, demonstrates unequivocally that there are few generalizations that can be made about

TABLE 17.3 Prevalence of Disabilities in U.S. Schools, Ages 6–17

Disability[a]	Number Age 6–11	Number Age 12–17	Total Number	Percent with Disabilities[b]	Percent of Population[c]	Variations Between States[d]
SLD	1,113,465	1,603,190	2,716,655	50.5%	5.73%	3.1% (KY) to 9.6% (RI) Factor of 3.1 ×s
Sp/L	955,505	126,317	1,081,822	20.1%	2.28%	0.9% (DC) to 3.7% (WV) Factor of 4.1 ×s
MR	238,323	308,106	546,429	10.2%	1.15%	0.3% (NJ) to 2.87 (WV) Factor of 9.6 ×s
ED	159,691	283,452	443,143	8.2%	0.94%	0.1% (AR) to 2.0% (MN) Factor of 20 ×s
Low incidence	326,445	268,515	594,960	11.1%	1.26%	—
All disabilities	2,793,429	2,589,580	5,383,009	100.1%	11.36%	9.2% (CA) to 16.5% (RI) Factor of 1.8 ×s

Note. Based on U.S. Department of Education (2001), Tables AA3, AA4, and AA11.
[a]SLD = specific learning disabilities; Sp/L = speech and language disabilities; MR = mental retardation; ED = emotional disturbance; Low incidence = combined total of multiple disabilities, hearing impairments, orthopedic impairments, other health impairments, visual impairments, autism, deafness, blindness, traumatic brain injury, and developmental delay. [b]Refers to the composition of the population with disabilities; for example, of all students aged 6–17, slightly more than half are in the category of SLD. [c]Refers to the risk level for each disability in the student population. For example, 5.73% of all students aged 6–17 in the general student population have SLD. [d]Provides the lowest and highest prevalence of each disability by state and the multiplicative factor by which they occur.

disability identification other than that it varies significantly across states (U.S. Department of Education, 2001). For example, Minnesota identifies about 20 times more students as ED as does Arkansas, Rhode Island identifies three times more in LD as does Kentucky, and so on. The common denominator for virtually all SWD is significant achievement problems—often further complicated by behavior problems. The categories per se do not mean very much (Bocian, Beebe, MacMillan, & Gresham, 1999; Gresham, MacMillan, & Bocian, 1998; MacMillan, Gresham, & Bocian, 1998). Disability classification across states and districts within states is unreliable (Gottlieb, Alter, Gottlieb, & Wishner, 1994; Gottlieb & Weinberg, 1999).

An even more fundamental problem is the validity of classification in terms of the identification of groups of students with unique needs and the relationship of disability group membership to treatment or intervention decisions. There is considerable skepticism about the reliability and validity of three of the disability categories with relatively high prevalence (SLD, MR, and ED; Reschly & Tilly, 1999; Tilly, Reschly, & Grimes, 1999). These disabilities are a large part of the typical school psychology caseload.

Determining an ability-achievement discrepancy is crucial in most states as part of the SLD classification criteria and constitutes a major part of the current role of most school psychologists. The appropriateness of the discrepancy method of determining SLD eligibility is criticized with increasing stridency by persons associated with the reading disability research centers funded by the National Institute of Child Health and Human Development (Lyon, 1996). The major criticisms are that IQ-achievement-discrepant and nondiscrepant poor

readers do not differ in the instructional interventions needed or in responsiveness to that instruction. Moreover, the discrepancy criterion often delays treatment until third or fourth grade, when in fact the vast majority of children that will be identified later as SLD in the area of reading can be accurately identified in kindergarten with relatively straightforward measures of phonological awareness. Delaying treatment allows reading problems to worsen and causes enormous frustration for children, teachers, and parents. Fletcher et al. (1998) summarized this case:

> Classifications of children as discrepant versus low-achievement lack discriminative validity. . . . However, because children can be validly identified on the basis of a low-achievement definition, it simply is not necessary to use an IQ test to identify children as learning disabled. . . . For treatment, the use of the discrepancy model forces identification to an older age when interventions are demonstrably less effective. (Fletcher et al., 1998, pp. 200–201)

Changes in the SLD classification criteria involving either the elimination of the discrepancy requirement through a noncategorical scheme or other alternative classification criteria will present enormous challenges to school psychologists. SLD accounts for over half of the disabilities identified in the public schools; it is therefore a significant part of most school psychologists' roles. Changes in SLD will almost inevitably require acquisition of new skills and the development of competencies more related to early identification of specific skills and the design of effective treatments. Models exist for the successful transition of school psychologists to these new roles (Ikeda et al., 1996; Reschly et al., 1999; Tilly et al., 1999), but the vast majority of school psychologists are not well prepared for alternative roles that place less emphasis on assessment of intellectual functioning. Acquiring those skills and embedding them firmly in continuing education and graduate programs constitutes one of the greatest challenges to the school psychology profession.

Empirically Supported Treatments-Interventions

The empirically supported treatments-interventions movement has multiple roots. In medicine and professional psychology, it is prompted by the policies of managed care health insurance companies that restrict reimbursements to physicians, psychologists, and others to treatments that have been proven effective with specific kinds of problems and patients (Benedict & Phelps, 1998; Phelps et al., 1998). In education, empirically supported interventions are prompted more by the accountability movement that can be traced to the mid-1980s and continues with increasing force today. The educational accountability standards-based reform procedures are increasingly applied to SWD and special education programs. Questions are raised regarding the specific contribution of school psychology and special education to improving academic achievement, increasing the safety of schools, improving dropout and graduation rates, and overcoming at-risk conditions. It no longer is sufficient to simply assume that description of problems and careful conformance to legal guidelines in assessment and placement decisions is sufficient. The further requirement that positive results are demonstrated places significant pressure toward a problem-solving approach and the implementation of empirically supported interventions.

Many traditional practices in school psychology are not empirically validated in terms of a direct relationship to positive outcomes for children and youth. In fairness to traditional methods, most of these practices were never designed to have a direct relationship to interventions. For example, the most widely used measure in school psychology—one of the Wechsler ability scales—has little relationship to the design of interventions or the assessment of intervention effects (Gresham & Witt, 1997; Reschly, 1997). The Wechsler scales are useful for classification of children and youth using traditional classification definitions and criteria such as MR and SLD. The use of these categories likely will change in order to improve the delivery of effective services to children and youth.

There are several well-established problem-solving approaches (e.g., Bergan & Kratochwill, 1990; Fuchs & Fuchs, 1989; Tilly, 2002; Upah & Tilly, 2002). The best of these

approaches involve a systematic, data-based series of stages that include behavioral definition of the problem(s), collection of baseline data, establishment of goals, analysis of conditions (including prior knowledge), selection of an experimentally validated intervention and development of a behavior intervention plan, progress monitoring with formative evaluation (Fuchs & Fuchs, 1986), assessment of treatment fidelity, and evaluation of outcomes. These problem-solving approaches require a different set of competencies from those stressed in many school psychology graduate programs and continuing education events. Competencies are needed in direct assessment of skills and social behaviors in natural settings, knowledge of empirically validated academic and behavioral interventions, applied behavior analysis, and consultation methods. Providing those competencies in the future will challenge school psychology faculty and practitioners for many years into the future.

Personnel Needs

School psychology personnel needs are intense. A sufficient supply of appropriately trained school psychologists has been a problem for many years, and it appears that the problem is increasing due to a number of factors (Lund et al., 1998). In 1998–1999, over 1,000 of the 26,000 school psychologists employed in U.S. public schools were not fully certified or licensed by the state in which they were employed. The number of unfilled vacancies as well as the employment of persons on temporary certificates or licenses appears to have increased in recent years. School psychology employment is affected by economic conditions, with expansion of employment in periods of economic growth and stable or slightly declining employment in recession periods (Lund et al., 1998). When this chapter was written, the United States had been in a recession for about 6 months. It is likely that school psychology employment will stabilize over the next few years, decreasing the number of unfilled vacancies and the employment of persons with temporary certificates or licenses.

Current and future shortages of school psychologists may be aggravated by the effects of the retirements of school psychologists who entered the field in the 1960s, 1970s, and 1980s. As noted earlier, the average age of school psychology practitioners grew significantly during the 1990s. Professional employees in public schools generally retire at an age younger than that of other professionals due at least in part to plans that permit early retirement when a criterion is met that combines age and years of experience (e.g., 90 years). For example, a 60-year-old school psychologist who has worked for 30 years is eligible in many states for full retirement benefits.

The shortages of appropriately prepared school psychologists experienced throughout the 1990s are likely to continue well into the next century barring significant changes in one or more of the factors that affect the supply and demand for school psychologists. The supply of new school psychologists from graduate programs has remained stable for about 20 years. The number of programs in institutions of higher education has not changed in that same time period, and it is not likely that a substantial number of new graduate programs will be established in the future. Personnel from other fields of professional psychology in which employment conditions are not as positive—particularly from clinical psychology—may augment sources of school psychology personnel. Programs to retrain clinical as school psychologists have been discussed, and a few are offered by universities with doctoral programs.

School psychology supply and demand phenomena are not understood completely. More information is needed on school psychology career choices, attrition, and retirement, as well as demand characteristics such as the impact of state and federal legal requirements, expansion of services to new populations, and alternative delivery systems (Fagan, 1995). The current situation suggests strong demand for school psychologists through the next decade. Factors that might change this picture are significant changes in economic conditions that produce more stringent school budgets or substantial changes in legal requirements reducing the need for the services of school psychologists.

Demands for Mental Health Services

There is increasing recognition of the strong need for improved comprehensive health services for many children and youth, particularly those at risk (U.S. Department of Health and Human Services, 2001). Comprehensive services delivered at a single site such as a public school have been developed in a few settings, and many more places need these services (Adelman & Taylor, 1993, 2000). Discussions of how comprehensive services might be delivered in schools have appeared in the literatures of clinical and school psychology (Adelman & Taylor, 1993, 2000; Carlson, Tharinger, Bricklin, Demers, & Paavola, 1996; Christenson & Conoley, 1992; Cowen & Lorion, 1976; Henggeler, 1995; Nastasi, 2000; Sheridan & Gutkin, 2000).

The principal barriers to expansion of wraparound services in schools are funding and reliable evidence that such services are indeed cost-effective. The funding problems associated with health and mental health services are well known and need no further discussion here. Bickman's (1997) controversial evaluation of comprehensive mental health services undermined the usual assumption that more of whatever service is provided by a professional association is better. In fact, more services and more comprehensive services do not necessarily lead to better outcomes—leading this discussion back again to the matter of empirically validated treatments. Questions still remain about the nature of these services and their costs and benefits. There are, however, a number of interventions that are effective in preventing later, more costly problems, and these interventions are cost-effective (Shinn et al., 2002). A major challenge to school psychology is developing expertise in these interventions and delivering them in cost-effective ways—perhaps as a replacement for part of the traditional role of special education eligibility evaluations and placements.

SUMMARY

School psychology's roots are long-standing and deep in American psychology. Educational psychology remains a fundamental part of those roots, and the current organization of school psychology programs usually enhances the intersection of school and educational psychology. School psychology has flourished over the last 25 years, in large part due to the legal guarantees of the educational rights of students with disabilities. These legal guarantees created the conditions for the rapid expansion of school psychology employment and the high demand for school psychology graduate programs. Changes are underway that likely will change school psychology from a heavy investment in the use of standardized tests to determine eligibility for special education disability classification and placement to greater reliance on problem solving, direct measures of performance over relevant domains of behavior, and implementation of experimentally validated interventions for problems in academic achievement, social behavior, and emotional regulation.

REFERENCES

Adelman, H. S., & Taylor, L. (1993). School-linked mental health interventions: Toward mechanisms for service coordination and integration. *Journal of Community Psychology, 21,* 309–319.

Adelman, H. S., & Taylor, L. (2000). Shaping the future of mental health in the schools. *Psychology in the Schools, 37,* 49–60.

American Psychological Association. (1996). *Guidelines and principles for accreditation of programs in professional psychology.* Washington, DC: Author.

Bardon, J. I. (1979). Debate: Will the real school psychologist please stand up? Part 1: How best to establish the identity of professional school psychology. *School Psychology Digest, 8,* 162–167, 181–183.

Bardon, J. I., Costanza, L. J., & Walker, N. W. (1971). Institutions offering graduate training in school psychology. *Journal of School Psychology, 9,* 252–260.

Bardon, J. I., & Walker, N. W. (1972). Characteristics of graduate training in school psychology. *American Psychologist, 27,* 652–656.

Bardon, J. I., & Wenger, R. D. (1974). Institutions offering graduate training in school psychology. *Journal of School Psychology, 12,* 70–83.

Bardon, J. I., & Wenger, R. D. (1976). School psychology training trends in the early 1970s. *Professional Psychology, 7,* 31–36.

Benedict, J. G., & Phelps, R. (1998). Introduction: Psychology's view of managed care. *Professional Psychology: Research and Practice, 29,* 29–30.

Bergan, J. R., & Kratochwill, T. R. (1990). *Behavioral consultation and therapy.* New York: Plenum.

Bickman, L. (1997). Resolving issues raised by the Fort Bragg evaluation: New directions for mental health services research. *American Psychologist, 52,* 552–565.

Bluestein, V. (1967). An analysis of training programs in school psychology. *Journal of School Psychology, 5,* 301–309.

Bocian, K. M., Beebe, M. E., MacMillan, D. L., & Gresham, F. M. (1999). Competing paradigms in learning disabilities classification by schools and the variations in meaning of discrepant achievement. *Learning Disabilities Research and Practice, 14,* 1–14.

Brown vs. Board of Education, 347 U. S. 483 (1954).

Brown, D. T. (1979). Debate: Will the real school psychologist please stand up? Part 2: The drive for independence. *School Psychology Digest, 8,* 168–173, 183–185.

Brown, D. T. (1987). Comment on Fagan's "School psychology's dilemma." *American Psychologist, 42,* 755–756.

Brown, D. T. (1989a). Commentary on NASP at twenty: Accreditation, public policy, and child advocacy. *School Psychology Review, 18,* 174–176.

Brown, D. T. (1989b). The evolution of entry level in school psychology: Are we now approaching the doctoral level? *School Psychology Review, 18,* 11–15.

Brown, D. T., & Lindstrom, J. P. (1977). *Directory of school psychology training programs in the United States and Canada.* Stratford, CT: National Association of School Psychologists.

Brown, D. T., & Minke, K. M. (1984). *Directory of school psychology training programs in the United States.* Stratford, CT: National Association of School Psychologists.

Brown, D. T., & Minke, K. M. (1986). School psychology graduate training. A comprehensive analysis. *American Psychologist, 14,* 1328–1338.

Cardon, B. W., & French, J. L. (1968–1969). Organization and content of graduate programs in school psychology. *Journal of School Psychology, 7,* 28–32.

Carlson, C. I., Tharinger, D. J., Bricklin, P. M., Demers, S. T., & Paavola, J. C. (1996). Health care reform and psychological practice in the schools: Implications for American psychology. *Professional Psychology: Research and Practice, 27,* 14–23.

Christenson, S. L., & Conoley, J. C. (Eds.). (1992). *Home-school collaboration: Enhancing children's academic and social competence.* Silver Spring, MD: National Association of School Psychologists.

Cowen, E., & Lorion, R. (1976). Changing roles for the school mental health professional. *Journal of School Psychology, 14,* 131–138.

Coulter, W. A. (1989). The entry level for professional school psychology: A modest proposal. *School Psychology Review, 18,* 20–24.

Curtis, M. J., Hunley, S. A., Walker, K. J., & Baker, A. C. (1999). Demographic characteristics and professional practices in school psychology. *School Psychology Review, 28,* 104–116.

Cutts, N. E. (1955). *School psychology at mid-century.* Washington, DC: American Psychological Association.

Diana vs. State Board of Education, No. C-70-37 (N.D. CA 1970).

Donovan, M. S., & Cross, C. T. (2002). *Minority students in special and gifted education.* Washington, DC: National Academy Press.

Education of the Handicapped Act. (1975, 1977). 20 U.S.C. §1400–1485 *et seq.,* CFR 300 (regulations).

Fagan, T. K. (1985). The quantitative growth of school psychology programs in the United States. *School Psychology Review, 14,* 121–124.

Fagan, T. K. (1986a). School psychology's dilemma: Reappraising solutions and directing attention to the future. *American Psychologist, 41,* 851–861.

Fagan, T. K. (1986b). The historical origins and growth of programs to prepare school psychologists in the United States. *Journal of School Psychology, 24,* 9–22.

Fagan, T. K. (1988). The historical improvement of the school psychology service ratio: Implications for future employment. *School Psychology Review, 17*(3), 447–458.

Fagan, T. K. (1992). Compulsory schooling, child study, clinical psychology, and special education: Origins of school psychology. *American Psychologist, 47,* 236–243.

Fagan, T. K. (1995). Trends in the history of school psychology in the United States. In A. Thomas & J. Grimes (Eds.), *Best practices in school psychology* (Vol. 3, pp. 59–67). Washington, DC: National Association of School Psychologists.

Fagan, T. K. (2000). Practicing school psychology: A turn-of-the century perspective. *American Psychologist, 55,* 754–757.

Fagan, T. K., & Wells, P. D. (2000). History and status of school psychology accreditation in the United States. *School Psychology Review, 29,* 28–51.

Fagan, T. K., & Wise, P. S. (2000). *School psychology: Past, present, and future* (2nd ed.). Washington, DC: National Association of School Psychologists.

Fletcher, J. M., Francis, D. J., Shaywitz, S. E., Lyon, G. R., Foorman, B. R., Stuebing, K. K., & Shaywitz, B. A. (1998). Intelligent testing and the discrepancy model for children with learning disabilities. *Learning Disabilities Research and Practice, 13,* 186–203.

French, J. L., & McCloskey, G. (1979). Characteristics of school psychology program directors and program production. *American Psychologist, 34,* 710–714.

French, J. L., & McCloskey, G. (1980). Characteristics of doctoral and nondoctoral school psychology programs: Their implications for the entry-level doctorate. *Journal of School Psychology, 18,* 247–255.

Fuchs, D., & Fuchs, L. S. (1989). Developing, implementing, and validating a prereferral intervention system. *School Psychology Review, 18,* 260–283.

Fuchs, L. S., & Fuchs, D. (1986). Effects of systematic formative evaluation: A meta-analysis. *Exceptional Children, 53,* 199–208.

Goh, D. S. (1977). Graduate training in school psychology. *Journal of School Psychology, 15,* 207–218.

Gottlieb, J., Alter, M. Gottlieb, B., & Wishner, J. (1994). Special education in urban America: It's not justifiable for many. *Journal of Special Education, 27,* 453–465.

Gottlieb, J., & Weinberg, S. (1999). Comparisons of students referred and not referred for special education. *Elementary School Journal, 99,* 187–199.

Gresham, F. M., MacMillan, D. L., & Bocian, K. M. (1998). Agreement between school study team decisions and authoritative definitions in classification of students at-risk for mild disabilities. *School Psychology Quarterly, 13,* 181–191.

Gresham, F. M., & Witt, J. M. (1997). Utility of intelligence tests for treatment planning, classification, and placement decisions: Recent empirical findings and future directions. *School Psychology Quarterly, 12,* 249–267.

Guadalupe Organization v. Tempe Elementary School District No. 3, No. 71-435 (D. AZ, 1972) (consent decree).

Henggeler, S. W. (1995). A consensus: Conclusions of the APA task force report on innovative models of mental health services for children, adolescents, and their families. *Journal of Clinical Child Psychology, 23,* 3–6.

Horner, R. H., & Sugai, G. (2000). School-wide behavior support: An emerging initiative [Special issue]. *Journal of Positive Behavioral Interventions, 2,* 231–233.

Hosp, J. L., & Reschly D. J. (2002). Regional differences in school psychology practice. *School Psychology Review, 31,* 11–29.

How do professional schools' graduates compare with traditional graduates? (1997). *APS Observer, 10*(5), 6–9.

Hyman, I. A. (1979). Debate: Will the real school psychologist please stand up? Part 3: A struggle of jurisdictional imperialism. *School Psychology Digest, 8,* 174–180, 185–186.

Ikeda, M. J., Tilly, W. D., III, Stumme, J., Volmer, L., & Allison, R. (1996). Agency-wide implementation of problem solving consultation: Foundations, current implementation, and future directions. *School Psychology Quarterly, 11,* 228–243.

Individuals with Disabilities Education Act. (1991, 1997, 1999). 20 U.S.C. §1400 *et. seq., C.F.R.* 300 (regulations), Regulations

Implementing IDEA (1997), (Fed. Reg., 1999, March 12, 1999, vol. 64, no. 48).

Kicklighter, R. H. (1976). School psychology in the U.S.: A quantitative survey. *Journal of School Psychology, 14,* 151–156.

Lund, A. R., Reschly, D. J., & Martin, L. M. (1998). School psychology personnel needs: Correlates of current patterns and historical trends. *School Psychology Review, 27,* 106–120.

Lyon, G. R. (1996). Learning disabilities. *The Future of Children: Special Education for Students with Disabilities, 6,* 56–76.

MacMillan, D. L., Gresham, F. L., & Bocian, K. M. (1998). Discrepancy between definitions of learning disabilities and school practices: An empirical investigation. *Journal of Learning Disabilities, 31,* 314–326.

Maher, B. A. (1999). Changing trends in doctoral training programs in psychology: A comparative analysis of research-oriented versus professional-applied programs. *Psychological Science, 10,* 475–481.

Magary, J. F. (Ed.). (1967). *School psychological services in theory and practice, a handbook.* Englewood Cliffs, NJ: Prentice-Hall.

McDonnell, L. M., McLaughlin, M. J., & Morison, P. (1997). *Educating one & all: Students with disabilities and standards-based reform.* Washington, DC: National Academy Press.

McMaster, M. D., Reschly, D. J., & Peters, J. M. (1989). *Directory of school psychology graduate programs.* Washington, DC: National Association of School Psychologists.

Nastasi, B. K. (2000). School psychologists as health care providers in the 21st century: Conceptual framework, professional identity, and professional practice. *School Psychology Review, 29,* 540–554.

National Association of School Psychologists. (2000). Standards for graduate programs in school psychology. Bethesda, MD: Author.

Pennsylvania Association for Retarded children v. Commonwealth of Pennsylvania, 343 F. Supp. 279 (E. D. PA 1972).

Pfeiffer, S. I., & Marmo, P. (1981). The status of training in school psychology and trends toward the future. *Journal of School Psychology, 19,* 211–216.

Phelps, L. (1998). *Health-related disorders in children and adolescents.* Washington, DC: American Psychological Association.

Phelps, R., Eisman, E. J., & Kohout, J. (1998). Psychological practice and managed care: Results of the CAPP practitioner survey. *Professional Psychology: Research and Practice, 29,* 31–36.

Phye, G., & Reschly, D. (Eds.). (1979). *School psychology: Perspectives and issues.* New York: Academic Press.

Pion, G. M., Mednick, M. T., Astin, H. S., Hall, C. C. I., Kenkel, M. B., Keita, G. P., Kohout, J. L., & Kelleher, J. C. (1996). The shifting gender composition of psychology: Trends and implications for the discipline. *American Psychologist, 51,* 509–528.

Prasse, D. P. (2002). School psychology and the law. In A. Thomas & J. Grimes (Eds.), *Best practices in school psychology IV* (4th ed., pp. 57–75). Washington, DC: National Association of School Psychologists.

Reschly, D. J. (1997). Utility of individual ability measures and public policy choices for the 21st century. *School Psychology Review, 26,* 234–241.

Reschly, D. J. (2000). The present and future status of school psychology in the United States. *School Psychology Review, 29,* 507–522.

Reschly, D. J., & Bersoff, D. N. (1999). Law and school psychology. In C. R. Reynolds & T. B. Gutkin (Eds.), *The handbook of school psychology* (3rd ed., pp. 1077–1112). New York: Wiley.

Reschly, D. J., Genshaft, J., & Binder, M. S. (1987). *The 1986 NASP survey: Comparison of practitioners, NASP leadership, and university faculty on key issues.* Washington, DC: National Association of School Psychologists.

Reschly, D. J., & Grimes, J. P. (1991). State department and university cooperation: Evaluation of continuing education in consultation and curriculum based assessment. *School Psychology Review, 20,* 519–526.

Reschly, D. J., & McMaster-Beyer, M. (1991). Influences of degree level, institutional orientation, college affiliation, and accreditation status on school psychology graduate education. *Professional Psychology: Research and Practice, 22,* 368–374.

Reschly, D. J., & Tilly, W. D., III. (1999). Reform trends and system design alternatives. In D. J. Reschly, W. D. Tilly III, & J. P. Grimes (Eds.), *Special education in transition: Functional assessment and noncategorical programming* (pp. 19–48). Longmont, CO: Sopris West.

Reschly, D. J., Tilly, W. D., III, & Grimes, J. P. (Eds.). (1999). *Special education in transition: Functional assessment and noncategorical programming.* Longmont, CO: Sopris West.

Reschly, D. J., & Wilson, M. S. (1995). School psychology faculty and practitioners: 1986 to 1991 trends in demographic characteristics, roles, satisfaction, and system reform. *School Psychology Review, 24,* 62–80.

Reschly, D. J., & Wilson, M. S. (1997). Characteristics of school psychology graduate education: Implications for the entry level discussion and doctoral level specialty definition. *School Psychology Review, 26,* 74–92.

Reynolds, C. R., & Gutkin, T. B. (1999). *The handbook of school psychology* (3rd ed.). New York: Wiley.

Sattler, J. M. (2001). *Assessment of children: Cognitive applications* (4th ed.). San Diego, CA: Jerome M. Sattler Publisher, Inc.

Shapiro, E. S. (Ed.). (1996). *Academic skills problems: Direct assessment and intervention* (2nd ed.). New York: Guilford Press.

Sheridan, S. M., & Gutkin, T. B. (2000). The ecology of school psychology: Changing our paradigm for the 21st century. *School Psychology Review, 29,* 485–502.

Shinn, M. R. (Ed.). (1998). *Advanced applications of curriculum-based measurement.* New York: Guilford Press.

Shinn, M. R., Walker, H. M., & Stoner, G. (2002). *Interventions for academic and behaviors problems: Vol. 2. Preventative and remedial approaches.* Bethesda, MD: National Association of School Psychologists.

Smith, D. K., & Fagan, T. K. (1995). Resources on the training of school psychologists. In A. Thomas & J. Grimes (Eds.), *Best practices in school psychology* (3rd ed., pp. 1257–1271). Washington, DC: National Association of School Psychologists.

Smith, P. C., Kendall, C. M., & Hulin, C. L. (1969). *The measurement of satisfaction in work and retirement.* Skokie, IL: Rand McNally.

Sugai, G., Horner, R. H., Dunlap, G., Hieneman, M., Lewis, T. J., Nelson, C. M., Scott, T., Liaupsin, C., Sailor, W., Turnbull, A. P., Turnbull, H. R., III, Wickham, D., Reuf, M., & Wilcox, B. (2000). Applying positive behavioral support and functional behavioral assessment in the schools. *Journal of Positive Behavioral Interventions, 2,* 131–143.

Thomas, A. (1998). *Directory of school psychology graduate programs.* Washington, DC: National Association of School Psychologists.

Thomas, A., & Grimes, J. (Eds.). (2002). *Best practices in school psychology IV* (4th ed.). Bethesda, MD: National Association of School Psychologists.

Tilly, W. D., III. (2002). Overview of problem solving. In A. Thomas & J. Grimes (Eds.), *Best practices in school psychology IV* (pp. 21–36). Bethesda, MD: National Association of School Psychologists.

Tilly, W. D., III, Knoster, T. P., & Ikeda, M. J. (2000). Functional behavioral assessment: Strategies for behavioral support. In C. F. Telzrow & M. Tankersley (Eds.), *IDEA amendments of 1997: Practice guidelines for school-based teams* (pp. 151–198). Bethesda, MD: National Association of School Psychologists.

Tilly, W. D., III, Reschly, D. J., & Grimes, J. P. (1999). Disability determination in problem solving systems: Conceptual foundations and critical components. In D. J. Reschly, W. D. Tilly III, & J. P. Grimes (Eds.), *Special education in transition: Functional assessment and noncategorical programming* (pp. 285–321). Longmont, CO: Sopris West.

Trachtman, G. M. (1981). On such a full sea. In J. Ysseldyke & R. Weinberg (Eds.), The future of psychology in the schools: Proceedings of the Spring Hill Symposium. *School Psychology Review, 10,* 138–181.

Upah, K. R. F., & Tilly, W. D., III. (2002). Designing, implementing and evaluating quality interventions. In A. Thomas & J. Grimes (Eds.), *Best practices in school psychology IV.* Washington, DC: National Association of School Psychologists.

U.S. Department of Education (1978–2001). *Annual report to Congress on the implementation of the Individuals with Disabilities Education Act.* Washington, DC: Office of Special Education Programs.

U.S. Department of Health and Human Services (2001, January). *Youth violence: A report of the surgeon general.* Washington, DC: Author.

Vensel, D. S. (1981). Assuming responsibility for the future of school psychology. *School Psychology Review, 10,* 182–193.

Walker, H. M., Horner, R. H., Sugai, G., Bullis, M., Sprague, J. R., Bricker, D., & Kaufman, M. J. (1996). Integrated approaches to preventing antisocial behavior patterns among school-age children and youth. *Journal of Emotional and Behavioral Disorders, 4,* 194–209.

White, M. A. (1963–1964). Graduate training in school psychology. *Journal of School Psychology, 2,* 34–42.

White, M. A., & Harris, M. W. (1961). *The school psychologist.* New York: Harper.

Ysseldyke, J., Dawson, P., Lehr, C., Reschly, D., Reynolds, M., & Telzrow, C. (1997). *School psychology: A blueprint for training and practice II.* Bethesda, MD: National Association of School Psychologists.

Yu, L. M., Rinaldi, D. I., Templer, D. I., Colbert, L. A., Siscoe, K., & Van Patten, K. (1997). Score on the examination for professional practice as a function of attributes or clinical psychology programs. *Psychological Science, 8,* 347–350.

CHAPTER 18

Learning Disabilities

LINDA S. SIEGEL

This chapter reviews the area of learning disabilities. The following issues are considered: definition of subtypes, reading disability, arithmetic disability, assessment, and remediation and accommodation.

DEFINITIONAL ISSUES

Historically, W. M. Cruickshank (1981) has suggested that the term *learning disabilities* is "one of the most interesting accidents of our professional times" (p. 81). It was never used before 1963 and developed from "prepared but informal remarks" (W. M. Cruickshank, 1981, p. 81) made by Samuel A. Kirk at a dinner for concerned parents of children with learning problems in Chicago. Shortly after the dinner, the parents organized themselves on a national level under the banner *Association for Children with Learning Disabilities.* Therefore, the term *learning disabilities* (LD) was adopted as a "functional term without precedents to guide those who attempted to define it and without research or common usage which would assist in its appropriate formulation as a functional term" (W. M. Cruickshank, 1981, p. 81).

The preparation of this manuscript was partially supported by a grant from the Natural Sciences and Engineering Research Council of Canada and was written while the author was a Scholar in Residence at The Peter Wall Institute for Advanced Studies. The author wishes to thank Sarah Kontopoulos and Stephanie Vyas for secretarial assistance.

This problem is complicated by the confusion in terms used to describe some or all of the LD population. W. W. Cruickshank (1972) observed that more than 40 English terms have been used in the literature to refer to some or all of the children subsumed under the LD label. Hammill, Leigh, McNutt, and Larsen (1981) also noted that a variety of terms—such as *minimal brain dysfunction or injury, psychoneurological learning disorders, dyslexia,* or *perceptual handicap,* to name a few—all have been used to refer to LD populations.

In response to the confusion surrounding the definitional issues, in 1981 the National Joint Committee for Learning Disabilities (NJCLD) adopted the following definitions:

> Learning disabilities is a generic term that refers to a heterogeneous group of disorders manifested by significant difficulties in the acquisition and use of listening, speaking, reading, writing, reasoning, or mathematical abilities. These disorders are intrinsic to the individual and are presumed to be due to central nervous system dysfunction. Even though a learning disability may occur concomitantly with other handicapping conditions (e.g., sensory impairment, mental retardation, social or emotional disturbanced) or environmental influences (e.g., cultural differences, insufficient/inappropriate instruction, psychogenic factors), it is not the direct result of these conditions or influences. (Hammill et al., 1981, p. 336)

However, as a number of investigators have suggested (e.g. Fletcher & Morris, 1986; Siegel & Heaven, 1986;

Wong, 1996), this definition also is difficult to operationalize because it is vague and unspecific. Wong (1996) and Keogh (1986, 1987) note that in spite of this definition and *The Rules and Regulations for Implementing Public Law 94-142* (Federal Register, 1977), special-education categories still differ from country to country, state to state, and even within states from district to district. To complicate matters further, Epps, Ysseldyke, and Algozzine (1985) found that states using different category names to classify learning disabled children may actually be using the same criteria to identify these children and some states using the same category names may be using different identification criteria.

Mann, Davis, Boyer, Metz, and Wolford (1983), in a survey of child service demonstration centers (CSDC), found that although most of the CSDCs used the federal criterion of academic underachievement, only two thirds of the centers used even two or three other criteria, and only 3 of the 61 centers used all of the diagnostic criteria. Furthermore, 36 CSDCs did not distinctly state discernible diagnostic criteria.

In 1985, the U.S. Congress passed an act (PL 99-158) forming the Interagency Committee on Learning Disabilities (ICLD) "to review and assess Federal research priorities, activities, and findings regarding learning disabilities" (Silver, 1988, p. 73). According to Silver (1988) three specific mandates were identified by Congress: (a) the determination of the number of people with learning disabilities and a demographic description of them; (b) a review of the current research findings on the cause, diagnosis, treatment, and prevention of learning disabilities; and (c) suggestions for legislation and administration actions that would increase the effectiveness of research on learning disabilities and improve the dissemination of the findings of such research, and prioritize research on the cause, diagnosis, treatment, and prevention of learning disabilities.

In 1987, the committee presented its report to Congress. In this report, the ICLD recommended a legislated definition of LD based on a revision of the 1981 NJCLD's definition. The new definition was to include (changes are in italics) "significant difficulties in . . . *social skills.*" Also, the final sentence was changed to read as follows: "with *socio*environmental influences (e.g., cultural differences, insufficient, or inappropriate instruction, psychogenic factors), and *especially with attention deficit disorder, all of which may cause learning problems, a learning disability* is not the direct result of those conditions or influences" (Silver, 1988, p. 79).

In addition, the committee argued that prevalence studies on learning disabilities should not and could not accurately be undertaken until there was national consensus on a definition of learning disabilities. However, since the publication of the report only one member of the NJCLD has supported

that revised definitions, whereas the others have voted for nonsupport. At issue appears to be the phrase *significant difficulties in . . . social skills.* In spite of all the work and research, Silver (1988) concludes that a lack of a uniform definition and set of diagnostic criteria is one of the most crucial factors inhibiting current and future research efforts. This problem must be addressed before further epidemiological, clinical, basic, and educational research can result in meaningful, generalizable findings.

Several aspects of these definitions are controversial and difficult to operationalize:

- *Exclusionary criteria.* One aspect of these definitions is that the learning difficulty is *not* a result of some other condition.
- *IQ-achievement discrepancy.* There must be a discrepancy between so-called potential and achievement such that achievement is significantly lower than would be predicted from achievement.
- *Specificity.* The learning problem is specific, generally confined to one or two cognitive areas.

Exclusionary Criteria

The presence of certain factors means that an individual will not qualify as learning disabled; these are called exclusionary factors. The definition of learning disabilities assumes that: (a) a learning disability is not the result of an inadequate education; (b) the individual does not have any sensory deficits, such as hearing or visual impairment; (c) the individual does not have any serious neurological disorders that may interfere with learning; and (d) the individual does not have major social or emotional difficulties that might interfere with learning. All of these exclusions seem reasonable, but they are rarely evaluated systematically; furthermore, it is not clear that there is any reason to do so. Consider, for example, a student with a seizure disorder. If the student is shown to be achieving poorly on some achievement test—similar to an individual pure learning disability without a neurological disorder—should the student be *denied* the remediations that are available to students with a learning disability? In the view of this author, the answer is no.

In regard to the issue of adequate education for students in a postsecondary institution, it is difficult to believe that a student would complete secondary school without an education in the basic skills of reading, spelling, writing, and arithmetic. The problems may not have been remediated, but there has been significant exposure to the teaching of these skills. Similarly, individuals with learning disabilities often report depression, social anxiety, low self-esteem, and other emotional difficulties. It is quite likely that these symptoms are a consequence—not a cause—of their problems. We do not know which came first, the emotional difficulty or the learning disability, and in most cases we will never know. However, these emotional difficulties appear to become more serious as the person gets older, indicating that the presence of the learning disability may be creating the emotional problem rather than the other way around; we can never be certain. There does not appear to be any longitudinal research that provides evidence on the causal direction of the relationship between learning disabilities and emotional problems. However, it seems unethical not to identify and treat the learning disability just because there are concurrent emotional difficulties.

IQ-Achievement Discrepancy

IQ tests are typically used in the identification of a learning disability. A great deal of weight is still given to the IQ score in the definition. In virtually all school systems and many colleges and universities, the intelligence test is one of the primary tests used in the identification of learning disabilities. In many cases, an individual *cannot* be identified as learning disabled *unless* an IQ test has been administered. One of the criteria for the existence of a learning disability is the presence of a discrepancy between IQ test score and achievement. I maintain that the presence of this discrepancy is not a necessary part of the definition of a learning disability; furthermore, it is not even necessary to administer an IQ test to determine whether someone has a learning disability. Many investigators (e.g., Fletcher & Morris, 1986; Reynolds, 1984–1985, 1985; Siegel, 1985a, 1985b, 1988a, 1988b, 1989a, 1989b) argue that not only is this assumption controversial, but it also may be invalid.

The intelligence test—and scores based on it—are not useful in the identification of learning disorders. There are both logical reasons for and empirical data to support this statement. It is often argued that we need IQ tests to measure the so-called potential of an individual. This type of argument implies that there is some real entity that will tell us how much an individual can learn and what we can expect of that person—that is, the IQ sets a limit on what the person can learn.

Lezak (1988) argues that IQ is a construct and does not measure any real function or structure. However, that argument has not prevented psychometricians from measuring this entity. But what is being measured? Presumably, intelligence means such skills of logical reasoning, problem solving, critical thinking, and adaptation to the environment. This definition appears to be a reasonable until one examines the content of the IQ test. IQ tests consist of measures of factual knowledge, definitions of words, memory, fine-motor coordination, and fluency of expressive language; they do not measure reasoning or problem-solving skills. They measure—for the most part—what a person has learned, not what he or she is capable of doing in the future. Typical questions on the IQ test consist of questions about definitions of certain words, about geography and history, tasks involving fine-motor coordination such as doing puzzles, memory tasks in which the person is asked to remember a series of numbers, and mental arithmetic problems in which individuals must calculate answers in their heads without the benefit of paper and pencil.

It is obvious that these types of questions measure what an individual has learned—not problem solving or critical thinking skills. In some of the subtests of the intelligence tests, extra points are given for responding quickly; therefore, the intelligence test puts a premium on speed. A person with a slow, deliberate style would not achieve as high a score as an individual who responded more quickly. Therefore, IQ scores do not represent a single entity; rather, are a composite of many skills. (For an extended discussion of the content of IQ tests, see Siegel, 1989a, 1989b, 1995.)

There is an additional problem in the use of IQ tests with individuals with learning disabilities. It is a logical paradox to use IQ scores with learning disabled individuals because most of these people have deficiencies in one or more of the component skills that are part of these IQ tests; therefore, their scores on IQ tests will be an underestimate of their competence. It seems illogical to recognize that someone has deficient memory, language, fine-motor skills, or any combination of these and then say that this individual is less intelligent because he or she has these problems.

One assumption behind the use of an IQ test is that IQ scores predict and set limits on academic performance, so that if a person has a low IQ score, educators should not expect much from that person's academic skills. In other words, by using the IQ test in the psychoeducational assessment of possible learning disabilities, we are assuming that the score on the IQ test indicates how much reading, arithmetic, and so on that we would expect from a person. However, some evidence does contradict this assumption. There are people who have low scores on IQ tests—that is, scores less than 90 or even 80; yet, they have average or even above average scores on reading tests. Even text comprehension may be more influenced by background knowledge (Schneider, Körkel, & Weinert, 1989) or phonological skills (Siegel, 1993b) than IQ scores (Siegel, 1988b); logically, this should not occur if level of reading were determined by IQ scores.

The most widely used IQ tests, the Wechsler Intelligence Scales for Children–III (WISC-III) and the Wechsler Adult Intelligence Scales–Revised (WAIS-R) are actually composed of two scales—a Verbal Scale in which the questions are largely based on language, from which one calculates a Verbal IQ, and a Performance Scale, from which one calculates a Performance IQ. It is also possible to calculate a total or full-scale IQ score. If a discrepancy between IQ and achievement is used, then which IQ score should be used—the Verbal, Performance, or full-scale score? It is quite possible to be categorized as dyslexic on the basis of one IQ score but not if another IQ score is used. For example, Valtin (1978–1979) found that it makes a difference which scale is used, the Verbal or Performance Scale. Children are often classified as dyslexic when the classification is based on one scale, but they are not considered dyslexic when the decision is based on the other. In addition, depending on the type of IQ scores, the difference between the good and poor readers could be significant or not significant, depending on which IQ score was used in the definition.

There is also empirical evidence that suggests it is not necessary to use the concept of intelligence in defining reading disabilities. When children with reading disabilities were divided into groups based on their IQ level and compared on a variety of reading, language, memory, spelling, and phonological tasks, there were no differences between the IQ groups on the reading-related tasks (Siegel, 1988b). Therefore, the reading-disabled group was quite homogeneous in relation to reading-related skills; administering an IQ would not provide useful information about performance differences on *reading*-related tasks.

One typical use of the IQ test is to use the IQ score to measure the discrepancy between IQ and academic achievement. If there is a discrepancy, then the individual is said to have a learning disability. If the individuals are poor readers but show no discrepancy between their IQ and reading scores, then they are not considered reading disabled. Fletcher et al. (1989) maintains that it has not been clearly demonstrated that children with discrepancies in IQ and achievement have more specific disabilities than do poor achievers whose IQ scores were not discrepant. In fact, they contend that there is relatively little empirical evidence to show that similarly defined children differ on measures other than IQ. In an epidemiological study on the influence of various definitions of learning disabilities on the selection of children, Shaywitz, Shaywitz, Barnes, and Fletcher (1986) found that although variations in the use of IQ indexes led to the identification of different children as learning disabled, there were few differences in cognitive abilities. Moreover, there were few differences among identified LD children with discrepant and nondiscrepant IQ scores.

A significant number of studies have found no difference in the reading, spelling, phonological skills, and even reading comprehension of learning disabled individuals with high and low IQ scores and no differences between individuals with dyslexia and poor readers on measures of the processes most directly related to reading (e.g., N. Ellis & Large, 1987; Felton & Wood, 1991; Fletcher, Francis, Rourke, Shaywitz, & Shaywitz, 1992; Fletcher et al., 1994; Friedman & Stevenson, 1988; Gottardo, Stanovich, & Siegel, 1996; Hall, Wilson, Humphreys, Tinzmann, & Bowyer, 1983; Jiménez-Glez & Rodrigo-López, 1994; Johnston, Rugg, & Scott, 1987a, 1987b; Jorm, Share, Matthews, & Maclean, 1986; Share, McGee, McKenzie, Williams, & Silva, 1987; Siegel, 1988b, 1992, 1998; Silva, McGee, & Williams, 1985; Stanovich & Siegel, 1994; Taylor, Satz, & Friel, 1979; Toth & Siegel, 1994). For example, Siegel (1992) compared two groups of children who had low reading scores. One group, which was composed of individuals with dyslexia, had reading scores that were significantly lower than were those that were predicted by their IQ scores; the other group, the poor readers, had low reading scores, but these reading scores were not significantly lower than would be predicted by their IQ scores. On a variety of reading, spelling, and phonological tasks, results showed *no differences* between these two groups in reading comprehension. In other words, there is no need to use IQ scores to predict the difference between the individuals traditionally called learning disabled and those who have equally poor achievement but also have lower IQ scores. These results have also been replicated in a study of adults with reading disabilities (Siegel, 1998). These findings suggest that there is no need to use IQ tests to determine who is learning disabled. We need to use only achievement tests. In addition, IQ scores do not predict who is able to benefit from remediation (Arnold, Smeltzer, & Barneby, 1981; Kershner, 1990; Lytton, 1967; Van der Wissel & Zegers, 1985; Vellutino & Scanlon, 1996; Vellutino, Scanlon, & Lyon, 2000). One study (Yule, 1973) found that reading disabled children with lower IQ scores made more gains than did reading disabled children with higher scores.

Other research shows that reading problems may actually interfere with the development of language, knowledge, and vocabulary skills, further complicating the issue of the relationship between IQ and reading; this is called the *Matthew effect*. The Matthew effect refers to the bidirectional relationship between reading and cognitive development. Stanovich (1986, 1988a, 1988b) has conceptualized the Matthew effect as "the tendency of reading itself to cause further development in other related cognitive abilities"—that is, IQ—such that the "rich get richer and [the] poor get poorer" (Stanovich, 1986, p. 360). Certain minimum cognitive capabilities must be present to begin reading; however, after reading commences, the act of reading itself further develops these same cognitive capabilities; this relationship of mutual reinforcement is called the Matthew effect. This Matthew effect of a reciprocal relationship between reading and other cognitive skills is reflected in performance on an IQ test; consequently, it undermines the validity of using an IQ-discrepancy-based criterion because children who read more gain the cognitive skills and information relevant to the IQ test and thus attain higher IQ scores. Children with reading problems read less; therefore, they fail to gain the skills and information necessary for higher scores on the IQ test.

If the Matthew effect as described by Stanovich were operating, it would be expected that IQ scores would decline with increasing age because vocabulary and knowledge increase as a result—at least in part—of experiences with print. If reading disabled children have less experience with print than do children without reading problems, then the chance to acquire new knowledge is reduced and the IQ scores are expected to decrease over time. In a cross-sectional study, Siegel and Himel (1998) found that the IQ scores—in particular, vocabulary scores—of older dyslexic children were significantly lower than were those of younger dyslexic children. Similar declines in IQ and vocabulary were *not* noted for the normally achieving readers—that is, children who showed age-appropriate reading skills. However, standard scores of the children with reading problems compared to chronologically age-matched children remained relatively constant with time, so that there was *not* an overall decline in skills. Scores on a subtest of the IQ test, Block Design, a test of visuospatial as opposed to verbal skills, also remained constant over time. This subtest measures visuospatial skills more than it does verbal skills, and it is not directly related to the knowledge required by reading. In addition, younger children were much more likely to be classified as dyslexic (as opposed to poor readers) than were older children because of the so-called decline in IQ scores that resulted from lack of print exposure. Finally, if intelligence is a measure of some stable construct of ability or potential and IQ tests measure it, then these test results should be stable over time. Elliot and Boeve (1987) found that the variable time has a statistically significant effect on both children's WISC-R verbal and performance scores. Therefore, for these students, it is questionable if the WISC-R is measuring a stable construct.

Ultimately, services may be denied to individuals who have not been administered an IQ test or who do not achieve a certain score on the IQ test (e.g., see Padget, Knight, & Sawyer, 1996). IQ scores are significantly correlated with socioeconomic status—that is, children from lower socioeconomic backgrounds are likely to have lower IQ scores probably because of a relative lack of experience with the vocabulary and knowledge measured by the IQ test. Children

from low socioeconomic backgrounds are more likely to be classified as poor readers than are dyslexics even though these children have the *same degree* of reading difficulty as dyslexics (Siegel & Himel, 1998); this means that the use of the discrepancy definition discriminates against children from low-SES backgrounds. Some argue that we should use IQ test scores because IQ is correlated with achievement (e.g., Wong, 1996). As Tunmer (1989) has noted, parental income is correlated with reading achievement (the correlations are almost identical in magnitude to those between reading and IQ); why not use a discrepancy between parental income and reading achievement as a measure of dyslexia? A significant discrepancy would be needed for the individual to get remedial help. The social consequences and unfairness of this suggestion are obvious, but the principle is the same as using a discrepancy between IQ and achievement.

The requirement for the use of the IQ score provides us with the dilemma of determining an IQ score that is necessary for an individual to achieve to be considered learning disabled. Some studies use 80, others 85, others 90, and some even use 100. For example, although they recognize that there are problems with the use of IQ in the identification of learning disabilities, Padget et al. (1996) argue that

> Clinical judgment may be needed when considering cases in which the Verbal IQ is below 90. Two cases in which this may be particularly important are older students who previously achieved a Verbal IQ above 90 and students who have low subtest scores only on the subtests that require significant auditory, sequential memory skills to perform the task. In most other cases when students score below these guidelines it strongly suggests that reading problems may be related to factors other than, or in addition to, dyslexia. (p. 59).

However, they present no evidence for this assertion. An opposing conclusion has been reached by G. Reid Lyon (1995) of the U.S. National Institute of Child Health and Human Development as follows:

> The assumption that a discrepancy between achievement and aptitude (typically assessed using intelligence tests) is a clear diagnostic marker for learning disabilities or can be considered a pathognomonic sign is at best premature, and at worst invalid. (p. 5121)

Often, it is recommended that instead of the IQ test, measures of listening comprehension be used presumably because this will assess an individual's level of cognitive processing (Aaron, 1991; Padget et al., 1996). Listening comprehension measures typically consist of the examiner's reading aloud a passage to the individual and then asking him or her questions about the text. This type of task places heavy demands on memory, and if an individual fails to answer a question correctly, the examiner does not know whether the individual did not understand the passage or has merely forgotten the answer. Ability to remember what has been heard also depends on one's background knowledge of the material in the text. Unlike when one reads text in which the material is available, one cannot refer back to the material in a listening comprehension task. Therefore, the time has come to abandon listening comprehension as an alternative to the IQ test.

Another assumption of many LD definitions—including US Public Law 94-142, Ontario's Bill 82, and the NJCLD's definition—is that there must be a discrepancy between IQ and achievement. In other words, the child's achievement is not commensurate with his or her ability or intelligence (IQ).

The second assumption of the discrepancy definition is that measures of intelligence and measures of achievement are independent. This assumption has been questioned by some investigators (see Lyon, 1987, for a complete discussion), but I maintain that it is necessary if a discrepancy definition is to be meaningful. If one accepts the argument that intelligence is not orthogonal to achievement, then there would be no reason to expect a discrepancy. Therefore, a discrepancy definition is logical if and only if the presence of a learning disability does not affect IQ test scores but does affect achievement test scores. Then children with LD would have a discrepancy between the scores on their IQ tests and the scores on their achievement tests, whereas normally achieving children and those with other disabilities will have scores on these tests that are similar (not discrepant).

A number of investigators (Green, 1974; Hopkins & Stanley, 1981; Siegel, 1988a, 1988b) have suggested that this assumption of independence is questionable. Green (1974) argues, for example, that comparisons of scores for ability and achievement are meaningful only to the extent to which unique elements are measured.

Hopkins and Stanley (1981) examined the overlapping variance in a well-constructed intelligence test (the Lorge-Thorndike) and in two subtests (the reading and the arithmetic) of a well-constructed achievement test (the Iowa Test of Basic Skills). On average, 47% of the variance was found to overlap. This finding suggests that when one ability test and one achievement test are used, about 50% of the time the same concept is being measured; this clearly violates the assumption of independence among concepts measured by the ability and achievement tests. It can only be hoped that the other 50% of the variance is tapping something different that can provide insight to the true differences revealed by the comparison.

Discrepancy definitions also have been questioned on statistical grounds. Reynolds (1984–1985, 1985) notes that many discrepancy models are based on grade equivalents. He points out that these models have problems in two areas. First, neither age nor grade-equivalent scores provide adequate mathematical properties (cannot be added, subtracted, multiplied, or divided) for use in discrepancy analysis. Second, the amount of retardation reflected by *2 years below grade level* changes with increasing grade level. A much greater level of retardation is reflected by a 2-year deficit at Grade 2 than at Grade 7, and even less retardation would be reflected at Grade 11. Therefore, a much greater deficit would be needed for a child in Grade 3 to be identified as LD than for one in Grade 10.

In summary, the weight of the evidence leads us to conclude that IQ scores are irrelevant to the definitions of learning disabilities.

Specificity

There are two types of specificity: The first involves the degree to which the individual's problem is specific to one or more cognitive areas, and the second involves the issue of whether all children with learning disabilities should be considered one homogeneous group. A number of authors (Hall & Humphreys, 1982; Stanovich, 1986, 1988a; Swanson, 1988b, 1989) have maintained that one of the essential concepts of a learning disability is its specificity—that is, a learning disability is presumed to be caused by a neurological inefficiency that affects a narrow group of subskills of cognitive processes; this affects a specific domain of academic skills but leaves intellectually ability intact. In other words, a learning disability reflects a cognitive deficit possibly due to a neurological dysfunction that is comparatively specific to a particular domain (e.g., reading or arithmetic). Swanson (1988a) has suggested that these specific deficits must not stray too far into other cognitive domains, or the concept of a specific learning disability will blend with other more generalized conditions (e.g., mental retardation). As well, Stanovich (1986) maintains that definitions of dyslexia must rest on an assumption of specificity. He contends that dyslexia results from a brain or cognitive deficit that is reasonably specific to reading.

Siegel (1988a) and Bryant and Brown (1985) argue that this type of specificity is unrealistic. Siegel (1988a) maintains that if children have problems in working memory, this condition could affect a variety of academic tasks—especially in areas such as reading, spelling, and arithmetic. Brown and Bryant (1985) suggest that if a child has a severe language problem, this condition could influence a large number of cognitive areas: reading, writing, speaking, listening, or any combination. Moreover, Siegel (1988a) contends that implicit in the specificity assumption is the assumption that domains such as reading and arithmetic are entirely independent cognitive processes. This assumption is invalid because working memory and recognizing and labeling abstract symbols are involved in both reading and arithmetic skills, and a child who has difficulty with these cognitive processes is likely to have problems with tasks involving such skills (Siegel, 1988a).

The second type of specificity involves questions about the degree to which all children with LD have the same problems or whether there are subtypes. On the basis of what is now known, the concept of a generalized homogeneous group labeled *LD children* should be abandoned; the child with LD should be considered as part of a smaller, more clearly defined subtype (Siegel, 1988a). As well, other theorists (e.g., Bateman, 1968–1969; Benton & Pearl, 1978; Boder, 1973; Kinsbourne & Warrington, 1963; Rourke, 1983, 1985) have contended that differences within the population of children with learning disabilities may reflect the existence of distinguishable subtypes. In other words, not all learning-disabled children have the same types of disabilities, and independent subtypes include distinctive characteristics and antecedent conditions that consistently predict specific patterns of learning difficulties. Therefore, failure to differentiate among types of learning disabilities can lead to inaccurate conclusions. For example, Siegel and Ryan (1984, 1988) found that children with reading disabilities have difficulty processing certain aspects of syntax, whereas specific children with specific arithmetic disabilities (and no reading disability) do not. Differences between the same two groups have been found in working memory (Fletcher, 1985; Siegel & Linder, 1984; Siegel & Ryan, 1989a). Swanson (1988b) found that children with a reading disability may be characterized by different patterns of memory dysfunction. These differences are reflected on measures of achievement in reading and arithmetic. If all these children had been considered together as a homogeneous group, these differences might have been obscured.

A Resolution of Definitional Issues

Clearly the field of special education continues to have problems defining and classifying children with learning disabilities. Current discrepancy definitions are problematic and should be reconsidered because they cannot be justified in light of their illogical nature. But where does that leave us and where can we go from there?

One way in which meaning is given to a concept is by defining it operationally. Specifically, an operational definition explains a concept solely in terms of the operations used to produce and measure it. Recognizing that there are problems inherent in operational definitions (e.g., the meaning of the concept is restricted to the narrowly described operations used for measuring it), I suggest that learning disabilities (a) need to have an IQ threshold because I recognize that the field is not ready to accept Siegel's (1989a, 1989b) challenge to the use of IQ tests; (b) should refer to a significant difficulty in a school-related area; and (c) should exclude only severe emotional disorders, second-language background, sensory disabilities, and specific neurological deficits.

Evidence (Siegel, Levey, & Ferris, 1985; Siegel & Ryan, 1989b) suggests that the type of operational definition used for the concept may influence the outcome and conclusions of the study. Siegel and Ryan (1989b) have argued that the actual definition used for a reading disability can make a difference in the conclusions that are drawn about information-processing characteristics of the children and whether there are reading-disability subtypes. In one study, poor readers (all with IQ scores equal to or above 80) were divided into four groups as follows: (a) those with deficits in phonological processing—inadequate phonological skills based on the reading of pseudowords, (b) those with word-recognition deficits, (c) those with comprehension-only deficits—inadequate reading comprehension skills but adequate word-recognition skills, and (d) those with rate-only deficits—slow reading speed but adequate word-recognition skills. When each disabled group was compared to an age-matched normally achieving group, distinct cognitive differences appeared. For example, children with a phonological deficit or a word-recognition deficit had scores that were significantly lower than were those of normal readers on short-term memory tasks but not on language tasks. The readers with rate-only deficits had cognitive profiles similar to those of normally achieving children. Therefore, the children with word-recognition problems are probably the ones with language deficits and those with only a reading comprehension problem probably do not have language problems.

In addition, there was approximately a 25% overlap between poor comprehenders and poor readers; therefore, had a reading comprehension test been used to define the learning-disabled group and word recognition not been used as a control, the reading-disabled group would have consisted of some children with word-recognition problems and some without.

This leads to the question *How should a reading disability be defined?* Stanovich (1986, 1989) has suggested that the core deficits in a reading disability are problems in phonological processing. Although reading is more than simply decoding and recognizing words (one has to remember what was read, put it into context, etc.), unfortunately currently there are no accurate tests to measure these variables (see Siegel & Heaven, 1986, for a complete discussion of this issue). Further empirical evidence suggests that when a difficulty with phonological processing, word recognition, or both is used as the basis of the definition of a reading problem, then disabled readers appear to have reasonably homogeneous cognitive profiles and—in particular—deficits in the language areas (e.g., Fletcher, 1985; Rourke & Finlayson, 1978; Rourke & Strang, 1978; Siegel & Ryan, 1984, 1988, 1989b; Strang & Rourke, 1983b). Therefore we and others (e.g., Siegel & Heaven, 1986; Siegel & Ryan, 1989a; Vellutino, 1978, 1979) argue that single-word or nonword reading constitute the purest measures of reading and that an operational definition of a reading disability should be based on nonword tests to measure phonological skills, single-word tests to measure word recognition skills, or both.

The classification of children with arithmetic problems is equally problematic. As Siegel and Ryan (1989a) note, it is almost impossible to find a group of reading-disabled children who also do not have severe deficits in arithmetic. At the same time, a number of investigators (Fletcher, 1985b; Rourke & Finlayson, 1978; Rourke & Strang, 1978; Siegel & Feldman, 1983; Siegel & Linder, 1984; Siegel & Ryan, 1984, 1988, 1989a) have found a group of learning-disabled children with difficulties in arithmetic but with average or above-average reading scores. Some evidence (e.g., Fletcher, 1985a; Rourke & Finlayson, 1978; Rourke & Strang, 1978; Siegel & Feldman, 1983; Siegel & Linder, 1984; Siegel & Ryan, 1984, 1988, 1989a) suggests that these children with arithmetic deficits but normal reading (word recognition) have cognitive profiles that are different from those of children with reading difficulties. Therefore, it is important that children designated as arithmetic LD not have problems that are confounded by difficulties in reading.

SUBTYPES

Given the heterogeneity of LD groups, Siegel (1988b) contends that if all LD children are grouped together, then inaccurate conclusions may be reached. Evidence in support of this position has been found by many investigators (e.g., Fletcher, 1985; McKinney, Short, & Feagans, 1985; Rourke & Finlayson, 1978; Siegel & Linder, 1984; Siegel & Ryan, 1984, 1988, 1989a, 1989b). For example, Siegel and Ryan (1984, 1988, 1989a, 1989b) and Fletcher (1985) found differences between specific arithmetic-disabled children without reading problems and reading-disabled children in both short-term and working memory. McKinney et al., using a cognitive battery designed to assess a wide range of linguistic and perceptual abilities, were able to classify 55 first- and second-grade, school-identified LD children into six subtypes. They then demonstrated that the three subtypes with

atypical cognitive profiles had poorer academic outcomes than did the three groups with normal or near-normal profiles. These differences might not have been evident had these children been grouped together and not divided into subtypes.

Because of this heterogeneity of LD groups, considerable effort has been made to identify specific subgroups of LD children who share common attributes that distinguish them from other subtypes. Not only do subtypes exist, but they also seem to take several forms in terms of achievement patterns, associated cognitive information-processing abilities, or both. Furthermore, these subtypes may vary as a function of etiology and age (e.g., McKinney et al., 1985; Rourke & Finlayson, 1978; Satz & Morris, 1981; Short, Feagans, McKinney, & Appelbaum, 1986; Siegel & Heaven, 1986).

Subtyping Models

Early subtype approaches are based on clinical inferences that have attempted to reduce complex data sets of subjects into presumably homogeneous classes largely based upon a priori considerations and visual inspection techniques. These methods have been criticized for their inability to manage simultaneously large quantities of information in an objective fashion as well as for the subjectivity that results from the bias of clinical decisions made at various stages during the subtype development and subject classification (see Satz & Morris, 1981, and Hooper & Willis, 1989, for a complete review).

More recently, with the availability of advanced computer technology, empirical classification models using applied descriptive multivariate statistics have been developed. This approach has involved a search for hidden structure in complex multidimensional data sets generally involving cognitive linguistic skills or direct measures of achievement or behavior (e.g., Doehring & Hoshko, 1977; Feagans & Appelbaum, 1986).

These methods also have difficulties. Hooper and Willis (1989) contend that standards of reliability and validity have frequently been overlooked or marginally addressed by investigators using these classification techniques. In addition, they suggest that "the adequacy and strength of models derived by empirical classification methods are influenced by many a priori clinical decisions including those regarding theoretical orientation, sample selection, and variable selection" (p. 104). Thus, the appropriate subtyping model remains an open question and may depend on the type of research undertaken.

Academic Performance Models

In spite of the difficulties inherent in subtyping models, a number of investigators (e.g., Fletcher, 1985; Rourke & Finlayson,

1978; Rourke & Strang, 1978; Siegel & Feldman, 1983; Siegel & Linder, 1984; Siegel & Ryan, 1984, 1988, 1989a, 1989b) have suggested that LD students in general can be divided on the basis of their academic achievement as measured by Wide Range Achievement Test (WRAT) scores in reading, spelling, and arithmetic. Although each investigator has created his or her own classification scheme, two broad categories of subtype groups have emerged. The first contains children with at least reading deficits, and the second contains children with at least arithmetic deficits and normal-to-above-normal reading scores. Some authors (e.g., Fletcher, 1985; Rourke & Finlayson, 1978; Rourke & Strang, 1978) have subdivided these groups further, basing their divisions on the presence of other deficits. For example, Siegel and Linder (1984) and Siegel and Ryan (1984, 1988, 1989a, 1989b) have used only two academic subtypes: (a) an arithmetic-disabled group, defined by scores equal to or below the 25th percentile on the WRAT Arithmetic subtest and scores equal to or above the 30th percentile on the WRAT Reading subtest and (b) a reading-disabled group, defined by scores equal to or below the 25th percentile on the WRAT Reading subtest and no cutoffs for the other two WRAT subtests. Fletcher (1985b) has developed the following four subtypes: (a) a reading-spelling-disabled group, (b) a reading-spelling-arithmetic-disabled group, (c) an arithmetic-disabled group, and (d) a spelling-arithmetic-disabled group. According to this categorization, the reading-spelling-disabled group is defined as consisting of children with (a) WRAT Reading and Spelling subtest scores below the 31st percentile, (b) WRAT Arithmetic subtest scores above the 30th percentile, and (c) the arithmetic score must be at least one-half standard deviation above the reading score on the appropriate WRAT subtest. The reading-spelling-arithmetic-disabled group is characterized by children with scores on all three WRAT subtests below the 31st percentile. The arithmetic-spelling-disabled group contains children who have (a) WRAT Spelling and Arithmetic subtest scores below the 31st percentile, (b) WRAT Reading subtest scores above the 39th percentile, and (c) at least one standard deviation between their reading and arithmetic scores. The arithmetic-disabled group consists of children who have (a) WRAT Reading and Spelling subtest scores above the 39th percentile, (b) WRAT Arithmetic subtest scores below the 31st percentile, and (c) difference of at least one standard deviation between their reading and arithmetic scores. In contrast, a series of studies by Rourke and his associates (Rourke & Finlayson, 1978; Rourke & Strang, 1978; Strang & Rourke, 1983a, 1983b) have identified the following three subtypes: (a) a general disabled group (reading-spelling-arithmetic-disabled), (b) a reading-disabled group, and (c) an arithmetic-disabled group. These investigators defined their reading-spelling-

arithmetic groups as consisting of children with WRAT subtest scores below the 19th percentile on all three subtests. The reading-spelling-disabled group consisted of children with (a) WRAT Arithmetic subtest scores at least 1.8 years higher than their WRAT Reading and Spelling subtest scores and (b) WRAT Reading and Spelling subtest scores below the 15th percentile. The arithmetic-disabled group contained children whose WRAT Reading and Spelling subtest scores were at least 2 years above the WRAT Arithmetic subtest scores.

Rourke and colleagues have developed subtypes of LD children based on patterns of academic performance (Fisk & Rourke, 1979, 1983; Ozols & Rourke, 1985; Porter & Rourke, 1985; Petrauskas & Rourke, 1979; Rourke & Finlayson, 1978; Rourke & Strang, 1978; Rourke & Fisk, 1981; Strang & Rourke, 1983, 1985a, 1985b; Sweeney & Rourke, 1978). Depending on the particular investigation, percentile cutoff scores of 20, 25, or 30 on the WRAT have been used to define a particular LD group.

In one study, Rourke and Finlayson (1978) investigated the performance of three groups of LD children on a neuropsychological battery. The subtypes were formed on the basis of their WRAT scores in reading, spelling, and arithmetic. The first subtype exhibited uniformly deficient performance in all three academic areas. They were found to be superior to a specifically arithmetic-disabled group on measures of visual-perceptual and visuospatial abilities. In the second subtype, children were relatively good at arithmetic as compared to their reading and spelling, but all areas were below average. Superior visuospatial abilities and Performance IQ scores were characteristic of this subtype. The third subtype was composed of children whose reading and spelling scores were average or above, but whose arithmetic score was at least 2 years below that. This group exhibited Verbal IQ scores that were higher than their Performance scores. Their performance on measures of visual-perceptual-organizational skills was somewhat deficient. Their performance on measures of verbal and auditory-perceptual abilities was superior to that of the first two groups, who were reading disabled and low achievers in arithmetic. Rourke and Strang (1978) found further deficiencies in this third subtype on complex psychomotor measures and differences in hand superiority on the Tactual Performance Test. Difficulties in visuospatial orientation, including right-left problems, and impaired bilateral tactile-perceptual abilities, including finger agnosia, were also characteristic of this group.

Strang and Rourke (1983a, 1983b) found that the specific arithmetic-disabled children made significantly more errors than did the reading and arithmetic disabled children on the Halstead category test. The arithmetic-disabled children had lower scores on those subtests, which "require a substantial degree of 'higher order' visual-spatial analysis" (Strang & Rourke, 1985b, p. 173). An analysis of the arithmetic errors made by the third group (specifically arithmetic disabled) on the WRAT subtest indicated a large number and variety of errors. The quality of errors, as expected, changed somewhat with age. The most prevalent types of mechanical errors were identified as follows: (a) spatial organization, (b) visual detail, (c) procedural errors, (d) failure to shift psychological set, (e) graphomotor, (f) memory, and (g) judgment and reasoning, indicating deficits in visuospatial and perceptual-motor abilities.

Ozols and Rourke (1985) compared the performance of two groups of LD children to a group of average-achieving children of the same age on four tasks—two verbal and two nonverbal. The groups were identified as follows: (a) a language-disorder group, who exhibited relatively well-developed visuospatial abilities but poor auditory-perceptual and language-related abilities (WRAT subtest percentile scores in reading, spelling, and arithmetic were all below 25); (b) a spatial-disorder group, who exhibited relatively well-developed auditory-perceptual and language-related abilities but poor visuospatial abilities (WRAT arithmetic subtest score was the only percentile score below 25). The language-disorder group performed significantly more poorly on the verbal tasks than did the controls, and the spatial-disorder group performed significantly more poorly than did the controls on the nonverbal tasks.

Siegel and Ryan (1984) used performance on achievement tests to subdivide LD children into more heterogeneous groups. Three LD groups were created and compared to a control group of normally achieving children. The LD groups were (a) reading-disabled children who had low scores on the WRAT Reading test, a test of word recognition skills; (b) children who were arithmetic written work disabled who had low scores on the WRAT Arithmetic test, a measure of computational arithmetic skills; and (c) children with attention deficit disorder (ADD; hyperactive) but with no other learning disabilities. Typically, the reading-disabled children had significantly below-average ability to understand the syntactic and morphological aspects of language and—at the youngest ages—memory for sentences. None of the other LD groups showed deficits in these areas. The reading-disabled children had a significant deficit in reading and spelling nonwords and in recognizing the visual form of a spoken sound. None of the other LD children had deficits in these areas, with the exception of the youngest, specifically arithmetic-disabled children, who had some difficulties with these phonological skills in spite of their normal word-recognition skills. This finding may be a result of the definition of arithmetic disability, which at the youngest ages involves memory skills in addition to computational skills. Thus, these younger arithmetic-disabled children may represent the more severely disabled children compared to older children who have a specific arithmetic disability. The children with ADD and no other difficulties with achievement did have significantly lower scores on a reading comprehension test (which is in reality a memory test and may require attentional skills), but these children showed no other deficits.

All of the reading-disabled children had a severe deficit involving phonological skills. They were quite homogeneous in this respect. In most cases there was no overlap in the scores of the reading-disabled and normally achieving children of the same chronological age. Furthermore, for the reading and spelling of nonwords, the reading-disabled children performed more poorly than did younger controls matched for reading level, indicating a very serious deficit. The children with an arithmetic writing disability and the children with a reading disability had significantly lower scores on a short-term memory task involving visually presented letters, but Siegel and Linder (1984) found that for auditorily presented letters, the arithmetic-disability group performed in the normal range, indicating that the deficit of this latter group was limited to short-term memory for visually presented information.

Fletcher (1985) used a verbal and nonverbal memory task to test the hypothesis that subgroups of disabled learners show different performance patterns. All tasks were based on selective reminding procedures (i.e., in subsequent presentations, items are repeated only if they were not recalled on the previous trial) to determine what inferences could be drawn concerning storage and retrieval skills in these subgroups. Control subjects had to obtain percentile scores above 39 on the Reading, Spelling, and Arithmetic subtests of the WRAT and show no history of achievement difficulties. Disabled learners were placed into one of four groups depending on their pattern of WRAT scores. The groups were (a) reading-spelling-disabled (R-S), (b) reading-spelling-arithmetic-disabled (R-S-A), (c) spelling-arithmetic-disabled (S-A), and (d) arithmetic disabled (A).

The findings indicated that not all LD children showed similar patterns of memory deficiencies. Children with reading problems showed only retrieval difficulties on verbal tasks, whereas children with arithmetic problems demonstrated both storage and retrieval problems on nonverbal tasks. Children with the R-S pattern had poorer verbal skills, whereas children with the arithmetic pattern showed poorer nonverbal skills. The R-S-A pattern had not been previously studied, but children demonstrating this pattern had relatively poor performance on the tasks used in this study.

Some studies were carried out in an attempt to determine the relative diagnostic power of a number of tests in discriminating between dyslexic children and those with other learning disabilities. In one study by Rudel and Denckla (1976), the performance of developmental dyslexic individuals was tested using visual-verbal tasks, such as naming pictured objects, letters, and numbers. A 2-year or greater lag in reading performance on a test of oral reading skill led to a classification of dyslexic. All participants were tested on rapid automatized naming tasks. Stimuli included colors, numerals, use objects (e.g., comb), and high-frequency lowercase letters. The naming speed on all four tasks for normally functioning individuals was faster than for nondyslexic LD participants, and nondyslexic participants were significantly faster than dyslexic subjects.

In this study, the experimental children were termed *learning disabled,* but no reference was made to how they were so designated. The authors stated that division of participants into dyslexic and nondyslexic groups was done post hoc by determining the difference between reading age and mental age. Reading grade level was based on a test of oral reading skill; no mention was made of what oral reading test was used. The problems associated with such tests have already been discussed. The lack of information on the measures used in this study raises questions about the heterogeneity and severity of the problems demonstrated by the group being studied.

In a second study (Denckla, Rudel, & Broman, 1981), a series of tasks was administered: a rapid automatized naming task, the Oldfield-Wingfield Pictured Object Naming Test, visual-Braille letter learning (a paired associate learning task), visual-temporal spatial matching (a *same* or *different* response was required of the participant after he or she watched a series of light flashes emitted from a single stationary point source in a black box), and finally the silent detection of repeated target symbols (a pencil-and-paper version of the visual matching task paradigm). The dyslexic group had a high percentage of dysphasic errors and prolonged times on repeated naming compared to the nondyslexic LD children.

In this study, the participants were defined as dyslexic on the basis of a discrepancy between the WISC-R score and the score on the Gray Oral Reading Test. The same problems as in the earlier study emerge. The latter test is an oral reading comprehension test that cannot be regarded as a pure test of reading skill. Failure to do well on this test could be the result of poor decoding skills, poor attention, poor memory, or poor comprehension. The result is a heterogeneous sample with findings that have limited external validity.

Another attempt at subtyping on the basis of achievement test scores is described by Satz and Morris (1981). Although

their subtyping scheme resembles Rourke's, it is flawed by the use of grade-level retardation on the WRAT subtests for classification. This scheme is particularly problematic with the many older children in the study.

Rather than finding significant heterogeneity on language and memory functioning, these studies found homogeneity within the population of disabled readers. It is important to note that the studies that have found homogeneity within the reading-disabled population have used retardation in word-recognition skills to define the reading-disabled population. In one very early study on subtyping that was unsuccessful, it was found that all reading-disabled children had difficulty with sound blending and short-term memory (Naidoo, 1972). As discussed later in this chapter, studies that have used other definitions (reading comprehension) do not find the same degree of homogeneity. As further evidence of this point, Siegel and Ryan (1989b) found that when a definition of reading disability was used that involved poor word-recognition or phonics skills, reading-disabled children had significant problems with phonological processing and understanding of syntax. However, children with low reading comprehension scores but good phonics, word recognition skills, or both did not show these problems. In summary, with achievement test definitions such as those used by Rourke and associates, Fletcher, and Siegel and colleagues, fairly homogeneous groups of reading-disabled children have emerged.

Regardless of the exact criteria used, this method of subtyping had identified groups of LD children whose arithmetic difficulties are not confounded by deficits in reading (word recognition). The emergence of a specific arithmetic-disabled subgroup has permitted investigators to clarify some of the characteristics that distinguish this group from other LD children with reading deficits.

Subtypes Within the Reading Disability Group

A number of investigators have assumed that a reading disability is not a single disorder but rather represents a group of more specific subtypes. Some of these conceptualizations are outlined in the following discussion. However, what appears to be heterogeneity is really not; because of definitional inadequacies, heterogeneity emerges. Several schemes have been used as subtyping systems. These schemes involve (a) the use of achievement tests to classify all LD children with the implicit assumption that all the children with a reading disability will show a reasonable similarity in cognitive performance and be different from those without a reading disability (as was described earlier), (b) the use of patterns of responses on reading tests to classify subgroups of disabled readers, (c) the use of neuropsychological measures to differentiate subgroups of disabled readers, and (d) the use of a large number of tests and elaborate multivariate statistical procedures to search for more homogeneous subgroups of disabled readers.

We examine attempts at subtyping according to these classification systems. It should be noted that there is a fundamental difference between the first type of subtyping scheme and the other three types. In the first type, patterns of achievement in other areas besides reading (e.g., spelling and arithmetic) are examined. Typically these studies—unlike the other three types—do not attempt to divide disabled readers into reading subtypes; rather, they try to differentiate disabled readers from other groups of LD children.

Classification Based on Reading Patterns.   Some classification schemes based on qualitative differences in reading performance have been attempted. For example, Lovett (1984) proposed that there are two subtypes of disabled readers: *rate disabled* readers who read slowly but have adequate decoding skills and *accuracy disabled* readers who have below-average decoding skills. Lovett found a number of differences between the accuracy and the rate disabled readers. However, the conclusions reached by Lovett may be a function of her definition. It seems to be quite possible that her rate disabled readers were not really reading disabled. For example, they had to be 1.5 years below grade level on four out of five of the rate measures. Grade level is an imprecise measure and represents an ordinal rather than an interval scale. Subtracting grade levels is not an appropriate way of defining individual differences. In addition, the same level of grade retardation may mean a different discrepancy at various levels in the developmental continuum. For example, a younger child with even a slight grade-level retardation would score at a low percentile or standard score level, whereas an older child might not necessarily have a low percentile score even at a 1.5- or 2-year grade-level retardation (see Siegel & Heaven, 1986, for detailed evidence on this issue). As many of the children in Lovett's study were at an older age level, in which a 1.5 grade level retardation does not necessarily indicate a serious impairment, the use of this criterion may mean that many of these children were not seriously reading disabled. The rate disabled children were not obviously impaired in spelling, language, comprehension, regular and exception word reading, or phonics, whereas the accuracy disabled children were. Although these rate disabled children may have been slower than average in reading speed (even this is unknown because of the grade-level criterion), it is not clear that they were different from normal readers. More important is that it is not clear that such children should be called disabled or dyslexic. They clearly have many good reading skills—for example, reading nonwords, reading exception words, and understanding syntax. They are probably below average in reading speed but not really disabled. Superficially, although it appeared that Lovett found subtypes, closer examination reveals that not all these children are truly reading disabled.

Vernon (1977) proposed a system for defining subgroups of poor readers based on variations in the level of the component skills involved in reading, such as letter discrimination, letter-sound correspondence, or slow reading. Unfortunately, such a system is not very useful without precise operational definitions or a methodology for separating these subgroups. Vernon's analysis of reading appears to represent sequential development of skills related to reading rather than skills that are absent or present simultaneously. Another attempt at defining groups of reading-disabled children was made by Boder (1968, 1971, 1973), who developed a screening procedure for diagnosing reading disabilities on the basis of three so-called reading (but actually spelling) patterns. Boder's screening procedure consists of a two-part test, flashed and nontimed presentation of words, and an individual spelling test based upon the child's reading performance. Spelling is assessed by asking the children to spell words from their sight vocabulary (at or below reading level) and then an equal number from their unknown vocabulary at grade level. The rationale for this method is that including words from the children's sight vocabulary allows for assessment of a child's ability to revisualize words and inclusion of unknown words taps the ability to spell phonetically (Boder, 1971). On the basis of this screening procedure, Boder outlined a categorization scheme to classify children with dyslexia based on three patterns. The first subgroup is called *dysphonetic* because these children are supposedly characterized by an inability to develop phonetic skills, have difficulty in sound-symbol integration, and read in whole-word gestalts—that is, they appear to see reading as a pattern recognition task. The second subgroup is called *dyseidetic;* children in this group are characterized by the opposite problem. They experience difficulty in forming so-called whole-word visual gestalts and must sound out every word as if they were encountering it for the first time. The third subgroup is called *alexic* and are characterized by the problems of both the other groups. It is important to note that the categorization of a child is based on *spelling*—not reading—patterns.

Camp and Dolcourt (1977) developed and tested two parallel standardized reading and spelling forms to increase the utility of Boder's concept utilization of subtypes. The word lists were revised to contain half phonetic (e.g., cave) and half dysphonetic (e.g., calf) words. In this new procedure, the examiner selected the list of spelling words that corresponded to the grade level the child could read 50% correctly. Camp and Dolcourt determined that dyseidetic individuals were diagnosed primarily by spelling performance, and because of Boder's definition (less than or equal to 50% of sight vocabulary correctly spelled and misspellings of known irregular words), several children would be classified as dyseidetic even though they were reading above grade level. Children who have good reading but poor spelling skills are common (e.g., Lennox & Sigel), but they are not really dyslexic.

A number of studies have been carried out using Boder's classification system, but many of them suffer from methodological and definitional problems that make their comparison extremely difficult and interpretation of their findings rather tenuous. For example, electrophysiological evidence for subgroups of developmental dyslexia has been reported by Fried, Tanguay, Boder, Doubleday, and Greensite (1981). Using Boder's diagnostic approach Fried et al. applied event related potential (ERP) techniques to the study of word and musical chord auditory information processing in the left and right hemispheres of their dyslexic participants and compared their performance with that of a normal control group. They found that latency differences between ERPs evoked by word and musical chord stimuli were greater for the left hemisphere of the normal children, as expected from studies conducted in adults (Brown, Marsh, & Smith, 1973). The dyseidetic children, all of who could phonemically decode and encode reading material well, also exhibited a normal pattern of greater waveform differences in the left as opposed to the right hemisphere, although the magnitude of these differences differed from that in the controls (a finding that the investigators attributed to differences in attentional factors between the groups). In contrast, the dysphonetic group did not show the greater word-musical chord ERP waveform differences in the left hemisphere. Fried et al. interpreted these data as suggesting that the left hemisphere may not have a fully developed capacity to process auditory information in the normal manner. An unexpected finding was that the alexic participants produced results similar to those of the normal readers, despite the fact that they were postulated to have problems with both the right and left hemispheres. It is possible that the waveform differences observed in this group were a matter of chance. In any case, the differential performance of the dysphonetic and dyseidetic readers may be a function of severity in that the dyseidetic individuals may not have been really reading disabled.

A study by Telzrow, Century, Whitaker, Redmond, and Zimmerman (1983) investigated the demographic and neuropsychological characteristics of children in the various reading categories defined by performance on the Boder Test

and found some differences between them. Unfortunately, the authors of this study fluctuated between calling their participants *learning disabled* and *reading disabled* to the extent that one does not really know much about the population under discussion. One is not told how the original diagnosis of developmental dyslexia was made, what measures were used, and what criteria for inclusion were adopted. Hence, it is possible that many were not really reading disabled.

A study by Nockleby and Galbraith (1984) compared the performance of dysphonetic individuals, those with non-specific reading disabilities, and normal readers on eight dependent-variable tasks—four of which were described as requiring analytic-sequential processing and four that required processing in a simultaneous gestalt fashion. The analytic sequential tasks included Auditory Sequential Memory (from the Illinois Test of Psycholinguistic Ability, or ITPA), Visual Sequential Memory (ITPA), the Lindamood Auditory Conceptualization Test, and Sound Blending (ITPA). Simultaneous gestalt tasks included a facial memory task using 40 photographs of men and women that had to be identified later, a tactile-visual recognition test in which children had to recognize shapes placed in their hand by viewing a response card of those shapes, the Benton Visual Retention Test, and the Raven Coloured Progressive Matrices. It was hypothesized that a subgroup of reading-disabled children categorized by the Boder test as dysphonetic would perform poorly on tasks requiring analytic-sequential processing and normally on tasks requiring simultaneous gestalt processing. A subgroup of disabled readers categorized as having nonspecific reading retardation were predicted to perform as well as a comparison group of normal readers on all perceptual and memory tasks. The dysphonetic and nonspecific groups did not perform significantly differently from the controls on any of the simultaneous gestalt processing measures. Dysphonetic individuals performed significantly below the control group on the visual and auditory memory test. Both dysphonetic and nonspecific groups performed significantly below the control group on the Lindamood test. Sound blending was the only analytic-sequential task that did not discriminate among the reader groups. The authors concluded that these results support the hypothesis that dysphonetic dyslexic children are deficient in one information-processing strategy (analytic-sequential) and normal in the other process (simultaneous gestalt) and that children identified by Boder as having nonspecific reading retardation may have essentially intact processing for both modes. However, the authors suggested that the absence of a difference between the non-specific and the dysphonetic groups on the Lindamood test appears to be evidence against Boder's classification system because the Lindamood has been found to be a valid indicator of problematic phonetic skills in poor readers. That both groups performed almost identically on this task suggests that both are phonetically disabled. Only one dependent variable—visual memory—actually distinguished these two groups. The present results suggest that many children classified as nonspecific in fact have difficulties processing the sounds of language.

This study suffers in the way that many of the subtype studies do: Their definition of a reading disability is questionable. As outlined by Siegel and Heaven (1986), grade scores or age levels are not as appropriate as percentiles for identifying a reading disability. In addition, the Gray Oral Reading Test (used to define the groups) consists of a series of graded oral reading passages. Although this study classified reading-disabled subjects into Boder's three subtypes, the dyseidetic group was ignored after the classification. It would be extremely valuable to know how the dyseidetic group performed on the Lindamood test, for example. If their performance was equally as poor as that of the other readers, considerable doubt would be cast on the dyseidetic category as a useful subtype. It is also important to know whether the dyseidetic group would in fact exhibit performance inferior to that of the other groups on the simultaneous gestalt processing tasks.

Malatesha and Dougan (1982) found that when Boder's scheme was used, dysphonetic and normal readers had different patterns of scores on a dichotic listening test. Again, this apparent heterogeneity appears to be a function of the definition used. First, 1-year grade-level retardation in reading was used as the criterion for reading disability. As noted earlier, grade-level retardation is not a valid measure because grade levels are ordinal rather than interval levels of measurement. Furthermore, it does not represent the true degree of difficulty at all developmental levels. Second, a reading comprehension test was used (Gates MacGinitic). Variables such as reading speed, vocabulary, prior knowledge, attention, and memory contribute to scores on this measure, and a child may achieve a low score for any or all of these reasons.

Evidence for the homogeneity of the reading-disabled population and a failure to validate the subtypes outlined by Boder comes from work by Van den Bos (1984). He predicted that the children Boder classified as dyseidetic should not have a deficit in processing auditorily presented letters because their problem is theoretically in processing visual information. In contrast, Van den Bos found that memory for auditorily presented or visually presented letters did not differentiate the dyseidetic from the dysphonetic dyslexic individuals by Boder's criterion. Conversely, Van den Bos predicted that according to Boder's criteria, dyseidetics should perform more poorly than do dysphonetic dyslexic

individuals on a letter-matching task because they presumably have difficulty with visual information processing. In fact, there were no significant differences between dysphonetic and dyseidetic participants on this task—all the dyslexic individuals performed significantly more poorly than did normally functioning individuals on this task. All the dyslexic participants had a particular problem with a task that involved determining whether two letters had the same name—a task that presumably relies on phonological processing skills. It should be noted that Van den Bos did not validate Boder's subtypes. Van den Bos used a criterion of poor word-recognition skills to define the dyslexic group. Therefore, he had poor readers in the sense that I believe the term should be used. A more appropriate definition of dyslexia resulted in homogeneity within the group.

In another reading performance-oriented system, Larsen and Parlenvi (1984) suggested that there may be significant individual differences and perhaps subtypes in groups of poor readers. In their study of reading in Sweden, they noted that some second-grade poor readers were not as disrupted as good readers in accuracy or rate of reading of inverted words, whereas others were more disrupted. However, these authors were not specific about the type of reading test used to define their groups; hence, they may have had a heterogeneous group of poor readers who represented a continuum of severity. Those readers whose performance was less disrupted or even possibly improved by the inverted stimuli may have been the very poor readers (dyslexic in the sense I support) who were reading through the visual route. The others may not have been really reading disabled in the traditional sense. As can be seen from the descriptions of the previously discussed studies, classification based on reading performance has not clearly differentiated valid subtypes of disabled readers.

Classification Based on Neuropsychological Models

A study by Kinsbourne and Warrington (1963b) represented one of the initial attempts to explore the possibility of distinct subgroups of dyslexic children. They divided children referred because of reading backwardness into two groups on the basis of WISC Verbal-Performance IQ discrepancies. Group 1 consisted of six children who had at least a 20-point Verbal-Performance (V-P) discrepancy in favor of performance. They were termed the language-retarded group. Group 2 consisted of seven children with a 20-point V-P discrepancy in favor of Verbal. These children were termed the Gerstmann group (Kinsbourne & Waningston, 1963a). Group 1 exhibited delays in speech acquisition, verbal comprehension, and verbal expression. Their mean reading and spelling ages were almost the same and were significantly lower than their arithmetic ages (WISC subtest). Group 2 exhibited finger agnosia as characterized by poor performance on tests of finger order and differentiation. They showed significant retardation in right-left orientation and in arithmetic difficulty. The mean spelling age was 1 year lower than the mean reading age. The mean arithmetic age was nearly the same as the reading age.

Although age levels rather than percentile scores were used in this study and therefore the exact severity of the academic skills deficit remains unknown, the findings are interesting because of the patterns they present. The language-disabled group with poorer reading and spelling performance; the Gerstmann group with poorer spelling, arithmetic, and handwriting performance; and a possible third group with both patterns of deficit have been identified by other investigators, such as the groups of Rourke et al., Siegel et al., and Fletcher et al. as elaborated earlier.

Johnson and Myklebust (1962, 1967) suggested that individuals can have auditory dyslexia and visual dyslexia. Their classification was based on clinical descriptions rather than empirical evidence. Persons with visual dyslexia appear to experience deficits in visual perception and in memory; consequently, they have visual discrimination problems that result in confusion of letters and words that look the same. They can make discriminations but only very slowly. Individuals with auditory dyslexia experience difficulty in remembering auditory stimuli and in stringing these stimuli into sequences. They experience problems in distinguishing similarities and differences in sounds, perceiving a sound within a word, synthesizing sounds into words, and dividing words into syllables. It is important to note that there is no reliable empirical evidence for these groups as distinct subtypes.

A similar attempt by Mattis, French, and Rapin (1975) and Mattis (1978) identified three subgroups of children with reading disorders: (a) language, (b) articulation and graphomotor, and (c) visual perception. The language-disordered group had difficulty discriminating similar sounds, repeating sentences, and following complex verbal commands (Token Test), but they had relatively intact visuospatial skills. The articulation and graphomotor group had adequate language skills, but people in this group had difficulties with articulation of speech sounds and copying shapes. A third group, the visuospatial-disordered group, had difficulty remembering visual stimuli, some problems with spatial concepts (Raven's Coloured Progressive Matrices), and relatively intact verbal skills. It is quite possible that the latter two groups were older and did not have reading problems that were as serious as those of the first group. The definition of reading disability used by Mattis et al. contributed to this apparent heterogeneity;

this is not to say that their classification scheme is incorrect. Rather, the heterogeneity in their sample may be a function of the *definition* of the reading-disabled group. Mattis et al. used children who were classified as retarded by two or more grades according to the WRAT. The problem with a grade-level retardation definition of reading disability has already been described. Although this scheme may not be a problem with younger children, it is with older children because a two-grade discrepancy between actual reading grade level and expected grade level may actually mean that the child has a relatively high score and therefore cannot be considered reading disabled. Information about the ages and reading percentile scores of the three subgroups was not presented, so we do not know if this is the case. The group called *visual-perceptual disorder* by Mattis et al. (1975) may have been older and may not have had as serious a reading problem (or even a reading problem at all). In addition, many of the skills measured by Mattis et al. (1975) seem to be deficient in this population; furthermore, without a normal comparison group, we do not know whether these results represent relative strengths and weaknesses or absolute low levels of performance by the groups.

Classification Based on Statistical Techniques

An example of a statistical approach to the definition of subtypes is that of Doehring, Trites, Patel, and Friedorowicz (1981), who investigated the interaction of subtypes of reading disabilities with language and neuropsychological deficits. A variety of tests of reading and reading-related skills were administered, and the results for the total sample and for a variety of subsamples were analyzed by factor analysis to ascertain the stability of the types of reading disabilities that were identified. Three factors emerged from the classification: Factor 1/Type O, difficulty with oral reading; Factor 2/Type A, auditory-visual association difficulty (difficulty in the types of silent reading skills that require the association of the spoken equivalents of printed letters, syllables, and words); and Factor 3/Type S, a sequencing deficit (difficulty with syllables and words as compared to letters and numbers).

After analyzing the reading test results, the authors attempted to explore the possibility that different types of language deficits might be involved in different types of reading disabilities. Twenty-two language measures were used to measure both lower level and higher level language skills. In general, it was found that individuals with reading problems were about as impaired in language skills as they were in reading skills. The pattern of language deficits suggested that the greatest difficulty was at relatively low levels of language skills (that is, phonemic segmentation and blending, serial naming, and morphophonemic knowledge). The language skills closest to normal involved the higher levels of semantic knowledge. The language test profiles of the three types were not as sharply differentiated as were their reading test profiles.

A battery of 37 neuropsychological tests was administered to determine the extent to which neuropsychological deficits interacted with each type of reading disability and to estimate the types of brain dysfunctions potentially associated with the reading disabilities. Factor analysis of the results did not differentiate any characteristic profiles of neuropsychological deficit. In addition, there was very little indication of any difference in relative incidence, localization, or severity of cerebral dysfunction among the three types of reading disabilities.

This study suffers from many of the same definitional problems as most other subtype studies do. A lag of approximately 2 years on reading measures defines the reading disability, and the study did not account for the fact that 2 years below grade level means very different things for a child in Grade 3 as opposed to a child in Grade 8. In this study, the age of the subjects sampled was extremely diverse (8–27 years), which means that there were enormous variations in the severity of the reading disability. It is hardly surprising that qualitative and quantitative differences in the reading performances of such a would emerge, but whether it makes sense to speak of subtypes rather than a range of performance depending on severity of deficits is questionable. The fact that normal readers scored below average in many related measures and individuals with reading problems scored in the normal range for some skills further confuses the interpretation. There seems to be a problem with the sensitivity of some of the measures used or alternatively with their relevance to a reading deficit. The volume of results at which one arrives after all these tests are administered is formidable but at the same time very confusing. It would probably make far more sense to break down the reading process itself into crucial areas and see how the participants performed in each area— for example, oral reading in context, word recognition, word attack, and silent reading. The findings from a more focused and detailed analysis of fewer measures might be more meaningful. The fact that 30–60% of the participants fell within the normal range on the oral reading tests makes one really wonder about the definition of *reading disability* in this study.

Furthermore, because a number of participants were classified into more than one type and had profiles characteristic of combined types, separation into three distinct groups becomes even more questionable. It seems that if one tested enough individuals (including normally functioning individuals) on enough measures, one would find enormous ranges of performances in both quality and quantity; it is questionable, however, how worthwhile it is to define them as different subtypes of a reading disability. The authors suggest that there seems to be a form of continuity between types, and I think that that is exactly what this study is all about. Most probably the authors have taken an extremely heterogeneous group of children in terms of reading performance and have emerged with three groups who are at different stages of the reading performance continuum. These styles of performing cannot be considered subtypes; rather, they represent different degrees of severity of a problem.

As with the language tests, the neuropsychological tests only reflected the heterogeneity of the group or in fact perhaps any reading-disabled group. With a more narrowed selection of measures and a detailed error analysis of actual reading performance (rather than a list of scores on so many measures), more meaningful subtypes might emerge. This study illustrates how inherent heterogeneity of the population under discussion affects subtypes. Doehring et al. found a significant overlap between reading-disabled and normal individuals on a variety of measures that tested the child's understanding of basic syntax using similar but not identical measures. There was also a great deal of variability within each of the subtypes that they identified. Siegel and Ryan (1984) have found virtually no overlap between reading-disabled and normally achieving children but found that the performance of the reading-disabled children was very significantly below that of normally achieving children of the same chronological age. Siegel and Ryan's subjects were homogeneous and selected on the basis of low scores on a word-reading test.

Rutter, Yule, and associates proposed the existence of two subtypes of reading disorders. They used a regression equation in which the expected reading level was predicted from a child's IQ score (e.g., Rutter, 1978; Rutter, Tizard, & Whitmore, 1970; Rutter & Yule, 1973; Yule, 1967; Yule, Rutter, Berger, & Thompson, 1974). According to these authors, if the child's reading level is significantly lower than that predicted from his or her IQ, then the child is said to be a *retarded reader.* They differentiate between backward readers (children who are at the bottom end of the reading attainment continuum) and retarded readers (children who are underachieving in relation to their chronological age and general level of intelligence) in sex distribution, neurological correlates, and association with speech and language disorders.

It should be noted that there was considerable overlap between the groups. Retarded readers who had (by definition) higher IQs were worse in their accuracy but not in comprehension and were worse in spelling but had higher scores in mathematics. We do not believe that these constitute meaningful subgroups. It is important to note that language measures (WISC) constituted part of the definition of IQ. Children with learning disabilities have language problems (Siegel, 1985a, 1985b; Siegel & Ryan, 1984; Vellutino, 1977, 1978, 1979); therefore, children will have lower IQ scores when a language-based test is used as a measure of IQ. It is impossible to measure IQ independently of language and reading skills. A definition in which subtypes are developed on the basis of IQ-reading level discrepancies therefore seems to be invalid (see previous discussion). The distinction between reading retardation and reading backwardness may represent a difference of severity in that children who are backward in reading have more cognitive deficits than do those who are retarded in reading (and hence have lower IQ scores).

Although Doehring (1984) notes that most subtype classifications of reading problems involve a visual nonverbal subtype, I contend that the appearance of this subtype is an artifact of the tests of reading used. When a subtype such as this one with visual nonverbal problems is used, I contend that they also have language problems, that they are the children with good phonics skills but low comprehension scores, or that their word recognition skills are adequate but because of attention difficulties they have problems with memory, speed, attention, strategies in relation to reading, or any combination of these problems.

Therefore, conclusive and convincing evidence of subtypes of reading disability has not emerged. In addition, there is homogeneity within the reading-disabled population. Apparent heterogeneity is a function of the definition used. As Doehring suggests, "The one simplifying assumption that I will continue to make for the present in my own work however is that the most profound reading disabilities involve difficulty in acquiring lower level coding and word recognition skills rather than higher-level skills and strategies" (Doehring, 1984, p. 211). If investigators use a word-recognition definition, phonics (nonword) definition, or both of reading disability, there will not be a significant amount of variability on relevant cognitive functions within the reading-disabled population.

Reading disability involves a problem with phonological processing, language, and memory for verbal information. Reading-disabled children can be differentiated from other LD children on these variables. Visuospatial and perceptual-motor problems may also occur in dyslexia, but they are not the basic problem, nor are they characteristic of all dyslexic individuals in the same way in which language problems are.

If a logically consistent definition of dyslexia is used, all dyslexic (reading disabled) children have problems with language.

A Simple Model of Subtypes

What emerges from this confusing array of studies is the fact that there are clearly two subtypes of learning disability—namely, a reading disability (dyslexia) and an arithmetic disability. These subtypes have been validated in child and adult populations (e.g. Rourke & Strang, 1978; Shafrir & Siegel, 1994b; Siegel & Ryan, 1988, 1989a, 1989b). Shafrir and Siegel (1994b) compared three groups—individuals with arithmetic disability (AD), reading disability (RD), and both reading and arithmetic disabilities (RAD), with a comparison group with normal achievement (NA)—on a variety of cognitive and achievement measures. The main findings were as follows: (a) Each of the groups differed significantly from the others on tests of reading, spelling, memory, and other cognitive measures; (b) both the RD and RAD groups showed a deficit in phonological processing, vocabulary, spelling, and short-term memory; (c) the AD group performed similarly to the NA group on pseudoword reading and phonological processing but performed more poorly than did the NA group on word reading and vocabulary; (d) on many tasks, the RAD group performed more poorly than did the other groups; and (e) the AD and RAD groups performed more poorly than did the NA and RD groups on a visuospatial task. Therefore, this classification scheme for the subtyping of learning disabilities in adults appears to have validity.

Spelling: A Digression

Problems with spelling do exist, but they can co-occur with either reading or arithmetic difficulties, and it is rare to find a child who has difficulties with spelling and no problems in any other areas of functioning. Some children may have specific difficulties with spelling when they are required to write the word from memory rather than when they are required to recognize the correct spelling of a word.

In addition, English words are characterized by both regular spelling (e.g., singing, print)—that is, words in which the letter-sound correspondences are predictable—and irregular spelling—that is, spelling that is not predicted from the rules of spelling-sound correspondence (e.g., island, knight). The possibility exists that children may be able to spell regular words but have more difficulty with the irregular words. In any case, spelling difficulties do occur but (as noted earlier) usually in combination with other problems. Furthermore, studies such as Jorm (1981), and Lennox and Siegel (1993, 1996) have found significant differences in the understanding of letter-sound correspondence rules and the orthographic awareness between children who were poor readers and spellers and children who were only poor spellers. On the basis of findings such as these and for the reasons discussed previously, reading and spelling need to be treated as separate variables.

TYPES OF LEARNING DISABILITIES

Over the past 30 years, it has become clear that there are two major clusters of learning difficulties. The most commonly known is a reading disability, sometimes called dyslexia. There is no difference in meaning between the terms *dyslexia* and *reading disability*. Another equally prevalent but less commonly known disability is an arithmetic (mathematics) disability, sometimes called *nonverbal learning disability, developmental output failure, writing-arithmetic disability,* or *visual-spatial disability*. Although there is, admittedly, some heterogeneity within the two major clusters, they do share enough common characteristics to be considered as specific entities.

Reading Disabilities

Depending on the theoretical bias of the particular investigator, the country, the circumstances, and so on, the word *dyslexia* may be used instead of *reading disability*. However, there is no difference between dyslexia and a reading disability; they are exactly the same.

Dyslexia involves difficulties with phonological processing, including such abilities as knowing the relationship between letters and sounds and phonological awareness—that is, the ability to segment the speech stream into separate elements. Over the years, a consensus has emerged that one core deficit in dyslexia is a severe difficulty with phonological processing (e.g., Rack, Snowling, & Olson, 1992; Siegel, 1993b; Snowling, 1980; Stanovich, 1988a, 1988b). Children with a reading disability have a core deficit in phonological processing. The evidence that is available clearly demonstrates that adults with dyslexia have deficits in phonological processing (e.g., Bruck, 1990, 1992; Elbro, Neilsen, & Petersen, 1994; Felton, Naylor, & Wood, 1990; Gottardo, Siegel, & Stanovich, 1997; Greenberg, Ehri, & Perin, 1997; Pennington, Van Orden, Smith, Green, & Haith, 1990; Pratt & Brady, 1988; Read & Ruyter, 1985; Russell, 1982; Scarborough, 1984; Shafrir & Siegel, 1994a, 1994b; Siegel, 1998). Most individuals with dyslexia show problems in the area of memory and language (Siegel & Ryan, 1984, 1988; Snowling, 1980; Stanovich, 1988a, 1988b; Vellutino, 1978). Usually individuals with dyslexia have spelling problems, but the presence of spelling difficulties *without* reading difficulties does not indicate dyslexia. A definition of dyslexia

that captures the other problems that often co-occur with it is illustrated in Padget et al. (1996):

> Dyslexia is a language-based learning disorder that is biological in origin and primarily interferes with the acquisition of print literacy (reading, writing, and spelling). Dyslexia is characterized by poor decoding and spelling abilities as well as deficit in phonological awareness and/or phonological manipulation. These primary characteristics may co-occur with spoken language difficulties and deficits in short-term memory. Secondary characteristics may include poor reading comprehension (due to the decoding and memory difficulties) and poor written expression, as well as difficulty organizing information for study and retrieval. (p. 55)

Current theories of the development of reading skills in English stress that phonological processing is the most significant underlying cognitive process (Stanovich, 1988a, 1988b, 1988c). Children and adults with a reading disability have difficulty with phonological processing. Phonological processing involves a variety of functions, but in the context of the development of reading skills, the most significant in the association of sounds with letters or combinations of letters. This function is referred to as the understanding of grapheme-phoneme conversion rules, and because of the irregular nature of the correspondences in English, the learning of these rules is a very complex process. The child who is learning to read must map oral language onto written language by decomposing the word into phonemes and associating each letter (or combination of letters) with these phonemes.

The task of the beginning reader is to extract these grapheme-phoneme conversion rules. The alternative is simply to memorize each word as a visual configuration and to associate a meaning with it. This kind of learning may occur, but it is inefficient and makes tremendous demands on visual memory. In English, no one-to-one correspondence exists between a letter (or letters) and a sound. The same letter represents different sounds, and the same sound may be represented by different letters.

In an alphabetic language such as English, the best measure of phonological processing skills is the reading of pseudowords—that is, pronounceable combinations of letters that can be read by the application of grapheme-phoneme conversion rules but that are, of course, not real words in English. Examples, include such pseudowords as *shum, laip,* and *cigbet*. Pseudowords can be read by anyone who is familiar with the grapheme-phoneme conversion rules of English even though they are not real words and have not been encountered in print or in spoken language before.

The development of the ability to read pseudowords has been studied extensively (e.g., Calfee, Lindamood, &

Lindamood, 1973; Hogaboam & Perfetti, 1978; Siegel & Ryan, 1988; Venezky & Johnson, 1973). Ample evidence indicates that children with dyslexia have a great deal of difficulty reading pseudowords. Studies such as those of Bruck (1988), Ehri and Wilce (1983), Snowling (1980), Siegel and Ryan (1988), and Waters, Bruck, and Seidenberg (1985) have shown that disabled readers have more difficulty reading pseudowords than do normal readers matched on either chronological age or reading level. For example, Siegel and Ryan (1988) studied the development of the ability to read pseudowords in normal and disabled readers aged 7–14 years. By the age of 9, the normal readers were quite proficient and performed at almost a perfect level for even the most difficult pseudowords, with—in some cases—as many as three syllables. Similarly, Backman, Bruck, Hebert, and Seidenberg (1984) showed that 10-year-olds perform as well as do adults on tasks involving the reading of pseudowords; however, Siegel and Ryan (1988) found that the performance of the reading-disabled children was quite different. These children appear to acquire these reading skills very late in development, and even reading-disabled children at the age of 14 were performing no better than were normal readers at the age of 7.

To control (at least partially) for experience with print, Siegel and Ryan (1988) used a comparison of disabled and normal readers matched on reading grade level. Even when the disabled readers and the normal readers were matched on reading level (hence, the disabled readers were considerably older than the normal readers), the performance of the reading-disabled individuals on a task involving the reading of pseudowords was significantly poorer than that of the normal readers.

Thus, difficulties with phonological processing seem to be the fundamental problem of children with reading disability, and this problem continues to adulthood. Many adults with a reading disability become reasonably fluent readers but still have difficulty reading pseudowords or read them very slowly (e.g., Barwick & Siegel, 1996; Bruck, 1990).

For children learning to read English, the learning of grapheme-phoneme conversion rules is a result of systematic instruction, and the extraction of the rules is a result of repeated encounters with print. No evidence is available as to how much of the development of decoding skills is a result of specific instruction in the grapheme-phoneme conversion rules and how much is a result of experience with print. In any case, the understanding of the grapheme-phoneme conversion rules develops rapidly in the first years of experience with print under normal conditions.

Some individuals have difficulties only with writing, spelling, or both. Because these written language problems usually occur in the context of problems with reading problems, arithmetic and mathematics problems, or both, the existence of a separate written language disability is not clearly established, nor is there a clear definition of it, especially in the adult population. Spelling difficulties can occur in the absence of severe reading disabilities (e.g., Bruck & Waters, 1988; Lennox & Siegel, 1993). There also may be problems with understanding or producing language. These problems have not been documented as distinct learning disabilities and are often components of dyslexia. If learning disabilities are to be treated as measurable entities and if individuals are to receive educational services based on the presence of a single or multiple learning disabilities, it is then obviously important to determine what these learning disabilities are.

Arithmetic Disabilities

Individuals with developmental output failure or writing-arithmetic disability have difficulty with computational arithmetic and written language, typically in the absence of reading difficulties, although this disability can co-occur with dyslexia. They often have difficulties with spelling and have problems with fine-motor coordination, visuospatial processing, and short-term and long-term memory (e.g., multiplication tables), but they usually have good oral language skills (Fletcher, 1985; Johnson & Mykelbust, 1967; Kinsbourne & Warrington, 1963; Kosc, 1974; Levine, Oberklaid, & Meltzer, 1981; Morrison & Siegel, 1991a, 1991b; Rourke, 1991; Rourke & Finlayson, 1978; Shafrir & Siegel, 1994b; Siegel & Feldman, 1983; Siegel & Linder, 1984; Spellacy & Peter, 1978). Rourke and his associates (e.g., Rourke, Del Dotto, Rourke, & Casey, 1990; Rourke & Tsatsanis, 1996) have described a syndrome called *nonverbal learning disabilities* that is similar to writing-arithmetic disability. However, the operational definition of this learning disability is problematic; it is not clear how a diagnosis can be made. Often, these individuals have verbal IQ scores significantly higher than performance IQ, but this discrepancy is neither necessary nor sufficient to make the diagnosis. Often, they have lower arithmetic scores than reading scores, but the differences between these scores are not always significant (e.g., Rourke et al., 1990). (For an extended discussion of the definitional issue and conceptualization of this disability, see Morrison & Siegel, 1991a.)

Investigators (e.g., Fletcher, 1985b; Rourke & Finlayson, 1978; Rourke & Strang, 1978; Siegel & Feldman, 1983; Siegel & Ryan, 1984, 1988, 1989a, 1989b) have found evidence that children with specific arithmetic deficits and average or above-average word recognition scores on the WRAT appear to have a variety of cognitive and neuropsychological deficits that differentiate them from children with at least reading deficits as defined by depressed scores on the Reading subtest on the WRAT. The cognitive and neuropsychological profiles of children identified as specific arithmetic-disabled are also different from those of normally achieving children.

Evidence (Fletcher, 1985b; Siegel & Linder, 1984; Siegel & Ryan, 1984, 1988, 1989a, 1989b) suggests that those children meeting the criteria of the specific arithmetic-disabled subtype have deficits in short-term and working memory that are dependent on the type of stimulus and the aspect of memory assessed. Specifically, Siegel and Linder (1984), in a study of the role of phonemic coding in short-term memory, compared three groups of children—one with reading disabilities (as defined by scores on the WRAT Reading subtest of equal to or below the 25th percentile and no cutoff on the other two WRAT subtests), a second with arithmetic disabilities (as defined by scores on the WRAT Arithmetic subtest of equal to or above the 30th percentile), and a normally achieving group (as defined by scores of greater than or equal to the 30th percentile on all three WRAT subtests). The children, aged 7–13, were administered a series of tasks that involved the visual or auditory presentation of rhyming and nonrhyming letters and either an oral or written response. Patterns and levels of performance were compared statistically across three age groups (i.e., 7–8, 9–11, 12–13) and between each subtype and normally achieving children. Due to statistical problems, noncomparable age distributions, and small sample sizes, it was not possible to compare across subtypes. Results indicated that both older disabled groups—like their normal counterparts—had significantly poorer recall of rhyming as opposed to nonrhyming letters (except for the oldest—12–13 years—arithmetic-disabled group, in which the authors suggest that the children may be functioning at the upper limit of their visual short-term memory). For stimuli presented visually, the overall performance levels of both LD groups were significantly lower than those of the normally achieving group. For the auditory stimuli, only the reading-disabled group differed significantly from the normally achieving peers.

Fletcher (1985b) found differences in memory tasks between LD groups as defined by WRAT scores. He compared four groups of LD children (a reading-spelling-disabled group, a reading-spelling-arithmetic-disabled group, a spelling-arithmetic-disabled group, and an arithmetic-disabled group) and a normally achieving group of children on storage and retrieval aspects of memory for verbal and nonverbal stimuli. He found that relative to the normally achieving controls, both the arithmetic and the arithmetic-spelling-disabled subgroups had significantly lower storage

and retrieval scores on the nonverbal task but did not differ from each other; the reading-spelling subgroup differed only on retrieval scores on the verbal task; and the reading-spelling-arithmetic subgroup differed on the retrieval scores on the verbal task and storage and retrieval scores on the nonverbal task. As with Siegel and Linder (1984), the differences between subgroups depended on the type of stimulus (verbal vs. nonverbal) and the aspect of memory (storage or retrieval) being assessed.

Siegel and Ryan (1988) also compared reading-disabled (as defined by WRAT subtest scores), specific arithmetic-disabled (as defined by WRAT subtest scores), and normally achieving children on a variety of skills involving grammatical sensitivity, phonology, and short-term memory. In general, it was found that older specific arithmetic-disabled children performed in a manner similar to that of the normally achieving group in grammatical sensitivity and phonological tasks. Some exceptions were found in that the arithmetic-disabled children in the 7–10 age group performed more poorly on a sentence repetition task; this difficulty was attributed to the short-term memory component of the task. Additionally, this age group performed more poorly than did normally achieving children on the nonword spelling sections (a writing task) of the phonics task. However, in tasks that measure short-term memory (phonological coding), the specific arithmetic-disabled group performed in a manner similar to that of the reading-disabled group and significantly more poorly than did the normally achieving group. The authors conclude that although both of the two disabled groups (compared with normally achieving children) have deficits in short-term memory, only the reading-disabled group had deficits in tasks said to represent a language disorder.

Siegel and Ryan (1989a) examined the same groups, using two working memory tasks—one involving sentences and the other involving counting. Again, the disabled groups differed from each other on the types of memory deficits observed. The reading-disabled group differed from the normally achieving children on both tasks, whereas the arithmetic-disabled children differed from their normally achieving peers only on the counting task. It appears from the research (Fletcher, 1985b; Siegel & Linder, 1984; Siegel & Ryan, 1988, 1989a, 1989b) that although both subtypes of LD children have deficits in short-term and working memory, problems in children with reading deficits are more generalized and involve both verbal and nonverbal aspects of memory, whereas those in children with arithmetic deficits and normal or above-normal reading are more limited to visual, nonverbal, and numerical material.

Evidence from a number of sources (Fletcher, 1985b; Rourke & Finlayson, 1978; Share, Moffitt, & Silva, 1988;

Siegel & Feldman, 1983; Spellacy & Peter, 1978; Webster, 1979) indicates that specific arithmetic-disabled children (as defined by deficient scores on the WRAT Arithmetic subtest and the age-appropriate scores on the WRAT Reading and Spelling subtests—Group 3) have age-appropriate auditory-perceptual and verbal abilities but are deficient on measures of visual-perception and visuospatial abilities. However, reading-disabled children (as defined by being relatively proficient at arithmetic as compared with their WRAT Reading and Spelling subtest scores—Group 2) have age-appropriate visual-perception and visuospatial abilities but are deficient on measures of auditory-perceptual and verbal abilities (Rourke & Finlayson, 1978). Also, Group 3 (arithmetic-disabled) children exhibit difficulty in tasks such as the Halstead Category Test, which require higher order visuospatial analysis and visual-perceptual organization (Strang & Rourke, 1983b). They also appear to exhibit deficits in measures of psychomotor abilities and on tests such as the Tactile Performance Tests (Reitan & Davison, 1974), the Grooved Pegboard Test, and the Maze Test designed to identify tactile-perceptual impairment (Rourke & Strang, 1978; Siegel & Feldman, 1983; Spellacy & Peter, 1978). On the other hand, Rourke and Strang (1978) and Strang and Rourke (1983) found that Group 2 children (relatively proficient in arithmetic, compared with their reading and spelling) are proficient at these tasks.

In addition, Rourke and Strang (1978) claim that the arithmetic subgroup (Group 3) exhibited normal right-hand performance but impaired left-hand performance—the exact opposite of the Group 2 children, who had impaired right-hand performance but normal left-hand performance. Strang and Rourke (1983a, 1983b) suggest that the arithmetic-disabled subgroup has deficiencies in nonverbal concept-formation compared with other disabled subgroups. Specifically, when the types of errors made of the Arithmetic subtest of the WRAT were analyzed, it was found that the specific arithmetic subtype tended to make a larger number of errors, make a greater variety of errors, and attempted to answer questions without an apparent understanding of the strategies needed to solve the problems (Strang & Rourke, 1985a, 1985b). This error pattern was not found in children with reading disabilities (Group 2).

As with the research with memory deficits cited earlier, Rourke and Finlayson (1978), Rourke and Strang (1978), and Strang and Rourke (1983a, 1983b) suggest that the characteristics described are different from those of other learning-disabled students (who showed deficits on all the WRAT subtests, Group 1, or just on the reading and spelling subtests compared with the arithmetic subtest, Group 2). This finding has led Rourke et al. (Rourke, 1982, 1983, 1985, 1987; Rourke

& Finlayson, 1978; Rourke & Fisk, 1988) to hypothesize that those children with arithmetic deficits belong to the larger nonverbal LD group with right-hemisphere processing problems, whereas those children with deficits in reading as well as arithmetic belong to the larger linguistic learning-disabled group with left-hemisphere processing problems. Clearly, however, children who only have severe deficits in arithmetic can be differentiated from children with reading difficulties and from normally achieving children on cognitive and neuropsychological profiles.

In light of the previously described controversy and research findings, the use of specificity assumptions in the definition of learning disabilities is questionable; this is true regardless of whether one refers to domain specificity (the limitation of the disability to one or two cognitive areas) or population specificity (failure to use subtypes).

ASSESSMENT OF LEARNING DISABILITIES

Determining who is learning disabled requires careful and systematic assessment. The three following questions address the assessment of learning disabilities: (a) How should achievement be measured; (b) which tests should be used; and (c) what cutoff scores should be used to identify a learning disability?

The Measurement of Achievement

The arguments about the definition of learning disability center on the determination of whether an individual meets specific criteria for the diagnosis of a disability. First of all, to measure whether there are significant difficulties, one must use a systematic assessment of these academic areas; standardized (norm-referenced) tests appear to be the best way to do this. Why use norm referenced tests? The answer is simple: Those making the assessment want to compare an individual with others of the same age and know whether that person has a *significant* problem. A standardized test is the best way to accomplish this task. Nonstandardized assessments can be used, but they do not provide normative information that can be used for the purposes of comparison. With a nonstandardized or informal assessment, it is impossible to know whether an individual has made the number and type of errors that are typical of his or her age group and therefore are normal and expected, or whether the errors are atypical and unexpected and indicative of a problem. Nonstandardized tests may play an important role (to be discussed later), but the core assessment should use standardized tests. However, nonstandardized assessments do have a role in the evaluation of writing; this role is discussed later in the chapter.

To assess learning disabilities, there are several types of tests that should be used. Specifically, an assessment of an individual for the possibility of a reading disability should include a measure of word-recognition skills. Word recognition is one of the critical building blocks in gaining meaning from print, and it is important to know whether these basic skills in this area are significantly below average (Stanovich, 1982). An assessment should include a reading test that involves the reading of what are called pseudowords—pronounceable combinations of English letters that can be sounded out with the basic rules of grapheme-phoneme correspondences. This type of test assesses the awareness of the phonological aspects of a language that is the key to decoding words in an alphabetic language such as English. Difficulties with these phonological skills are the basis of a reading disability (e.g., Bruck, 1990; Felton et al., 1990; Shafrir & Siegel, 1994a; Siegel & Ryan, 1988). A test of text reading—specifically, a reading comprehension test—should be included. Obviously, the measurement of text reading skills is particularly important to measure what individuals remember and understand from what they have read.

There should be a test of spelling involving the dictation of words; this parallels the type of spelling required in writing in the academic setting.

There should be a test of computational arithmetic skills to determine what the individual understands about the fundamental arithmetic operations. An assessment of mathematical problem-solving skills should be included.

There should also be an assessment of writing skills; this type of assessment is quite difficult for a variety of reasons. The time involved to allow someone to write may be extensive because one must allow time for planning as well as for the actual writing. Also, many individuals have learned to use a computer and prefer to write using a computer. Therefore, a proper assessment of writing might use a computer, which may not be feasible in most assessment contexts. It may be acceptable to ask the individual to bring in a sample of his or her writing, but some type of brief assessment in the context of the assessment is useful. The scoring of these written products is subjective and there does not appear to be agreement on what constitutes a widely accepted scoring system. However, Berninger (1994) has proposed a system that appears to have potential to consistently evaluate writing. She suggests six dimensions to evaluate writing: (a) handwriting quality (legibility), (b) handwriting fluency (number of words copied within time limits), (c) spelling single words from dictation (on standardized lists of increasing difficulty), (d) spelling in composition (percentage of correctly spelled words), (e) composition fluency (number of words produced within time limits), and (f) composition quality (content and organization of paragraph construction).

Identification of whether there is a learning disability should use a simple system. Brief tests of word recognition, decoding (pseudoword reading), reading comprehension, spelling, writing, and computational arithmetic and mathematical problem solving will detect most (if not all) of the learning disabilities. A low score on any of these tests is a danger signal. More detailed testing can then be conducted, but any testing should be related to remediation and not used without consideration of what new and useful information is provided by the test and whether it is really necessary—a point that is discussed in detail later in this chapter.

Types of Tests

There is considerable confusion in the field about how to measure achievement. Attempts at defining and studying learning disabilities suffer from a common fallacy of assuming that all tests that have the same label (e.g., intelligence test, reading test) measure the same skill (Siegel & Heaven, 1986; Siegel et al., 1985). When one considers the area of achievement tests, the labeling fallacy becomes even clearer. There appears to be almost an infinite variety of ways to measure reading, spelling, and arithmetic. The choice of which tests to use can determine whether a disability will be found. Consider the case of measuring reading achievement.

There are four types of material that are typically found in reading tests: (a) pseudowords, (b) single words, (c) sentences, and (d) paragraphs. For the reading of pseudowords, the individual is asked to read a set of pronounceable combinations of letters that test the understanding of the relationship between letters or groups of letters and their sounds. This type of test is simple and direct and measures a fundamental skill.

Tests of the reading of single, real words typically require that the individual read a set of words aloud. These words may vary on several dimensions, but usually these dimensions are not systematically assessed. For example, words may be regular—that is, they follow the letter-sound correspondence rules of English (e.g., *fat, block*)—or they may be exceptions to these rules—that is, they involve irregularity or unpredictable letter-sound correspondence (e.g., *have, said, island, sword*). A person may have difficulty with the irregular but not the regular ones. The words may be more familiar and in the person's vocabulary, such as *cat, book,* and *red,* or they may be less familiar, such as *predatory, terpsichorean,* and *oligarchy.* Obviously, what is familiar and what is unknown depends on the age, vocabulary, and experience of the individual. Some words may be read correctly because they have been encountered before, whereas others may be read incorrectly (but almost correctly; e.g., *intrigue* read *in-tri-gue* instead of *in-treeg*) because they are not part of the individual's vocabulary and have not been encountered before. The confounding of familiarity with other dimensions of a word makes the construction of a word-reading list a difficult task. In the case of each particular word, one simply does not know when a person reads a word correctly whether he or she has merely memorized it. Note that pseudowords do not present this difficulty.

The reading of both words and pseudowords assesses the basic problem in a reading disability—that is, difficulty with phonological processing; both tasks are relatively straightforward. However, the measurement of text processing becomes more complex. Text processing is typically measurable by tests that involve the reading of sentences and paragraphs. In both cases, there are often clues about the word from the surrounding context. Typically, nouns follow articles, verbs follow subjects, adjectives precede nouns, and so on. When an individual reads a word in context correctly, we do not know whether he or she has read the word or made a good guess from the context. Note that this problem is not an issue with the reading of single words or pseudowords.

The reading of sentences or paragraphs may occur silently or aloud. If the reading is silent, there is no way of assessing what the person is actually reading, although this type of reading may be more similar to what occurs in many reading situations. Questions about what has been read are the principal means to assess comprehension. In most cases, memory is a very important aspect of the testing of sentence and paragraph comprehension. Often, the material is removed so that it is not available when the questions are asked. The person may have read quite well but may forget the answer to the question. Even when the material is available, the individual's performance is timed, or a fixed time is allowed to complete the test. At least some of the variance between individuals may be caused by variations in reading rate or speed of task completion—not a differential understanding of the material. There is, however, a significant difference between a slow reader and one who may not even be able to decode the words in the first place. Some students are able to decode the words and answer the questions on a reading comprehension test but need more time. Some have a problem with decoding the words. An assessment should be able to differentiate these two difficulties.

Reading tests vary in the output or type of response that is required. Some require an oral output that may involve some degree of facility with expressive language, whereas others require a written output—for example, answering multiple-choice questions. Still others involve having the person select a synonym for a word; in reality, this test is a measure of vocabulary. An individual may select the incorrect word not because of poor reading skill, but because he or she is not sure of the correct synonym.

The actual comprehension questions themselves may vary in several dimensions. They may involve inferences, memory for details, or the general point of the passage. It is very likely that a large part of reading comprehension ability consists of memory skills (e.g., Tal & Siegel, 1996). The individual must decode words and obtain meaning from them, but also he or she must retain the information in working memory and be able to answer questions about the content of the reading passage. It seems apparent, however, that memory is still a significant factor in tasks in which recall of exact wording or details is not essential. In these cases, the meaning must be retained and then operated on in some manner to produce an expected answer.

The individual's familiarity with the material in the text can determine how the person will score on a reading comprehension test (e.g., Drum, Calfee, & Cook, 1981; Marr & Gormley, 1982; Schneider et al., 1989). For example, Schneider et al. found that background knowledge about soccer influenced comprehension of and memory for a story dealing with soccer, but there were no significant differences between children with high and low verbal aptitude skills. Therefore, background knowledge was a critical factor in text comprehension, but verbal ability was not.

Time to read can also be an integral part of the reading score. A number of factors can contribute to differences in the time taken to read a passage. For example, a person who recalled information about the story may have a faster time than does someone who could not recall the target information but who could remember its spatial location and look back quickly, who may in turn have a faster time than does a person who could not remember anything about the target information and had to search throughout the passage. Daneman (1984) has reported that much of the variance in reading comprehension scores disappears if individuals are allowed to look back at the passage that has just been read.

Another difficulty with reading comprehension tests is that frequently the questions can be answered with a reasonable amount of accuracy without reading or comprehending the passage (e.g., Tal & Siegel, 1996). Such questions as *Where was the cow kept?* can be answered by good guessing; cows are not likely to be kept in cars, closets, or bathtubs.

Obviously, the problem with having so much variability in the measurement of reading comprehension is that many different skills are assessed. Theoretically, there are many types of possible reading difficulties if this kind of measure of reading is used because the person could have a problem in any one or more of these components. Clearly, some of these combinations are more likely than others are, but the point is that it is unclear which dimensions are creating the problem when the individual achieves a low score on one of these sentence or paragraph reading tests. An individual may perform poorly on the more complex reading tests for any one of a number of reasons. For example, an individual may read a paragraph aloud correctly but forget the answer to a question or may read correctly but slowly. In reading single words, the person may produce a good phonetic but inaccurate rendering of a low-frequency word. The only reading task that is not confounded with other dimensions is the reading of pseudowords.

The Use of Cutoff Scores to Identify a Learning Disability

The question arises as to how low a score should be in order to identify a learning disability. One of the aspects of the definitional issues is that we are not dealing with a clearly identifiable entity when we speak of a learning disability. Andrew Ellis (1985) has noted, in regard to dyslexia, the proper comparison is with obesity, not measles:

> For people of any given age and height there will be an uninterrupted continuum for painfully thin to inordinately fat. It is entirely arbitrary where we draw the line between 'normal' and 'obese,' but that does not prevent obesity being a real and worrying condition nor does it prevent research into the causes and cures of obesity being both valuable and necessary. . . . Therefore, to ask how prevalent dyslexia is in the general population will be as meaningful, and as meaningless, as asking how prevalent obesity is. The answer will depend entirely upon where the line is drawn. (p. 172)

Measles is easy to diagnose because of the spots. People with learning disabilities have no spots, only some test scores. In a manner similar to the diagnosis of obesity, it is not clear at what point or how low the score is for the person to be considered learning disabled or how overweight a person must be before he or she is called obese. In the most extreme cases, it is clear. However, we are really dealing with degrees of severity and not with a clear question of absence or presence, except in the more extreme cases when the diagnosis is easy.

Deciding on the appropriate cutoff score below which one identifies a learning disability is problematic. As a guideline, many have typically used scores below the 25th percentile (e.g., Fletcher, 1985; Rourke, 1991). This cutoff is arbitrary, but there is some evidence of the validity of this score. First of all, a number of studies have found that this score separates learning disabled from normally achieving individuals on a variety of tasks (e.g., Fletcher, 1985; Rourke & Finlayson, 1978; Shaywitz, Fletcher, & Escobar, 1990; Siegel & Ryan, 1988). Does that mean that 25% of the population will be called learning disabled on the basis of that test? In reality, this is not the case, and this cutoff identifies about 7–8% of the population as learning disabled (Fletcher et al., 1994; Rourke & Finlayson, 1978; Shaywitz et al., 1990). Second, in this author's experience, this score is correlated with teachers' and parents' perceptions of children's problems in school and with the self-report of adults who report academic difficulties. Thus, the use of the 25th percentile as a cutoff score is correlated with observations in the real world. However, there is no way of knowing what is a valid cutoff score; there is no magic number to separate learning-disabled from non-learning-disabled individuals. An argument could just as easily be made for the 20th percentile or the 15th percentile instead of the 25th percentile. No blood test, X ray, or magnetic imaging technique can be used to diagnose a learning disability. However, for the educational system to identify who will receive the accommodations and remediation, we must take a continuous variable—for example, reading performance—and make it a dichotomous one.

A Simple Model

In this field there are issues of what constitutes appropriate assessment for learning disabilities. It certainly is the tradition to do extensive additional testing besides achievement testing. However, the usefulness of additional testing for the *identification* of learning disabilities is not clear. It is likely that the primary reasons for doing assessments are to document the existence of a learning disability and to recommend appropriate remediation and accommodations. In order to accomplish these aims, the achievement testing described previously is clearly needed. Typically, tests of cognitive processes and intelligence tests are included in many assessments. Do we really need tests of auditory memory, visual memory, language, and visual closure? Is there such an entity as auditory memory? Suppose the stimuli for an auditory memory task are words and the individual is asked to repeat them, or suppose they are musical phrases or melodies and the person is asked to discriminate them. Would conclusions about auditory memory be the same if these diverse stimuli were used? The question should always be *How does the task or test being used in the assessment relate to the determination of the learning disability and the provision of remediation or accommodations?* Of course, the individual may be interested in learning more about his or her strengths and weaknesses. An extended assessment may also be valid for these reasons. However, it is not necessary to define the learning disability to propose accommodations or remedial strategies.

Surber (1985) has summarized the problems with lengthy and detailed reports that include measures of cognitive processes and intelligence tests:

> At the opposite end of the continuum, some of the more lengthy reports include every detail of the evaluation process, whether relevant or not. Both novice and experienced readers are left to wade through the jargon, attempting to ferret out the key elements that have relevance for the student and the teacher in the classroom. Consequently, items of greatest relevance become diluted in the sea of information being washed ashore. (p. 162)

There were a number of problems with the assessments of learning disability. The evaluations that I have seen have resembled a patchwork quilt in which none of the squares were the same. Each evaluation uses different tests, different terminology, and different labels for the learning disability. Here are some examples of the types of learning disabilities that were reported to exist: language-based learning disability, subtle verbal processing, attentional and long-term memory limitations, difficulty in visual processing speed, statistically significant disparity between relative conceptual language strengths compared with mathematics and written output, slow processing speed, visuoperceptual processing inefficiencies, problems with the ability to process auditory and visual information, mild frontal lobe disorder, and poor auditory processing.

The process of assessing whether there is a learning disability has been made unnecessarily complex. Standardized tests of reading, spelling, arithmetic calculation, and mathematical problem solving as described earlier are essential. Obtaining a sample of writing is important. Other tests may be done for interest or research but they are *not* essential to the diagnosis of a learning disability.

In addition to the achievement tests discussed earlier, an important part of any assessment is the use of analyses of errors. Systematic analyses of errors may provide useful information about an individual's level of functioning in reading, spelling, and arithmetic, and they may provide information about appropriate accommodations. Numerous studies such as those of Barwick and Siegel (1996); Bruck and Waters (1988); Fowler, Shankweiler, and Liberman (1979); Guthrie and Siefert (1977); Lennox and Siegel (1993, 1996); McBride and Siegel (1997); Pennington et al. (1986); Siedenberg (1985); Smiley, Pascquale, and Chandler, (1976); Sprenger-Charolles and Siegel (1997); Tal and Siegel (1996); Weber (1970); Venezky and Johnson (1973); and Werker, Bryson, and Wassenberg (1989) have used analyses of errors as a means to understanding the nature of the difficulties in individuals with learning disabilities. A good assessment should systematically analyze the errors made by individuals.

Error analysis also provides some information about the types of questions the individual was able to answer correctly. For example, are the spelling errors good phonological equivalents of the word to be spelled (e.g., *nature* spelled as *nachure*)? Or are they good visual errors—that is, a close match to the visual form of the word (e.g., *nature* written as *natur;* e.g., Lennox & Siegel, 1993, 1996)? Analyses such as these help us understand the strategies that the individual is using and can provide guidelines for remediation.

Finally, an assessment should include a direct interview with the student to analyze strengths as well as weaknesses not detected by achievement tests. Many individuals with learning disabilities have talents in the areas of art, dancing, mechanics, music, sports, or any combination of these. For example, both Agatha Christie and W. B. Yeats had learning disabilities (Miner & Siegel, 1992; Siegel, 1988a) that can be documented but obviously were individuals with considerable talent. The recognition of these strengths is important to the development of educational strategies and to the self-esteem of the individual with learning disabilities (e.g., Vail, 1990).

REMEDIATION AND ACCOMMODATION

The following list includes some remedial techniques that are useful for helping individuals with learning disabilities.

For children, the following remedial measures are recommended for learning difficulties:

- To enhance word recognition skills, a word-family approach to draw attention to common word patterns (e.g., *cat, bat, sat, hat that, fat, rat, mat*) can be used.
- Talking books, books, or both can be used.
- Textbooks on tape should be provided if possible.
- The use of high-interest, low-vocabulary books.
- The use of procedures such as cloze tasks to improve the understanding of syntax.
- The use of a language experience approach—allowing the dictation of stories and then using the words from these stories as the basis for reading vocabulary.
- The use of a calculator should be considered to help with arithmetic facts and multiplication tables.
- The use of a computer (word processor) is encouraged; this may help improve the quality of written work. Using a computer spell check often and early in the writing process will ensure that the student sees correct spellings of words to enhance knowledge of common word patterns.

- Consideration should be given to the use of a tape recorder for projects, book reports, and so on, allowing the teacher to hear the quality of the ideas without relying on the written products.
- Copying from the blackboard is difficult; alternatives should be considered. For example, class handouts, photocopying other students' notes, or tape recording oral lessons may be an option.

The following *additional* recommendations should be considered for adults:

- Teaching metacognitive strategies to help individuals with learning disabilities enhances their learning (for a detailed discussion, see, e.g., Butler, 1995, 1998; Montague, 1997).
- Encouragement of self-monitoring strategies to organize information and to avoid confusion when doing more than one activity. Strategies could include drawing plans or making lists to follow sequential steps from a manual or verbal instructions.
- A literacy program and basic skills training in reading and arithmetic is a possibility for some individuals functioning at a very low level.
- Teaching people with learning disorders to make it clear when they do not understand is important. Even asking the person what they mean or to repeat the instructions in a different way may be helpful.
- If they have difficulty understanding, training people to ask the person to repeat the instructions in a different way can be helpful.
- Textbooks on tape should be provided.
- Tape recording of lectures should be allowed and encouraged if the instructor is willing to give permission. Consideration should be given to the use of a tape recorder for projects, reports, and so on; this would allow the teacher to hear the quality of the ideas without relying on the written products.
- If acceptable to the instructor, answers to essay questions should be completed in point form. Consideration should be given to a similar format for class assignments.
- Because of spelling difficulties, consideration should be given to not reducing grades for spelling errors.
- If possible, use a computer (word processor) for written work. This may help improve the quality of written work. Using a computer spell check often and early in the writing process will ensure that you see correct spellings of words to enhance your knowledge of common word patterns.

- Copying from the blackboard is difficult; alternatives should be considered. For example, class handouts, photocopying other students' notes, or tape recording oral lessons may be an option.
- Alternate modes of examination (e.g., oral exams) may be considered.

CONCLUSION

Until the field of learning disabilities resolves the definitional issues, significant progress will not be made. We must examine our basic concepts about the nature of learning disabilities and our current practices. Specific and clear operational definitions will help the field advance. However, this resolution will *not* happen automatically. It will take a concerted effort by the field.

REFERENCES

Aaron, P. G. (1991). Can reading disabilities be diagnosed without using intelligence tests? *Journal of Learning Disabilities, 24,* 178–186.

Arnold, L. E., Smeltzer, D. J., & Barneby, N. S. (1981). Specific perceptual remediation: Effects related to sex, IQ, and parents' occupational status; behavioral change pattern by scale factors; and mechanism of benefit hypothesis tested. *Psychological Reports, 49,* 198.

Backman, J., Bruck, M., Hebert, M., & Seidenberg, M. S. (1984). Acquisition and use of spelling-sound correspondences in reading. *Journal of Experimental Child Psychology, 38,* 114–133.

Barwick, M. A., & Siegel, L. S. (1996). Learning difficulties in adolescent clients of a shelter for runaway and homeless street youths. *Journal of Research on Adolescence, 6,* 649–670.

Bateman, B. (1968–1969). "Clinically" obtained IQs versus "production line" IQs in a mentally retarded sample. *Journal of School Psychology, 7,* 29–33.

Benton, A. L., & Pearl, D. (Eds.). (1978). *Dyslexia: An appraisal of current knowledge.* New York: Oxford University Press.

Berninger, V. (1994). Future directions for research on writing disabilities: Integrating endogenous and exogenous variables. In G. R. Lyon (Ed.), *Frames of reference for the assessment of learning disabilities: New views on measurement issues* (pp. 419–440). Baltimore: Paul H. Brookes.

Boder, E. (1968). Developmental dyslexia: A diagnostic screening procedure based on three characteristic patterns of reading and spelling. *Claremont College Reading Conference, 32,* 173–187.

Boder, E. (1971). Developmental dyslexia: A diagnostic screening procedure based on three characteristic patterns of reading and spelling. In B. C. Bateman (Ed.), *Learning disorders* (Vol. 4, pp. 298–342). Seattle, WA: Special Child Publications.

Boder, E. (1973). Developmental dyslexia: A diagnostic approach based on three atypical reading-spelling patterns. *Developmental Medicine and Child Neurology, 15,* 663–687.

Boder, E., & Jarrico, S. (1986). *Boder Test of Reading-Spelling Patterns.* New York: Grune & Stratton.

Brown, W. S., Marsh, J. T., & Smith, J. C. (1973). Contextual meaning effects on speech-evoked potentials. *Behavioral Biology, 9,* 755–761.

Bruck, M. (1988). The word recognition and spelling of dyslexic children. *Reading Research Quarterly, 23,* 51–69.

Bruck, M. (1990). Word-recognition skills of adults with childhood diagnosis of dyslexia. *Developmental Psychology, 26,* 439–454.

Bruck, M. (1992). Persistence of dyslexics' phonological awareness deficits. *Developmental Psychology, 28,* 874–886.

Bruck, M., & Waters, G. (1988). An analysis of the spelling errors of children who differ in their reading and spelling skills. *Applied Psycholinguistics, 9,* 77–92.

Bryant, B. R., & Brown, L. (1985). A critical review of four measures of paragraph reading. *Remedial and Special Education, 6*(2), 52–55.

Butler, D. L. (1995). Promoting strategic learning by postsecondary students with learning disabilities. *Journal of Learning Disabilities, 28,* 170–190.

Butler, D. L. (1998). The strategic content learning approach to promoting self-regulated learning: A report of three studies. *Journal of Educational Psychology, 90,* 682–697.

Calfee, R. C., Lindamood, P., & Lindamood, C. (1973). Acoustic-phonetic skills and reading: Kindergarten through twelfth grade. *Journal of Educational Psychology, 64,* 293–298.

Camp, B. W., & Dolcourt, J. L. (1977). Reading and spelling in good and poor readers. *Journal of Learning Disabilities, 10,* 300–307.

Cruickshank, W. M. (1981). A new perspective in teacher education: The neuroeducator. *Journal of Learning Disabilities, 14,* 337–341.

Cruickshank, W. W. (1972). Some issues facing the field of learning disability. *Journal of Learning Disabilities, 5,* 380–388.

Daneman, M. (1984). Acquiring vocabulary knowledge from text. Paper presented at the Second Meeting of Reading Researchers, University of Guelph, Guelph, Ontario, Canada.

Denckla, M. B., Rudel, R. G., & Broman, M. (1981). Tests that discriminate between dyslexic and other learning-disabled boys. *Brain and Language, 13,* 118–129.

Deshler, D. D., & Schumaker, J. B. (1993). Strategy mastery by at-risk students: Not a simple matter. *Elementary School Journal, 94,* 153–167.

Doehring, D. G. (1984). Subtyping of disorders: Implications for remediation. *Annals of Dyslexia, 34,* 205–216.

Doehring, D. G., & Hoshko, I. M. (1977). Classification of reading problems by the Q-technique of factor analysis. *Cortex, 13,* 281–294.

Doehring, D. G., Hoshko, I. M., & Bryans, B. N. (1979). Statistical classification of children with reading problems. *Journal of Clinical Neuropsychology, 1,* 5–16.

Doehring, D. G., Trites, R. L., Patel, P. G., & Fiedorowicz, C. A. M. (1981). *Reading disabilities: The interaction of reading, language, and neuropsychological deficits.* New York: Academic Press.

Drum, P. A., Calfee, R. C., & Cook, L. K. (1981). The effects of sentence structure variables on performance in reading comprehension tests. *Reading Research Quarterly, 16,* 486–514.

Ehri, L. C., & Wilce, L. S. (1983). Development of word identification speed in skilled and less skilled beginning readers. *Journal of Educational Psychology, 75,* 3–18.

Elbro, C., Neilsen, I., & Petersen, D. K., (1994). Dyslexia in adults: Evidence for deficits in non word reading and in the phonological representation of lexical items. *Annals of Dyslexia, 44,* 205–226.

Elliot, S. N., & Boeve, K. (1987). Stability of WISC-R IQs: An investigation of ethnic differences over time. *Educational and Psychological Measurement, 47,* 461–465.

Ellis, A. (1985). The cognitive neuropsychology of developmental (and acquired) dyslexia: A critical survey. *Cognitive Neuropsychology, 2,* 169–205.

Ellis, N., & Large, B. (1987). The development of reading. As you seek so shall you find. *British Journal of Psychology, 78,* 1–28.

Epps, S., Ysseldyke, J., & Algozzine, B. (1985). An analysis of the conceptual framework underlying definitions of learning disabilities. *Journal of School Psychology, 23,* 133–144.

Feagans, L., & Appelbaum, M. I. (1986). Validation of language subtypes in learning disabled children. *Journal of Educational Psychology, 78,* 358–364.

Federal Register. (1977). *The rules and regulations for implementing Public Law 94–142.* Washington, DC: U.S. Government Printing Office.

Felton, R. H., Naylor, C. E., & Wood, F. B. (1990). Neuropsychological profile of adult dyslexics. *Brain and Language, 39,* 485–497.

Felton, R. H., & Wood, F. (1991). A reading level match study of nonword reading skills in poor readers with varying IQ. *Journal of Learning Disabilities, 25,* 318–326.

Fisk, J. L., & Rourke, B. P. (1979). Identification of subtypes of learning-disabled children at three age levels: A neuropsychological, multivariate approach. *Journal of Clinical Neuropsychology, 1,* 289–310.

Fisk, J. L., & Rourke, B. P. (1983). Neuropsychological subtyping of learning-disabled children: History, methods, implications. *Journal of Learning Disabilities, 16,* 529–531.

Fletcher, J. M. (1985a). External validity of learning disability subtypes. In B. P. Rourke (Ed.), *Neuropsychology of learning disabilities: Essentials of subtype analyses* (pp. 187–211). New York: Guilford Press.

Fletcher, J. M. (1985b). Memory for verbal and nonverbal stimuli in learning disability subgroups: Analysis by selective reminders. *Journal of Educational Child Psychology, 40,* 244–259.

Fletcher, J. M., Espy, K. A., Francis, D. J., Davidson, K. C., Rourke, B. P., & Shaywitz, S. E. (1989). Comparisons of cutoff and regression-based definitions of reading disabilities. *Journal of Learning Disabilities, 22*(6), 334–338.

Fletcher, J. M., Francis, D., Rourke, B., Shaywitz, S., & Shaywitz, B. (1992). The validity of discrepancy-based definitions of reading disabilities. *Journal of Learning Disabilities, 25*, 555–561.

Fletcher, J. M., & Morris, R. (1986). Classification of disabled learners: Beyond exclusionary definitions. In S. J. Ceci (Ed.), *Handbook of social and neuropsychological aspects of learning disabilities* (Vol. 2, pp. 55–80). Hillsdale, NJ: Erlbaum.

Fletcher, J. M., Shaywitz, S. E., Shankweiler, D., Katz, L., Liberman, I., Steubing, K., Francis, D. J., Fowler, A., & Shaywitz, B. A. (1994). Cognitive profiles of reading disability: Comparisons of discrepancy and low achievement definitions. *Journal of Educational Psychology, 85*, 1–18.

Fowler, C., Shankweiler, D., & Liberman, I. (1979). Apprehending spelling patterns for vowels: A developmental study. *Language and Speech, 22*, 243–251.

Fried, I., Tanguay, P., Boder, E., Doubleday, C., & Greensite, M. (1981). Developmental dyslexia: Electrophysiological evidence of clinical subgroups. *Brain and Language, 12*, 14–22.

Friedman, G., & Stevenson, J. (1988). Reading processes in specific reading retarded and reading backward 13 year olds. *British Journal of Developmental Psychology, 6*, 97–108.

Gottardo, A., Siegel, L. S., & Stanovich, K. E. (1997). The assessment of adults with reading disabilities: What can we learn from experimental tasks? *Journal of Research in Reading, 20*, 42–54.

Gottardo, A., Stanovich, K. E., & Siegel, L. S. (1996). The relationships between phonological sensitivity, syntactic processing, and verbal working memory in the reading performance of third grade children. *Journal of Experimental Child Psychology, 63*, 563–582.

Green, D. R. (1974). *The aptitude-achievement distinction.* Monterey, CA: CTB/McGraw-Hill.

Greenberg, D., Ehri, L. C., & Perin, D. (1997). Are word-reading processes the same or different in adult literacy students and third-fifth graders matched for reading level? *Journal of Educational Psychology, 89*, 262–275.

Guthrie, J. T., & Seifert, M. (1977). Letter-sound complexity in learning to identify words. *Journal of Educational Psychology, 69*, 686–696.

Hall, J. W., & Humphreys, M. S. (1982). Research on specific learning disabilities: Deficits and remediation. *Topics in Learning and Learning Disabilities, 2*, 68–78.

Hall, J. W., Wilson, K. P., Humphreys, M. S., Tinzmann, M. B., & Bowyer, P. M. (1983). Phonetic similarity effects in good vs. poor readers. *Memory and Cognition, 11*, 520–527.

Hammill, D. D., Leigh, J. E., McNutt, G., & Larsen, S. C. (1981). A new definition of learning disabilities. *Learning Disability Quarterly, 4*, 336–342.

Hogaboam, T. W., & Perfetti, C. A. (1978). Reading skill and the role of verbal experience in decoding. *Journal of Educational Psychology, 70*, 717–729.

Hooper, S. R., & Willis, W. G. (1989). *Learning disability subtyping: Neuropsychological foundations, conceptual models, and issues in clinical differentiation.* New York: Springer-Verlag.

Hopkins, K. D., & Stanley, J. C. (1981). *Educational and psychological measurement* (6th ed.). Englewood Cliffs, NJ: Prentice-Hall.

Jiménez-Glez, J. E., & Rodrigo-López, M. R. (1994). Is it true that differences in reading performance between students with and without LD cannot be explained by IQ. *Journal of Learning Disabilities, 27*, 155–163.

Johnson, D. J., & Myklebust, H. R. (1962). Dyslexia in children. *Exceptional Children, 29*, 14–25.

Johnson, D. J., & Mykelbust, H. R. (1967). *Learning disabilities: Education principles and practice.* New York: Grune & Stratton.

Johnston, R. S., Rugg, M. D., & Scott, T. (1987a). The influence of phonology on good and poor readers when reading for meaning. *Journal of Memory and Language, 26*, 57–68.

Johnston, R. S., Rugg, M. D., & Scott, T. (1987b). Phonological similarity effects, memory span and developmental reading disorders: The nature of the relationship. *British Journal of Psychology, 78*, 205–211.

Jorm, A. (1981). Children with reading and spelling retardation: Functioning of whole-word and correspondence-rule mechanisms. *Journal of Child Psychology and Psychiatry and Allied Disciplines, 22*, 171–178.

Jorm, A., Share, D. L., Matthews, R. J., & Maclean, R. (1986). Behaviour problems in specific reading retarded and general reading backward children: A longitudinal study. *Journal of Child Psychology and Psychiatry, 27*, 33–43.

Keogh, B. K. (1986). Future of the LD field: Research and practice. *Journal of Learning Disabilities, 19*, 455–460.

Keogh, B. K. (1987). Response to Senf. In S. Vaughn & C. S. Bos (Eds.), *Research in learning disabilities* (pp. 97–101). Boston: College-Hill.

Kershner, J. R. (1990). Self-concept and IQ as predictors of remedial success in children with learning disabilities. *Journal of Learning Disabilities, 23*, 368–374.

Kinsbourne, M., & Warrington, E. K. (1962). Dyslexia in children. *Exceptional Children, 29*, 14–25.

Kinsbourne, M., & Warrington, E. K. (1963a). The developmental Gerstmann Syndrome. *Archives of Neurology, 8*, 490–501.

Kinsbourne, M., & Warrington, E. L. (1963b). Developmental factors in reading and writing backwardness. *British Journal of Educational Psychology, 54*, 145–156.

Kosc, L. (1974). Developmental dyscalculia. *Journal of Learning Disabilities, 7*, 164–177.

Larsen, S., & Parlenvi, P. (1984). Patterns of inverted reading and subgroups of dyslexia. *Annals of Dyslexia, 34*, 194–203.

Lennox, C., & Siegel, L. S. (1993). Visual and phonological spelling errors in subtypes of children with learning disabilities. *Applied Psycholinguistics, 14,* 473–488.

Lennox, C., & Siegel, L. S. (1996). The development of phonological rules and visual strategies in average and poor spellers. *Journal of Experimental Child Psychology, 62,* 60–83.

Levine, M. D., Oberklaid, F., & Meltzer, L. (1981). Developmental output failure: A study of low productivity in school-aged children. *Pediatrics, 67,* 18–25.

Lezak, M. D. (1988). IQ: R.I.P. *Journal of Clinical and Experimental Neuropsychology, 10,* 351–361.

Lovett, M. W. (1984). A developmental perspective on reading dysfunction: Accuracy and rate criteria in the subtyping of dyslexic children. *Brain and Language, 12,* 67–91.

Lyon, G. R. (1987). Learning disabilities research: False starts and broken promises. In S. Vaughn & C. S. Bos (Eds.), *Research in learning disabilities: Issues and future directions* (pp. 69–85). New York: Little, Brown.

Lyon, G. R. (1995). Toward a definition of dyslexia. *Annals of Dyslexia, 45,* 3–27.

Lytton, H. (1967). Follow up of an experiment in selection of remedial education. *British Journal of Educational Psychology, 37,* 1–9.

Malatesha, R. N., & Dougan, D. R. (1982). Clinical subtypes of developmental dyslexia: Resolution of an irresolute problem. In R. N. Malatesha & P. G. Aaron (Eds.), *Reading disorders: Varieties and treatment* (pp. 69–92). New York: Academic Press.

Mann, L., Davis, C. H., Boyer, C. W., Metz, C. M., & Wolford, B. (1983). LD or not LD, that was the question: A retrospective analysis of child service demonstration centers' compliance with the federal definition of learning disabilities. *Journal of Learning Disabilities, 16,* 14–17.

Marr, M. B., & Gormley, K. (1982). Children's recall of familiar and unfamiliar text. *Reading Research Quarterly, 18,* 89–104.

Mattis, S. (1978). Dyslexia syndromes: A working hypothesis that works. In A. Benton & D. Pearl (Eds.), *Dyslexia: An appraisal of current knowledge.* New York: Oxford University Press.

Mattis, S., French, J. H., & Rapin, I. (1975). Dyslexia in children and young adults: Three independent neuropsychological syndromes. *Developmental Medicine and Child Neurology, 17,* 150–163.

McBride, H., & Siegel, L. S. (1997). Learning disabilities and adolescent suicide. *Journal of Learning Disabilities, 30,* 652–659.

McKinney, J. D., Short, E. J., & Feagans, L. (1985). Academic consequences of perceptual-linguistic subtypes of learning disabled children. *Learning Disabilities Research, 1,* 6–17.

Miner, M., & Siegel, L. (1992). William Butler Yeats: Dyslexic? *Journal of Learning Disabilities, 25,* 372–375.

Montague, M. (1997). Cognitive strategy instruction in mathematics for students with learning disabilities. *Journal of Learning Disabilities, 30,* 164–177.

Morrison, S. R., & Siegel, L. S. (1991a). Arithmetic disability: Theoretical considerations and empirical evidence for this subtype. In L. V. Feagans, E. J. Short, & L. Meltzer (Eds.), *Subtypes of learning disabilities: Theoretical perspectives and research* (pp. 189–208). Hillsdale, NJ: Erlbaum.

Morrison, S. R. & Siegel, L. S. (1991b). Learning disabilities: A critical review of definitional and assessment issues. In J. E. Obrzut & G. W. Hynd (Eds.), *Neuropsychological foundations of learning disabilities: A handbook of issues, methods, and practice* (pp. 79–97). San Diego, CA: Academic Press.

Naidoo, S. (1972). *Specific dyslexia.* London: Pitman.

Nockleby, D. M., & Galbraith, A. A. (1984). Developmental dyslexia subtypes and the Boder Test of Reading-Spelling Patterns. *Journal of Psychoeducational Assessment, 2,* 91–100.

Ozols, E. J., & Rourke, B. P. (1979). Dimensions of social sensitivity in two types of learning disabled children. In B. P. Rourke (Ed.), *Neuropsychology of learning disabilities: Essentials of subtype analyses* (pp. 187–211). New York: Guilford Press.

Padget, S. Y., Knight, D. F., & Sawyer, D. J. (1996). Tennessee meets the challenge of dyslexia. *Annals of Dyslexia, 46,* 51–72.

Pennington, B. F., McCabe, L. L., Smith, S. S., Lefly, D. L., Bookman, M. O., Kimberling, W. J., & Lubs, H. A. (1986). Spelling errors in adults with a form of familial dyslexia. *Child Development, 57,* 1001–1013.

Pennington, B. F., Van Orden, G. C., Smith, S. D., Green, P. A., & Haith, M. M. (1990). Phonological processing skills and deficits in adult dyslexics. *Child Development, 61,* 1753–1778.

Petrauskas, R. J., & Rourke, B. P. (1979). Identification of subgroups of retarded readers: A Neuropsychological, multivariate approach. *Journal of Clinical Neuropsychology, 1,* 17–37.

Porter, J., & Rourke, B. P. (1979). Socioeconomic functioning of learning disabled children: A subtype analysis of personality patterns. In B. P. Rourke (Ed.), *Neuropsychology of learning disabilities: Essentials of subtype analyses* (pp. 257–280). New York: Guilford Press.

Pratt, A. C., & Brady, S. (1988). Relations of phonological awareness to reading disability in children and adults. *Journal of Educational Psychology, 80,* 319–323.

Rack, J. P., Snowling, M., & Olson, R. (1992). The nonword reading deficit in developmental dyslexia: A review. *Reading Research Quarterly, 27,* 28–53.

Read, C., & Ruyter, L. (1985). Reading and spelling skills in adults of low literacy. *Remedial and Special Education, 6,* 43–52.

Reitan, R. M., & Davison, L. A. (Eds.). (1974). *Clinical psychology: Current status and applications.* Washington, DC: Winston and Sons.

Reynolds, C. R. (1984). *Critical measurement issues in learning disabilities.* College Station: Texas A&M University Press.

Reynolds, C. R. (1984–1985). Critical issues in learning disabilities. *Journal of Special Education, 18,* 451–476.

Reynolds, C. R. (1985). Measuring the aptitude-achievement discrepancy in learning disability diagnosis. *Remedial and Special Education, 6,* 37–48.

Rourke, B. P. (1982). Central processing deficiencies in children: Toward a developmental neuropsychological model. *Journal of Clinical Neuropsychology, 4,* 1–18.

Rourke, B. P. (1983). Outstanding issues in research on learning disabilities. In M. Rutter (Ed.), *Developmental neuropsychiatry* (pp. 564–574). New York: Guilford Press.

Rourke, B. P. (1985). *Neuropsychology of learning disabilities: Essentials of subtype analysis.* New York: Guilford Press.

Rourke, B. P. (1987). Syndrome of nonverbal learning disabilities: The final common pathway of white-matter disease/dysfunction? *Clinical Neuropsychologist, 1,* 209–234.

Rourke, B. P. (1991). Validation of learning disabilities subtypes: An overview. In B. P. Rourke (Ed.), *Neuropsychological validation on learning disability subtypes* (pp. 3–11). New York: Guilford.

Rourke, B. P., Del Dotto, J. E., Rourke, S. B., & Casey, J. E. (1990). Nonverbal learning disabilities: The syndrome and a case study. *Journal of School Psychology, 28,* 361–385.

Rourke, B. P., & Finlayson, M. A. J. (1978). Neuropsychological significance of variations in patterns of academic performance: Verbal and visual-spatial abilities. *Journal of Abnormal Child Psychology, 6,* 121–133.

Rourke, B. P., & Fisk, J. L. (1981). Socio-emotional disturbances of learning disabled children: The role of central processing deficits. *Bulletin of the Orton Society, 31,* 77–88.

Rourke, B. P., & Fisk, J. L. (1988). Subtypes of learning-disabled children: Implications for a neurodevelopmental model of differential hemispheric processing. In D. L. Molfese & S. J. Segalowitz (Eds.), *Brain lateralization in children: Developmental implications* (pp. 547–565). New York: Guilford Press.

Rourke, B. P., & Strang, J. D. (1978). Neuropsychological significance of variations in patterns of academic performance: Motor, psychomotor, and tactile-perceptual abilities. *Journal of Pediatric Psychology, 3,* 22–62.

Rourke, B. P., & Tsatsanis, K. D. (1996). Syndrome of nonverbal learning disabilities: psyholinguistic assets and deficits. *Topics in Language Disorders, 16,* 30–34.

Rudel, R. G., & Denckla, M. B. (1976). Relationship of IQ and reading score to visual, spatial, and temporal matching tasks. *Journal of Learning Disabilities, 9*(3), 169–178.

Russell, G. (1982). Impairment of phonetic reading in dyslexia and its persistence beyond childhood: Research note. *Journal of Child Psychology and Psychiatry, 23,* 459–475.

Rutter, M. (1978). Prevalence and types of dyslexia. In A. Benton & D. Pearl (Eds.), *Dyslexia: An appraisal of current knowledge.* New York: Oxford University Press.

Rutter, M., Tizard, J., & Whitmore, K. (Eds.). (1970). *Education, health, and behavior.* London: Longmans.

Rutter, M., & Yule, W. (1973). Specific reading retardation. In L. Mann & D. Sabatino (Eds.), *The first review of special education.* Philadelphia: JSE Press.

Satz, P., & Morris, R. (1981). Learning disability subtypes: A review. In F. J. Pirozzolo & M. C. Wittrock (Eds.), *Neuropsychological and cognitive processes in reading.* New York: Academic Press.

Scarborough, H. (1984). Continuity between childhood dyslexia and adult reading. *British Journal of Psychology, 75,* 329–348.

Schneider, W., Körkel, J. & Weinert, F. E. (1989). Domain-specific knowledge and memory performance: A comparison of high- and low-aptitude children. *Journal of Educational Psychology, 81,* 306–312.

Shafrir, U., & Siegel, L. S. (1994a). Preference for visual scanning strategies versus phonological rehearsal in university students with reading disabilities. *Journal of Learning Disabilities, 27,* 583–588.

Shafrir, U., & Siegel, L. S. (1994b). Subtypes of learning disabilities in adolescents and adults. *Journal of Learning Disabilities, 27,* 123–134.

Share, D. L., McGee, R., McKenzie, D., Williams, S., & Silva, P. A. (1987). Further evidence relating to the distinction between specific reading retardation and general reading backwardness. *British Journal of Developmental Psychology, 5,* 35–44.

Share, D. L., Moffitt, T. E., & Silva, P. A. (1988). Factors associated with arithmetic and reading disability and specific arithmetic disability. *Journal of Learning Disabilities, 21,* 313–320.

Shaywitz, S. E., Fletcher, J. M., & Escobar, M. D. (1990). Prevalence of reading disability in boys and girls. *Journal of the American Medical Association, 264,* 998–1002.

Short, E. J., Feagans, L., McKinney, J. D., & Appelbaum, M. I. (1986). Longitudinal stability of LD subtypes based on age- and IQ-achievement discrepancies. *Learning Disability Quarterly, 9,* 214–225.

Siedenberg, M. S. (1985). The time course of information activation and utilization in visual word recognition. In D. Besner, T. G. Waller, & G. E. MacKinnon (Eds.), *Reading research: Advances in theory and practice.* (Vol. 5, pp. 199–252). San Diego, CA: Academic Press.

Siegel, L. S. (1985a). Deep dyslexia in childhood? *Brain and Language, 26,* 16–27.

Siegel, L. S. (1985b). Psycholinguistic aspects of reading disabilities. In L. S. Siegel & F. J. Morrison (Eds.), *Cognitive development in atypical children* (pp. 45–65). New York: Springer-Verlag.

Siegel, L. S. (1988a). Agatha Christie's learning disability. *Canadian Psychology, 29,* 213–216.

Siegel, L. S. (1988b). Evidence that IQ scores are irrelevant to the definition and analysis of reading disability. *Canadian Journal of Psychology, 42,* 202–215.

Siegel, L. S. (1988c). Definitional and theoretical issues and research on learning disabilities. *Journal of Learning Disabilities, 21,* 264–266.

Siegel, L. S. (1989a). IQ is irrelevant to the definition of learning disabilities. *Journal of Learning Disabilities, 22,* 469–478, 486.

Siegel, L. S. (1989b). Why do we not need IQ test scores in the definition and analyses of learning disability. *Journal of Experimental Child Psychology, 63,* 563–582.

Siegel, L. S. (1992). An evaluation of the discrepancy definition of dyslexia. *Journal of Learning Disabilities, 25,* 618–629.

Siegel, L. S. (1993a). Alice in IQ land or why IQ is still irrelevant to learning disabilities. In R. M. Joshi & C. K. Leong (Eds.), *Reading disabilities: Diagnosis and component processes* (pp. 71–84). Dordrecht, The Netherlands: Kluwer.

Siegel, L. S. (1993b). Phonological processing deficits as the basis of a reading disability. *Developmental Review, 13,* 246–257.

Siegel, L. S. (1995). Does the IQ god exist? *Alberta Journal of Educational Research, 41,* 283–288.

Siegel, L. S. (1998). The discrepancy formula: Its use and abuse. In B. K. Shapiro, P. J. Accardo, & A. J. Capute (Eds.), *Specific reading disability: A view of the spectrum* (pp. 123–135). Timonium, MD: York Press.

Siegel, L. S., & Feldman, W. (1983). Non-dyslexic children with combined writing and arithmetic difficulties. *Clinical Pediatrics, 22,* 241–244.

Siegel, L. S., & Heaven, R. (1986). Categorizing learning disabilities. In S. Ceci (Ed.), *Handbook of cognitive, social, and neuropsychological aspects of learning disabilities* (Vol. 1, pp. 95–121). Hillsdale, NJ: Erlbaum.

Siegel, L. S., & Himel, N. (1998). Socioeconomic status, age and the classification of dyslexic and poor readers: Further evidence of the irrelevancy of IQ to reading disability. *Dyslexia, 4,* 90–104.

Siegel, L. S., Levey, P., & Ferris, H. (1985). Subtypes of developmental dyslexia: Do they exist? In F. J. Morrison, C. Lord, & D. P. Keating (Eds.), *Applied developmental psychology* (Vol. 2, pp. 169–190). New York: Academic Press.

Siegel, L. S., & Linder, B. A. (1984). Short term memory processes in children with reading and arithmetic learning disabilities. *Developmental Psychology, 20,* 200–207.

Siegel, L. S., & Ryan, E. B. (1984). Reading disability as a language disorder. *Remedial and Special Education, 5,* 28–33.

Siegel, L. S., & Ryan, E. B. (1988). Development of grammatical sensitivity, phonological, and short-term memory skills in normally achieving and learning disabled children. *Developmental Psychology, 24,* 28–37.

Siegel, L. S., & Ryan, E. B. (1989a). The development of working memory in normally achieving and subtypes of learning disabled children. *Child Development, 60,* 973–980.

Siegel, L. S., & Ryan, E. B. (1989b). Subtypes of developmental dyslexia: The influence of definitional variables. *Reading and Writing: An Interdisciplinary Journal, 1,* 257–287.

Silva, P., McGee, R., & Williams, S. (1985). Some characteristics of 9-year-old boys with general reading backwardness or specific reading retardation. *Journal of Child Psychology and Psychiatry, 26,* 407–421.

Silver, L. B. (1988). A review of the federal government's Interagency Committee on Learning Disabilities report to the U.S. Congress. *Learning Disabilities Focus, 3,* 73–80.

Smiley, S. S., Pascquale, F. L., & Chandler, C. (1976). The pronunciation of familiar, unfamiliar, and synthetic words by good and poor adolescent readers, *Journal of Reading Behavior, 8,* 289–297.

Snowling, M. J. (1980). The development of grapheme-phoneme correspondence in normal and dyslexic readers. *Journal of Experimental Child Psychology, 29,* 294–305.

Spellacy, F., & Peter, B. (1978). Dyscalculia and elements of the developmental Gerstmann Syndrome in school children. *Cortex, 14,* 197–206.

Sprenger-Charolles, L., & Siegel, L. S. (1997). A longitudinal study of the effects of syllabic structures on the development of reading and spelling skills in French. *Applied Psycholinguistics, 18,* 485–505.

Stanovich, K. E. (1982). Individual differences in the cognitive processes of reading: 1. Word decoding. *Journal of Learning Disabilities, 15,* 485–493.

Stanovich, K. E. (1986). Matthew effects in reading: Some consequences of individual differences in the acquisition of literacy. *Reading Research Quarterly, 21,* 360–407.

Stanovich, K. E. (1988a). Explaining the differences between the dyslexic and garden variety poor reader: The phonological-core variance-difference model. *Journal of Learning Disabilities, 21,* 590–604, 612.

Stanovich, K. E. (1988b). The right and wrong places to look for the cognitive locus of reading disability. *Annals of Dyslexia, 38,* 154–177.

Stanovich, K. E. (1988c). Science and learning disabilities. *Journal of Learning Disabilities, 21,* 210–214.

Stanovich, K. E. (1989). Has the learning disabilities field lost its intelligence? *Journal of Learning Disabilities, 22*(8), 487–492.

Stanovich, K. E., & Siegel, L. S. (1994). The phenotypic performance profile of reading-disabled children: A regression-based test of the phonological-core variable-difference model. *Journal of Educational Psychology, 86,* 24–53.

Strang, J. D., & Rourke, B. P. (1983a). Arithmetic disabilities subtypes: The neuropsychological significance of specific arithmetical impairment in childhood. In B. P. Rourke, D. J. Bakker, J. L. Fisk, & J. D. Strang (Eds.), *Child neuropsychology: An introduction to theory, research, and clinical practice* (pp. 167–183). New York: Guilford Press.

Strang, J. D., & Rourke, B. P. (1983b). Concept-formation/nonverbal reasoning abilities of children who exhibit specific academic problems with arithmetic. *Journal of Clinical Child Psychology, 12,* 33–39.

Strang, J. D., & Rourke, B. P. (1985a). Adaptive behavior of children who exhibit specific arithmetic disabilities and associated neuropsychological abilities and deficits. In B. P. Rourke (Ed.), *Neuropsychology of learning disabilities: Essentials of subtype analysis* (pp. 302–328). New York: Guilford Press.

Strang, J. D., & Rourke, B. P. (1985b). Arithmetic disability subtypes: The neuropsychological significance of specific arithmetical impairment in childhood. In B. R. Rourke (Ed.), *Neuropsychology of learning disabilities: Essentials of subtype analysis* (pp. 167–183). New York: Guilford Press.

Surber, J. M. (1985). Best practices in a problem-solving approach to psychological report writing. In A. Thomas & J. Grimes (Eds.), *Best Practices in School Psychology*. Washington, DC: National Association of School Psychologists.

Swanson, H. L. (1988a). Memory subtypes in learning disabled readers. *Learning Disability Quarterly, 11,* 342–357.

Swanson, H. L. (1988b). Toward a metatheory of learning disabilities. *Journal of Learning Disabilities, 21,* 196–209.

Swanson, H. L. (1989). Phonological processes and other routes. *Journal of Learning Disabilities, 22,* 493–496.

Sweeney, J. E., & Rourke, B. P. (1978). Neuropsychological significance of phonetically accurate and phonetically inaccurate spelling errors in younger and older retarded spellers. *Brain and Language, 6*(2), 212–225.

Tal, N. F., & Siegel, L. S. (1996). Pseudoword reading errors of poor, dyslexic and normally achieving readers on multisyllable pseudowords. *Applied Psycholinguistics, 17,* 215–232.

Taylor, H. G., Satz, P., & Friel, J. (1979). Developmental dyslexia in relation to other childhood reading disorders: Significance and clinical utility. *Reading Research Quarterly, 15,* 84–101.

Telzrow, C. F., Century, E., Whitaker, B., Redmond, C., & Zimmerman, B. (1983). The Boder test: Neuropsychological and demographic features of dyslexic subtypes. *Psychology in the Schools, 20,* 427–432.

Toth, G., & Siegel, L. S. (1994). A critical evaluation of the IQ-achievement discrepancy based definition of dyslexia. In K. P. van den Bos, L. S. Siegel, D. J. Bakker, & D. L. Share (Eds.), *Current directions in dyslexia research* (pp. 45–70). Lisse, The Netherlands: Swets & Zeitlinger.

Tunmer, W. (1989). Mental test differences as Matthew effects in literacy: The rich get richer and to poor get poorer. *New Zealand Sociology, 4,* 64–84.

Vail, P. (1990). Gifts, talents, and the dyslexias: Wellsprings, springboards and finding Foley's rocks. *Annals of Dyslexia, 40,* 3–17.

Valtin, R. (1978–1979). Dyslexia: Deficit in reading or deficit in research? *Reading Research Quarterly, 14,* 201–221.

Van den Bos, K. P. (1984). Letter processing in dyslexic subgroups. *Annals of Dyslexia, 34,* 193.

van der Wissel, A., & Zegers, F. E. (1985). Reading retardation revisited. *British Journal of Developmental Psychology, 3,* 3–9.

Vellutino, F. R. (1977). Alternative conceptualizations of dyslexia: Evidence in support of a verbal-deficit hypothesis. *Harvard Educational Review, 47,* 334–354.

Vellutino, F. R. (1978). Toward an understanding of dyslexia: Psychological factors in specific reading disability. In A. L. Benton & D. Pearl (Eds.), *Dyslexia: An appraisal of current knowledge* (pp. 61–112). New York: Oxford University Press.

Vellutino, F. R. (1979). *Dyslexia: Theory and research.* Cambridge, MA: MIT Press.

Vellutino, F. R., & Scanlon, D. M. (1996). Experimental evidence for the effects of instructional bias on word identification. *Exceptional Children, 53,* 145–155.

Vellutino, F. R., Scanlon, D. M., & Lyon, G. R. (2000). Differentiating between difficult-to-remediate and readily remediated poor readers: More evidence against the IQ-discrepancy definition of reading disability. *Journal of Learning Disabilities, 33,* 223–238.

Venezky, R. L., & Johnson, D. (1973). Development of two letter-sound patterns in grades one through three. *Journal of Educational Psychology, 64,* 109–115.

Waters, G. S., Bruck, M., & Seidenberg, M. (1985). Do children use similar processes to read and spell words? *Journal of Experimental Child Psychology, 39,* 511–530.

Weber, R. (1970). A linguistic analysis of first-grade reading errors. *Reading Research Quarterly, 5,* 427–451.

Webster, R. E. (1979). Visual and aural short-term memory capacity deficits in mathematics disabled students. *Journal of Educational Research, 72,* 277–283.

Werker, J. F., Bryson, S. E., & Wassenberg, K. (1989). Toward understanding the problem in severely disabled readers: Pt. 2. Consonant errors. *Applied Psycholinguistics, 10,* 13–30.

Wong, B. Y. L. (1996). *The ABC's of learning disabilities.* San Diego, CA: Academic Press.

Yule, W. (1967). Predicting reading ages on Neale's analysis of reading ability. *British Journal of Educational Psychology, 37,* 252–255.

Yule, W. (1973). Differential prognosis of reading backwardness and specific reading retardation. *British Journal of Educational Psychology, 43,* 244–248.

Yule, W., Rutter, M., Berger, M., & Thompson, J. (1974). Over- and under-achievement in the general population. *British Journal of Educational Psychology, 44,* 1–12.

CHAPTER 19

Gifted Education Programs and Procedures

PAULA OLSZEWSKI-KUBILIUS

GIFTED EDUCATION PROGRAMS AND PROCEDURES

In this chapter I review research related to the practices within the field of gifted education. Talent-giftedness is a phenomenon that greatly interests our society. However, educators have a somewhat ambivalent attitude toward giftedness and gifted children. There is no agreed-upon definition of giftedness to guide practice and programs as there is with other special categories of children and no federal mandate to serve gifted children. As a result, the kinds of services available to gifted children in schools vary widely. I try to capture that variability and the issues that frame practice and theory within this emerging field of psychology and education.

Conceptions of Giftedness

The IQ Tradition

The field of gifted education has been dominated throughout its history by a conception of intellectual giftedness that emphasized individual differences in IQ. In practice, IQ is still widely used as a measure to identify giftedness in school children (Cox, Daniel, & Boston, 1985) and the research on giftedness is overwhelmingly done on groups defined as gifted on the basis of IQ scores (Tannenbaum, 1983).

The emphasis on IQ resulted largely from the work of Louis Terman. In 1921 Terman initiated a study of 1,500 children with IQ scores above 140 on the Stanford-Binet test. He and his colleagues studied these individuals longitudinally and prospectively resulting in numerous publications about the Termites (Cox, 1926; Terman, 1925; Terman & Oden,

1947; Terman & Oden, 1957). The Termites were found to be well-adjusted, high-achieving adults. Few of them, however, attained eminence in their fields.

Terman believed that giftedness involved quantitative but not qualitative differences in intellectual ability; gifted children are able to learn more quickly and solve problems more readily than are children with lower IQ scores, but their thinking and the organization of their intellectual abilities are not qualitatively different from those of other children. Terman also assumed that intelligence was a unitary construct, that it was constant and stable at least through the school years, and that heredity dominated over environment in influencing it. These beliefs and others of Terman regarding IQ have since been challenged and disputed, including the indispensability of IQ for adult success (Tannenbaum, 1983).

In response to the notion that intelligence is an indivisible, unitary construct, several researchers subsequently proposed multifactor theories of intelligence. Thurstone (Tannenbaum, 1983) proposed a list of seven primary abilities—verbal meaning, number ability, memory, spatial relations, perceptual speed, and reasoning abilities. Guilford produced the structure of the intellect model with 150 separate factors obtainable through the combinations of four different kinds of contents (e.g., figural), six different kinds of products (e.g., transformations), and five different kinds of operations (e.g., evaluation). In contrast to the IQ tradition, these multifactor theories have had very little influence on the practice of identifying or serving gifted children in schools although they have been used as identification rubrics in some research studies.

The last 15 years have brought a flurry of theories regarding intellectual giftedness. Only a very few of these new conceptions have yielded changes in school practices, however.

Cultural Perspectives on Giftedness and Talent

Tannenbaum (1990, 1983) proposes a psychosocial conception of giftedness. According to Tannenbaum, ". . . whereas the psyche determines the *existence* of high potential, society decides on the direction toward its fulfillment by rewarding some kinds of achievement while ignoring or even discouraging others" (1990, p. 21). Tannenbaum proposes four different categories of talents. *Scarcity talents* are those of which society is always in need and that are in short supply, such as the talents of a Jonas Salk or a Martin Luther King Jr. *Surplus talents* elevate and bring society to new heights, are not essential for life, and include individuals who make great contributions to art, literature, music, and philosophy. Individuals with surplus talents "are treated as 'divine luxuries' capable of beautifying the world without guaranteeing its continued existence" (Tannenbaum, 1990, p. 24).

Quota talents are those that require a high level of skill to produce goods and services needed by society, such as the talents needed to become physicians, lawyers, and engineers. These individuals typically do not provide creative breakthroughs, and society only needs a certain amount of them. Schools are most responsive to society's need for certain quota talents (e.g., current need for computer programmers and software engineers).

The last category is *anomalous talents;* this category includes specific, isolated, or idiosyncratic abilities such as speed-reading or great feats of memory. These talents provide amusement for others and may serve some practical purpose, but are examples of high-level or prodigious performance and are typically not recognized by society for excellence.

Tannenbaum (1990) is concerned with how ability in childhood is translated into adult achievement:

> Keeping in mind that developed talent exists only in adults, a proposed definition of giftedness in children is that it denotes their potential for becoming critically acclaimed performers or exemplary producers of ideas in spheres of activity that enhance the moral, physical, emotional, social, intellectual, or aesthetic life of humanity (p. 33).

Tannenbaum (1983, 1990) proposes five factors that link childhood potential to adult productivity—general intelligence such as high IQ or *g*, specific abilities, nonintellective factors such as personality and motivation, environmental factors such as support from the home, opportunities within the community or society's valuing of the talent area, and chance. The major contribution of Tannenbaum's theory is its emphasis on cultural context in defining talent.

Emphasis on Performance in Defining Giftedness

Renzulli (1990; see also Renzulli & Reis, 1986) proposes a model of giftedness that de-emphasizes the role of ability—particularly general ability as measured by IQ—and instead stresses achievement. Renzulli prefers to speak of gifted behaviors and gifted performances rather than gifted individuals. Renzulli believes that typically used IQ cutoff scores for the categorization of giftedness are somewhat arbitrary and too exclusive. Many more individuals who have lower IQs but who do have certain personality characteristics such as task commitment and high levels of motivation can produce gifted levels of performance in a particular domain.

Renzulli rejects the notion of schoolhouse or lesson-learning giftedness, the type most easily assessed by IQ and other cognitive tests, and instead focuses on creative productive giftedness—or giftedness recognized by the development of new products and new knowledge. According to Renzulli, the truly gifted are those who create knowledge, art, or music—not those who are able to consume it rapidly or at a very high level. Educational programs for children should concentrate on developing the characteristics and skills needed for adult creative productivity. School gifted programs should aim to produce the next generation of leaders, musicians, artists, and so on.

Renzulli emphasizes the role of nonintellective factors in achievement, such as task commitment and creativity, along with above-average but not superior general or specific ability. Task persistence includes perseverance, self-confidence, the ability to identify significant problems, and high standards for one's work. Creativity includes openness to experience, curiosity, and sensitivity to detail. For Renzulli, ". . . giftedness is a condition that can be developed in some people if an appropriate interaction takes place between a person, his or her environment, and a particular field of human endeavor" (Renzulli, 1990, p. 60). The interaction of the three components previously described leads to creative productive giftedness.

Renzulli very deliberately tries to show how his theory can be employed in schools. He and his colleagues have developed materials for both identification and curriculum to be used by educators who work with children. Specifically, Renzulli proposes an identification protocol that involves selecting students performing at the 80th or 85th percentile and giving them different kinds of enrichment opportunities. Students revolve into higher level, more complex activities that include independent research projects, and their placement is based on successful performance at lower levels.

Renzulli's model is frequently adopted by schools in the United States. Its appeal is twofold: It casts a wide net, so to speak, by including students with achievement levels that are lower than what is typical for gifted programs, and it comes with a ready-to-use set of curriculum and other materials.

Multiple Intelligence Perspective on Talent and Giftedness

Gardner (1983) postulates the existence of eight relatively autonomous human intellectual competencies or intelligences. These are linguistic, musical, logical-mathematical, spatial, bodily kinesthetic, interpersonal (knowledge of others) and intrapersonal (knowledge of self), and naturalistic (scientific knowledge). Each intelligence has distinct manifestations—such as poetry and writing for linguistic intelligence; dance for bodily and kinesthetic intelligence; and chess, painting, and sculpting for spatial intelligence. At the most fundamental level, each has a biological basis and a brain-based, neural substrate. Each intelligence has a unique computational capacity or information-processing device upon which more complex manifestations are based and built.

Gardner's criteria (1983) for the existence of a separate intelligence include the following: (a) that it can be found in relative *isolation* in special populations such as in individuals with brain damage or so-called idiot savants; (b) that it exists at very high levels in some individuals such as prodigies and is manifested in their performances of various tasks; (c) that it has an identifiable core operation or set of operations such as a sensitivity to pitch for musical intelligence; (d) that there is a distinct development history of the intelligence "ranging from universal beginnings through which every novice passes, to exceedingly high levels and/or special forms of training" (Gardner, 1983, p. 64) with a definable set of end state performances; (e) that it has an evolutionary history; (f) that there is support from experimental psychological tests for the intelligence; (g) that there is susceptibility of the intelligence to encoding as a symbol system; and (h) that there is support from psychometric studies for its existence (e.g. high correlations between measures of the same intelligence and low correlations between measures of different types of intelligence).

Gardner (1983) proposes that the types of intelligence are "'natural kinds' of building blocks out of which productive lines of thought and action are built" (p. 279). They can be combined to yield a variety of abilities, processes, and products. Normal human interaction typically requires that various types of intelligence work together in complex and seamless ways to accomplish human activities.

Many schools make reference to multiple types of intelligence within their mission statements. Multiple intelligences (MI) theory is increasingly being used as the basis of

gifted programs, affecting identification systems as well as programs (see Fasko, 2001). Gardner suggests that one can speak about the particular intelligences that are used in specific educational encounters. Additionally, one can characterize the material or content to be learned as falling within the domain of a particular intelligence: ". . . Our various intellectual competencies can serve as both means and as message, as form and as content" (Gardner, 1983, p. 334). The implications of Gardner's theory for identification of talents has been explored in several projects including the Key School in Indianapolis (in which MI theory is also being used by teachers as a basis for designing curricula and instructional activities) and Project Spectrum, which is directed by David Feldman of Tufts University (see Garner & Hatch, 1989). In research on Project Spectrum, Gardner found evidence that children who were assessed for the various intelligences in an intelligence-fair manner (e.g., using modes of assessment that respect the ways of thinking in the various intelligences, such as putting together household objects to assess spatial intelligence) exhibited profiles of relative strengths and weaknesses. Additionally, there was some evidence that more children were identified as talented in some domain than when more traditional measures were used. Although it is limited, this research supports Gardner's contention about the separateness of the various intelligences.

Gardner also asserts that a lengthy time period is required before the raw computational devices of an intelligence develop into expression in a mature, cultural mode. Part of that long time period is the natural process of development of the intelligence within an individual—a process of going through domain-specific developmental milestones. Another part is the less natural process of acquiring information that is deliberately transmitted via school or other agents such as parents or other adults. This latter part, which may be thought of as talent development, does not occur within a vacuum. Factors such as motivation, an affective state conducive to learning, and a supportive cultural context are also important—even necessary. Although Gardner does not deal with these factors in depth, he recognizes their contribution to the development of high levels of performance within each of the domains of the intelligences.

The Role of Training in Defining Talent and Giftedness

Gagne (1993, 1995, 1998, 1999) proposes a theory of giftedness and talent that has as its base the roles of training or learning. For Gagne, giftedness refers to exceptional "natural abilities which appear more or less spontaneously during the early years of children's development and give rise to significant individual differences without any clear evidence of any systematic learning, training, or practice" (1995, p. 105). There are four domains of natural abilities: intellectual abilities, physical abilities (which includes sensory and motor abilities), creativity, and socioaffective abilities (which includes leadership). A fifth possible domain of natural ability is the personal abilities, which include the ability to delay gratification, to focus one's attention on the task at hand, to perceive one's needs, and so on.

At the other end of the spectrum from natural abilities are talents, which are "systematically developed abilities which define the characteristic performance of an individual in a field of human activity: these are the abilities shown by competent pianists, teachers, carpenters, swimmers, journalists, pilots, and so forth" (1995, p. 105).

Gagne notes that whereas "natural abilities are defined in reference to characteristics of the person (intelligence, creativity, sociability, motoricity), systematically developed abilities or skills are labeled according to the field of human activities that governs the set of appropriate skills to master" (1995, p. 106). Also, natural abilities provide the component operations that are used to acquire the skills and knowledge associated with expertise in a particular domain or field. Thus, natural abilities are the building blocks or constituent elements of systematically acquired abilities.

According to Gagne, the growth of aptitudes or talents occurs through four developmental processes: maturation, daily use in problem-solving situations, informal training and practice, and formal training and practice. Gagne (1993) stresses that the relationship between aptitudes and talents is *co-univocal,* which means that one aptitude can be involved in the development of many different talents, and any talent can use abilities from more than one aptitude domain as its constituents.

For Gagne, gifted individuals are those who possess a natural ability in at least one of the four ability domains to a degree that places them in the top 10% of their age group. Similarly, talented individuals are those who possess levels of systematically developed abilities and skills that place them in the top 10% of individuals within the same field of endeavor. Gagne (1998) also advocates differentiation within this top 10% of individuals into categories (mild, moderate, high, exceptional, extreme) that are increasingly selective and consist of the top 10% of the previous category.

According to Gagne's theory, one can be gifted and not talented; however, one cannot be talented and not be gifted. A child could be intellectually gifted by virtue of high IQ or test scores but may not be academically talented if he or she does not display exceptional performance—via grades or awards—in an academic area. Giftedness is childhood promise, whereas talent is adult fulfillment of promise. The

process of talent development is then the systematic training and education sought by the gifted individual to develop talent to a high degree.

Gagne (1993, 1995) proposes the existence of catalysts that are both positive and negative influences that affect the development of childhood giftedness into adult talent. Intrapersonal catalysts include motivation, temperament, and personality dimensions of the individual such as adaptability, attitudes, competitiveness, independence, and self-esteem. Environmental catalysts include surroundings (home, school, community), persons (parents, teachers, mentors), undertakings (activities, courses, special programs), and events (significant encounters, awards, accidents such as the loss of a parent). For Gagne, catalysts, personality dimensions, or other nonintellective factors are not essential elements or components of a talent but are contributors to the results of the talented performance.

Triarchic Theory of Intelligence, Giftedness, and Talent

Sternberg (1986) proposes a general theory of intelligence that consists of three subtheories. The *componential subtheory* includes the processes that occur within the minds of individual—the "mental mechanisms that lead to more or less intelligent behavior" (p. 223). These mechanisms enable individuals to learn how to do things, plan what to do, and carry out their plans. The *experiential subtheory* deals with the role of experience in intelligent behavior. It specifies those points in an individual's continuum of experience at which a task or situation is novel and therefore requires intelligent behavior and those points at which the individual has so much experience that response to a particular task or situation is mostly automatic. The third subtheory, the *contextual subtheory,* has to do with how the individual deals with the external environment. It specifies three classes of acts—environmental adaption, selection, and shaping that constitute intelligent behavior in different contexts.

According to Sternberg, the componential subtheory addresses the question of how behaviors are "intelligent in any given setting" (p. 223). The experiential subtheory addresses the question of "when behaviors are intelligent for a given individual" (p. 224). The contextual subtheory addresses the questions of "what behaviors are intelligent for whom and where these behaviors are intelligent" (p. 224). Therefore, according to Sternberg, the componential subtheory is universal, and the mental mechanisms specified are used by all individuals—some better than others. The experiential subtheory is relativistic and the types of situations and activities that are novel or very familiar varies for each individual; however, it is universal that every person has a range of experience that varies from very familiar to very unfamiliar. The contextual subtheory is also relativistic with respect to both individuals (what is intelligent for one individual may not be the same for another) and the contexts in which they live and work (what is an intelligent thing to do in one situation may not be in another situation).

Sternberg (1986, 2000) asserts that giftedness can be obtained via different combinations of strengths among the skills that correspond to the three subtheories. For example, an individual who excels in utilizing the componential mechanisms in learning from school or books or in academic situations might be what we typically call a gifted learner. These individuals are most easily identified by educators and are typically selected for special gifted programs. They may excel on traditional achievement tests. Their strengths are in analytical skills. However, such persons may not necessarily be exceptional at "nonentrenched" tasks or display creativity in dealing with problems. Individuals who are adept at utilizing componential processes in novel situations might be characterized as exceptional problem solvers, as possessing unusual levels of insight, or as creative. These individuals are exceptional at generating new ideas of high quality. Individuals may be adept at both using componential mechanisms in prescribed learning situations and in novel ones, but may be unable to adapt successfully to different environments—what Sternberg refers to as practical intelligence or skills. Such individuals may be regarded as smart, creative, or both, but they may be unable to achieve at commensurately high levels in a career. More recently, Sternberg proposed and illustrated seven different patterns of intelligence involving different combinations of analytical, creative, and practical abilities (Sternberg, 2000).

Sternberg's componential theory has intrigued educators and researchers who work with and study gifted children. However, it has not been widely used as the basis for identification protocols for gifted children. Its major contribution has been to broaden the definition of intelligence beyond that defined by traditional IQ tests. See the chapter by Sternberg in this volume for a more complete description of this theory.

A Developmental Theory Approach to Giftedness and Talent

David Feldman (1986a, 1986b) proposes a conception of giftedness within the tradition of developmental psychology. Developmental psychologists are fundamentally interested in any kind of change and typically in broad changes experienced by all human beings; individual differences in intelligence or achievement have not traditionally been their

concern. Feldman asserts that reaching expert or gifted levels of performance in a field requires traversing a developmental path that involves moving through increasingly higher levels of stages—stages that are not reached by everyone and are therefore nonuniversal. Each stage is marked by a major mental reorganization of the domain. Nonuniversal development therefore accounts for gifted-level performances.

> For the average person, the number of stages or levels that he or she will master in a given domain is obviously fewer than for the 'gifted' individual. Another way of approaching the issues is to think of certain domains as being less likely to be selected for mastery than others; in so doing, 'giftedness' might be revealed not only by the number of levels one achieves, but also by the domain within which an individual chooses to pursue mastery. (Feldman, 1986a, p. 291)

Feldman (1981, 1986a) asserts that nonspecific environmental stimulation is sufficient for progress through broad universal stages of cognitive development such as those that Piaget proposes. However, he says that the development of expert levels of performance requires a more active and specific role for environmental forces. As individuals acquire expertise in a field, they do not rediscover all of the developmental history of the field; rather, they rely on teachers to instruct them. The role of environmental factors such as family support, schooling, and other opportunities to acquire the skills of the field are critically important to progress through nonuniversal stages of development. Moreover, unlike Piaget's stages, which assume that broad general intellectual structures must be present before their application to specific domains, Feldman posits that an individual child can move rapidly through the stages of intellectual development within a single domain (e.g., chess, mathematics) "without bringing all of cognitive development with it" (Feldman, 1981, p. 38).

For Feldman (1981, 1986a), the term *giftedness* refers to individuals who master all of the stages within a domain. *Creativity* is the extension of a field or domain beyond what it is at the present. *Genius* refers to individuals whose work results in a complete reorganization of a field or domain such as Darwin or Freud.

Feldman (1986a, 1986b) recognizes the contribution of other factors beyond education and training to the development of giftedness. He says that a strong desire to do a certain specific thing on the part of the individual must also be present as well as a sociohistorical time that values the talents of the gifted person. Feldman's main contribution is to present giftedness as a phenomenon with developmental characteristics that are similar to other developmental phenomena: "Giftedness . . . can best be comprehended within a framework of both broader and more specific stage transitions" (Feldman, 1986a, p. 291) and as a "sequential transformation of overall systems" (p. 302).

The Role of Emotional Characteristics in Defining Giftedness and Talent

Recent thinking about giftedness by a current group of psychologists, educators, and parents (the Columbus Group, named after their meeting place, Columbus, OH) has included an increased emphasis on the nonintellectual aspects of the phenomenon. According to this perspective, giftedness includes not only advanced or exceptional cognitive capacities, but also unique personality or social-emotional dimensions that are just as important to the phenomenological experience of being gifted. The Columbus Group (1991) proposed the following definition that gives equal weight to cognitive and emotional components of giftedness:

> Giftedness is asynchronous development in which advanced cognitive abilities and heightened intensity combine to create inner experiences and awareness that are qualitatively different from the norm. This asynchrony increases with higher intellectual capacity. The uniqueness of the gifted renders them particularly vulnerable and requires modification in parenting, teaching and counseling in order for them to develop optimally. (Columbus Group, 1991 as cited in Silverman, 1993, p. 634)

Note that this definition includes *heightened intensity* as an integral component. The notion of heightened intensity comes from the work of Dabrowski, a Polish researcher who proposed a theory of emotional development. Dabrowski's stage theory has two major components. One is that there are five levels of development, each of which represents a qualitatively different mode of relating to experience. At the lowest level are individuals whose main concern is immediate gratification; the highest level is characterized by harmony, altruism, lack of inner conflict, and universal values. Although the order of the levels is invariant, progression through the stages is not necessarily related to age. Advanced emotional development, which is the "commitment to live one's life in accordance with higher order values" (Silverman, 1993, p. 639), is determined by an individual's innate capacities to respond in a heightened manner to various stimuli—called *overexcitabilities,* which is the second major component of Dabrowski's theory. "The five overexcitabilities can be thought of as excess energy derived form physical, sensual, imaginational, intellectual, and emotional sources. Only when these capacities for responsiveness are higher than average do they contribute significantly to developmental potential" (Silverman, 1993, p. 641). See

Dabrowski (1964) for a more complete explanation of Dabrowski's theory.

The overexcitabilities have the potential to stimulate movement from a lower stage of emotional development to a higher one. Because gifted individuals, according to Dabrowski's research, are likely to possess one or more of these heightened sensitivities—particularly emotional overexcitabilities—they have greater potential to reach advanced levels of development. The overexcitabilities in combination with advanced intellectual ability makes gifted individuals unique and puts them at odds with the rest of the world. They are vulnerable to psychological stress because this combination of qualities results in rich but intense emotions that makes them feel out of synch with and different from others. According to Silverman (1993),

> The Columbus Group definition emerged in reaction to the increasing emphasis on products, performance and achievement in American thinking about giftedness. In the United States, it had gradually become politically incorrect to think of giftedness as inherent within the child and safer to talk about its external manifestations. Experts were recommending that 'gifted children' be replaced with 'gifted behaviors,' 'talents in different domains,' and 'gifted program children.' Something vital was being missed in these popular formulations: the child. (p. 635)

Conceptions of giftedness that emphasize social-emotional dimensions rest in part on the assumption that gifted children—by virtue of their intellectual giftedness and concomitant emotional characteristics—have increased vulnerability to emotional stress and psychiatric problems. However, the research on gifted children does not emphatically support that assumption (Neihart, 1999), although a number of studies suggest that creative adults (e.g., writers, artists) have increased risk for psychiatric mood disorders (Neihart).

Federal Definitions of Giftedness and Talent

The most often cited definition of giftedness appeared in the U.S. Commissioner of Education's 1972 report to Congress. Sidney P. Marland, Jr., then U.S. Commissioner of Education, was directed in 1969 to undertake a study to determine the extent to which gifted students needed federal educational assistance programs to meet their educational needs. Referred to as the *Marland report,* the definition he proposed for giftedness has been the mainstay of many local gifted programs.

> Gifted and talented children are those identified by professionally qualified persons who by virtue of outstanding abilities, are capable of high performance. These are children who require differentiated educational programs and/or services beyond those

normally provided by the regular school program in order to realize their contribution to self and society. Children capable of high performance include those with demonstrated achievement and/or potential ability in any of the following areas, singly or in combination: 1) general intellectual ability, 2) specific academic aptitude, 3) creative or productive thinking, 4) leadership ability, 5) visual and performing arts, 6) psychomotor ability. It can be assumed that utilization of these criteria for identification of the gifted and talented will encompass a minimum of 3–5%. (Marland, 1972, p. ix)

Later, Category 6 was dropped from the definition. The Marland definition has been criticized for the lack of emphasis on nonintellective factors and because the categories were not parallel (e.g., creative and productive thinking are skills, not abilities). It has been lauded because it included different domains of abilities and because it emphasized potential as well as demonstrated achievement (Gagne, 1993). Passow (1993) credits the Marland report with stimulating interest in gifted and talented children and initiatives to serve them in schools. Prior to the Marland report, only two states in the United States had mandated programs for gifted children and only three states had discretionary or permissive programs. By 1990, all 50 states had policies on the education of gifted children in place—a fact often attributed to the effects of the Marland report and definition of giftedness (Passow, 1993).

> Beyond the broadened definition, use of the phrase, 'gifted and talented' and the assertion that these children and youth had special needs which required differentiated educational experiences, the *Marland Report* began the formulation of a national strategy for identifying and educating this special population. (p. 30)

A more recent definition was released by the U.S. Department of Education in a report entitled *National Excellence: A Case for Developing America's Talent* (1993).

> Children and youth with outstanding talent perform, or show the potential for performing, at remarkably high levels of accomplishment when compared with others of their age, experience, or environment.
>
> These children and youth exhibit high-performance capability in intellectual, creative, and/or artistic areas, possess an unusual leadership capacity, or excel in specific academic fields. They require services or activities not ordinarily provided by the schools.
>
> Outstanding talents are present in all children and youth from all cultural groups, across all economic strata, and in all areas of human endeavor.

This definition, which is increasingly being adopted by individual states, also includes a broad definition of giftedness across different domains and emphasizes capability or potential.

An Educational Emphasis in Defining Giftedness and Talent

Gallagher and Courtright (1986) make a distinction between psychological and educational definitions of giftedness. Psychological definitions focus on individual differences or an individual's relative ranking on a continuum representing a particular ability. Giftedness from this perspective could be exceptional ability on almost any dimension of human performance, regardless of how narrow or specific. Educational definitions take into account the context of schools and specifically those abilities or areas of human performance that are under the purview of schools. Most typically, schools are concerned with those students whose abilities warrant some significant alteration in their education by way of grouping arrangements, grade placement, content being taught, and so on. Borland (1989) goes further to recognize that the specific context of a particular school affects the definition of giftedness: "For the purposes of education, gifted children are those students in a given school or school district who are exceptional by virtue of markedly greater than average potential or ability in some area of human activity generally considered to be the province of the educational system and whose exceptionality engenders special-educational needs that are not being met adequately by the regular core curriculum" (pp. 32–33).

Thus, there is not one fixed educational definition. Indeed, the educational definition will continue to change because what is considered to be the *purview of the schools* has changed historically and will continue to do so. The essential feature of the educational definition is that the school curriculum and school characteristics define the scope of abilities or domain within which exceptional performance should be considered.

Summary

As can be seen from the brief summary of conceptions of giftedness described previously, great variability surrounds many issues. Some conceptions emphasize demonstrated performance rather than high ability, such as Gardner (in adult domains of activity) and Renzulli (in children). Several theories give equal weight to nonintellective factors such as motivation and personality dimensions as to cognitive ones (e.g., Renzulli, the Columbus Group) or included them as important components in their model (e.g., Tannenbaum, Gagne). Some models include creativity as an essential component of giftedness (e.g., Renzulli), whereas others view it as a separate category or type of giftedness (e.g., Feldman, Marland definition) or natural ability (e.g., Gagne). Several theories emphasize the role of society and culture (e.g., Gardner, Tannenbaum) or the educative process of schools (e.g., Marland definition, Borland definition) in defining and recognizing different types or categories of giftedness. Other conceptions recognize and emphasize the contributions of more immediate environments such as the family, schooling, the community, and so on, and the process of developing talent as essential components of giftedness (e.g., Gagne, Tannenbaum).

Other Issues in Defining Giftedness and Talent

Adult Versus Childhood Giftedness

Currently, there are two separate research traditions within the field of gifted education—the study of childhood giftedness and the study of adult giftedness. Researchers who study gifted children are very concerned with issues surrounding educational practice, such as the identification of gifted children and appropriate educational interventions or models. Within this tradition, emphasis is given to general intellectual ability or IQ, above-level scholastic achievement, precocity of achievements with respect to age peers, identification through testing, and schooling as the main context for talent development (Olszewski-Kubilius, 2000). In contrast, those who study adult giftedness focus on domain-specific abilities, the creativity of achievements or products and their contribution to the field, and an individual's standing or stature as judged by other experts in the field (Olszewski-Kubilius, 2000). A major difference between child and adult giftedness is the emphasis on the field. A measure of the quality of adult achievements is the critical acclaim they receive from other experts—the extent to which they break new ground or move the field forward. Gifted children do not often typically create new knowledge; they discover what is already known— earlier and faster than most other children.

Generally, studies involving children examine short-term, developmental issues or issues regarding educational practice and use cross-sectional, multigroup designs. Finding an appropriate comparison group is a challenge if one of the aims of the study is to differentiate developmental or age-related effects from those due to differences in intellectual ability. To accomplish this goal, researchers use multiple comparison groups that are alternatively equivalent to the gifted group in either chronological or mental age. Few studies of children are prospective and longitudinal with the exception of the Terman studies, the Study of Mathematically Precocious Youth (SMPY), a study of more than 30 years of verbally and mathematically talented students identified in the late 1970s and early 1980s (Benbow, 1988; Benbow & Lubinski, 1994; Benbow & Stanley, 1983), and the Illinois

Valedictorian Project (Arnold, 1995), which is following high school valedictorians from the class of 1982 through adulthood. See Subotnik and Arnold (1994) for a more comprehensive listing of longitudinal studies.

There are many more retrospective studies of gifted adults than there are prospective studies of gifted children. Typically, the adults are identified as eminent or renowned in their field either by cultural impact of their work or by the judgments of other experts. These studies look back into the lives of these individuals, usually through analysis of historical documents, biographies, and autobiographies. Some of these studies include interviews with the individual (if still living) and with other family members. They present detailed case studies of the gifted individuals. The purpose of most of these studies is to determine what contributes to the development of high levels of talent and creative productive ability. Examples of these kinds of studies are Goertzel and Goertzel (1962), who studied the emotional and intellectual family environments of eminent individuals form the twentieth century; Roe (1953), who studied 23 eminent male scientists in different fields; Zuckerman (1977), who studied Nobel Laureates; Subotnik, Karp, and Morgan (1989), who studied high IQ individuals who graduated from the Hunter College Elementary School from 1948 to 1960; and Bloom (1985), who studied high achievers in six different talent areas.

Child Prodigies

Prodigious achievement by children has always fascinated our culture. Child prodigies are very rare and historically were regarded either as freaks or gods. Morelock and Feldman (1993, quoted from Feldman, 1986b) have studied child prodigies and define them as "a child who, before the age of 10, performs at the level of an adult professional in some cognitively demanding field" (p. 171). According to Feldman, child prodigies differ from geniuses and do not necessarily become geniuses, although "the prodigy's early mastery of a domain may put him in a better position for achieving works of genius, for he has more time to explore, comprehend, and experiment within a field" (Feldman, 1986b, p. 16). Prodigies are also distinguished from high-IQ children in that their talents are very narrowly specialized to a particular field of endeavor, whereas high-IQ children have intellectual abilities that enable them to function at high levels in a variety of different contexts. Prodigies are extreme specialists according to Feldman (1986b, p. 10) in that "they are exceptionally well tuned to a particular field of knowledge, demonstrating rapid and often seemingly effortless mastery."

The prodigious achievement of a child is evidence of a rare coming-together of a variety of supportive conditions— a process that is termed *co-incidence* (Feldman, 1986a,

1986b). The supportive conditions include a domain or field that is structured in a way and developed to the extent that it is available and comprehensible to a young child. The child's capacity and ways of learning must fit well with knowledge base of the domain and the forms in which learning and instruction occur. The talented child must be living in a historical time in which the domain is valued and high-level mastery of it is prized. Furthermore, the prodigy must come from a home with a family that recognizes and supports the ability and can obtain resources to insure its development (Feldman, 1986b).

According to Feldman (1986b) only some domains that can be described as developmental produce prodigies. Developmental domains typically have a long history of knowledge development and major changes over time in structure, technology, organization, and practice. They have several different levels of expertise to master in sequence—each level marked by a different set of skills. Feldman notes that the largest numbers of child prodigies have been found in chess and music, whereas many fewer have been found in writing, the visual arts, or mathematics. Child prodigies in fields such as physics or the natural sciences are virtually unheard of (Feldman, 1986b).

Although prodigies display exceptional capacity to master the levels of a particular field, their tremendously fast learning rate appears limited to a single domain. "Perhaps the purest essence of domain-specific talent is the ability to holistically intuit the syntactic core of rules and regularities lying at the heart of a domain of knowledge . . ." (Morelock & Feldman, 1993, p. 179). That these children do develop skills to such a high level in an area is a result of a delicate and rare interaction between the capabilities and developmental trajectory of the child and of the domain (Feldman, 1986b). And, despite early and rapid advancement in a field, Feldman's prodigies did not necessarily stay with the same field into adulthood. Most often, they gave up their commitment to that one field and branched out to others.

The Relationship Between Creativity and Intellectual Giftedness

The field of gifted education has had an ambivalent attitude toward the concept of creativity. Some, like Renzulli (described previously), believe that creativity is the essence of giftedness—one should not even speak about giftedness except to mean creative production. Alternatively, creativity is included as one of several categories of giftedness within the Marland definition (described previously) equal in status with other categories. Others believe that creativity is a phenomenon distinct from, yet larger than intellectual giftedness; creativity rests on the acquisition of skills and knowledge acquired

via intellectual giftedness but goes beyond it (see Feldman, described previously). Others believe that creativity can only be thought of within the context of a domain and in reference to adult work. It is "impossible to define creativity independently of a judgment based on criteria that change from domain to domain and across time" (Csikszentmihalyi, 1994, p. 143).

Definitions of creativity can be categorized according to four different emphases—personality, process, press (situation), and product (Fishkin, 1999). Work on the creative personality aims to illuminate the personality traits of creative producers, usually through retrospective research studies (examples of such studies are listed earlier in this chapter). Creative producers have been found to possess personality characteristics such as risk taking, flexibility, a preference for disorder, androgyny, the ability to tolerate ambiguity and delay gratification, and an introspective and introverted personality (Rogers, 1999).

Other researchers primarily focus their definition on the process of creativity, attempting to delineate the intellectual activities involved in creative thought such as use of imagery, problem-finding, and metacognitive components (Fishkin, 1999). Studies that focus on press are interested in the contextual determinants of creative productivity, particularly environmental factors. Work in this area has looked at aspects of the home environment such as encouragement of freedom of thought and risk taking, features of the work place such as leadership style of a supervisor, temperature, and physical climate, and other psychological and social variables that affect creativity (Keller-Mathers & Murdock, 1999).

Research on creative products has focused on determining how decisions about the uniqueness of products are made (e.g., criteria used, judgements by whom) within and across different domains, the relevance of creative production to the definition of creativity (e.g., can one be creative if one does not produce?), and the development of rating scales to make judgments about children's creative products (Keller-Mathers & Murdock, 1999).

Researchers who have tried to assess creativity have used a variety of instruments and techniques depending upon their theoretical perspective. Creativity measures include tests of divergent thinking, attitude and interest inventories, personality inventories, biographical analyses, ratings by teachers or others, judgments of products, criteria of eminence, and self-reports of creative activities or achievements (Johnson & Fishkin, 1999). The most extensively used and researched instruments to identify creative children are standardized measures of divergent thinking such as the Torrance Tests of Creative Thinking or several subtests of the Structure of the Intellect Test. Many assessments of creativity suffer from low reliability and questionable validity (see Johnson & Fishkin for a review).

An important issue of construct validity for creativity measures are their distinctiveness or independence from IQ. The relationship between IQ and divergent thinking measures has been described as nonlinear, with evidence of a threshold effect (Johnson & Fishkin, 1999). Across a wide range of IQ scores, the correlation between intelligence and creativity is about .40 (Johnson & Fishkin); however, beyond an IQ of 120, the correlation is negligible. The threshold relationship is interpreted to mean that greater creativity is associated with higher intelligence up to a certain point only. Beyond an IQ of 120, higher intelligence does not guarantee greater creativity, and other variables such as motivation and personality disposition are more influential. The relationship between creativity and academic achievement is complicated; some studies show a positive correlation, some show no correlation, and others indicate that the relationship is mediated by gender, type of creativity, and type of creativity assessment (Ai, 1999).

There have been many programs developed to advance the creative thinking skills of children. The assumption behind these programs is that creative thinking skills are not innate but instead are acquired through practice and deliberate teaching. Creative thinking programs include synectics, a form of analogical reasoning in which thinkers examine connections between seemingly unrelated objects; lateral thinking (e.g., the Cognitive Research Trust program or CoRt); Odyssey of the Mind (OM), a creativity training program in which teams of children practice skills such as brainstorming, suspending judgment, and listening to others in order to solve complex, open-ended problems in a competition; and the Future Problem Solving program (FPS), which teaches students to use creative problem-solving techniques applied to ill-defined, complex problems about futuristic issues in competition with other teams of students (Meador, Fishkin, & Hoover, 1999).

Pyryt (1999) reports on several meta-analyses that examined the effects of various types of creativity training on aspects of children's thinking. The outcome measure in these studies is typically performance on divergent thinking tests, mainly the Torrance Test of Creative Thinking. Pyryt found effects sizes averaging close to one standard deviation across a variety of groups of students, not just the gifted ones. Effect size correlated with the amount of training, and different types of training differentially affected performance on verbal versus figural divergent thinking measures.

An important issue for researchers and educators is the predictive validity of creativity measures for adult accomplishments. Cramond (1994), in a review of research on the Torrance tests, concludes that there are moderate correlations between childhood divergent thinking scores and adult accomplishments. However, Tannenbaum (1983) notes that Torrance's studies are the only ones that consistently support the predictive validity of divergent thinking measures for adult creative activities.

There is an accumulated body of research about highly creative, eminent individuals. These studies have sought to understand the factors that contribute to high levels of creative production. A major finding is that many creative producers experienced stressful and traumatic childhoods—particularly, the early loss of parents (Olszewski-Kubilius, 2000). Stressful childhoods are thought to contribute to the development of creativity by engendering strong motivations to express and thereby ameliorate childhood wounds through some creative outlet and to gain acceptance, love, or admiration from others. Early family environments that stress individual thought, expression, and independence, and those in which there is an emotional distance between parent and child and less vigilant parent monitoring and socialization of children create contexts for the development of personality traits (e.g., risk-taking) that are thought to be essential to the development of creativity (Subotnik, Olszewski-Kubilius, & Arnold, in press).

THE EDUCATION OF GIFTED CHILDREN

Identification

The identification of gifted children is a major issue for educators. It is inextricably tied to one's definition of and beliefs about the nature of giftedness and also to the programs and services that are put into place for children who have been identified as gifted. These two components serve as bookends to determine or bound the identification procedures.

For example, if you believe strongly that the aim of identification is to find children who have the potential to become creative producers in adulthood (see discussion of Renzulli earlier in this chapter), identification procedures might include a focus on demonstration of exceptionally creative work in school coupled with task persistence and motivation to produce unusual products at a high level. On the other hand, if your beliefs about giftedness are that it is exceptional intellectual ability regardless of actual achievement or performance, measures such as IQ scores could be used for identification, and you would aim to include children with high ability yet low school achievement. If you subscribe to an educational definition of giftedness and believe that gifted children are those for whom the typical school curriculum is inadequate, you would use measures of achievement to find students who are able to perform beyond their current school placement in the subjects typically taught in schools. If you subscribe to a multiple intelligences view of ability, you would want to establish identification procedures to find children with talent in the various domains and provide programs to help them develop that talent.

Programming or services affect identification procedures. If you believe that your goal is to prepare children to become creative producers in adulthood, you would build a program that gives them many opportunities to practice making or generating creative products. If you believe that your goal is to ensure that every child in school experiences academic challenges, you would design classes that through pacing or rigor of the content provide challenge to gifted learners.

In reality, identification procedures for gifted children are often put into place without a clear rationale or understanding of the beliefs about giftedness and its development upon which they rest. Moreover, there is often a mismatch between identification procedures and programming. A frequent and often valid criticism of gifted programs is that they often have very selective identification procedures that include high IQ and achievement scores, but the enrichment programs provide general enrichment appropriate for which most students could be successful.

Identification of Academic Talent

A national survey of school gifted programs conducted by the Richardson Foundation in the mid-1980s showed that teacher nomination was the most frequently used means to identify academically gifted students (91%), followed by achievement tests (90%), and IQ tests (82%; Cox et al., 1985). All other types of criteria—grades, peer or self-nomination, and creativity measures—were used significantly less often by schools (less than 10% in most cases).

Although it is frequently used, teacher nomination is not highly regarded as a method of identifying gifted students (Tannenbaum, 1983). Teachers tend to nominate children who are high achievers, polite, and well-behaved; sometimes use placement in a gifted program as a reward for high achievement; and often fail to identify underachieving gifted children (Borland, 1989). One of the problems in assessing the accuracy of teacher nomination is the lack of precise standards against which their judgments can be compared. Teachers improve in identifying children who turn out to be gifted as defined by IQ scores when they receive training about the behavioral characteristics of gifted children (Tannenbaum, 1983).

IQ tests, which are probably best viewed as predictors of aptitude for academic achievement, are relevant to educationally oriented definitions of giftedness. One of the problems with IQ tests is that the information is not very useful for programming planning because it does not relate well to the content areas

typically included in the school curriculum. Furthermore, IQ tests are limited in their prediction of adult success as well. However, IQ tests may reveal intellectual ability among underachieving students (Subotnik & Arnold, 1994).

Achievement tests and domain-specific aptitude tests do map onto the school curriculum better than do IQ tests and can indicate students' mastery of the in-grade curriculum. Due to severe ceiling problems, however, these tests do not reveal what students know beyond the information assessed on the test, which may be considerable. Sometimes, achievement tests are used off-level, so to speak, or tests (or test forms) designed for older students are given to younger ones, thereby eliminating the ceiling problems. However, it is also not clear to what extent achievement or special aptitude test performance predicts adult success in different fields (Tannenbaum, 1983). A substantial amount of evidence exists about this issue for mathematics; high mathematics scores on the Scholastic Achievement Test (SAT) in the seventh or eighth grade are associated with high academic achievement in high school and college and with the choice of mathematics as a career (Lubinski & Benbow, 1993).

Checklists for teachers and parents are also frequently used as part of an identification system. Very often, these are included primarily for political reasons—that is, to include the opinions of a particular group in the process. There are some published instruments available, including the Scales for Rating the Behavioral Characteristics of Superior Students (Renzulli, Smith, White, Callahan, & Hartman, 1976), which assesses abilities in 10 areas: learning, motivation, leadership, artistic, musical, dramatics, communication-precision, communication-expressive, planning, and creativity. Also available are the Purdue Academic Rating Scales, designed to identify secondary students for honors, advanced placement (AP), or accelerated classes: It focuses on signs of superior academic performance in mathematics, science, English, social studies, and foreign languages (Feldhusen, Hoover, & Saylor, 1990). See Johnson and Fishkin (1990) for a compendium of rating scales for creativity. Most often, schools devise their own questionnaires; hence, there is typically little or no validity or reliability information available on them.

Schools generally use multiple pieces of information about a student to make a decision about placement into a gifted program and employ some means or system of organizing and evaluating the data. Borland (1989) and others (Feldhusen & Jarwan, 1993) recommend that identification be viewed as a process consisting of several distinct phases. These phases include screening, which involves using available information about students to nominate them as potential candidates for the gifted program—candidates who need further scrutiny or examination to determine their match to the program. Sources of information for screening include existing student records, group tests, referrals, and nominations. At the screening phase, the goal is to cast a wide net, so to speak, using generous cutoffs so in order to include as many students as possible.

The second phase is selection or placement. This phase involves the gathering of more specific and reliable information, usually through additional testing (Borland, 1989). Tests to be used for selection or placement should be selected on the basis of their relevance to the educational program, their reliability and validity, the availability of normative data, and the extent to which they are free from ceiling effects and test bias (Feldhusen & Jarwan, 1993).

Placement decisions are usually based on the results of synthesizing the data in some fashion and typically involve one of the following mechanisms: constructing a matrix that involves assigning points to scores on different tests and summing them to yield a single giftedness index; computing standard scores for each measure in order to ensure comparability across measures; a comprehensive case study on each nominated student; or a multiple-cutoff method, which requires students to meet minimum score cutoffs for each measure included in the identification system (Feldhusen & Jarwan). More sophisticated methods such as multiple regression models that determine a formula based on the predictive validity of each identification instrument for program performance are rarely used (Feldhusen & Jarwan). Domain-specific measures may be used in areas such as the visual or performing arts and include portfolio assessment, product assessment or critique, auditions, and so on.

The third phase of the identification process that is rarely implemented is the evaluation of the viability of the identification protocol (Borland, 1989). This involves an analysis of students' performance in relation to the identification criteria and can involve a possible reformulation of the identification protocol. The questions being addressed at this phase of the identification process are *Are the students who were selected for the program succeeding in it?*, *Are the selection procedures excluding children who also could succeed in the program?*, and *Are the children in the program achieving at expected high levels over the long term?* Methods to assess the appropriateness of the selection protocol include the use of multiple regression to determine the extent to which identification criteria predict achievement in the program or the comparison of the achievement of children who were selected for the program to those who were nominated for the program but not selected. Schools infrequently evaluate their identification protocols.

In summary, typical problems with identification systems include the following: a lack of consistency between the philosophy of the program and the identification protocol; the overreliance on a single measure or instrument for identification; a mismatch between the identification protocol and the program being provided—most typically requiring high scores on measures of verbal and quantitative ability and providing a program in only one area or using very high cutoff scores on IQ or achievement tests and providing a general enrichment program suitable for mildly above-average learners; lack of evaluation of identification criteria to assess their predictive validity for program performance or outcomes; problems with instruments used, such as low reliability or validity and ceiling effects; use of some kind of summative score based on different selection criteria that has dubious validity; and the lack of procedures for periodic reassessment of students, both those in and those not in the program.

Recommended identification procedures include the use of multiple screening measures in an effort to be very inclusive and capture nontraditional students and underachievers, identification protocols tailored to the particular school domain (e.g. using math tests for an accelerated math program), placement decisions made by a committee using all available information, and off-level testing to deal with ceiling effects on on-level tests. See Feldhusen and Jarwan (1993) and Borland (1989) for a fuller discussion of recommended identification procedures for gifted students.

Identification of Underrepresented Students

A major issue within the field of gifted education is the typical underrepresentation of children of color within gifted programs or advanced classes (Olszewski-Kubilius & Laubscher, 1996) regardless of socioeconomic level (Ford, 1996). Reasons for this situation include lower performance on typically used identification instruments by minority students due to environmental factors such as fewer educational opportunities and qualitatively poorer educational environments, instrumentation problems such as cultural bias of tests and their lack of predictive validity for academic achievement of minority students, and the prejudices of teachers and other educational personnel making decisions about students. Ford (1996) recommends using alternative identification procedures that include nonverbal problemsolving tests (e.g., the Ravens Progressive Matrices tests or the Naglieri Nonverbal Ability Test), surveys and instruments specifically designed to identify giftedness among minority students, and training for educators regarding cultural sensitivity. Although the research evidence suggests that students of color are more likely to be identified as gifted when alternatives are used, they are still much less likely to be referred or nominated for such testing by their teachers (Sacuzzo, Johnson, & Guertin, 1994).

Musical and Artistic Talent

Systematic identification of musical and artistic talent within children is typically not done by schools. Some large urban school districts have performing arts high schools that draw students from a wide geographic area. Standardized tests for both music and art do exist; more often, however, teacher nominations, portfolios, and auditions are relied upon. As Winner and Martino (1993) note, very musically or artistically gifted children usually stand out and are easily identified by teachers.

The early signs of musical talent include exceptional sensitivity to the structure of music, including tonality, key, harmony, and rhythm; strong interest and delight in musical sounds; exceptional musical memory; quick and easy learning of an instrument; and early musical generativity or the ability to compose, transpose, and improvise (Winner & Martino, 1993). Perfect pitch and sight reading are less consistently associated with musical talent. Early signs of artistic talent include the ability to draw realistically at an early age and the ability to imitate the styles of other artists (Winner & Martino). More rare is an exceptional sense of composition, form, or color in childhood drawings. Artistically talented adolescents often produce drawings with elaborate imaginary settings and fantasy characters—a visual representation of a complex story (Winner & Martino).

Predictive Validity of Identification Tools

A major question underlying the identification of gifted students is whether these children do in fact achieve at expected levels in adulthood. It is very difficult to answer this question given that there is no agreed-upon definition of adult success. However, Subotnik and Arnold (1994) summarized the result of longitudinal studies of individuals identified as gifted (typically based on childhood IQ). They concluded that IQ accounted for little of the variability in adult outcomes. Neither did grades or other kinds of school-based, academic criteria. The fruition of childhood ability and promise is very tenuous, and social, environmental, and psychological variables play a huge role and interact in very complex ways (Olszewski-Kubilius, 2000). Researchers agree that beyond a certain point, ability is less important for adult achievement than are factors such as personality dimensions and motivation (Winner, 1996; Csikszentmihalyi, Rathunde, & Whalen, 1993).

Gifted Education and the Law

The federal government has historically, been reluctant to become involved in education; that is especially true for gifted education. Special educational services for gifted children are not required by law as they are for children with disabilities. There does exist an Office of Gifted and Talented in Washington DC (reestablished in 1988), and federal money currently supports a National Research Center for the Gifted and Talented. However, the federal government's primary role has been in providing definitions of gifted and talented children (Karnes & Marquart, 2000).

Currently, 48% of states in the United States have mandated both identification and the provision of special programs for gifted children, 17% have a mandate for identification but not programs, and 4% have a mandate for programs but not identification (Council of State Directors of Programs for the Gifted, 1996, as quoted in Karnes & Marquart, 2000). Many of these mandates (42%) were not by law, however; 6% were by administrative rule, 3% were by state department of education guidelines, 18% were by a combination of these, and 15% by some other means (Karnes & Marquart). In 1996, seventy-one percent of the states who reported in indicated that there were funds within the state budget specifically allocated for gifted education.

Administratively, most states have a designated state coordinator of services for gifted children (94%), although many have additional responsibilities; also, most of the state-level coordinators are placed under the departments of special education or curriculum (Karnes & Marquardt, 2000).

Almost all states (except five) in the United States have state definitions of gifted and talented students, and the majority use some version of the 1978 federal definition (Karnes & Marquardt, 2000). In terms of categories of ability included in state definitions, the focus is clearly on superior intellectual ability. Specific academic ability was mentioned in 33 states, creative ability in 30, visual and performing arts in 20, leadership in 18, and psychomotor in 3. Almost all of the states' definitions use the terms *demonstrated and/or potential achievement* (Karnes & Marquardt). Currently, only 28 states require that teachers have specific certifications or endorsements in order to teach gifted students (Karnes & Marquart).

Instructional Issues

Ability Grouping

One of the major strategies for dealing with gifted students in schools is ability grouping. Ability grouping as a technique to accommodate differences in learning rate is not used only by educators of gifted children. In the past, schools have used ability grouping widely, but its use tends to vary with the broader political climate at the time (see Kulik, 1992). Ability grouping was employed and hailed as successful after Sputnik; recently, however, it has been viewed negatively as another form of tracking—a major reform issue in the 1990s. The concerns about ability grouping among educators coalesce around several key issues—student achievement, teachers' expectations of students, instructional quality, racial and social discrimination and mobility, and social cohesion (Rogers, 1991). The concerns have to do primarily with whether ability grouping negatively affects students who are not in the highest group and specifically whether it lowers their achievement (due to a generally lowering of the intellectual level of the classroom when very bright students are removed or lowered teacher expectations or poorer instruction), self-esteem, or both. The main concerns about ability grouping often voiced by educators of the gifted but not by educators in general is whether placement with other bright students lowers individual gifted students' self-esteem, stresses them with unrealistic performance demands, or affects their sociability with children who are not as bright. Despite the concerns, the research on ability grouping mainly addresses only two issues—academic performance and self-esteem.

Kulik (1992) and Rogers (1991) agree that the effects of ability grouping vary greatly depending upon the type of program or curriculum that is given to the different groups of learners. Kulik's (1992) meta-analysis of studies in which students were ability grouped but given the same curriculum show that students in the lower and middle groups learn the same amount as do students of the same ability levels who were placed in heterogeneous classes. Students in the high group learned slightly more than did students of the same ability placed in heterogeneous classes—1.1 compared to 1.0 years on a grade-equivalent scale after a year of instruction. The results of meta-analyses of these types of grouping arrangements have often been used as evidence of the ineffectiveness of tracking by educators (Kulik, 1992). However, Kulik argues that these studies do not properly address the issue of tracking because no real differentiation of curriculum took place. These same groups of studies also revealed slightly negative effects for self-esteem for the high-ability students and slightly positive ones for less able students.

The results of meta-analyses of programs that involved within- or across-grade ability groupings of children who received different curricula showed some increased learning for all groups (Kulik, 1992). Typically, students who were ability grouped gained 1.2 to 1.3 years on grade equivalent scale compared to 1.0 years for students of comparable abilities in heterogeneous classes.

Meta-analysis of 23 studies that compared the achievement of gifted students placed in accelerated classes to students with equal abilities from nonaccelerated control classes showed that the accelerated students outperformed the nonaccelerated ones by nearly 1 year on a grade-equivalent scale of a standardized achievement test (Kulik, 1992). Substantial gains were also found for gifted students who were grouped full-time for instruction in gifted programs (Rogers, 1991). Rogers' analysis by type of accelerated gifted program showed that there were substantial academic gains for the following kinds of programs: nongraded classrooms, curriculum compression (compacting of the curriculum), grade telescoping (completing 2 years of school in one), subject acceleration, and early admissions to college. Also, these forms of acceleration did not have any substantial effect on the self-esteem of the gifted students (Rogers, 1991).

Academic gains of 4–5 months (on a grade-equivalent scale) were also found for gifted students grouped into enrichment classes compared to equally able students in regular mixed-ability classes (Kulik, 1992). Rogers (1991), in a review of research on ability grouping, concluded that there were also positive gains for gifted students who were receiving enrichment in cluster groups within their classes or in pullout programs on measures of critical thinking, general achievement, and creativity.

Rogers (1991) interpreted the results of various meta-analyses of ability grouping to indicate that negative changes found for self-esteem for gifted students are very small and appear only at the initiation of a program that involves full-time grouping. These effects are not present for other partial programs for gifted students, and some positive effects for self-esteem have been found for pullout types of enrichment programs.

Kulik (1992) concluded that the effects of grouping are strongest for gifted students because the adjustment of the content, curriculum, and instructional rate is more substantial. Rogers (1991) agrees that ability grouping takes many forms that are beneficial to gifted students. Despite the positive research findings regarding ability grouping for gifted students, educators of the gifted often have to vigorously defend their programs.

Acceleration Versus Enrichment

Acceleration and enrichment are the cornerstones of gifted education. These terms encompass the major educational strategies used with gifted children. Acceleration is defined as "progress through an educational program at rates faster or ages younger than conventional" (Pressy, 1949, p. 2, quoted in Southern, Jones, & Stanley, 1993, p. 387). Typically, acceleration is thought of as grade skipping, but it actually encompasses a large number of practices. Southern et al. list 17 accelerative practices including early entrance to any level of schooling, self-paced instruction, grade skipping, concurrent enrollment in two levels of schooling simultaneously, credit by examination, extracurricular programs, and curriculum compacting or compression of curriculum into shorter periods of time (see also Southern and Jones, 1991, for a thorough description and analysis of accelerative practices and options). Southern et al. note that these programmatic options vary along at least three dimensions: the degree to which the student is treated differently from his or her age peers (e.g., early entrance places students outside the normal grade for their age, whereas extracurricular programs and credit by examination involve little differentiation); the degree to which the accelerative option merely represents an administrative arrangement to recognize prior achievement (e.g., early admission to any level of schooling, grade skipping) versus active intervention to respond to students' learning needs (self-paced instruction or fast-paced courses); and the age at which a student could experience the accelerative program.

Despite its many forms, accelerative strategies are infrequently used by schools, and many educators have negative attitudes about them based on single experiences with individuals who were grade skipped (Southern et al., 1993). Acceleration actually involves two components—recognition of previous knowledge levels of the students that typically greatly exceed those of most same-aged students and a capacity to acquire new material at a rate faster than that of other students. Many accelerative strategies simply respond to the first component, whereas fewer are designed to address the latter. Most accelerative strategies bring content reserved for older students down to younger ones and assume that the content is appropriate for younger gifted students, which may or may not be true.

Proponents of accelerative strategies list many benefits for students, including less emphasis on needless repetition and drill, reduction of boredom, a closer match between level of instruction and level of achievement, increased productivity in careers in which early contributions are important, increased opportunity for academic exploration, and more appropriate level of challenge that engenders the acquisition of good study habits and avoidance of underachievement (Southern et al., 1993). Opponents of acceleration give the following as negative consequences of acceleration: academic problems stemming from gaps in content preparation; what has been called a specious precocity due to knowledge without appropriate experience; an undue focus on learning the right answers and short shrift to creativity and divergent production; social adjustment problems as a result of a

reduction of time for age-appropriate activities; rejection by older classmates; less opportunity to acquire social skills via interaction with same-aged peers; reduced extracurricular opportunities such as participation in sports or athletics due to age ineligibility; and emotional adjustment problems due to stress and pressure to perform (Southern et al., 1993).

The research evidence regarding the efficacy of acceleration for gifted students is the same research cited previously for grouping and is overwhelmingly positive. The research regarding specific accelerative strategies such as early admission to elementary school is much more varied, however, linking early admission to increased failure and retention rates and to more frequent referrals for placement in special education. However, Southern et al. (1993) characterize much of this research as suffering from serious methodological flaws. The research on early admissions to college is positive regarding both the academic performance and emotional-social adjustment of early entrants. Specifically, early entrants do as well as academically or better than do other gifted students who do not enter early, make friends easily and readily with older, typical-aged college students, and more frequently complete college on time, earn honors, and complete a concurrent master's degree (Olszewski-Kubilius, 1995).

Definitions of enrichment vary, but it is typically considered to be instruction or content that extends the boundaries of the curriculum. The assumptions behind enrichment as a focus of gifted education are (a) that the typical school curriculum leaves out a great deal of content and skill learning that is valuable for students to acquire and (b) that it focuses on lower level cognitive skills such as the learning of facts at the expense of more complex cognitive abilities (Southern et al., 1993). Practitioners attempt to provide enrichment to gifted students in a variety of ways—increasing the breadth of the curriculum by adding content that is not typically covered and perhaps is more abstract; adding depth by allowing students to study a topic more deeply and more thoroughly; adding opportunities for more real-world applications of the content learned through projects; infusion of research opportunities; or a focus on learning skills such as divergent thinking skills, heuristics, or problem-solving skills. Unlike acceleration, enrichment tries to meet the educational needs of gifted students by the addition of content rather than adjustments of pacing of instruction (Southern et al., 1993).

Acceleration and enrichment have often been pitted against each other as opposing educational strategies. In reality, the distinctions between them are often very blurred. Providing additional content via enrichment often results in a student's being ahead of or accelerated with respect to other students in achievement. Often the additional content provided is content reserved for older students. Programs that truly meet the needs of gifted students will be some combination of enrichment and acceleration—adjustments to content as well as adjustments to instructional pace. The preference for acceleration or enrichment as an educational strategy to serve gifted children often has to do with societal sentiments and political ideologies prevailing at the time (Southern et al., 1993).

Types of Gifted Programs: Elementary Level

Borland (1989) identified seven program formats as typical among program options available in schools for gifted children. These formats include special schools; a school-within-a-school, in which a semiautonomous educational program for gifted students exists within a school; multitracked programs, which involve grouping students by ability for each major subject; pullout programs, which are arrangements in which students spend most of their time within a regular classroom and are removed for a given time period each week for special instruction with other gifted students; resource room programs, in which students who are typically grouped within heterogeneous classrooms report to a special site on a part-time basis for instruction; and provisions within the classroom, which may include cluster grouping, special assignments, or some other curricular modification.

The various program options have different benefits and disadvantages for students and teachers. Part-time programs such as resource room and pullout programs have the advantage of giving students contact with both age-mates and intellectual peers in a single day. However, being pulled out of the regular classroom for a program makes the gifted students conspicuous, which they may not like. Part-time programs often fall victim to providing superfluous content as administrators struggle to define the curriculum for these programs and typically opt to not intrude on the traditional school subjects. And, typically, the program may involve only 2–4 hours of instruction and so are quite minimal in scope and impact. Partial, pullout types of programs can be logistical and scheduling nightmares, raise the ire of teachers whose students are being pulled out, and are expensive because they typically require an additional teacher (Borland, 1989).

Full-time programs—whether they involve special schools or a school-within-a-school—give students maximal exposure to intellectual peers and thus peer support for high achievement. If the school specializes in a particular area (e.g., math and science or the arts), students will have a rich and exceptional array of challenging courses and extracurricular activities from which to choose and instructors with exceptional content area expertise. Most of these programs are highly selective, and competition to gain entrance is fierce. In addition, after they are admitted, students can experience unhealthy levels of stress due to competition for grades (Borland, 1989). There is also the danger that students entering special schools may focus on a particular discipline too early without exploring other interests and options fully (Borland, 1989).

Programs that group students by ability for each subject can accommodate students with exceptional ability in only one or two areas and provide a good match between the identification criteria, subject-area achievement, and placement. However, these programs can be difficult for teachers because the class makeup changes for each subject. They can be scheduling nightmares, and very often a truly differentiated curriculum is not provided to the different groups of students (Borland, 1989).

Cox et al. (1985), in a national survey of practices in gifted education at both the elementary and secondary levels, found that the most frequently offered program option was the part-time special class or pullout model (72% of districts reporting). This option was followed by enrichment in the regular classroom (63%), independent study (52%), and resource rooms (44%). However, when criteria were applied to determine whether the program was substantial (e.g., a part-time special class had to meet for at least 4 hours a week in order to be considered substantial), only 47% of the part-time programs, 16% of the enrichment programs, 23% of the independent study programs, and 21% of the resource room programs were deemed substantial.

Less frequently employed program options (28–37% of total programs) were AP classes; continuous progress (defined as allowing students to proceed through the curriculum without age-grade distinctions for subjects); mentorships; full-time special class; itinerant teacher; moderate acceleration (defined as completion of grades K–12 in 10–13 years); concurrent or dual enrollment (defined as enrollment in high school and college simultaneously); and early entrance to any schooling level. The least frequently used program options (11% or less) were radical acceleration (i.e., completion of grades K–12 in 11 or fewer years), fast-paced classes (i.e., completion of two or more courses in a discipline in an abbreviated time frame), special schools, and nongraded schools (Cox et al., 1985). It is interestingly to note that the program options with the highest percentage of substantial programs were those less often employed by schools—early entrance, concurrent or dual enrollment, continuous progress, full-time special class, itinerant teacher, and special schools (Cox et al.).

Research about the efficacy of different program models is scant (Delcourt, Loyd, Cornell, & Goldberg (1994). Delcourt et al. cite only 10 studies (excluding their own study) within the last 20 years that examined academic outcomes of different types of gifted programs. These studies involved students primarily in Grades 2 through 6. These authors compared the performance of second- and third-grade students within four different types of gifted programs—full-time special schools, full-time separate classes, pullout programs, and within-class programs to groups of nongifted students and students nominated by teachers as potentially qualified for the gifted program (the gifted comparison group) but not currently placed in it. Students' prior performance on a standardized achievement test was used as a covariate, and differences between the gifted students in the four gifted programs and the two comparison groups were assessed. Results were that the students within the separate classes, full-time schools, and pullout programs had higher scores on a standardized achievement test than did students in either of the comparison groups and students in the within-class programs when starting levels of achievement were accounted for. The within-class students had the lowest scores in all areas of achievement of all the groups assessed. Delcourt et al. state, "since Within-Class programs are a popular model in gifted education, their curricular and instructional provisions for the gifted must be carefully maintained lest they disintegrate into a no-program format" (1994, p. xviii).

Delcourt et al. (1994) also found that students in the separate classes had the highest levels of achievement across the comparison groups and other program types but the lowest perceptions of their academic competence and sense of acceptance by peers. Students in the special schools also had lower perceptions of their academic competence than did the other groups of children. Delcourt et al. concluded that lowered self-esteem or perceptions of academic competence, which appear after initial placement and last for about 2 years subsequently, is a result of social comparison—that is, students comparing themselves to other very bright students. Students in all the groups studied reported that they felt comfortable with the number of friends they had in their own school and their popularity. "The type of grouping arrangement did not influence student perceptions of their social relations for gifted or nongifted students" (Delcourt et al., 1994, p. xix).

Archambault et al. (1993) studied a national sample of third- and fourth-grade teachers to determine what kinds of strategies they use to provide differentiated instruction to gifted students. The results showed that across different types of schools, teachers made only minor modifications in the regular curriculum to meet the needs of gifted students. These included eliminating already-mastered material and assigning advanced readings, independent projects, enrichment worksheets, or reports. In addition, gifted students were given no more opportunities to work at enrichment centers, work with other students on a specific interest, move to another grade for a particular subject, or work on an advanced curriculum unit than were average students within their classrooms (Archambault et al., 1993).

One strategy that has been proposed as appropriate for gifted students is curriculum compacting; this is a strategy whereby needless repetition and drill and already-learned concepts are eliminated from the curriculum through pretesting or some kind of preassessment. Research done by Reis et al. (1993) showed that 40–50% of the in-grade curriculum could be eliminated for gifted students in subjects such as math, social studies, and science without affecting achievement. Specifically these students still scored as well as or higher than did other gifted students who had not had curriculum compacting on achievement tests given above level. This study also showed that teacher training was critical to the implementation of curriculum compacting as a strategy to accommodate gifted students' higher levels of knowledge and faster learning rates. The quality of compacting was higher for teachers in this study who received more intensive training, including several hours of group compacting simulations and 6–10 hours of peer coaching.

Regardless of how well they compacted the curriculum, most teachers had a tendency to substitute nonacademic kinds of activities such as peer tutoring when content material was eliminated from instruction (Reis et al., 1993). They also preferred to substitute with enrichment rather than accelerative types of learning activities. The authors suggest that further training on substitution strategies was needed as well as access to and assistance with selecting appropriate advanced content materials to use with students.

Types of Gifted Programs: Secondary Level

Within the field of gifted education, the lion's share of the research and writing about programs is focused on elementary school-aged children. For children in this age range, both program models (e.g., Renzulli's model, multiple intelligences) and different kinds of administrative and grouping arrangements for the delivery of services (e.g., pullout programs, enrichment, cluster grouping, acceleration, resource room, etc.) abound. However, for secondary-level students, fewer models for programs exist, and creative service delivery options are rarely employed. In most secondary schools, honors-track and AP classes are the only options for students functioning above grade level. However, at the secondary level (in contrast to the elementary level) accelerative options are more readily accepted as a means to accommodate gifted learners owing in part to the success and wide acceptance of the AP program, which implies that students are working at least 1 year above grade level.

Special classes for advanced secondary students typically occur within departments that are organized around major content domains. This means that many opportunities may be available to students to develop high levels of talent within particular domains. It can also result in a program that has many good parts but no whole—no systematic means or process of identifying students who need special programming and no integration across the curriculum (VanTassel-Baska, 1998).

At the elementary level, there is often an individual responsible for the gifted program—the gifted coordinator. At the secondary level, this is rarely the case. Programs that are considered appropriate for gifted students at the secondary level are the AP program of the College Board, which enables students to take college-level courses while in high school and via examination thereby earn college credits; and the International Baccalaureate program (IB), which is a 2-year program of advanced courses taken in the junior and senior years. The IB program emphasizes multicultural perspectives and foreign language proficiency and is an international program designed to prepare high school students to be able to pursue college or university course work at any institution worldwide. The IB program was initially developed in the 1960s as a result of international school efforts to establish a common curriculum and university entry credentials for geographically mobile students. Schools opt to implement the IB program, a process that entails a detailed self-study and several years of planning and preparation. Students who enroll in the IB program take special courses and exams in order to earn the IB diploma. IB is considered to be an academically rigorous course of studies by U.S. colleges and universities (Tookey, 1999/2000).

In 22 states within the United States, legislation enables high school students to be simultaneously enrolled in high school and college—referred to as *dual enrollment, concurrent enrollment,* or *postsecondary option.* Students who partake of this option spend part of their day on a college campus taking a college course. The legislation across states varies considerably (McCarthy, 1999; Olszewski-Kubilius & Limburg-Weber, 1999) but typically requires high schools to use their per-pupil state funds to pay part or all of the college tuition. The legislation may stipulate what kinds of courses can be taken (typically only courses that the high school does not offer), the number of courses that can be taken, and the types of institutions (private vs. public) that students can attend. Some states specify the circumstances under which students can earn high school and college credit and the amount of credit that can be earned. Most states reserve dual enrollment for juniors and seniors who have already earned a certain number of high school credits or satisfied a specified

number of graduation requirements. Dual enrollment and AP are similar in that they both are ways in which high school students can take classes for college credit while in high school.

Other programmatic options for gifted secondary students include competitions and internships. These options are not exclusively for gifted students, although they typically require demonstration of a high level of interest in a specific area (internships) or require advanced skills in order to be competitive (competitions). Thus, they are often viewed as most appropriate for students who are gifted.

Competitions are typically extracurricular activities, and students can participate via the sponsorship of their school or on their own. There are many different kinds of competitions (see Olszewski-Kubilius & Limburg-Weber, 1999, for resources) in many different domains. The benefits of competitions include learning how to compete, acquiring and honing independent study skills, gaining opportunities for feedback and critique from professionals, and opportunities to work on real-world problems. Competitions also often have significant cash prizes. Several of the best known are the Intel Science Talent Search (formerly Westinghouse) and the Mathematics, Physics, and Chemistry Olympiads. Usually, students who get involved in team competitions prepare for them via a high school club. These extracurricular activities have many advantages for students; they provide socially supportive contexts within which students can learn a great deal of specific subject matter (Subotnik, Miserandino, & Olszewski-Kubilius, 1997).

Internships are typically available to college-aged students, although increasingly, these opportunities are being opened to high school students and being organized by high schools. The benefits of internships are primarily in the opportunities to participate in significant adult work and to connect with professionals who can assist with career and educational planning (Olszewski-Kubilius & Limburg-Weber, 1999).

Other options for gifted students include special schools. Currently there are 10 special high schools within the United States (six in the South or Southeast, two in the Midwest, one in the West, and one in the Northeast) designed for students who are mathematically and scientifically talented. These schools are supported by state education dollars, which means that tuition and room and board are free. Typically they are established by the state legislature after extensive lobbying efforts on the part of parents and state lawmakers. Most serve students in Grades 11 and 12 only. These schools offer an advanced curriculum and have a variety of courses in mathematics and science that is wider than the variety that would be found at a typical high school. They can also give students educational opportunities that are not usually available to most high school students, such as opportunities to work with scientists on research, access to state-of-the-art laboratories, and career counseling (Olszewski-Kubilius & Limburg-Weber, 1999). These schools are also home to some internationally ranked chess, debate, and academic teams.

A final option for gifted high school students is early entrance to college. Many students across the United States leave high school 1 year early and enter college; most colleges and universities accept younger students. However, a dozen or so special early college entrance programs exist that accept students 2–4 years early. These programs are often designed so that students simultaneously complete high school graduation requirements and earn college credits. Some are supported by state education dollars. These programs provide special support systems for students in the form of designated counselors, special dormitories, and social events (Olszewski-Kubilius & Limburg-Weber, 1999).

Many programs geared towards gifted and talented students are sponsored by organizations and institutions other than schools—predominantly universities and colleges. Parents have turned to these institutions for services for their gifted children because such services are not available from their local school and because they want their children to have additional academic opportunities. These extraeducational opportunities include summer programs, study abroad, and distance learning programs.

Summer programs have increased tremendously, and there are hundreds of such programs in the United States. Distance learning programs are also growing—for example, virtual high schools. Some distance learning programs offer a complete high school curriculum. Several programs are geared specifically towards advanced learners and offer AP courses or college-level courses in traditional by-mail formats or through online and Internet technologies (Olszewski-Kubilius & Limburg-Weber, 1999). Gifted students use distance learning courses to take advanced courses that they cannot fit into their schedule at high school or to take courses not offered by their school. Study abroad programs are generally not specifically targeted at academically gifted students but are often used by such students to enhance their high school studies or are used to fill a semester left vacant by accelerated studies.

In the United States, there exists a nationally available program called *talent search* that plays a substantial role in educating gifted children but is not sponsored by schools. Talent search programs involve testing children anywhere from Grades 3 through 9 who are performing at the 95th percentile or above on a standardized in-grade achievement test via standardized tests that are given off-level. The most well-developed programs involve having seventh- and eighth-grade students take the SAT or the American College Test (ACT). Other talent search programs involve younger students in taking tests such as the PLUS and EXPLORE. Comparable talent searches are carried out all over the United States by various universities that provide services to a single state or to several states. It is estimated that over 200,000 students across the United States participate in talent search programs annually.

The talent search programs increase families' access to educational resources specifically designed for gifted students, including special summer programs, distance learning programs, weekend courses for students, and conferences and workshops for parents. They give parents information about gifted children's developmental, social, psychological, and educational needs through newsletters and magazines (Olszewski-Kubilius, 1998).

Talent search programs are among the most researched models of identification of academic talent and service delivery that exist within the field of gifted education (Olszewski-Kubilius, 1998). Research has validated the use of the 95th percentile as a cutoff score for participation in the talent search and the predictive validity of scores on the SAT for performance in accelerated classes (Olszewski-Kubilius, 1998). Talent search scores provide a valid indication of level of developed reasoning ability and learning rate within several academic domains that can be matched to educational programs adjusted for pacing and content. Talent search scores are also predictive of future accomplishments such as grades and course taking in high school; they are also predictive of choice of field of study in graduate school (see Olszewski-Kubilius, 1998 for a review of this research).

Although research evidence about the long-term effects of participation in gifted programs is scant, the most substantial body of research exists surrounding the effects of participation in talent-search-sponsored educational programs. Specifically, students who had participated in special programs were more likely to pursue advanced courses in high school such as BC calculus and AP courses, chose more academically selective colleges, earned more honors, were more likely to accelerate their studies, and had higher educational aspirations than did students who did not (see Olszewski-Kubilius, 1997, for a review). These effects were especially potent for gifted females, enabling them to keep up with gifted boys in mathematics course taking (see Olszewski-Kubilius, 1998, for a review of this research). It is likely that participation in out-of-school educational programs that offer advanced and accelerated courses provides both social support for achievement and a safe setting in which to risk taking challenging courses. Achieving success in classes such as these does much to bolster students' confidence, thereby increasing the possibility that they will pursue advanced courses in their home school setting.

Although institutions other than the local schools are increasingly serving gifted students through programs and courses, there is very little articulation between in-school and out-of-school programs. Many students take courses in university summer programs for their own personal growth and enrichment and do not expect to receive credit from their school. Increasingly, however, students and families use summer programs to complete required high school courses or to complete advanced courses that can fulfill graduation requirements. Credit for summer courses or any outside-of-school program is infrequently given for a variety of reasons (Olszewski-Kubilius, Laubscher, Wohl, & Grant, 1996). At present, schools and out-of-school institutions that serve gifted students through programs work independently rather than cooperatively.

The Future of Gifted Education

Although it is difficult to make predictions about the future of gifted education, it is certain that there will be significant changes in both what is delivered to students and the manner in which it is given. At present, there is a shift away from offering gifted programs to serving gifted children within their heterogeneous classrooms; this is in part due to dwindling resources for special programs, the fact that the pullout program (the most typical gifted program) is expensive and cumbersome to run, and the current climate of inclusion regarding special needs students. Research cited previously suggests that although having the regular teacher meet the needs of gifted students within the classroom sounds good in theory, it is difficult to implement, and little real differentiation of curriculum and instruction actually takes place. However, this does not mean that this model cannot be salvaged or that the preference for inclusion will diminish. It requires a shift in the conception of the gifted coordinator and in the conception of the gifted.

Typically the gifted coordinator administers the single gifted program. However, a new conceptualization is that of coordinator of resources for children capable of working above grade level and for teachers who work with them. Gifted children cannot be served with a one-size-fits-all program. Research on talented children reveals no single profile of giftedness, and very few children are exceptional across all school subjects. Thus, a variety of programs and services needs to be in place for a variety of children with a variety of exceptional abilities. The talent development coordinator's role would be to devise and implement identification systems for various domains, assist teachers with grouping arrangements and differentiation of curriculum within the classroom for all children who are advanced, help teachers adjust the level of the curriculum to provide challenge for all students, make special arrangements for students with exceptional needs (learning disabled and gifted or highly gifted), help students access outside-of-school educational programs, coordinate with community organizations and institutions of higher education for services and programs, and design needed school or district programs.

Efforts to help more marginal students reach their potential through special programs could reasonably be considered under the rubric of the talent development program. The research on talent development has shown that schools and the process by which high levels of talent are developed are often at odds. For example, the retrospective literature on eminent adults shows a pattern of early specialization in the talent area and education more akin to apprenticeships and mentorships, unlike our current traditional schooling (Sosniak, 1999; Subotnik & Coleman, 1996). Shifting to a talent development approach to education will require dealing with strongly held beliefs that education—particularly early education—should promote well-roundedness. Can we take what the literature has to offer regarding how talent develops and incorporate it into our schooling process for all children? Gifted education and the talent development literature may have much to say to those who wish to reformulate schools so that all children are motivated to learn to their highest potential. The fundamental basis for gifted education is recognizing individual differences among children and responding to them so that all children are challenged intellectually in school.

The major issues facing gifted education as a field (as well as education generally) is the gap between the achievement of minorities and nonminorities at every socioeconomic level (*Reaching the Top;* College Board, 1999). Gifted programs have been criticized for underidentifying students of color and for contributing to the inequities that exist in schools regarding the education of poor and minority children (Sapon-Shevin, 1996). Gifted education needs to be responsive to this issue and see itself as an important part of the solution to the problem. More equitable ways of identifying talent need to be developed, and programs need to focus on potential for achievement as well as already developed ability. There are assessments available, such as the Naglieri Noverbal Ability Test (NNAT) that appear to be better at identifying minority children who are gifted than do the IQ and achievement measures currently in use (Sacuzzo et al., 1994). However, the NNAT and other similar measures are rarely included in gifted identification protocols. In addition, when more children with potential as opposed to actualized and demonstrated ability are included in the gifted program, the nature of the program will necessarily have to change. Verbally articulate, culturally enriched, middle- or upper-middle-class will not longer be the typical profile of characteristics of children within the gifted program, and curriculum content and instruction will need to respond to a more varied range of interests, abilities, strengths, and weaknesses. These issues will likely frame both research and practice in the upcoming decade.

Another lesson from the studies of talented individuals is the important role of out-of-school agencies in developing talent. Many parents who have financial resources seek additional services and programs for their talented children from universities, summer camps, and other organizations. However, tuition costs make lack of access an important issue and potentially can increase the inequities between talented students of varying economic levels. An important role for gifted education is forging a closer connection between schools and community organizations and institutions in the service of educating children. Communities can offer opportunities for students to connect with mentors and to have internships, additional classes, and enrichment experiences. Gifted education needs to move beyond the school walls to provide the kinds of experiences that talented children need to develop high levels of talent and to remain engaged, motivated, and challenged. Lauren Sosniak (1998) calls for children's involvement in communities of practice or adult worlds where they can work as novice yet contributing members. These kinds of experiences may be vital to the development of talent because they can affect both the acquisition of needed skills and attitudes and also increase motivation to succeed.

Articulation and cooperation between outside-of-school agencies such as universities and museums and schools is also critical if schooling moves beyond the school walls. It is not unusual for schools to deny students credit or appropriate placement for courses that they have taken outside their local school. Examples included denying high school credit for Algebra I taken in the eighth grade at the elementary or middle school or denying credit for a course taken at a university summer program (Olszewski-Kubilius et al., 1996). Concerns about the quality of outside courses certainly affect schools' decisions about credit and placement, but if schools cannot provide the needed courses at the appropriate time for gifted students (which may mean earlier than for most students), they must be more willing to work with outside agencies to do so. The boundaries between levels of schooling must become more fluid and the dependence on age for placement into classes less rigid to meet the needs of gifted children.

A theme that emerges from the research on practices in gifted education is the importance of teacher training. It is clear that teachers will improve in the identification of gifted students and provision of differentiated curriculum and instruction if given training. It is also clear that training must involve much more than is typically thought of as professional development—that is, attendance at a workshop or conference—and is more likely to succeed in changing teacher behaviors if modeling and mentoring are provided for an extended length of time. In the Archambault et al. (1993) study cited earlier, 61% of the teachers had not had any in-service training in gifted education despite the fact that their average length of teaching was 10 years. Little more than half of the states in the United States currently require teachers to have special endorsements or certificates to teach gifted students. Preservice training in gifted education typically consists of a few hours of instruction within the Exceptional Children course. Only when there is recognition that meeting the educational needs of gifted students does require special techniques and methods that must be specifically taught to and acquired by teachers will this situation change.

A final issue that will affect gifted education is the potential role of distance education in helping to serve gifted students. Already, virtual high schools and universities exist offering advanced curricula to learners from diverse schools and backgrounds. Distance education has the potential to completely reorganize the way special advanced classes can be offered and increase access to them dramatically. It also has the potential to relegate gifted education to outside agencies as schools find it easier to use these programs in lieu of making substantial accommodations in their basic curricula and programs.

Despite the research presented in this chapter, there is a paucity of studies on the effectiveness and outcomes of different types of program models—particularly at the secondary level. Specifically, research on cooperative programs between schools and community institutions or schools and universities is needed as well as research about program models that effectively serve a diverse group of gifted children. Many innovative approaches are being tried, but few are being tested and adequately evaluated. Although there is considerable research on several practices within the field, the literature on best practices is still relatively limited.

Along with best practices, more research is needed on the types of training and professional development models that help teachers to acquire the skills they need. And finally, more research is needed on why attitudes toward certain practices such as acceleration continue to be negative despite the overwhelming positive research support for the practice. Research is sorely needed on how to use research in this field to effect change and affect school policies and classroom practices.

REFERENCES

Ai, X. (1999). Creativity and academic achievement: An investigation of gender differences. *Creativity Research Journal, 12*(4), 329–338.

Archambault, F. X., Jr., Westberg, K. L., Brown, S. W., Hallmark, B. W., Emmons, C. L., & Zhang, W. (1993). *Regular classroom practices with gifted students: Results of a national survey of classroom teachers.* Storrs: University of Connecticut.

Arnold, K. D. (1995). *Lives of promise. What becomes of high school valedictorians.* San Francisco: Jossey-Bass.

Benbow, C. P. (1988). Sex differences in mathematical reasoning ability in intellectually talented preadolescents: Their nature, effects, and possible causes. *Behavioral and Brain Sciences, 11*(2), 169–182.

Benbow, C. P., & Lubinski, D. (1994). Individual differences amongst the mathematically gifted: Their educational and vocational implications. In N. Colangelo, S. G. Assouline, & D. L. Ambrosen (Eds.), *Talent development. Proceedings from the 1993 Henry B. and Jocelyn Wallace National Research Symposium on Talent Development* (pp. 83–100). Dayton: Ohio Psychology Press.

Benbow, C. P., & Stanley, J. C. (1983). *Academic precocity: Aspects of its development.* Baltimore: Johns Hopkins University Press.

Bloom, B. S. (Ed.). (1985). *Developing talent in young people.* New York: Ballantine.

Borland, J. H. (1989). *Planning and implementing programs for the gifted.* New York: Teachers College Press.

College Board. (1999). *Reaching the top: A report of the National Task Force on Minority High Achievement.* New York: Author.

Columbus Group. (1991, July). Unpublished transcript of the meeting of the Columbus Group, Columbus, OH.

Council of the State Directors of Programs for the Gifted. (1996). *The 1996 state of the states gifted and talented education report.* Helena, Montana.

Cox, C. (1926). *Genetic studies of genius: Vol. 1. The early mental traits of three hundred geniuses.* Stanford, CA: Stanford University Press.

Cox, J., Daniel, N., & Boston, B. O. (1985). *Educating able learners. Programs and promising practices.* Austin: Texas University Press.

Cramond, B. (1994). The Torrance Tests of Creative Thinking: From creation through establishment of predictive validity. In R. F. Subotnik & K. D. Arnold (Eds.), *Beyond Terman: Longitudinal studies in contemporary education* (pp. 229–254). Norwood, NJ: Ablex.

Csikszentmihalyi, M. (1994). The domain of creativity. In D. H. Feldman, M. Csikszentmihalyi, & H. Gardner (Eds.), *Changing the world. A framework for the study of creativity* (pp. 135–158). Westport, CT: Praeger.

Csikszentmihalyi, M., Rathunde, K., & Whalen, S. (1993). *Talented teenagers. The roots of success and failure.* Cambridge, England: Cambridge University Press.

Dabrowski, K. (1964). *Positive disintegration.* London: Little, Brown.

Delcourt, M. A. B., Loyd, B. H., Cornell, D. G., & Goldberg, M. D. (1994). *Evaluation of the effects of programming arrangements on student learning outcomes.* Storrs: University of Connecticut.

Fasko, D., Jr. (2001). An analysis of multiple intelligences theory and its use with the gifted and talented. *The Roeper Review, 23*(3), 126–130.

Feldhusen, J. F., Hoover, S. M., & Saylor, M. F. (1990). *Identification and education of the gifted and talented at the secondary level.* Unionville, NY: Trillium.

Feldhusen, J. F., & Jarwan, F. A. (1993). Gifted and talented youth for educational programs. In K. A. Heller, F. J. Monks, & A. H. Passow (Eds.), *International handbook of research and development of giftedness and talent* (pp. 233–251). New York: Pergamon Press.

Feldman, D. H. (1981). A developmental framework for research with gifted children. In D. Feldman (Ed.), *New directions for child development: Vol. 17. Developmental approaches to giftedness and creativity* (pp. 31–45). San Francisco: Jossey-Bass.

Feldman, D. H. (1986a). Giftedness as a developmentalist sees it. In R. J. Sternberg & J. E. Davidson (Eds.), *Conceptions of giftedness* (pp. 285–305). New York: Cambridge University Press.

Feldman, D. H. (1986b). *Nature's gambit. Child prodigies and the development of human potential.* New York: Basic Books.

Fishkin, A. (1999). Issues in studying creativity in youth. In A. S. Fishkin, B. Cramond, & P. Olszewski-Kubilius (Eds.), *Investigating creativity in youth* (pp. 3–26). Cresskill, NJ: Hampton Press.

Ford, D. Y. (1996). *Reversing underachievement among gifted black students.* New York: Teachers College Press.

Gagne, F. (1993). Constructs and models pertaining to exceptional human abilities. In K. A. Heller, F. J. Monks, & A. H. Passow (Eds.), *International handbook of research and development of giftedness and talent* (pp. 69–88). New York: Pergamon Press.

Gagne, F. (1995). From giftedness to talent: A developmental model and its impact on the language of the field. *The Roeper Review, 18*(2), 103–111.

Gagne, F. (1998). A proposal for subcategories within gifted or talented populations. *Gifted Child Quarterly, 42*(2), 87–95.

Gagne, F. (1999). My convictions about the nature of abilities, gifts, and talents. *Journal for the Education of the Gifted, 22*(2), 109–136.

Gallagher, J. J., & Courtright, R. D. (1986). The educational definition of giftedness and its policy implications. In R. J. Sternberg & J. E. Davidson (Eds.), *Conceptions of giftedness* (pp. 93–111). New York: Cambridge University Press.

Gardner H. (1983). *Frames of mind. The theory of multiple intelligences.* New York: Basic Books.

Gardner H., & Hatch, T. (1989). Multiple intelligences go to school. Educational implications of the theory of multiple intelligences. *Educational Researcher, 18*(8), 4–10.

Goertzel, V., & Goertzel, M. G. (1962). *Cradles of eminence.* Boston: Little, Brown.

Johnson, A. S., & Fishkin, A. S. (1999). Assessment of cognitive and affective behaviors related to creativity. In A. S. Fishkin, B. Cramond, & P. Olszewski-Kubilius (Eds.), *Investigating creativity in youth* (pp. 265–306). Cresskill, NJ: Hampton Press.

Karnes, F. A., & Marquart, R. G. (2000). *Gifted children and legal issues.* Scottsdale, AZ: Gifted Psychology Press.

Keller-Mathers, S., & Murdock, M. C. (1999). Research support for a conceptual organization of creativity. In A. S. Fishkin, B. Cramond, & P. Olszewski-Kubilius (Eds.), *Investigating creativity in youth* (pp. 49–71). Cresskill, NJ: Hampton Press.

Kulik, J. A. (1992). *An analysis of the research on ability grouping: Historical and contemporary perspectives.* Storrs: University of Connecticut.

Lubinski, D., & Benbow, C. P. (1993). The study of mathematically precocious youth. The first three decades of a planned 50 year study of intellectual talent. In R. F. Subotnik & K. D. Arnold (Eds.), *Beyond Terman: Longitudinal studies in contemporary gifted education* (pp. 255–281). Norwood, NJ: Ablex.

Marland, S. P. (1972). *Education of the gifted and talented: Report to the Congress of the United States by the U.S. Commission of Education.* Washington, DC: U.S. Government Printing Office.

McCarthy, C. (1999). Dual enrollment programs: Legislation helps high school students enroll in college courses. *Journal of Secondary Gifted Education, 11*(2), 24–32.

Meador, K. S., Fishkin, A. S., & Hoover, M. (1999). Research-based strategies and programs to facilitate creativity. In A. S. Fishkin, B. Cramond, & P. Olszewski-Kubilius (Eds.), *Investigating creativity in youth* (pp. 389–416). Cresskill, NJ: Hampton Press.

Morelock, M. J., & Feldman, D. H. (1993). Prodigies and savants: What they have to tell us about giftedness and human cognition. In K. A. Heller, F. J. Monks, & A. H. Passow (Eds.), *International handbook of research and development of giftedness and talent* (pp. 161–184). Oxford, England: Pergamon Press.

Neihart, M. (1999). The impact of giftedness on psychological well-being: What does the empirical literature say? *The Roeper Review, 22*(11), 10–17.

Olszewski-Kubilius, P. (1995). A summary of research regarding early college entrance. *Roeper Review, 18*(2), 121–125.

Olszewski-Kubilius, P. (1997). Special summer and Saturday programs for gifted students. In N. Colangelo & G. A. Davis (Eds.), *Handbook of gifted education* (2nd ed., pp. 180–188). Boston: Allyn and Bacon.

Olszewski-Kubilius, P. (1998). Research evidence regarding the validity and effects of talent search educational programs. *Journal of Secondary Gifted Education, 9*(3), 134–138.

Olszewski-Kubilius, P. (2000). The transition from childhood giftedness to adult creative productiveness: Psychological characteristics and social supports. *The Roeper Review, 23*(2), 65–71.

Olszewski-Kubilius, P., & Laubscher, L. (1996). The impact of a college counseling program on economically disadvantaged gifted students and their subsequent college adjustment. *Roeper Review, 18*(3), 202–207.

Olszewski-Kubilius, P., Laubscher, L., Wohl, V., & Grant, B. (1996). Issues and factors involved in credit and placement for accelerated coursework. *Journal of Secondary Gifted Education, 8*(1), 5–15.

Olszewski-Kubilius, P., & Limburg-Weber, L. (1999). *Designs for excellence: A guide to educational program options for academically talented middle school and secondary school students.* Center for Talent Development, Northwestern University. Evanston, IL.

Passow, A. H. (1993). National/state policies regarding education of the gifted. In K. A. Heller, F. J. Monks, & A. H. Passow (Eds.), *International handbook of research and development of giftedness and talent* (pp. 29–46). New York: Pergamon Press.

Pyryt, M. C. (1999). Effectiveness of training children's divergent thinking: A meta-analytic review. In A. S. Fishkin, B. Cramond, & P. Olszewski-Kubilius (Eds.), *Investigating creativity in youth* (pp. 351–366). Cresskill, NJ: Hampton Press.

Reis, S. M., Westberg, K. M., Kulikowich, J., Caillard, F., Hebert, T., Plucker, J., Purcell, J. H., Rogers, J. B., & Smist, J. M. (1993). *Why not let high ability students start school in January? The curriculum compacting study.* Storrs: University of Connecticut.

Renzulli, J. S. (1990). Three ring conception of giftedness. In R. J. Sternberg & J. E. Davidson (Eds.), *Conceptions of giftedness* (pp. 53–92). New York: Cambridge University Press.

Renzulli, J. S., & Reis, S. M. (1986). The enrichment triad/revolving door model: A schoolwide plan for the development of creative productivity. In J. S. Renzulli (Ed.), *Systems and models for developing programs for the gifted and talented* (pp. 216–266). Mansfield Center, CT: Creative Learning Press.

Renzulli, J. S., Smith, L. H., White, A. J., Callahan, C. M., & Hartman, R. K. (1976). *Scales for Rating the Behavioral Characteristics of Superior Students.* Wethersfield, CT: Creative Learning Press.

Roe, A. (1953). *The making of a scientist.* New York: Dodd, Mead.

Rogers, K. B. (1991).*The relationship of grouping practices to the education of the gifted and talented learner.* Storrs: University of Connecticut.

Rogers, K. B. (1999). Is creativity quantitatively measurable? In A. S. Fishkin, B. Cramond, & P. Olszewski-Kubilius (Eds.),

Investigating creativity in youth (pp. 217–237). Cresskill, NJ: Hampton Press.

Sacuzzo, D. P., Johnson, N. E., & Guertin, T. L. (1994). *Identifying underrepresented disadvantaged gifted and talented children: A multi-faceted approach.* (Document Reproduction Service No. ERIC Report 368095)

Sapon-Shevin. (1996). Beyond gifted education: Building a shared agenda for school reform. *Journal for the Education of the Gifted, 19*(20), 194–214.

Silverman, L. K. (1993). Counseling needs and programs for the gifted. In K. A. Heller, F. J. Monks, & A. H. Passow (Eds.), *International handbook of research and development of giftedness and talent* (pp. 631–647). New York: Pergamon Press.

Sosniak, L. (1998, May). *The development of talent: Welcoming youth into communities of practice.* Presentation at the 1998 Henry B. and Jocelyn Wallace National Research Symposium on Talent Development, Iowa City, IA.

Sosniak, L. (1999). An everyday curriculum for the development of talent. *Journal of Secondary Gifted Education, 10*(4), 166–172.

Southern, W. T., & Jones, E. D. (1991). *The academic acceleration of gifted children.* New York: Teachers College Press.

Southern, W. T., Jones, E. D., & Stanley, J. C. (1993). Acceleration and enrichment: The context and development of program options. In K. A. Heller, F. J. Monks, & A. H. Passow (Eds.), *International handbook of research and development of giftedness and talent* (pp. 387–410). New York: Pergamon Press.

Sternberg. R. J. (1986). A triarchic theory of intellectual giftedness. In R. J. Sternberg & J. E. Davidson (Eds.), *Conceptions of giftedness* (pp. 223–243). New York: Cambridge University Press.

Sternberg, R. J. (2000). Patterns of giftedness: A triarchic analysis. *Roeper Review, 22*(4), 231–234.

Subotnik, R. F., & Arnold, K. D. (1994). *Beyond Terman. Contemporary longitudinal studies of giftedness and talent.* Norwood, NJ: Ablex.

Subotnik, R. F., & Coleman, L. J. (1996). Establishing the foundations for a talent development school: Applying principles to creating an idea. *Journal for the Education of the Gifted, 20*(2), 175–189.

Subotnik, R. F., Karp, D. E., & Morgan, E. R. (1989). High IQ children at mid-life: An investigation into the generalizability of Terman's "Genetic Studies of Genius." *Roeper Review, 11*(3), 139–144.

Subotnik, R. F., Miserandino, A., & Olszewski-Kubilius, P. (1997). Implications of the Mathematics Olympiad studies for the development of mathematical talent in schools. *International Journal of Educational Research, 25*(6), 563–573.

Subotnik, R. F., Olszewski-Kubilius, P., & Arnold, K. D. (in press). Beyond Bloom: Revisiting environmental factors that enhance or impede talent development. In J. Borland & L. Wright (Eds.), *Rethinking gifted education: Contemporary approaches to meeting the needs of gifted students.* New York: Teachers College Press.

Tannenbaum, A. J. (1983). *Gifted children. Psychological and educational perspectives.* New York: Macmillan.

Tannenbaum, A. J. (1990). Giftedness: A psycho-social approach. In R. J. Sternberg & J. E. Davidson (Eds.), *Conceptions of giftedness* (pp. 21–53). New York: Cambridge University Press.

Terman, L. M. (1925). *Genetic studies of genius: Vol. 1. Mental and physical traits of a thousand gifted children.* Stanford, CA: Stanford University Press.

Terman, L. M., & Oden, M. H. (1947). *Genetic studies of genius: Vol. 4. The gifted child grows up: Twenty-five years follow-up of a superior group.* Stanford, CA: Stanford University Press.

Terman L. M., & Oden, M. H. (1957). *Genetic studies of genius: Vol. 5. The gifted group at mid-life; Thirty-five years' follow-up of the superior child.* Stanford, CA: Stanford University Press.

Tookey, M. E. (1999/2000). The International Baccalaureate program: A program conducive to the continued growth of the gifted adolescent. *Journal of Secondary Gifted Education, 11*(2), 52–66.

U.S. Department of Education. (1993). *National excellence: A case for developing America's talent.* Washington, DC: Office of Educational Research and Improvement. PIP 93-1201.

VanTassel-Baska, J. (1998). Key issues and problems in secondary programming. In J. VanTassel-Baska (Ed.), *Excellence in educating gifted & talented learners* (pp. 241–260). Denver, CO: Love.

Winner, E. (1996). *Gifted children: Myths and realities.* New York: Basic Books.

Winner, E., & Martino, G. (1993). Giftedness in the visual arts and music. In K. A. Heller, F. J. Monks, & A. H. Passow (Eds.), *International handbook of research and development of giftedness and talent* (pp. 253–282). New York: Pergamon Press.

Zuckerman, H. (1977). *Scientific elite: Nobel laureates in the United States.* New York: Free Press.

CHAPTER 20

School-Related Behavior Disorders

HILL M. WALKER AND FRANK M. GRESHAM

The focus of this chapter is on the behavior disorders of children and youth, which are increasingly manifested within the context of schooling. Children by the thousands now appear at the schoolhouse door showing the damaging effects of prior exposure to family-based and societal risks (abuse, neglect, chaotic family conditions, media violence, etc.) during the first 5 years of life. Our society has begun to reap a bitter harvest of destructive outcomes among our vulnerable children and youth resulting from such risk exposure and from our seemingly diminished capacity to rear, socialize, and care for them effectively. It is now not uncommon for as many as half of the newborns in any given state to suffer one or more risk factors for later destructive outcomes and poor health (Kitzhaber, 2001).

The characteristics, needs, and demands of these children and youth have overwhelmed the capacity of schools to accommodate them effectively. Ironically, our school systems have been relatively slow to recognize the true dimensions of the challenges that these students pose to themselves, to the social agents in their lives, and to the larger society. Recent estimates by experts of the number of today's youth with significant mental health problems reflect the destructive changes that have occurred in the social and economic conditions of our society over the past 30 years. Angold (2000) estimated that approximately 20% of today's school-age children and youth could qualify for a psychiatric diagnosis using criteria from the *Diagnostic and Statistical Manual of Mental*

Disorders–Fourth Edition (*DSM-IV;* American Psychological Association, 1994). Hoagwood and Erwin (1997) argued that about 22% of children and youth enrolled in school settings have mental health problems that warrant serious attention and treatment. Slightly less than 1% of the school-age population is served as emotionally disturbed under provisions of the Individuals with Disabilities Act (IDEA, 1997), which illustrates the enormous gap that currently exists between need and available supports and services for these students in the school setting.

In a recent *Washington Post* investigative report on the changed landscape of problem behavior and its impact on schooling, Perlstein (2001) provided elaborate documentation of the increasingly outrageous forms of behavior displayed by younger and younger children and concluded that our schools are "awash in bad behavior" (p. B1). She described elementary school students who defied their teachers and called them obscene names, who threatened them with physical violence, who attacked their peers for no apparent reason, who brought drugs and weapons to school, who destroyed classroom furnishings when disciplined, and whose parents denied their child's culpability in these incidents and refused to take ownership or responsibility for dealing with them. In addition, Perlstein provided compelling evidence of national trends involving the rising use of school suspensions and expulsions of very young children, the creation of school-based detention centers, and investment in alternative educational programs and personnel—all increasing dramatically at the elementary school level. Educators perceive the costs of these accommodations as taking dollars away from needed school reform efforts designed to increase educational accountability and achievement levels.

The larger society has finally begun to express concern about our troubled children and youth and to assemble experts from multiple disciplines to create policy, develop legislative initiatives, and construct action plans that will address this growing national problem. For example, in September 2000, the U.S. Surgeon General convened a national conference on children's mental health, involving a collaboration between the U.S. Departments of Health and Human Services, Education, and Justice, to develop a national action agenda that balances health promotion, disease prevention, early detection, and universal access to care. This conference produced an influential report titled *Report of the Surgeon General's Conference on Children's Mental Health: A National Action Agenda,* which provides a blueprint for action on this critically important topic.

In a more reactive vein, the widely publicized school-shooting tragedies of the 1990s have shocked us into action and cast a national spotlight on the problems that young people daily experience with bullying, emotional abuse, and harassment at the hands of their peers. It is estimated in media reports that approximately 160,000 U.S. students miss school each day because of bullying. When mixed with mental health problems (severe stress and anxiety, depression, paranoia) and the desensitizing effects of pervasive exposure to violence in the media, the toxic consequences of bullying can pose a real risk of tragic outcomes in the context of an abused student seeking revenge—a recurring pattern that we have seen in school shootings. Kip Kinkle, who went on a school-shooting rampage at Thurston High School in Springfield, Oregon, in 1998 after murdering his parents, was an exemplar of this combination of destructive attributes. The Thurston shooting prompted a collaborative effort between the U.S. Departments of Education and Justice (in which the senior author was a participant) that created a national panel of experts who produced two resource guides sent to every school in the country: *Early Warning/Timely Response: A Guide to Safe Schools* and *Safeguarding Our Children: An Action Guide. Implementing Early Warning, Timely Response.* The first document focused on warning signs and early detection; the second provided guidelines for implementing the *Early Warning/Timely Response* guide.

Schools have now realized that these complex problems cannot be dealt with through a business-as-usual approach. School administrators are searching for and considering an array of strategies that will help make schools safer and more effective; they are now open to prevention approaches in ways that have not heretofore been in evidence. The spate of tragic school shootings over the past decade prompted a strong investment in school security technology by educators and created pressures for the profiling of potentially dangerous, troubled students. Neither approach has been demonstrated as particularly effective in making schools safer or free of the potential for violence. Profiling has very serious downside risks for student victimization through damage to reputations (Kingery & Walker, 2002).

School administrators have been generally open to, but less enthusiastic about, investing in comprehensive, positive, behavioral-support approaches that (a) create orderly, disciplined school environs; (b) establish positive school cultures; and (c) address the needs of *all* students who populate the school. Perhaps this is the case because these programs require up to 2 years for full school implementation. Two of the best known and most cost-effective approaches of this type are the *Effective Behavioral Support* (EBS) and *Project Achieve* intervention programs developed respectively by Horner, Sugai, and their associates at the University of Oregon and Knoff and his associates at the University of South Florida. Both of these proven model programs are profiled in *Safeguarding Our Children: An Action Guide. Implementing Early Warning, Timely Response* (see Dwyer & Osher, 2000).

The development of comprehensive interagency collaborations that address primary, secondary, and tertiary forms of prevention is an investment that schools have yet to make to any significant degree. However, to reduce and actually reverse the harm caused by the broad-based risk exposure experienced by today's children and youth, it will be necessary to scale up and mount such collaborative initiatives with good integrity (Eddy, Reid, & Curry, 2002).

Behaviorally at-risk children and youth provide a funnel through which the toxic social conditions of our society spill over into the school setting and destructively impact the capacity of our schools and educators to provide for these vulnerable students the normalizing and protective influences of schooling. This growing student population increasingly stresses and disrupts the teaching-learning process for everyone connected with schooling. The peer cultures of schools grow ever more corrosive, and there are more incidents of challenges to school authority and operational routines by angry, out-of-control students. School personnel, perhaps understandably, regard members of this student population with suspicion because of the large number of school-shooting tragedies that have occurred over the past decade. At the other end of the spectrum, significant numbers of today's students experience severe anxiety and depressive disorders primarily of an internalizing nature.

This chapter focuses on the topic of behavior disorders (BD) in the context of schooling and is written from the perspective of the school-based professionals (school psychologists, special educators, school counselors, early interventionists, behavioral specialists) who are specialists in addressing the needs and problems of this behaviorally at-risk student population. Herein, we address three major topics as follows: (a) the critical issues that have shaped and continue to influence the field of behavior disorders; (b) the adoption and delivery of proven, evidence-based strategies that have the potential to divert at-risk students from a destructive path and that contribute positively to school engagement and academic success; and (c) the content of interventions for addressing the adjustment problems of BD students within the school setting. The chapter concludes with some brief reflections on the future of the BD field and directions it should consider for its future development.

CRITICAL ISSUES AFFECTING THE FIELD OF BEHAVIOR DISORDERS

BD professionals working in higher education and school and agency settings are uniquely positioned, and qualified, to have a positive impact on the needs, challenges, and problems presented by the behaviorally at-risk student population. They have intimate knowledge of schools and their cultures; they know instructional processes and routines; and they are experts in behavior change procedures. No other professional combines these types of skills and knowledge. As a rule, BD professionals are strongly dedicated to improving the lives of these children and youth through the direct application of the strategies and techniques that they have been taught for changing behavior in applied contexts. However, as our society's problems have worsened, the results of their intervention efforts look less and less impressive in the face of schools that have been transformed into fortress-like structures and student populations that continue to be out of control.

The BD field has developed some seminal contributions to our understanding of school-related behavior disorders along with methods for addressing them, but this knowledge base and these proven practices are often not in evidence in the daily operation of schools. The gap between what is known and proven and what is practiced is no where greater than in the field of school-related behavior disorders. This section is divided into two major topics that focus, respectively, on "What is Right with Behavior Disorders?" and "What is Wrong with Behavior Disorders?" We believe that the critical issues affecting the BD field can be effectively illustrated

using this dichotomy. Before dealing with this set of issues, however, we would like to put the BD field in context relative to its role as a resource to schools in dealing with behaviorally at-risk students and its status as a subspeciality of the larger field of special education.

The Current Landscape of Behavior Disorders as a Field

The field of behavior disorders, as a disciplinary subspecialty of general special education, is a relatively new field dating from the early 1960s. Frank Wood (1999) recently profiled the history and development of the Council for Children with Behavior Disorders (CCBD) in this regard.

Although encompassing diverse philosophical and theoretical approaches, the field has generally maintained a consistent focus on empirical research and has provided important journal and monograph outlets for the contributions of its researchers and scholars. The Journal of Behavioral Disorders, the CCBD Monograph Series, the *Journal of Emotional and Behavioral Disorders,* and *Education and Treatment of Children* are excellent examples of peer-reviewed publications that publish high-quality research and commentary in the BD field. These outlets and their respective editors have advanced the field's development and have contributed enormously to the cohesive knowledge base that we see today relating to the social, emotional, and behavioral status of at-risk children and youth in the contexts of school and community.

The field of behavior disorders can trace its roots to the use of behavior change procedures with mentally ill children and youth within highly restrictive settings (mental institutions, residential programs) and to the delivery of mental health services for the emotional problems of vulnerable children and youth within school and community settings. Over the past three decades the number and severity of the problems manifested by children and youth, who are referred to as having emotional disorders (ED) or behavior disorders, have changed substantially (Walker, Zeller, Close, Webber, & Gresham, 1999). Early in our field's development the children and youth referred and served as having emotional disorders had primarily mental and emotional problems (depression, social isolation, self-stimulatory forms of behavior, etc.). Problems representing critical behavioral events, sometimes involving a danger to self and others, such as severe aggression, antisocial behavior, vandalism, cruelty to animals, and interpersonal violence, were rarely dealt with by BD professionals.

It is clear that thousands of young children in our society are being socialized within chaotic, abusive family and community contexts in which they are exposed to a host of risk factors that provide a fertile breeding ground for the development of highly maladaptive attitudes, beliefs, and behavioral forms. These risk factors can operate multiply on an individual across family, community, school, and cultural contexts. They are registered in unfortunate life paths that are often tragic and involve huge social and economic costs. We now see comorbid mixtures of syndromes (conduct disorder and attention-deficit/hyperactivity disorder, or ADHD) in school-age children that are efficient predictors of adult psychopathology (see Gresham, Lane, & Lambros, 2000; Lynam, 1996).

Professionals in the field of behavior disorders are charged with effectively accommodating this changed population of children and youth within the context of schooling. The presence, risk status, and intense needs of these students place powerful stressors on the ability of schools to serve them; they present a continuing and significant challenge to BD professionals and to the field. Increasingly, educators are having to forge partnership arrangements with mental health and other social service systems in order to meet the needs of these individuals, their families, and their caregivers.

In our view, the field of behavior disorders possesses the knowledge and skills necessary to accommodate the majority of behaviorally at-risk children who must be served by schools. However, for those children who enter the schoolhouse door having severe tertiary-level involvements, schools will find it necessary to continue forging effective partnership arrangements with nonschool service systems such as mental health. We see this development as a positive one that should be promoted and enhanced. The advent of family resource centers, attached to school districts, provides an excellent vehicle for the coordination and delivery of such approaches.

Today, BD professionals at all levels are challenged as they have never been before. Continuing to serve students having mental health needs primarily under the aegis of the ED category of special education is no longer viable. The intensity of need and the sheer numbers of affected individuals are simply too great, and the consequences of not serving this growing student population are both tragic and ominous. Schools, in collaboration with community agencies, must find new ways of responding to this service need that continues to grow and expand. The BD professional can play a powerful role in building a new service delivery infrastructure for meeting this critical need and making sure that schools are key players in developing viable solutions to this societal problem that we all own collectively.

What Is Right With Behavior Disorders?

Because of the quality of the BD field's cadre of professionals, its consistently empirical focus, strong commitment to

best and preferred practices, and the diversity and rigor of its methodological tools and approaches, the field has a well-developed capacity to contribute innovations that can lead (a) to important outcomes in the lives of youth with emotional disorders and (b) to the enhancement of the skills and effectiveness of online BD professionals (Walker, Sprague, Close, & Starlin, 2000). Many of these contributions can be documented as they operate currently within general education contexts. Some examples include the following:

- The roots of many standards-based school reforms and performance-based assessment systems can be traced to behavioral psychology and applied behavior analysis.
- The current emphasis on teaching social skills as part of the regular school curriculum to reduce conflicts and prevent violence results from initiatives by BD and related services professionals.
- The development of behavior management approaches for managing student behavior in specific school settings results from prototype models developed by the BD field.

In recent years the BD field has contributed some advances that (a) increased our understanding of how behaviorally at-risk children and youth come to engage in and sustain their destructive, maladaptive behavior patterns over time; (b) documented how some of our interactions with students with emotional disorders in teaching-learning situations control both teacher and student behavior in negative ways; (c) provided for the universal screening and early identification of school-related behavior patterns that facilitate effective early intervention; (d) documented the relationship between language deficits and conduct disorder among at-risk children and youth; (e) investigated the metric of disciplinary referrals and contacts with the school's front office as a sensitive measure of the following school climate, the global effects of schoolwide interventions, and the behavioral status of individual students; (f) developed effective, low-cost models of school-based intervention that allow access to needed services and supports for *all* students in a school; (g) contributed schoolwide, disciplinary and positive behavioral support systems that improve outcomes for the whole school; (h) reported longitudinal, comprehensive profiles of the affective, social-behavioral status of certified, referred, and nonreferred students; and (i) developed the concept of resistance to intervention for use in school-based eligibility determination and treatment selection decisions (Walker et al., 2000). Ultimately, these advances will improve the BD field's capacity to meet the challenges and pressures of a changed population with emotional disorders and to address proactively the vulnerability of schools in preventing and responding to the violent acts of very disturbed youth such as Kip Kinkle (mentioned earlier). Descriptions of some of these advances and seminal contributions are briefly described below.

Functional Behavioral Assessment

The development and validation of functional behavioral assessment (FBA) techniques and approaches stands as perhaps one of the most important advances in the field of behavior disorders (O'Neill, Horner, Albin, Storey, & Newton, 1997). Functional behavioral assessment (a) provides a usable methodology for identifying and validating the motivations that drive maladaptive forms of student behavior in applied settings, (b) allows for the identification of the factors that sustain such behavior over time, and (c) provides a prescription for intervening on these sustaining variables with the goal of producing fundamental, enduring changes in the rate and topography of problem behavior.

Functional behavioral assessment, which is based on operant learning theory and its application to the learning and behavioral difficulties of children and youth, is derived from the field of applied behavior analysis. The dominant theoretical orientation of the BD field has historically been applied behavior analysis, and its many contributions to BD date back over 30 years. They were chronicled in the edited volume titled *Behavior Analysis in Education* (Sulzer-Azaroff, Drabman, Greer, Hall, Iwata, & O'Leary, 1988). In 1997 the amendments to IDEA required use of both FBA and *positive behavioral supports* (PBS) and interventions in evaluating and intervening with students having a possible disabling condition. Prior to this landmark legislation, many BD professionals and behavior analysts considered FBA and PBS to be best practices, but federal law did not mandate their use.

Based on a valid FBA, PBS programming has much to offer the BD community in fulfilling the mandates of IDEA. The 1997 IDEA amendments do not specify what constitutes a valid FBA, nor do they state the essential components of a positive behavioral support plan. However, in the few years since the passage of this law, the BD field has vigorously responded in developing a range of feasible FBA and PBS models and approaches.

FBA methods can be categorized as (a) indirect, using interviews, historical-archival records, checklists, and rating scales; (b) direct or descriptive in nature, using systematic behavioral observations in naturalistic settings; and (c) experimental, employing standardized experimental protocols that systematically manipulate and isolate contingencies that control the occurrence of problem behavior using primarily single-case experimental designs (Horner, 1994; O'Neill et al., 1997). Despite the methodological rigor of functional analysis approaches, there are limitations regarding the external validity of its findings as well as the amount of

time and expertise required to conduct a valid functional analysis (Gresham, Quinn, & Restori, 1998; Repp & Horner, 1999). Many of the studies using functional assessment procedures over the past decade were based on low-incidence disability groups, thus limiting the applicability of these results to high-incidence groups.

Walker and Sprague (1999) argued that there are two generic models or approaches to the assessment of behavior problems. One model, termed the *longitudinal or risk factors exposure model,* grew out of research on the development of antisocial behavior (Loeber & Farrington, 1998) and seeks to identify molar variables that (a) operate across multiple settings and (b) put students at risk for long-term, negative outcomes (e.g., drug use, delinquency, school failure). The second model, called the *functional assessment approach,* seeks to identify microlevel variables operating in specific situations that are sensitive to setting-specific environmental contingencies. Both models are useful in school-based assessment processes, but they answer quite different questions. If your goal, for example, is to understand and manage problem behavior in a specific setting, the FBA is valuable and should be the method of choice. However, if your goal is to understand the variables and factors that account for risk status across multiple settings and what the student's future is likely to involve, then knowledge about the student's genetic-behavioral history (risk factor exposure) is required. Admittedly, the FBA model (primarily functional analysis) suffers from several threats to its external validity; one should not assume that the same results could be generalized to other populations, methods, settings, and behavioral forms.

Despite these limitations, FBA methods represent a valuable tool for the BD professional working in school settings. They hold the potential to identify setting-specific causal factors that account for problematic student behavior, and their use may enhance the power and sustainability of behavioral interventions. However, this latter outcome remains to be demonstrated empirically. Although FBA has its share of critics (see Nelson, Roberts, Mathur, & Rutherford, 1999), this assessment methodology has been widely adopted by BD researchers and professionals and by other disciplines (e.g., school psychology).

Positive Behavioral Support Intervention Approaches

The development of PBS approaches is another significant contribution of the BD field in the area of creating well disciplined, orderly schools with positive school climates. Sugai and Horner (in press) along with their associates have been leaders in this effort and were recently awarded a 5-year center grant from the U.S. Office of Special Education Programs to investigate and promote the adoption of PBS approaches nationwide (see the ERIC/OSEP Special Project, winter, 1999 issue of *Research Connections in Special Education* for an extensive treatment of PBS). This approach has the advantages of (a) targeting all students within a school; (b) coordinating the implementation of universal, selected, and targeted intervention strategies; and (c) focusing on positive, proactive approaches as opposed to punitive, reactive interventions.

Sugai and Horner (in press) developed the EBS program, which is a combined universal-selected intervention that teaches behavioral expectations in both schoolwide and specific contexts (i.e., classroom, playground, lunchroom). EBS is a systems approach to creating and sustaining effective and orderly school environs, and it has now been implemented in over 400 schools nationwide. The program teaches generic behavioral expectations such as being responsible, respectful, and safe and requires complete buy-in from all personnel within the school. Full implementation of the EBS program usually requires 2 or more years.

Office discipline referrals from teachers has been the primary means used to evaluate the schoolwide impact of EBS. In one of the earliest evaluation studies of EBS, Taylor-Green and Kartub (2000) found that the number of disciplinary referrals in an at-risk middle school decreased by 47% in 1 year; after 5 years the initial number of office referrals had been reduced overall by 68% from the pre-EBS level. A study by Lewis, Sugai, and Colvin (1998) found that the EBS program also reduced problem behavior within specific school settings including the lunchroom, playground, and hallways. Hunter and Chopra (2001) recently reported a review of primary prevention models for schools, in which they endorsed EBS as a universal intervention that works.

Positive behavioral support is a popular intervention approach with regular educators, and PBS models will likely have a substantial school adoption rate over the next decade. Most significantly, PBS has been incorporated as a required best practice into the reauthorized legislation supporting the 1997 IDEA amendments for students suspected of having a behavior disorder or disability. When used in concert with more specialized intervention approaches that address secondary and tertiary prevention goals, PBS models have the potential to integrate qualitatively different interventions that will comprehensively impact the behavior problems and disorders of all students within a school setting (Walker et al., 1996). This is indeed a rare occurrence in the field of general education.

Analysis of Teacher Interactions With Students With Behavior Disorders

Two important lines of work have recently developed in the BD field relating to the interactions that occur between BD students and their teachers in classroom settings. Together, they shed considerable light on the interactive dynamics and processes occurring in these teacher-student exchanges wherein the behavior of each social agent is reciprocally controlled by the actions of the other. The resulting effects can damage the teacher-student relationship, disrupt the instructional process, and reduce allocated instructional time for everyone.

Colvin (1993) developed a conceptual model that captures the phases of behavioral escalation that a teacher and an agitated student typically cycle through in a hostile confrontation. It begins with the teacher's making a demand of an agitated student who appears calm but is not. The teacher's approach serves as a trigger that accelerates the agitation. This acceleration process typically occurs through a reciprocal question-and-answer exchange between the teacher and the student. There is an overlay of increasing hostility, emotional intensity, and anger during these exchanges until the interaction hits a peak, usually expressed as teacher defiance or a severe tantrum. This is followed by a rapid de-escalation and recovery of the calm state. However, seething anger is the usual by-product of this type of interaction, on the part of both teacher and student, which, as a rule, plays out in less than 60 s.

These escalated interactions are usually modeled for and learned by BD students in the family context as dysfunctional families often use a process of coercion to control the behavior of family members (see Patterson, 1982; Patterson, Reid, & Dishion, 1992). These same types of negative, destructive interactions typically occur between students with challenging behavior patterns and their teachers. They resemble behavioral earthquakes that come out of nowhere, do incredible damage, and require long periods for recovery. This behavioral escalation game is one that teachers should not play for two primary reasons: (a) Even if the teacher gets the better of the student in this public exchange, he or she will likely have created an enemy dedicated to revenge; and (b) if the reverse occurs, the teacher's ability to manage and control the classroom will be severely compromised and even damaged. It is best to avoid and escape from such escalated interactions whenever possible. Colvin explained how to recognize these developing episodes and how to avoid and short-circuit them (see Colvin, 1993; Walker, Colvin, & Ramsey, 1995).

Shores, Wehby, and their colleagues (see Shores, Gunter, et al., 1993; Shores, Jack, et al., 1993; Wehby, Symonds, Canale, & Go, 1998) have designed and conducted a series of observational studies that spotlight the interplay of precipitating stimuli, setting events and behavioral actions occurring within many of the interactions between BD students and their teachers that occur on a daily basis. Their work confirms key parts of the Colvin escalation model and should be required reading for all prospective teachers, and especially for teachers of students with behavior disorders. The results of their studies also replicate the findings of Patterson et al. (1992) and Wahler and Dumas (1986) with families who produce antisocial children; in these families family members learn to control each other's behavior through aversive means including punishment and coercion. This same coercive process spills over into the school setting and is replicated with teachers by these behaviorally at-risk children. That is, the effect of the student's behavior on the teacher is highly aversive, leading to reduced levels of praise, negative student recognition, and less instructional time. Ultimately, both teachers and students come to view these exchanges, and the classroom environment, as punishing. This can lead to escape and avoidance forms of behavior by both parties. Wehby et al. (1998) developed a set of teaching recommendations, based on results of this work, that should be incorporated into preservice teacher preparation programs and adopted by experienced teachers as well.

The Relationship Between Language Deficits and Conduct Disorder

Hester and Kaiser (1997) investigated the relationship between conduct disorder and language deficits and examined the conjoint risk factors (impoverished language environs, poverty, social stressors, and coercive family dynamics) that produce children who are both highly aggressive and very unskilled in their functional use of language. These investigators have developed an intriguing social-communicative perspective on the prevention of conduct disorder using early language intervention. This work involves both descriptive and experimental studies and has the potential to be a seminal contribution to the BD knowledge base relating to our understanding and accommodation of at-risk children having conduct disorders.

Analysis of Office Discipline Referrals as a Screening and Program Evaluation Tool

For the past decade a group of researchers at the University of Oregon have been investigating the metric of school discipline contacts or referrals to the principal's office for student infractions (teacher defiance, aggression, harassment, etc.) that merit more than just classroom-based sanctions (Sugai, Sprague, Horner, & Walker, 2000; Walker, Stieber, Ramsey, & O'Neill, 1993). Discipline referrals can be used to profile an entire school, small groups of students, and selected individual students within a school. Walker et al. (1993) found discipli-

nary referrals to be a powerful variable in discriminating low-risk from high-risk antisocial students. Tobin and Sugai (1999) reported that discipline referrals are associated with the outcomes of identification for special education, restrictive placements, and later school dropout. Walker and McConnell (1995) found a moderately strong relationship between discipline contacts and later arrests in a longitudinal study of a sample of high-risk boys. Loeber and Farrington (1998) cited research showing a similar relationship of moderate strength between these two variables among antisocial youth.

In addition to profiling a school and selected students therein, aggregated discipline contacts across school years can be a sensitive measure of effective schoolwide interventions that address disciplinary issues (see Sprague, Sugai, Horner, & Walker, 1999). One of the clear advantages of this measure is that it accumulates as a natural by-product of the schooling process and can be culled unobtrusively from the existing archival student records of most schools. Currently, there is a need to establish normative databases on this measure at elementary, middle, and high school levels. In our view, this is a very promising measure that will prove attractive to BD researchers, scholars, and practitioners in the future. Readers should consult Wright and Dusek (1998) for a recent critique of the advantages and limitations of this measure.

Resistance to Intervention as a Tool for Determining Eligibility and Treatment Selection

A relatively new approach to making eligibility determinations and selecting or titrating interventions is based on the concept of *resistance to intervention* or, alternatively, lack of responsiveness to intervention. Gresham (1991) defined this concept as a student's behavioral excesses, deficits, or situationally-inappropriate behaviors continuing at unacceptable levels subsequent to empirically supported interventions implemented with integrity. Resistance to intervention is based on the best practice of prereferral intervention and allows school personnel to function within an intervention context rather than a psychometric eligibility framework in identifying BD students.

Resistance to intervention results in a lack of change in target behaviors as a function of exposure to a proven intervention. This failure can be taken as partial evidence for a BD eligibility determination under auspices of the IDEA certification process. Moreover, this same concept can be used to modify, change, or titrate intervention procedures much like medications are titrated based on an individual's responsiveness to a drug dosage or type. Third, resistance to intervention can be used as a cost-effective basis for allocating treatment resources to those students whose lack of responsiveness indicates that they need more intensive intervention.

A number of factors are related to resistance to intervention. Some of the factors that seem most relevant for school-based interventions are (a) severity of behavior, (b) chronicity of behavior, (c) the generalizability of behavior change, (d) treatment strength, (e) treatment integrity, and (f) treatment effectiveness. All of these factors have been identified as being related to resistance of student behavior to intervention in past research (see Gresham, 1991, and Gresham & Lopez, 1996, for a discussion of these factors).

The notion of resistance to intervention provides BD professionals with a powerful method for managing school-based interventions in a cost-effective manner and for indirectly assessing the relative severity of a student's problematic behavior. It stands as one of the most useful and valuable innovations in behavior disorders within the past decade.

This list of contributions by the BD field is selective and not representative in that it reflects our biased views. In addition, it by no means exhausts the universe of innovative contributions of the highest quality and impact in the BD field. A perusal of the BD peer-reviewed journals over the past few years documents many varied examples of outstanding achievements by BD scholars, researchers, and on-line professionals. These contributions have led to many enhancements in the life quality of students with behavior disorders and their families and have improved the skills and competence of those professionals who work with them. They provide solid evidence about what is right with the BD field (see Walker et al., 2000, for a more detailed discussion of these contributions).

What Is Wrong With Behavior Disorders?

No discipline can claim to be virtuous and above reproach in its policy, directions, and management of its professional agenda. That is certainly true of the BD field. However, it is important to note that there is much more right about BD than wrong with BD.

This section discusses some of the decisions, directional changes, and failures that have occurred within the BD field and that we believe have not served the field well. The following topics in this regard are discussed next: (a) the BD field's failure to reference its interventions and achieved outcomes to societal issues and problems, (b) the adoption of a postmodern, deconstructivist perspective by some sectors of the BD field, (c) the failure to identify and serve the full range of K–12 students experiencing serious behavioral and

emotional problems in the context of schooling, and (d) the lack of evidence of BD leadership in developing a prevention agenda for behaviorally at-risk students.

Referencing BD Interventions and Results to Societal Issues and Problems

Recently, Walker, Gresham, and their colleagues provided commentary on some shortcomings of the BD field and suggested some new directions for its consideration (see Walker et al., 1998). These authors made the following major points in this commentary:

1. During the last several decades, the field of special education, of which BD is a subspecialty, has become politically radicalized and, unfortunately, fragmented as a result of internal strife and turf battles among professionals.
2. Due in part to this disciplinary conflict, special education is often perceived by professionals in other fields as strife-ridden, expensive, litigious, consumed with legislative mandates, bound by court orders mandating certain practices, and ineffective.
3. These external perceptions of special education have damaged its status and legitimacy, cast doubt on its ability to manage its affairs, and hindered its ability to pursue a professional agenda on behalf of individuals with disabilities and their families.
4. Though largely avoiding this political strife, the BD field, by association, has suffered from these generic, pejorative impressions about special education that have been widely disseminated in the public media and through the professional networks of related disciplines.

Though regarded as controversial, this article has stimulated an ongoing debate in the BD field regarding the role of science in its activities, ways of knowing, and the legitimate domains of influence that the field should seek to develop. A central point of this commentary was that the BD field has a specialized and well-developed knowledge base, much of which is empirically verified and reasonably well integrated, that deals with the adjustment problems of at-risk, vulnerable children and youth in the context of schooling. However, as a matter of practice, the BD field does not take advantage of opportunities to demonstrate its contributions to solving problems of great societal concern (e.g., school failure and dropout, preventing gang membership, addressing bullying and harassment, preventing school violence, participating in delinquency prevention initiatives, ensuring school safety, and controlling the transport of dangerous weapons across school boundaries). Further, the BD field does not promote its solutions to these problems with the audiences that count, including the general public, state and local policy makers, and the U.S. Congress.

The article argued that the gap between what is known in the BD field and what is applied in everyday practice is glaring and likely rivals that of any other field. BD professionals were urged to reference the outcomes of their research to these larger issues of great societal concern and to target their interventions in ways that impact them and their precursors. In our view, the BD field has a long way to go in establishing its value to the larger constituencies that it serves as the fields of medicine, engineering, psychology, and speech-language pathology have accomplished so successfully. However, given the concerns of the public and educators about youth violence, schooling effectiveness, and school safety, the time has never been better for the BD field to demonstrate its value and effectiveness through the promotion of many of its seminal contributions as solutions to these societal problems.

Behavior Disorders and the Postmodern, Deconstructivist Perspective

Postmodernism and deconstructivist philosophies have spread rapidly through the social sciences in the past decade (Wilson, 1998). These philosophies reject the scientific method and deny the possibility of common or universal forms of knowledge. The proponents of postmodern deconstructivism (PD) often criticize scientific understanding on the basis that it is decontextualized and does not acknowledge the construction of meanings. PD advocates have gained considerable influence in many institutions of higher education; their positions pose a significant threat to the BD field partly because a behavior disorder or emotional disturbance is known as a judgmental disorder (Walker et al., 1998). That is, the disorder is said to exist only if certain persons agree that it represents a departure from expected or normative patterns of behavior. Thus, the subject matter of behavior disorders is particularly vulnerable to postmodern constructions of reality. PD suggests that we can know nothing but our own experiences and that the realities of phenomena are determined more by our perceptions of them than by their actual physical, objective attributes.

Postmodernism, as Kauffman has noted, is receiving considerable press and attention in the social sciences (Kauffman, 1999). Recently, the journal, *Behavioral Disorders* devoted a special issue to postmodern perspectives and formulations

vis-à-vis behavior disorders (Hendrickson & Sasso, 1998). Reactions from BD scholar-researchers to the lead article by Elkind (1998) were not particularly supportive or in agreement with most of the key points made.

Elkind (1998), for example, argued that our conceptions and theories about behavior disorders are determined by the basic social and cultural tenets prevailing in our society at any given time. Elkind argued further that there has been a paradigm shift in this regard as reflected in the postmodern themes of difference, particularity, and regularity. Specifically, Elkind suggested that individual differences in behavioral characteristics and expression are so vast, complex, and unique that traditional classification systems are next to useless and artificial at best. Elkind recommended that we focus our efforts exclusively on the individual and said that BD professionals have at their disposal an array of therapeutic techniques, from differing theoretical approaches, and that we should apply combinations of them as the child's individual needs warrant. How we would select such combinations of techniques and evaluate the efficacy of our efforts remains a mystery to the present authors.

This case, albeit persuasively articulated by Elkind, has not and likely will not be well received by the BD field. Calls to focus on the unique characteristics and strengths of individual children and youth have always had appeal for BD professionals. However, adoption of this approach by some sectors of the BD field strikes us as the inverse of progress. In our view, the wide spread adoption of this perspective would result in a return to a focus on the single case, each of which is considered a unique event, which characterized the early beginnings of the field of applied behavior analysis over 30 years ago. Treating every student as a unique individual case means that we cannot generalize from one case to another and that each is essentially a new experiment, the results of which would have no meaning or relevance to those coming before or after. At present, we do not have the financial luxury of not treating at-risk students in group contexts within school settings.

Further, we have learned a great deal over the past two decades from studying problems and maladaptive conditions, among BD as well as non-BD student populations, that share certain commonalities of attributes and characteristics (e.g., ADHD, social isolation, instrumental aggression, antisocial behavior, depression, etc.). Our ability to develop interventions that produce similar outcomes, across children and youth representing these conditions, is critical to advancing the knowledge base in behavior disorders. It would be a mistake of gigantic proportions to abandon this approach in our research and development efforts in the future.

Ultimately, the postmodern perspective will likely occupy some space in the universe of accepted formulations about behavior disorders that currently exist in the BD field. However, because of the BD field's long commitment to research-based solutions and empirical approaches, we believe that it is doubtful that it will ever occupy a dominant or prevailing position in this regard.

Failure to Serve the Full K–12 Range of Students With Behavior Disorders

Historically, school systems have substantially underserved the K–12 student population with behavior disorders. As noted earlier, approximately 20% of the public school population is estimated to have serious mental health problems, but slightly less than 1% nationally of K–12 students are declared eligible annually for services under the ED category of the IDEA. Using the IDEA definition for ED, school psychologists have traditionally served as gatekeepers in determining which students referred for behavior disorders actually qualify as emotionally disturbed and thus are able to access the services, supports, and protections afforded through IDEA certification. School psychologists have typically used the IDEA definition for ED to rule out rather than rule in students referred for behavior disorders as emotionally disturbed; thus, the vast majority of students with school-related mental health problems is denied access to IDEA services and appropriate interventions tailored to their needs. The ED definitional criteria of IDEA require that an evaluative judgment be made regarding whether the referred student is emotionally disturbed versus socially maladjusted. If as a result of the IDEA eligibility evaluation process the student is considered to be maladjusted, then ED certification is denied; otherwise, the student is certified and can access IDEA supports, services, and protections.

The strict gatekeeping by school psychologists around the determination of ED eligibility is reflective of school administrators' extreme reluctance to extend the protections of IDEA to this student population. By so doing, it becomes very difficult to apply disciplinary sanctions to ED-certified students because of the protections built into IDEA. Furthermore, parents and advocates can sue school districts for not providing a free and appropriate education for an ED-certified student. Out-of-state residential placements for these students can easily exceed $100,000 annually, and school districts have to bear these costs if it is shown that they cannot provide a free, appropriate educational experience for an ED-certified student. Currently, the Hawaii state government is under a costly, court-ordered decree after losing a class action suit for denying services to ED-eligible students. Further, teachers

who refer students with behavior disorders for possible ED certification are sometimes negatively regarded by administrators as unable to manage their classrooms effectively. In the face of these strong barriers, it is unlikely that adequately serving students with behavior disorders will ever be accomplished under the aegis of the IDEA.

The ED eligibility definition and its application to the population referred for behavior disorders has been the subject of considerable debate over the past several decades. It has been severely criticized as invalid and arbitrary (Forness & Knitzer, 1990; Gresham et al., 2000). Recently, Walker, Nishioka, Zeller, Bullis, and Sprague (2001) reported results of a study in which no differences were detected between 15 ED-certified and 15 noncertified socially maladjusted (SM) middle school boys on a series of measures that assessed both positive and negative forms of adjustment within home and school settings. The dimensions on which the two groups were evaluated included demographics, school history, academic achievement, social competence, behavioral characteristics, personal strengths, ADHD symptoms, and attitudes toward aggression and violence using multiple measures and informants across home and school settings (see Walker et al., 2001, for details of these measures). Given these results, it is difficult to see on what basis the judgment was made in determining the ED or SM status of these students. This is especially significant, given that 12 of the 15 socially maladjusted students had previously been referred and certified as eligible for special education but were later decertified. However, all of the socially maladjusted boys in this study had been placed on a waiting list for placement in an alternative middle school program for students having severe behavior problems.

The observation has been made by some BD professionals that students should not be screened and identified for services that do not currently exist. However, it is difficult to know how the true need for services for this population can be determined unless systematic screening efforts are put in place to document the extent of need. Without such careful documentation, motivations to develop services and delivery mechanisms will continue to be weak among school personnel. Standardized definitional criteria and screening procedures would likely be required to accomplish this goal.

We are convinced that a different approach is necessary to meet the needs of the public school student population with behavior disorders. In our view, an integrated approach or model of the type proposed by Walker et al. (1996) will be required to address the needs of all students in a school setting. This model provides for the seamless integration of differing types of interventions for achieving primary, secondary, and tertiary prevention goals and outcomes. In this integrated approach, universal interventions are used to achieve primary prevention outcomes; small-group interventions are used to address secondary prevention goals; and individualized interventions with wraparound services are used to address the needs of tertiary level students and their families. A resistance to intervention procedure determines which students require secondary and tertiary prevention supports and services following their exposure to the primary prevention intervention. This integrated model is highly cost-effective and is perhaps the only way that the mental health and adjustment needs of all students in today's schools can be addressed, at some level, given the ongoing press on schooling dollars. A more detailed illustration of this model is presented in the section on evidence-based interventions.

BD Leadership in Developing a Prevention Agenda

In our view, there are two major opportunities or windows for mounting prevention initiatives that have a chance to divert behaviorally at-risk children from a destructive path. The two developmental periods or windows are the age ranges of 0 to 5 years and 6 to 10 years. Because BD professionals are primarily school based, they can have their greatest impact from kindergarten through the primary and intermediate grades. However, many behavioral specialists employed by school districts have the opportunity to work collaboratively with early childhood educators and Head Start personnel who deal with 3- and 4-year-olds. In the past decade there have been many anecdotal reports of very young children exhibiting more mature forms of destructive behavior (e.g., wearing gang colors, physically attacking teachers, plotting serious harm toward peers, engaging in inappropriate sexual behavior, etc.). Furthermore, larger numbers of children are coming to school lacking in specific school-readiness skills, and they are often very unprepared to cope with the normal demands and routines of schooling. In a recent survey Rimm-Kaufman, Pianta, and Cox (2000) documented the breadth and prevalence of school-readiness problems among kindergartners. In their survey, up to 46% of surveyed teachers reported that about half of their class entered kindergarten with problems in one or more areas, as follows: difficulty following directions, 46%; difficulty working independently, 34%; difficulty working as part of a group, 30%; problems with social skills, 20%; immaturity, 20%; and difficulty communicating/language problems, 14%. Longitudinal research indicates that these impairments in social competence and school readiness skills can serve as harbingers of future adjustment problems in a number of domains including interpersonal relations, employment, academic achievement, and mental health (Loeber & Farrington, 1998; McEvoy & Welker, 2000).

As noted earlier, increasing numbers of children are bringing antisocial, challenging behavior patterns with them to the schooling process. Moffitt (1994) referred to these children as early starters who are inadvertently socialized to an antisocial behavior pattern by their families and caregivers. Patterson et al. (1992) researched and illustrated the coercion processes operating among family members that lead to this unfortunate and destructive behavior pattern. In this family context, early starters learn to aggress, escalate, and coerce others to achieve their social goals. Most bring this behavior pattern with them to the schooling process, and this leads to social rejection by both teachers and peers within just a few years (Eddy et al., 2002). Unfortunately, a majority of these children will not access the school-based intervention supports and services that they need to succeed in school because of the practices of related services, school personnel who typically classify them as socially maladjusted which has the effect of denying them this access.

Thousands of our vulnerable children and youth are on a destructive path. The longer one remains on this path, the more serious are the outcomes the individual is likely to encounter. Longitudinal studies in Australia, New Zealand, Canada, the United States, and Western Europe converge in documenting this destructive pathway (Kellam, Brown, Rubin, & Ensminger, 1983; Loeber & Farrington, 1998; Patterson et al., 1992). Reid and his colleagues (Eddy, Reid, & Fetrow, 2000; Reid, 1993) have long argued that the earlier one addresses the problems of children who are on this path, the more likely it is that they will be successfully diverted from later destructive outcomes. Longitudinal follow-up studies of the long-term effects of early intervention provide clear evidence that this is indeed the case (see Barnett, 1985; Hawkins, Catalano, Kosterman, Abbott, & Hill; 1999; Strain & Timm, 2001). Further, in a randomized-control trial of early versus later intervention, Hawkins et al. (1999) found that a school-based early intervention that (a) targets and teaches social skills to students, behavior-management skills to teachers, and family-management skills to parents in a coordinated fashion; (b) facilitates bonding, engagement, and attachment to schooling; and (c) is delivered in the primary grades leads to strong protections against a number of health-risk behaviors at age 18, including delinquent acts, teenage pregnancy, heavy drinking, multiple sex partners, behavioral incidents requiring disciplinary action at school, low achievement, and school failure.

It is essential that BD professionals assume a more active role, and a leadership one when possible, in making sure that *all* behaviorally at-risk children are detected at the point of school entry and provided with the supports, services, and interventions that will help ensure a successful beginning to their school careers. Achieving this goal will require developing close working relationships with early childhood educators, parents, and mental health professionals, where appropriate. The school-based BD professional is ideally positioned to assume this role and to coordinate the universal screening and intervention delivery strategies that can divert many behaviorally at-risk students from this path. More specifically, as argued elsewhere (Walker et al., 1999), we believe that the BD professional's role should include the following functions at a minimum:

1. Promulgating best practices for students both with and without behavior disorders that are research based and cost efficient.
2. Advocating for educators' adoption of proven evidence-based approaches to intervention.
3. Forming true partnerships with general educators and professionals from other disciplines that create the commitment and breadth of knowledge necessary to address the complex needs and problems of the behaviorally at-risk school population.
4. Taking the lead in building multidisciplinary, interagency team approaches to providing integrated interventions for at-risk students and their families.

The BD field has a talented and knowledgeable cadre of professionals who, in our estimation, could perform these functions skillfully. However, at present they are not adequately supported by school systems in performing these functions.

ADOPTION AND DELIVERY OF EVIDENCE-BASED INTERVENTIONS

In traditional practice schools have not been strongly motivated to assume ownership and responsibility for solving the behavior problems and disorders of school-age children and youth. Rather than investing in proactive interventions to teach skills and to develop behavioral solutions, school administrators have relied primarily on a combination of sanctions (suspensions, expulsions) and assignment of problem students to self-contained settings in responding to the BD student population. The basic strategy has been to punish or isolate students with challenging behavior rather than to solve their problems and respond to their needs. Some educators have referred to these students as the schools' homeless street people, and, in a very real sense, they have typically been treated as such.

In addition, school systems historically have not been motivated to search for and apply proven, cost-effective interventions that can substantively affect the learning and adjustment of the full range of K–12 students. Walker et al. (1998) noted that in no field is there a more glaring lack of connection between the availability of proven, research-based methods and their effective application by consumers in education. The analysis, commentary, and writings of Carnine (1993, 1995) and Kauffman (1996) have been instrumental in highlighting the gaps that exist in the field of education. Kauffman (1996) observed that the education profession is characterized by continuous change but little sustained improvement because the relationship between reliable, effective practices and their widespread adoption remains obscure. This is the dominant educational context in which BD professionals have to work and advocate for the adoption of proven, effective practices for the student population with behavior disorders.

However, in the last few years the attitudes of school systems have shown signs of change in this regard probably as a function of the twin pressures generated by the school reform movement and the school-shooting tragedies of the 1990s. Now schools are beginning to embrace the following practices, which had, in the past, been infrequently adopted: (a) the universal screening of all students to detect those with emerging behavior disorders; (b) investment in primary, secondary, and tertiary forms of prevention; (c) developing proactive rather than reactive responses to child and youth problems in school; and (d) searching for evidence-based interventions and approaches that are proven to work. This may be the front edge of a paradigm shift for the field of general education. If so, the school-based BD professional is ideally positioned to serve as a leader and resource in facilitating this organizational change.

In our view, the problems attendant on serving the full range of K–12 students with behavior disorders do not stem from a lack of available, evidence-based interventions. Rather, it is much more a problem of knowing what works, having the will to implement effective practices with good integrity, and finding the resources necessary to support this effort. A number of reviews of best practices in the areas of school-related behavior disorders, school safety, and violence prevention have been developed recently. These reviews provide a valuable resource for school-based professionals and administrators who often have difficulty locating and evaluating the efficacy of differing intervention models and approaches—all of which claim to be effective.

One of the most valuable, thorough, and comprehensive reviews of effective, school-based interventions addresses the effectiveness of programs for preventing mental disorders in school-age children and youth and that are designed for use primarily in school settings (Greenberg, Domitrovich, & Bumbarger, 1999). These investigators reviewed the broad landscape of available programs numbering in the thousands.

It is instructive that they found only 34 evidence-based programs that met rigorous standards of efficacy. Their report provides the following valuable information for professional consumers:

1. It identifies critical issues and themes in prevention research with school-age children and families.
2. It profiles universal, selected, and indicated programs that reduce symptoms of both externalizing and internalizing symptoms.
3. It summarizes state-of-the-art programs in the prevention of mental disorders in school-age children.
4. It identifies the key elements that contribute to program success.
5. It provides suggestions to improve the quality of program development and evaluation.

Aside from its overall quality, there are a number of specific strengths to the report of Greenberg et al. (1999). Separating the review into universal, selected, and indicated interventions and then determining whether the interventions reviewed address primarily *externalizing* or *internalizing* behavior problems and disorders substantially increases the relevance of the review for school applications and provides needed clarity for consumers. In our view, the great majority of adjustment problems that students manifest in the school setting are either directed outwardly toward the external social environment (i.e., aggression, defiance, bullying, coercion) or internally (i.e., social withdrawal, anxiety, depression, phobias) representing problems with others versus problems with self. Externalizing disorders usually require a reduce-and-replace intervention strategy, whereas internalizing disorders typically call for a focus on skill development and performance enhancement.

Greenberg et al. (1999) found that the most effective interventions were those that (a) had multiple components, (b) involved multiple social agents (parents, teachers, peers), (c) were implemented across several settings (classroom, playground, home), and (d) were in place for a sufficient period of time to register socially valid outcomes—usually a minimum of 1 year. This review is being continuously updated and expanded as new evidence-based interventions come on line. It is highly recommended as a blueprint or roadmap for BD professionals to use in upgrading school-based practices for the behaviorally at-risk K–12 population. A special issue of the APA journal *Prevention and Treatment* (March, 2001) was devoted to the report and its findings.

The U.S. Public Health Service classification system for differing types of prevention is well suited for the delivery of these three types of interventions profiled in the Greenberg et al. (1999) review (i.e., universal, selected, indicated). As a

rule, universal interventions are used to achieve primary prevention goals and outcomes (i.e., to prevent harm); selected interventions are used for secondary prevention efforts (i.e., to reverse harm); and indicated interventions are used for tertiary prevention applications (i.e., to reduce harm). Walker et al. (1995, 1996) have adapted this classification schema for the delivery of proven interventions within school settings that address the needs of *all* students. Figure 20.3 illustrates this classification schema. School settings are ideally suited to implement this delivery structure because they are naturally organized to implement schoolwide interventions (e.g., a school discipline plan, a school safety plan, a school improvement plan), small-group interventions (e.g., resource and self-contained classrooms), and individually tailored interventions (e.g., counseling). In the last 5 years, this three-level intervention delivery system has been widely adopted by researchers and school personnel alike across the country.

School personnel are especially amenable to universal intervention approaches because they treat all students equitably and in the same manner. Thus, the fairness issue that resonates so strongly with most teachers is indirectly addressed as every student is exposed to the intervention in an identical fashion. Those students for whom the universal intervention is insufficient then receive secondary and possibly tertiary prevention interventions. One of the great advantages of a universal intervention is that it creates a context in which more intensive small-group and individually tailored interventions can achieve greater effectiveness, which are then applied only after the failure of a universal intervention approach for certain students. Another is that it addresses the problems of mildly involved, at-risk students in a cost-effective manner. The scaled-up adoption of this integrated delivery system, when combined with proven intervention models that have been adapted to and tested within the school setting, has the potential to improve substantially the effectiveness of schooling and to create much more positive school climates.

THE CONTENT OF SCHOOL INTERVENTIONS FOR STUDENTS WITH BEHAVIOR DISORDERS

When children begin their school careers, they are required to make two critically important social-behavioral adjustments *teacher-related* and *peer-related* (Walker et al., 1995). That is, they must negotiate a satisfactory adjustment to the academic and behavioral expectations of teachers and conform to the demands of instructional settings. Of equal importance, they must negotiate a satisfactory adjustment to the peer group, find a niche within it, and develop social support networks consisting of friends, affiliates and acquaintances. Walker, Irvin,

Noell, and Singer (1992) have developed an interpersonal model of social-behavioral competence for school settings. This model identifies the adaptive and maladaptive behavioral correlates of successful student adjustment in the domains of teacher-related and peer-related functioning. The model also describes the long-term outcomes that are commonly associated with the *adaptive* (e.g., school success, friendship-making, peer and teacher acceptance) versus *maladaptive* (e.g., school failure and dropout, assignment to restrictive settings, delinquency) pathways contained within it.

The adaptive and maladaptive behavioral correlates included in the teacher- and peer-related adjustment dimensions of this model are based on empirical evidence generated by the present authors and their colleagues as well as research evidence presented in the professional literature on social competence. The long-term outcomes listed for each path under these two forms of adjustment are based on longitudinal and cross-sectional studies reported in the literature over the past two decades (see Loeber & Farrington, 1998; Patterson et al., 1992; Strain, Guralnick, & Walker, 1986).

Failure in either of these critically important areas impairs a student's overall school adjustment and success; failure in both puts a student's overall quality of life at risk and is a harbinger of future problems of potentially severe magnitude. Students with behavior disorders are invariably below normative levels and expectations on the adaptive behavioral correlates of teacher- and peer-related adjustment and usually outside the normative range on the maladaptive behavioral correlates. In the great majority of cases, the intervention of choice for students with behavior disorders involves developing their social skills and overall social competence while teaching them alternatives to the maladaptive forms of behavior that tend to dominate their behavioral repertoires. In our view, the potential of social skills instruction (SSI) for students in general, and particularly for students with behavior disorders, has yet to be realized in spite of a substantial investment in SSI efforts over the past two decades by school personnel (Bullis, Walker, & Sprague, 2001; Elksnin & Elksnin, 1995).

Recent reviews of the efficacy of SSI with the K–12 school population with behavior disorders have not been encouraging (see Gresham, 1997, 1998a; Kavale, Mathur, Forness, Rutherford, & Quinn, 1997). These authors have conducted and reviewed meta-analyses of social skills interventions and concluded that the average effect sizes in the studies they reviewed are minimal to moderate at best, generally ranging between .30 and .45. Given the level of effort invested in these studies, these results do not appear to be terribly cost-effective. A number of reasons have been hypothesized for these disappointing outcomes, including (a) the failure to match deficits in social skills with the intervention, (b) the absence of theoretical models to guide SSI, (c) implementing the SSI

procedure in artificial instructional settings and expecting generalization of newly taught skills to natural settings, and (d) implementing the SSI for insufficient amounts of time for it to impact the student's behavioral repertoire. We believe that an equally powerful, but infrequently mentioned, reason concerns the failure to address the competing, maladaptive behavior problems of students with behavior disorders who are the targets of SSI. SSI alone is rarely sufficient to teach prosocial skills and simultaneously to address a well-developed maladaptive behavioral repertoire. Direct intervention techniques designed to reduce and eliminate maladaptive forms of behavior are required for this purpose. Some best-practice principles and guidelines for conducting SSI with students with behavior disorders are described next.

Social Skills Instruction for Students with Behavior Disorders

The school is an ideal setting for teaching social skills because of its accessibility to children and their peers, teachers, and parents. Fundamentally, social skills intervention takes place in school and home settings, both informally and formally, using either universal or selected intervention procedures. Informal social skills interventions are based on the notion of incidental learning, which takes advantage of naturally occurring behavioral incidents or events to teach appropriate social behavior. Most of the SSI in home, non-classroom school contexts, and community settings can be characterized as informal or incidental. Literally thousands of behavioral incidents occur in these naturalistic home, school, and community settings, creating rich opportunities for making each of these behavioral incidents a potentially successful learning experience. Formal SSI, on the other hand, can take place seamlessly within a classroom setting in which (a) the social skills curriculum is exposed to the entire class or it is taught to selected students within small-group formats and (b) social skills are taught as subject matter in the same way as are social science, history, biology, and other academic subjects. However, unless formal and informal methods of teaching social skills are combined with each other, there is likely to be a disconnect between conceptual mastery of social skills and their demonstration and application within natural settings.

Objectives of Social Skills Instruction

(From Kathleen L. Lane, Frank M. Gresham, & Tam E. O'Shaughnessy, *Interventions for Children with or At Risk for Emotional and Behavioral Disorders*. Published by Allyn and Bacon, Boston, MA. Copyright © 2002 by Pearson Education. Reprinted by permission of the publisher.)

SSI has four primary objectives: (a) promoting skill acquisition, (b) enhancing skill performance, (c) reducing or eliminating competing problem behaviors, and (d) facilitating generalization and maintenance of social skills. Most students with behavior disorders will likely have some combination of acquisition and performance deficits, some of which may be accompanied by competing problem behaviors. Any given student may require some combination of acquisition, performance, and behavior-reduction strategies. All students will require procedures to facilitate generalization and maintenance of previously learned social skills (see Gresham, 2002).

Table 20.1 lists specific social skills and behavior-reduction strategies for each of the four goals of SSI. Appropriate intervention strategies should be matched with the particular

TABLE 20.1   Objectives and Strategies of Social Skills Instruction

I. PROMOTING SKILLS ACQUISITION
  A. Modeling.
  B. Coaching.
  C. Behavioral rehearsal.
II. ENHANCING SKILLS PERFORMANCE
  A. Manipulation of antecedents.
    1. Peer initiation strategies.
    2. Proactive classroom management strategies.
    3. Peer tutoring.
    4. Incidental teaching.
  B. Manipulation of consequences.
    1. Contingency contracting.
    2. Group-oriented contingency systems.
    3. School-home notes.
    4. Verbal praise.
    5. Activity reinforcers.
    6. Token and point systems.
III. REMOVING COMPETING PROBLEM BEHAVIORS
  A. Differential reinforcement.
    1. Differential reinforcement of other behavior (DRO).
    2. Differential reinforcement of low rates of behavior (DRL).
    3. Differential reinforcement of incompatible behaviors (DRI).
  B. Overcorrection.
    1. Restitution.
    2. Positive practice.
  C. Time-out.
    1. Nonexclusionary (contingent observation).
    2. Exclusionary.
  D. Systematic desensitization (for anxiety-based competing behaviors).
  E. Flooding and exposure (for anxiety-based competing behaviors).
IV. FACILITATING GENERALIZATION
  A. Topographical generalization.
    1. Training diversely.
    2. Exploiting functional contingencies.
    3. Incorporating functional mediators.
  B. Functional Generalization.
    1. Identify strong competing stimuli in specific situations.
    2. Identify strong competing problem behaviors in specific situations.
    3. Identify functionally equivalent socially skilled behaviors.
    4. Increase reliability and efficiency of social skilled behaviors (build fluency).
    5. Decrease reliability and efficiency of competing problem behaviors.

Source: Gresham (1998b).

deficits or competing problem behaviors that the student exhibits. A common misconception is that one seeks to facilitate generalization and maintenance *after* implementing procedures for the acquisition and performance of social skills. The evidence is clear that the best and preferred practice is to incorporate generalization strategies from the beginning of any SSI program (Gresham, 1998b).

Promoting Skills Acquisition

Procedures designed to promote skill acquisition are applicable when students do not have a particular social skill in their repertoire, when they do not know a particular step in the performance of a behavioral sequence, or when their execution of the skill is awkward or ineffective (i.e., a fluency deficit). It should be noted that a relatively small percentage of students would need social skills intervention based on acquisition deficits; far more students have performance deficits (Gresham, 1998a).

Three procedures represent pathways to remediating deficits in social skill acquisition: *modeling, coaching,* and *behavioral rehearsal.* Social problem solving is another pathway, but it is not discussed here because of space limitations and because it incorporates a combination of modeling, coaching, and behavioral rehearsal. More specific information on social problem solving interventions can be found in Elias and Clabby (1992).

Modeling is the process of learning a behavior by observing another person performing it. Modeling instruction presents the entire sequence of behaviors involved in a particular social skill and teaches the student how to integrate specific behaviors into a composite behavior pattern. Modeling is one of the most effective and efficient ways of teaching social behavior (Elliott & Gresham, 1992; Schneider, 1992).

Coaching is the use of verbal instruction to teach social skills. Unlike modeling, which emphasizes visual displays of social skills, coaching utilizes a student's receptive language skills. Coaching is accomplished in three fundamental steps: (a) presenting social concepts or rules, (b) providing opportunities for practice or rehearsal, and (c) providing specific informational feedback on the quality of behavioral performances.

Behavioral rehearsal refers to practicing a newly learned behavior in a structured, protective situation of role-playing. In this way, students can enhance their proficiency in using social skills without experiencing adverse consequences. Behavioral rehearsal can be covert, verbal, or overt. Covert rehearsal involves students' imagining certain social interactions (e.g., being teased by another student or group of students). Verbal rehearsal involves students' verbalizing the specific behaviors that they would exhibit in a social situation.

Overt rehearsal is the actual role-playing of a specific social interaction.

Enhancing Skills Performance

Most social skills interventions involve procedures that increase the frequency of particular prosocial behaviors in specific social situations because most social skills difficulties involve performance deficits rather than acquisition deficits. This suggests that social skills interventions for most students should take place in naturalistic environments (e.g., classrooms, playgrounds) rather than in small, pullout-group situations. Failure to perform certain social skills in specific situations results from two fundamental factors: (a) inappropriately arranged antecedents and (b) inappropriately arranged consequences. A number of specific procedures can be classified under the broad rubric of antecedent and consequent strategies.

Interventions based on antecedent control assume that the environment does not set the occasion for the performance of prosocial behavior. That is, cues, prompts, or other events either are not present or are not salient in order for the child to discriminate these stimuli in relation to the performance of prosocial behavior. A cuing and prompting procedure uses verbal and nonverbal cues or prompts to facilitate prosocial behavior. Simple prompts or cues for some children may be all that is needed to signal them to engage in socially appropriate behavior (e.g., "Say thank you," "Ask Katrina to join your group"). Cuing and prompting represent one of the easiest and most efficient social skills intervention strategies (Elliott & Gresham, 1992; Walker et al., 1995).

Interventions based on consequent control can be classified into three broad categories: (a) reinforcement-based strategies, (b) behavioral contracts, and (c) school-home notes. Reinforcement-based strategies assume that the student knows how to perform a social skill but is not doing so because of little or no reinforcement for the behavior. The objective in using these strategies is to increase the frequency of reinforcement for prosocial behavior. Reinforcement strategies include attention, social praise, tokens and points, and activity reinforcers as well as group-oriented contingency systems. Extensive discussions of behavioral contracts, school-home notes, and group-oriented contingency systems can be found in more comprehensive treatments of these subjects (Kelley, 1990; Kohler & Strain, 1990; Stuart, 1971)

Removing or Eliminating Competing Problem Behaviors

The focus of SSI is clearly on developing and refining prosocial behaviors. However, the failure of some students to either acquire or perform certain social skills may be due to the presence of competing problem behaviors. This is particularly true of students having behavior disorders whose externalizing or internalizing symptoms compete with or block the acquisition and performance of prosocial behaviors. For example, aggressive behavior may be performed instead of a prosocial behavior because it may be more efficient and reliable in achieving one's social goals and producing reinforcement. A number of techniques that are effective in reducing competing problem behaviors are presented in Table 20.1.

Facilitating Generalization and Maintenance

Basically, there are only two processes that are essential to all behavioral interventions: discrimination and generalization (Stokes, 1992). Discrimination occurs within the context of stimulus control. A major problem confronting social skills interventions is that it is much easier to prompt the occurrence of some behaviors in one place, for a limited period of time, than it is to get those same behaviors to occur in a variety of other places for an extended period of time. That is, it is infinitely easier to teach discriminations than it is to teach generalization and maintenance.

Generalization of behavior change is related directly to the principle of resistance to intervention. If social skill deficits occur at low frequencies, competing problem-behavior excesses will likely occur at high frequencies, and both of these deficits and excesses tend to be chronic with students with behavior disorders (i.e., they have lasted a relatively long period of time), and they will tend to show less generalization across different nontraining conditions as well as less durability over time as SSI is withdrawn (Gresham, 1991). In effect, these students quickly discriminate training from nontraining conditions, particularly when training conditions are noticeably different from nontraining conditions.

Students with behavior disorders often show excellent initial behavior change in response to well-designed, powerful school interventions of a secondary or tertiary prevention nature, particularly in relation to their competing problem-behavior excesses, but they tend not to show generalization or maintenance of these behavior changes. One reason for this may be that exclusive attention often is focused on decreasing the momentum of undesirable behavior to the exclusion of facilitating the momentum of desirable behaviors such as critically important social skills. The primary reason for this frequently observed lack of generalization and maintenance is that essential components of behavior change are not actively programmed to occur as part of SSI.

Various generalization programming strategies are presented in Table 20.1 under the headings of topographical and functional generalization. The topographical description of generalization refers to the occurrence of relevant behaviors (e.g., social skills) under different nontraining conditions (Stokes & Osnes, 1989). These nontraining conditions can be settings or situations (setting generalization), behaviors (response generalization), or time-based (maintenance). A more detailed and now-classic treatment of topographical generalization is described by Stokes and Osnes (1989).

A functional approach to generalization consists of two types: (a) *stimulus generalization,* which is the occurrence of the same behavior under variations of the original training conditions (the greater the difference between training conditions and subsequent environmental conditions, the less the generalization), and (b) *response generalization,* which is the control of multiple behaviors by the same stimulus.

An extremely important goal of SSI is to determine the reliability and efficiency of competing problem behaviors relative to socially skilled alternative behaviors. Competing problem behaviors will be performed instead of prosocial behaviors if the competing behaviors are more efficient and reliable than the prosocial behavior. Efficient behaviors (a) are easier to perform in terms of response effort and (b) produce reinforcement more rapidly. Reliable behaviors are those that produce the desired outcomes more frequently than do prosocial behaviors. For example, pushing into the lunch line may be more efficient and reliable than politely asking to cut into line.

To program for functional generalization, school personnel should (a) decrease the efficiency and reliability of competing inappropriate behaviors and (b) increase the efficiency and reliability of prosocial behaviors. The former can be accomplished by many of the procedures listed in Table 20.1 under Removing Competing Problem Behaviors. The latter can be achieved by spending more time and effort in building fluency of trained social skills using combinations of modeling, coaching, and, most important, behavioral rehearsal with specific performance feedback (see Gresham, 2002).

We are convinced that SSI outcomes can be greatly enhanced by adopting these best-practice principles and strategies. They have been incorporated into a number of proven behavioral interventions (see Coleman & Webber, 2001; Elksnin & Elksnin, 1995; Shinn, Walker, & Stoner, 2002; Walker, Colvin, & Ramsey, 1995).

CONCLUSION

Throughout this chapter we have made the case (a) that the K–12 student population with behavior disorders is underserved by schools; (b) that powerful, proven interventions are available that are designed for and have been tested with students with behavior disorders in the contexts of both mainstreamed and specialized school settings; (c) that the BD professional is ideally positioned to assume a leadership role in coordinating these interventions while involving key social agents in the lives of students with behavior disorders (and their parents, teachers, peers); and (d) that the BD professional has the knowledge, expertise, and necessary role position to work effectively with other agencies and professionals in developing prevention initiatives at both the preschool and K–12 grade levels. As we noted earlier, the time and opportunities have never been better to pursue this agenda because of the more open receptiveness of school leaders and on-line personnel to effective interventions that can make the school safer, violence free, and more inclusive, positive, and effective. However, a missing link in this regard has been and continues to be the organized advocacy to promote and support adoption of this changed and relatively ambitious agenda for the BD professional and larger field.

Walker et al. (1998) have contributed and outlined a national agenda for the BD field that provides a template to assist in guiding its future development. Further, in June 2001 a group of 18 BD professionals in higher education, who are well-known scholar-researchers within the BD field, convened at the University of Virginia for a two-day meeting to further elaborate this agenda and develop an action plan to promote and support its implementation nationally over the next several years. In terms of content, this group of professionals focused its deliberations on three major areas: (a) the role of science in the affairs of the BD field, (b) the identification and promulgation of evidenced-based interventions that work for students with behavior disorders in school settings, and (c) development of interdisciplinary and interagency strategies for improving the effectiveness of both intervention and prevention initiatives. Two outcomes of this meeting involved the decision to create an academy of BD professionals devoted to the prevention of learning and behavior disorders in the context of schooling and the development of a monograph that will define best practices in the BD field and set evaluative standards for the same.

We are optimistic that these efforts will result in enhancements of schools' capacities to serve BD students and their families better. We look forward to participation in the achievement of this agenda for the BD field.

REFERENCES

American Psychological Association. (1994). *Diagnostic and statistical manual of mental disorders* (4th ed.). Washington, DC: Author.

Angold, A. (2000, December). *Preadolescent screening and data analysis.* Paper presented to the 2nd Annual Expert Panel

Meeting on Preadolescent Screening Procedures, Washington, DC.

Barnett, W. S. (1985). The Perry Preschool Program and its long-term effects: A benefit-cost analysis. *High/Scope Early Childhood Policy Papers* (No. 2). Ypsilanti, MI: High/Scope.

Bullis, M., Walker, H. M., & Sprague, J. R. (2001). A promise unfulfilled: Social skills training with at-risk children and youth. *Exceptionality, 9*(1 & 2), 67–90.

Carnine, D. (1993, December 8). Facts, not fads. *Education Week,* 40.

Carnine, D. (1995). *Enhancing the education profession: Increasing the perceived and actual value of research.* Eugene, OR: National Center to Improve the Tools of Educators.

Coleman, M., & Webber, J. (2001). *Emotional and behavioral disorders: Theory and practice* (4th ed.). Boston: Allyn & Bacon.

Colvin, G. (1993). *Managing acting out behavior.* Eugene, OR: Behavior Associates.

Dwyer, K., & Osher, D. (2000). *Safeguarding our children: An action guide.* Washington, DC: U.S. Departments of Education and Justice, American Institutes for Research.

Eddy, J. M., Reid, J. B., & Curry, V. (2002). The etiology of youth antisocial behavior, delinquency and violence and a public health approach to prevention. In M. R. Shinn, H. M. Walker, & G. Stoner (Eds.), *Interventions for academic and behavior problems: Vol. 2. Preventive and remedial approaches* (pp. 27–52). Bethesda, MD: National Association for School Psychologists.

Eddy, J. M., Reid, J. B., & Fetrow, R. A. (2000). An elementary school-based prevention program targeting modifiable antecedents of youth delinquency and violence: Linking the Interests of Families and Teachers (LIFT). *Journal of Emotional and Behavioral Disorders, 8*(3), 165–176.

Elias, M., & Clabby, J. (1992). *Building social problem-solving skills: Guidelines for school-based programs.* San Francisco: Jossey-Bass.

Elkind, D. (1998). Behavioral disorders: A postmodern perspective. *Behavioral Disorders, 23*(3), 153–159.

Elksnin, L. K., & Elksnin, N. (1995). *Assessment and instruction of social skills* (2nd ed.). San Diego, CA: Singular.

Elliott, S. N., & Gresham, F. M. (1992). *Social skills intervention guide.* Circle Pines, MN: American Guidance Service.

ERIC/OSEP Special Project. (winter, 1999). *Positive behavioral support.* Research Connections in Special Education (number 4). Reston, VA: The ERIC Clearinghouse on Disabilities and Gifted Education. Also available on the internet at http://ericec.org, under "Research Connections."

Forness, S., & Knitzer, J. (1990). *A new proposed definition and terminology to replace "serious emotional disturbance" in the Education of the Handicapped Act.* Washington, DC: The National Mental Health and Special Education Coalition.

Greenberg, M. T., Domitrovich, C., & Bumbarger, B. (1999). *Preventing mental disorders in school-age children: A review of the effectiveness of prevention programs.* Available from the Prevention Research Center for the Promotion of Human Development, College of Health and Human Development, Pennsylvania State University, State College, PA.

Gresham, F. M. (1991). Conceptualizing behavior disorders in terms of resistance to intervention. *School Psychology Review, 20,* 23–36.

Gresham, F. M. (1997). Social skills. In G. Bear & K. Minke (Eds.), *Children's needs: Psychological perspectives* (2nd ed., pp. 515–526). Bethesda, MD: National Association of School Psychologists.

Gresham, F. M. (1998a). Social skills training: Should we raze, remodel, or rebuild? *Behavioral Disorders, 24*(1), 19–25.

Gresham, F. M. (1998b). Social skills training with children: Social learning and applied behavior analytic approaches. In T. S. Watson & F. M. Gresham (Eds.), *Handbook of child behavior therapy* (pp. 475–498). New York: Plenum Press.

Gresham, F. M. (2002). Social skills assessment and instruction for students with emotional and behavioral disorders. In K. Lane, F. Gresham, & T. O'Shaughnessy (Eds.), *Children with or at risk for emotional and behavioral disorders* (pp. 242–257). Boston: Allyn & Bacon.

Gresham, F. M., Lane, K. L., & Lambros, K. M. (2000). Comorbidity of conduct problems and ADHD: Identification of "fledging psychopaths." *Journal of Emotional and Behavioral Disorders, 8*(2), 83–93.

Gresham, F. M., & Lopez, M. (1996). Social validation: A unifying concept for school-based consultation research and practice. *School Psychology Quarterly, 11*(1), 204–227.

Gresham, F. M., Quinn, M., & Restori, A. (1998). Methodological issues in functional analysis: Generalizability to other disability groups. *Behavioral Disorders, 24,* 180–182.

Hawkins, J. D., Catalano, R. F., Kosterman, R., Abbott, R., & Hill, K. G. (1999). Preventing adolescent health-risk behaviors by strengthening protection during childhood. *Archives of Pediatrics & Adolescent Medicine, 153,* 226–234.

Hendrickson, J. M., & Sasso, G. M. (Eds.). (1998). Postmodernism and behavioral disorders [Special issue]. *Behavioral Disorders, 23*(3).

Hester, P., & Kaiser, A. (1997). Early intervention for the prevention of conduct disorder: Research issues in early identification, implementation, and interpretation of treatment outcome. *Behavioral Disorders, 22,* 57–65.

Hoagwood, K., & Erwin, H. (1997). Effectiveness of school-based mental health services for children: A 10-year research review. *Journal of Child and Family Studies, 6,* 435–451.

Horner, R. H. (1994). Functional assessment: Contributions and future directions. *Journal of Applied Behavioral Analysis, 27*(2), 401–404.

Hunter, L., & Chopra, V. (2001). Two proactive primary prevention program models that work in schools. *Report on Emotional and Behavioral Disorders of in Youth, 1*(3), 57–59.

IDEA. (1997). *Reauthorization of the Individuals with Disabilities Education Act.* Washington, DC: U.S. Congress.

Kauffman, J. M. (1996). Research to practice issues. *Behavioral Disorders, 22,* 55–60.

Kauffman, J. M. (1999). How we prevent the prevention of emotional and behavioral disorders. *Exceptional Children, 65*(4), 448–468.

Kavale, K., Mathur, S., Forness, S., Rutherford, R., & Quinn, M. (1997). Effectiveness of social skills training for students with behavior disorders: A meta-analysis. In T. Scruggs & M. Mastropieri (Eds.), *Advances in learning and behavioral disabilities* (Vol. 11, pp. 1–26). Greenwich, CT: JAI Press.

Kellam, S., Brown, C., Rubin, B., & Ensminger, M. (1983). Paths leading to teenage psychiatric symptoms and substance use: Developmental epidemiological studies in Woodlawn. In S. B. Guze, F. J. Earls, & J. E. Barrett (Eds.), *Childhood psychopathology and development* (pp. 17–51). New York: Raven Press.

Kelley, M. (1990). *School-home notes: Promoting children's classroom success.* New York: Guilford Press.

Kingery, P. M., & Walker, H. M. (2002). What we know about school safety. In M. R. Shinn, H. M. Walker, & G. Stoner (Eds.), *Interventions for academic and behavior problems: Vol. 2. Preventive and remedial approaches* (pp. 71–88). Bethesda, MD: National Association of School Psychologists.

Kitzhaber, J. (2001, February). *A prevention agenda for Oregon's at-risk children.* Address given at a statewide early childhood conference, Portland, OR.

Kohler, F., & Strain, P. (1990). Peer-assisted interventions: Early promises, notable achievements, and future aspirations. *Clinical Psychology Review, 10,* 441–452.

Lewis, T., Sugai, G., & Colvin, G. (1998). Reducing problem behavior through a school-wide system of effective behavioral support: Investigation of a school-side social skills training program and contextual interventions. *School Psychology Review, 27,* 446–459,

Loeber, R., & Farrington, D. P. (Eds.). (1998). *Serious and violent juvenile offenders: Risk factors and successful interventions.* Thousand Oaks, CA: Sage.

Lynam, D. (1996). Early identification of chronic offenders: Who is the fledgling psychopath? *Psychological Bulletin, 120,* 209–234.

McEvoy, A., & Welker, R. (2000). Antisocial behavior, academic failure, and school climate: A critical review. *Journal of Emotional and Behavioral Disorders, 8*(3), 130–140.

Moffitt, T. (1994). Adolescence-limited and life-course-persistent antisocial behavior: A developmental taxonomy. *Psychological Review, 100*(4), 674–701.

Nelson, R., Roberts, M., Mathur, S., & Rutherford, R. (1999). Has public policy exceeded our knowledge base? A review of functional behavioral assessment literature. *Behavioral Disorders, 4,* 169–179.

O'Neill, R. E., Horner, R. H., Albin, R. W., Storey, K., & Newton, S. (1997). *Functional analysis of problem behavior: A practical assessment guide.* Pacific Grove, CA: Brooks/Cole.

Patterson, G. R. (1982). *Coercive family process: Vol. 3. A social learning approach.* Eugene, OR: Castalia.

Patterson, G. R., Reid, J. B., & Dishion, T. J. (1992). *Antisocial boys.* Eugene, OR: Castalia Press.

Perlstein, L. (2001, July 11). Schools awash in bad behavior: Area educators complain of students out of control. *The Washington Post,* p. B1.

Reid, J. B. (1993). Prevention of conduct disorder before and after school entry: Relating interventions to developmental findings. *Development & Psychopathology, 5,* 311–319.

Repp, A. C., & Horner, R. H. (1999). *Functional analysis of problem behavior: From effective assessment to effective support.* Belmont, CA: Wadsworth.

Rimm-Kaufman, S. E., Pianta, R. C., & Cox, M. J. (2000). Teachers' judgments of problems in the transition to kindergarten. *Early Childhood Research Quarterly, 15*(2), 147–166.

Schneider, B. (1992). Didactic methods for enhancing children's peer relations: A quantitative review. *Clinical Psychology Review, 12,* 363–382.

Shinn, M. R., Walker, H. M., & Stoner, G. (Eds.). (2002). *Interventions for academic and behavior problems: Vol. 2. Preventive and remedial approaches.* Bethesda, MD: National Association of School Psychologists.

Shores, R., Gunter, P., & Jack, S. (1993). Classroom management strategies: Are they setting events for coercion? *Behavioral Disorders, 18*(2), 92–102.

Shores, R., Jack, S., Gunter, P., Ellis, D. N., DeBriere, T., & Wehby, J. (1993). Classroom interactions of children with behavior disorders. *Journal of Emotional and Behavioral Disorders, 1,* 27–39.

Sprague, J. R., Sugai, G., Horner, R. H., & Walker, H. M. (1999, winter). Using office referral data to evaluate school-wide discipline and violence prevention interventions. *Oregon School Study Council Bulletin, 42*(2).

Stokes, T. (1992). Discrimination and generalization. *Journal of Applied Behavior Analysis, 25,* 429–432.

Stokes, T., & Osnes, P. (1989). An operant pursuit of generalization. *Behavior Therapy, 20,* 337–355.

Strain, P. S., Guralnick, M., & Walker, H. M. (Eds.). (1986). *Children's social behavior: Development, assessment, and modification.* New York: Academic Press.

Strain, P. S., & Timm, M. A. (2001). Remediation and Prevention of Aggression: An evaluation of the Regional Intervention Program over a quarter century. *Behavioral Disorders, 26*(4), 297–313.

Stuart, R. (1971). Behavioral contracting with families of delinquents. *Journal of Behavior Therapy and Experimental Psychiatry, 2,* 1–11.

Sugai, G., & Horner, R. (in press). The evolution of disciplinary practices: School-wide positive behavior supports. *Child and Family Behavior Therapy.*

Sugai, G., Sprague, J. R., Horner, R. H., & Walker, H. M. (2000). Preventing school violence: The use of office discipline referrals to assess and monitor school-wide discipline interventions. In H. M. Walker & M. H. Epstein (Eds.), *Special series: School safety: Pt. 1. Journal of Emotional and Behavioral Disorders, 8*(2), 94–101.

Sulzer-Azaroff, B., Drabman, R., Greer, D., Hall, R. V., Iwata, B., & O'Leary, S. (1988). Behavior analysis in education 1968–1987 from the *Journal of Applied Behavior Analysis* (Reprint series, Volume 3). Lawrence, KS: Society for the Experimental Analysis of Behavior.

Taylor-Green, S. J., & Kartub, D. T. (2000). Durable implementation of school-wide behavior support: The High Five Program. *The Journal of Positive Behavioral Interventions, 2*(4), 5–8, 18–20.

Tobin, T., & Sugai, G. (1999). Predicting violence at school, chronic discipline problems, and high school outcomes from sixth graders' school records. *Journal of Emotional and Behavioral Disorders, 7*, 40–53.

Wahler, R., & Dumas, J. E. (1986). "A chip off the old block": Some interpersonal characteristics of coercive children across generations. In P. Strain, M. Guralnick, & H. M. Walker (Eds.), *Children's social behavior: Development, assessment and modification* (pp. 49–91). Orlando, FL: Academic Press.

Walker, H. M., Colvin, G., & Ramsey, E. (1995). *Antisocial behavior in schools: Strategies and best practices*. Pacific Grove, CA: Brooks/Cole.

Walker, H. M., Forness, S. R., Kauffman, J. M., Epstein, M. H., Gresham, F. M., Nelson, C. M., & Strain, P. S. (1998). Macrosocial validation: Referencing outcomes in behavioral disorders to societal issues and problems. *Behavioral Disorders, 24*(1), 7–18.

Walker, H. M., Horner, R. H., Sugai, G., Bullis, M., Sprague, J. R., Bricker, D., & Kaufman, M. J. (1996). Integrated approaches to preventing antisocial behavior patterns among school-age children and youth. *Journal of Emotional and Behavioral Disorders, 4*, 193–256.

Walker, H. M., Irvin, L. K., Noell, J., & Singer, G. H. S. (1992). A construct score approach to the assessment of social competence: Rationale, technological considerations, and anticipated outcomes. *Behavior Modification, 16*, 448–474.

Walker, H. M., & McConnell, S. R. (1995). *The Walker-McConnell scale of social competence and school adjustment (SSCSA)*. San Diego, CA: Singular.

Walker, H. M., Nishioka, V., Zeller, R., Bullis, M., & Sprague, J. R. (2001). School-based screening, identification, and service delivery issues. *Report on Emotional & Behavioral Disorders in Youth, 1*(3), 51–52, 67–70.

Walker, H. M., & Sprague, J. R. (1999). The path to school failure, delinquency and violence: Causal factors and some potential solutions. *Intervention in School and Clinic, 35*(2), 67–73.

Walker, H. M., Sprague, J. R., Close, D. W., & Starlin, C. M. (2000). What is right with behavior disorders: Seminal achievements and contributions of the behavior disorders field. *Exceptionality, 8*(1), 13–28.

Walker, H. M., Stieber, S., Ramsey, E., & O'Neill, R. (1993). Fifth grade school adjustment and later arrest rate: A longitudinal study of middle school antisocial boys. *Journal of Child and Family Studies, 2*(4), 295–315.

Walker, H. M., Zeller, R.W., Close, D. W., Webber, J., & Gresham, F. M. (1999). The present unwrapped: Change and challenge in the field of behavior disorders. *Behavioral Disorders, 24*(4), 293–304.

Wehby, J., Symonds, F., Canale, J., & Go, F. (1998). Teaching practices in classrooms for students with emotional and behavioral disorders: Discrepancies between recommendations and observations. *Behavioral Disorders, 24*, 51–56.

Wilson, E. O. (1998, March). Back from chaos. *The Atlantic Monthly, 41–62.

Wood, F. (1999). CCBD: A record of accomplishment. *Behavioral Disorders, 24*(4), 273–283.

Wright, J., & Dusek, J. (1998). Research into practice: Compiling school base rates for disruptive behaviors from student disciplinary referral data. *School Psychology Review, 27*, 138–147.

PART SIX

EDUCATIONAL PROGRAM, RESEARCH, AND POLICY

CHAPTER 21

Learning and Pedagogy in Initial Teacher Preparation

JENNIFER A. WHITCOMB

Learning to teach is arguably one of the most cognitively and emotionally challenging efforts that humans attempt. Studies of teaching (e.g., Jackson, 1990; Lampert, 1985; McDonald, 1992) point out the uncertainty, complexity, and immediacy that characterize the practice of teaching. Over the last 25 years scholarly efforts to elevate the standing of teaching to a profession on par with medicine or law have identified both a knowledge base that teachers must understand in order to teach children well and the complex judgments teachers make on a regular basis; however, a contrasting camp has persistently sought to deregulate initial teacher preparation, arguing that the knowledge for teaching is comprised primarily of deep subject-matter knowledge and selected teaching techniques. The current context of public education poses many formidable challenges for teachers: Among them are the public's mandate to ensure that *all* children have deep, flexible knowledge and skills to succeed in an information-based society; teaching shortages in critical areas; the legacy of poverty that some children inherit; increasing ethnic and linguistic diversity that presses us to revisit our understanding and enactment of democratic principles; and increasing calls for accountability in the form of standardized test scores. How best to prepare teacher candidates to teach in this demanding context is a vexing question. Furthermore, it must be answered in a factious policy environment that is deeply divided in its responses to the challenges of designing and carrying out initial teacher preparation (e.g., Feistritzer,

1999; Finn, Kanstoroom, & Petrilli, 1999; National Commission on Teaching and America's Future, 1996).

Rigorous research plays an important role in navigating this contested terrain. The term *rigor* has the potential to be used loosely and rhetorically to imply high standards for research, whether or not they have been met. Cochran-Smith and Fries (2001) have critiqued the "evidentiary warrant" of rigorous, empirical research. Although they recognize that such research may help to resolve persistent problems in teacher education, they also argue that divisive ideological dilemmas in teacher education require additional deliberation. They further suggest that evidence alone will not resolve the normative debates about how best to prepare teachers. Also required, they say, is careful scrutiny and analysis of the "assumptions and motivations that underlie the establishment of different initiatives in the first place as well as the values and political purposes attached to them" (p. 13).

Contrasting this view, Levin and O'Donnell (1999) argued that educational research, in general, has a credibility gap that will only be resolved through the adoption of a research model resembling research in the field of medicine. They press for a four-stage process of educational inquiry that begins with pilot studies, proceeds to a combination of controlled laboratory experiments and classroom-based design experiments, moves next to randomized classroom trials, and culminates with informed classroom practice. Also calling for increased rigor, Wilson, Floden, and Ferrini-Mundy (2001) maintained that the research base in teacher preparation is "relatively thin." They established this claim after surveying research conducted in the last 20 years and identifying few

The author would like to thank Gloria Miller, Marti Tombari, and Irving Weiner for their commentary and critique. The responsibility for all ideas expressed, however, is hers.

studies that met their standards for rigorous, empirical research. They derived their standards using Kennedy's (1996, 1999a) framework of multiple genres of research in teacher education. Kennedy enumerated five genres, which include multiple-regression, follow-up surveys (e.g., to program alumni), comparative population studies (e.g., between credentialed and noncredentialed teachers), experiments and quasi experiments in teacher education, and longitudinal studies (e.g., case studies examining teacher change). Zeichner (1999) developed a similar list, although he includes two different research categories, conceptual/historical and self-study research. When introducing each genre, Kennedy outlined the aspects of teacher preparation examined, the outcomes found, and the logic of the genre's argument. For her, each of these genres has critical limitations, particularly when the goal is to document the impact of teacher preparation. Kennedy argued for methodological pluralism as a means of capturing the entire story, while at the same time expressing a preference for experimental and longitudinal studies. Above all, though, she maintained that research in teacher education must have stronger designs, particularly if teacher educators want to defend themselves from skeptics' challenges.

The precedence for inquiry initiated from multiple genres appears to be well established in teacher preparation (Kennedy, 1999a; Shulman, 1988; Zeichner, 1999). However, given this larger backdrop of persistent challenges to the quality of educational research, in this chapter the term *rigorous research* refers to empirical work that meets the highest standards of research methods. For example, a rigorous study outlines its conceptual framework, its normative assumptions, and its clear relationship to prior studies. Second, a rigorous study provides explicit and detailed description of its design, data, and analysis so that readers may assess the validity of the findings. This chapter focuses on research published in refereed journals because such studies have undergone the process of peer-review. Not all scholarship reviewed in this chapter, however, is empirical; also included is conceptual scholarship that either inspires a substantive body of empirical research or provides critical commentary on empirical work.

Although many disciplines comprise the field of education, educational psychology guides us toward the central role that teacher cognition plays in learning to teach. Giving definition to the discipline, Berliner and Calfee (1996) asserted that "educational psychology is distinctive in its substance: *the systematic study of the individual in context*" (p. 6). The discipline's particular ways of problem construction, theories, and methodologies have yielded insights into the nature and development of teacher beliefs, understanding of subject matter, problem solving, decision making, and reflection.

Scholarship from this vantage point has helped to shape an image of teaching as an intellectual profession that requires its practitioners to synthesize a sizable knowledge base, to deliberate and reason using this knowledge base, and to reconstruct and reflect upon lived experience in order to learn from it.

Handbook chapters, as a scholarly genre, offer selective, focused reviews of the literature. Although teaching and learning to teach have been studied from a range of disciplinary viewpoints, handbooks of educational psychology have typically addressed teaching processes and learning to teach and as such have informed the field in important ways (e.g., Borko & Putnam, 1996; Pressley et al., 2002). Even though the field of research on teacher education is fairly recent (Wilson et al., 2001), three handbooks synthesizing and codifying research in this area have been published since 1990 (Houston, Haberman, & Sikula, 1990; Murray, 1996c; Sikula, Buttery, & Guyton, 1996). Two handbooks of research on teaching have also been published (Biddle, Good, & Goodson, 1997; Richardson, 2001). Within all these handbooks many chapters review research conducted within a cognitive framework (e.g., Borko & Putnam, 1996; Calderhead, 1996; Feiman-Nemser & Remillard, 1996; Putnam & Borko, 1997; Richardson & Placier, 2001). Additionally, since 1996 several significant reviews of the research literature on learning to teach have been published (Ball & Cohen, 1999; Griffith & Early, 1999; Munby, Russell, & Martin, 2001; Putnam & Borko, 2000; Wideen, Mayer-Smith, & Moon, 1998; Wilson et al., 2001). To address the breadth of this field is beyond the scope of this, or any, chapter. Accordingly, this chapter focuses primarily on research conducted within a cognitive psychological framework that examines individual teacher candidate's learning to teach in the context of initial teacher preparation (ITP). In this chapter ITP refers to the bounded set of experiences comprised of the formal study of teaching, learning, and schools that is most typically conducted in both academic courses and field experiences. These experiences are designed to prepare individuals for initial teaching licenses. Such preparation programs may or may not be housed at a university and may be completed at either undergraduate or graduate levels.

The choices of conceptual framework, unit of analysis, and learning context are deliberate. First, they obviously reflect the theme of this volume. Second, they explicitly build on several recent comprehensive reviews within this same framework (e.g., Borko & Putnam, 1996; Putnam & Borko, 1997, 2000). Third, individual teacher candidate's learning is a relentless focus of teacher educators. At the conclusion of ITP institutions must be able to judge whether a particular candidate's knowledge, performance, and dispositions meet the entering standards of the profession. Although new conceptions of knowledge and learning emphasize the social and distributed nature of cognition, ultimately each individual must demonstrate his or her knowledge and practice. Finally, attention to context ensures that researchers consider the multiple and overlapping contexts in which ITP occurs. Indeed, the interaction between cognition and context is at the forefront of work in many domains of educational psychology.

As with any choice, there are attendant losses. By making the figure of this review cognitively framed studies of new teachers' learning, illustrative and important work that considers veteran teachers' learning in the contexts of professional development is relegated to the background (e.g., Wilson & Berne, 1999). Also left out are studies that reflect other disciplinary or theoretical orientations to the study of new teachers' learning—namely, philosophical, critical, historical, feminist, anthropological, and sociological approaches (Buchmann & Floden, 1993; Cochran-Smith, 1991; King, Hollins, & Hayman, 1997; Lucas, 1997; McWilliam, 1994; Tabachnick & Zeichner, 1991; Zeichner, Melnick, & Gomez, 1996).

Throughout the chapter rigorously conducted research is highlighted. Scholarship of learning to teach, in general, has no shortage of normative arguments for what teacher candidates should learn and how that preparation should be carried out. Indeed, there is speculation that conflicting visions of the purposes of teacher preparation may not be reconciled. A need exists, therefore, for systematically gathered, empirical evidence to study these arguments. The chapter has two major sections: The first synthesizes essential conceptualizations and empirical findings regarding what teacher candidates learn and how they do so; the second reviews promising research from a situative perspective and suggests future directions for research.

REVIEW OF THE REVIEWS: WHAT COLLECTIVE STORY DO THEY TELL?

In the latter part of the 1990s several handbook chapters and reviews of the literature on learning to teach synthesized a burst of cognitively oriented research conducted in the 1980s and early 1990s. That scholarship examined the nature and development of teacher thinking and teacher knowledge. The depth of these chapters suggests that formal inquiry into learning to teach is indeed a subdiscipline within the field of educational psychology (Borko & Putnam, 1996; Calderhead, 1996; Feiman-Nemser & Remillard, 1996; Murray, 1996b; Putnam & Borko, 1997, 2000). Much of the research reviewed reflects broader trends within educational psychology—for example, the establishment of cognitivism

as an overarching paradigm and the rise of constructivism as a theory of learning; a broadening of research methodologies, particularly the inclusion of qualitatively designed studies; and an emphasis on practice (Berliner & Calfee, 1996; Pressley & Roehrig, in press).

The development of a collective story from these reviews and other seminal studies in the area of teacher learning and pedagogy in teacher preparation was guided by the following questions: How has research conducted within a cognitive framework illuminated our understanding of both what new teachers should know and how they learn? How has research within a cognitive framework shaped and informed key dilemmas of ITP (e.g., teaching in ways that are responsive to diverse students, teaching for understanding, issues of transferring knowledge from one setting to another)? What does this literature on teacher learning have to say about best practices in ITP? To answer these questions, this section traces how a cognitive framework has evolved, noting in particular recent emphasis on a situative perspective; describes different approaches to defining a knowledge base for teaching; summarizes key findings from studies of how teachers learn; and reviews scholarly analysis of pedagogy in teacher preparation.

Evolving Conceptual Frameworks to Study Learning to Teach

A conceptual framework feeds a study's design because it shapes the questions posed, the methods used, the researcher's stance, and the settings in which inquiry is conducted. The scholarly team of Borko and Putnam (1996; Putnam & Borko, 1997, 2000) have produced several reviews that synthesize an evolution in conceptual frameworks used to study teachers' thought and learning. This evolution reflects shifts in perspective that have shaped and reshaped the broader field of educational psychology, notably a progression from behaviorist to cognitivist to sociocultural or situative perspectives. With each shift a revised understanding of what constitutes powerful student learning has emerged. In broad strokes there has been a movement from a receptive-accrual view of learning to a cognitive-mediational view (Anderson, 1989). The image of a good teacher has undergone similar changes (Clark, 1995), and thus out of necessity, so have the assumptions for the purposes and outcomes of ITP.

Behaviorist Perspective

Much of the process-product research, conducted in the 1950s through the 1970s, drew on behaviorism as its conceptual framework (Brophy & Good, 1986). Emphasizing the teacher's effective management of learning, process-product classroom-based studies sought to correlate specific teacher actions and talk with student achievement on standardized tests. It yielded a rather atomistic view of teaching, parsing teaching into specific behaviors or sequences of behaviors that were consistent with a receptive-accrual view of student learning. The image of good teaching that emerged from this research was of an individual who directs the flow of activities and talk so that all students are engaged and progressing in an efficient, orderly manner (Clark, 1995). The implications for ITP meant that teacher candidates were presented with discrete knowledge and practices that had been proven effective in process-product studies. Often these were introduced in teaching laboratories and simulations (Carter & Anders, 1996). Eventually, teacher candidates were expected to assemble separate skills together to execute effective practice.

Cognitive Constructivist Perspectives

In response to a growing sense of inadequacy regarding the findings and methods of process-product research (Calderhead, 1996), during the mid-1970s scholars shifted attention to teachers' cognitions or mental lives. This body of research, which is still thriving, initially reflected an information-processing view of the mind but subsequently adopted a constructivist view of cognition. Studies elaborated the complexity of teacher's intentions, planning, decision making, and problem solving (Clark & Peterson, 1986). Teacher thinking about classroom management, instructional choices, use of class time, and checking for understanding fueled research (Richardson-Koehler, 1987). Empirical evidence highlighting the powerful role that teachers' beliefs played in teachers' thought processes (Calderhead, 1996) began to mount. Images of good teaching were captured in metaphors such as the teacher as diagnostician, as decision maker, and as reflective practitioner (Clark, 1995).

Research on teacher thinking overlapped with studies of teacher knowledge. Shulman and his colleagues in the Knowledge Growth and Teaching Project (e.g., Grossman, Wilson, & Shulman, 1989; Wilson, Shulman, & Richert, 1987; Wilson & Wineburg, 1988) played a central role in shaping this line of research, which characterized the knowledge base that informs teacher's thinking and the dynamic, personalized manner in which each teacher comes to understand this knowledge. Shulman's (1986a) introduction to the third *Handbook of Research on Teaching* identified content as a "missing paradigm" of research on teaching. Shulman and his colleagues fleshed out an enormously generative concept, pedagogical content knowledge, which broadly speaking refers to the specialized knowledge that teachers have of how to represent content knowledge in multiple ways to learners.

In her landmark study, Grossman (1990) outlined four components of pedagogical content knowledge:

> (1) an overarching conception of what it means to teach a particular subject, (2) knowledge of instructional strategies and representations for teaching particular topics, (3) knowledge of students' understanding and potential misunderstandings of a subject area, and (4) knowledge of curriculum and curricular materials. (as cited in Borko & Putnam, 1996, p. 690)

For example, if a science teacher views teaching biology as a form of inquiry, she might emphasize open-ended lab experiences over lectures and textbook reading. That same biology teacher must have at her fingertips a range of ways to represent key concepts such as photosynthesis or the replication of DNA, and these representations must go beyond equations. She also needs to anticipate students' likely confusion regarding these concepts, particularly those that might arise in the process of completing scientific investigations. Finally, she needs to know the many curricular material resources available to help students grapple with and make sense of these concepts. Bruner's (1960) bold hypothesis "that any subject can be taught effectively in some intellectually honest form to any child at any stage of development" (p. 33), as well as Schwab's (1964) delineation between the substance and syntax of the disciplines, resonates in Shulman's writing.

Propelling the emphasis on teachers' understanding of their subject matter were two other large-scale, standards-based reforms. First, in 1987 the National Board for Professional Teaching Standards (NBPTS) was established, which developed rigorous standards for expert veterans and means of assessing them. Second, most national subject-matter organizations developed standards for what students should know and be able to do at the conclusion of K–12 education. The emerging "reform" vision challenged teachers to "teach for understanding" (Blumenfeld, Marx, Patrick, Krajcik, & Soloway, 1997; Cohen, McLaughlin, & Talbert, 1993; Darling-Hammond, 1997). In general, teaching for understanding emphasizes student's active, cognitive transformation of knowledge; it is typically contrasted with passive, receptive acquisition of knowledge. Several rhetorically loaded terms are also used as synonyms for teaching for understanding, for example, adventurous teaching (Cohen, 1989), reform-minded teaching, and ambitious teaching. Indeed, the term *adventurous* peppers the literature reviews on teacher learning (e.g., Ball & Cohen, 1999; Borko & Putnam, 1996; Feiman-Nemser & Remillard, 1996; Putnam

& Borko, 1997, 2001; Richardson, 1996). Putnam and Borko (1997) provided a thoughtfully concise explanation of this rhetorical term:

> [T]he sorts of teaching that are being promoted in most current, scholarly reform movements . . . [are] approaches that emphasize the importance of students' thinking and the development of powerful reasoning and understanding within subject-matter domains. In many cases, reformers are calling for teachers to enhance, and sometimes supplant, the "direct instruction" models of teaching that pervade today's public school classrooms by providing opportunities for students to explore ideas in rich contexts, rather than relying primarily on teacher presentation and student rehearsal. Because teaching for these goals entails thinking of subject-matter content in new ways and being attentive and responsive to the thinking of students, teaching cannot be prescribed in advance as a set of techniques to be carried out in a particular way. Rather, these approaches require teachers to think differently about students, subject matter, and the learning process and to become more "adventurous" in their teaching. (p. 1229)

It should be noted, however, that the concept of teaching for understanding, which is referred to by its proponents as a reform-minded approach, also has its opponents. In many ways, the progressive-traditional battle over both what should be taught and how persists in education. In the contested terrain of education, each side seeks to claim the high ground by claiming its favored approach as the reform-minded one. In this chapter the phrase "teaching for understanding" is preferred.

As the idea of teaching for understanding took hold, the image of the good teacher expanded the notion of a deliberative, or reflective, practitioner to include the image of an academic coach or intellectual guide shepherding communities of learners as they constructed an understanding of major ideas and ways of thinking within each discipline. To fulfill this role, the teacher must also engage as a practical scholar of his or her discipline.

As studies of teachers' knowledge flourished, a number of researchers, strongly influenced by interpretive methods in other disciplines, began to explore how teacher candidates' personal narratives and life histories influence learning to teach (e.g., Carter, 1990; Clandinin & Connelly, 1987; Elbaz, 1983; Kagan, 1992; Louden, 1991; Ross, Cornett, & McCutcheon, 1992; Zeichner, Tabachnick, & Densmore, 1987). Carter and Doyle (1996) synthesized this body of research, which emphasizes the centrality of the teacher candidate's personal construction of personal practical knowledge. They concluded,

> From an outside perspective of program policy, becoming a teacher is all too often seen as obtaining credentials and acquiring skills. From a biographical frame, however, becoming a teacher means (a) transforming an identity, (b) adapting personal understandings and ideals to institutional realities, and (c) deciding how to express one's self in classroom activity. . . . [T]his far more complex picture of the essence of the teacher education experience promises to transform fundamentally how teachers are viewed and perhaps even how they are valued (p. 139).

Collectively, studies of teacher thinking and teacher knowledge influenced ITP curriculum and pedagogy in several important ways, and many of these influences still prevail in ITP programs today. Varied approaches have been taken to help teacher candidates make explicit their tacit beliefs (e.g., Feiman-Nemser & Featherstone, 1992). For example, one strategy is the study of images of teaching in popular culture. Another involves providing teacher candidates with early experiences in classrooms where the veteran teacher engages in highly sophisticated teaching for understanding. Such experiences are intended to provoke dissonance and reflection that lead to a revised understanding of what learning might entail. With an emphasis on reflection, teacher educators have sought to engage new teachers in critical examinations of their beliefs about generic teaching strategies, children's learning and development, and the social conditions of schooling and issues of equity and social justice (Clift, Houston, & Pugach, 1990; Zeichner & Tabachnich, 1991). Such examinations have been elicited and structured through many activities, such as journal writing, child studies, and actual investigations into subject-matter concepts. Not surprisingly, teaching within the subject matters garnered much attention. Teacher educators have stressed the teacher candidates' need to recognize how disciplinary understanding differs from school knowledge, to represent complex concepts in multiple ways, to interpret children's naive misconceptions and coach them toward more accurate understandings, and to possess a robust theory of the discipline itself (e.g., its core concepts, rules of evidence, and ways of developing new knowledge; Ball & McDiarmid, 1990; Stengel & Tom, 1996). Finally, teachers are urged to both reconstruct and reflect on their autobiographies and narratives of lived experience as they build understandings of school and classroom events.

Social Constructivist and Situative Perspectives

Amidst this burst of research on how an individual teacher's knowledge and beliefs both develop and shape practice, researchers discovered, or rediscovered, the importance of context in cognition. This unfolded in several ways. First, teacher educators engaged teacher candidates in reflection about the contexts in which they worked and in which the learners lived (e.g., King et al., 1997; Ladson-Billings, 1999). Second, renewed attention to the situated nature of cognition mirrored the evolution of cognitive constructivism to social constructivism (Nuthall, 1997). Putnam and Borko (2000) synthesized the situative perspective thus:

> Situative theorists challenge this assumption of a cognitive core independent of context and intention (Brown, Collins, & Duguid, 1989; Greeno & the Middle School Through Applications Project Group, 1998; Lave & Wenger, 1991). They posit, instead, that the physical and social contexts in which an activity takes place are an integral part of the activity, and that the activity is an integral part of the learning that takes place within it. How a person learns a particular set of knowledge and skills, and the situation in which a person learns, become a fundamental part of what is learned. Further, whereas traditional cognitive perspectives focus on the individual as the basic unit of analysis, situative perspectives focus on interactive systems that include individuals as participants, interacting with each other as well as materials and representational systems (Cobb & Bowers, 1999; Greeno, 1997). (p. 4)

As a learning theory, situated cognition suggests that learning should be rooted in authentic activity; that learning occurs within a community of individuals engaged in inquiry and practice; that more knowledgeable "masters" guide or scaffold the learning of novices; and that expertise is often distributed across individuals, thus allowing the community to accomplish complex tasks that no single person could accomplish alone. In this view of learning, the good teacher is one who orchestrates the flow of information among individuals, as one who assists, rather than controls, the learning of others, as one who "rouses minds to life" (Tharp & Gallimore, 1988).

Scholars of teacher learning see great potential in this conceptual framework (Putnam & Borko, 2000). At the heart of the situative perspective is the issue of transfer of learning from one setting to another; as such, it informs an ongoing dilemma in teacher education regarding the bridge between theory and practice (Dewey, 1977). Finding sturdy ways to negotiate between theory and practice is even more important when the goal of teacher preparation is to ensure that new teachers can teach for understanding. Second, because a situative perspective focuses on interactive systems, it may help teacher educators develop theories of teacher learning that draw attention to the "interrelationship of knowledge and action in the classroom context and develop an understanding that more accurately captures the cognitive, affective, and behavioral aspects of teachers' work" (Calderhead, 1996,

p. 711). The situative perspective draws attention to settings, talk, and mediational tools. For instance, efforts to expand traditional classroom field experiences into community-based settings or to bring videotapes of exemplary teaching for understanding into university courses are under development. Efforts to create opportunities for authentic conversation and problem solving among teacher candidates and veterans are at the forefront of teacher education design. In addition, sociocognitive tools, such as hypermedia case materials, have been created to provide tasks that are more authentic. The nature of teacher candidates' learning in these new settings, in these conversations, and with these sociocognitive tools is a focus of research (Putnam & Borko, 1997; Richardson, 1997).

Summary of Conceptual Frameworks

In this overview to conceptual frameworks a chronological tidiness is implied that is not necessarily present in the many studies cited. What is clear, however, is that as cognitive psychologists' conceptual frameworks modulated, scholars of learning to teach quickly and easily appropriated them to conduct inquiries into learning to teach. As a psychological framework evolved from a behaviorist to a situative perspective, it inspired lines of research that provided broad empirical evidence for the cognitive complexity required to teach, particularly when the educative end is teaching for understanding. In this overview to conceptual frameworks the focus was on those aspects of teacher learning and practice to which each new framework has called attention. For lack of space, what has been left out is a discussion of how methods of inquiry into teaching and teacher learning have also evolved, particularly to include more interpretive studies. Calderhead (1996) offered an efficient review of the broadening of methods to study teacher thinking and learning.

Defining a Knowledge Base for Teaching

Although there have been many efforts to formulate a knowledge base for teaching (Grow-Maienza, 1996), during the 1980s a distinctive body of work sought to specify a knowledge base grounded in the findings emerging from cognitive constructivist studies of teaching. This work was initiated, for the most part, to distinguish teaching as a profession, with a distinct and complex body of knowledge mastered by expert teachers. Landmark publications by Shulman (1986b, 1987), along with *Knowledge Base for the Beginning Teacher* (Reynolds, 1989) and later *The Teacher Educator's Handbook: Building a Knowledge Base for the Preparation of Teachers* (Murray, 1996c), mapped out the substance or content that teachers and teacher educators need to know. The notion of a knowledge base, however, is not neutral (Donmoyer, 1996). A brief chronological survey reveals that approaches to formulating a knowledge base reflect the policy context in which a scholar writes, his or her unique authorial purposes and audiences, and differing philosophical traditions of teacher education. Tabachnick and Zeichner (1991) presented four traditions of reflection in teacher education, which they base on Kleibard's (1986) typology of major school reform movements. First, the *academic* tradition focuses on representations of subject matter to students to promote understanding. Second, the *social efficiency* tradition focuses on the intelligent use of generic teaching strategies suggested by research on teaching. Third, the *developmentalist* tradition focuses on the learning, development, and understanding of students. Fourth, the *social reconstructionist* tradition focuses on the social conditions of schooling and issues of equity and justice. These four traditions of reflective teaching have been used by others to describe the general orientation of a teacher preparation program (e.g., Carter & Anders, 1996; Grow-Maienza, 1996).

Overall, the domains of knowledge specified across the different approaches to a knowledge base for teaching are remarkably consistent. Variation, however, exists in terms of the sources consulted to elaborate a domain; furthermore, different scholars, given their philosophical orientation, privilege some domains over others. In general, the knowledge base for teaching has been a compelling metaphor, but this point will be revisited after delineating several state-of-the-art formulations of a knowledge base.

Categories of Knowledge Approach

Shulman's (1987) much-cited article laid out seven categories of teacher knowledge:

> If teacher knowledge were to be organized into a handbook, an encyclopedia, or some other format for arraying knowledge, what would the category headings look like? At minimum they would include: content knowledge, general pedagogical knowledge, curriculum knowledge, pedagogical content knowledge, knowledge of learners and their characteristics, knowledge of educational contexts, and knowledge of educational ends, purposes and values. (p. 8)

Shulman's introduction rests on the metaphor of handbook or encyclopedia headings, suggesting that a sizable and codifiable body of information exists. His phrase "at minimum" acknowledges that a knowledge base should not be viewed as exclusive, or even overly prescriptive. Of the seven categories, Shulman discerned pedagogical content knowledge as

the most important, arguing that this body of knowledge is uniquely within the purview of teachers. Shulman also broadened a definition of the sources that give rise to a knowledge base, moving beyond the research findings of process-product studies to include scholarship in the content disciplines, materials, and settings of the institutionalized educational process; research on schooling from multiple disciplines; and the wisdom of practice itself. Finally, Shulman advanced a model of pedagogical reasoning and action by describing how teachers make proper judgments using the knowledge base.

Shulman's seminal argument reflects the policy environment to which he spoke. Much of Shulman's work has served to elevate teaching to a profession resembling, in particular, medicine or law. He wrote at a time when policy makers had simplified the findings of process-product studies to a list of desired teacher behaviors. In many states and school districts, mandated observation protocols reduced teacher evaluation to specific observable behaviors (e.g., listing lesson objectives on the board), regardless of whether the targeted teacher actions were educative in a particular moment in time. Shulman (1987) wrote that

> teachers cannot be adequately assessed by observing their teaching performance without reference to the content being taught. The conception of pedagogical reasoning places emphasis upon the intellectual basis for teaching performance rather than on the behavior alone. . . . The currently incomplete and trivial definitions of teaching held by the policy community comprise a far greater danger to good education than does a more serious attempt to formulate the knowledge base. (p. 20)

As a result of Shulman's emphasis on subject matter, some have placed him in an academic tradition of practice in teacher education. However, if one merely considers the list of headings, it is clear that the knowledge domains that Shulman outlines are consistent with any of the traditions.

Confirmed Knowledge Approach

Feiman-Nemser and Remillard (1996) provided a thoughtful analysis of three state-of-the-art approaches to conceptualize this base. The three they selected examine respectively what a teacher knows, does, and values. They began with a review of *Knowledge Base for the Beginning Teacher* (KBBT in the following extract; M. C. Reynolds, 1989), which was commissioned by the American Association of Colleges of Teacher Education (AACTE). Here is their summary:

> The project organizers identified domains with which, in their judgment, every beginning teacher should be familiar. Then they invited experts associated with each domain to write a chapter

outlining "confirmed knowledge" appropriate for "professional responsible beginning teachers." The table of contents reveals topics that are part of the emerging work on professional knowledge for teaching (Shulman, 1987; Grossman, 1990): classroom organization and management, learners and learning, classroom instruction, the developmental needs of pupils, subject matter knowledge for teaching, subject specific pedagogy, knowledge about reading and writing, students with special needs, the social organization of classes and schools, the school district, ethical dimensions of teaching, to name about half of the chapter titles. KBBT reflects the range and richness of professional knowledge that bears on teachers' work, but it leaves open the question of what it means to know and use such knowledge in teaching. (Feiman-Nemser & Remillard, 1996, pp. 72–73)

The AACTE commissioned this monograph as one of its efforts to professionalize teaching; in that sense it is consistent with Shulman's purposes. Although on the one hand this might be viewed as self-serving, on the other hand, as Feiman-Nemser and Remillard pointed out, the result was a rich range of knowledge. As their summary suggests, M. C. Reynolds and his project colleagues produced a work that was consistent with the purposes of Shulman's (1987) categorization of teacher knowledge. If Shulman's categories were a minimum list of encyclopedia headings, then M. C. Reynolds's was the comprehensive version. M. C. Reynolds's emphasis on confirmed knowledge, however, differs substantively from Shulman's more broadly construed delineation of sources for the knowledge base. Referring again to Tabachnick and Zeichner's (1991) traditions of practice in teacher education, M. C. Reynolds's monograph is difficult to place because the sheer breadth of domains outlined touches on all four traditions. His criterion of confirmed knowledge, however, suggests some philosophical agreement with the social efficiency tradition.

Performance Tasks Approach

The second approach to a knowledge base for teaching that Feiman-Nemser and Remillard selected is A. Reynolds's (1992) enumeration of essential tasks that a beginning teacher should be able to do. They present it in the following way:

> A second approach . . . begins with the question, "What should teachers be able to do?" and reasons backward to the knowledge and skills required for performing these tasks. This is the tack taken by the Educational Testing Service in its recent efforts to design new performance assessments for beginning teachers. . . . These tasks [A. Reynolds] argues, fit any teaching situation regardless of the teacher's philosophy, subject matter, or students. Having an adequate knowledge base means being able to do the following: (1) plan lessons that enable students to relate

new learning to prior understanding and experience, (2) develop rapport and personal interactions with students, (3) establish and maintain rules and routines that are fair and appropriate to students, (4) arrange the physical and social conditions of the classroom in ways that are conducive to learning and that fit the academic task, (5) represent the subject matter in ways that enable students to relate new learning to prior learning and that help students develop metacognitive strategies, (6) assess student learning using a variety of measurement tools and adapt instruction according to results, and (7) reflect on their own actions and students' responses in order to improve their teaching. (Feiman-Nemser & Remillard, 1996, pp. 74–75)

A. Reynolds's approach was intended to inform the development of a standardized assessment for teacher licensure; as such, it frames teaching tasks as generic and separate from a normative vision of the means and ends of education. The list seems, in some ways, a throwback to teacher behavior lists of the process-product studies, for there is little effort to explain what assumptions about the character of good teaching undergird the performance of these tasks. A cognitive constructivist theory of learning is implied, however, particularly in points 1, 5, and 7. A. Reynolds's knowledge base seems to be in keeping with the social efficiency tradition of teacher preparation.

Values and Dispositions Approach

The third approach that Feiman-Nemser and Remillard (1996) provided is one developed by the NBPTS:

> As a first step in defining professional standards, the board adopted a policy statement entitled "What Teachers Should Know and Be Able to Do" (National Board for Professional Teaching Standards, 1990). The statement set out five course propositions that reflect what the board values in teaching and serve as a foundation for its work. (1) Teachers are committed to students and their learning. (2) Teachers know the subjects they teach and how to teach those subjects to students. (3) Teachers are responsible for managing and monitoring student learning. (4) Teachers think systematically about their practice and learn from experience. (5) Teachers are members of learning communities.
>
> The policy statement underscores the value and limits of formal knowledge in teaching. In relation to the first proposition, for example, we are told that highly accomplished teachers base their practice on prevailing theories of cognition and intelligence as well as on "observation and knowledge of their students' interests, abilities, skills, knowledge, family circumstances and peer relationships." We are also told that "teaching ultimately requires judgment, improvisation, and conversation about ends and means" (p. 13). (p. 77)

This approach to a knowledge base for teaching is couched in terms of a teacher's professional obligations. It rests on the assumption that teachers, as scholars of their practice, will synthesize ideas from multiple sources (e.g., content material, educational research, wisdom of practice) to make appropriate judgments that support all children's learning. The distinguishing feature of a professional is the ability to exercise wise and proper judgment. From this approach to a knowledge base, teacher educators emphasize how to critically evaluate and learn from academic scholarship and lived experience. In this sense it bears a strong resemblance to the developmental or personalistic tradition in teacher preparation.

Knowledge of Diversity Approach

Hollins, King, and Hayman (1994), Ladson-Billings (1999), and Zeichner (1996) identified several key domains of knowledge that teacher candidates must develop in order to be culturally inclusive in their classroom. Zeichner summarizes these knowledge domains as (a) sociocultural knowledge about child development, second-language acquisition, and the influences that socioeconomic, linguistic, and cultural characteristics have on students' performance in schools; (b) specific knowledge of their particular students' culture and background and how to apply this knowledge to foster student learning; and (c) a clear sense of their own ethnic and cultural identities. An approach to a knowledge base for teaching that emphasizes diversity is important because the demographic imperative suggests that in the future, a teaching force comprised of primarily White, middle-class women will teach an increasingly ethnically, racially, linguistically, and economically diverse student population. The track record for educating poor children of color is in all respects a failure; therefore, unless the teaching force becomes radically better educated about the lives and needs of these children, the system will serve increasingly more students in wholly inadequate ways. Thus, in many ways scholars who have elaborated these domains work within the social reconstructionist tradition.

Learning Profession Approach

In perhaps the most recent formulation of a knowledge base for teaching, Ball and Cohen (1999) framed the knowledge base as an answer to the question, "What do teachers need to know?" They asserted that a teacher must understand subject matter, know about children, become acquainted with cultural differences, develop and expand their ideas about learning, and know pedagogy. The five domains that they present elegantly synthesize previous articulations. Ball and Cohen

further stated that this professional knowledge must be developed in and from a teacher's practice; that is, learning must arise from genuine inquiry into the artifacts and actions of classroom practice. Ball and Cohen's formulation was part of a lead chapter in a policy volume devoted to the establishment of teaching as the "learning profession" (Darling-Hammond & Sykes, 1999). The premise of their volume is that unless and until teachers have, and avail themselves of, well-structured opportunities to develop the professional knowledge articulated in this formulation of the knowledge base, the kinds of complex learning advocated in most reform visions will never be realized. This approach integrates the academic, developmentalist, and social reconstructionist traditions of teacher preparation, for it rests on the assumption that the radically equitable goal of education today is to ensure that all children achieve high levels of academic understanding. To do so will require teachers to understand subject matter and child development in highly sophisticated ways.

Summary of Approaches to a Knowledge Base for Teaching

What may be concluded from these six different approaches to a knowledge base for teaching? First, all six show remarkable consistency in terms of the domains; moreover, these domains show a heavy influence from the field of educational psychology. For example, many common chapter titles in educational psychology textbooks—learning theories, motivation, child/adolescent development, exceptionality, and assessment/measurement—are reflected in the domains just mentioned. Second, the idea of a knowledge base contributes to efforts to establish teaching as a profession; thus, all six approaches are forms of political argument, for each scholar seeks to convince a suspicious audience that teaching is more than an intuitively learned endeavor. When viewed chronologically, they reveal subtle shifts in how specific knowledge distinguishes teaching as a profession. For instance, M. C. Reynolds pointed out the sheer volume of ideas and concepts that teachers draw upon, whereas the NBPTS emphasized the complex judgment that teachers use to navigate this breadth of information. Meanwhile, Ball and Cohen emphasized that professional knowledge is situated within the practice itself. Third, what is perhaps most critical in distinguishing the different approaches are the sources consulted to fill the different domains. M. C. Reynolds relies on confirmed knowledge, defining this as knowledge that derives from empirically designed studies. In this sense, M. C. Reynolds fits most closely with a positivist tradition of research and knowledge generation. Shulman and the others take a broader approach, valuing this knowledge but also valuing subject matter and the wisdom of practice. In this sense their approaches articulate with interpretive traditions or with traditions of social critique (Calderhead, 1996; Wideen et al., 1998).

This brings up an unfinished point: What are the connotations associated with the metaphor of a knowledge base? First, the image connotes construction, perhaps a building's foundation or perhaps a roughly framed building, but such an image leaves open the finishing of the structure, and these are potentially matters of taste or economic means. The approaches just described imply, with varying degrees of specificity, images of good teaching. The point is, however, that without a normative vision of good teaching practice, a knowledge base is an unfinished construction. In the current policy climate, competing, and indeed contradictory, normative visions of good teaching are promoted. Second, although a knowledge base connotes richness and depth of what should be known, it tends to underscore the interconnections among domains when engaging in teaching practice. More important, it does not acknowledge the political nature of knowledge and the different ways in which judgment may be exercised (Cochran-Smith, 2000; Donmoyer, 1996). In other words, a knowledge base may highlight relevant information, but it does not necessarily suggest how to use it in particular situations. One could argue that the knowledge base is not actually knowledge per se, but rather a characterization or description of the curriculum for learning to teach. Finally, descriptions of a knowledge base do not necessarily characterize the mental structures by which this knowledge is actually held. For instance, is the knowledge base a collection of propositions, a set of beliefs, stories, event structures, images or metaphors, or relational tags to what others in a community of practice know? Fenstermacher (1994) offered a probing analysis of these epistemological concerns. Cognitively oriented studies of learning to teach shed some light on how individuals actively construct a personal knowledge base that guides their everyday classroom judgments and decisions.

How Teacher Candidates Learn to Teach

The heart of learning to teach is the development of judgment, which involves the development and orchestration of various forms and domains of knowledge. The knowledge base for teaching enumerates approaches to the content or substance of ITP. Nevertheless, it sidesteps grander questions: What counts as teacher learning and growth? Who decides what counts? Judgment, after all, must be considered in a normative fashion. For example, does or must teacher learning involve altered beliefs or conceptual change, and if so, which beliefs, and in what ways are they altered? Does or must teacher learning involve the elicitation and reconstruction of

practical arguments, which are the post hoc examinations and justifications of actions (Fenstermacher & Richardson, 1993)? Or is teacher learning the ability to perform or enact certain complex skills or practices, such as a guided reading or writers' workshops? If so, who decides which practices? Or is teacher learning the development of pedagogical content knowledge—that is, building a conception of the discipline, of how to represent key concepts, of how and when students will likely stumble, of how to select appropriate curricular resources? Or has learning occurred when an individual has been enculturated into a community's ways of thinking (Putnam & Borko, 1997)? For instance, Montessori teachers and schools enact a particular curriculum and pedagogy that is based on a philosophy of child development; teacher learning might mean coming to participate in the classroom and school. Legitimate participation comes with understanding how that philosophy is instantiated in the classroom and teacher communities. If learning involves enculturation, how does one respond to the multiple communities that characterize educators? Finally, if one considers the notion of distributed cognition, has learning occurred when a community of educators knows where expertise lies and how to find and elicit that expertise in the service of resolving a dilemma of practice? For instance, when seeking to support a struggling reader, the necessary expertise may reside in the child's former teachers, parents, and the district's reading specialist. When considering the question of what kind of learning counts, for many teacher educators the likely answer is "all of the above," although, of course, not all teacher educators would agree, and others involved in setting policy for ITP tend to be more constrained in their response, focusing on enactment of predetermined specific skills or content knowledge.

One of the essential questions all teachers must answer is, "Am I primarily a transmitter or transformer of my society's values?" (Grant & Murray, 1999, p. 57). Most teacher educators resonate with the transformative side of the question. For them, the purpose of ITP is to prepare teacher candidates to teach for understanding and to do so with increasingly diverse students. Several recent reviews of the literature on learning to teach were consulted to synthesize what is known about learning to teach for understanding (Ball & Cohen, 1999; Borko & Putnam, 1996; Calderhead, 1996; Feiman-Nemser & Remillard, 1996; Kennedy, 1999b; Putnam & Borko, 1997; Richardson, 1996; Wideen et al., 1998; Wilson et al., 2001). One obvious conclusion reached by many teacher educators is that learning to teach for understanding will not be achieved by the provision of propositional knowledge (Wideen et al., 1998). In other words, both cognitive and social constructivist theories of learning have taken firm hold, leading researchers to view teacher candidates as active, social learners who must learn to perceive, interpret, and act with increasing sophistication (Resnick, 1991); however, the precise nature and content of that sophistication varies depending on one's normative or philosophical perspectives regarding the purposes of education. Thus, on the one hand, many of these scholars acknowledge that our understanding about learning to teach is fragmented, contradictory, and incomplete; on the other hand, some findings have coalesced around the respective roles that prior beliefs, content knowledge, mentors and colleagues, and setting play in learning to teach.

Role of Prior Beliefs

One of the most fertile areas of cognitively oriented research has addressed the role of prior beliefs and knowledge in learning to teach. Several reviews summarize this body of work (e.g., Calderhead, 1996; Nespor, 1987; Pajares, 1992; Putnam & Borko, 1997; Richardson, 1996). The term *belief* has a certain definitional slipperiness associated with it. Calderhead (1996) pointed out the range of terms used to refer to beliefs.

> The term *beliefs* has been used in research in numerous ways. As Pajares (1992) points out, such terms as beliefs, values, attitudes, judgments, opinions, ideologies, perceptions, conceptions, conceptual systems, preconceptions, dispositions, implicit theories, personal theories, and perspectives have frequently been used almost interchangeably, and it is sometimes difficult to identify the distinguishing features of beliefs and how they are to be separated from knowledge. (p. 719)

Drawing on philosopher's distinctions, Richardson (1996) argued that "the term *belief* . . . describes a proposition that is accepted as generally true by the individual holding the belief. It is a psychological concept and differs from knowledge, which implies epistemic warrant" (p. 104). That is, knowledge, unlike beliefs, must meet standards of evidence and does not have varying degrees of conviction. Perhaps the slipperiness in defining this term results from the fact that many teachers treat beliefs as knowledge (Kansanen et al., 2000).

A common starting point for research into the role of prior beliefs on learning to teach has been the recognition that teacher candidates arrive in teacher preparation settings having experienced 12 to 16 or more years of formal education; Lortie (1975) called this period the *apprenticeship of observation*. During this apprenticeship, individuals form robust schemas that shape interpretations and evaluations of later experiences in schools and classrooms. Other sources for frames of reference include cultural-media archetypes, other

personal experience that informs a worldview, and experience with formal knowledge (Richardson, 1996; Wideen et al., 1998). Often, these schemas support traditional notions of direct instruction and receptive-accrual learning; as such, they guide new teachers to teach in manners consistent with how they were taught, rather than in ambitious ways. Kennedy argued, "Reformers can change teaching practices only by changing the way teachers interpret particular situations and decide how to respond to them" (Kennedy, 1999b, p. 56). However, teacher candidates' entering beliefs have proven remarkably resilient. Thus, these schemas or beliefs are both filters of learning as well as targets of change (Borko & Putnam, 1996; Putnam & Borko, 1997; Richardson, 1996).

Scholars' inquiries into teacher beliefs have examined the characteristics of beliefs on a wide array of domains. Calderhead (1996) categorized teachers' beliefs into the following areas: beliefs about learners and learning, teaching, subject, learning to teach, and the self and the teaching role. Borko and Putnam do not separate knowledge and beliefs, and they organize their two published reviews into a teacher candidate's knowledge and beliefs about general pedagogy (which includes beliefs about teaching, conceptions of the self and teaching, learners and learning, and classroom management), subject matter, and pedagogical subject matter. Although providing a content analysis of beliefs is helpful, far more critical in this area of research is inquiry into how beliefs function as filters or frames of reference, why they are so resilient, and what relationship beliefs have with actual practice.

Studies that show how beliefs serve to filter teacher candidate learning have often been conducted in the context of programs whose purpose is to prepare teacher candidates so that they understand constructivist theories of learning and will engage in practices consistent with those theories. In general, researchers have reasoned that when teacher candidates do not embrace learner-centered theories and practices, their initial beliefs about teachers and learning serve as barriers to understanding knowledge-based theories that run counter to their beliefs. Beliefs filter teachers' perceptions, interpretations, and decisions about how to respond to particular classroom events. Most of these studies have used interpretive research designs and have tended to involve small participant populations. A few general findings follow.

Hollingsworth (1989) found that prior beliefs influenced both how teacher candidates interacted with information presented in the ITP program and, more important, with the depth of conceptual change. Hollingsworth conducted baseline interviews and observations to develop background profiles. Multiple data sources were collected, including audiotapes of teacher education courses, completed assignments and journals, systematic interviews, and observations of the teacher candidates' classroom teaching. Taxonomies of cognitive processing (e.g., Rumelhart and Norman's, 1976, categories of accretion, fine-tuning, and restructuring) were used to code the data and to determine cognitive change. Data were reduced into a case study of each participant. Cross-case analysis allowed Hollingsworth to show how beliefs about general classroom management, the teaching of reading, and of the academic task changed over in response to experiences in the teacher preparation program. Using inductive methods, Britzman (1991) conducted extensive interviews and observations of two individuals to show that beliefs have a high level of specificity. The Teacher Education and Learning to Teach (TELT) study found that belief systems, or frames of reference, depended on a particular situation. Indeed, in this study of writing instruction, the closer the teachers moved to actual practice, the more their frame of reference reflected a traditional view of writing instruction (Kennedy, 1999b).

A number of scholars have speculated about why teacher candidates' initial beliefs have proven to be so resilient. Frequently cited, Weinstein's (1989, 1990) studies involving questionnaires, interviews, and self-rating scales found that teacher candidates were unrealistically optimistic about the difficulties that teaching would pose for them. Weinstein speculated that such a stance may have given teacher candidates little motivation to engage in concepts introduced by teacher educators. Kennedy (1998) argued that most teachers' beliefs fall into the difficult-to-change category (e.g., formed early in life, containing an affective component, related to self-concept, and interconnected with other beliefs). Many have commented on the apparent disconnect between the agenda of teacher educators and that of teacher candidates (e.g., McDiarmid, 1990; Zeichner & Gore, 1990). That is, teacher candidates enter teaching with a strong belief that the teacher's role is to present knowledge to students; meanwhile, teacher educators seek to prepare them to view teaching as guiding students to construct understanding. Wideen et al. (1998) pressed teacher educators to question this fundamental tension by engaging in a critical examination of teacher educators' beliefs and normative views regarding the purposes of teacher education. Accompanying such an examination would be efforts on the part of teacher educators to understand, from the teacher candidates' perspectives, why teacher candidates' ideas about teaching make sense to them. Such inquiry might parallel studies like Ball and Wilson (1996) conducted in examining young children's misconceptions regarding core concepts in math and social studies; rather than view the children's thinking as errors, Ball and Wilson took their students' ideas seriously and viewed their misconceptions as genuine attempts to make sense of new ideas.

Wideen et al. (1998) reviewed a number of short- and long-term interventions designed to promote changes in beliefs, or conceptual change. Short-term interventions include specific courses, such as introductory seminars or content area methods courses, whereas long-term interventions spanned at least a full year and tended to reflect program-level orientations. Across these studies, a range of specific beliefs was examined, including beliefs about diverse students, conceptions of the subject matter, the role of the teacher, and so on. Many of the findings were based on inductive analyses of extensive interview data, artifact analysis, and observation in both university courses and field settings. Wideen et al. claimed that no conclusive findings emerged from this set of studies. One general trend is that studies seeking to document noticeable change within the context of one course have more often been less effective than longer-term interventions (Richardson, 1996; Wideen et al., 1998), thus suggesting that beliefs that have been constructed over long periods of time may not be so easily reconstructed in one experience within an ITP program. Wideen et al. (1998) concluded that those ITP programs that "build upon the beliefs of preservice teachers and feature systematic and consistent long-term support in a collaborative setting" are more successful in promoting genuine conceptual change (p. 130). Feiman-Nemser and Remillard (1996) named several basic conditions for bringing about conceptual change: opportunities to evaluate positively new practices when compared to traditional ones; opportunities to see examples of new practices in authentic settings, if possible; and direct experiences, as learners, when these approaches are enacted.

More longitudinal studies that carefully examine the arc of teacher learning from ITP through induction may be needed to understand fully changing belief systems and, by extension, teaching practices. Wideen et al. (1998) suggested that the "fixed nature of prospective teachers' beliefs should remain an open question rather than an accepted assumption until the impact of the more robust programs of teacher education has been fully analyzed" (p. 144). Robust, in this case, implies those programs that meet the conditions suggested in the previous paragraph. In many of these interpretive studies, there is no common metric for change even though researchers characterize the nature and degree of conceptual change. Thus, the ambiguous results of preservice teacher change may well reflect the researchers' normative biases regarding how much change counts as significant growth or development. One way researchers can respond is by providing detailed descriptions of data analysis. Adams and Krockover (1997) suggested an exemplar to guide future study designs.

Continued attention to beliefs will prevail as long as beliefs are psychologically found to interact with practice.

Although Calderhead (1996) held that relationships between beliefs and classroom practice are contestable, Richardson's (1996) review concluded that the relationship between beliefs and action is indeed complex and reciprocal; that is, not only do beliefs drive action, but also reflection upon action may change beliefs. The two "operate together in praxis" (Richardson, 1996, p. 105). What is still unclear, at least empirically, is whether changed beliefs will necessarily lead to changes in practice. Findings from the TELT study suggest that what a teacher espouses generally about her teaching practice is not necessarily consistent with how she decides to respond to a particular teaching situation (Kennedy, 1998). Wilcox, Schram, Lappan, and Lanier (1991) found that although experiences in a constructivist teacher education program led elementary teacher candidates to change beliefs about how they, as adults, learned math, their beliefs about how children learn mathematics did not change, remaining consistent with traditional, prescriptive views of math instruction. The methods used in the TELT study suggest that beliefs must be determined in the context of particular tasks, thus reflecting a situative perspective. The context plays a role not only in the teacher candidate's ability to change her beliefs, but also in her ability to have her practices align with her beliefs. In the mathematics example just provided, the researchers speculated that some reasons for the discrepancy between beliefs about personal learning and beliefs about children's learning may be the result of the heavy reinforcement of traditional pedagogy during student teaching and the initial years of teaching.

The resounding conclusion is that prior beliefs do shape teacher candidate's learning, serving variously as filters, frames, barriers, or perhaps gatekeepers to understanding knowledge-based, learner-centered theories and practices. Furthermore, because they are so salient, many teacher educators view them as targets of change, and thus an important objective of ITP is to shift teacher candidates' frames of reference toward reform-minded views of teaching and learning. Unfortunately, many teacher candidates do not expect that teacher preparation will involve changing frames of reference. Rather, they expect that teacher preparation will show them how to teach (i.e., provide them with the procedures of traditional practice); hence, they resist the ideas of teacher educators. There is, then, a normative tug-of-war between teacher candidates' expectations and teacher educators' objectives in ITP. Cognitive psychology might help resolve this clash by providing more nuanced understandings of the exact mechanisms by which these filters or frames operate. Although some studies indicate that the characteristics of the individual do indeed matter (e.g., traditional vs. nontraditional teacher candidates; see Richardson, 1996), less well

understood is how the substance of the belief itself shapes interpretation. For instance, do beliefs about racial or class matters work differently than those about subject matter? What emotions are associated with the beliefs and with the experience of dissonance, and how do those emotions shape the learning or unlearning experience? Motivation theory may contribute insights into how individuals choose to mediate significant dissonance. How do relationships among teacher educators and candidates and among teacher candidates themselves shape the process of conceptual change? Findings in the chapters by Pintrich and by Pianta in this volume may also inform teacher educators' practice and research. Finally, a situative perspective holds great promise, for empirical evidence suggests that belief systems, or frames of reference, are highly dependent on specific task situations and contexts.

Role of Subject Matter Knowledge and Pedagogical Content Knowledge

Shulman's identification of content as the missing paradigm launched a number of studies into how teacher candidate's prior understanding of subject matter shapes learning to teach. Some of this research falls within the larger framework of research on teacher beliefs; that is, studies examined how teacher candidates' conceptions of the subject matter, both as an academic discipline and as a school subject, play a role in learning how to teach. Other studies explored the relationship between the teacher candidates' formal knowledge of the subject matter and learning to teach specific content and concepts. Schwab's (1964) distinction between the substance and syntax of a discipline often appears in discussions of teachers' subject-matter content knowledge. Researchers have analyzed teachers' knowledge in terms of what they know about how the core concepts, ideas, and facts of a discipline are organized and relate to one another (substance), as well as what they know about the system of evidence by which inquiry is conducted within the discipline and by which new knowledge is added (syntax). As it turns out, what a teacher candidate knows shapes both the content and methods of a teacher's practice (Borko & Putnam, 1996). A number of in-depth research reviews have yielded several core findings (Putnam & Borko, 1997; Richardson, 1996; Wilson et al., 2001).

First, with regard to the substance of teacher candidates' subject-matter content knowledge, teacher candidates have often "mastered basic skills, but they lack the deeper conceptual understanding that is necessary when responding to student questions and extending lessons beyond the basics" (Wilson et al., 2001, p. 9). This finding stretches across all the academic disciplines and has been documented at the level of specific substantive, core subject matter concepts (e.g., understanding place value and fractions in mathematics; Ball, 1990). Teacher candidates' syntactic knowledge has been shown to have great variation (Grossman et al., 1989). For those interested in novice teachers' understanding of math and science, the evidence suggests that most teacher candidates do not have a deep grasp of the discipline's epistemology (Borko & Putnam, 1996). It should be noted, however, that teacher candidates may not be dramatically different from the general college-educated population. In one study examining career paths of 10,000 college graduates nationwide, secondary teacher candidates had comparable academic records to the group as a whole, although elementary candidates did have lower standardized test scores and weaker academic records, at least as measured by number of remedial classes and level of courses taken (Henke, Geis, Giambattista, & Knepper, 1996).

Second, those teachers who "have richer understanding of subject matter tend to emphasize conceptual, problem-solving, and inquiry aspects of their subjects, whereas less knowledgeable teachers tend to emphasize facts and procedures" (Putnam & Borko, 1997, p. 1232). These findings are significant because teachers without this robust understanding of substance and syntax of the discipline are more likely to teach uncritically those lesson plans taken from textbooks and colleagues and to miss opportunities to clarify and extend students' understandings of subject-matter knowledge.

Third, the empirical evidence is mixed regarding whether teacher candidates can develop deeper understandings of a discipline or beliefs about the nature of the discipline during ITP. It appears that when teacher candidates have opportunities to engage in solving real problems, to work in small groups, and to talk about their learning, they are more likely to improve their substantive content knowledge (Borko & Putnam, 1996). Given that many teacher candidates complete an academic undergraduate major (rather than a major in education), recent policy efforts have also sought to address how undergraduate programs of study influence potential teacher's substantive and syntactic understandings of the disciplines (American Council on Education, 1999; Murray & Porter, 1996). If these policy recommendations are enacted, their impact will need to be studied with rigor.

Finally, a number of studies were reviewed by Wilson and colleagues (2001) to examine the relationship between subject-matter knowledge and student learning. An interesting finding is that they identified no rigorous research that examined these two factors directly; rather, most studies used proxies for subject-matter knowledge (e.g., specific courses or academic majors). Indicators of student learning were often reduced to standardized test scores, which many argue are inadequate for assessing the kind of understanding promoted in many of the reforms. The few studies meeting their criteria reveal inconclusively how, specifically, teachers' subject-matter knowledge matters in shaping children's learning.

Related to inquiries into the role of subject-matter content knowledge in learning to teach have been numerous studies about how the teacher candidates develop pedagogical content knowledge. This form of knowledge has received much attention because it is, arguably, unique to teaching; furthermore, because few teacher candidates have well-developed pedagogical content knowledge when they begin teacher preparation programs, this domain of teacher knowledge must be developed within the purview of teacher preparation or during the induction phase of learning to teach. Most research reviews cite Grossman's (1990) landmark study when defining the key components of pedagogical content knowledge (see the previous section on cognitive constructivist perspectives, where these components were outlined).

Borko and Putnam (1996; Putnam & Borko, 1997) provided a thorough synthesis of research into all four components of Grossman's conceptualization. Several key findings emerge from the studies that they review. First, the teacher candidate's conception of the discipline directly influences instructional choices, resulting in dramatically different classroom experiences for learners even when the basic content is the same. For example, Grossman (1990) showed that two high school teachers' conceptions of teaching English dramatically shaped the way they taught *Hamlet*. One teacher emphasized close textual reading of the entire play, whereas another used film versions as the text. These different emphases stemmed, in part, from the teacher's different views about the purpose of high school English. One sought to introduce her students to the norms of literary criticism practiced in university English departments, whereas the other viewed high school English as an opportunity for students to forge personal connections between cultural works of merit and their lived experience. These conceptions of subject matter function much like beliefs do and thus are not easily changed. However, several rigorous studies have demonstrated that teacher preparation courses can help teacher candidates reconstruct their subject-matter knowledge into a conception of the discipline that is better suited for student learners. For example, Gess-Newsome and Lederman (1993) worked with preservice biology teachers. Initially, these teachers were only able to generate discrete topical lists of core biology topics; however, over the science methods course, the teachers were able to transform this topical list into one that established interconnections among topics. Thus, this experience influenced the organization of their knowledge of biology as a school subject matter. A second finding is that if a teacher candidate's subject-matter content knowledge is weak, then his or her pedagogical content knowledge will also be weak. This has interesting implications for the design of baccalaureate teacher preparation programs in particular, where the likelihood of working more closely with liberal arts and science faculty is higher than in postbaccalaureate programs. It raises the question of whether it is possible to develop simultaneously subject-matter content knowledge and pedagogical content knowledge. A third finding is that one of the great challenges for teacher candidates is to learn when children are likely to encounter confusion and difficulty in learning content. Much of the research has pointed out what teacher candidates do not know about students' understanding. Putnam and Borko (1997) called for more research to describe the processes by which teacher candidates develop this specific aspect of pedagogical content knowledge. Such knowledge is particularly important with a student population that is becoming increasingly more diverse.

Role of Mentors and Colleagues

Social constructivism has advanced, from a theoretical perspective, the importance of cognitive apprenticeship (Brown et al., 1989) and assisted performance (Tharp & Gallimore, 1988). As such, the theory directs researchers' attention to the critical role that dialogue with others plays in the process of learning to teach. Teacher educators and teacher candidates both recognize that conversations with mentors—both cooperating teachers and university supervisors—and with colleagues are a means for teacher candidates to mediate their understanding of the knowledge base for teaching and to refine their judgments and decisions (Cochran-Smith & Lytle, 1999). Talk with parents is also a potentially rich source of learning for teacher candidates. Potentially educative conversations occur both formally (e.g., through planning or evaluation conferences and through class activities and assignments) and informally (e.g., through voluntary associations, cohort groups, and in communities of practice such as those found in professional development schools, etc.). Many of the studies cited earlier in this chapter regarding conceptual change or changing content knowledge did in fact involve interventions that placed teacher candidates in small problem-solving groups.

To date, the research regarding the nature of the learning that occurs through these conversations has not been studied with the same depth and rigor as the research on prior beliefs and subject knowledge. These studies have tended to be focused more on how talk is a medium through which individuals become socialized into the norms of the discourse

community of teachers (McLaughlin & Talbert, 1993; Zeichner & Gore, 1990) than on the specific and substantive learning that occurs within the conversations and dialogue. Wilson and Berne (1999) reviewed a number of studies of projects in which experienced teachers engaged in talk about subject matter, learning, or teaching. Many of these studies analyzed the discourse, using analytic tools from psycho- and sociolinguistics, and made claims about knowledge gained in these settings. As such, this review is a helpful starting point for researchers interested in studying this phenomenon. If talk is both the medium for and an indicator of learning, it needs to be better understood; furthermore, because talk is by its nature evanescent, relationships between talk and practice must also be more clearly elaborated.

Some of the work in this area has characterized the discourse occurring in innovative communities of experienced teachers (Wilson & Berne, 1999). Other descriptive analyses have provided existence proofs of such communities (e.g., Goldenberg & Gallimore, 1991; Grossman, Wineberg, & Woolworth, 2001; Sherin, 2000). Fortunately, both Grossman and colleagues and Sherin collected systematic data; thus, we can look forward to their subsequent analyses and insights into how the talk fostered learning. As scholars turn to study the role that talk plays in teacher learning during initial preparation, they may well refer to this scholarship, particularly in designing tasks and settings that are more likely to promote educative discourse. Although it is still too early to draw generalizations from this area of research, some conceptual and synthetic scholarship suggests that if the goal of ITP is to prepare teacher candidates to teach for understanding, then unless teacher candidates are working in reform-oriented settings, their conversations with veteran and novice colleagues may serve to reinforce, rather than to reinvent, traditional or conventional practice (Richardson, 1997; Sykes & Bird, 1992). Whether a community has an inquiry stance may play a role in the substance and depth of learning (Cochran-Smith & Lytle, 1999). The role that conflict plays in the learning process is potentially an important variable. For example, conflict is often perceived as something to avoid, when in fact the dissonance may well be essential for deep learning (Achinstein, 2002; Sapon-Shevin & Chandler-Olcott, 2001). Teacher candidates may need to learn how to engage in constructive argument, a practice that runs counter to the norms of privacy, politeness, and nonjudgmental interactions found in the faculty communities of most schools (Wilson & Berne, 1999). This seems especially important if teachers are going to discuss the genuine challenges associated with understanding how matters of ethnicity, class, and gender shape children's learning. Focusing the talk on artifacts of teaching (e.g., student work or videotapes of classroom events) seems to lead to more focused interactions where participants wrestle with the learner's understanding (Allen, 1998; Sherin, 2000). Factors that may influence the quality of talk and, by extension, learning include an individual's role and authority within the group (group refers to two or more participants), the purposes and protocols for conversation, the length of time that the group has existed, the stability of membership in the group, the presence or absence of a facilitator who scaffolds discussion, and the rewards for participation in the group. Studies of the talk that occurs between mentors and teacher candidates and among colleagues has great potential to enhance our understanding of learning to teach.

Role of Settings for Learning

As a situative perspective takes hold, it has framed settings, or contexts, as central to the learning process. But as Putnam and Borko (2000) asked, "Where should teachers' learning be situated?" (p. 5). They suggested that well-designed experiences that link university courses and field experiences are one possible response, citing Wolf, Carey, and Mieras (1996) as an exemplar. Many teacher candidates and practicing teachers hold that field experiences are the sine qua non of settings in which teacher candidates learn to teach; however, Wilson et al. (2001) summarized research enumerating many well-recognized flaws of these experiences (e.g., disconnected from other components of teacher preparation, focused narrowly on mechanical aspects of teaching, reinforcing the status quo of traditional teaching, and overwhelming thus leading teacher candidates to teach in ways they were taught). Much of the conceptualization of professional development schools seeks to overcome these flaws (Darling-Hammond, Wise, & Klein, 1999; Sirotnik & Goodlad, 1988). Gallego (2001) described a novel blending of field experiences completed in both classroom and community-based settings in order to foster understanding of the complex relationships that support teaching and learning. For example, the field experiences in two settings provided a productive contrast so that the teacher candidates were able to recognize and critically reflect on the role that physical environment plays in ownership of learning. Others recognize that such structural changes will be slowly realized; therefore, teacher education programs must promote an inquiry orientation as a means to provide teacher candidates with "opportunities to engage in ongoing examination of self as teacher within the contexts of classrooms, schools, and the broader professional community" (Knowles & Cole, 1996, p. 665). At this time, a body of rigorous research elaborating what and how teachers learn in these structurally innovative settings is still in its formative stages.

Summary of Learning to Teach

What emerges from this cursory summary of studies of learning to teach is that if the central goal of ITP is to ensure that those teachers entering the profession are able to teach for understanding, then teacher educators must support new teacher candidates to develop new frames of reference and behavioral enactments that are consistent with these ideas (Kennedy, 1998, 1999b). This has proven difficult to accomplish on a widespread basis. The set of beliefs about general pedagogy and learning that candidates have constructed over many years as learners in classrooms proves to be quite resilient and serves to filter interpretations of experiences in ITP. For many teacher candidates, ITP aims to create occasions to develop a wholly new, and often contradictory, view of good teaching and good teaching practices. For new teachers to enact these reform-minded practices requires not only new beliefs about teaching and learning but also the ability to transform substantive content knowledge into pedagogical content knowledge. Like changing beliefs, this has also proven difficult. Rigorous studies that have been conducted yield contradictory results. Feiman-Nemser and Remillard (1996) observed rather sanguinely, "We know even less about the processes of learning to teach than we do about the content" (p. 78). Fortunately, theoretically driven models of professional development and reform in the settings in which teacher candidates learn to teach have led to powerful arguments for redesigning the experiences, tasks, and settings through which teacher candidates learn to teach. For example, researchers' attention to talk in the learning process and to the influence of context in the learning process has potential to illuminate some vexing dilemmas of learning to teach. Scholars in this field are just beginning to understand and evaluate the nature of learning that occurs in these newer frameworks.

Best Practices in Initial Teacher Preparation

Much of the above research has both obvious and subtle implications for pedagogy in ITP. The forms of teaching most desired by teacher educators, captured in the umbrella term *teaching for understanding,* often run counter to both teacher candidates' prior beliefs about teaching and the culture and core practices of many schools. ITP, then, must offer a strong intervention in order to bring about robust learning (or unlearning?). Many see teacher preparation as a relatively weak intervention poised between these far more enduring learning experiences (Richardson, 1996). Nevertheless, to decide what are *best* practices depends largely on what "one thinks the enterprise of teacher education is about and how it works" (Carter & Anders, 1996, p. 557).

The oft-heard expression "practice what you teach" refers to the normative proposition that teacher educators should model practices that promote teacher candidates' active and social construction of teaching and learning (Lauer, 1999; Richardson, 1997; see also chapter by McComb in this volume). There is no shortage of proposed practices, including case methods, simulations, observation guides, modeling, cognitive coaching, teacher research or action research or child studies, student work protocols, video clubs, problem-based learning, discourse communities, and narrative methods. Indeed, many of these practices have been recommended and described in work cited earlier in this chapter; researchers have also attempted to account for teacher candidate learning within these pedagogical activities.

What is known empirically about sound pedagogy in ITP? Carter and Anders (1996) offered a review that focuses exclusively on the pedagogy of teacher education. They broke down their review into three categories of pedagogy: teaching laboratories and simulations; field-based pedagogies, including observation guides, structured assignments, opportunities to write about teaching, and seminars and conversations; and cases and case methods. They located each of these pedagogical approaches within a framework for teacher education (i.e., practical/craft, technological, personal, academic, and critical social); then they reviewed the empirical base for each of these approaches. With regard to teaching laboratories and simulations, they concluded that this set of practices, which emerged in the 1970s and early 1980s, tended to highlight discrete teaching skills. Although teacher candidates could demonstrate or perform these skills in laboratory settings, such performances did not always transfer to genuine classrooms. They suggested that a reformulation of these practices to involve more deliberation and problem solving has potential. With regard to field-based pedagogies, they found "little solid evidence concerning the impact of field experience in general or of specific strategies" (p. 575). They cited findings from other studies that suggest that field experiences may engender a survival orientation and reinforce stereotypes, particularly of diverse learners. They argued that the selection and coordination of sites and the character of the supervisor's or mentor's feedback are important qualities in the framing of field experiences. With regard to case-based pedagogies, they summarized different approaches to case methods but acknowledged the need for more study of actual teacher candidate learning.

Carter and Anders (1996) ended their review with the observation that "research on program pedagogy is not a highly developed area" (p. 584). They expressed concern, however, that research conducted in the spirit of effectiveness studies that compare one pedagogical approach with another will lead to inconclusive results. Nonetheless, it seems evident that more systematic approaches to studying the nature, variation, and impact of teacher preparation pedagogy are sorely needed to guide the design of ITP. Levin and O'Donnell (1999) provided a stage model for how such inquiries might be conducted. Many of the important studies mentioned in this review as well as the current interest in self-study research (Zeichner, 1999) fall into Levin and O'Donnell's first stage. They offered the field an important starting point of hypotheses, preliminary ideas, and observations. But also needed are integrated studies linking design experiments in ITP with controlled laboratory experiments of teacher candidate learning, which are then followed by randomized program trial studies. Many in teacher education will find this proposal too rooted in a scientific or positivistic paradigm of educational research. However, without a more rigorous research base, teacher educators will continue to clash with a highly suspicious public over the importance of developing professional knowledge and judgment.

What Collective Story Do the Reviews Tell?

This cursory review of the flourishing field of cognitively oriented studies of learning to teach has underscored the intellectual complexity of teaching. New directions in cognitive psychology show promise in responding to ongoing questions and dilemmas about how teacher candidates learn to teach and how ITP programs can best foster such learning. Thus far, scholarship in the area of learning to teach has provided several approaches to a knowledge base for teaching. This knowledge base has in turn shaped the substance of ITP curriculum. However, constructivist theories of learning posit the "idea that teacher learning ought not to be bound and *delivered* but rather *activated*. This positions the 'what' of teacher knowledge in a much different place" (Wilson & Berne, 1999, p. 194). Given that teaching involves, at its core, professional judgment, emphasis on helping new teachers perceive, interpret, and respond wisely to classroom events has garnered the attention of teacher educators. Much research has been conducted examining how a teacher candidate's prior beliefs, life history, and subject-matter knowledge shape interpretations of events and decisions for action. Significant emphasis has gone in to finding ways to facilitate meaningful conceptual change, with the hope that this will in turn lead to reform-minded teaching practice. The track record has been uneven. Some well-structured interventions have shown modest success at facilitating conceptual change and at fostering critical reflection, but much of this research has not necessarily connected changes in teacher thinking with desired teacher actions. It appears, however, that as the situative perspective takes hold in cognitive studies, new and critical variables are emerging that may help researchers to develop more robust theories of learning to teach. Ball and Cohen (1999) suggested that the field lacks "carefully constructed and empirically validated theories of teacher learning that could inform teacher education, in roughly the same way that cognitive psychology has begun to inform the education of schoolchildren" (p. 4).

ONCE AND FUTURE RESEARCH

Given the genre conventions of a handbook chapter, readers expect, at this point, an argument regarding future research in this field. Two brief responses follow, one highlighting promising lines of research, the other commenting on potential questions and methodological approaches for future research. It is a given that the goal of such research is to inform the field regarding how best to prepare new teachers to engage and teach diverse students to understand content in deep, flexible ways so that they are, in turn, able to respond to complex issues and problems of the world in which we live. This is, without qualification, a tall order. It is one that the traditional grammar of schooling is unlikely to fulfill; hence, models of learning to teach for understanding are called for.

Promising Research from a Situative Perspective

In Berliner and Calfee's conclusion to the *Handbook of Educational Psychology* (1996), they predicted that "research flowing from situationist perspectives, concepts of distributed cognition, the development of new technologies, and methodologies such as design experiments, should keep educational psychologists quite busy as we enter the twenty-first century" (p. 1021). Putnam and Borko (2000) picked up on this foreshadowing, as they argued that a situative perspective brings important conceptual tools to bear on the process of learning to teach. This perspective radically reconsiders what it means to learn to teach, for it breaks down the conventional notion of first understanding a principle and then applying it in practice. Instead, a situative perspective suggests that professional knowledge, which often fuses principles and practices, is intimately connected to the contexts and settings in which individuals encounter principles and practices. Scholars of learning to teach already see the explanatory power of this perspective and also its potential to guide cycles of design and research in ITP. Studies of learning to teach writing and of case methods illustrate this point.

Learning to Teach Writing

Learning to teach writing is, arguably, a challenging task. First, writing is a complex cognitive tool that is not easily mastered. Second, writing instruction in school has traditionally been prescriptive and emphasized the acquisition of conventions (e.g., grammar, punctuation, and usage); in contrast, reformers see writing as an activity for making meaning, and they advocate writing instruction that guides students to become strategic, purposeful writers. Third, preparing teacher candidates to embrace this vision of the purpose of writing instruction is challenging because most teacher candidates have little experience as writers; their prior beliefs about writing in school coupled with the persistent presence of traditional writing instruction present challenges to teacher educators. In response, the TELT study (Kennedy, 1998, 1999b) examined how teacher preparation programs influenced adoption of reform ideas in writing instruction. Grossman and colleagues (Grossman, Smagorinsky, & Valencia, 1999; Grossman, Thompson, & Valencia, 2001; Grossman et al., 2000) studied how beginning teachers appropriated a set of pedagogical tools for teaching writing. Taken together, these studies are already making important contributions on empirical, methodological, and theoretical levels.

Empirically, a number of critical findings from TELT have already been mentioned. For example, Kennedy found that teacher candidates' espoused beliefs did not necessarily match the beliefs implicit in their immediate responses to particular teaching tasks or situations. More significantly, she found that teacher candidates had a set of interlocking, mutually reinforcing ideas about the nature of writing and writing instruction to which they were personally attached. These beliefs influenced how they responded to representative teaching situations, often in ways that maintained the status quo of traditional writing instruction. Equally important, using a carefully defined standard of evaluating pre- and postinterviews, she was able to show that ITP programs influence teacher learning through enrollment and through their substantive orientations. Grossman et al. (2000) found that during ITP courses, teacher candidates were introduced to conceptual tools (e.g., concepts of scaffolding and ownership in writing instruction). However, their appropriation of these tools during their first year of teaching varied depending on whether they received accompanying practical tools and on the activity settings in which they taught. An interesting finding was that the teacher candidates often attempted pedagogical practices in their second year that were much more consistent with reform ideas, thus suggesting that the impact of ITP may not be realized until after the first year of teaching. The teacher candidates appeared to have constructed powerful and guiding visions that took more than one year to be activated. The researchers also found that the district's policies, practices of support, and curriculum materials and assessments played an important role in how the first- and second-year teachers were able to construct understandings of what it means to teach in general, and language arts in particular (Grossman et al., 2001).

Methodologically, these two studies had much in common, and each represents the kind of rigorous research that is sorely needed in this field. First, both are longitudinal case studies of teacher candidates who were prepared in a range of ITP programs. Second, they offer detailed contextual information about these different ITP programs, which varied in both structure and substantive orientation. Third, they used repeated interviews and observations to gather data. Kennedy used the same pre- and postprogram interview protocol. Her measures merit significant attention: In addition to open-ended, biographical questions, she also asked each participant to respond to representative teaching situations (e.g., respond to a particular piece of writing, a student's statement of boredom, a particular question of English language usage). Finally, both are well grounded theoretically. Grossman and colleagues adopted the theoretical framework of activity theory, as have others in the field (e.g., Newell, Gingrich, & Johnson, 2001). The use of activity theory bears attention because this framework appears to have both broad explanatory power and the potential to shape ITP practice.

Case Methods in Initial Teacher Preparation

Case methods have both a long and short history in ITP. The use of cases or vignettes extends back for many years, but Shulman's (1986b) presidential address to the American Educational Research Association renewed teacher educators' attention. By the early 1990s the case idea was well established (Sykes & Bird, 1992), and by the mid-1990s there was sufficient activity with this pedagogy to warrant a complete chapter in the second edition of the *Handbook of Research on Teacher Education* (Merseth, 1996). Both Putnam and Borko (2000) and Carter and Anders (1996) feature case methods as a central pedagogy in ITP. One reason case methods took hold so quickly is that they are a relatively low-tech pedagogy. Although the development of casebooks is labor intensive (e.g., Shulman, Lotan, & Whitcomb, 1998) and the art of facilitating case discussions or case writing requires time to develop, weaving case methods into traditional university courses is a relatively simple addition. That the most recent edition of almost every standard educational psychology

textbook includes cases suggests that this practice is widespread. A far more compelling reason is that case methods are consistent with the situative perspective because they allow teacher candidates to have vicarious experiences. Well-crafted cases preserve the complexity of teaching, but at the same time, they allow teacher candidates to slow down their perception, interpretation, and analysis of the details. Although case methods are frequently promoted and appear to be widespread as an ITP pedagogy, calls for empirical support for this practice began to mount (Merseth, 1996; Sykes & Bird, 1992).

This call was met in 1999 with a full-length monograph on the research base for teaching and learning with cases (Lundeberg, Levin, & Harrington, 1999). The sections of the book review learning fostered through case-based pedagogy, structuring the learning environment with cases, and rethinking the concept of a case. In the foreword Merseth cited several reasons for the slow development of an empirical base for case methods. First, she observed that good research designs hinge on clearly targeted goals. Because cases have been employed for a variety of pedagogical purposes (e.g., to present the complexity of teaching, to teach teacher candidates how to problem solve, or to foster deeper reflection), it is sometimes difficult to make comparisons across studies because the pedagogical aims differ. Second, it is difficult to account for the many factors, or variables, that affect learning using case-based methods. Merseth's general critique of the empirical base for case methods suggests the need for the kind of rigorous designs that Levin and O'Donnell (1999) outlined. The range of research designs reflected in this collection of studies, however, is rather eclectic. As such, it provides the first stage of research in Levin and O'Donnell's approach. The studies reported provide strong initial hypotheses for understanding teacher candidate learning through experiences with cases. More multisite studies that richly capture the contextual variety of programs, group dynamics, and even instructor effects and at the same time employ common measures of learning may help the field strengthen the initial empirical claims.

Thoughts on Future Research

This concluding section offers a brief reflection on questions worth asking and on rigorous methods. It goes without saying that ITP will continue to engender high levels of suspicion and aspersion from an increasingly vocal group of individuals who believe that ITP is both unnecessary and quite possibly an impediment to a quality teaching force. The studies reviewed in this chapter provide some evidence that it does matter, but the answers are not unequivocal. Regarding the following few domains in need of more sustained inquiry, it should be noted that Cochran-Smith (2000, 2001), Putnam and Borko (2000), and Wilson et al. (2001) have framed well the sorts of questions that matter and research agendas that will move the field forward. The suggestions that follow embellish, rather than replace, their suggestions.

First, much more remains to be understood about how teacher candidates' beliefs shape learning to teach for understanding and to teach children whose backgrounds differ substantially from the teacher's. Similarly, we need to understand better the many well-considered interventions that teacher educators are developing to promote conceptual change and to enhance the impact of ITP on a teacher candidate's knowledge and beliefs. We need to understand much more clearly the "outcomes" matters (i.e., the relationships among a teacher candidate's knowledge and beliefs, her emerging practice, and the learning of her students). Studies conducted within a situative perspective, by changing the unit of analysis from the individual to the activity setting, may provide a new view on these dilemmas. The increasing emphasis on performance assessments and accountability within teacher preparation will likely add to the intensity and stress levels associated with participating in an ITP program. Gold (1999) suggested ways in which universities might be more attentive to teacher candidates' psychological maturity. The field will benefit from enhanced understanding of how the teacher candidates' emotional states affect learning to teach. To respond to these persistently unresolved questions research must be conducted using more rigorous methods. Many have argued for methodological pluralism (Kennedy, 1999a; Sleeter, 2001; Zeichner, 1999); that pluralism will be needed to establish a system of generating credible knowledge from education research (Levin & O'Donnell, 1999). Unfortunately, in the area of research on learning to teach, the field seems to get what it pays for. The works that appears to show the greatest promise (e.g., longitudinal, multisite studies that use well-defined and well-designed measures of teacher learning) are some of the few adequately funded research projects. More large-scale design and research efforts are needed.

In closing, the body of research on learning to teach, though still relatively new, has led to understandings of the knowledge base for teaching, the critical role that prior beliefs play in teacher learning, and the powerful role that talk and settings play in the process of learning to teach. Given the ambitious goal that many reformers have of ensuring that every child has a teacher capable of fostering deep, flexible understanding of content, scholars of learning to teach have considerable work to do. Fortunately, as we move into the twenty-first century, the field appears to be armed with promising conceptual tools that have the potential to provide important theoretical models of teacher learning. With well-supported, rigorous research, those models will be developed in concert with best practices for ITP.

REFERENCES

Adams, P. E., & Krockover, G. H. (1997). Beginning science teacher cognition and its origins in the preservice science teacher program. *Journal of Research in Science Teaching, 34,* 633–653.

Allen, D. (Ed.). (1998). *Assessing student learning: From grading to understanding.* New York: Teachers College Press.

American Council on Education. (1999). *To touch the future: Transforming the way teachers are taught.* Washington, DC: Author.

Anderson, L. M. (1989). Learners and learning. In M. C. Reynolds (Ed.), *Knowledge base for the beginning teacher* (pp. 85–99). Oxford, England: Pergamon.

Achinstein, B. (2002). Community, diversity, and conflict among schoolteachers: *The ties that blind.* New York: Teachers College Press.

Ball, D. L. (1990). The mathematical understandings that prospective teachers bring to teacher education. *Elementary School Journal, 90,* 449–466.

Ball, D. L., & Cohen, D. K. (1999). Developing practice, developing practioners: Toward a practice-based theory of professional education. In L. Darling-Hammond & G. Sykes (Eds.), *Teaching as the learning profession: Handbook of policy and practice* (pp. 3–32). San Francisco: Jossey-Bass.

Ball, D. L., & McDiarmid, G. W. (1990). The subject-matter preparation of teachers. In W. R. Houston (Ed.), *Handbook of research on teacher education* (pp. 437–449). New York: Macmillan.

Ball, D. L., & Wilson, S. M. (1996). Integrity in teaching: Recognizing the fusion of the moral and intellectual. *American Educational Research Journal, 33,* 155–192.

Berliner, D. C., & Calfee, R. C. (Eds.). (1996). *Handbook of educational psychology.* New York: Macmillan.

Biddle, B. J., Good, T. L., & Goodson, I. F. (1997). *International handbook of teachers and teaching.* Dordrecht, The Netherlands: Kluwer.

Blumenfeld, P. C., Marx, R. W., Patrick, H., Krajcik, J., & Soloway, E. (1997). Teaching for understanding. In B. J. Biddle, T. L. Good, & I. F. Goodson (Eds.), *International handbook of teachers and teaching* (Vol. 2, pp. 819–878). Dordrecht, The Netherlands: Kluwer.

Borko, H., & Putnam, R. (1996). Learning to teach. In D. C. Berliner & R. C. Calfee (Eds.), *Handbook of educational psychology* (pp. 673–708). New York: Macmillan.

Britzman, D. P. (1991). *Practice makes practice: A critical study of learning to teach.* Albany, NY: State University of New York Press.

Brophy, J. E., & Good, T. L. (1986). Teacher behavior and student achievement. In M. C. Wittrock (Ed.), *Handbook of research on teaching* (3rd ed., pp. 328–375). New York: Macmillan.

Brown, J. S., Collins, A., & Duguid, P. (1989). Situated cognition and the culture of learning. *Educational Researcher, 18*(1), 32–42.

Bruner, J. (1960). *The process of education.* Cambridge, MA: Harvard University Press.

Buchmann, M., & Floden, R. (1993). *Detachment and concern: Conversations in the philosophy of teaching and teacher education.* New York: Teachers College Press.

Calderhead, J. (1996). Teachers: Beliefs and knowledge. In D. C. Berliner & R. C. Calfee (Eds.), *Handbook of educational psychology* (pp. 709–725). New York: Macmillan.

Carter, K. (1990). Teachers' knowledge and learning to teach. In W. R. Houston (Ed.), *Handbook of research on teacher education* (pp. 291–310). New York: Macmillan.

Carter, K., & Anders, D. (1996). Program pedagogy. In F. B. Murray (Ed.), *The teacher educator's handbook: Building a knowledge base for the preparation of teachers* (pp. 557–592). San Francisco: Jossey-Bass.

Carter, K., & Doyle, W. (1996). Personal narrative and life history in learning to teach. In J. Sikula, T. Buttery, & E. Gutor (Eds.), *Handbook of research in teacher education* (2nd ed., pp. 120–142). New York: Macmillan.

Clandinin, D. J., & Connelly, F. M. (1987). Teachers' personal knowledge: What counts as "personal" in studies of the personal. *Journal of Curriculum Studies, 19,* 487–500.

Clark, C. (1995). *Thoughtful teaching.* New York: Teachers College Press.

Clark, C., & Peterson, P. (1986). Teachers' thought processes. In M. Wittrock (Ed.), *Handbook of research on teaching* (3rd ed., pp. 255–296). New York: Macmillan.

Clift, R. T., Houston, W. R., & Pugach, M. C. (Eds.). (1990). *Encouraging reflective practice in education: An analysis of issues and programs.* New York: Teachers College Press.

Cobb, P., & Bowers, J. S. (1999). Cognitive and situated learning perspectives in theory and practice. *Educational Researcher, 28*(2) 4–15.

Cochran-Smith, M. (1991). Learning to teach against the grain. *Harvard Educational Review, 61,* 279–310.

Cochran-Smith, M. (2000). The future of teacher education: Framing the questions that matter. *Teaching Education, 11*(1), 13–24.

Cochran-Smith, M. (2001). Desperately seeking solutions. *Journal of Teacher Education, 52,* 347–349.

Cochran-Smith, M., & Fries, M. K. (2001). Sticks, stones and ideology: The discourse of reform in teacher education. *Educational Researcher, 30*(8), 3–15.

Cochran-Smith, M., & Lytle, S. (1999). Relationships of knowledge and practice: Teacher learning in communities. *Review of Research in Education, 24,* 249–305.

Cohen, D. K. (1989). Teaching practice: *Plus que ça change.* In P. W. Jackson (Ed.), *Contributing to educational change:*

Perspectives on research and practice (pp. 27–84). Berkeley, CA: McCutchan.

Cohen, D. K., McLaughlin, M. W., & Talbert, J. E. (Eds.). (1993). *Teaching for understanding: Challenges for policy and practice.* San Francisco: Jossey-Bass.

Darling-Hammond, L. (1997). *The right to learn: A blueprint for creating schools that work.* San Francisco: Jossey-Bass.

Darling-Hammond, L., & Sykes, G. (Eds.). (1999). *Teaching as the learning profession: Handbook of policy and practice.* San Francisco: Jossey-Bass.

Darling-Hammond, L., Wise, A. E., & Klein, S. P. (1999). *A license to teach: Raising standards for teaching.* San Francisco: Jossey-Bass.

Dewey, J. (1977). The relation of theory to practice. In J. A. Boydston (Ed.), *John Dewey: The middle works, 1899–1924, Volume 3: 1903–1906* (pp. 249–272).

Donmoyer, R. (1996). The concept of a knowledge base. In F. B. Murray (Ed.), *The teacher educator's handbook: Building a knowledge base for the preparation of teachers* (pp. 92–119). San Francisco: Jossey-Bass.

Elbaz, F. (1983). *Teacher thinking: A study of practical knowledge.* London: Croom Helm.

Feiman-Nemser, S., & Featherstone, H. (1992). *Exploring teaching: Reinventing an introductory course.* New York: Teachers College Press.

Feiman-Nemser, S., & Remillard, J. (1996). Perspectives on learning to teach. In F. B. Murray (Ed.), *The teacher educator's handbook: Building a knowledge base for the preparation of teachers* (pp. 63–91). San Francisco: Jossey-Bass.

Feistritzer, C. E. (1999). *The making of a teacher: A report on teacher preparation in the U.S.* Washington, DC: National Center for Education Information.

Fenstermacher, G. (1994). The knower and the known: The nature of knowledge in research on teaching. *Review of Research in Education, 20,* 3–56.

Fenstermacher, G., & Richardson, V. (1993). The elicitation and reconstruction of practical arguments in teaching. *Journal of Curriculum Studies, 25,* 101–114.

Finn, C. E., Jr., Kanstoroom, M., & Petrilli, M. J. (1999). *The quest for better teachers: Grading the states.* Washington, DC: Thomas B. Fordham Foundation.

Gallego, M. (2001). Is experience the best teacher? The potential of coupling classroom and community-based field experiences. *Journal of Teacher Education, 52,* 312–325.

Gess-Newsome, J., & Lederman, N. G. (1993). Preservice biology teachers' knowledge structures as a function of professional teacher education: A year-long assessment. *Science Education, 77,* 25–45.

Gold, Y. (1999). The psychological dimensions of teacher education: The role of the university. In R. Roth (Ed.), *The role of the university in the preparation of teachers* (pp. 166–179). Philadelphia: Falmer Press.

Goldenberg, C., & Gallimore, R. (1991). Changing teaching takes more than a one-shot workshop. *Educational Leadership, 49*(3), 69–72.

Grant, G., & Murray, C. E. (1999). *Teaching in America: The slow revolution.* Cambridge, MA: Harvard University Press.

Greeno, J. G. (1997). On claims that answer the wrong questions. *Educational Researcher, 26*(1), 5–17.

Greeno, J. G., & the Middle School Through Applications Project Group. (1998). The situativity of knowing, learning, and research. *American Psychologist, 53,* 5–26.

Griffith, G., & Early, M. (Eds.). (1999). *The education of teachers: Ninety-eighth yearbook of the National Society for the Study of Education.* Chicago: University of Chicago Press.

Grossman, P. L. (1990). *The making of a teacher: Teacher knowledge and teacher education.* New York: Teachers College Press.

Grossman, P. L., Smagorinsky, P., & Valencia, S. (1999). Appropriating tools for teaching English: A theoretical framework for research on learning to teach. *American Journal of Education, 108,* 1–29.

Grossman, P. L., Thompson, C., & Valencia, S. (2001). *District policy and beginning teachers: Where the twain shall meet* (Document R-01-4). Albany, NY: State University of New York and Seattle, WA: University of Washington. Center on English Learning and Achievement and Center for Study of Teaching and Policy.

Grossman, P. L., Valencia, S., Evans, K. Thompson, C., Martin, S., & Place, N. (2000). *Transitions into teaching: Learning to teach writing in teacher education and beyond* (Report Number 13006). Albany, NY: State University of New York, National Research Center on English Learning and Achievement.

Grossman, P. L., Wilson, S. M., & Shulman, L. S. (1989). Teachers of substance: Subject matter knowledge for teaching. In M. Reynolds (Ed.), *Knowledge base for the beginning teacher* (pp. 23–36). Oxford: Pergamon.

Grossman, P. L., Wineburg, S., & Woolworth, S. (2001). Toward a theory of teacher community. *Teachers College Press, 103,* 942–1012.

Grow-Maienza, J. (1996). Philosophical and structural perspectives in teacher education. In F. B. Murray (Ed.), *The teacher educator's handbook: Building a knowledge base for the preparation of teachers* (pp. 506–525). San Francisco: Jossey-Bass.

Henke, R. R., Geis, S., Giambattista, J., & Knepper, P. (1996). *Out of the lecture hall and into the classroom: 1992–93 college graduates and elementary/secondary school teaching.* Washington, DC: Department of Education, National Center for Education Statistics.

Hollingsworth, S. (1989). Prior beliefs and cognitive change in learning to teach. *American Educational Research Journal, 26,* 160–189.

Hollins, E. R., King, J. E., & Hayman, W. C. (1994). *Teaching diverse populations: Formulating a knowledge base.* Albany, NY: State University of New York Press.

Houston, W. R., Haberman, M., & Sikula, J. (Ed.). (1990). *Handbook of research on teacher education.* New York: Macmillan.

Jackson, P. (1990). *Life in classrooms.* New York: Teachers College Press.

Kagan, D. M. (1992). Professional growth among preservice and beginning teachers. *Review of Educational Research, 62*(2), 129–169.

Kansanen, P., Tirri, K., Meri, M., Krokfors, L., Husu, J., & Jyrhämä, R. (2000). *Teachers' pedagogical thinking: Theoretical landscapes, practical challenges.* New York: Peter Lang.

Kennedy, M. (1996). Research genres in teacher education. In F. B. Murray (Ed.), *The teacher educator's handbook: Building a knowledge base for the preparation of teachers* (pp. 120–152). San Francisco: Jossey-Bass.

Kennedy, M. (1998). *Learning to teach writing: Does teacher education make a difference?* New York: Teachers College Press.

Kennedy, M. (1999a). The problem of evidence in teacher education. In R. A. Roth (Ed.), *The role of the university in the preparation of teachers* (pp. 87–107). Philadelphia: Falmer Press.

Kennedy, M. (1999b). The role of preservice education. In L. Darling-Hammond & G. Sykes (Eds.), *Teaching as the learning profession: Handbook of policy and practice* (pp. 54–85). San Francisco: Jossey-Bass.

King, J. E., Hollins, E. R., & Hayman, W. C. (1997). *Preparing teachers for cultural diversity.* New York: Teachers College Press.

Kliebard, H. M. (1986). *The struggle for the American curriculum: 1893–1958.* New York: Routledge & Kegan Paul.

Knowles, J. G., & Cole, A. L. (1996). Developing practice through field experiences. In F. B. Murray (Ed.), *The teacher educator's handbook: Building a knowledge base for the preparation of teachers* (pp. 648–688). San Francisco: Jossey-Bass.

Ladson-Billings, G. (1999). Preparing teachers for diversity: Historical perspectives, current trends, and future directions. In L. Darling-Hammond & G. Sykes (Eds.), *Teaching as the learning profession: Handbook of policy and practice* (pp. 86–123). San Francisco: Jossey-Bass.

Lampert, M. (1985). How do teachers manage to teach?: Perspectives on problems in practice. *Harvard Educational Review, 55,* 178–194.

Lauer, P. A. (1999, Dec.). *Guidelines for applying the learner-centered psychological principles to preservice teacher education.* Aurora, CO: Mid-Continent Research for Education and Learning, Aurora, CO.

Lave, J., & Wenger, E. (1991). *Situated learning: Legitimate peripheral participation.* Cambridge, England: Cambridge University Press.

Levin, J. R., & O'Donnell, A. M. (1999). What to do about educational research's credibility gaps? *Issues in Education, 5,* 177–229.

Lortie, D. (1975). *Schoolteacher: A sociological study.* Chicago: University of Chicago Press.

Louden, W. (1991). *Understanding teaching: Continuity and change in teachers' knowledge.* New York: Teachers College Press.

Lucas, C. J. (1997). *Teacher education in America: Reform agendas for the 21st century.* New York: St. Martins Press.

Lundeberg, M. A., Levin, B. A., & Harrington, H. (Eds.). (1999). *Who learns what from cases and how?: The research base for teaching and learning with cases.* Mahwah, NJ: Lawrence Erlbaum.

McDiarmid, G. W. (1990). Challenging prospective teachers' beliefs during early field experience: A quixotic undertaking? *Journal of Teacher Education, 41*(3), 12–20.

McDonald, J. (1992). *Teaching: Making sense of an uncertain craft.* New York: Teachers College Press.

McLaughlin, M., & Talbert, J. E. (1993). *Contexts that matter for teaching and learning: Strategic opportunities for meeting the nation's educational goals.* Stanford, CA: Center for Research on the Context of Secondary School Teaching, Stanford University.

McWilliam, E. (1994). *In broken images: Feminist tales for a different teacher education.* New York: Teachers College Press.

Merseth, K. (1996). Cases and case methods in teacher education. In J. Sikula, T. Buttery, & E. Guyton (Eds.), *Handbook of research on teacher education* (2nd ed., pp. 722–746). New York: Macmillan.

Munby, H., Russell, T., & Martin, A. K. (2001). Teachers knowledge and how it develops. In V. Richardson (Ed.), *Handbook of research on teaching* (4th ed., pp. 877–904). Washington, DC: American Educational Research Association.

Murray, F. B. (1996a). Beyond natural teaching: The case for professional education. In F. B. Murray (Ed.), *The teacher educator's handbook: Building a knowledge base for the preparation of teachers* (pp. 3–13). San Franciso: Jossey-Bass.

Murray, F. B. (1996b). Educational psychology and the teacher's reasoning. In F. B. Murray (Ed.), *The teacher educator's handbook: Building a knowledge base for the preparation of teachers* (pp. 419–437). San Francisco: Jossey-Bass.

Murray, F. B. (Ed.). (1996c). *The teacher educator's handbook: Building a knowledge base for the preparation of teachers.* San Franciso: Jossey-Bass.

Murray, F. B., & Porter, A. (1996). Pathway from the liberal arts curriculum to lessons in the schools. In F. B. Murray (Ed.), *The teacher educator's handbook: Building a knowledge base for the preparation of teachers* (pp. 155–178). San Francisco: Jossey-Bass.

National Board for Professional Teaching Standards. (1990). *Toward high and rigorous standards for the teaching profession: Initial policies and perspectives of the National Board for Professional Teaching Standards* (2nd ed.). Washington, DC: Author.

National Commission on Teaching and America's Future. (1996). *What matters most: Teaching for America's future.* New York: Author.

Nespor, J. (1987). The role of beliefs in the practice of teaching. *Journal of Curriculum Studies, 19*(4), 317–328.

Newell, G. E., Gingrich, R. S., & Johnson, A. B. (2001). Considering the contexts for appropriating theoretical and practical tools for teaching middle and secondary English. *Research in the Teaching of English, 35,* 302–343.

Nuthall, G. (1997). Understanding student thinking and learning in the classroom. In B. J. Biddle, T. L. Good, & I. F. Goodson (Eds.), *International handbook of teachers and teaching* (Vol. 2, pp. 681–768). Dordrecht, The Netherlands: Kluwer.

Pajares, M. F. (1992). Teachers' beliefs and educational research: Cleaning up a messy construct. *Review of Educational Research, 62*(3), 307–322.

Pressley, M., & Roehrig, A. (in press). Educational psychology in the modern era: 1960 to the present. In B. Zimmerman & D. Schunk (Eds.), *Educational psychology: A century of contributions.* Mahwah NJ: Lawrence Erlbaum.

Putnam, R., & Borko, H. (1997). Teacher learning: Implications of new views of cognition. In B. J. Biddle, T. L. Good, & I. F. Goodson (Eds.), *International handbook of teachers and teaching* (Vol. 2, pp. 1223–1296). Dordrecht, The Netherlands: Kluwer.

Putnam, R., & Borko, H. (2000). What do new views of knowledge and thinking have to say about research on teacher learning? *Educational Researcher, 29*(1), 4–15.

Resnick, L. (1991). Shared cognition: Thinking as social practice. In L. B. Resnick, J. M. Levine, & S. D. Teasley (Eds.), *Perspectives on socially shared cognition* (pp. 1–20). Washington, DC: American Psychological Association.

Reynolds, A. (1992). What is competent beginning teaching? A review of the literature. *Review of Educational Research, 62,* 1–35.

Reynolds, M. C. (Ed.). (1989). *Knowledge base for the beginning teacher.* New York: Pergamon.

Richardson, V. (1996). The role of attitudes and beliefs in learning to teach. In J. Sikula, T. Buttery, & E. Gutor (Eds.), *Handbook of research on teacher eduction* (2nd ed., pp. 102–119). New York: Macmillan.

Richardson, V. (Ed.). (1997). *Constructivist teacher education: Building new understandings.* Washington, DC: Falmer.

Richardson, V. (2001). *Handbook of research on teaching* (4th ed.). Washington, DC: American Educational Research Association.

Richardson, V., & Placier, P. (2001). Teacher change. In V. Richardson (Ed.), *Handbook of research on teaching* (4th ed., pp. 905–947). Washington, DC: American Educational Research Association.

Richardson-Koehler, V. (Ed.). (1987). *Educators' handbook: A research perspective.* New York: Longman.

Ross, E. W., Cornett, J. W., & McCutcheon, G. (Eds.). (1992). *Teacher personal theorizing: Connecting curriculum practice, theory, and research.* Albany: State University of New York Press.

Rumelhart, D. E., & Norman, D. (1976). *Accretion, tuning, restructuring: Three modes of learning* (Report No. 7602). La Jolla, CA: La Jolla Center for Human Information Processing.

Sapon-Shevin, M., & Chandler-Olcott, K. (2001). Student cohorts: Communities of critique or dysfunctional families? *Journal of Teacher Education, 52,* 350–364.

Schwab, J. (1964). The structure of disciplines: Meanings and significance. In G. W. Ford & L. Pugno (Eds.), *The structure of knowledge and the curriculum* (pp. 1–30). Chicago: Rand McNally.

Sherin, M. G. (2000). Viewing teaching on videotape. *Educational Leadership, 57*(8), 36–38.

Shulman, J. H., Lotan, R., & Whitcomb, J. A. (1998). *Groupwork in diverse classrooms: A casebook for educators.* New York: Teachers College Press.

Shulman, L. S. (1986a). Paradigms and research programs in the study of teaching: A contemporary perspective. In M. C. Wittrock (Ed.), *Handbook of research on teaching* (3rd ed., pp. 3–36). New York: Macmillan.

Shulman, L. S. (1986b). Those who understand: Knowledge growth in teaching. *Educational Researcher, 15*(2), 4–14.

Shulman, L. S. (1987). Knowledge and teaching: Foundations of the new reform. *Harvard Educational Review, 57*(1), 1–22.

Shulman, L. S. (1988). Disciplines of inquiry in education: An overview. In R. M. Jaeger (Ed.), *Complementary methods for research in education* (pp. 3–17). Washington DC: American Educational Research Association.

Sikula, J., Buttery, T., & Guyton, E. (Eds.). (1996). *Handbook of research on teacher education* (2nd ed.). New York: Macmillan.

Sirotnik, K. A., & Goodlad, J. I. (Eds.). (1988). *School-university partnerships in action: Concepts, cases, and concerns.* New York: Teachers College Press.

Sleeter, C. E. (2001). Epistemological diversity in research on preservice teacher preparation for historically underserved children. *Review of Research in Education, 25,* 209–250.

Stengel, B. S., & Tom, A. R. (1996). Changes and choices in teaching methods. In F. B. Murray (Ed.), *The teacher educator's handbook: Building a knowledge base for the preparation of teachers* (pp. 593–619). San Francisco: Jossey-Bass.

Sykes, G., & Bird, T. (1992). Teacher education and the case idea. *Review of Research in Education, 18,* 457–521.

Tabachnick, B. R., & Zeichner, K. M. (1991). *Issues and practices of inquiry-oriented teacher education.* London: Falmer.

Tharp, R., & Gallimore, R. (1988). *Rousing minds to life: Teaching, learning, and schooling in social context.* Cambridge, England: Cambridge University Press.

Weinstein, C. S. (1989). Teacher education students' preconceptions of teaching. *Journal of Teacher Education, 40*(2), 53–60.

Weinstein, C. S. (1990). Prospective elementary teachers' beliefs about teaching: Implications for teacher education. *Teaching and Teacher Education, 6,* 279–290.

Wideen, M., Mayer-Smith, J., & Moon, B. (1998). A critical analysis of the research on learning to teach: Making the case for an ecological perspective on inquiry. *Review of Educational Research, 68,* 130–178.

Wilcox, S., Schram, P., Lappan, G., & Lanier, P. (1991). *The role of a learning community in changing preservice teachers' knowledge and beliefs about mathematics education* (Research Report No. 91-1). East Lansing, MI: National Center for Research on Teacher Learning, College of Education, Michigan State University.

Wilson, S. M., & Berne, J. (1999). Teacher learning and the acquisition of professional knowledge: An examination of research on contemporary professional development. In A. Iran-Nehad & P. D. Pearson (Eds.), *Review of research in education* (Vol. 24, pp. 173–209). Washington, DC: American Educational Research Association.

Wilson, S. M., Floden, R. E., & Ferrini-Mundy, J. (2001). *Teacher preparation research: Current knowledge, gaps, and recommendations* (Document No. R-01-03). Washington: University of Washington, Center for Study of Teaching and Policy.

Wilson, S. M., Shulman, L. S., & Richert, A. E. (1987). 150 different ways of knowing: Representations of knowledge in teaching. In J. Calderhead (Ed.), *Exploring teachers thinking* (pp. 104–124). London/Philadelphia, PA: Cassell Educational.

Wilson, S. M., & Wineburg, S. (1988). Peering at history through different lenses: The role of disciplinary knowledge in teaching. *Teachers College Record, 89,* 525–539.

Wolf, S. A., Carey, A. A., & Mieras, E. L. (1996). "What is this literachurch stuff anyway?" Preservice teachers' growth in understanding children's literary response. *Reading Research Quarterly, 31*(2), 130–157.

Zeichner, K. (1996). Educating teachers for cultural diversity. In K. Zeichner, S. Melnick, & M. L. Gomez (Eds.), *Currents of reform in preservice teacher education* (pp. 133–175). New York: Teachers College Press.

Zeichner, K. (1999). The new scholarship in teacher education. *Educational Researcher, 28*(9), 4–15.

Zeichner, K., & Gore, J. (1990). Teacher socialization. In W. R. Houston, M. Haberman, & J. Sikula (Eds.), *Handbook of research on teacher education* (pp. 329–348). New York: Macmillan.

Zeichner, K., Melnick, S., & Gomez, M. L. (1996). *Currents of reform in preservice teacher education.* New York: Teachers College Press.

Zeichner, K., & Tabachnick, B. R. (1991). Reflections about reflective teaching. In B. R. Tabachnick & K. Zeichner (Eds.), *Issues and practices in inquiry-oriented teacher education* (pp. 1–21). London: Falmer.

Zeichner, K., Tabachnick, B. R., & Densmore, K. (1987). Individual institutional, and cultural influences on the development of teachers' craft knowledge. In J. Calderhead (Ed.), *Exploring teachers'thinking* (pp. 21–59). London/Philadelphia, PA: Cassell Educational.

CHAPTER 22

Educational/Psychological Intervention Research

JOEL R. LEVIN, ANGELA M. O'DONNELL, AND THOMAS R. KRATOCHWILL

The problems that are faced in experimental design in the social sciences are quite unlike those of the physical sciences. Problems of experimental design have had to be solved in the actual conduct of social-sciences research; now their solutions have to be formalized more efficiently and taught more efficiently. Looking through issues of the *Review of Educational Research* one is struck time and again by the complete failure of the authors to recognize the simplest points about scientific evidence in a statistical field. The fact that 85 percent of National Merit Scholars are first-born is quoted as if it means something, without figures for the over-all population proportion in small families and over-all population proportion that is first-born. One cannot apply anything one learns from descriptive research to the construction of theories or to the improvement of education without having some causal data with which to implement it (Scriven, 1960, p. 426).

In 1999 Joel R. Levin and Angela M. O'Donnell published an article, "What to Do About Educational Research's Credibility Gaps?" in *Issues in Education: Contributions from Educational Psychology,* a professional journal with limited circulation. With the kind permission of Jerry Carlson, editor of *Issues,* major portions of that article have been appropriated to constitute the bulk of the present chapter.

Education research does not provide critical, trustworthy, policy-relevant information about problems of compelling interest to the education public. A recent report of the U.S. Government Accounting Office (GAO, 1997) offers a damning indictment of evaluation research. The report notes that over a 30-year period the nation has invested $31 billion in Head Start and has served over 15 million children. However, the very limited research base available does not permit one to offer compelling evidence that Head Start makes a lasting difference or to discount the view that it has conclusively established its value. There simply are too few high-quality studies available to provide sound policy direction for a hugely important national program. The GAO found only 22 studies out of hundreds conducted that met its standards, noting that many of those rejected failed the basic methodological requirement of establishing compatible comparison groups. No study using a nationally representative sample was found to exist (Sroufe, 1997, p. 27).

Reading the opening two excerpts provides a sobering account of exactly how far the credibility of educational research is perceived to have advanced in two generations. In what follows, we argue for the application of rigorous research methodologies and the criticality of supporting evidence. And, as will be developed throughout this chapter, the notion of evidence—specifically, what we are increasingly seeing as vanishing evidence of evidence—is central to our considerable dismay concerning the present and future plight of educational research, in general, and of research incorporating educational and psychological treatments or interventions, in particular. We maintain that "improving the 'awful reputation' of education research" (Kaestle, 1993; Sroufe, 1997) begins with efforts to enhance the credibility of the research's evidence.

Improving the quality of intervention research in psychology and education has been a primary goal of scholars and researchers throughout the history of these scientific disciplines. Broadly conceived, intervention research is designed to produce *credible* (i.e., believable, dependable; see Levin, 1994) knowledge that can be translated into practices that affect (optimistically, practices that *improve*) the mental health and education of all individuals. Yet beyond this general goal there has always been disagreement about the objectives of intervention research and the methodological and analytic tools that can be counted on to produce credible knowledge. One purpose of this chapter is to review some of the controversies that have befallen psychological and educational intervention research. A second, and the major, purpose of this chapter is to suggest some possibilities for enhancing the credibility of intervention research. At the very least, we hope that our musings will lead the reader to consider some fundamental assumptions of what intervention research currently is and what it can be.

CONTEMPORARY METHODOLOGICAL ISSUES: A BRIEF OVERVIEW

Although there is general consensus among researchers that intervention research is critical to the advancement of knowledge for practice, there is fundamental disagreement about the methodologies used to study questions of interest. These include such issues as the nature of participant selection, differential concerns for internal validity and external validity (Campbell & Stanley, 1966), the desirability or possibility of generalization, the appropriate experimental units, and data-analytic techniques, among others that are discussed later in this chapter.

Evidence-Based Treatments and Interventions

Of the major movements in psychology and education, few have stirred as much excitement or controversy as have recent efforts to produce evidence-based treatments. With its origins in medicine and clinical-trials research, the evidence-based movement spread to clinical psychology (see Chambless & Ollendick, 2001, for a historical overview; Hitt, 2001) and, more recently, to educational and school psychology

(Kratochwill & Stoiber, 2000; Stoiber & Kratochwill, 2000). At the forefront of this movement has been the so-called quantitative/experimental/scientific methodology featured as the primary tool for establishing the knowledge base for treatment techniques and procedures. This methodology has been embraced by the American Psychological Association (APA) Division 12 (Clinical Psychology) Task Force on Evidence-Based Treatments (Weisz & Hawley, 2001). According to the Clinical Psychology Task Force criteria for determination of whether a treatment is evidence based, quantitative group-based and single-participant studies are the only experimental methodologies considered for a determination of credible evidence.

The School Psychology Task Force, sponsored by APA Division 16 and the Society for the Study of School Psychology, has also developed criteria for a review of interventions (see Kratochwill & Stoiber, 2001). In contrast to their clinical psychology colleagues' considerations, those of the School Psychology Task Force differ in at least two fundamental ways. First, the quantitative criteria involve a dimensional rating of various designs, including criteria of their internal validity, statistical conclusion, external validity, and construct validity. Thus, the evidence associated with each dimension is based on a Likert-scale rating and places responsibility on the consumer of the information for weighing and considering the support available for various interventions under consideration. Table 22.1 provides sample rating criteria for group-based interventions from the *Procedural and Coding Manual for Review of Evidence-Based Interventions* (Kratochwill & Stoiber, 2001).

A second feature that distinguishes the School Psychology Task Force considerations from previous evidence-based efforts is the focus on a broad range of methodological strategies to establish evidence for an intervention. In this regard, the School Psychology Task Force has developed criteria for coding qualitative methods in intervention research. At the same time, a premium has been placed on quantitative methodologies as the primary basis for credible evidence for interventions (see Kratochwill & Stoiber, 2000; Kratochwill & Stoiber, in press). The higher status placed on quantitative methods is not shared among all scholars of intervention research methodology and sets the stage for some of the ongoing debate, which is described next.

Quantitative Versus Qualitative Approaches

What accounts for the growing interest in qualitative methodologies? Recently, and partly as a function of the concern for authentic environments and contextual cognition (see Levin & O'Donnell, 1999b, pp. 184–187; and O'Donnell & Levin, 2001, pp. 79–80), there has been a press for alternatives

TABLE 22.1   Selected Examples of School Psychology Task Force Evidence-Based Intervention Criteria

I. General Characteristics
   A. Type of Basis (check all that apply)
      A1. ☐ Empirical basis
      A2. ☐ Theoretical basis
   B. General Design Characteristics
      B1. ☐ Completely randomized design
      B2. ☐ Randomized block design (between-subjects/blocking variation)
      B3. ☐ Randomized block design (within-subjects/repeated measures/multilevel variation)
      B4. ☐ Randomized hierarchical design
      B5. ☐ Nonrandomized design
      B6. ☐ Nonrandomized block design (between-subjects/blocking variation)
      B7. ☐ Nonrandomized design (within-subjects/repeated measures/multilevel variation)
      B8. ☐ Nonrandomized hierarchical design
   C. Statistical Treatment (check all that apply)
      C1. ☐ Appropriate units of analysis
      C2. ☐ Family-wise/experiment-wise error rate controlled
      C3. ☐ Sufficiently large N

II. Key Features for Coding Studies and Rating Level of Evidence/Support
   (3 = Strong Evidence   2 = Promising Evidence   1 = Weak Evidence   0 = No Evidence)
   A. Measurement (check rating and all that apply)   ☐3 ☐2 ☐1 ☐0
      A1. ☐ Use of outcome measures that produce reliable scores for the population under study:
          Reliability =
      A2. ☐ Multimethod
      A3. ☐ Multisource
      A4. ☐ A case for validity has been presented.

   B. ☐ Comparison Group (check rating)   ☐3 ☐2 ☐1 ☐0
      B1. Type of Comparison Group (check all that apply)
          B1.1. ☐ No intervention
          B1.2. ☐ Active Control (attention, placebo, minimal intervention)
          B1.3. ☐ Alternative Treatment
      B2. ☐ Counterbalancing of Change Agents
      B3. ☐ Group Equivalence Established
          B3.1. ☐ Random Assignment
          B3.2. ☐ Statistical Matching (ANCOVA)
          B3.3. ☐ Post hoc test for group equivalence
      B4. ☐ Equivalent Mortality with
          B4.1. ☐ Low Attrition (less than 20% for posttest)
          B4.2. ☐ Low Attrition (less than 30% for follow-up)
          B4.3. ☐ Intent to intervene analysis carried out

  • Key Findings ————
   C. Key Outcomes Statistically Significant (check)   ☐3 ☐2 ☐1 ☐0
      C1. Key Outcomes Statistically Significant (list only those with $p \leq .05$)

          ————————————————

   D. Key Outcomes Educationally or Clinically Significant (check)   ☐3 ☐2 ☐1 ☐0
      D1. Effect Sizes [indicate measure(s) used]

          ————————————————

   E. Durability of Effects (check)   ☐3 ☐2 ☐1 ☐0
      ☐ Weeks
      ☐ Months
      ☐ Years
   F. Identifiable Components (check)   ☐3 ☐2 ☐1 ☐0
   G. Implementation Fidelity (check)   ☐3 ☐2 ☐1 ☐0
      G1. ☐ Evidence of Acceptable Adherence
          G1.1. ☐ Ongoing supervision/consultation
          G1.2. ☐ Coding sessions
          G1.3. ☐ Audio/video tape
      G2. ☐ Manualization
   H. ☐ Replication (check rating and all that apply)   ☐3 ☐2 ☐1 ☐0
      H1. ☐ Same Intervention
      H2. ☐ Same Target Problem
      H3. Relationship Between Evaluator/Researcher and Intervention Program
          ☐ Independent evaluation

Source: Adapted from Kratochwill & Stoiber (2001).

to traditional experimental methodologies in educational research. Concerns for external validity, consideration of the complexity of human behavior, and the emergence of sociocultural theory as part of the theoretical fabric for understanding educational processes have also resulted in the widespread adoption of more qualitative methods. In terms of Krathwohl's (1993) distinctions among description, explanation, and validation (summarized by Jaeger & Bond, 1996, p. 877), the primary goals of educational research, for example, have been to observe and describe complex phenomena (e.g., classroom interactions and behaviors) rather than to manipulate treatments and conduct confirming statistical analyses of the associated outcomes.

For the past 10 years or so, much has been written about differing research methodologies, the contribution of educational research to society, and the proper functions and purposes of scientific research (e.g., Doyle & Carter, 1996; Kaestle, 1993; Labaree, 1998; O'Donnell & Levin, 2001). Some of these disputes have crystallized into the decade-long debate about quantitative and qualitative methodologies and their associated warrants for research outcomes—a debate, we might add, that is currently thriving not just within education but within other academic domains of the social sciences as well (e.g., Azar, 1999; Lipsey & Cordray, 2000). As has been recently pointed out, the terms *qualitative* and *quantitative* are oversimplified, inadequate descriptors of the methodological and data-analytic strategies associated with them (Levin & Robinson, 1999).

The reasons for disagreements between quantitative and qualitative researchers are much more than a debate about the respective methodologies. They are deeply rooted in beliefs about the appropriate *function* of scientific research. Criticism of quantitative methodologies has often gone hand in hand with a dismissal of empiricism. Rejection of qualitative methodologies has often centered on imprecision of measurement, problems with generalizability, and the quality and credibility of evidence. Failures to resolve, or even to address, the issue of the appropriate research function have resulted in a limiting focus in the debate between qualitative and quantitative orientations that trivialize important methodological distinctions and purposes. Unfortunately, the debate has often been ill conceived and unfairly portrayed, with participants not recognizing advances that have been made in both qualitative and quantitative methodologies in the last decade. The availability of alternative methodologies and data-analytic techniques highlights a key issue among researchers regarding the rationale for their work and the associated direction of their research efforts. Wittrock (1994) pointed out the need for a richer variety of

naturalistic qualitative and quantitative methodologies, ranging from case studies and observations to multivariate designs and analyses.

In addition, arguments about appropriate methodology have often been confused with a different argument about the nature of scholarship. Beginning with Ernest Boyer's (1990) book, *Scholarship Reconsidered: Priorities of the Professoriate,* institutions of higher education have sought ways to broaden the concept of scholarship to include work that does not involve generating new knowledge. This debate is often confused with the methodological debate between the respective advocates of qualitative and quantitative approaches, but an important feature of this latter debate is that it focuses on *methods* of knowledge generation (see also Jaeger, 1988).

RESEARCH METHODOLOGY AND THE CONCEPT OF CREDIBLE EVIDENCE

Our purpose here is not to prescribe the tasks, behaviors, or problems that researchers *should* be researching (i.e., the *topics* of psychological and educational-intervention research). Some of these issues have been addressed by various review groups (e.g., National Reading Panel, 2000), as well as by task forces in school and clinical psychology. As Calfee (1992) noted in his reflections on the field of educational psychology, researchers are currently doing quite well in their investigation of issues of both psychological and educational importance. As such, what is needed in the future can be characterized more as refining rather than as redefining the nature of that research. For Calfee, *refining* means relating all research efforts and findings in some way to the process of schooling by "filling gaps in our present endeavors" (p. 165). For us, in contrast, *refining* means enhancing the scientific integrity and evidence credibility of intervention research, regardless of whether that research is conducted inside or outside of schools.

Credible Versus Creditable Intervention Research

We start with the assertion, made by Levin (1994) in regard to educational-intervention research, that a false dichotomy is typically created to distinguish between basic (laboratory-based) and applied (school-based) research. (a) What is the dichotomy? and (b) Why is it false? The answer to the first question addresses the methodological rigor of the research conducted, and which can be related to the concept of internal validity, as reflected in the following prototypical pronouncement: "Applied research (e.g., school-based research) and other real-world investigations are inherently complex and therefore must be methodologically weaker, whereas laboratory research can be more tightly controlled and, therefore, is methodologically stronger."

In many researchers' minds, laboratory-based research connotes "well controlled," whereas school-based research connotes "less well controlled" (see Eisner, 1999, for an example of this perspective). The same sort of prototypical packaging of laboratory versus classroom research is evident in the National Science Foundation's (NSF) 1999 draft guidelines for evaluating research proposals on mathematics and science education (Suter, 1999). As is argued in a later section of this chapter, not one of these stated limitations is critical, or even material, as far as conducting scientifically sound applied research (e.g., classroom-based research) is concerned.

The answer to the second question is that just because different research modes (school-based vs. laboratory-based) have traditionally been associated with different methodological-quality adjectives (weaker vs. stronger, respectively), that is not an inevitable consequence of the differing research venues (see also Levin, 1994; Stanovich, 1998, p. 129). Laboratory-based research can be methodologically weak and school-based research methodologically strong. As such, the methodological rigor of a piece of research dictates directly the credibility (Levin, 1994) of its evidence, or the trustworthiness (Jaeger & Bond, 1996) of the research findings and associated conclusions (see also Kratochwill & Stoiber, 2000). Research credibility should not be confused with the educational or societal importance of the questions being addressed, which has been referred to as the research's creditability (Levin, 1994). In our view (and consistent with Campbell & Stanley's, 1966, sine qua non dictum), scientific credibility should be first and foremost in the educational research equation, particularly when it comes to evaluating the potential of interventions (see also Jaeger & Bond, 1996, pp. 878–883).

With the addition of both substantive creditability and external validity standards (to be specified later) to scientifically credible investigations, one has what we believe to be the ideal manifestation of intervention research. That ideal surely captures Cole's (1997, p. 17) vision for the future of "both useful research and research based on evidence and generalizability of results." For example, two recent empirical investigations addressing the creditable instructional objective of teaching and improving students' writing from fundamentally different credible methodological approaches, one within a carefully controlled laboratory context (Townsend et al., 1993) and the other systematically within the context of actual writing-instructed classrooms (Needels &

Knapp, 1994), serve to punctuate the present points. Several examples of large-scale, scientifically credible research studies with the potential to yield educationally creditable prescriptions are provided later in this chapter in the context of a framework for conceptualizing different stages of intervention research.

Components of CAREful Intervention Research

In our view, credible evidence follows from the conduct of credible research, which in turn follows directly from Campbell and Stanley's (1966) methodological precepts (for a contrasting view, see chapter by McCombs in this volume). The essence of both scientific research and credible research methodology can in turn be reduced to the four components of what Levin (1997b) and Derry, Levin, Osana, Jones, and Peterson (2000) have referred to as *CAREful* intervention research: *C*omparison, *A*gain and again, *R*elationship, and *E*liminate. In particular, it can be argued that evidence linking an intervention to a specified outcome is scientifically convincing if (a) the evidence is based on a *C*omparison that is appropriate (e.g., comparing the intervention with an appropriate alternative or nonintervention condition); (b) the outcome is produced by the intervention *A*gain and again (i.e., it has been "replicated," initially across participants or observations in a single study and ultimately through independently conducted studies); (c) there is a direct *R*elationship (i.e., a connection or correspondence) between the intervention and the outcome; and (d) all other reasonable competing explanations for the outcome can be *E*liminated (typically, through randomization and methodological care). Succinctly stated: If an appropriate *C*omparison reveals *A*gain and again evidence of a direct *R*elationship between an intervention and a specified outcome, while *E*liminating all other competing explanations for the outcome, then the research yields scientifically convincing evidence of the intervention's effectiveness.

As might be inferred from the foregoing discussion, scientifically grounded experiments (including both group-based and single-participant varieties) represent the most commonly accepted vehicle for implementing all four CAREful research components. At the same time, other modes of empirical inquiry, including quasi experiments and correlational studies, as well as surveys, can be shown to incorporate one or more of the CAREful research components. In fact, being attuned to these four components when interpreting one's data is what separates careful researchers from not-so-careful ones, regardless of their preferred general methodological orientations.

THE CONCEPT OF EVIDENCE

Good Evidence Is Hard to Find

If inner-city second graders take piano lessons and receive exercises that engage their spatial ability, will their mathematics skills improve? Yes, according to a newspaper account of a recent research study ("Piano lessons, computer may help math skills," 1999). But maybe no, according to informed consumers of reports of this kind, because one's confidence in such a conclusion critically depends on the quality of the research conducted and the evidence obtained from it. Thus, how can we be confident that whatever math-skill improvements were observed resulted from students' practicing the piano and computer-based spatial exercises, rather than from something else? Indeed, the implied causal explanation is that such practice served to foster the development of certain cognitive and neurological structures in the students, which in turn improved their mathematics skills: "When children learn rhythm, they are learning ratios, fractions and proportions. . . . With the keyboard, students have a clear visual representation of auditory space." (Deseretnews.com, March 15, 1999, p. 1). Causal interpretations are more than implicit in previous research on this topic, as reflected by the authors' outcome interpretations and even their article titles—for example, "Music Training Causes Long-Term Enhancement of Preschool Children's Spatial-Temporal Reasoning" (Rauscher et al., 1997).

In the same newspaper account, however, other researchers offered alternative explanations for the purported improvement of musically and spatially trained students, including the enhanced self-esteem that they may have experienced from such training and the positive expectancy effects communicated from teachers to students. Thus, at least in the newspaper account of the study, the evidence offered to support the preferred cause-and-effect argument is not compelling. Moreover, a review of the primary report of the research (Graziano, Peterson, & Shaw, 1999) reveals that in addition to the potential complicators just mentioned, a number of methodological and statistical concerns seriously compromise the credibility of the study and its conclusions, including nonrandom assignment of either students or classrooms to the different intervention conditions, student attrition throughout the study's 4-month duration, and an inappropriate implementation and analysis of the classroom-based intervention (to be discussed in detail in a later section). The possibility that music instruction combined with training in spatial reasoning improves students' mathematics skill is an intriguing one and one to which we personally resonate. Until better controlled research is conducted and more credible evidence presented, however, the possibility must remain just that—see also Winner and Hetland's (1999) critical comments on this research, as well as the recent empirical studies by Steele, Bass, and Crook (1999) and by Nantais and Schellenberg (1999).

In both our graduate and undergraduate educational psychology courses, we draw heavily from research, argument, and critical thinking concepts presented in three wonderfully wise and well-crafted books, *How to Think Straight about Psychology* (Stanovich, 1998), *Statistics as Principled Argument* (Abelson, 1995), and *Thought and Knowledge: An Introduction to Critical Thinking* (Halpern, 1996). Anyone who has not read these beauties should. And anyone who has read them and applied the principles therein to their own research should more than appreciate the role played by old-fashioned evidence in offering and supporting an argument, whether that argument is in a research context or in an everyday thinking context. In a research context, a major theme of all three books—as well as of the Clinical Psychology and School Psychology Task Forces—is the essentiality of providing solid (our "credible") evidence to support conclusions about causal connections between independent and dependent variables. In terms of our present intervention research context and terminology, before one can attribute an educational outcome to an educational intervention, credible evidence must be provided that rules *in* the intervention as the proximate cause of the observed outcome, while at the same time ruling *out* alternative accounts for the observed outcome.

If all of this sounds too stiff and formal (i.e., too academic), and maybe even too outmoded (Donmoyer, 1993; Mayer, 1993), let us restate it in terms of the down-to-earth advice offered to graduating seniors in a 1998 university commencement address given by Elizabeth Loftus, an expert on eyewitness testimony and then president of the American Psychological Society:

> There's a wonderful cartoon that appeared recently in Parade Magazine. . . . Picture this: mother and little son are sitting at the kitchen table. Apparently mom has just chided son for his excessive curiosity. The boy rises up and barks back, "Curiosity killed what cat? What was it curious about? What color was it? Did it have a name? How old was it?" I particularly like that last question. . . . [M]aybe the cat was very old, and died of old age, and curiosity had nothing to do with it at all. . . . [M]y pick for the one advice morsel is simple: remember to ask the questions that good psychological scientists have learned to ask: "What's the evidence?" and then, "What EXACTLY is the evidence?" (Loftus, 1998, p. 27)

Loftus (1998, p. 3) added that one of the most important gifts of critical thinking is "knowing how to ask the right questions about any claim that someone might try to foist upon you." In that regard, scientific research "is based on a fundamental insight—that the degree to which an idea seems true has nothing to do with whether it is true, and the way to distinguish factual ideas from false ones is to test them by experiment" (Loftus, 1998, p. 3). Similarly, in a recent popular press interview (Uchitelle, 1999), economist Alan Krueger argued for continually challenging conventional wisdom and theory with data: "The strength of a researcher is not in being an advocate, but in making scientific judgments based on the evidence. And empirical research teaches us that nothing is known with certainty" (p. C10). Stanovich (1998), in advancing his fanciful proposition that two "little green men" that reside in the brain control all human functioning, analogizes in relation to other fascinating, though scientifically unsupported, phenomena such as extrasensory perception, biorhythms, psychic surgery, facilitated communication, and so on, that "one of the most difficult things in the world [is to] confront a strongly held belief with contradictory evidence" (p. 29).

That intervention researchers are also prone to prolonged states of "evidencelessness" has been acknowledged for some time, as indicated in the following 40-year-old observation:

> A great revolution in social science has been taking place, particularly throughout the last decade or two. Many educational researchers are inadequately trained either to recognize it or to implement it. It is the revolution in the concept of evidence. (Scriven, 1960, p. 426)

We contend that the revolution referred to by Scriven has not produced a corresponding revelation in the field of intervention research even (or especially) today. Consider, for example, the recent thoughts of the mathematics educator Thomas Romberg (1992) on the matter:

> The importance of having quality evidence cannot be overemphasized. . . . The primary role of researchers is to provide reliability evidence to back up claims. Too many people are inclined to accept any evidence or statements that are first presented to them urgently, clearly, and repeatedly. . . . A researcher tries to be one whose claims of knowing go beyond a mere opinion, guess, or flight of fancy, to responsible claims with sufficient grounds for affirmation. . . . Unfortunately, as any journal editor can testify, there are too many research studies in education in which either the validity or the reliability of the evidence is questionable. (Romberg, 1992, pp. 58–59)

In the pages that follow, we hope to provide evidence to support Scriven's (1960) and Romberg's (1992) assertions about the noticeable lacks of evidence in contemporary intervention research.

The Evidence of Intervention Research

The ESP Model

Lamentably, in much intervention research today, rather than subscribing to the scientific method's principles of theory, hypothesis-prediction, systematic manipulation, observation, analysis, and interpretation, more and more investigators are subscribing to what might be dubbed the ESP principles of *E*xamine, *S*elect, and *P*rescribe. For example, a researcher may decide to *examine* a reading intervention. The researcher may not have well-defined notions about the specific external (instructional) and internal (psychological) processes involved or about how they may contribute to a student's performance. Based on his or her (typically, unsystematic) observations, the researcher *selects* certain instances of certain behaviors of certain students for (typically, in-depth) scrutiny. The researcher then goes on to *prescribe* certain instructional procedures, materials and methods, or small-group instructional strategies that follow from the scrutiny.

We have no problem with the *examine* phase of such research, and possibly not even with the *select* phase of it, insofar as all data collection and observation involve selection of one kind or another. We do, however, have a problem if this type of research is not properly regarded for what it is: namely, preliminary-exploratory, observational hypothesis generating. Certainly in the early stages of inquiry into a research topic, one has to look before one can leap into designing interventions, making predictions, or testing hypotheses. To demonstrate the *possibility* of relationships among variables, one might also select examples of consistent cases. Doing so, however, (a) does not comprise sufficient evidence to document the existence of a relationship (see, e.g., Derry et al., 2000) and (b) can result in unjustified interpretations of the kind that Brown (1992, pp. 162–163) attributed to Bartlett (1932) in his classic study of misremembering. With regard to the perils of case selection in classroom-intervention research, Brown (1992) properly noted that

> there is a tendency to romanticize research of this nature and rest claims of success on a few engaging anecdotes or particularly exciting transcripts. One of the major methodological problems is to establish means of conveying not only the selective and not necessarily representative, but also the more important general, reliable, and repeatable. (p. 173)

In the ESP model, departure from the researcher's originally intended purposes of the work (i.e., examining a particular instance or situation) is often forgotten, and prescriptions for practice are made with the same degree of excitement and conviction as are those based on investigations with credible, robust evidence. The unacceptability of the prescribe phase of the ESP research model goes without saying: Neither variable relationships nor instructional recommendations logically follow from its application. The widespread use of ESP methodology in intervention research and especially in education was appropriately admonished 35 years ago by Carl Bereiter in his compelling case for more empirical studies of the "strong inference" variety (Platt, 1964) in our field:

> Why has the empirical research that has been done amounted to so little? One reason . . . is that most of it has been merely descriptive in nature. It has been a sort of glorified "people-watching," concerned with quantifying the characteristics of this or that species of educational bird. . . . [T]he yield from this kind of research gets lower year by year in spite of the fact that the amount of research increases. (Bereiter, 1965, p. 96)

Although the research names have changed, the problems identified by Bereiter remain, and ESP methodology based on modern constructs flourishes.

The Art of Intervention Research: Examples From Education

If many intervention research interpretations and prescriptions are not based on evidence, then on what are they based? On existing beliefs? On opinion? Any semblance of a model of research yielding credible evidence has degenerated into a mode of research that yields everything but. We submit as a striking example the 1993 American Education Research Association (AERA) meeting in Atlanta, Georgia. At this meeting of the premier research organization of our educators, the most promising new developments in educational research were being showcased. Robert Donmoyer, the meeting organizer, wanted to alert the world to the nature of those groundbreaking research developments in his final preconference column in the *Educational Researcher* (the most widely distributed research-and-news publication of AERA):

> Probably the most radical departures from the status quo can be found in sessions directly addressing this year's theme, *The Art and Science of Educational Research and Practice*. In some of these sessions, the notion of art is much more than a metaphor. [One session], for example, features a theater piece constructed from students' journal responses to feminist theory; [another] session uses movement and dance to represent gender relationships in educational discourse; and [another] session features a

demonstration—complete with a violin and piano performance—of the results of a mathematician and an educator's interdisciplinary explorations of how music could be used to teach mathematics. (Donmoyer, 1993, p. 41)

Such sessions may be entertaining or engaging, but are they presenting what individuals attending a conference of a professional *research* organization came to hear? The next year, in a session at the 1994 AERA annual meeting in New Orleans, two researchers were displaying their wares in a joint presentation: Researcher A read a poem about Researcher B engaged in a professional activity; Researcher B displayed a painting of Researcher A similarly engaged. (The details presented here are intentionally sketchy to preserve anonymity.) Artistic? Yes, but is it research? Imagine the following dialogue: "Should the Food and Drug Administration approve the new experimental drug for national distribution?" "Definitely! Its effectiveness has been documented in a poem by one satisfied consumer and in a painting by another."

These perceptions of a scientific backlash within the research community may pertain not just to scientifically based research, but to science itself. In their book *The Flight From Science and Reason,* Gross, Levitt, and Lewis (1997) included 42 essays on the erosion of valuing rationalism in society. Among the topics addressed in these essays are the attacks on physics, medicine, the influence of the arguments against objectivity in the humanities, and questions about the scientific basis of the social sciences. Thus, the rejection of scientifically based knowledge in education is part of a larger societal concern. Some 30 years after making his case for strong-inference research in education (Bereiter, 1965), Carl Bereiter (1994) wrote the following in a critique of the current wave of postmodernism thought among researchers and educators alike:

> This demotion of science to a mere cognitive style might be dismissed as a silly notion with little likelihood of impact on mainstream educational thought, but I have begun to note the following milder symptoms in otherwise thoroughly mainstream science educators: reluctance to call anything a fact; avoidance of the term *misconception* (which only a few years ago was a favorite word for some of the same people); considerable agonizing over teaching the scientific method and over what might conceivably take its place; and a tendency to preface the word *science* with *Eurocentric,* especially among graduate students. (Bereiter, 1994, p. 3)

What is going on here? Is it any wonder that scholars from other disciplines, politicians, and just plain folks are looking at educational research askew?

Labaree (1998) clearly recognized the issue of concern:

Unfortunately, the newly relaxed philosophical position toward the softness of educational knowledge . . . can (and frequently does) lead to rather cavalier attitudes by educational researchers toward [a lack of] methodological rigor in their work. As confirmation, all one has to do is read a cross-section of dissertations in the field or of papers presented at educational conferences. For many educational researchers, apparently, the successful attack on the validity of the hard sciences in recent years has led to the position that softness is not a problem to be dealt with but a virtue to be celebrated. Frequently, the result is that qualitative methods are treated less as a cluster of alternative methodologies than as a license to say what one wants without regard to rules of evidence or forms of validation. (Labaree, 1998, p. 11)

In addition to our having witnessed an explosion of presentations of the ESP, anecdotal, and opinion variety at the "nouveau research" AERA conferences (including presentations that propose and prescribe instructional interventions), we can see those modes of inquiry increasingly being welcomed into the academic educational research community—and even into journals that include "research" as part of their title:

When I first began presiding over the manuscript review process for *Educational Researcher,* for example, I received an essay from a teacher reflecting on her practice. My initial impulse was to reject the piece without review because the literary genre of the personal essay in general and personal essays by teachers in particular are not normally published in research journals. I quickly reconsidered this decision, however, and sent the paper to four reviewers with a special cover letter that said, among other things: ". . . *The Educational Researcher* has published pieces *about* practitioner narratives; it makes sense, therefore, to consider publishing narrative work . . . I will not cavalierly reject practitioners' narratives and reflective essays." . . . [I]n my cover letter, I did not explicitly invite reviewers to challenge my judgment (implicit in my decision to send work of this kind out for review) that the kind of work the manuscript represented—if it is of high quality—merits publication in a research journal. In fact, my cover letter suggested this issue had already been decided. (Donmoyer, 1996, pp. 22–23)

We do not disregard the potential value of a teacher's reflection on experience. But is it research? On what type of research-based evidence is it based? We can anticipate the reader dismissing Donmoyer's (1996) comments by arguing that the *Educational Researcher* is not *really* a scholarly research journal, at least not exclusively so. It does, after all, also serve a newsletter function for AERA. In fact, in the organization's formative years (i.e., in the 1940s, 1950s, and 1960s) it used to be just that, a newsletter. Yet, in Donmoyer's editorial, he was referring to the Features section, a research-based section of the *Educational Researcher,* and he clearly regarded the contents of that section, along with the manuscripts suitable for it, in scholarly research terms. What *is not* research may soon be difficult, if not impossible, to define. In the 1999 AERA meeting session on research training, there was no clear definition of what research *is.*

Additional Forms of Contemporary Intervention Research Evidence

In this section we single out for critical examination three other methods of empirical inquiry, along with their resulting forms of evidence, which are thriving in psychological and educational intervention research today. These are the case study, the demonstration study, and the design experiment.

The Case Study

Case study research—consisting of the intensive (typically longitudinal) study and documentation of an individual's "problem" of interest, along with the (typically unsystematic) introduction of various intervention agents designed to address the problem—is not a new methodology in psychology and education. Examples can be observed throughout the history of these disciplines. Although limitations of the case study have been known for some time (see Kazdin, 1981; Kratochwill, 1985), it continues to flourish in intervention research. It is not the use of case study research that is problematic, but rather the claims and generalizations for practice that result from this methodology. An illustration of its application in research on treatment of children's disorders will alert the reader to case study concerns.

Considerable research has been conducted focusing on the treatment of posttraumatic stress disorder (PTSD) in adults, but treatment of children has not been as extensive. Nevertheless, children are very likely to experience PTSD; the disorder can be diagnosed in young children and needs to be treated. Although several treatments might be considered, eye movement desensitization and reprocessing (EMDR) therapy (Cocco & Sharp, 1993) seems to be getting increased attention as a particularly effective treatment for stress-related problems in children (see Greenwald, 1999). But does EMDR qualify as an evidence-based treatment of PTSD in children? In a recent review of research in that area (Saigh, in press), only one study could be found that offered empirical support for this form of therapy.

EMDR typically involves asking the person to imagine a traumatic experience while at the same time visually tracking

TABLE 22.2   Levels of Inference Generally Associated With Various Research Methodology and Outcome Features

Characteristics	Low Inference	High Inference
Types of data	Subjective data	Objective data
Assessment occasions	Single point measurement	Repeated measurement
Planned vs. ex post facto	Ex post facto	Planned
Projections of performance	Acute problem	Chronic problem
Effect size	Small	Large
Effect impact	Delayed	Immediate
Number of participants	$N = 1$	$N > 1$
Heterogeneity of participants	Homogeneous	Heterogeneous
Standardization of treatment	Nonstandardized treatment	Standardized treatment
Integrity of treatment	No monitoring	Repeated monitoring
Impact of treatment	Impact on single measure	Impact on multiple measures
Generalization and follow-up assessment	No formal measures	Formal measures

the finger movements of the psychologist. While this activity is going on, the child may be instructed to state negative and positive statements about him- or herself, with an emphasis on coping. In a case study in this area, Cocco and Sharpe (1993) used a variant of EMDR through an auditory procedure for treatment of a 4-year, 9-month-old child who was assaulted. Following the assault, the child was reported to experience nightmares, bed-wetting, carrying a toy gun, and sleeping in his parents' bed. During the therapy the child was told to imagine the event and track the therapist's finger movements. In addition, the child was asked to draw a picture of the assailants and a picture of a superhero for the treatment sessions. An auditory procedure was used in which the therapist clicked his finger at the rate of 4 clicks per second for 12 s. At the same time, the child was asked to look at the picture he had drawn and then to verbalize what the hero was doing to the assailants as the therapist clicked his fingers. It was reported that the child stabbed the picture while verbalizing that he was killing the assailants. The treatment was considered successful in that the child no longer experienced nightmares, no longer wet his bed, and did not need to sleep with his parents or carry a toy gun. At a six-month follow-up, however, the child was reported to wet the bed and sleep in his parents' bed.

What can be concluded from this case study? In our opinion, very little, if anything. In fact, the desperate clinician looking for an effective treatment might be misled into assuming that EMDR is an effective procedure for this childhood disorder when, in fact, more tightly controlled and replicated (i.e., CAREful) research would suggest effective alternatives. Among the variety of treatment procedures available for children experiencing PTSD, behavior-therapy techniques have emerged as among the most successful, based on clinical research (Saigh, Yasik, Oberfield, & Inamdar, 1999). In particular, flooding therapy, a procedure investi-

gated in a series of controlled single-participant research studies with replication of findings across independent participants (e.g., Saigh, 1987a, 1987b, 1987c, 1989), has emerged as an effective treatment for this serious disorder.

Again, our negative view of case studies is related to the generalizations that are often made for practice. Within a proper context, case-study research may be useful in generating hypotheses for future well-controlled investigations (Kratochwill, Mott, & Dodson, 1984). Moreover, not all case studies are alike on methodological dimensions, and the researcher using these methods has available options for improving the inference that can be drawn from such studies. Table 22.2 shows some of the methodological features that suggest levels of inference (varying from high to low) that can be applied to both design of case studies and interpretation of data from these investigations (see also Kazdin, 1998). Nevertheless, case studies fall into the "demonstration study" category (to be discussed next) and differ from another often-confused "single case" design, the systematically implemented and controlled single-participant study, in which replication and (in many instances) intervention randomization are central features (see Kratochwill & Levin, 1992).

The Demonstration Study

Two ubiquitous examples of demonstration studies in educational contexts include (a) an instructional intervention that is introduced within a particular classroom (with or without a nonintervention comparison classroom) and (b) an out-of-classroom special intervention program that is provided to a selected group of students. The critical issue here (which will be revisited shortly) is that with only one classroom receiving special instruction or only one group participating in a special program, it is not possible to separate the effects of the intervention or the program from the specific implementation of it.

Levin and Levin (1993) discussed interpretive concerns associated with the evidence derived from a demonstration study in the context of evaluating the outcomes of an academic retention program. They are encompassed in three CAREful-component questions rolled into one: Was the program effective? With an emphasis on "effective," one can ask, "Relative to what?" for in many program evaluation studies frequently lacking is an appropriate Comparison (either with comparable nonprogram students or with participants' pre-program data). With an emphasis on "the," one can ask, "Do you mean *this* single implementation of the program?" for generalization to other program cohorts or sites is not possible without an Again and again replication component. Finally, with an emphasis on "program," one can ask, "Can other, non-program-related, factors account for the observed outcomes?" for without program randomization and control, one cannot readily Eliminate other potential contributors to the effects. Levin, Levin, and Scalia's (1997) report of a college retention program for academically at-risk minority students provides an example of a demonstration study. Like our previous case study example, because of the uncontrolled nature of the study and the one-time implementation of the program, any of the documented positive outcomes associated with program participants cannot be regarded as either scientifically credible or generalizable to other implementations of the program. In that sense, then, and as Levin et al. (1997, pp. 86–87) pointed out, a report of their particular program and its outcomes can indicate only what happened under a unique and favorable set of circumstances. It clearly is not an indication of what to expect if a similar program were to be implemented by others with other college students elsewhere.

The Design Experiment

Also considered here is the classroom-based design experiment, originally popularized by Collins (1992) and by Brown (1992) and welcomed into the educational research community by Salomon (1995, p. 107) and by various research-funding agencies (e.g., Suter, 1999). In design experiments research is conducted in authentic contexts (e.g., in actual classrooms, in collaboration with teachers and other school personnel), and the experiment is not fixed in the traditional sense; rather, instructional-design modifications are made as desired or needed.

On closer inspection, one discovers that from a strict terminological standpoint, design experiments neither have a design nor are experiments. In particular, in conventional research usage, *design* refers to a set of pre-experimental plans concerning the specific conditions, methods, and materials to

be incorporated in the study. In a design experiment, however, any components may be altered by the researcher or teacher as the investigation unfolds, as part of "flexible design revision" (Collins, 1992): "It may often be the case that the teacher or researchers feel a particular design is not working early in the school year. It is important to analyze why it is not working and take steps to fix whatever appears to be the reason for failure" (p. 18).

Similarly, in conventional research terminology, *experiment* refers to situations in which participants are randomly assigned to the two or more systematically manipulated and controlled conditions of a study (e.g., Campbell & Stanley, 1966). In a design experiment, however (and as will be expanded upon shortly), appropriate randomization and control are conspicuously absent, which, in turn, does not permit a credible attribution of outcomes to the intervention procedures under investigation. Take, for example, Collins's (1992) description of a hypothetical design experiment (with numbers in square brackets added for identification in the subsequent paragraph):

> Our first step would be to observe a number of teachers, and to choose two who are interested in trying out technology to teach students about the seasons, and who are comparably effective [1], but use different styles of teaching: for example, one might work with activity centers in the classroom and the other with the entire class at one time [2]. Ideally, the teachers should have comparable populations of students [3]. . . . Assuming both teachers teach a number of classes, we would ask each to teach half her classes using the design we have developed [4]. In the other classes, we would help the teacher design her own unit on the seasons using these various technologies [5], one that is carefully crafted to fit with her normal teaching style [6]. (Collins, 1992, p. 19).

From this description, it can be seen that in a design experiment there are numerous plausible alternative explanations for the observed outcomes that compete with the intervention manipulation of interest. Consider the following components of Collins' hypothetical study:

Regarding [1], how can "comparably effective" teachers be identified, let alone defined? In [2], teachers differing in "teaching style" differ in countless other ways as well; one, for example, might have brown hair and the other gray, which could actually be an age or years-of-experience proxy. Regarding [3], again, how are student populations "comparable," and how are they defined to be so? For [4] through [6], assuming that the two teachers could both teach their respective classes in precisely the prescribed manner (a tall assumption for a within-teacher instructional manipulation of this kind) and that individualized teacher-style "crafting" could be accomplished (another tall assumption), any result of such a study would represent a confounding of the intervention manipulation and specific teacher characteristics (as alluded to in [2]), so nothing would be learned about the effects of the instructional manipulations per se. Even worse, in the rest of Collins's (1992, p. 19) example, the described instructional manipulation contains no less than *seven* sequentially introduced technology components. Consequently, even if teacher effects could be eliminated or accounted for, one would still have no idea what it was about the intervention manipulation that produced any outcome differences. Was it, for example, that students became more engaged by working on the computer, more attuned to measurement and data properties and accuracy by collecting information and entering it into a spreadsheet, more self-confident by interacting with students from other locations, more proficient writers through book production, and so on? There is no way of telling, and telling is something that a researcher-as-intervention-prescriber should want, and be able, to do.

The design experiment certainly has its pros and cons. Those who regard intervention research's sole purpose as improving practice also often regard research conducted in laboratory settings as decontextualized and irrelevant to natural contexts (see Kazdin, 1998). In contrast, the design experiment is, by definition, classroom based and classroom targeted. On the other side of the ledger, design experiments can be criticized on methodological grounds, as well as on the basis of design experimenters' potential to subordinate valuable classroom-instructional time to the (typically lengthy and incompletely defined) research agenda on the table. In our view, design experiments can play an informative role in preliminary stages of intervention research as long as the design experimenter remembers that the research was designed to be "preliminary" when reporting and speculating about a given study's findings. For a true personal anecdote of how researchers sometimes take studies of this kind and attempt to sneak them "through the back door" (Stanovich, 1999) into credible-research journals, see Levin and O'Donnell (2000).

In fact, design experiments and other informal classroom-based studies are incorporated into the model of intervention research that we propose in a later section. On a related note, we heartily endorse Brown's (1992, pp. 153–154) research strategy of ping-ponging back and forth between classroom-based investigations and controlled laboratory experiments as a "cross-fertilization between settings" (p. 153) for developing and refining contextually valid instructional theories (see also Kratochwill & Stoiber, 2000, for a similar view of research in school psychology). The reader must again be reminded, however, that scientifically credible operations (chiefly, randomization and control) are not an integral part of a design experiment, at least not as Collins (1992) and Brown (1992) have conceptualized it.

Summary

For much intervention research as it is increasingly being practiced today, we are witnessing a movement away from CAREful research principles, and even away from preliminary research models principally couched in selected observations and questionable prescriptions. Rejection of the scientific method and quantitative assessment may be leading to inadequate graduate training in rigorous research skills that are valued by many academic institutions and funding agencies. At the same time, it should not be forgotten that even qualitatively oriented researchers are capable of engaging in mindless mining of their data as well. Vanessa Siddle Walker (1999) recently distinguished between data and *good* data, which, in our current terminology, translates as, "Not all evidence is equally credible."

Just as in other fields informed by bona fide empirical inquiry, in psychology and education we must be vigilant in dismissing "fantasy, unfounded opinion, 'common sense,' commercial advertising claims, the advice of 'gurus,' testimonials, and wishful thinking in [our] search for the truth" (Stanovich, 1998, p. 206). Case studies, demonstration studies, and design experiments have their place in the developmental stages of intervention research, as long as the researchers view such efforts as preliminary and adopt a prescription-withholding stance when reporting the associated outcomes. We cannot imagine, for example, well-informed researchers and consumers taking seriously instructional prescriptions from someone who proudly proclaims: "Let me tell you about the design experiment that I just conducted. . . ."

In the next section we offer some additional reflections on the character of contemporary intervention research. In so doing, we provide suggestions for enhancing the scientific integrity of intervention research training and the conduct of intervention research.

ENHANCING THE CREDIBILITY OF INTERVENTION RESEARCH

Psychological/Educational Research Versus Medical Research

Very high standards have been invoked for intervention outcome research in medicine. The evidence-based intervention movement was initiated in medical research in the United Kingdom and embraced more recently by clinical psychology

(Chambless & Ollendick, 2001). An editorial in the *New England Journal of Medicine* spelled out in very clear and certain terms the unacceptability of admitting anecdotes, personal testimony, and uncontrolled observations when evaluating the effectiveness of a new drug or medical treatment:

> If, for example, the Journal were to receive a paper describing a patient's recovery from cancer of the pancreas after he had ingested a rhubarb diet, we would require documentation of the disease and its extent, we would ask about other, similar patients who did not recover after eating rhubarb, and we might suggest trying the diet on other patients. If the answers to these and other questions were satisfactory, we might publish a case report—not to announce a remedy, but only to suggest a hypothesis that should be tested in a proper clinical trial. In contrast, anecdotes about alternative remedies (usually published in books and magazines for the public) have no such documentation and are considered sufficient in themselves as support for therapeutic claims. Alternative medicine also distinguishes itself by an ideology that largely ignores biologic mechanisms, often disparages modern science, and relies on what are purported to be ancient practices and natural remedies. . . . [H]ealing methods such as homeopathy and therapeutic touch are fervently promoted despite not only the lack of good clinical evidence of effectiveness, but the presence of a rationale that violates fundamental scientific laws—surely a circumstance that requires more, rather than less, evidence. (Angell & Kassirer, 1998, p. 839)

Angell and Kassirer (1998) called for scientifically based evidence, not intuition, superstition, belief, or opinion. Many would argue that psychological research and educational intervention research are not medical research and that the former represents an inappropriate analog model for the latter. We disagree. Both medical research and psychological/educational research involve interventions in complex systems in which it is difficult to map out causal relationships. Reread the Angell and Kassirer (1998) excerpt, for example, substituting such words as "child" or "student" for "patient," "amelioration of a conduct disorder or reading disability" for "recovery from cancer of the pancreas," "ingested a rhubarb diet" for "ingested a rhubarb diet," and so on. Just as medical research seeks prescriptions, so does psychological and educational research; and prescription seeking should be accompanied by scientifically credible evidence to support those prescriptions (see, e.g., the recent report of the National Research Council, 2001). Furthermore, as former AERA president Michael Scriven poignantly queried in his contemplation of the future of educational research, "Why is [scientifically credible methodology] good enough for medical research but not good enough for educational research? Is aspirin no longer working?" (Scriven, 1997, p. 21).

Moreover, the kinds of researchable questions, issues, and concerns being addressed in the medical and psychological/educational domains are clearly analogous: Is one medical (educational) treatment better than another? Just as aspirin may have different benefits or risks for different consumers, so may an instructional treatment. And just as new medical research evidence may prove conventional wisdom or traditional treatments incorrect (e.g., Hooper, 1999), the same is true of educational research evidence (e.g., U.S. Department of Education, 1986; Wong, 1995). Citing the absence, to date, of research breakthroughs in psychology and education (in contrast to those that can be enumerated in medicine) is, in our view, insufficient cause to reject the analogy out of hand.

It is possible that many people's initial rejection of the medical model of research as an apt analogue for psychological/educational research results from their incomplete understanding of what constitutes medical research. In the development of new drugs, clinical trials with humans proceed through three phases (NIH, 1998). In Phase I clinical trials research is conducted to determine the best delivery methods and safe dosage levels (including an examination of unwanted side effects) of a drug. Phase II clinical trials address the question of whether the drug produces a desired effect. Phase III trials compare the effects of the new drug against the existing standards in the context of carefully controlled randomized experiments. Thus, although medical research includes various forms of empirical inquiry, it culminates in a randomized comparison of the new drug with one or more alternatives to determine if, in fact, something new or better is being accomplished (see, e.g., the criteria from the Clinical Psychology Task Force for a similar view). A recent example of this work is the evaluation of the effects of Prozac on depression in comparison to other antidepressants. The phases of clinical trials described here roughly parallel the stages in the model of educational research that we now propose.

A Stage Model of Educational/Psychological Intervention Research

Our vision of how to close one of intervention research's undamental credibility gaps, while at the same time better informing practice, is presented in Figure 22.1's stage model of educational/psychological intervention research. In contrast to currently popular modes of intervention-research inquiry and reporting, the present conceptualization (a) makes explicit different research stages, each of which is associated with its own assumptions, purposes, methodologies, and standards of evidence; (b) concerns itself with research credibility through high standards of internal validity; (c) concerns itself with research creditability through high standards of external validity and educational/societal importance; and, most significantly, (d) includes a critical stage that has heretofore been missing in the vast majority of intervention research, namely, a randomized classroom trials link (modeled after the clinical trials stage of medical research) between the initial development and limited testing of the intervention and the prescription and implementation of it. Alternatively, Stage 3 could be referred to as an instructional trials stage or, more generically, as an educational trials stage. To simplify matters, for the remainder of the chapter we continue to refer to Stage 3 as the randomized classroom trials stage of credible intervention research studies.

Stages 1 and 2 of the Figure 22.1 model are likely very familiar to readers of this chapter, as studies in those traditions comprise the vast majority of intervention research as we know it. In addition, throughout the chapter we have provided details of the two Stage 2 components of the model in our consideration of the research-first (controlled laboratory experiments) versus practice-first (case studies, demonstrations, and design experiments) perspectives. Both controlled

laboratory experiments and applied studies are preliminary, though in different complementary senses. The former are preliminary in that their careful scrutiny of interventions lacks an applied-implementation component, whereas the latter are preliminary in that their intervention prescriptions are often not founded on scientifically credible evidence. Stage 1 and Stage 2 studies are crucial to developing an understanding of the phenomena that inform practice (Stage 4) but that first must be rigorously, complexly, and intelligently evaluated in Stage 3. Failure to consider possibilities beyond Stages 1 and 2 may result in a purposelessness to research, a temptation never to go beyond understanding a phenomenon and determining whether it is a stable phenomenon with genuine practice implications. The accumulation of applied, scientifically credible evidence is precisely the function of the randomized classroom trials stage (Stage 3, highlighted in Figure 22.1) of the model. As in medical research, this process consists of an examination of the proposed treatment or intervention under realistic, yet carefully controlled, conditions (e.g., Angell & Kassirer, 1998).

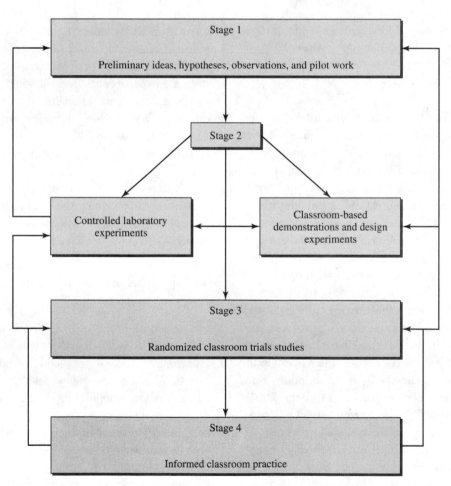

Figure 22.1   Stage Model of Educational/Psychological Intervention Research.   *Source:* From Levin & O'Donnell (1999).

"Realistic conditions" refer to the specific populations and contexts about which one wishes to offer conclusions regarding treatment efficacy (i.e., external validity desiderata). In medical research the conditions of interest generally include humans (rather than animals), whereas in psychological and educational research the conditions of interest generally include children in community settings and school classrooms (rather than isolated individuals). In addition, in both medical and psychological/educational contexts, the interventions (e.g., drugs or instructional methods, respectively) must be administered in the appropriate fashion (dosage levels or instructional integrity, respectively) for a long enough duration for them to have effect and to permit the assessment of both the desired outcome (e.g., an improved physical or social-academic condition, respectively) and any unwanted side effects (adverse physical, cognitive, affective, or behavioral consequences). In a classroom situation, an appropriately implemented instructional intervention of at least one semester, or even one year, in duration would be expected to satisfy the "long enough" criterion.

"Carefully controlled conditions" refer to internally valid experiments based on the random assignment of multiple independent "units" to alternative treatment-intervention conditions. Again, in medical research the randomized independent units are typically humans, whereas in educational intervention research the randomized independent units are frequently groups, classrooms, or schools (Levin, 1992, 1994). As with medical research, careful control additionally involves design safeguards to help rule out contributors to the effects other than the targeted intervention, such as including appropriate alternative interventions, incorporating blind and double-blind intervention implementations (to the extent possible) so that child, teacher, therapist, and researcher biases are eliminated, and being responsive to all other potential sources of experimental internal invalidity (Campbell & Stanley, 1966; Shadish, Cook, & Campbell, 2002).

The randomized classroom trials stage of this model is sensitive to each of the earlier indicated CAREful research components, in that (a) the inclusion of alternative interventions (including appropriately packaged standard methods or placebos) permits meaningful Comparison when assessing the effects of the targeted intervention; (b) the use of multiple independent units (both within a single study and, ideally, as subsequent replication studies) permits generalization through the specified outcomes being produced Again and again; and (c) with across-unit randomization of interventions (and assuming adequate control and appropriate implementation of them), whatever Relationship is found between the targeted intervention and the specified outcomes can be traced directly to the intervention because (d) with

such randomization, control, and implementation, one is better able to Eliminate all other potential explanations for the outcomes.

The randomized classroom trials stage of our proposed model possesses a number of critical features that are worth mentioning. These features represent the best of what CAREfully controlled and well-executed laboratory-based research has to offer applied and clinical research. First and foremost here is the inclusion of multiple units (or in single-participant research designs, multiple phases and within-phase observations per unit; see, e.g., Kratochwill & Levin, 1992) that are randomly assigned to receive either the targeted intervention or an acceptable alternative. For example, when classrooms are the units of analysis, the use of multiple independent classrooms is imperative for combating evidence-credibility concerns arising from both methodological and statistical features of the research. Each of these will be briefly considered here (for additional discussion, see Campbell & Boruch, 1975; Levin, 1985, 1992, 1994; Levin & Levin, 1993).

Methodological Rigor

Consider some examples from educational research to contextualize our perspectives on methodological rigor. In a typical instructional intervention study, the participants in one classroom receive new instructional methods or materials (including combinations of these, multicomponent versions, and systemic curricular innovations), whereas those in another classroom receive either alternative or standard instructional methods/materials/curricula. One does not have to look very hard to find examples of this type of study in the intervention research literature, as it is pervasive. The aforementioned Graziano et al. (1999) training study is an example of this methodological genre. The problem with such studies is that any resultant claims about intervention-produced outcomes are not credible because whatever effects are observed can be plausibly attributed to a myriad of other factors not at all connected with the intervention. In studies where there is only one classroom/teacher per intervention, for example, any potential intervention effects are inextricably confounded with classroom/teacher differences—even if "equivalence" can be demonstrated on a pretest. If students are not randomly assigned to classrooms and classrooms to interventions, intervention effects are confounded with selection biases as well. Indeed, as far as credible evidence is concerned, a reasonable case can be made that a "one classroom per intervention" study is just that—an individual case. Accordingly, one-classroom-per-intervention cases fall into our earlier discussion of intervention research that in actuality is a classroom-based demonstration.

With the addition of sequential modifications of the instructional intervention, the previously discussed design experiment also resembles the one-classroom-per-intervention prototype. Minor variations of that prototype include assigning a couple classrooms to each intervention condition (e.g., Brown, 1992) or having one or a few teachers alternately implement both interventions in a few classrooms (e.g., Collins, 1992). Unfortunately, methodological and statistical concerns (related to nonrandomization; contaminating teacher, student, classroom, and researcher effects; and inappropriate units of analysis, among others), analogous to the ones raised here, are associated with such variations as well. Recent methodological and statistical developments out of the behavior-analytic and clinical research traditions do, however, have the potential to enhance the scientific credibility of the one-or-few-classrooms-per-intervention study (e.g., Koehler & Levin, 1998; Kratochwill & Levin, 1992; Levin & Wampold, 1999) and, therefore, should be given strong consideration in classroom-based and other intervention studies.

Unfortunately, adding the sequential intervention-modification strategy of design experiments serves only to add confounding variables to the interpretive mix. Although some may regard confounding the effect of an intervention with other variables to be acceptable in a design experiment—"Our interventions are deliberately designed to be multiply confounded" (Brown, 1992, p. 167)—confoundings of the kind described here clearly are not acceptable in the classroom trials stage of educational intervention research. In Stage 3 of the model, the random assignment of multiple classrooms or other intact groups to interventions serves to counteract this methodological concern; for actual research examples, see Byrne and Fielding-Barnsley (1991); Duffy et al. (1987); and Stevens, Slavin, and Farnish (1991).

Consistent with the earlier presented *Comparison* component of CAREful research, the need for including appropriate comparison classrooms (or other aggregates) is of paramount importance in the Stage 3 model. As Slavin (1999) forcefully pointed out in response to a critic advocating the documentation of an intervention's effectiveness not by a comparison with a nonintervention control condition but through the presentation of what seem to be surprising outcomes in the intervention condition,

An experimental-control comparison between well-matched (or, ideally, randomly assigned) participants is to be able to provide powerful evidence for or against a causal relationship [attributable to the intervention], because the researcher establishes the experimental and control groups in advance, before the results are known, and then reports relative posttests or gains. In contrast, [the critic's] search for "surprising" scores or gains begins after the fact, when the results are already known. This cannot establish the effect of a given program on a given outcome; any of a thousand other factors other than the treatment could explain high scores in a given school in a given year. . . . If an evaluation has data on 100 schools implementing a given program but only reports on the 50 that produced the most positive scores, it is utterly meaningless. In contrast, a comparison of 10 schools to 10 well-matched control schools provides strong evidence for or against the existence of a program impact. If that experimental-control comparison is then replicated elsewhere in a series of small but unbiased studies, the argument for a causal relationship is further strengthened. (Slavin, 1999, pp. 36–37)

Slavin's hypothetical example should evoke readers' memories of the perils and potential for deception that are inherent in the examine aspect of the ESP model of educational intervention research. The example also well illustrates the adapted adage: A randomized experiment is worth more than 100 school demonstrations!

Analytic Appropriateness

Early and often in the history of educational research, much has been written on the inappropriateness of researchers' statistically analyzing the effects of classroom-implemented interventions as though the interventions had been independently administered to individual students (e.g., Barcikowski, 1981; Levin, 1992; Lindquist, 1940; Page, 1965; Peckham, Glass, & Hopkins, 1969). That is, there is a profound mismatch between the units of intervention administration (groups, classrooms) and the units of analysis (children, students) and conducting child/student-level statistical analyses in such situations typically results in a serious misrepresentation of both the reality and the magnitude of the intervention effect. [As an interesting aside, *units of analysis* is another term with a specific statistical meaning that is now being casually used in the educational research literature to refer to the researcher's substantive grain-size perspective: the individual student, the classroom collective, the school, the community, etc. (see, e.g., Cobb & Bowers, 1999, pp. 6–8).] Consider, for example, a hypothetical treatment study in which one classroom of 20 students receives a classroom management instructional intervention and another classroom of 20 students receives standard classroom protocol. It is indisputably incorrect to assess the intervention effect in that study on the basis of a conventional student-level t test, analysis of variance, chi-square test, or other statistical procedures that assume that 40 independently generated student outcomes comprise the data. Analyzing the data in that fashion will produce invalid results and conclusions.

Even today, most "one group per intervention" (or even "a couple groups per intervention") researchers continue to adopt units-inappropriate analytic practices, in spite of the earlier noted cautions and evidence that such practices lead to dangerously misleading inferences (e.g., Graziano et al., 1999). In a related context, Muthen (1989, p. 184) speculated on the reason for researchers' persistent misapplication of statistical procedures: "The common problem is that measurement issues and statistical assumptions that are incidental to the researchers' conceptual ideas become stumbling blocks that invalidate the statistical analysis."

In the randomized classroom trials stage of the model, the critical units-of-analysis issue can be dealt with through the inclusion of multiple randomized units (e.g., multiple classrooms randomly assigned to intervention and control conditions) in conjunction with the application of statistical models that are both appropriate and sensitive to the applied implementation nature of the experiment (e.g., Bryk & Raudenbush, 1992; Levin, 1992). In the medical and health fields, group-randomized intervention trials (Braun & Feng, 2001) have been referred to as *cluster randomization trials* (e.g., Donner & Klar, 2000), with the corresponding pitfalls of inappropriate statistical analyses well documented. The number of multiple units to be included in a given study is not a specified constant. Rather, that number will vary from study to study as a function of substantive, resource, and unit-based statistical power considerations (e.g., Barcikowski, 1981; Levin, 1997a; Levin & Serlin, 1993), as well as of the scope of curricular policy implications associated with the particular intervention. In addition, appropriate statistical methods to accompany multiple-baseline and other "few units per intervention" single-participant designs (alluded to earlier) are now available (see, e.g., Koehler & Levin, 1998; Levin & Wampold, 1999; Marascuilo & Busk, 1988; Wampold & Worsham, 1986).

Two additional critical features of the randomized classroom trials stage should also be indicated.

Intervention-Effect Robustness

The use of multiple randomized units in the randomized classroom trials stage permits legitimate intervention-effect generalizations across classrooms, teachers, and students—something that is not legitimate in the prototypical intervention study. With the additional feature of random selection of groups or classrooms within a school, district, or other population, statistical analyses that permit even grander generalizations are possible (e.g., Bryk & Raudenbush, 1992), a desirable and defining characteristic of Slavin's (1997) proposed design competition for instructional interventions.

(A design competition should not be confused with a design experiment, as has already occurred in the literature. The critical attributes of the former have been discussed earlier in this article; those of the latter are discussed in a following section.) Finally, replication of the randomized classroom trials stage of the model, across different sites and with different investigators, increases one's degree of confidence in the reality, magnitude, and robustness of the intervention effect. In summary, each of the just-mentioned sampling augmentations of the randomized classroom trials stage can be considered in relation to enhancing the research's external validity.

Interaction Potential

The randomized classroom trials stage lends itself not just to generalization, but also to specificity, in the form of determining whether a particular intervention is better suited to certain kinds of groups, classrooms, teachers, or students than to others. With one-unit-per-intervention and conventional analyses, investigating intervention-by-characteristics interactions is not possible, or at least *not* possible without the methodological shortcomings and statistical assumption violations mentioned earlier. Just as different drugs or medical treatments may be expected to affect different patients differently, different classroom interventions likely have different effects on students differing in academic ability, aptitude, motivational levels, or demographic characteristics. The same would be expected of instructional interventions delivered by teachers with different personal and teaching characteristics. That is, one size may not fit all (Salomon & Almog, 1998, p. 224), but that assumption can readily be incorporated into, and investigated in, the randomized classroom trials stage of intervention research (e.g., Bryk & Raudenbush, 1992; Levin, 1992; Levin & Peterson, 1984); for an actual research example, see Copeland (1991). Included in this analytic armament are adaptations for studying intervention by outcome-measure interactions, changes in intervention effectiveness over time, and other large- or small-scale classroom-based multivariate issues of interest (see also Levin & Wampold, 1999).

What Is Random in Randomized Classroom Trials Studies?

It is important to clarify exactly what needs to be random and controlled to yield scientifically credible unit-based evidence, for we have witnessed substantial confusion among intervention researchers concerning how to meet standards of internal, as opposed to external, validity in such studies. Reiterating that high internal validity alone is what makes an empirical study scientifically credible, we point out that in randomized classroom trials research,

- Classrooms and teachers do not need to be randomly selected.

- Participants do not need to be randomly assigned to classrooms.

- The only aspect that must be *random* is the assignment of candidate units (e.g., groups, classrooms, schools) to the different intervention conditions, either across all units or in a matched-unit fashion. By "candidate," we are referring to all units for which there is a priori agreement to be included in the study, which implies accepting the fact that there is an equal chance of the candidates' being assigned to any of the study's specified intervention conditions. A "wait-list" or "crossover" arrangement (e.g., Levin, 1992; Shadish, Cook, & Campbell, 2002) can also be implemented as a part of the nontargeted-intervention units' assignment.

- Scientifically credible studies based on whole unit random assignment operations can be performed on targeted participant subgroups. For example, classrooms containing students both with and without learning disabilities could be randomly assigned to intervention conditions, with the focus of the study's interventions being on just the former student subgroup.

- When either out-of-classroom or unobtrusive within-classroom *interventions* can be administered, within-classroom *blocked* random assignment of participants to intervention conditions represents a scientifically credible strategy—for an actual research example, see McDonald, Kratochwill, Levin, and Youngbear Tibbits (1998).

- Even if units are *initially* assigned to interventions randomly (as just indicated), *terminal* conditions-composition differences resulting from participant or group attrition can undermine the scientific credibility of the study (see, e.g., the Graziano et al., 1999, training study). In such cases, analyses representing different degrees of conservatism should be provided, with the hope of obtaining compatible evidence.

An important addendum is that statistical adjustments and controls (e.g., analysis of covariance, path models) do not represent acceptable substitutes for situations in which random assignment of classrooms to intervention conditions cannot be effected. Although this point has been underscored by statisticians and methodologists for many years (e.g., Elashoff, 1969; Huitema, 1980), educational researchers continue to believe that sophisticated statistical tools can resurrect data from studies that are inadequately designed and executed. Muthen (1989) aptly reminded us of that in

quoting Cliff (1983):

> [Various multivariate] methods have greatly increased the rigor with which one can analyze his correlational data, and they solve many statistical problems that have plagued this kind of data. However, they solve a much smaller proportion of the interpretational . . . problems that go with such data. These interpretational problems are particularly severe in those increasingly common cases where the investigator wishes to make causal interpretations of his analyses. (Muthen, 1989, p. 185)

When random assignment of units to interventions has been used, however, the concurrent application of analysis of covariance or other multivariate techniques is entirely appropriate and may prove to be analytically advantageous (e.g., Levin & Serlin, 1993); for actual research examples, see Torgesen, Morgan, and Davis (1992) and Whitehurst et al. (1994).

Summary

Conducting randomized classroom trials studies is not an easy task. We nonetheless claim that: (a) randomized experiments are not impossible (or even impractical) to conduct, so that (b) educational researchers must begin adding these to their investigative repertoires to enhance the scientific credibility of their research and research-based conclusions. Classroom-based research (and its resultant scientific credibility) can also be adversely affected by a variety of real-world plagues, including within-classroom treatment integrity, between-classroom treatment overlap, and construct validity, as well as other measurement issues (e.g., Cook & Campbell, 1979; Nye, Hedges, & Konstantopoulos, 1999). In addition, a variety of external validity caveats—superbly articulated in a persuasive treatise by Dressman (1999)—must be heeded when attempting to extrapolate educational research findings to educational policy recommendations. There can be no denying that in contrast to the independent and dependent variables of the prototypical laboratory experiment, the factors related to school or classroom outcomes are complex and multidimensional. Yet, others have argued compellingly that to understand the variables (and variable systems) that have implications for social policy, randomized experiments should, and can, be conducted in realistic field settings (e.g., Boruch, 1975; Campbell & Boruch, 1975). Here we present a similar argument for more carefully controlled classroom-based research on instructional interventions and on other educational prescriptions.

Implementing a Randomized Classroom Trials Study

Is there a need for either smaller or larger scale randomized intervention studies? Have any instructional interventions advanced to the point where they are ready to be evaluated in well-controlled classroom trials? Or, as was alluded to earlier, are such implementation-and-evaluation efforts the sole property of medical research's clinical trials? Yes, yes, and no, respectively, and the time is ripe to demonstrate it.

A similar research sequence could be followed in moving beyond classroom description, laboratory research, and one-unit-per-intervention studies to help settle the whole-language versus phonemic-awareness training wars in reading instruction (e.g., Pressley & Allington, 1999), to prescribe the most effective classroom-based reading-comprehension techniques (e.g., Pressley et al., 1992), to investigate issues related to optimal instructional media and technologies (e.g., Salomon & Almog, 1998), and the like—the list goes on and on. That is, there is no shortage of randomized classroom-intervention research leads to be explored, in virtually all content domains that promote cognitive or behavioral interventions. (Beyond the classroom, school and institutional trials experiments can help to bolster claims about intervention efforts at those levels.) In addition to a perusal of the usual scholarly syntheses of research, all one needs do is to take a look at something such as *What Works* (U.S. Department of Education, 1986) for research-based candidates with the potential to have a dramatic positive impact on instructional outcomes, classroom behavior, and general cognitive development. Randomized classroom trials research can provide the necessary credible and creditable evidence for that potential.

Commitment of Federal Funds to Randomized Classroom Trials Research

The notions we have been advancing are quite compatible with Stanovich's (1998, pp. 54–55, 133–135) discussions of the importance of research progressing from early to later stages, producing, respectively, weaker and stronger forms of causal evidence (see also Table 22.3). The notions are also in synchrony with the final evaluative phase of Slavin's (1997) recommended design competitions, in which an agency identifies educational problems and research bidders submit their plans to solve them. With respect to that evaluative phase (which roughly corresponds to our randomized classroom trials stage), Slavin (1997) wrote,

> Ideally, schools for the third-party evaluations would be chosen at random from among schools that volunteered to use the program being evaluated. For example, schools in a given district might be asked to volunteer to implement a new middle school model. This offer might be made in 5 to 10 districts around the country: some urban, some suburban, some rural, some with language-minority students, some large schools, some small

ones, and so on. Fifty schools might be identified. Twenty-five might be randomly assigned to use the program and 25 to serve as controls (and to implement their current programs for a few more years). Control schools would receive extra resources, partly to balance those given to the experimental schools and partly to maintain a level of motivation to serve as control groups. (p. 26)

The random assignment of volunteering schools to the program and control conditions, along with the allocation of additional resources to the control schools, exhibits a concern for the research's internal validity (see, e.g., Levin & Levin, 1993). Additionally, the random sampling of schools exhibits a concern for the research's external validity and also permits an investigation of program effectiveness as a function of specific school characteristics. Multiple high-quality randomized school or classroom trials studies of this kind would do much to improve both public and professional perceptions of the low-quality standards that accompany educational research today (e.g., McGuire, 1999; Sabelli & Kelly, 1998; Sroufe, 1997). Incorporating and extending the knowledge base provided by smaller scale Stage 2 empirical studies (e.g., Hedges & Stock, 1983), the decade-long Tennessee Project STAR randomized classroom experiment investigating the effects of class size on student achievement (e.g., Nye et al., 1999) is a prominent example of scientifically credible research that has already begun to influence educational policy nationwide ("Research finds advantages," 1999). The same can be said of the Success for All randomized schools experiments investigating the effects of systemic reform on student academic outcomes in schools serving traditionally low-achieving student populations (e.g., Slavin, Madden, Dolan, & Wasik, 1996). Of less recent vintage, an illustration of a scientifically credible intervention with educational creditability is Harvard Project Physics, a randomized schools experiment based on a national random sample, in which an innovative high school physics curriculum was carefully implemented and evaluated (e.g., Walberg & Welch, 1972).

Are federal funding agencies willing to support randomized classroom trials ventures? Such ventures appear to be exactly what at least some agencies want, if not demand:

> At one end of the continuum, research is defined by researcher questions that push the boundaries of knowledge. At the other end of the continuum, research is defined by large-scale and contextual experiments, defined by implementation questions that frame robust applications. . . . What is needed now, and what NSF is actively exploring, is to move ahead simultaneously at both extremes of the continuum. Basic learning about the process of learning itself—innovative R&D in tackling increasingly complex content and in the tools of science and mathematics

education—informs and must be informed by applied, robust, large-scale testbed implementation research. (Sabelli & Kelly, 1998, p. 46)

Thus, in contrast to detractors' periodic assertions that the medical research model does not map well onto the educational research landscape, we assert that randomized classroom trials studies have much to recommend themselves.

Additional Comments

We conclude this section with five comments. First, we do not mean to imply that randomized classroom trials studies are appropriate for *all* areas of intervention research inquiry, for they most certainly are not (see, e.g., Eisner, 1999). Systematic observation, rich description, and relationship documentation, with no randomized classroom component, may well suffice for characterizing many classroom processes and behaviors of both practical and theoretical consequence. For the prescription of instructional interventions (e.g., alternative teaching methods, learning strategies, curricular materials) and other school- or other system–based innovations, however, randomized classroom trials studies could go a long way toward responding to former Assistant Secretary of Education McGuire's (1999) call for rigorous educational research that "readily inform[s] our understanding of a number of enduring problems of practice" (p. 1).

Second, randomized classroom trials studies can be carried out on both smaller and larger scales, depending on one's intended purposes and resources. The critical issues here are (a) realistic classroom-based interventions that are (b) administered to multiple randomized classrooms. Scientifically credible classroom-based intervention research does not invariably require an inordinate number of classrooms per intervention condition, such as the 50 schools alluded to by Slavin (1997) in the final stage of his aforementioned design competition scenario. Initially, an intervention's potential might be evaluated with, say, three or four classrooms randomly assigned to each intervention condition. Even with that number of multiple classrooms (and especially when combined with classroom stratification, statistical control, and the specification of relevant within-classroom characteristics), classroom-based statistical analyses can be sensibly and sensitively applied to detect intervention main effects and interactions of reasonable magnitudes (e.g., Barcikowski, 1991; Bryk & Raudenbush, 1992; Levin, 1992; Levin & O'Donnell, 1999a; Levin & Serlin, 1993). This statement may come as surprise to those who are used to conducting research based on individuals as the units of treatment administration and analysis. With classrooms as the units, the ability to detect intervention

effects is a function of several factors, including the number of classrooms per intervention condition, the number of students per classroom, and the degree of within-classroom homogeneity (both apart from and produced by the intervention; see, e.g., Barcikowski, 1981). Each of these factors serves to affect the statistical power of classroom-based analyses. After an intervention's potential has been documented through small, controlled, classroom-based experiments (and replications) of the kind alluded to here, more ambitious, larger scale, randomized trials studies based on randomly selected classrooms or schools, consistent with Slavin's (1997) design competition notions, would then be in order.

Third, if we are to understand the strengths, weaknesses, and potential roles of various modes of empirical inquiry (e.g., observational studies, surveys, controlled laboratory experiments, design experiments), we need an overall model to represent the relationships among them. For Figure 22.1 to be such a model, one must believe that it is possible to have a generalized instructional intervention that can work in a variety of contexts. Testing the comparative efficacy of such an intervention would be the subject of a Stage 3 randomized classroom trials investigation. A substantive example that readily comes to mind is tutoring, an instructional strategy that has been shown to be effective in a variety of student populations and situations and across time (see, e.g., Cohen, Kulik, & Kulik, 1982; O'Donnell, 1998). For those who believe that interventions can only be population and situation specific, a unifying view of the reciprocal contributions of various research methodologies is difficult to promote.

Fourth, along with acknowledging that the classroom is typically a nest of "blooming, buzzing confusion" (Brown, 1992, p. 141), it should also be acknowledged that in the absence of Figure 22.1's Stage 3 research, the confusion will be in a researcher's interpreting which classroom procedures or features produced which instructional outcomes (if, indeed, any were produced at all). In that regard, we reiterate that randomized classroom trials research is equally applicable and appropriate for evaluating the effects of single-component, multiple-component, and systemic intervention efforts alike. With the randomized classroom trials stage, at least a researcher will be able to attribute outcomes to the intervention (however tightly or loosely defined) rather than to other unintended or unwanted characteristics (e.g., teacher, classroom, or student effects).

Finally, and also in reference to Brown's (1992, p. 141) "blooming, buzzing confusion" comments directed at classroom-based research, we note that not all research on teaching and learning is, or needs to be, concerned with issues of teaching and learning *in classrooms*. Consider, for example, the question of whether musical knowledge and spatial ability foster the development of students' mathematical skills. Answering that question does not require any classroom-based intervention or investigation. In fact, addressing the question in classroom contexts, and certainly in the manner in which the research has been conducted to date (e.g., Graziano et al., 1999; Rauscher et al., 1997), may serve to obfuscate the issue more than resolve it. Alternatively, one need not travel very far afield to investigate the potential of individually based interventions for ameliorating children's psychological and conduct disorders. Controlled large-scale assessments of the comparative effectiveness of various drug or behavioral therapies could be credibly managed within the randomized classroom (or community) trials stage of the Figure 22.1 model (see, e.g., COMMIT Research Group, 1995; Goode, 1999; Peterson, Mann, Kealey, & Marek, 2000; Wampold et al., 1997). Adapting Scriven's (1997, p. 21) aspirin question here, is the individual administration of therapeutic interventions applicable only for treating medical, and not educational, problems?

Closing Trials Arguments

So, educational intervention research, whither goest thou? By the year 2025, will educational researchers still regard such methodologies as the ESP investigation, the demonstration study, and the design experiment as credible evidence producers and regard the information derived from them as "satisficing" (Simon, 1955)? Or are there enough among us who will fight for credible evidence-producing methodologies, contesting incredible claims in venues in which recommendations based on intervention "research" are being served up for either public or professional consumption?

A similar kind of soul searching related to research purposes, tools, and standards of evidence has been taking place in other social sciences academic disciplines as well (e.g., Azar, 1999; Thu, 1999; Weisz & Hawley, 2001). Grinder (1989) described a literal fallout observed in the field of educational psychology as a result of researchers' perceived differences in purposes: In the 1970s and 1980s many researchers chose to withdraw from educational psychology and head in other disciplinary directions. In the last decade or so we have seen that sort of retreat in at least two kindred professional organizations to the AERA. Perceiving the American Psychological Association as becoming more and more concerned with clinical and applied issues, researchers aligned with the scientific side of psychology helped to form the American Psychological Society (APS). Similarly, International Reading Association researchers and others who wished to focus on the scientific study of reading rather than on reading practitioners' problems founded a professional

organization to represent that focus, the Society for the Scientific Study of Reading. Will history repeat itself, once again, in educational research?

Our message is a simple one: When it comes to recommending or prescribing educational, clinical, and social interventions based on research, standards of evidence credibility must occupy a position of preeminence. The core of the investigative framework we propose here is not new. Many educational researchers and methodologists concerned with the credibility of research-derived evidence and prescriptions have offered similar suggestions for years, if not decades: Harken back to Bereiter's (1965) trenchant analysis of the situation. Why, then, do we believe it important, if not imperative, for us to restate the case for scientifically credible intervention research at this time? Perhaps it is best summarized in a personal communication received from the educational researcher Herbert Walberg (May 11, 1999): "Live long enough and, like wide ties, you come back in style—this in a day when anecdotalism is the AERA research method of choice." A frightening state of affairs currently exists within the general domain of educational research and within its individual subdomains. It is time to convince the public, the press, and policy makers alike of the importance of credible evidence derived from CAREfully conducted research, delineating the characteristics critical to both its production and recognition. In this chapter we have taken a step toward that end by first attempting to convince educational/psychological intervention researchers of the same.

REFERENCES

Abelson, R. P. (1995). *Statistics as principled argument.* Mahwah, NJ: Erlbaum.

Angell, M., & Kassirer, J. P. (1998). Alternative medicine: The risks of untested and unregulated remedies. *New England Journal of Medicine, 339,* 839–841.

Azar, B. (1999). Consortium of editors pushes shift in child research method. *APA Monitor, 30*(2), 20–21.

Barcikowski, R. S. (1981). Statistical power with group mean as the unit of analysis. *Journal of Educational Statistics, 6,* 267–285.

Bartlett, F. C. (1932). *Remembering: A study in experimental and social psychology.* Cambridge, England: Cambridge University Press.

Bereiter, C. (1965). Issues and dilemmas in developing training programs for educational researchers. In E. Guba & S. Elam (Eds.), *The training and nurture of educational researchers* (pp. 95–110). Bloomington, IN: Phi Delta Kappa.

Bereiter, C. (1994). Implications of postmodernism for science, or, science as progressive discourse. *Educational Psychologist, 29,* 3–12.

Boruch, R. F. (1975). On common contentions about randomized field experiments. In R. F. Boruch & H. W. Riecken (Eds.), *Experimental testing of public policy* (pp. 107–145). Boulder, CO: Westview Press.

Boyer, E. L. (1990). *Scholarship reconsidered: Priorities of the professoriate.* Princeton, NJ: Carnegie Foundation.

Braun, T. M., & Feng, Z. (2001). Optimal permutation tests for the analysis of group randomized trials. *Journal of the American Statistical Association, 96,* 1424–1432.

Brown, A. L. (1992). Design experiments: Theoretical and methodological challenges in creating complex interventions in classroom settings. *Journal of the Learning Sciences, 2,* 141–178.

Bryk, A. S., & Raudenbush, S. W. (1992). *Hierarchical linear models.* Newbury Park, CA: Sage.

Byrne, B., & Fielding-Barnsley, R. (1991). Evaluation of a program to teach phonemic awareness to young children. *Journal of Educational Psychology, 83,* 451–455.

Calfee, R. (1992). Refining educational psychology: The case of the missing links. *Educational Psychologist, 27,* 163–175.

Campbell, D. T., & Boruch, R. F. (1975). Making the case for randomized assignment to treatments by considering the alternatives: Six ways in which quasi-experimental evaluations in compensatory education tend to underestimate effects. In C. A. Bennett & A. A. Lumsdaine (Eds.), *Evaluation and experiment: Some critical issues in assessing social programs* (pp. 195–296). New York: Academic Press.

Campbell, D. T., & Stanley, J. C. (1966). *Experimental and quasi-experimental designs for research.* Chicago: Rand-McNally.

Chambless, D. L., & Ollendick, T. H. (2001). Empirically supported psychological interventions: Controversies and evidence. *Annual Review of Psychology, 52,* 685–716.

Cliff, N. (1983). Some cautions concerning the application of causal modeling methods. *Multivariate Behavioral Research, 18,* 115–126.

Cobb, P., & Bowers, J. (1999). Cognitive and situated learning perspectives in theory and practice. *Educational Researcher, 28*(2), 4–15.

Cocco, N., & Sharpe, L. (1993). An auditory variant of eye-movement desensitization in a case of childhood posttraumatic stress disorder. *Journal of Behaviour Therapy and Experimental Psychiatry, 24,* 373–377.

Cohen, P. A., Kulik, J. A., & Kulik, C. C. (1982). Educational outcomes from tutoring: A meta-analysis of findings. *American Educational Research Journal, 19,* 237–248.

Cole, N. S. (1997). "The vision thing": Educational research and AERA in the 21st century: Pt. 2. Competing visions for enhancing the impact of educational research. *Educational Researcher, 26*(4), 13, 16–17.

Collins, A. (1992). Toward a design science of education. In E. Scanlon & T. O'Shea (Eds.), *New directions in educational technology* (pp. 15–22). New York: Springer-Verlag.

COMMIT Research Group. (1995). Community intervention trial for smoking cessation (COMMIT). *American Journal of Public Health, 85,* 183–192.

Copeland, W. D. (1991). Microcomputers and teaching actions in the context of historical inquiry. *Journal of Educational Computing Research, 7,* 421–454.

Derry, S., Levin, J. R., Osana, H. P., Jones, M. S., & Peterson, M. (2000). Fostering students' statistical and scientific thinking: Lessons learned from an innovative college course. *American Educational Research Journal, 37,* 747–773.

Donner, A., & Klar, N. (2000). *Design and analysis of cluster randomization trials in health research.* New York: Oxford University Press.

Donmoyer, R. (1993). Yes, but is it research? *Educational Researcher, 22*(3), 41.

Donmoyer, R. (1996). Educational research in an era of paradigm proliferation: What's a journal editor to do? *Educational Researcher, 25*(2), 19–25.

Doyle, W., & Carter, K. (1996). Educational psychology and the education of teachers: A reaction. *Educational Psychologist, 31,* 23–28.

Dressman, M. (1999). On the use and misuse of research evidence: Decoding two states' reading initiatives. *Reading Research Quarterly, 34,* 258–285.

Duffy, G. R., Roehler, L. R., Sivan, E., Rackliffe, G., Book, C., Meloth, M. S., Vavrus, L. G., Wesselman, R., Putnam, J., & Bassiri, D. (1987). Effects of explaining the reasoning associated with using reading strategies. *Reading Research Quarterly, 22,* 347–368.

Eisner, E. (1999). Rejoinder: A response to Tom Knapp. *Educational Researcher, 28*(1), 19–20.

Elashoff, J. D. (1969). Analysis of covariance: A delicate instrument. *American Educational Research Journal, 6,* 381–401.

Goode, E. (1999, March 19). New and old depression drugs are found equal. *New York Times,* pp. A1, A16.

Graziano, A. B., Peterson, M., & Shaw, G. L. (1999). Enhanced learning of proportional math through music training and spatial-temporal training. *Neurological Research, 21,* 139–152.

Greenwald, R. (1999). *Eye movement desensitization and reprocessing (EMDR) in child and adolescent psychotherapy.* Northvale, NJ: Jason Aronson.

Grinder, R. E. (1989). Educational psychology: The master science. In M. C. Wittrock & F. Farley (Eds.), *The future of educational psychology: The challenges and opportunities* (pp. 3–18). Hillsdale, NJ: Erlbaum.

Gross, P. R., Levitt, N., & Lewis, M. W. (1997). *The flight from science and reason.* Baltimore: Johns Hopkins University Press.

Halpern, D. F. (1996). *Thought & knowledge: An introduction to critical thinking* (3rd ed.). Mahwah, NJ: Erlbaum.

Hedges, L. V., & Stock, W. (1983). The effects of class size: An examination of rival hypotheses. *American Educational Research Journal, 20,* 63–85.

Hitt, J. (2001, December 9). Evidence-based medicine. In "The year in ideas," *New York Times Magazine* (Section 6).

Hooper, J. (1999). A new germ theory. *Atlantic Monthly, 283*(2), 41–53.

Huitema, B. E. (1980). *The analysis of covariance and alternatives.* New York: Wiley.

Jaeger, R. M. (Ed.). (1988). *Complementary methods for research in education.* Washington, DC: American Educational Research Association.

Jaeger, R. M., & Bond, L. (1996). Quantitative research methods and design. In D. C. Berliner & R. C. Calfee (Eds.), *Handbook of educational psychology* (pp. 877–898). New York: Macmillan.

Kaestle, C. F. (1993). The awful reputation of education research. *Educational Researcher, 22*(1), 23–31.

Kazdin, A. E. (1981). Drawing valid inferences from case studies. *Journal of Consulting and Clinical Psychology, 49,* 183–192.

Kazdin, A. E. (1998). *Research design in clinical psychology* (3rd ed.). Boston: Allyn & Bacon.

Koehler, M. J., & Levin, J. R. (1998). Regulated randomization: A potentially sharper analytical tool for the multiple-baseline design. *Psychological Methods, 3,* 206–217.

Krathwohl, D. R. (1993). *Methods of educational and social science: An integrated approach.* White Plains, NY: Longman.

Kratochwill, T. R. (1985). Case study research in school psychology. *School Psychology Review, 14,* 204–215.

Kratochwill, T. R., & Levin, J. R. (Eds.). (1992). *Single-case research design and analysis: New developments for psychology and education.* Hillsdale, NJ: Erlbaum.

Kratochwill, T. R., Mott, S. E., & Dodson, C. L. (1984). Case study and single-case research in clinical and applied psychology. In A. S. Bellack & M. Hersen (Eds.), *Research methods in clinical psychology* (pp. 55–99). New York: Pergamon Press.

Kratochwill, T. R., & Stoiber, K. C. (2000). Empirically supported interventions and school psychology: Pt. 2. Conceptual and practical issues. *School Psychology Quarterly, 15,* 233–253.

Kratochwill, T. R., & Stoiber, K. C. (Eds.). (2001). *Procedural and coding manual for review of evidence-based interventions.* Task Force on Evidence-Based Interventions in School Psychology. Division 16 of the American Psychological Association and the Society for the Study of School Psychology. Available from Thomas R. Kratochwill, School Psychology Program, 1025 West Johnson St., University of Wisconsin-Madison, Madison, WI 53706–1796.

Kratochwill, T. R., & Stoiber, K. C. (in press). Evidence-based interventions in school psychology: Conceptual foundations of the Procedural and Coding Manual of Division 16 and the Society for the Study of School Psychology Task Force. *School Psychology Quarterly.*

Labaree, D. F. (1998). Educational researchers: Living with a lesser form of knowledge. *Educational Researcher, 27*(8), 4–12.

Levin, J. R. (1985). Some methodological and statistical "bugs" in research on children's learning. In M. Pressley & C. J. Brainerd (Eds.), *Cognitive learning and memory in children* (pp. 205–233). New York: Springer-Verlag.

Levin, J. R. (1992). On research in classrooms. *Mid-Western Educational Researcher, 5,* 2–6, 16.

Levin, J. R. (1994). Crafting educational intervention research that's both credible and creditable. *Educational Psychology Review, 6,* 231–243.

Levin, J. R. (1997a). Overcoming feelings of powerlessness in aging researchers: A primer on statistical power in analysis of variance designs. *Psychology and Aging, 12,* 84–106.

Levin, J. R. (1997b, March). *Statistics in research and in the real world.* Colloquium presentation, Department of Psychology, University of California, San Diego.

Levin, J. R., & Levin, M. E. (1993). Methodological problems in research on academic retention programs for at-risk minority college students. *Journal of College Student Development, 34,* 118–124.

Levin, J. R., & O'Donnell, A. M. (1999a). Educational research's credibility gaps, in closing. *Issues in Education: Contributions from Educational Psychology, 5,* 279–293.

Levin, J. R., & O'Donnell, A. M. (1999b). What to do about educational research's credibility gaps? *Issues in Education: Contributions from Educational Psychology, 5,* 177–229.

Levin, J. R., & O'Donnell, A. M. (2000). Three more cheers for credible educational research! *Issues in Education: Contributions from Educational Psychology, 6,* 181–185.

Levin, J. R., & Peterson, P. L. (1984). Classroom aptitude-by-treatment interactions: An alternative analysis strategy. *Educational Psychologist, 19,* 43–47.

Levin, J. R., & Robinson, D. H. (1999). Further reflections on hypothesis testing and editorial policy for primary research journals. *Educational Psychology Review, 11,* 143–155.

Levin, J. R., & Serlin, R. C. (1993, April). *No way to treat a classroom: Alternative units-appropriate statistical strategies.* Paper presented at the annual meeting of the American Educational Research Association, Atlanta, GA.

Levin, J. R., & Wampold, B. E. (1999). Generalized single-case randomization tests: Flexible analyses for a variety of situations. *School Psychology Quarterly, 14,* 59–93.

Levin, M. E., Levin, J. R., & Scalia, P. A. (1997). What claims can a comprehensive college program of academic support support? *Equity & Excellence in Education, 30,* 71–89.

Lindquist, E. F. (1940). Sampling in educational research. *Journal of Educational Psychology, 31,* 561–574.

Lipsey, M. W., & Cordray, D. S. (2000). Evaluation methods for social intervention. *Annual Review of Psychology, 51,* 345–375.

Loftus, E. (1998). Who is the cat that curiosity killed? *APS Observer, 11*(9), 3, 27.

Marascuilo, L. A., & Busk, P. L. (1988). Combining statistics for multiple-baseline AB and replicated ABAB designs across subjects. *Behavioral Assessment, 10*, 1–28.

Mayer, R. E. (1993). Outmoded conceptions of educational research. *Educational Researcher, 22*, 6.

McDonald, L., Kratochwill, T., Levin, J., & Youngbear Tibbits, H. (1998, August). *Families and schools together: An experimental analysis of a parent-mediated intervention program for at-risk American Indian children.* Paper presented at the annual meeting of the American Psychological Association, San Francisco.

McGuire, K. (1999). *1999 request for proposals.* Washington, DC: U.S. Department of Education, Office of Educational Research and Improvement.

Muthen, B. (1989). Teaching students of educational psychology new sophisticated statistical techniques. In M. C. Wittrock & F. Farley (Eds.). *The future of educational psychology: The challenges and opportunities* (pp. 181–189). Hillsdale, NJ: Erlbaum.

Nantais, K. M., & Schellenberg, E. G. (1999). The Mozart effect: An artifact of preference. *Psychological Science, 10*, 370–373.

National Institutes of Health. (1998). *Taking part in clinical trials: What cancer patients need to know* (NIH Publication No. 98-4250). Washington, DC: Author.

National Reading Panel. (2000). *Report of the National Reading Panel: Teaching children to read: An evidence-based assessment of the scientific research literature on reading and its implications for reading instruction: Reports of the subgroups.* Rockville, MD: NICHD Clearinghouse.

National Research Council. (2001). *Scientific inquiry in education* (R. J. Shavelson & L. Towne, Eds). Washington, DC: National Academy Press.

Needels, M. C., & Knapp, M. S. (1994). Teaching writing to children who are underserved. *Journal of Educational Psychology, 86*, 339–349.

Nye, B., Hedges, L. V., & Konstantopoulos, S. (1999). *The effects of small classes on academic achievement: The results of the Tennessee class size experiment.* Unpublished manuscript, Tennessee State University.

O'Donnell, A. M. (1998, February). *Peer tutoring: A review of the research on an enduring instructional strategy.* Colloquium presentation, Center for Assessment, Instruction, and Research, Fordham University, New York.

O'Donnell, A. M., & Levin, J. R. (2001). Educational psychology's healthy growing pains. *Educational Psychologist, 36*, 73–82.

Page, E. B. (1965, February). *Recapturing the richness within the classroom.* Paper presented at the annual meeting of the American Educational Research Association, Chicago.

Peckham, P. D., Glass, G. V., & Hopkins, K. D. (1969). The experimental unit in statistical analysis. *Journal of Special Education, 3*, 337–349.

Peterson, A. V., Jr., Mann, S. L., Kealey, K. A., & Marek, P. M. (2000). Experimental design and methods for school-based randomized trials: Experience from the Hutchinson Smoking Prevention Project (HSPP). *Controlled Clinical Trials, 21*, 144–165.

Piano lessons, computer may help math skills. (1999, March 15). *Deseret News.*

Platt, J. R. (1964). Strong inference. *Science, 146*, 347–353.

Pressley, M., & Allington, R. (1999). What should reading instructional research be the research of? *Issues in Education: Contributions From Educational Psychology, 5*, 1–35.

Pressley, M., El-Dinary, P. B., Gaskins, I., Schuder, T., Bergman, J. L., Almasi, J., & Brown, R. (1992). Beyond direct explanation: Transactional instruction of reading comprehension strategies. *Elementary School Journal, 92*, 513–555.

Rauscher, F. H., Shaw, G. L., Levine, L. J., Wright, E. L., Dennis, W. R., & Newcomb, R. L. (1997). Music training causes long-term enhancement of preschool children's spatial-temporal reasoning. *Neurological Research, 19*, 2–8.

Research finds advantages in classes of 13 to 17 pupils. (1999, April 30). *New York Times*, p. A23.

Romberg, T. A. (1992). Perspectives on scholarship and research methods. In D. A. Grouws (Ed.), *Handbook of research on mathematics teaching and learning* (pp. 49–64). New York: Macmillan.

Sabelli, N. H., & Kelly, A. E. (1998). The NSF Learning and Intelligent Systems research initiative: Implications for educational research and practice. *Educational Technology, 38*(2), 42–46.

Saigh, P. A. (1987a). In vitro flooding of an adolescent's posttraumatic stress disorder. *Journal of Clinical Child Psychology, 16*, 147–150.

Saigh, P. A. (1987b). In vitro flooding of a 6-year-old boy's posttraumatic stress disorder. *Behaviour Research and Therapy, 24*, 685–689.

Saigh, P. A. (1989). The development and validation of the Children's Posttraumatic Stress Disorder Inventory. *International Journal of Special Education, 4*, 75–84.

Saigh. P. A. (in press). The cognitive-behavioral treatment of child-adolescent posttraumatic stress disorder. In S. E. Brock & P. Lazarus (Eds.), *Best practices in school crisis prevention and intervention.* Bethesda, MD: National Association of School Psychologists.

Saigh, P. A., Yasik, A. E., Oberfield, R. A., & Inamdar, S. C. (1999). Behavioral treatment of child-adolescent posttraumatic stress disorder. In P. A. Saigh & J. D. Bremner (Eds.), *Posttraumatic stress disorder: A comprehensive text* (pp. 354–375). Boston: Allyn & Bacon.

Salomon, G. (1995). Reflections on the field of educational psychology by the outgoing journal editor. *Educational Psychologist, 30*, 105–108.

Salomon, G., & Almog, T. (1998). Educational psychology and technology: A matter of reciprocal relations. *Teachers College Record, 100*, 222–241.

Scriven, M. (1960). The philosophy of science in educational research. *Review of Educational Research, 30,* 422–429.

Scriven, M. (1997). "The vision thing": Educational research and AERA in the 21st century: Pt. 1. Competing visions of what educational researchers should do. *Educational Researcher, 26*(4), 19–21.

Shadish, W. R., Cook, T. D., & Campbell, D. T. (2002). *Experimental and quasi-experimental designs for generalized causal inference.* Boston: Houghton Mifflin.

Simon, H. A. (1955). A behavioral model of rational choice. *Quarterly Journal of Economics, 69,* 99–118.

Slavin, R. E. (1997). Design competitions: A proposal for a new federal role in educational research and development. *Educational Researcher, 26*(1), 22–28.

Slavin, R. E. (1999). Yes, control groups are essential in program evaluation: A response to Pogrow. *Educational Researcher, 28*(3), 36–38.

Slavin, R. E., Madden, N. A., Dolan, L. J., & Wasik, B. A. (1996). *Every child, every school: Success for All.* Thousand Oaks, CA: Corwin.

Sroufe, G. E. (1997). Improving the "awful reputation" of education research. *Educational Researcher, 26*(7), 26–28.

Stanovich, K. (1998). *How to think straight about psychology* (5th ed.). New York: Longman.

Stanovich, K. E. (1999). Educational research at a choice point. *Issues in Education: Contributions from Educational Psychology, 5,* 267–272.

Steele, K. M., Bass, K. E., & Crook, M. D. (1999). The mystery of the Mozart effect: Failure to replicate. *Psychological Science, 10,* 366–369.

Stevens, R. J., Slavin, R. E., & Farnish, A. M. (1991). The effects of cooperative learning and direct instruction in reading comprehension strategies on main idea identification. *Journal of Educational Psychology, 83,* 8–16.

Stoiber, K. C., & Kratochwill, T. R. (2000). Empirically supported interventions in schools: Rationale and methodological issues. *School Psychology Quarterly, 15,* 75–115.

Suter, L. (1999, April). *Research methods in mathematics and science research: A report of a workshop.* Symposium presented at the annual meeting of the American Educational Research Association, Montreal, Quebec, Canada.

Thu, K. M. (1999). Anthropologists should return to the roots of their discipline. *Chronicle of Higher Education, 45*(34), A56.

Torgesen, J. K., Morgan, S. T., & Davis, C. (1992). Effects of two types of phonological awareness training on word learning in kindergarten children. *Journal of Educational Psychology, 84,* 364–370.

Townsend, M. A. R., Hicks, L., Thompson, J. D. M., Wilton, K. M., Tuck, B. F., & Moore, D. W. (1993). Effects of introductions and conclusions in assessment of student essays. *Journal of Educational Psychology, 85,* 670–678.

Uchitelle, L. (1999, April 20). A real-world economist: Krueger and the empiricists challenge the theorists. *New York Times,* pp. C1, C10.

U.S. Department of Education. (1986). *What works.* Washington, DC: Author.

U.S. Government Accounting Office. (1997). *Head Start: Research provides little information on impact of current program.* Washington, DC: Author.

Walberg, H. J., & Welch, W. W. (1972). A national experiment in curriculum evaluation. *American Educational Research Journal, 9,* 373–384.

Walker, V. S. [Speaker]. (1999, April). *Research training in education: What are the essentials and can we agree?* (Cassette Recording No. 2.39). Washington, DC: American Educational Research Association.

Wampold, B. E., Mondin, G. W., Moody, M., Stich, F., Benson, K., & Ahn, H. (1997). A meta-analysis of outcome studies comparing bona fide psychotherapies: Empirically, "All must have prizes." *Psychological Bulletin, 122,* 203–215.

Wampold, B. E., & Worsham, N. L. (1986). Randomization tests for multiple-baseline designs. *Behavioral Assessment, 8,* 135–143.

Weisz, J. R., & Hawley, K. (2001, June). *Procedural and coding manual for identification of beneficial treatments.* Draft document of the Committee on Science and Practice Society for Clinical Psychology, Division 12, American Psychological Association, Washington, DC.

Whitehurst, G. J., Epstein, J. N., Angell, A. L., Payne, A. C., Crone, D. A., & Fischel, J. E. (1994). Outcomes of an emergent literacy intervention in Head Start. *Journal of Educational Psychology, 86,* 542–555.

Winner, E., & Hetland, L. (1999, March 4). Mozart and the S.A.T.'s. *New York Times,* p. A25.

Wittrock, M. C. (1994). An empowering conception of educational psychology. *Educational Psychologist, 27,* 129–141.

Wong, L. Y.-S. (1995). Research on teaching: Process-product research findings and the feeling of obviousness. *Journal of Educational Psychology, 87,* 504–511.

CHAPTER 23

Research to Policy for Guiding Educational Reform

BARBARA L. McCOMBS

As I look across the impressive collection of work in this volume on the contributions of educational psychology to our understanding of teaching and learning, I am struck with how important these contributions are to effective educational reform. I am also struck by what others have identified as the challenges we face in applying what we have learned—challenges that span making our work more visible, accessible, and credible to educators, policy makers, and the public. In this chapter, my focus is on how educational psychology's knowledge base can best be applied to twenty-first-century educational reform issues and—in so doing—discuss what policy implications arise. I address this topic in five parts:

1. What we have learned.

2. How work in educational psychology has contributed to effective reform.

3. What research directions are still needed.

4. How our knowledge base can best address issues of concern in the current reform agenda.

5. What policy issues must be addressed in twenty-first-century educational reform efforts.

Prior to beginning these topics, however, I would like to clarify what I understand to be the purpose and function of educational psychology as a credible knowledge base and science.

The definitions of educational psychology have been varied over the past century of psychological research on learning, but one commonality exists: There is widespread agreement that educational psychology is by definition an applied science. What that means to me is that it functions to conduct applications-driven research, development, and evaluation in the areas of human motivation, learning, and development. This research creates knowledge that informs practice and can be applied to the teaching and learning process in school settings in ways that enhance human potential and performance.

Applications of educational psychology's knowledge base must of necessity acknowledge the complexities of individuals and the educational systems and structures within which they operate throughout kindergarten to adult school settings. Systemic and multidisciplinary attention to how what we have learned about teaching and learning from diverse areas of research—including cognitive, motivational, social, and developmental—must be integrated with applications in schooling areas that include curriculum, instruction, assessment, teacher development, and school management (to name a few). Those of us working in this arena must therefore understand the context of schools as living systems—systems that operate at personal, technical, and organizational levels and that support personal, organizational, and community levels of learning; this places a responsibility on those working in the field of educational psychology to have both a breadth and depth of knowledge—not only about teaching and learning at the individual or process levels, but also about how this knowledge can be comprehensively integrated for application in diverse school settings and systems.

Given its applied nature and broad function, educational psychology also has to satisfy the tension between scientifically defensible research and research that has ecological validity in pre-K–20 school settings. This tension has been with the field since the beginning, and we have learned much in over a century of research. One of our biggest challenges will be to educate others about what we have learned and in the process help them recognize our current and future roles in twenty-first-century educational reform efforts.

WHAT HAVE WE LEARNED ABOUT LEARNING, TEACHING, COGNITION, MOTIVATION, DEVELOPMENT, AND INDIVIDUAL DIFFERENCES?

To establish a context for discussing what we have learned that is applicable to educational reform issues, this section begins with a brief review of major educational reform initiatives occurring nationally and internationally in the areas of assessment, standards, and accountability. It includes my perceptions of how educational psychology has been involved in reform movements and how the growing knowledge base can address reform issues in the twenty-first century. An example of a comprehensive project to define and disseminate the psychological knowledge base on learning, motivation, and development is then provided. This example involves the work of the APA Task Force on Psychology in Education (1993) and the APA Work Group of the Board of Educational Affairs (1997)—notably, their development and dissemination of the *Learner-Centered Psychological Principles* as a set of guidelines and a framework for school redesign and reform.

Defining Educational Reform and the Status of Twenty-First-Century Reform Efforts

Education reform has been a topic in the forefront for educators, researchers, policy makers, and the public since the 1983 *Nation at Risk* report. From the 1990s into this century, reform efforts have focused on a number of issues, including state and national academic standards, standardized state and national testing, and increased accountability for schools and teachers. The overall goal of all these efforts has been to create better schools in which more students learn to higher levels (Fuhrman & Odden, 2001). In the process of moving toward this goal, there has been increased recognition that improvements are needed in instruction and professional development and that transformed practices rather than more of the old methods are needed. A current focus on high-stakes testing has produced results in some schools but not in all. There is growing recognition that many practices need to be dramatically changed to reflect current knowledge about learning, motivation, and development. Educators and researchers are beginning to argue that a research-validated framework is needed to guide systemic reform efforts and that credible findings from educational psychology provide a foundation for this emerging framework.

Links between school reform and research in educational psychology are discussed by Marx (2000) in an introduction to a special issue of the *Educational Psychologist* on this topic. He points out that over the past quarter century, considerable progress has been made in providing new conceptions, principles, and models that can guide thinking about reforms that match what we know about learning, motivation, and development. Applying what we know to existing schools is not a simple matter, however, and requires the field to navigate through political and social issues and to attend to the best of what we know concerning the reciprocity of learning and change from a psychological perspective.

For example, Goertz (2001) argues that for effective reform we will need ways to balance compliance and flexibility in implementing standards-based reform that is sensitive to federal, state, and local contexts and needs. Educators will also need ways to ensure that substantial learning opportunities are provided for all learners in the system—including teachers, school leaders, students, and parents (Cohen & Ball, 2001). New policies will be needed as well as increased resources for capacity building if performance-based accountability practices are to be successful (Elmore & Fuhrman, 2001); ways to bridge the divide between secondary and postsecondary education will also be needed (Kirst & Venezia, 2001). Wassermann (2001) contends that the debate about the use of standardized tests to drive teaching must be balanced with collaborative efforts to define what is important to us in the education of our youth. Others are arguing for the increased use of assessment data to guide reform efforts, the need to attend to cultural changes, and the importance of strengthening the role of effective leadership and support for reform efforts (Corcoran, Fuhrman, & Belcher, 2001). To support these changes, Odden (2001) argues that new school finance models are needed to incorporate cost findings into school finance structures such that adequate fiscal resources are available to districts and schools for effective programs. Finally, these challenges must be met in an era of increased localization of funding.

The Role of Educational Psychology in Reform Efforts

The past century of research on learning has journeyed through a variety of theories that have alternately focused on behavioral, emotional, and cognitive aspects of learning. This range of theoretical perspectives, and the ways in which knowledge that is derived from these theories has been applied to school and classroom practices, have had (at best) a checkered history of successes and failures. For many educators, *research-based* has become a dirty word—a word that connotes something that is here today and gone tomorrow when the next research fad appears. Since the past decade or two of research, the picture appears to be changing. Current research in educational psychology is looking at learning from a more integrative perspective.

This integrative focus—shared by many authors in this volume—is based on a growing recognition from various perspectives (e.g., neurological brain research, psychological and sociological research) that meaningful, sustained

learning is a whole-person phenomenon. Brain research shows that even young children have the capacity for complex thinking (e.g., Diamond & Hopson, 1998; Jensen, 1998; Sylwester, 1995). Brain research also shows that affect and cognition work synergistically, with emotion driving attention, learning, memory, and other important mental activities. Research evidence exists on the inseparability of intellect and emotion in learning (e.g., Elias, Zims, et al., 1997; Lazarus, 2000) and the importance of emotional intelligence to human functioning and health (e.g., Seligman & Csikszentmihalyi, 2000). For example, brain research related to emotional intelligence, reported by Goleman (1995), confirms that humans have an emotional as well as an intellectual (or analytical) brain, both of which are in constant communication and involved in learning.

Recent research highlighted by many of the chapters in this volume is also revealing the social nature of learning. In keeping with this understanding, Elias, Bruene-Butler, Blum, and Schuyler (1997) discuss a number of research studies, including those in neuropsychology, demonstrating that many elements of learning are relational—that is, based on relationships. Social and emotional skills are essential for the successful development of cognitive thinking and learning skills. In addition to understanding the emotional and social aspects of learning, research is also confirming that learning is a natural process inherent to living organisms (APA Work Group of the Board of Educational Affairs, 1997).

From my research and that of others who have explored differences in what learning looks like in and outside of school settings, several things become obvious (e.g., McCombs, 2001b; Zimmerman & Schunk, 2001). Real-life learning is often playful, recursive, and nonlinear—engaging, self-directed, and meaningful from the learner's perspective. But why are the natural processes of motivation and learning seen in real life rarely seen in most school settings? Research shows that self-motivated learning is only possible in contexts that provide for choice and control. When students have choice and are allowed to control major aspects of their learning (such as what topics to pursue, how and when to study, and the outcomes they want to achieve), they are more likely to achieve self-regulation of thinking and learning processes.

Educational models are thus needed to reconnect learners with others and with learning—person-centered models that also offer challenging learning experiences. School learning experiences should prepare learners to be knowledge producers, knowledge users, and socially responsible citizens. Of course, we want students to learn socially valued academic knowledge and skills, but is that sufficient? In the twenty-first-century world, content is so abundant as to make it a poor foundation on which to base an educational system; rather, context and meaning are the scare commodities today. This situation alters the purpose of education to that of helping learners communicate with others, find relevant and accurate information for the task at hand, and be colearners with teachers and peers in diverse settings that go beyond school walls.

To move toward this vision will require new concepts defining the learning process and evolving purpose of education. It will also require rethinking current directions and practices. While maintaining high standards in the learning of desired content and skills, the learner, learning process, and learning environment must not be neglected if we are to adequately prepare students for productive and healthy futures. State and national standards, however, must be critically reevaluated in terms of what is necessary to prepare students to be knowledgeable, responsible, and caring citizens. Standards must move beyond knowledge conservation to knowledge creation and production (Hannafin, 1999). The current focus on content must be balanced with a focus on individual learners and their holistic learning needs in an increasingly complex and fast-changing world.

The needs of learners are also changing and an issue of concern given its relationships to problems such as school dropout is that of youth alienation. Ryan and Deci (2000) maintain that alienation in any age population is caused by failing to provide supports for competence, autonomy, and relatedness. Meeting these needs are also essential to healthy development and creating contexts that engender individual commitment, effort, and high-quality performance. Unfortunately, there are too many examples in the current educational reform agenda of coercive and punitive consequences for students, teachers, and administrators when students fail to achieve educational standards on state and national tests. Educational psychologists' attention to these issues is obvious in several of the chapters in this volume.

Educational psychology's growing knowledge base supports comprehensive and holistic educational models. A current challenge is to find these models and link their successful practices to what has been demonstrated relative to the needs of learners in research on learning, motivation, and development. The stories of teachers and other educators must also become part of our credible evidence. For example, Kohl, founder of the open school movement, shares his 36-year experience as a teacher working in dysfunctional, poverty-ridden urban school districts (in Scherer, 1998). He emphasizes the importance of teachers projecting hope—convincing students of their worth and ability to achieve in a difficult world. Kohl advocates what he calls *personalized*

learning based on caring relationship and respect for the unique way each student perceives the world and learns. Respecting students, honoring their perspectives, and providing quality learning are all ways that have been validated in research from educational psychology and related fields. Research from a multitude of studies and contexts has demonstrated the efficacy of these strategies for engaging students in learning communities that encourage invention, creativity, and imagination.

The Learner-Centered Psychological Principles

In keeping with an awareness of these trends, proactive efforts have been made in the past decade to make educational psychology's knowledge base more visible and accessible to educators and policy makers. One such example is the work of the American Psychological Association (APA). Beginning in 1990, the APA appointed a special Task Force on Psychology in Education, one of whose purposes was to integrate research and theory from psychology and education in order to surface general principles that have stood the test of time and can provide a framework for school redesign and reform. The result was a document that originally specified twelve fundamental principles about learners and learning that taken together provide an integrated perspective on factors influencing learning for *all* learners (APA Task Force on Psychology in Education, 1993). This document was revised in 1997 (APA Work Group of the Board of Educational Affairs, 1997) and now includes 14 principles that are essentially the same as the original 12 principles, except that attention is now given to principles dealing with learning and diversity and with standards and assessment.

The 14 learner-centered principles are categorized into four research-validated domains shown in Table 23.1. Domains important to learning are metacognitive and cognitive, affective and motivational, developmental and social, and individual differences. These domains and the principles within them provide a framework for designing learner-centered practices at all levels of schooling. They also define *learner-centered* from a research-validated perspective.

Defining Learner-Centered

From an integrated and holistic look at the principles, the following definition of learner-centered emerges: The perspective that couples a focus on individual learners (their heredity, experiences, perspectives, backgrounds, talents, interests, capacities, and needs) with a focus on learning (the best available knowledge about learning and how it occurs

TABLE 23.1   The Learner-Centered Psychological Principles

Cognitive and Metacognitive Factors

Principle 1: Nature of the learning process.
The learning of complex subject matter is most effective when it is an intentional process of constructing meaning from information and experience.

Principle 2: Goals of the learning process.
The successful learner—over time and with support and instructional guidance—can create meaningful, coherent representations of knowledge.

Principle 3: Construction of knowledge.
The successful learner can link new information with existing knowledge in meaningful ways.

Principle 4: Strategic thinking.
The successful learner can create and use a repertoire of thinking and reasoning strategies to achieve complex learning goals.

Principle 5: Thinking about thinking.
Higher-order strategies for selecting and monitoring mental operations facilitate creative and critical thinking.

Principle 6: Context of learning.
Learning is influenced by environmental factors, including culture, technology, and instructional practices.

Motivational and Affective Factors

Principle 7: Motivational and emotional influences on learning.
What and how much is learned is influenced by the learner's motivation. Motivation to learn in turn is influenced by the individual's emotional states, beliefs, interests and goals, and habits of thinking.

Principle 8: Intrinsic motivation to learn.
The learner's creativity, higher-order thinking, and natural curiosity all contribute to motivation to learn. Intrinsic motivation is stimulated by tasks that have optimal novelty and difficulty, are relevant to personal interests, and provide for personal choice and control.

Principle 9: Effects of motivation on effort.
Acquisition of complex knowledge and skills requires extended learner effort and guided practice. Without learners' motivation to learn, the willingness to exert this effort is unlikely without coercion.

Developmental and Social Factors

Principle 10: Developmental influence on learning.
As individuals develop, they encounter different opportunities and experience different constraints for learning. Learning is most effective when differential development within and across physical, intellectual, emotional, and social domains is taken into account.

Principle 11: Social influences on learning.
Learning is influenced by social interactions, interpersonal relations, and communication with others.

Individual Differences Factors

Principle 12: Individual differences in learning.
Learners have different strategies, approaches, and capabilities for learning that are a function of prior experience and heredity.

Principle 13: Learning and diversity.
Learning is most effective when differences in learners' linguistic, cultural, and social backgrounds are taken into account.

Principle 14: Standards and assessment.
Setting appropriately high and challenging standards and assessing the learner and learning progress—including diagnostic, process, and outcome assessment—are integral parts of the learning process.

Note. Summarized from the APA Work Group of the Board of Educational Affairs (1997, November). *Learner-centered psychological principles: Guidelines for school reform and redesign.* Washington, DC: American Psychological Association.

and about teaching practices that are most effective in promoting the highest levels of motivation, learning, and achievement for all learners). This dual focus then informs and drives educational decision making. The learner-centered perspective is a reflection in practice of the learner-centered psychological principles in the programs, practices, policies, and people that support learning for all (McCombs & Whisler, 1997, p. 9).

This definition highlights that the learner-centered psychological principles apply to all learners—in and outside of school, young and old. Learner-centered is also related to the beliefs, characteristics, dispositions, and practices of teachers. When teachers derive their practices from an understanding of the principles, they (a) include learners in decisions about how and what they learn and how that learning is assessed; (b) value each learner's unique perspectives; (c) respect and accommodate individual differences in learners' backgrounds, interests, abilities, and experiences; and (d) treat learners as cocreators and partners in teaching and learning.

My research with learner-centered practices and self-assessment tools based on the principles for teachers and students from K–12 and college classrooms confirms that what defines learner-centeredness is not solely a function of particular instructional practices or programs (McCombs & Lauer, 1997; McCombs & Whisler, 1997). Rather, it is a complex interaction of teacher qualities in combination with characteristics of instructional practices—as perceived by individual learners. Learner-centeredness varies as a function of learner perceptions that in turn are the result of each learner's prior experiences, self-beliefs, and attitudes about schools and learning as well as their current interests, values, and goals. Thus, the quality of learner-centeredness does not reside in programs or practices by themselves.

When learner-centered is defined from a research perspective, it also clarifies what is needed to create positive learning contexts and communities at the classroom and school levels. In addition, it increases the likelihood of success for more students and their teachers and can lead to increased clarity about the requisite dispositions and characteristics of school personnel who are in service to learners and learning. From this perspective, the learner-centered principles become foundational for determining how to use and assess the efficacy of learner-centered programs in providing instruction, curricula, and personnel to enhance the teaching and learning process. The confirm that perceptions of the learner regarding how well programs and practices meet individual needs are part of the assessment of ongoing learning, growth, and development.

CONTRIBUTIONS OF EDUCATIONAL PSYCHOLOGY TO EFFECTIVE REFORM

In looking across the chapters in this volume and other recent work in the field of educational psychology, a number of trends emerge. Most significant from my perspective are the following:

- Acknowledging the *complexity of human behavior* and the *need for integrative theories and research* that contextualize teaching and learning in *schools as living systems* that are themselves complex, dynamic, and *built on both individual and relational principles.*

- *Looking at humans and their behavior holistically* and focusing not only on cognitive and intellectual processes, but also on social and emotional processes that differentially influence learning, motivation, and development.

- *Situating the study of teaching and learning* in diverse school contexts and in particular content domains with a mix of quantitative and qualitative methodologies.

- Seeing *teachers as learners* whose own professional development must mirror the best of what we know about learning, motivation, and development.

- *Rethinking critical assumptions about human abilities and talents,* reciprocity in teacher and learner roles, and the function and purpose of schooling so that we can better prepare students for productive contributions to a global world and lifelong learning with emerging technologies.

- *Acknowledging the central role of learners' thinking and perceptions of their experiences* in learning and motivation—for all learners in the system, including teachers, administrators, parents, and students.

We are in an exciting era of transformation and change—an era where the knowledge base in educational psychology has the opportunity to play a significant role in shaping our K–20 educational systems for the better. Particularly relevant to educational reform is knowledge being gained in the following areas, many of which have been highlighted in prior chapters in this volume. My intention here, however, is to describe more broadly how other areas of research in the field of educational psychology are informing issues in educational reform and the design of more effective learning systems.

Dealing With Increased Student Diversity

An issue of growing concern is the record number of students entering public and private elementary and secondary schools (Meece & Kurtz-Costes, 2001). This population is more diverse than ever before, with almost 40% minority students in the total public school population. Wong and Rowley (2001) offer a commentary on the schooling of ethnic minority children, cautioning that researchers should be sensitive to the cultural biases of their research with populations of color, recognize the diversity within ethnic groups, limit comparisons between groups, integrate processes pertaining to ethnic minority cultures with those of normative development, examine cultural factors in multiple settings, balance the focus on risks and problems with attention to strengths and protective factors, and examine outcomes other than school achievement. There is a need for comprehensive and coherent frameworks that allow differentiation of common issues (e.g., all children being potentially resistant to school because of its compulsory nature) to identify additional factors (e.g., cultural dissonance between school norms and ethnic culture norms) related to resistance to school. Multiple contexts should be studied, longitudinal studies undertaken, and sophisticated statistical tools applied.

Okagaki (2001) argues for a triarchic model of minority children's school achievement that takes into account the form and perceived function of school, the family's cultural norms and beliefs about education and development, and the characteristics of the child. The significant role of perceptions, expectations for school achievement, educational goals, conceptions of intelligence, and self-reported behaviors and feelings of efficacy are discussed as they influence successful strategies for the education of minority children. Home, school, and personal characteristics must all be considered, with particular attention paid to practices that facilitate positive teacher-child and child-peer interactions. The culture of the classroom must be made more visible and understandable to children from different cultural backgrounds—carefully considering the depth and clarity of communications with parents, helping students and parents see the practical relevance of obtaining a good education, thinking through how what we do in schools might have stereotyping effects for students, and recognizing that families have different theories about education, intelligence, parenting, and child development.

It is generally recognized that unacceptable achievement gaps exist between minority and nonminority children and that dropout rates are higher for some ethnic groups. Longitudinal research by Goldschmidt and Wang (1999) using National Educational Longitudinal Study (NELS) database on student and school factors associated with dropping out in different grades shows that the mix of student risk factors changes between early and late dropouts, with family characteristics being most important for late dropouts. Being held back was the single strongest predictor of dropping out for both early and late dropouts, but misbehaving was the most important factor in late dropouts. Hispanics are more likely to drop out than are African Americans and African Americans are more likely to drop out than are Whites. These differences are partly accounted for by differences in family, language, and socioeconomic factors. Associations between racial groups and factors such as being below expected grade levels, working while in school, and having poor grades also contribute to the differences in cultural groups.

Interventions that show promise for reversing these negative trends include social support and a focus on positive school climates. Lee and Smith (1999) report research on young adolescents in the Chicago public schools that indicates there needs to be a balance of challenging and rigorous academic instruction with social support in the form of smaller, more intimate learning communities. Such a balance tends to eliminate achievement differences among students from different racial and socioeconomic backgrounds—particularly in math and reading. The biggest disadvantages in achievement are for students who attend schools with both little social support and low academic challenge and rigor; thus, social support is particularly effective when students also are in schools that push them toward academic pursuits. The balance needs to be one with a focus on learning and on learner needs.

Studying Development of Academic Motivation

Ryan and Patrick (2001) studied the motivation and engagement of middle school adolescents as a function of their perceptions of the classroom social environment. Changes in motivation and engagement were found to be a function of four distinct dimensions of the environment: (a) promoting interaction (discuss with, share ideas, get to know other students), (b) promoting mutual respect (respect each other's ideas, don't make fun of or say negative things to others), (c) promoting performance goals (compare students to others, make best and worst test scores and grades public, make it obvious who is not doing well), and (d) teacher support (respect student opinions, understands students' feelings, help students when upset or need support in schoolwork). In general, if students perceived teacher support and perceived that the teacher promoted interaction and mutual respect, motivation and engagement were enhanced. On the other hand, if students perceived that their teacher promoted performance goals, negative effects on motivation and engagement occurred. Students with supportive teachers reported higher self-efficacy and increases in self-regulated learning, whereas with performance-goal-oriented teachers, students reported engaging in more disruptive behaviors. Ryan

and Patrick conclude that becoming more student-centered means (a) attending to social conditions in the classroom environment as perceived by students and (b) providing practices that enhance students' perceptions of support, respect, and interaction.

Our work with kindergarten-through college-age students over the past 8 years has revealed that learner-centered practices consistent with educational psychology's knowledge base and the learner-centered psychological principles enhance learner motivation and achievement (McCombs, 2000a, 2001a; McCombs & Whisler, 1997; Weinberger & McCombs, 2001). Of particular significance in this work is that student perceptions of their teachers' instructional practices accounts for between 45–60%, whereas teacher beliefs and perceptions only account for between 4–15% of the variance in student motivation and achievement. The single most important domain of practice for students in all age ranges are practices that promote a positive climate for learning and interpersonal relationships between and among students and teachers. Also important are practices that provide academic challenge and give students choice and control, that encourage the development of critical thinking and learning skills, and that adapt to a variety of individual developmental differences.

Using teacher and student surveys based on the learner-centered psychological principles, called the Assessment of Learner-Centered Practices (ALCP), teachers can be assisted in reflecting on individual and class discrepancies in perceptions of classroom practice and in changing practices to meet student needs (McCombs, 2001). Results of our research with the ALCP teacher and student surveys at both the secondary and postsecondary levels have confirmed that at all levels of our educational system, teachers and instructors can be helped to improve instructional practices and change toward more learner-centered practices by attending to what students are perceiving and by spending more time creating positive climates and relationships—critical connections so important to personal and system learning and change.

For students who are seen as academically unmotivated, Hidi and Harackiewicz (2000) provide insights from a review of research related to academic motivation. The literature on interests and goals is reviewed and integrated, and the authors urge educators to provide a balance of practices that are sensitive to students' individual interests, intrinsic motivation, and mastery goals—with practices that trigger situational interest, extrinsic motivation, and performance goals. This balance helps to shift the orientation to an internalization of interests and motivation and to promote positive motivational development for traditionally unmotivated students. The importance of the roles of significant others (e.g., teachers, parents, coaches) is also highlighted in terms of eliciting and shaping interests and goals in their students and children. Such an intrinsic-extrinsic motivational balance is deemed essential if educators are to meet diverse student needs, backgrounds, and experiences—that is, to adapt to the full range of student differences, we need the full range of instructional approaches, and these approaches need to be flexibly implemented.

The effects of student perceptions of their classroom environment on their achievement goals and outcomes was studied by Church, Elliot, and Gable (2001). The relationship between student perceptions and achievement outcomes was indirect; their influence first affected achievement goals, which in turn influenced achievement outcomes. If undergraduate students perceived that their instructor made the lecture interesting and engaging (compared to a situation in which they perceived that the instructor emphasized the importance of grades and performance evaluations or had grading structures that minimized the chance of being successful), they adopted mastery goal orientations (intrinsic motivation) versus performance goal orientations (extrinsic motivation). The authors conclude that stringent evaluation standards can lead to the adoption of performance-avoidance goals and hinder mastery goal adoption. For this reason, a study of both approach and avoidance orientations is needed because it moves research toward a broader framework that involves more complex integration of multiple constructs.

On the other hand, Midgley, Kaplan, and Middleton (2001) argue that the call to reconceptualize goal theory to acknowledge the positive effects of performance-approach goals is not warranted. They review studies that indicate the negative effects of performance-approach goals in terms of students' use of avoidance strategies, cheating, and reluctance to cooperate with peers. They stress that it is important to consider for whom and under what conditions performance goals are good. Emphasizing mastery goals needs to be an integral part of all practices—particularly in this era, in which standards, testing, and accountability dominate educational practices and deep meaningful learning is in short supply.

In a longitudinal study of changes in academic intrinsic motivation from childhood through late adolescence, Gottfried, Fleming, and Gottfried (2001) found that not only is intrinsic motivation a stable construct over time, but academic intrinsic motivation declines—particularly in math and science—over the developmental span. For this reason, Gottfried et al. argue that early interventions are needed to identify those students who may be at risk for low motivation and performance. Practices such as introducing new materials that are of optimal or moderate difficulty; related to student interests; meaningful to students; provide choice and autonomy; and utilize incongruity, novelty, surprise, and complexity are recommended.

Developing Students' Metacognitive and Self-Regulation Competencies

Lin (2001) describes the power of metacognitive activities that foster both cognitive and social development. To accomplish this goal, however, knowledge about self-as-learner must be part of the metacognitive approach. Knowing how to assess what they know and do not know about a particular knowledge domain is not sufficient, and Lin's research shows that knowledge about self-as-learner as well as supportive social environments help promote a shared understanding among community members about why metacognitive knowledge and strategies are useful in learning. The knowledge of self-as-learner can also be expanded to helping students know who they are and what their role is in specific learning cultures and knowledge domains or tasks; thus, this research highlights the application of the knowledge base on metacognition in ways that are holistic and assist in the development of both cognitive and social skills.

Another example of applying research that integrates cognitive, metacognitive, motivational, and social strategies in the form of self-regulated learning (SRL) interventions is provided by Paris and Paris (2001). After reviewing what we have learned in this area, Paris and Paris define a number of principles of SRL that can be applied in the classroom, including the following:

- Helping students use self-appraisal to analyze personal styles and strategies of learning as a way to promote monitoring of progress, revising of strategies, and enhanced feelings of self-efficacy.

- Teaching self-management of thinking, effort, and affect such as goal setting, time management, reflection, and comprehension monitoring that can provide students with tools to be adaptive, persistent, strategic, and self-controlled in learning and problem-solving situations.

- Using a variety of explicit instructional approaches and indirect modeling and reflection approaches to help students acquire metacognitive skills and seek evidence of personal growth through self-assessments, charting, discussing evidence, and practicing with experts.

- Integrating the use of narrative autobiographical stories as part of students' participation in a reflective community and as a way to help them examine their own self-regulation habits.

Additional principles are suggested by Ley and Young (2001, pp. 94–95) for embedding support in instruction to facilitate SRL in less expert learners. These principles are

- Guide learners to prepare and structure an effective learning environment; this includes helping learners to manage distractions by such strategies as charts for recording study time and defining what is an effective distraction-free study environment for them.
- Organize instruction and activities to facilitate cognitive and metacognitive processes; this includes strategies such as outlining, concept mapping, and structured overviewing.
- Use instructional goals and feedback to present student monitoring opportunities; this includes self-monitoring instruction and record keeping.
- Provide learners with continuous evaluation information and occasions to self-evaluate this includes helping students evaluate the success of various strategies and revising approaches based on feedback (Ley & Young, 2001, pp. 94–95).

Redefining Intelligence and Giftedness

As pointed out in this volume (see chapters by Sternberg and by Olszewski-Kubilius), there is a growing movement in theory and practice to reconceptualize what is meant by intelligence and giftedness. For example, Howard Gardner, in an interview by Kogan (2000), strongly argues that schools should be places where students learn to think and study deeply those things that matter and have meaning; schools should also help students learn to make sense of the world. He advocates a three-prong curriculum aimed at teaching—through a multiple intelligences approach—truth, beauty, and goodness. To teach truth, Gardner believes children need to understand the notion of evolution—including species variation and natural selection—and an appreciation of the struggle among people for survival. To teach beauty, Gardner would choose Mozart's *The Marriage of Figaro* as a pinnacle of beauty that portrays characters with deeply held emotions, offers the opportunity to help students appreciate other works of art, and inspires new creations. To teach goodness, Gardner chooses helping students understand a sequence of events such as the Holocaust, which shows what humans are capable of doing in both good and bad ways and provides a way for students to learn how others deal with pressures and dilemmas. Methods such as dramatic, vivid narratives and metaphors are recommended for involving students in their learning.

Other new developments influencing our understanding of intelligence are interdisciplinary fields of research that can offer multiple perspectives on complex human phenomena. Ochsner and Lieberman (2001) describe the emergence of social cognitive neuroscience that allows three levels of analysis: a social level concerned with motivational and social factors influencing behavior and experience; a cognitive level concerned with information-processing mechanisms that underlie social-level phenomena; and a neural level concerned with brain mechanisms that instantiate cognitive processes. Although still in its infancy, this multidisciplinary field promises to provide new insights about human functioning that can be useful in studying learners and learning in complex living systems such as schools. It also follows the trend toward more integrative and holistic research practices.

Consistent with this integrative trend is work by Robinson, Zigler, and Gallagher (2000) on the similarities and differences between people at the two tails of the normal curve—the mentally retarded and the gifted. As operationalized in tests of intelligence, deviance from the norm by performance two standard deviations from the mean (IQ of 70–75 or lower or IQ of 125–130 or higher) typically defines individuals who are mentally retarded or gifted, respectively. In looking at educational issues, Robinson et al. raise the following points:

- A one-size-fits-all paradigm for education does not accommodate individual differences in level and pace of learning—creating major problems for meeting the needs of diverse students in the current system designed for the average student.
- Strategies and approaches that work well with gifted children need to become models for improving the school experiences of all children.
- The basic philosophies and values of American schools are in keeping—at least theoretically—with the concept of adapting to individual differences in abilities, thereby providing an opportunity for our schools to become models of how best to deal with students in the two tails of the normal curve.
- More work is needed to solve the problems of economic and ethnic disadvantages that skew distributions of IQ scores and lead to discrimination by gender, race, and ethnic origin in terms of overplacement of minority students in special services and underrepresentation of minority students in gifted services.
- Research agendas in areas such as neurodevelopmental science, brain function, and genetics need to look at both ends in longitudinal studies that can provide insight into how to design interventions that overcome current maladaptive approaches to learning and performance that can hinder retarded and gifted students.

Understanding Components of Effective Teachers, Teaching, and Teacher Development

The past decade of research has seen an increased focus on teaching, teachers, and teacher education. Part of this increased attention is due to a growing understanding of the nature of learning and the role of teachers as lifelong and expert learners. Hoy (2000) argues for the need to place learning at the center of teaching, which means that teachers must have both deep content knowledge and a deep understanding of learning, motivation, and development. She also describes shifts in teacher education toward more integrative study that contextualizes content and pedagogical knowledge in social environments and inquiry-based curricula. Collaboration between and among students and teachers at all levels of schooling is another trend, along with encouraging reflection and field-based experiences. The concern is raised that educational psychology may get lost or marginalized in these trends, challenging us to think through how to situate and integrate our knowledge base and make processes of learning, motivation, and development more visible and accessible to teacher education students.

A specific look at the impact of teacher education on teachers of secondary mathematics is described by Borko et al. (2000). They argue that for teacher education to make a difference, both university experiences and field placements need to share comparable visions of reformed practice and teacher learning as situated in reformed practice. Such practice has methods situated (i.e., taught in the context of) in the content area (e.g., mathematics) and uses learning tasks that encourage multiple representations, solution strategies, and actively involve students in the learning process (e.g., having them make conjectures, provide justifications and explanations, and draw conclusions). Similarly, Zech, Cause-Vega, Bray, Secules, and Goldman (2000) describe a professional development model, content-based collaborative inquiry (CBCI), that engages educators in inquiring and constructing their own knowledge with a focus on their own and their students' understanding and learning processes. Sustaining communities of inquiry to support lifelong teacher learning and educational reform is discussed as a way to shift practicing teachers' orientations toward knowledge and knowing. By helping teachers focus on students' understanding in content domains, teachers' critical reflection and assessment of their content knowledge and practice occurs. Collaborative inquiry helps uncover assumptions and build communities of practice based on trusting relationships.

Van den Berg and Ros (1999) remind us that teachers have individual questions, needs, and opinions about innovations and reform initiatives that must be attended to in any reform process. Using a concerns-based approach, different types of concerns were revealed at different stages of the innovation process and pointed to the need to attune innovation policies to these factors. Three clusters of concerns were identified: self-worries (e.g., amount of work involved in the innovation), task worries (e.g., classes too big to accommodate the innovation), and other worries (e.g., getting older colleagues to implement the innovation). The teachers' concerns varied as a function of stage of the innovation (adoption, implementation, institutionalization), with self-worries more apparent in the adoption stage, task worries emphasized more in the implementation stage, and more other worries present in the institutionalization stage. The authors conclude with a plea to include opinions of teachers as well as orientation toward uncertainty in reform efforts and to provide explicit opportunities for reflection and dialogue in ongoing workshops and seminars.

The importance of collective teacher efficacy for student achievement is explored by Goddard, Hoy, and Hoy (2000). *Collective teacher efficacy* is defined as the perceptions of teachers in a school that the efforts of the faculty as a whole will positively affect students. A measure was developed and validated, and it was shown to have a positive relationship with student achievement in both reading and mathematics. It was also shown to differentiate achievement differences between schools; higher levels of collective teacher efficacy were related to gains in reading and mathematics achievement. When teachers share a sense of efficacy, they act more purposefully to enhance student learning and are supported organizationally to reflect on efforts that are likely to meet the unique needs of students.

Another critical variable is the degree to which teachers believe that instructional choice promotes learning and motivation. In spite of a large literature documenting the positive effects of choice—particularly on affective areas such as interest, ownership, creativity, and personal autonomy—many teachers continue to limit student choice. Flowerday and Schraw (2000) interviewed 36 practicing teachers to examine what, when, where, and to whom teachers offer choice. Among the findings were that teachers with high self-efficacy are more likely to provide instructional choices, as are teachers who themselves feel intellectually and psychologically autonomous and who are more experienced in particular subject areas. Most or all teachers agreed that choice should be used (a) in all grades, with older students needing more choices; (b) in a variety of settings, on different tasks, and for academic and social activities; and (c) in ways that offer simple choices first, help students practice making good choices, use team choices for younger students, provide information that clarifies the choice, and offer choices within a task.

New learner-centered professional development models for teachers focus on examining beliefs, empowerment, teacher responsibility for their own growth, teachers as leaders, and development of higher-order thinking and personal reflection skills (e.g., Darling-Hammond, 1996; Fullan, 1995; McCombs & Whisler, 1997). A key to teachers' abilities to accept and implement these learner-centered models is support in the form of self-assessment tools for becoming more aware of their beliefs, practices, and the impact of these practices on students. Information from teachers' self-assessments can then be used by teachers to identify—in a nonthreatening and nonjudgmental context—the changes in practice that are needed to better serve the learning needs of all students. In this way, teachers can begin to take responsibility for developing their own professional development plans.

A number of researchers are creating instruments to help teachers at all levels of the educational system (K–16) look at their own and their students' perceptions of their learning experiences. To date, however, these tools are available in innovative teacher preparation programs and are not used in higher education in general largely because of reluctance among many college administrators to change current evaluation procedures that are based on direct instruction rather than holistic and constructivist models of teacher classroom practices.

Changes in evaluation procedures are occurring in teacher education, and current approaches support teacher growth with learning opportunities that (a) encourage reflection, critical thinking, and dialogue and (b) allow teachers to examine educational theories and practices in light of their beliefs and experiences. For teachers to change their beliefs to be compatible with more learner-centered and constructivist practices, however, they need to be engaged in reflective processes that help them become clearer about the gap between what they are accomplishing and what needs to be accomplished. Reflection is defined by Loughran (1996) as a recapturing of experience in which the person thinks about an idea, mulls it over, and evaluates it. Thus, Loughran argues that reflection helps develop the habits, skills, and attitudes necessary for teachers' self-directed growth.

The work of my colleagues and me in developing a set of self-assessment and reflection tools for K–16 teachers (ALCP), in the form of surveys for teachers, students, and administrators, combines aspects of these approaches (McCombs & Lauer, 1997; McCombs, Lauer, & Pierce, 1998; McCombs & Whisler, 1997). However, the focus, is on identifying teacher beliefs and discrepancies between teacher and student perspectives of practices that can enhance student motivation and achievement—as a tool to assist teachers in reflecting on and changing practices as well as identifying personalized staff development needs.

Our research (McCombs & Lauer, 1997; McCombs et al., 1998; McCombs & Whisler, 1997) looked at the impact of teacher beliefs on their perceptions of their classroom practices as well as how teacher perceptions of practice differ from student perceptions of these practices. In a large-scale study of teachers and students, we confirmed our hypothesis about the importance—for student motivation, learning, and achievement—of those beliefs and practices that are consistent with the research on learners and learning. We also found that teachers who are more learner-centered are both more successful in engaging all students in an effective learning process and are themselves more effective learners and happier with their jobs. Furthermore, teachers report that the process of self-assessment and reflection—particularly about discrepancies between their own and their individual students' experiences of classroom practices—helps them identify areas in which they might change their practices to be more effective in reaching more students. This is an important finding that relates to the *how* of transformation—that is, by helping teachers and others engage in a process of self-assessment and reflection, particularly about the impact of their beliefs and practices on individual students and their learning and motivation, a respectful and nonjudgmental impetus to change is provided. Combining the opportunity for teacher self-assessment of and reflection on their beliefs and practices (and the impact of these practices on individual students) with skill training and conversations and dialogue about how to create learner-centered K–16 schools and classrooms can help make the transformation complete.

Our research also revealed that teachers were not absolutely learner-centered or completely non-learner-centered. Different learner-centered teachers had different but overlapping beliefs. At the same time, however, specific *beliefs* or *teaching practices* could be classified as learner-centered (likely to enhance motivation, learning, and success) or non-learner-centered (likely to hinder motivation, learning, and success). Learner-centered teachers are defined as those whose beliefs and practices were classified more as learner-centered than as non learner-centered. For example, *believing all students learn* is quite different from *believing that some students cannot learn,* the former being learner-centered and the latter being non-learner-centered. Learner-centered teachers see each student as unique and capable of learning, have a perspective that focuses on the learner's knowing that the teacher's beliefs promote learning, understand basic principles defining learners and learning, and honor and accept the student's point of view (McCombs, 2000a; McCombs & Lauer, 1997). As a result, the student's natural inclinations—to learn, master the environment, and grow in positive ways—are enhanced.

Capitalizing on Advances in Teaching and Learning Technologies

In a review of emerging Web-based learning environments, McNabb and McCombs (2001) point out that recent efforts to infuse electronic networking into school buildings via the Internet promise to promote connections among teachers and students in classrooms and those in the community at large. At the same time, uses of electronic networks for educational purposes cause large disturbances to the closed-ended nature of twentieth-century classroom practices (Heflich, 2001; Jones, 2001; McNabb, 2001). What becomes apparent are misalignments among curricular goals and resources, instructional practices, assessments, and accountability policies governing learning activities. The current shortage of qualified teachers available to the nation's children on an equitable basis provides an additional challenge and opportunity for systemically transforming the nature of schooling to better meet the needs of twenty-first-century learners.

Haywood (personal communication, University of Edinburgh and Open University, June 15, 2001) argues that to overcome built-in inertia in traditional systems and the people they serve (students, teachers, administrators) requires new forms of learning, assessment, and community. New forms of communication that emerge in electronic-learning cultures may lead to new and better forms of socialization. Some of the bigger challenges in distance learning have been in how to help people handle change and in supporting new educational processes while working within the dominant traditional systems. The implementation issues range from determining the number of computers needed to how computers are used and how much they are used.

Current research at the Open University and other European institutions supporting some form of Web-based learning is now focusing on identifying the range of individual and group learning outcomes that must be assessed in both formative and summative ways. Other issues include finding new ways of communicating (Barnes, University of Bristol, personal communication, June 19, 2001) and identifying new social learning outcomes that result. Current challenges include communicating across several mediums in electronic-learning environments, looking at change over time, and finding ways to reward risk-taking at the personal and institutional levels as traditional K–20 systems make steps to change current learning and assessment paradigms.

Taking up the challenge of building learner-centered and technology-based classrooms, Orrill (2001) describes how

teachers can be supported toward this goal with professional development that includes reflection, proximal goals, collegial support groups, one-on-one feedback, and support materials for teachers. The framework was based on the assumption that change is individual but must be supported over time in the social context of schools. Data were collected on 10 middle school teachers using simulations in project-based learning over a 4-month period. Refinements to the professional development framework included helping teachers to develop reflective skills prior to using proximal goals to focus reflection activities. Outside resources, one-on-one feedback, and collegial group meetings are then used to enhance the interplay between reflection and proximal goals. Guidance is essential as part of the development of reflection such that teachers see the importance of focusing on learner-centered goals that can be enacted immediately in refining the simulation activities.

Significant in using emerging technologies are personalization strategies. Just as Lin (2001) found higher levels of social development and achievement when metacognitive activities included self-as-learner knowledge, Moreno and Mayer (2000) report that personalized multimedia messages can increase student engagement in active learning. In a series of five experiments with college students, personalized rather than neutral messages resulted in better retention and problem-solving transfer. The importance of self-reference to student engagement and motivation has a long-standing research base, but it appears to be especially important in technology-based learning, particularly because it also influences higher learning outcomes.

The issue of scaling up technology-embedded and project-based innovations in systemic reform is addressed by Blumenfeld, Fishman, Krajcik, Marx, and Soloway (2000). Studying urban middle schools, a framework is used to gauge the fit of these innovations with existing school capabilities, policy and management structures, and the organizational culture. The authors argue that the research community needs to create an agenda that can document how innovations work in different contexts and how to select reforms that match outcomes that are valued in their community and that are compatible with state and national agendas. Collaboration with teachers and administrators not only can help them adapt the innovation to make it achievable, but such collaboration also can promote an understanding of what will be require for sustainable systemic innovations that challenge traditional methods.

Of significance in this work with technology-based teaching and learning systems is the growing agreement that what we know about learning, motivation, development, and effective schooling practices will transfer to the design of these new systems (McNabb & McCombs, 2001). What we have learned that is particularly applicable includes findings summarized earlier in this chapter and in many of the other chapters in this volume: Comprehensive dimensions of successful schools and learning environments must be concerned with (a) promoting a sense of belonging and agency, (b) engaging families in children's learning and education, (c) using a quality and integrated curriculum, (d) providing ongoing professional development in both content and child development areas (including pedagogy), (e) having high student expectations, and (f) providing opportunities for success for all students.

Building New Learning Communities and Cultures

In most institutions of elementary, secondary, and higher education and progressively within professional development programs, teachers, administrators, policy makers, and those in content-area disciplines are isolated from each other. It is difficult to find examples of cross-department collaborations in course design, multidisciplinary learning opportunities, or organizational structures and physical facilities that allow interactions and dialogue among a range of educational stakeholders. Schools are isolated from emerging content in professional disciplines. Change is often mandated from above or from outside the system. Critical connections are not being made, and it is not difficult to foresee that change is then difficult and often resisted because of personal fears or insecurities. Those fears and insecurities disappear when people participate together in creating how their work gets done.

In developing effective learning communities and cultures, it is important to see the role of educational psychology's knowledge base and the principles derived from this knowledge base in a systemic context. It is important to understand that education is one of many complex living systems that functions to support particular human needs (cf. Wheatley, 1999). Even though such systems are by their nature unpredictable, they can be understood in terms of principles that define human needs, cognitive and motivational processes, interpersonal and social factors, and development and individual differences. A framework based on research-validated principles can then inform not only curriculum, instruction, assessment, and related professional development but also organizational changes needed to create learner-centered, knowledge-centered, assessment-centered, and community-centered practices that lead to more healthy communities and cultures for learning.

Effective schools function as a healthy *living system*— an interconnected human network that supports teachers, students, and their relationships within communities of expert practice. In placing emphasis on the learner-centered developments of both students and teachers (as expert learners) within the context of emerging technologies, educational psychology's knowledge based can be applied to building a fully functioning living system. This system supports a community network of members who are connected and responsive to each other. Community members interact in ways that precipitate learning and social development on all levels of the system. With the recent infusion and development of new and innovative technologies, researchers and scientists have imagined and implemented a wide range of methods for making this goal attainable.

Studies about the impact of the Internet on society and communities show that people in general are using the Internet at home, at the library, and at work for a variety of purposes including informal learning (Bollier, 2000; English-Lueck, 1998; Nie & Erbing, 2000; Shields & Behrman, 2000). Children are finding connections to basic and advanced knowledge available in and generated through the community; some of this knowledge can conflict with that in textbooks. Youth's career exploration and teachers' professional development is best served in the community arena. Geographic cultures are converging electronically with other cultures via networks that allow easy movement in and out of many cultures. McNabb (2001) points out that historically research shows that positive cultural experiences based on mediated interactions with others are a vital part of children's personal and interpersonal development that fosters one's overall ability to learn (Boyer, 1995; Dewey, 1990; Feuerstein & Feuerstein, 1991; Vygotsky, 1978).

Wilson (2001) explains that *culture* refers to the set of artifacts and meanings (norms, expectations, tools, stories, language and activities, etc.) attached to a fairly stable group of people associating with each other; thus, as humans, each of us is (in a sense) multicultural and multilingual as we adapt to different cultural norms required by different groups and allegiances, a phenomenon that can proliferate on the Internet. It is community that helps bring coherence to our multicultural experiences. Wilson identifies belonging, trust, expectation, and obligation as defining characteristics of community. A sense of *belonging* within the community pertains to common purposes and values; *trust* pertains to acting for the good of the whole. Community carries an expectation among its members that the group provides value—particularly with respect to each other's learning goals and with that a sense of *obligation* to participate in activities and contribute to group goals.

In addition, evidence shows that electronically networked cultures and communities are causing shifts related to control of these new cultures for learning. In the twentieth-century industrial era, the focal point within school systems tended to pertain to goals generated externally (top-down) with mass production designs for curriculum, instruction, and assessment purposes (Reigeluth, 2001). In twenty-first-century culture, the focal point is shifting to customized learning experiences and personal learning plans with goals based on each learner's personal needs and interests facilitated by learner-centered pedagogy, content area understanding along a continuum from novice to expert developed through access to knowledge-centered materials and human resources in the community, and learners' needs and achievements identified by formative assessments aligned to personal learning plans using assessment-centered feedback loops.

Finally, the foregoing research, needs, and challenges facing today's learners in K–20 systems also face preservice and in-service teachers. Researchers are increasingly calling for learning and professional development approaches that lead to what they call emerging communities of practice. This idea is in keeping with the recognition that electronic-learning technologies allow for nonlinear emergent learning and new paradigms of assessment. Emerging technologies also allow for a variety of learning communities and cultures, including communities of interest, communities of sharing, and communities of caring—all of which can be part of the experience at various points in time and contribute to both higher engagement and higher learning outcomes.

WHAT RESEARCH DIRECTIONS ARE NEEDED?

This section provides what I see as basic and applied research directions that can foster the usefulness of educational psychology's contributions to education and educational reform during the twenty-first century. Although educational psychology is generally thought of as an applied field, basic as well as applied research directions suggested in Handbook chapters are summarized and others added from my perspective. All of these directions are then considered in light of implementation and evaluation implications as they are applied in the context of school and teacher accountability issues.

Basic Research Directions

In making the knowledge base from educational psychology more visible and accessible to educators and policy makers, some basic research directions are needed. From the preceding chapters in this volume and from my own perspective, a number of suggestions can be made, including the following:

- Research that can further refine and elucidate alternative conceptions of ability and intelligence and broaden our

understanding of the interplay between cognitive, affective, neurobiological, and social factors that influence the development of competencies.

- Research on voluntary study groups, effective uses of problem-based learning, intersections of cooperative learning and curriculum, strategies for professional development and follow-up support for cooperative learning, and how well cooperative learning works for gifted students or other students at the margins.

- Research on adult literacy, along with more research on how teaching word recognition also affects normal and gifted readers (not just struggling readers) and how to develop teachers to deliver motivational reading and writing programs.

- Research on the cultural aspects of learning and contrasts between activity theory and contextualism as alternative views for understanding the sociocultural context of the teaching and learning process.

- Research that explores relations between self-regulation and volition, the development of self-regulation in children, self-regulation and the curriculum, and self-regulation across the life span.

Applied Research Directions

Along with these basic research directions, more research is needed on the contexts of learning environments and the complex interactions between personal, organizational, and community levels of learning in schools as living systems; this includes attention to applied research in the following areas:

- Research on teacher development, including what teachers cite as the biggest challenge—the students themselves. Excellent teaching is a complex balancing act, and there are no quick fixes to producing excellent teachers.

- Research on what can be learned about learning and human adaptability to change during the implementation phase as new and existing teachers and others in our existing places called school begin to increasingly use electronic-learning technologies in new ways. These new ways of learning promise to be the catalyst for systems change and to a new paradigm for learning and assessment within electronically networked schools.

- Research to better understand the comprehensive dimensions of successful schools as (a) promoting a sense of belonging and agency, (b) engaging families in children's learning and education, (c) using a quality and integrated curriculum, (d) providing ongoing professional development in both content and child development areas (including pedagogy), (e) having high student expectations, and (f) providing opportunities for success for all students.

- Research to identify the best socialization experiences for positive adjustment with diverse student populations—examining how children's understanding of rules and norms change, how these rules are complementary or compatible with peer and adult norms, what differential impacts reward structures that teachers establish have depending of students' age and family environment, and further work on student beliefs and perceptions of social support from teachers and peers.

- Research that identifies teacher preparation practices that can foster of the development of metacognition in students and the application of metacognition to their own instruction.

- Research on school-based methodologies for studying the complex interrelationships between and among individual, organizational, and community levels of learning and functioning that can provide solid and credible evidence to support conclusions about causal connections between variables.

Producing Credible Research: Implementation and Evaluation Considerations

Educators, researchers, and policy makers are recognizing the need for new evaluation strategies and assessment methods that are dynamic measures of learning achievement and learner development aligned with multiple types of formative and summative outcomes (Broadfoot, 2001; Gipps, 2001; McNabb, Hawkes, & Rouk, 1999; Popham, 2001; Stiggins, 2001). As people increasingly use the Internet for educational purposes, evaluation strategies and assessment methods that can fully capture the complexity, flexibility, and open-ended nature of the learning processes and outcomes in networked communities are needed. Shepard (2000) calls for recognizing that different pedagogical approaches need different outcome measures. Most of our current accountability systems are based solely on high-stakes scores pertaining to knowledge-transmission outcomes, whereas research findings on how people learn and what is needed for twenty-first-century citizenry pertain to achieving knowledge-adaptation and knowledge-generation, higher-order thinking, technological literacy, and social-emotional outcomes (Bransford, Brown, & Cocking, 1999; Carroll, 2001; Groff, 2001; Mc-Combs, 2001a; McNabb, 2001; Ravitz, 2001; Repa, 2001). Evaluation and assessment designs need to be based not only on knowledge-centered principles but also on a combination of community-centered and learner-centered principles. Some learning communities thrive, whereas others get started and dissipate. Development of new evaluation strategies and assessment methods will lead to an understanding of what makes particular communities viable and how best to support learning in both on- and off-line learning communities. Assessment measures can be designed to provide data about the balance between individualized and group learning processes, instructional strategies and activity structures, and outcomes within different types of learning communities (McCombs, 2000b).

A host of other issues that will expand into the twenty-first century concern the growth of technology-based learning environments. In such environments, educational psychologists can play a central role in defining research and evaluation data requirements. For example, data collected in technology-based environments may be required to calibrate the online school climate and address research-based concerns about the negative effects of the distal nature of online relationships and the amount of time these distal relationships take away from close, more nurturing relationships (Mc-Combs, 2001a; McNabb, 2001; Repa, 2001). Research conducted by Kraut et al. (1998) indicates that a unit of measure with which to assess social ties in cyberspace is needed to foster the development of children's overall mental, social, and physical health and well-being. Building such measures on what we have learned is essential.

Other measurement and evaluation challenges concern the balancing of content knowledge gains against other, nonacademic educational goals. Currently our educational systems have a proliferation of standards competing for the attention of teachers and students. Dede (2000) points out that no one person can possibly meet all the standards that many states are now requiring of teachers and students. This phenomenon is indicative of a knowledge transmission mode of operating. In a traditional transmission-of-knowledge learning situation, not knowing has resulted in disadvantages to some learners in terms of future learning opportunities and decisions made based on high-stakes assessment scores. In a knowledge-generation learning situation, however, not knowing provides the foundation for the inquiry and calls for *assessment-centered* practices for feedback and revision (Bransford et al. 1999; Carroll, 2001). The new types of assessments for which researchers and evaluators are calling rely on communities in which learners have trusting relationships; in such relationships, learners feel comfortable enough to admit that they didn't understand a task, and they are willing and feel safe in exposing their uncertainty (Bransford, 2001; McLaughlin, 2001; Rose, 2001; Wilson, 2001).

Our present accountability system has created an overemphasis on summative assessments with little useful feedback at the personal, organizational, and community levels. Ravitz (2001) points out that current high-stakes and summative assessments are performed solely for Big Brother and do not provide feedback helpful to learners and leaders. According to Braun (2001), the present systems tend to focus on collecting summative data needed by those most removed from schools and the learning process—that is, policy makers. Little time is afforded to efforts needed to collect more formative data to serve the needs of those involved in shaping the learning process and thus its outcomes—that is teachers, students, and parents. However, issues pertaining to summative assessment need to be addressed because as a society, we want students to show some ability to transfer their learning to new situations (Bransford, 2001). There are important differences between static assessments of transfer (e.g., in which people learn something and then try to solve a new problem without access to any resources) versus dynamic assessments (e.g., assessments that allow people to consult resources and demonstrate the degree to which they have been preparing for future learning in particular areas). Portfolios properly designed can support formative data needed for learning and summative data for accountability within the community (Braun, 2001).

Formative assessment needs to combine input from all three levels of the learning community (i.e. personal, organizational, and community levels) through self-evaluation, peer critique, and expert feedback focused on conceptual understandings and skills that transfer. New evaluation strategies and assessment methods suitable for digital learning can capture learner change, growth, and improvement as it occurs in networked learning communities. This will involve issues of scale, as pointed out by Honey (2001). She suggests the real work of reform involves rethinking at the local level. She points out that we need to take seriously the challenge of working in partnership with schools and districts on terms that are meaningful to the people ultimately responsible for educating students—administrators, teachers, parents, and the students themselves (Cohen & Barnes, 1999; Meier, 1999; Sabelli & Dede, in press; Schoenfeld, 1995; Tyack & Cuban, 1995). This process can perhaps best be understood as one of diagnosis—an interpretive or deductive identification of how particular local qualities work together to form the distinctive elements of the learning community. The process of adaptation through experimentation and interpretation—what Nora Sabelli calls the *localization of innovation*—is critical to the work of reform (Honey, 2001).

Confrey and Sabelli (2001) call for programmatic evaluations and assessment to be informed by implementation research that builds upon and contributes to increasingly more successful implementations of innovation. Implementation research expects the system to react adaptively to the intervention and documents how the intervention and the system interact, changing both the approach and the system. Confrey and Sabelli identify two scales of implementation research needed for sustainable, cumulative education improvements: within-project and across-project implementation research. Within-project implementation research implies the need to devote resources to *project-level research*. Across-project implementation research implies thinking hard about how to revise and refine funding efforts to ensure maximum learning from current efforts; it also implies becoming able to use this knowledge to inform the next round of *programmatic research*. These and other issues are areas in which educational psychology's knowledge base will be needed.

HOW CAN EDUCATIONAL PSYCHOLOGY'S KNOWLEDGE BASE BEST BE APPLIED TO EDUCATIONAL REFORM ISSUES IN THE TWENTY-FIRST CENTURY?

This section builds on issues introduced in the prior sections and discusses them within a living-systems framework for education —that is, my focus here is to discuss what I believe are ways in which educational psychology's knowledge base can be applied in whole-school or systemic reform efforts (in terms of both the overall organizational and personal domains in living systems); in reform efforts aimed at curriculum, instruction, and assessment (in terms of both the personal and technical domains of living systems); and in reform efforts aimed at creating new learning communities and cultures, including those in electronic-learning environments (in terms of both the personal and community levels of living systems). The dominance of people (the personal domain) in all levels of living systems is then discussed as the fundamental rationale for the role educational psychology can and should play in educational reform in the twenty-first century.

Implications for Application in Systemic Reform Efforts

A focus on the learner and the personal domain emerges from those who see schools as living systems (Wheatley & Kellner-Rogers, 1998). As people in living systems such as educational environments are given more opportunities to be creatively involved in how their work gets done, standards of functioning are not imposed or mandated from outside; rather, these standards, measures, values, organizational structures, and plans come from within—through an ongoing dialogue in which people share perceptions, seek out a diversity of interpretations, and agree on what needs to be done. In this process of learning and change, research-validated principles that are agreed upon can be guides to determine what will work well in the current situation or context such that the system is designed to take care of itself, others, and the place (Wheatley & Kellner-Rogers, 1998).

A key implication is that the larger context of education must support and value individual learners as well as learning outcomes. The culture and climate must acknowledge the purpose of education as going beyond academic competence and content knowledge alone. There must be a shared vision, values, and sense of inclusive ownership among all stakeholders about purpose of education. Restoring a sense of schools as caring communities is a fundamental way to provide social and emotional support.

Similar concerns in the moral dimensions of school are described by Berreth and Berman (1997). These dimensions attempt to nurture empathy and self-discipline and to help students develop social skills and moral values. The practices of small schools, caring adults, community service, and parent involvement are recommended along with processes and practices of modeling, direct instruction, experience, and continual practice. The learner-centered framework can be used to accomplish these purposes. Individuals can be assisted to learn and develop high levels of self-awareness, self-control, empathy, perspective taking, and social skills in handling relationships. One guideline stressed is that students should be active partners in creating a caring classroom climate and community (Elias et al., 1997).

Another critical implication for practice is that attention should be given to the role of student perceptions and input. Freiberg (1998) acknowledges that few climate measures use students as a source of feedback but believes each student's perspective is critical—particularly during transitions from one school level to the next. Given the importance of this feedback, Freiberg argues that using measures that assess student perceptions and worries about school should be part of all school reform efforts. A case is also made for the importance of caring to positive development. For example, Elias et al. (1997) believe that caring is central to the shaping of meaningful, supportive, rewarding, and productive relationships. Caring occurs when children believe that adults unconditionally accept and respect them and when the community believes that everyone is important and has something to contribute. But can the importance of caring be acknowledged as a critical part of the current reform agenda?

Palmer (1999) argues that we need to acknowledge that not only do teaching and learning involve intellect and emotion, but they also involve the human spirit. He underscores the point that teaching and learning are not either-or in the sense of being intellectual or spiritual. He contends that teachers—regardless of their subject matter and who their students are—end up teaching *who* they are. The biggest challenge is to provide teachers with adequate time and support to reflect on questions worth asking. Time for self-reflection can renew and transform practices and ways of relating to self and others. Teachers need opportunities to learn and change their minds.

To accomplish trusting relationships among and between teachers and students, strategies for promoting school cultures of caring need to be implemented gradually and be guided by student voices. Research by Battistich, Soloman, Watson, and Schaps (1997) shows that middle school students' perceptions of sense of school as community were consistently associated with a positive orientation toward school and learning—including attraction to school, task orientation toward learning, educational aspirations, and trust and respect for teachers. The data also indicated that students' perceptions of community were positively associated with prosocial attitudes, social skills, and sense of autonomy and efficacy; they were negatively related to students' drug use and involvement in delinquent behavior. When these communities satisfy basic psychological needs, students become bonded to such schools and accept their values.

According to Schaps and Lewis (1999), the structural changes necessary to create caring school cultures are relatively simple and inexpensive to bring about. The larger issue is to achieve a fundamental attitude shift among educators, policy makers, and the public. They must be convinced that in addition to responding to pressure to produce high test scores, it is legitimate and necessary to focus on the development of caring and competent people. School time spent developing trusting relationships, talking with students, and guiding them to be more competent across all domains of caring must also be deemed valuable.

Implications for Application in Curriculum, Instruction, and Assessment

According to Sadker and Sadker (1994), "most educators regard the formal curriculum as the organization of intended outcomes for which the school says it is responsible" (p. 163). The twentieth-century curriculum was primarily focused on knowledge transmission (Berryman, 1993; Carroll, 2000; Judy & D'Amico, 1998; Shephard, 2000) and the instruction practices and assessments aligned with the transmission of established knowledge in content areas. Jones (2001) points out that educational technology clearly brings to the forefront debates about education as the transmission of information versus education as learning and experience—formal versus natural education.

Bransford (2001) points out that being *knowledge-centered* includes looking at the world in which people will eventually operate and then designing learning opportunities by working backwards from that perspective. Carroll (2000, 2001) describes how a networked community can support three types of knowledge-centered outcomes: knowledge transmission, knowledge adaptation, and knowledge generation. Designs for knowledge-centered curricula assumes that the learners are immersed in current events that highlight topics and issues from which they can learn and to which they can contribute through active engagement with others in the networked community who are also actively addressing the topics and issues. Educators and community members can provide leadership by thinking more deeply about the knowledge and skills applicable to living and working in the twenty-first-century society and taking very seriously questions about *what* should be taught by helping learners prioritize the focus of their learning activities (Bransford, 2001).

Personal and interpersonal development features of curriculum also emerge from the social interactions among those in the networked community. An integrated focus on the personal, organizational, and community levels of learning clarifies the need for a holistic and integrated curriculum characterized by core standards for basic content knowledge and skills, for career development, and for social-emotional and physical development. Underlying this framework is the thinking of those who work with *living systems* and seek to center on human needs and natural processes that must be supported in the systems that address technical issues (curriculum, instruction, assessment) and organizational issues (management structures, decision making, policies). Thus, increased attention is needed to the research-based living-systems framework and issues relevant to the personal, technical, and organizational domains of electronic-learning cultures and communities (see McCombs, 2000b, and McCombs & McNabb, 2001).

Closely intertwined with the holistic, community-based curriculum is instruction that is essentially *learner-centered* in the sense of connecting with the knowledge, skills, attitudes, and beliefs of learners (APA Task Force of Psychology in Education, 1993; APA Work Group of the Board of Educational Affairs, 1997; Bransford, Brown, & Cocking, 1999; McCombs, 2001a; McCombs & Whisler, 1997). McCombs (2000a) points out that both students and teachers are colearners with changing roles as the learning content, context, and community shape individual expertise in nonlinear learning approaches. As Peck explains, the notion of teacher no longer

seems like the appropriate term for the leaders in these networked communities. Leaders—or expert learners, as Carroll (2001) describes them—will need to view a large part of their responsibility as the creation of the social conditions that will promote learning.

Twenty-first-century instruction needs to focus on fostering self-directed learning habits along a development continuum, from novice to mature learner and expert. Rose (2001) explains that development of higher-level thinking skills—learning that can be applied to a variety of situations, rather than just recitation of facts—happens best when the learners interact both with the information and with others to discuss their understanding. Accepting this idea requires an understanding that learning happens in the context of interaction with other humans. When the interactions are an important part of the learning process, then developing the learning community is important to the process (Rose, 2001).

Balancing a focus on learners with a focus on the desired academic, social, and personal knowledge domains required of responsible twenty-first-century learners and citizens promises to offset traditional learning system problems with learner motivation, engagement, and social development (McCombs, 2001b). Instructional practices within a holistic curriculum that is knowledge-centered also involves a serious examination of how to help students learn with understanding rather than only memorization. This practice can help students organize their knowledge, skills and attitudes in ways that support transfer—where transfer includes the idea of preparing people for future learning (see Bransford & Schwartz,1999).

A shift in assessment practices to support a learning culture is advocated by Shepard (2000). She argues that it is essential to move the current paradigm to one that blends current ideas from cognitive, constructivist, and sociocultural theories because of the corruption of the standards movement into a heavy-handed system of rewards and punishments. Dynamic, ongoing assessments that can help determine what a student is able to do independently and with adult guidance are needed to guide optimal development. By placing learners in communities of practice, individuals can become increasingly adept and competent while developing robust understandings of concepts. Good assessments, Shepard argues, are those that help students rethink old understandings, draw new connections, and create new applications. Self-assessments that help students monitor their own progress also helps them share responsibility for learning with teachers while developing increased ownership of students' own learning. The evaluation of teaching should include helping teachers make their own investigations and reflections visible to students as part of the teaching and learning dialogue. For these changes to occur, however, teacher development must include an understanding of motivation and how to develop classroom cultures in which learning and learners are at the center. Attention must also be focused on helping teachers reflect on their beliefs and undergo a personal change process.

Implications for Application in New Learning Communities and Cultures

Honey (2001) addresses the unrealized promise of emerging technologies to create new types of learning communities and cultures. Although technologies can provide powerful scaffolds to complex processes like inquiry and computational reasoning and the interpretation of media artifacts, she points out that we also know that school organizations are powerful mediators and frequently powerful resisters of learning innovations. Honey reports that when student learning does improve in schools that become technology-rich, those gains are not caused solely by the presence of technology or by isolated technology-learner interactions. Rather, she says such changes are grounded in learning environments that prioritize and focus on *core educational objectives* at the organizational level (Center for Children and Technology, 2000; Chang et al., 1998; Hawkins, Spielvogel, & Panush, 1997; Honey, Hawkins, & Carrigg, 1998).

Witherspoon (2001) has outlined several issues for which educational psychology's knowledge base could be helpful in designing effective learning communities and cultures. These issues center on ethical governance practices that are relevant to both on- and off-line applications. They include the following:

- Designing civil interchange into system functions and promoting intercultural sensitivity.
- Developing rigorous standards to protect and enforce the privacy of participants, to assure the identity of students taking tests, and to determine that inquiries for student-related information come from those authorized to have that information.
- Providing accessibility of communities and programs to those with disabilities as well as to those in poverty areas.

Wilhelm (2001) raises another organizational issue associated with networked learning, the central issue of equity. In terms of achieving greater equality in students' opportunity to learn, technological innovation often drives a deeper wedge between the haves and have-nots; thus less affluent districts are often playing catch-up to cohorts with higher per-pupil expenditures. While acknowledging the digital divide, Peck (2001) contends that if the student-to-student interactions were expanded and electronic support was provided to scaffold students in the process of providing feedback to each other, the costs of electronic learning could be dramatically reduced, making it accessible to everyone possessing the necessary learning to learn skills.

WHAT POLICY ISSUES ARE IMPLIED FROM THE APPLICATION OF EDUCATIONAL PSYCHOLOGY'S KNOWLEDGE BASE IN TWENTY-FIRST-CENTURY REFORM EFFORTS?

This final section integrates prior sections by summarizing major future issues likely to be faced by educational psychology, including political realities and the role of educational psychologists in educating the public about its knowledge base and how it can best be used in transformative ways to create the most effective teaching and learning environments for all learners in the twenty-first century. Major changes in how education is viewed, its purpose, and its structures as we enter into a century with more opportunities for the use of emerging technologies for education are highlighted. Policy issues that surfaced in chapters of this Handbook are discussed along with others from my own work in school reform.

Policy Issues Related to Definitions of Intelligence and Ability

Without rethinking definitions of intelligence and ability, Sternberg (in this volume) argues that societal invention may play more of a role in sorting than does nature because society places high value on test scores for sorting and placement decisions. This practice can lead to disenfranchisement and the narrowing of skills valued, not to mention disregarding the value of creative and practical skills. Because of links to power structures, such social systems tend to perpetuate themselves and become endlessly looping closed systems. Policies thus need to emphasize multiple measures and reexamination of selection and placement criteria.

In general, policies are needed that recognize the growing knowledge base on alternative conceptions of intelligence and ability. These policies must emphasize the valuing of diversity and pluralism at all levels of the educational system. They must embrace Banks' (2000) plea for new conceptions of race and ethnicity, intellectual ability, and knowledge systems, such that these concepts do not privilege particular racial, ethnic, social class, or gender group; that is, new conceptions are needed that reflect the experiences of all groups. They must also embrace new notions about learning and learners that unite rather than divide people and groups, derived from research-validated principles such as those defined in the APA Work Group of the Board of Educational Affairs' (1997) Learner-Centered Psychological Principles.

Policy Issues Related to New Teacher and Student Roles in Teaching, Learning, and Assessment

The spirit of vitality in learner-centered schools is that aspect of the culture committed to learning and change. Teachers' needs to be learners must be part of the culture that supports student motivation, learning, and achievement. The nature of the culture formed among teachers committed to high achievement for all learners is one that is also committed to ongoing learning, change, and improvement. The process must be one that supports continuous examination and critical inquiry into ways of helping students learn better; it must become a normal activity that involves the whole faculty and builds community. The vision is subject to change, and the whole system maintains flexibility and openness to new learning, transformation, and change.

Policies are needed that provide for flexibility in programs that support learning and change for all learners, including teachers and other adults. Roles must be subject to change and one-size-fits-all thinking must be eliminated. Allowing students to become teachers and listening to and respecting the perspectives of all learners must be part of the culture and embedded in policies that govern school functioning.

Policy Issues Related to Individualization of Learning Content and Experiences

Integrated instructional programs must themselves be a model of the very process and quality they want to engender in teachers as learners. To produce quality teaching and learning, learners must experience both quality content and processes. Systems that foster quality by fear-based or punitive measures engender fear, withdrawal, and halfhearted compliance. Unfortunately, this situation is coloring much of today's reform agenda. Principles of respect, fairness, autonomy, intellectual challenge, social support, and security must guide the standard-setting and implementation process. Time for learning and change—to share successful practices, experiment, and continually improve must be acknowledged.

Policies to deal with these issues must be guided by an understanding of schools as living systems as well as an understanding of individual, organizational, and community learning needs. Punitive and coercive practices should be avoided, and collaborative and inclusive practices should be encouraged. Trust building and relationship building through

dialogue need to be explicitly acknowledged in federal, state, and local school policies.

Policy Issues Related to Content and Curriculum That Meet Whole Learner Needs

From a broad systems view, many educators, researchers, and policy makers agree that the current educational, judicial, and social systems are not working (e.g., Nissen, 1999; Norris, 1999; Wheatley, 1999). They see the systems as not only unconnected but also based on outdated thinking and old models of human learning, growth, and development. Furthermore, these current systems are often based on principles applicable to nonliving, mechanical systems and do not match the uncertainty and complexity of living, human systems; thus, it is time to explore a new model that includes what is needed in living systems to bring the system into balance. It is time to support a cycle of positive teacher and youth development and learning.

When successful school reform efforts are analyzed (e.g., Fullan, 1997), the critical difference is in *how* these practices are implemented and in whether there is explicit and shared attention given to individual learners and their unique cognitive as well as social and emotional learning needs. *The critical difference is thus in whether practices are learner-centered and focus on the people and the personal domain.* This focus, however, must be balanced with challenging academic content and standards and attention to social and emotional development.

Policies are therefore needed that address this balance through integrative curricula, multiple assessment measures, and a focus on school climate. Practices that encourage student responsibility for academic and nonacademic outcomes and that provide learners with choice and control should be explicitly addressed in policies.

Policy Issues Related to Diversity and Inclusion of All Learners

Healthy learning communities have the further defining qualities of accepting, incorporating, and honoring all diverse views. Individuals welcome divergent perspectives because they understand that the underlying outcome is learning and change in a context of respect and caring. Individuals also understand that learning communities broaden their perspectives to make room for the learning that can occur to encompass all points of view without making anyone wrong. When different world views and beliefs are held, inclusive dialogue becomes the process for learning; relationships become the vehicle for change in beliefs and assumptions about learning, learners, and teaching. Self-organizing learning communities then meet individual needs for safety, and they encourage new relationships and ways of generating new relationships. Each learner's perspective is a valued medium of learning and a catalyst for change and improvement.

Policies must acknowledge the relational aspects of learning and the value of each person in the system. Practices that exclude individuals—be they students, teachers, parents, or others who have a stake in the educational system—must be avoided. Policies must acknowledge the knowledge base on effective communication and organizational development in outlining guidelines for dealing with diversity and inclusion.

Policy Issues Related to Testing and Accountability

Practices such as grading of schools, teachers, and administrators based on the quality of student achievement can misplace the responsibility for learning (cf. McCombs, 2000a). Even if teachers are held responsible for student learning, *it is the student who makes the decision to learn.* Teachers *cannot make learning happen;* they can encourage with a variety of incentives, but teachers know well that many incentives (e.g., grades, fear of discipline) work only for some students. When teachers overly control the learning process, they may get compliance, but they won't get responsibility.

Responsibility begins with making choices. Without the opportunity to choose and face the consequences of those decisions, there is no sense of ownership. Ownership, which results from choices, is empowering. Without empowerment and ownership, there is no responsibility or accountability—there is blaming and compliance. With ownership, learning is fun and exciting for students and teachers, and both share in the pleasures and responsibilities of control. When responsibility and power are shared, the natural response is empowerment, ownership, and responsibility. *We own what we create*—an important implication of the learner-centered principles and framework when they are applied to policy recommendations.

To summarize, the following are what I see as specific policy recommendations that can further the application of educational psychology's knowledge base to school reform:

- Policies must capture individual and organizational purposes directed at continuous change and learning as a holistic process that involves intellect, emotion, and spirit.
- Policies must emphasize new leadership roles that empower teachers and students alike to take increased control over their own learning and development.

- Policies must emphasize a balance between concerns with high achievement and concerns with meeting individual learning, motivational, and social needs of diverse students.
- Policies must emphasize change strategies focused on inclusive dialogue, building respectful relationships, and practices that are owned by all participants.
- Policies must value outcomes that go beyond academic achievement to emotional and social outcomes that include increased personal and social responsibility.

In conclusion, we have a responsibility upon which many in our profession are increasingly recognizing and acting—the responsibility to educate policy makers, parents, and the public about what we know that can create both effective educational experiences and a positive change or educational reform process. Not only do we need to help others understand new conceptions of learning, motivation, and development, but we also need to help them understand that learning and change are flip sides of the same social-psychological process—the process of changing one's mind. Processes and contexts that support learning are also those that support change. Change—like learning—is an ongoing, dynamic, and lifelong process of continuous improvement. It can be motivating, invigorating, and challenging, or it can be fearful, intimidating, and punitive. As we embark on a new decade of school reform, educational psychology promises to provide more insights into not only how to enhance individual learning, motivation, and development. It also promises to assist in understanding the conditions, contexts, and processes for effective change and educational reform. This is a challenge that I believe the field is ready to accept. Based on the contributions to educational psychology in this volume and in the field in general, this is also a challenge on which I believe we are prepared and ready to deliver.

REFERENCES

APA Task Force on Psychology in Education. (1993, January). *Learner-centered psychological principles: Guidelines for school redesign and reform.* Washington, DC: American Psychological Association and Mid-Continent Regional Educational Laboratory.

APA Work Group of the Board of Educational Affairs. (1997, November). *Learner-centered psychological principles: A framework for school reform and redesign.* Washington, DC: American Psychological Association.

Banks, J. A. (2000). The social construction of difference and the quest for educational equality. In R. S. Bandt (Ed.), *Education in a new era* (pp. 21–45). Alexandria, VA: Association for Supervision and Curriculum Development.

Battistich, V., Soloman, D., Watson, M., & Schaps, E. (1997). Caring school communities, *Educational Psychologist, 32*(3), 137–151.

Berreth, D., & Berman, S. (1997). The moral dimensions of schools. *Educational Leadership, 54*(8), 24–27.

Berryman, S. E. (1993). Learning for the workplace. *Review of Research in Education, 19,* 343–401.

Blumenfeld, P., Fishman, B. J., Krajcik, J., Marx, R. W., & Soloway, E. (2000). Creating usable innovations in systemic reform: Scaling up technology-embedded project-based science in urban schools. *Educational Psychologist, 35*(3), 149–164.

Bollier, D. (2000). *Ecologies of innovation: The role of information and communications technologies.* Washington, DC: Aspen Institute.

Borko, H., Peressini, D., Romagnano, L., Knuth, E., Willis-Yorker, C., Wooley, C., Hovermill, J., & Masarik, K. (2000). Teacher education does matter: A situative view of learning to teach secondary mathematics. *Educational Psychologist, 35*(3), 193–206.

Boyer, E. L. (1995). *The basic school: A community for learning.* Princeton, NJ: Carnegie Foundation for the Advancement of Teaching.

Bransford, J. (2001). *Toward the development of a stronger community of educators: New opportunities made possible by integrating the learning sciences and technology.* Paper prepared for the PT3 Vision Quest on Assessment in e-Learning Cultures. Retrieved from www.pt3.org. Retrieved October 3, 2001.

Bransford, J., Brown, A. L., Cocking, R. R. (Eds.). (1999). *How people learn: Brain, mind, experience, and school.* Washington, DC: National Academy Press.

Bransford, J. D., & Schwartz, D. (1999). Rethinking transfer: A simple proposal with multiple implications. *Review of Research in Education, 24,* 61–100.

Braun, H. (2001). *PT3: Assessment and evaluation.* Paper prepared for the PT3 Vision Quest on Assessment in e-Learning Cultures. Retrieved from www.pt3.org. Retrieved October 2, 2001.

Broadfoot, T. (2001, April 22). *Assessment for an uncertain age.* Paper presented at the Cultures of Learning Conference, Session 3.32, University of Bristol, Bristol, UK.

Carroll, T. G. (2000, March). *Thinking outside the box about technology evaluation.* Paper presented at the North Central Regional Educational Laboratory's Regional Conference on Evaluating Technology in Education, Chicago.

Carroll, T. G. (2001). *Do today's evaluations meet the needs of tomorrow's networked learning communities?* Paper prepared for the PT3 Vision Quest on Assessment in e-Learning Cultures. Retrieved September 2001, from www.pt3.org

Center for Children and Technology. (2000, August). *The transformation of Union City: 1989 to present* (CCT Report). New York: EDC/Center for Children and Technology.

Chang, H., Henriquez, A., Honey, M., Light, D., Moeller, B., & Ross, N. (1998, April). *The Union City story: Education reform and technology. Students' performance on standardized tests* (CCT Report). New York: EDC/Center for Children and Technology.

Church, M. A., Elliott, A. J., & Gable, S. L. (2001). Perceptions of classroom environment, achievement goals, and achievement outcomes. *Journal of Educational Psychology, 93,* 43–54.

Cohen, D. K., & Ball, D. L. (2001). Making change: Instruction and its improvement. *Phi Delta Kappan, 83*(1), 73–77.

Cohen, D., & Barnes, C. (1999). Research and the purposes of education. In E. Lagemann & L. Shulman (Eds.), *Issues in education research* (pp. 17–41). San Francisco: Jossey-Bass.

Confrey, J., & Sabelli, N. (2001). *Research and evaluation in and on "Preparing Tomorrow's Teachers for Technology."* Paper prepared for the PT3 Vision Quest on Assessment in e-Learning Cultures. Retrieved September 2001, from www.pt3.org

Corcoran, T., Fuhrman, S. H., & Belcher, C. L. (2001). The district role in instructional improvement. *Phi Delta Kappan, 83*(1), 78–84.

Darling-Hammond, L. (1996). The quiet revolution: Rethinking teacher development. *Educational Leadership, 53*(6), 4–10.

Dede, C. (2000, October 13). *Expert panel on technology and educational reform.* Panel presentation at the North Central Regional Educational Laboratory First Annual Conference, Chicago.

Dewey, J. (1990). *The school and society and the child and the curriculum.* Chicago: University of Chicago Press.

Diamond, M., & Hopson, J. (1998). *Magic trees of the mind.* New York: Dutton.

Elias, M. J., Bruene-Butler, L., Blum, L., & Schuyler, T. (1997). How to launch a social and emotional learning program. *Educational Leadership, 54*(8), 15–19.

Elias, M. J., Zims, J. E., Weissberg, R. P., Frey, K. D. S., Greenberg, M. T., Haynes, N. M., Kessler, R., Schwab-Stone, M. E., & Shriver, T. P. (1997). *Promoting social and emotional learning: Guidelines for educators.* Alexandria, VA: Association for Supervision and Curriculum Development.

Elmore, R. F., & Fuhrman, S. H. (2001). Holding schools accountable: Is it working? *Phi Delta Kappan, 83*(1), 67–72.

English-Lueck, J. A. (1998, June 19). *Technology and social change: The effects on family and community* (COSSA Congressional Seminar Report). Retrieved September 2001, from http://www.sjsu.edu/depts/anthropology/svcp/SVCPcosa.html

Feuerstein, R., & Feuerstein, S. (1991). Mediated learning experience: A theoretical review. In R. Feuerstein, P. S. Klein, & A. J. Tannenbaum (Eds.), *Mediated learning experience: Theoretical, psychosocial and learning implications* (pp. 3–51). London: Freund Publishing.

Flowerday, T., & Schraw, G. (2000). Teacher beliefs about instructional choice: A phenomenological study. *Journal of Educational Psychology, 92*(4), 634–645.

Freiberg, H. J. (1998). Measuring school climate: Let me count the ways. *Educational Leadership, 56*(1), 22–26.

Fuhrman, S. H., & Odden, A. (2001). Introduction to a Kappan special section on school reform. *Phi Delta Kappan, 83*(1), 59–61.

Fullan, M. (1995). The limits and the potential of professional development. In T. R. Guskey & M. Huberman (Eds.), *Professional development in education: New paradigms and practices* (pp. 253–267). New York: Teachers College Press.

Fullan, M. (1997). Emotion and hope: Constructive concepts for complex times. In A. Hargreaves (Ed.), *Rethinking educational change with heart and mind* (pp. 216–223). Alexandria, VA: 1997 ASCD Yearbook.

Gipps, C. (2001, April 22). *Sociocultural perspectives on assessment.* Paper presented at the Cultures of Learning Conference, Session 3.32, University of Bristol, Bristol, UK.

Goddard, R. D., Hoy, W. K., & Hoy, A. W. (2000). Collective teacher efficacy: Its meaning, measure, and impact on student achievement. *American Educational Research Journal, 37*(2), 479–507.

Goertz, M. E. (2001). Redefining government roles in an era of standards-based reform. *Phi Delta Kappan, 83*(1), 62–66.

Goldschmidt, P., & Wang, J. (1999). When can schools affect dropout behavior? A longitudinal multilevel analysis. *American Educational Research Journal, 36*(4), 715–738.

Goleman, D. (1995). *Emotional intelligence.* New York: Bantam Books.

Gottfried, A. E., Fleming, J. S., & Gottfried, A. W. (2001). Continuity of academic intrinsic motivation from childhood through late adolescence: A longitudinal study. *Journal of Educational Psychology, 93*(1), 3–13.

Groff, W. (2001). *Career development paradigms for digital dividends.* Paper prepared for the PT3 Vision Quest on Assessment in e-Learning Cultures. Retrieved September 2001, from www.pt3.org

Hannafin, M. (1999). *Learning in open-ended environments: Tools and technologies for the next millennium* (ITFORUM Paper 34) http://itech1.eoe.uga.edu/itforum/paper34/paper34.html

Hawkins, J., Spielvogel, R., & Panush, E. (1997). *National study tour of district technology integration summary report* (CCT Report). New York: EDC/Center for Children and Technology.

Heflich, D. (2001). *Breaching the walls of a cell: Changes brought about by electronic networking.* Paper prepared for the PT3 Vision Quest on Assessment in e-Learning Cultures. Retrieved September 2001, from www.pt3.org

Hidi, S., & Harackiewicz, J. M. (2000). Motivating the academically unmotivated: A critical issue for the 21st century. *Review of Educational Research, 70*(2), 151–179.

Honey, M. (2001). *Issues in using technology to support local school-change.* Paper prepared for the PT3 Vision Quest on Assessment in e-Learning Cultures. Retrieved September 2001, from www.pt3.org

Honey, M., Hawkins, J., & Carrigg, F. (1998). Union City Online: An architecture for networking and reform. In C. Dede (Ed.), *The 1998 ASCD Yearbook: Learning with technology* (pp. 179–191). Alexandria, VA: Association for Supervision and Curriculum Development.

Hoy, A. W. (2000). Educational psychology in teacher education. *Educational Psychologist, 35*(4), 257–270.

Jensen, E. (1998). *Teaching with the brain in mind.* Alexandria, VA: Association for Supervision and Curriculum Development.

Jones, S. (2001). *Community and culture in education.* Paper prepared for the PT3 Vision Quest on Assessment in e-Learning Cultures. Retrieved September 2001, from www.pt3.org

Judy, R. W., & D'Amico, C. (1998). *Workforce 2020: Work and workers in the 21st century.* Indianapolis, IN: Hudson Institute.

Kirst, M., & Venezia, A. (2001). Bridging the great divide between secondary schools and postsecondary education. *Phi Delta Kappan, 83*(1), 92–97.

Kogan, M. (2000). Teaching truth, beauty, and goodness: An interview with Howard Gardner. *Monitor on Psychology, 31*(11), 66–67.

Kraut, R., Patterson, M., Lundmark, V., Keisler, S., Mukopadhyay, T., & Scherlis, W. (1998). Internet paradox: A social technology that reduces social involvement and psychological well-being? *American Pscyhologist, 53,* 1017–1031.

Lazarus, R. S. (2000). Toward better research on stress and coping. *American Psychologist, 55*(6), 665–673.

Lee, V. E., & Smith, J. B. (1999). Social support and achievement for young adolescents in Chicago: The role of school academic press. *American Educational Research Journal, 36*(4), 907–945.

Ley, K., & Young, D. B. (2001). Instructional principles for self-regulation. *Educational Technology Research and Development, 49*(2) 93–103.

Lin, X. (2001). Designing metacognitive activities. *Educational Technology Research and Development, 49*(1), 23–40.

Loughran, J. (1996). *Developing reflective practice: Learning about teaching and learning through modeling.* London: Falmer Press.

Marx, R. W. (2000). School reform and research in educational psychology. *Educational Psychologist, 35*(3), 147–148.

McCombs, B. L. (2000a, August). *Addressing the personal domain: The need for a learner-centered framework.* Paper presented at the symposium, "Learner-Centered Principles in practice: - Addressing the personal domain," American Psychological Association, Washington, DC.

McCombs, B. L. (2000b, September 11–12). *Addressing the role of educational technology in the teaching and learning process: A learner-centered perspective.* Paper presented at the Secretary's Conference on Educational Technology, Alexandria, VA.

McCombs, B. L. (2001a). *The learner-centered perspective on teaching and learning in electronically networked cultures.* Paper prepared for the PT3 Vision Quest on Assessment in e-Learning Cultures. Retrieved September 2001, from www.pt3.org

McCombs, B. L. (2001b). Self-regulated learning and academic achievement: A phenomenological view. In B. J. Zimmerman & D. H. Schunk (Eds.), *Self-regulated learning and academic achievement: Theory, research, and practice* (2nd ed., pp. 67–123). Mahwah, NJ: Erlbaum.

McCombs, B. L. (in press). The Learner-Centered Psychological Principles: A framework for balancing a focus on academic achievement with a focus on social and emotional learning needs. In J. E. Zins, R. P. Weissberg, M. C. Wang, & H. J. Walberg (Eds.), *Building school success on social and emotional learning*. New York: Teachers College Press.

McCombs, B. L., & Lauer, P. A. (1997). Development and validation of the Learner-Centered Battery: Self-assessment tools for teacher reflection and professional development. *The Professional Educator, 20*(1), 1–21.

McCombs, B. L., Lauer, P. A., & Pierce, J. (1998, July). *The learner-centered model of seamless professional development: Implications for practice and policy changes in higher education.* Paper presented at the 23rd International Conference on Improving University Teaching, Dublin, Ireland.

McCombs, B. L., & Whisler, J. S. (1997). *The learner-centered classroom and school: Strategies for increasing student motivation and achievement.* San Francisco: Jossey-Bass.

McLaughlin, C. (2001, April 22). *Learning-to-learn, live, and choose.* Paper presented at the Cultures of Learning Conference, Session 3.32, University of Bristol, Bristol, UK.

McNabb, M. L. (2001). *In search of strategic designs for mediating e-learning.* Paper prepared for the PT3 Vision Quest on Assessment in e-Learning Cultures. Retrieved September 2001, from www.pt3.org

McNabb, M., Hawkes, M., & Rouk, U. (1999*). Critical issues in evaluating the effectiveness of technology.* Washington, DC: U.S. Department of Education Retrieved from http://www.ed .gov/Technology/TechConf/1999/

McNabb, M. L., & McCombs, B. K. (2001). *Designs for e-learning: A vision and emerging framework.* Paper prepared for the PT3 Vision Quest on Assessment in e-Learning Cultures. Retrieved September 2001, from www.pt3.org

Meece, J. L., & Kurtz-Costes, B. (2001). Introduction: The schooling of ethnic minority children and youth. *Educational Psychologist, 36*(1), 1–7.

Meier, D. (1999). Needed: Thoughtful research for thoughtful schools. In E. Lagemann & L. Shulman (Eds.), *Issues in education research* (pp. 63–82). San Francisco: Jossey-Bass.

Midgley, C., Kaplan, A., & Middleton, M. (2001). Performance approach goals: Good for whom, under what circumstances, and at what cost? *Journal of Educational Psychology, 93*(1), 77–86.

Moreno, R., & Mayer, R. E. (2000). Engaging students in active learning: The case for personalized multimedia messages. *Journal of Educational Psychology, 92*(4), 724–733.

Nie, N. H., & Erbing, L. (2000). *Internet and society: A preliminary report.* Stanford, CA: Stanford Institute for the Quantitative Study of Society.

Nissen, L. B. (1999, June). *The power of the strength approach.* Paper presented at the 8th Annual Rocky Mountain Regional Conference in Violence Prevention in Schools and Communities, Denver, CO.

Norris, T. (1999, June). *Healthy communities for healthy youth.* Paper presented at the 8th Annual Rocky Mountain Regional Conference in Violence Prevention in Schools and Communities, Denver, CO.

Ochsner, K. N., & Lieberman, M. D. (2001). The mergence of social cognitive neuroscience. *American Psychologist, 56*(9), 717–734.

Odden, A. (2001). The new school finance. *Phi Delta Kappan, 83*(1), 85–91.

Okagaki, L. (2001). Triarchic model of minority children's school achievement. *Educational Psychologist, 36*(1), 9–20.

Orrill, C. H. (2001). Building technology-based, learner-centered classrooms: The evolution of a professional development framework. *Educational Technology Research and Development, 49*(1), 15–34.

Palmer, P. J. (1999). Evoking the spirit in public education. *Educational Leadership, 56*(4), 6–11.

Paris, S. C., & Paris, A. H. (2001). Classroom applications of research on self-regulated learning. *Educational Psychologist, 36*(2), 89–101.

Peck, K. (2001). *Electronically networked learning cultures as and within living systems.* Paper prepared for the PT3 Vision Quest on Assessment in e-Learning Cultures. Retrieved September 2001, from www.pt3.org

Popham, W. J. (2001, April 10–14). *Standards-based assessment: Solution or charade?* Paper presented as part of the symposium "Creating classroom and large-scale assessment that enhance instructional decision-making," American Educational Research Association, Seattle, WA.

Ravitz, J. (2001). *Will technology pass the test?* Paper prepared for the PT3 Vision Quest on Assessment in e-Learning Cultures. Retrieved September 2001, from www.pt3.org

Reigeluth, C. (2001, June 8). *High-performance high-technology learning communities: What works?* Panel presentation at the NCREL National Conference on Technology, Naperville, IL.

Repa, T. (2001). *The Internet and social and emotional learning.* Paper prepared for the PT3 Vision Quest on Assessment in e-Learning Cultures. Retrieved September 2001, from www. pt3.org

Robinson, N. M., Zigler, E., & Gallagher, J. J. (2000). Two tails of the normal curve: Similarities and differences in the study of mental retardation and giftedness. *American Psychologist, 55*(12), 1413–1424.

Rose, R. (2001). *e-learning communities and cultures.* Paper prepared for the PT3 Vision Quest on Assessment in e-Learning Cultures. Retrieved September 2001, from www.pt3.org

Ryan, A. M., & Patrick, H. (2001). The classroom social environment and changes in adolescents' motivation and engagement during middle school. *American Educational Research Journal, 38*(2), 437–460.

Ryan, R. M., & Deci, E. L. (2000). Self-determination theory and the facilitation of intrinsic motivation, social development, and well-being. *American Psychologist, 55*(1), 68–78.

Sabelli, N., & Dede, C. (in press). *Integrating educational research and practice: Reonceptualizing the goals and process of research to improve educational practice.*

Sadker, M. P., & Sadker, D. M. (1994). *Teachers, schools, and society* (3rd ed.). Yew York: McGraw-Hill.

Schaps, E., & Lewis, C. (1999). Perils on an essential journey: Building school community. *Phi Delta Kappan, 81*(3), 215–218.

Scherer, M. (1998). A conversation with Herb Kohl. *Educational Leadership, 56*(1), 8–13.

Seligman, M. E. P., & Csikszentmihalyi, M. (2000). Positive psychology: An introduction. *American Psychologist, 55*(1), 5–14.

Shepard, L. A. (2000). The role of assessment in a learning culture. *Educational Researcher, 29*(7), 4–14.

Shields, M. K., & Behrman, R. E. (2000). Children and computer technology: Analysis and recommendations. *The Future of Children, 10*(2), 4–30. Retrieved from www.futureofchildren.org

Stiggins, R. J. (2001, April 10–14). *Making classroom assessment instructionally relevant.* Paper presented as part of the symposium "Creating classroom and large-scale assessment that enhance instructional decision-making," American Educational Research Association, Seattle, WA.

Sylwester, R. (1995). *A celebration of neurons: An educator's guide to the brain.* Alexandria, VA: Association for Supervision and Curriculum Development.

Tyack, D., & Cuban, L. (1995). *Tinkering toward utopia.* Cambridge, MA: Harvard University Press.

Van den Berg, R., & Ros, A. (1999). The permanent importance of the subjective reality of teachers during educational innovation: A concerns-based approach. *American Educational Research Journal, 36*(4), 879–906.

Vygotsky, L. S. (1978). *Mind in society: The development of higher psychological processes.* Cambridge, MA: Harvard University Press.

Wassermann, S. (2001). Quantum theory, the uncertainty and alchemy of standardized testing. *Phi Delta Kappan, 83*(1), 28–40.

Weinberger, E., & McCombs, B. L. (2001, April). *The impact of learner-centered practices on the academic and non-academic outcomes of upper elementary and middle school students.* Paper presented at the symposium, "Integrating what we know about learners and learning: A foundation for transforming preK-20 practices," American Educational Research Association, Seattle, WA.

Wheatley, M. J. (1999). *Leadership and the new science: Discovering order in a chaotic world* (2nd ed.). San Francisco: Berrett-Koehler.

Wheatley, M. J., & Kellner-Rogers, M. (1998). Bringing life to organizational change. *Journal of Strategic Performance Measurement, April–May,* 5–13.

Wilhelm, T. (2001). *First principles in e-learning: The "e" stands for equity.* Paper prepared for the PT3 Vision Quest on Assessment in e-Learning Cultures. Retrieved September 2001, from www.pt3.org

Wilson, B. (2001). *Sense of community as a valued outcome for electronic courses, cohorts, and programs.* Paper prepared for the PT3 Vision Quest on Assessment in e-Learning Cultures. Retrieved September 2001, from www.pt3.org

Witherspoon, J. P. (2001). *e-learning: Ethics and governance considerations.* Paper prepared for the PT3 Vision Quest on Assessment in e-Learning Cultures. Retrieved September 2001, from www.pt3.org

Wong, C. A., & Rowley, S. J. (2001). The schooling of ethnic minority children [Commentary]. *Educational Psychologist, 36*(1), 57–66.

Zech, L. K., Gause-Vega, C. L., Bray, M. H., Secules, T., & Goldman, S. R. (2000). Content-based collaborative inquiry: A professional development model for sustaining educational reform. *Educational Psychologist, 35*(3), 207–217.

Zimmerman, B. J., & Schunk, D. H. (Eds.). (2001). *Self-regulated learning and academic achievement: Theory, research, and practice* (2nd ed.). Mahwah, NJ: Erlbaum.

CHAPTER 24

Future Perspectives in Educational Psychology

GLORIA E. MILLER AND WILLIAM M. REYNOLDS

Educational psychology is an applied science dedicated to applying psychological principles to the study of important educational issues and problems with a focus on learners, learning, and teaching (Slavin, 2000). McCombs (this volume) emphasizes the important role of educational psychology and its promise to deepen our understanding of learning, motivation, development processes, and the contexts and conditions that can effect change and reform. Another distinction that characterizes research traditions in educational psychology is the emphasis on understanding cognition and learning and—more recently—how these related domains are reciprocally influenced by the contexts in which they occur.

Current Changes in the Field

Educational psychology as a field has matured and advanced significantly over the last century and in particular in the last two decades. A well-defined, empirically based body of literature in educational psychology has grown dramatically in breath and depth. This proliferation of research is evidenced by increased manuscript submission rates at leading journals

representing the field, by the number of new educational psychology journals and books, and finally by heightened societal interest in education—especially in political arenas. Although the sheer quantity of research in educational psychology published over the last two decades is impressive, another notable trend is the broad scope of this research. A review of the chapters in this volume suggests that the field of educational psychology cannot be defined by a single line of inquiry. Educational psychologists are conducting research across a wide range of topics and across a variety of learning contexts and settings. The published work within many domains is so vast as to require focused compendium volumes in order to adequately capture the expanding literature (e.g., *Handbook of Self-Regulation,* Boekaerts, Pintrich, & Zeidner, 2000; *Handbook of Mathematics and Computational Science,* Harris & Stocker, 1998; *Handbook of Reading Research,* Kamil, Mosenthal, Pearson, & Barr, 2000; *Handbook of School Psychology,* Reynolds & Gutkin, 1999; *Handbook of Research on Teaching,* Richardson, 2001). Contributors within each of these volumes are heavily identified with the field of educational psychology.

The diversity of philosophies, theories, and practices encompassed in the field of educational psychology suggests that the discipline is broadening and changing as quickly as our expanding knowledge base; this has led some researchers to suggest that the modern era of educational psychology is at a crossroads. Key shifts in theory have contributed to attempts to blend research across major frames of reference (Calfee & Berliner, 1996; also see the chapter by Reynolds & Miller in this volume). To heed the call by Cronbach in 1957 to merge the study of individual differences (differential psychology) and cross-individual commonalties (experimental psychology), contemporary research in educational psychology seeks to merge general laws of behavior with individual variations in behavior. Bruner (1990) suggests that the field has moved from a focus on stimuli and responses to a focus on information processing—and most recently, to models of learning and cognition that emphasize meaning and the construction of meaning. Stronger conceptual links between behavioral, Piagetian, and Vygotskiian theories have led to studies of individual human capacities that also strive to understand the impact of contexts on learning and cognition. Contemporary researchers seek more global foundations that capture how external environments modify or affect the individual as well as what goes on in the minds of learners as they explore and interact in their world. Individual processes are studied with an eye towards understanding the significant impact of social, interpersonal, and cultural environments on learner's beliefs, attitudes, and cognition. These trends have led to significant new advances in theory, research, and practice.

The contributors to this volume reviewed important historical contributions to the emergence of contemporary work within five domains. Authors were asked to synthesize current issues and trends and to present impressions of future issues likely to have a major impact on theory and application in the twenty-first century. Innovations and developments with the most promise for the future were identified, as were unresolved theoretical, methodological, and practical issues in need of further clarification and research. The work reviewed here reflects the considerable changes and accumulated understanding that have developed in the latter half of the twentieth century. This work has had a profound influence on our understanding of learners, learning, and instruction. Because these authors represent some of the most prominent educational psychologists active in the field today, their ideas are likely to have an enduring effect on future research. As instructors and mentors in institutions of higher education, their ideas will not only influence a whole new generation of educational psychologists but will also inform key decision-makers responsible for educational reforms and policies.

Organization of This Chapter

The goal of this chapter is to highlight and synthesize the salient future implications forwarded by our contributors. By closely examining and integrating their ideas and recommendations, we hope to identify critical theoretical, research, and practical issues likely to inform and direct the field of educational psychology well into the twenty-first century. A framework was developed to capture the key future issues that surfaced across a majority of chapters. In doing so we were struck by the consistency of promising perspectives highlighted across the five research domains used to organize and structure the content of this volume. That there was greater uniformity than divergence across chapters clearly emphasizes the importance of these issues in guiding the nature and role of educational psychology in the future. The future issues integrated into this chapter reflect those with the greatest potential for advancing our understanding of individual learners and learning contexts, including interpersonal, relational, and instructional processes; curriculum development; and teacher preparation. Consequently, these issues are likely to have a substantial impact on prospective practice, research, and policy.

This chapter is organized into three sections. The first section presents theoretical issues likely to receive continued refinement and elaboration. Notable areas of consensus are highlighted, as are remaining differences in philosophical orientation and ideas for translating theory into educational practice. The second section reviews current methods of inquiry most likely to inform and enhance future educational research. Key methodological concerns that represent pressing issues for future researchers are presented, including the need to balance basic and applied research. The third section consolidates central themes with the greatest potential to influence educational research, practice, and policies. Notable areas in need of further investigation and key recommendations for training a new generation of educators and educational psychologists are forwarded. The issues reviewed here are developed primarily with exemplars from the chapters included in this volume. Accordingly, the reader is referred to specific chapters in this volume for further elaboration and more in-depth analysis.

A strong consensus among our contributors was that the significant knowledge-base established by educational psychologists must be transformed into sound educational policy and practice and consequently should play a major role in directing future educational reform. Accordingly, this chapter concludes with impressions of the prospective status of the field of educational psychology. We focus on the contributions as well as the limitations of our knowledge base. We agree with many of our authors who caution against the tendency to overgeneralize or look for magic bullets or easy answers to very complex challenges in education today. However, we concur with McCombs (in this volume), who suggests that we need to do more to highlight the significant contributions of educational psychologists. Indeed, the future promise of educational psychology will likely depend upon how well this body of work is understood by educational consumers and policy makers and on how easily it can facilitate the ongoing work of educators seeking to increase student learning, enhance teacher preparation, and improve schooling practices.

THEORETICAL ADVANCES

In the last two decades, significant theoretical advances have been made in almost every area of study reviewed in this volume. Advances include expanded, ecological models, greater refinement and clarification of key concepts, and more precise specification of interrelationships between constructs. There are also new areas of investigation that have emerged in the past decade, such as the role and nature of new technologies, including the Internet, as a dynamic force in the learning process. Future work based on these advances ultimately will lead to highly integrated areas of inquiry.

Broader Models of Cognition and Learning

Educational researchers increasingly have studied how learners construct meaning within broader social and cultural environments; this has been accompanied by a focus on reciprocal processes—how learning is affected by and results in modification of external environments. Recent models of intelligence and memory processes (see chapters by Mayer and by Sternberg in this volume) include multidirectional theories that focus on socially situated learning, practical aspects of intelligence, and implicit theories of intelligence. The work reviewed by Mayer (this volume) supports the notion that the human mind seeks to build and manipulate mental representations.

The recognition that social environments are critical to the study of cognition and early development has increased since the mid-1950s with the rising influences of constructivism and the integration of Vygotskiian, Brunerian, and Piagetian models of learning. Cognitive theorists have moved from individually focused roots to more socially situated frameworks from which to study learning. Socially mediated conceptualizations of learning have transformed hierarchical information-processing models to ones in which intellectual behavior is studied as learners adapt to and modify their environments. Models of cognition now incorporate both individually focused study and the study of situated learning embedded within contexts (Bruner, 1990, 1996).

Future researchers will continue to investigate areas of cognition beyond conventional aspects of intelligence, leading to reconceptualizations of how socialization experiences shape learning and cognitive development (see chapter by John-Steiner & Mahn in this volume). Models of how the mind works will be integrated with models of how students perform authentic tasks in educationally relevant settings. As Mayer (this volume) suggests, in the future we must continue to be informed by more comprehensive theories of individual learners, yet we must continue to recognize that individually focused theories will be substantially improved when they are situated in and informed by examinations of environmental and contextual variables. In the future there will be little room for unidirectional notions of learning and cognition or isolated models with little input from the individual. Instead, reciprocal and multidimensional models of learning will focus on how basic internal processes are transformed by and with input from the environment.

Sensitivity to Sociocultural Contexts

The variables of race and gender as well as family, school, and community contexts and their effects on learning processes have been examined across many of the domains reviewed here. Sociocultural theories and approaches have led to new constructs and methodologies for studying the complexity of human learning across diverse learners and settings. John-Steiner and Mahn (this volume) review the increasing interdisciplinary literature on teaching and learning processes guided by Vygotsky's sociocultural framework. Within this framework, interrelationships between social and individual processes are explored during the construction of knowledge, and teaching-learning processes emphasize ethnically relevant aspects of behavior. This research's emphasis on language, culture, social interaction, and context is particularly relevant to the study of cognition and learning in today's multicultural society.

Sociocultural influences have had a strong impact on contemporary studies of cognition and learning. Western conceptualizations and interpretations of intellectual competence have been extended to include culturally defined analytical as well as creative and social abilities and implicit versus explicit notions of intelligence. Theories of intelligence have increasingly sought to capture logical, largely verbal abilities typically stressed in educational settings and practical abilities that focus on how individuals adapt and shape their environments (see chapter by Sternberg in this volume).

Analyses of gender-based learning have led to contrasting perspectives of scientific inquiry as a deeply personal and relational activity versus an objective, rationalist, depersonalized style of inquiry. Research suggests that females may seek to make sense of the world through interpersonal connections and attachments, in contrast to males, who use more analytical stances (see chapter by Koch in this volume). Sociocultural influences are also reflected in broader models of peer- and adult-mediated learning within new media learning environments (see chapter by Goldman-Segall & Maxwell in this volume).

The study of relationships between teachers and students and the individual and contextual factors that influence such relationships are additional domains that have benefited from sociocultural influences (see chapters by Pianta, Hamre, & Stuhlman and by Pressley et al. in this volume). Research on teacher-student and peer group contexts has led to a greater understanding of key relational and interaction variables that contribute to learning and adjustment. Cooperative learning researchers have investigated how cultural background might affect decision-making and accountability processes in collaborative learning groups involving cultures that stress harmonious and stable intergroup relations versus individualistic and competitive processes (see chapter by Slavin et al. in this volume). These findings are particularly relevant for teaching linguistically and culturally diverse learners (see chapter by John-Steiner & Mahn in this volume).

To further establish conditions under which personal and sociocultural characteristics mediate the effects of particular learning strategies and classroom conditions, studies are needed that identify specific components most responsible for learning and affective outcomes. For example, future work is needed to determine whether cooperative learning is as effective with high school and early childhood populations (see chapter by Slavin et al. in this volume) and whether differential benefits are found with normal versus high-achieving or gifted students (see chapter by Olszewski-Kubilius in this volume). The question for future researchers is how to best design group and individual incentives to match critical person, setting, and contextual demands. At the same time, researchers should not ignore the potential for aptitude by treatment interactions (Cronbach & Snow, 1977; Snow, 1986, 1989; Snow & Lohman, 1984) that may be particularly relevant in understanding sociocultural relationships in learning and cognition.

The next century will be replete with research to further our understanding of the role of sociocultural variables and systems that affect learning and teaching relationships. This work will expand upon the range of sociocultural variables studied by educational psychologists and will involve studies of group and individual variation across school and home environments. Future researchers are less likely to encourage the compartmentalization of culture, race, or gender; instead, they are more likely to design studies that allow for flexible and situated points of view. Koch (this volume) exemplifies this idea by suggesting the need for gender-flexing policies to acknowledge that boys may benefit from practices traditionally associated with girls and vice versa.

Integration of Metacognition, Self-Regulation, and Motivation

A burgeoning literature over the last two decades has led to substantial advances in our knowledge of metacognition, self-regulation and motivation processes and constructs, and their impact on learning and teaching. Metacognition is viewed as a primarily conscious, distinct subcomponent of self-regulation that contributes to a learner's knowledge of and control over cognition (see chapter by McCormick in this volume). Self-regulation processes are broadly defined as systematic thoughts and behaviors that students initiate, modify, and sustain in order to attain personally relevant learning and social goals (see chapter by Schunk & Zimmerman in this volume). Motivational processes are viewed as those that instigate or get people going, keep them going in a particular direction, and help them finish tasks (see chapter by Pintrich in this volume; Pintrich & Schunk, 2002). Normative comparison, performance monitoring, and evaluative judgments of progress have been tied to self-regulatory performance cycles before, during, and following a task. One's goal orientation and representations of the purpose of a task, beliefs about the importance of a task, interest in a task, and ideas about the ultimate utility of a task are all motivational constructs with a strong impact on cognition and learning outcomes (see chapter by Pintrich in this volume). Self-efficacy has gained increasing prominence as a key mediator of regulatory and motivational processes (Bandura, 1977, 1986). Self-efficacy—viewed as prospective beliefs influential before a task is begun—differs from older attribution theories that view such expectancies as post hoc explanations of performance (see chapter by Pintrich in this volume). Self-efficacy positively affects self-regulation and cognitive engagement and has been linked to improved learning performance over time. Self-efficacy beliefs comprise one of the strongest predictors of actual course achievement, even after accounting for variance associated with a student's previous knowledge or general intellectual ability (see chapter by Schunk & Zimmerman in this volume). A strong research base exists that shows the reciprocal influence of self-efficacy beliefs, behavioral choices, and personal goal-setting processes.

The increased integration of cognitive, self-regulatory, and motivational research has led to ecologically valid interpretations of academic and classroom learning. The conclusion to be drawn from this body of work is that it is not enough to be behaviorally engaged in learning; students also must be cognitively and motivationally engaged for deeper understanding and learning to occur. We agree with both Pintrich and McCormick (both in this volume), who suggest that future researchers will increasingly identify key self-regulatory and personal motivational constructs related to academic achievement and competencies. Future work will focus on how metacognition, self-regulation, and motivation differ across individuals, across tasks, and with the type of skill assessed. Continued efforts will strive to clarify the domain specificity or generality of such skills. Furthermore, because we know little about how such processes change over the lifetime, there will be an emphasis on developmental shifts in metacognition, self-regulation, and motivation and how these processes emerge in young children (see chapter by Schunk & Zimmerman in this volume; Schunk & Zimmerman, 1997; and Zimmerman, 2000, for more specifics on such developmental progressions). Studies also will be designed to assess how such processes are exemplified in practical life tasks over time—for example, how adults make choices to balance personal and professional goals. Finally, continuing efforts to clarify the interrelationships between these constructs and cognitive outcomes will help determine the reciprocal contributions of academic success, metacognitive awareness and regulation, motivational intent, and personal goal setting.

Focus on Relational and Motivational Processes in Schooling

Contemporary research on classroom learning has established the importance of relational processes between children and adults in predicting success and risk in school settings. In the quest for understanding student learning and adjustment, socially mediated goal structures and relationships that students have while in school with other students and adults have taken on new prominence. The inclusion of two chapters on these issues (see chapters by Pianta, Hamre, & Stuhlman and by Wentzel in this volume) is a sign of the vast literature that has accumulated on these topics over the last decade.

Educational psychologists have demonstrated that child-teacher relationships have a positive and reciprocal effect on students' learning, achievement, enjoyment, involvement, and school engagement and on teachers' sense of well-being, efficacy, job satisfaction, and retention (Pianta, 1999). Work on classroom relationships and teaching processes has been strongly influenced by developmental systems theory

(Lerner, 1998). In this framework, student-adult and student-student relationships are viewed as interrelated units functioning reciprocally to motivate successful adaptation and development (see chapter by Pianta, Hamre, & Stuhlman in this volume). Students' beliefs about relationships in school are strongly associated with general feelings about the school climate, which in turn contributes to greater trust in and use of teachers and peers as sources of support. Teachers rated by students as demonstrating greater care are more effective in structuring and managing classroom processes and tend to set higher goals for student performance (see chapter by Wentzel in this volume). The implication of these findings is that positive student-teacher relations reciprocally influence classroom expectations and behaviors. Exposure to positive adult and peer interpersonal relationships also can motivate achievement and coping in behaviorally at-risk students (see chapter by Walker & Gresham in this volume). That such relationships play a central role in overall school climate has led some to suggest that teaching may require interpersonal involvement at a level higher than that of most other professions (Calderhead, 1996).

Educational psychologists also have been at the forefront in identifying what motivates and mediates individuals' goals for leaning and the classroom or school factors that support and promote the expression of these personal attributes (see chapter by Wentzel in this volume). Critical student attitudes and beliefs and the fit between a student's social goals and those of teachers and peers are strongly related to social and school adjustment. In the case of students who evidence severe behavioral problems, it is now known that impaired relations between students' social goals and academic accomplishments may contribute to escalation of violence (see chapter by Walker & Gresham in this volume). Moreover, studies of socially adjusted versus less adjusted individuals point to differences in their ability to set and achieve goals that are sanctioned by the larger community as valuable and desirable. Successful students have been described as having socially integrative (helpfulness, sharing), learning (persistence, intrinsic motivation, interest), and performance (completing assignments, organization) characteristics (see chapter by Wentzel in this volume). Students identified as gifted are more likely to express these behaviors and also are more likely to set goals that correspond to teacher objectives (see chapter by Olszewski-Kubilius in this volume).

In the future, researchers will examine comprehensive theoretical models of school- and home-based relations to better understand the links between social motivation, prosocial behavior, and academic performance. A broader array of social goals related to school adjustment will be investigated beyond those associated with academic achievement. Individual and contextual factors that affect students' goal selection and pursuit will be identified. Continued work will focus on how multiple personal goals are negotiated and coordinated to guide social as well as intellectual development (Wentzel, 1998). Although available data support the developmental systems perspective of teacher-child relations, the means by which such information is transmitted in schools must be more clearly elaborated. Pianta, Hamre, and Stuhlman (this volume) predict that such evaluations will require comprehensive means of assessing quality and types of relationships. This process would involve in-depth analyses of mechanisms that affect relational exchanges and relationships, with the use of multiple methods, across multiple occasions and contexts, and over extended periods of time. Comprehensive evaluations would allow researchers to map out under what conditions certain motivational goals will become adaptive or maladaptive (see chapter by Wentzel in this volume).

Finally, greater knowledge of the interdependence of interpersonal relations, motivational systems, and personal goals will be used to improve our ability to serve different populations of students. Studies involving students with severe learning and behavior difficulties will be designed to determine whether family and community influences on motivation and learning can be enhanced or positively modified by schooling experiences. Prevention efforts and interventions with at-risk students will be enhanced through a greater understanding of how such constructs relate to increased social competence and self-determination and contribute to improved group approval and peer acceptance (see chapters by Siegel and by Walker & Gresham in this volume). Reschly (this volume) similarly predicts that the field of school psychology will place more emphasis on early identification, which in turn will lead to mutually supportive home, school and community interventions to enhance academic achievement, prosocial behavior, and emotional regulation.

Attention to Gender

Educational psychologists interested in studying classroom and instructional processes increasingly have stressed the impact of gender in understanding motivation, cognition, and interpersonal classroom processes. A growing number of studies have identified specific curriculum content, classroom interactions, and school climates that promote gender equity (see chapter by Koch in this volume). Gender equity in education refers to educational practices that are fair and just toward both females and males. This work has led to teacher training efforts designed to promote more equitable classroom learning environments. Such training specifically

targets attitudinal changes through increased awareness and knowledge of hidden curriculum and gender-differentiated instruction.

Current researchers view uniform or one-size-fits-all responses to create equitable classroom climates as oversimplifications. Instead, recent attempts to develop more equitable environments are designed to uncover the needs and social issues behind gendered behavior rather than simply to ensure equal treatment. These approaches seek to level the playing field by encouraging all children to be contributors to class environments, which can lead to different (vs. similar) experiential offerings for girls and boys. Future researchers will continue to focus on what it means and how to best achieve gender equity in daily classroom interactions and curriculum choice considerations and how to best prepare teachers in this area.

Significance of Early Childhood and Developmental Research

Although much of the work in educational psychology has focused on kindergarten through Grade 12, educational psychologists have begun to play a larger role in studying preschool learning and early childhood settings. This literature has helped to further illuminate the significance of the birth-to-five period and the role of play in early literacy, musical, artistic, and mathematical skills and in affective and social development (see chapter by Goelman et al. in this volume). The increasing contributions of educational psychology researchers in this area reinforced the decision to include a chapter focused exclusively on early childhood in this volume.

Educational researchers have increasingly sought to examine developmental progressions in many of the domains reviewed here. For example, motivational researchers are seeking to isolate the complex influence of the task, current situational characteristics, past relational experiences, prior beliefs, and ongoing beliefs that develop during a task (see chapters by Pintrich; by Pianta, Hamre, & Stuhlman; and by Wentzel in this volume). One general observation is that there may not be a single developmental trajectory to explain how certain abilities unfold. Different trajectories of development may arise depending on individual and contextual influences. These ideas were expressed by Goelman and his colleagues (this volume), who distinguished between newer map versus stage theories of development. In the former, interactive developmental processes are studied by examining a repertoire of skills over time to determine how a wide range of expressions and representations develop depending on reciprocal individual and environmental factors. Examinations of such developmental progressions also are prevalent in the literature on early literacy and mathematics learning (see chapters by Pressley and by Lehrer & Lesh, respectively, in this volume).

Most authors, however, point to the clear need for more extensive examinations of how key constructs develop over time and are influenced by contextual factors. As McCombs (this volume) points out, much more work is needed to integrate concepts of learning and development with evolving processes and theories of education and teaching. Instead of proposing tight developmental sequences and stages, future educational psychology researchers will need to examine a range of different acquisition repertoires; this will entail work directed beyond individual or group progressions to instead look for continuums of diverse abilities and differential contexts that promote development. It also will require an even greater emphasis on early childhood populations and a commitment to studying key constructs across a wider range of ages.

Advances in Neurobiology

Contemporary neurobiological theories are poised to have a substantial influence on theories of learning and cognition in the future. Early studies that related basic laboratory procedures (i.e., measures of glucose metabolism, speed of nerve conduction) with formal psychometric tests or learning tasks have been replaced with more sophisticated assessments of brain functioning and neural processing and with complex testing of cognitive and learning abilities (see chapter by Sternberg in this volume). It may be that analogous research with more sophisticated laboratory tools—like the early studies of brain-behavior relationships undertaken in the 1940s, 1950s, and 1960s to provide researchers with an understanding of brain functioning and psychopathology—can provide insights into learning and cognitive skills.

There also has been a strong emphasis on understanding early neurobiological influences on development. Examinations of such interactions were found in many educational applications reviewed here but most specifically in studies of language and literacy development (Shaywitz, 1996). The role of phonological awareness (i.e., the ability to segment the speech stream into its constituent parts) in early literacy acquisition is a good example of research that jointly emphasizes developmental and neurological processes (see chapters by Goelman et al. and by Pressley in this volume). Motivational researchers have increasingly bridged biological, cognitive, and affective constructs (see chapter by Pintrich in this

volume). We will continue to see even stronger ties between ongoing theory building within a domain and the growing knowledge base in genetics and neurobiology. Such integration will reduce competing notions of underlying biological, cognitive, and emotional psychological processes and will help to more precisely determine how these interact to affect learning.

Impact of Technology

Educational psychologists increasingly have been involved in investigations of learning and instruction within emerging media and technology environments (see chapter by Goldman-Segall & Maxwell in this volume). Contemporary research has focused less on how individual cognition is affected by technology and more on examining effects with technology. New models of computer instruction view computers as flexible and student-directed versus static and expert-driven learning approaches. Prior advances in software technology that originally stressed constructivist processes to make learning and thinking processes more concrete have been broadened to allow children to add animation to pictures, rotate graphics, and link hypertext to audio and video information. Technological and software advances now allow learning to occur on demand with simulations, visualizations, and concept mapping. Students can manipulate variables and instantly see results, can participate in setting up dynamic interactive systems, and can apply sophisticated data analysis tools. Each of these advances provides new avenues for researchers to investigate how students design, construct, and understand complex systems and representations in mathematics and science.

Although investigations of individual learning benefits with educational technology will continue, there are likely to be fewer investigations of simple outcomes or isolated person effects. Recent studies of computer learning are focused on how students make sense of complex systems, how learning occurs during jointly constructed computer interactions, and how teachers can mediate and expand the effects of technology—especially regarding mathematical learning (also see chapter by Lehrer & Lesh in this volume). New software programs allow learners to explore problems in cooperation with others and not just to concretize and experience problems. It now is possible for users to engage in sophisticated real-time data sharing processes whereby a variety of learners contribute to and compare points of view and collaborate on gathering and constructing knowledge. Goldman-Segall and Maxwell (this volume) review several ongoing investigations in which learners across the nation and world concurrently collect, communicate, and analyze data from large-scale environmental projects. These programs are capable of tracking how communities of students make decisions and open up a new methodology for exploring formative learning.

Advances in software and technology will continue to broaden our ability to investigate how students think and construct knowledge individually and in collaboration with others (Brown & Duguid, 2000). In the twenty-first century, these advances are likely to enhance our ability to study distributed and situated learning and subsequently our understanding of learning with technology. Goldman-Segall and Maxwell (this volume) have proposed a new perspectivity theory for studying learning processes that occur when a community of minds is engaged in real-life inquiry using computers. Within this framework, computers are viewed as a partner in the learning process and as a tool that encourages thinking in relationship with others. In effect, synchronous telecommunication capabilities that allow groups of learners to be networked for collaborative inquiry may improve our knowledge of cooperative partnerships in ways that were never before possible. By stressing interpersonal relationships, these programs suggest a move to blend studies of cognitive components with affective components of online learning.

Individuals learning through new media contexts and engaging in collective learning discussions will provide exciting new means to study learning and cognition, self-regulation, motivation, affect, and relationships across time, place, and culture. Technology and media advances have the potential of creating unique and previously unfathomable research opportunities in educational psychology as future researchers investigate new approaches, configurations, and environments for studying learners and learning. Expanding on Papert's (1980) ideas, Goldman-Segall and Maxwell (this volume) suggest that in the future we must develop learning environments that encourage diverse styles of studying and understanding.

Value of Continuing Debates

Notwithstanding the remarkable advances observed across the many domains reviewed here, clashes in theoretical paradigms and differences in what constitutes evidence will continue to influence future research within the field. Several examples clarify how such ongoing controversies are positive influences that have helped to broaden our knowledge base and have led to new insights regarding relevant contexts for learning and teaching.

Debates about the relative importance of mastery over performance goals and other self-regulatory constructs have led to the identification of alternative performance goals that differentially affect student achievement. One such externalized

goal that focuses on a student's desire to outperform others to get higher grades has been found to contribute to higher levels of academic performance. Researchers also have sought to clarify debates concerning the domain or situational specificity of motivational constructs such as self-efficacy or control beliefs. Research motivated by such debates has led to greater specificity of key motivational constructs and constructs of self related not only to generalized achievement but also to motivation and self-regulatory activities, such as choice, judgments of value, cognitive engagement, and task persistence (see chapters by Pintrich and by Schunk & Zimmerman in this volume). This work has important implications concerning qualifications for how to help students set personal goals and for how to provide specific motivational feedback that will promote both short- and long-term academic and social competencies. That individual beliefs, expectancies, and attributions can be changed through teacher feedback is an especially exciting area of future research for students exhibiting learning and behavioral dis-abilities (see chapters by Siegel and by Walker & Gresham in this volume).

The controversy over the domain specificity or generalizability of cognitive abilities has led to studies that move beyond this simple dichotomy. Researchers have sought to determine how learning and metacognitive processes emerge initially within specific domains of knowledge and then advance to broader general abilities across domains (see chapter by McCormick in this volume for further elaboration of these issues). In the cooperative learning literature, there are continuing debates as to what affects motivation for learning and how incentives are employed to structure or influence learning (see chapter by Slavin et al. in this volume). These debates have contributed to studies that move beyond whether greater learning occurs with individual as well as collective learning goals. Slavin et al. have called for more focused studies to determine situations in which group goals and individual accountability may not both be necessary. Such hypothesized occasions might be when students are working collaboratively on higher level cognitive tasks that lack a single right answer, those in which students voluntarily join groups and are already strongly motivated to perform, or in highly structured situations in which learning is likely a result of simply participating. Another context in which individual accountability may not be as essential is during communal learning groups composed of homogeneous ethnic minority members who already demonstrate high levels of interdependence functioning (Hurley, 1997).

There is a trend to move beyond proving simple dichotomies; research now seeks to examine multiple paths between personal goal structures and various cognitive, self-regulatory, and achievement outcomes (see chapters by

Pintrich and by Wentzel in this volume). Researchers will seek to more accurately determine the directional and causal precedence of motivational components on cognition and learning. This work will link affective, motivational, and cognitive processes—possibly by integrating prior research on the effect of emotions on test performance with assessments of self-esteem and self-identity. Debates about the impact of development, experience, and culture will help expand the ages and places in which we study critical learning and relationships and the practices and policies that influence such processes (Pianta & Walsh, 1996).

Finally, with no clear consensus in sight as to what constitutes intelligence or optimal cognitive, problem-solving, or learning behavior, researchers will continue to contrast and distinguish the strengths and weaknesses of competing alternatives that bridge classical and constructivist information-processing views. Future work will carry on the century-old debate that intelligence is not a fixed, genetically based trait, but rather is strongly affected by environmental influences that transpire over an individual's lifetime as well as across generations (see chapter by Sternberg in this volume on the Flynn effect). Competing concepts and constructs proposed to account for important individual differences will be integrated into more comprehensive models that combine social and cultural contexts with the biological and affective bases of cognition. Theoretical ties will be strengthened by linking the literature on cognition, self-regulation, and learning to other motivational constructs involved in predecision processing and volition, which is invoked in postdecision processing (see chapters by Pintrich and by Schunk & Zimmerman in this volume).

RESEARCH IMPLICATIONS

The longevity of emerging theories and research domains in educational psychology will depend largely upon future empirical documentation that will incorporate new methodologies and levels of inquiry.

Expanded Methods of Inquiry

Methodological expansions in the new century will extend beyond a focus on individuals in decontextualized settings to include examinations of group learning in situations in which newly acquired knowledge must be applied and adapted. This will require descriptions and assessments of interactive and multidirectional relationships situated in broader social and cultural contexts. Such inquiry calls for the incorporation of advanced methodologies and psychometric procedures that

allow for the study of interdependent individual and social variables during problem solving in natural settings. Data collection traditions will be blended across anthropology, linguistics, psychology, and education using a variety of observational, interview, and participant methodologies (see chapters by Sternberg and by John-Steiner & Mahn in this volume). Traditional statistical analyses also will be broadened to include more rigorous models of item analysis such as IRT (Item Response Theory) and path and survival analyses that can capture multiple complex latent and direct relationships within changing populations.

These advances would not be trivialized by debates about the value and relevancy of qualitative versus quantitative methodologies. Instead, future researchers would move beyond this debate to discussions of how these two traditions can coexist and be profitably combined (Levin & Robinson, 1999). Recognition of the contribution of both would lead to integrated designs that capture qualitative and quantitative attributes. One such approach that permits legitimate generalization and prescription is the randomized classroom trial discussed originally by Levin (1992), elaborated by Levin and O'Donnell (1999), and further captured by Levin, O'Donnell, and Kratochwill (this volume). Also in the past two decades there has been greater acceptance of rigorous single-subject and quasi-experimental designs and a growing recognition of their instructional and evaluative relevance (Kratochwill & Levin, 1992; Levin & Wampold, 1999; Neuman & McCormick, 2000).

The push to enhance our understanding of educationally relevant constructs must be based on robust theory and credible evidence (see Levin & O'Donnell, 1999; also see chapter by Levin et al. in this volume). These researchers suggest that this goal will best be accomplished when we utilize a continuum of methodologies that abide by high standards of investigative quality and rigor. Expanded investigative repertoires will include innovations that involve contextually based inquiry, individual experimental study, and large-scale experimental implementation designs. A continuum of research within a domain would embrace and merge findings from naturalistic and laboratory approaches using longitudinal and cross-sectional designs and individual and group methods that take place in a variety of culturally relevant and culturally distinct contexts.

A few examples would serve to highlight how these advances have been incorporated in contemporary work. Experimental methodologies complemented by descriptive or correlation methods and ethnographic approaches have provided rich understandings about the complexities of literacy instruction (Florio-Ruane & McVee, 2000; Juel, 1988) and other teaching and classroom processes (see chapter by

Pressley et al. in this volume). Integrated approaches have been reflected heavily in the study of literacy and mathematics development and instruction (see chapters by Lehrer & Lesh and by Pressley in this volume). One example is a longitudinal ethnographic study of family communication and subsequent language and literacy development (Hart & Risley, 1995) in 42 families of emergent readers in preschool who were observed in a variety of settings over 2 years. Another is a year-long nationally conducted observational study of expert versus typical teachers who were selected based on administrator nomination, parent ratings, and student outcomes (Pressley, Allington, Wharton-McDonald, Block, & Morrow, 2001). Key findings associated with these combined methodologies have contributed to the design of innovative instructional strategies that are currently under empirical investigation, using randomized classroom designs to assess the strategies' impact on teacher communication and student performance (see chapter by Pressley et al. in this volume). Quasi-experimental methodologies also have contributed to broader, more ecological validations of ongoing classroom instructional strategies (Brown, Pressley, Van Meter, & Schuder, 1996). Future attempts to combine methodologies will lead to further insight about the holistic contexts that improve student learning.

In the technology field, Goldman-Segall and Maxwell (this volume) review how formal experimental methods that stress quantifiable enhancements for learning have been balanced with more descriptive, introspective studies of learners' perceptions and ongoing decision-making strategies. These researchers point to new technological advances that stress community sharing and learning and the need to employ anthropological observation and participatory techniques to answer very different sets of questions from within the learning environment rather than studying it from without (Wenger, 1998). Indeed, researchers exploring new technological learning domains have been at the forefront of such expanded methodologies that allow for dense and realistic explanations and descriptions (Salomon, Perkins, & Globerson, 1991) in combination with more conventional scientific, experimental approaches that isolate independent variables to determine causality and generalizability across settings.

Finally, Goelman and colleagues (this volume) discuss how play has been studied across a number of disciplines, including biology, linguistics, sociology, anthropology, art, literature, and psychology, using an array of naturalistic and experimental methodologies (see chapter by Goelman et al. in this volume). Such an interdisciplinary focus has strongly augmented our comprehension of this key learning process and has led to important advances in early childhood theory, research, and practice. Expanded investigative repertoires

that lead to complimentary efforts can greatly enhance our understanding and contribute to more valid recommendations for addressing critical educational issues in the future.

Advances in Assessment

Theory-driven assessment strategies that capture complex interrelationships and processes have led to a wider array of measurement alternatives within and across studies. McCormick (this volume) points to progress in the assessment of metacognition through measures taken before, during, and after task performance (e.g., Feelings of Knowing, Test Readiness, and Test Judgment measures). She encourages future researchers to overcome the limits and criticisms raised against subjective reflection judgments of ongoing monitoring in order to develop broader metacognitive assessments. Such recommendations have also been forwarded across the domain of self-regulatory and motivational assessment. Mayer and Pintrich (this volume) recommend more precise appraisals of cognitive mental representations by merging cognitive laboratory tasks with metacognitive and motivational outcomes.

Assessment innovations will lead to greater integration and combinations of physiological measurement to tap elementary cognitive information processing and affective behavioral reactions. For example, comprehensive assessments of physical reactions (heart rate), brain functioning (blood flow), and cognitive behavioral reactions (visual scanning, verbal responses during problem solving) might be recorded during instruction and learning. Traditional intellectual testing would be pooled with an array of other assessments that might vary depending on whether a given problem requires analytical, creative, or practical thinking abilities (see chapter by Sternberg in this volume). Pintrich (this volume) predicts that the discovery of links between motivation and cognition will occur through combinations of lab and naturalistic studies that track basic motivational processes in addition to cognitive and metacognitive processing.

A variety of new measures and approaches to measurement have been developed in many of the areas reviewed. In the early childhood and literacy field, advances have included increased use of play-based procedures and the development of reliable early assessments of innate abilities and aptitudes like those currently used to study infants' audition and phonological awareness (see chapters by Goelman et al.; by Lehrer & Lesh; and by Pressley in this volume). In the future, such assessments will help establish how early literacy, numeracy, communication, and artistic or musical skills emerge and are reflected in children's primary learning and living environments. This will require extended observations in home and school settings and will also require the use of dynamic assessment methods. Dynamic assessments and design experiments—in which students receive guided adult feedback as they are exposed to a variety of task demands, instructional strategies, and learning contexts—are critical for discovering the effects of scaffolded, transactional instruction (see chapters by John-Steiner & Mahn; by Lehrer & Lesh; and by Pressley in this volume). Such methods will help establish parameters of performance malleability and will lead to more valid instructional recommendations. Finally, Reschly (this volume) discusses a number of contemporary and future diagnostic challenges facing the field of school psychology, including a push towards direct versus standardized measures of educational and behavioral skills in relevant domains.

Advances in technology have increasingly added to our repertoire of alternative assessments for gathering comprehensive learning-based observations (also discussed later in this chapter). Many newly emerging computer environments require fresh ways to judge how children develop, process, and represent their thinking. The recent advent of structured conferencing and online multimedia sharing allows for renegotiated and interlinked information use and reuse during dynamic collaborations. Currently this innovation is used in several ongoing research projects to connect multiple classrooms across the world. See discussions of the National Geographic Kids Network (NGKNet) project, in which thousands of students collaborate on data collection and research of local and global significance (i.e., acid rain; Feldman, Konold, & Coulter, 2000, cited in the chapter by Goldman-Segall & Maxwell in this volume). These new environments that take advantage of technology to enable collaboration may be the wave of the future for studying both the effects of and effects with technology (see chapter by Goldman-Segall & Maxwell in this volume). Such innovations will necessitate new assessment methodologies, such as longitudinal digital ethnographies of children's thinking that can allow one to examine individual and collaborative learning processes and relations (see chapter by Goldman-Segall & Maxwell in this volume). Future studies of computer environments also would move beyond examinations of behavior and cognition to consider the emotional and relational support required and affected by such learning environments. In fact, the affective capacity and impact of computers are the main focus of an ongoing project pioneered by Rosalind Picard (1997) at MIT (cited in the chapter by Goldman-Segall & Maxwell in this volume).

In the future, educational psychologists will continue to forge and evaluate comprehensive methods to assess an array of learning, behavioral, affective, motivational, and interpersonal outcomes. Immediate and long-term indexes of performance will include some combination of physiological responses, psychometric testing, introspective and third-party interviews, direct observation, contextual manipulation, and dynamic instruction of key processes expected to affect learning and development.

Authentic Outcomes and Developmental Considerations

Across many of the domains reviewed here, there was a common call for the replication of key findings using authentic tasks in authentic contexts. To move beyond fixed notions of abilities, researchers expect that newer psychometric tests will be designed to capture both typical, real-world performance and maximal, conventional performance (see chapter by Sternberg in this volume); this would involve measures of idiosyncratic and alternative intellectual skills that more adequately capture indexes of out-of-school success. Skills related to schooling would be supplemented with those needed for successful functioning within families, work, and community settings. Such assessments will allow for the exploration of interpersonal problem-solving and intellectual behavior during ongoing, practical life endeavors or simulations. Sternberg (this volume) also predicts that future intellectual assessments will be relatively independent of current psychometrically defined intelligence tests as they begin to provide more comprehensive evaluations of contemporary constructs.

Replication and extensions of research with authentic tasks are essential for educational and curriculum improvements. Researchers have begun to generalize and investigate key findings within relevant curriculum domains. Information-processing and metacognitive researchers in particular have studied theoretical applications through instructional programs in mathematics, writing, and reading. Students taught using empirically derived instruction evidence significantly improved performance over those students taught through more traditional methods (especially see the chapters by Lehrer & Lesh; by Mayer; and by McCormick in this volume).

There was a call for advances in the early identification of children with exceptional needs or talents (see chapters by Olszewski-Kubilius; by Siegel; and by Walker & Gresham in this volume). Difficulties associated with assessing younger children and the limitations of traditional and standardized intelligence measures will be overcome by an array of diverse procedures. Reschly (this volume) discusses the push toward new conceptual definitions and classification criteria for educationally funded disabilities that rely on noncategorical criteria, especially for specific learning disabilities (also see chapter by Siegel in this volume). Developmental assessment in the future will more accurately capture both synchronous and asynchronous development patterns and recognize idiosyncratic progressions of development across tasks, settings, and persons (see chapter by Goelman et al. in this volume). Such approaches are critical to identify giftedness and learning disabilities because restricted testing in one domain often compromises early identification (see chapters by Olszewski-Kubilius and by Siegel in this volume).

Another area of continued research is a focus on developmental foundations and trajectories across the domains reviewed here. Researchers increasingly are addressing how critical competencies are modified or moderated by enduring characteristics—such as ethnicity, gender, and exceptionality—and by critical contextual variables. These trends will lead to future studies of dynamic functional relationships over extended periods of time—for example, to determine how motivation and cognition interrelate over time and how personal characteristics and interpersonal relationships affect such processes across a variety of settings. Developmental investigations will help clarify the characteristics of schooling contexts, including relationships that promote social skills and learning (see chapters by Koch; by Pianta, Hamre, & Stuhlman; and by Wentzel in this volume). Furthering our understanding of developmental mechanisms responsible for altering or harnessing critical contextual and relational resources (i.e., the influence of parents, teachers, and peers) will lead to more effective school-based prevention and early intervention programs (see chapters by McCombs and by Walker & Gresham in this volume).

Research Synthesis and Integration

Researchers in the next century will probably address the complexities of synthesizing and integrating research methods and findings on a much broader level, which will help refine our predictions of academic and social performance. Key constructs within a domain often are studied independently within one theoretical paradigm. Self-regulation, for example, has been represented by distinctly separate lines of research across operant, information processing, developmental, social-constructivist, and social cognitive theories. These orientations have led to diverse explanations of self-regulatory constructs and the reciprocal interactions that define when and how self-regulation processes are invoked (see chapter by Schunk & Zimmerman in this volume). In other cases, completely different constructs and factors are used to explain an area of study, as in motivation and metacognition (see chapters by McCormick and by Pintrich in this volume).

Although enormous knowledge has been gained through such theoretical autonomy, continued separation may lessen our ability to discriminate and detect tandem variables not directly under investigation. Kuhn (1972) suggested that

competing paradigms can produce a divided community of researchers whose differences in terminology, conceptual frameworks, and ideas about legitimate questions of inquiry can hinder rather than foster advances in theory, research, and practice. Researchers across many of the domains presented here have called for future integration of theories and methodologies in order to avoid conducting research simply to establish settings and conditions that favor one's own theoretical perspective (see chapter by Schunk & Zimmerman in this volume).

Finding ways to bridge research paradigms might be accomplished through the use of consistent variable definitions, instruments, sample ages, and criterion measures. Not only would building such connections help reconcile similar concepts labeled differently, but it also would help clarify differences between concepts labeled with similar terms and lead to synthesis methodologies that might encourage a closer review of construct dependency (see chapter by Schunk & Zimmerman in this volume). Domains of research across reading, writing, and literacy (Adams, Treiman, & Pressley, 1998) and writing, science, and mathematics (see chapter by Lehrer & Lesh in this volume) have been profitably combined in recent years. Innovative consolidation and integration will arbitrate and expand our understanding of the conditions under which various forms of learning and social experiences affect students' development and achievement. For example, play might be simultaneously examined as a medium through which to study children's intellectual, cognitive, metacognitive, and self-regulatory behavior; affective and motivational growth; and interpersonal relationships in order to discover how children make sense of who they are in relation to their world and to others.

The next generation of theorists will be more knowledgeable of cross-domain findings. Collective studies collaboratively designed will constructively combine different theoretical viewpoints, resulting in a wider spectrum of criterion and predictor variables investigated within one study. There also will be an increase in longitudinal investigations using a common framework to compare key variables in learning and development. Many examples of such synthesis and integration were forwarded by our authors. An array of individual attributes (e.g., gender, ethnicity, temperament), perceptions of relationships, self-regulatory and motivational constructs, and verbal and nonverbal communication exchange processes employed in one study would enhance our understanding of child-teacher relationships (see chapter by Pianta et al. in this volume). Integrated methodologies would help illuminate how different personal constructs facilitate or impede various achievement or motivational outcomes across home and school contexts (see chapter by Wentzel in this volume) and male and female populations (see chapter by Koch in this volume). Cooperative learning outcome assessments would involve a range of memory, comprehension-monitoring, motivation, goal-setting, and adult-student or peer-student relationship variables (see chapter by Slavin et al. in this volume). Calls also were made to merge what we know across the domains of intelligence, cognition, metacognition, self-regulation, motivation, and affect (see chapters by Mayer, by McCormick, by Pintrich, and by Sternberg in this volume). Finally, Pintrich (this volume) suggests that synthesis and appraisals of generalized constructs over extended periods and divergent situations would enhance our knowledge of the enduring, global nature versus the domain specificity of motivational beliefs.

PRACTICE INITIATIVES

The work of educational psychologists has transformed and inspired educational practice and policies and has stimulated dynamic instructional strategies, curriculum innovation, and teacher education programs. Educational psychologists also have contributed to high standards of credible pedagogical evidence. Although important cautions have been made against blind translations to practice, educational psychologists have been at the forefront in helping to make this important knowledge base more visible and accessible to educators and educational policy makers in the future.

Strategies for Instruction

Instructional innovations for diverse learners and settings have been developed through comparative studies of expert learners engaged in cognitive pursuits, controlled experiments that demonstrate gains in performance following instruction, and observations of exceptional teachers in classrooms in which students prosper and develop advanced academic skills. Content-area instruction in mathematics, science, reading, and writing has consistently been bolstered by research on cognitive, metacognitive, and self-regulatory strategies that focuses on how students monitor, modify, and adapt ongoing processes during learning (see chapters by Mayer, by McCormick, and by Schunk & Zimmerman in this volume). Instruction has also been influenced by sociocultural studies of teaching processes that foster critical argument, cooperative learning, and individual expression (see chapters by John-Steiner & Mahn, by Lehrer & Lesh, and by Pressley et al. in this volume). Work on motivational and social relational strategies also have been forwarded that can deeply influence learning behavior in the classroom (see chapters by Pintrich; by Pianta et al.; by Wentzel; and by McCombs in this volume). Several examples of this burgeoning literature are noted in the following discussion.

Emerging strategy research in mathematics emphasize how individual students think about concepts like units of measure and also how students collectively come to participate in mathematical conversations and arguments in a classroom (see chapter by Lehrer & Lesh in this volume). Researchers of mathematics learning have moved beyond strategies of early number and arithmetic learning; they now include investigations of central mathematical concepts in geometry and measurement and data modeling and statistics. There is a strong focus on how students form mathematical habits of mind by learning symbols and arguments. The emphasis is now on teaching formats that emphasize multiple forms of mathematics rooted in practical activity and adult- or peer-guided activity and that foster the growth of mathematical reasoning (see chapters by Lehrer & Lesh and by Mayer in this volume). Similar strategy approaches are used extensively within technological environments to foster problem-solving and science inquiry (see chapter by Goldman-Segall & Maxwell in this volume).

Work on literacy development is an excellent example of psychological theory and research informing meaningful educational practice (see chapter by Pressley in this volume). Instructional strategies in phonemic awareness have a substantial impact on reading immediately and several years later in comparison to other cognitive and conceptual training. Context and instructional strategies to promote infant and toddler prelanguage (i.e., babbling, repetition, rhythm, and tonal play) and communicative ability have focused on important literacy prerequisites embedded in functional adult-child relational strategies (see chapter by Goelman et al. in this volume). As one example, early childhood researchers have established that singing to infants without (vs. with) words and using only repetitive neutral syllables appear to concentrate their auditory attention, leading to better vocal reproductions. The effectiveness of broad repertoires of reading comprehension strategies also have been studied that encourage students to transact with text, construct interpretations with other readers, and react to multiple perspectives (Pressley & El-Dinary, 1997).

Integrative strategies to enhance writing have been developed that focus on planned, higher-order messaging processes (also see chapters by McCormick and by Mayer in this volume) and connections between discussion, collaboration, reading, and writing (Flower et al., 1990). There also is a growing emphasis on dialogue, argument, writing, and inscription strategies that highlight the integral connections between literacy and mathematical thinking processes (see chapter by Lehrer & Lesh in this volume). One area for future collaborative endeavors is the blending of effective strategies for reading, writing, and mathematics with special attention given to systems of inscription used in mathematics and literacy that help students integrate their cognitive and social resources to better develop arguments (see chapter by Lehrer & Lesh in this volume).

Motivational strategies have been forwarded that positively influence self-regulation of thinking and learning. Learning engagement and achievement are thought to occur best when children are given the choice and control to create personally meaningful outcomes (see chapters by McCombs and by Pintrich in this volume). Strong evidence exists to confirm the impact of teacher attitudes, characteristics, and connections with students that promote more persistent academic engagement and greater literacy and mathematics performance (see chapters by Pianta et al. and by Wentzel in this volume). New strategies of cooperative learning have contributed to our knowledge of how to present and design group instruction to effectively enhance learning and motivation for a variety of learners and contexts (see chapters by Schunk & Zimmerman and by Slavin et al. in this volume).

Although tremendous gains have been made in the design of effective instructional strategies across the domains of research reviewed here, evidence of significant short-term improvements must be bolstered in the future by evidence of maintenance and generalization to group and classroom settings and across domains of learning. Work is needed to design integrative and holistic strategies to enhance cognitive and information-processing mechanisms as well as social, motivational, and interpersonal processes that underlie human performance. Greater understanding of student learning and development would also benefit from collaborative endeavors across content areas on the role of conjecture, proof, and argument in classroom discussion and in the formation of relationships that promote higher engagement and motivation. Progress in these areas will add to our ability to design more effective strategies for instruction that capitalize on students' strengths and compensate for weaknesses. Continued studies of exemplary practices will help guide principles of instruction and will lead to instruction better matched to meet the needs of the diverse student populations of the twenty-first century.

Tensions in Designing Instruction

Current debates exist as to whether it is better to teach critical strategies or to facilitate a student's discovery of them. Undoubtedly the role of systematic instruction in identified skills and abilities has long been a contentious issue in many areas of study (Shulman & Keislar, 1966). Tensions between advocates of direct versus indirect instruction are present in discussions of content learning, self-regulatory skills, and instructional approaches for reading and writing. On the one hand is the notion that abilities are contained within the child as an innate need to grow and explore, and such abilities will unfold given supportive environments without direct intervention. Constructivist theories posit that the learner actively and consciously engages in building his or her own knowledge base. On the other hand is the view that more structured pedagogical approaches can nurture opportunities for learning and development.

Contemporary researchers appear to have moved from a focus on settling this argument in an either-or, all-or-none fashion to a more centrist focus. Increasingly, evidence suggests that a multitude of cognitive and self-regulatory processes develop more successfully over time with some direct and systematic environmental intervention. Arguments from a middle-ground stance are reflected in contemporary views of play in education. Children are hypothesized to construct their understanding of the world through freely expressed forms of play but also through play activity facilitated by teachers, who create a scaffolded environment for inquiry (see chapter by Goelman et al. in this volume). This centrist view also is reflected in contemporary calls for balanced literacy instruction, in which explicit instruction in critical phonological and language skills is embedded within meaningful, contextualized, and functional contexts (see Pressley, 1998; also see chapter by Pressley in this volume). Finally, greater recognition of the heterogeneity within identified groups of exceptionalities also have pointed to the need to recognize the differential effectiveness of various learning and instructional approaches (Gagne, 1998; also see chapter by Siegel in this volume).

The consensus view was apparent across many chapters. Vygotskiian theoretical notions of adult guidance, scaffolding, and guided learning within the zone of proximal development (Vygotsky, 1978; Wertsch, 1985) were referenced in chapters on interpersonal, instructional, and relational processes and also were vital to chapters on learning, curriculum applications, and exceptional learners. Effective teachers sensitively guide children toward important discoveries, support children's efforts at mastery, and translate learning experiences so that students gain a sense of accomplishment that contributes to their sustained interest and desire for further growth and mastery (see chapter by John-Steiner & Mahn in this volume; Wertsch, 1998). Classroom practices based on constructivist and relational notions are contributing to our knowledge of how to create motivating, exciting, and inviting environments that facilitate students' achievement and social-emotional performance (see chapters by Pianta et al. and by Pressley et al. in this volume). Researchers in mathematics have found important links between teaching practices that revoice or transform student comments during discovery learning into mathematical references that draw attention to central concepts (see chapter by Lehrer & Lesh in this volume for more on these practices). Consequently, teachers are learning how to balance the need for children to freely explore with their need to be encouraged by adults and provided assistance that will help them master a range of cognitive, metacognitive, and motivational abilities.

Teacher Impact and Preparation

Teachers create environments that nurture and enhance children's learning as well as their mental and moral development. Studies of the role of the teacher have moved beyond simple outcome assessments of student achievement. Contemporary research on teaching has helped delineate an essential teaching knowledge-base and most recently has shifted to studies that focus how teachers' beliefs, values, attitudes, and strategies guide everyday classroom judgments and decisions (Feiman-Nemser & Reimillard, 1996). Educational researchers have begun to recognize and assess the multiple challenges faced by initial and veteran teachers (see chapter by Pressley et al. in this volume; Roehrig, Pressley, & Talotta, 2002) and increasingly are studying contexts that foster teachers' development and improvement—especially during programs of initial teacher preparation (see chapter by Whitcomb in this volume).

Contemporary work views teaching as an active, social, and sophisticated interpretive activity reciprocally influenced by a intricate array of person-internal and contextual variables (Darling-Hammond & Sykes, 1999). The demands of today's diverse and politicized climates have led researchers to conclude that teaching is a highly challenging and complex process (see chapter by Pressley et al. in this volume). A growing number of studies have focused on how teachers become committed to and effective at meeting individual student needs (see chapter by Whitcomb in this volume). Educational psychologists have helped clarify the important role of mediated interpersonal interactions between peers, teachers, and students (see chapters by Pianta et al.; by Slavin et al.; and by Wentzel in this volume) and scaffolded teaching opportunities (see chapter by John-Steiner & Mahn in this volume). Overwhelming evidence points to improvements in reading and writing when teachers prompt, coach, and scaffold learning and personally model their own reading and writing processes (see chapter by Pressley in this volume).

Increasingly, educational researchers have clarified the critical impact of teacher attitudes, characteristics, and classroom management on interpersonal relations, academic engagement, and achievement levels. Teachers who highlight personal goals of value, utility, and interest effect more cognitive engagement, self-regulation, and achievement in students (see chapters by Pintrich, by Pressley et al., and by Wentzel in this volume). The quality of interpersonal processes and relationships between students and teachers has been shown to predict evaluations of self-efficacy and learning (see chapter by Pianta, Hamre, & Stuhlman in this volume). Teachers also play a critical role in creating equitable climates that lead to consistent performance across males and females (see chapter by Koch in this volume). Furthermore, student motivational beliefs have been positively enhanced through teachers' attributional feedback, and teachers who promote strong self-efficacy beliefs play a key role in boosting individual cognitive and self-regulatory strategies and subsequent classwide achievement (see chapter by Pintrich in this volume).

Educational psychology researchers have begun to translate current theory and models of learning into recommended best practices for teacher education reform (see chapter by McCombs in this volume). For example, researchers have recommended that new teachers be trained on how to incorporate effective, empirically validated practices (i.e., cooperative learning) in the classroom (see chapter by Slavin et al. in this volume). McCormick (this volume, citing Hartman, 2001) stresses the need to prepare teachers to teach with and for metacognition. The former refers to getting teachers to use metacognitive processes to enhance their own learning through reflection on their goals for teaching and on student characteristics in relation to these goals. The latter refers to making teachers aware of how to activate metacognitive processes in their students and infuse these principles into their daily instruction. It is also clear that pedagogical content knowledge alone is insufficient for producing competent teachers. Just as critical to a teacher's success is the ability to manage the flow of information in a classroom—especially in the diverse and intellectually heterogeneous classrooms of today's society (see chapter by Pressley et al. in this volume). Teachers need to become more aware of their own attitudes and beliefs and recognize their role as relationship builders in making personal connections among and with students (see chapter by Pianta et al. in this volume) and in creating culturally relevant (see chapter by John-Steiner & Mahn in this volume) and gender-equitable classroom climates (see chapter by Koch in this volume). Teachers also must know how to produce challenging and positive learning and interpersonal climates. Climates that encourage choice, self-control, and self-reflective thinking (see chapter by McCombs in this volume) and foster proof-based discussions in which cycles of conjecture and revision in light of evidence is promoted (see chapter by Lehrer & Lesh in this volume) have been found to promote literacy processes and mathematical understanding in students of all ages.

Whitcomb (this volume) reviews the growing literature on how new teacher candidates develop such views of teaching and teaching practice. She also points to the ongoing politicized debates about the best means of changing and directing the practice of teaching—especially during initial teacher preparation programs. Growing evidence exists that initial teacher preparation programs must do more to ensure that teachers are able to flexibly respond and effectively adapt classroom instruction to meet diverse student needs (Kennedy, 1999). The most promising models of initial teacher preparation emphasize modeling of newly learned practices in authentic contexts, encourage constructive evaluations of personal judgment and decision-making, and incorporate reflective discussions with communities of experienced teachers (Borko & Putnam, 1996; Putnam & Borko, 2000). However, Whitcomb (this volume) and others have called for more comprehensive and rigorous studies designed to help clarify how knowledge, beliefs, and values filter an initial teacher candidate's perceptions, interpretations, and subsequent responses to classroom events. It remains to be seen whether currently proposed teacher preparation reforms translate to modifications in actual teaching practice and ultimately to impacts on student achievement.

It is very likely that in the future, educational research will be more effectively translated into preservice and in-service teacher preparation programs. Indeed, teachers need to be viewed as continuing learners whose own performance and professional development should mirror the best of what we know about learning, motivation, and development (see chapter by McCombs in this volume). Until recently, researchers knew little about which issues and topics were entering into the lexicon of teaching practice or why certain information entered and not others. Whitcomb (this volume) predicts that future teacher training and development models will seek to build a richer conceptual content knowledge, a deeper appreciation of and belief system about the pedagogy of teaching, and a broader array of instructional decision-making and judgment processes in teacher candidates. She and McCombs (this volume) predict that core professional skills, judgments, and values will increasingly be based upon and guided by well-founded, learner-centered principles arising from the educational psychology literature; this also will involve training teachers to use and analyze rules of credible evidence to enhance their ability to ask critical questions about and make informed judgments on the relative impact of interventions (see chapter by Levin, O'Donnell, & Kratochwill in this volume).

A critical opportunity exists for educational psychologists to have a strong impact on strengthening our knowledge of the complex processes, challenges, and self-reflective abilities of highly competent teachers. This potential will increase because of the predicted shortage of new teachers and because of a greater emphasis on student performance accountability standards. Competent teachers will be in great demand, increasing the importance of our burgeoning knowledge base and the need for sound pedagogy and more rigorous research to inform and transform the field of teaching and teacher preparation. Whitcomb (this volume) suggests that these goals will best be accomplished through a greater integration of work across the individual traditions studied in educational psychology and the work currently underway to study initial teacher preparation and continued teacher learning.

Technology and Its Role in Practice

The emergence of the widely available public Internet has led to unheard-of possibilities for long-distance and other forms of collaborative learning. Goldman-Segall and Maxwell (this volume) posit the emergence of the Internet as the beginning of a new research field in computer-assisted learning. Virtual environments in which students can meet and interact and collaboratively work on research are more readily available as a new learning format. These researchers call for a move beyond an individual focus to one of a community of minds in which the focus is on how knowledge is constructed between people engaged in real-life inquiry. Their newly proposed perspectivity theory corresponds to a move from viewing a computer as an object with which to think to a view of the computer as a partner or as a tool that allows people to think and rethink in relationship with others. Their ideas build upon past work that views the computer as a cognitive partner in learning, as part of the cultural milieu, and as a convivial tool (Illich, 1972). Innovations such as collaborative design boards, real-time meeting space, scaffolded conferencing and note-taking, hypertext and media, and video conferencing have provided the medium for studying how groups of learners work together to create an ecology for learning. These innovations also will help us to rethink the kinds of human relations that can be built with multimedia tools.

One controversial future question is whether these new online environments are as effective as direct collaborative engagement with others during learning. Future research is needed to establish whether there are links between what we know about face-to-face cooperative learning groups and those offered through new media and technology advances (see chapters by Goldman-Segall & Maxwell and by Slavin et al. in this volume). We hope that future researchers will move beyond dichotomous questions that pit one modality over another. As Lehrer and Lesh (this volume) note, the teaching environments within which technology is embedded also are critical to facilitating greater understanding of mathematics—particularly concepts found in geometry. These researchers review studies that demonstrate advantages of technology that heighten learning when paired with concomitant instruction, dialogue, and joint explanation. We agree with Goldman-Segall and Maxwell, who suggest that the most profitable work of the future will be to determine what types of learning environments—media or otherwise—promote processes and representations that are better for particular knowledge and tasks, across different contexts, and with different types of learners.

Other questions regarding how best to integrate technology into the curriculum relate to concerns regarding access and inequity. McCombs (this volume) and others point out that such issues arise when certain members of the population are systematically denied equal access because of vast differences in monetary or personnel resources. Technology integration also is difficult when innovation and reforms misalign with current practice and capability or accountability policies; this might occur if content standards or technology competencies work against collaborative efforts and learning. Finally, the availability of qualified teachers and personnel who are willing and able to readily adapt new technological advances can be problematic. Teachers need much support and training before technology is applied in the ways envisioned by key researchers in the field.

Curriculum Development

Many of the research findings in educational psychology in the latter part of the twentieth century have provided a strong theoretical basis for how critical constructs can be fostered in educational settings. Curriculum developers have begun to take notice of many of these findings. Knowledge of key content domain strategies and skills has stimulated curriculum development across many of the domains reviewed here.

Notable developments in reading and writing research and curriculum have been made (see Gaffney & Anderson, 2000; chapter by Pressley in this volume). Balanced literacy practices have been developed that mimic processes and self-questions characteristically found in expert readers and writers (Pressley, 1998); in writing curriculum, this has meant teaching students directly how to plan, draft, and revise materials (Harris & Graham, 1996). Curriculum for early education has been developed to foster the contemporary use of art, play, and music. Childhood technology has moved beyond the original constructivist LOGO environ-

ments pioneered by Seymour Papert (1980); children and adults now use media that helps them learn to explore, express, and participate in knowledge construction and exploration while learning about advanced mathematical concepts such as fractions (see chapters by Goldman-Segall & Maxwell and by Lehrer & Lesh in this volume). Findings regarding the individual profiles and stability of giftedness suggest the need to find optimal curricular matches for these students earlier than once thought. Olszewski-Kubilius (this volume) points to the importance of early instruction that captures higher-level conceptual ability to increase motivation and lower resistance. She points to work that suggests when such approaches are introduced to older gifted students, they become frustrated with the new demands and subsequently will not be motivated for complex learning.

Unfortunately, many published curriculum materials have not adequately incorporated methods to foster motivation, self-regulation, or cooperative learning. Pintrich (this volume) and others have called for future work that merges key learning and motivational constructs into curriculum designed for the content area domains of writing, science, and mathematics. The challenge is how to best incorporate our broad knowledge base about motivation and relational constructs into classroom curriculum that not only enhances learning but also leads to high levels of engagement and persistence in the face of failure. Finally, we anticipate that in the future there will be even more curriculum transformation research on how to encourage participation of women and minorities and on how to overcome sexual stereotypes and harassment (see chapter by Koch in this volume). Educational psychologists will continue to design and evaluate practices and attitudinal changes that will help close the glaring gender gaps in education captured in several national reports (AAUW; American Association of University Women Educational Foundation, 1998).

Cautions on Translations to Practice

Much of the work represented in the chapters in this book has had a significant impact on educational practice, innovation, and reform. Research in the field of educational psychology has contributed to moving educational reform to the forefront of political discussions (e.g., National Council of Teachers of Mathematics, 2000; National Reading Panel, 2000). Educational psychologists have the potential to capture the attention both of the public and of policy makers (see chapter by McCombs in this volume). Nevertheless, there is a need to be cautious about how work within the field is translated to practice.

There is a great tendency for the public to jump on quick, unidimensional solutions when bending to political pressures that overlook important counterevidence or unintended outcomes. When educational advances are touted for their positive affects on learning and development, rarely are important concomitant impacts recognized. For example, Goelman et al. (this volume) point out that much of what is marketed today as educational programming for young children is more in line developmentally with the preferences and skill levels of older students. Another example is the current tendency to succumb to the idea that educational software or web-based resources can provide an efficient modality for all learning woes. Goldman-Segall and Maxwell (this volume) note that misinformation as well as good information can be found on the Internet and that educators should remember that gathering information online is not the same as learning.

Too often, initial promising findings are translated into easy fixes and educational answers by mandates of packaged curriculum, courseware, and programs for all learners. Such one-size-fits-all thinking overlooks the diversity that exists in today's learners and learning contexts (see chapter by McCombs in this volume). Mandated solutions to students' learning needs often have not been scrutinized with the same rigor called for to establish credible evidence by educational researchers and may not be easily transferable across settings (Levin & O'Donnell, 1999). Current school reform movements and mandates are rarely evaluated for how they may change an array of outcomes, including impacts on learning as well as on motivation and interpersonal processes between teachers and students. For example, teaching driven by performance testing and learning-based outcomes should be evaluated for its impact on collaborative efforts that promote relationships in school settings (see chapters by McCombs and by Pianta et al. in this volume).

Another issue is that many reforms have not attended to all segments of the population. Appropriate early education for young gifted children or young children experiencing significant learning or behavioral problems are just a few of the neglected groups of students with exceptional needs (see chapters by Olszewski-Kubilius, by Siegel, and by Walker & Gresham in this volume). A number of factors influence how children with exceptional needs are educated, including ideological beliefs, current economic and demographic trends, issues of educational classification, and ideas about when appropriate programming should begin (also see chapter by Reschly in this volume). Notions about the malleability of abilities and the stability of behaviors can influence acceptability notions about how and when to offer services.

Moreover, when early and remedial intervention services are offered, many educators are badly equipped to meet the individual needs of exceptional students (see chapters by Reschly, by Siegel, by Walker & Gresham, and by Whitcomb in this volume).

The increasing globalization of our society will raise important policy and research issues over the next century. Social and cultural contexts have been incorporated by educational psychologists into the study of a broad range of processes and contexts contributing to learning and development (see chapter by John-Steiner & Mahn in this volume). Reforms arising from this work must be careful not to allow sociocultural differences to connote deficiencies within certain groups. For example, remedial home-based programs to strengthen early literacy skills can be developed and delivered in such a way as to imply deprived notions of parenting practices. Alternatively, these programs can be developed from the mindset that different literacy purposes are reflected in culturally diverse families; some such purposes are less suited for successful transitions into school. The later approach would demonstrate a greater understanding of important contextual factors contributing to school deficiencies in culturally different students (see chapter by Goelman et al. in this volume). Reforms to meet the needs of culturally diverse students must be designed to match what we know about general learning, motivation, and development and the complex array of contextual factors that can influence such processes (see chapters by John-Steiner & Mahn and by McCombs in this volume).

Finally, educational psychologists will need to fight reform pressures and politics that reduce complex notions into easily defined yet constrained concepts that have not been comprehensively appraised for their positive and negative effects. In the future, more work may be needed to further evaluate less psychometrically strong theories that are likely to influence key educational policies (see chapter by Levin et al. in this volume; Levin & O'Donnell, 1999). Educational psychologists will be at the forefront, countering the demands for quick answers by advocating models and methods that capture the diversity and complexity necessary to understand human learning and development. Educational psychologists will lead efforts cautioning against looking for any single magic bullet to solve all learning and instruction problems (see chapter by Pintrich in this volume). As McCombs (this volume) suggests, educational psychologists are likely to be instrumental in the identification of a continuum of potential solutions for our pressing educational challenges—solutions that take into account both individual capacities and social and cultural environments.

EDUCATIONAL PSYCHOLOGY'S FUTURE: CONCLUSIONS

Since 1848, almost every educational policy statement proposed for public education has included explicit objectives for the development of intellectual, scholastic, and cognitive competencies as well as character development, moral values, conformity, and cooperation as social competencies for producing model citizens (see chapter by McCombs in this volume and Wentzel, 1998). Educational psychology researchers have contributed theory and practice to further our knowledge in each of these pursuits.

Over the next two decades, educational psychology researchers are likely to integrate comprehensive models of learning and cognition with affective, motivational, social, and biological influences. Moreover, ecological and sociocultural frameworks will increasingly influence our understanding of individual cognitive and social pursuits, behavioral and academic competence, and social-interpersonal relationships. The next generation of theorists will be more interested in describing interactive relationships that are multidirectional and situated in broad ecological frameworks. Indeed, in the future complex systems, frameworks will be used to build more comprehensive models for understanding individual cognitive and social pursuits, behavioral and academic competence, and social-interpersonal relationships. Theoretical ties will be strengthened by linking the literature on cognition, self-regulation, and learning to relational, motivation, and classroom processes. Wentzel (this volume) concurs when she suggests that educational researchers and policy makers will benefit from continued work on the dynamic, multilevel interactions that take place in schools in order to further our understanding of the complex phenomena of classroom adjustment and achievement.

At times it is clear that various theoretical perspectives within a domain widely differ in the location of key criterion variables. These differences in theory and constructs have led our authors to call for more collaborative efforts in the future. The critical question is how willing and successful educational psychology researchers will be in finding fruitful connections for consolidating dominant theories in the hopes of identifying more comprehensive theoretical models in the future. Such thinking is sure to advance the field so that educational practice can benefit more fully from the contributions of educational research across various fields and orientations. Such collaboration will go far in making our knowledge base more visible and accessible to educators and policy makers. (see Lambert & McCombs, 1998, and chapter by McCombs in this volume for a discussion of a collaborative Task Force

on Psychology in Education sponsored by the APA that resulted in the publication of *14 Learner Centered Practice Principles*).

It is important to note that a push for greater synthesis also has its drawbacks—especially if it results in a de-emphasis on work that seeks to clarify and isolate discrete constructs and processes. Integrative models across increasingly broad domains might contribute to a less distinctive knowledge base associated with the field of educational psychology. In fact, historically, rigorous empirical investigations of independent concepts and processes have helped distinguish many areas of research within educational psychology. Thus, a significant challenge for the next generation of researchers is how to encourage the pursuit of critical and enduring constructs while expanding into new areas of inquiry with the goal of establishing interrelationships across a wide corpus of research. Theoretical integration notwithstanding, controversy and debates across and within many domains will contribute to vigorous refinements and expansions of independent as well as integrated constructs that will continue to improve our understanding of important influences on learning and schooling.

In 1992, Calfee reflected on the field of educational psychology and noted that what was needed in the coming century was a refinement of more credible and convincing educational research. Levin and O'Donnell (1999) have recently reframed this suggestion as a call for future efforts to enhance the credibility of educational psychology as a discipline, which will in turn enhance the quality and societal value of educational research (also see chapter by Levin et al. in this volume). Trustworthy and credible research to assess the relative impact of educational and psychological treatments or interventions is of critical importance for policy makers. Levin, O'Donnell, and Kratochwill (this volume) call for future educational reforms based on clearly delineated standards of credible evidence. Such calls are receiving wide recognition in national research funding. In the future, innovative continuums that draw both from contextually based inquiry and from robust, rigorous large-scale implementation studies will be a top priority for educational researchers. Although frustrations have been voiced about the widely divergent quality and rigor associated with the past era of educational research (Sroufe, 1997), it is clear that educational psychology more than any other field offers research validated frameworks to guide systematic reform efforts in education (see chapter by McCombs in this volume). The many research successes in the areas of study reviewed here should go far in stimulating a great deal of additional research in the twenty-first century. Such work will permit progress not only by augmenting our understanding of academic success, but also by providing more definitive research to increase our understanding about how to intervene and prevent schooling difficulties and failures.

We concur with the assertion forwarded by the majority of the authors here—that educational psychologists have an important opportunity to play a significant role in shaping K–20 education in the twenty-first century. Work within the field of educational psychology is poised to address the challenges posed by the vast achievement differences across students from diverse backgrounds and the pressing expectations of promoting higher levels of achievement for all students. As the researcher-contributors in this volume point out, an important reciprocal relationship exists between psychology and education that is best reflected in the contributions of educational psychologists historically and is even more visibly represented in the last two decades. We are in an exciting era of transformation and change. We anticipate that research in educational psychology will continue to provide the practical, theoretical, and intellectual underpinnings that will enable students to achieve their fullest potential.

Summary

Our perspectives for the future as presented in this volume are in large part based on recent past efforts in educational psychology, emerging trends identified by the contributors to this volume, and the integration of advances across domains covered in this volume. It sometimes occurs that the most interesting predictions for *things to come* are made by historians (e.g., Wells) who are able to synthesize cyclical historical trends with current status to arrive at best guesses for the future. We did not use historical antecedents to derive our future perspectives and are less inclined to view our suggestions for the future as predictions as much as fruitful avenues and venues for future research, practice, and policy. We have attempted to extrapolate meaningful trends in educational psychology to elucidate short- and long-term goals—some of which have been specific and others of which have been broadly defined. Above all, we view the field of educational psychology as an exciting area of psychological research that has made and will continue to make important contributions to the understanding and promotion of human learning, cognition, and the schooling process.

REFERENCES

Adams, M. J., Treiman, R., & Pressley, M. (1998). Reading, writing, and literacy. In I. Sigel & A. Renninger (Eds.), *Handbook of child psychology: Vol. 4. Child psychology in practice* (pp. 275–355). New York: Wiley.

American Association of University Women Educational Foundation (1998). *Gender gaps executive summary*. Washington, DC: Association of University Woman Educational Foundation.

Bandura, A. (1977). Self-efficacy: Toward a unifying theory of behavioral change. *Psychological Review, 84,* 191–215.

Bandura, A. (1986). *Social foundations of thought and action: A social cognitive theory.* Englewood Cliffs, NJ: Prentice-Hall.

Boekaerts, P. R., Pintrich, P. R., & Zeidner, M. (Eds.). (2000). *Handbook of self-regulation.* San Diego, CA: Academic Press.

Borko, H., & Putnam, R. (1996). Learning to teach. In D. C. Berliner & R. C. Calfee (Eds.), *Handbook of educational psychology* (pp. 673–708). New York: Macmillan.

Brown, J. S., & Duguid, P. (2000). *The social life of information.* Boston: Harvard Business School Press.

Brown, R., Pressley, M., Van Meter, P., & Schuder, T. (1996). A quasi-experimental validation of transactional strategies instruction with low-achieving second grade readers. *Journal of Educational Psychology, 88,* 18–37.

Bruner, J. (1990). *Acts of meaning.* Cambridge, MA: Harvard University Press.

Bruner, J. (1996). *The culture of education.* Cambridge, MA: Harvard University Press.

Calderhead, J. (1996). Teachers: Beliefs and knowledge. In D. C. Berliner & R. C. Calfee (Eds.), *Handbook of educational psychology* (pp. 709–725). New York: Macmillan.

Calfee, R. C. (1992). Refining educational psychology: The case of the missing links. *Educational Psychologist, 27,* 163–175.

Calfee, R. C., & Berliner, D. C. (1996). Introduction to a dynamic and relevant educational psychology. In D. C. Berliner & R. C. (Eds.), *Handbook of educational psychology* (pp. 1–11). New York: Macmillan.

Cronbach, L. J., & Snow, R. E. (1977). *Aptitudes and instructional methods: A handbook for research on interactions.* New York: Irvington.

Darling-Hammond, L., & Sykes, G. (Eds.). (1999). *Teaching as the learning profession: Handbook of policy and practice.* San Francisco: Jossey-Bass.

Feiman-Nemser, S., & Remillard, J. (1996). Perspectives on learning to teach. In F. B. Murray (Ed.), *The teacher educator's handbook* (pp. 63–91). San Francisco: Jossey-Bass.

Feldman, A., Konold, C., & Coulter, B. (2000). *Network science, a decade later: The internet and classroom learning.* Mahwah, NJ: Erlbaum.

Florio-Ruane, S., & McVee, M. (2000). Ethnographic approaches to literacy research. In M. L. Kamil, P. B. Mosenthal, P. D. Pearson, & R. Barr (Eds.), *Handbook of reading research* (Vol. 3, pp. 153–162). Mahwah, NJ: Erlbaum.

Flower, L., Stein, V., Ackerman, J., Kantz, M. J., McCormick, K., & Peck, W. C. (1990). *Reading to write: Exploring a cognitive and social process.* New York: Oxford University Press.

Gaffney, J. S., & Anderson, R. C. (2000). Trends in reading research in the United States: Changing intellectual currents over three decades. In M. L. Kamil, P. B. Mosenthal, P. D. Pearson, & R. Barr (Eds.), *Handbook of reading research* (Vol. 3, pp. 53–74). Mahwah, NJ: Erlbaum.

Gagne, F. (1998). A proposal for subcategories within gifted or talented populations. *Gifted Child Quarterly, 42*(2), 87–95.

Harris, J. W., & Stocker, H. (Eds.). (1998). *Handbook of mathematics and computational science.* New York: Springer.

Harris, K. R., & Graham, S. (1996). *Making the writing process work: Strategies for composition and self-regulation.* Cambridge, MA: Brookline Books.

Hart, B., & Risley, T. R. (1995). *Meaningful differences in the everyday experience of young American children.* Baltimore: Brookes.

Hartman, H. (Ed.). (2001). *Metacognition in learning and instruction: Theory, research and practice.* Norwell, MA: Kluwer.

Hurley, E. (1997, April). *The interaction of communal orientaion in African American children with group processes in cooperative learning: Pedagogical and theoretical implications.* Paper presented at the annual meeting of the American Educational Research Association, Chicago.

Illich, I. (1972). *Deschooling society.* New York: Harrow Books.

Juel, C. (1988). Learning to read and write: A longitudinal study of 54 children from first through fourth grades. *Journal of Educational Psychology, 80,* 417–447.

Kamil, M. L., Mosenthal, P. B., Pearson, P. D., & Barr, R. (Eds.). (2000). *Handbook of reading research* (Vol. 3). Mahwah, NJ: Erlbaum.

Kennedy, M. (1999). The role of preservice education. In L. Darling-Hammond & G. Sykes (Eds.), *Teaching as the learning profession: Handbook of policy and practice* (pp. 54–85). San Francisco: Jossey-Bass.

Kratochwill, T. R., & Levin, J. R. (1992). *Single-case research design and analysis: New developments for psychology and education.* Hillsdale, NJ: Erlbaum.

Kuhn, D. (1972). Mechanism of change in the development of cognitive structures. *Child Development, 43,* 833–844.

Lambert, N., & McCombs, B. L. (1998). *How students learn: Reforming schools through learner-centered education.* Washington, DC: APA Books.

Lerner, R. M. (1998). Theories of human development: Contemporary perspectives. In W. Damon & R. M. Lerner (Eds.), *Handbook of child psychology: Theoretical models of human development* (5th ed., pp. 1–24). New York: Wiley.

Levin, J. R. (1992). On research in classrooms. *Mid-Western Educational Researcher, 5,* 2–6.

Levin, J. R., & O'Donnell, A. M. (1999). What to do about educational research's credibility gaps? *Issues in Education, 5,* 177–229.

Levin, J. R., & Robinson, D. H. (1999). Further reflections on hypothesis testing and editorial policy for primary research journals. *Educational Psychology Review, 11,* 143–155.

Levin, J. R., & Wampold, B. E. (1999). Generalized single-case randomization tests: Flexible analyses for a variety of situations. *School Psychology Quarterly, 14,* 59–93.

National Council of Teachers of Mathematics. (2000). *Principles and standards for school mathematics.* Reston, VA: Author.

National Reading Panel. (2000). *Teaching children to read: An evidence-based assessment of the scientific research literature on reading and its implications for reading instruction: Reports of the subgroups.* Washington, DC: National Institute of Child Health and Development.

Neuman, S. B., & McCormick, S. (2000). A case for single-subject experiments in literacy research. In M. L. Kamil, P. B. Mosenthal, P. D. Pearson, & R. Barr (Eds.), *Handbook of reading research* (Vol. 3, pp. 181–194). Mahwah, NJ: Erlbaum.

Papert, S. E. (1980). *Mindstorms: Children, computers, and powerful ideas.* New York: Basic Books.

Pianta, R. C. (1999). *Enhancing relationships between children and teachers.* Washington, DC: American Psychological Association.

Pianta, R. C., & Walsh, D. (1996). *High-risk children in the schools: Creating sustaining relationships.* New York: Routledge.

Picard, R. (1997). *Affective computing.* Cambridge, MA: MIT Press.

Pintrich, P. R., & Shunk, D. H. (2002). *Motivation in education: Theory, research and applications* (2nd ed.). Englewood Cliffs, NJ: Prentice Hall Merrill.

Pressley, M. (1998). *Reading instruction that works: The case for balanced teaching.* New York: Guilford.

Pressley, M., Allington, R., Wharton-McDonald, R., Block, C. C., & Morrow, L. M. (2001). *Learning to read: Lessons from exemplary first grades.* New York: Guilford.

Pressley, M., & El-Dinary, P. B. (1997). What we know about translating comprehension strategies instruction research into practice. *Journal of Learning Disabilities, 30,* 486–488.

Putnam, R., & Borko, H. (2000). What do new views of knowledge and thinking have to say about research on teacher learning? *Educational Researcher, 29*(1), 4–15.

Reynolds, C. R., & Gutkin, T. B. (1999). *The handbook of school psychology* (3rd ed.). New York: Wiley.

Richardson, V. (Ed.). (2001). *Handbook of research on teaching* (4th ed.). Washington, DC: American Educational Research Association.

Roehrig, A. D., Pressley, M., & Talotta, D. (2002). *Stories of beginning teachers: First year challenges and beyond.* Notre Dame, IN: University of Notre Dame Press.

Salomon, G., Perkins, D. N., & Globerson, T. (1991). Partners in cognition: Extending human intelligence with intelligent technologies. *Educational Researcher, 20,* 2–9.

Schunk, D. H., & Zimmerman, B. J. (1997). Social origins of self-regulatory competence. *Educational Psychologist, 32,* 195–208.

Schunk, D. H., & Zimmerman, B. J. (1998). *Self-regulated learning: From teaching to self-reflective practice.* New York: Guilford Press.

Shaywitz, S. E. (1996). Dyslexia. *Scientific American, 275*(5), 98–104.

Shulman, L. S., & Keislar, E. R. (Eds.). (1966). *Learning by discovery: A critical appraisal.* Chicago: Rand McNally.

Slavin, R. E. (2000). *Educational psychology: Theory and practice* (6th ed.). Needam Heights, MA: Allyn & Bacon.

Snow, R. E. (1986). Individual differences and the design of educational programs. *American Psychologist, 41,* 1029–1039.

Snow, R. E. (1989). Aptitude-treatment interaction as a framework for research on individual differences in learning. In P. L. Ackerman, R. J. Sternberg, & R. Glaser (Eds.), *Learning and individual differences: Advances in theory and research* (pp. 13–58). New York: Freeman.

Snow, R. E., & Lohman, D. F. (1984). Toward a theory of cognitive aptitude for learning from instruction. *Journal of Educational Psychology, 76,* 347–376.

Sroufe, G. E. (1997). Improving the "awful reputation" of educational research. *Educational Researcher, 26*(7), 26–28.

Vygotsky, L. S. (1978). *Mind in society: The development of higher psychological processes.* Cambridge, MA: Harvard University Press.

Wenger, E. (1998). *Communities of practice: Learning, meaning, and identity.* Cambridge, MA: Cambridge University Press.

Wentzel, K. R. (1998). Social support and adjustment in middle school: The role of parents, teachers, and peers. *Journal of Educational Psychology, 90,* 202–209.

Wertsch, J. V. (1985). *Vygotsky and the social formation of mind.* Cambridge, MA: Harvard University Press.

Wertsch, J. H. (1998). *Mind as action.* New York: Oxford University Press.

Zimmerman, B. J. (2000). Attaining self-regulation: A social cognitive perspective. In M. Boekaerts, P. R. Pintrich, & M. Zeidner (Eds.), *Handbook of self-regulation* (pp. 13–39). San Diego, CA: Academic Press.

Author Index

Koedinger, K. R., 357–358, 362, 381, 382
Koehler, M., 364, 365, 382
Koehler, M. J., 572, 573
Koestner, R., 187
Kogan, M., 591
Koh, J., 11, 304, 614, 615, 618, 620, 621, 622, 626
Kohlberg, L., 156, 157, 158
Kohler, F., 526
Kohler, W., 48
Kohn, A., 187
Kohout, J., 443, 448
Kohout, J. L., 435
Kolligian, J., 251
Kolpakowski, T., 369
Kolstad, A., 333
Konold, C., 379, 401, 414, 619
Konstantopoulos, S., 574, 575
Kontos, S., 319
Koontz, J. E., 167
Kopp, C. B., 63
Körkel, J., 457, 477
Korzenik, D., 288
Kosc, L., 473
Koschmann, T., 394, 395, 417
Kosiewicz, M. M., 61
Kostelinik, M. J., 305
Kosterman, R., 521
Kotovsky, L., 360
Kovach, R., 72
Kowalski, T. J., 167
Kozulin, A., 127, 139, 145
Krabbe, E. C., 363
Krajcik, J., 536, 594
Krajcik, J. S., 406
Krampe, R. T., 160
Krapp, A., 113
Krathwohl, D. R., 50, 560
Kratochwill, T., 574
Kratochwill, T. R., 14, 16, 60, 448, 558, 559,
    561, 565, 566, 568, 571, 572, 617, 624,
    626, 627
Kraus, C., 87
Kraut, R., 597
Krechevsky, M., 35, 37
Kress, G., 145
Kreuzig, H., 37
Krockover, G. H., 544
Kroeber, A. L., 394
Krokfors, L., 543
Kruger, J., 82
Kruglanski, A., 112
Kruithof, A., 86
Krumboltz, J., 237
Krummerheuer, G., 364
Kuhl, J., 74
Kuhn, D., 81, 182, 361, 362, 363
Kuhn, T., 417
Kulik, C. C., 576
Kulik, J. A., 500, 576
Kulikowich, J., 503
Kupersmidt, J. B., 240, 242, 247
Kurland, D. M., 405, 417
Kurowski, C. O., 245, 251
Kurtz-Costes, B., 588
Kusche, C., 225, 227

Labaree, D. F., 560, 565
Labbo, L. D., 333
LaBerge, D., 343
Lacerenza, L., 338, 339
Lachman, J. L., 48, 49
Lachman, R., 48, 49
Ladd, G. W., 204, 209, 210, 212, 217, 218, 219,
    220, 228, 235, 242, 246
Ladson-Billings, G., 538, 541
LaFreniere, P. J., 204
LaGrange, A., 302
Lajoie, S. P., 404
Lakatos, I., 357
Lakoff, G., 360, 363, 376
Lamb, M. E., 318, 320
Lambermon, M. W. E., 218, 219
Lambert, N., 627
Lambert, N. M., 240
Lambert, S., 167
Lambert, W. E., 95, 303
Lambros, K. M., 514
Lampert, M., 365, 533
Lan, W. Y., 60
Landow, G. P., 398, 405
Lane, K. L., 514
Lange, R., 302
Langer, J., 144
Langer, J. A., 335, 345
Lanier, P., 545
La Paro, K., 204, 206, 212, 213
Lappan, G., 545
Lapsley, D. K., 156
Large, B., 458
Larkin, J., 276
Larouche, C., 110, 111
Larreamendy-Joerns, J., 365
Larsen, S., 468
Larsen, S. C., 455
Lasley, T., 167
Latane, B., 186
Latham, G. P., 68, 69, 109
Latour, B., 367, 368, 370, 371
Laubscher, L., 498, 506, 507
Lauer, P. A., 549, 587, 593
Laurel, B., 397
Lave, J., 36, 134, 418, 421, 538
Lawrence, L., 303
Laychak, A. E., 242, 243
Leary, D. E., 48
LeCompte, M., 245
Leder, G., 277
Lederer, J. M., 190
Lederman, N. G., 546
Lee, C., 127, 144
Lee, D.-S., 157
Lee, K., 369
Lee, O., 380, 381
Lee, R., 305
Lee, V. E., 589
Leerner, R. M., 199, 201, 202, 203, 205, 206,
    215, 216
Leevers, H. J., 361
Lefcourt, H., 106
Lefebvre, M. L., 302
Lefly, D. L., 479

Leggett, E. L., 109, 110, 111, 112, 237
Lehman, J. F., 381
Lehmann, F., 305
Lehr, C., 432, 444
Lehrer, M., 615, 618, 619, 620, 621, 622, 623, 625
Lehrer, R., 12, 13
Lehrer, R., 364, 365, 366, 371, 372, 373, 374,
    375, 376, 377, 378, 379, 380, 381, 382,
    383, 404
Lehto, A., 112
Leigh, J. E., 455
Leikin, R., 191
Leinhardt, G., 358
Lemann, N., 25
Lemke, J., 398
Lennox, C., 467, 471, 473, 479
Leontiev, A. N., 127
Lepper, M., 113, 245
Lepper, M. R., 72, 156, 158, 159, 187, 246
Lerner, R. M., 11, 201, 613
Lero, D., 319, 320, 321
Lesgold, A., 161, 395
Lesh, R., 12, 13, 383, 384, 615, 618, 619, 620,
    621, 622, 623, 625
Lesh, R. A., 384
Leslie, A., 361
Leslie, A. M., 359
Levey, P., 461, 476
Levi, I., 360
Levin, B. A., 551
Levin, H., 338
Levin, J., 401, 574
Levin, J. R., 5, 14, 16, 65, 85, 86, 90, 343, 533,
    549, 551, 552, 558, 560–561, 563, 566,
    567, 568, 570, 571, 572, 573, 574, 575,
    576, 617, 624, 626, 627
Levin, M. E., 567, 571, 575
Levine, E. Z., 262, 272
Levine, L. J., 293, 562, 577
Levine, M. D., 473
Levine, W. H., 83
Levinowitz, L. M., 294, 295
Lévi-Strauss, C., 406
Levitt, N., 564
Levy, C. M., 54
Levy, V. M., 156
Lewis, A. B., 54, 55
Lewis, C., 224, 599
Lewis, J., 31
Lewis, L., 167
Lewis, M., 300
Lewis, M. W., 55, 564
Lewis, R., 375
Lewis, T., 516
Lewis, T. J., 432
Ley, K., 591
Lezak, M. D., 457
Liaupsin, C., 432
Liberman, D., 338
Liberman, I., 458, 478, 479
Licht, B. G., 65, 67
Lidz, C., 146
Lie, A., 336
Lieberman, A. F., 205
Lieberman, M. D., 591

Subject Index